For all who have been members of No 45 Sqn in the past so that later generations of Flying Camels, should there continue to be some, will know of their exploits.

First published in Great Britain, 1995
by C G Jefford

Flying Camels
PO Box 45
High Wycombe
Bucks
HP10 9SB
UK

ISBN   0 9526290 0 3

Printed and bound by Unwin Brothers Ltd.,
The Gresham Press, Old Woking, Surrey, GU22 9LH.
A member of the Martins Printing Group.

The Flying Camels

THE HISTORY OF No 45 Sqn, RAF

BY

Wing Commander C G JEFFORD MBE BA RAF Retd

Contents

Maps

The maps in the this book are intended to provide an indication of the whereabouts of the locations mentioned in the main narrative and in the Annexes, apart from those in the British Isles and contemporary airfields in Europe, all of which are relatively easy to find.

In view of the complexity of the squadron's movements and activities and in order to avoid excessive duplication the provision of maps has been rationalised. As a result the reader will find that several of them cover quite lengthy periods, making it sometimes necessary to refer back and forth between chapters in order to locate a particular place, eg the map of Iraq provided in Chapter 4 is also relevant to Chapters 5 and 7 and the map of India included in Chapter 9 covers the squadron's whole period in the Far East. Due apology is made for this inconvenience.

It should be noted that place names, particularly those in the 'third world' (as rendered by westerners) have a tendency to change with time. For instance, Qotafiya and Muqeibila are used in this book, although veterans of the squadron's days in the Middle East may remember them as Qu'ttaf and Mukebele; similar changes may be noticed in the chapters dealing with the war in Burma. In recent, post-colonial, years many once familiar places, and even countries, have had their names changed completely, eg Ceylon is now Sri Lanka and Negombo reverted to its original name of Katanuyake in the 1950s. Confusion can also arise in finding locations of significance to the squadron in Flanders as a result of Belgium's being bilingual; thus, for instance, what the squadron noted as Neuve-Église is more likely to appear as Nieuwkerke on a modern map.

Foreword

by Air Chief Marshal Sir Anthony Skingsley GBE KCB MA

I am very pleased that Wing Commander 'Jeff' Jefford has decided to compile a history of No 45 Sqn, and that, having taken on the project, he has not been daunted when the magnitude of the undertaking became fully apparent! '45' has an outstanding record, full of incident and variety. The word 'unique' is much overworked nowadays, and I shall not be tempted into it; but there is no doubt that 45 Squadron has been a very special unit and has packed an enormous amount into a space of not much more than 75 years.

After its unrivalled success with the Sopwith Camel in World War I, it is not quite clear why the Powers that Be decided to send the Squadron ever further away from the UK. But they did; and because of this, 45 played a leading part in some of the innovative air operations overseas that are now part of the history of the development of air power. Now, unfortunately, it is only a 'shadow' squadron. Once planned to be a Tornado squadron, it fell victim to the cutbacks of recent years. That I deeply regret. We have to remind ourselves of the reasons for those cutbacks; we are no longer menaced by the Warsaw Pact, and defence can rightly be given a lower priority than before, permitting more to be spent on hospitals, education, and the other services that the citizen looks to his Government to provide. Nevertheless most of us will feel a deep sadness at the operational demise of a splendid unit that we were proud to belong to.

I am often asked which tour in my long Service career was the best. Impossible to answer; the Commander-in-Chief at 52 is a different man to the Squadron Commander at 32, finding different rewards and satisfactions. But 45 was my first command, and will always have a special place. About one thing I have always been entirely clear: it was without doubt the most fun!

Preface

In the course of researching the story of the Flying Camels it has become very apparent to me that the squadron's history means different things to different people. To any ex-member, but especially to those who saw active service with the unit, it tends to mean the period which they personally remember. Thus to some of its veterans No 45 Sqn was only ever a Blenheim squadron in the North African desert while others are no more than vaguely aware of this and can only conceive of it as having being a Venom outfit in Malaya. But, whenever they served with it, what these people remember is their colleagues and they are often recalled even more vividly than incidents. On the other hand, the typical student of air force history tends to be more concerned with events and hardware, rather than people, and his interest may well be confined to some specific type of aeroplane or a particular period, usually the First or Second World Wars but rarely both.

It follows that in view of the potential readership, in attempting to present a squadron's entire history one must try to satisfy several 'markets'. One group wants to be reminded of its own experiences during a discrete two or three year period, these periods overlapping over nearly eighty years; others wish to know the intimate details of the service records of the various types of aircraft which the squadron flew while another's primary interest may be to learn of the part played by the unit in a particular campaign. Relatively few people are concerned with the squadron's history as a continuous chronicle - but that is what it is. The people and the aeroplanes come and go. Dramatic events occur and then fade into obscurity. Only the squadron, as an entity, provides a coherent link between these ephemera - the whole of its history is greater than the sum of its parts.

In writing this book I have attempted to be all things to all men and have, therefore, probably failed to satisfy any of them. My primary aim has been to establish and present the facts while still endeavouring to reflect something of the 'flavour' of squadron life as it has changed over the years by noting the exploits of the constantly changing kaleidoscope of personalities. Despite its limitations, what emerges is I believe a story which is full of interest and one of which to be proud. It is certainly a story which should have been told before. Had it been it would surely have been appreciated that, if only because of its longevity, the history of the Flying Camels is an integral part of that of the RAF and that without No 45 Sqn in its Order of Battle the character of the whole service is diminished. No 45 Sqn was one of the mere handful of units which kept the air force's flag flying in the critical era between the wars and as such it is the holder of one of the original thirty Squadron Standards which were awarded in 1943. It is surely inappropriate that junior, not necessarily lesser, but certainly very junior squadrons should still be in the front line while the Flying Camels are relegated to a shadowy quasi-existence as a reserve squadron. Since this is a point which tends to crop up periodically in the following narrative the reader may regard this book as something of a polemic. I make no apology for this. If being the squadron's historian does not entitle me to be partisan, then what does?

In places the squadron's official records are very patchy and there is no surviving documentation at all for some periods. To fill in these gaps and to flesh out others I am indebted to the many ex-members and their relatives and colleagues who have given me access to their flying log books, diaries and other personal papers, loaned me their photographs and contributed their reminiscences. Without their help this story could not have been told. I wish to acknowledge in particular the assistance that I have received from Mrs Mollie Abbott, A D Allen, J J Alt, R J Armstrong, E Ashton, A D Ashworth, R M Barclay, R Barrett, T H Bartlett, Mrs Joyce Bayly, Wg Cdr D K Bednall, C E Birkbeck, Mrs Faye Blenkhorne, L N Boot, D Brereton, C G Briggs, N A Bruce, D J Butler, J Byrne, L J Charlton, S Chick, R I Clark, D J Clarke, M A Clarke, D Cliffe, Wg Cdr W E Close, Sqn Ldr R Collis DFC, Air Cdre G S Cooper OBE, J Coughlin, O Cowell, R M Cowley, P G Crayden, D Davies, Wg Cdr F G Daw DFC AFC, Wg Cdr M J Dawson, Sqn Ldr W M Drake, L H Durrant, J Eades, A M Eckel, V A Emson, D G Eve, P Farley, S J Findley, C E French, E F French, R W Fussell, H Gardener, AVM M J Gibson CB OBE, J Gillan, N Gittins, W G A Glaze, D Godfrey, Mrs Babs Golder, D Goodrich, G A Gowing, C Haggarty, E J Hallett, G J Hancox, Sqn Ldr K Hargeaves, Gp Capt T A Hastings OBE, H C Hatherly, E R Henman, R D Hilditch, Sqn Ldr C A Hodder, P Hodkinson, Sqn Ldr K G Hodson OBE, A Holden, Sqn Ldr R T Holloway MBE, L E Howard, Gp Capt R F G Howard BEM, Mrs Betty Hughes, Mrs Daphne Hughes, A N Huon, Sqn Ldr W J A Innes, R G Jackson, Sqn Ldr V K Jacobs, E T Johnson, G T Jones, R Jones, T J Jones, K U Keel, Sqn Ldr M E Kerr, D W Ketteringham, Gp Capt G C O Key OBE DFC, J A H Kirkpatrick, H C Langrish, A J Lamb, Wg Cdr F J O Lasbrey, R Lea, D Leggatt, W Lindsay, A Lowe, Sqn Ldr W F T Lucas, R McAusland, A G McCandlish, B T McDade, Sqn Ldr J W Maloney DFC RAAF, A J Martin, Sqn Ldr P J Mason, C S Matthews, Wg Cdr P Miller, AVM L E Moulton CB DFC, N D Murrell, F G Neale, M W Neale, H M Nicholls, Sqn Ldr S O'Connor DFC AFC AFM, H Osborne, Sqn Ldr L R J Ovenden AFC, D A Owen, Wg Cdr D McL Paton, A M Pedlar, D Pells, A R Pinches, Gp Capt H P Pleasance OBE DFC*, A H Pridmore, M Retallack, E G Rivers, Air Cdre D F Rixson CVO OBE DFC

AFC, AVM M M J Robinson CB, J Scanes, F Scholfield, ACM Sir Anthony Skingsley GBE KCB MA, Air Cdre I S Stockwell CBE DFC AFC, Sqn Ldr P D Stonham MBE, G Taylor, W G M Taylor, B Terry, F G Terry, Wg Cdr C W S Thomas AFC, G A Tibbs, F Umdasch, G W Underwood, J Vigar, G Viner, C Webster, S B Whitely, F Whitlock, Gp Capt R Whittam, L Wilde, G F Williams, Sqn Ldr R S Williams, A Winston-Smith, Sqn Ldr H Witton, Gp Capt D Wood LVO AFC, Wg Cdr R Wood, W Worrall, C J Yeo and P L Young

In addition to the above I am very grateful to the staffs of the Air Historical Branch of the Ministry of Defence, the Royal Air Force Museum, the Royal New Zealand Air Force Museum, the Imperial War Museum, the National Maritime Museum, the Public Record Office, the Map Rooms of the British Library, the India Office and the Royal Geographical Society, to OC No 45(R) Sqn and to the CRO at RAF Wittering, all of whom made substantial contributions to my research by helping me to track down particularly elusive facts. Considerable help was also provided by members of Cross & Cockade and of these I must especially thank Jim Brown for his generosity in sharing with me the results of his many years of research into the exploits of No 45 Sqn during WW I. I also gratefully acknowledge the help that I have received from the Mafia of aviation historians, who can be so unstinting in their help with a project of this nature; these included Chaz Bowyer, Jack Bruce, John Grech, Peter Green, Chris Hobson at the RAF Staff College, Philip Jarrett, Andrew Kemp, Stuart Leslie, Howard Levy, Don Neate, Brian Pickering of MAP, Bruce Robertson, Wg Cdr J Routledge, Ray Sturtivant, Andy Thomas, Geoff Thomas, Dick Ward, Joe Warne, Alan Webb of the Mosquito Museum and George H Williams. I wish also to record my gratitude to Michael Turner for his kindness in granting me permission to reproduce his splendid painting of Vengeances of No 45 Sqn on the dustjacket.

Last but not least, I must express my appreciation of the contribution made my wife, who ploughed through ever-lengthening successive drafts of this opus, correcting my sometimes innovative spelling, finding more appropriate associations for my misrelated participles, enhancing the status of my inadequate commas and attempting to simplify some of my more laboured prose. But, since I have a tendency to use three long words where one short one would do, have an overdeveloped predilection for convoluted constructions, involving numerous subordinate clauses, an affinity for the subjunctive and a tendency to indulge in the past imperfect, often complicated by a conditional qualification, she was not entirely successful in her efforts to streamline all of the text. If this book is difficult to read then it is entirely my fault and not Gill's.

I should perhaps add a word of explanation regarding the quality of many of the photographs which appear in the following pages. Ideally one would have liked to have used only professionally-produced "8x10 glossies" but the reality is that, where they exist, most pictures of this type have been seen many times before; furthermore, their very perfection makes them somehow impersonal. The majority of the pictures in this book have been contributed by ex-squadron members and in many cases they have been blown up from very small, often faded and/or sepia-tinted and sometimes crumpled, snapshots printed on low-grade stock. It is hoped that what they may lack in definition is at least partly offset by the intimacy and spontaneity which they convey and by the fact that many are being published for the first time.

May 1995   C G Jefford
                                                                                              Loudwater
                                                                                              Bucks

Chapter 1. In the beginning - an uncertain start.

When the RFC first deployed to France in 1914 it left behind an element from which additional units were formed. After a work-up period, during which most of them served as quasi-flying training schools, these new squadrons moved overseas in their turn, leaving behind nuclei from which yet more units were created and so the Corps expanded. By February of 1916 the forecast position was that within a month thirty-two squadrons would have been mobilised and despatched overseas. In order to maintain the flow of reinforcements and to sustain what had become an established sequence it was now necessary to raise and designate the next wave of units. In letter 87/4469 of 1st March 1916, Lt Col Marindin authorised, on behalf of the Deputy Director of Military Aeronautics, the inclusive formation of Nos 37 to 48 Service Squadrons. Thus was No 45 Sqn conceived. Once it had been provided with a nucleus from its parent unit, originally nominated to be No 15 Reserve Squadron at Doncaster, it was to work up at Sedgeford.

Following the almost inevitable amendment of the plan, No 45 Sqn actually came into being at Gosport with No 22 Sqn as its parent. It was to be a unit of 7th Wing (Wg) within VI Brigade (Bde). Although no specific date had been promulgated for this momentous event to take place, the administrative wheels began to turn and on 16th March Sgts Walsh and Walters along with seven mechanics, all of No 22 Sqn, were earmarked for transfer to No 45 Sqn but, pending its embodiment, they were temporarily attached to No 28 Sqn, which was also working up at Gosport. Three days later Capt C E Ryan of No 28 Sqn was appointed Acting CO of the new unit. He was joined that same day by a substantial group of officers, including Lts H T Shaw and E F P Lubbock and 2/Lts D V Armstrong, P Pralle, P Beanlands, R L H Laye, P C Morgan, E G Manuel, J H Parry, W L Scandrett, E Pearson, J Sowrey, M L Taylor and H C G Watney; most if not all, of these men were being inherited from No 22 Sqn and they were initially attached to No 45 Sqn, pending formal War Office postings. They were joined on March 21st by a draft of forty-two brand new groundcrew.

The squadron began to acquire some aeroplanes too. A VI Bde letter, 6BT/84 of 28th March, directed that twelve aircraft were to be transferred from No 22 Sqn to No 45 Sqn and this authorisation was published in 7th Wg's Daily Routine Orders two days later, although the first of these aeroplanes had probably already changed hands a week before. It is interesting to note that by 1994, when these words were being written, considerably in excess of a thousand aeroplanes would have passed through the squadron's hands (see Annex L) - the first dozen of these were a Bristol Scout (5294), a Martinsyde S.1 (5442), four BE 2cs (1761, 2062, 2069 and 2073) and six Avros (793, 2890, 4047, 4048, 4052 and 4759). This initial batch of aeroplanes was accompanied by sixteen spare engines (ten 80hp Gnomes and six 70hp Renaults).

No 45 Sqn was gradually taking shape, but in a slightly haphazard fashion as there was still some doubt about its formal status. HQ VI Bde wrote to the War Office on April 14th requesting clarification as to the official formation date

for its new unit. On the 17th Capt B C Fellows of the Directorate of Air Organisation replied that No 45 Sqn (*had!*) formed on 1st March. Better late than never, and in order to keep the bureaucratic books straight, VI Bde despatched its C/6.B/32 of 18th April, a formatted letter, informing the Directorate of Military Aeronautics that No 45 Sqn had indeed been formed on 1st March 1916.

While this uncertainty was being resolved the squadron continued to grow and it began to function as an element of the training system. Before the end of March Lt Shaw, Lt Morgan and 2/Lt Parry had been elevated to the status of temporary flight commanders. On 23rd March Capt Robert Loraine, late of the pre-war West End stage and war service with No 5 Sqn, joined the squadron as its first substantive flight commander; on the 28th 2/Lt H T Birdsall arrived to take up his appointment as Assistant Equipment Officer (AEO)[1] and, finally, on 15th April, Lt G Alchin was posted in to oversee the instruction of the squadron's observers. Training was well under way by this time and on 25th April Pearson, Parry, Shaw and Beanlands were all promulgated as having passed their Graduation 'A' Examinations. The flow of incoming trainees continued and before the end of that month 2/Lts W A Porkess, J G Aronson, E Mark, R True and S McLure along with F/Sgts Lawford and Webb had joined the squadron to undergo instruction in 'Higher Aviation'.

The colourful Major L A Strange had been attached to No 45 Sqn as CO, vice Capt Ryan, on March 27th, pending a formal posting which was effected on 6th April. Louis Strange was among the RFC's most experienced and capable flyers. Having qualified as a pilot before the war, he had gone to France in August 1914 and had subsequently flown operationally for over a year with Nos 5, 6 and 12 Sqns. He returned to England to form and work up No 23 Sqn but just as they were about to move to France he had been stricken with appendicitis and obliged to relinquish his command. Nominally carried on the books of No 40 Sqn while he was being attended to in Cosham Military Hospital, on his release Strange was given No 45 Sqn but, since he was still restricted to light duties, he was in no condition to work up another unit. Fortunately, a convenient solution was to hand.

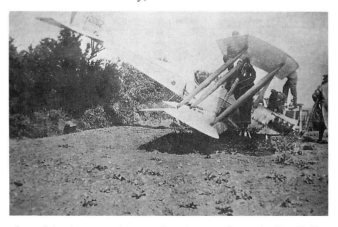

One of the first aeroplanes to be taken on charge by No 45 Sqn, BE 2c 2062, parked in an undignified fashion at Burnham Market on 25th June 1916 by 2/Lt Turner-Bridger, then a pilot under instruction with the unit. (J M Bruce/G S Leslie)

Maj William Ronald Read MC, 1st (King's) Dragoon Guards, who became OC No 45 Sqn on 24th April 1916, a few weeks after its formation; he remained in command for exactly a year. (Imperial War Museum)

No 41 Sqn was on the point of forming, also at Gosport, and Major W R Read of the 1st (King's) Dragoon Guards had been nominated to command it. Since No 45 Sqn's formation had already been under way for some six weeks, its need for a full-time CO was far more pressing so it was decided simply to exchange COs. War Office letter 112/RFC/34(MA1) of 11th April transferred Read from his appointment as OC Designate for No 41 Sqn to become OC No 45 Sqn while at the same time posting Strange in the opposite direction. Thus Willie Read came to be the first permanent CO of No 45 Sqn, actually taking up his appointment on 24th April.

Read was another very experienced pilot. Having gained his Aero Club certificate (No 463) at Larkhill in January 1913, he first went to France with No 3 Sqn at the beginning of the war. Wounded in November 1914, he spent most of the following year flying with No 5 Sqn before returning to England to command No 3 Reserve Squadron. He had thus acquired practical experience of both combat and instructional flying by the time he arrived at Gosport.

On the same day that the CO had been appointed, Capt C M Crowe became the second substantive flight commander giving the unit an almost full complement of executive officers, although neither of the original flight commanders was to become a permanent fixture.

On 2nd May Read took the squadron to Thetford where it came under the auspices of the Dover-based 6th Wg. On the 21st it moved again, this time to Sedgeford, and back to 7th Wg whose HQ had by then transferred to Norwich. By this time the original pair of flight commanders had already moved on, their places having been taken by Capt G Mountford and 2/Lts L H D Henderson and H G P Lowe, only Mountford (who had joined the squadron on 21st April) being substantive in post. When the squadron arrived at Sedgeford Maj Read found that its new home had very little to offer. The only other inhabitants were some RNAS personnel who looked after a single flight shed which occasionally housed a solitary BE 2c intended to counter the nocturnal incursions of Zeppelins. Read found himself having to establish the camp more or less from scratch, including such fundamentals as erecting huts and hangars and laying on water.

Once the squadron was up and running it was incorporated into the anti-Zeppelin defences and tasked with providing a stand-by aircraft. Thereafter one of No 45 Sqn's BEs, the only one notionally equipped for night flying, was prepared every evening, picketed facing into wind and primed for take off. It was only 'scrambled' once, when a Zeppelin was reported to have been illuminated by searchlights over Sandringham. Willie Read rushed out to the aerodrome and clambered aboard but the aeroplane refused to start and the intruder made off. Despite this lack of success, there were several subsequent invitations for officers of the squadron to partake of tea and cucumber sandwiches on the lawn at Sandringham with Queen Alexandra and on one occasion she came to Sedgeford to pay them a return visit.

When No 45 Sqn arrived at Sedgeford the intention (as reflected in the RFC Programme of Development published on 20th May 1916) was for it to become an artillery observation unit. The plan called for the squadron to be fully equipped with either RE 8s or Armstrong Whitworth FK 8s by August 16th. In the meantime, as was normal in 1916, the squadron's task was to prepare itself for mobilisation by functioning as a cross between a modern basic flying training school and an operational training unit. For this task it was equipped with a variety of obsolescent aircraft and from time to time No 45 Sqn operated Henri Farmans, BE 2bs and at least one FE 2b in addition to the types already mentioned. By mid-June the squadron had twenty-three trainees under instruction. Many of the pilots among them would probably have had little more than five hours of flying time to their credit when they arrived at Sedgeford, this having been acquired, almost invariably on Farmans, at one of the Reserve Squadrons.

The experience of 2/Lt G H Cock, later to become one of No 45 Sqn's most successful wartime aviators, provides a typical example of the pattern of flying training in 1916. He began his course at Thetford where he made his first flight on 28th June in a Farman Shorthorn (A327). Having amassed a little over three hours of dual experience, he went solo on his thirteenth flight, which he made on 13th July - not an auspicious combination but it was not a Friday so superstition was confounded and the trip was evidently a success. He graduated from No 25 Reserve Squadron on the 25th, by which time he had 10hrs 33mins of flying time recorded in his log book (accumulated in the course of thirty-three flights) of which 7hrs 17mins had been flown solo. Cock was then posted to No 45 Sqn to undergo his Higher Aviation course, making his first flight from Sedgeford in a BE 2c on 27th July. After progressing via Avros to Bristol Scouts he finally gained his wings on 7th September, flying a 1½ Strutter for the first time three days later.

While Cock and his colleagues were developing their crude flying skills, they also had some academic studies to take care of. Under the guidance of appropriate specialist instructors (or qualified pilots labelled as such) the fledglings were required to consolidate their familiarity with the Lewis and Vickers machine guns (following an initial acquaintance gained by attendance at one of the courses run by the School of Aerial Gunnery at Hythe) and to develop their awareness of the mysteries of the internal combustion engine, the arts of aerial navigation and photography and so on.

It all sounded plausible enough but in practice the concept was deeply flawed. The majority of experienced pilots were serving in France and most of those who were being 'rested' in the UK were instructing at the Reserve Squadrons, where their expertise was crucial. As a result there were very few pilots with substantial flying experience available to assist the Service Squadrons with their work up to operational status. In the case of No 45 Sqn, only the CO could reasonably be considered as being competent to act as a flying instructor. The log book of 2/Lt K L Caldwell illustrates this point very clearly. While qualifying in Higher Aviation with No 45 Sqn between 3rd June and 22nd July he flew dual trips with Lt McArthur, 2/Lt Henderson, 2/Lt Beanlands and F/Sgt Webb, none of whom had had their wings for more than a few months themselves (McArthur gained his on 31st May).

This was very much a case of the blind leading the blind. The fact that a pilot was able to control his aeroplane did not necessarily mean that he also understood exactly what he was doing and, even if he did, it certainly did not automatically follow that he possessed the skills required to enable him to pass whatever knowledge he did have on to anyone else. In other words, while there may have been a notional training syllabus, there was little training doctrine or method to back it up[2]. From the trainee's point of view, instruction in Higher Aviation was a matter of passing examinations in a number of technical subjects and flying as many trips as he could, during which, if he did not kill or injure himself, he would learn from his own mistakes. The training philosophy could be summed up as 'practice, with a dash of good luck, would make perfect - and if you could already ride a horse then you were off to a good start.'

Primitive as it was, even this approach might have produced satisfactory results if adequate opportunities for practice had been provided but the war's appetite for fresh pilots was such that few were able to acquire much flying experience before they had to be committed to combat. This was not, of course, peculiar to the graduates of No 45 Sqn; it was simply the only way to satisfy the demands of the RFC's constantly expanding front-line whilst making good the considerable losses being sustained in combat and through accidents. Once No 45 Sqn had moved to France and found itself on the receiving end of this system the professional inadequacies of some of his aircrew, especially pilots, were to cause Willie Read considerable heartache. Significant deficiencies were exhibited by many of the replacements he was sent, but it was even more galling in the early days to discover that some of the pilots who had been trained at Sedgeford under his own supervision also fell far short of the mark.

The facilities available for training observers in 1916 were even more rudimentary than those provided for pilots. There was no dedicated school and prospective observers were simply posted to Service Squadrons where they were expected to pick up what they could by tagging on to the

A group of airmen of No 45 Sqn's HQ Flight at Sedgeford in the summer of 1916. From the left: 2/AM A J Carter (Clerk), 2/AM H B Rich (Motor Cyclist), 2/AM B H Coker (Clerk), Sgt F Mawby (Storeman), 2/AM H C Godfrey, 2/AM R A Northcote (Clerk) and 2/AM R D Fleming. The latter would appear originally to have been a Motor Cyclist, although he later flew with the squadron as a gunner; he was killed in action on 26th January 1917. (D Godfrey)

A formal photograph of No 45 Sqn's officers taken at Sedgeford circa late September 1916. From the left, back row: 2/Lt A G Cardwell, 2/Lt J A Vessey, 2/Lt A S Carey, 2/Lt W J Thuell; 2/Lt H Johns and Lt F Surgey. Second row: 2/Lt N G Arnold, 2/Lt J N Baker, 2/Lt L F Jones, 2/Lt O J Wade, 2/Lt M J Fenwick, 2/Lt G H Cock, 2/Lt V B Allen, 2/Lt W Nicholls, 2/Lt L Beer and 2/Lt C S Emery. Third row: Lt L R Wright (Wireless Officer), 2/Lt H H Griffith; 2/Lt H T Birdsall (Assistant Equipment Officer), Capt Hon E F P Lubbock (OC B Flt), Capt G Mountford (OC A Flt), Maj W R Read (OC No 45 Sqn), Capt L Porter (OC C Flt), Lt R C Morgan (Recording Officer), 2/Lt H G P Lowe, Capt H S Lees-Smith and Lt C S J Griffin. Front row: 2/Lt F H Austin, 2/Lt E G Manuel, 2/Lt G Ross-Soden, 2/Lt H D W Debenham, 2/Lt D E Greenhow and 2/Lt J C H Ferme. Nine of these men (Cardwell, Johns, Baker, Nicholls, Beer, Lees-Smith, Ross-Soden, Debenham and Ferme) did not accompany the unit to France; the others formed the core of the squadron when it was mobilised. (Imperial War Museum)

4

pilots and flying when/if a trip was offered; thereby, it was hoped, they would acquire a modicum of practical expertise via an essentially osmotic process. Initial indoctrination training in aviation-related subjects was provided at the School of Military Aeronautics at Reading, which ran a course (which was also attended by pilots) covering basic aerodynamics, the construction and rigging of aeroplanes, the workings of the aero-engine and other technical topics. For those observers earmarked to serve with artillery co-operation units, as was the case with No 45 Sqn's men in mid-1916, the Wireless School at Brooklands offered another appropriate course, which a number of the squadron's first generation of back-seaters attended. Since the unit's role was subsequently changed, however, the aeroplanes which it eventually took to France were not fitted with wireless so the core of the Brooklands course proved to be somewhat irrelevant. Nevertheless, much valuable incidental knowledge will no doubt have been acquired. The only formal instruction of direct value was provided by the machine gun course at Hythe.

2/Lt J A Vessey's progress was typical of an observer's *ab initio* training at this time. After active service in the trenches, among the ranks of the Royal Fusiliers, Vessey returned to England and was commissioned into the RFC in 1916, reporting to its school at Reading on 7th July. Posted from there to No 45 Sqn, he was at Hythe from 25th July until 15th August and at Brooklands between 17th August and 7th September. He was formally graded as an observer on 15th October - the day that the squadron arrived in France.

A broadly similar situation prevailed among the groundcrew, and the squadron had a cadre of seasoned NCOs to train its young Air Mechanics (AM). In this case, however, most of them were being taught to apply basic crafts and engineering skills which were both better understood and more easily demonstrated than the art of flying. Some of the later arrivals may have passed through the RFC's School of Instruction which opened at Reading in July 1916 and began to turn out qualified fitters and riggers after a five-week course. The squadron also needed a variety of other specialist craftsmen, most of whom were recruited as ready-qualified civilians; these included drivers, storemen, blacksmiths, carpenters, sailmakers and the like, as well as cooks and butchers to keep them fully fuelled.

Air Mechanics were not being consumed by the meatgrinder in and above the trenches of France, however, so there was less demand for urgent replacements and those posted to the squadron tended to become a fixture, many of them remaining on its strength until 1919. By contrast the aircrew, particularly the officers, were something of a floating population as any experienced men tended to be promoted and posted away to take up executive posts with units already in France or with one of the additional new squadrons which were constantly being formed in the UK. France was also the destination for the majority of the students passing through the system, there being an insatiable and always urgent demand for them to take the places of the fallen.

While the squadron was at Sedgeford one of its student pilots displayed a little enterprise which is worthy of note, just for the record. By mid-1916 the RAF 4 engine had already been installed in substantial numbers of BE 12s and

RE 7s and had been earmarked as the power plant for the new RE 8 which was destined to become one of the mainstays of the RFC. Despite its already being in operational use, this engine was still suffering from a number of teething troubles, one of which was overheating of the rear pair of its four in-line cylinders. Lt McLure devised a means of improving the flow of cooling air to the back of the engine and submitted his idea for consideration. On July 25th a letter from HQ 7th Wg acknowledged his initiative, although his design was rejected on the grounds that it would have induced too much drag and would have been too heavy.

As the summer passed, the personalities who were to constitute the operational No 45 Sqn gradually began to appear on its strength and by mid-July the two acting flight commanders had been relieved by Capt L Porter and Capt Hon E F P Lubbock who, with Mountford, were to accompany the squadron to France. On 1st August, maintaining the practice of siring the next generation of units, an element was hived off to form the nucleus of No 64 Sqn and No 45 Sqn began to prepare for its impending move across the Channel. Eric Lubbock transferred to No 64 Sqn for a time but returned to the fold before the squadron left for France. By this time its role had been changed and it was now to be a fighter-reconnaissance squadron equipped with

One of the squadron's original observers, 2/Lt John Arthur Vessey survived a remarkable eight months of combat operations before he and his pilot, Capt Gordon Mountford, were killed in a flying accident, a mid-air collision, on 12th June 1917. By that time Vessey had taken part in five successful engagements with enemy aircraft and he was thus technically entitled to be considered an 'Ace'. (Geo H Williams)

A few days before it deployed to France, the squadron began to collect its operational 1½ Strutters from Ruston Proctor of Lincoln. This manufacturer's shot of 7777 will have been taken in about September of 1916 and clearly shows the Nieuport mounting for the rear gun which was fitted to early production aircraft. Camouflage was just being introduced at this time and, although this one is obviously wearing PC 10, several of the squadron's original aeroplanes were finished in clear dope. Like many of the squadron's two-seaters, 7777 had a short life. It was shot down on 22nd October 1916, just eight days after it had reached France. Its crew, Capt Porter and Lt Samuels, were killed. (J M Bruce/G S Leslie)

the Sopwith Two-Seater, technically designated as the LCT (Land Clerget Tractor) by its parent company but universally known throughout the RFC and to posterity as the 1½ Strutter. The 1½ Strutter had originally been sponsored by the RNAS but the RFC soon came to appreciate its potential as a counter to the Fokker Monoplane and arranged for some to be transferred to its charge while placing further orders on its own behalf. Ruston, Proctor & Co of Lincoln received a War Office contract; production aeroplanes began to appear in June 1916 and on 22nd July the first four off the line (7762-7764) were allotted to No 45 Sqn who used them for familiarisation flying.

Still working to the published schedule, by 16th August the squadron's personnel were as ready as they were ever going to be but the unit still had no operational aeroplanes. To remedy this deficiency arrangements were made for the pilots to collect some more aircraft direct from the manufacturers in Lincoln. On one such trip, while crossing the Wash on his way back to Sedgeford, Major Read was disconcerted to find his aircraft becoming increasingly, inexplicably, and thus alarmingly, unstable in pitch. When he tried to inform his passenger of the deteriorating situation he was startled to find that the rear cockpit was empty. Despite the random control inputs, Read descended towards the sea and began to search for the missing man. After a while the out-of-balance condition began to correct itself and the passenger reappeared. It transpired that he, a member of Ruston's design staff, had decided to make an examination of the aeroplane's structure under flight loading at first-hand and had burrowed his way into the bowels of the fuselage with unfortunate effects on the centre of gravity!

By the beginning of September the squadron had three combat ready Sopwiths (including 7774 and 7786) and more

followed during the month. In a letter dated 28th September the Director of Air Organisation ordered the squadron, "...to proceed overseas on 7.10.16. The aeroplanes will proceed overseas on 9.10.16." The main party, under the command of the Squadron Adjutant, Lt R C Morgan, left as ordered, sailing from Southampton on the *Duchess of Argyll*, and reached Rouen on 9th October. There they were joined on the 12th by the Wireless Officer, Lt L R Wright, with the squadron's MT echelon. Two days later they set out for Fienvillers. Travelling via Amiens, they reached their destination on the 16th, having spent the intervening night bivouacked in their vehicles. Incidentally, shortly after the squadron landed in France it was pointed out that only wings were entitled to have an Adjutant and Morgan was accordingly 'demoted' to the status of a mere Recording Officer.

For the transit to France the back seats of nearly all of the aircraft were occupied by mechanics, it presumably being hoped that they might be able to get their aeroplane moving again in the event of a forced landing - a strong possibility in 1916. This left the observers and a number of 'spare' pilots to make their way across the Channel with the main party. When the squadron first established itself in France the observers on its strength were: Lt F Surgey, 2/Lts N G Arnold, F H Austin, G H Bennett, A S Carey, C S Emery, F Fullerton, D E Greenhow, W Jordan, G B Samuels, W J Thuell and J A Vessey and Sgt P S Taylor; there were also at least two gunners, Cpl R D Fleming and Pte W Chandler. Pilots on strength at this time, but who do not appear to have flown an aeroplane across to France, included Lt G L Rodwell, 2/Lt V B Allen, 2/Lt N H Read and Sgt Malcolm.

The aircraft and crews involved in No 45 Sqn's initial deployment are listed at Figure 1.1. Their move was far from straightforward as poor weather caused it to be postponed by 24 hours and disrupted its execution when it did take place; furthermore, since the squadron was still not fully equipped, Lt L W McArthur, Lt L A Chamier and 2/Lt H H Griffith had been sent to Farnborough to collect additional aeroplanes and they were to make the crossing to France from there. Four pilots failed to get off from Sedgeford when the squadron began its move on 10th October, Capt Mountford, 2/Lts Cock and Fenwick and F/Sgt Webb; a fifth, 2/Lt Wade, crashed on take off. Cock did not manage to get away until the 13th, and even then he only got as far as Thetford. Despite these tribulations, over the next few days the majority of the aeroplanes succeeded in reaching France, crossing the Channel between Lympne and Clairmarais (St Omer), before making the last hop to Fienvillers (Candas). By close of play on the 15th ten pilots had reached their destination to be joined by Cock the following day. The stragglers trickled in over the next ten days. Since he wrecked 7776 at Bertangles on the 18th while flying with 2/Lt J A Vessey, it is probable that 2/Lt E E Glorney was the first of the latecomers to turn up, possibly in 7776 on the 17th.

Cpl H W Grimmitt's experience of the transit to France provides an informative commentary on the difficulties that were inevitably encountered when half-trained pilots were committed to tasks that were clearly beyond their competence. Flown by Lt Chamier, their first aeroplane had been damaged during an unsuccessful attempt to take off from Sedgeford[3]. The pair were promptly despatched to Farnborough to pick up a replacement, Grimmitt carrying the guns which he had dismounted from their original aeroplane. En route these were deposited for a time in the cloakroom at Waterloo Station while the crew went for a cup of tea! Farnborough found them a new aeroplane and they set off to join the squadron in France. This time Chamier failed to pump sufficient pressure into the fuel system before taking off and shortly after the machine had become airborne its engine stopped. With minimal excess speed to play with the pilot should have landed straight ahead but he attempted to make a 180° flat turn and a downwind deadstick landing. He made a reasonable fist of what was an inherently difficult, in fact dangerous, manoeuvre but lost it towards the end and the aircraft was wrecked. It had not been a bad effort all the same, considering that the pilot had just 20 minutes total flying time on Sopwiths! When the local CO learned of this he decided not to risk another 1½ Strutter and he rustled up a less demanding aeroplane for Lt Chamier to ferry across to France. This turned out to be a BE 12 (6174) which he flew over to No 1 Aircraft Depot (AD) at Clairmarais on 21st October.

Since the BE 12 was a single-seater, this left Grimmitt and his guns still stranded in England. Another Sopwith was prepared and, flown by a Lt Phillips (not of No 45 Sqn), Cpl Grimmitt set out for France again; but they only got as far as Kent before engine trouble forced them to land, buckling a wheel in the process. After these problems had been sorted out they continued on their way and on October 26th they eventually delivered 7790

to Clairmarais, whence it was issued to No 45 Sqn two days later. Almost as soon as the crew had landed Grimmitt was winkled out by Lt Griffin who was at the Aircraft Depot to pick up a new aeroplane. He flew him down to Fienvillers that same day in A1071, one of the squadron's first replacement aircraft. There were to be many, many more.

No 45 Sqn, with a reported strength of twenty-seven officers and 183 other ranks, was now an element of the 9th Wg[4]. Uniquely, 9th Wg was not assigned to a Brigade; it functioned under the direct operational control of GHQ RFC, this being exercised through its Advanced HQ which was also located at Fienvillers. This very crowded aerodrome was about 6 miles WSW of Doullens and already housed Nos 19, 27 and 70 Sqns, flying BE 12s, Martinsydes and 1½ Strutters respectively, while also serving as the airfield for No 2 AD at Candas; accommodation was therefore at a premium.

Few preparations had been made for the arrival of the new squadron and Maj Read was most unimpressed by the state of the camp. The newcomers were allocated a single hut and three bell tents to serve as offices, and little else - no rations, no water, no blankets, no accommodation; it was all far too much like a repeat of the Sedgeford experience. What was worse, it soon became apparent that Willie Read was going to find it difficult to establish a working relationship with the wing commander, Lt Col H C T Dowding[5].

While all this housekeeping had been going on Dowding had been complaining that not enough flying was being done. In view of the amount of effort that was having to be expended on domestic affairs Read considered this hardly surprising, and said so! In any case it was not really a fair comment. The squadron had in fact begun flying the day after the second wave of aircraft had arrived, 2/Lt Griffith and Lt Surgey having flown the first in-theatre practice flight in A1066 on 16th October.

On October 20th No 45 Sqn flew its first operational mission, a patrol over the Somme Front as the battle of that name, which had begun on 1st July, was drawing to its close. The participants were Lubbock and Samuels (7782), Manuel and Fullerton (7783), Lowe and Jordan (7786) and Griffin and Greenhow (7780). They flew a Defensive Patrol in the vicinity of Péronne in the course of which they had a brief skirmish with four aircraft, identified as LVGs, possibly damaging one of them. There was a price to pay, however, and with his 7782 already badly shot about, Eric Lubbock, hit a fence on landing which effectively put his aeroplane out of

Date of Arrival	Serial	Pilot	Passenger
14 Oct	7778	Maj W R Read	1/AM W C Dodwell
14 Oct	7777	Capt L Porter (OC C Flt)	Cpl G Warren
14 Oct	7782	Capt E F P Lubbock (OC B Flt)	Sgt A S Rollo
14 Oct	7780	2/Lt H G P Lowe	1/AM D W Bozman
14 Oct	7786	Lt C S Griffin	Cpl R H Lee
15 Oct	7775	Capt G Mountford (OC A Flt)	1/AM Voysey
15 Oct	A1064	2/Lt M J Fenwick	?
15 Oct	7783	2/Lt E G Manuel	1/AM W Bendall
15 Oct	7788	2/Lt H H Griffith	1/AM Mackenzie
15 Oct	A1066	2/Lt O J Wade	1/AM A Saunders
16 Oct	7774	2/Lt G H Cock	1/AM W Snelling

Fig 1.1. The first eleven aircraft of No 45 Sqn to reach their destination when the unit deployed to France and their dates of arrival at Fienvillers.

Capt Hon *Eric Fox Pitt Lubbock MC. Having joined the army as a private soldier in September 1914, Lubbock was commissioned in the following February. In August he transferred to the RFC and, flying with No 5 Sqn, became a qualified observer in October 1915. He returned to England for pilot training and joined No 45 Sqn at Gosport on 20th April 1916, gaining his wings in July. Thereafter he commanded the squadron's B Flight from before its arrival in France until his death in combat on 11th March 1917. (J G Muir)*

action for several weeks. Since it was delivered to No 1 AD in a wrecked condition on 21st October, it appears that someone also damaged 7779 on or about the 20th but the culprit's name does not appear to have been recorded. A second patrol flown on the 20th was successful but uneventful. The following day several further uneventful Defensive Patrols were flown, including solo sorties by Capt Lubbock and 2/Lt Carey in 7777 and by the CO and 2/Lt Jordan in 7786, the latter in co-operation with some DH 2s. October 21st was also notable for the squadron's first in-theatre casualties when 2/Lts Fenwick and Bennett wrecked 7778 while attempting to land from a reconnaissance patrol after their engine had failed, both of them sustaining injuries in the process.

On October 22nd disaster struck. The squadron was briefed to carry out a five-aircraft patrol of the Bapaume, Péronne, Marcoing area; a sixth aeroplane was prepared to act as a reserve. Four took off between 0830hrs and 0840hrs but within five minutes Wade and Thuell were down again, 7788's Clerget having shed a cylinder. The remaining pair were having trouble starting. The three crews that were still airborne should have waited for their companions and it was probably an indication of their inexperience that they did not, nor did they manage to stay together. They were initially misled by a formation of No 70 Sqn's 1½ Strutters, possibly mistaking them for the rest of their own team, since the squadron had no distinguishing markings at the time. They tagged on to them but, presumably realising their mistake, Griffin and Greenhow in 7780 later gave up and returned to base. Cock and Arnold stuck with it and followed No 70 Sqn around in 7774 for more than three uneventful hours. 2/Lt Griffith and Lt Surgey spotted another formation and went off to investigate them. Unfortunately these aircraft turned out to be German. In the ensuing one-sided fight the observer claimed to have driven one of their assailants down out of control (OOC) before suffering a severe stomach wound himself. A1066 had been quite badly shot up and its petrol tank had been holed but Geralt Griffith succeeded in breaking off the engagement and made an emergency landing near Bryas.

In the meantime the two late starters had taken off but, realising that things had gone awry, the CO signalled to them to land again and succeeded in recalling both of them (the aircraft had no radio so such signals were transmitted visually, in this case by the use of a flare). The major then relaunched the mission using the two recalled crews, Capt Gordon Mountford with 2/Lt Claude Emery in 7775 and Sgt Percy Snowden with 2/Lt William Fullerton in A1061, plus 2/Lts Oliver Wade and William Thuell, now remounted in 7786; this time they were accompanied by Capt Leslie Porter and 2/Lt George Samuels in 7777. They took off at 1015hrs and this time all four managed to keep track of each other. About an hour into the patrol Mountford had problems with a jammed gun; he withdrew 7775 from the formation to return to base leaving the other three crews to continue with the patrol. None of them returned. On only its third day of operations the squadron had had the misfortune to run up against some of the best pilots of Jastas 2 and 4. The victors of the engagement were Hpt Oswald Boelcke, Ltn Erwin Böhme and Ltn Wilhelm Frankl. All three were already established 'Aces' whose final victory scores were to be forty, twenty-four and twenty, respectively. No 45 Sqn's green crews had had little chance against seasoned air fighters of this calibre.

In its first week in France, which had involved just three days of operations, the squadron had had six men killed in action; a seventh had been severely wounded and two others had been injured in a flying accident - yet all that the wing commander seemed able to do was complain! Of the fourteen aeroplanes (including replacements) which had reached Fienvillers thus far, eight were already out of action[6]. Before the day was out another aeroplane had been lost. A1069 had never even reached Fienvillers; flown by 2/Lt L F Jones and Cpl S Betts, it was a latecomer from England which had arrived at Clairmarais on 20th October. Shortly after taking off on its delivery flight to the squadron on the 22nd, its engined failed and the aeroplane was significantly damaged in the ensuing pile up, although its crew emerged unhurt. These substantial losses meant that the squadron was already desperately in need of both aircraft and crews and the situation was to get worse over the next few days.

Lt McArthur and Sgt J A Morton, arrived from Farnborough on the 25th in A1070, the sixteenth and last aeroplane known to have been flown over from England by pilots of No 45 Sqn[7]. But that same day the squadron suffered another fatality. Lt Ernest Glorney had been sent home a few days before to collect a new aeroplane from the manufacturers in Lincoln. He was on his way back to France when his aircraft crashed in Kent and he was killed[8].

By this time the inadequacies of some of his pilots were becoming all too apparent to the CO and in his diary Willie Read described some of them as "cruel bad". He applied to have several sent home for further training and, after some initial resistance from the staff at Wing HQ, 2/Lt Allen, 2/Lt Jones and Sgt Malcolm were posted away between October 24th and 28th, as was one of the air gunners, Pte Chandler; 2/Lt Read followed them three weeks later. Two more pilots who were on Read's short-list, Lts Chamier and Rodwell, were both admitted to hospital on the 27th; neither ever rejoined the unit. Although they are not thought to have been among the CO's marked men, the squadron's strength was further reduced by the loss of 2/Lts Fenwick and

Manuel, both of whom were also in hospital by the end of the month; neither of them ever returned to the fold either. To offset these losses just two replacement pilots had reached the squadron in late October, both being transferred from No 70 Sqn. One of them, 2/Lt H G C Bowden, reported sick within four days of his arrival; he did eventually come back to the squadron but not until the following February.

The squadron probably hit its lowest point on October 27th when the CO recorded that its effective strength stood at just seven pilots (Mountford, Lubbock, Lowe, McArthur, Griffith, Griffin and Bowden - Cock was away on a machine gun course), thirteen observers and seven aeroplanes. The apparent surplus of observers had been created by the arrival of a batch of new faces, most of them on the 26th; they were Lts J Senior and M Moore and 2/Lts T F Northcote, F G Truscott and W G Scotcher. They were joined by another, Sub Lt J Thomson RNVR, on the 28th along with a pair of air gunners, Cpl R C Jenkins and Pte J Gagne. Willing as these men may have been, most will have been more of a liability than an asset at the time and they will have done little to restore the squadron's immediate fighting potential. Several of these new arrivals had reported to No 45 Sqn, quite literally, the day after they had transferred in the field to the RFC. In effect they were soldiers, straight from the trenches; it is doubtful whether many of them had even flown in an aeroplane at this stage. Although the need to provide observers with a more substantial training course was slowly being realised, at this stage of the war they still received scant attention and it was up to their units to prepare them for combat as best they could. Before the new arrivals could be expected to function adequately, they had to be turned into aviators and several were promptly despatched to Camiers to attend a week's machine gun course.

On 28th October the squadron was notified of its unit identity marking which was to be a single band painted around the rear fuselage aft of the roundel, and this was duly applied in white on camouflaged aircraft and in black (or red?) on those with a clear-doped natural linen finish. Shortly after this the Sopwiths' wheel covers began to be painted in flight colours. It is not known exactly when this embellishment was introduced but it was certainly before March 1917 and possibly much earlier; it appeared on both clear-doped and camouflaged aircraft. Photographic evidence shows that the wheel covers of A Flight's aircraft were painted in a dark colour, most probably red, and one picture suggests that A Flight may have applied the fuselage band in red as well. B Flight's wheel covers and fuselage band were in white and the wheels of C Flight's aeroplanes were painted in red and white halves. At least one picture of an A Flight aeroplane indicates that its fin may have been painted in red and it is known that C Flight's 1½ Strutters sported red and white fins. To conform to this pattern, it is possible that B Flight may well have painted the fins of their aeroplanes in white but the author has seen no photographic evidence to support this surmise.

Meanwhile, Willie Read's relationship with the wing commander had become increasingly strained. The crux of the problem lay in their differing priorities. Read's chief concern at this stage was for the welfare and well-being of his men; Dowding was more concerned with achieving the operational task. The chief bone of contention was accommodation. In the absence of adequate domestic facilities and in view of the autumnal conditions, Read permitted his men to use one of the squadron's Bessonneau hangars as a mess. In Dowding's view these were to be reserved for the aeroplanes and the men would have to make do with an RE 7 hangar. Both were made of canvas but the Bessonneaus were far more substantial structures and thus less prone to splitting, and they did not leak (as much). The dispute hinged on which resources should be provided with the best protection - the men or the machines. It came to a head on 31st October when Read noted his most recent confrontation with Dowding (whom he privately referred to as "the Cherub") as follows: "I said what I thought of them (*the men*) pigging it in the tent when they might be in the Bessonneaus and the damned old fool said I was impertinent. I was. I do not know whether I dislike him more than I despise him. There will be a big row one day and the old fool will court martial me for insubordination, and I shall deserve it." Inevitably Dowding's wishes prevailed, but as Willie Read saw it, his efforts to improve the conditions under which his men worked were constantly being blocked or disapproved of and he became increasingly disenchanted with higher authority.

Read's earlier protests had not been without effect, however, and it had already been acknowledged that the camp's accommodation was indeed inadequate. On 24th

When he was shot down on 22nd July 1917 Geoffrey Cock was the last of the original group of aircrew of No 45 Sqn who had crossed over to France in October 1916. With twelve, possibly more, victories to his credit he was easily the most successful 1½ Strutter pilot in the RFC. (J A Brown)

9

A Vickers-built 1½ Strutter, A1083. This aeroplane was flown by No 45 Sqn between 11th December 1916 and 12th May 1917. When this picture was taken the wings, the tailplane and the forward upper decking were in PC 10 but most of the fuselage was clear-doped. The fin is in red and white, indicating ownership by C Flight, and necessitating the repainting of the serial number in contrasting colours. No 45 Sqn's fuselage band identity marking is clearly shown but it is difficult to tell whether it is red or black. (Imperial War Museum)

October all of the wing's NCOs and ORs and the officers of Nos 45 and 70 Sqns had moved into billets in Fienvillers village, the officers of Nos 19 and 27 Sqns being obliged to remain at the aerodrome. Even so the billets found for the men were far from satisfactory and there was still much to be done on camp. After the required amount of nagging six small huts were delivered on the 26th for the unit to erect for use as additional offices and technical accommodation and two days later Sgt Maj Higginbottom (not thought to have been of No 45 Sqn) was despatched with a fistful of francs to locate and purchase two kitchen ranges.

Fienvillers was visited by no less a personage than the King of Montenegro on 31st October. He spent some time with No 45 Sqn and showed considerable interest in its aeroplanes. Willie Read volunteered to take him for a flip but the offer was not taken up, either because of the weather conditions, which were far from ideal, or because the staffs did not want to expose the royal personage to any unnecessary risks

The provision of some half- or untrained observers had gone some way towards restoring the unit's notional strength and a lick of paint and a royal visit had probably done something for morale but these were hardly enough to have transformed the squadron into an effective fighting unit. If it was going to be rebuilt properly a period of in-theatre consolidation training was essential. On 5th November the squadron moved to Boisdinghem, eight miles to the west of St Omer, where, temporarily withdrawn from operations, it was to be permitted to regain its balance. With mechanics occupying their rear cockpits, the eight available aeroplanes which were flown to the squadron's new aerodrome were 7774, 7775, 7780, 7783, 7788, 7790, A1070 and A1071. 2/Lt Cock and Cpl Ward had to have two stabs at the trip as they were obliged to turn back with engine trouble during

their first attempt, bending 7774's axle on landing. Cock did succeed in delivering his aircraft to Boisdinghem later in the day, but not without bending its axle again. A1064, the only other aeroplane which had been on the squadron's charge up to this time, but which has not been accounted for previously, had been wrecked by F/Sgt Webb and 2/Lt Scotcher on 24th October.

While it was at Boisdinghem the squadron was to be temporarily attached to the 11th (Army) Wg, under Lt Col F W Richey, within II Bde - but, so far as Read was concerned, any move away from Dowding was an improvement! The unit still seemed to be dogged by ill-fortune, however, and in the course of the move 2/Lt Birdsall was involved in a motor-cycle accident and sustained a broken leg. His replacement, Lt T M Wheeler, lasted less than six weeks before he too was admitted to hospital to be succeeded by 2/Lt M P Mullery who arrived to fill the post of Assistant Equipment Officer on December 16th, by which time the squadron had moved forward again. Further instability in the support echelon had been caused by the loss of the squadron's one and only Wireless Officer, Lt Wright, who had been transferred to 15th Wg on 30th October, presumably because someone in authority had finally noticed that No 45 Sqn's Sopwiths had no wireless.

Having set up shop at Boisdinghem, a training programme was soon established. This included exercises in formation flying, air-to-ground gunnery, practice combat, map reading, photography and, for the new pilots especially, lots of circuit work to practise the crucial art of landing the delicate and sometimes capricious Sopwiths. This latter activity kept the mechanics busy, straightening a succession of bent undercarriages and rerigging aeroplanes which had been twisted out of true by awkward landings. On November 8th the unit's strength stood at a nominal ten crews (at least, it had ten pilots) and with a new aeroplane, 7793, having been collected by 2/Lt Lowe on the 6th and 7782 restored to use it also had ten aeroplanes. Even this depleted state was to be short-lived, however, for tragedy struck again that day when both Lowe and his observer, 2/Lt Jordan, were killed while attempting a forced landing in 7783 after its engine had failed. The following day the CO and six other crews flew the short distance to St Omer to attend the funeral.

While this intensive training period was under way Sgt Malcolm reappeared. He was given a dual ride on 12th November and then flew solo on the 13th and 14th, all three trips being made in 7788. Both of the solo flights ended when the undercarriage axle was bent and in the second case the propeller was damaged as well. Sgt Malcolm did not fly with the squadron again. At much the same time it appears that the squadron was also trying to make gunners out of some of its own groundcrew. Among those who were given a number of practice flights during November were Cpls Betts, Grimmitt and Lee and 2/AMs Deakin, Hill and Saunders but by the end of the month the attempt seems to have been largely abandoned, although Betts and Grimmitt were still flying the odd patrol as late as January 1917. At much the same time two of the squadron's back-seaters were commissioned. The recently arrived Pte Gagne left, presumably for an appropriate course, on 25th November while Sgt P S Taylor became a subaltern on 15th December, departing for HQ V Bde a week later.

After ten days of the training regime operational sorties began again and missions were flown by formations of up to six aircraft on 15th, 16th, 17th, 21st and 26th November. The Squadron Record Book (Army Form W3343) describes these missions as "reconnaissances" but none of them actually involved crossing the lines and they appear to have been more in the nature of defensive patrols. Nevertheless they were very valuable in that they permitted the crews to accumulate what they were most in need of, experience, and as this increased so did their confidence. Beyond fruitlessly giving chase to some "Huns" over St Omer on the 26th, none of these missions was remarkable apart from being punctuated by the sort of technical difficulties which characterised all flying in that era - chiefly engine failures of varying severity and problems with fuel flow due to loss of pressure in the system, which was provided by air driven pumps, or to blocked fuel lines. Whenever operations were not called for the training programme continued but Willie Read gave himself a day off on the 17th and flew over to Dunkirk to have a look at one of the RNAS' impressive new Sopwith Triplanes.

Despite the change of command to 11th Wg, the CO was still finding the staffs unco-operative. The squadron's accommodation at Boisdinghem was very cramped as a large contingent of Royal Engineers was resident there as well. Read failed to see why it was necessary for the REs to be quartered on an aerodrome at all, especially as their presence was interfering with the operation of his unit. On 17th November he formally requested that the sappers be billeted elsewhere. This request upset the staff and a ten-day wrangle ensued. In the end Read won and the REs moved out, but he had made himself unpopular again and he was now having rows with Richey almost every day.

By this time the staff at II Bde were pressing for the squadron to be moved forward again, but before it did so Read was to cross swords with his superiors yet again, this time with the brigade commander himself, Brig T I Webb-Bowen. With the aim of fostering his unit's corporate identity, the CO had endorsed and encouraged the introduction of a squadron emblem, the head of a ferocious breed of sheep sporting a magnificent set of curly horns. This had been painted on various of the squadron's vehicles, but probably not on its aeroplanes. Webb-Bowen decided to disapprove and ordered Read to have the offending motif removed before the squadron redeployed, this edict arriving on 29th November. Wearily the CO was obliged to obey - *Ovis poli* ('scrub the sheep'), as he wrote ruefully in his journal. It is interesting to note that No 45 Sqn was one of the relatively few RFC units to adopt a badge but once this initiative had been frustrated the emblem appears to have faded rapidly into obscurity. In fact the sheep's head was to return to haunt the squadron briefly some twenty years later, although it is unlikely that anyone serving with the unit in 1936 was aware of it (see page 116).

The squadron made its move on December 4th, this time to what was to become its permanent home, Ste-Marie-Cappel. This aerodrome was a field, about 400 yards square, located some fifteen miles east of St Omer. It was a great improvement on Fienvillers, since it had proper hangars for the aircraft and huts for both technical and domestic accommodation. There was a good deal of metal construction in the aircraft sheds and this made it advisable to swing the aircraft compasses. A captain from wing came over to do this and, having completed the first to his satisfaction, he observed to one of the pilots that it was just as well that his valuable services had been retained because the compass had been 30⁰ in error. "Thank God I never use it!" was all the thanks he got. When Leslie Porter had been shot down on 22nd October Lt A W Keen had been attached from No 70 Sqn to take his place as OC C Flight. This arrangement was formalised on October 31st when he was officially transferred to No 45 Sqn's books as a captain but on 3rd December, just before the squadron moved forward again, Keen was posted back to England. His replacement was Capt W G B Williams who took up his appointment on December 6th. On that same day the squadron flew its first operation over the Ypres Front under the auspices of 11th Wg, to which the squadron was now permanently assigned. Three patrols, involving eleven sorties, were flown that day, all without loss, although two aeroplanes were obliged to put

Lt James Dacres Belgrave joined the squadron on 30th November 1916 and took part in six victorious engagements between February and May 1917 while flying 1½ Strutters with No 45 Sqn. Posted home at the beginning of June he returned to France a year later to join No 60 Sqn with whom he raised his score to eighteen in less than a month before being killed in action on 13th June 1918. The award of the first of his two MCs was officially promulgated on 18th July 1917; it was the first decoration to be formally gazetted to a member of No 45 Sqn. (J A Brown)

down at Abeele with technical problems.

Shortly after its arrival at Ste-Marie-Cappel the squadron's establishment was raised to a full eighteen aircraft and crews. The last four new aeroplanes (7800, A1075, A1076 and A1077) were delivered on 16th December but on that date the squadron still had only sixteen pilots and twelve observers actually available to fly them. Not before time, there was also an intake of additional and replacement pilots to make up the shortfall that had prevailed since late October. These men came from all over the empire, and by the end of December the officers who had recently joined No 45 Sqn's ranks included Capt J E Mackay, a Canadian, Lts J D Belgrave, J D F Keddie and E V C Hamilton and 2/Lts F T Courtney, J A Marshall, J V Lyle and E E Erlebach plus 2/Lts C StG Campbell and F G Garratt from Canada, H E R Fitchat from South Africa and H P Solomon from New Zealand. Once again Maj Read was dismayed at the flying abilities of some of the new arrivals and lamented that he was still getting "dud pilots who aren't fit to wear the pilots' badge and have to be taught to fly when they come to me." Again he made representations to have some of them sent home. In their defence it has to be said that, in view of the cursory

7792 sporting B Flight's white wheel covers and showing the Scarff ring which became the standard mounting for the Lewis gun in the rear cockpit. This aeroplane was taken on charge in November 1916 and survived for over four months, by which time it had become Frank Courtney's personal mount; he called it Little 'Erbert. It was wrecked on April 3rd, following an engine failure shortly after take off; 2/Lt Barker was injured but his observer, 2/Lt Selby, walked away unhurt. (J A Brown)

preparation they had been given, the lack of finesse exhibited by some of the newcomers was hardly their fault. This time none were sent away but it was quite clear that the squadron's in-house training programme would need to be sustained whenever operational tasking permitted.

While the squadron absorbed this influx of new people operations continued, although the winter weather was now a further adverse factor with which it had to contend. A particularly successful reconnaissance mission was flown on December 19th, but there were no plaudits from Wing HQ to counterbalance what Willie Read perceived to be their constant sniping. The following day two more successful reconnaissances were flown by nine aircraft and on Christmas Eve a four-aircraft Defensive Patrol became involved in the first direct engagement with the enemy since the disastrous mission of 22nd October[9]. This time all the aircraft returned, although one was obliged to land at Bailleul. On the 23rd three crews (the CO with Cpl Robert Fleming in A1072, Lawrence McArthur with John Vessey in A2381 and Gordon Mountford with Claude Emery in 7793) flew to St Omer to "test" a Triplane. Some of the pilots were lucky enough to get a quick trip in it and also to sample a Pup and a Nieuport scout. These were the shapes of things to come - but not for No 45 Sqn.

Preparations for the imminent Christmas festivities were complicated by the demolition of several RE 7 hangars by a gale on 23rd December. One of these had been serving as the men's mess and it had already been rigged up with a stage for the squadron party. Nevertheless repairs were made in time and Christmas was celebrated in the traditional fashion with the officers and NCOs ministering to the troops. There was an ample supply of alcohol to lubricate the proceedings and the party was greatly assisted by the squadron's two newly acquired pianos, one of which had been purchased for Fr950, the other being rented for Fr50 per month.

On Boxing Day the squadron had another inconclusive clash with the enemy, even though the crews had given chase with some determination. Wing, however, was outraged when it learned that the patrol had crossed the lines, which the squadron had not yet been authorised to do. Even such small successes seemed to turn sour once the staff learned of

2/Lt Frank Courtney, joined the squadron in December 1916, shortly after it moved to Ste-Marie-Cappel. He was to become OC B Flight for a short time in March/April 1917 which is the approximate date of this picture. Something of a maverick he, like Macmillan, was to become a test pilot after the war. (J A Brown)

them. Since his crews had been in hot pursuit of the enemy at the time, Read reacted very adversely to the colonel's tirade, which had included the threat that if it happened again the offending pilot would be sent back to England forthwith. Read viewed this ultimatum with considerable distaste but was obliged to relay the message to a perplexed Eric Lubbock, the leader of the offending patrol, who promptly composed the following piece of insubordinate doggerel, to which the CO turned a Nelsonian blind eye[10].

A real good bit of straffing fun
Was when we tried to straff the Hun,
But funnier than anything
Was the straffing we got from the Wing.
"We'll send you home", they said to me,
"If you attack the enemy".

They'll send me home! Oh what a threat,
It really makes me whine and fret.
It puts me in a clammy sweat.
I tremble at the damned disgrace.
Don't send me to that awful place!
I'll turn my back on every Hun
And won't let Austin fire his gun.

"Oh love the Boche plane as your friend.
Let all this vulgar brawling end",
I heard our peaceful Colonel shout.
"When nearing Wipers, turn about.
As for this fighting, cut it out
And never put the Hun to rout".

Lt Col Richey was succeeded as OC 11th Wg by Lt Col G B Stopford on December 30th and Read found that he was able to work reasonably well with the new OC. By now the squadron had largely overcome its initial teething troubles and, after a further week's delay before they were cleared to cross the lines - a penance for the infringement of the 26th - regular operations began. In the meantime intensive training continued, as on 2nd January when, in the course of twenty-five flights, the squadron amassed a total of more than twenty-three hours of airborne time. These sorties included practice formation flying, two four-aircraft reconnaissances (flown on the friendly side of the lines), and sundry gunnery and photography trips. Only one pilot experienced any difficulty at all; as luck would have it, it was the CO. Flying alone, Maj Read was forced to land at Poperinghe with an engine snag. This was sorted out over night and with Michael Mullery in the rear cockpit he took off again at first light the next morning and flew A1075 safely back to Ste-Marie-Cappel. Apart from this one minor incident, what was significant about 2nd January was that nobody had broken anything and nothing important had fallen off. Things were definitely starting to look up. The flying of some of its pilots may still have lacked a certain polish but the squadron was finally beginning to turn the corner.

Thereafter, whenever the winter weather permitted missions were flown on most days throughout January 1917, usually in twos and threes but occasionally in formations of as many as eight. Contacts with the enemy were infrequent and inconclusive but life was not without incident - undercarriages were still being damaged at a rate of one or

two per day. At this juncture the squadron was also making a concerted effort to bring its gunners up to scratch, several new faces having joined Cpl Fleming at the turn of the year, including Gnr F A R C Lambert, Bdr A Harrison, 2/AM B G Perrott, 2/AM F J Ridgway and Gnr T Falconer.

On January 23rd the squadron had its first major engagement for three months. It was a busy day all round. The squadron, operating throughout the hours of daylight, launched its first pair at 0730hrs, another at 1000hrs, a formation of four at 1135hrs, two more pairs at 1215hrs and 1410hrs and a final four-ship at 1520hrs. The two four-aircraft missions were the squadron's first attempts at photographic reconnaissance, using an oblique camera, although both were unsuccessful due to weather conditions. In the course of the day Capt Williams and 2/Lt Senior in A1083 claimed one HA OOC and one damaged while Gnr Lambert (piloted by Lt Eric Hamilton in 7774) claimed to

The outer cover of No 45 Sqn's 1916 Christmas dinner menu. It is of particular interest as it includes what is probably the only surviving representation of the short-lived sheep's head motif that might have become the squadron's badge, had it not been suppressed by Brig Webb-Bowen (see Chapter 5). The card was printed in full colour and is a reproduction of a painting by one of the squadron's original observers, 2/Lt N G Arnold. Norman Arnold evidently decided that he had made a mistake in joining the RFC; he applied to cease flying on 16th December 1916 and three weeks later he was permitted to transfer to the 1st Btn of the Royal Fusiliers. (Imperial War Museum)

have damaged another. To offset these successes 2/Lt Thomas Northcote (a New Zealander, flying as observer to 2/Lt Frank Courtney in 7792) was wounded and A1078 failed to return from the final mission of the day, 2/Lt James Lyle and Bdr Alfred Harrison being posted missing. Three days later F/Sgt Webb and Cpl Fleming were lost when A1074 was shot down in flames over Halluin[11].

At about this time Major Read sustained another blow. A regulation was introduced which prohibited all squadron commanders from flying over the lines. The rationale was that, in view of the RFC's appalling loss rate, anyone who had survived long enough to have attained the rank of major represented so much accumulated experience and expertise that he was virtually irreplaceable, and certainly too valuable an asset to be put at risk. While there was an undeniable logic behind this policy it was deeply resented by those, Read among them, who believed that their squadrons should be led from the front, that is, in the air. Increasingly disillusioned and frustrated, Willie Read soldiered on.

Notes.

1. Assistant Equipment Officer was a rather misleading term as it tends to conjure up the impression of a senior storeman. Stores accounting was certainly part of an AEO's duties but he was also the squadron's technical officer. He was therefore required to be familiar with aero-engines, aircraft rigging, MT and so on and was responsible to the CO for the supervision of all maintenance carried out at squadron level.

2. The most recent standing instruction specifying the minimum qualifications for a pilot to be considered fully trained had been published on 23rd March 1916. This required him to have: flown fifteen hours solo; flown a service (as distinct from a training) aeroplane "satisfactorily"; made a cross-country flight of at least sixty miles, making two landings en route, and to have landed twice in the dark with the assistance of flares. The most searching test was that he had also to have climbed to 6,000ft and remained there for at least fifteen minutes before descending to land, with his engine switched off, touching down within a circle of 50 yards diameter. Significantly there was no mention of combat manoeuvring, indeed of manoeuvring of any kind. There were further recommended exercises for those fortunate enough to spend more time in training, but completion of these was not mandatory. In essence, if he could get an aeroplane off the ground, keep it in the air and then land again, with or without power, a pilot was fit to fight.

3. There may be some doubt over some of the details of this saga. When Grimmitt first recounted the tale to Norman Macmillan some years later his recollection was that his initial crash had occurred as the squadron was leaving Sedgeford for France, which would have made the most likely date 10th October. In one of his notebooks, however, Maj Read noted that when the squadron began its move Chamier had already been sent to Farnborough, and he named the pilot who crashed as Oliver Wade. From various notes among Macmillan's papers it appears that he may have subsequently persuaded Grimmitt to acknowledge, albeit reluctantly, that he *might* have been mistaken over the identity of his pilot, ie that it could have been Wade.

This writer believes that Grimmitt's recollection was substantially correct, as much of it can be confirmed from other documentary sources. The only error might be in his dating of the first crash, at Sedgeford; it is possible that this took place just before, rather than as, the squadron was moving to France, since Read noted that it was Wade who crashed as the squadron was leaving. If Wade did crash, however, the damage can have been only slight as he succeeded in reaching Fienvillers a few days later in what was almost certainly his original aeroplane (there would have been no spares at Sedgeford, hence the need to send pilots to Farnborough to collect additional aircraft). Alternatively, Read may have been mistaken and it may well have been Chamier who crashed on or about 10th October; in which case Grimmitt was correct on all counts.

4. These figures have been taken from an entry made in the War Diary of HQ 9th Wg on 15th October, although there is some reason to doubt their accuracy and it is suspected that the information recorded by the wing's scribe may have been what Fienvillers expected to receive rather than the result of an actual head count. For instance, the records of No 1 AD indicate that of the seven aircraft which had reached Clairmarais between the 11th and 13th October, all of which are identified by their serial numbers, five left

for Fienvillers on the 14th, one on the 15th and the last on the 16th (which accords with the information at Fig 1.1); other aircraft not noted by No 1 AD will either not have landed at Clairmarais or will have flown on the same day and thus not been in residence when the daily return was compiled. The astute reader will also have noted that in this Chapter some thirty-three officers are identified by name as having been on the squadron's strength at or about the time that it set up shop in France, rather than the twenty-seven noted by 9th Wg. It is possible that the six 'wild' officers may have been a group of surplus aircrew who were already in France and had been waiting for the next squadron to arrive.

In one of Maj Read's contemporary notebooks he identifies the squadron's officers at the time of its deployment to France. It is not clear exactly when this list was compiled, but it was almost certainly in arrears, so this does not preclude the possibility of a few people having actually joined the squadron *in* France. There is some evidence to support this contention as nine of the thirty-three named officers do not appear in the pre-deployment photograph taken at Sedgeford and reproduced on page 4. Of these nine, two (Chamier and McArthur) are known to have been on the squadron's strength before it left Sedgeford and a third (Glorney) is believed to have been. The remaining six 'original' officers who are missing from the photograph are Bennett, Fullerton, Jordan, N H Read, Rodwell and Samuels and this writer has been unable to find any other reference to them in the admittedly sparse documentation relating to the squadron while it was still in England. It is suspected, therefore, that these six, two pilots and four observers, actually joined the squadron as, rather than before, it arrived in France.

There is some circumstantial evidence to support this conjecture in 9th Wg's daily pilot state returns for 15th and 17th October. The first notes that 1/AM (*sic*) Malcolm was "insufficiently trained" and the second that 2/Lt Read had "not yet flown a Sopwith". The normal procedure was for a pilot to be transferred to another unit working up in the UK if he had not completed his training when his squadron mobilised, since there was obviously little point in taking such people to France. This suggests that Read and Malcolm (and Samuels?) had crossed the Channel earlier, either with another squadron or as replacements and, having become 'spare' for various reasons, were available for posting to No 45 Sqn when it arrived.

5. Later, as Air Marshal Sir Hugh Dowding GCVO KCB CMG, to be AOCinC Fighter Command during the Battle of Britain.

6. The fourteen aircraft which had reached the squadron by 22nd October were 7774, 7775, 7776, 7777, 7778, 7779, 7780, 7782, 7783, 7786, 7788, A1061, A1064 and A1066. Those which were out of action were 7777, 7786 and A1061 (lost in combat), 7778, 7782 and A1066 (damaged in or as a result of combat) and 7776 and 7779 (wrecked in accidents).

7. The thirteen aircraft flown to France by identified pilots of No 45 Sqn were 7774 (Cock), 7775 (Mountford), 7777 (Porter), 7778 (Read), 7780 (Lowe), 7782 (Lubbock), 7783 (Manuel), 7786 (Griffin), 7788 (Griffith), A1064 (Fenwick), A1066 (Wade), A1069 (Jones) and A1070 (McArthur). The pilots of three other aircraft have not been positively identified. There is some circumstantial evidence to connect Glorney with 7776 and Snowden with A1061. If these associations are correct this only leaves 7779 which must have been ferried across by Webb, who is known to have flown to France.

8. The identity and fate of Glorney's companion (there would almost certainly have been someone in the rear cockpit) have not been discovered and the serial number of the aeroplane involved appears not to have been recorded either.

9. The term Defensive Patrol, as used here, was changed to Line Patrol on or about 25th January 1917. As explained in Chapter 2, the tactical significance of both of these labels was that such operations did not involve penetration of enemy airspace.

10. It was fairly common for the RFC In the Field to send back to England those of its members who were deemed to be miscreants, malcontents or misfits, and anyone else who had offended the staff. Needless to say, anyone serving in England who transgressed in such ways was sent to France. It was a classic case of pragmatism masquerading as policy, a peculiar practice to which the military is particularly prone. As Lubbock's poem suggests, such inconsistencies did not escape the notice of the civilians-in-uniform who constituted the bulk of the wartime army.

11. The loss of F/Sgt Walter George Webb was particularly sad as he had been virtually a founder member both of the RFC and of No 45 Sqn. He had transferred to the infant Corps from the Royal Engineers as early as 26th June 1912 and thus had a Service No comprising just three digits, 191. He went to France as a mechanic with No 3 Sqn in August 1914 but the following year entered pilot training, gaining his initial 'wings' in September 1915 and joining No 45 Sqn in April 1916 to undertake his training in Higher Aviation. Completing this course two months later, he remained on strength to become a fully-fledged squadron pilot.

Chapter 2.   1½ Strutters - operational success, but at a cost.

The squadron's routine operations fell into three broad categories: Line Patrols were flown directly over the trenches; Defensive Patrols were mounted some four to five miles behind the German positions and Offensive Patrols operated about eight miles beyond that. Ideally these patrols were flown throughout the hours of daylight by the squadrons of the Army Wings to a co-ordinated pattern, typically at this stage of the war by formations of two to four aircraft at heights of 8,000-10,000 feet. The aim was to provide a permanent defensive umbrella for the observation aircraft of the Corps Wings, which were engaged in co-operation with the artillery and infantry units on the ground, and a defensive barrier to counter the intrusion of German reconnaissance flights. It will be apparent from the above that the RFC's overall concept of operations was essentially aggressive and involved its aircraft being deployed forward into enemy airspace, even on "defensive" operations. The underlying philosophy was to retain the initiative and to carry the fight to the enemy as much and as often as possible. As a result British aircraft were constantly exposed to 'Archie' - German anti-aircraft artillery (AA) - and often directly in the line of fire of friendly guns bombarding German positions. Inevitably the majority of aerial combats took place on the German side of the lines, minimising the chances of a successful recovery to friendly territory in the event of an aircraft being damaged or, and just as likely, suffering a technical failure.

On 23rd February 1917 the squadron's aircraft began to be modified to mount a camera rigged to take vertical photographs through an aperture cut in the underside of the fuselage. From then on patrol work was increasingly supplemented by reconnaissance tasks. Inherently dangerous as combat patrols were, these reconnaissance missions, which often involved relatively deep penetrations of enemy airspace, well beyond the mutual support of other squadrons' patrols, were far more demanding, and costly.

By this time the 1½ Strutter was already becoming seriously outclassed as a combat aircraft. When it had been introduced in mid-1916 (the first ones for the RFC had reached France in May when No 70 Sqn's A Flight had arrived, although it was to be August before the squadron was fully up to strength) it had been the first British aircraft to enter service with a practical interrupter gear for the front gun and was expected to be a great advance on contemporary pusher types. It was of well-proportioned, workmanlike design and as a pure flying machine its handling characteristics were pleasant enough. It was certainly more manoeuvrable than the BE types with which much of the RFC was still equipped, but it lacked the agility to be a really effective dog-fighter. Its major failing, however, was its slow introduction into service, which robbed it of the chance to exploit the technological advance which it undoubtedly represented and prevented it from fulfilling its initial promise. While it might have provided a worthy opponent for the German aircraft which it had been intended to counter, by the time that the second and third units (Nos 45 and 43 Sqns) had become fully operational in France it was early 1917 and aviation technology had moved on. By then the opposition was beginning to deploy the third variant of the highly successful series of Albatros scouts, the D III, colloquially known to the RFC as the 'Vee Strutter'. There were only a dozen or so of these formidable new fighters at the Front in January 1917 but by April there were over 300 of them and the 1½ Strutter had had its day.

The two-seater Sopwith weighed about 2,150 lbs loaded and was powered by a 110 hp Clerget. Each crew member

The flightline at Ste-Marie-Cappel circa March 1917. By this date PC 10 camouflage was becoming increasingly common but, as this picture shows, some of the squadron's 1½ Strutters were still finished in clear dope and on these the squadron's fuselage band marking was applied in some dark colour. The nearest aeroplane has a painted cowling, probably a replacement taken from a camouflaged machine, and the first three aircraft all sport C Flight's red and white wheel covers. (Geo H Williams)

15

On the left of this picture is 2/Lt F H Austin and on the right, Lt J D Belgrave; the two observers in the middle are, unfortunately, unidentified. (J A Brown)

had a single machine gun. By contrast the single-seat Albatros, powered by a 160 hp Mercedes, was slightly smaller dimensionally and weighed some 200 lbs less. Thus the Albatros, being more compact and having nearly 50% more power, was both faster and more manoeuvrable. Equally as important, it could deliver twice the weight of fire from its twin forward-firing machine guns. What the RFC needed for its two-seat Army squadrons was the Bristol Fighter, but it was to be April 1917 before they would become available at all and another three months before they would appear in significant numbers and before the RFC had evolved the appropriate tactics to exploit fully that type's considerable potential.

In the meantime No 45 Sqn had to persevere with its Sopwiths. What might have made a difference was the provision of single-seat escorts, at least to the extent that was feasible, for the RFC's Pups and Nieuports could not match the 1½ Strutter's range and endurance. 'The staffs', however, took the view that, since the Sopwiths were classified as *fighter*-reconnaissance aircraft, they should be able to take care of themselves. The increasing obsolescence of the Sopwiths when compared to the opposition appeared to make no impression on those at Wing and Brigade and they were rarely prepared to authorise escorts, yet they continued to task the squadron with reconnaissances involving deep penetrations of enemy airspace. In their defence it has to be acknowledged that at the time the staffs had little option; there was nothing else available to do the job. Once again Maj Read, who had been vociferously demanding escorts for his crews, found himself at loggerheads with his superiors.

The squadron's crews fought on doggedly, putting their faith in good formation keeping to provide mutual covering fire from the rear cockpits. After some experiment an arrowhead eventually emerged as the most satisfactory arrangement, typically with five aircraft in a vic and a sixth 'in the box'. Whatever formation was adopted, however, if the enemy succeeded in disrupting the group it was every man for himself. The weather in February restricted operations but there was a notable engagement on the 7th when five 1½ Strutters on a photographic mission to Menin at 10,000 feet fought several enemy single-seaters. The final score may have been two-to-one in the squadron's favour, but, since it was not possible to verify the British claims, it may well have been one:nil to the Germans. The following is the text of the

Combat Report (Army Form W3348) submitted by Capt Lubbock (observer 2/Lt Frank Austin, in A1084), who was confirming his early promise as an aggressive air-fighter.

As we were taking the first photograph four machines dived on the machine on our left rear. The machine was piloted by 2/Lt Erlebach with 2/AM Ridgway gunner observer. The Sopwith fell out of control, and the wings folded up. We attacked one of the Germans. Altogether our machine had 6 combats with 4 different enemies but it is hard to say where one fight ended and the next began. After our third fight the pilot's gun jammed. There were then three Sopwiths, one having fallen out and crossed the lines safely. After that there were 4 HA over Menin. The three Sopwiths turned and attacked over Menin. While we were fighting violently with one HA, Lt Belgrave and Sub Lt Thompson attacked him also and he was driven down in a vertical nose-dive South of Lille. After two more combats in which one HA dived vertically and apparently out of control into Menin, the enemy went down. When no more HA were in sight we returned home.

Edward Erlebach was killed following the catastrophic collapse of 7789. Amazingly, Frederick Ridgway survived the aircraft's fall, although he succumbed to his injuries later that day. The GHQ War Diary for 7th February credits the squadron with two OOC. The destruction of 7789 was credited to Ltn Walter von Bülow-Bothkamp of Jasta 18. He was eventually to claim a total of twenty-eight victories, three of them being Sopwiths of No 45 Sqn; he had previously been responsible for the losses of A1078 and A1074 on January 23rd and 26th.

Lubbock, again with Austin in A1084, escorted by Lt Belgrave and Sub Lt Thompson in 7780, had another fight two days later during a photographic mission and the following extract from his Combat Report is illuminating.

....we were then attacked by an HA. He dived on our tail. The observer's gun jammed. The pilot turned rapidly from right to left but was unable to throw off the HA which was very well piloted. We thereupon looped the loop and were able to fire 4 shots at the enemy while doing so. But the HA again got on our tail. The Sopwith looped a second time. All this time the observer was mending his gun with the greatest calmness. During the second loop one half of the Sopwith's tail folded back. The fore and aft controls were thereby rendered almost useless. The machine dived steeply but the pilot was able to flatten out slowly. Luckily the observer had now finished his gun and fired one drum into the HA who turned east and dived for Houthulst Forest.

Although this combat produced no claims it graphically illustrated two of the factors which complicated combat flying in early 1917, the relative fragility of the aircraft themselves and the unreliability of their equipment. Despite the structural failure, Lubbock was able to carry out a forced landing at Chateau Louvie, although A1084 never flew again, at least not with No 45 Sqn. Incidentally, Lubbock and Austin brought back thirty-six exposed photographic plates so the aim of the mission had been achieved.

Poor weather persisted throughout late February and on

into early March. No Combat Reports were submitted to HQ 11th Wg by any of its squadrons between 16th February and 1st March, indeed there was no flying at all between February 19th and 23rd. Nevertheless sorties were flown whenever possible, and further losses were sustained. On 6th March the squadron had a fight with three Siemens-Schuckert D Is, which, since they were copies of the French Nieuport (as flown by No 1 Sqn), were not initially perceived to be hostile. Engine trouble had already obliged Capt Mackay to leave his companions; he was making his way back to base when he was attacked by the apparently friendly aircraft. His aircraft was badly shot about and his observer, 2/Lt Greenhow, was severely wounded. John Mackay managed to put A1072 down successfully at Abeele but Denys Greenhow died shortly afterwards. Meanwhile the SSW D Is had found the remaining two Sopwiths and again succeeded in making an initially unopposed attack from above and behind. Eventually both observers, Sub Lt Thompson and 2/AM Perrott, opened fire and one of the HA broke away, but the other two dived under the Sopwiths and exposed themselves to their front guns whereupon they were fired on by Capt Lubbock and 2/Lt Marshall. One of the HA dived away and was observed to crash in the enemy lines but it was impossible to say who

Despite the tear in the original of this photograph it still reveals several interesting details. The aeroplane is wearing the squadron's fuselage band and this, its fin, and a large and rather elaborate figure 2 all appear to have been painted in the same colour. Since A992 belonged to A Flight it is probable that all of these embellishments were in red, but evidently of a slightly different hue to that used in the roundels (perhaps because they had been applied directly over PC 10 without a neutral base coat). A992 was with No 45 Sqn for only three weeks, making its final flight with the unit on 28th April 1917 when an engine failure precipitated a forced landing near Béthune with 2/Lt Findlay and 2/AM Harries on board. (Geo H Williams)

The life expectancy of an aviator was very short in early 1917. A typical example is provided by this officer, Capt D W Edwards RASC, who joined No 45 Sqn as an observer on 17th February. He and his pilot, 2/Lt C StG Campbell RFC were posted 'missing presumed killed' just six weeks later when they were shot down in A2381 on 6th April. (Geo H Williams)

had shot it down. Curiously the RFC War Diary for that date credits only Mackay (who had made no claim!) with one OOC. Marshall's A1086 was able to make it home to Ste-Marie-Cappel but the engine of Lubbock's A1082 packed up and, in attempting to follow Mackay into Abeele he eventually crash landed just short of the airfield.

Despite his growing expertise, Eric Lubbock was to survive for only four more days. On 11th March, again flying with Sub Lt John Thompson in the repaired A1082, accompanied by 2/Lts Horace Bowden and John Marshall with 2/Lts D B Stevenson and F G Truscott as their respective observers, he set off on a Line Patrol during which Thompson had also been briefed to take some photographs. Shortly after take off Marshall was forced to put down in a field with engine trouble, leaving the other two to carry on as a pair. After an hour on station they were attacked over Ypres by two Albatros D IIIs. The fight was observed from the British trenches and one of the D IIIs was reported to have fallen OOC into the enemy lines but both of No 45 Sqn's Sopwiths were shot down. Lubbock's machine broke up and fell just behind the Allied trenches. Horace Bowden had been shot through the head and the violence of the uncontrolled manoeuvres of his aircraft had caused its wings to fold; the wreckage of A1071 fell into the moat at Ypres. Both observers were seen to fall from their aircraft as they came down. All four bodies were retrieved and buried at Poperinghe on 12th March, alongside Greenhow. John Thompson had exposed five plates which were salvaged from the wreckage of A1082. The mission had been a success....

Six days later, on the 18th, Lt James Belgrave, with 2/Lt Francis Truscott in A2384, shot down an enemy two-seater in flames over Ploegsteert Wood but this was small compensation for the five men who had died in March. In the meantime, on the 12th, Frank Courtney had been promoted to captain to take over Lubbock's B Flight. His reign was but brief, however, as he was transferred to No 70 Sqn at Vert Galand the very next day. B Flight passed into the hands of Capt C H Jenkins who had arrived at Ste-Marie-Cappel on 9th March.

Norman Macmillan was to become a successful combat flier and a respected post-war test pilot and aviation writer but when he first joined No 45 Sqn at the end of March 1917 Willie Read despaired of his ever becoming a competent aviator. This is one of Macmillan's early efforts, possibly A8281 on May 19th. (J A Brown)

It may appear from the foregoing that the squadron's record thus far was hardly one of unrivalled success. It must be stressed, however, that it was par for the course for a new unit arriving in France in the autumn of 1916. Apart from being afforded only a bare minimum of flying hours, trainee aircrew were given virtually no insight into tactics. In any case, at this stage tactical doctrine was still evolving and lacked definition. The older hands who were now serving as instructors in the UK had gained their experience when aerial warfare had been in its infancy. Although the early two-seater observation types, typified by the ubiquitous BE 2-series, were being increasingly supplemented by single-seat scouts, SPADs, Nieuports and Pups, lingering adherence to the very term 'scout' underlined the fact that, in the minds of many of those in the upper strata of the RFC hierarchy, reconnaissance was still perceived to be the primary function of the aeroplane. The veterans of 1915 and 1916 were passing on what they had learned as best they could, but much of it was already out of date and basic flying training was still an amateurish affair. By now, however, it was becoming apparent that there were some basic rules to the art of flying instruction and that the use of proper dual-controlled training aircraft was essential. Once this was recognised the service began to respond but it was to be the summer of 1917 before Smith-Barry's 'Gosport System' of flying training was to be introduced. At much the same time a whole range of specialised operational training schools began to be established to teach specific role-related skills and techniques. Thenceforth things would begin to improve but by that time No 45 Sqn would have been in France for nearly a year and would have won its spurs the hard way.

In fact the squadron had by now overcome its uncertain start and was playing its full part in the air war within the constraints imposed by its aircraft. Natural leaders were beginning to emerge and those who still survived from the early days, notably Cock and Belgrave, were becoming seasoned air fighters, but the problem of inadequately prepared newcomers remained. To the extent that operational tasking permitted, under Read's guidance it continued to be squadron policy to ease, rather than thrust, a new man into combat. He would first be given one or two flights in the local area accompanied by an experienced pilot or observer, as appropriate, to familiarise himself with the local geography and landmarks. New pilots would also be given a couple of solo trips to practice circuit work. For their first few operational sorties it was also the aim to fly a tyro with an old hand before the new men were paired off as crews.

As the air war expanded, statistics were clearly beginning to show that if he could survive his first month of operations a pilot had a reasonable chance of becoming competent, even successful, and that, with luck, he might then even complete a tour of combat duty. One of the fundamental lessons of military aviation was being learned - that there is no substitute for sound and realistic training. Unfortunately, circumstances in 1916-17 simply did not permit an extension of the time devoted to training. The Corps was constantly expanding and the consequent requirement for additional new crews, added to the constant demand for replacements for those lost in combat, overstretched the capacity of the training machine. As General Henderson, the first commander of the RFC In the Field observed paradoxically, "The loss rate is high because training is short, but training is short because the loss rate is so high".

Nearly all of the pilots joining the squadron at about this time were newly trained and, as usual, Read regarded them as a pretty poor lot. On 3rd April he wrote in his diary, "Forbes, Evans, Harriman, Macmillan and Forrest are the absolute edge in rottenness - as pilots". During the next week he applied for several of them be sent back for further training and on 11th 2/Lts C H Harriman and H B Evans did go home. Another of his candidates for repatriation was 2/Lt

N Macmillan. He was allowed to stay, however, and he soon matured to become a skilful fighter pilot and a flight commander. Macmillan remained in the aviation business after the war and went on to pursue a highly successful career as a test pilot, author and war correspondent.

In view of Norman Macmillan's underlying potential one must conclude that Read may have been a trifle intolerant, or at least hasty, in making his judgements. Nevertheless it could be fairly argued that as the CO of an operational unit he was entitled to expect that replacement pilots should display a reasonable degree of competence. The training provided, however, simply did not furnish this. During this period many of the pilots arriving in France had not been taught to loop, to roll, to initiate and recover from a spin, to fly in formation or even to use bank angles of greater than 45°. A typical example is provided by Sgt E A Cook who reported to the squadron on 1st April with a grand total of just 34 hrs and 55 mins flying time in his log book of which only 65 minutes had been on Sopwiths. He had two dual trips with Capt McArthur (OC C Flight since 30th January in succession to Williams) on 10th and 11th and then flew solo sorties on 12th and 13th, damaging his aircraft on both occasions. Thereafter he got the hang of it and went on to become a sound squadron pilot until he was shot down on 5th June. Read's point was that it was not (or at least that it should not have been) the squadron's function to carry out this sort of basic training or to have to accept the consequent significant accident rate, which simply depleted the number of aeroplanes available for operational flying. Needless to say he was even more concerned about the rate at which his crews were being killed in action[1]. His disenchantment deepened.

The CO was not alone in perceiving many of his new crews to be inadequate. Lt Maurice Moore, who had himself joined the squadron as an untrained observer in the previous October was by now a seasoned aviator; he recorded his personal impressions of this situation while studying at the RAF Staff College as a flight lieutenant in 1928. The following observations are extracted from his paper.

A very low standard of flying skill was evident in the pilots arriving to replace casualties during the first five months of 1917. Some had done only ten or fifteen hours solo and did not know how to 'throw their aircraft about'. Officer observers were very scarce and increasing use was made of air gunners. Though some of these were very efficient they were unable to 'mother' fresh pilots in their work as could the experienced observer, and consequently (*they*) were at a disadvantage in a fight. The use of these inexperienced personnel cost us dearly and heavy losses were not without effect on the morale of newcomers. Short of curtailing operations, however, it is difficult to see how it could have been avoided.

The weather continued to interfere with flying from time to time and these interludes permitted the squadron's football team to take to the field on several occasions during March. On the 17th Willie Read had the satisfaction of seeing his squadron beat HQ 11th Wg 3:0, although there were some who found this hardly surprising as OC No 45 Sqn had been the referee. A rematch on the 25th (which Read did *not* referee) settled the matter; this time the squadron beat Wing

Capt Lawrence McArthur, OC C Flight from late January 1917 until his death on 27th May when he and 2/Lt Carey were shot down near Ypres in A8226 by Ltn Ritter Max von Müller. (J A Brown)

by six goals to nil.

The early spring brought improved weather and the 'campaigning season' opened with the Battle of Arras. This was also perhaps the greatest period of ascendancy that the German air force was to enjoy throughout the entire war. To the RFC it came to be known as 'Bloody April'; 316 aircrew were to die in that month alone. April was not to be No 45 Sqn's worst month however; that was yet to come. Nevertheless they did not escape unscathed. Their first combat losses occurred on the 6th. On that day the squadron despatched eight aircraft, two of them carrying cameras, on a long-range mission to photograph Lille, Roubaix and Tournai. A ninth aeroplane took off as an airborne reserve and, when one crew was obliged to turn back with engine problems, 2/Lt J E Blake and Capt W S Brayshay in 7806 duly took their place. Not long after crossing the lines A1077 sustained a near miss from Archie which blew one blade off its propeller. Fighting the terrible vibration which resulted from the consequent imbalance, 2/Lt R M Findlay succeeded in re-crossing the lines and putting the aeroplane down at Steenwerke, flipping it onto its back in the process and ending its flying career; both he and his observer, Lt Moore, were fortunate to escape without serious injury. As the remaining seven aeroplanes proceeded eastwards, enemy aircraft gathered behind them until there were six of them, a two-seater plus two Albatros and three Halberstadt scouts. They attacked from the rear but the British formation held together, repelled the onslaught without loss and forged on. While over the target area the enemy formation was joined by six more Albatros D IIIs. Photography complete, the squadron turned for home and the Germans struck, led by the

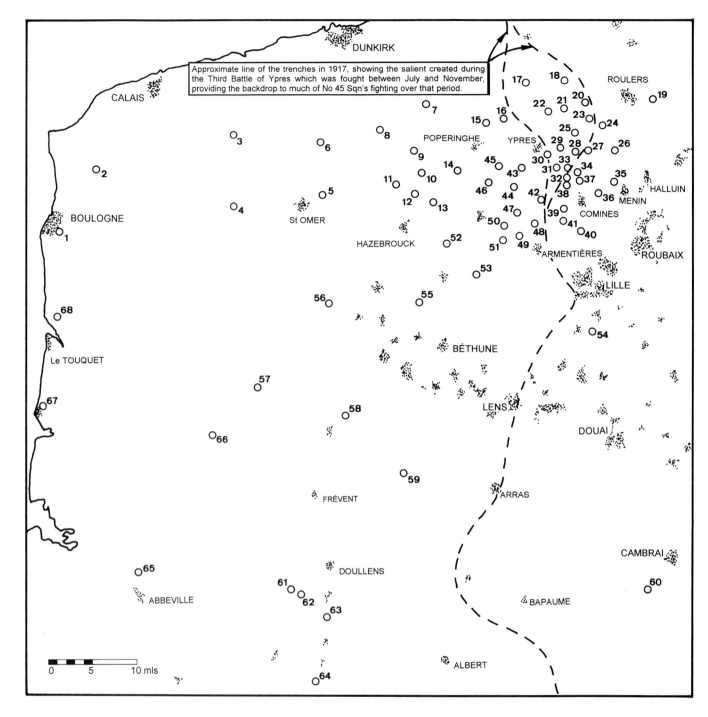

DUNKIRK

Approximate line of the trenches in 1917, showing the salient created during the Third Battle of Ypres which was fought between July and November, providing the backdrop to much of No 45 Sqn's fighting over that period.

CALAIS

ROULERS

○17   ○18
        ○19

○7
        ○22 ○21 ○20
          ○23
○16   ○24
○3   ○6   ○15   ○25
        ○8   POPERINGHE   YPRES   ○29 ○28 ○27 ○26
○2   ○9   ○30 ○33 ○34
        ○14   ○45   ○31 ○37   ○35
○4   ○5   ○11   ○10   ○43   ○32   HALLUIN
        ○12   ○13   ○46   ○44 ○42 ○38 ○36   MENIN
St OMER   ○47   ○39   COMINES
BOULOGNE   ○50   ○41
○1   HAZEBROUCK   ○52   ○51 ○49 ○48 ○40
                ARMENTIÈRES   ROUBAIX

○68   ○53
                LILLE
        ○56   ○55
                ○54
Le TOUQUET   BÉTHUNE

○67   ○57
        ○58   LENS
○66   DOUAI

        ○59
    FRÉVENT   ARRAS

                CAMBRAI
○65   ○60
ABBEVILLE   DOULLENS
    ○61
    ○62   BAPAUME
    ○63

0   5   10 mls   ALBERT
○64

Map 2.1, Northern France and Flanders, showing locations and localities of significance to No 45 Sqn.
Note that this map is also relevant to Chapter 3.

65	Abbeville	43	Dickebusch Lake	60	Marcoing	54	Seclin
14	Abeele	9	Droglandt	2	Marquise	12	St Sylvestre Cappel
3	Audricq	53	Estaires	17	Merckem	11	Ste-Mare-Cappel
27	Becelaere	61	Fienvillers	42	Messines	10	Steenvoorde
29	Bellewerde Lake	66	Hesdin	24	Moorslede	51	Steenwerke
67	Berck-sur-Mer	19	Hooge	47	Neuve-Église	37	Tenbrielen
64	Bertangles	38	Houthem	49	Nieppe	63	Vert Galand
4	Boisdinghem	18	Houthulst Forest	7	Oost Cappel	52	Vieux-Berquin
58	Bryas	33	Kastelhoek	1	Ostrove Camp	39	Warneton
13	Caestre	44	Kemmel	45	Ouderdom	36	Wervicq
68	Camiers	32	Kortewilde	23	Passchendaele	46	Westouter
62	Candas	50	La Crèche	48	Ploegsteert Wood	20	Westroosebeke
5	Clairmarais	22	Langemarck	21	Poelcappelle	16	Woesten
15	Coppernollehoek	59	Le Hameau	28	Polygon Wood	8	Wormhoudt
35	Coucou	56	Liettres	40	Quesnoy	34	Zandvoorde
26	Dadizeele	57	Maisoncelle	31	Railway Wood	30	Zillebeke
41	Deulemont	6	Marckeghem	55	Robecq	25	Zonnebeke

six D IIIs. The reserve aeroplane, 7806, was the first to fall, to the guns of the commander of Jasta 30, Oblt Hans Bethge; James Blake and William Brayshay were both killed. The rest of the formation clung together while their leader, Capt McArthur, manoeuvred it as best he could to disrupt the repeated attacks. 2/Lt Cock's Combat Report (which is quoted verbatim) gives his perception of the rest of the engagement as he saw it from A1075:

> The first hostile machine came up on the right of the formation, flew along at the side and slightly in front, firing at about 300 yards range; he then crossed well in front of the formation, and I got a burst of about 70 rounds from the front gun. Then the other hostile machines came up behind the formation and attacked the rear and middle machines of the formation. The two middle machines were attacked from below, and both went down completely wrecked. The attacking hostile machine then flew up and turned and 2/Lt Murison fired 50 rounds into him at about 30 yards range. He fell to pieces and went down on top of our two wrecked machines. Every hostile machine <u>completely outmanoeuvred</u> us and were capable of beating us, climbing, turning and speed. At the end of the combat, there were two hostile machines left which then flew off.

The underlining is Cock's and was, presumably, yet another attempt to drive home to the staff the inadequacy of the 1½ Strutter as a combat machine. The two aeroplanes which he had seen go down (some reports indicated that they had first collided) were A1093 (2/Lts John Marshall and Francis Truscott) and A2381 (2/Lt Colin Campbell and Capt Donald Edwards); both were credited to Ltn Joachim von Bertrab of Jasta 30. The four aeroplanes remaining from the original formation of eight fought their way home without further loss and landed with their photographs. Six men and four aeroplanes was a high price to have paid for just eleven exposed plates, but the staff still declined to provide escorts, or even to co-ordinate scout patrols to provide some form of protection for outbound and inbound missions.

In the meantime Frank Courtney had returned to the fold to resume command of B Flight on March 19th, his stay with No 70 Sqn having lasted less than a week. It seems that he had been too outspoken in his criticism of the 1½ Strutter for the staff of the GHQ-controlled 9th Wg and it was evidently decided that he would be less of an embarrassment back in 11th Wg. They could move Courtney about but they could not keep him quiet and he spoke his mind again on 6th April when the Brigade Commander, Brig Webb-Bowen, was visiting Ste-Marie-Cappel. The general made some remark which appeared to imply that the squadron's aircrew might not have been fighting hard enough; OC B Flight took exception to this - and said so (although accounts differ as to whether his objection was voiced *sotto voce* or as a direct protest). In either case, since the unit had had six men killed in combat on that day alone, something like a 17% loss rate, the point was well made. The general did not pursue the matter any further at the time but it may have been no coincidence that three weeks later Courtney was on his way back to England.

2/Lt J T G Murison was given the credit for having destroyed the HA which went down on the 6th April mission and 2/AM Perrott, gunner to Lt P T Newling, for having driven another down OOC. These would prove to be the only victories claimed by the squadron during April, although they engaged the enemy on several more occasions. But that day's losses were not the only casualties. On the 3rd 2/Lt G B Barker had been injured in a forced landing in 7792 following an engine failure immediately after take-off, and on the last day of the month 2/Lt Wright was forced to land A1080 near Lillers due to battle damage; his gunner, Burnaby Perrott, had sustained a bullet wound to the head and was already dead. In between times 7774, 7762 and A992 had all been damaged as a result of the forced landings which were almost routine, although none of their crews had sustained injury.

As if things were not already bad enough in April 1917, industrial disputes at home were holding up the supply of replacement aircraft. No 46 Sqn, which had moved to France at about the same time as No 45 Sqn, had been unfortunate enough to have been mounted on the Nieuport 20, a French two-seater, similar in concept to the 1½ Strutter, but of an earlier and even less combat-worthy design. Since No 46 Sqn was now re-equipping with Pups, there was a surplus of Nieuports available and they were issued to No 45 Sqn as stop-gaps. They proved to be at least 20 mph slower than the Sopwiths and quite incapable of keeping station with them in a climb. Their control responses were leaden and they displayed an apparently inherent tail heaviness when fully loaded. Describing his personal impression of the Nieuport, Norman Macmillan wrote that it had "little power of manoeuvrability, except in a spin, into which it fell with astonishing agility." The inferior performance and poor manoeuvrability of the Nieuports would have made them a liability in mixed formations with the 1½ Strutters and their general inadequacy would have made it virtually suicidal to have attempted significant penetrations of enemy airspace with Nieuports alone.

The first of these practically useless aeroplanes arrived on 13th April when Capts McArthur and Mountford fetched A6731 and A6742 from St Omer. Strong winds interfered with flying on the 14th and 15th but training sorties began on the 16th and over the next few days four more Nieuports were acquired; Mountford collected A6736 on the 19th and Maj Read, Capt Courtney and 2/Lt Cock brought in A6735, A6741 and A6740, respectively, on the 20th. The CO allocated two to each flight where their use was initially restricted to training sorties. This was the Nieuports' greatest value to the squadron as they could be used for flying

One of the seven Nieuports issued to No 45 Sqn, A6740 sports a dark (red?) fuselage band and C Flight's red and white wheel covers. (Geo H Williams)

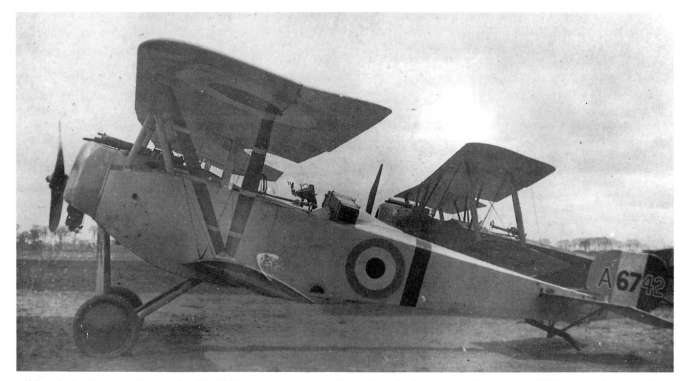

Although the Nieuport 20s issued to No 45 Sqn as stopgaps were flown for only three weeks, they acquired full unit markings as shown by this one, A6742, which displays both the squadron's marking of a fuselage band (in red) and A Flight's red wheel covers. The unsatisfactory Nieuports were initially confined to training sorties but A6742 is fully rigged for operations with a forward-firing Vickers gun, a Scarff ring and Lewis gun in the rear cockpit and a camera mounted on the rear fuselage decking to permit oblique photography. (J A Brown)

practice by newly arrived pilots which meant that the Sopwiths could be preserved for combat missions and spared some of the unfair wear and tear that the half-trained newcomers tended to inflict on their mounts during their first few flights. Among the new pilots who flew these aeroplanes during April were 2/Lts W A Wright, H Forrest, G M Robertson and N Macmillan; recently arrived observers and gunners who sampled the Nieuport included 2/Lts C G Stewart and E T Caulfield-Kelly and 2/AM W Pocock. Another of this latest batch of pilots, 2/Lt J H Forbes, did his best to torpedo the unpopular Nieuports, albeit unintentionally, by damaging A6736 on 21st April but Willie Read collected A6732 as a replacement the next day. On the 26th John Forbes bent that one too and, for his pains, the CO had him sent home for further training.

When they were eventually committed to operations the Nieuports were confined to Line Patrols and oblique photography, ie taking pictures of the German trenches from a reasonably safe distance. The first such sorties were flown on April 23rd and thereafter, so far as can be ascertained, they continued to fly one or two missions per day, usually operating as pairs. Since the squadron's records for this period are incomplete, it is not possible to be precise but the Nieuports certainly flew at least twenty-one operational sorties, of which three were photographic tasks - the actual total could well have been twice this figure as the missing pages cover half of the period during which the Nieuports were being used operationally[2]. It was with some relief that the squadron began to receive replacement Sopwiths again at the beginning of May and on the 6th the five surviving Nieuports were ferried back to St Omer; their passing was not regretted.

There were two other significant events during April, a

Above: Another of the interim Nieuports, C Flight's A6731. (Imperial War Museum). Below: Capt Mountford collected A Flight's Nieuport A6736 from St Omer on April 19th. Two days later Lt Forbes broke it. (Geo H Williams)

change of address and a change of command. It had been decided to move No 20 Sqn into Ste-Marie-Cappel and, perhaps because they were the senior unit, they were to have the better accommodation. No 45 Sqn was obliged to move to the far side of the airfield and operate under canvas. They duly set about erecting tents, marquees, four Bessonneau

The arrival of No 20 Sqn's big FE 2bs at Ste-Marie-Cappel on 14th April 1917 displaced No 45 Sqn who were obliged to erect a tented camp on the other side of the aerodrome. From the lack of foliage on the trees it looks as if it was still pretty chilly for living under canvas. The large banner is the rarely illustrated RFC flag - see Footnote 3. (J A Brown)

hangars and a few pre-fabricated huts and laying down timber dispersals for the aeroplanes. On 14th April the squadron took up residence in 'tent city'. The following day No 20 Sqn's ground echelon motored in, their FE 2bs arriving the next day. The resentment that might have been caused by No 45 Sqn's having been obliged to move did not materialise and the two units quickly established a mutual respect and friendly relations which were to last until No 45 Sqn moved to Italy at the end of the year.

Willie Read had hoped that having a fighter squadron on the same aerodrome might make it possible to arrange escorts and on the 16th six of No 20 Sqns 'Fees' were detailed to accompany six of No 45 Sqn's two-seaters on a mission but the weather intervened and the operation was cancelled. This single example of a co-ordinated mission did not indicate any far-reaching change of policy, however, and thereafter the two squadrons rarely if ever flew together.

The change of command was a very low-key affair. Maj Read had become deeply disillusioned by his later experience of service in the RFC and was saddened by the heavy losses which he felt powerless to prevent, partly because he was denied the right to lead his men personally and partly because of the constant resistance to his pressure for escorts. Having by now completed a year as a squadron commander, six months of it on active service in France, he requested that he be permitted to return to his own regiment. The Corps was not accustomed to receiving what amounted to a resignation from a squadron commander and Read's request created something of a stir. His release was eventually agreed to, however, and on 24th April he relinquished command to his successor, returning to the Dragoons, who were then located in the Albert/Péronne sector[4].

In the few days granted them for a handover the old and new COs conferred in private for long periods; then Read quietly withdrew and left without ceremony. In the event Willie Read stayed with the cavalry for only four months before returning to the RFC. He went on to have a successful career in Trenchard's Independent Force as CO of No 216 Sqn, flying HP 0/400s in France. After a short post-war break he rejoined the unit, moved it to Egypt and

From the left, 2/Lts Arthur Selby, Allan Carey, Geoffrey Cock, John Vessey and Robert Bennie at the tented site at Ste-Marie-Cappel circa April 1917. (G Muir)

remained in command until it had converted to DH 10s. He eventually retired in 1932 as Wg Cdr W M Read MC DFC AFC**.

The new CO was Maj H A Van Ryneveld MC, a South African, who had accumulated extensive operational experience flying with the RFC in Palestine and Salonika and on Home Defence duties in the UK. He too was barred from flying with his men but, since this was by now accepted as the norm, he was accustomed to this constraint and thus better able to work within it. He had some constructive ideas about

the best formations to adopt and made a point of personally briefing missions whenever possible. Thereafter he would frequently take an aircraft up himself, ostensibly to 'check the weather' or to 'inspect a patrol' in flight, but actually hoping that he would find a stray enemy aeroplane. As to escorts, Van Ryneveld fully recognised the need for them but he also accepted that he was no more likely to succeed in getting them authorised than Read had been and he declined to adopt Read's rather truculent attitude towards higher authority. He preferred to try working around the staffs, rather than confronting them, and endeavoured to co-ordinate operations at unit level, informally arranging for No 1 Sqn's Nieuports to provide cover if they happened to be about when his Sopwiths were operating. Tasking was such, however, that this sort of dovetailing was not often achieved in practice. Life went on much as before. In fact, on the few occasions that escorts were provided they proved to be a disappointment, as Lt Maurice Moore later recalled:

> During this period (*ie May, June and July*) we encountered strenuous opposition, and casualties were very heavy. The use of single aircraft and aircraft in pairs, in order to evade attention, only succeeded once or twice. We tried every sort of formation up to nine aircraft, and we several times tried escorts of scouts. These proved no real help; their presence - provided they arrived at the rendezvous and did not subsequently become detached in the AA fire - certainly gave a pleasing moral support at the outset, but when the enemy attack came they were either too high to be able to intercept or so low as to be unable to take the offensive; and in the latter case we had to defend them. On the whole we found that an unescorted formation of six aircraft, in the form of a closed triangle, with the rear middle aircraft somewhat below those on its right and left, worked best, though engine trouble and enemy action rarely allowed us to maintain those numbers.

Perhaps the most significant legacy left by Read was the squadron-based training which he had introduced. This was now paying off and the earlier wholesale destruction of undercarriages was down to, a perhaps irreducible, rate of about one per week. When an aircraft was damaged,

whether by accident, through a technical defect or in combat, the squadron workshops were generally able to repair it. The unit's own tradesmen were perfectly capable of changing engines, patching or replacing holed fuel tanks, rebuilding undercarriages, mending torn fabric and re-rigging distorted airframes but they lacked the capacity to do this wholesale. When a wrecked aircraft had to be salvaged from a remote site, when the squadron already had a backlog of repair work or if a repair was likely to take longer than 36 hours, a damaged aircraft would be passed to No 1 Aircraft Repair Section (ARS), an element of No 1 AD, for their attention at St Omer.

In this context an examination of Annex L is instructive. The squadron flew the 1½ Strutter in France for ten and a half months. Including the seven Nieuports, at least 147 aeroplanes have been positively identified as having served with the squadron during that time. Even allowing for a few serviceable aircraft being returned when the unit was eventually re-equipped that would still indicate an average rate of consumption of approaching fourteen aircraft a month, nearly one every two days. It is also interesting to note the recurrence of some names in the listing at Annex L. For example, in June alone: 2/Lt R S Bennie crashed A8222 taking off on the 2nd, collapsed the undercarriage of A991 landing the following day and was forced to land A8269 off the aerodrome on the 5th; Lt W R Winterbottom broke A8788 on the 7th and A8307 on the 9th; and 2/Lt M P Lewis crashed A8278 on the 21st and A8790 four days later. In all these instances the aeroplanes were sufficiently badly damaged to require the attention of No 1 AD's workshops and they never returned to the squadron. In most cases these incidents occurred in the first few flights made after a new pilot had arrived and before he had mastered the Sopwith. Willie Read used to complain that his pilots "broke aeroplanes faster than they could be built"; in truth, however, it is doubtful whether any pilot managed to complete his time on the 1½ Strutter without experiencing some sort of incident although those occurring later in a career were more often due to a technical failure or combat damage, than to mishandling.

Up to the end of April the squadron's casualties had amounted to twenty-four missing or killed in combat with a further two accidental deaths and five wounded. Statistically this represented just about the entire squadron strength in six months. The return for this carnage had been just two confirmed victories, on 18th March and 6th April. The tide

A8225 was taken on charge by No 45 Sqn on 6th May but was wrecked on the 12th by 2/Lts Wright and Caulfield-Kelly. When this picture was taken the aeroplane had yet to acquire its white fuselage band but it already wears C Flight's colours on its wheel covers. (J A Brown)

of success turned just as Read was leaving and he missed gaining the satisfaction of seeing his efforts bear fruit. With a steady improvement in flying weather May was to be a hectic first month for the new CO, Combat Reports being submitted on fourteen days, but the final balance would clearly demonstrate that No 45 Sqn had now matured into a significant fighting force, and this with one hand figuratively tied behind its back owing to the limited combat potential of its 1½ Strutters.

In all some nineteen aeroplanes would be written off in one way or another during May, mostly through the usual run of accidents. On the other hand, the squadron would destroy twelve German aircraft for certain and claim a further fifteen driven down OOC: The cost in aircrew was three missing, five wounded, two of whom subsequently died, and three POWs, one of whom was also wounded. During the month 2/Lt Cock (on the 20th) and Lt Belgrave (on the 24th) were both to score their fifth victories (including claims made by their gunners) and thus became the first of the squadron's eventual, and quite remarkable, total of thirty-two 'Ace' pilots[5]. After claiming one more OOC, James Belgrave left the squadron on 1st June and, after a period with a Home Defence squadron in the UK, returned to France as a flight commander with No 60 Sqn. Before being shot down himself on 13th June 1918, he was to claim another twelve victories on SE 5as and gain a bar to the MC which he had earned while flying with No 45 Sqn.

There was a remarkable incident on May 7th. On that day 2/Lt Forrest and Gnr Lambert were flying alone over the lines in A1075 when they were attracted towards a British AA barrage directed at a pair of German aircraft. Being unable to gain the last few feet of altitude necessary to bring his front gun to bear, Forrest passed about 200 feet beneath the intruders to permit his gunner to fire upwards. Quite reasonably, he had anticipated that the AA Battery would hold their fire when the friendly aircraft appeared on the scene. But they did not. The Sopwith was hit by two shells. Fortunately they were not impact-fused so neither exploded but the first damaged the aircraft's tailplane and the second passed right through the rear fuselage, severing all the control lines to the tail surfaces and leaving the pilot with only the ailerons with which to attempt to control the aircraft. The

stricken aeroplane dived, accelerated than pulled up into first one spontaneous loop (the first that either man had ever experienced) and then another. In the course of the second of these involuntary gyrations, four spare ammunition drums for Lambert's Lewis gun slid into the rear fuselage and became lodged there. This redistribution of weight went some way towards balancing the aeroplane and thenceforth it confined itself to a succession of self-induced climbs, stalls and dives. It had already lost about 2,000 feet during the loops and it fell another 7,000 feet in the series of zooms and stalls. With no means of influencing longitudinal stability the crew could only cling on to something and wait. In the event the aeroplane hit the ground towards the end of one of its dive recoveries; its wheels tangled with a fence and it flipped over onto its back. The crew survived and were physically unharmed but they were deeply shocked by their nightmarish experience. Frederick Lambert was transferred to ground duties within the squadron, as an armourer, and Harry Forrest was repatriated for a lengthy period of recuperation. As it happened, the few rounds which Lambert had managed to get off had done their work and one of the HA was seen to fall OOC although its eventual fate could not be confirmed.

The first major engagement in May took place on the evening of the 9th. Six aircraft on an Offensive Patrol led by Capt McArthur and Lt Senior in A8226 were engaged by about a dozen Albatros single-seaters near Menin. Lawrence McArthur's machine was badly damaged; the observer was wounded, although he maintained his defensive fire until his pilot was able to escape and put the aircraft down at Bailleul. Joseph Senior died of his injuries shortly after being admitted to hospital. The squadron's second loss was 7803, flown by Lt W L Mills and 2/AM J W Loughlin. Since both were relatively new arrivals, it was quite early for them to have been flying together and, if further evidence were needed, the speed with which they were shot down served only to reinforce Read's policy of not committing new crews to combat without first providing them with one or two supervised sorties to permit them to acclimatise. Mills was posted missing (in fact he died within hours of the crash) but Loughlin was thrown clear on impact and survived to became a POW. It is probable that their aeroplane had been the twenty-sixth victory of Ltn Karl Schäfer, the CO of Jasta 28.

Taken on or about 10th May 1917, a panoramic view of Ste-Marie-Cappel aerodrome, framed by the canvas of C Flight's hangar. From the left, the aeroplanes are A8750, A8226 and A991. (J A Brown)

On the credit side Geoffrey Cock and John Murison in A8260 continued to build their scores, claiming one HA each, the pilot's victim going down in flames while the wings of the observer's were seen to fold, although Murison was obliged to share the credit for this one with 2/Lt Wright and Lt Caulfield-Kelly in A8225. To round off the day's balance sheet 2/Lt J Johnstone and 2/AM T M Harries in A963 claimed one HA OOC (although it was almost certainly destroyed) and Lt A E Charlwood and Lt A S Selby in A991 drove down two others, although they made no specific claims. The squadron had fought this engagement at odds of two to one against and had emerged the victors. There were more defeats to come, but the squadron was now demonstrably holding its own. It had come of age.

On 12th May No 45 Sqn put up nine aircraft and an airborne reserve for an Offensive Patrol. The spare aircraft and two others were obliged to turn back, leaving six to carry out the mission. There were several inconclusive clashes but in the one engagement which did develop one HA was driven down in a spin which was later confirmed by a ground observation from 109 Coy RE as having crashed in flames. Three crews might have been responsible for this victory, since all had recorded firing on and hitting an HA, although none made a specific claim. In the event it was formally credited to the all-Canadian crew of 2/Lt R S Watt and Lt G W Blaiklock in A8173.

May 12th also brought another victory for James Johnstone and Thomas Harries, in A963, although this is not always credited to them in surviving records. On that date a two-seater Albatros C V had been forced to land, more or less intact, on the British side of the lines, the pilot, Ltn Haubolt, having been mortally wounded. Its demise had been claimed by a British AA battery which had fired on the aircraft. The following day, however, two reports from the trenches stated that the aircraft had been seen to fall after being fired on by a British two-seater. Furthermore the surviving observer, Ltn Mohr, reported that Haubolt had been killed by a machine gun bullet and not by AA fire and this was subsequently confirmed. Van Ryneveld concluded that this victory rightly belonged to one of his crews. He personally submitted a post-dated Combat Report on behalf of his men, initialled by Johnstone, describing what had at the time appeared to have been an inconclusive engagement

which had not warranted formal comment, and claiming the victory.

The next major engagement was on 20th May and involved, after one had fallen out, a six aircraft Offensive Patrol which became embroiled in a fight with some fifteen Albatros and Halberstadt scouts. It was another success for No 45 Sqn and also produced a remarkable feat of airmanship. 2/Lt Cock in A8226, flying this time with 2/Lt Allan Carey, claimed one OOC and Sgt Ernest Cook with Lt George Blaiklock in A8268 each claimed one destroyed, a Halberstadt and an Albatros. A third confirmed kill was achieved by 2/Lt D C Eglington, observer to Capt Jenkins (who had been reinstated as OC B Flight when Frank Courtney left on 30th April) in A8246. However, Jenkins had been hit during the engagement and he subsequently fainted. Eglington climbed out of his cockpit and standing precariously on the oil-slick lower wing, clinging with one hand to one of the centre-section struts, he leaned into the pilot's cockpit, seized the control column and succeeded in pulling off a successful crash landing near Neuve Église. Dudley Eglington, previously wounded twice during his time in the trenches, was awarded the MC for this exploit. Sadly, Christopher Jenkins' wounds proved to have been mortal and he died three days later. Geoffrey Cock now became OC B Flight in the rank of temporary captain, which automatically accompanied the appointment, this being confirmed in the London Gazette of 26th June[6].

Four days later the squadron emerged victorious again. Lt Edward Caulfield-Kelly, observer to 2/Lt William Wright in A8269, shot down one HA in flames and claimed another OOC. Lt Newling with Lt W E Holland in A1095 and Lt Belgrave with 2/Lt Stewart in A8223 shared in the latter claim and on a later sortie Capt Gordon Mountford and 2/Lt John Vessey claimed two more. The day's balance sheet stood at four victories in all, one of them definitely confirmed, and no losses, although Charles Stewart had been wounded as had Frank Austin when A8279, piloted by Cock, had been hit by AA fire. A crew was lost the following day, however, when A963 failed to return; 2/Lt James Johnstone had been wounded and both he and his observer 2/Lt Thomas Millar (who had been with the squadron for just one week) were taken prisoner.

The squadron added to its growing game bag on May

27th but this time there was a higher price to pay. In one engagement Cock and Caulfield-Kelly in A1016 claimed one OOC and James Belgrave (with 2/Lt G A H Davies in A8280) another. Later in the day 2/Lt Fitchat in A1099 (observer 2/Lt R Hayes) shot down one HA for certain and Capt Mountford in A8299 (observer 2/Lt Vessey) and 2/AM H V Shaw in A8268 (pilot Sgt Cook) each claimed one OOC. Another five victories, but two more of the dwindling band of veterans who had been with the squadron since 1916 had been lost; Capt Lawrence McArthur and 2/Lt Allan Carey, were posted missing in A8226; a German aeroplane later dropped a message confirming their deaths near Ypres[7]. Their aeroplane had been the thirteenth (of an eventual thirty-six) victory of Ltn Max Ritter von Müller of Jasta 28. Command of McArthur's C Flight passed to Capt A N Benge who arrived to fill the appointment on 3rd June, although he stayed for only three weeks before being posted back to England.

Two more confirmed kills, both flamers, occurred on 28th May. Both fell to the guns of observers: Lt Caulfield-Kelly, who was wounded, in A8269 (pilot 2/Lt Wright) and 2/Lt W G Corner in A1095 (pilot Capt Cock). On the last day of the month there was one more fight. 2/Lt Vessey in A8299 (pilot Capt Mountford) claimed one OOC and 2/Lt Findlay and Lt Blaiklock in A8295 claimed another, although neither of these claims appears to have been substantiated.

An examination of the results of the squadron's most recent combats (see Annex E) reveals that an interesting pattern was beginning to develop. If equal credit is given to both crew members in those cases where it cannot be readily apportioned between them, and accepting the double-accounting which inevitably arises from such shared victories, it becomes clear that more of the twenty-eight HA claimed during May had probably fallen to the guns of observers than to those of pilots. There were a possible twenty-one claims by observers as against seventeen by pilots. The explanation for this lay largely in the combat constraints imposed by the 1½ Strutter. An initial display of aggression at the beginning of an engagement might give a pilot the opportunity to open fire, although doing this almost certainly meant abandoning the principal aim of the mission, usually the taking of photographs. Taking such an initiative would also involve breaking formation, never a wise move, and in all probability the more nimble German scouts would quickly evade and outmanoeuvre their attackers. Once the roles had been reversed, or from the outset if the formation stuck together as briefed, it would be the defensive fire from the rear cockpits of the Sopwiths which would inflict the most damage. In the majority of engagements the initiative lay with the enemy and, unless they attacked from head on, the Sopwith's relative lack of manoeuvrability would make it difficult for a pilot to bring his gun to bear. This appreciation of the tactical situation is substantiated by another passage extracted from Maurice Moore's 1928 Staff College paper:

A compact formation, good leadership, and good shooting from the observer's cockpit were our surety against the enemy and, save in dog fights, alterations in height and course of a slow nature only were the only tactics open to us.......The nature of our work and the superior performance of the enemy aircraft precluded the front gun from being of much effect in fighting. A single

On 20th May 1917 the pilot of A8246 was wounded and incapacitated but, by climbing out onto the wing in order to gain access to the controls, the observer succeeded in landing the aircraft for which feat he was awarded an MC. Sadly the pilot, Capt Christopher Hutchinson Jenkins (Sussex Regt), seen on the left in this picture, died three days later. His observer, Lt Dudley Charles Eglington (Black Watch) is on the right. The third figure is Capt William Allan Wright RFC who joined the squadron on 10th April and survived for over six months before leaving for England on 24th October. By that time he was OC B Flight and had eight victories to his credit. (Geo H Williams)

Lewis on a Scarff mounting was the rear armament. The vane sights we had on these guns were designed for a speed of 100 mph. The Sopwith 2-seater in formation flew at 75-80 mph, so some skill was required in allowing for this. The tracer bullet, so often condemned as being of no use in aiming, I found very useful for aiming at close ranges, provided you used both eyes when sighting; at anything but short ranges it was of course unreliable......Given good marksmanship, the effectiveness of back seat gunnery depended almost entirely on the amount of trust reposed in the gunner by the pilot. Good pilots, with efficient observers in the back seat, manoeuvred their aircraft in flight as the observer directed; but with air gunners behind them pilots were, perhaps not unnaturally, inclined to act without reference to the back seat. It was generally agreed that more casualties were due to unskilled piloting than to failure on the part of the back gunner; the commonest fault of the inexperienced pilot was to dive steeply away from his attacker on a straight course, rendering his gunner powerless to use his gun. As an assistance to intercommunication between pilot and observer in flight the mirror fitted on the centre-section in front of the pilot was most useful.

It is worth noting here that subtle differences were becoming apparent among the replacement observers who were arriving on the squadron in mid-1917. A substantial proportion of them were still coming from the trenches but, rather than simply being posted to an operational squadron to

Previously wounded twice while serving in the trenches with the King's Shropshire Light Infantry, Lt J C B Firth had just 35 flying hours in his log book when he reported to No 45 Sqn on 3rd May 1917. After an uncertain start he was to serve with the squadron for just under a year and would return to the UK as Capt John Firth MC, a flight commander with twelve victories to his credit. (J A Brown)

find their feet as best they could, they were now being sent back to England first to do a four-week course at Hythe. An element of flying had been added to the gunnery course by this time; Lt T A Metheral, for instance, had already spent eight hours in the air before he reported to Ste-Marie-Cappel in May. Over the next few months this figure slowly crept up and by August new observers were turning up with as many as thirteen flying hours recorded in their log books. It was not much, but it was infinitely more than some of the first wave of replacements had had in late 1916. The increasingly valuable contribution that its back-seaters were now making to the squadron's success in combat was in large measure a result of this steady improvement in both the quality and the quantity of the training that they were being given. This was also true of air gunners but, as Maurice Moore's previously quoted observation suggests, some pilots may have been reluctant to recognise and take advantage of the increasing expertise being displayed by these non-commissioned personnel[8].

The pattern of observers' guns accounting for more victories than those of pilots that emerged in May was sustained throughout June and July. In August, as the Sopwith's relative inferiority became even more marked, the rear gun became absolutely critical and the squadron's entire bag for that month was chiefly attributable to its observer/gunners. However, it appears to be in the nature of things that credit tends to accrue to pilots so the names of

Like many of the barely proficient pilots sent to France in 1917, Lt Firth bent a few 1½ Strutters before he mastered the art of flying them. This is one of three that he damaged during May, his first month on the squadron; it is either A991, A2385 or A8260. (J A Brown)

few of the men who occupied the rear cockpits are known to posterity, even though the squadron's observers actually inflicted more damage on the enemy than its pilots did. Two observers, Lt George Blaiklock, a Canadian, and Sgt Thomas Harries, who had respectively five and six victories to their personal credit, technically gained the status of being Aces in their own right. The lack of recognition afforded to observers was reflected in the distribution of honours and awards. Despite their vital contribution, none of No 45 Sqn's observers was decorated for his efforts, apart from the two who were given awards for specific individual feats so remarkable that they could hardly be ignored. It is possible that this is a syndrome which may be familiar to many 'back-seaters' of later generations - although it is also possible that this observation may simply be due to the writer's allowing his prejudices to corrupt his objectivity! The fact is that during the two-seater period the squadron's pilots gained precious little formal recognition either.

June was a less busy month. Many missions were flown, many of them being to photograph the German rear areas opposite the British 2nd Army, but combats occurred on only four days; each time the squadron came off worst as the odds against them grew due to the increasing tendency of the Germans to operate in large formations. Compared to the previous month losses were to be much heavier and successes fewer. In fact, with a total of twenty-one casualties of all kinds sustained, seventeen of them fatalities, June 1917 was to take the place of 'Bloody April' in the annals of No 45 Sqn - this monthly loss rate was never to be exceeded throughout the squadron's subsequent history[9]. These losses were only partly offset by a total of eleven claimed victories of which at least seven, including the two confirmed kills, were attributable to observer/gunners. The score was opened on the evening of June 3rd in a fight with possibly as many as twenty-five HA. Cpl Harries (gunner to 2/Lt Watt in A8244) shot down one HA and 2/Lt Hayes (observer to 2/Lt Fitchat in A1093) drove another down OOC. 2/Lts E D Haller and F H Foster were posted missing in A8272 - yet another very new crew; neither of them had been with the squadron for much more than a fortnight.

June 5th was a particularly bloody day for the squadron. In a fight over Menin with some eighteen Albatros scouts, the leader of which was painted red, the squadron lost 2/Lt B Smith and 2/AM S Thompson in A8280, 2/Lt Bennie and Lt Metheral (another Canadian) in A1925, and Sgt Cook and AM Shaw in A8268. The last two aircraft went down in flames and the only survivor from all three was Bernard Smith who became a POW. In addition, Lt Philip Newling and 2/Lt Wilfred Corner were both wounded and obliged to force land A8293 at Westouter while Lt J C B Firth had to put A8291 down at St-Sylvestre-Cappel with a holed fuel tank. Finally, 2/Lt M B Frew damaged A8279 on landing back at base. Only two aircraft had survived unscathed. On the credit side 2/Lt Macmillan's observer, 2/Lt P F H Webb, claimed one HA OOC while 2/Lt Frew had driven one down himself while his back-seater, 2/Lt M J Dalton, had despatched another in flames. These were the first claims submitted by Matthew 'Bunty' Frew who had joined the squadron on 28th April; he was eventually to become the squadron's top-scorer. Claims against No 45 Sqn that day were credited to Ltn Karl Allmenröder, Ltn Otto Brauneck and Ltn Alfred Niederhoff, all of the élite Jasta 11; by that date these three pilots had already jointly accounted for thirty-eight victories. A fourth claim, his first, was allowed to Ltn Richard Runge of Jasta 18; he was to run up against No 45 Sqn again.

There was another fight on 7th June in which no claims were made but during which 2/Lts A E J Dobson and G A H Davies were lost in A8296. The last engagement of the month, on 16th, took place near Comines and resulted in five HA being claimed OOC but at a cost of two more crews. 2/Lt T StG Caulfield and Rfn G Edwards went down in A381. This aircraft was the tenth victim of Oblt Eduard Ritter von Dostler, the recently appointed CO of Jasta 6. The second crew, Capt I G Elias and Rfn P C Hammond, had both been wounded and the pilot was forced to land A1019 at Blawre Port Farm; Percy Hammond died shortly afterwards. This crew had been with the squadron for only ten days. Vzfw Kurt Wusthoff of Jasta 4 claimed a Sopwith that day as the first of his twenty-seven victories; it was probably A1019.

In wartime it is perhaps even more distressing to lose people through accidents than in combat and the squadron experienced just such a grievous loss on 12th June. Capt Mountford and 2/Lt Vessey were returning to base from a trip to St Omer in A8299 when they collided with A8244 in which 2/Lt Watt and 2/AM Pocock had just taken off as part of the escort to a six-aircraft reconnaissance mission. Both aircraft were destroyed and all four men died. With the loss of Gordon Mountford and John Vessey, Geoffrey Cock was now the sole survivor of the original No 45 Sqn air echelon which had deployed to France in the previous October; he was to last for another five weeks. There was one other fatality during June when Rfn Edward Sharp died in action on the 27th but, beyond the fact that he was killed by machine gun fire from the ground, the circumstances are obscure, since no details of the incident appear to have survived. To take Mountford's place, 2/Lt Robert Findlay was made up to captain to become the second OC A Flight.

It is perhaps worth noting here that in mid-June the term 'EA', standing for Enemy Aircraft, superseded the previous 'HA', perhaps because the earlier initials had come to be widely understood to stand for Hun, rather than Hostile,

2/Lt Matthew Brown Frew joined No 45 Sqn in April 1917 and made his first claims, an Albatros D III destroyed and another OOC, on June 5th; by the time he left the squadron in the following February he would have participated in the shooting down of twenty-three more enemy aeroplanes, making him the squadron's most successful pilot. This outstanding combat record won him a DSO and two MCs. (J A Brown)

Aircraft and the authorities wished to discourage this practice. It was at about this time that some excitement was occasioned by an attack on the airfield. A lone German aeroplane had been seen flying over at a considerable height under fire from British AA guns. Shortly afterwards a projectile landed on the airfield and buried itself in the ground but failed to detonate. With some trepidation the missile was very gingerly unearthed. It turned out to be not the anticipated German bomb but an unexploded British shell!

During June the squadron had been completely re-equipped with new aircraft powered by 130hp Clergets. The extra 20hp conferred a slight improvement in the aircraft's altitude performance but, since the squadron continued to be tasked at the same heights as before, little practical advantage was gained from the notional upgrade. By this time, however, No 70 Sqn had already begun to re-equip with Camels and the 1½ Strutter was destined to soldier on with Nos 43 and 45 Sqns for only another two months. Despite the limitations of their aeroplanes, July was to be the squadron's most successful month while operating the type. Twenty-eight claims were made, seven of which were confirmed as kills. This success was tempered, however, by further substantial losses, thirteen men killed or missing, another wounded and two more becoming POWs.

Aerial activity intensified considerably during July as the Anglo-French armies prepared to launch another offensive. No 45 Sqn clashed with the enemy on numerous occasions.

The claims which resulted are listed at Annex E but particularly significant events are highlighted here. The month's first casualty was L/Cpl Fred Russell who died of wounds sustained in action on the 2nd but details of the incident are lacking and it is not known which aeroplane he had been flying in or who his pilot had been. A few days later, on the 7th, Capt A T Harris, who had been transferred from No 70 Sqn on 18th June to command C Flight, opened his score with one OOC near Comines and claimed another over Kortewilde on the 12th. Cpl Harries also had a good day on the 7th when, flying with Sgt R A Yeomans in A8292, he claimed one EA in flames and two OOC on a single sortie. These were to be the last of Thomas Harries' six personal victories (it is not possible to say to what extent a seventh, shared, claim on May 12th had been attributable to his gun). He was posted home on 16th July and after being commissioned and retrained as a pilot he would shoot down one more aircraft and win a DFC while flying SE 5As with No 24 Sqn. The successes of July 7th were offset by the loss of two more crews on that same day. Lt Frederick Snyder, a Canadian, having survived a crash the previous day (in A1023 flown by Lt R Musgrave), was posted missing with his Australian pilot, Lt Thomas Hewson, when A1029 failed to return. The second missing aeroplane was A8281, flown by 2/Lt John Gleed and Lt John Fotheringham. Of these four men, only Fotheringham had been with the squadron for more than a month.

Among the several losses in July was Geoffrey Cock, the last and most successful of the originals. He increased his score on the 6th, 7th and 13th before, flying with Lt Moore on the 22nd, he fought his last combat. As it happened both the Brigade and Squadron Commanders had gone forward to the trenches that day to observe the mission which had initially involved eleven Sopwiths, although this had reduced to eight by the time that the engagement began. In his book *Into the Blue*, Norman Macmillan describes this fight as it was recounted to him by Cock himself some years later.

About 30 Huns attacked and the leader's first burst of fire put his, Cock's, engine out of action. After one shot by his observer, Moore's Lewis gun jammed and he could not get it going again because he had let the spring tension down and had forgotten to bring a spare. Five Huns continued to shoot at them all the way down from 15,000 feet and Cock had the luck to set one on fire with

For a 1½ Strutter A1095 was a relatively long-lived aeroplane, serving with No 45 Sqn from February to June 1917. It was eventually returned to No 1 AD as being unfit for further operational flying. Judging from the rather tatty paintwork, this photograph was probably taken quite late in the aeroplane's career. (J M Bruce/G S Leslie)

his front gun after his engine had stopped, a marvellous feat which he said Webb-Bowen and Van Ryneveld confirmed. The propeller must have stopped where the cam allowed the gun to fire freely. Cock was soaked in petrol from his riddled tank and has never known why his B2576 did not catch fire. Possibly the dead engine saved them from this fate. The left side of the rudder-bar was smashed by a bullet that might have been explosive and part of this bullet penetrated his ankle (and was later extracted with a penknife).

Lt Moore's Staff College paper of 1928 includes another post-dated, but first-hand, account of this engagement which differs in detail from Cock's. Having first commented on the growing German practice of concentrating their fighters in large numbers and then operating them in separate, but co-ordinated, groups he went on....

...our formation of six (*sic*) aircraft was engaged by four formations of eight or nine each just as we got to our photographic beat, about fifteen miles over (*the lines*), beyond the Menin-Roulers road. One formation led off on our left rear from slightly below; next came a dive by lot No 2 from our right rear and above, followed immediately by lots No 3 and 4, one from above on the left, the other from the right and on the same level as ourselves. The whole attack, I regret to say, was excellently timed, and the two aircraft on each side of us (the leading aircraft) went down in flames at once. Our engine was put out of commission; shortly afterwards my foresight was broken, the top being shot off, and I got a jamb in the cartridge guide spring which I could not succeed in getting clear before we crashed gently into a shell-hole just on the wrong side of the lines.

Apart from Cock's lucky shot, two other claims were made during this engagement. Lt George Blaiklock, flying as observer to Lt E F Crossland, gained his sixth and last personal victory with one OOC and Lt Firth scored his third, although his observer, 2/Lt James Hartley, whose gun had actually been responsible for the OOC which they had claimed ten days earlier, was killed during the fight. Contrary to Moore's recollection, only one other aeroplane had actually been lost, 2/Lts R H Deakin and R Hayes going down in flames in A1032.

Although both Geoffrey Cock and Maurice Moore survived to become POWs their combat careers were over, for this war at least. Cock's record had been quite outstanding. In his log book he had indicated that he personally calculated his overall tally to have been nineteen, of which he regarded fifteen as having been 'confirmed', nine falling to his front gun and six to those of his various observers. Using the more conventional yardsticks of Combat Reports and communiqués his overall score is more realistically considered to have been twelve, including the one that he took down with him on the 22nd July. Regardless of which figure one accepts, the inescapable conclusion is that Geoffrey Cock was far and away the most successful exponent of the 1½ Strutter in the entire RFC. The loss of B2576 was credited to Oblt Wilhelm Reinhard of Jasta 11; it was the first of his eventual total of twenty victories. With the loss of Cock, Alexander Charlwood was promoted to succeed to the command of B Flight.

The squadron was to sustain several more casualties before the month was out. 2/Lt H N Curtis and Sgt W S Wickham were posted missing in A1020 on July 25th and A1031 failed to return on the 28th, taking with it Lt G H Walker and 2/Lt B G Beatty. As was so often the case all four men were relatively new and inexperienced, George Walker, for instance, had arrived six weeks before with just 30 hours of solo flying under his belt and Benjamin Beatty, a Dubliner, had been with the squadron for only four days before being shot down. There was another casualty on the 28th. After it had been badly shot about, Sgt Robert Yeomans managed to get A8766 down at Bailleul; he was not seriously injured himself (although he never flew with the squadron again) but his gunner, Dvr William Fellows, had been mortally wounded and he died the next day. Despite the constant losses, however, the squadron was still having its successes and, having added to his score with a flamer destroyed by his observer, 2/Lt G A Brooke, on the 16th, 2/Lt Frew achieved another confirmed kill, which fell to his own gun, on the 28th bringing his overall score to five and making him the squadron's third Ace pilot.

The squadron's days as a two-seater outfit were now numbered. Its first Camel, B3755, was collected from No 70 Sqn by Maj Van Ryneveld on 24th July and he and Arthur Harris ferried in the next two, B3871 and B3971, from No 1 AD on the 27th. But even as they were being replaced the 1½ Strutters kept on fighting and August was not without incident.

On 31st July the British Second and Fifth Armies opened the Third Battle of Ypres. This was eventually to create a salient five miles deep and eight miles wide, but it would not succeed in breaking through the German line. The fighting cost more than half a million casualties, went on for over three months and finally ended when the Canadians took what remained of Passchendaele. This bloodbath provided the backdrop for No 45 Sqn's operations for the rest of its time in France.

Despite its now thoroughly outmoded equipment, before the squadron finally dispensed with their services its dwindling band of observers claimed a remarkable eleven victories in August (five of them confirmed kills, two in flames). By comparison with the recent loss rate the price paid was relatively light. 2/Lt E J Brown was killed and his observer 2/Lt L Cann wounded when they made a forced landing in A8771 at Poperinghe on 17th and 2/Lts C M Ross and J O Fowler were posted missing in A8298 two days later. A8298 had been part of a six-aircraft patrol and was seen by other participants to rear up violently and shed its wings. There had been no 'Archie' at the time and it seems highly probable that the aircraft had been struck by an artillery shell, but whether outbound or inbound it was impossible to say. Charles Ross and John Fowler were the squadron's last fatalities on 1½ Strutters but six more men were wounded during August. They were: 2/Lts J W Mullen (in A1056) and A E Peel, a South African, (in A1004) on the 10th; 2/Lt P F H Webb in A1044 on the 13th; 2/Lt J C Lowenstein, another South African, and Lt A J F Bawden in A1064 on the 15th and Pte W Whittington in B2560 on the 16th. Of these all except Lowenstein were observers.

A number of squadrons can tell tales of observers who climbed out on the wing to save their aeroplanes but on No

Seen here after leaving No 45 Sqn, Willie Read's successor was Maj Pierre Van Ryneveld MC. He commanded the unit from April 1917 until his narrow escape from death on 18th August while flying B3871, one of the squadron's first Camels. (J A Brown)

45 Sqn this was done twice, Dudley Eglington's exploit in May having been the first; it happened again in August. The second incident occurred following an engagement between two Sopwiths and a pair of Albatros scouts near Deulemont on August 11th. The following extract is taken from the Combat Report submitted by the CO:

....while passing under a gap in the clouds 2 Albatros Scouts dived at them from above the clouds firing continuously. Cpl Jex (Observer to Lt McMaking) shot down one enemy scout, which burst into flames at 2,000 feet from the ground, and crashed on the canal immediately to the left (sic) of Deulemont. The second enemy scout attacked Capt Pender's machine from the side, and one bullet passed through both main petrol tanks and wounded Capt Pender seriously in the back. Pioneer Smith (Capt Pender's Observer) got in a full double drum at the enemy scout from very close quarters. The enemy scout crashed 4 fields to the left (sic) of the first machine. Capt Pender then fainted and his machine got into a spin. As Pioneer Smith could not make him hear he climbed over the side and forward along the plane to the pilot's cockpit, and found the stick wedged between Capt Pender's legs. He pulled Capt Pender back, and pushed the stick forward. The machine came out of the spin and Capt Pender almost immediately recovered. Capt Pender then brought the machine (down) and landed his Observer safely near Poperinghe. Members of the 16th Divisional Ammunition Column, where Capt Pender came down, saw Pioneer Smith standing on the side of the machine and heard him encouraging Capt Pender saying "Pull her up Sir", as they were about to crash into some hop poles Capt Pender did pull her up and landed on the other side with very little damage.

Ian Pender had joined the squadron only a fortnight before this incident occurred and it is a mute comment on the pressure under which the RFC was working at that time that he had a grand total of just 26 flying hours recorded in his log book when he presented himself at Ste-Marie-Cappel as an operational pilot. Previously wounded twice while serving with the Seaforth Highlanders, he had, thanks to his gunner, survived a third time. Van Ryneveld immediately cited Pnr William Smith for a Distinguished Conduct Medal (he already wore the ribbon of the MM for earlier actions in the trenches) which was formally gazetted on October 22nd.

As August drew to a close the Camels began increasingly to eclipse the old two-seaters as the new fighters began to make their first operational sorties. The last 1½ Strutter claims were made on the 23rd and the final photographic mission was flown on 30th by 2/Lt H M Moody and Lt Blaiklock in B2596 and Lt R L Clegg and 2/Lt R S V Morris in B2583. They were escorted by a pair of Camels, B3917 and B3775, flown by 2/Lt R J Dawes and Lt A O MacNiven, but the mission was uneventful and it was eventually abandoned due to low cloud.

In view of the progressive re-equipment programme, no replacement observers had joined the squadron for some time and, in addition to the crop of casualties that had occurred during August, Lt A S Selby had been posted back to England on the 11th. When the last three 1½ Strutters (A1051, A1053 and B2596) were ferried away on September 1st only a dozen back-seaters remained on the effective strength. That same day seven of them, Lts C T R Ward and G A Brooke along with 2/Lts V R S White, R C Purvis, T W McLean, R S V Morris and H Dandy, were posted across the aerodrome to join No 20 Sqn. With them went a number of the squadron's specialist ground tradesmen, including its entire Photographic Section. When he was discharged from hospital after recovering from the wound he had received on 13th August, they were joined by 2/Lt Paul Webb. At the same time three more observers, Lt G W Blaiklock and 2/Lts

L M Copeland and M J Dalton, went back to England to be followed by the recently-promoted Sgt A Jex a few weeks later. That left Capt J W Higgins as the last man in. James Higgins elected to give up flying and to stay with the squadron as its third Recording Officer in succession to Lt W E G Bryant, who had held the appointment since 2nd November 1916 but who had now joined the exodus to No 20 Sqn. By this time the incumbents of the other two established non-flying posts were 2/Lt W T H Hocking, who had taken over as the squadron's Assistant Equipment Officer early in March, and Lt M A H Fell, who had become its (first?) Armament Officer in May.

It is difficult to assess the squadron's overall performance while flying 1½ Strutters, since any such assessment must consider the unit's combat record and the relationship between claims and victory scores is a notoriously contentious topic. The author's interpretation of the squadron's 'score' is presented at Annex E. This amounts to a total of eighty-four claims of which twenty-eight were kills. No 43 Sqn, which had moved to France at much the same time as No 45 Sqn, is normally considered to have destroyed about half that number. No 70 Sqn, which had flown 1½ Strutters for by far the longest period, some fifteen months, all of which had been spent operating under the aegis of the GHQ Wing, destroyed about half of No 43 Sqn's total. Such comparisons are, of course, misleading, since different forms of tasking and operations over different sectors were bound to produce differing opportunities. Nevertheless, in absolute terms No 45 Sqn clearly inflicted more damage on the enemy during its two-seater phase than did either of its contemporaries. The cost had been terrible. A total of sixty-four men had been killed in action or in flying accidents, had

An informal group of two-seater crews photographed at Ste-Marie-Cappel in July 1917. From the left, they are: Capt A T Harris, Capt V R S White MC (obs), 2/Lt A S Selby (obs), Capt W T Wood, Capt J W Higgins (obs) with 'Peter', Lt C A Barber and Lt G H Walker. (J A Brown)

died of wounds or had been posted missing; a further nineteen had been wounded and six more (two of them wounded) were to spend up to eighteen months in captivity. This amounted to the loss of the squadron's entire fighting strength nearly three times over in less than a year.

What recognition had there been for this considerable achievement and sacrifice? Just two MCs awarded to Belgrave and Cock in June (gazetted in July) and the previously noted MC and DCM won by Lt Eglington and Pnr Smith. No 45 Sqn was on the threshold of becoming a single-seat fighter squadron, however, and the associated glamour would ensure that, henceforth, it would attract its fair share of decorations.

Notes:

1. In this context it is informative to consider what happened to the thirty-five aircrew (thirty of them officers) who had been with the squadron when it first arrived at Fienvillers in October 1916, although the process was not yet complete as the last of the 'originals' served with the squadron until as late as July 1917. Five were rejected and sent away for further training or returned to their units; four were struck off strength on admission to hospital (sick); two returned to the army at their own request; one observer was transferred to Home Establishment, ie the UK, to train as a pilot and one pilot was posted back to England where he was subsequently killed in a flying accident. The remaining twenty-two men all became casualties: one was taken prisoner; four were wounded in action, five were killed in flying accidents and twelve were posted killed or missing in action.

2. Most regrettably, as a result of a spate of thefts in the late 1980s, numerous enclosures were stolen from many of the files held by the Public Record Office. No 45 Sqn's WW I documents were among those which attracted the attention of one or more thieves and although some of the papers have been recovered (and there has been a prosecution) some pages of the Squadron Record Book and of the Daily State Book are still missing as are a number of Combat Reports. If any reader knows the whereabouts of any of these missing documents he is urged to contact the PRO or the author.

3. The familiar RAF Ensign, which was introduced in December 1920, was preceded by an RFC flag but the precise origins of the latter remain obscure. In 1961 Peter Hering stated in his *Customs and Traditions of the Royal Air Force* that in 1947 research at the War Office revealed "....that orders issued to the British Army in the field on 1st July 1917 authorised the use of a Royal Flying Corps Headquarters flag, and that this was flown only on the RFC Commander's car. It was light blue, edged with dark blue, and had a red stripe running lengthways across the centre and the letters 'RFC' in dark blue." It is quite clear from this description and the photograph on page 23 that this flag was being flown by No 45 Sqn at Ste-Marie-Cappel well in advance of the date on which it was endorsed as a decoration for a general's motor car; the lack of foliage on the trees suggests that the picture was probably taken in April, when the tented camp was first set up.

4. The way in which Willie Read's effective rank fluctuated in mid-1917 provides a classic example of the practical approach that was taken to such matters in wartime. Having relinquished command of No 45 Sqn, as a temporary major, Read returned to the Dragoons as a temporary captain. When he gave up flying he had done so partly in the expectation that an offensive was about to be launched, enabling him to gain first hand experience of a contemporary cavalry action. In this ambition he was to be disappointed, however, and after a few months of entirely static warfare he itched to fly again. Not surprisingly, his application was coldly rejected at first, but after he had succeeded in buttonholing General Higgins, to whom he addressed a personal appeal, Read was grudgingly accepted back into the fold on the understanding that he would return as a lieutenant. This offer was gratefully accepted and Willie Read went back to England to rejoin the RFC's game of snakes and ladders.

5. Despite its having no official standing, the term 'Ace' (denoting the victor of five or more air engagements) gained considerable currency during WW I and it has remained in use ever since. For the remainder of this narrative it is used without the inverted commas.

6. As Footnote 4 suggests, it is sometimes difficult to keep track of the ranks of some of the squadron's officers during WW I. In 1917 some of its pilots were directly recruited members of the RFC but others, and most of its observers, were attached from other arms of the service, with one or two having originated within the RN. A few of the transferees were substantive lieutenants, or even captains, but the majority of the squadron's aircrew were temporary second lieutenants, often at first, in the case of those who had only recently been commissioned, with the proviso 'on probation'. Regardless of rank, the employment standard of a squadron pilot was that of a Flying Officer (not a *rank* until August 1919), but he could be upgraded to become a Flight Commander, which carried with it (while actually filling an appropriate appointment) virtually automatic promotion to the rank of temporary captain, or temporary major on being advanced to Squadron Commander grade. Such changes in status were usually authorised in the field with immediate effect, formal endorsement (generally backdated) following several weeks later in the London Gazette.

This pattern was replete with anomalies; for instance, while a Flight Commander was always a captain (usually a temporary one), a captaincy did not automatically confer Flight Commander status. To illustrate this point, a 'real' captain, recently transferred to the RFC (like John Mackay), would be a relative novice as an aviator and his position within the squadron's parochial hierarchy would be below that of an established Flight Commander who, although wearing the insignia of a (temporary) captain, might in reality be a mere subaltern (like Geoffrey Cock); both of them would, of course, be subordinate to their CO who was a major only in the eyes of the RFC (as far as the Dragoons were concerned, Willie Read was still only a lieutenant).

This problem was less acute during WW II, as the RAF had by then established its own system which removed the complication of residual regimental ranks. Even so the complexities of backdated seniority can sometimes make it difficult to be precise about a person's rank in 1939-45 and this is especially true of those who joined the squadron as sergeants and advanced all the way to flight lieutenant before leaving the unit. In most cases, of course, as in 1914-18, these ranks were effective only for the duration of the war and most of the officers who remained in uniform in the post-war era shed several ranks; some even forfeiting their wartime commissions.

Throughout the whole of this narrative the aim has been to reflect each individual's contemporary effective rank, ie that in which he was actually serving and the insignia of which he was most likely to be wearing. (*I readily acknowledge the possibility that I may not have got it right in every case, all of the time! - CGJ*).

7. The immaculate replica of a Sopwith 1½ Strutter currently (1995) displayed in the RAF Museum at Hendon is marked as A8226 of No 45 Sqn.

8. In view of the significantly enhanced training that air gunners were now receiving, in June 1917 2/Lt W T Douglas of the Aerial Gunners Office in Lympne proposed that they should be permitted to wear an appropriate badge; a further letter followed containing a selection of suggested designs. The various gunnery emblems were all rejected but it was agreed that from 12th July 1917 qualified air gunners would be entitled to wear the observers' flying badge. The minimum qualifications were completion of the one-month course at the Aerial Gunnery School at Hythe and participation in eight operational sorties overseas.

9. No 45 Sqn was actually to suffer similar losses in May 1941 and, since all seventeen of those who died that month were lost as a result of combat, this could be regarded as the squadron's blackest month in absolute terms. On the other hand, since the Blenheim was a three-seater, the squadron was rather larger in 1941 so this loss involved a smaller proportion of its total manpower. The casualties sustained in June 1917 represented 58% of the squadron's established fighting strength at that time and, proportionally, this was certainly the squadron's worst ever monthly casualty rate.

Chapter 3. Camels in France and Italy then into limbo.

As more Camels became available more pilots began to convert to the new aeroplanes. There was no training course such as today's pilots would expect. Just, "Get in and have a go", with perhaps a warning about the extremely responsive controls compared to those of the old two-seater. As a precaution, Van Ryneveld wisely insisted that before flying the Camel each pilot had to fly over the aerodrome in a 1½ Strutter and demonstrate to him personally his ability to enter and recover from a spin.

The Camel was undoubtedly a bit of a handful and in *Into the Blue* Norman Macmillan provides a graphic account of his own hazardous initiation into the exhilarating handling characteristics of this feisty little fighter. He describes a twenty-five turn spin in which only 2,500 feet were lost and which left him so disorientated that he lost another 400 feet in a form of skewed, side-slipped 'level' flight while he tried to re-establish a more familiar relationship with the horizon. On an early formation practice on 12th August he learned another lesson. Conditioned to relatively sluggish control responses, in attempting to follow his leader into a dive he followed his previous practice on the 1½ Strutter of thrusting the stick hard forward and trimming nose down. The Camel responded instantly and bunted so violently that Macmillan's seat belt broke and he was thrown clean out of the cockpit, finishing up on top of the cowling clinging to the business ends of the twin Vickers guns. As Macmillan had parted company with the stick, the g forces eased and he was able to scramble back into the cockpit, although not without

damaging some of its fixtures and fittings, and recover the situation. He returned to Ste-Marie-Cappel a much wiser man and was very lucky to have survived to become an older one as well.

Although the order prohibiting COs from crossing the lines was still extant there was nothing to say that they could not engage in combat on their own side and on four occasions during August Maj Van Ryneveld attempted to intercept German two-seaters which had penetrated Allied airspace. The last time was on the 18th and it nearly cost him his life. The CO had taken-off in B3871 and climbed to engage a high flying EA. This time it began to look as though he might succeed in engaging the enemy but, as the range closed, the intruder's gunner opened fire first and the major took four bullets in the chest, a fifth grazing his head. Despite the loss of blood he was able to remain conscious and land his machine intact at Bailleul where he dismounted before collapsing. He was taken to hospital and was fortunate to make a full recovery. In time he was to command 11th Wg and he ended the war a full colonel at twenty-seven years of age. In 1920 he and Major Quintin Brand, both of them South Africans, undertook a trail-blazing epic flight back to their native land for which both were to be knighted. No 45 Sqn's second CO went on to become the founding father of, and the driving force behind, the South African Air Force, finally retiring in 1949 as General Sir Pierre (Helperus Andrias) Van Ryneveld KBE CB DSO MC, Chief of the General Staff of the Union Defence Forces.

B2321/5 in a shell hole at 'Clapham Junction' near Zillebeke after a forced landing by 2/Lt George Bush on September 26th. The use of individual aircraft identification numbers was short-lived and they were soon replaced by letters. (J A Brown)

Meanwhile, back in France the senior flight commander, Arthur Harris, took over the squadron pending the appointment of a new CO.

The next CO arrived on 22nd August and assumed command two days later. Maj Awdry 'Bunny' Vaucour had been flying since 1915, first as an observer with No 10 Sqn and then as a two-seater pilot with No 70 Sqn. He had won an MC during each of these tours. Since January 1917 he had commanded B Squadron of the Central Flying School at Upavon where a number of the squadron's pilots had passed through his hands. The day after he arrived he made his first acquaintance with the squadron's new Camels - and wrecked B3792 on take-off, damaging several other parked aircraft in the process. A trifle embarrassing to say the least, but not a true reflection of his ability as a pilot.....after all he already had three victories to his credit, and he was to score again with No 45 Sqn.

Along with the departure of the observers came a policy under which all of the squadron's pilots would henceforth be commissioned. The switch to single-seaters had meant that the squadron had shed several of its specialist tradesmen. At the same time the number of aircrew had automatically been halved and those that remained now all messed together. The result was that the squadron became a more compact and intimate unit and its new Recording Officer, James Higgins, who was already very familiar with all of the squadron's personnel, was able to ease the new CO into the chair and relieve him of much of the burden of routine administration.

In late August, while the 1½ Strutters were carrying out their last few missions, the intensity of Camel flying steadily increased. Climbing tests were conducted with each aeroplane to check its performance and numerous air-to-ground gunnery, formation, practice combat and general handling sorties were flown with surprisingly few aeroplanes being damaged. On the 16th four pilots, Van Ryneveld,

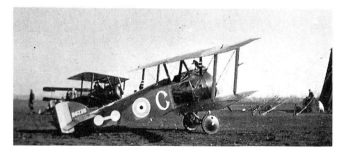

Above: Another September picture showing one of the squadron's earliest Camels identified by a numeral rather than a letter. (J A Brown) Below: B6238/C was one of the squadron's first Camels, being taken on charge on 4th September 1917. Moody and Hand were to claim seven victories in it over the next few months. (J A Brown)

Findlay, Firth and Montgomery flew individual sorties in fruitless attempts to intercept intruders. There were several more of these thereafter but none came to anything, apart from Van Ryneveld's sortie on the 18th. On August 22nd, on which day the unit's ninth Camel was delivered, the squadron crossed the lines for the first time on their new mounts but no contact was made with the enemy.

While familiarity with the new aeroplanes was growing they had still to be blooded in combat and as yet the pilots flew them with a respect arising from a vague uncertainty. During the evening of 25th August Norman Macmillan, flying B3917, took part in a six-aircraft Offensive Patrol. His engine was not running as well as it might have been and he found himself trailing behind the rest of the formation and eventually lost them. Alone, he ran into a bunch of about ten black and white Albatros Scouts. A sharp engagement ensued and before both of his guns jammed he had managed to fire on two of the enemy. He made good his escape and H Battery, RA subsequently reported "...having seen 1 Camel put up a magnificent fight with several EA and drive one down completely out of control". The ice was broken. The Camel's first victory had been chalked up. Two days later Arthur Harris got another one.

Since it was the usual practice for unit markings to be applied to new aeroplanes almost as soon as they were taken on charge it is just possible that No 45 Sqn's earliest Camels wore the white band. There appears, however, to be no concrete evidence to support this conjecture. What is known is that all unit identification markings, all of which consisted of a variety of fuselage bands or geometric shapes painted in white, were in the process of being revised and on 25th August new ones were promulgated. No 45 Sqn was allocated a dumb-bell which was to be painted on each side of the fuselage aft of the roundels[1]. These were duly applied and a third was added on top of the fuselage spine. Initially each aeroplane also carried an individual number in front of the roundel and on the upper mainplane but the numerals were soon superseded by individual letters[2]. The style of the lettering varied considerably from aeroplane to aeroplane, those of A and B Flights tending to be rather more ornate than those of C Flight. It is perhaps worth noting that, while No 45 Sqn was the only unit within II Bde to use the dumb-bell, the same symbol was also allocated to other units, eg No 21 Sqn in V Bde and No 56 Sqn in (the HQ RFC controlled) 9th Wg. Other units which were allocated the dumb-bell as their identity marking at one time or another included Nos 19, 49, 79, 92 and 210 Sqns and the American 17th Aero Sqn. Although several units have subsequently adapted their WW I markings for use in later years, only No 45 Sqn has reclaimed the dumb-bell and, by precedent at least, it is now the squadron's exclusive preserve.

As the last three two-seaters were being flown away on 1st September, the squadron's seventeenth and eighteenth Camels were delivered, bringing it fully up to strength. On the same date two flight commanders, Capt Robert Findlay and Capt Alexander Charlwood were posted home, both having served with the squadron for over six months. The new OCs were to be Norman Macmillan for A Flight and William Wright for B Flight, both assuming captaincies. In just two weeks the squadron had re-equipped, lost all of its observer/gunners, some of its familiar groundcrew, its old

CO and two of its three flight commanders. It had been an unsettling period. No 45 Sqn was now a single-seat fighter squadron and it had, at last, been given the tools to do the job. But there was still something lacking. What was needed was a confidence builder to cement the remodelled unit together. They had not long to wait.

On September 3rd, in the course of three patrols, Macmillan, Harris and 2/Lt E D Clarke all got confirmed kills, while Lts W C Moore and O L McMaking and 'Bunty' Frew drove down three more OOC. Macmillan was sure that he had destroyed a second over Dadizeele but it proved impossible to confirm this victory. The squadron did not escape unscathed, however, and Lt Robert Clegg, who had been with the unit for only a fortnight, received a bullet in the knee during the second patrol and was killed when his B2306 crashed while he was attempting to get it down at Bailleul. Lt A T Heywood, who had been with the unit about three weeks longer, was posted missing in B3917. 2/Lt Richard Dawes, another relative newcomer, had his machine badly shot about but succeeded in making it back to base intact. The pattern, so clearly established in the two-seater days, was holding true. If a pilot was going to be shot down it was most likely to happen at the beginning of his tour, especially if, on an early sortie, he were unlucky enough to run up against an opponent of the calibre of Ltn Werner Voss, one of the most formidable of German fighter pilots. This is exactly what had happened to Aubrey Heywood and he had become Voss' thirty-ninth victim. Nevertheless the balance sheet for the day was definitely in the squadron's favour: six victories, possibly seven, three of them confirmed kills, and only two losses. Confidence was now firmly re-established and morale rose.

Throughout September the squadron continued to score regularly, claiming nine more definite kills and nineteen further probables making the overall total for the month thirty-four. Losses also continued to mount, however, and it was still almost always the 'new boys' who went down. Lt W Shields was killed on September 5th, just four days after joining the unit. 2/Lt E B Denison, a Canadian, was shot down to become a POW on the 11th, ten days after arriving, as was 2/Lt E A Cooke on the 21st after only three days with the unit. Four other pilots were posted missing, all of their deaths later being confirmed. Three of them were newcomers: Lt Alister MacNiven on the 5th (arrived on 18th August); Lt B R Davis on the 20th (arrived 6th September) and another Canadian, 2/Lt C F Risteen, on the 26th (arrived 21st). The fourth missing pilot was an exception to the inexperience rule. Lt Oscar McMaking had been with No 45 Sqn for four months and was by now a seasoned combat veteran with five victories to his credit, three of them having fallen to the guns of his observers during the two-seater days. Even he met his match on 11th September, however, when he too came up against Voss, the commander of Jasta 10, flying a Fokker Triplane. Oscar McMaking's B6236 was his forty-seventh victim. But, while experience is undoubtedly a major factor in ensuring a pilot's survival in combat it cannot guarantee it. After claiming just one more victory, Werner Voss himself succumbed to a group of SE 5as of No 56 Sqn on 23rd September after a very closely fought engagement.

September also produced an instance of an inexperienced pilot coming out on top. 2/Lt R J Brownell joined the squadron on 4th September and was assigned to Macmillan's A Flight. He was actually just a shade less green than most newcomers since he had managed to accumulate about 60 hours of flying time before going out to France, significantly more than the average. After the customary familiarisation trip and a few abortive missions which were cancelled due to weather, he flew his first patrol on September 9th. He was carefully briefed for this operation by his flight commander whose chief concern was that the tyro did not become separated from the rest of the patrol, as so often happened. Brownell was instructed not to worry about shooting down

Seen at Ste-Marie-Cappel in front of one of the recently erected Nissen huts in October 1917, from the left: 2/Lt J E Child, 2/Lt R J Brownell, 2/Lt P Carpenter, 2/Lt T F Williams and 2/Lt D W Ross. (J A Brown)

aeroplanes and just to concentrate on sticking close. He did exactly as he was told and, much as his overconfidence had led him to expect, he succeeded in staying with his leader. He followed all his manoeuvres, even when these became quite violent in bumpy air and while avoiding Archie. At one stage his leader had fired his guns, so Brownell had let rip a burst as well. When they landed Macmillan was full of praise - "Damn good show Brownell! I saw you shooting at the Hun. Don't think you got him though." "What Hun?" said a nonplussed Brownell, "I thought you were just keeping your guns warm, so I fired mine too." This 'new boy' had just had his first dogfight and didn't even know it! The very next day, however, on only his third patrol, he shot down a DFW two-seater in flames which put a stop to any further merriment at his expense. Brownell, an Australian (a Tasmanian to be pedantic) who had previously won the MM as a sergeant artilleryman at Gallipoli, was to become one of the squadron's many high-scoring pilots and would remain in uniform after the war, finally retiring from the RAAF, as Air Commodore R J Brownell CBE MC MM.

At about this time several pilots were experimenting with hi-tech gadgets to improve the efficiency of their machines. For instance Harris had devised a counter to indicate how many rounds had been fired, and a selection of gun sights was being experimentally fitted to various aircraft. During a visit to the squadron Trenchard was particularly impressed by John Firth's aeroplane which sported no fewer than three such devices. He commented favourably, but Firth airily said that he never used any of them; he just "got up close and fired point blank". The great man observed frostily that the gun sight was actually there to be used, not just to plug the hole in the windscreen, and moved on.

There had been some domestic changes at Ste-Marie-Cappel during the late summer. While No 45 Sqn had been exchanging its 1½ Strutters for Camels, the neighbouring No 20 Sqn had begun to dispose of its big 'Fees' and by mid-September it had been re-equipped with the very potent Bristol Fighter. In the same month No 60 Sqn had arrived with their SE 5as and had settled in on the same side of the airfield as the two-seater squadron. Having spent a not too uncomfortable summer under canvas, the CO made representations about the approach of winter and some Nissen huts were erected for No 45 Sqn so that by the end of the month not only was Ste-Marie-Cappel home to three of the most successful and famous fighter squadrons that the RFC was to produce, but they were now equipped with war-winning aircraft and their pilots and men were reasonably warm and dry as well. Things were definitely looking up. It is interesting to note that half a century later these same three squadrons would again be stationed together; this time at Tengah where they would constitute the sharp end of the Far East Air Force of the 1960s.

October produced another nineteen victories, eleven of them confirmed kills. There were five combat casualties. 2/Lt K H Willard was shot down and killed on the 12th. Capt H B Coomber and 2/Lt C I Phillips were posted missing on the 12th and 27th respectively. Phillips had been with the squadron for four weeks when he was lost, Coomber for less than a fortnight and Willard a mere four days. Both of the other pilots who were shot down survived. Lt Clarke's Camel was hit by ground fire on the 26th and, although he managed to reach friendly territory before he was obliged to put his damaged B2327 down in the mud, he was unfortunate enough to be injured in the resultant pile up. Edward Clarke, who had previously accounted for six EA, was decorated with an MC six weeks later but he did not fly with the squadron again. He remained in aviation after the war, finally retiring in 1960 with a CBE after twenty-three years as Managing Director of Saunders-Roe. The second of October's survivors was one of the squadron's Canadian pilots, 2/Lt Emerson Smith, who was wounded when his B5152 was hit by ground fire during a strafing attack on the 27th. He had the misfortune to crash on the wrong side of the lines and was taken prisoner; he had scored seven victories since joining the squadron on 12th August.

One other squadron pilot died in October 1917, but he was not lost in combat. On 29th 2/Lt Gerald Pearson was seen to dive into the ground in B2350 from about 3,000 feet for no accountable reason. He had arrived at Ste-Marie-Cappel only two days before and was still involved in local familiarisation flying. As he had crashed attempting to take off in B2388 only three hours earlier, it seems quite likely that his unfamiliarity with the Camel might well have been aggravated by the onset of delayed shock from this earlier incident.

One of the latest batch of new arrivals was to make a name for himself in October - literally. 2/Lt T F Williams had joined Harris' C Flight on September 24th. A month later he flew on a patrol being led by Frew but he failed to keep station and, although they were still in sight, he became separated from the formation. A group of seven Albatros spotted the straggler and attacked. There was a brief skirmish and, before regaining the safety of the rest of his patrol, Williams managed to despatch the Albatros' leader, who crashed near Coucou. On returning to Ste-Marie-Cappel, Frew congratulated the Canadian on his achievement in having fought seven EA single-handed and emerged the victor, comparing him to Werner Voss in his speed of reaction and marksmanship. The name stuck and he remained 'Voss' Williams for the rest of his remarkably long life.

The most successful day's fighting during October was on the 27th when ten Camels, operating in two flights of five, became embroiled in a fight with a similar number of Albatros fighters. This resulted in the squadron's being credited with three victories, all confirmed kills. Apart from the pilots' initials having been deleted for brevity, the Combat Report covering this engagement is reproduced below verbatim (an

Lt Earl Hand claimed the first enemy aeroplane to fall to B2430/B, an Albatros shot down OOC on 15th November 1917 during the squadron's last patrol over France before it was withdrawn from ops to prepare for its move to Italy. Lt Raymond Brownell claimed four victories over Italy while flying B2430 after which Hand used it to down three more victims before the aeroplane was passed on to No 28 Sqn with whom it achieved one more victory. (J A Brown)

2/Lt Peter Carpenter joined No 45 Sqn on 15th September 1917 and had shot down eight enemy aircraft by the time he was posted to No 66 Sqn as a Flight Commander on 27th February 1918. He was to claim a further sixteen victories with his new unit, making him No 66 Sqn's top scorer. (J A Brown)

NOP is a Northern Operational Patrol).

Whilst on an NOP, three RE 8s were seen being very badly Archied and making for our lines. An E Scout was preparing to attack the rear machine when 2/Lt Frew flew at it nose on and after firing a good burst straight into it, its right wing collapsed and it went down in a slow spin. 2/Lts Child and Brownell followed it down, fired several shots into it, and saw it crash smoking badly NE of Comines. Meanwhile, as this machine was obviously being protected, judging by its daring, 2/Lt Frew, being now all alone, was attacked with great determination by 8 Albatros Scouts. He managed, however, by dint of employing every imaginable manoeuvre, to hold his own until the other Camel formation of 5 machines led by Lt Firth arrived on the scene. The odds being now more equal, the EA were in turn attacked with great fury. Lt Firth shot one down in flames almost at once and it was seen by 2/Lt Frew to fall to pieces in the air. 2/Lt Frew then noticed a Camel about 3/4,000 feet below him going down smoking, and being sorely pressed by 3 E Scouts which were firing into it. He immediately dived right down amongst them and singling out the most aggressive opponent fired about 20 rounds into it at about 15 feet range. It burst into flames at once, went down and crashed E of Moorslede; confirmed by Lt Firth. He then turned on the other two but they, after a few rounds were fired, refused combat and dived East. 2/Lt Frew then looked about for the Camel but it had disappeared altogether. Lt Firth had meanwhile, along with some Nieuports, chased the remainder, and saw one E Scout going down completely out of control SE Westroosebeke about 1040am.

On 11th November 1917 the recently arrived 2/Lt H J Watts made this quite respectable attempt at demolishing the Squadron Office. B2393 was eventually rebuilt and it flew again, but not with No 45 Sqn. (No 45 Sqn archives)

Some sources credit Child and Brownell with having shared in shooting down the first of the three enemy aircraft to fall but, since it had already been substantially destroyed by Frew before they engaged it, this has not been reflected in the list of victories tabulated at Annex E. It is significant that, while Brownell noted the engagement in his journal, from what he wrote it is quite clear that he did not consider that his contribution had been critical. The Camel which had been observed going down was 2/Lt Cecil Phillips' B2382.

There had been two changes of command in October. Arthur Harris, having by then accounted for five enemy aeroplanes (and of whom more anon) was admitted to hospital on the 8th and command of his C Flight had passed to John Firth. At that time Firth already had four victories to his credit, two of them on two-seaters; he was to add eight more. B Flight had also changed hands when 'Bunty' Frew had taken over from Wright on the 24th. Capt William Wright had returned to England, having flown with No 45 Sqn for six months, during which he had scored eight victories, half of them on two-seaters and six of them confirmed as destroyed. When Frew became a flight commander he already had fourteen victories to his credit; he added another three before the end of the month.

Another new pilot, 2/Lt H J Watts (yet another Canadian) achieved some early notoriety on 11th November when, on his tenth day on the squadron, he lost control while landing in B2393 and rammed the Squadron Office. Fortunately, although the aeroplane was quite badly damaged, no one was hurt and, perhaps in the light of his own escapade in August, Vaucour chose not to make too much of it. November produced six more kills for the squadron's game book, and six more OOCs. There was only one casualty, 2/Lt R G Frith who was wounded and shot down on 5th, spending the rest of the war as a POW. The last claims for the month, two destroyed and two OOC, were made in the morning of the 15th. Two German Aces fell that day, Ltn Richard Runge of Jasta 18, who had raised his total score to eight since opening it by claiming one of No 45 Sqn's 1½ Strutters on June 5th, and Ltn Hans Ritter von Adam, CO of Jasta 6 and victor of twenty-one engagements. It seems probable that Runge may have fallen to the guns of Kenneth Montgomery in B3929, although some sources suggest that his victim may have been Adam in a joint action with No 29 Sqn. That afternoon the squadron was withdrawn from operations.

In the autumn of 1917 the Italians were losing the Twelfth Battle of the Isonzo, better known as the defeat of Caporetto. The army appeared to be on the point of collapse in the face of the Austro-German offensive and eleven divisions, six French and five British, were earmarked to go to Italy to stiffen the resistance. This Expeditionary Force was to be accompanied by both French and British air echelons; only the British committed fighters, although there was already a small autonomous French fighter unit in Italy dedicated to the aerial defence of Venice. In the event the Italians checked their retreat themselves once they had crossed the River Tagliemento and they then made a further, planned, withdrawal to establish and hold a new defensive line on the Piave. The administrative wheels were already turning, however, and the Allied reinforcements continued to deploy. The British air element was an RFC Brigade, the VIIth, commanded by Brig Webb-Bowen. Its single subordinate Wing was the 51st, under Lt Col R P Mills, and

A Flight preparing for its last patrol over France, 15th November 1917; B2376/E in the foreground with B6238/C next in line followed by B6383/A and B4609/F. (J A Brown)

39

the flying units were Nos 34 and 42 Sqns with RE 8s and Nos 28, 45 and 66 Sqns with Camels.

The movement plan called for Nos 42 and 45 Sqns to be the last to go and they were scheduled to leave France in four daily trains departing between 25th and 28th November. On November 15th the squadron was struck off the strength of 11th Wing. That night they gave a farewell party which ended, according to Brownell's memoirs, with the Officers' Mess being set on fire by some departing guests; fortunately those who had already retired were roused from their slumbers before they came to any harm. He also recounts how the squadron's aeroplanes flew off the next day with an assortment of awkward articles of personal kit tied to their undercarriages for want of anywhere else to stow them. Prominent among these were a number of 'Pots, Chamber, Officers for the use of', which led to the unit's being christened the 'Pee Pot Squadron' - fortunately they left France shortly afterwards and the name did not stick!

On the 16th the squadron flew its sixteen serviceable Camels to Fienvillers where they were dismantled and prepared for transportation under the direction of No 2 Aeroplane Supply Depot. No 2 Aircraft Depot at nearby Candas provided additional aeroplanes to bring the squadron up to its established strength of eighteen plus one reserve. They also issued eighteen RE hangars, 10,000 gals of aviation spirit, 4,000 gals of MT petrol and 1,500 gals of castor oil. All of this plus the unit's vehicles, stores, spares, tools and personal kit was to be packed into 20-ton trucks to make up two trains of thirty-five wagons each, plus two similar trains for No 42 Sqn.

The preparations went well and the trains were ready to move when the Battle of Cambrai began on 20th November. Thereafter the fighting in France took priority over that in Italy and, although No 42 Sqn managed to get away on time, no engines could be found for No 45 Sqn's trains and

the move stalled. With its aeroplanes already dismantled the squadron was unable to take part in the fighting and it was obliged to while away the time in its billets in Fienvillers village. To keep them occupied the pilots were sent off to Berck-sur-Mer for a short gunnery refresher course. The squadron ran through three Armament Officers in quick succession during this interlude. Lt B C Lester had replaced Maurice Fell in October but he left on posting on November 20th. His replacement, Lt L C Herne, lasted for only a day as he went straight into hospital as soon as he arrived but Lt R Buck took over on December 1st to restore some stability. In the event Ronald Buck, who had flown as a pilot with No 60 Sqn until he had been wounded in October 1916, was to stay with No 45 Sqn for the rest of its active service. Two locomotives eventually became available and the squadron's trains finally set off on 12th December, HQ and A Flight in one, B and C Flights in the other.

The journey, via the Rhone valley and the Riviera, took six days and the squadron was more or less self-sufficient en route. One wagon had been rigged up as a field kitchen and the cooks endeavoured to have a hot meal ready whenever the train stopped. At least two of the squadron's dogs, 'Crash' and 'Beattie', accompanied the unit but 'Crash' wandered off during one stop and went permanently AWOL. As the squadron moved further south its arrival tended to be greeted at each halt by excited Italians who insisted on impromptu but semi-formal welcoming ceremonies. Norman Macmillan, who commanded the first of the trains, was suffering from 'flu and disinclined to take part in one particularly extravagant occasion at Savona. Not wishing to give offence, however, he was finally inveigled into making a token diplomatic appearance in greatcoat and pyjamas to receive the good wishes of the local Colonel Commandant. Inevitably this developed into a lengthy series of speeches, Lt H D O'Neill doing the honours for the away team, and numerous toasts. In the meantime the train pulled out.

B Flight's B3929/L plus three of C Flight's Camels, B5158/M, B2494/S and B6354/N. Note that the first two aircraft have their identities painted on their rudders while B2494 wears its serial on its fin, although there is a white scar on its rudder where it (or some other number?) used to be. (Imperial War Museum)

Overruling the protests of the stationmaster the colonel insisted that the train be brought back to pick up the commander of his gallant allies. This was achieved at the expense of considerable disruption to the Italian rail system, although this was before Mussolini had made the trains run on time, so perhaps no one noticed (see *Into the Blue*).

On arrival at Padua on December 18th the squadron detrained and unloaded all its kit. The Camels were transported to the south western outskirts of the city where they were re-erected at the Caproni aerodrome at San Pelagio, test flying beginning on the 23rd. Slightly behind schedule, having been delayed by adverse weather, the squadron eventually moved by road to its operational airfield at Istrana on Christmas Day. No 42 Sqn had recently moved its RE 8s to Grossa to make room for the newcomers, leaving No 34 Sqn and an Italian fighter squadron to become the squadron's neighbours at its new base, which was located about six miles west of Treviso. The squadron found its billets in Fossalunga village and began to settle in.

On Boxing Day the Germans carried out a bombing raid on Istrana. The official record indicates that this was a riposte to two attacks on San Felice airfield made by the RE 8s of Nos 34 and 42 Sqns on the 15th and 16th of December. It is more likely, however, that it was provoked by an unauthorised (and officially unrecorded) strafing attack made by Capt Barker and Lt Hudson of No 28 Sqn on Motta aerodrome on Christmas Day. In any event, without their Camels, No 45 Sqn could not participate in the reaction to the Austrian raid but its personnel were able to enjoy the spectacle of the Italian Hanriots getting airborne and wreaking havoc on the raiders. There were actually two attacks and with No 28 Sqn joining the fray as well the intruders lost at least nine out of about forty-five aircraft involved. It was later reported that many of the shot-down crews were found to have been inebriated, since they had been ordered off on operations at short notice in the middle of their seasonal festivities! There were five casualties on the ground, four Italian mechanics and one of No 34 Sqn's. That afternoon No 45 Sqn's pilots returned to San Pelagio, collected their eighteen aeroplanes and flew them to Istrana in flight formations. 2/Lt J P Huins damaged B2400 on landing and evidently damaged himself at the same time as he was subsequently listed as 'Wounded in Action', although

'Accidentally Injured' would appear to have been a more appropriate classification. Whatever his categorisation 'Proc' Huins made a full recovery and he rejoined C Flight on January 12th.

The squadron flew its first practice flights in Italy on December 27th and was then grounded again by weather. On New Year's Eve it flew its first operational missions and drew first blood when a three-aircraft patrol, comprising Raymond 'Brownie' Brownell in B2430 and Richard 'Dickie' Dawes (a Canadian) in B6412 led by Henry 'Mike' Moody in B6238, encountered three Albatros D IIIs over Pieve di Soligo. The Combat Report reads:

...2/Lt H M Moody succeeded in enticing them down to attack. As soon as they did this he went for the leader head on and forcing him underneath got onto his tail and followed him down from 11,000 to 5,000 ft firing about 400 rounds into him at about 20 yards range. The machine then went down completely out of control (confirmed by 2/Lt R J Brownell). Meanwhile 2/Lt R J Brownell having singled out another opponent followed it down from 11,000 ft to about 200 ft firing continuously into it until it crashed nose first into the ground. (Confirmed by 2/Lt H M Moody). 2/Lt R J Dawes attacked the third enemy machine and fired about 350 rounds into it at close range and when last seen (*it*) was going down slowly out of control. The enemy Pilots showed no inclination to fight and when attacked immediately tried to seek safety by diving away.

Thus was the squadron's Italian game book opened with one destroyed and two OOC. For both Moody and Brownell these were their fifth victories. They were to share a second kill later that same day when they shot down Ltn Alwin Thurm of Jasta 31 who had been attacking Italian observation balloons near Asolo. Their eventual totals would be eight and eleven respectively.

The closing sentence of the report on this first engagement is interesting, but it could be misleading to read too much into this single observation as it was certainly not the case that the opposition faced by the squadron in Italy was always less resolute than that to which they had been accustomed in France. Nevertheless, the three Camel squadrons fighting in Italy were to establish a remarkable

The innards of the Clerget from Macmillan's B6383 receiving some attention. Moody and Brownell are second and third from the left; Dawes is standing immediately below the gun muzzles. (J A Brown)

combat record which ultimately came to represent an overall victory-to-loss ratio of the order of 10:1 and the relative calibre of the enemy pilots and their machines must surely have been a contributory factor. If the RFC did have a qualitative edge, however, its value was not so much that it enabled the British pilots to shoot down the enemy but that it prevented the enemy from shooting down the British. This was crucial, as it permitted fledgling aviators to survive for long enough to get their bearings and actually become competent fighter pilots instead of being killed on their first or second missions.

The contrast between the casualty rate sustained by the squadron in France and that in Italy is quite remarkable, and very significant. In the twelve months during which the squadron had flown 1½ Strutters and Camels in France it had sustained a total of 106 aircrew casualties, from all causes. During its nine months in Italy only eleven pilots were killed, wounded, injured, posted missing or taken prisoner. The fact there was only one man in a Camel, as against two in a 1½ Strutter, will have made an obvious contribution to these statistics but this alone is hardly sufficient to account for the startling contrast between these figures.

One significant contributory factor was that the progressive improvements introduced into the training system from the summer of 1917 had begun to feed through to the squadrons. Apart from replacement pilots being *better* trained, they had also received *more* training and by mid-1918 they were arriving with roughly twice the flying experience that their predecessors had had - something over

sixty hours being typical. This meant that new pilots were less likely to have accidents. But in this context it was far more important that there were so few combat losses because that meant that the squadron had to accept and train relatively few replacement pilots during 1918. This, in turn, meant that the squadron's complement of aircrew remained relatively stable which permitted the pilots to become familiar with each other's strengths and weaknesses. As each individual became more and more experienced and mutual trust developed, the corporate fighting potential of each flight became greater than the sum of its individual parts. It was this stability and familiarity which permitted so many of the squadron's pilots to become so successful.

All of this is not to say that aerial combat in Italy was a soft option. Far from it. It was, for instance, the usual practice for the British fighters to operate in three-aircraft patrols, as a result of which they were frequently outnumbered when they engaged the enemy. Nevertheless, despite their numerical inferiority, their ever-increasing skill and experience generally enabled them to emerge as the victors.

Webb-Bowen, under whose command the squadron had fought in France, had found that using a single subordinate formation to exercise operational and administrative control over five squadrons, operating in two very different roles, was an unsatisfactory arrangement. He therefore proposed that the original 51st Wg should become a Corps Wing, dedicated to controlling the RE 8s, and that an Army Wing should be set up to look after the fighters. This suggestion was approved and on 5th January HQ 14th Wg was established at Villalta under Lt Col P B Joubert de la Ferté and all three Camel squadrons were immediately transferred to its control[3]. The officers on the strength of No 45 Sqn on that date, by which time they had already claimed four more victories, are listed at Figure 3.1.

On January 6th King Victor Emmanuel of Italy visited Istrana. Since Major Vaucour was at Villalta that day, his deputy, Capt Macmillan, found himself playing host to royalty. Maturity came fast in wartime. Just eight months earlier Norman Macmillan had been a very green newcomer to No 45 Sqn under threat of being sent home to learn how to fly properly! He was now the senior flight commander of the same unit with ten victories to his credit, the tenth, an Albatros driven down OOC, having been claimed on New Year's Day. Unfortunately, January 6th was to end badly for Macmillan. That evening he directed one of the men, AM A Heley, a batman, to douse an open cooking fire so that it would not act as a beacon for night raiders. The can of water used to do this turned out to contain petrol and Macmillan's face was badly burned in the ensuing flash fire. Fortunately he did not lose his eyesight and eventually made a full recovery but he had now done his bit and was posted home on 18th January, having temporarily bequeathed A Flight to Raymond Brownell a week before. His carelessness subsequently cost the unfortunate Heley seven days 'Field Punishment No 1'.

January 1918 was a very a fruitful month for No 45 Sqn; it suffered only two casualties while claiming a remarkable thirty-one victories, all but eight of them being confirmed as kills. 'Bunty' Frew's score continued to mount and another famous name also

Maj A M Vaucour MC*		
A Flight	**B Flight**	**C Flight**
Capt N Macmillan	Capt M B Frew MC*	Capt J C B Firth
Lt M D G Drummond	Lt H D O'Neill	Lt H T Thompson
2/Lt R J Dawes	2/Lt H J Watts	2/Lt G H Bush
2/Lt E McN Hand	2/Lt J E Child	2/Lt J P Huins
2/Lt C E Howell	2/Lt P Carpenter	2/Lt D W Ross
2/Lt R J Brownell MM	2/Lt A J Haines	2/Lt J Cottle
2/Lt H M Moody	2/Lt J R Black	2/Lt T F Williams
Capt J W Higgins - Recording Officer		
Lt R Buck - Armament Officer		
2/Lt W T H Hocking - Assistant Equipment Officer		

Fig 3.1. The officers of No 45 Sqn as at 5th January 1918.

began to figure in the squadron's Combat Reports, 2/Lt C E Howell. Cedric 'Spike' Howell had joined the squadron on 27th October 1917. He had been a slow-starter but in January he began to hit his stride, shooting down his first EA on the 14th and a second on the 26th. Just as the squadron was gaining a prospective Ace it lost an established one. On 2nd January 2/Lt Montgomery, who had accounted for eleven enemy aircraft since joining No 45 Sqn in June 1917, was elevated to flight commander status and two days later he was posted to No 66 Sqn as a captain. He was to score only once more before being shot down himself to become a POW.

The squadron's two losses for the month both occurred on January 11th. Shortly before mid-day six Camels, escorting an RE 8 of No 42 Sqn, became embroiled with ten Albatros of which one was destroyed and three were driven down OOC, but 2/Lt Douglas Ross' B2436 failed to return to base. No one actually saw what had happened to him but a few days later his death was confirmed by a message dropped by an Austrian aircraft. Lt H T Thompson, claimed the one confirmed kill in the engagement (probably Oblt Hans Kummetz, CO of Jasta 1 and victor of at least seven aerial combats) but then found himself alone and the object of the undivided attention of five or six enemy aircraft. He headed south west and eventually shook off his attackers, but not before his aircraft had sustained some damage and he himself

had been hit, although his wound was only superficial. Lost and short of fuel he finally landed B2494 in a field. Henry Thompson, an Australian from New South Wales, eventually found his way back to Istrana and after a short stay in hospital resumed operational flying. Despite these two early losses, 11th January was still a good day for the squadron with three more kills being claimed in the afternoon.

Capt Frew's greatest combat success was achieved on January 15th when he shot down three enemy aircraft in a single engagement. The Combat Report describing this remarkable feat, reads:

Whilst on the Central Patrol Capt.M.B.Frew observed 4 Albatross Scouts protecting a 2/seater being heavily engaged by anti-aircraft fire, on our side of the Lines. He immediately led his formation round to intercept them coming back. By careful manoeuvring, and by taking every advantage of the sun, he was able to select the most opportune time and place to attack, besides having informed the other two pilots by means of signals exactly what was to take place. When the moment arrived, he dived down from 12,000 ft. at the 2/seater which was flying with one Scout higher than the other 3, and after having fired about 4 shots from point blank range, with only one gun working, it went down in flames and crashed at RAI S. VAZZOLA (confirmed by 2/Lt.P.Carpenter.) 2/Lt.P. Carpenter had meanwhile

The squadron's officers dining on or about 30th January 1918. At the left hand side of the table, front to rear, are: 2/Lt G H Bush, 2/Lt R J Brownell, 2/Lt J P Huins and 2/Lt W T H Hocking. On the right are 2/Lt J Cottle, Lt M D G Drummond, Lt C K Attlee, 2/Lt R R Renahan, Capt Thompson, Lt D G McLean, Lt R Buck and Capt N C Jones. The three stewards in the background are, from the left, AM Huband, Cpl Ames and AM Bye. Most of the officers' names feature in the narrative apart from: 2/Lt Robin Renahan, who joined No 45 Sqn on 12th January but reported sick almost immediately and was struck off strength on 9th February prior to being sent back to the UK; Lt Attlee, one of the MOs belonging to the wing, who was periodically attached to No 45 Sqn and Capt Thompson whose connection with No 45 Sqn is not known. (Imperial War Museum)

B6372/H, awaiting a salvage party after Frew's forced landing at Saletto, following his epic engagement on 15th January 1918. Clearly visible are sundry tears in the fabric, indicative of the fragile conditions of the wing structure as a result of the damage it had sustained. Despite the state of its starboard wheel, the aeroplane stayed the right way up and it was soon back in action. After Frew's departure B6372 took part in the destruction of a further six enemy aircraft (making a total of nineteen) while being flown by Lts H D O'Neill and C G Catto and its new 'owner', Capt N C Jones. The ultimate fate of this remarkable aeroplane is somewhat obscure. Its last recorded sortie, a bombing mission, was flown by Jones on 16th June 1918; there is no indication of anything having gone awry during this flight. One usually reliable source says that B6372 was crashed on the 17th by Lt Drummond. This seems unlikely, however, as No 45 Sqn recorded that poor weather precluded any flying at all that day and because Drummond had been with No 28 Sqn since February. No 45 Sqn's Daily State return does list the aircraft as being unserviceable on the 17th, referring to an associated, but untraced, Casualty Report - there may be some connection here with 1/AM F Hitchin's having been admitted to hospital that day. B6372 was transferred to No 7 AP on June 24th. One authority states that by October it was at No 4 ASD in France, although it is definitely recorded as being with No 66 Sqn that same month, remaining with them in Italy until early 1919. (J A Brown)

dived on one of the 3 E.A. underneath and after a short but sharp encounter, in which the pilot of the E.A. handled his machine very skilfully, shot it down and on following saw it crash in close proximity to the 2/seater. Capt M.B.Frew was in the meantime fighting the 2 Scouts, using only one gun as it was impossible to rectify the stoppages in the other, and succeeded after a very hotly contested combat in shooting both down in turn, one bursting into flames and crashing and the other spinning into the ground in the vicinity of RAI.S.VAZZOLA. He then noticed 2/Lt.P.Carpenter aggressively attacking an E.A. nose-on, and just on the point of colliding, the E.A. split-aired round and in trying to get on his tail, was noticed by Capt.M.B.Frew who dived down about 1,000 ft. and shot it down completely out of control and when last seen by 2/Lieut.J.R.Black who had followed Capt.M.B.Frew throughout the encounter, was in a spin about 50 ft. from the ground; but it flattened out and succeeded in getting away owing to all ammunition being expended. The formation then after having a look round and only seeing one E.A. well North started for the Aerodrome. Immediately the return journey was commenced, the hostile anti-aircraft which had hitherto been silent, opened up a very heavy and accurate fire on the 3 Camels, which were now flying at a height of 3,000 ft. and about 5 miles from the Lines. Capt.M.B.Frew's machine was struck by a direct hit and very severely damaged. The rear main plane connecting rod being severed, allowing the plane to tilt up, centre section damaged and wheel shot off. He immediately shut off his engine and started to glide for the Lines, the anti-aircraft gunners putting up barrage after barrage in front of him which he could only glide through owing to the weak state of his machine. On nearing the PIAVE, the case seemed hopeless, as the machine was close to the ground and the River in front. Capt.M.B.Frew however as a last chance momentarily switched on his engine, thus giving him the necessary impetus to skim over the River and land behind the Italian Front Line at SALETTO without further damage to his machine. The Italian Officers who gathered round, informed him they had observed the whole combat and had seen 4 E.A. go down and crash, two being in flames. The pilots in the E.A. put up a great fight, the remaining one even following the Camels back to the Lines, but at a safe distance.

These were 'Bunty' Frew's twentieth, twenty-first and twenty-second victories and Peter Carpenter's seventh. Despite the damage it had sustained, B6372, Frew's personal mount, was salvaged and patched up. Before the end of the month both pilot and aeroplane would be back in the air together and on the 27th this combination would account for yet another Albatros which fell in flames over Conegliano. Frew's remarkable exploits on January 15th were used as the basis of a citation for a DSO, which was gazetted on March 4th.

Meanwhile 'Voss' Williams' score had been mounting. On January 26th he had taken part in a decisive engagement just to the east of Treviso in which he, Carpenter and Howell had attacked six Albatros DIIIs escorting a two-seater. They had completely disrupted the enemy formation, each of the squadron's pilots gaining a confirmed kill, William's victim falling in flames near Roncade. He was credited with a share in another victory on 2nd February, the eighth of his eventual total of nine. On this occasion, while patrolling on the far side of the Piave river near Conegliano, the three Camels had come across a Rumpler two-seater accompanied by a scout, tentatively identified as a Halberstadt. The patrol leader, 2/Lt G H Bush, another Australian, attacked the single-seater which promptly began to spiral down. As the enemy scout appeared to be making for the safety of its own lines, Williams headed it off and the luckless pilot eventually raised his hands above his head and glided down to land in Italian-held territory near Montello. In the meantime, the remaining member of the patrol had engaged the two-seater but without a positive result. The pilot of this third Camel was 2/Lt J Cottle who had joined the squadron shortly before it had moved to Italy. Having now mastered his aeroplane he would shortly begin to score slowly but steadily and by the end of the war Jack Cottle would have become the squadron's third ranking Ace.

On 4th February Lt D G McLean, a young Canadian who had arrived at Istrana only ten days before, was part of a section of four aircraft led by Frew which engaged eight Albatros D Vs. McLean shot one down, but during the flight back to base his aircraft, B2494, was hit by a passing artillery

Capt Frew and B6372/H, in which he claimed his last thirteen victories. After a successful wartime career 'Bunty' Frew was to remain in the RAF until 1948, eventually retiring as an air vice marshal. (J A Brown)

Most of C Flight's aeroplanes appear to have worn their individual letters in a slightly less ornate style than those of A and B Flights. B6354/N was originally Firth's aeroplane, when he was OC C Flight, but Bush, Cottle, Thompson and Vaucour also claimed victories while flying it. This Sopwith-built aeroplane would originally have had its serial number painted in a white 'box' on its rear fuselage but this would have been obscured by the application of the squadron's dumb-bell marking. The number would therefore have been reapplied either on the fin, in white, or on the rudder in black. When this picture was taken B6354's number was actually on its fin, but the rudder bore a white scar where it (or some other number?) had previously been. B2494/S also displayed these symptoms and other photographs show that B2430's serial number migrated from its fin to its rudder at some stage. It is surmised that these anomalies all occurred when the aeroplanes were reassembled at San Pelagio; some components may have been switched between airframes, the correct identities being restored or sustained by some ad hoc work with a paintbrush. (No 45 Sqn archives)

shell and he was killed - the second (possibly third) aircraft lost to No 45 Sqn in this fashion. Sad though this loss was, it was to be the unit's last casualty for over three months. The fight that saw Donald McLean score his first and only victory also saw 'Bunty' Frew score his last. Frew claimed one confirmed and another OOC, making him the squadron's top-scorer with a total of twenty-five victories. He was still suffering some discomfort from a displaced neck sustained when his aircraft had been hit by AA fire on January 15th and, in any case, he had by this time been flying with the squadron for just over nine months in the course of which he had been awarded a DSO and two MCs. He was due to go home. He remained in the RAF after the war and finally retired in 1948 as AVM Sir Matthew Frew KBE CB DSO* MC* AFC. Brownell, having relinquished A Flight to Capt N C Jones on 28th January was now promoted to take over Frew's B Flight. Norman Jones had been posted in from No 28 Sqn on being regraded to flight commander and had arrived with one victory to his credit; he was to claim eight more with his new unit. Presumably because hitherto Brownell had always been an A Flight man, he and Jones exchanged flights on 12th February.

February's game bag amounted to some fourteen claims in all, most of them destroyed. Two of these victories fell to 'Bunny' Vaucour. Although squadron commanders were still

2/Lt R J 'Dickie' Dawes plays with 'Beattie', 'Spud' and 'Stinker'. At times No 45 Sqn seems to have resembled a kind of canine refuge. (J A Brown)

technically barred from crossing the lines there was a growing tendency to disregard this regulation, and it was probably rather easier to do this in Italy than in France where the ruling had originated. The major flew a number of formal combat missions, his leading of a six-Camel escort to a bombing raid on February 4th being an early example. More often, however, he chose to fly alone rather than usurp the proper functions of his flight commanders. It was on one such lone patrol in B6354 that Vaucour got into a fight on 27th February, during which he racked up the squadron's 200th victory. The Combat Report reads:

Whilst flying at about 15,000 feet on the West bank of the Piave Major Vaucour saw 3 E Scouts preparing to attack 3 Camels which were flying at about 13,000 feet in vicinity of Oderzo. The EA dived down on the Camels, Pilots of which were seemingly unaware of their presence. Major Vaucour, realising the danger the Camels were in, dived in amongst the EA picking out the leader into which he put a burst of about 200 rounds, finishing up at about 10 yards range. This EA went straight down. He then attacked a second one and fired several good bursts into it from the closest of ranges and sent it down also between Oderzo and Ponte di Piave. Having lost sight of the EA, he flew alongside of the three Camels and saw that they had No 28 Squadron markings. Lt Jarvis confirms seeing a Camel with No 45 Squadron markings engaged in a fight with 3 EA, sending one down which crashed about 12.57 pm between Oderzo and the Lines; and another going down completely out of control from a height of 12,000 feet, same time and place.

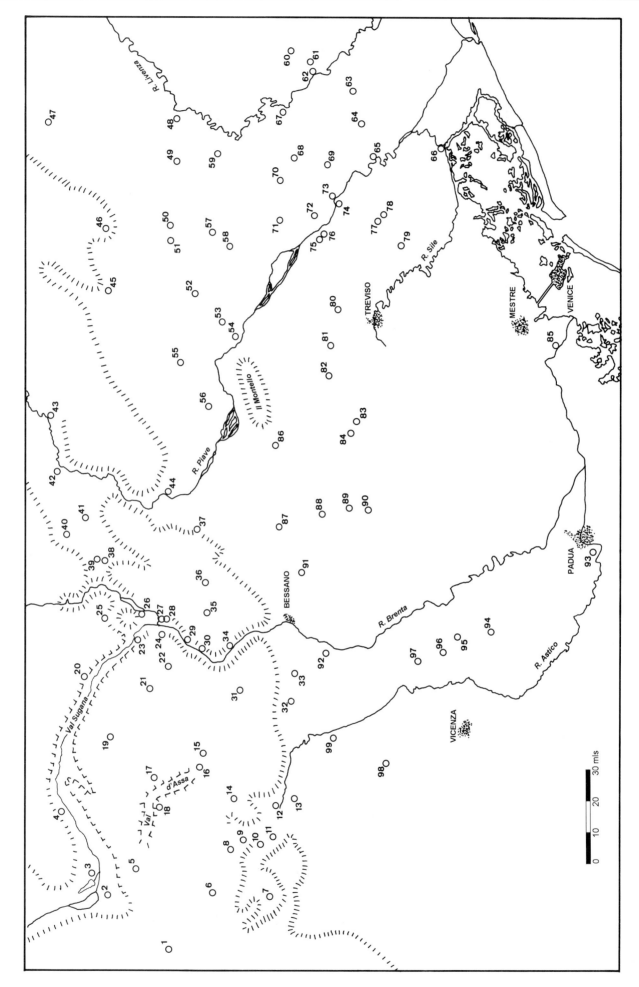

Map 3.1. *North eastern Italy, showing locations and localities which were of significance to No 45 Sqn and which are mentioned in Chapter 3 and/or Annexes E and L.*

10	Arsiero	22	Frisoni	55	Pieve di Soligo
39	Arten	64	Grassaga	13	Piovene
15	Asiago	20	Grigno	73	Ponte di Piave
87	Asolo	95	Grossa	27	Porteghetti
11	Astico	83	Istrana	59	Portobuffole
47	Aviano	32	Lavarda	18	Poselaro
50	Borgo	3	Levico	7	Posina
49	Brugnera	60	Loncon	82	Postioma
2	Caldonazzo	85	Malcontenta	48	Prata di Pordenone
94	Camisano	54	Marcatelli	88	Riese
16	Camporovere	43	Mel	26	Rocca
66	Capo Sile	77	Monastier de Treviso	79	Roncade
91	Casoni	31	Montaga Nuova	4	Roncegno
90	Castelfranco Veneto	35	Monte Asolone	75	Saletto
89	Castello di Godego	6	Monte Campomolon	74	Salgareda
38	Caupo	19	Monte Chiesa	51	San Fior
63	Ceggia	21	Monte Forcellona	33	San Luca
42	Cesana	36	Monte Grappa	30	San Marino
57	Cimetta	17	Monte Meatta	34	San Nazario
28	Cismon	8	Monte Seluggio	69	San Nicolo
12	Cogollo	37	Monte Tomba	93	San Pelagio
23	Coldarco	56	Moriago	97	San Pietro in Gu
46	Collalto	67	Motta di Livenza	62	Santo Stino di Livenza
29	Collicello	72	Negrisia	99	Sarcedo
52	Conegliano	92	Nove	44	Segusino
61	Corbolone	65	Noventa	76	Sette Casoni
24	Costa	70	Oderzo	53	Susegana
5	Costa Alta	71	Ormelle	14	Tresche
41	Feltre	40	Padavena	58	Vazzola
25	Fodatti	81	Paderno	78	Villa Dona
1	Folgaria	86	Pederiva	96	Villalta
80	Fontane	9	Peralto	98	Villaverla
84	Fossalunga	68	Piavon	45	Vittorio

Key to Map 3.1.

That same day 2/Lt Peter Carpenter was made up to captain and posted to No 66 Sqn as a flight commander. He had joined No 45 Sqn in the previous September since when he had shot down eight enemy aeroplanes. He was to claim a further sixteen victories with his new unit and gain a DSO and a Bar to the MC that he had already won while he had been flying with No 45 Sqn.

Shortly before this, on February 22nd, Brownell had had a very lucky escape. In the course of leading a seven-aircraft escort to an RE 8 reconnaissance, the British formation was intercepted and in the fight which followed Lt 'Paddy' O'Neill and 2/Lts Jack Child and George Bush all claimed confirmed victories while 2/Lt James Black and Lt Henry Thompson (now recovered from the minor wounds he had sustained a few weeks before) each claimed one OOC, all of this being without loss to the squadron. On the way back to Istrana, however, Brownell's engine threw a cylinder which carried away with it much of the support for the wing centre section while pieces of debris from the engine cowling jammed the tail controls of his B6238. He was eventually able to establish sufficient control authority to crash land the aeroplane the right way up, although it was a complete write off. Brownell himself was only slightly hurt and was flying again after a week's recuperation.

In one of his books, *Offensive Patrol*, Macmillan tells a another Brownell-story which occurred at about this time. It appears that he encountered a flight of ducks at about 500 feet over the aerodrome and promptly 'engaged' them, claiming two confirmed kills. Whether he was shooting for the pot or just for sport is not clear. What is clear, however, is that he happened to be lined up with the accommodation occupied by the Italian groundcrew at the time and he inadvertently strafed their billets. Fortunately no one was hurt, but the ducks were not the only ones to have their feathers ruffled that day.

Italian ducks aside, in his memoirs, *From Khaki to Blue*, Raymond Brownell recounts how he actually shot down an Italian aeroplane at about this time. Although flying over Venice was not permitted, it appears that it was a fairly common practice for pilots to infringe this prohibition from time to time and go sight-seeing at the end of a patrol. On one such occasion, on March 5th, while Brownell was indulging himself in this fashion, he was startled to find tracer bullets coming over his shoulder from an Italian fighter. He tried to indicate that his was a friendly aeroplane but the Italian pilot persisted in behaving aggressively. Brownell had little alternative but to engage him, restricting his fire to his opponent's wings rather than actually trying to hit the pilot. He eventually succeeded in forcing the Italian aeroplane down on the water where its wings came off. Seeing that the pilot was still moving, Brownell vacated the scene forthwith only to find a full scale witch hunt well under way by the time he got back to Istrana. Still outraged at having been fired on by an ally, Brownell told the CO the whole story, including the fact that he had shot him down. "Damn good show!", said Vaucour and proceeded to telephone wing HQ to flatly deny that any of his pilots had been in the vicinity or had had anything to do with the incident. Surprisingly the dust settled and no more was heard of the Italian complaint. Needless to say this 'victory' is not listed at Annex E!

There is another, probably apocryphal, variation on this story. The surviving French squadron dog, 'Beattie', of which 'Bunty' Frew was particularly fond, had been accidentally run over and killed by an Italian MT driver, probably in February. The officers held a formal 'wake' to mourn her passing. Late in the evening, by which time the participating pilots were all somewhat 'tired and emotional', Frew is alleged to have persuaded them to pledge that they would each shoot down an Italian to avenge their sad mutual loss. This anecdote probably contains more texture than substance but, if there is any truth in it, it did predate Brownell's 'victory' over Venice and it just might have been a contributory factor....

Seen here being recovered after its final flight on 22nd February 1918, Moody and Hand scored seven victories in B6238/C before it became Capt Brownell's aeroplane. (J A Brown)

An A Flight group at Istrana (or possibly Grossa) circa March 1918. From the left: 2/AM J W Clarke, Sgt A High, Sgt R H Lee, 2/AM Lee, F/Sgt J A Morton, 1/AM W C Dodwell, Capt R J Brownell MC MM (with his head still bandaged as a result of his crash on 2nd February), 2/Lt C E Howell, 1/AM M C Hansell, 2/AM W Ferguson, 2/Lt A F Lingard, 2/Lt M R James, 2/Lt E M Hand and 2/Lt R J Dawes. (Geo H Williams)

By March 1918 it was clear that the Italian army was not going to collapse after all. On the other hand there were indications that the Germans were about to launch an offensive in France so two of the British Divisions in Italy were withdrawn and No 42 Sqn went with them as did VII Bde and 51st Wg HQ. The senior RFC formation remaining in northern Italy was thus 14th Wg whose HQ now took command of all four remaining squadrons, the balloon units and all their supporting services with effect from 26th March.

By this time No 45 Sqn was at Grossa, having moved there on 15th and 16th March to share the aerodrome with No 28 Sqn. After two days billeted in Camisano village, while a number of huts were transported across from Istrana, the officers moved onto camp into accommodation which was rather Spartan compared to the comfortable villa at Fossalunga which had previously functioned as their mess. The squadron was soon operational again and on March 21st it mounted its first mission from Grossa, an uncontested escort to an RE 8 of No 34 Sqn flying a reconnaissance sortie in the vicinity of Aviano. In this same month the first Bristol Fighters became operational in Italy with No 34 Sqn's Z Flight and they began to take over the reconnaissance role, although they still needed to be escorted until there were enough of them to provide their own support; by this time it was July and the flight had expanded to become No 139 Sqn. This new unit would then be operating much as No 45 Sqn had done a year earlier, but it had the right aircraft to do the job, a type which was capable of holding its own against enemy single-seaters.

While they been operating from Istrana the bulk of No 45 Sqn's patrols had been flown to the north and east of Treviso over the plain between the Piave and Livenza rivers. The move to Grossa involved a change of sector and most, though not all, of the squadron's subsequent combats took place over very different terrain. No 45 Sqn's main hunting ground was now the southern foothills of the Italian Alps

bordering the Trentino. The squadron's new aerodrome was on flat, low-lying ground roughly half-way between Padua and Vicenza, but only ten miles to the north the ground begins to rise steeply into high and very rugged mountain country. Many of the squadron's engagements later in the year took place over the Brenta Valley, a deep rift running between peaks up to 7,500 feet high. Seen from the air, this country presented a spectacular panorama but in the winter it could often be obscured by cloud and in 1918 instrument flying was not a realistic option.

Operations were severely constrained by wintry weather conditions during March and the month yielded few combats; the squadron sustained no losses but its bag amounted to only two confirmed kills and four OOC. Among these victories were Jack Cottle's first and 'Voss' Williams' last, at least his last with No 45 Sqn. On May 30th, by then wearing the ribbon of the MC, Williams was transferred to No 28 Sqn as a captain to assume command of a flight; he would score six more victories with his new squadron. When Thomas Frederic Williams had taken part in his first aerial engagement he had been 32 years old, which was positively middle-aged for a combat pilot in 1917. After the war he returned to his native Canada to pursue a successful career as a professional pilot and he continued to fly until he was 72 years of age; he died in 1985, just two months before his 100th birthday.

Earlier in March, on the 10th, there had been another brush with the Italians when a patrol had been attacked in error by several Italian aircraft and a brief skirmish had ensued before the mistake was appreciated; it is possible that 2/Lt Child may have shot down one of the assailants but this allegation (or claim?) was not ratified. At that time James Child had already claimed three victories since joining the squadron in September 1917; he would score once more, on 7th July, just before he was posted back to England, making his total four (unless credit is given for his participation in Frew's kill on 27th October 1917).

April 1st 1918 saw the creation of the Royal Air Force but, although this portentous change was formally announced at a parade, as elsewhere in the combat zones, it passed with little further comment. Within the microcosm of the squadron far more attention will have been paid to the transfer of command of C Flight from John Firth to Mike Moody ten days later when Firth returned to England having flown with the squadron for eleven months. Otherwise April was chiefly significant for a continuation of March's poor weather and 14th Wg's three squadrons of Camels were involved in only four combats during the entire month. No 45 Sqn made only four claims: Raymond Brownell drove down an Albatros D III OOC on 17th and flamed a kite balloon on the 18th while 'Spike' Howell and 2/Lt Hand shot down two more 'Albatrii' on the 23rd.

Bomb racks had begun to be fitted to the Camels during March but, although a few bombing missions had been planned, as on the 8th and 9th, the weather intervened and none was actually carried out until May 4th when the squadron flew its first offensive strike. They were ordered to attack a hydro-electric plant north of Lake Garda. The six aircraft duly dropped their bombs on and around the target but, using 20 pounders, any damage that they might have inflicted could have been only slight. The formation had been led by Capt Bush who had been promoted to take over A Flight when Brownell left on April 21st. At that time 'Bushie' had claimed four confirmed kills; he would add one more to his total on May 22nd, two weeks before leaving for England as yet another No 45 Sqn Ace.

Although the weather was steadily improving, early morning fog was still causing problems, especially with dawn patrols. On several occasions, once the pilots had taken off they found that the ground was obscured and, since map-reading was the only means of navigation, they would be obliged to abandon their patrol and concentrate on finding somewhere to land. This happened on May 12th, for

instance, when the aeroplanes finished up at San Pietro in Gu and Castello di Godego where they waited for the sun to burn off the fog before flying back to Grossa.

The highlight of the month occurred on 13th May when, in a single combat with two LVG two-seaters escorted by ten Albatros scouts, 'Spike' Howell claimed to have shot down three of the EA, plus another OOC. Lt E H Masters also shot one down and shared another with the recently-arrived Lt F S Bowles. Six days later Lt C G Catto, the first of three American pilots to fly with the squadron (the other two were Lts M Gibson and J R O'Connell who were to join the unit in June and August, respectively), was to claim his first victory.

Lt Watts had a very close shave on May 24th. Low flying down the Brenta valley on his way back to Grossa after a patrol in B6282 he had reached Bessano when he flew into some overhead cables which cartwheeled his aeroplane into the river. Weighed down by his sodden flying clothing he nearly drowned. In an initial attempt to save the Canadian from the fast flowing water, two Italian soldiers were swept over a weir and died. Just before suffering the same fate, Henry Watts was finally rescued by Bayard Wharton, an American Red Cross volunteer. A little later the squadron's officers entertained Wharton in their Mess to express their gratitude.

Although this account of No 45 Sqn's time in Italy may give the impression that life was all flying and fighting this was not really the case. There were many lighter moments and, with the coming of spring, there was a spate of extracurricular activity in May. The officers arranged the permanent loan of two horses, so riding was one popular way of passing the time and, with the arrival of warmer weather, a swimming pool was constructed. The first plunge was taken on May 25th but it is not known to whom that honour fell. For the musically minded a concert was staged in the evening of May 22nd.

Sport was always high on the agenda and even during the spell of winter weather there had been fixtures, as on 7th March when there was an inter-squadron athletics competition which was won by No 66 Sqn. On May 14th the squadron organised a well-handicapped paper chase, the hares being within sight, but still ahead, of the hounds when

Originally an observer on 1½ Strutters from June 1917, Capt J W Higgins (right) stayed on as Recording Officer when the squadron converted to Camels; he filled this appointment until June 1918 when he was relieved by Lt D J Fryer. The chap on the left is Korp Andreas Kulczar, pilot of a Berg scout forced down by Bush and Williams on 2nd February 1918. The picture was taken on the balcony of the rather palatial villa which served as the Officers' Mess at Fossalunga. (J A Brown)

Lts H M Moody (left) and R J Brownell encumbered by the sort of flying clothing that was necessary when operating in draughty open cockpits with air temperatures well below zero. (J A Brown)

Lt Earl McNabb Hand, a Canadian, claimed five (possibly seven) victories while flying with No 45 Sqn between October 1917 and his final sortie on 1st June 1918 when he was shot down by the Austrian ace, Obltn Linke-Crawford. He is seen here with AM W C Dodwell and B2430/B. (J A Brown)

they reached home. Not to be cheated of their prey, however, the pack promptly 'dug them out' and threw them in a nearby stream. There was a full-blown sports day on the 19th. Most of the formal track and field events were won by mechanics but the prize for putting the shot went to Lt Charles 'Bollicky Bill' Catto, the big Texan from Dallas, who was not averse to the odd impromptu bout of fisticuffs when the occasion demanded (and sometimes when it did not). The needle event was the tug-of-war, A Flight beating C Flight in the final. This victory was not enough, however, to permit A Flight, the current holders, to retain the Challenge Cup and the overall winners of the meeting were the men of HQ Flight. The programme featured the usual selection of less serious events, including a veterans' race, which was won by

Sgt Lowe, and a gas mask race which provided AM H C Godfrey with a fleeting moment of glory.

Despite these diversions, now that the weather had finally broken, the squadron found itself engaged in frequent aerial fighting during June. There were two losses. On the first day of the month Lt Francis Jones was killed after he was seen to fall out of B7307. Jones had been with the squadron for five weeks during which he is known to have been experiencing some difficulty in mastering the Camel; it was assumed that he had lost control of his aircraft, possibly as a result of his having been taken ill in the air. That same day Lt Hand was shot down by the Austrian Ace Obltn Frank Linke-Crawford. Hand's B6423 fell in flames and he was badly burned but he recovered and survived the war as a POW. By this time Earl McNabb Hand, a Canadian from Ontario, was an Ace himself, having five official victories to his name; he had also claimed two Albatros scouts on January 11th but confirmation of these was lacking and these victories were never ratified. Hand had received his captaincy that very day and was to have succeeded to the command of either A or C Flights, since both Bush and Moody were due to be posted home on the 2nd. The brief hiatus caused by his loss was resolved by the return of Dickie Dawes, who had recently been transferred to No 28 Sqn, with whom he had scored another victory. He came back as a captain and assumed command of A Flight while 'Spike' Howell was promoted to become OC C Flight.

The following is a typical Combat Report from this period. Lest there be any lingering doubts, it illustrates quite clearly that, although many of the RFC/RAF's victims fell in enemy territory, it was just as necessary to obtain some form of corroboration before a claim could be recognised in Italy as

2/Lt George Harold Bush in B6423/T. Both long-servers with No 45 Sqn, the aeroplane was taken on charge in November 1917, two months after the pilot had joined C Flight. B6423 was lost when Hand was shot down while flying it on 1st June 1918 and the following day Bush, by then a captain and OC A Flight, left the squadron bound for the UK. (J A Brown)

2/Lt Alfred John Haines with B3929/L in the spring of 1918.
(J A Brown)

All three of the pilots engaged in this fight were to become Aces while flying with No 45 Sqn. Mansell James would score eleven, Dickie Dawes eight (and another with No 28 Sqn) and Charles Catto six. Incidentally, the description of the high-powered Lt James does not, of course, refer to the officer himself but to his aeroplane. On 13th May the squadron had begun a progressive re-equipment programme involving the delivery of new

Above: 2 Lt Ernest Harold Masters with B7307 R. Could the vertical stroke of that R be meant to represent a shapely leg? B7307 was eventually lost on 1st June 1918 when it crashed after Lt Francis Joseph Jones had been seen to fall out of its cockpit. (G Muir). Below: Lt Charles Gray Catto, one of three Americans to fly with No 45 Sqn in 1918. He joined the squadron on 16th March and scored the first of his six victories on 19th May. (Geo H Williams)

it was in France. It describes an Eastern Offensive Patrol (EOP) flown in the morning of 7th June and led by Dawes:

Whilst on EOP Capt R J Dawes saw one 2/Seater and 5 D III scouts about 17,000 feet at 9.30 am in the vicinity of Cismon. He then manoeuvred to get between the sun and the EA and attacked. Capt Dawes singled out one EA scout and fired a long burst into him at close range; the EA went down out of control, Capt Dawes followed him down firing and saw him crash at Piovena. Confirmed by Lt M R James. Lt M R James, with 140hp engine, singled out another EA and fired a burst of 100 rounds into the EA. The EA then went down out of control and crashed in vicinity of San Marino. Lt Catto confirms this. Lt M R James easily outmanoeuvred this EA and getting on another EA's tail fired a long burst into it. The EA was seen to crash by Capt Dawes in the vicinity of Collicello. Lt C G Catto dived on the 2/Seater and fired a short burst, but had to break off the combat owing to engine failure, making a forced landing at Nove aerodrome. Lt Catto was therefore prevented from observing what happened to the EA 2/Seater he had been firing at. Information was subsequently received that a 2/Seater Aviatik[4] had come down on this side of the Lines in the vicinity of Montagna Nuova just after the combat had taken place. This machine was identified by Capt R J Dawes and Lt M R James as being the same 2/Seater originally encountered. As no other combat took place at this time and place, there is therefore no doubt that this machine was brought down by Lt C G Catto.

An informal group at Grossa circa May 1918. From the left: Lts J E Child, C E Howell, J P Huins, H D O'Neill, T F Williams, H M Moody, G H Bush and C G Catto. (J A Brown)

aeroplanes with 140 hp Clergets, 10 hp more than the original models. This process was essentially complete by early August, although one or two of the 130 hp machines continued to be held on the squadron's charge for some time thereafter, their use being largely confined to practice flights and the familiarisation of new pilots.

June 7th was a particularly productive day for the squadron and on an earlier patrol Capt Norman Jones had destroyed a DFW two-seater while Lt G McIntyre had driven down a second OOC and Lt Alfred Haines had despatched two Albatros D IIIs in flames. Further multiple victories occurred on June 8th, 15th and 19th and there was a steady accumulation of single claims. In all the squadron scored twenty-three confirmed kills during June plus a further nine OOC.

The second half of June proved to be particularly hectic as the Austrians launched an offensive along the entire front on the 15th. The assault was checked in the Asiago (British) sector, but further downriver the attack threatened to break through via a series of pontoon bridges which were being thrown across the Piave. News of this development first reached 14th Wg after it was reported by one of No 45 Sqn's early patrols led by Howell. The RAF was immediately committed to help to block the Austrian advance and mounted a series of bombing and strafing attacks on the bridges themselves and on troop concentrations on the east bank. On the first day of the battle, out of a total of 350 bombs delivered by units of 14th Wg, No 45 Sqn dropped 112 on the Piave bridges, plus another twenty in the Asiago sector. Against such soft targets the 20 lb bombs were quite effective and the attacks caused considerable disruption,

This picture shows a number of C Flight personalities at Grossa. While Sgt Lambert (on the right) steadies the propeller, Sgt Wyatt kneels on it to gain access to the guns. The pilot on the extreme right is Lt Catto and the figure with an arm around his shoulders is probably Capt Dawes. (Geo H Williams)

although the enemy were able to repair the damaged bridges under cover of darkness. Although further attacks were mounted on the 16th, flying was constrained by extensive mist and low cloud. On the 17th no flying was possible at all but the heavy rains on that day raised the level of the river and the bridges were swept away. The attack faltered;

70,000 enemy soldiers were marooned on the wrong side of the river and the offensive petered out. The Italians counter-attacked on June 20th and by the 24th those Austrians who had not been killed or captured were back on the left bank of the river. No 45 Sqn had continued to be tasked with occasional offensive missions throughout this period. On 24th June, for instance, they dropped forty-four 20 lb bombs on Conegliano railway station.

Major Vaucour, still indulging in his lone 'inspections of patrols', had taken an active part in the fighting during June, his successful engagement on the 19th having a faintly regal aftermath:

> Whilst inspecting patrols, Major A M Vaucour observed a machine at about 17,000 feet crossing our Lines from the direction of Conegliano. Its movements being rather suspicious Maj Vaucour stalked this machine for 10 minutes, climbing from 14,000 ft to 18,000 ft. He then obtained a good position above the machine which turned out to be an EA 2/Seater, dived on to its tail, and opened fire at 50 yards range. After 50 rounds the EA went down with engine on, pieces falling off in all directions (the Pilot and Observer, holding on to a machine gun, finally falling out) and crashed close to Postioma, 8 miles NW of Treviso.

> Maj Vaucour then landed at San Luca to get a guard put on the machine, and ascertained personally that it could be salved. On arrival at the machine, HM the King of Italy's personal guard was found to be in possession, with instructions to allow no one to touch the machine. In the meantime, owing to the heat of the sun, the machine suddenly caught fire and most of the wreckage was burnt to cinders. Maj Vaucour handed over a revolver and speedometer as souvenirs for His Majesty, and left a guard on the remains of the wreckage.

In all 'Bunny' Vaucour was to claim five of his eight victories while commanding No 45 Sqn, the last on 25th June. On 16th July he was killed. An Italian fighter pilot, Tenente Alberto Moresco of the *78ª Squadriglia*, was carrying out a lone patrol in a Hanriot HD 1 when he encountered a machine of unfamiliar type, slightly above him and coming out of the sun. Unable to identify it, he assumed the aircraft to be hostile, turned onto its tail and opened fire. After only five rounds the aeroplane pulled up sharply into a loop and for the first time Moresco saw D8102's roundels and realised his awful mistake. Sadly, it was too late. No 45 Sqn's much loved CO was dead with a bullet in his head. The squadron was deeply shocked - such was the affection and regard felt for him that grown men wept at Vaucour's funeral. The Italian authorities were mortified, but casualties to friendly fire are an inevitable consequence of war and nothing could be done to redress the tragedy. Command of the squadron passed to Dawes, while his A Flight was taken over by the very experienced Lt H B Hudson MC, who had arrived on transfer from No 28 Sqn at the end of May. But these were temporary arrangements to hold the various forts; both of these men were due to be repatriated before the end of the month and by that time Dickie Dawes had already relinquished the position of Acting CO to Norman Jones.

The fourth officer to be appointed to command No 45 Sqn was Maj J A Crook who arrived at Grossa on 27th July

Major Awdry Morris Vaucour relaxes in the sun. With three earlier victories already to his credit, despite the prohibition on a squadron commander's flying over the lines, 'Bunny' Vaucour claimed five more victims while CO of No 45 Sqn. He died tragically on 16th July 1918 when he was shot down in error by an Italian pilot. (J A Brown)

and took up his appointment the following day, just as Jack Cottle was taking command of A Flight. At twenty-one years of age Joseph Crook was probably the youngest major in the RFC but, despite his youth, he was a very experienced combat pilot; he had logged over 850 flying hours and wore the ribbon of an MC, won in France in 1916 while he had been flying with No 21 Sqn as a mere nineteen year old.

Although marred by the death of Vaucour, July was otherwise another very successful month, the squadron's pilots adding twenty-seven more victories to the growing tally. A particularly notable fight took place on 12th July when a patrol attacked a group of ten EA which were later reinforced by five more, the initial numerical imbalance being somewhat redressed by the intervention of a flight of Italian SPADs and Hanriots. In the course of the mêlée 'Spike' Howell shot down two Phönix D Is, two Berg D Is and an Albatros D V, three of them confirmed kills, two in flames. Lt A Rice-Oxley, another rising star who would eventually claim a total of six victories, got two others in the same engagement and Cottle added one more later in the day.

Cottle scored once more in July, on the 31st, and the outcome of this fight was to be the subject of controversy for many years. On that day Linke-Crawford, the victor of at least twenty-seven (and possibly as many as thirty) engagements, was shot down and killed. For many years Cottle was a contender for the credit for this achievement; others advanced at various times have included Major

B2443/K flew with No 45 Sqn from 22nd October 1917 until 15th June 1918 when Lt Haines damaged it in a landing accident; between those dates it was involved in three successful combats, two with 2/Lt Jack Child and one with Lt Gordon McIntyre. (J A Brown)

Barker, late of No 28 Sqn and by then CO of No 139 Sqn, and a group of Italian pilots. Expert opinion currently favours the view that, while Linke-Crawford was engaged first by No 45 Sqn's Camels and then by a pair of Italian Hanriots, none of their pilots had really managed to defeat the Austrian. During a prolonged engagement with the Italians, his aircraft suddenly stopped manoeuvring and flew straight and level until, still under attack but taking no evasive action, it eventually broke up. It is believed that this indicates that the Aviatik had sustained a structural failure so critical that its pilot could neither fight nor run; what is certain is that Linke-Crawford's body bore no bullet wounds. Credit for having downed this redoubtable fighter pilot belongs most appropriately to one of the Italian pilots, Caporale Pilote Aldo Astolfi of the *81ª Squadriglia* and, while subscribing to the structural-failure thesis, most authorities on Austro-Hungarian aviation during the First World War now endorse this view. There is no doubt that Cottle did score on July 31st, however, but the latest research indicates that, while his victim came from Linke-Crawford's unit, Flik 60J, the Phönix D I which he shot down, was actually being flown by Fw J Acs.

There had been another epic engagement on July 15th when three of the squadron's aircraft had encountered a formation of sixteen enemy fighters near the Brenta Valley. Undeterred by the odds, Capt Howell led his formation straight in. Spike Howell shot down two EA himself, Proc Huins one and Alan Rice-Oxley one, plus another OOC. All of these claims were confirmed, one of them by 'Voss' Williams who joined in the scrap with his flight of No 28 Sqn's Camels, adding two more kills to his personal tally in the process.

Although, as has been noted previously, the squadron suffered relatively few losses as a result of enemy action during its time in Italy, flying was still an inherently dangerous business in 1918. While they were not as prone to failure as the old 1½ Strutters had been, the Camel could still

On 5th July 1918 Gordon McIntyre rode his damaged Camel, B7381/J, all the way down from 18,000 feet with a dead engine; it ended up on its back in marshland at Capo Sile, its pilot being somewhat shaken but physically unhurt. This picture shows the aeroplane being recovered and was probably taken the following day. (Geo H Williams)

let its pilot down, as had happened to Lt McIntyre on July 5th. A Canadian from Montreal, who had been with the squadron since March, he had been flying as escort to an RE 8 operating over the southern sector of the Front when his engine had seized[5]. Since he had 18,000 feet in hand, the pilot was able to stretch the subsequent glide to carry him back to friendly territory, where he attempted to land at the extreme eastern end of the Venice lagoon. Unfortunately this region is largely marsh and his aeroplane, B7381, suffered substantial damage when its wheels dug in. The aeroplane finished up on its back in shallow water, leaving Gordon McIntyre effectively submerged; he was able to disentangle himself from the rudder bar, however, and emerged substantially intact, if damp and only a little shaken.

This incident had occurred during the second mission flown by the squadron to protect RE 8s of No 34 Sqn operating from Malcontenta in support of the 3rd Italian Army. This inter-allied co-operative arrangement had begun the day before, when Nos 28, 45 and 66 Sqns had each furnished a pair of Camels to escort one of the three reconnaissance sorties flown that day, No 45 Sqn's contribution having been provided by Lts Child (D1975) and Black (D8169). For the duration of this undertaking all of the participating aircraft continued to be based on their own aerodromes, flying down to Malcontenta at about dawn and returning to their own roosts before nightfall. Nevertheless, Malcontenta was too far away to permit totally unsupported extended operations so, on 6th July, 14th Wg directed that a small detachment be set up at the forward airfield. This was to comprise an aerodrome party, including photographic processing facilities, of eleven men - three photographers plus a fitter and rigger from each of the four squadrons involved.

Operations in support of the Italians in the south continued until 11th July, No 45 Sqn taking part on all except the last two days, after which the detachment was withdrawn. In addition to those already mentioned, the pilots who took part in these operations were Bowles (twice), Oxley (twice), Hughes (twice), Haines, Hudson, Cottle, Howell, Masters, Crowe, Gibson, Huins and Catto. Although the Austrians appear to have made little attempt to interfere with the RE 8s as they trundled back and forth, these sorties were not without incident and, apart from Gordon McIntyre's narrow escape on the 5th, two other pilots were to have problems. Max Gibson damaged B6214 landing at Malcontenta at the end of his positioning flight on the 8th and the following day Ernest Masters was obliged to land back there when D1974's engine seized. Thanks, presumably, to the presence of the small handling party, the problem was sorted out and Masters was able to fly back to Grossa the next day.

By this time the focus of attention had moved north,

where No 34 Sqn's RE 8s had begun flying in support of the 4th Italian Army on 9th July, using Casoni as an advanced landing ground. Amusingly, however, it seems that No 66 Sqn had not been paying sufficient attention and when they were required to escort a mission on the 12th they sent their Camels down to Malcontenta instead of to Casoni where they were needed!

To begin with the routine was much the same as it had been at Malcontenta with the participating aircraft flying in and out each day to carry out what were cryptically described as "Special Missions". These were mostly artillery shoots and reconnaissance sorties, often carrying an Italian officer as observer in the rear cockpit. Interestingly, however, in a letter dated 12th July, 14th Wg directed that any photographic sorties were always to be flown by all-RAF crews and that the plates were to be brought back to Villaverla for processing - so much for inter-allied co-operation. The same letter also directed that "under no circumstances" would such missions be flown without an escort of at least two Camels but, whereas at Malcontenta all three fighter squadrons had flown on most days, at Casoni each unit was to take it in turns, providing all of the escorts required for the day(s) that they were assigned to the task. No 45 Sqn covered the Casoni commitment for the first time on 14th July when Lts Jack Child, Gordon McIntyre, James Black and Asa 'Susie' Lingard (all of B Flight) flew from there, only the first two actually being required to carry out an escort mission.

Compared to Malcontenta, Casoni was only half the distance from Villaverla, but even so a considerable amount of time and effort had to be expended on the daily deployment of the aircraft and their necessary ground support

This photograph of No 45 Sqn's D8237/D is believed to have been taken at Casoni during the brief period (14th-27th July) that 14th Wg's Camels flew from there as escorts to the RE 8s of No 34 Sqn's D Flight operating in support of the 4th Italian Army. The Squadron Record Book indicates that the only time that D8237 was involved in this operation was on 16th July when it was flown by Lt H B 'Steve' Hudson. It is said that some (all?) of the Camels taking part in these "Special Missions" had their unit identity markings painted out and replaced by a white band as seen here, the aim possibly being to create the impression that another British fighter squadron had arrived in Italy. (Author's collection)

- two mechanics from No 34 Sqn and four from the nominated Camel squadron. Since there was no sign of an early decline in the level of activity, to minimise the time being wasted No 34 Sqn established a permanent three-aircraft detachment at Casoni from 23rd July; this became the squadron's D Flight. By then No 45 Sqn had already covered the commitment several more times. Lts Hudson, Bowles, Oxley and Catto went to Casoni on 16th July, Lts Oxley, Davis, Dewhirst[6] and Milborrow on the 19th, Lts Haines, Crowe, Lingard and Hughes on the 21st and Lts James, Bowles, Oxley and Gibson on the 22nd but a combination of reduced tasking and adverse weather meant that only three more escort missions had actually been flown.

In his *Offensive Patrol*, Norman Macmillan indicates that No 45 Sqn mounted a detachment at Casoni late in July but it is doubtful whether this was a very substantial or long-lived affair - *if* it happened at all. The squadron operated from Casoni only once after No 34 Sqn had established its D Flight there. This was on 27th July when four pilots, Capt Cottle and Lt Oxley of A Flight and Lts Milborrow and Dewhirst of C Flt, spent the day there, only the first pair actually being called upon to fly an escort mission. The only untoward incident was that Cottle broke D8238's tailskid and James Dewhirst spent most of the day flying to Villaverla and back in B5813 to collect a spare.

While a small party of No 45 Sqn's groundcrew *may* have been established at Casoni for a few days, the requirement for dedicated escorts lapsed thereafter. The RE 8s of No 34 Sqn's D Flight continued to operate from Casoni in support of the Italian army until the last three aeroplanes were withdrawn to Villaverla on 5th September but no further 'special missions' were flown by any of the Camel squadrons. It would seem very unlikely therefore that any of No 45 Sqn's aeroplanes ever spent a night away from base. There exists, however, an interesting photograph (reproduced here), which is said to have been taken at Casoni, showing a Camel (D8237) in unusual markings, which may indicate that it had originally been intended to mount a prolonged detachment

there[7]. The aeroplane is displaying, in place of the usual dumb-bell, a white fuselage band, similar to that worn by the squadron's old 1½ Strutters. It has been suggested that this change of marking may have been a cunning plan to seduce enemy spies into concluding that an additional, fourth, British fighter squadron had arrived in Italy. Specific documentary evidence to support this conjecture is lacking but such ruses do seem to have been employed by the RAF in Italy (see below) so it is not an unlikely explanation - it would be interesting to know whether any of Nos 28 and/or 66 Sqns' aeroplanes were similarly marked at this time.

August was to be No 45 Sqn's last full month of operations in Italy. By the beginning of that month only seven pilots remained on strength from those who had made the journey from France. Three of the older hands had only just left, Lts Jack Child, Dickie Dawes and Paddy O'Neill, having set off for England on 29th July, accompanied by Lt 'Steve' Hudson. One of these stalwarts was to remain in the service after the war and would eventually retire as Air Commodore H D O'Neill CBE AFC. The squadron's officers as at August 1st are listed at Figure 3.2. The next men to arrive, on the 6th, would be Lt R J O'Connell and 2/Lt A V Green with 2/Lt L B Irish following three days later. The three officers who constituted HQ Flight at this time, Ronald Buck, Charles King and Douglas Fryer (the last two having been in post since February and July 1918, respectively) would continue to oversee all essential support services for the rest of the unit's career as a Camel squadron.

'Spike' Howell relinquished command of C Flight to Alan Rice-Oxley on August 9th and went home with nineteen victories to his credit; his achievements with the squadron were eventually to be recognised by the award of a DSO, an MC and a DFC. Sadly, he was drowned off Corfu in 1919 while attempting to fly a Martinsyde back to his native Australia.

Patrols were flown throughout August in the course of which a further twenty-two victories were added to the squadron's tally. On August 29th the squadron mounted another bombing raid but it was frustrated by cloud and only three of the six aeroplanes attempted to attack anything, let alone the nominated target in the Brenta Valley. Two days later the squadron had its last successful fight in Italy. Capt Cottle, with Lts James and Davis, encountered a formation of six Albatros D IIIs and proceeded to shoot down the lot; Jack Cottle was credited with three kills, Mansell James with two and Randall Davis with one OOC. The wreckage of three of their victims fell in friendly territory while that of a

A squadron group on leave in August 1918. From the left: Lt C G Catto, Capt M R James, Lt J R Black, Lt F S Bowles, Lt H T Smith and Lt A Rice-Oxley. Charles 'Bollicky Bill' Catto was one of the squadron's three American pilots and he was to be the most successful of them, shooting down six aeroplanes by November. 'Doc' Smith, an American who had enlisted in the British army, was attached to No 45 Sqn as its MO between 27th July and 12th August. (J A Brown)

Maj J A Crook MC		
A Flight	**B Flight**	**C Flight**
Capt J Cottle	Capt N C Jones	Capt C E Howell
Lt F S Bowles	Lt J R Black	Lt J H Dewhirst
Lt M Gibson	Lt A J Haines	Lt J P Huins
Lt M R James	Lt R M Hughes	Lt E H Masters
Lt F H Oxley	Lt A F Lingard	Lt E L Milborrow
Lt R G H Davis	Lt G McIntyre	Lt A Rice-Oxley
Lt C G Catto	Lt H F Crowe	Lt H T Thompson
Lt D J Fryer - Recording Officer		
Lt R Buck - Armament Officer		
2/Lt C F King - Assistant Equipment Officer		

Fig 3.2. The officers of No 45 Sqn, 1st August 1918.

Sgt MacNally, one of C Flight's groundcrew. (J A Brown)

the Western Front and the growing confidence of the Italians led to nine British battalions being recalled to France. No 45 Sqn was to go with them. On 12th September it was withdrawn from operations and on the 14th it began to dismantle its aircraft and pack its kit. Six days later the squadron began its return journey to France by train. During its nine months in Italy, No 45 Sqn had claimed the remarkable total of 154 aerial victories, 114 of them having been confirmed as 'kills'. As it set off for France the squadron left behind an unrivalled record of success and an enviable reputation.

There is an interesting footnote to the story of the squadron's service in Italy. It has been reported that, in order to disguise No 45 Sqn's departure, Nos 28 and 66 Sqns were both directed to apply dumb-bells to some of their aircraft in place of their own unit markings. To this author's knowledge no documentary evidence has yet come to light to substantiate this story but photographs, taken after No 45 Sqn had left Italy (one of which is reproduced here), show that at least two of No 66 Sqn's Camels were marked with a slightly modified form of the dumb-bell. It would seem therefore that there may well be some substance to this tale.

The journey back to France was uncomfortable but, compared with the trip to Italy in the previous December, it had the merit of being relatively short. On 22nd September the squadron arrived at Bettoncourt where it was assigned to VIII Bde's 41st Wg and began to re-erect its aeroplanes.

fourth was visible in the Austrian lines. Recent research suggests that, while there had originally been six aircraft in the Austrian formation, by the time that they were engaged by Cottle's flight there were only four, all flown by inexperienced pilots who had failed to keep up when the leading pair had dived away to attack a British two-seater; the four men who were shot down were Ltns Pürer, von Tomicki and Kubelik and Stfw Förster. In the course of this engagement the squadron's running total of victories claimed since leaving England in October 1916 had passed the 300 mark.

The squadron sustained three casualties in August, only one of them in combat. Lt Haines' D9412 was hit by AA fire while flying near Asiago on the 10th. His body fell between the lines and was later retrieved by the Austrians under a white flag and brought to the British positions. Alfred Haines, who had joined the squadron just before it left France, had previously accounted for six enemy aircraft; he was to be No 45 Sqn's last combat fatality of WW I. The other two incidents were both the result of night flying accidents. Lt James Black was injured in a crash on the 15th; the following night Capt W C Hilborn was similarly injured and he died in hospital ten days later. William Hilborn had been the victor of seven combats with Nos 28 and 66 Sqns and had been transferred to No 45 Sqn on 13th August to take over Howell's C Flight, which had been temporarily in the hands of Alan Rice-Oxley. With Hilborn's death Rice-Oxley resumed command but, although he was made up to captain, his second stint as a flight commander was also to be brief as Capt C H B Readman was posted-in to take over on the 20th.

The need to counter Ludendorf's summer offensive on

Capt Norman Jones joined the squadron as OC A Flight in January 1918 but transferred to B Flight a month later, remaining in command until September. By then he had eight victories to his credit. (J A Brown)

This picture shows Camel E7167/S of No 66 Sqn after it had been shot down behind the Austrian lines near Conegliano on 22nd October 1918, a month after No 45 Sqn had left for France. No 66 Sqn's own marking consisted of a vertical bar in front of and a horizontal bar behind the fuselage roundels but this aeroplane is obviously wearing a slightly modified form of No 45 Sqn's dumbbell, lending substance to reports that Nos 28 and 66 Sqns were required to display dumb-bells on some of their aircraft to disguise the fact that the RAF's fighter force in Italy had been reduced by a third. (Philip Jarratt)

The squadron was now a part of Trenchard's Independent Air Force (IAF)[8], the growing bomber force based to the south of Nancy which was paving the way for the employment of massive strategic air power that was to realise its full potential a quarter of a century later. In the course of its incursions into Germany, attacking war industries, rail communications and airfields, the bombers had suffered heavy losses. In other words the intruders had found themselves with exactly the same problem that No 45 Sqn had had a year or more before, and their recommended solution was the same - they wanted escorts. Ironically it was to be No 45 Sqn which was earmarked to fulfil this role. The Camel's successor, the Sopwith Snipe, was about to enter squadron service and a long-range variant of the aircraft was being developed with sufficient fuel tankage to permit it to accompany the bombers. The squadron was earmarked to receive these new Snipes but, as yet, none was available and in the meantime the squadron was to carry out normal patrols to protect the IAF's base area.

There was another reshuffle of flight commanders as the squadron was moving to its new theatre of operations. Capt Readman had not stayed long; on September 14th, just before the squadron left Italy, he had been transferred to No 7 AP and Mansell James been promoted to take over C Flight. Capt Rice-Oxley had stepped into yet another breach to become OC B Flight on Norman Jones' departure for England on 1st September. Unfortunately, he was admitted to hospital on the day that the squadron reached Bettoncourt and Catto stood in for him until a permanent successor could be appointed. The new OC B Flight arrived on September 29th; he was Capt J W Pinder, an ex-RNAS man who already had twelve victories to his name. These were to be the last changes of flight commander, A Flight remaining in Cottle's capable hands to the end. The squadron spent the last few days of September rebuilding its aeroplanes and becoming accustomed to its new surroundings. Flying was initially confined to air tests, local area familiarisation sorties and shakedown flights for a batch of new pilots.

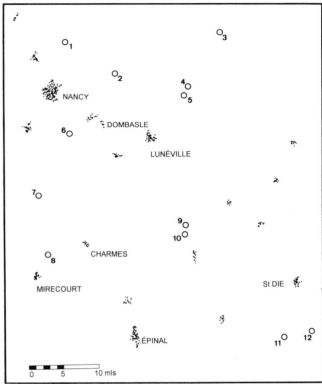

6	Azelot	3	Dieuze	5	Parroy
8	Bettoncourt	2	Erbéviller	10	Roville-aux-Chênes
4	Coincourt	12	Fraize	7	Tantonville
11	Corcieux	1	Montonoy	9	Xaffévillers

Map 3.2. *Eastern France, showing localities and locations of significance to No 45 Sqn in September-November 1918.*

No 45 Sqn flew its first operational patrol since its return to France on 1st October but it proved to be uneventful. On the 9th Capt Pinder drove down a Rumpler two-seater OOC and 2/Lt Leslie Irish did the same the following day, but otherwise the squadron found little trade at first. Their luck changed on October 23rd. A patrol engaged a group of German aeroplanes and made four claims. John Pinder shot down one Rumpler, which fell in friendly territory, damaged another and drove down an Albatros two-seater OOC. In the same engagement Lts Masters and Thompson also claimed Rumpler two-seaters OOC. Henry Thompson's victory was his fifth, making him the last of No 45 Sqn's pilots to gain the status of being an Ace.

The squadron had arrived back in France just as the Spanish influenza pandemic was developing. Over 27,000 British servicemen were admitted to hospital with either the 'flu' or pneumonia during October 1918; 1,463 of them died. It has not been positively confirmed but it seems highly probable that this was the cause of nine deaths among No 45 Sqn's groundcrew that month. They were: 2/AM E W Strong who died on the 4th; 2/AMs A Blease and W Radford on the 5th; 1/AM J Laughland on the 6th; 2/AM G C Cheetham and 1/AM W J Robinson on the 8th; 1/AM W Ritchie on the 11th; 1/AM H Molyneux on the 12th and 2/AM S Evans on the 19th.

Aerial activity in the squadron's sector appears not to have been very intense and the young pilots found other ways of expending their surplus energy. In a letter home, dated 13th October, Charles Catto wrote:

A South African, Major Allister Mackintosh Miller, made two recruiting tours of his native land during the war. On one of them his road show was given considerable impact by this BE 2e, A3110, a 'Presentation' aircraft which bore the inscription Rio de Janeiro Britons, No 2. *(via J A Brown)*

Seen here on the range at Istrana in early 1918, Capt Jack Cottle remained with No 45 Sqn until 1919 by which time he was OC A Flight and the victor of fourteen engagements. (J A Brown)

....we amused ourselves by knocking the chimneys off each other's huts with cinders from the cinder path. It was good sport but the cinders were sharp and my first two fingers are cut to ribbons. The Flying Corps boys are all like a lot of schoolboys, even our CO Major Crook joined in the fun today. Then in the Mess tonight we turned the place upside down, giving a couple of officers a shampoo with tomato sauce. I got a big ladle of hot cabbage on the head. The whole crowd often breaks out like that!

Although there had not been a great deal of combat in October there had been a number of significant events towards the end of the month. On 20th October Maj A M Miller DSO arrived to assume command and, having handed over the reins, Joe Crook left for England the following day. Allister Mackintosh Miller, a South African, had been flying since 1915 and had over 1,400 flying hours under his belt when he arrived at Bettoncourt but, surprisingly, since he was to command a fighter squadron, he had never flown a

Camel. Although it is quite unconnected with No 45 Sqn, there is an interesting tale attached to Miller's earlier flying experience. He had been serving with No 3 Sqn when Max Immelmann, 'The Eagle of Lille', was killed on 18th June 1916 and on 1st July Miller and his observer flew over the lines to drop a wreath on Vélu airfield near Bapaume. This tribute was accompanied by a note expressing the respect which the RFC had had for the fallen German Ace. Only two weeks later Miller's companion, Howard Long, was shot down and taken prisoner. Both crew members had signed the note which they had dropped and once Long's identity was clearly established he was granted certain concessionary privileges during the remainder of his time as a POW - which just goes to show that it pays to be chivalrous.

Shortly after the new CO had arrived there was a change of controlling authority when, on 28th October, the squadron was reassigned to 88th Wg. This did not involve a change of location, however, and in the event this arrangement proved to be short-lived; after only five days, control over the squadron was restored to 41st Wg.

In the meantime John Pinder had collected the squadron's first Snipe, E8081, on October 30th and the next day Jack Cottle brought in E8017. Neither of these aeroplanes was modified for long-range work but they were perfectly adequate for type familiarisation and the pilots were eager to try them out. In the event, however, they were to be the only Snipes that the squadron ever took on charge.

On 3rd November Jack Cottle scored his fourteenth and last victory by driving down a Fokker D VII OOC near Erbéviller. On the same day Lt Bowles failed to return, making him the last of No 45 Sqn's pilots to be lost in combat during WW I. His E7168 had fallen to the guns of

A Flight of No 45 Sqn shortly after the end of the war; the location is uncertain but the picture was probably taken at Bettoncourt. Seated, from the left: 2/Lt J C Williams, 2/Lt C W Verity, Lt M Gibson, Lt C G Catto, Capt J Cottle, Lt A F Lingard, 2/Lt L B Irish and Lt G Exley. Standing, from the left: F/Sgt J A Morton, next two unidentified, AM W Ferguson, AM W Green, AM W G Hansell, AM W C Dodwell, next three unidentified, Cpl Maidment, AM E Van Coevorden, Sgt H Heald. (Geo H Williams)

Ltns Kurt Seit and Karl Romeis of Jasta 80. Francis Bowles was the baby of the squadron, having turned nineteen years of age only four days before being shot down. Despite his youth he was an accomplished pilot, however, and he had claimed his fifth victory on 5th August. Fortunately he survived and became a POW - although not for long. The squadron's final victory claims were submitted two days later. At about mid-day on November 5th Capt Cottle destroyed a Rumpler C-type to the east of Dieuze and in the afternoon Capt Pinder and Lt Dewhirst shot down two more EA. No 45 Sqn's last Combat Report reads as follows:

When at 17,500 ft Capt J W Pinder observed 1 EA at 3,000 ft just over our lines on N side of forest of Parroy. The Patrol immediately dived to engage the EA but the EA saw their approach and dived down to the ground. The Camels then flying at 2,000 ft turned back to the Line and saw a 2/Str Rumpler coming nose on slightly below them. Capt Pinder engaged from the front and fired 100 rounds at almost point blank range passing right over the top of it. At this moment Lt Dewhirst who was behind observed a large white object like a tail plane fall from EA. Immediately after this Lt Dewhirst attacked a single seater from the rear at about 20 yards range firing a long burst. The pilot of the EA seemed to collapse in his machine the EA doing a (*left or right, the original is indecipherable - CGJ*) turn under the Camel's wing and was then lost to view. It was impossible to observe further results of these combats owing to the proximity of the ground. Camels were being fired at heavily by both

rifles and machine guns from the ground. Capt Pinder fired 240 rounds. Lt Dewhirst fired 190.

Both claims were subsequently confirmed as kills, a Rumpler and a Fokker D VII. They were John Pinder's fifth kill with No 45 Sqn (his seventeenth overall) and James Dewhirst's seventh.

On November 10th 2/Lt Cyril Robertshaw, a South African who had arrived in September, had his second trip on one of the Snipes (E8081) and wrecked it. The following day the Armistice became effective. The squadron flew on November 11th but all was quiet. There was no flying at all on the 12th and only sporadic sorties were mounted over the next few days. On 22nd November the IAF dispensed with the squadron's services and it moved to Le Hameau where it came under the aegis of 89th Wg of III Bde. No details of the incident (incidents?) appear to have survived but something fairly dramatic must have happened during the move because D8240, E1501 and F3979 all crashed on the 22nd, although no pilots seemed to have suffered any serious injuries that day. Apart from the move there was still very little flying, the only flight recorded between 17th November and 6th December being an air test which Cottle carried out on his D8237. On each of the 7th, 8th and 9th December there were two six-aircraft formation practices but flying then lapsed again. Concerned at the lack of activity the military mind scuttled to its last refuge and ordered the men off on a route march on the 16th while the officers were sent on a cross-country run. How well this went down with the long-suffering and long-serving groundcrew, like Sgt Maidment,

Sgt Morton, Sgt Lambert, Cpl Grimmitt and others who had been with the squadron since Sedgeford, has not been recorded!

On the 17th December the squadron flew fourteen sorties in formations of three and four and there was a parade followed by a football match. There was no more flying for a week after that - but there was another route march on the 19th. The squadron flew another series of formation practices on December 24th but this time it ended in disaster. Lt Milborrow in E1500 and Lt Masters in C54 collided. Edgar Milborrow, another South African, escaped with his life, although he had been injured; Masters was killed. The date made this unfortunate accident seem all the more tragic. Ernest Masters had been with the squadron since March and had thus survived eight months of combat flying, in the course of which he had shot down eight enemy aircraft, only to die in a flying accident on the first Christmas Eve after the guns had fallen silent.

There was no more flying until New Year's Day when four practice flights were laid on and two replacement aircraft were ferried in. On January 3rd an Education Officer, Lt R Platt, was attached to the squadron for a nine day stint, probably to offer advice on civilian resettlement and guidance on the procedures governing discharge and release from the service. In the meantime there was a little intermittent flying but even this seems to have petered out on January 18th. The last Snipe was flown occasionally during this period but its utilisation was now the exclusive preserve of the CO, Jack Cottle and John Pinder. Two more Camels were lost, both in landing accidents and both on the 6th. 2/Lt Alban Green, a Canadian who had been with the squadron since August, was admitted to hospital after crashing D9392 at Maisoncelle and Lt Dewhirst wrote off E7204 at Béthencourt.

While this desultory activity had been taking place at Le Hameau, and all the other once busy airfields in France, the staffs had been hard at it, working out how the huge air service, which had taken four years to build, could be dismantled again in a matter of weeks. The details of the first stage of the overall demobilisation plan were published on 14th January. The section relevant to No 45 Sqn required that all Clerget-engined Camels were to be flown to Liettres where they were to be reduced to produce by the resident Nos 151 and 152 Sqns, both of which had been designated as 'Demobilisation Units' (there were eight others). Once they had completed this task, the Demobilisation Units were required to self-destruct and demobilise themselves in the same way. No 151 Sqn was nominated to accept the aeroplanes of Nos 45, 54 and 65 Sqns. Having disposed of their aircraft and equipment, the personnel of these three units were to remain under the command of their original Brigade HQs but it would fall to HQ Reserve Brigade to keep them occupied and entertained until they could be disposed of. It was intended that the whole process (this first phase of demobilisation would dispense with forty-nine fully operational squadrons) should be carried out within just seven weeks - a whole squadron every day. Speed was of the essence.

Under another section of the plan Le Hameau had been designated as the collection point for the SE 5as of Nos 24, 40, 56 and 94 Sqns; their aeroplanes were to be handed over

to No 1 Sqn, another of the Demobilisation Units, and were eventually to be ferried back to England. To make room for the incoming flocks of SEs it was necessary for No 45 Sqn to move out as soon as possible. On the 17th January the squadron was reassigned to III Bde's 90th Wing and two days later it moved to Liettres.

Since the squadron's return to France a number of new faces had appeared to replace pilots who had been killed, admitted to hospital or posted. Of the eighteen line pilots, only seven of those shown as having been on strength on 1st August 1918 (Figure 3.2) still remained. The pilots and aircraft listed at Figure 3.3 are those who flew from Le Hameau to Liettres on 19th January 1919; they represent a final snapshot of the squadron's air echelon as it came to the end of its first period of active service.

There were a few more pilots still on strength, including Capt J W Pinder, Lt J H Dewhirst, 2/Lt A V Green, 2/Lt S J B Callcott and 2/Lt L F Hawley and the squadron's logistic and administrative affairs were still in the hands of the three officers who had looked after these matters in Italy, Lt Fryer, Lt Buck and 2/Lt King.

On their arrival at Liettres the aeroplanes were promptly transferred to No 151 Sqn and the groundcrew began disposing of portable hangars, tentage, tools, MT and the rest of their impedimenta in accordance with the instructions which had been issued by 'Q' Branch. Someone appears not to have read the small print in the demobilisation plan, however, and it was pointed out that Snipes were among the types which were not to be broken up. E8017 was not wanted at Liettres and the CO was obliged to take it back to Le Hameau. Once he had found out where it should have gone, he delivered the squadron's sole surviving Snipe to Marquise on the 21st. There was one last Camel still languishing at Le Hameau, E7244, and Lt Eric Nuding ferried it across to Liettres on January 22nd. This, for the time being, was probably the last flight made by a pilot of No 45 Sqn.

All of the squadron's personnel were put at the disposal of 'A' Branch on January 20th and they began to be posted away in batches almost immediately. Most of the groundcrew returned to England to be released from the service. Before the end of the month, eight pilots had been sent to Berck-sur-Mer, where they were attached to the staff of the Aerial Range, and four others went to Setques but in both cases these were probably only temporary assignments on the way home. Capt Cottle was in the UK on leave when the squadron began to be dispersed and it is doubtful that he ever rejoined it. During the first few days of February, Capt James was posted to No 15 Sqn; Lt

Pilot	Aircraft
Maj A M Miller DSO	E8017
Capt J Cottle DFC	D8237
Capt M R James DFC	E7212
Lt A F Lingard	D8211
Lt G McIntyre	F6443
Lt C G Catto	E1580
Lt R N Hughes	D8113
Lt M Gibson	D8243
Lt H Crowe	F6225
Lt J R O'Connell	F6281
Lt E G Nuding	D9430
Lt G Exley	F6497
2/Lt C A Robertshaw	E7230
2/Lt C W Verity	D9394
2/Lt J C Williams	E1539
2/Lt L B Irish	D9386
2/Lt J C S Masters	F6200

Fig 3.3. Pilots and aircraft of No 45 Sqn as it was reducing to cadre in late January 1919.

Fryer went to HQ 89th Wg; 2/Lt King joined No 5 Sqn and Lt Buck was attached to Hesdin. On January 19th the squadron had had twenty-one officers and 135 NCOs and Other Ranks on its books. By the 23rd the latter figure had already been whittled down to 110 but three days later the position was temporarily reversed when twenty-nine men of No 94 Sqn, which was also demobilising, were posted-in. The process started all over again, but it was very rapid, and by February 5th the squadron's total strength stood at just thirty-two men, of whom five were officers.

While all this had been going on Maj Miller had been admitted to hospital and Capt Pinder became CO of the rapidly dwindling unit on February 3rd. Two days later the squadron was formally declared to have been reduced to cadre status[9]. Most of the squadron's MT was transferred to No 1 AD on February 9th and on the 15th the rump of the squadron made its way to Boulogne in its remaining vehicles which it handed over to the authorities at the Port Depot before embarking for Folkestone. This small party had been provided with rail warrants to get them as far as Cirencester and from there they found their way to Rendcomb to join the cadre of No 46 Sqn which had arrived three days earlier.

There the two nominal squadrons were to await developments.

At this time it was still not entirely certain that the war was actually over. The Armistice of 11th November had been just that, an Armistice, and arriving at a formal Peace Settlement was proving to be problematical. Initially the Air Ministry's contingency plans provided for virtually the whole of the wartime RAF to be retained, at least in cadre form, and No 45 Sqn was pencilled in to re-equip with Sopwith Salamanders should it be reactivated. As 1919 wore on more cadres returned to England as further demobilisation measures were put into effect and by mid-year many of them began to be disbanded, but a handful lingered on. On the 18th December 1919 Air Organisation Memorandum AO 1445 announced that a batch of twenty-eight cadres, almost the last of them, would disband on 31st December. The remnant of No 45 Sqn, which had moved to Eastleigh on 15th October, was one of these units. It was not to be dormant for long however.

Before embarking on the squadron's post-war history it is appropriate to review briefly just what it had achieved in its two years of active service. Much of this is tabulated in some

The squadron's officers posed in front of one the squadron's two Snipes, probably at Le Hameau. Unfortunately, while the names of all of those present are known, it has been possible to match these to faces in only a few cases. Seated third from the left is Lt Ronald Buck; qualifying as a pilot in May 1916, he had accumulated some 250 flying hours before being wounded in action and grounded, eventually to become No 45 Sqn's Armament Officer. The figure to his left is thought to be Capt John William Pinder, OC B Flt (although, since Pinder was ex-RNAS, he just might be the standing figure wearing naval uniform). Centre left, wearing a formidable pair of furry gloves, is Maj Allister Mackintosh Miller DSO, a South African, who became OC No 45 Sqn on 21st October 1918; at that stage he had logged some 1,400 flying hours but, surprisingly under the circumstances, none of them on Camels. Centre right is Capt Jack Cottle DFC, OC A Flt. The figure on Cottle's left is believed to be Capt Mansell Richard James DFC, OC C Flt. Next to him is 2/Lt Charles Frederick King, another South African and the squadron's Assistant Equipment Officer. Standing, two places to the right of the officer in naval uniform and wearing a dark shirt, is the squadron's Recording Officer, 2/Lt Douglas Johnson Fryer. (J A Brown)

detail in various Annexes to this book but a short summary is provided here. Since October 1916 the squadron had claimed a grand total of 316 victories in aerial combat, of which 177 aircraft were regarded as having been destroyed or captured. Thirty-two of its pilots had claimed, or shared in, five or more victories and had thus conformed to the popular definition of having become Aces. To these may be added two observer/gunners whose guns had also accounted for at least five victories. Three other observers had participated in five victorious engagements, although some of the victims of these had fallen to the guns of their pilots. Early in 1918 it became official policy for both members of a two-seater crew to be given equal credit for an aerial victory, regardless of who had actually inflicted the damage, and if this yardstick is applied in retrospect then, technically, these three men should also be regarded as Aces, making the squadron's total a remarkable thirty-seven.

In the course of establishing this exemplary record very heavy losses had been sustained, particularly in the first year of operations. In all, seventy-four men had died during, or as a result of, combat missions. Sixty-six of them had been posted missing or killed in action; six more, one of them a POW, had succumbed to wounds which they had sustained and two (Watt and Pocock) were listed as 'accidentally killed', although they had actually been flying on an operational sortie. Sixty of these losses had occurred during the two-seater era. Eight more lives had been lost in flying accidents; twenty-three further men had been wounded and twelve others had been taken prisoner after having been shot down.

As has previously been observed the award of decorations in recognition of achievement was a rarity while the squadron was flying 1½ Strutters, yet it was during this period that losses were heaviest. It follows that the crews who flew with the squadron at that time were required to display just as much dogged courage as their single-seater successors, if not more, since the latter did at least have a fighting chance. The total recognition afforded to squadron personnel during a period in which the unit lost its entire strength nearly three times over, consisted of just three MCs and a DCM. Once the squadron had converted to Camels, however, decorations were awarded more generously and the squadron's pilots went on to win two DSOs, ten more MCs plus a Bar to an MC and ten DFCs plus a Bar to a DFC. In addition one MSM was awarded and seven individuals were Mentioned in Despatches. On top of that, eight Italian, three French and two Belgian awards were made to officers of the squadron.

Notes:

1. The original location of the serial number on a Sopwith Camel was determined by its manufacturer. Most Camels built by the parent company, for instance, and those built under contract by Nieuport & General, displayed their serial numbers in black within a neat white box on each side of the rear fuselage; those manufactured by Boulton & Paul had their serials painted on the rudder in black *and* in a box on the fuselage while early production batches from Ruston Proctor had their serials painted on the fin in black (making them quite difficult to distinguish against the PC 10 background). Production by other contractors and the passage of time introduced several variations on this theme, eg later aircraft produced by Ruston Proctor still had their serials on the fin but painted in a more legible pale grey, and in-service modifications by units were very common. No 45 Sqn's mechanics

became dab hands in the art of moving serial numbers about, primarily because the location of the fuselage dumb-bell marking behind the roundel interfered with the white serial number boxes. These boxes had to be obliterated and, where necessary, the serial number was repainted on the fin, either in a single line, eg B6238, or in larger characters with the letter on top, as on Frew's B6372. There is photographic evidence to show that they also repainted many of Ruston Proctor's early black fin-serials in white, eg on B2430, B2434 and B2443, and that when they had a mood to do so they were not beyond then moving it to the rudder in black, eg B2430.

2. It has been suggested that A and B Flights' Camels used letters from the outset and that the early use of numerals was confined to C Flight. This is possible but, with an establishment of only eighteen aircraft, the alphabet was well able to accommodate the squadron's entire strength so it not clear why C Flight's aeroplanes should have been marked differently, unless it was simply to show that they were indeed different - that *they* were C Flight and thus particularly distinctive and privileged. If that was the case then this drift towards some form of enhanced autonomy appears to have been short-lived.

3. Later to become Air Chief Marshal Sir Philip Joubert de la Ferté KCB CMG DSO, AOCinC Coastal Command in 1941-43.

4. The aeroplane which was credited to Charles Catto was not actually an Aviatik but a Brandenburg C I of Flik 8D, its crew being Zgsf A Gnamusch and Ltn R Huss (see photograph at Annex E).

5. In describing this incident to George Williams some fifty-five years later, McIntyre attributed the failure of his engine to AA fire. The Squadron Record Book makes no mention of 'Archie' having been a factor and specifically identifies the cause of the problem as being a seized-up engine. Furthermore, as McIntyre remembered the event he had been engaged on a solo escort mission, whereas it is known that he had actually been accompanied by Lt Bowles in B5181. It would seem, therefore, that during the half-century that had elapsed since the event, McIntyre's memory of it had become somewhat clouded.

6. This officer's name is rendered as 'Dewhurst' where it appears in the Air Force List and the London Gazette but it is invariably 'Dewhirst' in more mundane contemporary documentation, including Combat Reports, the Squadron Record Book, the Daily State returns, Routine Orders, etc and in references to him made in the writings of others. It is hardly likely that his name would have been consistently spelled wrongly on a daily basis from his arrival on No 45 Sqn in February 1918 right through to the end of the war and after, so 'Dewhirst' is considered to have been the correct version. It is assumed that his name must have been misspelled on some key document on enlistment, causing it to appear incorrectly in all subsequent *official* publications.

7. Macmillan's caption to this photograph claims that it shows an aeroplane of "Cottle's D Flight". Beyond this, however, there is no evidence to indicate that No 45 Sqn ever established a D Flight; there is certainly no reference to it in the surviving records of HQ 14th Wg or in those of any of its four constituent squadrons. The Squadron Record Book shows that Cottle himself did fly from Casoni, but only once - on 27th July when he used D8238. D8237 was undoubtedly one of No 45 Sqn's aeroplanes (one of A Flight's to be precise) and it too is noted as having been at Casoni, but again only once - on 16th July when it was flown by Lt Hudson, then Acting OC A Flight. If it is accepted that the picture of D8237 actually was taken at Casoni then it would appear to have been photographed a week *before* even No 34 Sqn's D Flight had been set up, ie when all of the aircraft and aircrews involved in operations from Casoni and all of their supporting personnel were still deploying on a daily basis and returning to their own aerodromes in the evenings. Cottle, incidentally, did not become a flight commander until 29th July when he was made up to captain to take over A Flight which had been in the hands of Lt Hudson since Capt Dawes had assumed temporary command of the squadron following the death of Maj Vaucour.

In the light of the above, it is suggested that a more accurate caption to the photograph might have read - "A Camel of No 45 Sqn's A Flight at Casoni where it was supporting the operations of RE 8s of No 34 Sqn, the latter eventually establishing a D Flight there as a permanent detachment."

8. Strictly speaking Trenchard's Command was styled the Independent Force, RAF, but colloquially (and in many official documents) it was known as the Independent Air Force and this is the term which will be used here.

9. A cadre notionally comprised two officers, two warrant officers, one SNCO and twelve men.

Chapter 4. The Baghdad Air Mail and Air Control - Vernons.

One of the consequences of the First World War was the total collapse of the Ottoman Empire, leaving a power vacuum in the Near East. It is not necessary to discuss here the British Government's reasons for wanting to fill this gap; suffice to say that at San Remo in April 1920 the French and British divided the region between them and the latter became the *de facto* rulers of the territory that now comprises Israel, Jordan and Iraq[1]. This outcome was contested, however, both by the previous rulers, the Turks, and by various elements of the indigenous populations. Fired by emergent nationalism, some of the latter were prepared to fight to establish their claims for recognition. This was a familiar imperial problem to the British, but the recent war had been very costly and financial resources were limited. Furthermore the need to make concessions to growing Indian nationalism meant that the government in Delhi was considering placing constraints on the previous British practice of employing the Indian Army as a colonial police force, free of charge. The problem faced by the British Government was how to devise a means of establishing its authority in the Near East without reducing the nation to penury in the process.

At the same time the RAF also had a problem. It was fighting for its very survival. It had been created in response to a public outcry against the success of German bombing attacks on England in 1917. Although these raids were mere pinpricks in absolute terms, they had caused considerable alarm and General Smuts had been appointed to investigate the situation. He reported that the lack of an appropriate single controlling agency had allowed the RFC and RNAS to evolve along parallel but quite separate lines and that there was inadequate co-ordination of their effort. As a result roles were being duplicated and resources dissipated. This was as true in other fields as it was in that of air defence, but air defence was the focus of immediate concern. Smuts recommended that a dedicated Air Ministry should be established and that the two flying services should be amalgamated under its aegis. All of this was implemented by 1st April 1918. Within a year, however, stringent post-war budgetary restrictions were already leading the RN and the army to question the continuing need for a separate third service, since its independence meant that the limited military budget had to be divided three ways instead of just two. In any case, it was argued, there was no longer an air threat to the UK and official Government policy was that there would be no war for at least ten years. It followed that the RAF's *raison d'être* had evaporated and that its continued existence was therefore both unnecessary and unaffordable.

If the RAF was to survive, the Chief of the Air Staff (CAS), Air Marshal Sir Hugh Trenchard, needed to demonstrate that a separate air service really was essential, even in peacetime. The key lay in its cost-effectiveness. He argued that, while aeroplanes could not do the job entirely alone, a handful of squadrons could be used to police huge areas and maintain order through appropriate offensive action when necessary. Alternatively, or if direct intervention failed, aeroplanes could also be used to convey troops rapidly from central locations to trouble spots. This would significantly reduce the residual number of soldiers required, since their

rapid deployment would enable them to contain unrest before it spread, thus obviating the need to maintain large and expensive garrisons 'up-country'. It was contended that air power would be a more effective way of maintaining imperial control than more traditional methods and, more convincingly to the Treasury, that it would be cheaper. The RAF's survival problem was to be neatly solved by making it the solution to the Government's imperial problem.

The CAS fought his case and won it. The 'Trenchard Memorandum' of 25th November 1919 was presented to Parliament and endorsed by the Commons the following month. On 5th January 1920 the Directorate of Air Organisation and Training published its plans for the strength and disposition of the peacetime RAF. Of the thirty-four squadrons which were to be maintained (of which only thirty-two were immediately available), twenty-two were to be based abroad in an imperial role: ten in Egypt; eight in India; three in Mesopotamia and one in Malta. Considerable thought had been devoted to the selection of the squadron identities which should be carried forward to constitute the peacetime RAF; the CAS chose No 45 Sqn to be one of the two additional units needed to complete the proposed force.

Developing the idea of using aeroplanes as instruments of imperial authority, Trenchard further refined his concept of air control and argued that, if air power was to predominate, then it followed that an RAF officer should be in command. In March 1921 a conference was convened in Cairo to examine the current problems in the Middle East. At this meeting, chaired by Winston Churchill and attended by Trenchard, it was agreed, although not without some dissent, that air control would be tried, that Mesopotamia would be the proving ground and that an RAF officer would be in overall command. It was also agreed that the number of squadrons to be based in the country should be raised to eight. The three units allocated to Mesopotamia in the initial plan had been Nos 6, 30 and 84 Sqns. To these had already been added Nos 55 and 8 Sqns; the latter, having reformed in Egypt in the previous October, was actually en route to Baghdad at the time of the Cairo Conference. The three additional units were to be Nos 1 and 70 Sqns, transferred from India and Egypt respectively, and one new squadron. The new unit was to be No 45 Sqn.

Sqn Ldr E M Murray DSO MC was nominated to command the reformed No 45 Sqn and he took up his appointment at Helwan on 23rd March 1921. He was accompanied by Flt Lt W F Anderson DSO DFC and Flt Lt C C Clark, who were to be the interim commanders of A and B Flights respectively. For a week the only junior officer available for them to order about was Fg Off R F Wallas but on 1st April, on which date the new squadron officially came into being, he was joined by Fg Offs C N Ellen DFC and M C Trench. More aircrew reported during May including Flt Lt G Bowen and Fg Offs W H Markham, G R O'Sullivan, J K A Jeakes DFC, C D Pyne, R J Rodwell, W J McDonough, F J Islip, G Archer and H J Bradley. On June 1st the squadron acquired its own MO, Sqn Ldr A J O Wigmore, and three weeks later it gained a Technical Officer, Flt Lt R T Nevill. As a result of a change in policy, however, the latter was not to stay for long. Technical Officers were about to be deleted

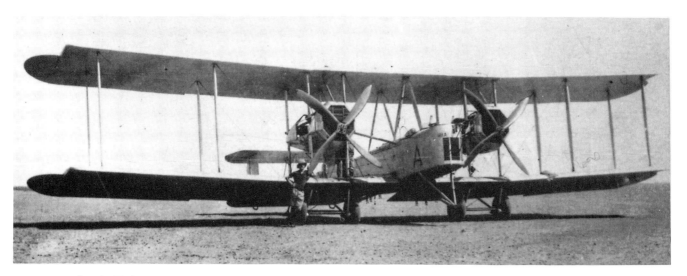

One the Vickers Vimys used by No 45 Sqn as interim equipment pending receipt of Vernons. (No 45 Sqn archives)

from squadron establishments and in September Richard Nevill was posted to Baghdad; by the end of the year the Technical specialisation had been abandoned altogether and the 'T' annotation no longer appeared in the Air Force List.

At first the squadron had no aeroplanes on charge and such flying as was done was carried out on DH 9As borrowed from the neighbouring No 47 Sqn. On 22nd June Fg Off H A Williams arrived to be the squadron's Stores Officer, which indicated that they might actually be about to receive some equipment of their own. Sure enough, on July 11th the squadron moved to Almaza where, later that month, it took on charge its first Vickers Vimy, F9191. The squadron was starting to take shape.

In 1919 the Italian Government had struck a large gold medallion which they had presented to their king as "national testimony for the proofs of heroism and sacrifice with which the army and navy went forth to glory and victory". The

Sqn Ldr E M Murray DSO MC, first CO of No 45 Sqn when it reformed in Egypt. (No 45 Sqn archives)

Italian Embassy letter dated 6th April 1920, from which the foregoing translation is taken, covered a facsimile of the original in silver, which was to be presented to HM King George V to commemorate the assistance which Great Britain had extended to Italy during the recent war. It was accompanied by twelve further replicas in bronze which were intended to be distributed among formations or individuals who had rendered particularly distinguished service on Italy's behalf. Four went to the RN, seven to the army and one to the RAF. On the personal recommendation of Air Commodore T I Webb-Bowen, the erstwhile commander of the RFC Brigade in Italy, the unit selected to receive this honour was No 45 Sqn, the most successful of the British air units to have served in that theatre. In fact Webb-Bowen had originally been given the medal himself, but when the RAF learned that the other eleven were being awarded to units, rather than to individuals, they had asked for it back! On August 10th 1921, at a parade attended by the Italian consul in Cairo, the medal was formally accepted by Sqn Ldr Murray from the AOC Middle East Area, AVM Sir Geoffrey Salmond KCMG CB DSO. Sadly this memento seems to have disappeared shortly afterwards. Years later, contemporary members of the squadron could remember the parade but none had any recollection of the squadron actually having had the medal in its custody thereafter. Its present whereabouts is unknown.

The acquisition of Britain's Middle Eastern empire had created an immediate demand for a communications network linking Cairo, the hub of British power in the region, to the outlying territories. In addition it opened up the longer-term prospect of its extension to India to supplement the sea routes via the Suez Canal or the Cape. Consideration was given to the construction of a railway between Baghdad and Amman and thence to the coast. Although this was technically feasible it would have been a daunting civil engineering project and prohibitively expensive. Once again aeroplanes were proposed as the answer. In due course it was envisaged that there would be a civil air route from London via Cairo, Amman, Baghdad, Basrah and the Persian Gulf to India, and ultimately through to Rangoon, Singapore and Australia. This was a trifle ambitious in the early 1920s, however, as aeroplanes still lacked the necessary reliability for sustained long-range commercial operations and it fell to the RAF to prove the concept by establishing a reliable connection between Cairo, Amman and Baghdad.

The overall distance from Cairo to Baghdad is roughly the same as that between London and Rome or Warsaw. So far as navigation was concerned, the first stage was relatively straightforward, since it followed the coast and railway line from Cairo to Ramleh before heading inland for about 60 miles across Palestine to Amman. The second stage, from Amman to Baghdad, was a very different matter as it covered well over 500 miles of desert terrain with very few distinctive features.

In those days the only practical means of navigation was map-reading and over such empty wastes there was simply no reliable way to fix an aircraft's position. Since there were no worthwhile landmarks in the desert the obvious solution was to provide some, and when the matter had been discussed at the Cairo Conference consideration had been given to using explosives to create a series of craters. The ultimate answer to the problem of the trackless waste, however, was the more modest one of simply providing a track. A partial reconnaissance of the eastern end of the desert sector was begun in April 1921 under the direction of Maj A L Holt OBE MC. In the course of this the party established a series of Landing Grounds (LG) to permit No 30 Sqn's DH 9As to support the expedition. This survey work continued into June by which time there were five designated LGs to the west of Ramadi at roughly 50 mile intervals and air reconnaissance flights had ventured out as far as 280 miles.

Authority for an RAF team to survey the route from the Amman end was granted at the end of May and on June 10th a group of Crossley tenders escorted by three Rolls-Royce armoured cars set out from Azrak under the command of Wg Cdr P B C Fellowes DSO of HQ Palestine Group. Maj Holt's resources were also put at the disposal of the RAF and he had returned to the desert in late May. Dragging a chain harrow behind one of the vehicles to define the track and marking out LGs as they went, the RAF team, which was supported by three DH 9As of No 47 Sqn, rendezvoused with Maj Holt to the east of El Djid whence he guided them to Ramadi. They reached Baghdad on June 26th, the three DH 9As having flown on ahead to land there on the 22nd.

They were not actually the first aircraft to cross the desert. It had first been done by a Handley Page V/1500 which had had to make two unscheduled landings during its direct flight from Egypt to Baghdad on 29th December 1918. Palestine and Baghdad had also been linked previously, in both directions, by a Handley Page 0/400 and a few DH 4s, DH 9s and DH 9As, but all of these connections had been flown via Damascus and a variety of other intermediate stops. No 47 Sqn's three aeroplanes were the first to make the direct crossing from Palestine without making the politically undesirable detour via French-controlled Syria and they had thus pioneered what was to become the standard British air mail route.

On June 30th three 'Ninaks'[2] of No 30 Sqn took off from Baghdad and headed west. Two stopped at Amman but the third flew on to Cairo, landing there the same day, having spent eleven hours in the air. On July 11th a DH 9A with Sir Geoffrey Salmond on board left Cairo at 0415hrs and, having picked up an escort of three more Ninaks at Amman, reached Baghdad at 1750hrs. The route was open and it had been flown from end to end in both directions.

Fg Off Robert Rodwell was one of the founder members of the new No 45 Sqn, being posted to the unit with effect from 21st May 1921; he retired from the RAF in 1952 as Air Cdre R J Rodwell CB. (No 45 Sqn archives)

The Amman-Baghdad sector was flown by a total of fourteen aeroplanes in July 1921, many of them carrying letters, but the first official consignment of mail did not leave Baghdad until 28th July, reaching London on August 9th. The first eastbound consignment left London on August 4th and was delivered to Baghdad on the 17th. The four-week transit time required by surface mail had been halved. Thereafter the air mail became a regular fortnightly schedule and from October the public were permitted to use the RAF-operated service at an initial surcharge of one shilling per ounce, although this was progressively reduced to threepence over the next two years.

The initial service was provided by 0/400s of No 70 Sqn, DH 10s of No 216 Sqn and DH 9As of Nos 30 and 47 Sqns. But all of these aircraft were either too old, too unreliable or too small and the probability of engine failure meant that the desert crossing was a particularly high risk operation for the single-engined Ninaks. Even though contemporary twins were barely able to stay airborne on one engine, its residual power gave them a reasonable chance of reaching one of the intermediate LGs which made rescuing them much easier, since a relief aeroplane could land alongside without too much danger of being damaged itself by having to alight on an unsurveyed surface. Twin-engined aeroplanes were deemed to be essential for flying the route and ideally they should be more powerful and more capacious than those which were available.

To enable the RAF to move troops by air to support it in its air policing role, two of its units were planned to be dedicated transport squadrons and the Vickers Vernon had been ordered to equip them. The Vernon was essentially a military adaptation of the Vickers Vimy Commercial which had in turn been derived from the wartime Vimy bomber with its original slim, square-section fuselage replaced by a cavernous oval one, capable of accommodating up to a dozen passengers or over a ton of freight. Powered (some of its pilots might have said under-powered) by a pair of Rolls-Royce Eagle VIII engines, this was the type which was to carry out most of the mail flying from 1922 onwards. The first six Vernons reached Egypt in the December of 1921 where they were to be erected by the Aircraft Depot at Aboukir.

While all this had been going on further improvements had been made to the desert sector of the air mail route by Maj Holt who, in the course of several forays into the desert, enhanced the visibility of the track and established additional LGs so that there was one every 15-30 miles. These were cleared of the more prominent boulders and marked. Running east from Amman they were lettered from A to R (omitting I and Q) while working west from Ramadi they were numbered as I to XI (with the exception of 8 which was written in Arabic). These designations were actually ploughed into the desert surface within a 20 yard diameter circle. By February 1922 the work was complete, although the route was re-marked in 1923 and thereafter as required whenever it began to become indistinct.

From an early stage the northern dog-leg via Amman and Ramleh was usually omitted. This permitted the Dead Sea to be crossed without the heavily-laden aeroplanes having to

When the original desert track had been marked in 1921 it had been done with a chain harrow dragged behind a Crossley tender. When it was renewed in 1923 a more substantial furrow was made using this Fordson tractor and plough. (Author's collection)

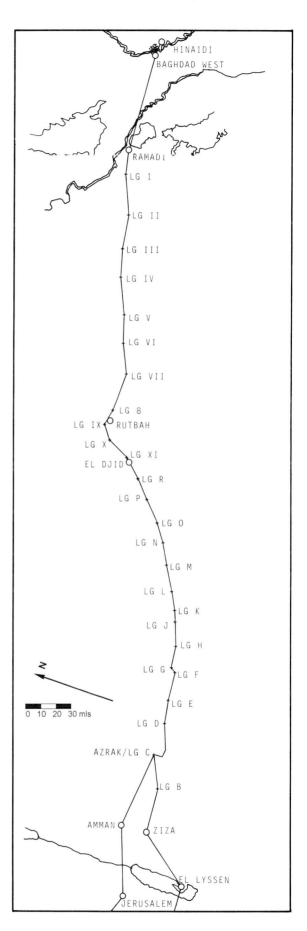

Map 4.1. *The desert sector of the Air Mail Route ran from Azrak to Ramadi. The surface track followed much the same course but meandered where necessary to avoid rocky areas.*

It is not certain who actually owned H653 when this picture was taken but it was one of the aircraft used by No 45 Sqn for a few months in 1921-22 before it was rearmed with Vernons and passed most of its Vimys on to No 216 Sqn. (Eric Harlin)

contend with the mountainous terrain which flanks the Jordan valley and has peaks reaching to over 3,500 feet. The amended route used Ziza as the drop off/delivery point for Transjordan and Palestine, and the mail was ferried from there to Amman and Ramleh by road or by No 14 Sqn's DH 9As. To begin with, the smaller mail carriers were obliged to fly with up to a dozen four-gallon cans of petrol slung beneath their wings to provide their own en route refuelling capability. This unsatisfactory procedure was superseded by the early provision of intermediate fuel dumps at LG V and LG D. The rescue of aeroplanes forced to land to the west of LG R was the responsibility of Middle East Area, this usually being delegated to HQ Palestine and Transjordan at Amman, while those which came down further to the east were looked after by HQ Iraq Group[3].

In the meantime No 45 Sqn had been slowly expanding. When the RAF's June expedition had been forming No 45 Sqn's then still small pool of manpower had been made available to Wg Cdr Fellowes but it is not known whether any of them actually took part in the desert crossing. By late October 1921 three more officers had arrived, Fg Offs S C Black MM, F McB Paul and H I T Beardsworth, and the squadron had four Vimys on charge. During that month the squadron flew its first practice bombing sorties, dropping four 112 lb bombs, and completed the erection of a second hangar to provide accommodation for four more aeroplanes. In November one of the squadron's Vimys led a formation over HMS *Renown* as she passed through the Suez Canal. Throughout this period No 45 Sqn maintained a low intensity

training programme, flying, for instance, just 30 hours in January 1922.

While No 45 Sqn had still been gradually finding its feet, No 70 Sqn had begun the planned move to Iraq, most of its personnel having left by sea in late December. The air echelon followed in January, the unit's seven Vimys flying out to join their groundcrew at Baghdad West aerodrome between 16th and 19th January. In February the first Vernons began to become available. While No 70 Sqn's new aeroplanes were ferried to Iraq progressively over the next several months, No 45 Sqn was able to accept its initial allotment at Almaza and completed its re-equipment programme before it moved. A Flight received their first Vernon in February 1922 and on March 16th they transferred their last Vimy, F9192, to B Flight who passed it on to the Depot the following month whence it found its way to No 216 Sqn.

Meanwhile there had been a problem over flight commanders as a result of Flt Lt Walter Anderson being posted to No 55 Sqn while Cecil Clark was in the throes of resigning his commission. In their absence the recently arrived Flt Lt H S Scroggs was holding the fort. By now, however, the flight commanders who were to run the squadron in Iraq had been nominated. They were to be Flt Lt Hon R A Cochrane AFC and Flt Lt R H M S Saundby MC DFC. Both arrived early in 1922. Both were to have particularly distinguished careers. No 45 Sqn's OC B Flight, after wartime service as Deputy AOCinC Bomber Command, would retire as Air Marshal Sir Robert Saundby KCB KBE

MC DFC AFC while OC A Flight would become Air Chief Marshal Hon Sir Ralph Cochrane GBE KCB AFC.

Saundby felt strongly that the squadron needed a distinguishing badge, some form of motif to encourage a corporate identity. In view of the squadron's record in the recent war it seemed appropriate to capitalise on the outstanding reputation which it had established on Sopwith aeroplanes and the Camel in particular. Coincidentally, the camel was also very appropriate for a squadron serving in the Middle East so what better than to add wings to the 'ship of the desert'? Other units were also devising emblems at this time, however, and there were several other ex-Camel squadrons still serving in the much reduced RAF, No 70 Sqn to name but one, and it was necessary to move fast if No 45 Sqn was to 'copyright' the bactrian beast as its insignia. Bob Saundby and Gordon Archer designed an appropriate heraldic device and the workshops at Almaza were prevailed upon to produce beaten aluminium shields featuring the winged camel in beaten copper, one for each aeroplane. As the Vernons were delivered, the shields were promptly fixed to their bulbous noses. Every badge has to have a motto; a suitably inspiring one, *Per Ardua Surgo* (Through Difficulties I Rise), was agreed upon, and this also featured on the aeroplanes' nose plates.

Pursuing the theme of identification it was also decided to give each aeroplane an individual name. A Flight elected to use names beginning with the letter 'A' while B Flight adopted the names of the trawlers in Kipling's wartime poem *Minesweepers*. The name of each aircraft was spelled out in brass letters, about three inches tall, mounted on polished wooden battens which were fixed either side of the nose. There was another difference between the flights. Saundby's team ruled that the selected names were unique to a specific aeroplane and thus not transferable while A Flight was content that a name could be reused on a replacement aeroplane, if and when the first came to grief. Later in the Vernon era it became common for the aeroplanes to have either a name beginning with the letter 'V' or one drawn from Greek mythology. Unfortunately, while many of the individual names are known, as are most of the serial numbers of the aeroplanes which the squadron used, it has not proved possible to correlate these in every case. What is known is indicated at Annex L.

With the arrival of four more pilots, Flt Lt A L Messenger AFC and Fg Offs J F Horsey, C Bousfield and S W Smith, by early 1922 the squadron's build up was complete and on 21st February Flt Lt Henry Scroggs set off with the main party of about 100 men, bound for Iraq. Having sailed around Arabia, the groundcrew reached Basrah on 14th March, later moving on to the large new air base at Hinaidi which was to be the unit's new home. The squadron's initial complement was seven aeroplanes, although in the fullness of time this was to rise to twelve. On April 2nd the first pair left Almaza for Hinaidi carrying AVM Sir Edward Ellington, who had just taken over from Salmond as AOC Middle East. The AOC inspected the aeroplanes and pronounced himself not best pleased to have found them overloaded with the personal effects of the crews, shot guns, fishing tackle, golf clubs and other such essentials. He directed that all this excess baggage was to be removed forthwith and went off to lunch leaving the crews unloading their kit. Once he was out of sight they

21st February 1921; the boat party at Almaza waiting for transport to take them to Port Tewfik, point of embarkation for the sea journey to Iraq. (No 45 Sqn archives)

promptly restowed their suitably camouflaged goodies and the air marshal was flown to Baghdad overweight but, since he did not know it, content.

The remaining five aeroplanes, captained by Sqn Ldr Murray, Flt Lts Cochrane and Saundby and Fg Offs Beardsworth and Ellen, having reached Ziza on the 14th April set out on the long desert leg the following day. They were carrying a consignment of mail. Bearing in mind that the Vernon had only just been introduced into service, that their airframes were newly erected, that their engines were barely 'run-in' and that the pilots had had little time to become accustomed to the idiosyncrasies of their new mounts, the story of their trip to Baghdad provides a fair indication of the difficulties involved in long-range flying in those days.

The first incident occurred when Ellen boiled a radiator. All five aeroplanes set down on a mud flat about five miles east of Azrak. After solving the problem they resumed their journey but Eric Murray immediately lost an engine and was forced to land again, damaging his undercarriage in the process. Ralph Cochrane landed alongside to ascertain the extent of the problem, then took off again in pursuit of the other three, whom he succeeded in overhauling. One of the engines of Cyril Ellen's Vernon now began to run rough so he made another precautionary landing, in the vicinity of LG K; again Cochrane went down with him and they both stayed where they were for the night. Meanwhile Bob Saundby and Herbert Beardsworth, with the all-important mail, had pressed on to LG II where they camped overnight but found themselves pinned down there on the 16th by a dust storm. After an intermediate stop at Ramadi they both reached Hinaidi on the 17th.

Although the Vernons had no R/T, they did carry a wireless set and, once down on the desert floor, the drill was to erect the portable mast and communicate with someone by W/T. The three stranded aeroplanes had done this to let the world know where they were. On the 16th one of No 14 Sqn's DH 9As flew out to Cochrane and Ellen with instructions for the former to fly back to Azrak, confirm the need for spares for Murray, then fly up to Amman to fetch them. This he did but he came down with scarlet fever en route and remained on the ground with Murray while his co-pilot, Fg Off Horsey, did the trip up to Amman. The spares were eventually delivered to Murray on the 18th by an MT convoy which evacuated Cochrane to hospital when it returned to its base. In the meantime, John Horsey delivered Ellen's spares and then flew on to Hinaidi alone. Murray and Ellen limped in separately several days later. Cochrane did not rejoin the squadron until July when he arrived by ferrying-in J6883 from Egypt. In his absence Henry Scroggs had looked after A Flight.

While the squadron had been carrying out its move there had been some major changes in the RAF's regional organisation. On 1st February 1922, in a first step towards the planned assumption of overall control by the RAF, the Iraq Group had been divorced from Middle East Area to become an independent formation under Gp Capt A E Borton CB CMG DSO. On 1st April, in a general revision of nomenclature, the group was renamed Royal Air Force Iraq while Middle East Area became RAF Middle East (RAFME). By late April No 45 Sqn was well established at Hinaidi and on 15th May it was formally deleted from HQME's books to become a subordinate unit of the new HQ Iraq the following day. On the last day of May No 70 Sqn, still with a mix of Vernons and Vimys, moved across from Baghdad West to Hinaidi. From then on the two Iraq-based squadrons shared the air mail commitment with No 216 Sqn also working the route from the Cairo end.

Apart from the mail run the squadron was also available for moving people and freight to wherever they were required. For instance, one aeroplane flew up to Mosul on May 15th, returning three days later and another took a W/T pack-set up to Kingerban on the 19th. On May 31st two aeroplanes took some fuel out to a No 70 Sqn Vernon which had come down in the desert between LG VII and LG 8.

Many of the air transport tasks arose from the air mail commitment, since there was a constant demand for spares for aircraft which had been damaged in forced landings or for fuel for pilots who had failed to make it to the next dump. Furthermore there was a constant need to ferry petrol out to LG V to top up the reserve fuel, either because passing mail aeroplanes had depleted the stock or because a party of Bedouin had helped themselves - they wanted the cans rather than the petrol. Eventually the dumps were made more secure by the provision of a steel tank encased in concrete, the whole thing being sunk in the ground and provided with a pump.

Nothing was ever easy in the early days of the mail run, as the following example shows. On 2nd June a No 45 Sqn aeroplane was tasked to take some replacement components out to an incoming mail Vernon which had damaged an elevator in a forced landing between LG VII and LG 8. The relief aeroplane lost its W/T generator en route, however, and was obliged to put down at Ramadi. On the 3rd a second relief aeroplane flew a replacement generator out to the first one and returned to base. The original rescue aeroplane now carried on to LG 8 but broke its tailskid on landing, a very frequent occurrence. On the 4th a third relief aeroplane flew a replacement skid out to the first one, spent the night at LG 8, and returned to Hinaidi on the 5th. Also on the 5th, however, the incoming unserviceable Vernon taxied to a slightly better site, breaking its tail skid in the process. A fourth relief aeroplane now flew out with more spares for the incoming aeroplane but also broke its skid on landing. By the 6th the (third) relief aeroplane at LG 8 had fitted its new skid and it returned to Hinaidi, leaving the original incoming mail aircraft and the fourth relief aeroplane still stranded in the desert, both with broken skids. On the 7th a fifth aeroplane flew out to LG 8 with another elevator for the incoming Vernon and replacement tailskids for both it and the fourth rescuer. All three aeroplanes remained in the desert effecting repairs on the 8th and took off together for Hinaidi on the 9th. Two arrived that day but one was obliged to land at Ramadi with an engine problem which it was able to rectify overnight without further assistance, finally reaching Hinaidi on the 10th. In 1922 this was all in a day's work, or rather in eight days' work.

While this saga had been unfolding those members of the squadron who were not involved in the rescue operation were practising formation flying. On June 6th the squadron took part in a flypast to commemorate HM King George V's birthday, the salute being taken by King Feisal of Iraq.

By mid-year the army was engaged in operations to counter Turkish irregulars who had already occupied Rowanduz and were advancing southwards. By September, with the assistance of the local Pishder tribesmen, they would have taken Rania and infiltrated as far south as Koi Sanjak.

Robert Saundby's Stormcock, *J6868. (Author's collection)*

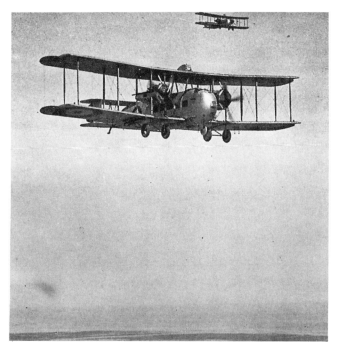

A pair of No 45 Sqn's Vernon Is progress in their stately fashion over the desert circa 1922/23. (No 45 Sqn archives)

To assist the troops who were attempting to stem this advance it had been decided to provide them with air support by detaching elements of Nos 1 and 8 Sqns to the northern sector. In preparation for this deployment, in late June and early July No 45 Sqn flew three aeroplane-loads of stores and bomb components up to Kirkuk. The Snipes and DH 9As flew there on the 6th and 9th July respectively. Thereafter No 45 Sqn flew resupply missions for the detachments as and when required. An urgent demand for spares signalled to Hinaidi could be satisfied by air in about sixteen hours. By road and rail it would have taken between five and seven days. In this context the Vernons were invaluable since their significant payload and large holds could accommodate quite bulky pieces of equipment. Without the Vernons an aircraft needing an engine change, for instance, would have been grounded for a week. With them, it could be flying again in a day; no other aircraft available in Iraq could carry a spare aero-engine. Resupply missions and the evacuation of sick and wounded soldiers from Kirkuk to the Base Hospital at Hinaidi became regular tasks for the next six months as the situation slowly deteriorated.

In July the squadron flew its first scheduled air mail run and this first trip went (almost) like clockwork. The outbound itinerary was to Ramadi on the 7th, Ziza on the 8th

and Heliopolis on the 9th. In the event it was necessary to make a precautionary landing at Ismailia on the 9th and Cairo was not reached until the following day. The eastbound run reached Ziza on the 21st and Hinaidi the next day, the captain of the mail carrier having been James Jeakes. This was a fairly typical example. The round trip covered some 1,720 miles and took about 25 hours of flying time at an average groundspeed of some 70 mph. With the prevailing westerly wind it was theoretically possible to complete the Cairo-Baghdad run in a day, but this would have allowed insufficient time for the transfer of mail at Ziza or for the crew to rest and made no provision for contingencies - and contingencies were the rule, not the exception. Besides which, the ultimate aim of the air mail service was to achieve reliability. It was not a race; speed would come later. To ensure that the mail got through, the service was always flown by at least two aeroplanes, one carrying the mail and the other acting as reserve. Three or more aeroplanes would be laid on if the amount of freight or number of passengers required this, or if an aeroplane needed to be escorted back to Hinaidi after overhaul by the depot at Aboukir. It was unusual, but not unknown, for an aeroplane to fly the route alone, but not if it was carrying the mail. Mail runs were routinely mounted once per fortnight and crews could be away for anything between one and two weeks, depending upon whether the next return run was to be flown by No 216 Sqn or whether the outbound aeroplanes were required to turn round and fly back straight away. Sometimes, in the early days, the two aeroplanes would be a joint formation, eg a No 45 Sqn Vernon and a Vimy from No 216 Sqn, the latter progressively trading in its DH 10s for Vimys between June and October 1922.

In the course of July 1922 the route was flown by five twin- and one single-engined aeroplane which between them carried eleven passengers and 1,100 lbs of mail and freight. Thereafter only twins were used and in September the mail run was flown by ten Vernons and one Vimy, carrying twenty-three passengers and 1,732 lbs of freight. The peak load was achieved in July 1923 when 2,200 lbs of mail was conveyed, but the figures quoted for September 1922 are more typical. The advantage conferred by twin-engined aeroplanes can be seen by comparing the figures for October 1921 when it had taken twenty-three aeroplanes to move just 700 lbs of mail with no capacity to carry passengers at all, except at the expense of leaving one of the crew behind.

There was a positive development in the summer of 1922 when, in August, the first Lion-engined Vernon II was flown at the Depot at Aboukir. Mounted lower in the gap between

It was unusual, but not unknown, for mail flights to be a joint undertaking as suggested by this picture of one of No 45 Sqn's Vernon Is and a Vimy of No 216 Sqn. (No 45 Sqn archives)

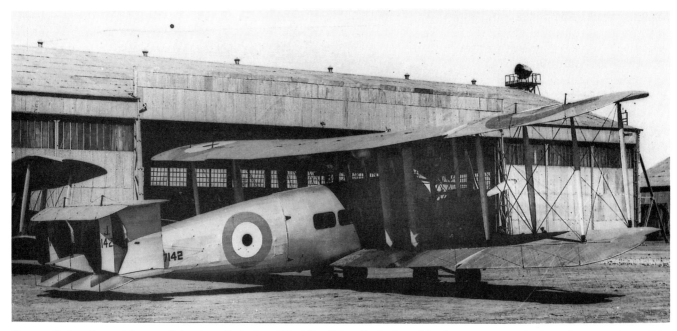

Vernon II, J7142, outside one of the aircraft sheds at Hinaidi. Although shadowed by the upper wing, the low-slung mounting of the Napier Lion can be seen. (No 45 Sqn archives)

the upper and lower mainplanes than the original Eagle engines had been, each Napier Lion II was rated at 450 hp, 30% more than the earlier engines. This additional power was very welcome as most of the desert stage of the route was about 2,000 feet above sea level and all operations were therefore routinely conducted under 'hot and high' conditions. The "built-in headwind", resulting from the Vernon's substantial bulk, prevented there being much of an improvement in overall performance, although taking off in high temperatures was less of a struggle and the new engines did offer significantly greater reserves of power and increased safety margins. The first of the new Vernons did not reach No 70 Sqn until January 1923, however, and No 45 Sqn did not start to receive theirs until much later in the year, probably in December.

The next few months were unremarkable, with air mail runs and associated rescue sorties being punctuated by occasional air transport tasks, mostly involving trips to Mosul and Kirkuk. Forced landings were as much a feature of these trips as they were of the air mail, but without the advantage of prepared LGs. On September 9th, for instance, an aeroplane on a Kirkuk run ran out of fuel and came down at Bazul. It was rescued the following day by another of the squadron's Vernons carrying a load of petrol. It happened again on 3rd October when an aeroplane on the way to Mosul with priority freight forced landed at Istablat. No 70 Sqn sent an aeroplane up to pick up the payload while the problem was sorted out. Two days later another aeroplane on a run to Kirkuk was obliged to land at Abu Bakr. The squadron sent up the necessary spares in another Vernon the same day and both aeroplanes flew back to Hinaidi on October 6th. It will be apparent from this that the crews had to be very self-sufficient and the aircraft carried water, survival rations and camping kit, since unscheduled night stops were not unusual. Furthermore the pilots needed to be reasonably competent mechanics, although they usually carried a fitter with them. Even so it was not unusual for rectification to be carried out on a do-it-yourself, get-you-home basis involving a degree of ingenuity and copious

quantities of sticky tape and string.

Not all Vernon incidents were as benign as those described above. On October 4th Flt Lt Messenger crashed taking off from Kirkuk in J6865 and the aircraft caught fire. Messenger was badly burned and died ten days later. AC1 A A Milne died of his injuries six hours after the crash; the sole passenger on board, Flt Lt R C L Holme of No 1 Sqn, had died instantly.

Although the most common cause of trouble was engine failure, the groundcrew were beginning to discover problems with the structure of the aeroplanes as well. The Vernons were built largely of wood and, writing at Staff College in 1925, Ralph Cochrane noted that in the heat of the summer it was found that their various components were subject to considerable shrinkage (a problem that the squadron was to encounter again some twenty years later when it was operating Mosquitos in India - in that case with fatal consequences). Within the Vernons' wings the width of the spars could contract by as much as 1/8th inch which, spread across the entire span, caused a general slackening of the internal drift wires. Unfortunately the aeroplane's designer had made no provision for internal examinations so that at every inspection the fabric had to be cut in no fewer than eighty-eight places, the wires tensioned and the fabric patched.

AVM Sir John Salmond KCB CMG CVO DSO (brother of Sir Geoffrey) had arrived in Baghdad on 11th July and on 1st October RAF Iraq was restyled Iraq Command. Salmond now commanded all in-theatre forces which comprised RAF units, British and Indian troops and locally recruited levies. The experiment in air control had begun. To avoid any potential inter-service disputes, Salmond was also gazetted as a temporary major general. It would not be long before the system was put to the test. Mustafa Kemal's resurgent Turks were still making headway and were hoping to regain control of the vilayet of Mosul; to this end they were fomenting unrest among the tribesmen in northern Iraq. At the same time Sheikh Mahmud, the governor of the Sulaimaniyah district, was promoting Kurdish independence. Trouble was brewing. On November 18th one of No 45 Sqn's aeroplanes flew Sir John back to Hinaidi from Mosul where he had been to confer with his subordinates in the field.

At this stage Eric Murray, who had been promoted to wing commander in June, departed for service on the North West Frontier with No 2 (Indian) Wing at Risalpur. His replacement was the squadron's erstwhile OC C Flight, Sqn Ldr A T Harris AFC. Arthur Harris had just come from India where he had commanded No 31 Sqn. Always forthright, he had said what he thought about his men's poor barrack accommodation, the awful condition of his old aeroplanes and the dangerous inadequacy of the spares back-up. In effect he emulated Frank Courtney who, five years earlier, had also spoken his mind. True to form, the RAF 'establishment' did to Harris in 1922 exactly what their RFC predecessors had done to Courtney in 1917; they posted him. Harris was transferred to Iraq Command where he cooled his heels at Basrah for a while until, presumably suitably rehabilitated, he was given command of No 45 Sqn and he took up his new post on 20th November. Three days later he was checked out on the Vernon by Ralph Cochrane in J6883 before laying claim to J6871 as his personal aeroplane.

The new CO foresaw that the squadron might shortly be committed to action and he set about turning his "trucking outfit" into a bomber squadron. There were some who found it difficult to take seriously the idea of treating the portly, lumbering Vernons with their saloon cabins as bombers. If there were any on No 45 Sqn, however, 'Bert' Harris quickly disabused them of the idea that this was some kind of joke. He had quickly appreciated that each Vernon could lift the same disposable load as at least three DH 9As and he saw no reason why this load should not be bomb-shaped. The squadron's Armament Officer was Fg Off D H Geeson and, with his team of six armourers, he was set to work devising ways and means of giving the Vernons an offensive capability. Under the supervision of WO Wilkinson, apertures were cut in the noses of each aircraft, bombsights were installed, underwing racks and release gear were designed, manufactured and fitted and by early January 1923 a training programme was under way. According to Bob Saundby, No 45 Sqn was the first unit to start using bombsights in Iraq. The designated bomber squadrons were simply "eyeballing it". To quote Saundby, writing at the RAF Staff College in 1928, "...I could not imagine how Bristol Fighters and DH 9As managed ever to hit without using their sights. It was not until later that I realised, when watching their bomb raids, that they never did hit, except by a lucky accident." Arthur Harris was about to show them how it was done.

One aeroplane was initially fitted with a Wimperis Course Setting Drift Sight which theoretically permitted an attack to be made from any direction. To be really effective, however, this sight required an accurate assessment of all the variable parameters necessary to solve the bombing equation, including the speed and direction of the wind, the aeroplane's airspeed, the height of the target above sea level and the height of the aircraft above the target. None of these could be gauged with much confidence, particularly target height, which could only be guessed at from the inadequate mapping which was available. The squadron soon abandoned this relatively sophisticated device and opted to use the much

A fully armed Vernon I bomber, unidentified but wearing No 45 Sqn's distinctive noseplate. The fabric sidescreens over the windows were a local modification fitted to some aircraft in an attempt to keep out sand and dust while they were on the ground. (No 45 Sqn archives)

simpler HAD (Home Aircraft Depot) Sight which was intended for use only in direct up-wind attacks, errors being corrected by the adjustment of just one bar on the sight. As Ralph Cochrane noted: "Even with the HAD sight a crew would have to practise together for at least three weeks before they could hope to get the mean error of eight shots within thirty yards of the centre point of the target, the whole difficulty being to bring the machine on to the target truly up wind."

Meanwhile the Turkish forces which had been infiltrating across the border since the summer were growing stronger and intelligence reports indicated that attacks were imminent on Koi Sanjak, Kirkuk and Erbil. It was decided to reinforce the northern sector on January 24th and then to take the offensive. A total of thirty-nine aeroplanes was accordingly deployed to Mosul and Kirkuk in addition to the twelve which were already in situ. This force included most of the Vernon fleet, its activities being co-ordinated by Sqn Ldr Francis Don on attachment from HQ Iraq. No 45 Sqn's commitment was eight aircraft which were based at Mosul. Fg Off Garth O'Sullivan in J6870 was forced to land at Shergat en route but a replacement was provided the following day. In all, the squadron's detachment numbered nineteen officers and sixty-six airmen, all of whom had been airlifted to Mosul.

Almost as soon as they arrived the newly deployed units began to undertake offensive air action against both the Turks in the north and the dissident Sheikh Mahmud in the Sulaimaniyah district. No 45 Sqn's Vernons flew bombing missions on February 3rd and 5th and again on March 7th and 9th, attacking several villages between Sargali and Sitak; it is known that Arthur Harris participated in the first two raids and that Bob Saundby flew on all four. For the most part, however, the Vernons were employed on casualty evacuation and resupply missions in support of the designated bomber squadrons and the troops of KOICOL as they moved north through the mountains. Meanwhile the rump of the squadron at Hinaidi continued to fly the mail run and to meet ad hoc transport tasks, most of which involved resupply trips to Mosul. The squadron lost one of its pilots on 6th February when Fg Off Harold Bradley was killed when a No 216 Sqn Vimy in which he was flying on an air mail run nosed over on landing at Ziza.

On February 9th Saundby's B Flight withdrew to Hinaidi, leaving A Flight to hold the fort. A short while later the Vernon's troop-lifting capabilities were put to the test when it became necessary to move two companies of the 14th

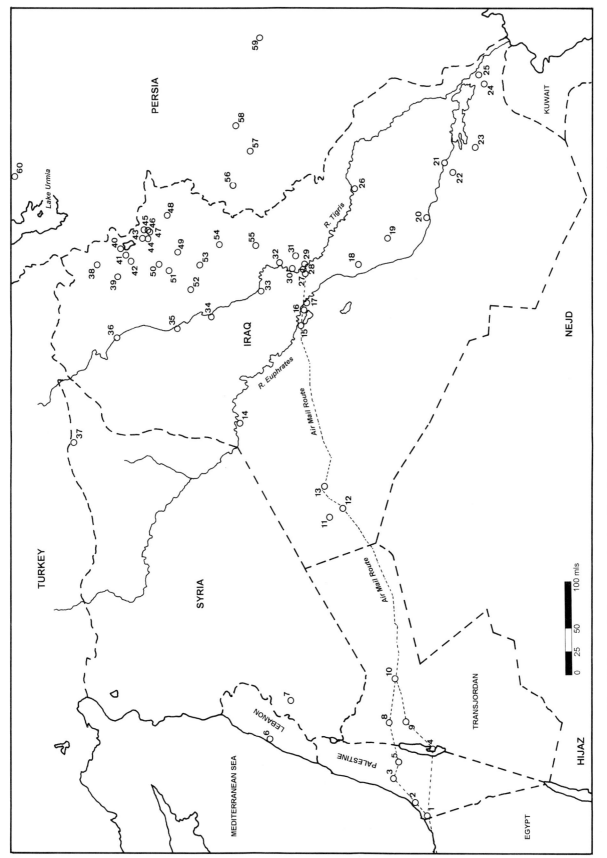

Map 4.2. Iraq and adjacent territories. Note that some of the locations shown are applicable to Chapters 5 and 7.

74

53	Abu Bakr	52	Erbil	1	Rafah
8	Amman	17	Falluja	15	Ramadi
14	Annah	2	Gaza	3	Ramleh
10	Azrak	11	H3	40	Rania
28	Baghdad	16	Habbaniyah	38	Rowanduz
27	Baghdad West	18	Hillah	13	Rutbah
34	Baiji	29	Hinaidi	20	Samawah
25	Basrah	33	Istablat	45	Sargali
32	Bazul	5	Jerusalem	41	Serkhuma
6	Beirut	47	Kanimiran	46	Shadalha
49	Betwata	58	Kermanshah	57	Shahabad
59	Burujird	54	Kingerban	24	Shaibah
31	Cassel's Post	51	Kirkuk	35	Shergat
7	Damascus	42	Koi Sanjak	50	Sitak
55	Delli Abbas	26	Kut	48	Sulaimaniyah
39	Diana	30	Mashahida	44	Surdash
19	Diwaniyah	36	Mosul	60	Tabriz
23	Djaliba	21	Nasiriyah	22	Ur
12	El Djid	56	Payitak Pass	37	Zerka
4	El Lyssen	43	Qamchugha	9	Ziza

Key to Map 4.2.

Sikhs from the railhead at Kingerban to Kirkuk. The first Vernon arrived at Kingerban at 0830hrs on the 21st, and by 1325hrs the following day the move was complete. The airlift had involved two British officers with their kit and their three bearers, 320 combat ready imperial soldiers, thirteen other passengers and 30,000 rounds of rifle ammunition. This had been accomplished by five Vernon Is of No 45 Sqn's B Flight, recalled from Hinaidi, and five of No 70 Sqn's new Vernon IIs. The squadron's contribution is summarised at Figure 4.1; it involved 28 hours flying time.

Two days later, on February 24th, a show of force was mounted over Sulaimaniyah involving twelve Bristol Fighters of No 6 Sqn, five Snipes of No 1 Sqn, two DH 9As of No 30 Sqn and three aircraft from each of the Vernon units. A similar demonstration was mounted the following day with eleven Brisfits[4] and four of No 45 Sqn's Vernons. Things then quietened down for a while but on 23rd March the squadron was employed in the bombing role again, a dozen aeroplanes drawn from Nos 6, 8, 45 and 70 Sqns dropping bombs on Qamchugha, Surdash and Shadalha.

In view of the criticism which has sometimes been levelled at the RAF's conduct of its air policing role it is worth noting here that, while the same could not be said for all of the units operating in Iraq at the time, No 45 Sqn's raids were carried out with the utmost precision. Quite apart from any moral scruples, the total weight of bombs being delivered made indiscriminate area bombing hopelessly ineffective, which is precisely why Arthur Harris had insisted on his pilots training with proper bomb sights. During this campaign, the first in which they had been employed as bombers, the Vernons carried up to ten 112 pounders on each sortie. Each one was dropped individually, the aiming on each successive bomb run being refined in the light of previous results with a progressive improvement in accuracy.

The next day, 24th March, Cochrane took his A Flight back to Hinaidi where its machines could be given some much needed attention. They had spent sixty days in the open, on fifteen of which it had rained heavily. Before deploying, however, the hulls had been painted with a protective coat of white lead and this had minimised the effects of prolonged exposure.

The only serious damage being that the three-ply wooden skin of the lower fuselage had begun to delaminate as a result of water accumulating in the bilges. The long detachment had taught many lessons about aircraft maintenance in the field, for those prepared to learn them. The following passage is another extract from Ralph Cochrane's 1925 Staff College paper:

One day two machines crashed their undercarriages, one on the aerodrome at Mosul and one at Shergat, the railhead 60 miles south of Mosul. One damaged various metal fittings in the tail and the control column levers, the other smashed all the compression ribs of one lower centre section. Spare parts for the first were not available in the country and for the second could only have been transported to the site with difficulty. Both machines

Air Chief Marshal Sir Ralph Cochrane GBE KCB AFC is seen here as an immaculately turned out flight lieutenant commanding A Flight of No 45 Sqn at Hinaidi in 1923. (No 45 Sqn archives)

Pilot	Aircraft	Number of passengers per sortie					
		1st	2nd	3rd	4th	5th	Total
Flt Lt Saundby	J6868	11	12	13	-	-	36
Fg Off O'Sullivan	J6870	12	10	10	-	-	32
Flt Lt Beardsworth	J6877	11	13	12	12	10	58
Flt Lt Matheson	J6882	11	10	-	-	-	21
Fg Off Jeakes	J6874	6*	-	-	-	-	6
*plus three bearers and their officers' kit						**Total**	153

***Fig 4.1.** No 45 Sqn's contribution to the troops movement between Kingerban and Kirkuk, 21st-22nd February 1923.*

were serviceable in three days thanks to two NCOs who were skilled tradesmen who knew how to improvise and how to make parts from raw materials if spares were not available to hand. The value of these skilled NCOs throughout the whole operation was immense for, although in theory it is not economical to repair crashed aircraft in a unit or to make parts which appear in the vocabulary, in practice it is often essential if operations are to be continued. Had the remainder of the personnel in the flights possessed equal skill even the most hopeless crash might have been repaired. As it was, the policy of overhauling and rebuilding all machines and engines in the squadron was introduced, partly because the Depot was too busy to take on the work and partly to train the Riggers and Fitters. Thus, during a period of twelve months, eight 300 hour machine overhauls and seven 400 hour rebuilds were undertaken in the squadron ARS, without any assistance from outside, while in the same period the ERS completed the overhaul of thirty-two engines.

Cochrane went on to criticise other aspects of contemporary logistic practice. He particularly lamented the economic folly of a policy which restricted the provision of raw materials in preference for the issuing of spare parts, pointing out that a lower centre section could be repaired with a sheet of plywood costing a few shillings while a replacement unit cost £200[5]. He was also critical of the fact that the air force lacked specialist technical officers who, he believed, could have increased both serviceability and efficiency through better organisation and management while also improving the supervision of the further training of newly qualified tradesmen. In this context it is interesting to note that the officers responsible for engineering on No 45

Sqn in 1923 were Fg Offs Denis Geeson (Armament), Gordon Archer (Electrics) and Ernest Attwood (Signals), all of whom were junior pilots; it is even possible that some of them *may* even have done an appropriate specialist course.

Throughout March and April the squadron maintained its detachment at Mosul, providing airlift as required, which was often. Most trips were to Hinaidi or Kingerban but some were to such obscure destinations as Mashahida, Erbil, Baiji and Shergat. The tasks were to deliver food, ammunition, clothing, fodder and whatever else was needed by the troop columns. A typical load delivered by Saundby in J6879 on April 16th consisted of such essentials as soap, dubbin, nosebags (horses for the feeding of) and bed ropes. Back at Hinaidi the air mail went on and two aircraft flew down to Shaibah, a relatively infrequent port of call, on the 24th April, returning the following day with a consignment of boots which were urgently needed by the soldiers in the north. It is significant that in the course of these operations the Vernons were air-dropping supplies to troops in inaccessible places, without the aid of parachutes, thus pre-dating a technique employed by the air transport force in Burma by some twenty years.

By the end of April the troops of KOICOL had reoccupied Rowanduz and ejected the Turkish incursion. While the column was withdrawing southwards, however, it was stricken by an epidemic of dysentery. The Vernons were called in to evacuate the sick. This involved a series of flights in an operation which lasted from 28th April to 2nd May. Again this was a joint 45/70 Sqn affair, this time commanded by Sqn Ldr Harris. No 45 Sqn's individual contribution, which represented about 60% of the total, involved the airlifting of 121 soldiers to Baghdad. There were nine return sorties from Kirkuk to Betwata and another nine to Koi Sanjak plus fifteen round trips between Kirkuk and Hinaidi.

J6882, Golden Gain, *down in the mountains of northern Iraq somewhere between Kirkuk and Serkhuma on 28th April 1923. Although not badly damaged the aeroplane could not be salvaged from such a remote site and even if it had been repaired in situ it could not have been flown out. The aircraft had to be burned but not before Flt Lt Ian Matheson had removed its badge and nameplate as souvenirs. (No 45 Sqn archives)*

Vernon, J6876, Pelican, *was a Mk I with its Eagle engines mounted in mid gap. Since it is flying the Iraqi flag the aeroplane was probably involved in one of the occasional Royal Flights undertaken by the squadron. (No 45 Sqn archives)*

The squadron employed six aeroplanes, which flew a little over 88 hours and covered 6,420 route miles. There were two forced landings, one near Cassel's Post on the 28th and another at Delli Abbas on the 30th. Both aircraft were flown out after on-site repairs and neither incident resulted in any injuries. There had been a third accident, however, and this one had resulted in the loss of an aeroplane.

The service ceiling of a Vernon was no more than 6,500 feet on a good day, and in the high temperatures experienced in Iraq there were no good days; 5,000 feet was a more realistic figure, and it took a considerable time to reach such an altitude. Northern Iraq is extremely mountainous with peaks reaching to over 8,000 feet and correspondingly deep valleys. Crossing this sort of country in the 1920s meant threading one's way between the mountains rather than flying over them and in such rugged terrain the wind can do strange things. On April 28th Flt Lt Matheson, with a load of sick soldiers on board, was flying his *Golden Gain* (J6882) on a route which involved crossing a sharp ridge, some 3,000 feet high. It was normal to fly over it at 5,000 feet (if the height could be gained) to minimise turbulence but on this occasion Matheson attempted to do it lower down. His aircraft was caught in a strong down current and began to loose height. The application of full power on the 360 hp Eagles was insufficient to counter the loss of altitude and, otherwise under full control, the aeroplane was forced lower and lower until Matheson was obliged to attempt to convert a collision with the ground into a quasi-landing on a rocky slope. He succeeded, after a fashion, but the inadvertent landing was hard enough to collapse the undercarriage. The flight up to then had been so rough, however, that the impact was not particularly remarkable; one of the passengers managed to sleep right through the incident and had to be woken up to get him out of the aeroplane! A rescue expedition led by an MO, Wg Cdr Henry Threadgold, eventually reached the crash site and evacuated the crew and their sick passengers by mule.

Had the aircraft been repaired it could not have taken off again from the rocky hillside where it lay and the site was so inaccessible that salvage was not a realistic option. *Golden*

Gain had to be burned. Before destroying his aeroplane, however, Ian Matheson salvaged the squadron badge from the nose and one of its nameplates. He later captained *Unity* and *The Flying Inn* and when he was finally posted back to England in late 1924 he took all three nameplates with him as souvenirs, mounted on a wooden shield along with the badge. Thirty-five years later the squadron was to get them back.

The HQ of the temporary Mosul Wing moved to Kirkuk on 1st May and the detachment began to run down, most of No 45 Sqn returning to Baghdad on the 10th. Four of the squadron's aeroplanes collected forty-eight 'unfit marching' Sikhs from Kirkuk on the 17th and flew them down to Hinaidi. The following day another four evacuated twenty stretcher cases. By the end of the month these tidying up operations were virtually complete and the squadron had settled itself down again in the relative comfort of Hinaidi.

In June 1923 the squadron began night flying for the first time and on the 2nd aeroplanes from both Vernon squadrons flew low over Baghdad during a fireworks display in celebration of HM King George V's birthday. As operations in the north petered out so the demand for resupply sorties and casualty evacuation declined but the air mail remained a constant commitment. On July 27th the squadron was tasked with flying King Feisal and five members of his household to Amman. On that day, escorted by a pair of Brisfits from No 6 Sqn, the two Vernons flew to Ramadi and stopped for the night. The following day, with Fg Off Bob Rodwell acting as the royal pilot, the Vernons flew on alone to Amman via an intermediate landing at Azrak where they topped up from a cache of pre-positioned petrol.

Several authors have testified to the considerable impact that the arrival of the dynamic 'Bert' Harris had on the squadron, among them Basil Embry who provides several recollections in his autobiography, *Mission Completed*, and Dudley Saward who includes a number of anecdotes from contemporaries, including Ralph Cochrane and Harris' rigger, Cpl George Thompson, in *Bomber Harris*, his authorised biography of the man. Apart from converting his transport aeroplanes into bombers the new CO had, or stimulated, numerous other innovative ideas. For instance, he had a

"Mad dogs and Englishmen", protected by their Wolseley helmets and spinepads, work on a Lion engine. All of Harris' junior pilots had to spend a good deal of their time in the workshops to become familiar with their aeroplanes and to establish a close working relationship with their airmen. (No 45 Sqn archives)

Under Bert Harris No 45 Sqn established an enviable reputation on the sports field. This is the winning Boxing Team in 1923. Standing, from the left, LAC Ballentyne, AC1 Lindley, Cpl Harrison, Cpl Rowed, AC1 Armstrong, AC1 Higgins and AC1 Simpson. In the foreground are AC2 Donovan and LAC Bull. The officers are Fg Off Embry and Sqn Ldr Harris.
(No 45 Sqn archives)

small electrically powered luggage trolley adapted so that it could be fitted under the tail of a Vernon, enabling one man to manoeuvre it on the ground. Previously the aircraft, which weighed nearly four tons, even when they were empty, had had to be manhandled in and out of the hangars and in summer temperatures of well over 100°F this was no joke. Ralph Cochrane later noted that it had previously taken his whole flight over an hour to clear the hangar; with the truck one man could do it alone in half the time. Another labour saving device for the groundcrew introduced during Harris' time was an air compressor to replace the hand pumps previously used to inflate aircraft tyres. Both obvious ideas perhaps, but it was Harris who implemented them.

Technical innovations were not confined to the world of the hangar and flightline. As previously observed, the Vernon's climbing performance was very poor (Cochrane noted that at a slightly reduced all up weight of 12,000 lbs it was no more than 100 ft/min) and it needed all the help it could get to gain height. Help was at hand in the form of thermals - as any glider pilot knows, there are up-currents within the atmosphere and a free ride can be obtained if an aircraft circles within them and allows itself to be carried upwards - the trick is to *find* these invisible updraughts. Based on an empty, but airtight, two-gallon petrol tin with a length of rubber tubing connected to an indicator, Ralph Cochrane and Flt Lt F M Rope, a pilot serving on the Technical Staff at HQ Iraq, devised a primitive variometer which could detect sudden changes in atmospheric pressure and thus locate the sought after free rides.

The domestic scene was equally vulnerable to Bert Harris' scrutiny and he took a close interest in what went on in the cookhouse to improve the quality of the airmen's messing. To lower the temperature in the barrack blocks he introduced a form of evaporative cooling used in India - water sprayed onto matting which was hung over the windows. He had the officers' mess redecorated and tightened up its administration.

Harris was a strict disciplinarian, a martinet according to his detractors, but he understood that being a CO was not a popularity contest and that laxity was inherently dangerous in a military organisation, especially one on active service. He instituted daily parades and required all his young officers to partake in physical training activities. There were ample sporting facilities at Hinaidi and under Harris' leadership No 45 Sqn came to dominate Command sports in 1923 when it won the Soccer Cup, while the squadron's pugilists took the RAF Open Boxing Championship. Harris demanded a very professional attitude from his aircrew and all newcomers spent a great deal of time in the squadron workshops at first, finding out just how their aeroplanes were put together. In the process they learned much that would be of value when they were forced to land somewhere in the desert, while at the same time establishing a rapport with the airmen which reinforced the unit's cohesion and identity. After the initial shock of Arthur Harris' dynamism, as Embry puts it, "Morale soared, *esprit de corps* rose to a great height and each member of his unit was proud to say, 'I belong to 45 Squadron.'"

While the squadron had been up at Mosul earlier in the year a few of the squadron's junior pilots, who had taken exception to Harris' rather brisk, new broom, approach, thought they would let him know how they felt. One evening they dropped a couple of revolver bullets down the chimney of the CO's hut and then covered the vent with a wet sack. Shortly afterwards the fire began to smoke and then the cartridges exploded in the fireplace, scattering hot coals and ashes around the room. At first Harris did nothing, but at about 1030pm he summoned Fg Off Beardsworth and politely asked him to go out to the landing ground, check that the aircraft were properly picketed and then report back. It was about a mile each way and very cold, the weather throughout the detachment being characterised by frequent heavy rain, gales and even snow, but Beardsworth's request for transport was firmly denied. Shortly after his return, Harris summoned Fg Off Jeakes and gave him the same task, then came Fg Off Rodwell's turn. When the cycle was complete it was repeated, the errand this time being to fetch a map from the squadron office. He kept it up until the small hours of the morning. That was the last time that anyone on No 45 Sqn tried to buck Arthur Harris.

It should be noted that this brush with the CO had little impact on the long-term prospects of the obstreperous young officers concerned and two of them were to have notably successful careers, Air Commodore H I T Beardsworth CBE retiring in 1946 and Air Commodore R J Rodwell CB in 1952. As further graduates of the Flying Camels' school of excellence they were just two more of the remarkable total of ten officers who, having served with No 45 Sqn during its five years in Iraq, subsequently rose to air rank.

Building on the experience gained while his aeroplanes had first been employed as bombers, the CO was determined to enhance the squadron's operational potential in this field. Another intensive programme of bombing training was implemented, this being accompanied by further examples of technical ingenuity. The Vernon was normally crewed by two pilots and Harris was convinced that the more experienced of them had the potential to be a better bomb-aimer than a comparative tyro, thus it was usually the aircraft captains who tended to find themselves peering through the cut-out in the nose of the Vernons trying to direct the second pilot to go left or right via instructions bellowed down the speaking tube. Engine and wind noise could make this form of communication inadequate and Fg Off Geeson devised a system whereby a wheel, controlled by the bomb-aimer, moved a pointer, to which it was connected 'by a suitable

system of linkages', along a rail fixed to the front of the cockpit coaming. All the pilot had to do was turn in the direction demanded by the pointer which would stop moving about once drift had been neutralised and the aeroplane was tracking steadily up wind towards the target.

Practice bombing was usually carried out at heights of between 2,000 and 3,000 feet, but (very) occasionally up to 6,000 feet, using empty 20 lb Cooper bombs against a target circle marked on a suitable area of desert. The problem was that it was difficult to observe where the bombs landed. Denis Geeson had Verey cartridges, with the explosive charge removed, fitted to the tails of the bombs with a percussion cap which would ignite the flare on impact so that the strikes could be seen. The bombing programme moved into high gear in July and the CO's log book shows that between the 10th and the 23rd he flew ten practice sorties, all with Fg Off Bob (or 'Bones', as his captain called him) Ragg acting as pilot and Harris aiming the bombs. Their average score was of the order of 26 yds..

Having worked his squadron up, Harris wanted to show what it could do and he proposed an inter-squadron Command Bombing Competition; Salmond approved. The competition was scheduled to take place between July 30th and August 2nd 1923. The target was to be a 30 yard diameter circle. The single-engined squadrons were each to

A fully modified and armed Vernon I bomber of No 45 Sqn. The rail for Denis Geeson's remote bomb-aiming pointer can just be discerned in front of the cockpit sill. The aluminium and copper noseplate bearing the Flying Camel motif and the bomb-aimer's cut-out are plainly visible and a row of five spotlights to assist in night landings can also be seen mounted below the nose. Beneath the lower wing a 112lb bomb is hung behind each undercarriage unit; there is a 230 pounder under the port inner wing and a pair of 112 pounders under the starboard inner wing. A container for BIBs is mounted under the starboard outer wing balanced by at least two 20 lb bombs on the port side. (No 45 Sqn archives)

A pair of Vernon Is somewhere 'down the route' in 1923; J6879 in the foreground is flying the Royal Mail pennant. The three figures on the right are, from the right: Fg Off H I T Beardsworth, Flt Lt R F L Dickey and Flt Lt I M Matheson. Walking towards them is Flt Lt R H M S Saundby. (No 45 Sqn archives)

enter four aircraft carrying four 20 lb bombs apiece. The Vernon units would both enter two aircraft, each armed with seven bombs. Two details would be flown, one at 2,000 feet and one at 3,000 feet. No 1 Sqn's single-seater Snipes would be permitted to dive-bomb. The results wiped the smiles off the faces of the sceptics. No 45 Sqn's transport pilots won easily with an average error of 24.9 yards, which was almost half of that achieved by the professional bomber crews of No 84 Sqn who came second with 45.8 yards. The Flying Camels' most obvious rivals, No 70 Sqn, were third with 57.5 yards and thereafter the remaining four squadrons trailed off to bottom out at 88.5 yards. While the Snipes, with their inherently accurate dive delivery, came close to No 84 Sqn with a score of 46 yards, even they presented no competition for No 45 Sqn. Arthur Harris had taken a competent but unremarkable transport squadron and had transformed it into the most formidable offensive unit in Iraq, arguably at that time therefore the best in the RAF - and they knew it.

Since the bombing range was already manned for the competition, the AOC took the opportunity of laying on a bombing demonstration for the benefit of the army on August 3rd, but this time using live 112 pounders. The squadron bettered its previous performance, just to show that it had not been a fluke.

The CO kept the pressure on throughout August and September and sought to extend the squadron's operational capability even further by investigating the feasibility of night bombing, using flares to illuminate the target. Harris flew the first night bombing experiment himself on September 28th. It was a success and, once the other pilots had had a go and the techniques had been refined a little, No 45 Sqn was able to offer Iraq Command a night attack capability. For this to be a realistic option, however, the crews needed to be able to find their way about in the dark and this was probably the limiting factor in the 1920s; it certainly was in Iraq where, unless one stuck to following the Tigris or Euphrates, it was easy enough to get lost in daylight. Nevertheless, despite the limitations of contemporary instrumentation and the total lack of navigation aids, night navigation exercises became an occasional feature of the squadron's training programme. Once again it was No 45 Sqn that was leading the way and its enterprise had been recognised - the next time that an aeroplane was needed to make a show of force, the job was given to the Flying Camels in preference to one of the 'proper' bomber units[6]; Harris had made his point. On

Fg Off Yvon Burnett in working dress. Burnett joined No 45 Sqn in Iraq in September 1924 and remained on strength until May 1928, by which time the unit was flying DH 9As in Egypt. He was eventually killed in Rhodesia on 18th March 1929 in the crash of a Fairey IIIF of No 47 Sqn. (No 45 Sqn archives)

September 10th a Vernon was detached to Annah and the following day it made a demonstration flight over the camp of Murdhi al Rufidi, a tribal leader who had been causing a local disturbance. On this occasion, however, it proved unnecessary to drop any bombs.

While Harris had been turning his squadron into a fighting unit, routine training flying and operational transport tasking had continued. There was a spot of excitement on September 10th when J6871 shed a wheel on take off but the Vernon was generously provided for in that department and the CO was able to land again without further drama. Meanwhile there were still occasional casualties to bring down from Kirkuk, Mosul and Kingerban and on 22nd September an aeroplane delivered some rations to LG XI to sustain a motor convoy which was re-marking the air mail track. On October 5th a pair of Vernons on the return run from Cairo came across a lone motor car stranded in the desert near LG III. They landed to investigate and found it to be full of Armenians who had been there for three days and were in a pretty poor state. Flt Lt Scroggs flew out later in J6891 with an MO, Sqn Ldr d'Arcy Power, on board. They rendered appropriate assistance, got the car going again and, refuelled and revictualled courtesy of the RAF, the little expedition resumed its journey - there was a benign aspect to the application of air power in a colonial context; it was not

An immaculate line-up at Hinaidi. The nearest two aeroplanes are Mk Is but most of the remainder appear to be Lion-engined which would date the photograph no earlier than mid-1924. (MoD)

all 'blood and bullets' as some commentators would have one believe.

A week later, on the 29th, the squadron hosted a Fancy Dress Dance in the Officers' Mess, raising Rs310 for charity. Another notable event in September had been the arrival of Flt Lt Jack Cottle MBE DFC who had had such a successful career flying Camels with the squadron in Italy. He was only to stay for a month, however, before moving over to No 8 Sqn to fly DH 9As but it was long enough for him to have been credited with having originated the suggestion that the squadron's motto was not so much a comment on its indomitably determined corporate spirit as an observation on the climbing performance of its aeroplanes!

In November 1923 the Quetta Staff College visited Hinaidi and a fire-power demonstration was laid on for them. This included an assault landing by a pair of No 45 Sqn's Vernons, which delivered twenty-five armed troops, followed by a display of bombing in which three other units participated. Once again No 45 Sqn showed its ascendancy with an average error of just 14 yards. By comparison, the other squadrons involved, which shall be nameless, scored 21, 41 and 46 yards. In reality 46 yards was no bad score, but the point was that the Flying Camels were the best. On the 16th Sqn Ldr Harris with seven of the squadron's Vernons, accompanied by three of No 8 Sqn's Ninaks, flew the thirty-one visitors and their hosts up to Mosul to continue

A view of Hinaidi aerodrome as at 20th March 1924. No 45 Sqn's hangars are at top right, marked with an X. (No 45 Sqn archives)

their tour of the unique RAF-run Command.

Towards the end of November trouble broke out again, this time among the Marsh Arabs of the middle Euphrates where the Beni Hucheim tribe were proving to be particularly reluctant to acknowledge the authority of King Feisal's administration. Various of the tribe's clans were refusing to pay their taxes and they were interfering with the railway to Basrah, more than 300 track spikes having been lifted to be turned into daggers. Disciplinary action was called for. On the 29th two trains deployed a mobile W/T station and sufficient men, fuel, bombs, ammunition and rations to maintain an RAF Armoured Car Section and four of No 45 Sqn's Vernons at Diwaniyah, and the Snipes and DH 9As of

Unit	Bombs (lbs)	SAA[7]	BIB[8]
No 1 Sqn	1,700	9,550	-
No 8 Sqn	11,016	2,300	2,000
No 30 Sqn	6,688	1,200	-
No 45 Sqn	20,288	-	5,600
No 84 Sqn	16,572	2,200	1,000

Fig 4.2. Offensive effort against the Beni Hucheim, north of Samawah, 30th November-1st December 1923

Nos 1 and 8 Sqns at Samawah. At the same time No 84 Sqn deployed forward from its base at Shaibah to Ur. Iraq Command's Gp Capt Arthur Longmore DSO was in overall command of the operation and attacks were carried out on the 30th November and 1st December. The total effort is summarised at Figure 4.2.

Led by its CO, who flew three sorties himself, No 45 Sqn's contribution was directed chiefly at the village occupied by Sheikh Qushan al Ajaza and it had been very significant, as Harris had known that it would be. It dropped a far greater weight of bombs than any other squadron, yet it had deployed only four aeroplanes. A typical load for a single Vernon sortie comprised one 520 lb, four 112 lb and four 20 lb bombs plus a considerable number of BIBs. Although it could not release them all in flight, the Vernon could actually lift up to 2,600 lbs of BIBs in the transport role and on occasion did so when resupplying other detachments. Furthermore, only No 45 Sqn was trained in night bombing and this capability was exercised during the brief campaign thus maintaining the pressure by preventing the tribesmen from sleeping. Heavy casualties had been inflicted. Intelligence subsequently reported 115 killed and 29 wounded plus the loss of over 750 head of assorted livestock, which represented much of the tribesmen's wealth.

The detachments were withdrawn in early December but it soon became apparent that the tribes were still restive and on the 17th five of No 45 Sqn's Vernons and three Brisfits of No 6 Sqn moved back to Diwaniyah while three Snipes went to Samawah. The squadron mounted several harassing raids on the night of 17th/18th December and on the 23rd the aeroplanes were withdrawn again, although this time the trains and the detachment infrastructure remained in place for a time.

1924 was a rather quieter year, at least to start with. During January the squadron was doing acceptance checks on new Lion-engined Vernon IIs which had now begun to arrive in significant numbers. No 70 Sqn had been given

A village in flames following an attack by one of No 45 Sqn's Vernons, December 1923. (No 45 Sqn archives)

priority in taking delivery of the Vernon II and had been largely re-equipped for some months. As a consequence of their having the higher-powered machines, since the previous September No 70 Sqn's effort had been more or less exclusively directed towards maintaining the air mail service. This had permitted No 45 Sqn to concentrate on in-theatre transport tasks, which now included a regular weekly mail run to Kirkuk, and honing its offensive capabilities. The only notable task in January was on the 3rd when three Vernons supported the rotation of No 30 Sqn's Kirkuk detachment, B Flight being moved up and A Flight brought back to Hinaidi. On the 22nd a mobile W/T station was deployed to Falluja in preparation for a period of night cross-country flying which the squadron undertook in February. Another development during February was the receipt of proper bomb release gear to replace the original home-made contraptions, and the crews checked these out with practice bombing details both by day and by night.

Previous experience of moving troops by air, still a novel experience for most people in the 1920s, indicated that this needed a more formal approach. A training programme was devised under which soldiers were to be given instruction and practice in enplaning and deplaning procedures (so that they would be able to do this without sticking their bayonets through the cabin walls) followed by a short familiarisation flight. The first of these sessions was laid on for the officers and men of the Royal Inniskilling Fusiliers (RIF) in February 1924 and from then on similar events became a regular feature of the training calendar.

The squadron suffered a fatality on 17th March when Plt Off Walter Ryder was killed. Since the official term 'killed' is used (rather than the alternative 'died') this would suggest an accident of some kind but no other details appear to have survived.

In March the squadron airlifted a detachment of No 30 Sqn from Kingerban to Kirkuk and, on the 23rd, three Vernons were deployed to Djaliba to reinforce No 84 Sqn who were keeping an eye on the dissident southern tribes. All appeared quiet, however and the aeroplanes returned to Hinaidi on the 24th without having taken any offensive action, although they had flown reconnaissance sorties on both days.

On April 6th Sir John Salmond left Iraq, having established that air power could indeed be instrumental in imposing imperial authority and that the RAF was perfectly

The squadron's Vernons (J6979 nearest to camera), by now a mix of Mk Is and Mk IIs, are seen here at Kingerban in June 1924 during their deployment for operations against Sheikh Mahmud. This detachment took place early in the Mk II era and, as can just be made out on the second and third aircraft, their Lion engines were still housed in neat cowlings; problems with overheating engines soon led to these being discarded. (No 45 Sqn archives)

competent to take the lead in peacekeeping operations. Trenchard's case had been proved. The reprieve of the 'Third Service' became increasingly secure as it continued to demonstrate its worth. The threat of its being absorbed back into the RN and the army continued to recede, although it was not until the mid-1930s that the grumblings of the last of its die-hard opponents finally lapsed into acquiescence once the navy had succeeded in regaining control of the Fleet Air Arm. Salmond departed in triumph escorted by a formation drawn from Nos 1, 6, 8, 30, 45 and 70 Sqns. The new AOC was AVM John Higgins CB DSO AFC.

* * *

This would seem to be an appropriate point to insert a 'commercial'. Whenever the RAF undergoes one of its periodic peacetime contractions, considerable effort is expended in selecting the squadron numbers which ought to be retained. Regardless of whatever distinctions other units may have earned during their service, if squadron histories are to have any real significance, it would seem to be axiomatic that the identities of the squadrons which served between the wars should be the first to be preserved and the last to be dispensed with. This is especially true of the mere handful of units which flew during the 1920s, and particularly so of those which were based in Iraq where the great experiment in air control was conducted. If they had not succeeded in meeting the challenge that was offered, it is unlikely that the RAF would have remained a separate organisation. These few squadrons represent the bedrock upon which the service was built and the individual contributions of the personalities who flew with them are reflected in the histories of these units. In broad terms these factors have been taken into account during deliberations over the preservation of squadron numberplates, but it is notable that since 1976 no place has been found in the front-line for No 45 Sqn. This writer considers this to be a most regrettable omission which cannot be dismissed as a mere oversight. At best, it is an error, arising from a lack of familiarity with, and a poor appreciation of, the history of the RAF and of its individual units. At worst it is evidence of susceptibility and partiality on the part of those whose responsibility it is to select unit identities.

* * *

The 1920s were the pioneering years of long-distance flying and several of the trail-blazers passed through Hinaidi.

One of the first was Sqn Ldr A S C MacLaren who night-stopped on 21st/22nd April 1924 during his attempted world flight. Overnight No 45 Sqn's airmen tuned the engine of his Vickers Vulture and redoped its wings before sending him on his way.

Towards the end of the month there was more unrest in the south and on April 26th a Section of No 6 Armoured Car Company was moved by train to Diwaniyah where they were joined the following day by eight of No 45 Sqn's Vernon bombers and nine of No 1 Sqn's Snipes. The Vernons had been bombed-up before they departed and they carried out their first attack en route. A further raid was flown during the afternoon. Most of the Vernons were then withdrawn but two stayed at Diwaniyah and one of them carried out a night attack on the 2nd/3rd May. The last two aeroplanes returned to Hinaidi on the 5th.

May was to see another outbreak of Kurdish unrest. The spark was provided by a minor domestic incident in the bazaar in Kirkuk on the 4th. It rapidly got out of control and led to a three-way ethno-religious conflict between Assyrian Levies, Kurds and local Christians. That same day six Vernons and one of the new Victorias which were beginning to reach No 70 Sqn airlifted a detachment of sixty-six men of the 1st Btn RIF and a quantity of machine guns and ammunition to Kirkuk. The aeroplanes returned to Hinaidi on the 5th and flew more troops up the following day. In all, 152 soldiers were deployed and the trouble was quickly brought under control. This had been a classic demonstration of Trenchard's concept of cost-effectiveness. It was not, however, to be the end of the affair.

Sheikh Mahmud saw the outbreak of unrest as another opportunity to press his case for Kurdish independence and immediately exploited the situation by instigating a propaganda campaign inciting the northern tribesmen to violence. For good measure he declared a *Jihad*. From May 7th patrolling troops and armoured cars began to find themselves under sniper fire from the hillsides. On the 19th two of No 45 Sqn's Vernons assisted No 6 Sqn to move up to Mosul but they were not to stay there for long. The deteriorating internal security situation called for decisive action and the RAF moved out into the field again. On May 26th Nos 6 and 8 Sqns joined No 30 Sqn at Kirkuk while Nos 45, 55 and 70 Sqns concentrated at Kingerban. The Kingerban force peaked at forty-two aircraft with the Vernon element under the overall control of Sqn Ldr Harris. In the meantime, on the 20th, No 30 Sqn had dropped leaflets on

Unit	Weight of bombs dropped					Number of BIBs
	520 lbs	230 lbs	112 lbs	20 lbs	Total	
No 8 Sqn	-	9,200	4,032	-	13,232	4,800
No 30 Sqn	-	2,760	9,744	1,140	13,644	4,000
No 45 Sqn	7,800	10,580	5,488	440	24,308	6,200
No 55 Sqn	-	4,370	-	-	4,370	2,200

Fig 4.3. Bombing effort against Sulaimaniyah, 27th/28th May 1924.

Sulaimaniyah warning that Mahmud's HQ was likely to be bombed and advising the people to evacuate the city. Three days later further leaflets publicly delivered an ultimatum. The Sheikh was to surrender himself by noon on the 25th or the town would be bombed. He did not comply and the threatened attack was carried out. Fourteen raids were flown on the 27th and 28th, involving a total of 101 sorties; each squadron's weapons expenditure is recorded at Figure 4.3.

Once again Harris' Vernons had shown their worth; not only had No 45 Sqn delivered a greater weight of bombs than any other unit, it had repeatedly demonstrated that it could do this with considerable precision. Over twenty-eight tons of bombs had been dropped in two days; No 45 Sqn had delivered 43% of this total, including fifteen of the big 520 pounders which only the Vernon could carry. Extensive material damage had been done but the majority of the population had already evacuated the town. At the time it

Still the pride of the squadron's silver collection, the Flying Camel first graced the dinner table at Hinaidi in 1924. (Author's collection)

was believed that there had been no direct casualties, although fifteen lives were lost in subsequent looting incidents. On May 29th the RAF returned to its bases. Sheikh Mahmud sustained a brief guerrilla campaign but then withdrew across the border into Persia and lay dormant, at least for a time.

By this time J6871 had been retired, with ten minutes under 404 hours of flying to its credit. Harris had adopted J7134, *Valkyrie*, as his personal Mk II during May and this was to be his mount for another bombing competition which was held at Hinaidi the following month. On two practice sorties on June 15th the CO's overall bombing accuracy was a remarkable six yards. The competition was held two days later and this time all the bombs were to be delivered as First Run Attacks; furthermore COs were given discretion to decide what aiming methods would be employed. It made no difference; the Flying Camels still came out on top. This event had been part of another fire-power demonstration laid on for the army and, for the first time in Iraq, for the general public. A dummy village had been erected on the airfield and at 0600hrs (tropical working day) on the 27th June four of No 45 Sqn's Vernons attacked. The very first bomb struck the centre of the 'village' which promptly burst into flames. A number of Snipes then strafed the 'escaping inhabitants', represented by strips of white cloth flapping in the breeze, before armoured cars closed in with machine guns blazing. Finally, the cars' crews dismounted and finished off the job with mortars and rifle grenades. It had certainly been spectacular. To anyone who had seen an RAF Pageant at Hendon it might have been old hat but few Iraqis had been to Hendon and they were deeply impressed, especially after the object lesson of the destruction recently visited on Sulaimaniyah.

In early July Sulaimaniyah was occupied by the 4th Btn Assyrian Levies and at the end of the month the two Vernon squadrons began airlifting Iraqi troops up from Baghdad to establish an administration and reassert central government control. During the month No 45 Sqn moved No 1 Sqn up to Kirkuk and mounted a short detachment at Kingerban for a few days to handle a troop movement. There were also the usual casualty evacuations and the weekly Kirkuk mail run.

While the campaign against the Kurds had been going on Bob Saundby had been on leave in the UK, leaving A flight, his personal aeroplane, *Stormcock*, and his co-pilot, Fg Off Embry, in the hands of Flt Lt J K Summers MC. Saundby was charged with conducting some important squadron business while he was at home. By mid-1924 the squadron silver fund, to which all current officers made a monthly payment and to which contributions from some of the wartime veterans were also added, was fairly well established. It had long been the squadron's ambition to have a Flying Camel in silver as a table decoration for formal occasions and Saundby had undertaken to have it made while he was in England. He called at the Goldsmiths' and Silversmiths' Company in London and commissioned them to produce it. They set about making a prototype in clay and Saundby made several visits to advise on the crucial positioning and styling of the wings. The model-maker was not happy with some features of the camel itself, however,

A real Flying Camel! (No 45 Sqn archives)

Only scant details of this incident have come to light. It involved J7140 and took place in August 1924 somewhere near Sulaimaniyah; Flt Lt John Summers did it. Other photographs indicate that the damage only involved the main undercarriage units, both of which had completely collapsed, presumably as a result of a forced landing following a loss of power. The aeroplane is seen here well on its way to being completely dismantled. Of particular interest are the large, but rarely visible, hatch in the side of the forward fuselage and the modified ram's horn air intake on the dismounted engine. This design of intake faced to the rear and was intended to cut down the ingestion of sand. With the aeroplane in this state the damage looks terminal but it was salvaged and eventually flew again. (No 45 Sqn archives)

particularly its feet, and he asked for some photographs of a typical beast to be sent from Iraq. Saundby had a better idea - he gave the man sixpence and suggested that he visit Regents Park Zoo! In the end they did a magnificent job and the piece still takes pride of place in the squadron's silver collection. This collection became quite extensive during the squadron's service in Iraq as it became a common practice for departing officers to present the squadron with a suitable token. These included a number of tankards engraved with the signature of the presenter, many of which are still in the possession of the squadron today.

The rest of the summer remained fairly quiet. Competitive bombing continued in August and September but the Flying Camels were unbeatable. There were also two major troop movements in August; a personnel rotation for the 1st Btn RIF's garrison at Kirkuk and the redeployment of 121 Iraqi soldiers from Kingerban to Sulaimaniyah, or 'Sul' as it was now known to old Iraq hands. Flt Lt Summers came to grief during the latter operation when J7140's undercarriage collapsed but the aeroplane was eventually rebuilt and returned to service.

In 1923 Harris had demonstrated that, despite some significant limitations, under certain conditions night operations were a realistic proposition. In the year that had elapsed since he had first introduced night bombing the techniques had been refined and the squadron's pilots had become familiar with the problems involved. The CO now sought to develop this capability further by introducing what amounted to night formation bombing, the aim being to concentrate the effects of an attack. On five nights in August up to five aircraft at a time carried out practice attacks in line astern, at least two of these sorties being flown at 6,000 feet, virtually the Vernon's ceiling. On the last day of this session, on the 24th, Harris took AVM Higgins up on a four-aircraft detail to show him how it was done, the AOC subsequently congratulating the squadron on its performance. Another significant event that month was the arrival of the squadron's first batch of NCO pilots: Sgts Frank Page, Frederick Fry, Samuel Muir, Alfred Reeve and Howard Alger.

In late September there was some VIP work. On the 24th the Secretary of State for Air, Lord Thompson, was flown in by No 70 Sqn. His aircraft was met over Ramadi by a joint No 45/70 Sqn formation and escorted into Hinaidi. On the 30th Saundby and Harris flew the minister back to Egypt via Amman, finally delivering him to Aboukir on October 2nd.

From October, having by now been largely re-equipped with Lion-engined Vernons, it became No 45 Sqn's turn to run the air mail and No 70 Sqn became the in-theatre transport squadron. Thereafter there was to be rather less excitement as the next fourteen months were mainly devoted to route-flying. The first outbound air mail run was flown to Cairo between 2nd and 4th October. The return flight was made by Flt Lt Dalzell in *Aurora* (J7141) and Flt Lt Saundby in *Valkyrie* (J7134), the latter already being in Egypt having been the aircraft in which Lord Thompson had been flown to Aboukir a few days before. They left on the 7th with the new CO, Sqn Ldr R M Hill MC AFC, on board. He arrived at Hinaidi the following day and assumed command of the squadron on the 14th. The much respected Sqn Ldr Harris, who had done so much to build the squadron's by now formidable reputation, left Iraq on the same day, sailing from Basrah on HMT *Glengorm Castle* bound for the UK where he was to take up the post of OC No 58 Sqn. He was to be AOCinC Bomber Command for much of WW II, finally retiring as Marshal of the RAF Sir Arthur Harris Bt GCB OBE AFC.

By late 1924 the air mail run had been developed into a fairly smooth running operation and the itinerary was now standard. Outbound: Hinaidi to Ramadi (night stop) - to Ziza (night stop) - to Heliopolis. Inbound: Heliopolis to Ziza - to a convenient LG (night stop) - to Ramadi - to Hinaidi. The selection of an LG on the return flight was at the captain's discretion and largely dictated by the time of sunset. Although the pilots were kept current in night flying there was still no reliable instrumentation, and navigation was still totally dependent on map reading. It would have been foolhardy to have attempted to fly the route at night without being able to see the track and it was not acceptable to expose the Royal Mail to any such unnecessary risks. Some early consideration had been given to night operations, however, and in the wave of enthusiasm which had

Photographed shortly after landing, the pennants flying from the rear outer struts of this Vernon II indicate that it is the mail-carrier. In the background, its companion and back-up still has its engines running. Note that both of these aeroplanes have been fitted with a pair of large fuel tanks under their upper wings, a modification that was introduced circa 1924. The location is LG 5 and the secure fuel storage bunker can be seen in the foreground along with a scatter of discarded petrol tins, presumably left for the benefit of passing Bedouin. (Author's collection)

Period	Completed as planned	Completed late	Failed	Total Attempts	Failure Rate
8-12/21	36	21	13	70	19%
1-6/22	31	46	12	89	14%
7-12/22	12	33	5	50	10%
1-6/23	15	29	4	48	8%
7-12/23	12	51	3	66	4%
1-6/24	31	21	2	54	4%
7-12/24	39	31	0	70	0%
Total	**176**	**232**	**39**	**447**	**9%**

Fig 4.4. *The improvement in the reliability of the Air Mail service between August 1921 and December 1924.*

accompanied the successful inauguration of the air mail service in 1921 it had been proposed that a series of lighthouses should be provided. By mid-1922, however, it had been appreciated that the logistic problems associated with installing and maintaining such devices (not to mention protecting them from disenchanted Arabs) outweighed any operational advantage that might be gained. After all, the air mail was only a fortnightly schedule so what was the hurry? It was not a race; the aim was to achieve reliability and dependability - speed would come later.

Although the air mail was now a comparatively routine undertaking and the squadron was flying the more powerful Vernon IIs, this did not mean that life was entirely without incident and forced landings were still quite common. The cause was nearly always engine failure which, on No 45 Sqn, ran at a rate of one failure per 136 flying hours for a total of fourteen incidents in the first six months of 1924 (the comparative figures for No 70 Sqn over the same period were one failure per 84 flying hours for a total of twenty incidents). Sound maintenance practices could go only so far towards alleviating this situation, however, as most failures were a reflection on the contemporary state of the engineering art and the robustness of the materials being used to build aeroplane engines at that time. Problems occurred with camshaft casings, the camshafts themselves, reduction gears, magnetos and, especially, the cooling systems; very

often the unscheduled landing would then result in damage to the undercarriage. Fortunately, and because of the generous provision of emergency LGs, these incidents were rarely serious, although it often meant that a crew would be stuck out in the desert for several nights. In fact, while the route is commonly described as being over desert, a more appropriate term is probably steppe, but whichever word is used the message is the same: a vast, treeless, virtually uninhabited tract of land. In his book *Baghdad Air Mail* Roderic Hill provides a graphic impression of the terrain and recounts many of the incidents which occurred during his two years in command of No 45 Sqn.

Despite the occasional incidents which still enlivened the air mail run, the aim of reliability was slowly being achieved. Figure 4.4 indicates the progress that had been made. The failure rate had been progressively reduced, from an order of 1 in 5 to zero. Although this aspect was now satisfactory the number of aircraft which completed the journey only after experiencing delays (which could be of several days' duration) was still too high. It was now becoming clear, however, that the required overall level of reliability was attainable. The RAF had devised the appropriate procedures, refined the operating techniques and accumulated a wealth of experience. What was needed now was a generation of better, more robust, aeroplanes which would be less likely to experience technical problems and be more capable of

Of the four Vimy Ambulances that were built, J7143 was the one most usually associated with No 45 Sqn. (No 45 Sqn archives)

Fg Off Bob (or 'Bones' as Arthur Harris called him) Ragg in his Sunday best. One of No 45 Sqn's ten ex-Vernon men who became air officers, he eventually retired as AVM R L Ragg CB CBE AFC. (No 45 Sqn archives).

withstanding adverse conditions of wind and weather. The first of these would be the RAF's Victoria, a transport derivative of the Virginia bomber - in effect, a stretched Vernon. The RAF would carry on flying the mail for a while yet, but it now looked as if civilian airliners might well be able to take over in a year or so.

Despite being committed to the mail run the squadron continued to maintain its operational capability, and night flying and bombing exercises were still regularly undertaken. On 1st January 1925 a new Vimy Ambulance was delivered to the squadron. In all, four of these aeroplanes passed through the hands of the two Vernon squadrons and each usually had one on charge. Despite their official designations they were often referred to as Vernon Ambulances since, with their saloon hulls, they were barely distinguishable externally from the standard Vernon, although their role was clearly advertised by the red crosses painted on their wings and superimposed on the centre spot of the large roundels on the aircraft's flanks. The main differences were that the ambulances had a nose hatch, in place of the bomb-aimer's station to permit the loading of stretchers, and their interiors were optimised for the carriage of casualties[9]. A doctor would accompany the crew when appropriate but a medical orderly usually sufficed. The aircraft taken on charge on New Year's Day was J7143 and responsibility for flying it was shared by Fg Offs Basil Embry and Denis Geeson.

There were no further events of note until March 29th when J7142 was obliged to crash land on an air mail run. Captained by Percy Maitland, the aircraft had had a difficult eastbound passage and on the 27th, inbound from Ziza, it had been forced to land at LG F with a port engine failure. After a temporary repair it only got as far as LG H before it had to put down again. Following a further application of self-help the aeroplane took off once more and limped on to LG J where Maitland decided to call it a day and stay put. A replacement engine was flown out and fitted on the 28th and the following day the aeroplane resumed its homeward journey. The new engine failed between LG O and LG P provoking yet another unscheduled landing, this time one which caused significant airframe damage, although no one was injured.

The following month there was another VIP trip. Four aeroplanes, captained by the CO, Sqn Ldr John Summers, Flt Lt Maitland and Fg Off Embry, departed for Egypt on the 18th April to pick up the Secretaries of State for Air and for the Colonies, Sir Samuel Hoare and the Rt Hon Leo Amery, with a party of MPs and appropriate escorting officers. They were delivered to Hinaidi without incident on the 26th, Fg Off H W R Banting having replaced Percy Maitland for the return trip.

Once the VIPs had seen all that there was to see, No 70 Sqn dropped them off at Ramadi where five of No 45 Sqn's aeroplanes, one of them a spare, had been positioned to fly them to Ramleh, finally returning them to Egypt on May 21st and 22nd. Basil Embry flew the two Ministers in J7143, the marginally more comfortable Vimy Ambulance. He recounts (*cf Mission Completed*) how Amery's private secretary came forward on the first leg and sought reassurance that in-flight meals had been arranged. The captain assured him that all was in hand and gestured airily towards the ration-box on top of which were several raw onions; what was inside was not much more appetising. In fact these were the crew's standard rations, more palatable sandwiches and flasks of cool drinks having been provided for the passengers. The message seemed to get through, however, and three months later a new and much improved scale of in-flight catering was issued. Another small coup for the Flying Camels!

It is instructive to consider the pilots involved in this trip. One of the aeroplanes was flown by the CO who was, in the fullness of time, to become Air Chief Marshal Sir Roderic Hill KCB MC AFC. Another was flown by Sqn Ldr 'Uncle' Lees, later Air Marshal Sir Alan Lees KCB CBE DSO AFC. The humble pilot of the Ambulance was to finish his career as Air Chief Marshal Sir Basil Embry GCB KBE DSO DFC AFC. Among the other junior officers on the squadron at

A familiar picture of Vimy Ambulance J7143 flying over Hinaidi. Note that the aeroplane lacks the bumper nosewheels which it certainly had when it was first delivered. (No 45 Sqn archives)

J7141, Aurora, *after an unscheduled landing at El Lyssen in October 1925. Details are lacking but, since the radiator has been removed from the port engine, the incident was probably caused by a coolant leak. From the left: Sqn Ldr F Graves (of HQ Iraq), Fg Off J V Kelly doing a 'Lawrence of Arabia', another (unidentified) horseman, LAC Lewis, AC Hayes and Sgt Godfrey. The varying styles of working dress make an interesting contrast. (No 45 Sqn archives)*

Whenever possible pilots and groundcrew worked as a recognised team and had a personal aeroplane to fly and maintain. Inter-flight and inter-crew competition was encouraged as a means of raising overall standards. This team won the inter-aircraft Lewis Gun Cup for 1925-26. From the left: LAC Lillywhite, LAC Lewis, Cpl Black, Fg Off J V Kelly, Fg Off J E Davies and LAC Henderson. The aeroplane is J7141, the second to bear the name Aurora. *(No 45 Sqn archives)*

this time, Flt Lt Percy Maitland and Fg Off Bob Ragg were also to have highly successful careers and were to retire as Air Vice Marshal P E Maitland CB CBE MVO AFC and Air Vice Marshal R L Ragg CB CBE AFC. Of such men was No 45 Sqn made in the 1920s.

The establishment of both Vernon squadrons was increased to twelve aircraft each during 1925 and the rank of their COs was accordingly raised to wing commander; Roderic Hill was promoted on July 1st. Ralph Cochrane and Bob Saundby had left in November 1923 and February 1925, their places being taken by Flt Lts Lees and Summers who continued to run A and B flights respectively, although both were squadron leaders by mid-1925. The following year, when sufficient aeroplanes finally became available, a C Flight was established under Sqn Ldr Evelyn Whitehouse, his appointment being the last change among the executive officers while the squadron was stationed in Iraq. Being heavily committed to the air mail left insufficient time for the squadron to practise in its bombing role to the extent that it would have liked but it still maintained its operational skills, and night bombing remained a No 45 Sqn speciality. By this time the incidence of forced landings was almost, but not quite, negligible and reliability had replaced uncertainty as the characteristic feature of the mail run.

The RAF's air mail had been provided with some commercial competition ever since the summer of 1923 when the Nairn Transport Company had inaugurated an alternative service between Baghdad and Damascus using fast cars. It was alleged that these eight-cylinder Cadillacs travelled at speeds of up to 70 mph - much the same as a Vernon, and somewhat faster if the latter was bucking a headwind. The two routes converged somewhere to the west of Rutbah and from there to Baghdad the visibility of the air mail track was maintained by the wheels of the Nairn cars. In August 1925, however, another advantage of air travel became apparent. There was an outbreak of banditry and several of the Nairn vehicles were ambushed and robbed; this could hardly happen to an aeroplane. Although a form of rival, the car service was certainly meeting a need and when it was interrupted it became necessary to add some relief flights to move the excess mail to and from Amman and Cairo.

The mail run was so regular by this time that it was

beginning to look more like an airline operation than a military activity, which had been the objective all along. In September 1925 Sir Sefton Brancker, the Director of Civil Aviation, accompanied by a number of Imperial Airways representatives, spent two weeks examining the Iraq Command sector of a proposed UK-India air link. The end was in sight.

Almost as if to confound the growing air of confidence in the mail run, Sgt Alger set off from Cairo in *Vagabond* (J7135) on October 22nd and did not reach Hinaidi until 4th November, having been forced to land five times en route with a series of engine and radiator problems. But this sort of thing was now exceptional. Another Royal Flight came the squadron's way in November when King Feisal and a number of his personal attendants were picked up in Egypt on the 11th and flown to Baghdad. The two Vernons arrived on the 15th having been escorted in from Ramadi in style by nine of No 55 Sqn's DH 9As.

An indication of the extent to which the air mail dominated the squadron's activities can be seen from an analysis of the hours flown in 1925. 2,034 hours had been spent on the route, which was 71.5% of the overall annual total of 2,842 hours. The balance was made up by 273 hours of air tests and ferry trips, the remainder being training flying,

An early example of a No 45 Sqn graffito. Fg Off Frank North gives scale to the work of an unknown artist at Ramadi in 1926. (No 45 Sqn archives)

Hinaidi, 26th February 1926. The pilot uses the tailplane of J7135, Vagabond, as a makeshift table to effect the ritual exchange of signatures as custody of No 45 Sqn's last consignment of Air Mail is transferred to a chap in a trilby, a raincoat and an elegant pair of socks. Note that this aeroplane has a row of hooks above its windows to permit it to be fitted with fabric sidescreens while on the ground. (No 45 Sqn archives)

446 hours by day and 89 hours by night. The training flying had been devoted to the same sort of tasks that occupy a squadron today - circuit work, practice emergencies, general handling, cross countries, range bombing and familiarisation trips for soldiers. Incidentally, while 89 hours of night flying may not seem to have been much spread over a whole year, it should be noted that this was more than any other squadron in Iraq Command had done.

Just as he was leaving the squadron on being posted to No 30 Sqn, Fg Off Embry was awarded an AFC in the 1926 'January List' in recognition of his work as captain of the squadron's Vimy Ambulance. No doubt his overall contribution to the life of the squadron had also been a factor, since he had been prominent in the sporting field from the outset and his Squadron Boxing Team had won the Open Championships again in 1925.

The squadron flew its last air mail trip in early 1926, the final pair, of which J7135 had been the mail-carrier, landing at Hinaidi on the 26th February after a trouble-free passage. Since the summer of the previous year No 70 Sqn had been progressively re-equipping with the Vernon III, which had additional fuel tankage, high-compression Lion III engines and dispensed with the characteristic bumper nosewheel. More significantly, they had also been receiving the altogether bigger and better Victorias. Once again No 70 Sqn was better equipped than No 45 Sqn and they reassumed responsibility for the air mail commitment, maintaining it until January 1927 when it was finally taken over by Imperial Airways. At Heliopolis No 216 Sqn was also gradually re-equipped with Victorias during 1926 and it flew its last mail run with a Vimy on August 22nd. Two months later, on October 22nd, No 70 Sqn flew the last Vernon service. For the few remaining months during which the desert air mail service remained an RAF responsibility the fortnightly schedule was maintained by a shuttle of Victorias and the new aeroplanes proved to be so reliable that from September onwards the requirement for the route to be flown in pairs was waived; for the last two months of 1926 Victorias droned across the empty wastes alone.

For No 45 Sqn it was back to bombing practice and in-theatre tasking in 1926, although they too now began to receive some of the 'fastback-model' Vernon IIIs. There was

Above: J7139, Venus, after Fg Off John Dick had stood it on its nose during an attempted take off from Hinaidi bound for Kirkuk on 19th July 1926. No one was seriously hurt but shortly after the aeroplane had been evacuated, under the weight of the engines, the whole wing structure collapsed forwards, completely destroying the cockpit section. (No 45 Sqn archives). Below: Vimy Ambulance J7143 was eventually rebuilt and converted into a Vernon III. It ended its days when it crashed into No 1 Sqn's hangar at Hinaidi on 26th July 1926. Plt Off G P Mee and LAC Henderson escaped with injuries but seven others on board were killed. This aeroplane probably should have been reserialled as JR7143 when it was rebuilt but it was plainly not wearing this identity when it crashed. (No 45 Sqn archives)

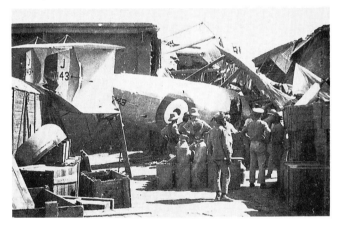

no more real excitement until July when, on the 4th, Sir Alan Cobham and his crew (A B Elliot, mechanic, and B W G Emmott, cameraman/photographer) who were surveying the air route to Australia, landed on the Tigris in his Jaguar-engined DH 50J floatplane, G-EBFO. The squadron helped turn the aircraft round and the following day the trail-blazers took off to fly on down to Basrah. An unknown tribesman aimed a casual shot at the aeroplane as it passed by and Elliot was killed. Such a lesson was hardly necessary but the incident served as a sharp reminder to all concerned that Iraq could still be a very inhospitable place. Despite this tragedy Cobham borrowed a mechanic from No 84 Sqn and pressed on to Melbourne. Having left England on June 26th he finally alighted again on the Thames at Westminster on October 1st. Cobham's exploit was of little direct concern to No 45 Sqn but it was another portent - the civilians were coming.

July 1926 was also notable for two accidents. Landing at Hinaidi on the 19th, Fg Off J S Dick tipped J7139 up on its nose and shortly afterwards, unable to sustain the weight of the engines, the whole wing structure collapsed, the upper mainplane falling forwards and completely destroying the cockpit section. Fortunately the crew had already vacated the aircraft and they escaped, shaken but otherwise unharmed. A week later J7143[10], the erstwhile Ambulance by now converted to Vernon III standard, suffered an engine failure shortly after taking-off on a routine mail run to Kirkuk

The officers of No 45 Sqn in the summer of 1926. Front row, from the left:- Fg Off Guy G H DuBoulay, Flt Lt Charles E Horrex AFC, Flt Lt Evelyn R Whitehouse, Sqn Ldr John K Summers MC, Fg Off John V Kelly, Wg Cdr Robert M Hill MC AFC, Sqn Ldr Alan Lees, Flt Lt Louis G Paget AFC, Flt Lt Ernest H Attwood, Fg Off Joe Davison (Stores). Back row, from the left:- Mr Woofenden, Fg Off Frank E North, Fg Off John E Davies, Fg Off Yvon W Burnett, Fg Off Reginald W Freeman (Accts), Fg Off John S Dick, Fg Off Maurice W J Boxall, Fg Off Leslie L Potter, Fg Off Gerard L Gandy, Fg Off Oswald K Stirling-Webb, Fg Off Cecil G C B Woledge, Plt Off George P Mee. (No 45 Sqn archives)

with nine on board. In what proved to be the worst accident in the squadron's entire history, it crashed into No 1 Sqn's hangar and was destroyed. Fg Off Oswald Stirling-Webb and six passengers were killed; only Fg Off Percy Mee and LAC Jock Henderson survived, although both had sustained injuries. These were not the last Vernons to be written off by the squadron, however, and in September both J7141 and J7547 were to be scrapped after sustaining damage in night landing accidents.

Shortly after this there was another outbreak of unrest. In the course of Abdul Aziz ibn Saud's campaign to consolidate his control over Nejd, groups of dissident tribesmen from Ha'il had fled across the border into Iraq whence they were making raids back into Saudi territory, sometimes reinforced by other groups of recalcitrant Ikhwan whom ibn Saud was trying to discipline. Their presence was a political embarrassment to Feisal's regime in Iraq, besides which they tended to provoke disturbances wherever they happened to be. In October 1926 the Shammar were causing trouble to the west of Baghdad and on the upper Euphrates and action was taken against them. One flight of No 55 Sqn and a section from No 4 Armoured Car Company were deployed to Rutbah and Annah respectively. No 45 Sqn moved both units. The total lift amounted to some 30 tons,

J7135, Vagabond, with its flag at half mast and draped in mourning for the departure of its pilot, Sqn Ldr Alan 'Uncle' Lees in November 1926. Note the spare wheel fixed to the fuselage above the lower wing root and the battery-powered baggage trolley, one of Arthur Harris' labour saving innovations. (P Baillie)

including 5,600 gals of petrol, 155 gals of oil, 10,395 lbs of miscellaneous stores and two spare engines with their associated lifting tackle. In addition some forty-five assorted personnel were airlifted out to the two detachments. Between October 13th and 28th sixteen sorties were flown to Rutbah and three to Annah. There was some action on the 20th and 21st and three additional trips to Rutbah were laid on, one to evacuate the wounded and two to fly out some prisoners. In all, the undertaking consumed some 230 flying hours. It was to be the Flying Camel's last significant operation with Vernons.

There was, however, one last piece of enterprise. Curious about the capabilities of the Mk III Vernons, the CO authorised some endurance flights and on October 21st Fg Off Yvon Burnett and Sgt Bennet flew one for 9 hrs and 20 mins. This creditable performance did not, however, come close to that which had been put up five days earlier when Fg Off John Kelly and Sgt Dingwall had kept J7545 airborne for exactly one hour longer, a tribute to their engine handling and quite possibly a record for the type.

Following ratification of a Turco-Iraqi Treaty on 5th November 1926, 'active service' in Iraq was terminated. With the external Turkish threat to the northern provinces removed, future operations would be more to do with internal security than with defending the borders of the Iraqi state. It could hardly be claimed, however, that Iraq had been completely pacified and there were to be several more campaigns before the Anglo-Iraqi Treaty of 1930 was signed, leading to the country becoming substantially independent in 1932. As yet Sheikh Mahmud was far from being a spent force (in some circles he was referred to as the 'Director of RAF Training' in recognition of the periodic bursts of activity which he continued to generate) and even when he did fade from the scene the centre of militant Kurdish nationalism simply moved from Sulaimaniyah to Mosul where it continued to flourish under the leadership of Sheikh Ahmad Barzani. There were also to be further occasional incidents on the southern border provoked by bands of Ikhwan die-hards from Nejd. Nevertheless the situation was slowly becoming more stable and there was an easing of tension. With Imperial Airways' assumption of responsibility for the air mail in January 1927, No 70 Sqn's big Victorias had been diverted to in-country transport tasking and there was now an excess of airlift available within Iraq Command. Since No 45 Sqn was still equipped with the less capable Vernons it had already been decided to run it down before withdrawing it to England where it was to be re-established with Vickers Virginias as a night-bomber unit. Before this plan could be

As he described in his book Baghdad Air Mail, *when Wg Cdr Roderic Hill relinquished command of No 45 Sqn he was driven away in a garland bedecked Rolls-Royce. (No 45 Sqn archives)*

The elephants' graveyard at Hinaidi. These two aeroplanes are J7135 (on the left) and J7141; also noted as being present at the same time were the remains of JR6872, J6977, J7139, J7140, J7143 and J7547. Note that J7135 has been fitted with a large forward access hatch. This door may have been an in-service modification as it was not fitted to all Vernons - photographs of J7141 show it both and without a door and J7547 never acquired one. It is difficult to detect in photographs but its presence is revealed by the number of fuselage windows, Vernons with a door having two forward windows, smaller than the others, on the port side. (No 45 Sqn archives)

implemented, however, it was decided to move No 47 Sqn to the Sudan, creating a need for a light bomber squadron to take its place in Egypt and No 45 Sqn was diverted to meet this new requirement.

Air Organisation Memorandum (AO) 1658 of 11th December 1926 announced that the HQ and one flight of No 45 Sqn had been struck off the strength of the Iraq Command with effect from November 1st and that its residual cadre was awaiting embarkation for Egypt pending transfer of the squadron to the Middle East Command. With appropriate informal ceremony, the popular Wg Cdr Hill relinquished his command and departed by air for Egypt where he was to take up an appointment on the technical staff of HQME. One of his flight commanders, Sqn Ldr Summers, assumed command of the remaining flight of the squadron which was attached to No 70 Sqn. AO 1672 of 1st February 1927 announced that the cadre of No 45 Sqn had been taken on the strength of the Middle East Command on 1st January and that the flight attached to No 70 Sqn had been disbanded on the 17th. So ended the Flying Camels' memorable first stay in Iraq. They would return in 1941 - with twenty-one Blenheims.

Notes:

1. This neo-colonial arrangement was made in the name of the League of Nations which august body subsequently (in 1922) ratified British and French responsibility for their new acquisitions under the terms of formal mandates.
2. RAF phonetic patois for the DH 9A.
3. The name Mesopotamia was officially superseded by that of Iraq on 29th September 1921.
4. RAF patois for the Bristol Fighter, also known as the 'Biff'.
5. Seen from the perspective of an officer in the field, trying to keep a squadron flying, Cochrane's point of view is easily understood. It may be, however, that in its wisdom, the Air Ministry, prevented from placing substantial orders for new aeroplanes by the parsimonious Defence Budgets of the 1920s, was doing what it could to sustain a national aircraft industry by procuring inessential, but relatively inexpensive, spare components (which, having been purchased, had then to be consumed) instead of promoting more economical do-it-yourself practices.
6. Technically, despite its primary task being that of a transport unit, No 45 Sqn was already actually classified as bomber unit, largely because air transportation was not a role that was officially recognised by the RAF's bureaucracy at the time. This was confirmed in 1924 when, following the promulgation of AMWO 218 on 27th March, roles were incorporated into unit designations, the squadron's full title then becoming No 45 (Bombing) Squadron. 'Bomber-Transport' would clearly have been a more appropriate description but this role did not gain official endorsement until 1931. The term 'Bombing' was later changed to 'Bomber' by AMWO No 221 of 4th April 1929 and the squadron continued to be known as No 45 (B) Sqn until May 1939 when AMO A.185 deleted roles from squadron designations altogether. They have never been formally reinstated, although a few units have resurrected their pre-war titles and brought them back into use, albeit unofficially.
7. SAA = Small Arms Ammunition, ie machine gun rounds.
8. BIB = 6½ oz Baby Incendiary Bombs, usually carried by the Vernon in containers of two hundred.
9. Apart from the nose hatch fitted to at least some Vimy Ambulances, several of the later Vernons had a large door, hinged at the top, in the port side of the fuselage above the leading edge of the wing (see some of the accompanying illustrations). This was presumably intended to permit loading of large items and may have had some application in the casualty evacuation role.
10. During the 1920s and early 1930s when an aircraft was substantially rebuilt after a major accident, was reconditioned after having flown a predetermined number of hours or was extensively modified by being converted into a later variant the letter R (for Rebuilt) was incorporated into its original serial number. Thus J7143 should have become JR7143 and some sources maintain that it did. This may well have been the case but the aeroplane was certainly marked as J7143 when it finally crashed so if the R ever was actually inserted it would seem that it must have been deleted again.

Chapter 5. Now these things befell in Egypt - Ninaks, Faireys, Vincents and Wellesleys.

Although it took several months for the arrangements to be formally promulgated, it had long been known on the grapevine that the squadron was to be re-established at Heliopolis with DH 9As and that the change from twin- to single-engined aircraft implied that the rank of the CO would revert to squadron leader. Sqn Ldr Summers, who had been minding the store since Roderic Hill's departure, was offered the post. Having been with the squadron since September 1923 he could have elected to return to the UK but he eagerly grasped the opportunity to command the unit. As CO Designate he immediately proposed that the squadron, or its still substantial remains, be moved from Iraq to Egypt as a going concern and re-equipped. This, he argued, would be preferable to running it down and starting all over again, thus wasting all the splendid work that the two previous COs had done in establishing the unit's identity and its unrivalled reputation. He was overruled.

When the squadron's cadre first set up shop at Heliopolis on 11th February 1927 it numbered just six men - John Summers, Fg Offs John New, Yvon Burnett and John Kelly (the latter acting as Adjutant), Sgt McKenzie (the Orderly Room NCO) and one Aircraft Hand, Cpl Collins. Nominally attached to No 47 Sqn for the time being, Summers immediately put them to work trying to keep track of the whereabouts of as many old No 45 Sqn hands as possible. Since his Plan A, that the squadron should stay together, had been rejected he reverted to Plan B, which was to reassemble it. In the meantime he visited the UK on leave and, as a new squadron commander, he was summoned to the Air Ministry to be briefed. This process included an interview with the CAS, still Trenchard but now a Marshal of the Royal Air Force, the first officer to hold this rank. In the course of the interview 'Boom' Trenchard stressed that his aim was to foster an RAF, rather than a squadron, spirit. Summers countered that the squadrons were the building blocks and that if they had *esprit de corps* then that of the service would look after itself. They agreed to differ but Summers emerged from the interview with Trenchard's endorsement of his plan to recover as many of the old hands as possible. Now that he had the CAS's personal sanction, on his return to Egypt, Summers prevailed upon the personnel staff at HQ RAFME to start arranging postings for as many ex-Flying Camelmen

as possible and sufficient were eventually rounded up to create a sound core for the resurgent unit.

The official announcement of the squadron's re-emergence was contained in AO 1687 of 9th May 1927 which declared that "as from 25th April 1927 No 45 Sqn has become a Day Bombing Squadron and has been increased from a Cadre to a Headquarters and one Flight". Three weeks later this was amended to read "...to full squadron establishment".

With the arrival of an initial batch of new groundcrew on April 27th the squadron began to come to life again and, having received its first few 'Ninaks', it managed to fly 7 hours before the month was out. Three more pilots were posted-in during May and the work up began to gain momentum; 45 hours were flown that month. In June, with the start of bombing training, the monthly flying effort rose to 93 hours and in July to 138 hours. On the 22nd of that month the squadron's first flight commander arrived, Flt Lt H K Goode DSO DFC, who promptly set about organising A Flight. Endurance flying was a major preoccupation in those days and the squadron made its first attempt at this on July 26th putting up four DH 9As on a 5 hrs 40 mins trip. One aeroplane had to land twice with a leaking cylinder and a second accompanied it so that only two aircraft managed to fly the exercise non-stop, the others limping home a few hours later.

By August the monthly total of flying was up to 172 hours, which was more than that flown by the well-established No 47 Sqn, and for good measure the squadron achieved the best bombing average as well. The Flying Camels were back in business. Conscious of the value of sport in building a unit's identity and morale, Summers had encouraged the formation of various teams and by September the squadron was making its presence felt in that arena too. In that month they beat both the Norfolk Regiment and the RAMC at soccer and No 47 Sqn at hockey and a start was made on establishing a rugby team. Another device which John Summers employed to rebuild the squadron was an entirely unofficial Squadron Fund. The 'book' lays down that the handling and expenditure of any funds, public or otherwise, is subject to certain constraints and requires that all transactions be subject to audit. In the early days at least

A line up of the squadron's DH 9As. Nearest the camera is HR3501, followed by JR7339 and JR7093. This photograph was taken at Heliopolis quite early in the Ninak era and before any squadron markings had been applied. Note that JR7339 has a letter B on its fin. Since No 45 Sqn usually identified its aeroplanes with numbers, it is probable that this letter-code was inherited from a previous user and that it will have been short-lived. (MOD)

the CO took charge of the squadron's illegal hoard of private cash himself and personally ensured that it was spent where it would do most good, on the airmen's welfare.

No 47 Sqn, who had long maintained a detachment in the Sudan, moved their HQ to Khartoum on 21st October and a week later No 45 Sqn took their place at Helwan on the right bank of the Nile about eighteen miles south of Cairo. It was a sand and gravel airfield, with three Bessonneau hangars, windowless huts built of thin stone slabs for barrack accommodation and a few brick-built bungalows for the comparatively small number of married personnel. The squadron had the place to itself. By this time Flt Lt Vincent Buxton OBE and Flt Lt Thomas C Luke MC had joined the unit as OCs B and C Flights and the arrival on November 1st of a final draft of airmen from Iraq, many of them ex-No 45 Sqn people, brought the squadron up to full strength at last. Reflecting this, the squadron, which by now had fifteen pilots on strength, six of them NCOs, flew 347 hours in December. The training routine consisted of bombing and gunnery, a little photography, visits to the numerous landing grounds which were scattered all over eastern Egypt, and endurance flying. From early 1928 onwards the squadron regularly accumulated between 300 and 400 flying hours every month. This was achieved from a total of twelve aeroplanes, each flight normally having three available and one undergoing maintenance. Sport was still a major preoccupation and on February 18th the Flying Camels beat the 'Flying Eyes' of No 208 Sqn to win the Middle East Command Hockey Cup.

To advertise the squadron's resurgence its aeroplanes soon began to display the squadron's emblem. Photographs of No 45 Sqn's Ninaks are relatively scarce but those which are available suggest that two styles of marking were applied. One was painted directly onto the sides of the engine cowling; the other was applied on some form of panel, possibly in imitation of the copper and aluminium badge carried by the Vernons. While the device carried on the DH 9As was unmistakably a Flying Camel, it has to be said that it was a less graceful rendering than the original version.

By this time Abdul Aziz ibn Saud had largely succeeded in suppressing the Ikhwan rebellion but the Hashemite ruler of the mandated British client state of Transjordan, the Emir Abdullah, was not averse to harbouring militant remnants of the Wahhabi movement, since their periodic cross-border raids back into Nejd were a thorn in the side of the Saudi leader who had only recently conquered the Hijaz and deposed Sharif Hussein, Abdullah's father. The British sought stability in the region, however, and whenever necessary acted to pacify these turbulent tribesmen. Trouble broke out in the spring of 1928 and two flights of No 45 Sqn were deployed to Palestine to reinforce No 14 Sqn's more or less permanent detachment at Ramleh. The Ninaks moved on March 15th; two days later three Victorias followed with the groundcrew and stores. On the 26th one flight redeployed to Amman. Several reconnaissances were flown but the squadron never became involved in any offensive action and both flights were withdrawn to Egypt on 10th April.

This exercise in redeployment epitomised the role of the squadrons based in Egypt. Unlike the units in Transjordan, Iraq, India and Aden, those stationed in Egypt had no immediate operational commitments and represented a strategic reserve which could be used wherever and whenever the need arose. But it was no good having a reserve if it could not reach a trouble spot in one piece, promptly and in a fit state to go into action. To encourage the development of the necessary reliability, in 1928 Lord Lloyd of Dolobran, the High Commissioner for Egypt and the

Most published sources maintain that No 45 Sqn wore no distinctive markings on its Ninaks. In fact most of its aeroplanes carried a Flying Camel motif on the sides of their engine cowlings. This picture shows one variation on this theme which was to have the Flying Camel painted in silhouette straight onto the cowling, probably in blue to judge from the tones of the roundels. In order to face in the aeroplane's direction of travel, this camel is proceeding from left to right, in contrast to the original design It is not known who was responsible for parking J7823 in a ditch or when it happened. (via A J Thomas)

Sqn Ldr John Summers, previously a flight commander on Vernons, remained with No 45 Sqn as its caretaker when it was reduced to a cadre at the end of 1926 and then became CO when it was re-established in Egypt in early 1927. He is seen here with his trophies after becoming the squadron's rifle shooting champion in 1928. (No 45 Sqn archives)

On behalf of No 45 Sqn, Sqn Ldr Summers accepts the Lloyd Trophy from His Excellency Lord Lloyd of Dolobran, High Commissioner for Egypt and the Sudan, at Heliopolis on 15th May 1928. (No 45 Sqn archives)

Sudan, sponsored an inter-squadron competition and presented a trophy that would be awarded to the most successful unit.

The first competition was relatively straightforward and required each squadron to put up all of its aeroplanes and fly a three-day exercise around Egypt. No 45 Sqn competed in the last week of April. It succeeded in launching all twelve of its aeroplanes on the 27th when they flew from Helwan to Assiut, then on to Aswan where they night-stopped. The following day they flew back to Assiut then on to Heliopolis where they spent another night. On the 29th the final day's itinerary took them to Suez, to Amman, to Ismailia and finally back to Helwan where they arrived at 0835hrs having flown overnight. One aeroplane had its throttle jam and was obliged to drop out during the last day but this was the only fault awarded to the squadron and it was declared the outright winner. The trophy was presented at Heliopolis on May 15th. It was a major ceremonial occasion. Nos 45, 208 and 216 Sqns were all on parade under the command of the station commander, Gp Capt C T Maclean DSO MC, with the officers of HQME and No 4 FTS in attendance. In other words, the prestige associated with this first competition was such that absolutely everybody was required to be there to see Sqn Ldr Summers accept the trophy from Lord Lloyd.

The remainder of the year passed without any untoward incidents, although there was a break in the routine during September when HMS *Eagle's* Flycatchers, Bisons and Darts came ashore. They visited various RAF installations, including Helwan, where they were hosted by the Flying Camels on the 17th.

A VIP task came the squadron's way during November when, on the 9th, it collected the AOC, AVM Sir Robert Brooke-Popham KCB CMG DSO AFC, from Heliopolis and flew him to Amman, then on to Hinaidi on the 12th. By this time John Summers had done five years in Iraq and Egypt and he was overdue for repatriation. On 14th November he handed over command of the squadron to Sqn Ldr F J Vincent DFC, who had just completed an eighteen month stint as OC No 84 Sqn at Shaibah. The first significant task to come the new CO's way was Middle East Command's 1929 air display which was to be held at Heliopolis on February 7th and from mid-January all participating units became involved in a programme of practices and rehearsals.

The event itself comprised the standard fare of formation flying, the bombing of a moving tank, an 'attack on a desert fort' and sundry aerobatics displays by No 4 FTS. It all went off without a hitch in front of an audience of some six thousand people.

During the late 1920s and early 1930s RAFME sponsored an irregular series of long-distance flights, partly as exercises in endurance flying and partly as a means of "showing the flag". These cruises, as they were often called, were generally undertaken by semi-autonomous flights formed for the purpose within a nominated parent squadron. In early 1929 reports appeared in the aviation press to the effect that a flight to the Cape was shortly to be carried out by No 45 Sqn. This may have been a result of a premature press release by the Air Ministry or simply a misunderstanding but, as it was still equipped with 1918-vintage DH 9As, No 45 Sqn was hardly the best choice for such an exercise. In the event the Cape Flight was carried out by four of No 47 Sqn's far more robust Fairey IIIFs. There was a tenuous connection with the Flying Camels, however, in that Fg Off Yvon Burnett was one of the pilots. Sadly, he was to be killed, along with Sgt Turner, when, during the return flight, their aircraft crashed shortly after taking off from Gwelo (Southern Rhodesia) on 18th March 1929.

Early in December 1928 No 45 Sqn had managed to get its hands on a Fairey IIIF, S1141, but the squadron was not yet due to be re-equipped and the aeroplane was withdrawn again on 9th January 1929 when it was flown back to the Depot at Aboukir by Flt Lt R H Carter, OC B Flight since Buxton had left for the UK in mid-1928. Nevertheless a number of pilots had had an opportunity to fly the aeroplane and this brief initial acquaintance with the IIIF was to pay dividends when the squadron was eventually rearmed with the type in rather unusual circumstances. It is of some interest to note that the prototype of the Fairey IIIF had made its first flight on 19th March 1926 in the hands of Norman Macmillan, onetime commander of No 45 Sqn's A Flight.

Whenever a senior RAF officer wanted to visit somewhere he would arrange to be flown to his destination by one of the squadrons. Apart from being the fastest and most efficient way to travel, these trips provided excellent training in long distance flying and were also a welcome break from the routine. One such task which came No 45 Sqn's way began on 22nd February 1929 when Flt Lt Luke took Air Cdre F W Bowhill (Chief of Staff at Iraq Command) down to Khartoum, returning him to Egypt on 2nd March. A second DH 9A, flown by Sgt F V W Foy, escorted the VIP aircraft throughout the exercise.

Trouble began to brew in Palestine in March 1929. This was not the first time that friction had occurred between the resident Arab community and Jewish settlers but it was the first time that it had been of any significance to No 45 Sqn. They waited for the order to move but it never came. Meanwhile there was the Lloyd Competition to keep people busy. The 1929 event had been extensively revised compared to that of the previous year and it had been extended to cover specific operational skills as well as reliability. In May the squadron won the Lloyd Trophy for gunnery. The reliability course was to be flown twice and the squadron did its summer run between the 7th and 9th of June.

Tension was still high in Palestine and the call to arms finally came on August 27th when B and C Flights, with seven Ninaks between them, moved to Ramleh, arriving at 1000hrs and 1100hrs. The aeroplanes were E917, J7829, J7832, J7874, J8186, J8188 and J8202; J8189 joined them a few days later. There were at least eight pilots in the initial detachment: the CO, Flt Lts Harry Goode, Ron Carter and Tom Prickman (OCs A, B and C Flights respectively), Fg Offs Ronald Wilson, Guy Stanley-Turner and Hubert Patch and Sgts C A Price and Stratton. Within two hours of their arrival in Palestine two crews were ordered to fly back to Gaza to protect a DH 66 Hercules airliner of Imperial Airways which was on the ground being refuelled; their task complete, they landed back at Ramleh again at 1430hrs. Fifteen minutes later Fg Off Stanley-Turner took four aircraft to Zikhron Ya'aqov village which was under attack by Arab guerrillas. The flight went straight into the attack and the Arabs withdrew leaving an estimated thirty dead. At 1620hrs Sqn Ldr Vincent led two aircraft, one of them from No 14 Sqn (flown by Flt Lt Cecil Riccard who, until April 1929, had been OC No 45 Sqn's B Flight in succession to Buxton), on a reconnaissance of the Gaza area to verify reports of 5,000 Arabs massing but they found nothing. By dusk all the aircraft were back on the ground at Ramleh.

August 27th had been a busy day and had provided a classic example of the capabilities that Lord Lloyd had been seeking to develop when he had presented his Reliability Trophy the previous year. By winning the cup The Flying Camels had clearly shown their ability to perform to the highest standards under competition rules. Now they had done it under operational conditions as well; they had deployed to a trouble-spot and had arrived able to go straight into action. This was entirely due to the calibre of the squadron's personnel, not least its groundcrew who were adept at keeping what were now rather tired old Ninaks serviceable. In this context it is notable that one of the aggressive young pilots who had gone into action with Stanley-Turner's formation on that first day of the campaign had been Fg Off Patch. After spending 1928-30 with No 45 Sqn he was to go on to become yet another distinguished Flying Camels alumnus, retiring as Air Chief Marshal Sir Hubert Patch KCB CBE. Furthermore he was not the only

officer of the detachment to have a notable career; Tom Prickman would eventually become Air Commodore T B Prickman CB CBE

The following day was spent dropping leaflets on a large group of Arabs encamped at Bureir and keeping an eye on the Gaza area. The Bureir Arabs were later seen to be folding up their tents. Similar missions were flown on the 29th with the squadron's aeroplanes at various times overflying Tiberias, Nazareth, Affule, Semakh, Kolundia, Artuff, Safed, Beisan, Hebron and various crossing points over the Jordan, some of these sorties being provided with an escort of three Flycatchers from HMS *Courageous*. On

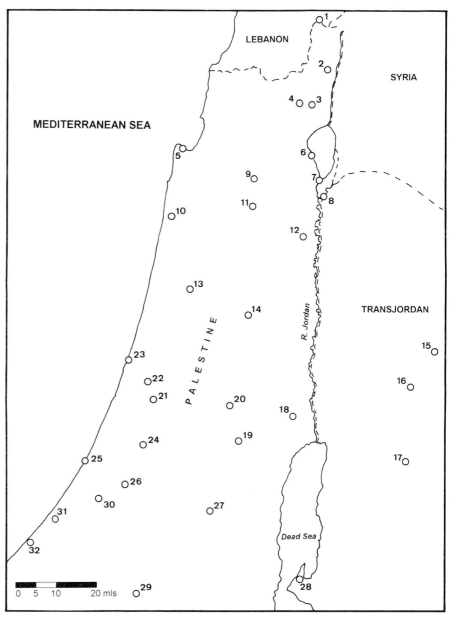

11	Affule	25	El Majdal	8	Jisr Mejamie	4	Safed
16	Amman	26	Falluja	20	Kolundia/Ramallah	22	Sarafand
24	Artuff	31	Gaza	2	Lake Huleh	7	Semakh
29	Beersheba	5	Haifa	1	Metullah	6	Tiberias
12	Beisan	27	Hebron	14	Nablus	13	Tulkeram
30	Bureir	23	Jaffa (Tel Aviv)	9	Nazareth	15	Zerka
32	Deir el Ballah	18	Jericho	21	Ramleh	10	Zikhron Ya'aqov
28	El Lyssen	19	Jerusalem	3	Rosh Pina	17	Ziza

Map 5.1. Palestine in 1929; note that the conventional spelling of many of these names and some of the names themselves have subsequently changed.

Apparently wearing its Flying Camel on a (metal?) plate fixed to the engine cowling, J7832 was one of the DH 9As used by the squadron in Palestine. Later to become famous as a photographer of aeroplanes, Charles Sims was an airman with No 45 Sqn in 1927-28 and although there is no evidence to connect him with this picture it is just possible that it is an early example of his work. (MOD)

August 30th the CO picked up the police chief from Beersheba, flew him to Ramleh for a conference and then returned him to his HQ. By 1200hrs Sqn Ldr Vincent was back at Ramleh and taking off again to lead a formation of eight DH 9As, a single Bristol Fighter, four Fairey IIIFs and three Flycatchers, drawn from Nos 14, 45 and 208 Sqns and the Fleet Air Arm, in a demonstration over Jerusalem. Meanwhile, following up an earlier report from No 14 Sqn of a group of Arab insurgents moving down from the north in the vicinity of Safed, Flt Lt Carter had taken two Ninaks and three Flycatchers up to the Syrian border to attack them. They found nothing of particular significance, however, and after firing a few rounds over a group of Bedouin tents near Lake Huleh, without intending to inflict casualties, the Flycatchers were led to Semakh as they were running short of fuel. In the afternoon Carter led another two-aircraft patrol (E917 and J8188) to locate a reported band of 1,000 Arabs crossing the Jordan. It was another false alarm. They found eight Bedouin encampments, but they all appeared to be engaged in nothing more aggressive than grazing their flocks. No camels or horses were observed, so if these groups were at all warlike then the warriors were certainly not at home. The patrol returned to Semakh where it spent the night. In all the squadron had flown seventeen sorties that day.

The pattern of patrols, reconnaissances and communication flights, some escorted by Flycatchers, continued on the 31st, Carter's two aeroplanes returning from Semakh via another patrol of the Jordan valley. The squadron saw action again that day when the CO in J7874, accompanied by Patch in J7832, observed a group of Arabs looting a burnt-out village north of El Majdal; the two DH 9As attacked and the pilots reported having killed four of the looters and a camel.

There was another show of strength on 1st September

when the squadron contributed six to a total of nine DH 9As which overflew Semakh, Tiberias, Safed and Metullah accompanied by six Fairey IIIFs of the FAA. On the same day Sgt Price dropped leaflets over Jerusalem while Stanley-Turner flew to Kolundia to pick up a couple of spare tyres for an armoured car which was stranded near Ziza. Two more pilots arrived on the 2nd when Sgts Kirlew and Horton delivered a pair of Avro 504Ns from No 4 FTS, these aeroplanes promptly being tasked with communications sorties. By dusk Kirlew had been to Amman and back while Horton had done a return trip to Haifa. By this time a routine had been established and from the 3rd onwards the squadron flew two patrols per day, although these were now largely uneventful.

While all this had been going on A Flight had been rearming with Fairey IIIFs at Helwan. On September 8th Flt Lt Goode brought his re-equipped flight up to Ramleh to add J9641, J9642 and J9645 to the squadron's Order of Battle. Their arrival permitted a detachment of naval aircraft which had been temporarily based ashore at Gaza to rejoin HMS *Courageous.*

A Flight flew its first patrol on the 9th, despatching all three Faireys to carry out a reconnaissance of the Safed district. Only J9642 flew the whole mission successfully as Sgt Tribe was forced to land in J9641 and Harry Goode landed alongside in J9645 to keep him company. The problem was quickly solved, however, and both crews were back at Ramleh before dusk. More IIIFs were delivered over the next few days and by the 15th conversion was complete, B and C Flights having been re-equipped in Palestine while still meeting all their operational commitments. Led by Ron Carter, the squadron's last patrol with Ninaks had been flown on September 10th. Throughout this period the squadron had continued to maintain its two daily patrols and its

J9640 was one of the original batch of Fairey IIIFs taken on charge by No 45 Sqn in the autumn of 1929 when it was operating in Palestine. It is seen here in 1930 after becoming the first of the squadron's Faireys to accumulate 500 flying hours. The presence of a cheat line edging the black decking of the upper fuselage can be detected above the exhaust stubs; comparison with the tones of the roundels suggests that the colour is neither red nor blue. The most likely alternative is yellow, for B Flight, although this does not sit very comfortably with the individual number 4. (No 45 Sqn archives)

A flight of No 45 Sqn's early Fairey IIIFs over Jaffa in October 1929. (No 45 Sqn archives)

aeroplanes had been seen over Jaffa, Jerusalem, Semakh, Tiberias, Tulkeram, Safed, Beisan, Hebron, Jisr Mejamie, Nablus, Gaza and Beersheba. This pattern continued for the next week but by the 21st calm had been largely restored and the situation permitted the frequency of patrols to be reduced to two per day, one being flown by each of Nos 14 and 45 Sqns. Patrols were not the only activities, however, and other aircraft were used to visit LGs to assess their suitability for use by the Faireys; there were also occasional requirements for aircraft to fly passengers to Amman or to Egypt and there was routine continuation training to be carried out in photography, gunnery and the like.

As noted earlier, it is not clear whether or not No 45 Sqn had ever been pencilled in to form the 1929 Cape Flight but, now re-equipped with Faireys, it had definitely been nominated to form the West Africa Flight later in the year. This event was far too important to cancel or postpone, despite the squadron's preoccupation with activities in

Palestine. To support the preparations for the enterprise, C Flight was temporarily withdrawn to Egypt and on September 21st Fg Off Stanley-Turner and Sgts Price and Bowen flew their aeroplanes back to Helwan. On the same day a Victoria of No 216 Sqn collected Fg Off George Fachiri and nine of C Flight's groundcrew and flew them down to Helwan as well. Sadly, one of C Flight's airmen, LAC Parker, did not make the trip; he died in Ramleh Hospital that day. The CO flew back to Helwan on the 22nd in J9640 with F/Sgt Matthews but he returned to Ramleh the next day.

During September the squadron's nine aircraft had flown 720hrs, representing an average of something like 2½ hours per day per aeroplane. Bearing in mind that two different types had been involved and that the groundcrew had been learning about the workings of the Faireys as they went along, this was a quite remarkable achievement.

From early October Sqn Ldr Vincent spent most of his time in Egypt preparing for the long-range flight which was scheduled to depart on the 19th under his command. On the 15th Flt Lt Goode flew back to Helwan in J9645 to take over as Acting CO, leaving Ron Carter in charge of the two flights at Ramleh. There was a general strike in Palestine between the 19th and 21st of October but this passed without turning into a crisis and the squadron's detachment was called upon to do no more than fly its daily patrol. The only other occurrence of particular note was Sgt Tribe's forced landing at Semakh on October 23rd when J9643 burst an oil pipe. The crew were able to fix the problem themselves, however, and they returned to Ramleh under their own steam.

With the long-range flight safely on its way, C Flight's work was done in Egypt and on October 25th Fg Off Patch (who had returned to Helwan on the 18th) led its three Faireys back to Palestine. This gave B Flight the chance to snatch a short break at Helwan and the two formations passed each other as Flt Lt Carter led his three aircraft in the

With the Nile and Gezirah Island forming the background, the IIIF Mk Is which equipped the 1929 West Africa Flight formate over Cairo Nearest the camera is SR1171/N2, then SR1174/N1 and SR1172/N3. The colours of the fins can be gauged from the rudder striping (blue leading prior to 1930). (No 45 Sqn archives)

opposite direction. On the 29th it was A Flight's turn and as Stanley-Turner took them back to Helwan, their place was taken by a presumably refreshed and reinvigorated B Flight. A Flight returned to Ramleh on November 4th, restoring the squadron's presence in Palestine to a full three flights. Harry Goode had flown his J9645 back with A Flight and, in the continued absence of Sqn Ldr Vincent, he now assumed command of the whole squadron.

Regular patrolling ceased during November, the squadron flying its last one on the 7th. They were kept on stand-by in Palestine for a further month, however, and a number of odd jobs came their way, including several communications flights, shuttling VIPs and senior staff officers between Jerusalem, Amman and Ma'an. The first of these had cropped up on October 31st when Flt Lt Carter, with an escort of two more Faireys, had collected Sir John Chancellor, High Commissioner for Palestine, from Kolundia and flown him to Amman to confer with the Emir Abdullah. On November 6th Carter took two aeroplanes to Aboukir to provide an escort for Sir Percy Loraine, the new High Commissioner for Egypt. Other prominent personalities who flew in the squadron's Faireys during November were Mr Luke (Secretary to Sir John Chancellor), Gp Capt Playfair, Cdr Archdale and Lt Col Shute. The pilots employed on these duties included Flt Lt John Drabble, who succeeded Carter as OC B Flight on 16th November, Fg Off Stanley-Turner and Plt Offs Arthur Combe and Charles Howes.

Fg Off Patch took four Faireys to Amman on November 10th, remaining there until the 13th to relieve No 14 Sqn's detachment while they flew a Lloyd Trophy reliability exercise, the competition having been broadened to permit the inclusion of units based in Palestine. While they were in Transjordan No 45 Sqn's detachment flew several reconnaissance sorties and airlifted a spare wheel out to an armoured car at LG D.

On December 8th No 45 Sqn was withdrawn to Egypt, their place being taken by No 6 Sqn's Brisfits which arrived the following day. The squadron had deployed to Palestine with old DH 9As of wooden construction and came back with shiny new all-metal Fairey IIIFs. It is not often that a squadron is re-equipped while deployed away from its main base and to have done it within a week, while responding to operational tasking and without a major incident, was a considerable tribute both to its aircrew and to its groundcrew.

Meanwhile the West Africa Flight had been to Nigeria and back. Three additional Fairey IIIFs had been provided to undertake the venture. These were Mk Is, with the earlier, more angular, style of fin and rudder. The fin of each aircraft was painted in a different colour and carried an identification number. The participating crews and their aircraft are listed at Figure 5.1.

The route they had followed was Helwan - Wadi Halfa - Khartoum - El Fasher via El Obeid - Fort Lamy - Kano via Maidugari - Katsina - Sokoto - Kaduna - Ilorin - Lagos - Accra - Tamale via the Volta River - Accra via Koomassie - Lagos - Minna - Jos - Bauchi - Kano - Yola - Maidugari - Fort Lamy - El Fasher - Khartoum via El Obeid - Aswan - Helwan.

Army co-operation exercises had been flown at Kano, Katsina, Sokoto and Yola with troops of the 1st Btn,

Flight No	Aircraft	Crew
N1 (red fin)	S1174	Sqn Ldr F J Vincent DFC Flt Lt T B Prickman
N2 (white fin)	S1171	Fg Off R C Wilson Sgt C F Spillard
N3 (blue fin)	S1172	Sgt L F Humphrey A/Sgt (LAC) G Wiles

Fig 5.1. Composition of the 1929 West Africa Flight

Officers of No 45 Sqn photographed on 1st February 1930. Seated, from the left: Flt Lt F O Hall (Accts), Flt Lt J E L Drabble, Sqn Ldr F J Vincent, Flt Lt T B Prickman; Flt Lt E P Carroll (MO, locum from No 4 FTS). Standing, left to right: Fg Off G Fachiri, Fg Off H L Patch, Fg Off J A P Harrison, Fg Off Albert E Connelly (Stores), Fg Off R C Wilson, Fg Off A R Combe, Fg Off G N J Stanley-Turner. (No 45 Sqn archives)

Nigerian Regiment and, in response to requests from the British Residents, a number of short 'joyrides' had been given to local notables. No RAF assistance had been available beyond Khartoum; in fact the Faireys may have been the first aeroplanes ever to have landed at some of their waypoints and the six men had been entirely self-sufficient for the maintenance and repair of their aircraft. Having flown twenty-nine stages and covered 8,685 route miles, (ie exclusive of the numerous in-theatre trips), since setting out on October 19th, the flight landed back at Helwan on 29th November, exactly on schedule, as they had been throughout the whole six weeks.

Once re-established back at base the squadron's priority task was to carry out the second, winter, reliability flight for the Lloyd Trophy. Starting early on December 14th the squadron flew to Wadi Halfa via Assiut and Aswan. The next day's stages took them to Atbara then on to Khartoum and back to Atbara. On the 16th they retraced their steps via Wadi Halfa to Aswan and on the 17th they returned to Helwan via Assiut and El Rus, the last short leg being flown at night. In an elapsed time of 3½ days the crews had spent twenty-four hours in the air, the longest flight being the northbound leg to Wadi Halfa which had taken over four hours. They had done well, but not quite well enough and the Trophy went to No 14 Sqn. Thereafter, perhaps because the point had been made or because Lord Lloyd had left Egypt, the competition appears to have lapsed, or at least declined in prominence.

By comparison with 1929 the next year was comparatively uneventful. Apart from participation in manoeuvres with the army in March there was little to disturb the routine in early 1930 and, since these exercises took place between Cairo and Helwan, this was hardly demanding. In that same month, on the 3rd, the squadron participated in the annual RAFME Display at Heliopolis. This included the usual demonstrations of aerobatics and bombing and a display of formation drill by nine Fairey IIIFs from each of Nos 45 and 47 Sqns, the latter having flown up from Khartoum for the occasion. The finale was a flypast of forty-eight aircraft led by the only Grebe in the Middle East (J7571) which was followed by the eighteen participating Faireys of the two bomber squadrons, nine Brisfits of No 208 Sqn, three Vimys and seven Lynx-Avros from No 4 FTS with ten of No 216 Sqn's stately Victorias bringing up the rear.

Although it was fairly quiet, from time to time the odd unusual task did come the squadron's way. On 23rd July, for

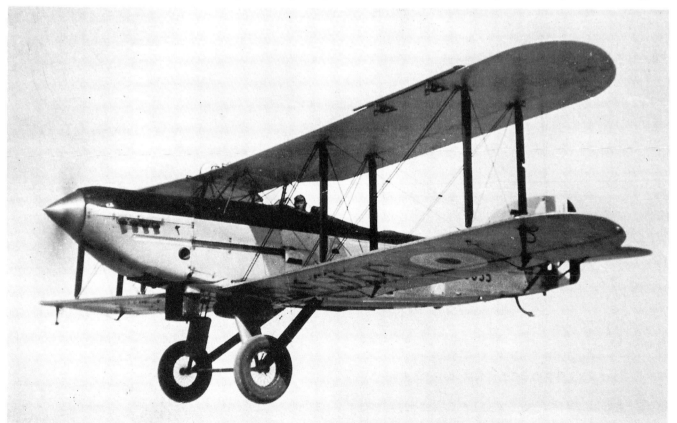

Sgt Tompkins airborne in B Flight's J9655/7 over the Nile near Wadi Halfa in 1930. A cheat line can be detected just behind the spinner; this may have been in yellow. (Philip Jarratt)

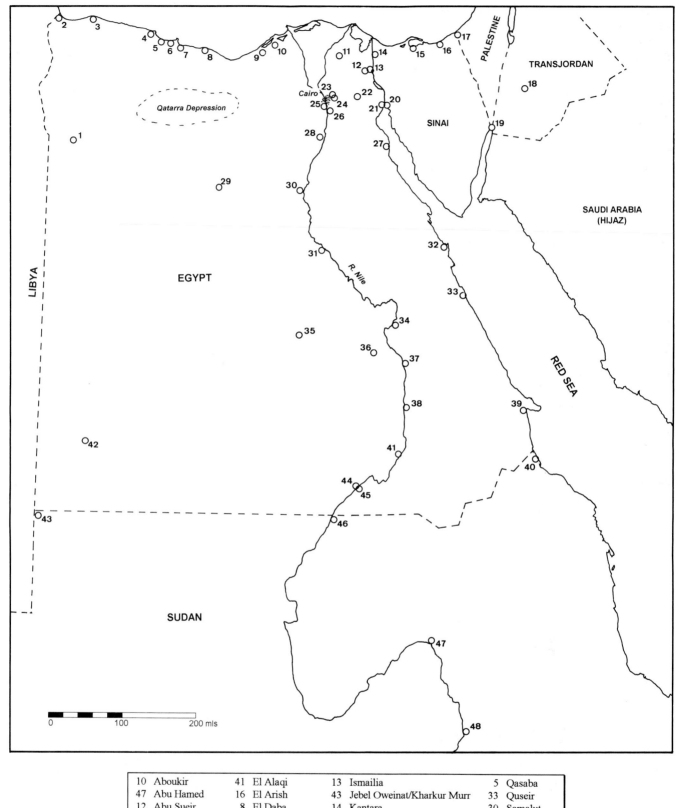

10	Aboukir	41	El Alaqi	13	Ismailia	5	Qasaba
47	Abu Hamed	16	El Arish	43	Jebel Oweinat/Kharkur Murr	33	Quseir
12	Abu Sueir	8	El Daba	14	Kantara	30	Samalut
24	Almaza	28	El Rus	35	Kharga Oasis	3	Sidi Barrani
9	Amiriya	11	El Simballawen	34	Luxor	1	Siwa
19	Aqaba	7	Fuka	25	Ma'adi	2	Sollum
31	Assiut	17	Gaza	18	Ma'an	21	Suez
38	Aswan	42	Gilf Kebir	6	Maaten Bagush	22	Suez Road
48	Atbara	40	Hassa Lagoon	4	Mersah Matruh	44	Toshka
29	Bahariya Oasis	23	Heliopolis	15	Moseifig	45	Toshki Garb
39	Berenice	26	Helwan	36	Nagh Hammadi	46	Wadi Halfa
37	Edfu	32	Hurghada	20	Port Tewfik	27	Zaffarana

Map 5.2. *Egypt and the Nile valley, the area covered by No 45 Sqn's local operations during the 1930s.*

instance, Flt Lt Prickman set off with three aeroplanes on a lengthy flight down to Hurghada and Quseir, this expedition taking several days, and on August 7th another section of three aircraft conveyed a party of staff officers to Khartoum. Three more, led by Flt Lt Cyril Greet, took Capt De Wet (the appropriately named Sea Transport Officer) to Amman, via Suez and Aqaba, and back between the 12th and 15th of September. At the same time three more aeroplanes were detached to Aboukir for three days to provide an escort to the AOC. At the end of the month the CO and C Flight flew down to the Bahariya Oasis to photograph it. Beyond such minor diversions there was endless routine training. As an example, in June 1930 the squadron flew 452 hours, during which they visited four LGs, did some night flying, dropped 496 practice bombs, exposed 110 vertical and 111 oblique photographs and fired 250 rounds of ammunition from the pilots' Vickers guns, while the gunners shot seventy-six camera gun films from the rear cockpits. This was a typical month's work. Occasionally a long range navigation exercise would be laid on as on 13th May when seven aircraft had flown to Suez, waited until nightfall and then flown back in the dark via Abu Sueir and Heliopolis. There was another on 23rd July when Flt Lt Tom Prickman led three aircraft down to Hurghada, returning the following day.

Long-range flying was a key element of the squadron's role and this implied good engine handling and sound fuel management. Since there had been several forced landings due to people running out of petrol, Sqn Ldr Vincent was not entirely satisfied with the way that some of his pilots, particularly the younger ones, were performing. One morning he ordered a no-notice squadron call-out and instructed the groundcrew to prepare as many aeroplanes as possible. The CO picked the more junior pilots, some of whom were still wearing pyjamas under their hastily-donned

flying overalls, and briefed them for a formation cross-country "and back in time for breakfast". Nine aircraft took off at 0630hrs. About an hour and a half later they were over Aboukir and turning onto a reciprocal track. But they did not land at Helwan. The CO led them all the way to Assiut before he turned back towards base at about noon. Shortly

C Flight up for a spot of formation practice in 1930, J9653/10, J9662/11 and J9650/9. At this stage the squadron's aircraft wore no distinctive unit markings, each aeroplane simply carrying a number between 1 and 12 in black on its fin and repeated in white on the rear fuselage decking. (P G Crayden)

The start of a tradition. In June 1930 the squadron created this memorable image by arranging all twelve of its aeroplanes to represent a clockface and, after the SWO had no doubt spent some considerable time being suitably innovative with his pace stick and marking out the ground with tape and chalk, parading its men to form the squadron's number. Since the trouble was even taken to arrange the aeroplanes, all with their props neatly dressed horizontally, in numerical order, it seems odd that Number 12 was at 3 o'clock - perhaps it all took so long to set up that the sun had moved! One or two other units in the Middle East took up the idea during the 1930s but the practice then lapsed. It was revived by No 45 Sqn with its Venoms in 1957 and since then it has become a tradition, the exercise subsequently being repeated with Canberras, Hunters, Tornados and Jetstreams. (No 45 Sqn archives)

The No 45 Sqn party which surveyed the route of a projected Amman-Baghdad railway. Using two Faireys to carry out the associated photography the task took from 3rd November 1930 until 30th April 1931 and involved a total of 695 flying hours. (No 45 Sqn archives)

afterwards the first aeroplane ran short of fuel and was obliged to make a forced landing. As the formation flew on its numbers steadily dwindled. When the CO finally reached Helwan, after a total flight time of some 7½ hours, only Sgt Stratton was still with him. The rest were strung out along the Nile waiting for one of the senior pilots to fly out to them with enough petrol to get them home. Frank Vincent later recalled that several of his pilots would not speak to him for days, but the lesson was learned; thenceforth fuel management became an art. This was to make a major contribution to the unrivalled reputation that the squadron was establishing for getting the most out of its aeroplanes.

Something a little out of the ordinary came the squadron's way in the autumn of 1930 when, on 3rd November, two aircraft were detached to Amman to assist in surveying the route for a projected Haifa-Baghdad railway. This task, which included the creation of a photographic mosaic from about 15,000 feet, was to take six months and would keep the crews involved fully occupied. In November alone the two aircraft flew 92 hours on eight photographic sorties, forty communications flights and eighteen air tests and practice trips. Four days after the Amman detachment began, another aircraft was detached to Ismailia to start a similar photographic survey of the Suez area. In three weeks this aeroplane flew 36 hours. This too was to be a lengthy task which would not be completed until February 13th.

There was one more significant development towards the end of the year when the squadron adopted a distinctive unit marking for its aeroplanes. Prior to this they had worn only an individual aircraft-in-squadron number in black on each side of the fin and in white on the top decking of the fuselage. By the end of 1930 most of these had been deleted and the aircraft now sported a diagonal red/blue (red uppermost) stripe across the fin with a rectangular break in the middle containing a small pale blue Flying Camel and the squadron's motto, very much in the style that had been displayed by the Vernons. Another subtle touch, which has not been noted previously, is that at least some of No 45 Sqn's Faireys had a narrow cheat line edging the black fuselage decking. This line is not apparent in all photographs of IIIFs which suggests either that it was not universally applied or that it may have been painted in flight colours[1].

The squadron was given another VIP job in January 1931 when it flew Sir Percy Loraine and his entourage to Wadi

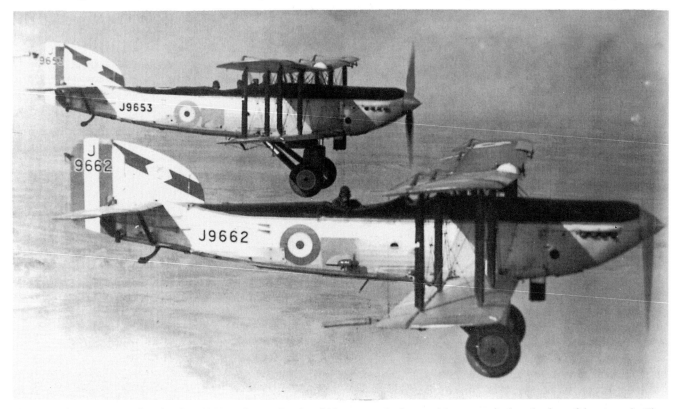

A unit marking was introduced in late 1930, a diagonal red and blue stripe (red on top) being applied to the fins of the aircraft. There was a rectangular gap in the middle of the stripe where a representation of a Flying Camel, accompanied by the unit's motto on a scroll, was painted in pale blue in a style very similar to the original Vernon motif. Thereafter the aircraft ceased to carry an individual number. An early application of this marking is seen here on C Flight's J9662 and J9653; the latter is still wearing its old number 10 on its fuselage decking. (P G Crayden)

two photographic aeroplanes at Amman finally completed their task and returned to Helwan having flown a total of 695 hours.

The CO took three aircraft all the way to Shaibah and back successfully between the 4th and 11th of May 1931 but a week later the squadron lost an aeroplane. Starting at about 2,000 feet, Sgt Pitcher got his Fairey, J9662, into a flat spin from which he was unable to recover. He and LAC Fraser abandoned the aircraft at about 800 feet thus carving for themselves a small niche in the squadron's history as they were its first members to make parachute descents.

Above:- 1930 Xmas dinner menu. Below:- J9662 did not wear its new fin stripe for very long. This photograph was taken on 18th May 1931 after Sgt Pitcher and LAC Fraser had been obliged to abandon their aeroplane, becoming in the process the first Flying Camels to make parachute descents. (both P G Crayden).

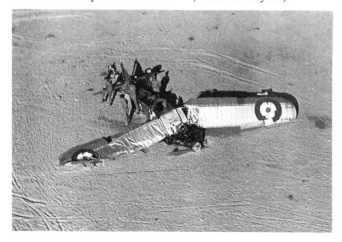

Halfa on the 12th then on to Khartoum the following day. The 1931 RAFME Display was held on 20th February and the squadron played its usual part. Between 2nd and 5th April four of the squadron's Faireys picked up the CAS, now Sir John Salmond, at Sollum and flew him to Heliopolis then on to Kolundia and back to Egypt via Ramleh. Although of no direct concern to the squadron, quite a stir was caused by the appearance of the airship *Graf Zeppelin* which visited Almaza and Heliopolis shortly after this and many squadron members made the trip up to Cairo to see the monster. Between the 13th and 17th April two aeroplanes flew the AOC to Amman and back. On the last day of the month the

Above:- No 45 Sqn practising for the 1931 RAFME Display. It would seem that the squadron must have been scraping the barrel to get nine aircraft up. The upper wing of the nearest aeroplane is clearly not painted silver and is probably still in primer; this is not a trick of the light as the same difference in tone is apparent in other pictures taken on the same occasion. The fact that the digits are missing from the fuselage serial number (SR????) is further evidence to suggest that the aeroplane was pressed into service before its pre-display wash and brush up had been completed. Below:- On 7th July 1931 J9642 became the first of the squadron's aeroplanes to complete 1,000 flying hours, this total having been accumulated in less than two years. The aeroplane is seen here being ferried to the Depot at Aboukir by Flt Lt Cyril Greet. It is known that J9642 had worn the red and blue fin stripe so this had presumably been painted out when the aircraft was prepared for despatch. A (red?) cheat line can be seen running the length of the black decking of the upper fuselage. (both No 45 Sqn archives)

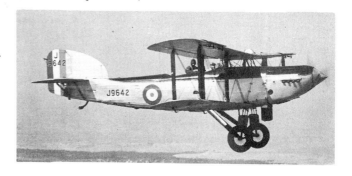

The second of the squadron's aeroplanes to accumulate 1,000 flying hours was J9653. It is seen here on that occasion with, from the left: Cpl Tibble, F/Sgt Ottoway, Sgt White, Sqn Ldr Francis Vincent and Fg Off Arthur Combe. (No 45 Sqn archives)

Some months earlier J9640 had become the first of the squadron's Faireys to complete 500 flying hours and it had been flown back to the Depot at Aboukir for overhaul as was then the standard practice. On completion of this inspection it was apparent that the combination of the more robust metal construction of the Fairey IIIF (all of the squadron's previous aeroplanes had been made of wood) and the squadron's meticulous maintenance standards made it unnecessary to recall aircraft at this stage. No 45 Sqn was the first unit in the Middle East to be authorised to retain its aircraft until they had flown 1,000 hours, the first airframe to reach this milestone being J9642 on 7th July 1931. Sqn Ldr Vincent later recalled that he had taken particular pride in this achievement which had attracted the personal attention of the CAS who sent the squadron a congratulatory message.

To keep in touch with the long-range flying game the squadron sent three Faireys to Iraq during May. They left for Amman on the 7th and reached Hinaidi, via a refuelling stop at Rutbah, the next day. After visiting Shaibah they retraced their steps to arrive back at Helwan on the 11th. By this time, however, the squadron had learned that it was to provide the West Africa Flight again in 1931 and training for

No 45 Sqn *was selected to form the West Africa Flight again in 1931. Allocated specific identities for the undertaking the four aircraft, K1703/1, K1704/2, K1705/3 and K1713/4, are seen here getting in a little formation practice over Cairo. (No 45 Sqn archives)*

this was put in hand. This time four aircraft were to undertake the cruise, with a fifth accompanying them as far as the Sudan as a reserve. In the event the spare aircraft was not needed and at Khartoum it was handed over to No 47 Sqn, its crew making their way back to Helwan by Nile steamer and rail. The aeroplanes and crews involved are listed at Figure 5.2.

The itinerary this time was even more ambitious than in 1929 and it was intended to take the flight right through to the Gambia on the Atlantic coast, emulating No 47 Sqn who had done this in 1930. Under the overall command of Air Cdre Ross (SASO at HQ RAFME), the formation left on October 14th and, routeing via Assiut, Wadi Halfa, Khartoum, Atbara, El Fasher, El Obeid, El Geneina, Ati, Fort Lamy and Maidugari reached Kano on the 23rd. A week was spent in Nigeria and the opportunity was again taken to run some exercises with the army to give them experience of co-operating with aeroplanes. On November 1st the flight moved on to Katsina and two days later to Sokoto. Here they learned of an epidemic of yellow fever that had broken out further to the west and concluded that it would be foolish to press on. It was decided to try to outflank the problem by flying round it to the north, through French territory. Henry Walker and Sgt Pitcher in K1704 and K1713 flew the Air Commodore up to Niamey in the French Sudan to investigate the feasibility of reaching

Flight No	Aircraft	Crew
1	K1703	Sqn Ldr F J Vincent DFC Fg Off A R Combe
2	K1704	Flt Lt H E Walker MC DFC Air Cdre R P Ross DSO AFC
3	K1705	Sgt R D Kemsley A/Sgt (LAC) A W Jones
4	K1713	Sgt D J Pitcher A/Sgt (LAC) C G Johnson A/Sgt (Cpl) C H Tibble
-	K1715	Sgt Tompkins A/Sgt Bickley A/Sgt Bearne

Fig 5.2. *Composition of the 1931 West Africa Flight.*

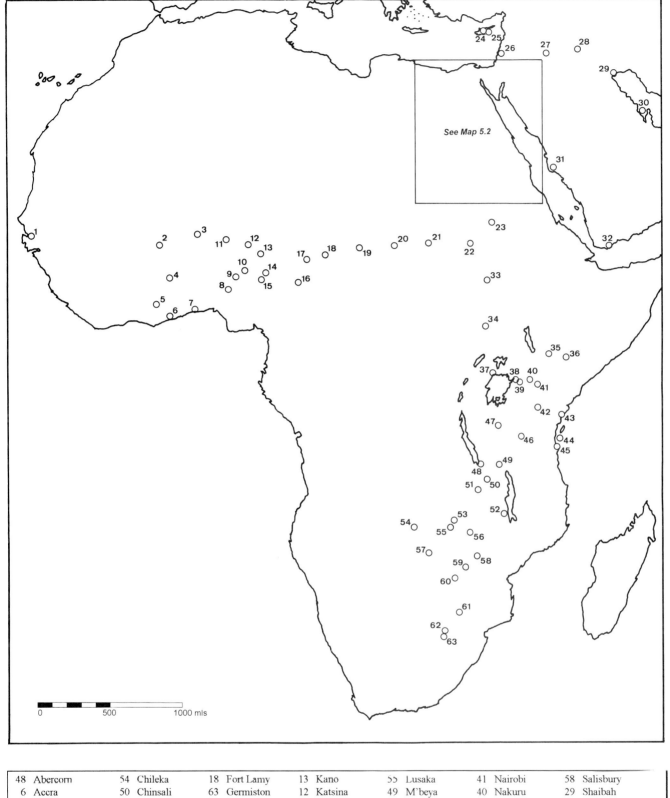

48	Abercorn	54	Chileka	18	Fort Lamy	13	Kano	55	Lusaka	41	Nairobi	58	Salisbury
6	Accra	50	Chinsali	63	Germiston	12	Katsina	49	M'beya	40	Nakuru	29	Shaibah
19	Ati	45	Dar es Salaam	59	Gwelo	23	Khartoum	51	M'pika	3	Niamey	11	Sokoto
30	Bahrein/Muharraq	46	Dodoma	28	Hinaidi	32	Khormaksar	17	Maidugari	24	Nicosia	47	Tabora
1	Bathurst	21	El Fasher	8	Ilorin	38	Kisumu	33	Malakal	39	Njoro	4	Tamale
14	Bauchi	20	El Geneina	31	Jeddah	5	Koomassie	35	Marsabit	2	Ougadougo	36	Wajir
26	Beirut	22	El Obeid	15	Jos	7	Lagos	9	Minna	61	Pietersburg	16	Yola
53	Broken Hill	37	Entebbe	34	Juba	52	Lilongwe	43	Mombassa	62	Pretoria	44	Zanzibar/Dumba
60	Bulawayo	25	Famagusta	10	Kaduna	57	Livingstone	42	Moshi	27	Rutbah	56	Zomba

Map 5.3. Africa, showing the area covered by No 45 Sqn's long range cruises during the 1930s.

Above:- No 45 Sqn's pilots circa December 1931. From the left, back row: Sgt D J Pitcher, Sgt Owens, Sgt Tompkins, Fg Off A F McKenna, Fg Off J B Tatnall, Fg Off A H Marsack, Fg Off J Boston, Sgt Roberts, Sgt R D Kemsley and Sgt Knights. Front row: Flt Lt P deC Festing-Smith, Flt Lt H E Walker MC DFC, Sqn Ldr F J Vincent DFC, Flt Lt J C Belford, Flt Lt J A P Harrison and Fg Off D H Marsack. (No 45 Sqn archives). Below:- Accidents of this nature were not uncommon in the 1930s. J9817 is seen here after Fg Off Frank Hewitt had flipped it onto its back sometime in 1931. The aeroplane was straightened out again and was finally written off after a similar incident in December 1936. (P G Crayden)

Bathurst via Ouagadougou. The French authorities were co-operative but advised that the unsupported desert crossing would be extremely hazardous and strongly recommended against any attempt to reach Bathurst via the suggested route - after all if anything did go wrong it would be up to the French to mount the rescue operation. Reluctantly, it had to be accepted that the northern route was not a practical proposition and the attempt to reach the Gambia had to be abandoned. The flight re-traced its steps and arrived back at Helwan on November 21st to be met by the AOC, AVM Cyril Newall. Between them the four aircraft had flown 330 trouble free hours in covering some 7,000 miles.

While the CO had been away there had been a spot of excitement for the rest of the squadron. There had been some civil disturbances on Cyprus and, on October 24th, seven Victorias of No 216 Sqn had flown a company of the King's Regt across to the island to restore order. The following day they were joined by C Flight of No 45 Sqn which, led by Flt Lt James Belford, had flown out to Nicosia via Ramleh and Beirut; two of the other pilots were Plt Off Austin McKenna and F/Sgt Tompkins. The four Faireys (J9827, J9828, J9640 and JR9652), were placed at the

disposal of the army commander and thereafter they operated as required, carrying out numerous patrols, reconnaissances, photographic and mail-dropping sorties and communications flights. The situation was rapidly brought under control and two of the aircraft returned to Helwan on November 6th, leaving the other pair unserviceable due to lack of spares (J9640 had crashed while landing at Famagusta on October 27th). These two aeroplanes were eventually dismantled and shipped back to Egypt by sea, both rejoining the squadron after repair. In view of the attention focused on Cyprus by this incident it was decided to upgrade the available mapping of the island and Flt Lt J A P Harrison was detached with a single IIIF to begin the necessary photographic survey on November 25th.

1931 ended on a distinct note of triumph. The Lion was one of the stalwart British aero-engines of the inter-war period. It had, for instance, powered the squadron's later Vernons and it now drove its current Faireys. In 1931 the Lion's manufacturers, D Napier & Sons, presented a Challenge Trophy to be awarded to the squadron which achieved the best overall performance using aeroplanes powered by their highly successful product. Inherent in this competition was the prevailing contemporary policy of fostering reliability and endurance. The Flying Camels excelled themselves and in 1931 they flew over 7,300 hours, ie over 600 hours from each of its twelve engines. This was a considerable achievement and resulted in the squadron's being declared the outright winners. The trophy was a handsomely mounted representation of a Lion engine in silver. Curiously the engraved plate on the plinth actually credits the squadron with having flown only 7,346 hours, rather than the 7,356 reflected by the monthly statistics compiled by HQME. It is not known which of these figures was the 'typo' but the squadron's lead was such that the odd ten hours was neither here nor there.

Although the squadron's performance in 1931 had been particularly notable it had been steadily making a name for itself in this field for some time and *The Aeroplane* of 20th May 1931 had carried an item noting that No 45 Sqn had flown 6,382 hours in 1929, 6,250 in 1930 and that by the end of April it had already amassed 2,500 flying hours in 1931[2]. The item went on to point out that this had been achieved with just twelve aeroplanes, supported by fourteen pilots and only forty-one workshop personnel.

The winning of the Napier Trophy was undoubtedly a factor which contributed to the Fairey Company's presenting the squadron with a silver model of a IIIF the following year. The engraved plate on the plinth reads: "Commemorating their record service, 1928-1932" - a little odd as the squadron did not re-equip with Faireys until late 1929. Both of these splendid pieces are still in the squadron's silver collection.

By January 1932 the CO, who was eventually to retire as Air Cdre F J Vincent CBE DFC, had spent well over four years in Iraq and Egypt and his successor, Sqn Ldr H W L Saunders MC DFC MM, reached Helwan on the 20th. The new CO arrived just as the squadron was working up for another air display at Heliopolis. This event was held on 12th February and the following day 'Dingbat' Saunders, a successful wartime fighter pilot who had claimed fifteen victories while flying SE 5as with No 84 Sqn, assumed command. It was No 84 Sqn's CO, Sholto-Douglas, who had given him his nickname. Saunders often used the term 'dingbat' in conversation. When he explained, in response to his CO's enquiry, that it was a word used in his native Australia to identify anything unknown, Douglas promptly declared, "Well, I don't know what you are, so I'll call you Dingbat". The name stuck.

There were no operational commitments in 1932 and life consisted largely of a continual round of training flying. As

Above:- The location of this photograph of J9805 is not known but it was not Helwan, which had only Bessonneau hangars while the squadron was operating IIIFs. Since the aeroplane is wearing squadron markings and its fin stripe has red leading, the picture cannot have been taken before late 1930. It probably dates from 1931 as most IIIFs had been fitted with exhaust manifolds by 1932. Again, the presence of a cheat line of indeterminate colour can be detected. (Philip Jarratt). Below left:- In March 1932 No 45 Sqn took part in trials to assess the suitability of the long-range tanks fitted under the lower wings of this Fairey, J9164. The modification was not a success as the aeroplane was too heavy and its overall performance was significantly degraded. (Author's collection). Below right:- On completion of the long-range trials J9164 reverted to standard and was absorbed into the squadron. It is seen here, minus its big 'jugs', after acquiring full unit markings. Note the complexity of the exhaust manifolds by comparison with the neat stubs shown in earlier photographs. (No 45 Sqn archives)

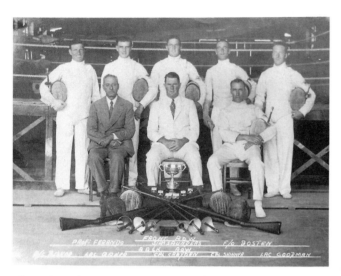

Throughout the 1930s the squadron maintained high standards in the sporting field. This is the fencing team circa 1932. From the left, back row: AC Bishop, LAC Baker, Cpl Crayden, Cpl Skinner and LAC Goodman. Front row: Prof Fernando (coach?), Sqn Ldr Hugh 'Dingbat' Saunders and Fg Off John Boston. (P G Crayden)

an example of the sort of bombing accuracies being achieved, LAC Fraser's log book records that he flew three eight-bomb classification details with his pilot, Fg Off James Tatnall, on the 11th and 12th of July in JR9652. When averaged and converted to a common bombing height of 10,000 feet his overall accuracy worked out at 41.3 yards.

If life was routine this did not mean that it was boring and there were frequent out of the ordinary tasks to be fulfilled. In March, for instance, the squadron completed a series of trials on a Fairey (J9164) which had been fitted with long-range fuel tanks beneath the lower wings. On April 6th Flt Lt Joe Harrison returned to Helwan having finally completed the Cyprus survey. Between 10th and 12th May three aircraft began to explore a coastal route following the Red Sea down to Aden. This first expedition involved landings at Hurghada and Berenice before returning via Aswan. On the 23rd there was a spot of salvage work when a party of groundcrew administered the last rites to one of No 47 Sqn's Faireys (J9809) which had come down at Nagh Hammadi. The aircraft was assessed as being beyond economic repair and, its carcass having been stripped of useable components, the remains were cremated where they lay. In June a reinforcement exercise was held which involved a full battalion of troops being moved from Egypt to Iraq by air.

Propeller spinners were optional on the Fairey IIIF and from about 1933 onwards, when this picture of J9831 was probably taken, they were often discarded. (M W Payne)

Three of the squadron's aeroplanes conveyed the battalion commander and his principal staff officers from Ismailia to Hinaidi, the round trip being carried out between the 23rd and 25th. Between May and July the squadron provided a taxi service for the High Commissioner and the GOC on several occasions which involved trips to Amman and Kolundia as well as more mundane watering holes in Egypt.

The tempo increased a little in the autumn. A weekly mail run between Heliopolis and Amman via Ramleh was instituted - out on Thursday, back on Saturday. This was to become a regular squadron commitment. No 5 Armoured Car Coy conducted an exercise in south eastern Egypt during November and two Faireys were assigned to support it. They carried out an initial reconnaissance on November 9th then flew in direct support of the cars during the field phase, which took place between 14th and 24th, frequently landing alongside the column to deliver spares or to advise on the nature of the terrain ahead. On November 25th spares were flown down to a Victoria which had damaged its undercarriage landing at Wadi Halfa. The following day the same aeroplane was forced to land again before it had reached Aswan. Several of the squadron's Faireys flew down to the site to pick up the passengers and ferry them to their destination. The final significant event of 1932 was a long-distance bombing exercise conducted by three aircraft which flew non-stop from Helwan to Amman, carrying out a First Run Attack on the range at Zerka before landing at their destination.

The membership of the RAF between the wars consisted predominantly of unmarried men and those stationed overseas had few distractions beyond the camp boundaries. One of the consequences of being obliged to make their own entertainment was the proliferation of squadron songs. Most were extremely bawdy; a few were laments for the lot of the poor benighted airman. A typical example of one of the latter, penned by 'Anon' and entitled "Helwan", was published in 1933:

> Those with ambition to follow Tradition,
> That's worthy of keeping alive,
> Need never despair that the feature is rare -
> They can find it in old "45".

> The Squadron reposes where old-fashioned Moses
> Was found by a bynt in the rushes,
> The sweet-smelling water that pleased Pharaoh's daughter
> Still flows in a series of gushes.

> With each little gush in the sulphurous slush
> Comes a sweet little old-fashioned odour;
> It floats on the breeze like the song of a cheese
> But is tasteless in whiskey and soda.

1933 was another quiet year, although the weekly air mail run to Palestine provided frequent opportunities for crews to land away and there was a steady series of unusual commitments. On April 18th, for instance, the squadron rendezvoused with the Fairey Long-Range Monoplane, which was returning from South Africa after having broken the world's long distance record, and escorted it to Heliopolis. A photographic survey of the Bahariya and Kharga Oases was carried out between 24th and 29th April and the Red Sea route was flown three times, in April, November and

December, in the course of which it was extended south to the Hassa Lagoon. There were occasional VIP flights and, on June 3rd, a flypast over Gezirah to mark the King's Birthday. In October there was another armoured exercise in the south east, this time with the Royal Tank Corps, and again the squadron provided support, flying 50 hours on the task between the 5th and 10th.

The year's biggest project was a tour of Iraq. This was undertaken by six aircraft between 2nd and 8th May. Led by Flt Lt Ivor Dale, other participating pilots were Fg Off Charles Moore, Plt Off Donald Evans and Sgt Hubbard. It was a punishing schedule: Amman - Rutbah - Hinaidi - Kirkuk - Mosul - Hinaidi - Shaibah - Hinaidi - Ramadi - Rutbah - H3 - Amman and back to Helwan; en route the aircraft had overflown the LGs at Sulaimaniyah, Diana, Kut, Nasiriyah, Ur, Samawah and Hillah (see Map 4.2). Each aircraft had made thirteen landings and flown nearly 33 hours in just seven days. There were no snags and the whole exercise had been conducted precisely to the planned schedule.

A regular activity which took aircraft away from base was the standing commitment to inspect landing grounds. A typical example is provided by Plt Off Don Evans who called at Assiut, Kharga, Aswan, Wadi Halfa, Edfu, El Alaqi, Toshki Garb, Luxor, Samalut, El Rus, Hurghada and Zaffarana between 7th and 16th September 1933. He was accompanied by Cpl Thompson and LAC Hughes and the expedition was mounted in JR9644. The following month Evans was back at Zaffarana for three days, taking part in the previously noted tank co-operation exercise; his aeroplane was again JR9644 but this time he was accompanied by LAC Marchant. Later in October he did another tour of LGs, this one lasting only three days. While this sort of thing was quite routine, and therefore unremarkable, it will be appreciated that such exercises were actually quite demanding; operating independently, for several days at a time with minimal resources, fostered self-reliance and encouraged initiative, qualities which were to be of enormous value in the years ahead.

By early 1934 it was becoming clear that the Italians had extravagant imperial ambitions in Africa. They already administered Eritrea, part of Somaliland and Libya, where their absolute authority was confined to the coastal strip of Tripoli and Cyrenaica. The following year they were to launch their brutal conquest of Abyssinia. Their strategic plans led the Italians to show an overt interest in the southern reaches of Libya, where their territory abutted that of the south western corner of Egypt and the north western tip of the Sudan. To dispel any doubts as to whose authority prevailed in this wasteland the Foreign Office was concerned to define the point to which Egyptian, ie *de facto* British, jurisdiction extended. This was the Jebel Oweinat, a rocky outcrop some 5,500 feet high, projecting above the general terrain which was at some 1,500-3,000 feet above sea level. It was deemed necessary to fly the flag in this God-forsaken spot and No 45 Sqn was ordered to do it.

Fg Off A H Marsack[3] was given the task and on January 11th he took a pair of Faireys down to the Kharga Oasis, the second aircraft being flown by Sgt Cheesewright. Four of No 216 Sqn's Victorias airlifted in sufficient petrol to permit the stocking of a fuel dump at a temporary LG which was

Above:- No 45 Sqn's imperial outpost at Kharkur Murr with the mass of the Jebel Oweinat looming in the background. Below:- The little band that occupied one of the remoter corners of the British Empire in January 1934. From the left: LAC Poll, LAC Banks, Fg Off Alfred Marsack, Sgt Cheesewright and LAC Mansfield. Not shown (because he was taking the picture?) is LAC Burge. (both No 45 Sqn archives)

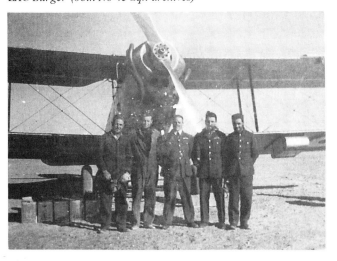

established to the south west at Gilf Kebir. This phase was completed by the 15th and the following day the Faireys, carrying OC No 216 Sqn, Wg Cdr C W Mackey, and another Victoria pilot as passengers, left the advanced base and flew down to the Oweinat in search of a suitable location at which to establish the required British presence. Several landings were made in dried up wadis but without finding water. At dusk another likely site was spotted from the air, and early on the 17th Marsack and OC 216 Sqn flew back there, landed, confirmed the presence of water and hoisted the RAF Ensign at Kharkur Murr. A Victoria delivered tents and supplies then withdrew, leaving Marsack, Cheesewright and LACs Poll, Burge, Mansfield and Banks (two fitters, a W/T operator and a medical orderly, respectively) to hold the notional fort. Some days later a truckload of Italians materialised out of the north and set up camp on an adjacent rock of their own. There was some mild fraternisation, but it was accepted that the British had been there first and that the question of whose authority held sway over which rocks had already been clearly decided. More to the point, however, the British controlled the only source of water so they were quite definitely in charge.

Alfred Marsack and company remained encamped at the Jebel Oweinat until 12th February when a machine gun battery of the Sudan Defence Force arrived to relieve them. The squadron's detachment had constituted a remote outpost of the British Empire. It was the first time that the RAF had been called upon to establish such an occupation force, thus securing for the Flying Camels a permanent, if somewhat obscure, footnote in the chronicle of Great Britain's late imperial history. Although now long-forgotten, this incident was of considerable contemporary significance. Once British possession had been clearly demonstrated and acknowledged by the Italian government, the Foreign Secretary himself, Lord Simon, communicated his personal gratitude to the AOCinC ME, ACM Sir Robert Brooke-Popham, who relayed to the squadron London's formal acknowledgement of their services.

In the meantime the squadron had been working up for Heliopolis' 1934 display with ten practices in January and seven more the following month. before the big event on February 23rd. As usual the squadron laid on nine aeroplanes, the participating pilots being the CO, Flt Lt Harold Martin, Fg Offs Herbert Dale, John Boston, Alfred Marsack and Arthur Hicks, Plt Off Donald Evans and Sgts Hall and Hubbard. They flew a total of six formations: three vics abreast; a single broad vic; a diamond nine; nine in line abreast; a broad arrowhead and a letter T.

There was another long-range flight in early 1934. The Union of South Africa was also concerned about the long term implications of Italian territorial ambitions and the aim of the exercise was to demonstrate the RAF's ability to reinforce the SAAF by deploying a force of five Faireys of No 45 Sqn and four Victorias of No 216 Sqn to Pretoria. They were to use Imperial Airways' Cairo-Cape route which had been opened in 1932, but without its being especially pre-stocked. The formation was to make its best speed on the outbound flight but would make a more leisurely return journey, showing the flag as widely as possible. Wg Cdr R T Leather AFC, from HQME, was in overall charge of the force, X Sqn as it was called, with Sqn Ldr P H Mackworth DFC commanding the Victoria Flight and Hugh Saunders commanding the Fairey Flight. No 45 Sqn's crews were:

Sqn Ldr H W L Saunders and Fg Off C S Moore
Fg Off H R Dale and A/Sgt (LAC) Jacquemet
Fg Off J Boston and F/Sgt Girdwood
Plt Off D R Evans and A/Sgt (Cpl) Hamlin
Sgt Hubbard and A/Sgt (Cpl) Bearne

Fg Off Charles Moore was to look after navigation; Jacquemet was to handle W/T communications and F/Sgt Girdwood was the detachment's photographer (*Where, oh where, are his photographs now? - CGJ*). The two remaining crewmen were fitters who would try to solve any technical problems which might crop up en route. X Sqn had an overall strength of thirty-eight men. Seventeen of them were drawn from No 45 Sqn, seven of its groundcrew being on board the Victorias in addition to the ten men who flew in the Faireys. As on previous off-route, long-range sorties, airmen (at least those who were flying as aircrew) were given acting rank as SNCOs, partly to reflect their considerable

The Fairey Flight of X Sqn which undertook the practice reinforcement of the SAAF in early 1934. Seated, from the left: F/Sgt Girdwood, Fg Off C S Moore, Flt Lt H R Dale, Sqn Ldr H W L Saunders, Fg Off J Boston, Plt Off D R Evans and Sgt Hubbard. Standing, from the left: Sgt Gurn, Sgt Marchant, unknown, unknown, Sgt Hamlin, Sgt Pragnell, Sgt Jacquemet, two more unidentified participants, and Sgt Wood. (45 Sqn archives)

responsibility but also to ensure that they would be provided with adequate accommodation and appropriate entertainment should any semi-diplomatic functions occur. The Faireys, which were numbered from 5 to 9, included JR9677, JR9793, KR1158 and JR9640.

The outbound itinerary was as follows (see Map 5.3):

26th February	Wadi Halfa via Heliopolis and Assiut
27th February	Khartoum via Atbara
1st March	Juba via Malakal
2nd March	Nairobi via Kisumu
3rd March	Moshi
4th March	M'beya via Dodoma
5th March	Broken Hill via Chinsali and M'pika
7th March	Bulawayo via Salisbury
8th March	Pretoria via Pietersburg

Pretoria was reached on schedule and without untoward incident. After a few days rest the Faireys flew out to Germiston on March 11th and gave a flying demonstration, returning to Pietersburg on the 14th. The following day they began the more relaxed return journey:

15th March	Bulawayo; air display
19th March	Livingstone
23rd March	Lusaka
26th March	Salisbury; air display and bombing demonstration
30th March	Zomba; co-operation exercise with the King's African Rifles (KAR)
2nd April	Chileka
4th April	Lilongwe
6th April	Abercorn via M'pika
8th April	Tabora; exercise with KAR
10th April	Dar es Salaam via Dodoma; exercise with KAR
13th April	Dumba (Zanzibar)
15th April	Mombassa; exercise with Kenya Defence Force
17th April	Nairobi; exercise with KAR

20th April	Njoro; air display
21st April	Entebbe via Kisumu; exercise with KAR
25th April	Juba
26th April	Khartoum via Malakal
28th April	Wadi Halfa via Atbara
29th April	Aswan
30th April	Helwan via Assiut and Heliopolis

When this exercise is compared to the situation only ten years before, when the squadron had been flying the Baghdad Air Mail, it can be seen what remarkable progress had been made in aviation. In 1924 it had been far from certain that the well-surveyed and supported four-day trip from Baghdad to Cairo and back could be flown without experiencing problems. The return flight to the Transvaal had involved operating away from base for over two months during which more than 9,000 route miles had been flown, to which must be added the substantial amount of local flying which was undertaken on the way back. There had been only one serious incident, on 6th April, when Plt Off Don Evans and Cpl Hamlin had crashed taking off from Lilongwe in JR9793; the aeroplane was severely damaged and, being so far off the beaten track, it could not be salvaged and had to be written off. The crew had escaped unscathed, however, and Evans commandeered Sgt Hubbard's JR9640 for the rest of the journey home. Overall the expedition had reflected exactly what Lord Lloyd had been so keen to develop - sustained reliability.

The summer of 1934 was quiet and there were few events of particular note. During April two aircraft co-operated with HMS *Ormonde* which was continuing the survey of the Red Sea route. On the 24th May nine aircraft carried out formation drill over Alexandria to celebrate Empire Day. In September, two five-aircraft ceremonial ship-escorts were provided; on the 1st to HMS *Queen Elizabeth* as she entered Alexandria and on the 10th to HMS *Sussex* as she left Suez and headed off into the Red Sea bound for Australia with HRH the Duke of Gloucester on board.

In October the Flying Camels were called upon to carry out another redeployment exercise to rehearse their reinforcement role, this time at full squadron strength. Temporarily provided with three additional aeroplanes, the whole unit left for Iraq on the 16th. This undertaking involved fifteen Faireys, eleven officers and seventy-two NCOs and airmen, with sufficient spares to sustain operations for thirty days, the support element being moved by five Victorias. A tented camp was established out on the airfield at Hinaidi and the squadron set about familiarising itself with the region by liaising locally with No 55 Sqn. In addition, short in-theatre detachments were mounted to call on No 30 Sqn at Mosul and No 84 Sqn at Shaibah during which the visiting pilots were able to acquaint themselves with some of Iraq's more remote LGs. All went according to plan and, having plainly demonstrated its abilities, the squadron returned to Helwan on November 6th.

There were several notable occurrences in early 1935, the first being another RAFME Display at Heliopolis. It is in the nature of such events that they tend to grow from year to year and to sustain this momentum by 1935 it had become necessary to rope in Nos 14 and 55 Sqns from Transjordan and Iraq. There had been a significant change in the types of aeroplanes involved since the squadron had first taken part in

The weekly mail run to Palestine and Transjordan was a regular feature of No 45 Sqn's routine from 1932 onwards. This photograph was taken during a run carried out between 22nd and 24th September 1934 and shows three of the squadron's Faireys at Ramleh. The nearest aeroplane is JR9677 and the next in line is JR9826. The three officers in the foreground are, from left to right: Fg Off Donald Evans, Fg Off Heather (of RAF Ramleh) and Plt Off Derek Atkinson. (No 45 Sqn archives)

one of Heliopolis' air days. Apart from its own DH 9As having been replaced by IIIFs, No 208 Sqn's Brisfits had been superseded by Atlases and there were now squadrons of Gordons and Wapitis participating plus the odd Audax and Demon. Only No 216 Sqn's Victorias provided continuity, but it was still an air force of silver biplanes. No 45 Sqn's contribution was its standard repertoire of formation flying, the participants this time being Flt Lts Ernest Barlow and Donald Fleming, Fg Offs Alfred Marsack, William Turner and Henry Graham, Plt Off Donald Evans and Sgts Hall and Hubbard led, of course, by 'Dingbat' Saunders.

Another event to break the routine was the temporary attachment to the squadron of several reserve pilots so that they could fulfil their annual training commitment. They were on strength during February and March and included Fg Off C S Brown, Fg Off A D L Carroll, Plt Off H Spooner, Fg Off B C Mason (who worked for Shell) and Sgts J C Harrington and F V W Fry (who had been with No 45 Sqn in 1928-29), both of the latter being Imperial Airways pilots.

A VIP trip came up in March when three of the squadron's aeroplanes were required to convey the CIGS, General Sir Archibald Montgomery-Massingberd, and his ADC down to Khartoum on the 8th and bring him back again on the 13th. The next special event occurred during the morning of May 6th when there was a mass formation flypast over Cairo by Nos 6, 45, 208 and 216 Sqns and No 4 FTS to mark the silver jubilee of HM King George V, the squadron contributing nine aircraft. The Flying Camels and the Flying Eyes did a repeat performance over Alexandria in the afternoon. Finally, on August 3rd the squadron took part in a search for a missing Italian aircraft and found its burnt-out wreckage only 12 miles south of Almaza, its departure point.

A little variety had been added to the standard training curriculum in November 1934 when four of the squadron's aeroplanes had been detached to Ismailia to provide some crews with their first experience of live air-to-air gunnery. This initial exercise was repeated on a larger scale in 1935 when one flight spent 17th to 24th June at Ismailia firing at drogues, the other two flights being provided with similar opportunities between 1st and 12th July. Beyond this, life

An aerial view of Helwan taken on 9th September 1935. In the foreground are the watchtower, an Avro 504N and three Bessonneau hangars, one for each flight. Out on the airfield the five Faireys of Flt Lt Barlow's B Flight's are being prepared for their trip to Nairobi during which they will be supported by No 216 Sqns Victorias, three of which are also present. (No 45 Sqn archives)

was a fairly constant round of bombing, photography and navigation exercises, leavened with a little night flying and visits to LGs like those at Mersah Matruh, Sollum, Siwa, Qattara and others in the Sinai desert. To break the monotony there was still the weekly mail trip to the Levant, Kolundia being added to the itinerary from April. If not exactly idyllic, it was a fairly comfortable existence and, for those whose pockets were deep enough, the fleshpots of Cairo were not too far away. But the fascist dictatorships started to flex their muscles during 1935; international relations deteriorated steadily and by the end of the year these developments were beginning to disturb the squadron's long-established peacetime routine.

The next notable event, however, was of domestic rather than global significance. Sqn Ldr Saunders had now been CO for 3½ years and it was time for him to move on. He was eventually to retire in 1953 as Marshal of the RAF Sir Hugh Saunders GCB KBE MC DFC MM, yet another senior commander who carried the Flying Camel stamp of approval. Many years later when asked to recall his time in command of No 45 Sqn Sir Hugh stressed the excellent training that it had provided and was able to point out, with some pride, that four of his junior pilots, all on their first tour after graduating from the RAF College at Cranwell, had become air officers: Air Chief Marshal Sir Donald Evans KBE CB DFC; Air Vice Marshal H R Graham CB CBE DSO DFC; Air Vice Marshal C S Moore CB OBE and Air Commodore C Widdows CB DFC. 'Dingbat' Saunders' successor was Sqn Ldr A R Churchman DFC who took over on September 14th.

The Italians launched their invasion of Abyssinia in October 1935 but tension had already been increasing in East Africa and there had been some instability on the Kenyan frontier. Sqn Ldr G E Gibbs MC, previously OC No 47 Sqn, was despatched to Nairobi in September to command an RAF detachment, identified initially as the Kenya Frontier Control Flight. On September 18th Flt Lt E C Barlow headed south with five Faireys of No 45 Sqn's B Flight, accompanied by four Victorias of No 216 Sqn led by Flt Lt H P Fagan. It was a partial replay of the previous year's Transvaal exercise, but this time it was for real. The detachment, which included thirty-eight of No 45 Sqn's groundcrew, had been briefed to expect a stay of up to four weeks and they took appropriate spares and personal effects plus a mobile W/T station to permit direct communication with Cairo. The recently promoted Flt Lt J Lambie, who had been No 45 Sqn's resident Accountant Officer since early 1933, accompanied the detachment to serve as its all-singing, all-dancing administrator, before being transferred to No 47 Sqn in March 1936.

The formation more or less followed the Nile to Lake Victoria, except for the great bend between Wadi Halfa and Abu Hamed; this leg was flown by following the railway line across the desert. Fuel was picked up at intermediate LGs and the first night was spent at Wadi Halfa. The detachment spent two days at Khartoum, taking advantage of the last hangar facilities that would be available, then pressed on via Malakal and Juba to Kisumu. The last stage was flown on September 25th and involved overflying very mountainous

KR1713 of the squadron's Kenya-based B Flight in 1935. The aeroplane displays three interesting features. First, it is still wearing rudder stripes; these were officially deleted with effect from 1st August 1934 but it took time for this instruction to be implemented and they were still adorning some aeroplanes in the Middle East well into 1936. Secondly, the aircraft has a well-defined cheat line, presumably in B Flight-yellow (it is certainly not red or blue). Finally, like all of the Faireys deployed to Nairobi, the aeroplane has been fitted with Type G wheels with the low pressure 'balloon' tyres which were standard on Gordons but comparatively unusual on IIIFs. (K Smy)

terrain in severe thunderstorms, but everyone made it and formation was rejoined before arrival at their destination - the Imperial Airways airstrip located about five miles outside Nairobi and at a height of some 5,500 feet above sea level.

After unloading, two of the Victorias returned to Egypt, leaving a total of seven aircraft to form the detachment. The airfield had a wire perimeter fence but it was found that this failed to keep out the abundant wild life and there were to be several incidents involving lions during B Flight's stay - which turned out to be rather longer than the briefed three or four weeks! Sqn Ldr Gibbs had already prepared a tented camp site and had secured the use of a corrugated iron shed to house stores. At first the officers were accommodated in the Nairobi Club while the airmen lived under canvas at the airfield but after a short time the officers joined them there. Within a few days the little force had settled in and began patrolling the northern border, particularly that with Italian Somaliland. They also selected and surveyed a scattering of LGs and began co-operation exercises with the Kenya Defence Force and the King's African Rifles.

The Abyssinian crisis had also led to a number of squadrons being redeployed from the UK to reinforce Middle East Command. At the same time the Command itself began to grow as a result of the succession of RAF Expansion Schemes. One of the mechanisms employed was to form a fourth flight within an existing squadron. When these flights were fully worked up they were hived off to form new squadrons or transferred to other units. Within RAFME D Flights were formed by Nos 6, 8, 14, 45 and 208 Sqns and these were eventually transferred to Nos 29, 41, 45, 6, and 29 Sqns respectively, the two flights absorbed by No 29 Sqn later being used to form No 64 Sqn. All of this was accomplished while many of the parent squadrons were themselves being re-equipped.

So far as No 45 Sqn was concerned its D Flight was established on September 19th and equipped with Harts, the first (of an eventual six) arriving on the 26th. The flight's pilots were Plt Offs O H D Blomfield, T B Hunter and K J Rampling with Flt Lt A N Luxmoore as their CO. Just as the squadron was absorbing these Hawker cuckoos into their Fairey nest the problem was compounded by the re-equipment of A and C Flights, the first ten Vincents for No 45 Sqn arriving in Egypt on board the SS *Sabian* on 29th October. Deliveries to the squadron began on November 28th and on December 12th the last two Fairey IIIFs left for Nairobi to restore the somewhat depleted strength of B Flight.

In the meantime, while No 6 Sqn had been exchanging its old Gordons for Harts at Ismailia, it had formed a D Flight mounted on Demons. At Amman No 14 Sqn, also with Gordons, also formed a D Flight but was not itself re-equipped. In January 1936 everyone changed partners. No 45 Sqn passed its Hart-equipped D Flight to the by now Hart-flying No 6 Sqn on the 6th. This displaced their Demon-equipped D Flight which was transferred on the same

An early Vincent line-up, K4677 nearest the camera. (Author's collection)

day to the Demon-flying No 29 Sqn. No 14 Sqn's Gordon-equipped D Flight (Flt Lt J G Franks, Fg Off D P McKeown and Plt Offs W I Collett and F J O Lasbrey) joined the Vincent-equipped No 45 Sqn on the 10th. It all seems to have been very complicated and it is difficult now to understand why the establishment of each squadron was not simply increased by one permanent flight. There must have been a sound rationale behind the adoption of such a convoluted procedure at the time but it is no longer clear why it was considered necessary to indulge in this curious game of 'musical flights'.

While all this flight-swapping had been going on, B Flight had been going through a bad patch down at Nairobi. They had lost an aircraft, SR1175, on November 19th. It had been caught by a severe downdraught while flying in the vicinity of the Rift Valley and forced down in circumstances which recall the loss of *Golden Gain* in 1923. Although the pilot and his crewman were unhurt, the aircraft was a complete write-off. A second accident had occurred on 29th December and this time there had been casualties, the squadron's first fatalities since 1926. J9827 had spun and

crashed, killing Fg Off Conrad Francis. Cpl Beyant in the rear cockpit survived but died in hospital the following day. Only a day later, the gloom arising from these losses was deepened by the death of the commander of the Victoria Flight who accidentally killed himself in one of his own aircraft parked out on the airfield when he mishandled a loaded shotgun. On January 4th a third Fairey was lost when JR9640 hit a tree while Fg Off Clair Byram was attempting to land at the LG at Wajir but, fortunately, this time there were no casualties.

Despite these setbacks, positive progress was being made at Nairobi. In January 1936 huts began to be erected at the airfield and shortly afterwards the detachment was able to begin moving into more permanent accommodation. As previously noted, re-equipment was in vogue throughout the RAF at this time and this even extended to No 45 Sqn's B Flight which received its first Gordon on 15th January, all five of its new aircraft having been delivered by the end of the following month. In view of the altitude of the aerodrome at Nairobi the additional power provided by the Gordon's Panther engine was much appreciated. On the last day of February Flt Lt Ernest Barlow returned to Helwan to take over C Flight, displacing Flt Lt G R Beamish who took his place in Kenya. The activities of the detached flight continued to consist of the classic 'colonial' tasks of periodic LG visits and border patrols, the latter now being enlivened by the occasional fusillade of rifle fire from Abyssinian tribesmen who, having suffered badly at the hands of the Italian Air Force, were inclined to regard any aircraft as hostile.

Meanwhile, back at Helwan, Sqn Ldr Churchman had been settling in and shaking down the squadron's sturdy new Vincents. On 19th December he led five aircraft on a tour of western LGs, landing at Mersah Matruh and Sidi Barrani before returning to base. On January 17th four aircraft flew a

Above:- B Flight's K4677 undergoing maintenance in one of Helwan's canvas hangars. Below:- Seen here before unit markings were applied, K4666 was one of the initial batch of Vincents delivered to No 45 Sqn in November/December 1935. (both 45 Sqn archives)

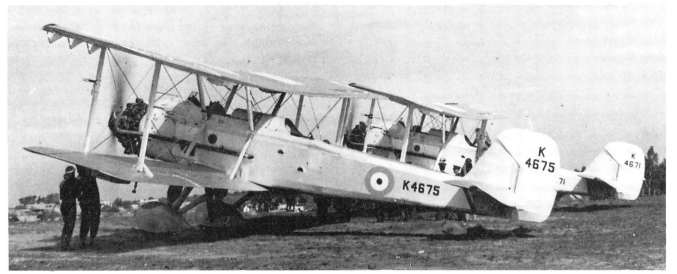

The mail run to Palestine continued to be a part of the routine during the Vincent era. K4675 and K4671 are seen here at Ramleh early in 1936. The second of these aeroplanes came to a slightly sticky end as one of the accompanying pictures shows. (45 Sqn archives)

very demanding navigation exercise - 9½ hours around Sinai at 1,000 feet with no intermediate landings. The squadron lost its standing commitment to fly the weekly air mail run in early 1936 and the last of the regular trips to Amman was flown on 27th February. On the same day two aircraft flew to Hinaidi, returning on 2nd March. On March 27th the whole squadron moved out into the desert with ten aircraft and set up camp at Fuka LG for an exercise in bombing and army co-operation. This detachment was to last for only four days but Fuka was to become all too familiar to No 45 Sqn in a few years' time. On March 20th the squadron put up six Vincents to escort HMS *Queen Elizabeth* as she sailed from Alexandria with the outgoing CinC Mediterranean Fleet on board. In late April the German Ambassador, Baron von Stöhrer, who had allegedly been participating in a car race, was reported missing out in the desert. The squadron flew 104 hours between 21st and 23rd searching for him. As it happened he was not in the sector allotted to the squadron and he was eventually found by No 216 Sqn in the vicinity of the Bahariya Oasis. At much the same time three of the squadron's aircraft went on one of the periodic long cross-countries, flying to Luxor, via Assiut and Kharga Oasis on the 20th, to Hurghada, via Aswan and Quseir, on the 21st and returning to Helwan the following day.

Several of the reinforcement squadrons which had been deployed to the Middle East in response to the Abyssinian crisis had been stationed at unsophisticated LGs in the Western Desert, where they had had few support facilities, and by this time their aircraft were in need of attention. With the fall of Addis Ababa on 6th May the Italians' bloody campaign was drawing to a close and the slackening of tension permitted No 142 Sqn to be pulled back to Helwan where, hosted by No 45 Sqn, its Harts were overhauled and its personnel rested. They flew back to Mersah Matruh on June 6th to be replaced by the bulk of No 29 Sqn from Amiriya six days later, the rest of the unit joining them on 20th July. No 29 Sqn was not required to return to the desert, however, and its Demons remained at Helwan until August 6th when the unit moved to Aboukir on the first stage of its journey back to the UK.

Although some of the reinforcement squadrons were being withdrawn it should be noted that RAFME's own units

had been considerably expanded during the recent crisis. In July 1935 No 45 Sqn had had a total of nineteen pilots available; a year later it had twenty-nine, eleven of them NCOs. It is worth observing here that few pilots stayed with the squadron for a full tour during the 1930s. After anything from six months to two years, most junior pilots moved on to fly with one of RAFME's other resident bomber units, Nos 6, 14 or 47 Sqns, while a few, generally flight lieutenants, were 'promoted' to twins by being transferred to No 216 Sqn. The Air Ministry was also concerned to develop other aspects of a junior officer's potential and some spent the latter part of their overseas tours in ground appointments as the adjutant at one of the larger stations or with one of the

Above:- K4665 being recovered after an incident at Kolundia on 1st August 1936. Sgt J D T Taylor-Gill had the misfortune to encounter a pot-hole while landing and the aeroplane's port undercarriage leg sheared off. (Philip Jarratt). Below:- In pulling up to avoid hitting his leader during a formation take off from Aboukir on 24th March 1936 Sgt R C Hyett stalled K4671. The aeroplane stayed the right way up but the impact was sufficient to break the engine bearers and collapse the undercarriage, which did the port lower wing no good at all. (Author's collection)

Above:- The shadows indicate that the sun was relatively low when this picture of K4663 was taken, suggesting that it had probably just emerged from its lair in anticipation of the first trip of the day. (Philip Jarratt).

Armoured Car Companies - it was all good character building stuff.

By this time the staff at RAFME had decided that the Cyprus survey was in need of further refinement and on August 6th Flt Lt C S Cadell led three Vincents, supported by a Valentia of No 216 Sqn, to Nicosia where the detachment remained until 16th September carrying out numerous photographic sorties.

It was now the turn of B Flight at Nairobi to do a long-range trip, Flt Lt Beamish leading three Gordons down to Salisbury and back between August 11th and 24th. Sqn Ldr Gerald Gibbs had departed for the UK on promotion on June 15th and Beamish had assumed command in Kenya pending the formal appointment of a new CO. This did not occur until October 10th, when Sqn Ldr J W Jones was added to the nominal strength of No 45 Sqn; he arrived at Nairobi to take up the reins eight days later. The experience gained while commanding the Flying Camel's East African branch stood Beamish in good stead and he eventually retired as Air Marshal Sir George Beamish KCB CBE.

The new CO has recalled that he continued a previous policy which required that whenever his little air force went off on a flag-waving trip they would arrange a football match with the local village. Everyone took their soccer kit and a pair of Victorias and three Gordons carried sufficient men to produce a reasonably competent team. On an early sortie, while George Beamish was still showing him round his new patch, they called at Marsabit, where the RAF had beaten the local police team on their previous visit. Since this was only a small detachment making an informal visit it could not field 'the team' and no one had brought their kit. Nevertheless the locals demanded a rematch, paced out a pitch and jabbed four spears into the ground to make goalposts. Protocol did not permit the challenge to be refused so the match duly began with the RAF playing in uniform or overalls and the village's Arab school teacher acting as referee, charging about the pitch clad in a flowing robe. The RAF quickly established a 1:0 lead but thereafter neither side was able to score and the game dragged on until the sun set. In the darkness the Africans skilfully exploited their inherent tactical advantage and soon obtained an equalising goal, permitting the game to be terminated in an honourable draw. This early display of diplomatic skill marked the CO out for promotion and he was eventually to retire as Air Chief Marshal Sir John Whitworth Jones GBE KCB.

The question of RAF squadron badges had been under consideration by the Air Ministry for several years and in

January 1936 AMO A.14 introduced the now familiar standard badge frame. At the same time units were invited to submit their individual designs for approval by J C Heaton-Armstrong who, as Chester Herald, had been appointed as Inspector of Royal Air Force Badges. In company with other squadrons with long-established emblems, No 45 Sqn submitted its Flying Camel along with its motto, *Per Ardua Surgo*. There were some initial problems in deciding how best to represent a camel within conventional heraldic constraints but once these had been overcome the College of Heralds produced an interpretation which portrayed a blue camel, presumably to represent the colour of the sky, with golden wings. The design was forwarded to the squadron for its approval. This was duly forthcoming, the only proviso being that the wings were to be in red, presumably to reflect the colours of the diagonal fin stripe which had adorned the squadron's aircraft since 1930. After receiving the formal endorsement of the sovereign, the squadron's badge was officially promulgated by AMO A.256 on 29th October 1936. It was one of the very few to be sanctioned by HM King Edward VIII.

But this was not quite the end of the story. It appears that the Flying Camel motif was still regarded with some aesthetic distaste in certain circles. In November 1937 Sqn Ldr V R Gibbs, a member of the Air Ministry's Organisation Staff whose business specifically included squadron badges, obtained a copy of the card which had enclosed No 45 Sqn's Christmas dinner menu in 1916. As recounted in Chapter 1, this had featured a representation of the sheep's head motif (tentatively identified as being of the Argalis variety) which Willie Read was evidently still doggedly trying to sustain in use as a unit badge. His efforts were doomed to failure, however, as Brig Webb-Bowen had already insisted that the emblem be removed from the unit's vehicles. Since the brigade commander had effectively banned its public display, the badge soon fell into disuse and faded into obscurity. Sqn Ldr Gibbs forwarded the menu to Heaton-Armstrong with the suggestion that it might be preferable to "that awful flying camel" and that the change could be justified on the grounds of its being an older emblem.

Based on the emblem on the 1916 menu, this is the badge that might have been.

Whether Gibbs liked it or not, however, the camel was a particularly relevant motif for No 45 Sqn as it neatly symbolised both the unit's outstanding record while flying the Sopwith Camel and its later service in the transport role in Iraq - and in any case, it was the squadron's choice! Nevertheless, the College of Heralds prepared a sketch of the prospective new badge and sent it to the Air Ministry. Gibbs realised that if he was going to succeed in torpedoing No 45 Sqn's badge this would ultimately require the personal intervention of the King. This made it essential that he first gain support for his plan from the CAS and the Secretary of State for Air. Very wisely, the Private Secretary to CAS declined to take the matter up with his master, on the grounds that it would set an unfortunate precedent and might

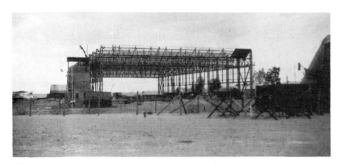

Above:- Seen here with construction well under way, a permanent hangar was built at Helwan in the course of 1936. Below:- OC A Flight, Flt Lt Victor Streatfeild, shortly after landing from a mail run to Ramleh. Streatfeild was posted to No 223 Sqn in November 1936, by which time the new hangar was evidently already in use, although the old Bessonneaus were still going strong until at least 1938. (both W Lucas)

well encourage other units to have second thoughts about their badges. Furthermore, he did not relish the prospect of having to suggest to a squadron that its current badge, with which the unit clearly identified and which already represented a significant accumulation of history and tradition, was unacceptable - particularly as no less an authority than the King himself had previously indicated that it was! Finally it would then be necessary to tackle the problem of persuading the unit to adopt a totally unfamiliar and, to them, quite meaningless emblem. Gibbs tried once more by forwarding the matter to his own chief, the Air Member for Supply and Organisation (AMSO), who sat on the Badges Committee. His outer office also declined to pursue the matter, for exactly the same reasons. The campaign collapsed. No 45 Sqn's camel flew serenely on, blissfully unaware of the dastardly bureaucratic attempt to shoot it down - with a sheep.

By late 1936 further symptoms of the Expansion Schemes were becoming evident and on December 15th No 45 Sqn's B Flight at Nairobi was raised to squadron status. It was redesignated as No 223 Sqn which was initially established to have a Headquarters and one flight, operating four Gordons with a fifth in reserve. Thereafter No 223 Sqn's story diverges from that of the Flying Camels and it went on to build a history and traditions of its own. Having already provided the new unit's nucleus, however, before the ties were finally cut No 45 Sqn provided the new squadron with one more transfusion of manpower by replacing its entire air echelon. Sqn Ldr Jones, who had spent little if any time in

Egypt in any case, remained at Nairobi as CO where he was joined by Flt Lt V C F Streatfeild, Fg Off D P Frost, Fg Off E M Withy and Fg Off W Lyons from Helwan, the latter being an Accountant Officer; for the first few months of its existence these were the only officers on No 223 Sqn's strength. The permanent loss of B Flight permitted No 45 Sqn to rationalise its internal organisation as A, B and C Flights and the D Flight that had been acquired from No 14 Sqn in January disappeared.

On 1st January 1937 Allan Churchman was promoted to

Above:- Sgt H Morris, one of No 45 Sqn's many NCO pilots, about to set off for India with K3611, one of No 216 Sqn's supporting Valentias, in the background. Below:- A brief stop at Bahrein on January 18th to refuel the aeroplanes and crews. (both P Hodkinson)

117

K4704 threading its way through the Khyber Pass. (No 45 Sqn archives)

wing commander but remained in command of the squadron which was about to set off on yet another major long-range flight. It was to exercise its reinforcement role again, but this time it was to bolster a more distant Command and fly all the way to India. Twelve Vincents were to take part, supported by three Valentias. The latter would be furnished by No 216 Sqn as far as Hinaidi with No 70 Sqn handling the latter half of the trip. The itinerary for the flight was as follows:

12th January	Ramleh via Gaza
14th January	Amman
15th January	Hinaidi via Rutbah
17th January	Shaibah
18th January	Sharjah via Bahrein
19th January	Karachi via Gwadur, (crossing the Gulf between Ras el Kaimah and Jask)

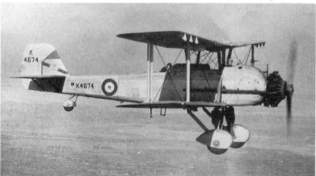

When unit markings were applied to the Vincents they were similar to those worn by the Faireys, a red and blue diagonal fin stripe with a Flying Camel in the middle as seen here on K4674. The tip of the fin is painted in a flight colour, in this case A Flight red. Flight colours were also applied in a vertical stripe on the front of the wheel spats. Below:- At a later stage of its career with the squadron K4674 was fitted, unusually, with a fixed-pitch, three-bladed metal propeller. In this picture the aeroplane appears to have triangular plates fitted to its rear interplane struts, possibly flight commander's pennants. (both W Lucas)

K4664 after having been stood on its nose at Helwan by an unknown pilot after its brakes had been overadjusted (at least, that was the pilot's explanation). This is a particularly good picture of the Flying Camel emblem carried on the nose of some, if not all, of the squadron's Vincents. (W Lucas)

| 20th January | Lahore via Khanpur |
| 21st January | Risalpur |

Three weeks were spent in India becoming familiar with the many LGs, taking part in patrols of the tribal areas, carrying out bombing exercises at Miranshah and Kohat (the latter by night as well as by day) and flying navigation exercises by flights. The return trip went further east before heading back towards Egypt, as follows:

13th February	Delhi via Lahore
15th February	Karachi via Jodhpur
17th February	Sharjah via Gwadur
18th February	Shaibah via Bahrein
19th February	Hinaidi
21st February	Amman via Rutbah
22nd February	Helwan

Excluding in-theatre flying, the round trip had covered 7,387 miles. It was conducted almost exactly to schedule, the only departure from the plan being caused by some problems with weather at the outset which had caused an unscheduled stop at Gaza and a day's delay at Ramleh. The only untoward occurrence had been on January 18th when Sgt Dixon ran into a patch of soft sand at Bahrein and tipped K4675 gently onto its nose; no one was hurt and after a new propeller had been fitted and the engine had been given a quick going over by the fitters the aeroplane continued on its way.

The early Vincents had been virtually anonymous but within a few weeks they had adopted the markings previously worn by the Faireys, a diagonal fin stripe in red and blue with a small blue Flying Camel in the middle. Other dabs of colour were provided by the tips of the fins and a vertical stripe on the fronts of the wheel spats being painted in appropriate flight-colours: red, yellow and blue for A, B and C Flights respectively. Some aircraft, certainly those of A Flight, also had a Flying Camel applied on the port side of the nose (possibly both sides, but confirmation is lacking); this appears to have been painted in red on some aeroplanes but it has been reported that on some the device was rendered in beaten copper and riveted in place. By the time of the India reinforcement exercise the squadron's badge had been formally approved and the Flying Camels on the fins were in

A view of the rows of relatively comfortable bungalows on Helwan's domestic site circa 1937. (Author's collection).

red and blue within a grenade-shaped frame[4]. The flames at the top of the grenade were picked out in red and the fin stripe was retained. The frame was applied with a stencil but the Flying Camels were painted by hand by each aeroplane's fitter and rigger so there were considerable variations in style.

On its return to Egypt the squadron quickly picked up the routine again and in March it flew squadron formations on five occasions in preparation for an air display to be held at Heliopolis on April 16th. Prior to this, two Vincents had been detached to the south west to co-operate with the Royal Tank Corps who were exercising in the vicinity of the Bahariya and Kharga Oases. In May the squadron joined Nos 208 and 216 Sqns in a flypast over Cairo to mark the coronation of HM King George VI. In that same month, on the 14th, Sqn Ldr N V Moreton took over as the new CO. He was soon involved in the regular round of bombing and photographic exercises, cross-countries and visits to LGs. From August regular weekly night bombing exercises were added to the standard training pattern. In mid-1937 there was a flurry of survey and reconnaissance work covering both the Western Desert and the Arabian side of the Red Sea in the vicinity of Jeddah.

In August 1936 there had been another outbreak of Arab-Jewish (and anti-British) unrest in Palestine which was to

K2617, one of the ex-D Flight Gordons retained at Helwan and used by the squadron for support tasks. The pilot may be Plt Off Patrick Troughton-Smith. The crewman is LAC Finlayson. (No 45 Sqn archives)

continue sporadically into the war years. Although the squadron had not been called upon to intervene directly, the regular air mail run had been reinstated and was periodically increased in frequency. Reg Collis (later Sqn Ldr R A Collis DFC) was serving on No 45 Sqn as a junior pilot officer in early 1937; he recalls:

Our most interesting duty was, I think, the weekly mail run to Palestine carrying the official mail for HQ Palestine and Transjordan. This consisted of picking up mail at Heliopolis, Ismailia and Gaza and dropping it off at Kolundia. The run was followed by a weekend off at Ramleh which enabled us to visit Tel Aviv and other places. Landing at Kolundia was quite a palaver. On arrival we had to dive on the armoured car depot in Jerusalem to wake them up and let them know that we were there. We then flew about until a couple of cars had

The squadron's Vincents jostle for a place in the new hangar at the end of the working day. Note that the tip of K4666's fin is coloured (K4666 belonged to B Flight so this marking should have been in yellow) and that it has metal pennants fitted to its rear interplane struts, as does the aircraft on the right. The Flying Camel badge can be seen on the nose of the aircraft on the right. (via A J Thomas)

Date and location are both unknown, as is the pilot's identity, but the aeroplane is No 45 Sqn's K4672. The pyramids in the background and the kit bags being unloaded suggest that the incident occurred in Egypt, not very far from Helwan, and that the aeroplane had been on its way to or from a remote destination, involving a night stop, and not on a local flight. The problem appears to have been a major oil leak. (No 45 Sqn archives)

driven out to the landing ground to stop the traffic on the Jerusalem-Ramallah road. The engine was kept running after landing; the mail was rapidly unloaded and, as quickly as possible, the aeroplane was airborne again for Ramleh. The aim of the game was to spend as little time as possible at a standstill as discontented Arabs and/or Jewish activists had a tendency to take pot shots at vulnerable British targets and a stationary aeroplane was a sitting duck.

By this time the infrastructure at Helwan had begun to be updated and during 1936 a permanent hangar had been built to house the squadron's Vincents. When they were not towing drogues for people to shoot at, the odd Gordon, legacies of the now defunct D Flight, could still be found lurking in there as well.

Two large scale bombing exercises were flown in October. On the 26th nine aircraft flew to El Arish where they were turned round and flown back to Helwan via the Suez Road Range, being intercepted by No 33 Sqn on the way in. Three days later a major fire power demonstration was mounted for the benefit of some 400 army officers. All three of the bomber squadrons based in Egypt took part. No 45 Sqn led, with each aircraft carrying eight 112 lb bombs. They pattern-bombed a dummy river crossing with a ferry, a jetty and some buildings. Bombing from 3,000 feet, thirty of the squadron's seventy-two bombs actually fell inside the small aiming circle within the target complex. It was a most impressive demonstration of accuracy although it was considered that the insubstantial construction of the simulated

Vincent K4676 was retained in service as a hack until at least July 1938, which was well into the Wellesley era, and several of this newer type can be seen in the background to this photograph. K4676 is seen here, looking a trifle middle-aged and shabby, as B Flight's duty crew prepare it for the day's flying. On the left is Cpl M B F Mackenzie, one of the many tradesmen who flew as gunners and wireless operators. He was killed on 2nd October 1940 when his Blenheim was shot down by Italian fighters during the East African campaign. In a white shirt, behind the bowser, is LAC F S White who was killed two months later in an accidental fall on a Nile paddle steamer. (L Wilde)

target probably failed to convey the real destructive power of the bombs.

After only two years with Vincents it was time to re-equip again, this time making the transition to monoplanes with retractable undercarriages and variable pitch propellers.

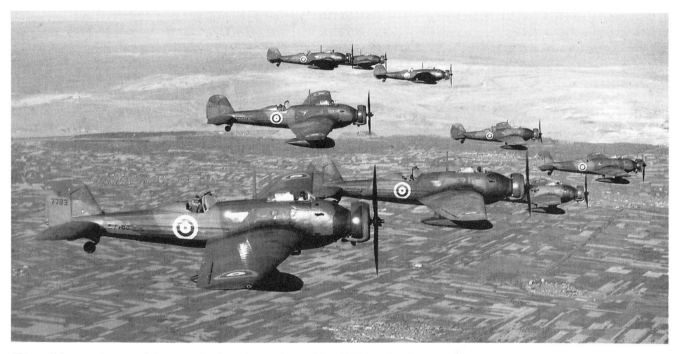

This well known photograph is reputed to have been taken in May 1938 but the absence of unit markings suggests that it was probably earlier and it is known that photographs were taken during formation-flying exercise on 27th January and 16th March. The nearest vic is led by K7773 with K7777 on its left and K7783 on its right (nearest to camera). The leader of the front vic is K7775. (MAP)

A neat line-up (possibly at Heliopolis in October 1938) showing the markings that were applied to the squadron's Wellesleys from mid-year. Each aeroplane has the Flying Camel motif in a grenade-shaped frame on its fin and sports the squadron number and an individual letter on its fuselage. 45.G is L2650, next in line is K7779/45.C. (R L Ward)

A few days before the squadron began to trade in its last biplanes it put up one last Vincent formation - eighteen of them. The first Wellesley was collected by Sqn Ldr Moreton on November 25th and on December 13th 'Mutt' Summers, Vickers' chief test pilot, visited Helwan to advise on the handling characteristics of the big new aeroplane and especially on the use of its flaps, subsequently underlining what he had been saying with an impressive flying demonstration By Christmas type-conversion was complete and between 7th and 8th January 1938 the CO showed off the squadron's new aeroplanes by taking three of them to Dhibban[5] and back. A week later two more followed them.

Although the squadron was now flying monoplanes, one Vincent was retained until well into 1938, K4676 being used as a hack and to give newly arrived pilots a couple of local familiarisation trips, and there was still the odd Gordon target-tower knocking about. Despite the presence of these reminders of the past, with the advent of the Wellesley the days of silver biplanes were over and the drab camouflage of the new bombers (Dark Green and Dark Earth on top with black undersides) provided a constant reminder that war was becoming increasingly likely. Although they had a much more sombre appearance than their predecessors, ownership of the unit's new aeroplanes was still clearly advertised since the squadron number, along with an individual code letter, was soon painted on the fuselage sides in large letters and the Flying Camel emblem was carried on the fin in a grenade-shaped frame.

Range was the Wellesley's strongest suit (it was to capture the World Long Distance Record later that year) and the squadron began to exploit this potential by undertaking much longer non-stop trips. On February 4th Sqn Ldr Moreton with Plt Off H P Pleasance and Sgt R T Shaw in K7774, K7776 and K7786 set off for Kenya with Air Cdre A A Walser MC DFC (Air Officer Administration at HQ RAFME) in overall command of the enterprise. K7786 was obliged to put down at El Rus with engine trouble. This was quickly diagnosed as oily plugs and the aircraft was soon airborne again and heading south in pursuit of the other two. Unfortunately, on landing at Wadi Halfa, Harold 'Flash' Pleasance was unable to throttle back and his extended run-out came to an abrupt halt with the Wellesley straddling the wall of a cemetery. No one was hurt (although LAC Charnley and AC Beer doubtless had something to write home about that week) but K7786 was out of action and it had to be replaced. Flt Lt W J H Ekins left Helwan at short notice in K7775 and was able to catch up with the CO at Khartoum. After a night stop there, and another at Juba, the three aircraft reached Nairobi on the 7th and paid a visit to Zanzibar on the 10th before retracing their track to Helwan where they arrived on the 18th.

A Wellesley returning from a mail run to Palestine on March 26th was unable to lower its undercarriage and Sgt Grant was obliged to land K7777 at Helwan using the underwing bomb nacelles as skids. The nacelles bore the

An informal A Flight group circa August 1938. From the left: AC Peacock, Cpl Patterson, AC Strudwick, AC Simpson, AC Clarkson and AC Lanyon; the two on the right are unidentified. Archie Strudwick was another of the squadron's airmen gunners; he became a fully-fledged sergeant WOp/AG in 1940 and continued to fly with the squadron until May 1941. (R McAusland)

brunt of the damage; the crew were unhurt and the aeroplane was back on the flightline in fairly short order. As can be seen from Annex L, several more Wellesleys were to suffer undercarriage malfunctions and/or collapses but the crews generally walked away from these incidents little the worse for wear. Writing to the author in 1994, Leslie Moulton, who joined the squadron as a sergeant pilot in the summer of 1938, recalled that, "It became almost a habit for certain pilots to pull up the undercarriage lever, mistaking it for the flap control," adding cryptically, "Rixson and Thomas will be able to tell you more about it that I can." Leslie Moulton was yet another ex-45 Sqn man who was to attain a very senior rank in the service; he eventually retired in 1971 as Air Vice Marshal L H Moulton CB DFC, his last appointment being as AOC No 90 (Signals) Gp.

The change of aeroplanes had not meant a change in role so the squadron's daily round remained much as it had been for the previous ten years, bombing, gunnery, photography and general flying practice but with the ominous recent addition of a requirement to carry out the occasional landing encumbered by having to wear a gas mask. Visiting LGs continued to feature in the routine, this occupation being quite demanding, not least because some of the more obscure Emergency LGs were very hard to find. Many were merely areas of relatively flat terrain, often no more than 400 yards in length, with a minimum of obstructions, whose status as

LGs was indicated solely by a white painted designation marking. The aim of the exercise was to find the place and then, if the marking had been obscured by sand, to land and clear this away or perhaps repaint it. Another traditional activity carried on since the days of the Fairey IIIFs was running consignments of official mail up to Ramleh and/or Amman and occasionally as far as Habbaniyah. This was still a sought after trip as it provided a useful long-range navigation exercise, a change of scene and an opportunity to restock the messes with fresh citrus fruit. The unrest in Palestine was still simmering, however, and there were occasional reports of the Stern Gang shooting at aeroplanes approaching to land at Ramleh, but none of No 45 Sqn's was ever hit.

From Monday to Friday during the summer the working day began at 0545hrs with the first aircraft airborne by 0615hrs; breakfast was snatched as and when possible and work ceased at about 1200hrs except for Thursdays when there was night flying. There was a formal parade every Saturday morning and a Church Parade every third Sunday. Beyond this one's time was more or less one's own but, cash being in relatively short supply, sorties into Cairo were fairly rare. For the more affluent there were trips to the Gezirah Sports Club and the Ma'adi Club both of which provided pleasant surroundings and comfortable facilities. Helwan itself also offered ample opportunities for sport and this occupied a great deal of most people's spare time. Participation was encouraged and there was a constant round

Above:- LAC Jack Eades of B Flight leans proprietorially on L2658/45.O. Below:- Collapsed undercarriages were not uncommon during the Wellesley era. This is L2658/45.O, after Sgt M C Thurlow undershot while landing at Helwan on 11th November 1938. The Wellesleys were quite robust aeroplanes, however, and most returned to the flightline after this sort of incident - some of them more than once. (both J Eades)

Not as expensive as it looks! This is K7781/45.L after it had been forced to land at Toshka on 7th July 1938. Three days later this Victoria (JR9675) of No 216 Sqn delivered a new engine. Of particular interest are the Victoria's collapsible radio mast which has been erected to establish long-range W/T communications and the lifting tackle rigged on its port engine bearers to act as a crane to change the Wellesley's engine. (D F Rixson)

of inter-flight competitions. It is worth observing that rivalry between the flights was intense, particularly among the airmen, and it is notable that right up to 1946 the flights tended to be quite insular and to work, live and spend their leisure time in exclusive groups. They could, however, always be relied upon to overlook their differences and unite whenever the squadron's honour was challenged, as in an inter-station sporting fixture - and in effect No 45 Sqn was 'Helwan' for much of the 1930s. Other light relief was furnished by a do-it-yourself camp cinema, the programme often being enlivened by a sort of cabaret between reels which consisted largely of scurrilous stories and 'in jokes' which Helwan's residents found wildly amusing but which totally mystified visitors. Few officers were married and the dozen or so commissioned bachelors lived in the small Officers' Mess where they shared a bearer, one between two, and dined formally in either Mess Dress or Dinner Jackets every night except weekends.

Although the Flying Camels continued to be the only residents for a while, with an eye to the future, in April 1938 RAFME raised the status of Helwan to that of a fully fledged station. No 45 Sqn was now expected to use the station's resources and as a result it lost the services of the support staff element which had been an integral part of its organisation since 1916. At the time the squadron's MO was Flt Lt I K McKenzie; its Accountant Officer was Fg Off W J R Cann and its Equipment Officer, Fg Off McD B Manson[6] - all three had been transferred from No 45 Sqn's books to those of RAF Helwan by mid-May. In the event this turned out to be only a brief interlude as the war soon demonstrated that a mobile tactical unit operating overseas had to be fully

autonomous and needed more, not less, organic support. By the summer of 1940 the squadron's MO and Equipment Officer had been re-established and it had acquired a full time Adjutant and Engineering, Intelligence and Cypher Officers as well.

The routine continued to be punctuated by the odd task involving brief detachments. Between 27th and 30th May a section of three aircraft toured the Western Desert inspecting some of the more remote LGs. On July 1st another three flew to Khartoum non-stop, in formation, in a flight time of about 7½ hours. Plt Off D F Rixson was No 3 on this flight and has recalled that his aircraft had "terrible fuel flow problems as the wing tanks did not feed evenly. We could only counter the consequent out-of-balance condition by anchoring elastic parachute cord to the cockpit light fittings and then running it round the control column to ease the physical strain". This was not the only lesson learned on these long trips. Lacking a 'pee-tube' (a curious oversight in an aeroplane with such a remarkable endurance), pilots resorted to filling an empty Verey cartridge case and then dumping the contents over the side. Unfortunately the slipstream caused it to re-enter the aeroplane at the wireless operator's station so this practice had to be suitably modified, with the containers being gingerly passed back to the rearmost crew position!

A week later the Khartoum trip was repeated but this time K7781 experienced engine trouble and Sgt S A G Abbott was forced to land at Toshka. A new engine was needed and this and an engineering team were flown down to the site on July 10th in a Valentia of No 216 Sqn. It took five days to change the engine in the field, with the working party based at Wadi Halfa and being flown to and from the site each day by a pair of Wellesleys. The aircraft was flown back to Helwan on the 16th. That same month the squadron underwent an intensive period of gunnery training, both air-to-ground and air-to-air.

Various references to the RAF's pre-war expansion have already been made in this Chapter and it is worth pausing here to consider the impact that one particular aspect of these developments was having at squadron level. The substantial and rapid increase in the size of the service had inevitably created a situation broadly analogous to that which had pertained when the squadron had first been raised in 1916. As flying training was now both a well-established and a very thorough procedure, the problems were far less acute but, as in 1916-17, the creation of so many new squadrons in 1936-37 had progressively siphoned off the majority of older pilots to fill executive appointments, considerably diluting the overall experience level within existing units. This pattern was common to all squadrons, of course, but it is appropriate to consider here how these changes affected the Flying Camels.

Some of its more seasoned pilots (like Flt Lt Victor Streatfeild) had gone to help supervise the formation of new squadrons or had been promoted and posted to take up supervisory positions in existing units (like Sqn Ldr G B Keily); some (like Flt Lts Donald Fleming and Ernest Barlow) had been transferred to instructional duties while others (like Flt Lts John Franks and Thomas Dickens) had been promoted to help administer the constantly growing service. In May 1938, with the posting of Flt Lt William Ekins, the last of the squadron's really experienced men had gone. In place of the traditional three flight lieutenant flight commanders the squadron was left with Fg Off George Fidler as its senior pilot and, although he was still on his first tour, he was promptly made up to acting flight lieutenant to fill the

gap - but even he left in August. By then, apart from the CO, *all* of the squadron's pilots were on their first tours and most of them were either acting pilot officers or equally green sergeants.

In October of 1938, less than three years after he had first joined the squadron as a brand new pilot officer, Fg Off G J Bush was granted an acting flight lieutenancy to restore some sort of hierarchical structure; he was assisted in his supervisory tasks by two newly created acting flying officers, P P Troughton-Smith and H P Pleasance, both of whom had arrived (as acting pilot officers) as recently as April 1937; this inexperienced but capable triumvirate was responsible for much of the day to day running of the unit from then until the outbreak of war. It says much for them as individuals, and (in stark contrast to the situation in 1916) for the quality of the training which this generation of pilots had received, that there were so few incidents during this period and none of those that did occur proved to be serious.

One factor which contributed to the squadron's successful passage through this transition stage was its length. If nothing else, the Government's policy of appeasing Hitler at least served to buy sufficient time to allow many of the RAF's freshly trained pilots to mature into reasonably competent aviators. Another positive influence was the emergence of a degree of stability within the ranks of the air echelon. There were still a lot of comings and goings but many of the men who arrived in 1938 would still be on the squadron when it finally went into combat two years later. Among the personalities who arrived at about this time and who would constitute the backbone of the squadron when the war finally began, were J H Williams, J S Davies, D F Rixson, G C B Woodroffe, W J Swire-Griffiths, C L Wright, C W S Thomas, and D K Bednall; apart from the first three, who were pilot officers, they were all acting pilot officers at the time of their arrival.

The squadron's officers in March 1939 . Back row, from the left: Plt Off C W S Thomas, Plt Off R W A Gibbs, Plt Off A S Smith, Plt Off C L Wright, Plt Off G C B Woodroffe, Plt Off D K Bednall and Plt Off E G Rands. Front row: Plt Off W J Swire-Griffiths, Plt Off J S Davies, Plt Off D F Rixson, Flt Lt G J Bush, Sqn Ldr N V Moreton, Fg Off H P Pleasance, Fg Off P P Troughton-Smith and Plt Off J H Williams. (D F Rixson)

Above and below - Oops! This incident occurred on 1st September 1938 when K2745, one of the odd Gordons still floating about at Helwan, taxied into K7774; The culprit was Sgt Nicholls. (both D K Bednall)

Frequent long-range training sorties provided a change of scene and some light relief. This picture was taken at Hurghada in the autumn of 1938 and shows three of the squadron's pilots being entertained by a group of British 'expats'. Plt Off Dundas Bednall is standing fifth from the left. Sgt Shaw is on the extreme right and next to him (KD shorts and a towel) is Sgt Leslie Moulton. (D K Bednall)

By long-established precedent Wednesday was formation day on No 45 Sqn and this continued to be the case into the Wellesley era. There being no runway as such the whole width of the airfield was used on these occasions, the normal practice being to take off in three vics abreast. This had been easy enough with IIIFs and Vincents, but the wings of the Wellesleys spanned some seventy-five feet which made it a bit of a tight squeeze to get nine aeroplanes fitted into the gap between the watchtower and an inconvenient ditch. No concessions were made to modernity, however, and the traditional formation take-off remained the order of the day, the only differences being the whiteness of the knuckles and some agitated, even frantic, hand signals between aeroplanes in an effort to persuade everyone else to keep their distance.

Aside from its potential for being a bit of a problem on the ground, the Wellesley's immense wing span gave it an aspect ratio approaching that of a glider. Thus, in addition to its remarkable range capability, the type had a significant high altitude performance. On 13th October Plt Off Bednall tried this out when, in the course of an oxygen test, he persuaded L2640 to climb to 32,000 feet which, for a standard service aeroplane, was not at all bad in 1938.

In September the CO, with four aircraft, flew the AOC, AVM H R Nicholl CB CBE, down to Nairobi to conduct his annual inspection. By this time, the summer of 1938, international tension had increased again to be defused, albeit temporarily, by the Munich Agreement. The squadron had been issued with a number of extra aircraft and on September 27th, at the height of the crisis, the squadron had no fewer than twenty-seven Wellesleys on charge and serviceable. On the 28th nine of them were loaded with 500 lb and 250 lb bombs and picketed out on the aerodrome on stand-by. This posture was sustained until October 2nd when the increased state of readiness was relaxed. Preparations for war

continued, however, and a session of anti-gas training was implemented for everyone. In the meantime the bomber force based in Egypt had been reinforced by the redeployment of No 211 Sqn's Hinds which flew in from Palestine on September 29th. Thenceforth they were to be based at Helwan, which had been the exclusive preserve of the Flying Camels for ten years.

In view of the still tense international situation it was deemed necessary to demonstrate to the Egyptians that the British had adequate strength to defend their country (or, alternatively, to impress upon them that it was not worth considering being too friendly with the Italians) and to this end a mass flypast was staged over Cairo on October 18th. This involved four Wings totalling 127 aircraft. The third formation was by far the largest, consisting of eighteen of No 45 Sqn's Wellesleys and thirty-six Gladiators drawn from Nos 33 and 80 Sqns. The following day the squadron capped that by flying no fewer than twenty-four aircraft to Heliopolis where the British Ambassador, Sir Miles Lampson, was reviewing both the RAF and the Royal Egyptian Air Force (REAF). All of these aircraft, plus No 211 Sqn's Hinds, took off from Helwan within a hectic seven minutes and they all landed again in eleven minutes, no doubt leaving everything and everybody covered in a fine coating of dust. An illuminating insight into the robustness of contemporary attitudes towards aviation medicine and flight safety is provided by Plt Off Dundas Bednall's experience. While standing in front of K7776 in the sun, waiting for the great man to pass by, he fainted. He was promptly picked up, dusted down and propped up again; the rows of chaps had to be both neat *and* complete! When it was all over, still a trifle green about the gills, he climbed into his aeroplane and flew it back to Helwan in formation with the rest of the gaggle.

Long-range sorties continued. On October 28th, for instance, three Wellesleys piloted by Plt Off Bednall and Sgts Shaw and Moulton, flew down to Hurghada, returning three days later. Five more aircraft flew to Habbaniyah and back between November 15th and 19th and on December 1st the CO led four aircraft to Port Sudan, returning via Atbara and Wadi Halfa to reach Helwan on the 5th. One aircraft had to land with a fuel problem on the last leg but its crew was able to effect a repair and they made it back to base under their own steam. Later that month a Blenheim of No 30 Sqn was reported missing and on the 9th and 10th the squadron contributed a total of nineteen sorties to the subsequent

After twelve happy years at Helwan the squadron moved to Ismailia in January 1939. Above, a view of the airmen's bungalows at Ismailia and, below, Ismailia's pundit light being trundled out onto the airfield in preparation for a session of night flying. (both J Eades)

large-scale search. The squadron first swept the Sinai Desert repeatedly but found nothing. Its allocated area was then moved north and nine aircraft were detached to Amman on the 12th to help cover Palestine and Transjordan. After a further week an aircraft of another unit located the wreckage of the Blenheim in Iraq; No 45 Sqn had flown a total of 231 hours in connection with this task. While this had been going on three other aircraft had flown a long-range cruise to Nairobi and back, setting out on the 13th and returning on the 22nd.

In early 1939 there was a reshuffling of units in Egypt and on January 3rd No 45 Sqn began a leisurely exchange of bases with the Gladiators of No 80 Sqn at Ismailia, both squadrons having been relocated by the 16th. Before the end of the month No 211 Sqn's Hinds had also moved to Ismailia to join No 45 Sqn and the resident Gladiator-equipped No 33 Sqn. The Wellesleys resumed their long-range trips as soon as they arrived and gas training continued to feature in the training programme, as on January 30th, for instance, when all personnel wore respirators for 30 minutes. In February four aircraft flew a rugby team to Habbaniyah and two others visited Khartoum. Later that month Aden was added to the squadron's destinations when Flt Lt Bush with Plt Offs Wright and Rixson flew the AOC down to Khormaksar and back between the 13th and 18th.

Another diversion was provided early in 1939 when a Vildebeest IV was made available to the squadron. The Mk IV was powered by the innovatory Perseus engine, the first of Bristol's sleeve-valve radials to enter service, and it is presumed that K8087, the penultimate Mk IV to be built, had

When No 45 Sqn moved to Ismailia at the beginning of 1939 it acquired this Vildebeest IV, K8087, which was probably in Egypt to accumulate operating experience with its sleeve-valved Bristol Perseus engine under desert conditions. Its career with No 45 Sqn came to an end when Sgt L H Moulton used it to collect Padre Cox from Heliopolis and flipped the aeroplane over onto its back on landing back at base. It was Leslie Moulton's only significant accident in an eventual total of over 4,000 flying hours. (R McAusland)

126

been sent out to Egypt to see how the new engine stood up to the demanding local environmental conditions. A number of pilots had an opportunity to fly the aeroplane until Leslie Moulton flipped it onto its back while landing at Ismailia; his only significant accident in an eventual total of over 4,000 flying hours. The incident had occurred at the end of a flight from Heliopolis, the Vildebeest having been used to pick up Padre Cox[7]. Apart from the padre bumping his head, as a result of releasing his straps while hanging upside down in them, no one was hurt.

Sqn Ldr E B Webb took command of the squadron on March 1st and on the 29th nine of its Wellesleys flew over the SS *Strathaird* to bid farewell to Noel Moreton as he sailed for the UK, where he was to take up a staff appointment at HQ Coastal Command as a wing commander. Now that No 45 Sqn was part of a wing there was more direct competition to stimulate it in the sporting field. The squadron rose to the challenge and on 31st March walked off with the Inter-Squadron Cup at the Ismailia Sports Day. On April 1st the squadron put up another formation, this time of twelve aircraft, to escort AVM Mitchell, the visiting Air Member for Personnel, as his Empire flying boat left Alexandria.

The Alexandria district staged a major exercise between 22nd and 26th April. This required the squadron's Wellesleys to fly out to Mersah Matruh each day then take off to mount simulated night attacks on the Nile delta from the west. Dundas Bednall (later Wg Cdr D K Bednall) has provided an impression of this event in his book, *Sun on my Wings*. The relevant passage reads:

> The idea was for the squadron to attack Alexandria by simulated bombing runs from, I believe, 10,000 feet then to carry on and land back at Ismailia. All this, so far, was quite simple and offered no problems even though the night was moonless. But there was one quite astonishing snag; we had to fly in close formations of three aircraft each with no navigation or other lights, except a very dim red interior light in each of the Wellesleys which was supposed to be visible from the neighbouring aircraft. This was unbelievable! No one had tested this 'visibility' on the ground and never, to my knowledge, was any close (very close) formation bombing ever done on a moonless night.
>
> The whole thing was disastrous; the dim light in the other aircraft could hardly be seen and, in any case, a single light gives no idea of distance whatsoever. There was no communication between aircraft and, shortly after take off, I deemed that discretion was the better part of valour and decided to 'bomb' the target as a single aircraft. All the others, I believe, did the same and all except Plt Off Thomas, arrived safely back at Ismailia.

'Cubby' Thomas (later Wg Cdr C W S Thomas AFC) had had an engine problem. He has described the incident as follows:

> With AC1 Cooper as my wireless operator, at about midnight on April 26th my aircraft, L2640, was the last to take off from Mersah Matruh. We had to overfly the camera obscura equipment at Aboukir and then fly direct to Ismailia. All was well until we were about twenty minutes from base when I noticed a big drop in oil

K4779/45.C, with Ismailia's airship mooring mast in the background. As the aeroplane is still wearing its original Type A1 roundels the photograph was probably taken sometime between January 1939, when the squadron moved to Ismailia, and May 1939, at which time Type B roundels, ie with yellow and white deleted, began to be applied. (via A J Thomas)

This photograph of K7782 illustrates the colours being worn during the last two months of the Wellesley's service with No 45 Sqn. The fuselage roundels are now the red/blue Type B and, although not actually visible, it is probable that the aeroplane is sporting its recently allocated DD code in place of the numeral 45. Interestingly, the picture also shows that, although a desert colour scheme was not formally introduced until August 1941, an interim scheme (or large-scale field experimentation) was implemented as early as mid-1939. The very obvious difference in tones indicates that this aeroplane has had the Dark Green areas of its original camouflage pattern repainted in a much lighter colour, presumably a light tan. This has obscured the serial numbers on both the rear fuselage and the rudder (in direct contravention of published instructions) but not the squadron badge on the fin. (via R C Sturtivant)

pressure and had little or no power when I opened the throttle. I was losing height quite quickly and got Cooper to send a message to Ismailia - 'Unable to maintain height; am going to force land in cotton field at El Simballawen.' I did a quick circuit, dropping a parachute flare at about 1,000 feet and then, with wheels and flaps down, we made a perfect landing by the light of the flare which went out just after we touched down. While the engine was still running Cooper sent off another message - 'Landed safely, no damage to crew or aircraft.' You can imagine the scene at dead of night when we were surrounded by Arabs, all thinking that we were Italians come to bomb them! Luckily I spoke enough kitchen-Arabic to convince them that I was only an English officer who had run out of petrol. Actually we had plenty of petrol but when I started the engine again at first light there was still no oil pressure. The oil tank proved to be dry as a bone; some airmen or other had failed to refill it at Mersah Matruh, although he had signed up the F.700[8]. The local mayor turned up on his donkey early in the

Many of the squadron's cast off Wellesleys were passed on to Nos 47 and 223 Sqns. This one, coded DD.I, is seen arriving at Khartoum in June 1939 on transfer to No 47 Sqn. The photograph is particularly interesting as it the only one to have come to light clearly showing the application of No 45 Sqn's pre-war identification code. This aeroplane has also had the Dark Green areas of its camouflage overpainted in a much lighter tone, obscuring the serial numbers. (Courtesy of OC No 47 Sqn)

Seen here at Ismailia, one of the squadron's early Blenheim Is, L8520, with its cowlings off. (via A J Thomas)

morning accompanied by his entourage and we all sat under the Wellesley's wing while he got his slaves to brew up some revolting Turkish coffee, very thick and consisting largely of grounds.....Eventually my CO arrived and pronounced himself delighted with my airmanship. He decided to fly the aeroplane out himself, however, once some oil had been put in and some petrol taken out. There was not much space available but Eric Webb was a determined character and he successfully got the Wellesley off again. Despite the odd spot of excitement that this exercise had evidently generated it was considered to have been a success and the squadron had certainly excelled itself, having flown the remarkable total of 100 hours at night that week.

During the previous summer, at the time of the Munich crisis, many of the silver biplanes, especially fighters, still in service in the UK had been hastily camouflaged and there had been a rather inadequately co-ordinated attempt to 'tone down' national markings so that several variations on the roundel theme were being displayed. In March 1939 German troops crossed the border into Czechoslovakia and Hitler then demanded Danzig and various territorial concessions from the Poles. The UK's appeasement policy was abandoned and preparations for war accelerated. One symptom of this was a directive (promulgated on 27th April by AMO A.154/39) which was intended to rationalise and standardise the rather haphazard state of aircraft markings. Fuselage roundels were now to be in red and blue only and,

Another of the squadron's early Blenheims, L6663, wearing a Flying Camel in a grenade frame on the opaque panel beneath the windscreen. The underwing serial numbers were soon to be painted out, which is just as well as this one may have been applied as L8883. This could have been a mere trick of the light but at least one pilot (Plt Off Bednall) logged a flight in "L8883". NB the serial L8883 fell in the unallotted block L8876-L9020 and this number should not, therefore, have appeared on any airframe. (D K Bednall)

while a discreet squadron badge could still be displayed, all earlier forms of unit identification were to be replaced by a two letter code group. No 45 Sqn was allocated the letters DD and these began to be applied to its aeroplanes in place of the previous large number '45' on the sides of their fuselages.

Photographic evidence indicates that at much the same time, ie circa May 1939, some of No 45 Sqn's Wellesleys were also repainted in an *ad hoc* desert colour scheme. This was probably created by overpainting those areas of the camouflage pattern which had originally been Dark Green with a much lighter colour, presumably a tan shade[9]. This appears to have been applied somewhat hurriedly as the fresh paint obscured the serial numbers, in direct contravention of AMO A.154. It is not known how many of the squadron's aircraft underwent this transformation but photographs of two are reproduced here and it seems reasonable to assume that most, if not all, of the fleet was repainted.

In between bouts of slapping on paint, training continued and on May 13th it was Cairo's turn to sponsor an exercise. This one was held in daylight and the squadron flew 82 hours of troop co-operation sorties while participating in this event. There was another Aden trip for the benefit of the AOC between 19th and 27th May; it was the squadron's last major undertaking with Wellesleys. It was time to re-equip yet again and Blenheims had begun arriving at Ismailia earlier that month, the first of these having gone to No 211 Sqn.

The CO picked up the first Blenheim I for the squadron in June 1939 and began the conversion programme with a demonstration flight on the 26th. With no dual-controlled variant the conversion was personally supervised by Eric Webb who sat on the jump-seat with a copy of the pilots' handbook and a long black ruler. The latter was used to draw the pilot's attention to taps which needed turning, tits which needed pressing and knobs which needed pulling, and to administer a sharp rap over the knuckles of any hands straying towards the wrong controls at the wrong time! In little more than a week all the pilots had gone solo on the new type and by early July the pilots were consolidating their acquaintance with the Blenheim and becoming accustomed to the added complications which arose from having two engines. It was not so much that having two engines was a problem in itself but, for pilots who had never flown twins before, life could become a little difficult when one of them stopped - the Blenheim's Mercuries were not particularly

On 10th July 1939 Plt Off Robert Gibbs distinguished himself by perpetrating the squadron's first Blenheim prang when he swung on landing at Amman and L8500's port undercarriage leg gave up in protest. (R L Ward)

prone to stopping but they could be induced to do so if the throttles were handled over-enthusiastically. Although the squadron had already been through the tribulations associated with adapting to variable pitch props with the Wellesleys, unfamiliarity with the Blenheim produced another crop of prematurely grey hairs as the odd pilot regressed and attempted to take off in coarse pitch! Nonetheless the conversion was completed without anyone making any terribly expensive noises out on the airfield and the redundant Wellesleys were passed on to Nos 47 and 223 Sqns for use in the Sudan and Kenya.

The advent in the late 1930s of relatively sophisticated multi-seat aeroplanes, like the Blenheim, was of considerable significance to flying personnel other than pilots. Traditionally the back seats of the bombers that the RAF had been flying for the previous twenty years had been filled by the squadrons' groundcrew, and those airmen who wished to fly as gunners or as W/T operators had been encouraged to do so. They were rewarded by a daily allowance of a few pence and those who became formally qualified as gunners were entitled, indeed were proud, to wear a winged bullet made of brass on the right sleeve of their tunics. The increasingly complex equipment being installed in new and forthcoming types of aeroplanes made it necessary, however, to provide properly trained specialist personnel to man the various crew stations. In any case the same technical complexity was making it more difficult to release ground tradesmen from their primary duties to allow them to go gallivanting about in the sky.

Initially the training system was simply unable to meet the enormous demands for professional observers, gunners and wireless operators being made by the rapid pre-war expansion and re-armament programmes. For a while the 'amateurs' were permitted to fly on under the old rules, but their days were numbered; if they wanted to continue flying they would eventually have to remuster to one of the new aircrew trades. Like all squadrons, No 45 was affected by the implications of this new manning policy; the first few formally trained NCO observers had begun to arrive while the squadron was still flying Wellesleys but for a while yet most of the bombs dropped by the squadron would continue to be aimed by eager fitters and riggers. The Wireless Operator/Air Gunner (WOp/AG) fraternity were one jump

L8482	L8475
Sqn Ldr E B Webb	Flt Lt G J Bush
F/Sgt Birchall	Sgt N Maryon
Sgt C A Hodder	Sgt C Wordsworth
Sgt Grant	AC J K Copeland
AC G Munson	AC Jackson
L8477	**L8481**
Flt Lt H P Pleasance	Flt Lt P P Troughton-Smith
Cpl Jones	Sgt Chambers
Cpl M B F Mackenzie	Sgt Hill
LAC Price	AC Kaye
AC Beer	
L8479	**L8478**
Plt Off J S Davies	Plt Off G C B Woodroffe
LAC Evans	Sgt Ely
LAC Hodkinson	Cpl Smith
AC Crook	LAC J E Nutt
AC Pizzey	LAC J Eades
L6663	**L8476**
Plt Off R W A Gibbs	Sgt M C Thurlow
Sgt Butterfield	Cpl R F Coatsworth
LAC Wright	LAC Brockes
LAC Cole	LAC A Strudwick

Fig 5.3. The first element of No 45 Sqn to deploy to the Western Desert, 4th August 1939.

ahead of the observers and, under the terms of AMO A.17, all fully qualified volunteer airmen gunners had been formally designated as such since January 1939 and effectively remustered as full-time aircrew which had created some significant, if temporary, vacancies among the ground trades. As yet, however, few (if any) of No 45 Sqn's gunners were formally qualified and they continued to fly under their original status.

By July the squadron was undertaking long range training flights with its new aircraft and on one of these, on the 10th, Plt Off R W A Gibbs bent the squadron's first Blenheim when he swung on landing at Amman and collapsed the undercarriage of L8500. On July 31st the CO showed how it should have been done by flying a consignment of priority mail to Habbaniyah and back without breaking his aeroplane.

By this time it was clear that the Munich Agreement had been a false dawn. International tension was rising again and

The squadron deployed to its forward base at Fuka on 4th August 1939. Eight aircraft of B Flight moved up that day to be followed by others shortly afterwards. Six of these aeroplanes are seen here; nearest the camera is L8477 followed by L8476, L6665 and L8475. The aeroplanes are wearing no unit identity markings. (L Wilde)

operational imperatives had to take priority over consolidation training on the new aircraft. The wing was to be moved forward to pre-empt any possible initiatives by the Italians in Libya. No 45 Sqn moved eight aircraft forward to Fuka on August 4th, each one carrying one or two tradesmen and an assortment of stores and tools. Most of the groundcrew travelled by road and four more aircraft joined the others over the next few days. The first eight aircraft and those on board are listed at Figure 5.3. On the same day No 33 Sqn went to Qasaba and No 211 Sqn to El Daba. SHQ Ismailia provided the controlling formation, Advance Wing HQ, and moved out to Maaten Bagush.

The wing, which was redesignated No 253 Wg shortly after its arrival, was supported by No 1 (ME) Air Stores Park (ASP)[10] and No 1 Advanced Repair Section (ARS)[11]. Both of these units were collocated with No 45 Sqn at Fuka but provided facilities for all three squadrons and the HQ. Each squadron furnished a permanent detachment of airmen to the ARS to assist with the engine and airframe overhauls which it undertook.

Alexandria sponsored another exercise on the 15th/16th August during which each pilot flew 2 hrs 50 mins at night. This turned out to be the last major training event conducted in peacetime.

On 3rd September 1939 Great Britain declared war on Germany. On that date the squadron was commanded by Sqn Ldr Eric Webb, the respective commanders of A, B and C Flights were Flt Lts P P Troughton-Smith, H P Pleasance and G J Bush and the Adjutant's duties were in the hands of Fg Off D F Rixson. Engineering was under the supervision of WO S C Mounsey with F/Sgts Chambers, Bates and Birchall running the three flights. The squadron could field twelve Blenheim Is, with a further three in reserve, and its total strength in manpower amounted to fourteen officers and 150 NCOs and airmen, which was well below its proper establishment of manpower. Nevertheless, if so ordered, the squadron was ready to go to war. In the meantime they could only wait to see what would happen.

Notes:

1. Flight colours, officially red, yellow and blue for A, B and C Flights respectively, were standardised with effect from 18th December 1924. Regrettably, it is not always possible to identify (or even to detect) these colours in black and white photographs because, depending on the emulsion used, their representation can be very misleading. With orthochromatic film blue is rendered as a pale grey while red and yellow appear as dark tones whereas panchromatic film makes blue appear dark while yellow and red are light. Several examples of these anomalies can be found among the pictures illustrating this chapter where the tonal balance between the red and blue of the roundel can differ markedly from one photograph to the next.

Unfortunately, in black and white terms 'dark' can be virtually black and, whatever the actual colour of the cheat line (if there is one), if it is reproduced as near-black it will provide little or no contrast with the black decking of the fuselage, creating the impression that it is not there at all.

2. The squadron's records confirm the figure of 6,382 flying hours for 1929, although the monthly totals for No 45 Sqn contained in HQME's War Diary actually add up to 6,400. Both sources agree that the actual figure for 1930 was 6,260 and HQME notes the running total for 1931 as being 2,534 hours by the end of April.

3. Alfred Marsack and his younger brother, Dudley, were New Zealanders. They had joined the RAF together, trained together and, on 10th October 1931, they had reported to No 45 Sqn together. Both were eventually to retire as group captains.

4. AMO A.14 of 1936, which had introduced the standard frame for official badges, had also stipulated that approved squadron emblems could thenceforth be marked on a unit's aeroplanes in one of three standard frames, a grenade for bombers, a spearhead for fighters and a star for reconnaissance aircraft.

5. Opened in March 1937 this station retained the name of Dhibban for only a year; it was renamed Habbaniyah on 1st May 1938.

6. Presumably in an attempt to improve its image, at the end of 1936 the Stores Branch had redesignated itself as the Equipment Branch. In the 1960s it tried again and changed its name to the Supply Branch. These changes of nomenclature may have reflected more precisely what was intended to be the central function of the branch but a cynic might suggest that nothing has ever really changed and that 'equippers' have always been better at storing their goodies than supplying them.

7. It seems likely that Moulton's ill-treated passenger was shortly to become The Rev Sqn Ldr James Ernest Cox (74806), who was commissioned as a chaplain on 11th September 1939. If so, in 1941 he was to fly with No 45 Sqn again, but this time with fatal consequences.

8. The RAF Form 700 was, and still is, the key document in which the detailed technical history of an aeroplane is recorded throughout its life. Kept almost like a diary, it is signed by all the responsible tradesmen who have worked on an aeroplane on completion of their tasks, including such routine activities as Daily Inspections (DI) and refuelling and re-arming between flights. Prior to take off the aircraft captain inspects the F.700 to see what 'snags' the aeroplane is still carrying, whether its recent history gives any clues as to what might be expected to go wrong and to ensure that all necessary work has been done. Once satisfied, the captain signs for the aeroplane and assumes responsibility for it. After landing any technical problems are reported at the debrief and noted in the F.700. Responsibility for the aeroplane reverts to the groundcrew and the cycle begins again.

9. During the early 1930s the RAE evolved a range of desert paint colours for use in the Middle East. They (or locally mixed equivalents) are known to have been used on Malta during the Abyssinian crisis of 1935 and stocks may also have reached Egypt. The final variants of these desert colours (Dark Sand, Red Sand and Light Sand) were abandoned in mid-1939 but it is likely that existing stocks would have been used up, since, at much the same time, it became necessary to apply camouflage to the remaining silver aeroplanes in the Middle East (Victorias, Audaxes, Gauntlets, Gordons, etc). There is a possibility, therefore, that when No 45 Sqn's Wellesleys were repainted, one, or possibly both, of the colours used came from the Sand-series.

10. No 1 (ME)ASP was redesignated No 31 (ME)ASP on 28th November 1939.

11. No 1 ARS was redesignated No 51 Repair and Salvage Unit (RSU) on 4th July 1940.

Chapter 6. Short-Nosed Blenheims - the opening rounds in Egypt; the Sudan and COMPASS.

The outbreak of war proved to be something of an anti-climax. Nothing much happened, or at least nothing very warlike. There was certainly tension, but there was no action. The squadron was initially ordered to prepare nine aircraft and stand by at two hours' notice for a strike against Libya. This order was promptly executed and the squadron waited. This, however, was the period of the 'Phoney War' in Europe and, as yet, the British had no direct quarrel with the Italians in Africa. On September 5th the readiness state was relaxed to four hours and on the 9th to six hours. Training was resumed.

Before the war the only identification marking carried by the Blenheims had been a Flying Camel in a grenade-frame painted on the flat nose panel beneath the pilot's windscreen. The squadron's pre-war DD identification code appears never to have been applied to its Blenheims and they had certainly not been wearing code letters when they had moved out to Fuka. With the declaration of war all the original code combinations were withdrawn and replaced by a fresh allocation. No 45 Sqn's new letters were OB and this became its logo on and off for the next fifteen years. The new code letters were applied very promptly, along with an interim coat of 'desert' camouflage similar to that which had adorned the Wellesleys in May/June. As before, a coat of tan paint was applied over the Dark Green areas of the temperate scheme in which the aircraft had been delivered, producing something like the desert colour scheme which was to be introduced two years later; the undersides remained in the original black[1].

This chore was completed within ten days. On September 13th there was another Review of the RAF and REAF, this time by King Farouk at Mersah Matruh. The squadron paraded nine aircraft, all in the rather scruffy new paint scheme which presented the OB codes by contrasting the camouflage colours, ie the letters were in tan on brown and in brown on tan. This experiment in desert camouflage was not persevered with and by early 1940 the aircraft were back in their original colours with the code letters applied more neatly in pale grey; this remained the squadron's basic warpaint for the rest of its time on short-nosed Blenheims. From the summer of 1940, however, Blenheim Is operating in the Middle East began to appear with Sky (or perhaps a locally concocted shade of pale blue) undersides and some of No 45 Sqn's machines were certainly sporting this style by the end of that year.

While the stalemate persisted in Western Europe and an uneasy peace still prevailed in the Middle East several crews were usefully employed ferrying Blenheims and Wellesleys out from the UK. Patrick Troughton-Smith had been the first to go, sailing on the SS *Chitral* on August 13th and flying back via Manston, Marseilles and Malta in a new Blenheim to arrive on September 30th. Trips like this one continued on an occasional basis until the fall of France closed the route in 1940. Other squadron pilots known to have gone home to fetch aeroplanes out from the UK included Flt Lts Bush and Pleasance, Plt Offs Collins and Thomas and Sgt Bateman. These ferry flights were not all without incident and the squadron's Plt Off W J Swire-Griffiths, who was collecting a

On 13th September 1939 No 45 Sqn paraded nine of its Blenheims at Mersah Matruh where they were to be inspected by King Farouk. As can be plainly seen, by this time the aircraft had been temporarily repainted in a desert camouflage scheme. The code letters appear to have been applied in the same two contrasting colours. Dark Earth on the locally applied tan and vice versa. The line of Gladiators on the right appear to be in a broadly similar scheme while the Lysanders on the left are in darker tones, probably still the temperate Dark Earth Dark Green scheme in which they had been delivered. (R L Ward)

131

Blenheim earmarked for No 203 Sqn, was killed on 16th March 1940 when L9385 crashed before it had even cleared the UK.

LAC P Hodkinson, then one of the squadron's fitters, accompanied Sgt G J C P Bateman on his trip and he recalls that it was quite an adventure. Originally sent home to collect a Blenheim from Ternhill this eventually turned into a Wellesley which had to be picked up from Sealand. Having positioned at Boscombe Down, they set out on the return trip on Boxing Day 1939 in company with three others, the leader being a Flt Lt Burnett (not of No 45 Sqn). 'Cubby' Thomas, who had been in the UK since July, was returning to the Middle East in another of these Wellesleys, K8525. His account of the first disastrous leg is as follows:

> Flying in line astern, to meet a French requirement for wartime transits over their territory, we approached a weather front and our leader climbed up into the clouds and promptly disappeared from view. I was flying stepped down as Number Four and quickly lost sight of all the aircraft in front of me. I was too low for comfort and my wireless operator, AC Mackenzie, was yelling at me that our trailing aerial had wrapped itself around a tree. Result - no W/T, and we had no R/T anyway. In my endeavours to find somewhere to land I met another Wellesley flown by Frank Collins who had already made a precautionary landing somewhere, found his bearings and taken off again. I formated on him as closely as I could and he gave me a reassuring 'thumbs up' and pointed to his map. He led us to a French flying training school near Angers where we landed safely. In the meantime Pat Burnett in K8524 had landed at an airfield near Nantes and Sgt Bateman had attempted to get down in a field near Angers but he had hit some telephone wires or something on his approach and had damaged his aircraft.

Three of the crews were able to get going again once the weather had cleared and they eventually delivered their Wellesleys to Egypt. L2682 was no longer a going concern, however, and 'Junior' Bateman and Peter Hodkinson found their way back to the UK where they were eventually given another Wellesley to ferry, again one of four. The formation set off on 4th April 1940 and again the first leg proved to be difficult with a steadily lowering cloud base forcing the aircraft down to 50 feet. It would have been prudent to have

One of the squadron's Blenheims at Fuka. (L N Boot)

turned back but the leader forged on - to disaster. Plt Off J D Porter disappeared in K7754 somewhere over the Bay of Biscay and Sgt J A Lewis crashed into the sea off l'Aiguillon (near La Rochelle) in K7740. There were no survivors from either of these aircraft. Sgt Bateman, the only No 45 Sqn pilot involved, successfully put his K7775 (one of No 45 Sqn's original 1937 vintage Wellesleys) down at Nantes while the fourth, K8528, was forced to land at La Roche-sur-Yon. As K7775 was the only aeroplane in a fit state to continue, Bateman carried on alone but found the rest of the trip hampered by 'Phoney War' nerves. They were seriously delayed at Marignane by a regulation requiring them to have an escort for the sea crossing to Malta. This was eventually provided by a passing Bombay, but on reaching Hal Far they were obliged to hold off while obstacles, which had been erected to deter the Italians from making an assault landing, were removed from the airfield. They finally delivered the aeroplane to No 4 FTS at Abu Sueir whence it found its way to No 47 Sqn in the Sudan. Sgt Bateman and LAC Hodkinson finally rejoined the squadron on 5th May 1940.

Recounting this tale has taken us ahead of events and it is necessary to return to September 1939 to pick up the narrative. On the 17th of that month there was a large-scale fire power demonstration. The Blenheims of Nos 113 and 211 Sqns, with No 45 Sqn's nine aircraft leading, formed up over El Daba and flew to El Arish before turning back to make a high level attack on the Suez Road Range, each aircraft delivering a pair of 250 lb bombs. It was the first of several such demonstrations laid on for the benefit of the army during September. This series of events culminated in a large scale air-land exercise held in the desert between 24th October and 4th November. The squadron participated for

A general view of the domestic site at Fuka. (I. Wilde)

There were a number of crashes while the squadron was at Fuka. It is not known for certain which one this was but it may well have been Flt Lt George Bush's L8482 which crashed on the airfield on 19th February 1940. (L Wilde)

five days beginning on the 26th October during which period they used Maaten Bagush as a Forward Operating Base. In the meantime 'Flash' Pleasance[2], who was in the UK on a ferry trip when war was declared, had been 'press-ganged' into No 107 Sqn, creating a need for a new OC B Flight; this was satisfied by the transfer of Flt Lt G O Mills from No 211 Sqn on September 28th.

A feature of the early days in the desert was the friendly rivalry between the wing's two bomber squadrons. This began with No 211 Sqn mounting a surprise 'attack' on Fuka. The home team reacted in the approved fashion and took cover in their recently dug slit trenches to avoid the mass of toilet paper which was gently descending all over the camp site. Some days later the Flying Camels retaliated and

raised the stakes by depositing (by air) a number of lavatory buckets in the middle of the aerodrome at El Daba. Thereafter beat-ups of the rival aerodromes became increasingly frequent and progressively lower. Ultimately Eric Webb was to remove the radio aerial from the roof of the hut which served as El Daba's Officers' Mess with his tailwheel! This sort of thing was an accident looking for somewhere to happen and, very wisely, the two COs agreed to a truce before any real damage was done. Thereafter, in their efforts to impress the groundcrew, the more irresponsible pilots had to content themselves with making low passes over their own camp in an attempt to blow down the odd bell tent. This was only impressive once, however; after that it became a trifle wearing and John Dallamore put a stop to it when he became CO.

Although a good deal of routine training flying was carried out, there were few events of particular note at this time, although Fg Off A J H Finch did have a narrow escape

It does rain in the desert - as the squadron found out in November 1939. Flash floods could occur and the lower lying parts of what was an apparently flat area could suddenly be inundated. This atmospheric sunset shot of Fuka shows that the sand and gravel could very rapidly, albeit briefly, be transformed into a lake. (L Wilde)

Fuka's cinema. (L Wilde)

The interior of the Officers' Mess. The rough and ready bar stools made of reinforced crates make a stark contrast with the silver tray coffee table in the foreground. (D F Rixson)

on December 8th. He had experienced an engine failure in L8479 and during his approach he hit a stationary lorry inconveniently parked on the airfield perimeter. The damage was relatively light, however, and the aircraft was returned to service after repair.

The next out of the ordinary event was a search for an army truck lost out in the desert, to which the squadron committed five aircraft on January 19th. It was found by Fg Offs Rixson and Wright during the Blenheims' second sweep. Another sortie was laid on to drop food and water and the two soldiers were later picked up by a Valentia. The other features which made January 1940 memorable were two severe sandstorms. Although many of the squadron's personnel had been in Egypt for some time and were already well acclimatised, there were still many tricks to be learned about living and operating under canvas in the desert and sandstorms such as these taught many practical lessons. Another practical lesson had been learned a couple of months earlier when a torrential downpour had washed out the camp, obliging the squadron to spend the 9th and 10th of November re-erecting their bell tents on a site which would be less prone to flash floods. The camp, incidentally, was not entirely tented. Like any military unit obliged to live under primitive conditions for any length of time the squadron sought to improve its environment and several fairly substantial huts were cobbled together out of the timber from discarded and/or misappropriated packing cases. The best of these, since they provided the social focus for the squadron, were those which served as the Officers' Mess and the airmen's canteen. At this time the Flying Camels boasted the best pub in the Western Desert. It had to be the best; it was the only one.... Further entertainment was provided by an open air cinema on the ASP site which showed a film once per week. The weather in February continued to be troublesome and on the 19th Flt Lt George Bush crashed L8482 attempting to land at Fuka in a sandstorm. The aeroplane was a complete write-off but the crew and all five passengers walked away.

The quite substantial airmen's canteen, complete with electric light, built at Fuka by No 45 Sqn. The skull and crossbones over the door are real! The murals include a painting of a troopship and the perennial cry of the overseas airmen, "ROTB", plus the statutory pin-up clipped from Men Only. *(L Wilde)*

By this time No 253 Wg's bomber squadrons had been established to have eighteen Blenheims each and in March there was a change of servicing policy; thenceforth the 16th squadrons were to carry out all inspections up to 180 hours themselves. As a result the detachments of tradesmen from Nos 33, 45 and 211 Sqns were released by the ARS on the and returned to their parent units. Despite regaining these men the shortage of manpower continued to be a problem since, at the same time, No 45 Sqn was notified that it was to become a mobile unit. This meant that it had to be equipped to an expanded scale and was entitled to a significantly increased establishment. An 'establishment', however, represents only an ideal numerical strength; what really matters is the manning level against that ideal. The squadron had started the war below strength and the original shortfall had not yet been redressed. Increasing the notional establishment only exacerbated the actual undermanning problem but additional manpower was now in the pipeline.

In the meantime the shortage of people could not be allowed to prevent the squadron from developing its operational flexibility and on March 18th Plt Off Frank Collins led a five-vehicle convoy down to Siwa Oasis to set up a squadron deployment exercise. On the 21st three

The No 45 Sqn detachment at Siwa Oasis in March 1940. (D F Rixson)

Fg Off 'Sooty' Wright outside No 45 Sqn HQ/Ops at Fuka in early 1940. (D F Rixson)

Blenheims (Flt Lt Garth Mills, Fg Off Dennis Rixson and Fg Off Charles 'Sooty' Wright) flew down to join them and spent two days undertaking photographic sorties from this primitive base.

An initial batch of thirty new tradesmen had arrived on February 29th and on April 4th another draft of twenty-three additional personnel was posted in, just in time to take part in a major trench digging programme. They were followed on the 26th by nine fully qualified NCO observers to swell the ranks of the few, like Sgts Hodder and Hill, who had joined the squadron on Wellesleys. The influx of more 'proper' observers was regarded with mixed feelings in some quarters as their arrival displaced several of the squadron's volunteer bomb-aimers, some of whom had been flying as such for over two years. Within a few months, however, several of these old hands would have remustered as air observers and once their qualifications had been endorsed they would fly with the squadron again.

Since December 1939 qualified WOp/AGs had been entitled to wear a standard pattern cloth flying badge which superseded the old 'winged bullet'; completion of the appropriate qualifying courses also carried automatic promotion to the rank of sergeant. As yet, however, none of the squadron's home-grown gunners had been formally trained. By mid-1940 most of the unit's observers (several of them ex-groundcrew) were formally qualified NCO aircrew but many of the Blenheims' turrets continued to be manned by increasingly experienced, but still technically unqualified, airmen gunners until August. The manning pattern reflected by the constitution of the crews which participated in No 45 Sqn's first operational mission (*see Figure 6.1*) was typical for a Middle East bomber squadron at this early stage of the war.

Additional personnel continued to trickle in, among them a new Canadian CO, Sqn Ldr J W Dallamore, who took over from Eric Webb on April 20th. By the end of that month the squadron numbered twenty-one officers, thirty-four NCOs and 265 other ranks to operate and maintain its fifteen short-nosed Blenheim Is. It was nearly, but not quite, up to strength. On May 3rd Plt Off A G Sheppard was posted-in. The first batch of observer officers had been commissioned as recently as March and Alfred Sheppard was the first of this new breed to join the Flying Camels.

While this expansion was under way there had been a brief burst of excitement on April 23rd when Plt Off J S Davies was despatched to investigate a report of an unidentified submarine. This was not the first panic of this type, hunts for phantom submarines having been ordered several times since Christmas. It proved to be as fruitless as all the others, however, and after spending three hours searching the designated area Jock Davies returned to Fuka having found nothing. Training events were still being mounted and between May 7th and 13th Nos 30, 45, 55 and 211 Sqns took part in a prolonged air exercise over various targets in the Nile delta to test their defences and to familiarise the population with air-raid precautions. On the 9th nine of No 45 Sqn's aircraft 'raided' Alexandria and Ismailia. After landing at Ismailia to refuel they flew back to the desert by night, exercising searchlight batteries en route. One aeroplane failed to arrive at Fuka.

Fg Off Thomas, Sgt Davies and AC1 Richardson were missing in L8472. Having failed to join up with the other aircraft after taking off for the return flight to Fuka, the crew had flown west alone but had become uncertain of their position. In 1994 'Cubby' Thomas provided the following account of this incident:

...we ploughed on in Black Out conditions, still no sign of Fuka. When the ETA came up I said, "Navigator where are we?" He replied, "I don't know, Sir. I think we are lost!" Whereupon I took the situation into my own hands and began a square search. Suspecting that we were south of track, I descended to put on my landing

lamp to see whether we were over land or sea. Just as I put my hand on the lamp switch we hit the deck at about 180 mph and still at 1,000 feet AMSL on my altimeter. We ricocheted off the ground and landed again in an ugly heap in the sand. Luckily I had taken my hands and feet off the controls and curled up in a ball in my seat. When we came to rest there was no part of the aeroplane remaining in front of me. My navigator, who had been sitting on my right, had disappeared. I found him with an awful gash in his knee caused by the jagged edge of the Blenheim as he had fallen out on impact. In the rear of the aircraft Richardson had had the instep of one foot trapped by one of the turret struts. We got him out and I dressed all the wounds as best I could using the first aid kit and then found that I too had a gashed knee which needed attention. I used the crash axe to remove the signal pistol which was fitted in the floor of the aircraft and we just waited to be found.

The following morning nine aircraft were launched to search for the missing Blenheim. It was not found at first but a second sweep located it near El Qattara when Fg Off Finch spotted a Verey light. He promptly landed alongside to render assistance and found the crew suffering from cuts and bruises but otherwise unhurt. F/Sgt Broadhurst also landed but hit a boulder which collapsed the stern frame of his L6664. Arthur Finch airlifted out the stranded crew and

After several months of interim colour schemes and experiments the situation had stabilised by early 1940 with the Blenheims reverting to their original Dark Green and Dark Earth with black undersides and codes neatly applied in pale grey. OB.X. seen here at Fuka. is a typical example. This was evidently a full power check on the engines as the wheels are still chocked and there are a couple of sand-blasted 'erks' perched on the tailplane to keep the back end firmly on the deck. (L N Boot)

136

Broadhurst was left sitting in the desert instead. A salvage party from No 1 ARS, led by the squadron's Fg Off J H Williams and WO Mounsey, set out from Fuka and by the 13th had L8472 dismantled and loaded for transportation. Repairs were also made to L6664 and on the 15th Broadhurst was able to fly it out.

The start of the German offensive against France and the Low Countries on May 10th made it seem increasingly likely that Mussolini would join in to take advantage of Hitler's success in the hopes that Italy would then be able to claim a share of the spoils. More trenches were dug; a blackout was imposed and the aircraft were dispersed about the airfield. Fifty airmen were checked out on the Lewis gun, a number of which had been provided for anti-aircraft defence and installed in gun pits. Defensive positions were manned from

"A competent NCO" demonstrates the correct way to dig a trench to an apparently bemused audience who were no doubt intent on keeping him at it solo for as long as possible. (L Wilde)

Anti-gas training was an occasional feature of the routine at Fuka. This is the recently arrived AC2 Les Boot getting his knees brown in May 1940. (L N Boot)

Two of the squadron's Arab bearers who had accompanied the squadron to Fuka. They were all sent back to Helwan in May 1940 when it looked as if the shooting was about to start. (I. Wilde)

Inside the Ops Tent at Fuka, early 1940. From the left Plt Offs George Cockayne, Dick Shepherd, Frank Collins and Ted Scoones. The figure at lower right has not been positively identified. (D F Rixson)

May 16th.

At about this time the locally-employed Egyptian labourers and bearers who had accompanied the squadron when it had moved forward from Helwan, many of whom had been with the squadron for several years and felt a considerable loyalty to the Flying Camels, were sent back to civilisation. They had done a good deal to lighten the airmen's load, especially while the squadron had been seriously undermanned, by undertaking many low-grade but essential tasks including, under suitable supervision, the onerous mounting of guards. With their departure the now increased guarding commitment had to be absorbed into the squadron's working pattern. A far more dramatic consequence of the departure of the bearers was that the whole squadron, including the 'erks', had to get used to getting out of bed without the luxury of an early morning mug of char being brought to them by 'Abdul'. There was talk of a second unit joining No 45 Sqn at Fuka so yet more trenches had to be dug for their benefit.

On May 20th Fg Off Dennis Rixson ('Tubby' as he was to be affectionately known by his airmen) took over C Flight from Flt Lt George Bush, relinquishing the post of Adjutant to Fg Off 'Cubby' Thomas. This relieved Thomas of the interminable chore of amending the Adj's copy of King's Regulations as he was now able to delegate this to lesser mortals. Flying training began to be restricted during May as the situation in France deteriorated, although a photographic survey was made of the aerodromes and camp sites at Mersah Matruh, Qasaba and Fuka on the 20th and the squadron contributed nine aircraft to yet another morale boosting flypast over Cairo on the 22nd. On landing back at Fuka from the second of these events the opportunity was taken to conduct a refuelling and rearming practice under operational conditions. There was also some limited night flying to keep the pilots current but apart from this the emphasis was on defensive preparations culminating in a practice air raid warning on June 5th and a mock attack on the airfield for the benefit of all the Fuka-based units on the 6th.

On 10th June 1940 Italy declared war on Great Britain. That evening the airmen assembled in their home-made canteen to be addressed by Sqn Ldr Dallamore. He explained the situation, told the men what was expected of them and wished them luck.

The squadron (and No 211 Sqn) flew its first raid early on June 11th. It was the first offensive air action of the war in North Africa. The aircraft and crews scheduled to fly the mission are listed at Figure 6.1. One of L6664's engines refused to start but the other eight aircraft took off at 0415hrs. Most carried a selection of 40, 20 and 4 lb bombs, although L8466 had two 250 pounders on board. In echelon starboard, the formation followed the coast to Maaten Bagush and Mersah Matruh then flew out to sea, coasting in again near Bardia. As they neared Tobruk at 0610hrs they turned to port and dived towards their target, El Adem airfield. Apart from the contents of two Small Bomb Containers which hung up, all bombs were dropped among the parked aircraft and the 4 lb incendiaries could be seen burning all over the camp site, which was also machine-gunned for good measure but several of the aircraft failed to rejoin formation after the attack.

One, L8476, was seen to be on fire as it left the target area. It crashed into the sea about 10 miles off Tobruk; there were no survivors. It was later learned that L8519 had crashed at Sidi Barrani with the loss of all three on board. Two other aircraft, L8469 and L8478, had sustained slight damage, from either shrapnel or AA fire, but both made it back to Fuka without difficulty. One of L8466's engines failed shortly after leaving the target but, by jettisoning all excess equipment, Fg Off Finch managed to keep it going for over 100 miles over the sea before the second engine packed

AC2 Les Boot perched on the tail of L8481, one of the aeroplanes which took part in No 45 Sqn's first mission of WW II. (L N Boot)

up just as the aircraft was crossing the coast and he crash-landed the aircraft near Buq Buq. The crew, who were shaken but otherwise unharmed, were picked up by a patrol from the 11th Hussars who took them to Sidi Barrani whence they were flown back to Fuka. Three aircraft had been lost; two had been damaged and six men were dead. The Flying Camels' first operation of WW II had truly been a baptism of fire.

The pace did not slacken; apart from having to patch up its own aeroplanes, nine Blenheims of No 55 Sqn from Ismailia arrived at Fuka requiring a quick turn-round by No 45 Sqn so that they could fly their first mission that afternoon. In fact No 55 Sqn then took up residence at Fuka and one hopes that they were suitably grateful for the trenches that 45 Sqn had already dug for them, and for the tents which had been erected in anticipation of their arrival by the ASP boys.

On 12th June the squadron took part in a night attack on Tobruk in conjunction with a naval bombardment. Led by OC B Flight, Flt Lt Garth Mills, six aircraft took off at 0245hrs. The weather was poor and only three aircraft succeeded in joining formation; they failed to locate the target and were obliged to bring their bombs back to Fuka. Fg Off G C B Woodroffe in L8481 never found the others and returned independently. L6663 suffered an engine failure and Sgt Grant was forced to abandon the sortie altogether. Having become airborne, after the rather unnecessary excitement of a night take-off in formation, Fg Off Rixson had problems synchronising his engines. He did not know it at the time but this was because he had kissed the ground with a propeller, bending a blade, during the take off run. His preoccupation with this problem prevented him from joining up with the others. He elected to press on alone and although he too failed to identify Tobruk he eventually dropped his bombs on a troop concentration at Bardia. Short of fuel and still having problems with his engines, Rixson eventually landed at Mersah Matruh and returned to Fuka by road, L8524 being ferried over later, after the bent prop had been sorted out.

The squadron was tasked with a series of small-scale attacks on June 13th. At 0700hrs Flt Lt Troughton-

Aircraft	Pilot	Observer	WOp/AG
L8478	Sqn Ldr J W Dallamore	Sgt C A Hodder	Cpl M B F Mackenzie
L8519	Sgt M C Thurlow	Sgt B A Feldman	AC1 H Robinson
L8524	Fg Off D F Rixson	Sgt J Sears	LAC G Munson
L8466	Fg Off A J H Finch	Sgt R Dodsworth	LAC Fisher
L4923	Plt Off R W A Gibbs	LAC A Strudwick	AC1 A A Meadows
L8469	Fg Off J H Williams	Sgt C Wordsworth	AC1 R W Reader
L8476	Sgt P Bower	Sgt S G Fox	AC1 J W Allison
L8481	Flt Lt P P Troughton-Smith	Sgt E B Ryles	LAC Cooper
L6664	Sgt I D F Grant	Cpl H Vipond	LAC H Ellis

***Fig 6.1.** Crews and aircraft detailed for No 45 Sqn's (and the RAF's) first offensive mission of the North African campaign, 11th June 1940.*

Smith and Plt Off Collins raided Sidi Azeiz aerodrome. Finding no aircraft on the LG they dropped their bombs on some MT vehicles instead. Half an hour later L8524 took off alone for Giarabub. It failed to return and Fg Off J S Davies, Sgt G E Negus and LAC J K Copeland were all posted missing. A third raid was launched at 0815hrs; the CO in L8478, Fg Off Williams in L6665 and Fg Off Wright in L8502. The target was Fort Maddelena. No fighters were encountered and the formation carried out a successful attack in the face of some AA fire. On landing at Fuka the same three aircraft were turned round and took off again at 1245hrs flown by the same crews. They delivered a second attack on Fort Maddelena then returned to base via Giarabub in the hopes of seeing some sign of John Davies and his crew. They observed that one of the hangars had been damaged and also saw the wreckage of an aeroplane; it may well have been L8524. It was later confirmed that there had been no survivors from the missing crew.

In its first twenty-three operational sorties the Flying Camels had been particularly unfortunate and had suffered much higher losses than the other Blenheim units; four aircraft and three crews represented something like 22% of its aeroplanes and 17% of its fighting men gone in just three days. On June 15th the squadron was stood down from operations and, their place at Fuka having been taken by No 55 Sqn, three days later they were transferred to reserve. The advance party of four vehicles set off for Helwan on the 18th under Plt Off Collins to be overtaken en route by the air echelon conveying ten officers, eleven SNCOs and forty-four airmen. They were followed by the main road party and the whole squadron was reunited at its pre-war base by the 22nd.

Being the reserve squadron did not mean that the Flying Camels were out of the war, however. To reinforce No 113 Sqn, three crews were detached to Maaten Bagush on June 26th to fly operations. Four days later the squadron was notified that Sgt R C Lidstone had been posted missing after his No 113 Sqn aircraft had been shot down into the sea off Bardia. Initial reports indicated that some of the crew might have been captured by the Italians after having taken to their dinghy but it was not until September 9th that confirmation was received that Sgt Lidstone was a POW.

Four more crews, this time taking their own B Flight aeroplanes with them, were loaned to No 211 Sqn at El Daba. The detachment is listed at Figure 6.2; note that there were still airman observers flying ops. These crews flew back to Helwan on July 6th having taken part in a successful raid on the LG at El Gubbi (Tobruk) the previous day.

In the meantime the squadron had been accepting some replacement crews and carrying out continuation training. On one of the latter trips Plt Off G A Cockayne burst a tyre on take off in L8478 on July 8th. Since this was a check ride Fg Off Williams was on board, as well as Plt Off Sheppard and AC1 Reader. John 'Red' Williams took over control and made a successful wheels-up landing, although both engines were damaged. While the squadron was rebuilding its strength there were still tasks to be fulfilled. For instance, two aircraft spent some time on a fruitless search for the CO of No 33 Sqn whose Gladiator had come down somewhere and on July 16th four aircraft were detached to Maaten Bagush to

search for the WOp from a No 216 Sqn Bombay who had wandered off into the desert after his aircraft had been forced to land; he was not found. Nos 55, 113 and 211 Sqns also provided some trade for the groundcrews since stood-down aviators would fly into Helwan on week-end leave and No 45 Sqn would oblige them by turning their aircraft round.

On July 9th the Blenheim in which AC1 A A Meadows was flying as gunner (he was then attached to No 113 Sqn) was hit by AA fire, the pilot being wounded in both arms and legs. Albert Meadows rendered first aid and kept the pilot from loosing consciousness during the flight back to El Daba. Operating the flaps and undercarriage, he then assisted the pilot in making a safe landing. Three days later he was awarded the DFM. He was the first member of No 45 Sqn to be decorated in WW II and one of the very few men to win a DFM in the rank of AC1.

In addition to the campaign in Libya, the Italians were also being engaged in East Africa and a request for reinforcements for the local air offensive had been sent to HQME. No 45 Sqn was nominated to answer the call and on July 21st they were warned to prepare six aircraft for deployment to the Sudan. An advance party of fifteen men led by Sgt Gwyther set off on the 27th, arriving in the Sudan on August 5th, and on the 29th six Blenheims of A Flight with a total of thirty men on board flew down to Erkowit via Wadi Halfa and Atbara. Led by Patrick 'Trout' Troughton-Smith the aircraft took off at 0630hrs and reached their destination nine hours later. The other pilots were Fg Off G C B Woodroffe, Plt Off R W A Gibbs, Plt Off C deW Richardson, Plt Off J M Dennis and Sgt W Beverley. Their aircraft were L6663, L6664, L8461, L8469, L8475 and L8537.

The first operation was flown on July 30th when Flt Lt Troughton-Smith bombed the railway station at Kassala. On the 31st this raid was repeated in conjunction with Wellesleys of No 14 Sqn; this time the detachment's three aircraft were led by Fg Off Woodroffe. Troughton-Smith led another three-aircraft raid on August 1st, obtaining several direct hits and starting fires at the fuel storage depot at Archiko, near Massawa. Several Italian fighters were seen taking off but there were no interceptions. The following day poor weather with a cloud base occasionally down to 300 feet disrupted a repeat performance. Despite the formation's having split up, the aircraft flown by Carlton Richardson and Gordon Woodroffe made individual attacks on Archiko while Sgt William Beverley unloaded his four 250 pounders among a group of Italian tri-motors, identified as Savoia-Marchetti SM 79s or SM 81s, at Asmara. The aircraft which had been to Massawa reported the presence of some submarines moored alongside the Abdul Kadar jetty in the harbour.

No 254 Wg decided to exploit the squadron's report. A Valentia delivered some anti-submarine (A/S) bombs from Port Sudan on the 3rd and the following day Fg Off

Aircraft	Pilot	Observer	WOp/AG
L8477	Flt Lt G O Mills	Plt Off A G Sheppard	Sgt E Fletcher
L6665	Fg Off J H Williams	Sgt C Wordsworth	Sgt T A Ferris
L8481	Plt Off R W A Gibbs	LAC A Strudwick	Sgt L C Murray
L8538	Sgt I D F Grant	Cpl H Vipond	Sgt H Ellis

Fig 6.2. Crews and aircraft of No 45 Sqn attached to No 211 Sqn 28th June-6th July 1940.

Woodroffe made a dawn reconnaissance of the harbour to confirm that the submarines were still there, dropping half a ton of bombs on Zula airfield while he was about it. The presence of the target boats having been confirmed, five Wellesleys from each of Nos 14 and 47 Sqns were despatched to carry out diversionary attacks near the town while No 45 Sqn's three Blenheims attacked the submarines. Led by Troughton-Smith the formation approached the target area at 12,000 feet before diving to 2,500 feet to deliver their weapons in the face of an intensive barrage of AA fire. All went according to plan; three submarines were observed and a direct hit was claimed on a submarine depot ship while another bomb exploded between two of the subs. On the 6th Gordon Woodroffe reconnoitred the harbour again and later that day three aircraft set off for Port Sudan to load up with more A/S bombs. The return flight, via the target, was hampered by poor visibility and Plt Off Richardson was forced to turn back with engine trouble. The remaining pair carried out successful attacks, Sgt Beverley's crew claiming a hit on a destroyer. Fg Off Woodroffe's Blenheim was hit in the cockpit by AA fire, the pilot being wounded in the left arm and shoulder, although he was able to fly the aircraft back to Erkowit. A final three-aircraft raid was flown against Massawa harbour on the 9th, all three aircraft claiming near misses on shipping.

On that same day the detachment was ordered to return to Egypt. They moved back piecemeal beginning with three aircraft flown by Troughton-Smith, Gibbs and Dennis on the 13th, the groundcrew finally reaching Helwan by rail on the 21st. In the course of this detachment the squadron's bombs were aimed by airmen for the last time, LAC Archie Strudwick having been responsible for the direct hit on a ship on August 4th.

During their short stay the detached flight had flown twenty-one sorties without loss and all but one of them had been successful. No 254 Wg had been very impressed with the squadron's performance and had appreciated the additional striking power which the six Blenheims had

represented. A formal appeal was made for them to be retained in the Sudan but this was overruled, although with the proviso that they would be sent back if and when operations in the desert permitted. While they had been at Erkowit the squadron had also been on show to the media. Two war correspondents, Messrs Matthews and Moorhead, had flown on the Kassala raid on the July 31st; a newsreel cameraman from Paramount had been carried in one of the aircraft which had attacked the submarines at Massawa on August 4th and, prior to the repeat attack on the 6th, three Blenheims flown by Troughton-Smith, Gibbs and Beverley had laid on an impressive display of low-level flying over the airfield for the benefit of the cameras of the press. Plt Off Bob Gibbs evidently gained a taste for this sort of ultra-low flying and after the detachment had returned to Helwan he was caught doing it again in L6664, but this time without authorisation. Since he had damaged his aircraft by striking the mast of a felucca sailing on the Nile a very dim view was taken of his exploit!

Whatever the pressing need for the detachment's urgent recall to Egypt had been, it seemed to have evaporated by the time they got there and the squadron was not called on for operations. They resumed their reserve status and carried on with training flying. In the meantime the opportunity was taken to avail themselves of Helwan's sports facilities and a squadron swimming gala was held on August 18th with a station event four days later, Mrs Dallamore distributing the prizes on both occasions. There was some excitement on the 23rd when Flt Lt McWhirter and Plt Off Sheppard were reported overdue in L2379, a Magister to which they had temporarily gained access. The carburettor float had stuck, obliging them to make a dead stick landing, but they were able to correct the fault and eventually returned to Helwan under their own steam, but not before a search had been started.

There had been another unfortunate incident earlier in the month, on August 8th. A number of the officers had been entertained at Ma'adi, just to the south of Cairo, by the 19th

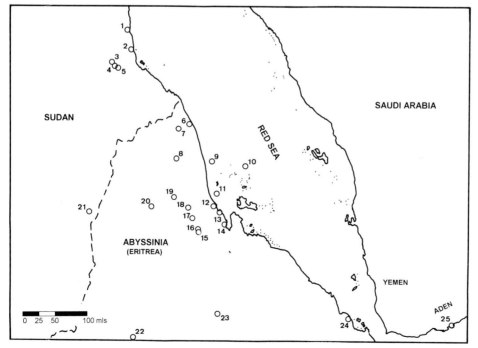

20	Agordat
23	Amba Alagi
13	Archiko
17	Asmara
24	Assab
10	Difnien Island
11	Dohol Island
7	Elghena
5	Erkowit/Carthago
22	Gondar
16	Gura
9	Harmil Island
21	Kassala
19	Keren
25	Khormaksar
15	Mai Edaga
12	Massawa
6	Mersa Taclai
8	Nackfa
1	Port Sudan
2	Suakin
3	Summit
18	Teclezan
4	Wadi Gazouza
14	Zula

Map 6.1. Abyssinia and the Sudan, the area covered by No 45 Sqn's operations in July-November 1940.

Btn of the New Zealand Regt. On their way back to base there was a road accident; the car rolled and inside it the rather substantial Dennis Rixson fell on top of 'Red' Williams. The upshot was that Williams' spine was damaged and, although not permanently disabled, he was declared temporarily unfit for operational flying and two days later he was packed off to the Pilots' Pool at Ismailia. August 8th had also seen a change among the squadron' executives, Flt Lt A G Dudgeon having arrived to command B Flight in succession to Garth Mills who had been posted to Aden. Tony Dudgeon was not to stay for long, however, as he was made up to squadron leader on September 24th and he left the squadron shortly afterwards.

The squadron developed quite a close relationship with the New Zealanders during the summer of 1940 and, while the Battle of Britain was being fought in the skies over England, in the Middle East they were playing cricket. Len 'Oscar' Wilde, then an LAC fitter, remembers taking part in a UK-NZ 'test match' which was held at Ma'adi at about this time:

> New Zealand batted first and the first wicket fell after a couple of overs. This was the cue for the appearance of a Kiwi who dashed around the field with a glass of *Stella* beer, the local brew, for each and every fielder, the umpires and the remaining batsmen. Two overs later two more wickets fell and two further glasses of *Stella* were downed by one and all. The fall of each wicket was lubricated by a glass of *Stella* and after six wickets the proceedings were getting a bit hectic. One bowler became very belligerent and had to be taken off 'drunk in charge of a ball'. A batsman refused to leave the field when out, owing to the absence of an umpire who had left to attend to a call of nature. The hilarious proceedings drew to a close at about 89 all out and, after sandwiches and refreshments, the Kiwis took the field. If the wicket had been three oak trees it is doubtful whether the bowlers could have hit it by this time! Highly dangerous though; most runs came from 'byes', rather than the impact of ball on bat. The trouble was that, as the wickets fell, the *Stella* flowed. Finally an honourable draw was declared and both teams got down to some serious drinking.

Since there was evidently no immediate call for the squadron's services in Egypt, HQME acceded to No 254 Wg's request and on the last day of August the squadron was warned for a return to the Sudan, this time at full strength. The crews which had been attached to No 113 Sqn since late June were recalled, the last ones returning to the fold on September 1st. On the 9th A Flight's six Blenheims took off for Wadi Halfa again; this time their ultimate destination was to be Summit. While preparations for this move were getting under way, a total of seventeen new NCO pilots and observers was being taken on strength. By this time most of the ex-groundcrew who had been manning the squadron's Blenheims since 1939 had already been regraded as NCOs and those who were still flying as airmen were now formally remustered as air observers or WOp/AGs and promoted to sergeant. When the squadron moved to the Sudan all of its aircrew were either officers or NCOs.

On the 13th an advance party of two officers and forty men with all the heavy kit set off for Suez to embark on the

LACs Jones and Toogood, AC Newbould and Cpl Eades setting up camp at Wadi Gazouza - bell tents again, but a little more vegetation than at Fuka. (L Wilde)

'A friend in need' - LAC Len Wilde helps LAC Jimmy Toogood to make his three pints of water per day go as far as possible at Wadi Gazouza. (L Wilde)

SS *Harpanicus* bound for Port Sudan. On the 19th Flt Lt Bush with four others on board headed south in L8525 to join A Flight. The main party of six officers and 214 NCOs and airmen began their journey on the 21st. They travelled by train from Cairo via Luxor to Aswan where they transferred to an ancient Nile steamer which took them as far as Wadi Halfa. There the kit had to be off-loaded and transferred to another train which carried them, in considerable heat and discomfort, across the Nubian Desert at about 20 mph via Atbara to Erkowit. Here they switched to trucks for the last leg to Wadi Gazouza where they set up camp under canvas on the 27th. The air party, led by Sqn Ldr Dallamore, and consisting of eleven officers and thirty-nine NCOs and airmen, had flown down in the remaining

C Flight at Wadi Gazouza. Front row, from the left: Cpl Peter 'Rastus' Hodkinson, Plt Off Eric Scoones, Fg Off 'Cubby' Thomas, Flt Lt Dennis Rixson, Fg Off Frank Collins, F/Sgt 'Twitcher' Birchall; Sgt Searle and two unidentified faces. C Flight named its aeroplanes for pubs in the Nottingham area. Providing the backdrop to this photograph is The Black Boy; other named aircraft included The Chequers, The Red Lion and The Cheshire Cheese. (C W S Thomas)

eleven Blenheims on the 25th. With the transfer of A Flight from Summit the squadron was once again united - eighteen aircraft and about 340 men in all. It is interesting to note that the squadron had more than doubled in size in the year since the war had begun.

In the meantime the 'old Sudan hands' of A Flight had been hard at it operating from Summit. The first three-aircraft mission had been mounted on September 11th, the crews having been briefed to bomb a fuel dump at Gura at 30 minute intervals. Unfortunately the weather was poor and two of the aircraft were obliged to attack the alternative target at Asmara and then divert to Erkowit[3] where they spent the night. Two days later another three aircraft did succeed in bombing Gura. Three more Blenheims scattered incendiaries and light bombs on the airfield at Asmara on the 14th, encountering some inaccurate light AA fire but suffering no casualties. On the 16th Plt Off Richardson returned to Asmara with Sgts Davies and Meadows in L8461 to carry out an armed reconnaissance, taking a number of photographs and delivering four 250 pounders and four 25 lb incendiaries while they were about it. The Blenheim was engaged by a Fiat CR 42 and although it sustained some damage the crew was unharmed and Richardson succeeded in bringing it back to Summit. On the 18th three more aircraft bombed Kassala and were intercepted by a pair of CR 42s, one of which was believed to have been hit by return fire from the Blenheims. There was a lull until the 23rd when three aircraft attacked Gura again, having another inconclusive engagement with some CR 42s in the process. The following day Plt Off Gibbs with Sgts Strudwick and

Murray flew a lone reconnaissance of Gura in L8475; they were twice intercepted by CR 42s but their attacks were not pressed home and the Blenheim returned to Summit unscathed. The last mission mounted from Summit, a raid on the airfields at Mai Edaga and Gura was flown on the 25th, again by three aircraft. The leader, Patrick Troughton-Smith, experienced engine trouble in L8469 and was obliged to return to base but Fg Off Woodroffe in L6664 and Flt Lt Bush in L8475 completed the mission in the face of some ineffective harassing attacks by CR 42s.

It fell to the experienced A Flight to fly the squadron's first missions from Wadi Gazouza on September 27th when a pair of aircraft, Plt Off Dennis with Sgts Ellis and Richardson in L8481 and Sgts Beverley, Ryles and Meadows in L8502, were despatched to reconnoitre Gura. They were intercepted by a pair of CR 42s which then failed to press home their attacks and both Blenheims returned to base undamaged. The following day three aircraft, flown by the CO (with Plt Off Sheppard and Sgt Mackenzie in L8473), Sqn Ldr Dudgeon (with Sgts Hodder and Fletcher in L8477) and Plt Off Collins (with Sgts Street and Crook in L8481), returned to Gura to deliver a total of 3,000 lbs of bombs. They were engaged by some light flak and a CR 32, but again the Italian fighter failed to press its attack. Gura was the target again when the CO, Flt Lt Rixson and Plt Off Cockayne (flying respectively with Plt Off Sheppard and Sgt Mackenzie in L8502, Sgts Sears and Munson in L8481 and Sgts Ferris and Reader in L8463) went back there on the 29th to drop another ton and a half of bombs.

A total of nine aircraft (L6664, L6665, L8452, L8463,

Photographed from a No 14 Sqn aeroplane, Fg Off Rixson flying The Cheshire Cheese *over Abyssinia. (D F Rixson)*

L8467, L8473, L8477, L8502, and L8538) flying in waves of six and three, hit Gura yet again on the 30th, delivering some 4½ tons of bombs. Both formations reported seeing Italian fighters and it had to be assumed that L6665, which failed to return, had fallen to their guns. The recently promoted Sqn Ldr Bush and Sgts J C Usher and J Corney were posted missing. It is probable that L6665 was shot down by Tenente Mario Visintini of the *412ª Sqa*; he was the most successful Italian fighter pilot of the East African campaign with a total of at least fifteen victories, one of them a Blenheim on September 30th. The loss of George Bush was felt particularly keenly by many of the airmen who remembered him from Helwan and the early days at Fuka. He had first joined the squadron when the Vincents had arrived, as long ago as December 1935. When he had been posted away in May 1940 he had promised that he would get back to the Flying Camels when the balloon went up. As good as his word, he had returned on September 4th only to be killed less than four weeks later.

On October 2nd the CO led a three aircraft strike against Mai Edaga, each aircraft delivering four 250 pounders and incendiaries. They were attacked by six CR 42s and this time the Italian pilots were far more aggressive and tenacious. L8452 was hit and crashed in flames, killing Sqn Ldr Dallamore and Sgt Mackenzie. Plt Off Sheppard succeeded in taking to his parachute and became a POW, although he was to be liberated in April 1941, a few weeks before the Italian Viceroy surrendered at Amba Alagi (although the East African campaign did not finally end 27th November). Flt Lt Rixson flying L8464 and Plt Off Gibbs in L8461 found themselves engaged in a fifteen-minute running fight with the persistent Fiats but eventually managed to shake off their

pursuers without sustaining any major damage. Had Sqn Ldr Dudgeon still been available he would doubtless have taken over the squadron but only the day before he had been posted back to Fuka to assume command of No 55 Sqn. On 30th September the squadron had had three squadron leaders; by October 2nd it had none. It thus fell to Flt Lt Troughton-Smith, as senior flight commander, to assume command pending the appointment of a new CO and the arrival of Flt Lt James Paine to succeed Tony Dudgeon's as OC B Flight.

The loss of John Dallamore shocked the squadron, especially the younger airmen. His concern for their well-being was widely acknowledged and half a century later those who remembered him still spoke of this and recalled that he could always find the time to give a quiet word of encouragement to a homesick young AC, disorientated by suddenly finding himself living in a tent in the middle of the desert thousands of miles from home. Some wept when they learned of his death.

Len Wilde has recorded some impressions of life in the Sudan. A particularly painful memory is the fact that only one beer ration reached the squadron during its entire two months in theatre - it was *Allsop's* lager, three bottles per man. There were occasional opportunities to hitch a ride on a gharry (truck) to pay a visit to the local metropolis at Erkowit. The chief attraction here was the 'swimming pool'. This was actually a flooded railway turntable filled with a murky fluid of uncertain origin, but it was the nearest, indeed the only, pool for hundreds of miles so it was plunged into with reckless abandon and no one appears to have caught anything incurable. The other luxury on offer in Erkowit was a mutton chop 'banjo' (sandwich), such tasty morsels being quite unobtainable at Wadi Gazouza. Len also recalls a more

A group of No 45 Sqn's NCO aircrew at Wadi Gazouza in front of one of the huts which had begun to appear before the squadron returned to Egypt. Left to right:- Sgt D Cliffe, Sgt J E Everington, Sgt E J Street, Sgt R H C Crook, Sgt I D F Grant, Sgt J McGurk and Sgt H Vipond. (D Cliffe)

operational activity:

Another busy chore was dummy flarepath duty. Every night a dummy flarepath would be laid out, miles away from the actual aerodrome, with the aim of confusing the enemy. It consisted of dozens of goose neck flares, laid out on an open stretch of scrub, which were lit and patrolled by the odd airmen unlucky enough to have been selected. It was a quite eerie. No wind, a starlit sky and a strong chance of an encounter with a wandering band of fuzzy-wuzzies who, being sensible chaps, travelled in the cool of the night. At 1130 pm prompt an Italian mail plane would drone overhead maintaining communications with Libya hundreds of miles to the north west. We were convinced that our flarepath served as one of its navigation aids! This flarepath business ceased after we left the Sudan and we never heard of its use again.

Operations continued on October 3rd with a successful six-aircraft raid on Agordat railway station, a further three aircraft making harassing attacks on a variety of LGs the following day. On the 6th Massawa aerodrome was the target for three more Blenheims. The next sorties were two individual reconnaissance missions flown on the 8th by Troughton-Smith in L8461 and Rixson in L8473. The former ran short of fuel and was obliged to put down on the coast at Suakin although the aircraft was flown out again once it had been refuelled. Gura was the target again for three aircraft on the 9th, on which date Plt Offs Gibbs and Dennis returned to Egypt with their crews to collect two aircraft from Helwan to replace those which had been lost. On the 10th Gura was again hit by three Blenheims in the face of some light AA; Italian fighters intercepted but failed to attack. The next day three aircraft flew a successful reconnaissance mission to Gura without delivering any bombs. Two bombing missions, each of three aircraft, were despatched to Mai Edaga and Asmara on the 12th; apart from Sgt Bain's being obliged to abort his sortie when L8469 developed technical problems, these raids were all successfully executed.

October 13th was a black day for the squadron. An initial three aircraft raid on Gura was intercepted, but not attacked, and was otherwise uneventful. A second strike at the same

target was a disaster. To start with, Sgt V J Griffiths experienced engine trouble in L8477 and was obliged to return early. The other two crews pressed on. Both failed to return. Fg Off Woodroffe with Sgts Ryles and Meadows went down with L8463; the squadron's Intelligence Officer, Plt Off L S Roberts, had been flying with them and he too was lost. Plt Off Cockayne with Sgts Ferris and Reader in L8502 were also missing. No raids were flown on the succeeding two days while an extensive search was made for the missing crews but nothing was found.

The new CO, Sqn Ldr V Ray, arrived in the Sudan on October 15th although he did not formally assume command of the squadron until November 5th. This must have left something of a vacuum as the Acting CO, Flt Lt Troughton-Smith, was posted to HQ No 252 Wg on October 22nd, command of A Flight falling to Fg Off A C H Haines who had been with the squadron since September 12th.

Operations were resumed on the 19th with a three-aircraft strike against Massawa. The next day two missions were flown, both involving three aircraft, the first to Difnien Island, the second to Agordat. In the meantime an Italian destroyer had been reported beached at Harmil Island and on the 21st three aircraft, each armed with four 250 lb bombs, were despatched in an effort to deliver the *coup de grâce*. The attack was made in line astern from 4,000 feet. The sticks dropped by the first two aircraft (Plt Off Gibbs with Sgts Strudwick and Murray in L8525 and Plt Off Dennis with Sgts Ellis and Cordy in L8549) both overshot the target. The bomb aimer in the third crew (Sgts William Beverly, Ronald Gentry and Victor Harrison in L8461) noted this and elected to release only his first bomb to avoid wasting the rest in similar overshoots. It struck the ship squarely on the stern, producing clouds of white and black smoke. The destroyer was later reported to have been scuttled and the squadron's star marksman was thenceforth known as Sgt 'One-Bomb' Gentry[4].

Len Wilde recalls an incident which occurred at about this time:

The fastest man in the world was a rigger on C Flight. He was a 5'4" LAC Fitter/Rigger; a pugnacious Scot known as Jock McKillop. A Blenheim was being refuelled and bombed up. The armourers were about to leave when an electrician who was testing circuits jettisoned the delayed-action fused bombs. The armourers' truck driver, hearing the thump of the bombs hitting the deck, slammed the lorry into gear and took off with sundry armourers clinging to any available hand hold. Little Jock, perched on top of the engine cowling checking the oil level, leapt through the prop; his legs, already working like the clappers, got instant traction as soon as he hit the sand and he took off like a proverbial greyhound. The truck driver, Cpl McLaughlin, swore he was in third gear, foot hard down and still accelerating when he glanced out of the window to see Jock overtake him. In fact the bombs had not dropped far enough to activate and all was well once the blue air had evaporated.

An attempt was made to neutralise Italian listening posts on October 23rd with an attack by three aircraft on two sites in the vicinity of Mersa Taclai. These targets were very small and dispersed, however, and were thus particularly difficult both to detect and to hit and none of the crews claimed to have been successful. Later in the day another three Blenheims successfully bombed Massawa which was a far more substantial target; No 254 Wg later reported that the bombs dropped by Dennis Rixson's crew (Sgts Jimmy Sears and David Cliffe in L8473) had hit the post office, which must have caused some disruption to Italian communications. Sqn Ldr Ray (with Sgts Hodder and Murray in L8469) flew his first sortie on the 25th, leading another three-aircraft strike against the Mersa Taclai listening post. Again an attack was carried out but, as before, the results were uncertain. There was a short break before the next mission, a raid by three aircraft on a supply dump at Teclezan on the 30th. Although the attack was delivered, once again the crews were not confident of the results since the target intelligence had proved to be poor and the aiming point had been difficult to distinguish.

On October 30th Sqn Ldr Ray set off in L8538 on a singleton raid against a W/T station at Nackfa. After spending over half an hour stooging about in the alleged target area without being able to find it, the crew selected what Intelligence had identified as an MT yard and attacked that instead. Since it looked more like a stable, however, they dropped only one bomb on it. With fuel still to spare they went on to have a look at the elusive listening post at Mersa Taclai. They found it but decided that it had already sustained significant damage, presumably from the attack delivered on the 23rd. One bomb was dropped on it, for luck, and the crew brought their remaining two bombs back to Wadi Gazouza. On the last day of the month Plt Off Collins (with Sgts Street and Crook in L6663) carried out another singleton strike against a W/T station at Elghena and three other aircraft bombed a suspected supply dump near Agordat, Flt Lt Rixson's L8473 returning with a single neat bullet hole drilled through its fuselage.

By November an air of semi-permanence had begun to percolate through to Wadi Gazouza and a few wood-framed rattan-walled buildings began to be erected. Nevertheless some sections, and most people, remained under canvas throughout their stay in the Sudan. One or two enterprising airmen, among them AC1 Dick Holloway, an armourer, paid some of the locals to build them native-style huts, reasoning that over the previous few thousand years they had probably evolved the most comfortable and appropriate style of accommo-dation. For a total outlay of about £3 a concrete floor was thrown in and the reed structures proved to be both cool and dry. Since the Sudan is such an arid region, 'dry' turned out to be a sur-prisingly worthwhile characteristic. The previous November's object lesson in the art of desert camping had already been forgotten by some. Despite there having been no rain at Wadi Gazouza for years, the airmen's tent lines had been prudently established on a low ridge but the officers had erected theirs (or could it be that they had been erected for them?) within the wadi itself. The inevitable happened on November

Some of the squadron's more enterprising airmen, among them AC1 Dick Holloway, paid some of the locals to build them native style 'hayshacks'. (R T Holloway)

12th when a sudden storm saw the officers washed out again. If there had previously been any doubt, this incident demonstrated quite conclusively that, however skilled the squadron's officers might have been as aviators, they certainly could not walk on water!

During November a further thirty-six bombing sorties were flown, many of them as singletons but occasionally in groups of three. Targets included Teclezan, Elghena, Zula, Dohol Island and Gura, but Agordat and Keren received most attention. On the 19th a lone Blenheim flown by Sqn Ldr Ray with Sgts Hodder and Fletcher bombed the railway station at Keren but was then intercepted by a pair of particularly persistent CR 42s of the *412ª Sqa*, although one of them was severely shaken by the explosion of the Blenheim's remaining 250 pounder which was jettisoned at low level in the path of the pursuing fighters. After a twenty-minute running fight, in the course of which the Blenheim sustained extensive damage, Vernon Ray being slightly wounded, the Fiats eventually broke off and the aircraft returned to Wadi Gazouza without further incident. Four days later, on November 23rd, the squadron made its last contribution to the campaign in East Africa when Fg Off Haines (with Sgts Wordsworth and Cordy), Plt Off Traill-Smith (with Sgts Hoyle and Liggins) and Sgt Beverley (with

This photograph was taken from the cockpit of Sgt Forder's L8377 as he followed OB.G back to Egypt at the end of November 1940. (L Wilde)

145

LAC Francis Stuart White of No 45 Sqn who was killed in an accidental fall from the upper deck of a Nile steamer on 30th November 1940 during the squadron's return to Egypt from the Sudan. (L Wilde)

Sgts Davies and Harrison) flew a successful bombing mission against Agordat.

While the squadron had been busy in the Sudan the Italians had been advancing into Egypt and they were now digging-in at Sidi Barrani. General Wavell was about to take action to eject them and the Flying Camels were required to support this desert offensive. In all the squadron had flown 121 sorties from Wadi Gazouza which, with the twenty-one flown from Summit by the initial A Flight detachment, made a total of 142 for the second deployment to the Sudan. Four aircraft had been lost in combat; twelve men had died and one had been taken prisoner.

As usual it took several days to accomplish the change of base, the first to leave being Dennis Rixson who, with Sgts Jimmy Sears and George Munson, had flown L8467 back to Helwan as early as November 11th, picking up Fg Off Thomas and Sgts Dodsworth and Fisher at Wadi Halfa on the way. The bulk of the squadron began its move back to Egypt on November 27th. The heavy kit, which included forty-eight vehicles, was driven in convoy to Port Sudan and

Cpl 'Donny' Brown, an armourer, was one of the mainstays of No 45 Sqn's football team for the three years up to 1943. He is seen here in late 1940, probably at Qotafiyah, sitting on a clutch of four 250 pounders, the standard load for the Blenheim I in the background. (A G McCandlish)

shipped to Suez on board the SS *Tyndareus*. For the main party the return journey was a replay of the uncomfortable experience of two months earlier, but this time it was marred by the death en route of LAC F S White who fell from the upper deck of the Nile steamer on November 30th. The first of the remaining eleven serviceable Blenheims reached Helwan on the 29th to be joined by the bulk of the squadron's manpower on December 1st and the heavy kit on the 4th. Since it provides an indication of the aircrew personalities at that time, the crews for the return flight are listed at Figure 6.3 (note that F/Sgt Birchall and all those with the rank of corporal or below were groundcrew tradesman - all groundcrew known to have been on strength are listed at Annex N.)

In addition to those listed as having flown back to Egypt,

Below:- The 500 pounder was an unusual weapon for Blenheims in the Middle East but the squadron dropped some while it was operating from Qotafiyah in late 1940. This is LAC Len Wilde with one of the big bombs. (L Wilde)

L8469	L8538	L8473
Sqn Ldr V Ray	Fg Off F G Collins	F/Sgt I D F Grant
Sgt C A Hodder	Sgt E J Street	Sgt H Vipond
Sgt E Fletcher	Sgt R H C Crook	Sgt J McGurk
F/Sgt Birchall	AC1 G R Aldhurst	LAC Easingwood
L8481	**L8479**	**L8525**
Plt Off B CdeG Allan	Plt Off E V G Scoones	Fg Off A C H Haines
Sgt A W Smith	Sgt J E Everington	Sgt C Wordsworth
Sgt L W Morling	Sgt D Cliffe	Cpl Eden
Cpl Anderson	LAC Starr	Cpl Wright
L8537	**L8464**	**L1534**
Flt Lt J Paine	Plt Off P J B Griffiths	Plt Off F W Chadwick
Sgt Chaplin	Sgt A C Tadhunter	Sgt Burns
Sgt C P Edwards	Sgt C Blackshaw	Sgt T Turnbull
Cpl J Eades	Cpl Burr	LAC Beer

L8477	L6663
Sgt G D Forder	Sgt W Bain
Sgt J Holdaway	Sgt Turnbull
Sgt Lidbury	Sgt Corcoran
LAC L Wilde	LAC Jones

Fig 6.3. *The crews and aircraft of No 45 Sqn which left Wadi Gazouza for Helwan on 28th November 1940.*

two other aircraft, L6664 and L4923, were left behind with No 52 RSU having their engines changed while L8475 was being stripped for salvage. Other pilots on strength at that time, but not allocated a Blenheim to fly back to Egypt, included Plt Offs R W A Gibbs, P C Traill-Smith, J M Dennis and R A Vinson and Sgts W Beverley and Harley. Additional observers, all of whom travelled with the main party, were Sgts S Davies, A G Grocott, H C T Holmans, H Ellis, R W Gentry, Hoyle and A Strudwick. They were accompanied by the following WOp/AGs: Sgts S C Cordy, Collins, V W J Harrison, Inganni, J Bullock, T O Liggins DFM, J P Charlton, Hall, J S McLaren, C Richardson, L C Murray and K Mills. To complete the picture the following officers, who also travelled with the main party, were filling ground appointments at that time: Flt Lt C E G Wickham (MO); Fg Off G M Darling (Equip); Plt Off C J Kirlew (Adj) and Plt Off S W Hodge (Cyphers).

On its arrival in Egypt the squadron was to be granted little respite. A group of newly posted airmen which had been assembled at Helwan to await the squadron's return was rapidly taken on strength and on December 8th the air party flew out to the desert again, this time to Qotafiya (also sometimes referred to as Qu'ttaf) where they rendezvoused with the groundcrew who had set off the day before. On the

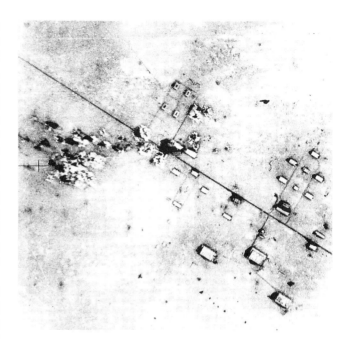

Bomb strikes on El Adem from a Blenheim of No 45 Sqn. 9th December 1940. (Author's collection)

Fg Off 'Cubby' Thomas with C Flight's L6663. The Chequers. The photograph was taken at Qotafiyah on 9th December 1940 shortly after the aeroplane had landed after a raid on Menastir. Although it had returned safely it had thirty-six bullet holes in its fuselage courtesy of a bunch of Italian CR 42s. Note that by late 1940 at least some of the Blenheims had had their black undersides repainted in a much lighter colour, probably a pale blue or something akin to the Sky which was becoming standard in the UK. (L Wilde)

A group of B Flight's airmen at Qotafiyah in December 1940. Standing, left to right: LAC Stone. Cpl Bassett Burr. AC1 Teddy Finlayson. Cpl Jack Eades. Cpl Jock Adams. Cpl Jock Leslie. unidentified. LAC Jimmy Toogood. LAC Durrant(?). Seated, from the left: Cpl Teddy Nutt. F Sgt 'Chiefy' Bates. LAC Tubby Beer. LAC Wylie. (L Wilde)

L1534/OB.K at Qotafiyah in December 1940. This aeroplane was damaged by Italian fighters during a raid on Menastir on 9th December and the pilot was obliged to make a single-engined belly-landing at Sidi abd el Raniman (between El Daba and El Alamein). The crew, Flt Lt Paine and Sgts Chaplin and Edwards, were not seriously hurt. (R T Holloway)

9th a flight of No 39 Sqn was attached to the squadron and on that day operations were begun. Ten sorties were flown, Sollum, Menastir and Gambut all being attacked. At least ten enemy fighters were encountered and there were several brushes with CR 42s. All of the Blenheims returned but Flt Lt Paine had to belly-land L1534 at Sidi abd el Raniman on the way back and several other aircraft sustained significant damage, notably Fg Off Thomas' L6663 which sported no fewer than thirty-six bullet holes in its fuselage.

This was the opening of the big push by "Wavell's 30,000", Operation COMPASS, and it was to involve the squadron in its most intensive period of operations so far. In the ten days between December 9th and 18th the squadron flew eighty-four sorties involving raids of up to nine aircraft at a time. Targets, in addition to those visited on the 9th, were nearly all airfields or seaplane bases and included Sidi Azeiz, Bomba, El Adem, Bardia, Tobruk, El Gubbi, Gazala and Tmimi, most of these attacks being delivered from between 10,000 and 18,000 feet. One aircraft and crew had been lost, L8465 having failed to return from a raid on Sollum on the 12th; Plt Off P C Traill-Smith, Plt Off V D Fry

Sgt Colin Blackshaw boarding a Blenheim. He was killed on 3rd January 1941 when his aircraft was shot down by CR 42s near Gazala. (L Wilde)

The Regia Aeronautica's Fiat CR 42s gave the squadron some problems in December 1940. This one, looking rather less fearsome than it once had, was one of several found at Menastir when the squadron moved in. (I. Wilde)

and Sgt T O Liggins were posted missing. There was a decline in the intensity of ops towards the end of the month, only two more raids being ordered. Three aircraft operated on Christmas Day but there was enough of a break to permit the traditional celebrations to take place, enlivened by the presence of the French Foreign Legion troops who were providing airfield defence at that time. On New Year's Eve the squadron despatched three aircraft to bomb Bardia, making the total for December ninety sorties.

There was no let up in early January 1941. The month began with a nine aircraft strike against Gazala, at least two large aircraft being destroyed on the ground. The following day it was the turn of MT concentrations at Bardia. Four missions were flown for a total of nineteen sorties to which No 39 Sqn's detachment added another two. On the 3rd another three aircraft attacked Bardia and two more bombed Gazala. This time the Italians reacted. A CR 42 engaged Flt Lt Paine's aircraft and succeeded in putting a bullet through the spar, although the aeroplane regained its base in one piece. L8479 was less fortunate, however, and was shot down into the sea in flames taking Plt Off P J B Griffiths, Sgt A C Tadhunter and Sgt C Blackshaw with it. On the 4th another pair of Blenheims taking part in one of several raids on Tobruk was attacked by seven CR 42s but this time they succeeded in shaking off their pursuers without damage.

Tobruk now became the focus of attention. Three aircraft went there on the 5th but were obliged to bring their bombs back due to adverse weather. Further, more successful, three-aircraft missions were launched against Tobruk on the

6th, 8th and 9th. On January 11th the squadron's air echelon and a groundcrew support party were redeployed to a benighted airstrip with the imposing designation of LG 81. The 'aerodrome' proved to be far too small to permit take offs by fully loaded Blenheims and no operations were (could be) flown during the six days that the squadron was effectively marooned at LG 81. That did not mean, however, that they had a pleasant break. Far from it. Because they fully expected to be moved to a more sensible site at any time the squadron did not even attempt to make camp and they slept in and under their aircraft. Their stay there was extremely uncomfortable. Furthermore, the logistic system failed to provide either water or rations and, to keep body and soul together, the groundcrew were eventually obliged to break into the emergency packs carried by the aircraft. It was with great relief that the air echelon learned on January 17th that it was to move again, this time to Menastir where an advance party from Qotafiya had gone on the 13th and where the whole squadron was now to be concentrated.

Menastir had previously been occupied by *the Regia Aeronautica* and was littered with unexploded sixteen-inch shells from a naval bombardment and numerous wrecked Italian aeroplanes. The next raid, again three aircraft to Tobruk, was mounted on the 18th, the day after the squadron arrived at its new airfield. On January 21st the demand was for a maximum effort during the final push on the town. The squadron responded splendidly. Operating in close co-operation with the ground forces, with a constantly advancing bomb line and with just eight serviceable aeroplanes the squadron put up the remarkable total of thirty-two sorties. The participating crews are listed at Figure 6.4.

Pilot	Observer	WOp/AG
Flt Lt A C H Haines	Sgt C Wordsworth	Sgt Eden
Flt Lt J Paine	Sgt H C T Holmans	Sgt C P Edwards
Flt Lt D F Rixson	Sgt J Sears	Sgt G Munson
Fg Off C W S Thomas	Sgt R Dodsworth	Sgt Fisher
Fg Off F G Collins	Sgt E J Street	Sgt R H C Crook
Plt Off J M Dennis	Sgt H Ellis	Sgt S C Cordy
Plt Off B CdeG Allan	Sgt A W Smith	Sgt L W Morling
Plt Off R W A Gibbs	Sgt A Strudwick	Sgt L C Murray
Plt Off F W Chadwick	Sgt Burns	Sgt T Turnbull
F/Sgt W Overell	Sgt T Gomm	Sgt Bishop
Sgt W Bain	Sgt Turnbull	Sgt Corcoran
Sgt G D Forder	Sgt J Holdaway	Sgt Lidbury
Sgt W Beverley	Sgt S Davies	Sgt V W J Harrison

Fig 6.4. *The thirteen crews of No 45 Sqn who between them flew thirty-two sorties during the final assault on Tobruk, 21st January 1941.*

Most people were content to acquire an Italian rifle at Menastir but LAC 'Oscar' Wilde went one better with this Breda light anti-aircraft gun. (L Wilde)

The camp site at Menastir with a couple of captured Italian motorcycles parked outside the tent. (L Wilde)

Three 'Italians' of C Flight, from the left: Cpl R Anderson, Cpl 'Rastus' Hodkinson and LAC Jimmy Starr. (L Wilde)

When operations were not being mounted, scavenging became an almost full time occupation as the victors helped themselves to the booty left behind by the retreating enemy army. Chianti and tinned tuna were found in abundance and every tent at Menastir had its own cache of such goodies. Among the more sought after prizes was one of the small Italian rifles. Scores of these were acquired along with ample stocks of ammunition and impromptu "shooting competitions on a scale to rival Bisley", as 'Oscar' Wilde describes them, were mounted out in the desert. Another manifestation of the British victory was the acquisition of Italian uniforms and for a while many of the squadron's airmen went about their business wearing these, B Flight's F/Sgt 'Chiefy' Bates, running his outfit tricked out in the regalia of an Italian general. Motoguzzi and Benelli motorcycles were also popular trophies. Several of these were found and the squadron's fitters found themselves besieged by hordes of wheedling aircrew bent on begging or bribing them to get them working. The high spirits were dampened a little on January 19th when two of the squadron's pilots, F/Sgt 'Lofty' Grant and Sgt Harley, were severely injured when they rode over a landmine on one of these machines.

Despite the sense of pride and achievement engendered

General 'Chiefy' Bates of the 45a Squadriglia Autonomo's B Flight. (L Wilde)

Each of them flew twice that day and several flew three times. Tobruk was taken on the 22nd. As the Italians continued to retreat the squadron harried them constantly, mounting a series of almost daily attacks on their airfields at Derna, Marawa, Appollonia and Barce for the rest of the month.

Ever since the squadron had moved to the west of Sidi Barrani just after Christmas the scale of the Italian defeat had become increasingly evident. The single road paralleling the coast was choked by thousands of demoralised and dejected Italian prisoners being shepherded back towards Egypt.

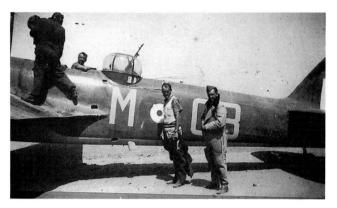

A crew boards OB·M before a desert sortie. The pale undersides indicates that this picture was taken quite late in the Mk I era, probably after the squadron's return from the Sudan. (I. Wilde)

On the way back to Helwan in February 1941 a group of the squadron's airmen pose by a marker stone erected by the Italians. The Desert Air Force was to take a fierce pride in its unconventional style of dress - No 45 Sqn were evidently trend-setters in this respect. (I. Wilde)

by the success of the British offensive and the almost festive air created by the windfall of luxuries and 'toys' which fell into the squadron's hands, it was never possible to forget that it was not really a game. Constant grim reminders of the fighting which had recently taken place were everywhere provided by the scores of Italian bodies that had been hurriedly buried in shallow graves but were then uncovered by the frequent sandstorms.

Peter Hodkinson writes of the sandstorms at Menastir:

Our flight had a marquee to live in and McKillop, in search of something to eat, left the tent during a storm. He was, of course, quite unable to see where he was going and got completely lost. Eventually he decided to stop wandering about and stay put where he was until the storm blew itself out. A truck found him sitting at the side of the desert road, still clutching his mug and 'irons', and gave him a lift back to camp. I remember that on another occasion I was working on a Mercury engine. I was trying to fit new pistons and already had the 'pots' off when the storm blew up - the crankcase just filled up with sand. As far as I can recall we had to abandon the aircraft.

As the British and imperial troops, the 'Benghazi Harriers', raced westwards the squadron maintained its contribution to the offensive. On February 4th two of the squadron's aircraft attacking Barce were bounced by CR 42s, and L8538 was shot down in flames. Sgt H C T Holmans and Sgt C P Edwards were killed but the pilot, Flt Lt James Paine, managed to bale out (this was his third major incident in eight weeks). He landed in territory which was still notionally held by the Italians but, with the aid of some co-operative Senussi tribesmen, he succeeded in making contact with friendly troops and was returned to the squadron. Having already put in several more sorties against Barce and Marawa, No 45 Sqn's last raids of the campaign were flown against Benghazi on the 5th. The town was taken the next day and on February 9th the offensive stopped at El Agheila. The Flying Camels had made a major contribution to the success of Operation COMPASS having flown at least 212 sorties since December 9th[5]. On the day that the advance halted the squadron began to withdraw to Helwan where it was to be re-equipped with 'long-nosed' Blenheim IVs, the

first of which was delivered on February 22nd.

So far as can be positively ascertained the squadron had flown 398 sorties with its Blenheim Is. This broke down into an initial twenty-three flown from Fuka when the North African war began in June 1940; a total of 163 contributed to the East African campaign, by A Flight's detachments to Erkowit and Summit and the subsequent deployment of the whole unit to Wadi Gazouza, and the 212 sorties flown in support of 'Wavell's 30,000'. The cost had been twenty-nine men killed in action.

Notes:

1. These early flirtations with desert camouflage were not confined to No 45 Sqn. The previously silver Gauntlets and Gladiators of RAFME's resident fighter squadrons had been hastily repainted in a variety of *ad hoc* schemes during 1939 and No 113 Sqn began a series of trials with a new colour scheme as late as March 1940. That a range of specific desert colours was required had been recognised since at least 1933, but those that had been developed to meet this need by the RAE were deleted in 1939 in favour of the prevailing temperate scheme. Despite the obvious need for a system of desert camouflage, and apparently quite extensive experimentation in the field in the months preceding Italy's declaration of war, by the middle of 1940 most combat aircraft were in UK-style green and brown and it was not until August 1941 that a desert scheme of 'Sand and Stone' with Azure undersurfaces was authorised.

2. 'Flash' Pleasance was to have a successful wartime career on night fighters, commanding No 25 Sqn and being credited with five confirmed victories plus one probable and two damaged. He retired in 1960 as Gp Capt H P Pleasance OBE DFC*.

3. The airfield at Erkowit had been officially renamed Carthago on 7th July 1940 but most references to it in the squadron's documentation still used the original name and this has been reflected here.

4. This ship was the *Nullo* which had been seriously damaged in a night action with the Royal Navy. It had not actually been beached but was seeking protection from the friendly shore batteries on Harmil Island. It was to no avail, however, and the ship could not be saved; her captain went down with her. Although credit for sinking the *Nullo* must go to the RN, that in no way minimises Ronald Gentry's achievement in gaining a direct hit.

5. The squadron's Operational Record Book (ORB - the RAF Form 540) for February 1941 contains a note to the effect that the unit had flown 270 sorties since its return to the desert on 8th December. This writer has not been able to validate this figure. The ORB appears to be reasonably comprehensive for this period and the author's total of 212 sorties is based on the information that it contains.

Chapter 7. Long-Nosed Blenheims - Cyrenaica, Crete, Syria, Iraq and CRUSADER.

Despite the scale of their recent triumph in Cyrenaica the British were not to retain the initiative for long. On February 12th General Rommel arrived in Tripoli to be followed two days later by the first units of what was to become the *Deutsche Afrika Korps* (DAK). This was not the only problem on the horizon, however, as General Wavell's Middle East Command was vast and many other demands were being made on his limited resources. One priority was to bring the East African campaign to a successful conclusion but even more pressing was the situation in Greece. *Il Duce's* invasion of that country from Albania in October 1940 had backfired somewhat; the front line was now on Albanian, rather than Greek, soil and it was anticipated that Hitler would soon intervene to redress the balance. It was therefore considered essential that Greece be reinforced. In early 1941 it was decided to despatch an Expeditionary Force and to strengthen the initial RAF contingent of Nos 30, 80, 84 and 211 Sqns, which had already been in Greece for four months. Nos 11, 33 and 112 Sqns were added in January/February 1941; now Nos 45 and 113 Sqns were to join them.

At Helwan preparations for the move were immediately put in hand. Thus, even as the squadron was taking delivery of its new Blenheim IVs and disposing of its old Mk Is, it was simultaneously packing its kit. There were some significant personnel changes too. Dennis Rixson, who was to end his career as Air Commodore D F Rixson CVO OBE DFC AFC, had left to join No 113 Sqn early in February, temporarily bequeathing C Flight to Fg Off Ted Scoones. With the squadron's withdrawal from the desert James Paine had also departed and command of B Flight had passed to 'Cubby' Thomas. Another change was the arrival on March 21st of Sqn Ldr J O Willis to relieve Vernon Ray who set off for Australia on April 1st, the new CO taking over his predecessor's very experienced rear crew, the newly commissioned Plt Off C A Hodder and Sgt E Fletcher.

By this time the squadron's main party was already en route for Alexandria and preparing to embark for Greece. Meanwhile Rommel's *Afrika Korps* had opened its offensive by taking El Agheila on March 24th. For a few days the

Germans were held but eventually they broke through. Agedabia fell on April 2nd and two days later Benghazi was back in enemy hands. No 45 Sqn was urgently redirected back to the desert to try to stem the flood. The next few days were pandemonium.

When the new orders arrived the bulk of the squadron's groundcrew were in two parties. One had already reached Alexandria, the other was in transit at Ikingi. There was a hurried reshuffling of personnel and the parties were reassembled as technical and support echelons. The former headed off 'up the Blue' by road with Plt Offs E R Butcher (Eng), A W Bennett (Admin), R D Culverwell (Equip), L Code-Lewis (Int) and S W Hodge (Cyphers). They reached Qasaba on 6th April, Sollum on the 7th and Gambut, where they made contact with the air echelon, on the 8th. The MO at this stage was Flt Lt F L E Musgrove; it is assumed that he will have accompanied the road party but confirmation of this is lacking.

The ninety-six men of the sea party under the Adj, Plt Off C J Kirlew, and Sgt N Maryon embarked at Alexandria, but instead of heading for Greece they sailed west, for Tobruk, where they came ashore on April 8th. Among this group was Wilf Worrall, then an LAC storeman. The following account of their experiences is based predominantly on his recollections.

They arrived late at night and were driven to a deep wadi which came to be known as 'Duff Gen Valley', owing to the many rumours and counter-rumours which it spawned. In the vehicle in which Worrall travelled there had been a Guardsman who tendered his warm congratulations on the party's having reached Tobruk but he was curious to know how they proposed to get out again, since the DAK was busy surrounding the town! Domestic accommodation in the wadi was a matter of staking a claim to a reasonably level area on which to spread a groundsheet. Come daylight it was discovered that the squadron was sharing the wadi with infantrymen who were using it to catch a nap between stints at the front. Two days after arriving the party was briefed that the town might well fall and that everything identifying the squadron was to be destroyed. After another two days an

This Blenheim IV of No 45 Sqn was photographed at Helwan and, judging from the Mk Is in the background, it probably shows one of the first examples of the long-nosed version to be taken on charge by the squadron. (I. Wilde)

army patrol identified one of the last gaps in the German lines just as the noose around Tobruk was being drawn tight. The squadron party boarded three trucks with the aim of making a run for it. While waiting on the edge of the town for an armoured car escort they were buzzed by two Bf 109s, which gave everyone a fright, although no one was hurt[1]. The convoy having been spotted, however, it was decided that the escape plan was now too risky and they returned to Duff Gen Valley.

Since they were now well and truly trapped it was decided that they should start to earn their keep and from then on the squadron's 'Tobruk echelon' was employed on the docks either as stevedores, unloading supply ships, or as lightermen, ferrying stores ashore. "It was a hair-raising experience to be working throughout the night deep down in a floodlit ship's hold surrounded by tons of ammunition with our presence clearly advertised by a spotlight at the masthead illuminating the lighter moored alongside." In all, the support echelon was in Tobruk for nearly two weeks before they were evacuated by a small freighter. Even this was a nerve-racking episode: "We were very puzzled at being told to remove our boots before boarding the ship. On crossing the gangplank the reason became very apparent - the deck was completely covered by live 250 lb bombs which had been salvaged from the airstrips." A day later the party was put ashore at Mersah Matruh and shortly afterwards they were

Photographed circa March 1941, Sgt Inganni, flew with squadron as a WOp/AG from 9th September 1940 until he was posted to No 113 Sqn on 9th June 1941. (L Wilde)

greatly relieved to be reunited with the rest of the squadron which had by then taken up residence once more at Fuka.

In the meantime the aircrew had been having adventures of their own. Led by James Willis, on what was only his second flight since taking command of the squadron, eight aircraft (R3733, T2049, T2174, T2249, T2339, V5573, V5592 and Z5898) and crews, mostly of B Flight, headed west in two groups of four on April 4th. Landing first at Marawa, they were immediately obliged to pull back to Derna where they arrived at about 1730hrs to supplement No 55 Sqn. The following day five of the squadron's Blenheims, accompanied by two of No 55 Sqn's, bombed Marble Arch. On the 6th the two squadrons began a fighting withdrawal. A six-aircraft mission was flown from Derna against Agedabia, the aircraft landing at Gazala whence a further four sorties were put up against MT concentrations at Mechili. The squadron despatched seven Blenheims from Gazala to attack Mechili again on the 7th. From this raid the aircraft recovered to Gambut and then launched four more sorties, again to Mechili. Mechili was the target for another six aircraft on the 8th.

Between the 5th and 8th April B Flight's eight aircraft had flown six missions, all led by Sqn Ldr Willis, for a total of thirty-two operational sorties while moving its base three times. The only available groundcrew had been the handful who could be crammed into the eight Blenheims and their contribution to sustaining the offensive effort can hardly be overstressed. LAC Len Wilde was a member of this party and he has provided the following graphic account of some of his personal experiences:

We flew from Helwan to Marawa, stayed about an

Sgt Forder poses with one of the squadron's early Mk IV's while LAC 'Oscar' Wilde appears to be administering a light flick of a feather duster to the top hatch. The photograph was taken at Helwan in March 1941. (L Wilde)

hour, and were then redirected to Derna. We operated from Derna and were refuelling and rearming when a bunch of six '110s arrived. The only road passed by the boundary of Derna 'drome and was crowded with retreating army units. The first sign of trouble was a loud bang as one of the trucks was hit and exploded as the planes strafed the road. Then they swung away, towards the juicier targets presented by our aircraft, and headed for us! I jumped off the mainplane and grovelled my way back to take cover under the tailplane. Bursts of gunfire passed overhead and as the last of the fighters zoomed away I sprinted for a slit trench. The rear gunners of the '110s sprayed us as we ran and the bullets were like bees around us! I looked up from the trench and saw a '110 within a few yards of the tail of a 55 Sqn Blenheim which was trying to land. The AG in the Blenheim was firing back. They seemed to be glued together but finally the '110 broke away and the Blenheim landed safely. They were lousy shots though as only one of our planes had been shot up[2].

During this period we would see the squadron off on a raid, all pile aboard the remaining planes and retreat to a 'drome further back, to which the raiders would recover. After Derna we went to Gazala. At dusk we were bedding down under the planes' wings when an Australian padre arrived in a staff car. He gave each of us a tin of peaches and a wonderful bottle of beer! To this day I still remember it as the finest beer of my life - absolute nectar! Sadly the padre was killed in one of our squadron 'planes. Shortly after taking off from inside Tobruk at dawn, with him as a passenger, it was shot down into the sea[3].

The following day was unique. The squadron had a raid to do. All the groundcrew, with their tools and kit couldn't fit in the one remaining plane. F/Sgt Bates volunteered to stay behind and kindly volunteered Cpl Jack Eades and myself to be his companions! One of the planes flying the raid was detailed to drop in at Gazala on the way back to pick us up. Off they went and we sat, alone and a trifle disconcerted, on our tool boxes. The escarpment to the west was alive with the movement of trucks and other vehicles; heliographs were flashing and there were the constant thuds and thumps of explosions. A staff car and a lorry circled the 'drome salvaging oil and petrol and eventually reached us. The officer in charge of the party advised us to go with them or to walk due east 'a bit sharpish'. We put our faith in the squadron and elected to wait for our promised pick-up. The salvage party set fire to a crashed Blenheim and went on their way. By this time Chiefy was getting decidedly restless but then we heard a familiar drone in the sky - our lovely squadron. One Blenheim broke away and landed and Plt Off Chadwick taxied over to us. He kept the engines running while we scrambled aboard in double quick time with (most of) our gear. Then we took off, right over the burning Blenheim. No sooner were we airborne than Chiefy Bates, who had been checking over the toolboxes, announced that one of the ones we had abandoned had contained his pistol. On balance, however, he decided to accept whatever retribution might come his way rather than ask the pilot to return to Gazala! We landed at

Plt Off Leonard Code-Lewis, a Rhodesian tobacco-farmer who joined the squadron early in 1941 and served as its Intelligence and Briefing Officer until October. Known informally as 'Felix', he was rarely without his pipe. (L E Durrant)

Gambut to find that most of the rest of the groundcrew had now arrived. I spent the next hour shooting them the biggest line possible!

The road party from Egypt had reached Gambut on April 8th but the advancing Axis forces obliged them to retrace their steps to Qasaba on the 9th. That day most of the aircraft pulled back to Qasaba as well but two crews (those of Sqn Ldr Willis and Plt Off Allan) flew to the LG at El Gubbi, within the Tobruk perimeter, whence they made another attack on Mechili. At dusk they took off again and flew to Maaten Bagush for the night, rejoining the rest of the air echelon and the groundcrew at Qasaba on the 10th. Additional crews had arrived from Egypt by this time and four aircraft had attacked MT at El Adem that day. On the 11th a pair bombed Acroma while another five aircraft attacked enemy troops who were fast closing the ring around Tobruk, three of the latter formation being hit by shell splinters from accurate AA fire. The following day the squadron despatched a three-aircraft raid against MT near Gambut, landing at El Gubbi whence a second raid (involving only twenty minutes of flight time, out and back) was launched against MT near El Adem. Having first landed again at El Gubbi the Blenheims finally flew back to Qasaba late in the afternoon.

The air echelon moved yet again on the 13th, this time right back to its old stamping ground at Fuka. On the way all eight aircraft attacked the besiegers of Tobruk at El Adem and, having delivered their bombs, landed at El Gubbi to rearm, subsequently taking off again under shell fire to carry out yet another attack before heading for Fuka where the rest of the squadron was concentrating and had already begun to mount raids.

By the time that the squadron reached the comparative safety of Fuka on April 13th it had flown sixty-seven bombing sorties since its hurried redeployment to the desert

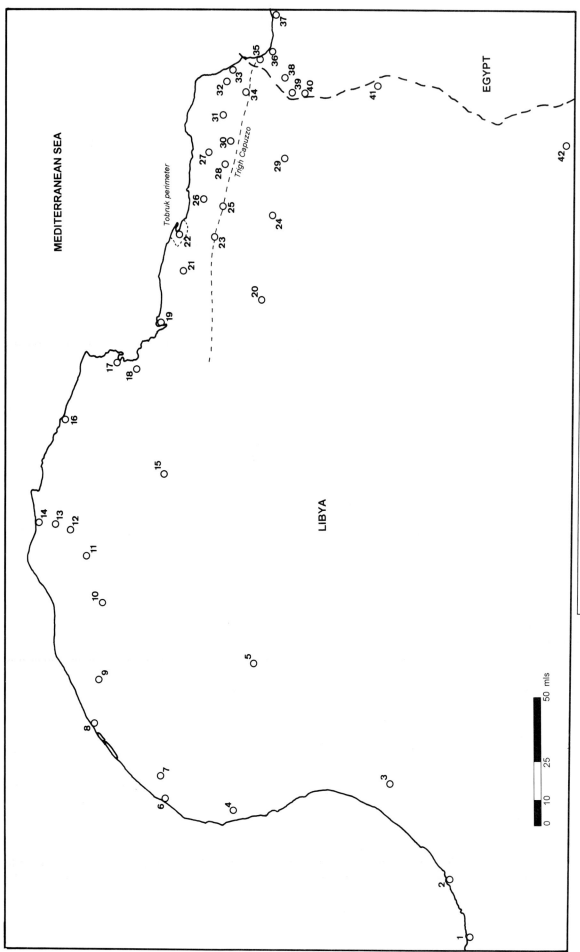

MEDITERRANEAN SEA

Tobruk perimeter

Trigh Capuzzo

LIBYA

EGYPT

| 0 | 10 | 25 | 50 mls |

Map 7.1. Cyrenaica, the area of North Africa over which the squadron fought in 1940-41. This map is also relevant to Chapters 6 and 8.

21	Acroma	1	El Agheila	27	Gambut	10	Marawa	39	Sidi Omar
3	Agedabia	12	El Faidia	30	Gasr el Arid	15	Mechili	25	Sidi Rezegh
14	Appollonia	22	El Gubbi	19	Gazala	32	Menastir	11	Slonta
9	Barce	38	Fort Capuzzo	4	Ghemines	2	Mersa Brega	35	Sollum
33	Bardia	41	Fort Maddelena	42	Giarabub	5	Msus	18	Tmimi
6	Benghazi	29	Gabr Saleh	36	Halfaya	34	Sidi Azeiz	8	Tocra
7	Benina	28	Bir Chleta	31	Bir el Baheira	24	Bir el Gobi	20	Bir Hacheim	40	Bir Sheferzen
17	Bomba	26	Bu Amud	37	Buq Buq	13	Cyrene	16	Dema	23	El Adem

154

on the 4th, to which could be added a number of non-operational flights as they moved from airfield to airfield. In those ten days its aeroplanes had flown from Marawa, Derna, Gazala, Gambut, El Gubbi, Maaten Bagush and Qasaba under conditions of extreme confusion and with minimal technical support. Sgt David Cliffe recalls that trucks would arrive at the aircraft, drop off a clutch of 250 pounders and a heap of four-gallon petrol tins and drive off, leaving the aircrews to prepare their own aeroplanes for the next sortie. There were no hoists or winches so the bombs had to be manhandled into the bomb bays. The squadron's performance throughout this period had been quite remarkable but it has never received the recognition that it deserved, perhaps because it was associated with a retreat rather than a victory. Nevertheless it is a record of which the squadron can be proud and it ranks high among No 45 Sqn's many fine achievements.

Under the circumstances it was surprising that there had been no casualties. One or two aeroplanes had been hit by ground fire, including Plt Off Allan's Z5898 on April 9th, but the only loss appears to have involved one of the aircraft from the rear party operating from Fuka. Z5894 was damaged by enemy fighters on the 12th and, after the crew subsequently lost their bearings in a sandstorm, the newly arrived Plt Off Paul Vincent was forced to land in the desert.

It would be another week before the return of the Tobruk party would see the squadron restored to its full strength but, by now reinforced by the arrival of further aircraft from Helwan and safely out of reach of the DAK, it was at least able to draw breath. Despite the continuing shortage of manpower, the relative stability permitted the squadron to redouble its efforts, many of the raids flown during the remainder of the month being mounted as joint shows with No 55 Sqn who were also based on one of the Fuka airstrips.

The recovery of the original party from Tobruk was not to be the squadron's last involvement with the besieged port as a party of about thirty men, many of them armourers, was later flown back there. They remained in the town for several weeks, acting as a rearming and refuelling party for aircraft, of any unit, operating into and out of the airstrips within the perimeter. Like the first Tobruk party they too found themselves occasionally working in the docks and they eventually got out on a small motor vessel which they had just unloaded.

The first joint No 45/55 Sqn raid mounted from Fuka was flown on April 13th when both squadrons attacked MT on the 'road' between Sollum and Msus. On the 14th, flying in formations of three, the squadron contributed twelve aircraft to raids on the Tobruk perimeter. The following day Tobruk was attacked again as were El Adem and Bardia. On the 16th a further twelve sorties were flown, the targets being parked aircraft at Derna, and concentrations of MT and armour at Acroma and El Adem. Over the next two days a further nineteen sorties were flown against MT at El Adem, Bardia and Derna. V5438 failed to return from one of the missions flown on the 18th. Fg Off F G Collins, Sgt E J Street and Sgt R H C Crook were posted missing. On the 19th and 20th the squadron, operating in pairs rather than threes, flew a further sixteen sorties, mostly against enemy transport at Gazala, Derna, Tobruk, Bardia and Acroma. On the 21st the squadron put up two major raids, each of nine aircraft. The objectives this time were the enemy's airfields at Derna and Gazala. Both attacks were highly successful and in the latter case the crews believed that they had accounted for at least six aircraft on the ground.

Thereafter the pace slackened a little, although daily raids continued to be flown. Four aircraft bombed Benghazi harbour on the 22nd, one of them failing to return. Sgt W Beverley, Sgt R W Gentry and Sgt V W J Harrison were posted missing in V5625. The following day the target was parked aircraft at Derna and on the 24th a total of eight Blenheims was despatched to attack Derna again and MT near Fort Capuzzo and Acroma. Returning at night from the last of these raids Fg Off Chadwick's T2170 lost one of its propellers but he was able to get the aeroplane down in one piece at Mersah Matruh. No bombing raids were flown on April 25th and 26th as the squadron spent both days flying in and out of El Gubbi under fire to evacuate personnel of No 73 Sqn and the staff of No 258 Wg from the beleaguered Tobruk enclave, a total of seventy-five personnel being airlifted to safety.

On April 27th an unidentified crew flew an important courier into Tobruk but their aircraft was subsequently damaged by enemy fire while it was on the ground within the perimeter and they were unable to complete their task. The following day Plt Off Bruce Allan and Sgt Len Morling were despatched in Z5898 to bring the courier out. By this time the *Luftwaffe's* I/JG 27 had reached North Africa; its

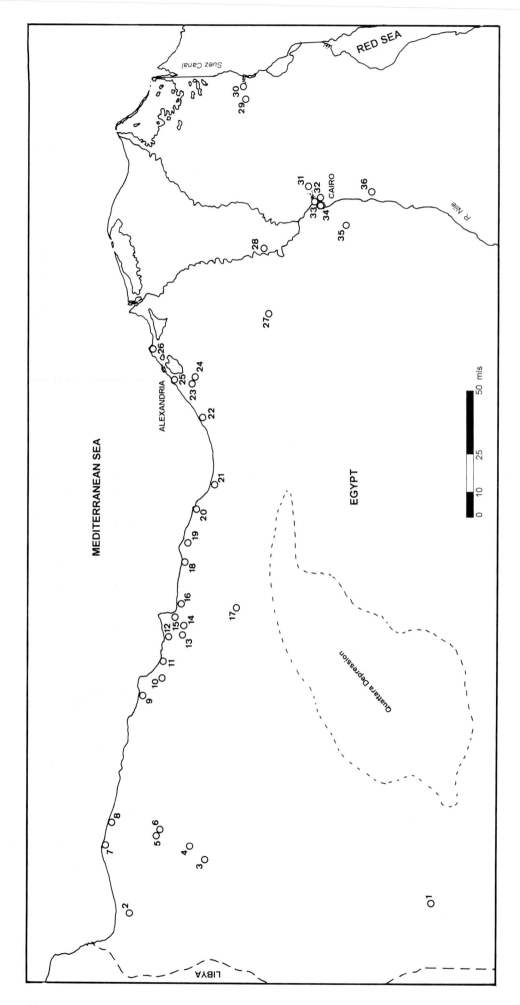

MEDITERRANEAN SEA

RED SEA

Suez Canal

ALEXANDRIA

CAIRO

R. Nile

EGYPT

LIBYA

Qattara Depression

0	10	25	50 mls

26	Aboukir	21	El Alamein	28	Gezai
29	Abu Sueir	19	El Daba	34	Gezirah
32	Almaza	35	Fayoum Road	31	Heliopolis
24	Amiriya	16	Fuka	36	Helwan
22	Burgh el Arab	15	Fuka Satellite (LG 16)	23	Ikingi
25	Dekheila	10	Gerawala	30	Ismailia

17	LG 53	13	LG 116	18	Qotafiya
5	LG 75	8	LG 121	20	Sidi abd el Rahman
6	LG 76	3	LG 128	7	Sidi Barrani
2	LG 81	12	Maaten Bagush	1	Siwa Oasis
14	LG 103	9	Mersah Matruh	33	Tura
4	LG 110	11	Qasaba	27	Wadi Natrun

Map 7.2. Northern Egypt showing locations and localities of significance to No 45 Sqn between June 1940 and February 1942. ie the period covered by Chapters 6-8 inclusive

156

Two of the three refugee Yugoslav SM 79s which caused a stir when they landed at Fuka on 19th April 1941 loaded, it was said, with gold bullion. They flew on to Heliopolis the same day and were later pressed into service with RAF as transports; this one became AX704.
(L Wilde)

Messerschmitts were now fully operational and as soon as No 45 Sqn's aeroplane began its take off run for the return flight it was spotted by a patrol of Bf 109Es. Five of them pounced on the unfortunate Blenheim, chased it out to sea and shot it down. All seven men on board were lost (the passengers being Wg Cdr D V Johnson, Sqn Ldr D P Barclay, the Rev Sqn Ldr J E Cox, Plt Off S E Beloe and Capt R S Oughwright). The victorious pilot was the legendary Hans-Joachim 'Jochen' Marseille, who was eventually to be credited with 151 aerial victories in Africa and was arguably the most naturally gifted of all *Luftwaffe* fighter pilots.

Four aircraft took part in a joint attack with No 55 Sqn on parked Ju 52s at Derna on the 28th; one of them, T2345 piloted by Sgt Naldrett-Jays, ran out of fuel on the way back and was forced to land in the desert about 20 miles south of El Alamein. It is believed that Sgt John Prockter was injured in this incident as Sgt Bissett later took his place within the crew, Sgt Dann continuing to fly as gunner.

Although neither had any impact on the squadron's operations, there had been two memorable diversions in late April. With the fall of Yugoslavia a handful of the Royal Yugoslav Air Force's aircraft had escaped to North Africa, some of them allegedly laden with bullion, the country's gold reserves. While of no direct consequence to No 45 Sqn, the arrival of three Yugoslav Savoia-Marchetti SM 79s in their midst at Fuka on April 19th certainly caused a stir. The second incident was a press visit by the prominent American journalist, Miss Clare Boothe-Luce. As the only female for miles around, her presence excited considerable interest. Len Wilde's account of her visit reads: "Tools were dropped, activities ceased and dozens of scurrying figures dashed to admire this vision. Our lords and masters, the officers, arrived en masse and, as was their right, took charge of the beauty! One or two of the more ambitious chaps arrived on the scene a little late, with traces of shaving lather around their ears, hopeful of attracting the lady's attention!" Since the lady in question was shortly to become a Senator and was later US Ambassador to Italy, it can be safely assumed that relations during her visit remained on an entirely diplomatic level and that they were conducted with the utmost decorum throughout; nevertheless her brief visit was still a topic of fevered discussion several months later.

April 1941 had been a hectic month. Some idea of the intensity of activity can be gauged from Flt Lt 'Cubby' Thomas' log book which shows that in the twenty-seven days beginning on 4th April he made forty-two flights, of which twenty-four had been bombing raids, accumulating 89 flying hours. On most of these trips, including all of the operational sorties, he had been accompanied by his regular crew, Sgts Dodsworth and Fisher. Another example is provided by Sqn Ldr Willis who had made thirty flights, including twenty-two raids. The crews on strength during this intensive period of operations are listed at Figure 7.1. It is interesting to note that RNZAF and SAAF personnel had begun to appear on the squadron for the first time during April 1941. This early trickle of aircrew from the Commonwealth was to become a flood by the end of the year.

The Axis thrust ran out of steam in early May and the

No	Pilot	Observer	WOp/AG
1	Sqn Ldr J O Willis	Plt Off C A Hodder	Sgt E Fletcher
2	Flt Lt C W S Thomas	Sgt R Dodsworth	Sgt Fisher
3	Fg Off F G Collins	Sgt E J Street	Sgt R H C Crook
4	Fg Off E V G Scoones	Sgt J E Everington	Sgt D Cliffe
5	Plt Off B CdeG Allan	Sgt A W Smith	Sgt L W Morling
6	Plt Off F W Chadwick	Sgt Burns	Sgt T Turnbull
7	Sgt W Bain	Sgt Turnbull	Sgt Corcoran
8	Sgt G D Forder	Sgt J Holdaway	Sgt H Marshall
9	Flt Lt A C H Haines	Sgt C Wordsworth	Sgt S C Cordy
10	Fg Off R W A Gibbs	Sgt A Strudwick	Sgt L C Murray
11	Fg Off J M Dennis	Sgt S Davies	Sgt C Richardson
12	F/Sgt W Overell	Sgt T Gomm	Sgt Bishop
13	Sgt E W McClelland	Sgt H Vipond	Sgt J McGurk
14	Sgt W Beverley	Sgt R W Gentry	Sgt V W J Harrison
15	Fg Off N W Pinnington	Plt Off H F Irving RNZAF	Sgt R J Martin
16	Fg Off J Beveridge	Plt Off A H Wise RNZAF	Sgt V J Griffiths
17	Lt D Thorne SAAF	Plt Off D Brooks	Sgt M Grant
18	Lt E Jones SAAF	Plt Off L P Bourke RNZAF	Sgt S B Whiteley
19	Plt Off P J Vincent	Plt Off S C Niven RNZAF	Sgt O B Thompson
20	Sgt P Naldrett-Jays	Sgt J R Prockter	Sgt A W Dann
21	Sgt N H Thomas	Sgt G R Adams	Sgt G K Grainger
22	Sgt G L Sulman	Sgt D Rhodes	Sgt D Thacker
23	Sgt S F Champion	Sgt G F Jones RNZAF	Sgt A W Phillips

Note. Crews Nos 1-8 constituted the squadron's forward echelon in Cyrenaica, 4th-8th April. Crews Nos 9-14 were those already on strength which took part in operations from 9th April onwards and Crews Nos 15-23 joined the squadron on various dates during the month.

***Fig 7.1.** No 45 Sqn crew state during April 1941.*

V5573 after Lt Thorne's successful one-wheel landing at Fuka on 6th May 1941. (L Wilde)

front stabilised in the vicinity of Buq Buq. Operations continued, but at a rather more measured pace. On May 1st two aircraft were despatched to find and bomb a tanker reported to be off Benghazi. They failed to locate it and attacked the harbour instead, achieving a direct hit from about 50 feet on a ship which was left burning fiercely. The following day it was back to attacks on MT; singletons harassing vehicle concentrations near Gambut and Tobruk while pairs went to Capuzzo and Bir Chleta. On the 3rd another attempt was made to find the tanker off Benghazi. Again nothing was found and while one aircraft dropped its incendiaries on two small motor vessels, claiming a direct hit on one, the other deposited its load on a concentration of MT near Ghemines. Four more aircraft, with others from No 55 Sqn, all loaded with 40 pounders, attacked the LG at Benina. The airfield was crowded with Ju 52s, possibly as many as seventy-five of them, delivering German reinforcements; much damage was inflicted.

May was particularly notable for the introduction of Blenheim IVFs. These 'fighter' aircraft carried a gun pack in the bomb bay with four forward-firing .303 Brownings. It was perhaps stretching a point to classify these aeroplanes as fighters, but their battery of machine guns certainly provided these Blenheims with an enhanced ground attack capability. On May 4th four aircraft went after MT again, two bombers to Gambut and two strafers to Marawa. One of the latter was obliged to abort with a technical problem but Sgt E W McClelland carried out a very successful ground attack sortie. Until the squadron's withdrawal from the Desert in June, the Mk IVFs were concentrated in A Flight which became the 'Fighter' Flight. Since no bombing aiming was involved, the Mk IVFs were sometimes flown by two-man crews, no observer being carried.

Operations were severely curtailed in early May by sandstorms which took a week to blow themselves out. This hampered flying activities considerably and although a few crews did occasionally manage to take off, none was able to complete its mission. One of these aircraft was involved in an accident on the 6th when V5573's undercarriage malfunctioned, Lt Thorne pulling off a successful landing on the one available wheel.

During May a revised War Establishment for light bomber squadrons (WE/122A), which had been published by HQME towards the end of April, was implemented. This involved reorganising these units on a two-flight basis, each to be commanded by a squadron leader, and raising the rank of their COs to wing commander. Since the squadron had effectively been operating as two flights since re-equipping with Mk IVs in March, matching itself to the new establishment was a relatively straightforward process. It was to be some time, however, before officers of the appropriate rank were posted-in to fill the new slots. Associated with this change was a restructuring of the squadron's deployment. Henceforth, only the aircrew, the first-line servicing teams and the armourers were to be forward at the operational LG. The rest of the squadron with the maintenance and repair facilities, for both aircraft and MT, its stores, medical facilities, administrative back-up and so on were to be located to the rear. To conform with this concept, in early May the squadron established its Base LG at Wadi Natrun under the command of Flt Lt G D Jones DFC with Flt Lt J P Brazil as MO, Lt A H R George as Assistant Adjutant and Plt Off W L V Logan as Cypher Officer. As this major reshuffle was taking place the squadron lost another of its stalwarts when F/Sgt C W Bates, B Flight's erstwhile 'Italian general', was commissioned into the Technical Branch; he departed on the 17th on posting to Helwan.

A break in the weather allowed Fg Off Gibbs, with Sgts Strudwick and Murray, to deliver 180 4 lb incendiaries on Agedabia LG on the night of 10/11 May in V5422. The following day three Mk IVFs, operating as singletons, went strafing in the vicinity of Sollum and that night the squadron made its first attempt to use the Desert Air Force's new secret weapon - the 'spike' (or 'prickle' as they were known in No 55 Sqn). Spikes were steel plates - basically triangular in shape, with about four-inch sides, but with barbed corners which were twisted so that whichever way up the objects

The Blenheim's bomb bay doors were normally held shut by bungee cord and were opened simply by the weight of the bombs falling on them. This aeroplane, Z9888/OB.A, is believed to be rigged for a 'spiking' mission as it has a number of containers in its bomb bay, the doors of which have been removed as the 'spikes' lacked the weight to ensure that they would open satisfactorily. (A Winston-Smith)

landed they would come to rest with one point sticking upwards. About 3,000 of these could be packed into containers carried in the Blenheims' bomb bays and, when the lids were released, they tumbled out to be spread liberally over enemy LGs to inhibit surface movement. The initial mission was flown by Sgts Forder, Holdaway and Marshall in T2056 but extensive low cloud over the target, Gambut, frustrated their efforts and they brought their load back to Fuka.

A second attempt at spiking was more successful when Fg Off Dennis, Sgt Davies and Sgt Richardson in T2339 deposited their cargo in a swathe across El Adem on 13th May, although a second aircraft, T2350 (Fg Off Pinnington, Plt Off Irving and Sgt Martin), was obliged to return early with a technical problem. That night it was Gambut's turn and the CO, with Plt Off Hodder and Sgt Fletcher in T2428, and Sgt Forder's crew in T2056 both completed their sorties successfully, despite encountering concentrated AA fire. Bu Amud received the same treatment just before dawn on May 15th. Plt Off Vincent, Plt Off Niven and Sgt Thompson were successful in T2056 but Norman Pinnington's crew were again obliged to abandon their mission, this time in Z5888. A few more spiking missions were flown but the tactic was soon abandoned. It could certainly be effective, however, as the squadron found to its cost when a 'spiker' inadvertently released its load at Fuka. Within hours much of the squadron's MT was immobilised with punctured tyres. The whole squadron had to turn out and sweep the airstrip line-abreast to retrieve the offending objects.

Another innovation introduced at about this time was the 'howler'. This was an air-driven fan mounted under the nose of the aircraft. Normally stowed with the vanes aligned with the aircraft's longitudinal axis, it could be rotated by the observer so that it faced the airflow. It then spun up and acted as a siren, emitting a high-pitched, and hopefully terrifying, wail - it probably unnerved the crew, who had to live with the noise permanently, as much as the enemy who only had to put up with it briefly as the aircraft passed by!. Like the spikes, this war-winning invention did not last long but Les Boot, then an AC1, recalls them being fitted on a number of No 45 Sqn's aircraft in May 1941.

Operation BREVITY was launched on May 15th with the immediate aim of regaining control of the Halfaya Pass and then, if possible, of relieving Tobruk. On the first day of the campaign four of No 45 Sqn's Blenheims participated directly in the attack by bombing, in concert with others from Nos 14 and 55 Sqns, a concentration of enemy infantry south of Halfaya. Thereafter the squadron concentrated on interdicting the enemy's lines of communication and attacking his MT. On the 16th four fighter Blenheims machine-gunned a convoy of between 50 and 100 vehicles on the Barce-El Gubbi road and caused extensive damage. A second sortie, by two strafers attacking MT between Tobruk and Bardia, was intercepted by three Bf 109s. V5817 was last seen being chased out to sea. The very experienced two-man crew, Flt Lt Haines and Sgt Stan Cordy (WOp/AG) were both posted missing; (by the time he was shot down Tony Haines had already flown the remarkable total of forty-eight bomber sorties and twenty-seven fighter patrols - many, but not all, of them with No 45 Sqn). Two aircraft attacked Derna LG at dawn on the 18th. T2056, with Fg Off Beveridge, Plt Off Wise and Sgt Griffiths, failed to return; Allan Wise, a New Zealander, was the first member of the squadron's Commonwealth contingent to lose his life. Later that day four Mk IVFs strafed MT between Barce and Slonta.

A total of twelve sorties was flown on May 19th. The first mission of the day saw five of A Flight's fighters inflicting heavy damage on enemy MT between Agedabia and Ghemines but one of them, T2179, was seen to crash into the ground and burst into flames. Its crew had joined the squadron only three days earlier and this had been their first

Seen here later in 1941, Sgt Harry Langrish was shot down over Crete in V5592 on 26th May. He found his way to the coast and after being evacuated on board HMS Kandahar he rejoined the squadron a few days later. (H C Langrish)

sortie; Plt Off D Carter[4] and Sgt H J Cassar were killed but Sgt G W Swanbo survived to become a POW. In the early afternoon four fighters strafed MT between Barce and Slonta and in the early evening three bombers attacked another MT concentration near Fort Capuzzo with 20 lb incendiaries, starting numerous fires. The following day two fighters machine-gunned Mechili LG, claiming to have destroyed one SM 79, a Ju 52 and a CR 42.

Meanwhile things had not been going well in Greece and the British and imperial forces had fallen back on Crete. On May 20th Germans paratroops landed at Maleme and No 45 Sqn's effort was diverted to the island's defence. Fg Off John Dennis had taken over A Flight after the loss of Tony Haines and, with Sgts Davies and Richardson, he flew the first mission of the squadron's brief campaign over Crete on the 22nd. They returned with valuable intelligence concerning an enemy convoy approaching the island from the north. This was subsequently attacked by other forces and a second reconnaissance later in the day found the convoy heading away from the island with several vessels on fire. A third mission failed to locate the ships.

Led by the CO in V5422, five aircraft set out to bomb Maleme airfield at dawn on May 23rd but the formation became separated in the darkness. Pressing on as singletons, the aircraft ran into a storm over the target and two crews were unable to carry out their attacks; the others managed to get their bombs away but only one crew was able to observe its bomb strikes. Four more bombers attacked Maleme with a mix of 40 pounders and 20 lb incendiaries in the afternoon.

This mission was more successful but the formation leader flew into cloud over the target and disappeared. Plt Off Vincent, with Plt Off Niven and Sgt Thompson in V5624, failed to return. One other aircraft was despatched on a shipping escort, although it failed to find its charges.

Escorted by four Hurricanes of No 274 Sqn from Gerawala, a pair of A Flight's Mk IVFs was briefed to strafe Maleme airfield on the 25th. This mission was only partially successful. To begin with, while positioning for the operation late on the 24th, Sgt McClelland crash landed Z5766 near Sidi Barrani; he was unhurt, as were Sgts Vipond and McGurk, but the aeroplane was definitely out of action. The second aircraft, T1823, took off as planned but again the formation was hampered by bad weather and only one Hurricane managed to stay with the lone Blenheim all the way to the target. Nevertheless the crew's perseverance and determination had been noted and it drew a personal message of congratulation for Sgts Champion, Jones and Phillips from the AOC 204 Gp (Air Cdre Raymond Collishaw CB DSO OBE DSC DFC). At about the same time a six-aircraft formation from Fuka bombed Maleme, claiming to have damaged at least a dozen large aircraft on the ground. In the afternoon, a second wave, this time of four aircraft, was less successful as three of them were obliged to return to base with a variety of technical snags. Meanwhile, other of the squadron's Blenheims shared with Nos 15 SAAF, 73 and 274 Sqns the responsibility for maintaining a protective patrol over the damaged HMS *Formidable*.

The Blenheim was never an aircraft that was able to cope with a determined fighter attack and two of the four which were despatched to bomb Maleme on May 26th were badly mauled when they were bounced by three Bf 109Es of JG 77. T2339 was shot down with the loss of Sgts N H Thomas, G R Adams and G K Grainger. V5592 was also shot down, although its crew survived. Fg Off T F Churcher and Plt Off R D May (who hailed from British Guiana) became POWs in Greece but Sgt H C Langrish, the gunner, evaded successfully for two days and three nights before reaching friendly troops and being evacuated to Egypt on the destroyer HMS *Kandahar*; he returned to the squadron on the 30th. The third aeroplane, T2350, escaped the fighters but got lost on its way back to base and the crew finally elected to bail out. Plt Off J Robinson and Sgt A F Crosby were eventually picked up after four days and five nights in the desert. Unfortunately their observer, Sgt W B Longstaff, wandered off on the first day; he was never seen again.

A three-aircraft mission was briefed to 'spike' Maleme on May 27th but Z5896 crashed on take off and burst into flames, killing Fg Off Norman Pinnington and Plt Off Howard Irving and causing the raid to be cancelled. Despite the explosions of 40 lb bombs and .303" ammunition, the gunner was successfully rescued from the blazing wreckage under the direction of Plt Off 'Felix' Code-Lewis. Sadly, however, Sgt Richard Martin had already suffered extensive burns and two weeks later he died.

For the rest of the month the squadron was tasked with escorting Hurricanes to Crete and then mounting standing patrols over the ships which were evacuating the troops by maintaining a shuttle between the island and Alexandria. These missions were flown twice daily by single Blenheims with as many Hurricanes as could be mustered, often only one or two. Considering the Blenheim's strictly limited capability as a day fighter these sorties were surprisingly successful and on 27th May Lt Thorne, flying T2243, engaged a Ju 88 and succeeded in damaging it. Sgt McClelland was even more successful two days later when he shot down a Ju 88 on the 29th while flying T2252. Confirmation of his claim was provided by the squadron's own Sgt Harry Langrish. In 1993 he recalled the incident as follows: "...on HMS *Kandahar* I had taken up position in the Signals Office. I heard the 45 Sqn call sign and knew that one of the aircraft was in the vicinity. The destroyer was then attacked by Ju 88s then the message came down saying that the Blenheim and the Hurricane escort had both destroyed a Ju 88 each."

Only three replacement crews had arrived during May and, although some of the nine men involved had survived, all had been shot down. With these added to its other losses, the squadron's fighting strength had been severely reduced[5]. By the end of the month No 45 Sqn could muster only six crews and eight serviceable aircraft and it had more or less fought itself to a standstill. On June 1st the AOC signalled his personal acknowledgement of their efforts and the squadron was declared non-operational. Two days later the main party left Fuka for Wadi Natrun followed by the air party the next day. By the 7th the squadron was established at its Base LG where it learned that Sqn Ldr Willis had been promoted to wing commander with seniority backdated to March 1st, ie three weeks before he had assumed command. The squadron now had a CO of the appropriate rank but there was still no sign of any squadron leader flight commanders so Fg Off John Dennis and Flt Lt 'Cubby' Thomas continued to fill the posts of OCs A and B Flights respectively. The groundcrew began to overhaul the few remaining aeroplanes but the shortage of aircrew grew steadily worse with the transfer of Lt Thorne and Sgt Sulman, complete with their crews (Plt Off Brooks and Sgt Inganni, and Sgts Rhodes and Thacker respectively), to No 113 Sqn on June 9th.

During May the squadron had received several formal messages of appreciation acknowledging their substantial contribution to the countering of Rommel's offensive. A more tangible form of recognition had been the award of a DFC to the CO, James Willis, on 18th May, this being formally gazetted on the 30th. By the end of that month the squadron had been at war for almost a year and actively engaging the enemy for all but a few weeks of that time. It had flown the first raid of the North African campaign, contributed significantly to the Italian defeat in East Africa, played a major role in supporting General Connor's rout of the Italians in Libya, and in blunting Rommel's subsequent counter-attack, and it had done its best to relieve the pressure on the troops in Crete and to protect their evacuation. In the course of these operations the squadron had had fifty-four men killed in action with many others wounded, taken prisoner or killed in flying accidents. Apart from Meadows' DFM, which had been awarded for a specific act of gallantry, the CO's DFC was the only other decoration to have been won by the squadron thus far, although a few of its personnel were later to be Mentioned in Despatches. This lack of official recognition was common in the Middle East; the work of many other squadrons, especially bomber squadrons,

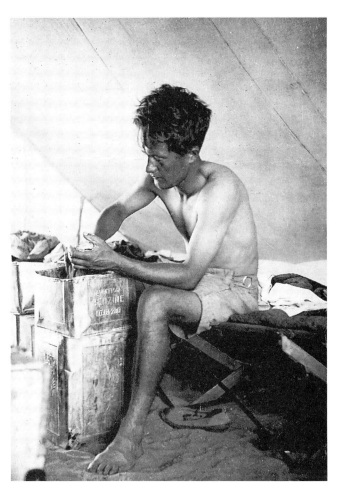

Cpl Pellow, one of the squadron's Fitter IIs, doing his dhobi at Wadi Natrun with the aid of a couple of petrol tins. (L N Boot)

was afforded much the same official indifference. For No 45 Sqn this was not a unique experience - it very closely duplicated the pattern of 1917 when, despite very heavy losses, its considerable achievements while flying 1½ Strutters had gone largely unrewarded.

The squadron's refit in Egypt was to be overtaken by developments elsewhere in the Middle East and it was to be committed to action again before it had been even notionally restored to operational status. On April 1st the pro-German Raschid Ali had staged a coup in Iraq and seized control of that country. After some initial hindrance of the movement of British troops (in contravention of the Anglo-Iraqi Treaty of 1930) the Iraqi army deployed first to threaten and then to attack the RAF base at Habbaniyah, and to cut the oil pipeline to Palestine. Fighting ensued but by the end of May Raschid Ali had fled to Persia and shortly afterwards the Regent was restored to the throne.

The Iraqi revolt had been provided with limited air support by the Italians and Germans and a composite force (the *155ª Squadriglia* of the *Regia Aeronautica* and the *Luftwaffe's Sonderkommando Junck*) had been deployed to Mosul to take part in the action. To do this they had staged through Syria and the pro-Axis sympathies of the Vichy regime there represented a considerable threat to Britain's already precarious position in the Middle East. With the collapse of the Iraqi revolt the French authorities had asked the Germans to withdraw their forces from Syria and by June 6th they had complied. Despite this, however, it was decided

LAC Kelly and AC2 Burrows brewing up on the way to Palestine in June 1941. (A G McCandlish)

to take pre-emptive action to preclude the possibility of a further Axis deployment and on June 8th British, Australian, Indian and Free French forces invaded Syria. On June 19th No 45 Sqn was ordered to move to Palestine to support this operation. Two days later most of the groundcrew left by road and rail, heading for Ramleh. LAC F Rushton had to be left behind in hospital at Wadi Natrun where, sadly, he died on the 22nd, the day the air echelon, such as it was, flew to Aqir.

One advantage of Ramleh and Aqir was that they did at least provide hutted accommodation, something of a novelty for the desert warriors of No 45 Sqn who were by now more accustomed to living like Bedouin and, to judge from contemporary photographs, looking like them too at times.

The squadron was still well below its fighting strength when it moved to Palestine, its overall experience level having been further diluted by the loss of several more of its stalwarts, including Fg Off Chadwick, Plt Offs Sears and

Plt Off John Kingsley 'Eddie' Edmonds joined No 45 Sqn on 26th June 1941 and found himself instantly appointed to be a flight commander. He is seen here flying over Palestine in July, "at 25,000' and -35°C". (L E Durrant)

Hodder and Sgts Fisher, Dodsworth, Richardson, Davies, Bain and Shalom, all of whom had been posted away while the squadron was at Wadi Natrun. In fact only five pilots, five observers and six gunners who had been with the squadron in May were still on its strength but within this small residual pool of manpower there was only one recognisable crew. With the numbers hastily made up by a few early replacements the air echelon consisted of just four nominally operational crews when it moved to Aqir on 22nd June. Until the 28th these twelve men flew all of the missions allocated to No 45 Sqn, a total of some twenty-two sorties.

Operations began on June 23rd when Wg Cdr Willis (with Sgts Wordsworth and Carthy) led two more of his hastily assembled crews (Sgts McClelland, Jones and Whiteley and Sgts Naldrett-Jays, Bissett and Dann) in a raid against Fort Soueida. The release gear on one of the aircraft turned out to be faulty and its crew had to abort the raid and fly out to sea to jettison their bombs. The other two crews attacked but without doing any observable damage.

While this first bombing operation was being flown, the only other available crew (Plt Offs Sam Champion and Lawrence Bourke with Sgt John Bullock) was carrying out a reconnaissance of Beirut in the course of which their Blenheim was bounced by four French fighters. They were very fortunate to escape being shot down, although their aircraft was damaged and a bullet through a tyre caused V5440 to ground loop on landing and its undercarriage folded up. The following day two more raids, in formations of three and four aircraft, were mounted against Fort Soueida, but neither succeeded in hitting it. On the 25th a single Blenheim reconnoitred Beirut and the following day another covered the coast as far north as Latakia while a second dispensed leaflets over Soueida.

By this time reinforcements were becoming available and the first three replacement crews checked in on June 26th with another three arriving two days later; all were relatively new arrivals in the Middle East, most having recently ferried Blenheims out from the UK. As the squadron's ranks swelled it became necessary to re-establish the two-flight organisation and one of the first of the new arrivals, Plt Off J K Edmonds, was nominated as OC B Flight in succession to Flt Lt Thomas, another of the very experienced men who had left the squadron at Wadi Natrun. The appointment of John Edmonds, a pilot officer who had only just arrived in theatre, to fill a squadron leader post on the very day that he reported to the squadron (June 26th) was a symptom of the unsettled state of the unit and it would be early July before sufficient new crews had arrived to restore it to anything like its established strength. Despite the previous operational experience of the replacement crews, which was in some cases quite substantial, most were new to the Middle East. They had had little time to become familiar with local conditions and operating procedures or to acclimatise themselves, and none at all to work with the rest of the squadron or to get to know its groundcrew. Nevertheless they had to be committed to operations immediately and with the considerable changeover in aircrew, for the first few days of the Syrian campaign, the squadron was not a very cohesive unit[6].

There had been little opportunity for training flying while the much depleted squadron had been at Wadi Natrun and

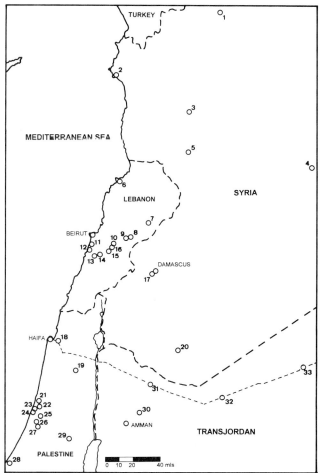

Map 7.3. Syria and Palestine, the combat zone during
the brief campaign of 1941.

16	Ain Zalta	32	H5	19	Muqueibila
1	Aleppo	3	Hama	4	Palmyra
18	Aqir	10	Hammana	22	Petah Tiqva
7	Baalbeck	21	Herziliya	27	Ramleh
14	Beit ed Dine	5	Homs	8	Rayak
13	Beit er Ramal	24	Jaffa	26	Sarafand
11	Chalde	29	Jerusalem	20	Soueida
12	Damour	2	Latakia	23	Tel Aviv
15	El Barouk	25	Lydda	6	Tripoli
28	Gaza	31	Mafraq	9	Zahle
33	H4	17	Mezze	30	Zerka

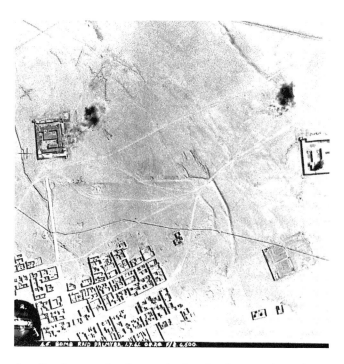

*A strike photograph taken as the first bombs went down during
the squadron's successful attack on Palmyra on 1st July.
(L E Durrant)*

there was certainly no time for a work up now; as a result
operational efficiency was somewhat below par to begin with
and the CO was disappointed with the bombing accuracy
achieved during the first few missions. He attributed the
poor early results partly to the relatively unfamiliar nature of
medium-level bombing and partly to the lack of experience of
the mere handful of 'scratch' crews that was initially
supposed to represent an eighteen-crew squadron. While
most of these desert veterans had already seen a considerable
amount of action as individuals, mostly on low-level
operations with No 45 Sqn, few of them had actually flown
together as crews before and it took a few trips before they
began to get the measure of each other's idiosyncrasies.
After a few days things began to settle down and when the
influx of new crews from the UK began to join in as well
bombing results improved rapidly. For old and new crews
alike, however, bombing was sometimes problematical in
Syria because of the paucity of relief information on the
available mapping. Most of the early attacks were conducted

from about 10,000 feet and, since it was often impossible to
determine the altitude of the targets with any accuracy, and
several of them were at a significant height above sea level,
this was bound to cause aiming errors and produce
systematic overshoots or undershoots.

Another coastal reconnaissance was flown on the 27th
while four aircraft attacked MT and gun positions near
Damascus. The bombers were engaged by AA fire and Sgt
John Bullock, a veteran of the Sudan, was severely wounded.
Plt Off Bourke attended to him as best he could while Plt Off
Champion landed V5968 at Mezze (Damascus) in the hope of
getting him to hospital. Sadly, their gunner died before
professional medical assistance could be rendered and his
place in the crew was taken by another old hand, Sgt
Lidbury. Three other aircraft, operating in conjunction with
No 11 Sqn, attacked French artillery positions on the
Damascus-Beirut road but again the bombing was inaccurate.
On the 28th one aircraft flew a reconnaissance to Tripoli
which also covered airfields in the vicinity of Homs and the
Baalbek Valley and five aircraft bombed Palmyra with
disappointing results. That afternoon three more aircraft
bombed railway sidings at Rayak and succeeded in straddling
the tracks.

The following day the new arrivals began to operate in
earnest and the squadron was able to put up a ten-aircraft
raid against Palmyra barracks. Again the bombing lacked
precision, but a repeat performance on the 30th was better.
Later that day three aircraft bombed, and finally hit, Fort
Soueida then strafed it and delivered leaflets; one aircraft was
damaged by AA fire but was able to get home. After a week
of 'on the job training' things were beginning to improve.
One other sortie was flown that day; a reconnaissance of the
area between Latakia and Aleppo.

July began with another ten-aircraft raid on Palmyra, a
successful one this time. On the same day the squadron's
base party moved up from Ramleh to join the operational

163

Pilot	Observer	WOp/AG
Wg Cdr J O Willis DFC	Sgt C Wordsworth	Sgt M F Carthy
Fg Off J M Dennis	Sgt H Ellis	Sgt J S McLaren
Plt Off J K Edmonds	Plt Off L E Durrant	Sgt K J Chapman
Plt Off R A Brown	Plt Off J Wright	Sgt J McGurk
Plt Off S F Champion	Plt Off L P Bourke RNZAF	Sgt Lidbury
F/Sgt L T Wilton-Jones	Sgt J C Wimhurst	Sgt D J Lowe
Sgt E W McClelland	Sgt G F Jones RNZAF	Sgt S B Whiteley
Sgt P Naldrett-Jays	Sgt Bissett	Sgt A W Dann
Sgt J H Tolman	Plt Off A W Hutton	Sgt D S J Harris
Sgt C Melly	Plt Off F L Rippingale	Sgt J Halsall
Sgt J Burns	Sgt J A H Kirkpatrick	Sgt J E White
Sgt Percival	Sgt Ainslie	Sgt V Day
Sgt F N Scott	Sgt Fry	Sgt D Catty
Sgt G M Hardy	Sgt J Newhouse	Sgt R Waddington
Sgt R Wood	Sgt R A Turton RNZAF	Sgt J E Wilcock
Sgt C G Hockney	Sgt Topping	Sgt Keating
Sgt L R W Howell RNZAF	Sgt K G Hodson	Sgt W Armour
Sgt Stewart	Sgt Colway	Sgt Catton
Sgt W M Osborne DFM	Sgt Martin	Sgt H Garfath
Sgt D A Cawthen	F/Sgt K R Cornford	Sgt W D Capewell
Sgt C E O'Neill	Sgt Bradford	Sgt Greenwood

Fig 7.2. Crews who flew on operations with No 45 Sqn during its participation in the Syrian campaign, 23rd June-11th July 1941.

echelon at Aqir. Also on July 1st, HQME fired a rocket in the direction of No 45 Sqn over the state of its Operational Record Book (*a criticism with which this chronicler has some sympathy*). In the squadron's defence the CO pointed out that over the last few months the squadron had been both highly mobile and almost constantly in action and that the succession of people appointed to maintain the ORB (under the overall supervision of the Adj and the Int Off) had displayed an unfortunate tendency to go missing! Nevertheless, he informed Group that he had chewed out Cyril Kirlew and Felix Code-Lewis and assured them that the Form 540 would be better kept in future. It was - for a while.

By now the squadron had largely shaken itself down again and bombing accuracy had been restored to acceptable levels. On July 2nd four aircraft bombed Soueida again while another carried out a long reconnaissance at 18,000 feet covering Tripoli-Homs-Rayak-Beirut. On the same day Sgt Pat Melly and Plt Off Fred Rippingale were despatched to search for and attack a suspected enemy convoy off Tyre. They found what they identified as three destroyers, two merchant vessels and one other large ship, radioed their location and attacked in the face of a heavy AA barrage, although they were unable to observe the results. In fact they had not hit anything, which was fortunate as the ships turned out to have belonged to the RN - which goes some way towards explaining why the Navy are often accused of being trigger-happy! Four other aircraft already en route were recalled. Later in the day, three aircraft obtained direct hits with their 250 lb bombs in yet another raid on Fort Soueida.

More new crews arrived early in July and by this time the squadron's strength had been substantially restored. The crews who flew on operations over Syria with the squadron are listed at Figure 7.2[7].

Three more reconnaissance missions were flown on the 3rd and 4th, the last of which was intercepted over Aleppo by three Vichy-French MS 406s of GC I/7. After a ten-minute running fight the Blenheim, which had been hit several times,

succeeded in escaping, Lt de la Taille being credited with a 'probable'. In fact the aeroplane, V6503, regained its base. The pilot and observer, Sgts J Burns and J A H Kirkpatrick, were unhurt but their gunner, Sgt John White, died as a result of the wounds he had sustained.

Two bombing missions were also flown on July 4th; four aircraft attacked parked aircraft at Hama, claiming to have destroyed at least two Martin 167s and damaged hangars, while six others attacked a suspected HQ in a chateau at Beit ed Dine. On the 5th twelve aircraft bombed Beit ed Dine again and although some bombs missed altogether, others did significant damage. On the same day the squadron was ordered to work in close support of the 7th Australian Div and A Flight, with twelve aircraft, was moved forward to Muqeibila where the crews and airmen resumed their familiar practice of living under canvas.

Sgt (later Wg Cdr) Ron Wood, one of the recent arrivals from the UK, recalls the *ad hoc* but quite effective tasking set up.

The field telephone rang and someone with the army moving up the coast asked, for instance, if we could put a gun out of action which was giving them trouble at Map Ref XXXXXX. I arrange to call back and then contact Jerusalem who authorise the operation and ask if we want a fighter escort - Yes please - OK, could you get onto 3 Sqn RAAF and arrange it with them. I call 3 Sqn and they agree to take off and join us when we fly over their airfield. It was all done in about 30 minutes - at the expense of some mild disturbance to the Aussies' permanent two-up school.

On the 6th a total of fourteen aircraft in three raids attacked targets in the vicinity of Damour with mixed results, although all the bombs fell in the designated target areas. The following day the HQ at Beit ed Dine was attacked, for the third time, by a total of eight aircraft, one formation of four putting ten of its sixteen 250 pounders on or near the designated aiming point. Three other aircraft attacked a bridge at Ain Zalta with unobserved results. On the 8th four

The air echelon (A Flight) moved up to Muqeibila on July 5th. This is the Officers' Mess. (L E Durrant)

The aircrew of A Flight shortly after their arrival at Muqeibila. Standing at the extreme left is Sgt Francis 'Scotty' Scott; third from the left is Sgt Gordon Jones and next to him is Sgt Pat Melly. Sixth from the left is Plt Off Fred Rippingale. Fourth from the right is Sgt Ron Wood. Of the group wearing the splendid Victorian-style Wolseley helmets (a sure sign of new arrivals in-theatre; most people who wished to wear some form of topee soon replaced these with the less overstated 'Bombay bowler'), Sgt Halsall is on the left and Sgt 'Tubby' Fry on the right. Seated, front and centre, is Sgt Mac McClelland with Sgt Ben Whiteley on his right (with a towel turban). (L E Durrant)

Peak-loading for Kiwis on No 45 Sqn was five, first in April 1941 and again in July. Seen here at Muqeibila are, from the left, Sgt Bill Howell, Sgt Bert Turton, Sgt Gordon Jones, Plt Off Lin Durrant and Plt Off Lawrie Bourke; all were RNZAF apart from Durrant who had enrolled in the RAFVR but eventually transferred to his 'own' air force in 1944. (L E Durrant)

aircraft bombed and started fires at a W/T station at Chalde (near Damour) while the bombs of four more aircraft straddled a bridge near Beirut. Another four-aircraft mission was aborted due to cloud cover over the target. On the 9th

ten aircraft were despatched to bomb an ammunition dump near Zahle. Only one attempted to attack through the 9/10ths cloud cover, the remainder attacking an alternative target with inconclusive results. Later in the day eight more aircraft made a successful raid on an ammunition dump at El Barouk while a singleton bombed another at Hammana. Meanwhile, back in the relative calm of Aqir the squadron's base party found time to field its football team for the first time in months and proceeded to beat No 11 Sqn 2:0.

July 10th was one of the blackest days of the entire war for the Flying Camels. Twelve aircraft were sent to attack the ammunition dump at Hammana with an escort of six Tomahawks from No 3 Sqn RAAF. The attack was a great success with many hits appearing to trigger further huge explosions. Shortly afterwards, however, the formation was bounced by six Dewoitine D.520s. The Tomahawks engaged them and claimed to have shot down all but one of the Vichy fighters but not before they had inflicted severe damage on the bombers. Three Blenheims were shot down. Sgts G M Hardy, J Newhouse and R Waddington were lost in Z9547. Sgts D A Cawthen, K R Cornford and W D Capewell went down in Z6455. The third loss was Z6433 with F/Sgt L T Wilton-Jones with Sgts J C Wimhurst and D J Lowe. Other crews reported seeing three parachutes which turned out to have been Cawthen, Waddington and Wilton-Jones, all of whom became POWs. F/Sgt Wilton-Jones suffered burns but was well-treated and was in hospital when he was liberated shortly afterwards by Australian occupation troops. He reported that his observer, Sgt Wimhurst, had also escaped from their burning Blenheim before it exploded, but that his parachute had failed to open. Six more aircraft had sustained varying degrees of battle damage and a seventh, V5926, was

165

This aeroplane, Z6155/K, began flying ops with No 45 Sqn during the Syrian campaign. It later found its way out to India (possibly with No 113 Sqn) and was eventually lost about 50 miles south of Imphal on 8th July 1942 while being flown by a No 45 Sqn crew on attachment to No 113Sqn. (L Wilde)

Z7509/S taxies in at Muqeibila. The airstrip was originally a melon field and the first order of business for the advance party was to clear it of its crop. (L E Durrant)

obliged to make a belly-landing; Sgts W M Osborne and H Garfath were slightly injured but the observer, Sgt Martin, was unhurt.

One further aircraft was written off that day after the squadron's last raid of the campaign. Three aircraft attacked troops at a road block at Beit er Ramal with a total of seventy 40 lb General Purpose (GP) bombs. V5968 had two hang ups which came loose at 50 feet as the aircraft was approaching to land. The aircraft was wrecked and its crew, Sgts Stewart, Colway and Catton, who had only recently joined the squadron, were lucky to escape without being seriously injured.

During the five days that the squadron had operated in close support of 7th Division they had flown seventy-one sorties in the course of which they had delivered a total of 53,560 lbs (about 24 tons) of ordnance comprising 124 x 250 lb bombs, 510 x 40 lb bombs and 540 x 4 lb incendiaries. Subsequently Maj Thomas Whittaker, who had been attached to the squadron as Army Liaison Officer, was able to visit some of the targets which had been attacked to assess the damage. In some cases, it was difficult to distinguish bomb craters from those which had been made by mortar and artillery shells, but in the case of the suspected HQ at Beit ed

Dine (which turned out to have been a chateau housing only a platoon of Lebanese troops) he was able to identify at least twelve direct hits. As the crews' reports had indicated, the arms dump at Hammana had been well plastered and the southern half had self-destructed as a result of sympathetic detonations among the stored ammunition. On the other hand, while the squadron's bombs had straddled the dump at El Barouk nothing vital had actually been hit and damage had therefore been negligible.

The primary conclusion of the major's report was that the destructive power of the 250 lb GP bomb, which was the squadron's heaviest offensive weapon, was simply inadequate. This was undeniably true, particularly where 'hard' targets were involved, and the problem had long been recognised. The abrupt dissipation of the dynamic energy built up by a bomb in flight will result in some damage when it strikes it target (like a cannonball) and, in order to prevent its breaking up on impact, the casing needs to be reasonably robust. But the real destructive power of a bomb lies in its explosive content. The bomb designer's problem is to get the balance right and the basic limitation of the GP series was that they were too much bomb and not enough bang; they were less than 30% by weight explosive and this simply was not enough. By late 1941 the more efficient Medium Capacity (MC) bombs began to appear, the explosive content of these rising to about 50%. It would be late in the war, however, before the MC series became available in overseas commands and there were huge stockpiles of GP bombs to be expended first. The squadron would just have to soldier on, but they were not alone.

The Vichy French authorities had agreed to a cease-fire which had come into effect at midnight on 11/12th July. All of the squadron's aircraft were prepared for further operations in the event that the cease-fire failed to hold, but the readiness state was sufficiently relaxed to permit the squadron to field its football team again at Aqir. On the afternoon of the 12th they played a local team from the

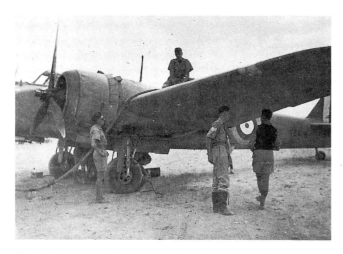

T2428/P being refuelled prior to the show of strength mounted on 28th July. This aeroplane was flown by Sgt O'Neill and his crew but Sgt K J Chapman (in flying boots) went along for the ride; Ken Chapman was killed in action when, by then crewed with O'Neill, he was shot down on 22nd November 1941.
(L E Durrant)

| Name | Trade | Raids flown | |
		Since 5/4/41	Total
Wg Cdr J O Willis	P	48	48
Fg Off J M Dennis	P	39	68
Flt Lt A C H Haines	P	22	48
Plt Off C A Hodder*	O	31	40
Sgt S Davies*	O	25	55
Sgt C Richardson*	WAG	25	44
Sgt C Wordsworth	O	38	72
Sgt E W McClelland	P	23	36
Flt Lt C W S Thomas	P	23	48
Sgt L C Murray*	WAG	29	45
Sgt J S McLaren	WAG	27	27
Sgt E Fletcher*	WAG	27	60
Sgt P Naldrett-Jays	P	24	24
Sgt A W Dann	WAG	24	24
Sgt G D Forder*	P	23	35
Sgt J Holdaway*	O	23	34
Sgt H Marshall*	WAG	23	23
Sgt S B Whiteley	WAG	22	22
Sgt G F Jones RNZAF	O	22	22
Sgt M F Carthy	WAG	23	28
Sgt R Dodsworth*	O	22	48
Sgt Fisher*	WAG	21	56
Appended to this list are the names of six more aircrew who, while they had not completed the stipulated twenty sorties within the specified period (the first three having been shot down) had also made notable contributions to No 45 Sqn's operational effort. They were:			
Fg Off F G Collins	P	12	43
Plt Off CdeG Allan	P	18	31
Sgt L W Morling	WAG	18	31
Sgt H Vipond	O	12	49
Sgt H Ellis	O	9	50
Sgt J McGurk	WAG	17	51

***Fig 7.3.** Summary of operational sorties flown by selected aircrew of No 45 Sqn as at 25th July 1941.*

Herzilian Sporting Club and beat them 1:0. Later the team and its large number of supporters were entertained to tea and a dance organised by a local committee, this unaccustomed light relief being much appreciated by all concerned. On the 14th the readiness state was further relaxed, although the Muqeibila echelon was still required to remain in situ. In the hope of avenging their defeat of 9th July, No 11 Sqn's footballers had requested a rematch and on the 15th the squadron obliged, this time beating them 4:1! On the same day a corporal and ten men were flown up to Palmyra in a Bombay to inhibit a number of Vichy aircraft which had been captured there.

On the 16th the Muqeibila detachment was reduced to a section of three Blenheims. Apart from one unserviceable aircraft, the remainder of A Flight returned to Aqir. On the same day a second party of groundcrew, under F/Sgt Chambers and Sgt Griffiths, joined the others at Palmyra while the squadron put up a twelve-aircraft formation from Aqir to make a lengthy (4 hrs 50 mins) demonstration flight over Palestine and Syria, being accompanied for part of the way by six Hurricanes of No 80 Sqn. Four aircraft flew up to Muqeibila on the 17th to relieve the detachment there but before the day was out they too were recalled. The squadron was now on stand-by to move into Syria and was required to have nine aircraft immediately available for operations. The remainder were at the CO's disposal for training, although all were to be ready to move anywhere within forty-eight hours.

Having begun the campaign seriously below strength, the squadron had been rapidly built up again but it had suffered a number of casualties and the first of another influx of new faces began to arrive on July 17th. Wg Cdr Willis took the opportunity provided by this quiet period to reorganise the unit. It had now been operating on a two-flight basis for some time, the flight commanders being Fg Off J M Dennis, still OC A Flight, and Fg Off L F Penny, who had relieved John Edmonds on the 11th to become OC B Flight. Most of the officers filling ground appointments at this stage had been with the squadron since it had re-equipped with Mk IVs or earlier, including Plt Offs Ernest Butcher (Eng), Arthur Bennett (Admin), Ron Culverwell (Equip), Leonard Code-

Lewis (Int) and Stan Hodge (Cyphers). There were two temporary shortfalls but a new MO, Fg Off P J Kelly, joined the squadron on July 31st and the Adj, Plt Off Cyril Kirlew, who had been admitted to hospital in Sarafand on July 10th, was replaced on August 3rd by Flt Lt P P Butters.

Although training flying continued, the brief period of calm allowed the squadron to indulge in some much needed relaxation. They were able to sample the delights of Tel Aviv and to swim, both in the sea and in a swimming pool. The football team, which appeared to be having a problem finding worthy opponents, played No 80 Sqn on July 17th and beat them 3:0, although they were held to a draw the following day in a match with the local champions from the Petah Tiqva Sporting Club.

On July 24th an eighteen-aircraft formation, nine each from Nos 11 and 45 Sqns, flew another demonstration over Jerusalem and Soueida as troops moved in to occupy the latter. On the 25th six aircraft flew a practice mission to the Amman bombing range and on the 26th the squadron flew yet another demonstration and played a return soccer match with the Petah Tiqva team - another draw. On that day the squadron was warned for a move to Iraq. On the 28th they put up a formation of eighteen aircraft to fly a demonstration covering Beirut, Homs, Hama and Aleppo.

Shortly after the Syrian campaign ended, HQ 204 Gp

The convoy stops for a breather on the way to Iraq. The rearmost of these three trucks has a novel numberplate which reads "CHRISSY". (R T Holloway)

A group of No 45 Sqn's support staff in front of the tent lines on Habbaniyah's polo ground, August 1941. From the left, back row, are AC2 Whybrow, Cpl O'Meara, LAC Coughlin and LAC Osborne; in front are LAC Morris and Cpl O'Keefe. O'Keefe was an accounts clerk, the others, all ACHs, worked in Ops apart from Whybrow who is thought to have been in the admin office. (J Coughlin)

Sgts Mac McClelland, Gordon Jones and Ben Whiteley (left to right) joined the squadron as members of three different crews in March/April 1941. In June they combined to make up one of the four scratch crews which constituted the squadron's total fighting strength when it was hurriedly redeployed to Palestine; thereafter they flew together until the end of October. (R Wood)

circulated its units asking for a list of those who had completed more than twenty missions since April 5th, roughly the date on which Rommel's initial eastward probe towards Mersa Brega had turned into the major thrust which had resulted in the loss of Cyrenaica. Since it presents an overall impression of the squadron's work over that period Wg Cdr Willis' response, dated July 25th, is reproduced at Figure 7.3. Note that only five of those listed had been with the squadron for the entire period under review. Flt Lt Haines had been shot down on May 26th; those marked with an asterisk had left the squadron before July 25th and most of the rest, including all of those whose sortie totals are the same in both columns, had arrived after April 5th.

The CO also took this opportunity to cite a number of other squadron personalities for a variety of specific personal achievements. If he had been hoping that this might have attracted some form of official recognition, he was to be disappointed. His other nominations were as follows.

a. Plt Off J Robinson for ensuring his own survival and that of Sgt Crosby after their crash in the desert on May 27th.

b. Plt Off L Code-Lewis for his direction of the rescue of Sgt Martin on May 27th.

c. Plt Off E R Butcher for the initiative he had displayed as Engineering Officer over a prolonged period involving

particularly difficult conditions.

d. Plt Off A W Bennett for his energy and administrative ability in co-ordinating, without loss of equipment or personnel, the squadron's sudden redeployment to Cyrenaica in April 1941 and its subsequent hasty withdrawal.

e. WO A W Brock for his devotion to duty which had contributed significantly to the large number of sorties flown by the squadron.

f. F/Sgt J F Chambers for his loyalty, energy and devotion to duty.

g. Sgt N Maryon for his leadership and resourcefulness, especially during the unscheduled period spent in Tobruk by a number of the squadron's airmen.

The move to Iraq began on August 3rd with the departure of the ground echelon. Travelling in the squadron's own MT, their route took them via Haifa, Mafraq, the pumping stations at H5, H4 and H3 on the oil pipeline from Iraq to the coast, and LG V (on the old Air Mail route) to Habbaniyah which they reached on the 7th. Fifty-one vehicles had set out and they all made it, bar one; the squadron's ancient crane, driven by LAC Peter Hodkinson, gave up the ghost trying to climb out of the Jordan valley. A vivid memory retained by some of the airmen who undertook this journey is of being shaken awake in the mornings by the Squadron Warrant Officer, Mr Dwyer, immaculately turned out with his buttons gleaming and presenting a marked contrast to the grimy, dishevelled appearance of the majority of the travellers. Despite being of the 'old school', however, the SWO was no martinet and his chief concern was to see that the job, whatever it was, got done and, although he always set a splendid example himself, he never let 'bull' get in the way.

It is interesting to note that in the six weeks that it had been in Palestine the squadron's fleet of aircraft had roughly quintupled in size. Before setting heading for Iraq on August 10th, it flew all of its Blenheims over Jerusalem in formation; there were twenty-one of them. On reaching Habbaniyah the squadron found that it was joining Nos 11 and 14 Sqns both of which had also just been redeployed from Palestine.

Habbaniyah was among the largest military bases in the Middle East and was well equipped with sports facilities, including a large swimming pool. It had, however, recently been knocked about a bit in the course of the Iraqi nationalists' unsuccessful attempt to oust the British. As a result it was unable to cope adequately with the large influx of bodies. Much to their disgust the squadron's airmen found themselves back under canvas again, on the (sand) polo field. A large proportion of the squadron promptly went down with sandfly fever. The inability of 'Hab' to make room in its ample barrack accommodation meant that its medical staff were to be severely overtaxed. In view of the numbers who succumbed to the fever, a hangar was converted into a sick bay. The patients were given a dose of 'the mixture', wrapped in a blanket, then a groundsheet and left to sweat it out in the heat of the Iraqi summer. Since most people were back at work in a couple of days it seemed to work - perhaps because the cure was worse than the symptoms?

Out on the airfield it was hot and uncomfortable, and conditions were trying to say the least; by late morning the metal skins of the aircraft were too hot to touch. Nevertheless the CO kept the squadron at it with a 'tropical' working day involving an early morning start and flying until about lunch time. Not wishing to be caught out by a short-notice tasking, as had happened in June, Wg Cdr Willis was concerned to get the new crews properly worked up before they were committed to operations. The aircrew were reshuffled to balance the experience levels in the two flights and a daily regime of formation flying and bombing, photography and navigation training sorties was instituted.

The reason for the move to Iraq had been British concern over the attitude of Iran. As Syria had done before, she was showing signs of being sympathetic to the Axis and there was concern over maintaining access to Iranian oil. The Iranian government was presented with a demand that all German advisers be expelled. This ultimatum was rejected and on August 21st the squadron was warned to expect operations to commence the following day.

In the event the British did not move into Iran until the night of 24/25th August so there was no tasking until the 25th when twelve aircraft flew leaflet raids over western Iran and one aircraft carried out a photographic reconnaissance of the Payitak Pass. The Payitak is on the road via Kermanshah to Teheran and was the objective of the 21st Indian Infantry Brigade. The pass, with its steep sides and hairpin bends, is an ideal defensive position which could be, and in the past had been, held by a handful of men against forces of up to division strength. Two further reconnaissances of the pass were flown on the 26th and it was then heavily bombed by Nos 11, 14 and 45 Sqns. Led by Wg Cdr Willis, the squadron contributed twelve Blenheims to the attack. Exactly how much damage was done is unclear but the raid was certainly spectacular and when the squadron flew a post-strike reconnaissance mission on the 27th it was apparent that the Iranians had withdrawn. The Gurkhas took the Payitak Pass without opposition.

Since Hitler's launching of Operation BARBAROSSA on June 10th the Russians had become allies of the British and they too were concerned about Axis activity in Iran, which represented their southern flank. The British and Russian governments had decided on a pre-emptive occupation of Iran to secure their vital interests and the Red Army had launched its invasion in the north at the same time as the British had moved in from the west. There was, however, a need to improve co-ordination between the two forces, and on August 26th Flt Lt Penny flew some British negotiators up to Mosul to rendezvous with a Russian aircraft. The pair then flew up to Tiflis where a Russian delegation was waiting to set up a joint two-way communication channel. The outbound trip went according to plan but on the return flight one of the Blenheim's engines caught fire and Leonard Penny was obliged to crash land Z6156 near Lake Urmia. He was

In May 1941 this Bf 110 (WNr 4035) of II ZG 76 had been deployed to Mosul as part of Sonderkommando Junck in support of the Iraqi rebellion. It was forced to land in the desert whence it was later salvaged by the RAF and restored to airworthiness. It is seen here generating some interest among No 45 Sqn's personnel at Habbaniyah. Wg Cdr Willis flew in this aeroplane three times, once on a check ride and twice as pilot. (L Wilde)

V5967/V was taken on charge by No 45 Sqn on 26th June 1941 and subsequently flew ops over Syria, Iran and Cyrenaica until January 1942. (R G Jackson)

The Nairn Transport Company had offered the Flying Camels some competition over the carriage of mail to Baghdad in the 1920s. When the squadron returned to Iraq in 1941 the company was still going strong and operating 'desert cruisers' like this one, seen at Habbaniyah, which the RAF appears to have commandeered. The link with No 45 Sqn is tenuous but these remarkable vehicles impressed themselves on squadron members at the time, hence the photograph. (R T Holloway)

unhurt but the other crew members, Sgts John Kirkpatrick and 'Taffy' George, were both injured and were subsequently admitted to hospital in Tabriz, Penny himself finally getting back to Habbaniyah on the 30th. In his absence his post as OC B Flight had been taken over on the 27th by the recently arrived, but more senior, Flt Lt A Hughes DFC who had previously been flying with the Free French Blenheim squadron.

On the 28th, in support of the advancing troops, eleven Blenheims dropped leaflets over Burujird and Gulpaigan and another aircraft flew a reconnaissance of Shahabad but found little of significance to report. On the 29th the Iranian government indicated that it was ceasing to offer any further resistance and the squadron reverted to stand-by. A considerable stock of leaflets had been issued which, with the Iranian capitulation, were now surplus to requirements. Just for once the supply of toilet paper was to be adequate!

There had been some direct, if limited, participation by the *Luftwaffe* in the Iraqis' ill-fated attempt to neutralise Habbaniyah back in May and in the course of the fighting a Bf 110 had been forced to land in the desert. Afterwards it had been salvaged and restored to airworthiness. After an initial check ride with Wg Cdr Bocking of No 11 Sqn, the CO was able to make two further flights to sample the handling characteristics of this aeroplane[8].

Although peace and stability had been re-established in Iraq, the temporary availability of three Blenheim squadrons provided an opportunity to remind the local populace that the British meant business. A convincing demonstration of British power was duly laid on for September 8th. Thirty-six Blenheims, twelve each from Nos 11, 14 and 45 Sqns, flew in vics of three, line astern, over Mosul, Kirkuk and Baghdad. The formation was led by James Willis and attracted numerous plaudits.

On September 12th the squadron was warned for a return to Egypt. Three days later Flt Lt Butters and Fg Off Butcher led the MT convoy away on the cross-country marathon via LG V, H3, H4, Mafraq, Haifa, Ramleh and El Arish to Ismailia, then on to Fuka (LG 16) which was reached on the 24th; a total journey of over 1,300 road miles completed in nine days - except that for much of the route there was no road. This time forty-nine of the fifty-two vehicles which started out, completed the trip. That they were able to keep the trucks moving under the worst possible field conditions says something about the squadron's high standards of maintenance but probably even more about the ingenuity and resourcefulness of its tradesmen. Few other squadrons can have made as long and as gruelling a journey as this, as a

The squadron's straggle of vehicles seems to stretch to the horizon during this stop on the way back to Egypt. (L Wilde)

Sgt Ron Wood was another of the replacement crews who ferried a Blenheim (Z9547) out from the UK and then joined the squadron shortly after it had been deployed to Palestine. He was wounded and shot down, on 22nd November by which time he had flown thirty-three ops, sixteen of them with No 45 Sqn. (R Wood)

T2124/F	Z6439/Y	V6149/A
Sgt W M Osborne DFM	Wg Cdr J O Willis DFC	Sgt Stewart
Sgt Martin	Plt Off L P Bourke RNZAF	Sgt Colway
Sgt K Mills	Sgt M F Carthy	Sgt Catton
AC1 G R Aldhurst	LAC Smith	LAC Mills
T2185/N	**V5948/X**	**Z6155/K**
Sgt P Bartlett	Flt Lt J M Dennis	Sgt E W McClelland
Sgt Williams	Sgt J Tozer	Sgt G F Jones RNZAF
Sgt A R Field	Sgt J S McLaren	Sgt S B Whiteley
Cpl Davies	F/Sgt Hyatt	LAC Pownall
V5991/B	**V5435/W**	**V5587/E**
Sgt J H Tolman	Fg Off R A Brown	Sgt F N Scott
Plt Off A W Hutton	Sgt Jenkins	Sgt Fry
Sgt D S J Harris	Cpl R McAusland	Sgt D Catty
Cpl T J Cant		LAC C Higgins
V6180/Q	**V5586/C**	**T2318/H**
Sgt P Naldrett-Jays	Flt Lt A Hughes DFC	Sgt C Melly
Sgt Bissett	Flt Lt F J Austin	Plt Off F L Rippingale
Sgt A W Dann	Sgt D Cliffe	Sgt J Halsall
AC2 Thomas	Cpl H Sharpe	AC1 H Gardner
V6143/T	**V6132/R**	**T2428/P**
Sgt F Scott	Flt Lt L F Penny	Sgt R Wood
Sgt G E Sully	Sgt Hall	Sgt R A Turton RNZAF
Sgt J R Mansfield	Sgt Griffiths	Sgt J E Wilcock
LAC Cushing		LAC J Toogood
V5899/U	**Z7509/S**	**V5967/V**
Sgt C E O'Neill	Fg Off J K Edmonds	Sgt Percival
Sgt Bradford	Plt Off L E Durrant	Sgt Ainslie
Sgt Greenwood	Sgt K J Chapman	Sgt V Day
LAC G Bell	AC1 D Huntley	Cpl J E Nutt
Z6440/Z	**V6467/G**	**V5992/L**
Sgt C G Hockney	Sgt L R W Howell RNZAF	Sgt G T Bennett
Sgt Topping	Sgt K G Hodson	Sgt Pritchard
Sgt Keating	Sgt W Armour	Sgt H W Twydell
LAC E Pidduck	Cpl Easingwood	LAC Inglis

Fig 7.4. No 45 Sqn's air echelon as it left Iraq for Egypt, 26th September 1941.

completely self-contained unit, moving itself over such a distance entirely under its own arrangements. Len 'Oscar' Wilde provides an impression of what the journey across Iraq was like:

There was no road as such, and transport making the trip simply followed the pipeline which traversed the desert carrying oil to Haifa. About every 150 miles there was a pumping station and these were the daily 'targets'. The 'road' could be up to half a mile wide as each lorry tried to avoid the soft churned up sand and stay clear of the clouds of dust. Fifteen to 20 mph was good going, and travelling in the back of a bumping, swaying lorry, covered in swirling dust for hours at a time was a journey of some considerable discomfort, not to say hardship. Water was available at the pumping stations and after a swill and a meal everyone would crawl under the trucks in an effort to take shelter from the sun. The only other vehicles we encountered were the RAF

Regiment's Armoured Cars which constantly patrolled the pipeline. Daytime temperatures were always well over 100°F and once reached 128°F. A peculiarity of a convoy was the fact that if the leading truck set the pace at, say, 20 mph, the breakdown vehicles bringing up the rear would often have to do 30 mph just to keep up. This was due to the varying speeds and constant deviations of the vehicles in between, which never maintained a constant speed or heading. At times the whole business would look like a cavalry charge as each truck edged outwards, away from the dust and debris of the one in front so that what started out as a column would often turn into line abreast.

Two days after the ground echelon had set up shop at LG 16 (Fuka Satellite) the twenty-one Blenheims of the air party

On the night of 30th September, after a 3½ hour mission to Gambut, Fg Off John 'Eddie' Edmonds was obliged to carry out a belly-landing at Fuka. This 'morning after' picture shows Plt Off Lin Durrant posing in front of the wreckage of Z7509 S. The third member of the crew was Sgt Ken Chapman; none of them were much the worse for wear. (L E Durrant)

171

2/Lt Doug Allen (left) and 2/Lt Trevor Evans, two South African pilots who joined the squadron on 4th October 1941. (A D Allen)

Another of No 45 Sqn's South Africans. 2/Lt H R L 'Gus' Alder displays his 'proper' RAF moustache, ie one that can be seen from behind. (L E Durrant)

Flt Lt Arthur Hughes DFC joined No 45 Sqn on 8th August 1941 as OC B Flight. He was made up to squadron leader (as seen here) in October and stayed with the squadron until August 1942, by which time he was a wing commander and CO. (L E Durrant)

flew to Lydda and the squadron was reunited on the 27th. Figure 7.4 lists the aircraft and crews which flew back to Egypt from Habbaniyah. It identifies all of the squadron's aeroplanes and most of its aircrew as it deployed into the Western Desert for the fourth time. Note that twenty of the squadron's airmen also appear in this list (all groundcrew known to have been on strength at this stage are named at Annex N) and that Flt Lt Austin was not an observer but a pilot who had just joined the squadron and was being given a lift to Egypt by Arthur Hughes. Although they do not reflect all of the squadron's subsequent losses, of the aircrew listed, ten would be dead before Christmas, five would be POWs and one would have been seriously wounded; nine of the aircraft shown would have been lost or written off.

The reason for the squadron's having been recalled to Egypt was that they were to be part of the build up for Operation CRUSADER which was scheduled to be launched in November. This would succeed in evicting the enemy from Cyrenaica and driving him back to El Agheila, his start line of the previous April. In the interim the squadron was to take part in the daily round of bombing missions and, after a brief period to settle in, operations began on September 30th with the CO leading a six-aircraft raid on Gambut. All the aircraft returned safely although Z7509 crashed while landing in the dark, fortunately without injury to the crew, Fg Off John 'Eddie' Edmonds, Plt Off Lin Durrant and Sgt Ken Chapman.

On September 17th, shortly before the squadron had left Iraq, Flt Lt F J Austin had been posted in to take over A Flight and on October 10th his predecessor, Flt Lt John Dennis, left for AHQ Western Desert[9], his departure being marked by the award of a DFC - possibly the sole result of Wg Cdr Willis' submission of July 25th. Early in October 'Bunny' Austin and Arthur Hughes were both promoted to squadron leader. It had taken five months from the publication of the revised War Establishment, but the squadron finally had all three of its executive posts filled by officers of the appropriate ranks.

More personnel changes followed during October as a number of new crews were taken on strength and the squadron began to display an increasingly international character. No 45 Sqn had had a leavening of 'colonials' for some time, of course, notably Sqn Ldr John Dallamore, a Canadian, and Plt Off Leonard 'Felix' Code-Lewis who had been a tobacco farmer in Rhodesia. None of the initial intake of South Africans who had arrived in April 1941 was still with the squadron, however, and of the first batch of 'Kiwis' only Plt Off Lawrie Bourke and Sgt Gordon Jones were still

"One man and his dog...."; Sgt Garfath and 'Tiger'. Henry 'Tubby' Garfath acquired 'Tiger', who was to become quite an experienced Blenheim aviator, in Malta circa May 1941. (L E Durrant)

A gaggle of No 45 Sqn's Blenheims over the desert circa October 1941. (Mrs Daphne Hughes)

This multinational crew joined the squadron on 17th October 1941, from the left: Sgt John Pannifer RAF, Sgt Ced Birkbeck RAAF and Sgt Ted Pulford RCAF. (Mrs Daphne Hughes

on strength. Their numbers had been partially restored in June by the arrival of Fg Off Edmonds, who hailed from New Guinea, and in July by two more RNZAF men, Sgts Turton and Howell. The influx of new crews in July had included several other colonials disguised in RAF uniforms; Plt Off Lin Durrant, for instance, was another New Zealander and Sgt John Kirkpatrick was a Canadian. Now, however, there was a virtual flood of new aircrew from all over the Commonwealth. Three South Africans, 2/Lts A D Allen, T C Evans and H R L Alder arrived during October while Sgts E B Pulford and W A Gaudet came from Canada and, among others, Plt Offs P E Graebner, W J Corbett and Sgts C G Briggs and K A Gardiner joined the squadron's ranks from Australia. More RAAF men, among them Plt Offs D G Eve and J W Maloney and their crews, swelled the squadron's imperial ranks during November. These are but examples, there were many, many more, particularly Australians. For the remainder of the war, while the Flying Camel's groundcrew would continue to be almost exclusively British, at times over half of its aircrew contingent would be Australian, and a Canadian and New Zealand presence was also maintained until 1945.

The influx of replacement crews brought with them a rash of Commonwealth shoulder flashes, accompanied by varicoloured headgear, slouch hats and other odd bits of 'different' kit, all of which contributed further variety to the hotchpotch of outfits which passed for air force 'uniform' in the desert. Apart from this, however, there was another, even more obvious, change in the squadron's appearance during October when its aircraft were repainted. The original Mk IVs had been delivered in Dark Earth/Dark Green/Sky but in August 1941 a more appropriate scheme was promulgated for aircraft operating in the Middle East. From the late summer onwards replacement aircraft were delivered with Light Earth and Middle Stone upper surfaces and Azure undersides. In the autumn those aircraft which were still in

the earlier scheme were sent to Heliopolis to be repainted. V5948, for example, acquired its new colours between 26th and 27th October while Z9609 was repainted between 6th and 8th November. Another change in the squadron's warpaint had been the deletion of its identity code at some time during the year. At the beginning of the Mk IV era the Blenheims had certainly carried the OB combination but this was later deleted and by the time that the squadron moved to Palestine at the end of June its aeroplanes displayed only an individual identification letter painted ahead of the fuselage roundel.

With the large number of new crews, a great deal of training flying and bombing practice was undertaken during October to shake the squadron down yet again. This was complemented by fighter affiliation exercises and a lecture programme which included advice on escape and evasion. Time was also found to experiment with bombing techniques. In general it is true to say that the lower the height from which a bomb is released the more accurate it will be. On the other hand, a bomb is released in a horizontal attitude and

This crew, from the left, 2/Lt Doug Allen SAAF, Sgt Ned Hammat RAAF and Sgt Geoff Gowing RAAF, arrived at LG 16 from No 70 OTU on 4th October 1941. They had several close shaves while flying with No 45 Sqn, the first of them on October 29th. (G A Gowing)

The squadron then reckoned that with three aircraft in line abreast 150 yards apart, each dropping a stick of four 250 lb bombs from 150 feet, they could take out any soft target in an area measuring 300 yards by 450 yards.

Despite the repainting programme, the intensive training schedule and arcane experiments in weapons delivery, the squadron still found time to fly sixty-six sorties during the month; the targets included Gazala, Bardia, Gambut, Derna, Gabr Saleh and Gasr el Arid. An attack against Gabr Saleh on October 22nd was provided with an escort of three squadrons of fighters operating from LG 110. Since the raid was intercepted, this protection undoubtedly saved the squadron from loss, although one of the Tomahawks was shot down. Forty-eight of the October sorties were flown at night. Two of the night raids, one against supply dumps on the Bardia-Tobruk Road on October 26th, the other on Gazala on the 30th, were supported by the flare-dropping Albacores of No 826 Sqn of the FAA, shore-based at Maaten Bagush.

Late in the month the squadron began to use LG 53 (about twenty-five miles south of Fuka) as a dispersal base, both to launch missions and to park aircraft overnight. This initiative was prompted by an air raid on LG 16 on October 26th which had demolished one of B Flight's tents; fortunately, it had been unoccupied at the time. Two operational missions were mounted from LG 53 during October, both involving incidents. On the 29th 2/Lt Allen with Plt Off E L Hammat and Sgt G A Gowing, on their third operational mission, were one of six crews briefed to attack Gambut. In the event two aircraft went unserviceable so only four flew the raid. A tailwheel snag delayed V6467's positioning flight to LG 53 and by the time this had been rectified the sun had gone down. Fuka had not expected to be night-flying so no flarepath had been laid out and, with his aeroplane laden with sundry groundcrew and their toolboxes, Doug Allen eventually took off in the dark. Just as it became airborne the aircraft's port mainwheel hit a pile of sand on the aerodrome boundary, slightly damaging the hydraulic mechanism. This damage was not severe but it was enough to prevent the undercarriage from retracting and with its wheels stuck down the aircraft would only maintain height at the expense of the

needs a finite time of fall before it has reoriented itself more or less vertically so that it will stay put where it hits the ground. The squadron tried delivering 250 pounders at 180 mph from fifty feet with an eleven-second delayed action fuse, reasoning that they would be well clear of the target before the bombs detonated. This was certainly accurate enough but, predictably, the weapons hit the ground horizontally, ricocheted and were still underneath the aircraft when they went off. Fortunately no damage was done. The armourers tried bending the fins to persuade the bombs to 'tuck' as soon as they were released but this only made their flight behaviour erratic and they remained a hazard to the aircraft. Ultimately they found that by unwinding the vanes on the tail pistols by 10 turns they could ensure a safe release (*at least that is what it says in the squadron's ORB, although the rationale underlying the procedure escapes this writer*).

Left:- From the left, 2 Lt Gus Alder, Plt Off Bill Corbett and Sgt Cliff Briggs. The aeroplane is V6180/Q in which they were obliged to make forced landings on two occasions, the first being on 31st October. (C G Briggs) Right:- Fg Off R A 'Dicky' Brown was one of the influx of new pilots who arrived from the UK in June 1941. He flew with the squadron until the end of its time in the Middle East, having a lucky escape from V5435 on 1st November; this picture was taken later that month. (A D Allen)

cylinder head temperatures going 'off the clock'. Allen was obliged to abandon the flight and try to get down again where he thought (hoped?) the darkened airfield might be. The ORB describes his effort as "a fine belly-landing in the dark". It was not quite a true belly-landing, however, as the undercarriage was down but it must have been exciting enough even so, especially at night. The aeroplane actually touched down, as the pilot recalls, "in the squadron bomb disposal area, without hitting anything, but we came close to colliding with the dhobi tent before finally coming to rest." No one was hurt and damage to the airframe was only superficial; V6467 was air tested on November 12th and shortly afterwards it was back flying ops.

The second incident occurred after a night raid on Gambut on October 30th/31st when 2/Lt Alder and his crew, Plt Off Corbett and Sgt Briggs, found themselves 'uncertain of their position' and short of fuel. Gus Alder pulled off a successful, if bumpy, wheels-down night landing in the desert and before the batteries went flat Cliff Briggs was able to send enough of a transmission to let people know that they were down and alive. They spent a day waiting by the aircraft but the only aeroplane they saw was a Heinkel so the next night they started walking. The following morning they came across an Arab goat-herd who led them to a salvage team from No 54 RSU which was picking over the carcass of a wrecked Valentia (K2808) of No 216 Sqn. The NCO in charge of the working party, Sgt May, laid on a truck which took the stranded crew as far as Burgh el Arab whence they made their way back to the squadron. In the meantime, knowing that the crew was down safely, the squadron had mounted no further raids as its flying effort had been devoted to searching for V6180 which was eventually located on November 2nd. It was refuelled and flown out and by the 11th was back with the squadron. In the meantime, there had been little opportunity for the footsore crew to recuperate from their experience and on November 5th they flew a stores run to Amiriya and back; two days later they were back on ops flying a raid on Bir Hacheim.

Operating from the bumpy surface of LG 53 led to several more accidents, including the loss of V5435 on November 1st. This was to have been a ferry flight back to base and apart from his normal crew of Fg Off John 'Paddy' Wright and Sgt Bert Jenkins, Fg Off R A Brown had a number of passengers on board. One of them was 2/Lt Doug Allen:

Dicky Brown had quite a lot of people in that aircraft that evening. I was on the jump seat next to the pilot up in the nose with two ground staff chaps forward in the nav position. Trevor Evans was in the back with two or three others near the turret. During the take off run the starboard tyre burst on the stony surface and Dicky was unable to keep the aircraft straight. As the speed fell off the starboard wheel dug into the surface and, unable to stand the load of the resulting ground loop, the port undercarriage collapsed and, as the engine hit the ground, it burst into flames. A great lick of flame came up through the wing root and burnt all the hair off my left arm! The chaps in the back soon had the hatch open and shot out like champagne corks but up front we were not so lucky. It was standard practice in the Blenheim to take off with the sliding perspex hatch over the cockpit open. For some reason on this occasion Dicky had closed it

Sgt Charles Edward O'Neill rides on the jump seat of Z9609 during a tactical exercise with fighters on November 6th. Sqn Ldr Hughes is at the controls. (L E Durrant)

before starting his take off run. After the aircraft came to a standstill we found to our horror that the hatch had jammed; probably the whole fuselage had twisted in the crash. I can still picture Dicky with both feet on the dashboard, hauling like hell on the hatch handle with panic-stricken me egging him on. Finally the hatch relented and slid back and we were out. A three-ton truck raced out to our rescue but the driver, in the mistaken belief that we had bombs on board, did not stop. He only slowed down and after passing close to the burning aircraft accelerated away with several of us clinging to the tailgate, unable to get on board and taking gigantic leaps at about 30 mph! No one was hurt in this incident but the Blenheim burned all night.

On the night of November 2nd/3rd five aircraft flew a raid via LG 53 against a supply dump on the Tobruk-Bardia Road with target illumination again being provided by No 826 Sqn's Albacores; fires were started. This mission was repeated the following night but this time LG 53 was to claim two lives. While the five aircraft were away a dense fog settled on the LG. One of the Blenheims, V6143, had a 250 lb bomb hang-up and, while attempting to land on the bumpy surface in poor visibility, one of the aircraft's wingtips

No 45 Sqn began to move forward to LG 75 on 14th November 1941. As the background to this photograph of a bomb train indicates, it was a just another patch of featureless desert. (C G Briggs)

175

touched the ground and there was an explosion. All three crew members were seriously injured and Sgts G E Sully and J R Mansfield died very shortly afterwards; only the pilot, Sgt F Scott survived. Of the other pilots involved only Sgt

Above:- Sgt Dennis Owen had lost all his kit when he had been in Greece with No 84 Sqn. He is seen here at LG 103 in November 1941 wearing-in a newly issued replacement uniform, hence the sharp creases. The uniform was khaki, rather then blue, which became more or less standard in the Desert Air Force, although they did not stay as smart as this for very long.

Below:-Quenching their thirst with Stella beer atop Berchtesgarten, *a swastika-bedecked crew dugout at LG 75, are, from the left: Sgt 'Gerry' Osborne, Sgt Ken Mills and Sgt 'Tubby' Garfath, as always, with 'Tiger'. Note the Lewis gun with which most bunkers were equipped. (D A Owen))*

Tolman succeeded in getting down at LG 53; Sqn Ldr Austin landed at Bagush Satellite and Sgts Percival and Melly recovered to main base at Fuka Satellite. Another aircraft, T2185, had been written off the previous evening when Sgt P Bartlett had hit an obstruction while making a night take off from LG 16 without the aid of a flarepath; fortunately there were no casualties. Apart from these incidents, an attack by the *Luftwaffe* on Fuka railway station had made the night of the 3rd memorable for everyone at LG 16. The bombers hit an ammunition train and explosions went on for the rest of the night; few people managed to get much sleep, despite the fact that this was the third successive night that Fuka had been visited by the *Luftwaffe*.

There was a brief lull in ops and then another five-aircraft raid was launched on the night of 6th/7th November. The target this time was a large concentration of MT and tanks near Bir Hacheim and, again assisted by the navy's Albacores, the attack was very successful with numerous secondary explosions being observed. Three more night ops were flown on the 9th/10th, all armed recces of roads between Barce and Derna. All three aircraft, operating as singletons, carried mixed loads of 250 lb and 40 lb bombs and these were dropped on parked MT found in the vicinity of El Faidia and Cyrene. The crews involved were: Sqn Ldr Hughes, Plt Off Durrant and F/Sgt Cliffe; Flt Lt Penny, Sgt Bruce and Sgt George and Sgts Stewart, Colway and Catton.

In preparation for Operation CRUSADER, which was to be launched on November 18th, A and B Flights began to move forward to LG 75 on the 14th. LG 103 was the squadron's new dispersal airfield while Fuka Satellite, where the rear echelon remained, now became the Base LG. LG 75 turned out to be just another patch of featureless sand, indistinguishable from the rest. Dennis Owen, then a sergeant observer flying with Sgt W M 'Gerry' Osborne DFM and Sgt H 'Tubby' Garfath, has provided the following random impressions of the domestic arrangements at LG 75 (or LG 103 or Fuka or LG 53 or Gambut - it did not make much difference):

At LG 75 we had the occasional night raid by the Hun and it was surprising how much digging went on in the dark when everybody suddenly decided that it would be a good time to deepen one's slit trench. Most tents possessed one. We had a Lewis gun on a tripod outside our dugout and even a pan of ammo. I don't recall where it came from, but we never had occasion to use it.

The Sergeants' Mess consisted of a large depression about three feet deep, open to the air, in which we stood propped up against the 'walls', ie the sides of the depression, and ate our grub from tin plates. No tables or anything like that. I think there was a tent at one end which served as a bar. The cook - Sgt 'Topsy' Turner - did the best he could with the rubbish that he was sent, so that we existed for a long time on bully beef, tinned butter, tinned, very salty, bacon and hard biscuits. The tins were the usual cylindrical type but of a khaki colour, presumably to prevent them from shining in the sun and attracting the enemy? We didn't get many potatoes and when we did they were the sweet variety. The bully beef came stewed, cold, fried and in a variety of more mysterious forms, but it was always unmistakably bully beef.

The glasses from which we drank our beer were made from the lower halves of beer bottles which had been made by some cunning process involving a hot wire around the barrel of the complete bottle and oil - although I never saw this actually being done. The beer ration came at irregular intervals and, of course, it did not last long. Now and again we could buy small tins of New Zealand lamb tongues which we ate straight from the tin. I can taste them now - delicious.

The sanitary arrangements were quite simple, and not too insanitary. The main bog consisted of a wooden vaulting horse type of structure set over a long hole of indeterminate depth. The top had half-a-dozen or so holes down its length, each hole being covered by a lid. The lids were cunningly balanced so that they opened to the rear against some kind of stop, so that if a bod was sitting on the hole, the lid was propped against the lower part of his back, but as soon as he stood up the lid automatically fell shut. In theory this prevented the ingress of flies and confined smells. The whole device stood out in the open with no screening at all and was provided with a supply of khaki 'Forms Blank' which usually blew all over the place if there was any wind. It was a great social leveller to sit out in the fresh air, admiring the view and being viewed in turn by all and sundry. The were also a few solo bogs out at the dispersal sites.

One day there arrived on the squadron an attractive woman - YES! a real woman - a journalist, for an American magazine I think[10]. She had come to see how the doughty men of the RAF were waging war against the forces of tyranny. She happened to walk by one of the solo bogs while it was being perched upon by one of the groundcrew. There he was and there she was and neither of them could do much about it. So the airman just raised his topee and wished her a good morning - now that's what I call sang-froid. There were, incidentally, malicious rumours circulating to the effect that the said very attractive lady was sharing the tent of the CO of one of the neighbouring squadrons, but that was sheer fantasy and could not possibly have been true - could it?

At such times as the water supply allowed, and if the desire coincided, we would have a bath. This was achieved with the aid of the ubiquitous four-gallon petrol can. It was cut in half and the two halves placed side by side. You stood in one half and washed the upper part of the body with such water as was available,

which ran down and collected around your feet. You then transferred to the other tin and reused the water to attend to your nether regions. Once in a while someone would organise a gharry and we would drive to the sea for a really refreshing swim.

The last few missions had been relatively uneventful but as soon as CRUSADER's ground offensive was launched the squadron's loss rate began to increase markedly. The first incident occurred during a raid against the enemy LG at Bir el Baheira on November 18th. T2124 was hit by flak and sustained damage to its tail unit, although the crew, Sgts Francis Scott, Reg Jackson and Dennis Catty, were uninjured and the aeroplane returned to LG 75. The next day, operating as singletons and taking advantage of cloud cover, six more Blenheims attacked Sidi Rezegh. Z7510 failed to

Pilot Sgt Frank Scott (centre) and WOp AG Dennis Catty (right) joined the squadron in June 1941. Their original observer, Sgt 'Tubby' Fry, was replaced in November by Sgt 'Jackie' Jackson (left). (R G Jackson)

Crews on stand-by, perched on top of the Ops dugout at LG 75, November 1941. From the left, back row: Plt Off Geoff Furmage, Fg Off 'Paddy' Wright, Sgt 'Gerry' Osborne, Sgt Doug Harris, Sgt James Tolman, Sgt Ainslie, Plt Off Tony Hutton. Front row: Plt Off Jimmy Fraser, Plt Off Chas Pailthorpe, Sgt Dennis Owen, F/Sgt David Cliffe, Sgt Percival, Fg Off Dicky Brown and, bottom right, Sgt Bob Barclay. (A D Allen)

Sgt Cliff Briggs in his turret - he was credited with a confirmed Fiat CR 42 on November 19th. (C G Briggs)

Following their forced landing in the middle of a tank battle on November 19th, (from the left) Fg Off Lin Durrant, F/Sgt Dave Cliffe and Sqn Ldr Arthur Hughes passed through Piccadilly *(about 25 miles SSE of Sidi Barrani) while wending their way back to LG 75 and found time to pose in front of the Western Desert's own petrol tin rendering of Eros. (L E Durrant)*

return; its newly arrived Australian crew, Plt Off Eric Magor, Plt Off Alex Cain and Sgt Thomas MacLiver, were posted missing from their first operational mission. A second aircraft, V5943 (Sqn Ldr Hughes, Plt Off Durrant and F/Sgt Cliffe), was shot down near Sidi Omar; David Cliffe provides the following account of this incident:

We ran out of cloud cover after leaving the target and our port engine was hit by flak. Hughes initially ordered us to prepare to bail out but changed his mind and crash landed the aircraft on its belly. In my hurry to get out of the aeroplane I did not realise that my flying helmet was still attached to the intercom plug. I found myself hanging in mid-air and had to scramble back inside to disconnect myself. We could hear the sound of heavy gunfire and saw a tank heading straight for us. We could not tell whether it was an enemy or an allied tank and could only wait anxiously to find out. The tank stopped beside our aircraft. Its top hatch opened and a head emerged wearing what appeared to be a German officer's

hat. The person then spoke to us and said, "I say chaps, are you all right?" You can imagine our relief! He was from the Dragoon Guards and he informed us that we had crash landed in the middle of a battle. We quickly scrambled into his tank which took us to the gun positions of the RHA whence we were transported to Brigade HQ. An RASC truck then took us to a forward supply depot and from there, by various means, we made our way back to the squadron which we eventually reached two days later. During our absence we had been posted missing and our next of kin had been notified. My few personal effects had been divided up by the other crews; this had included my camp bed and primus stove - two very valuable possessions in the desert. Fortunately I was able to reclaim these.

The enemy had not had it quite all his own way and the score had been evened slightly by Sgt Cliff Briggs who, flying with his usual crew of 2/Lt Alder and Plt Off Corbett, had claimed a CR 42 from the turret of T2393.

The following day, the 20th, in company with seven of No 14 Sqn's Blenheims and a fighter escort, the squadron put up nine aircraft to attack an MT concentration at El Adem; one of No 45 Sqn's aeroplanes was slightly damaged by AA fire but made it safely back to LG 75. This mission was repeated on November 21st by a similar joint force of Blenheims which staged through LG 128 to strike at an MT park at Bir Hacheim and, although they were unescorted this time, they suffered no losses.

The next mission was to demonstrate just how vulnerable the Blenheim had become by late 1941. In the early days of the North African campaign the opposition had been provided by the *Regia Aeronautica* flying lightly-armed biplanes. While Blenheims were not impervious to rifle calibre machine guns they could withstand a certain amount of damage and, since the Italian fighters did not have that great an edge in performance, the bombers had had a reasonable chance of holding their own in 1940. With the arrival of units of the *Luftwaffe* in April 1941, however, particularly I/JG 27 with its Bf 109Es, the balance of probabilities had started to tilt in the enemy's favour. During September I/JG 27 began to return to Germany, one *Staffel* at a time, to re-equip with the more powerful and faster Bf

Of the six unescorted Blenheims despatched to attack MT on the Acroma-El Adem road on 22nd November 1941 only two returned to base. This crew, from the left, Plt Off Phil Graebner, Sgt Ken Gardiner and Plt Off Stuart Muller-Rowland, made it back safely but their Blenheim had three holes in its port wing. (C E Birkbeck)

Only recently repainted in desert colours, as seen here, Z6439/Y was one of the four aircraft lost on 22nd November 1941. Its crew, Wg Cdr J O Willis DFC, Plt Off L P Bourke RNZAF and Sgt M F Carthy were all killed. (G A Gowing)

109F. To avoid any shortfall in the *Luftwaffe's* fighter force, all three *Staffeln* of II/JG 27 had been withdrawn from Russia to Germany, rearmed with '109Fs and then redeployed to North Africa. The first of these late-model Messerschmitts arrived in Libya with 4./JG 27, which flew its first patrols on September 26th, and over the next few weeks the force grew steadily. The presence of these substantially more capable aeroplanes had not gone undetected by British Intelligence and on 20th October Sgt Geoff Gowing had noted in his diary: "S/Ldr Austin discussed with A Flt crews decisions from Group of future tactics and report of 25 109F aircraft around the forward area yesterday." The arrival of the new Messerschmitts had altered the tactical picture considerably; if unescorted Blenheims were to be caught in daylight by these fast and very potent fighters there was only one likely outcome. There were strong echoes of 1917 and unescorted missions in 1½ Strutters. Was history about to repeat itself?

It was. On November 22nd six of No 45 Sqn's Blenheims were despatched on a 'cloud cover' raid to attack MT between Acroma and El Adem. They had an escort of Tomahawks from No 3 Sqn RAAF but south of El Adem these were drawn off by a group of Messerschmitts, three of the Australian fighters being shot down. This left the bombers to forge on unprotected and they were bounced by about twenty Bf 109s. Having recently arrived in Egypt by ferrying a Blenheim out from the UK via Gibraltar and Malta, Sgts J E Pannifer, C E Birkbeck and E B Pulford had joined the squadron on October 17th; they were one of only two crews to return from this mission. This is how Ced Birkbeck recalls it:

> In the first few moments of the attack the CO's plane was shot down as were three others. Our own plane had large shell holes in the port wing, completely wiping out the aileron. As we raced for cloud cover we noticed that some of the chaps had baled out and a few even walked back from the desert. Fortunately there was enough cloud around to offer some protection; we were throttled back as far as possible and we stayed in cloud as long as we could. As soon as we emerged a couple of fighters would attack and we would race for the next cloud. This kept on for quite some time and resulted in our more or less flying in circles. Eventually the fighters must have run short of petrol; there were no more attacks and we were able to return to base. I don't think that our plane ever flew again. The other crew to return safely was that of Stuart Muller-Rowland with Phil Graebner and Ken Gardiner. Their aircraft had also been shot up.

Birkbeck's recollection is substantially accurate. Wg Cdr James Willis with Plt Off Lawrie Bourke and Sgt Michael 'Paddy' Carthy had gone down in Z6439 and Sgts Charles O'Neill, Lionel Smith and Kenneth Chapman in Z7686; all six men died. T2318 had also been lost, but Sgt Pat Melly and

Sgt Pannifer and Sqn Ldr Austin examining the damage inflicted on Z6440's port aileron by a Bf 109 on 22nd November. (C E Birkbeck)

his crew, Plt Off Rippingale and Sgt Halsall, survived to become POWs. The crew of Z9609 also managed to bale out but the pilot and gunner, Sgts Wood and Whiteley, had both been wounded, (Whiteley, not normally a member of this crew, had been flying in place of Sgt Jimmy Wilcock who was sick that day). As Ron Wood recalls:

> After a bitterly cold night in the desert, my navigator, Bert Turton, set off on foot for a Bedouin camp which he had seen during his descent and at about mid-day he arrived back with a donkey for me. He had persuaded the owner that our need was greater than his - his .38 revolver having helped in the persuasion.

Now mobile, Ron Wood set off alone for the Bedouin camp while Whiteley and Turton headed east in an attempt to regain friendly territory. The Arabs promptly handed Wood

Another picture of Z6440 with Sgt Ted Pulford RCAF in the turret. Although it cannot be seen too clearly in this reproduction, the original photograph reveals extensive damage to the fuselage from machine gun fire; the manuscript annotation reads "full of holes like a pepperpot". (C G Briggs)

over to the Italians and shortly afterwards Ben Whiteley was rounded up too; they spent the next three and a half years in a series of POW cages in Italy and Germany. Their Kiwi observer was more fortunate. He avoided capture and, perhaps even more remarkably, survived successfully for six days in the desert (reportedly by eating snails) before he was picked up by a South African MO who, ironically, was lost himself but he did have a vehicle and supplies and they eventually made their way to safety.

The two aircraft which succeeded in returning to base had both sustained sufficient damage to warrant their withdrawal to an RSU for repairs. The *Luftwaffe* pilots who had cut such a swathe through the squadron had all belonged to 1./JG 27 which had only recently returned from Germany with its formidable new F-model Messerschmitts; they were Hpt Karl-Wolfgang Redlich (who claimed one near Gazala and another near Bir Hacheim), Obfw Albert Espenlaub (one near

Bir el Gobi) and Uffz Josef Grimm (one near Gazala).

With the loss of Wg Cdr Willis, who had flown fifty-eight operational sorties in his time as OC No 45 Sqn, command of the squadron fell to OC A Flight and Sqn Ldr Austin took over, pending the appointment of a new CO. In the first three weeks of November the squadron had lost seven aircraft on operations. Of the twenty-one men involved only four had rejoined the squadron; eleven were dead, one was wounded and the remaining five were POWs. Two more aircraft had been lost in accidents while several others had

An increasing number of Australian crews joined the squadron in late 1941. This one is, from the left Plt Offs Kemp, Eve and Bain with Blenheim V5587/E in which they flew three sorties during December 1941. (A D Allen)

One of the men shot down on 22nd November (with Sgts Melly and Halsall in T2318) was Plt Off Fred Rippingale who had been with the squadron since late June. He was to spend the next three years as a prisoner of war. Released on 10th December 1944, he was made a MBE on 1st June 1945, presumably in recognition of his activities as a POW. (L E Durrant)

Impressed by the bushy beards sported by some of their compatriots flying with No 3 Sqn RAAF, permission was sought to emulate them. The CO turned this proposal down flat and insisted that all of his aircrew were to be clean shaven. Plt Offs Eve, Kemp and Bain took him at his word. This is Dudley Eve making his protest. (D G Eve)

suffered substantial battle damage and had had to be taken off strength. Despite these setbacks operations continued unabated. In fact the intensity increased towards the end of the month as the campaign against enemy transport in Cyrenaica continued. These later raids were usually provided with fighter escorts and were often larger as they were frequently flown in concert with Free French Blenheims and those of No 14 Sqn. Sqn Ldr Hughes, who had previously spent a year with the Free French, was very useful at the planning stage of these joint missions as he was able to brief the crews in English and then run through it again in flawless French.

No 45 Sqn flew forty-four sorties, nearly half of its monthly total of ninety-six, during the last week of November, the peak occurring on the 25th when four missions, involving eighteen individual sorties, were mounted against concentrations of MT and armour at Sidi Omar and Bir Sheferzen. All of these later raids were successful except for that mounted on the 28th in concert with No 14 Sqn, the Free French 'Lorraine Sqn' and a fighter escort; the force encountered 10/10ths cloud over the target area on the Trigh Capuzzo and was obliged to bring its bombs back to base. On the last mission flown during November, on the 29th, to which the squadron contributed six aircraft to a total of sixteen, the pilot of T2393, Sgt J Robinson, sustained leg injuries when his aircraft was slightly damaged by enemy action but he succeeded in bringing it back and landing safely; Sgts 'Pat' Paterson and 'Joe' Gaudet escaped injury.

Operation CRUSADER was proving to be a somewhat confused affair on the ground and there was a great deal of very mobile fighting between Bardia and Tobruk. This, amplified by the relative slowness and unreliability of communications in 1941, meant that it was almost impossible to define a bomb line and as a result the Blenheim squadrons were not tasked as heavily as might have been expected. Even so they flew a substantial number of sorties. Bomb lines were the business of the Army Intelligence Liaison Officer (AILO) who had been attached to the squadron, Capt Field; he attended the debriefing of crews after each mission and was always delighted if they could tell *him* where any friendly units were! The battle hung in the balance for some time but after two weeks Rommel was eventually obliged to relax the stranglehold in which he had held Tobruk for eight months.

When the squadron had lost a number of its crews over Crete during May the system had been unable to replace them (or their aeroplanes) and eventually it had had to be withdrawn from the line to refit. Six months later the situation had been completely transformed. By now the Empire Air Training Scheme was turning out a constant stream of aircrew and sufficient reserves of manpower were available in the Middle East to make good losses as they occurred. As a result the constitution of the squadron's air echelon was constantly changing but Figure 7.5 provides an indication of its status during the last few days of November 1941. As always, a number of supernumerary people was also held on strength, recovering from injuries or awaiting replacements for missing crew members; at this time these included, for instance, Sgts Turton, Robinson, Field and Scott. In addition, two complete crews, Sgts Hockney, Topping and Keating and Sgts Naldrett-Jays, Bissett and Dann, were away flying Marylands on attachment to No 21 Sqn SAAF. Of these only Cyril Hockney was to return to the fold, in December when, their original pilot still being out of action, he took over

This is the rest of Dudley Eve. (D G Eve)

Pilot	Observer	WOp/AG
Wg Cdr C B B Wallis	Sgt D Page	Sgt B T McDade
Sqn Ldr F J Austin	Plt Off F J Fraser	F/Sgt K Mills
Sqn Ldr A Hughes DFC	Plt Off L E Durrant	F/Sgt D Cliffe
Flt Lt L F Penny	Sgt G L Bruce	Sgt G George
Fg Off R A Brown	Fg Off J Wright	Sgt Jenkins
Plt Off C W Head RAAF	Plt Off R H Reeves	Sgt Butler
Plt Off J S Muller-Rowland	Plt Off P E Graebner RAAF	Sgt K A Gardiner RAAF
Plt Off J H Tolman	Fg Off A W Hutton	Sgt D S J Harris
Plt Off D G Eve RAAF	Plt Off G E Kemp RAAF	Plt Off N Bain RAAF
Plt Off G G Furmage RAAF	Plt Off C D Pailthorpe RAAF	Sgt R M Barclay RAAF
Plt Off J W Maloney RAAF	Sgt D McK Carew-Reid RAAF	Sgt W R Wilson RAAF
2/Lt A D Allen SAAF	Plt Off E L Hammat RAAF	Sgt G A Gowing RAAF
2/Lt T C Evans SAAF	Plt Off N W Bayly RAAF	Sgt K E Edwards RAAF
2/Lt H R L Alder SAAF	Plt Off W J Corbett RAAF	Sgt C G Briggs RAAF
F/Sgt J Burns	Sgt R E J Reeves	Sgt J E Wilcock
Sgt G W Hartnell RAAF	Plt Off P C Lahey RAAF	Sgt D Thornton RAAF
Sgt F N Scott	Sgt R Jackson	Sgt D Catty
Sgt Stewart	Sgt Colway	Sgt Catton
Sgt G T Bennett	Sgt H C Nullis	Sgt H W Twydell
Sgt Percival	Sgt Ainslie	Sgt V Day
Sgt W M Osborne DFM	Sgt D A Owen	Sgt H Garfath
Sgt R P Curtis RAAF	Sgt L J Charlton RAAF	Sgt J L Brinkley RAAF
Sgt J E Pannifer	Sgt C E Birkbeck RAAF	Sgt E B Pulford RCAF
Sgt J Robinson	Sgt J Paterson	Sgt W A Gaudet RCAF
Sgt W S McLellan RAAF	Sgt J R Vernon RAAF	Sgt J Nankervis RAAF

Fig 7.5. No 45 Sqn crew state in late November 1941.

Sgt Robinson's rear crew of Sgts 'Pat' Paterson and 'Joe' Gaudet. There had also been a few changes among the ground appointments since they were last noted. Nuts and bolts were now the preserve of Flt Lt T H Jones who had been transferred in from No 70 Sqn to become Engineering Officer on October 5th; Plt Off H W Pickering had relieved 'Felix' Code-Lewis as Intelligence Officer on 22nd November and custody of cyphers was now the responsibility of the recently-arrived Plt Offs A Hassall and K J W Josling[11]. Flt Lt 'Paddy' Kelly continued to serve as the squadron's MO; Flt Lt Philip Butters was still the Adjutant and Fg Off Ron Culverwell was still minding the stores.

By this time the squadron also had its new CO, Wg Cdr C B B Wallis having assumed command on November 26th. Previously OC A Flight with No 55 Sqn, he had brought his old crew of Sgts D Page and B T McDade with him. As Dennis Owen recalls, the new wing commander soon made his presence felt: "We had used the paucity of the water supply - the official ration was two pints per day, if you were lucky - as an excuse for growing beards. For most of us this meant a dusting of fluff around the jowls; in my case it looked like half an ounce of light shag cigarette tobacco! The first thing Wallis did was to storm through the unit to bring us into shape, like getting some sort of proper messing arrangements instead of a glorified hole in the ground and, of course, giving us a communal rocket about not shaving." As the accompanying photographs of Plt Off Dudley Eve show, the 'no beards' edict did not go down too well with some.

November had been notable for the amount of enemy offensive air activity; the squadron had been bombed several times, both at Fuka and at LG 75, although it had sustained neither damage nor casualties. On December 1st the squadron was bombed again by a number of Ju 88s but this time it had the satisfaction of being able to watch the intruders being engaged by RAF night fighters. There was a fireworks display of tracer and one of the bombers fell less than a mile from LG 75 and exploded. Most of the squadron hared off across the desert to investigate, capturing the three German aircrew in the process. Another enemy raider, presumably looking for the airstrip, bombed the burning wreckage while many of the squadron's airmen were still at the crash site but, fortunately, no one was hurt.

December having begun with a spectacular incident, the rest of the month was to be equally as eventful. The squadron contributed six aircraft each time to raids flown on the first three days of the month, the targets being MT at Sidi Rezegh, Bir el Gobi and on the Trigh Capuzzo. All of these missions were flown in concert with other Blenheim units, No 84 Sqn now joining in as well, so that the attacking force often numbered twenty-four bombers. Close escort fighters were provided on the 1st and 3rd, the raid on the intervening day being aborted before the target due to adverse weather conditions.

A particularly tragic accident occurred on December 4th. All four squadrons of No 270 Wg based at LG 75, Nos 14, 45 and 84 Sqns plus the Free French unit, were to take part in a thirty-aircraft raid on MT at Sidi Rezegh. There was little wind to disperse the heavy haze of dust which interfered with visibility or to dictate the direction of take off and there appears to have been some confusion over which 'runway' was in use. Sqn Ldr Hughes was leading the squadron that day and as he became airborne with the first vic he was horrified to see that the French were taking off in the opposite direction. The leading formations had missed colliding by seconds but the squadron's second vic was less fortunate. This is 2/Lt Doug Allen's perception of what happened next:

I was flying Z6446, with Ned Hammat in the nose and Geoff Gowing in the turret, in the Number 2 position on Tolman's right. Muller-Rowland and his crew were in the Number 3 position when we began our take off run. The Free French flight, whom we met about half way down the runway, came at us head-on. I was trying, with a somewhat ropey engine, to keep station on the leader when Ned, his eyes wide with horror, yelled something to me and pointed towards the nose of the aircraft. A glance in that direction and I was just in time to see the two lead aircraft lift off the ground and almost immediately collide! The Free French machine came cartwheeling down the runway - wingtip, nose, wingtip and so on, until it stopped right way up. We were none of us going as fast as we should have been but Muller-Rowland managed to pull his Blenheim into the air and went into a 'split-arse' turn, right on the deck and somehow escaped. Lagging as I was with my oiled-up engine, I slammed both throttles shut and kicked on right rudder. Luckily for all six of us the FF bloke decided to fly and pulled the +9 boost override. I can still see those four yellow 250 pounders passing only a couple of feet overhead![12] Many months later I was to meet the French pilot who flew

The wreckage of the Ju 88 brought down by RAF night fighters a short distance from the squadron's camp site at LG 75 on 1st December 1941. (L E Durrant)

The remains of V5991 in which Plt Off Tolman, Fg Off Hutton and Sgt Harris died following a collision with a French Blenheim taking off from LG 75 on 4th December 1941. (G A Gowing)

Left:- F/Sgt Dave Cliffe reads an old copy of Life *magazine while keeping an eye on the clutch of bombs destined for the next mission. (Mrs Daphne Hughes). Above:- Bomb loading procedure the Desert Air Force way - a 250 pounder being hoisted into the bomb bay of one of No 45 Sqn's Blenheims using the most advanced technology available. (A D Allen)*

opposite to me (in the FF No 3 position) in an American PX near Khartoum - small world!

The flight's leading Blenheim, V5991, exploded, killing Plt Off James Tolman, Fg Off Antony Hutton and Sgt Douglas Harris outright. The crew of the Lorraine Sqn's Blenheim was badly injured, particularly de Maismont and the pilot, Fifre, who died shortly afterwards. The carnage on the airfield prevented eleven aircraft from getting off but the remaining seventeen Blenheims formed up and doggedly continued with the mission which resulted in a particularly successful operation.

A severe sandstorm on the 5th precluded flying. The squadron diarist wrote: "Visibility, even inside the tents, was almost nil and a thick layer of sand covered everything. Dinner consisted of sand with bully beef and sand and biscuit sandwiches. A most depressing day." Conditions improved on the 6th and the squadron contributed five aircraft to another joint attack on German armour at Bir el Gobi. This raid was carried out at low-level and, as he skimmed a rise and dropped down the far side, Gus Alder was confronted with a line of six camels plodding across the desert. The crew felt a slight thump as V6180 hit something but it kept going. When they got back to LG 75 the groundcrew found the head of one of the unfortunate beasts jammed between the cylinders of one of Blenheim's engines - a real Flying Camel, after a fashion!

The Japanese attacked Pearl Harbour on December 8th and within hours of the news reaching the desert rumours began to circulate about No 45 Sqn being redeployed to the Far East. On the same day the arrival of another new crew, Plt Off P U A Keel, Plt Off L G George RAAF and Sgt J F Jennings RAAF, further broadened the squadron's international composition as the pilot was the unit's first and only Dane. Four singletons were launched on the 10th to harass MT at Mechili but all were frustrated by the weather. By this time the Axis forces had finally been pushed further back into Cyrenaica (Tobruk had been relieved on December 7th) and they were establishing themselves in the vicinity of Gazala. On the 12th six aircraft carried out an attack, staging through the recently captured airfield at El Adem on the way out and on the way back. Only five aircraft actually flew the mission as Hughes' V5967 had damaged its tailwheel landing at El Adem on the outbound positioning flight. One aircraft, regarded by Doug Allen's crew as their personal Blenheim, was hit by flak. Geoff Gowing's diary entry for December 13th reads, "P/O Paul Keel and crew took our V6467 on a raid yesterday, south of Derna, and brought it back with the turret seat smacked by a cannon shell. Sgt Jennings collected the shell in his rear; it fortunately didn't explode, but he was

From the left, Plt Off Lloyd George RAAF, Sgt Bill 'Titch' Fylan and Plt Off Paul Keel at Gambut in December 1941. (Mrs Daphne Hughes)

The domestic arrangements at Gambut were somewhat primitive although Sgt McAusland seems to have acquired a particularly desirable hole in the ground. (R McAusland)

As at Menastir a year before, Gambut was found to be littered with wrecked enemy aircraft. This picture shows some of No 270 Wg's men picking over the remains; note the Free Frenchman on the left. The swastika from the fin of this aeroplane, a Bf 109E of JG 27, has already been removed to decorate someone's dugout and the white tailband has acquired a curious graffito - not sure what it says; it is probably written in Australian.... (G A Gowing)

badly enough injured. The blood cleaned up today; the hole in the fuselage patched beneath the turret where I sit and a new seat fitted." Keel and Lloyd George had not been hurt; Sgt Jennings was admitted to hospital in Tobruk, his place within the crew being taken by Sgt Bill 'Titch' Fylan. The crews spent the night of the 12th at El Adem before returning to LG 75 the following day.

With the *Afrika Korps* now well to the west it was time for the squadron to move forward again and on the 13th an advance road party and some of the aircraft set off for El Adem, although the latter returned before nightfall. Peter Hodkinson recalls "going into Tobruk to get some fuel for the trucks and being told that the big bang during the previous night's raid had been the petrol dump going up - so, no petrol." He also remembers sleeping under a lorry and waking up in the morning covered with hoarfrost; the desert could be surprisingly cold as well as hot. The enemy had departed in considerable haste, leaving, much as they had a year before, a substantial quantity of abandoned goodies but the weather was harsher than it had been last time and there was not quite the same elation as there had been at Menastir in the previous January. Something of the prevailing atmosphere can be detected in another extract from Geoff Gowing's diary written on December 15th.

Started 0445 for 0700 take off for El Adem. Heavy rainstorm - delayed and airborne at 0820 in 35 (*ie* Z7635 - *CGJ*). On standby all day at El Adem, nothing doing. Finished up with very heavy dust storm so couldn't take off from El Adem or land at 75. Spent a bugger of a night with 270 Wing at El Adem. Cold as hell, lay down in my flying suit with an Italian overcoat over me in an Italian tent. Water salted and not drinkable so had two large mugs of Chianti wine, which was in abundance, with German bread. Made my head spin. Collected enemy rifle, ammo & bayonet while there.

In the afternoon of the 16th the weather cleared somewhat and a number of aircraft were able to get off from El Adem to attempt an escorted raid but the fighter leader aborted the mission after they had passed Gazala and before the bomb run. The formation returned to El Adem but they were airborne again shortly afterwards to attack an enemy force which had been by-passed and cut off at Bardia. This strike was successful and the crews flew back to LG 75 for the night.

At this point the squadron's destination was changed from El Adem to Gambut and, while the advance party was being redirected, the groundcrews of both flights moved to the new LG on December 18th and 19th. To take their place the squadron's rear party left Fuka and moved forward to LG

Among the abandoned enemy aircraft found at Gambut was this captured Hurricane, V7670. Photographs of this aeroplane have appeared in print before but they have usually shown the port side and none have featured one of No 45 Sqn's airmen; he is LAC 'Dizzy' Day, an armourer. (I. Wilde)

75 which now became the Base LG. Gambut proved to be a pretty inhospitable area of rocky desert about eight miles from the coast. The surface being too hard to permit digging-in, the previous occupants had erected some low stone walls which provided at least some protection, which is more than could be said for many of the desert 'airfields' to which the squadron was by now well accustomed. More significantly, Gambut proved to be infested with fleas which resulted in the CO having to burn his trousers! The ORB again: "Water is very scarce and what there is salt. Tea made with salt water is a most unpleasant drink. A bath is out of the question and it is too cold for a dip in the sea - even if operations were limited to permit it". Another significant feature of Gambut was the quantity of abandoned German equipment and aircraft which littered the LG, mostly damaged Bf 109s and Ju 87s with the odd Bf 110 and Ju 88 and even a captured *'Luftwaffe'* Hurricane. The squadron found two German petrol bowsers among this booty and, restored to working order, these valuable acquisitions were duly absorbed into the unit's MT pool.

By this time Rommel had decided to pull back to El Agheila and the German and Italian forces were streaming back towards Agedabia and El Agheila. As a result there had been no respite from operations while the squadron had been moving forward and it had contributed up to nine aircraft to raids, usually flown in company with other Blenheim squadrons and with fighter cover, on December 17th, 19th and 20th against MT in the vicinity of Barce, Mechili, Ghemines and Tocra. The last of these missions was intercepted by about twenty Bf 109Fs and a fierce engagement ensued. F/Sgt David Cliffe, flying as usual with Arthur Hughes and Lin Durrant (but in Gus Alder's V6180), provides this personal impression of their sortie:

We had been briefed that the enemy had retreated to Benghazi but as we were passing Barce I saw two single-engined fighters taking off. I advised Hughes and asked if we were expecting to pick up an additional fighter escort. He said that we weren't and told me to keep an eye on them. The Blenheim's hopelessly inadequate TR9B radio did not even permit us to notify the other bombers of this potential threat, let alone warn our escorts. I watched helplessly as the enemy fighters climbed above and behind our top cover. They came diving down, hitting a Tomahawk on the way, and then engaging the bombers, the Blenheim on our left suddenly erupting in an orange ball of fire. I had opened up on the Jerries as soon as I saw the first Tomahawk go down but after that confusion reigned, our escort dispersing in all directions and the bomber formation beginning to break up as more enemy fighters appeared on the scene. I saw at least four of them. As Hughes headed for some heavy cloud I spotted an Me 109 at '6 o'clock, high', diving to attack someone below us. I gave it a long deflection burst and it began to pour heavy black smoke as it passed out of sight. The Germans had succeeded in disrupting the raid, however, and the mission was aborted. We dropped down to low level and made our way back to Gambut without encountering any further fighters. I had about fifty rounds left in each magazine when we landed.

Another of the crews who flew on that mission was the all-RAAF team of Plt Offs Furmage and Pailthorpe and Sgt

Barclay. Bob Barclay recalls events as seen from the turret of Z7588:

My guns packed up and as each '109 attacked I screamed my head off to Geoff (*Furmage*) to turn hard into them. This was successful on three occasions and, despite a few holes and being fired on by our lot residing in Tobruk, we made it back to LG 75.

F/Sgt Dave Cliffe whose guns probably destroyed one of JG 27's Bf 109Fs on 20th December 1941. (Mrs Daphne Hughes)

The Officers' Mess at Gambut, December 1941. On the left are Plt Offs George Kemp RAAF, Stuart Muller-Rowland, Norm Bain RAAF, Alan Tidswell RAAF and Dudley Eve RAAF; at the head of the table is the Adj, Flt Lt Philip Butters (or possibly the squadron's equipper, Fg Off Ron Culverwell) and on the right, Fg Offs John 'Paddy' Wright and T H Jones (Eng), an unidentified pilot officer, Plt Offs Phil Graebner RAAF and Fg Off Dicky Brown. Note that Kemp, Bain and Eve have begun to sprout a more conventional thatch after their protest at Wg Cdr Wallis' "no beards" rule. (Mrs Daphne Hughes)

In the course of this engagement seven Tomahawks and four Blenheims were lost, two of the latter from the Lorraine Squadron and two from No 45 Sqn. V6132 went down with no survivors from its crew of Sgts J Burns, R E J Reeves and J E Wilcock. The second of the squadron's crews, Sgts G T Bennett, H C Nullis and H W Twydell crash landed in V5948 not far from Barce but none of them was seriously hurt. They made contact with some Arabs who escorted them to Derna where they linked up with friendly troops and eventually rejoined the squadron on the 25th. Three of the attacking fighters were claimed as having been shot down, Dave Cliffe's '109 being credited as a 'probable'. As his crew had themselves been shot down only a month before, this went at least some way towards settling their particular score.

By now the squadron had recovered from its heavy losses during November and its tail was well up again. Much of this was due to Wg Cdr Wallis. A cheerful Irishman who usually wore a green spotted scarf when he flew, he had a zest for life and an enthusiasm for fun and parties and was already impressing his personality on the squadron. It was Christmas

The squadron bar. All set to crack the first bottles are OC B Flight, Sqn Ldr Arthur Hughes (left) and the CO, Wg Cdr Brian Wallis, wearing his green polka-dot scarf. (I. Wilde)

Christmas Day 1941 and a group of No 45 Sqn's aircrew model a typical selection of desert outfits: the battledress blouses are army, rather than air force, issue. From the left, standing: Sgt 'Pat' Paterson, Plt Off Bill Corbett RAAF, F Sgt Dave Cliffe, Sgt Ted Pulford RCAF, Sgt John Pannifer, Sgt Cliff Briggs RAAF and Sgt Bill Wilson RAAF; kneeling, Sgt Ken Gardiner RAAF and Sgt 'Taffy' George. (D Cliffe)

time and the CO was not going to let a little thing like a war interfere with the celebrations. Sqn Ldr Hughes took V7588 to Cairo on December 22nd to fetch some booze. He flew back on Christmas Eve with all available space packed with sixty cases of beer, twenty dozen bottles of liquor and two passengers, Gus Alder and LAC Adams, in addition to the crew. Hughes noted in his journal that his Blenheim had seemed to take forever to unstick when it took off from Heliopolis - which was hardly surprising! Just to be on the safe side, a lorry had also been sent to Alexandria to bring further supplies and this returned to Gambut on Christmas Day to a tumultuous welcome from the squadron's airmen. Christmas Day 1941 was a great success with the officers and NCOs serving the airmen their dinner of turkey and roast pork in the traditional fashion.

Christmas Day was also memorable for a visit by the *Luftwaffe*. At about lunch time a single Bf 109 suddenly appeared at very low level. Everyone immediately dived for cover. The German pilot appears not to have been in an aggressive mood, however, and he made two or three further passes, apparently waving from the cockpit. Since the '109 had not opened fire, the squadron's airmen emerged from their hidey-holes and waved back. Peter Hodkinson, who was then living with three other airmen in an abandoned aircraft packing case (and who is not alone in recalling this incident), remembers taking refuge in a small cave and emerging covered by big black fleas like the ones which had cost Brian Wallis his trousers! It would seem that the *Luftwaffe* pilot may have been mixing business with pleasure, however, and that his sortie had actually been a recce, as his visit was followed by an air raid at about 2100hrs. Fortunately the attack proved to be ineffective and the bombs fell harmlessly about a mile from the camp.

Jock McCandlish, then an LAC, recalls Christmas back at LG 75 and the subsequent journey west:

Petrol drums were converted into ovens; the essential food and drink was obtained and all was going well when the news came through that the Base Party was to move up to rejoin the rest of the squadron at Gambut and that the move was to start on Christmas Day! The solution was to bring Christmas forward by one day and it was well and truly celebrated. Due to its success - or was it

Another group of Christmas revellers at Gambut, all of them RAAF. From the left: Sgt L S Powell, Sgt L W H Connor, Sgt J J Eden, Sgt D J Smyth and Sgt D A Golder; of these five, only Golder would survive the Burma campaign. (Mrs Babs Golder)

excess? - the loaded trucks were a bit late in getting away next morning and the journey was then made somewhat longer because the Germans still held the port of Bardia. This meant that the town had to be by-passed, obliging us to leave the coastal road and take to the desert. An early stop was made when we met a small army convoy coming in the opposite direction. Seasonal greetings were exchanged and we shared our beer with them, the squadron acquiring at least one large swastika-bedecked flag in return. As we travelled west it became obvious from the many burnt-out tanks and other debris that we were travelling across what had only recently been a battlefield. As darkness fell it became necessary to make camp for the night. Some got their heads down under the gharries but some of the armourers, still full of Christmas cheer, laid on a pyrotechnic display which lit up the scene and drowned out the carol service being broadcast on our one and only radio. All was going well when the carol service was interrupted to announce that a small German force had broken out of Bardia. The Germans could not have been very far away but they probably gave the lunatic revellers of No 45 Sqn, capering about in the desert, a wide berth.

The squadron was reunited on Boxing Day as operations began again with three of the squadron's aircraft joining eleven others in an attack on MT at Agedabia. Then the squadron really moved into high gear. By now the main Axis force was well to the west but the isolated pocket at Bardia had still to be neutralised. On the 27th the squadron flew three missions against this target, each of six aircraft. The following day it put up no fewer than thirty-three sorties against the same objective.

On the 29th the focus was temporarily shifted further west and the first of that day's four missions was flown against Agedabia, which involved staging through Msus to pick up a fighter escort. The weather over the target proved to be too bad for bombing, however, so the Blenheims flew back to Gambut and dropped their three tons of bombs on Bardia before landing. A second three-aircraft raid against Agedabia, flown in company with about a dozen French Blenheims and again staging through Msus, was more successful and a direct hit was observed on a single-engined aircraft on the LG. The two remaining missions, mounted by three and two aircraft, were both against Bardia and all were successfully carried out, although it was difficult to assess what damage was being caused to the sand fortifications. Bardia was hit five more times on the 30th by a total of twenty-three aircraft and a further five bombed Agedabia. A sixth aircraft on the Agedabia mission, T2393, developed an engine problem and was obliged to land at Msus. On New Year's Eve the squadron hit its daily peak for the entire war. Thirty-nine sorties were flown in seven missions, all against Bardia, the largest being a twelve-aircraft strike.

During the last five days of 1941 the squadron had flown the remarkable total of one hundred and thirty-three sorties. In order to maintain this effort crews had been flying up to three times per day although, since the majority of missions had been mounted against Bardia, many of these trips had been of less than an hour's duration. Since this mini-campaign was being fought well behind the front line, there was little risk of encountering the *Luftwaffe* and a number of

unauthorised personnel, including several of the squadron's groundcrew, succeeded in persuading some of the pilots to take them along for the ride. The only person to get caught at this illicit practice was the MO who had a splendid strip torn off him by Wg Cdr Wallis, much to the amusement of the assembled aircrew and those (including the padre) who shared 'Doc' Kelly's guilt but had escaped detection.

No 45 Sqn made its last direct contribution to the North African campaign on New Year's Day 1942. In five hours the squadron mounted a further thirty-one sorties against the 9,000 or so luckless German and Italian soldiers pinned down at Bardia. A press reporter accompanied the CO's crew on

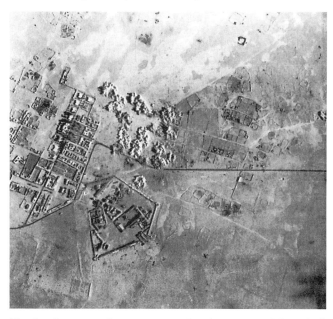

The bomb pattern beginning to take shape - Agedabia, 30th December 1941. (L E Durrant)

From the left, the padre, 2 Lt Trevor 'TC' Evans, Plt Off Norman Bayly and Sgt Ken Edwards after one of the sorties against Bardia during which a number of illegal passengers were carried. The padre has not been identified for certain but he may be the Rev Sqn Ldr U P Perring who was attached to the squadron on 20th October 1941. (A D Allen)

The squadron's final effort in the desert was a sustained three-day blitz against an isolated German enclave at Bardia. This photograph shows a formation of No 45 Sqn's Blenheim IVs during this brief but intensive campaign. (Mrs Daphne Hughes)

R3777 flew with No 45 Sqn for the last month of its participation in the North African campaign, evidently not long enough for it to acquire an individual code letter. The picture is of particular interest as it illustrates the practice, not uncommon in the desert, of operating Blenheims without their bomb bay doors, presumably because the bungee cord had became too perished to keep the doors closed. (Mrs Daphne Hughes)

one of the raids flown by Z7635 that day. Doug Allen took part in one of these final missions (also using Z7635) and the following is extracted from his recollection of his sortie, which was.....

.......a 'piece of cake' - like circuits and bumps back home, except that we off-loaded 4 x 250 pounders on 'the downwind leg', so to speak. We were at that time aiming our bombs from horizontal flight and we very seldom, I think, ever hit anything we were aiming at except by sheer good luck now and again. This lack of success bugged my Nav/Bomb Aimer, Ned Hammat, more than somewhat and he talked to me quite often about trying a little dive-bombing with the old Blenheim. [*The opportunity presented itself on January 1st when the squadron was allocated a specific blockhouse within the Bardia perimeter as its target.*] My crew, with Ken Edwards as WOp/AG in place of Geoff Gowing who was sick that day, was one of about six selected for this raid. Ned came to see me, all excitement - this he maintained was the perfect dive-bombing target and I agreed to give it a try. Ned planned to lie forward on the cockpit floor.

Having located the target I was to put the aircraft into a 45° dive, using the ring and bead sight to aim just short of the target. When Ned signalled to me by kicking one of his legs up I was to begin a nice steady pull out while he released the bombs in quick succession. On the way in I could see about three of our aircraft ahead of us and watched their bombs exploding all around the target but there were no actual hits. Throttling right back, I put the Blenheim into a fairly steep dive and at about 1,000' Ned signalled to me to pull out. We must have been back at about 1,000' in a steep climb when I got the shock of my life! The aircraft was hit by an enormous explosion, followed just seconds later by another. My first thought was that we had been hit by an 88mm 'Flak' shell and I looked over my shoulder back down the fuselage to see whether we still had a tail unit left! Ken Edwards was grinning at me delightedly from his turret and signalling a 'thumbs up' with both hands. In level flight once more I was amazed to see an enormous cloud of black smoke already above us and going on up to about 3,000 feet. A second one, at an angle to the first, probably went up to 5,000 feet. Ned had placed his first bomb just short of the blockhouse wall and the second had gone straight through the roof. The remaining two just hit the ground but, I would think, only yards beyond the building. The remaining two aircraft brought their bombs home!

The enemy enclave at Bardia surrendered on January 2nd. The Flying Camels' work in North Africa was (almost) done and on that same day they began to pull back to Helwan to prepare for a move to a destination which was, as yet, unspecified but with the Japanese swarming across South East Asia and the Pacific it was obviously going to be a lot further east than the squadron had ever been before.

Record keeping was not as precise in 1940-41 as it was to become in later years so it has been difficult to quantify the squadron's effort precisely during this period. Apart from recording being more of an art than a science before about 1943, especially in overseas Commands, the problem was complicated by the fact that the squadron was often divided between forward and rear bases. Furthermore, when the squadron was swept up in the tides of war, as alternating British and Axis offensives surged back and forth across Cyrenaica, maintaining the ORB sometimes took a low priority when the imperative was hot pursuit or hasty retreat. The Flying Camels were not unique in this respect, of course; indeed some units, particularly those which went to Greece and Crete, lost much of their documentation altogether (as No 45 Sqn was to do in Burma). The upshot is that there are some inconsistencies within No 45 Sqn's own records and occasional discrepancies between these and the corresponding fragmentary accounts maintained by the HQs of its controlling wings and groups; further anomalies are evident when aircrew log books are compared to the official record. Despite these constraints, however, it has been possible to quantify No 45 Sqn's effort on Blenheims to what is believed to be a reasonable degree of accuracy.

In ten months of operations on Blenheim Mk IVs the squadron flew at least 899 operational sorties. These can be broken down as: 277 desert sorties in April-May 1941; 172 sorties in the Syrian campaign of June-July; thirty-nine sorties over Iran in August and a further 411 after the squadron's return to the Western Desert for CRUSADER in September. To these can be added the 398 sorties flown on Mk Is, and summarised at the end of Chapter 6, to give an overall total for Blenheims in North and East Africa, the Levant and Iraq of 1,297.

The standard load for a Blenheim was four 250 lb GP bombs but 40 lb GPs, 20 lb fragmentation bombs and 25 lb and 4 lb incendiaries were frequently carried as were leaflets and 'spikes' and the occasional 500 pounder. Actual weapon loads per sortie were rarely noted so it is not possible to do more than make an estimate of what was dropped, and it must be remembered that the sorties flown by the Mk IVFs carried only light external bomb loads on an underfuselage rack as the bomb bay was taken up by the gun pack. Bearing all of this in mind, it is estimated that the squadron's overall offensive bombing effort while operating both short- and long-nosed Blenheims in the Middle East amounted to the delivery of perhaps 1,180,000 lbs of bombs, about 590 short tons.

If the squadron's offensive effort can only be estimated, the cost can be established with more precision. In a little over eighteen months, most of its spent living and fighting under the most arduous of conditions, seventy-nine of its men had died in combat. In other words the squadron had lost the equivalent of its entire fighting strength roughly twice over; three times over if those who had been wounded or who had become POWs are added to the total. Over the same period its personnel had been awarded just two DFCs and a single DFM. The squadron was now to move to the Far East where it would eventually operate with the XIVth Army, the 'Forgotten Army'. No 45 Sqn had already had more than its share of being 'forgotten', however, and in time its new masters in India would show themselves to be far more demonstrative in their recognition of the squadron's efforts than their counterparts in the Middle East had ever been.

Notes:

1. In point of fact there were no *Luftwaffe* fighters in North Africa on April 12th. The first Bf 109s did not reach Cyrenaica until I/JG 27 arrived on the 18th; they flew their first sorties over Tobruk two days later. This would suggest either that the incident described by Wilf Worrall occurred several days later than he recalls or that the 'Messerschmitts' which frustrated the attempted break out were actually Hurricanes (or, just possibly, Italian Fiat G.50s).

2. Contemporary records indicate that the Bf 110s were rather more successful than Len Wilde recalls. Although No 45 Sqn may have escaped relatively lightly, five Blenheims, two Lysanders and a Hurricane sustained damage and two of the Blenheims and a Lysander had to be destroyed when the LG was abandoned.

3. If the padre whom Len Wilde encountered at Gazala and the one who was shot down in one of No 45 Sqn's Blenheims (on 28th April) were one and the same then he was the Rev Sqn Ldr James Ernest Cox of HQ 204 Gp. He was not an Australian, however; he came from Croydon.

4. Carter was a pseudonym for a Free Belgian whose real name was George Henri Mathieu Reuter.

5. Only the losses which No 45 Sqn sustained in June 1917 come close to comparing with those which it suffered in May 1941 which, with a total of twenty-one casualties, seventeen of them killed in action, produced the worst monthly combat casualty rate in the unit's entire history.

6. Based solely on the evidence of correspondence with *some* ex-squadron members from this period, it is suspected that this early (and temporary) lack

of cohesion may have arisen partly from the limited respect which a few of the recent arrivals may at first have had for the handful of remaining veterans from the desert. After their previous experience of flying Blenheims with No 2 Gp some of the newcomers were apparently of the opinion that operating in the Middle East was "a bit of a rest cure". It is suspected that this may still be a common misconception today and, in case it is, the matter warrants examination. While it is true that No 45 Sqn's losses were relatively light between June and September 1941 (during which period some of the ex-2 Gp men moved elsewhere after a relatively short stay with the unit) this was an interlude of relatively low-intensity operations and did not reflect the pattern of the rest of that year. The publication of the second volume of W R Chorley's *Bomber Command Losses of the Second World War* permits a revealing statistical comparison to be made. Chorley lists aircraft losses by unit under three headings, those quoted at Figure 7.6 refer to those squadrons of No 2 Gp which flew Blenheims throughout 1941.

Squadron	Flying losses		Ground	Total
	Op	Non-Op	Incidents	Losses
No 21 Sqn	37	6	-	43
No 139 Sqn	34	7	1	42
No 82 Sqn	32	4	2	38
No 18 Sqn	27	5	1	33
No 105 Sqn	18	4	-	22
No 110 Sqn	16	4	-	20
No 114 Sqn	13	6	-	19
No 107 Sqn	15	2	-	17

Fig 7.6. *Aircraft losses by Blenheim squadrons of No 2 Gp in 1941.*

Applying Chorley's fairly rigorous yardstick, which excludes aircraft that were damaged but subsequently repaired (regardless of whether the incident had involved casualties or even deaths), the corresponding figures for No 45 Sqn that year were thirty-four aircraft lost on operational sorties and five on non-operational flights, for a total of thirty-nine. That puts the squadron third in a 'league table' of nine, indicating fairly conclusively that by 1941 flying Blenheims in the Middle East was just as likely to damage one's health as it was in Europe. It is suspected that analysis of the losses sustained by other Blenheim squadrons in the Middle East would reveal very similar rates to those suffered by No 45 Sqn.

7. As with all of the crew lists which appear periodically within this narrative, Figure 7.2 cannot represent a comprehensive picture of the crew state as this was constantly subject to minor changes. Others who flew during the Syrian campaign and whose names do not appear in Figure 7.2 included, for instance: Sgt Vipond, who stood in for McLaren on July 4th and 5th; Sgt R Bultitude, who arrived on the squadron with Plt Off Dicky Brown's crew but whose place was taken by Jim McGurk from July 7th onwards and Sgt John Bullock, who was killed on June 27th and replaced by Sgt Lidbury.

8. Alfred Llewellyn Bocking was an ex-Flying Camel. He had joined the squadron as an acting pilot officer in February 1936 and had flown from Helwan for over a year before transferring, unusually, to India where he joined No 28 Sqn.

9. HQ 204 Gp was redesignated AHQ Western Desert with effect from 9th October 1941.

10. The lady was probably Eve Curie who was in the Western Desert in late November 1941, accredited to the New York Herald Tribune and reporting on the British campaign.

11. It will have been noted that the squadron's administrative tail had been substantially larger since the introduction of the revised establishment of April/May 1941. Depending on circumstances, from time to time thereafter the squadron sometimes had two Adjutants/Administrators and/or two Cypher Officers on strength; it is believed that this was to cater for the periods during which the unit was operating on a split basis with one element at a Base LG while the operational echelon was at a forward strip.

12. It was not unusual for Blenheims in North Africa to be flown without their bomb bay doors, which accounts for Doug Allen's vivid recollection. It is not known for certain why this was done but it would seem likely that the doors may have been removed once the bungee cords which kept them closed had become too perished to function adequately.

Chapter 8. A desert swansong and pastures new - Burma.

The squadron was ordered back to Helwan on January 2nd, its intermediate destination being Wadi Natrun where its aeroplanes were to be dropped off to be given a wash and brush-up. It was not a smooth withdrawal. As soon as the first Blenheim landed it became evident that someone had neglected to inform the denizens of Wadi Natrun of the plan and, since neither fuel nor food nor accommodation was available, the Station Commander would not accept the aircraft or their crews. A fuming Brian Wallis had no alternative but to take his squadron elsewhere. He and Sqn Ldr Austin took most of A Flight to the naval airfield at Dekheila for the night; other crews went to Amiriya and to Heliopolis. Abandoning the Wadi Natrun option, most of the aircraft were flown to Helwan over the next few days and most of the aircrew were there by January 5th. This reshuffle was not achieved without incident. Landing at Dekheila on the 2nd, Plt Off Eve had ground-looped Z9573, and it took the FAA most of the next day to pull the aircraft (and a succession of bogged towing vehicles) out of the soft sand alongside the runway.

Despite Wadi Natrun's domestic problems, a few crews did succeed in spending the night of January 2nd there. Several of the crews who had headed for Alexandria found that they were unable to land (presumably because of Eve's aeroplane) so they flew back and presented themselves at Wadi Natrun again. These crews included: Plt Off Geoff Furmage in Z7588 with Plt Off Chas Pailthorpe and Sgt Bob Barclay; Plt Off Bill Maloney in V5938 with Sgts Des Carew-Reid and Bill Wilson, plus Plt Off Head as a passenger, and 2/Lt Gus Alder in V6180 with Plt Off Bill Corbett and Sgt Cliff Briggs. The next day V6180 set off for Helwan with six passengers squeezed into the back (these included another new all-Australian crew, Plt Off E G Christensen, Sgt B Pearce and Sgt R D Hilditch). On the way the port propeller parted company with the rest of the Blenheim and Alder was obliged to execute a successful wheels-down, asymmetric forced landing near one of the clusters of pyramids which litter the desert to the south and west of Cairo. No one was hurt and all nine men set off on foot, hiking for what Bob Hilditch calculated to be seventeen miles before they reached a road and were able to thumb a lift to civilisation. This was Alder's second unplanned landing in V6180 but, as in the first instance, the aeroplane had not been seriously damaged and in due course it was salvaged and restored to use, although not with No 45 Sqn.

There was a third accident in the course of the squadron's reshuffle and, sadly, this one resulted in a fatality. Taking off from Heliopolis on January 4th, Plt Off C W Head RAAF crashed in Z7588 and was killed. As the sortie had been only a short ferry trip to Helwan, Colin Head is believed to have been the only person on board.

Over the next few days several Blenheims shuttled back and forth between the Delta and Gambut ferrying people back to Egypt as on January 5th when Bill Maloney collected Cyril Hockney and his crew. The following day the bulk of the road convoy reached Helwan where the squadron came under the aegis of No 23 Personnel Transit Centre (PTC). Having returned to what was by rights No 45 Sqn's 'own' airfield, the older hands among the airmen were not best pleased to find that they were obliged to erect their tents yet again and live under canvas while interlopers occupied 'their' bungalows.

At this stage everyone knew that the squadron was being prepared for a move to the east but no one knew exactly where they would be going. Rumours abounded. Singapore and Australia seemed to be the most likely destinations, the latter probably being promoted by a whispering campaign fostered by the large number of RAAF crews now on strength. In fact the squadron's destination had yet to be finally decided but an Air Ministry signal of 10th January indicated that, of the four Blenheim squadrons that it was proposing to redeploy during that month, Nos 45 and 113 Sqns were intended to go to Burma while Nos 84 and 211 Sqns were expected to reinforce Singapore. A little later No 11 Sqn was also earmarked to move east, but by that time Singapore would already be in Japanese hands, the Dutch East Indies would be on the point of collapse and the British would be in full retreat in Burma - in view of the increasing threat to southern India, No 11 Sqn was sent to Ceylon.

The lack of hard information at squadron level was of no real consequence, however, and the remainder of January was spent preparing for the move. This involved a significant turnover of personnel. The South Africans were given the options of staying with the squadron or of remaining in Egypt and transferring to SAAF units. 2/Lts Allen and Evans decided to stay in North Africa; Allen converted to fighters and went on to fly Tomahawks with No 2 Sqn SAAF while Evans joined No 12 Sqn SAAF and eventually won a DFC on Bostons. Their departure broke up their crews and, although they all stayed on the squadron, only Plt Off Norman Bayly and Sgt Ken Edwards managed to stay together by joining up with Flt Lt I S Beeston, a newly arrived prospective flight commander. Gus Alder, the squadron's third long-serving South African, decided to remain with the unit where he was soon joined by another SAAF man, 2/Lt F A L DeMarillac.

While these and other crew changes were going on many

"There's a home for tired aircrew..."; Hurricane House on Cairo's Sharia Soliman Pasha. (D A Owen)

of the airmen who were already approaching their overseas tour expiry dates were posted off the squadron and replaced with fresh faces and there was a substantial intake of newcomers, both aircrew and groundcrew. In fact the squadron's strength was being more than restored; it was being considerably increased and a C Flight was re-established under (now Sqn Ldr) Leonard Penny. There were several old faces among the 'newcomers', including Fg Off John Edmonds who had been recalled from No 72 OTU. Similarly the crew of Sgts Osborne, Owen and Garfath, who had been on their way to Nakuru where they were to have become instructors, found their orders changed and they were directed to rejoin the squadron. They had had a good break, however, as Dennis Owen remembers:

In the middle of December Gerry, Tubby and I were sent to 'rest' on our way to Kenya. We stayed at Hurricane House, which was a rest home for NCOs with a group captain padre in charge and an Albanian called Alec Zog as

This picture was taken in January 1942 while a number of the squadron's aircrew were taking a break in Cairo before setting off for the Far East; this group all stayed at Hurricane House. From the left: Sgt Ken Gardiner; Sgt Ced Birkbeck; Sgt 'Taffy' George and F/Sgt Dave Cliffe. Gardiner's uniform is a bit of a puzzle as it appears to be in the darker 'RAAF blue' (compared to Cliffe's and George's RAF tunics) but it probably ought to have had 'Australia' shoulder flashes. The flying badge is also inappropriate as it appears to be an 'O' and Gardiner should have been wearing an 'AG' brevet. The style of this particular 'O' badge is very curious as it appears to have been modified to incorporate a laurel wreath. The observer's flying badge dated from WW I and the design of its wing differed from that of all other single-winged brevets (compare with the two on the right); it was also unique in that it lacked laurel wreaths - Ced Birkbeck's (army?) battledress blouse displays the correct, unmodified pattern. (C E Birkbeck)

general factotum. No bull, good food, proper baths and Arab bearers to do the chores, wait on tables, etc - and all right in the middle of Cairo with bars and restaurants virtually on the doorstep. There were probably about a dozen bods there at any one time, three to a room - with real beds, and sheets! We would go out every night to a posh hotel called Groppi's and pinch meals and drinks from waiters as they emerged from the kitchens with their trays held above their heads; we got quite good at it - a kind of shoplifting really. There was scope for other mischief too. Apart from decorating our room with purloined traffic signs (much to the distress of Alec Zog) we discovered that Cairo was built so that anyone could gain access to the roof of each block via a staircase and once up there you could come down again via another part of the building. This provided us with endless entertainment until the night we found ourselves in some sort of high class gambling club - the management called the MPs and threw us out. Our most successful 'night op' was when Tubby and I scaled the front of a hotel and lifted two large flags, one Egyptian and one Greek. I still have the latter *(this was written in 1994 - CGJ)*. All this came to an end when we were suddenly recalled to the squadron. There was a lot of reshuffling of crews and, while Gerry flew out to Burma, Tubby and I joined the sea party.

Throughout January as many aircrews as possible were released to get themselves into trouble in downtown Cairo in this fashion. Meanwhile, at Helwan, all the equipment for a

very large, fully mobile, light bomber squadron was being acquired and everything had to be packed. 'Everything' included the squadron silver but, since the news from the Far East was pretty depressing, rather than taking these valuables with them they were deposited in a bank vault in Cairo to await collection at some unspecified date in an uncertain future; it would be some five years before the squadron reclaimed them.

There was still some flying being done as an effort was made to provide new arrivals with a couple of shake down trips and a handful of crews were kept on call for any routine tasks which cropped up, such as air tests and ferries. One of these crews was that of Sgts R J Armstrong RCAF, A F Gooding and G B Whittaker who had ferried a Blenheim out to Fayoum via Portreath, Gibraltar and Malta during December. Shortly after their arrival in Egypt they were posted to No 45 Sqn and in the course of January they returned to the storage site at Fayoum three times, on the 16th, 18th and 30th, to collect Z7981, Z7913 and V5957 respectively.

One or two less mundane flying tasks also came the squadron's way, as on January 17th when there was a requirement to convey the AOCinC Middle East to the forward area. A couple of scratch crews were rounded up and two aircraft were prepared, which was just as well as the one crewed by Plt Off Rowe, Plt Off Bayly and Sgt Edwards declined to start. The second Blenheim (Z9668, flown by Sqn Ldr Penny with Plt Off Hammat and Sgt Gowing) left Helwan at 0710 hrs for the short hop to Heliopolis where their passenger was to be collected. Having first loaded his

If you are at a loose end in Cairo you just have to do it! Among the new arrivals at the beginning of 1942 were, from the left: Sgt A F Gooding; unidentified; Sgt G B Whittaker; Sgt H C Jewell; Sgt J R Hurley RCAF; Sgt F G Terry and Sgt R J Armstrong RCAF. All of these men had reached Egypt by ferrying Blenheims out from the UK. (R J Armstrong)

kit (which, as Sgt Gowing noted in his diary, included such delicacies as fresh green vegetables and "five bottles of whiskey") they flew him west to Tmimi. There they landed within earshot of gunfire and a marshaller jumped up on the wing to guide the aircraft to a dispersal. Geoff Gowing, still recalls the startled look on the corporal's face when the head and shoulders of Air Marshal Tedder emerged from the top hatch to accept his instructions! During the return flight to Cairo on the 19th, at the CinC's request the aircraft flew low across the recent battlefield at Sidi Rezegh; the sight of the carnage and the stench which pervaded the aircraft was still vividly recalled by Geoff Gowing half a century later. The air marshal was flown back to Tmimi on the 25th, nightstopping at Dekheila on the 28th on the way back and finally being delivered safely to Heliopolis the next day. The crew for this second trip was Bill Maloney, Des Carew-Reid and Bill Wilson; the aeroplane was Maloney's new Z9821 which he had collected himself from Fayoum on January 13th on a solo round trip during which he had delivered T2393 on the outbound leg.

There was yet another VIP trip on January 27th when Plt Offs Geoff Furmage, Chas Pailthorpe and Sgt Bob Barclay began a jaunt around the desert with Gen Sir Claude Auchinleck, Brig Shearer and Lt Stewart. They called at Tmimi, Gazala, El Adem and Mechili before finally returning their passengers to Heliopolis on February 3rd. Bob Barclay recalls that part of the final leg was flown with a Bf 110

keeping station about half a mile to the rear but, presumably out of ammunition, the German fighter never engaged the Blenheim.

Meanwhile the squadron's relatively relaxed period of pre-deployment preparations had been rudely interrupted. At 2130hrs on January 24th urgent orders had been received for twelve crews to pick up a dozen Blenheim 'fighters' from Wadi Natrun and return to Cyrenaica where they were to join Nos 11 and 14 Sqns at Bu Amud. The cause of the panic was the opening of a new German offensive and it was intended to use No 45 Sqn's 'new' Blenheim IVFs, each of which had been armed with a nose-mounted 20mm cannon in addition to the four machine guns in the belly pack and the fixed gun in the port wing, as makeshift tank-busters! While Sqn Ldr Hughes despatched runners to round up the necessary aircrew from downtown Cairo, a party of thirty-one airmen was assembled at Helwan and flown to Bu Amud in DH 86s and Lodestars. The aircrews known to have taken part in this hasty, and not exactly productive, return to the desert are listed at Figure 8.1.

Blowing sand made life very difficult on the 25th and the twelve Blenheim IVFs, which proved to be somewhat

This is Sqn Ldr Hughes' Z6094, one of the dozen or so Blenheim IVF 'tank busters' with which the squadron was temporarily equipped at the end of January 1942. The four-gun belly pack is clearly visible, as is the installation of the 20mm cannon; note that the transparency on the port side of the nose has been blanked out with a crudely tin-bashed sheet of metal which is wrapped around the pitot mast. With a fifth machine gun in the port wing these aeroplanes had some potential as strafers but it is doubtful whether they would have been very effective against tanks - even if the cannon could have been coaxed into working. (Mrs Daphne Hughes)

Z9668/N which was taken on charge by No 45 Sqn on 7th December 1941. It did not go to Burma with the squadron but was flown by a number of its crews while preparations for departure were being made at Helwan. This was the aeroplane used by Sqn Ldr Penny to fly Air Marshal Tedder to Tmimi on 17th January 1942. (F G Terry)

Pilot	Observer	WOp/AG
Sqn Ldr A Hughes DFC	Flt Lt L E Durrant	F/Sgt D Cliffe
Sqn Ldr F J Austin	Plt Off F J Fraser	F/Sgt K Mills
Fg Off J S Muller-Rowland	Plt Off P E Graebner RAAF	Sgt K A Gardiner RAAF
Lt H R L Alder SAAF	Plt Off W J Corbett RAAF	Sgt C G Briggs RAAF
Plt Off D G Eve RAAF	Plt Off G E Kemp RAAF	Plt Off N Bain RAAF
Plt Off J H Rowe RAAF	Plt Off E L Hammat RAAF	Sgt A A Fraser RAAF
Plt Off F W Guy	Plt Off A H Tidswell RAAF	Plt Off R V Alford
Plt Off P U A Keel	Plt Off L G George RAAF	Sgt W Fylan
Plt Off E G Christensen RAAF	Sgt B Pearce RAAF	Sgt R D Hilditch RAAF
2/Lt F A L DeMarillac SAAF	Sgt R Southorn RAAF	Sgt G A Gowing RAAF
Sgt R P Curtis RAAF	Sgt L J Charlton RAAF	Sgt J L Brinkley RAAF
Sgt C G Hockney	Sgt J Paterson	Sgt W A Gaudet RCAF

Fig 8.1. Crews known to have been involved in No 45 Sqn's final desert deployment, 25th January-7th February 1942.

battered examples, only made it as far as Amiriya. Led by Sqn Ldrs Austin and Hughes, they tried again on the 26th and again found sand up to 2,000 feet once they had passed Sidi Barrani. The crews pressed on as best they could but became scattered. Five landed at Qasaba; two got into LG 121 and another pair landed at Maaten Bagush; Plt Off Eve put T2349 down alongside the coast road west of Mersah Matruh while an aircraft which had been left at Amiriya with a major unserviceability returned to Wadi Natrun. The twelfth aeroplane, N3581, was the only one to succeed in getting down at Bu Amud but that sustained major damage while attempting to land in virtually zero visibility; fortunately the crew, Plt Off Edwin 'Chris' Christensen and Sgts Beau Pearce and Bob Hilditch emerged unscathed. Later that day the section at Qasaba, after another unsuccessful attempt to fly further west, moved to Maaten Bagush and by dusk on the 27th the squadron had eleven Blenheims concentrated there. Wg Cdr Wallis had attempted to join the detachment on the 26th but, frustrated by the awful flying conditions, he had been obliged to return to Helwan. The sandstorms persisted over the next two days and it was not until the 29th that conditions improved sufficiently to permit the detachment to proceed to its planned destination. Plt Off Rowe's and Sgt Hockney's aircraft were both unserviceable so, by the time that it eventually reached Bu Amud, the squadron was down to nine aeroplanes. Nos 11 and 14 Sqns proved to be very hospitable and fed everyone, while the Wing HQ provided a selection of tentage.

Intermittent heavy sandstorms continued over the next few days but, when conditions permitted, most of the squadron's crews managed to get in a couple of trips to practise the art of tank-busting on the plentiful supplies of burned out vehicles along the Trigh Capuzzo. Few of the pilots had any previous experience of ground attack operations and some hasty lectures were laid on to give them some idea of what was involved. As A Flight had found in May 1941, flying along a convoy of lorries while spraying them with machine-gun fire from the belly-pack was an exhilarating occupation but none of those pilots were still with the squadron and, in any case, tank-busting was a rather more precise business.

In essence tank-busting required two things; the direction of a constant and accurate stream of fire at a specific, and possibly moving, target as the range rapidly decreased, while avoiding being seduced into flying into the ground as the target's depression angle increased equally rapidly. The

pilots' attempts to master this unfamiliar technique were seriously hampered by the poor condition of their aeroplanes and the difficulties which the armourers were experiencing in keeping the unfamiliar cannons working without the appropriate tools.

On January 31st 2/Lt Freddie DeMarillac's gunner came down with pneumonia and he was flown back to Helwan. His place in the crew was taken by Sgt Geoff Gowing but, although attempts were made to rejoin the detachment on February 3rd and 4th, it was the 5th before they succeeded in getting back. Meanwhile, using the eight remaining Blenheims, training flying began in earnest on January 31st. The most successful crew managed to get six rounds off before their cannon jammed; most of the big guns failed to fire at all! Even if everything had gone smoothly, however, it is doubtful whether a 20mm cannon shell would have inflicted that much damage on a Panzer. The situation would have had to have become pretty desperate to have justified committing this ill-equipped, inadequately armed, poorly supported and virtually untrained force to action. Fortunately Rommel's offensive was beginning to flag by late January and he was to get no further than Gazala, the front eventually stabilising on a line between Tmimi and Mechili.

Dave Cliffe has a vivid memory of an incident which occurred during this interlude:

...when we were 'bunked' with 14 Squadron in the desert, a navigator (can't recall his name) got into the pilot's seat

One of the crews involved in No 45 Sqn's last desert deployment. Following his attachment with No 21 Sqn SAAF, Sgt Cyril Hockney (left) rejoined the squadron in late December 1941 (when this picture was taken) and crewed up with Sgts 'Joe' Gaudet RCAF (centre) and 'Pat' Paterson (right). The aeroplane in the background is V5967, a standard Blenheim IV bomber, not one of those armed with a cannon.. (L E Durrant)

193

Another of the crews involved in the squadron's eventful but inconclusive final deployment into the Western Desert: let to right:- Sgts Les Charlton, 'Rusty' Curtis and John Brinkley, all Australians. (L E Durrant)

of one of these fighters while I was underneath checking the forward-firing machine guns. Pretending that he was shooting-up the enemy, he pressed the firing button, not realising that the safety switches were in the firing position, and a hail of bullets missed me by about six inches!

Orders were received on February 2nd for the Blenheim Wing to withdraw further to the east and Nos 11 and 14 Sqns promptly began to pull back to LG 76. The following day No 45 Sqn was ordered back to LG 76 as well. Two more aeroplanes had joined the squadron by this time but the groundcrew echelon had been increased as well in the hope of improving serviceability so that the detachment now numbered eighty-eight men in all. Including their personal kit, recently acquired tentage and stock of ammunition, there were some three tons of freight to be moved. Apart from the ten aeroplanes, the only other available transport was three trucks! Blowing sand made the withdrawal as disjointed as the deployment had been and by dusk on the 3rd only three of the aeroplanes had made it to their planned destination; the others were scattered between LG 75, Maaten Bagush, Fuka, Qasaba, Mersah Matruh, Helwan and Wadi Natrun. The following day, while most of the crews were still attempting to rejoin the others at LG 76, Plt Off Bill Corbett arrived with the road convoy, one of the Chevrolets being towed by a captured Italian lorry. The tents were re-erected; a semblance of order began to reappear and preparations were made to resume training.

Brian Wallis made another attempt to join the detachment on February 4th but was again defeated by the sand. He got through on the 5th, however, bearing orders for the squadron's immediate return to Helwan. This was just as well as the other Blenheim units were moving to LG 116 and without their support the squadron's detachment simply could not have hoped to have continued operating. Over the next few days the squadron returned to base, a few of its tatty, second-hand Blenheims being flown to Gambut where they were passed on to No 14 Sqn. With the assistance of several Blenheim sorties mounted from Helwan to collect some of the surplus personnel, everyone was back at Helwan by the evening of the 7th, much relieved that the ill-conceived shambles was all over. Sqn Ldr Hughes wrote a first hand impression of these events in 1950 and this is reproduced verbatim at Annex H.

The squadron had been recalled because of the increased priority now being afforded to its redeployment to counter the Japanese offensive in the east, the hasty return to the desert having significantly delayed its intended departure date. The non-arrival of No 45 Sqn in Burma was now causing considerable concern and Rangoon and Delhi were urgently pressing for the squadron to be released by RAFME and despatched forthwith. The movement orders were hurriedly revised and the rescheduled plan now envisaged the squadron leaving Egypt in five elements, departing on consecutive days beginning on February 9th. The first flight of six aircraft was to be led by Wg Cdr Wallis followed by Flt Lt Beeston with five aircraft, Sqn Ldr Penny with five more, Sqn Ldr Hughes with another five and Sqn Ldr Austin with three. There was some slight readjustment of these arrangements but all twenty-four Blenheims were successfully despatched. 'Bunny' Austin left on schedule on the 13th but taking off from Lydda the following day he crashed in Z7913. None of the crew had been hurt so he decided to commandeer one of the accompanying aeroplanes. The other two crews tossed for it. The RAAF won, so Sgts Lance Powell, Les Connor and John Eden carried on. Sqn Ldr Austin took over Z9573 and the dispossessed crew, Sgts Bob Armstrong, Bert Gooding and George Whittaker, along with their passenger, LAC Aldridge, were obliged to make their way back to Egypt where they arrived on the 16th in time to join the sea party.

Before recounting the story of the air echelon it is convenient first to consider what happened to the main party. The bulk of the squadron, which consisted of ten officers, about twenty-five NCO aircrew and nearly four hundred groundcrew, was to travel to Burma by sea under the overall command of its Equipment Officer, Fg

Pilot	Observer	WOp/AG
Fg Off G G Furmage RAAF	Plt Off C D Pailthorpe RAAF	Sgt R M Barclay RAAF
Plt Off J H Rowe RAAF	Plt Off E L Hammat RAAF	Sgt A A Fraser RAAF
Sgt W S McLellan RAAF	Sgt J R Vernon RAAF	Sgt J Nankervis RAAF
Sgt R J Armstrong RCAF	Sgt A F Gooding	Sgt G B Whittaker
Sgt C G Hockney	Sgt J Paterson	Sgt W A Gaudet RCAF
Sgt G W Hartnell RAAF	Fg Off P C Lahey RAAF	Sgt D Thornton RAAF
Sgt F L Butcher RCAF	Sgt J A H Kirkpatrick	?
Sgt J E Pannifer	Sgt C E Birkbeck RAAF	Sgt E B Pulford RCAF

Fig 8.2. Crews of No 45 Sqn who are known to have reached India by sea.

Off Ron Culverwell. The aircrew known to have travelled by sea are listed at Figure 8.2 (although at least two of them, Furmage and Pailthorpe, sailed on a separate ship a few days behind the others). An advanced party set off for Port Tewfik on February 16th. At Helwan, the following day was spent loading the kit onto a train in the camp's own railway siding. Once it was all safely stowed the squadron boarded, only to have to wait four hours before the train finally moved off on the six hour journey to Port Tewfik which they reached at 0600 hrs on the 18th.

The vessel on which they were to sail was HMT *Orestes*, a middle-aged 8,000 ton ex-cargo boat of the Ocean Steamship Co Ltd, the 'Blue Funnel Line'. The Orderly Room staff boarded first, to check the men on board, then the stores were loaded and the ship finally sailed at 1700 hrs on February 19th. A ship's routine was quickly established with two sittings for meals. The only duty requirements were the manning of guns and the mounting of guards and picquets so a programme of lectures and deck sports (although there was precious little deck space!) was laid on to relieve the boredom. The inevitable periodic lifeboat drills provided further variety. In the evenings there was 'Housey-Housey' (Bingo), and two concert parties were cobbled together and performed to great acclaim. Stops were made on the 21st/22nd at Massawa and on the 25th at Aden, where some of the officers and NCOs were allowed a brief run ashore.

No 45 Sqn was not the only unit heading east at this time and, coincidentally, among the other passengers was a Plt Off V K Jacobs RNZAF. Then a Hurricane pilot with No 136 Sqn, he was to command the Flying Camels some twelve years later. In his unpublished memoirs he has given an impression of conditions on board ship:

As the ship had been a cargo vessel before it had been pressed into service as a trooper, the accommodation below decks was makeshift in the extreme and for us (the officers) became uninhabitable, since our cabins were constructed against the casing over the engine room and, once the ship put to sea, that wall was simply too hot to touch. Couple that internal heat with that generated by the latitude of the Red Sea and imagine the cramped quarters with some six officers to a tiny cabin in two-tier bunks, then some idea may be gained of the conditions under which we travelled. God knows how the airmen coped, cooped up in what had been the ship's holds.... Six days out of Tewfik, one of our engines gave up the ghost (a comfort to know that at least *Orestes* had two of them!) reducing our speed to 7-9 knots - and we were unescorted. *Orestes* was six months overdue for a refit so at this reduced speed our voyage would take us twelve days instead of seven to reach our anticipated destination, Colombo.

Dennis Owen has also commented on the appalling conditions under which the groundcrew travelled and the overwhelming heat. He also recalls that the ship had been fitted with makeshift gun positions mounted on 'pylon-like structures'...:

....the heat and humidity got so bad that I took my hammock each night, climbed into the steel latticework which formed the nearest pylon, and slung it directly underneath the gun platform. Fine, until the night I was

Home to No 45 Sqn and sundry other souls for four weeks, a pre-war shot of the SS Orestes *which conveyed the bulk of the squadron from Suez to Calcutta in early 1942. By that time she was not quite as spick and span as she appears here and she had acquired a few makeshift modifications and excrescences to adapt her for her role as a trooper and to provide her with notional short-range air defence capability. (National Maritime Museum)*

peacefully trying to get to sleep as a gentle, if warm, breeze blew over me, when I heard curious noises from the gun position over my head and after a while liquid started to drip through gaps in the floorboards. I climbed up the ladder to investigate and found the 'gunner' flat on his face and vomiting. There had been an issue of beer to the troops that evening and this one had overindulged!

Jock McCandlish has offered another observation on an aspect of life below decks:

To cope with the large number of passengers, an extra toilet had been erected up in the bows. It was a wooden structure with four or five cubicles, built over a sluice of sea water. It soon became evident that the trap to use was the one nearest the bow, ie upstream of the others. One bright spark discovered that if he dropped a piece of burning paper in the bow cubicle he could cause a fair amount of panic downstream. Fortunately there was a shortage of toilet paper on board so this practice soon died out.

The *Orestes* finally reached Colombo at 1230hrs on March 4th and entered harbour six hours later. The ship stayed in Ceylon for eight days and during this time shore

Shore-leave was granted while the Orestes *was in Colombo harbour in March 1942. Seen here at Mount Lavinia Beach during this interlude are, left to right, Sgts Pannifer, Rogers, Copcutt, Campbell and (in front) Hill. (D A Owen)*

leave was granted for all personnel. The only untoward incident occurred on the 8th when two MT drivers dived over the side of the ship for a swim. This unseamanlike behaviour upset the skipper and earned them four days confinement somewhere in the unsavoury bowels of the ship.

The news from Burma was bad; Rangoon fell while the squadron was still in Ceylon and the British forces were pulling back to the north. The squadron's destination was changed first to Akyab then to Calcutta. Escorted by HMIS

Above:- Sgt Bob Barclay, the big Tasmanian, outside a tent in the grounds of La Martinière School, late March or early April 1942. (G A Gowing)
Below:- Tents erected in the grounds of La Martinière School when the squadron set up shop on 26th March 1942. (L Wilde).

Indus, a 1,600 ton sloop, the *Orestes* chugged out of Colombo on the 12th and headed up the Coromandel Coast to drop anchor off the mouth of the Hooghly on the 17th. The following day she docked in Calcutta, 60 miles upriver.

Sqn Ldr Hughes was waiting to meet the ship and came aboard. A party of forty men was immediately told off to go to Burma to support the remaining aircraft. Another forty were to go to Dum Dum to act as a refuelling and rearming (R&R) party. The remainder were to move to Fyzabad by train. The latter group, which still numbered well over 300 men, comprised the majority of the technical and support personnel, including Fg Off R D Culverwell, Plt Off C Wilks (Cypher Officer), Plt Off B Lilly (Admin) and Flt Lt P J Kelly (MO). (*Although he is not specifically mentioned in the ORB at this juncture, Plt Off K J W Josling was still on strength and he was with the squadron in India until mid-1942, but it is not known how he made the journey from Egypt.*) They were to join Plt Offs Guy, Tidswell and Alford and a substantial number of NCO aircrew who had recently been withdrawn from Burma and who had already left Calcutta on the 12th. Once at Fyzabad everyone was to stand fast and await developments. The bulk of the sea party reached their destination on the 21st and set about occupying themselves with sports while acclimatising and recovering from the privations of their journey.

There was to be no such respite for those remaining in Calcutta. On the 19th the Burma party moved out to Dum Dum in the hopes of finding air transport to Magwe while the R&R party made a start on unloading the ship. The aircrew were temporarily quartered in the Grand Hotel and at Dum Dum pending a move to Magwe. For the next few days they assembled each morning, ready to start the journey but when news came through that the squadron had been effectively wiped out and that the RAF was pulling out of Burma, the move was abandoned (although, as related below, a few crews did get as far as Akyab). In the meantime, since there was a shortage of native labourers, most of the party of airmen earmarked for Burma had also found themselves working in the docks. As the squadron had been scaled as a fully mobile three-flight squadron there was a considerable amount of equipment to be unloaded, including the two German petrol bowsers which the squadron had 'liberated' from Gambut; other evidence of their recent success in Libya was provided by the fact that much of the squadron's complement of small arms was of Italian origin. It took until March 26th to get all the kit off the ship, reloaded onto a train and conveyed to No 304 MU at Kanchrapara where it was placed in storage.

On March 26th No 45 Sqn HQ was set up in Calcutta at No 11 Loudon Street. It was located in La Martinière School where room was made for it by the incumbents, the staff of the recently reconstituted HQ 221 Gp under whose auspices the squadron now came. In the absence of Wg Cdr Wallis, who was still in Burma, Arthur Hughes took command and, with Plt Off Furmage acting as Adjutant, established the whereabouts of all the squadron's personnel. At the end of March the situation was broadly as follows. Fifteen

Shortly after the Orestes *docked in Calcutta the squadron set up a Refuelling and Rearming Party to support the fighters defending the city. This photograph shows one of the squadron's armourers, LAC Dick Holloway, at Dum Dum with one of No 135 Sqn' Hurricanes (BM935). (R T Holloway)*

officers and some NCO aircrew (some from the sea party and some ex-Burma) were billeted-out in and around Calcutta awaiting developments while another substantial contingent of aircrew, mostly NCOs, was at Fyzabad with the bulk of the groundcrew. Flt Lt Durrant was attached to HQ 221 Gp as Group Navigation Officer. Of the remains of the operational echelon, the CO with Flt Lt Butters, Fg Off Pickering, twenty-four assorted aircrew and twenty-one groundcrew were at Lashio[1]. Sqn Ldr Penny was "somewhere in the field" attached to 17th Division as RAF Liaison Officer. Three aircrew, Sqn Ldr Austin, Fg Off Muller-Rowland and Plt Off Keel, were in various hospitals while 2/Lt DeMarillac and Sgt Southorn were recuperating at Dum Dum as 'walking wounded'. Four other aircrew had been killed in action. The squadron already had three detachments of groundcrew working in India: WO G W Adam had a party supporting Hurricanes at Alipore; F/Sgt 'Darkie' Hughes had another servicing Blenheims, Hudsons and the few remaining Buffalos at Dum Dum and Sgt Blasdale-Holmes, initially with just two airmen, was helping to turn round aeroplanes at Chittagong.

The billets provided for the NCOs and airmen who had originally been accommodated at Dum Dum airfield were condemned as being unsatisfactory and on March 21st they had moved back into the city and set up camp temporarily at La Martinière School, some inside the building others under canvas in the grounds. This fairly palatial establishment had previously been a convent school for girls and boasted an indoor swimming pool among its other facilities. It had been requisitioned for military use but, regrettably, this had involved the girls' moving out! McCandlish again:

> We dined in the school, but as soon as we queued up for our first meal we realised that we had a problem. The cookhouse was across the courtyard and we had to carry our plates and mugs of tea about twenty yards or so back

to the Mess. This involved running the gauntlet of a large flock of kite hawks or vultures. Apparently they were a protected species, probably because of their value as scavengers. These voracious birds would dive-bomb us as we crossed the courtyard and literally steal food right off our plates. I remember watching two airmen make this trip, eyes on the sky and evidently prepared to retaliate. As a bird attacked his plate, one of them let fly with his steaming mug of char. The bird dodged; his companion didn't, and was drenched! Fortunately he wasn't scalded; we Desert Rats were tough!

An element of the party destined to go to Burma appears to have become separated from the rest of the squadron, and indeed from the RAF, for a time and was left to its own devices. Eventually they presented themselves at Dum Dum where there was plenty of work to do before they were detached to Asansol to join No 353 Sqn. In their first few days in Calcutta, however, they had found themselves short of money and, since they did not have an appropriate 'chit', the army units they found would not advance them any cash. They were obliged to take matters into their own hands. Ernest Henman, then a sergeant Wireless and Electrical Mechanic (WEM) who had joined the squadron at Helwan immediately before it sailed for India, tells the following tale:

> We were aware that an army office in Calcutta issued certificates which authorised a bank to exchange £2 per man into rupees. However, the army declined to provide this service for RAF personnel. We were left with no alternative but to make a direct approach to a bank in the hopes that the manager would take pity on us and change some money without the crucial chit. We chose Barclays. In our travel-stained khaki and carrying our rifles, we arrived at the bank, which had several doors. The party split up and a group entered through each door. We must have given a good impression of a bunch of armed bandits

bent on holding the place up. The customers fled into the street and the tellers all disappeared too, leaving us in sole possession of the deserted premises. After about five minutes we became impatient and a started a chorus of 'Why are we waiting!' beating time on the floor with our rifle butts. The terrified Anglo-Indian manager eventually made an appearance. I explained our predicament but, without a chit, the manager, speechless with fright, would only shake his head in refusal. I advised him that if he was not more co-operative I might not be able to restrain my men from wrecking his establishment. This seemed to do the trick and he agreed to exchange our sterling at a rate of 13 rupees to the pound.

Having outlined the adventures of the sea party it is now necessary to go back in time to pick up the story of the air echelon. Although no formal documentation originated by No 45 Sqn during its time in Burma has survived, sufficient information has been gleaned from flying log books and from the diaries and recollections of many of the veterans who served with the squadron at that time to identify almost all of the personalities who were involved. In addition to the aircrews listed at Figure 8.2, ie those who sailed on the *Orestes*, those who are known to have flown out to Burma are listed at Figure 8.3. To complete the picture, other aircrew who are known to have been on strength at the time, but who appear not to have been formally constituted as crews and whose names do not therefore appear in either of these tabulations, are listed below. Most, if not all, of these men will have been with the sea party and an asterisk indicates those cases where this has been positively confirmed.

Pilots: Fg Off F G Daw* and Sgts G F Hayley and N T Taylor RCAF.

Observers: Plt Off R H Reeves and Sgts F R Haylock*

and D A Owen*.

WOp/AGs: Sgts H Garfath* and R Sparks RAAF.

It is interesting to note that No 45 Sqn had (at least) 103 aircrew on its strength when it left Egypt. Some sixty per cent of them came from the air forces of the dominions: fifty-one were RAAF; eight were RCAF; two were SAAF and one was RNZAF. When allowance is made for the fact that several of the others were in the 'wrong' air forces, eg Kirkpatrick was a Canadian, Goss an American, Durrant a New Zealander and Keel a Dane, the overseas contribution to the squadron's fighting strength was even more striking.

Most of the Blenheims had a passenger on board, competing for space with an assortment of kit, blankets, spares, tools and other paraphernalia, although it is known that some aircraft, eg Maloney's, carried two passengers while others, eg those of Eve and Curtis, had none. Of the total of twenty-three groundcrew and support staff of No 45 Sqn who are known to have reached Burma in this fashion, three were officers: Flt Lt P P Butters (Adj); Plt Off J T Arklay (Eng) and Plt Off H W Pickering (Int). Of the twenty ground tradesmen it has been possible to identify the following: Engines - Sgt J Toogood (also NCO in charge), Cpl T J Cant and LACs H Gardner, G Bell, G R Aldhurst, C Higgins and J Flynn; Airframes - Cpl H Sharpe and LACs L G Wilde, G Adkin, D Huntley, Anderson, Lansley, D Taylor and G Stanley; Armourers - LACs J Morris and G Newbould plus LAC J Gowers to look after the radios. There were two other engine fitters whose names have not been traced.

Apart from what could be shoe-horned into the Blenheims the bulk of the squadron's spares back-up was escorted out to Burma (solo!) by Cpl Wilf Worrall who set out by road from Helwan for Cairo on February 13th. He and his cargo reached Dum Dum about five days later having been flown there by a pair of DC-2s of No 31 Sqn. After a delay of several days an ancient Valentia was tasked with ferrying the kit down to Akyab, but that was as far as air transport would move it. Towards the end of February Worrall spotted one of the squadron's Blenheims landing and disgorging a load of civilian evacuees. He was able to attract the attention of the pilot and let him know that he, and the stores, were there. The next day Sqn Ldr Austin and Sgt Toogood flew in and a Blenheim shuttle was set up which was able to ferry nearly all the stores across to Magwe. Once established in Burma as the twenty-first and last member of the squadron's groundcrew echelon, Worrall located a stores park where he hoped to find others of his fraternity and an Aladdin's cave of equipment[2]. He was disappointed to find the cupboard almost bare, as whatever kit there might once have been had already been shipped out to India. He did not come away entirely empty-handed, however,

Pilot	Observer	WOp/AG
Wg Cdr C B B Wallis	Sgt D Page	Sgt B T McDade
Sqn Ldr F J Austin	Plt Off F J Fraser	F/Sgt K Mills
Sqn Ldr A Hughes DFC	Flt Lt L E Durrant	F/Sgt D Cliffe
Sqn Ldr L F Penny	Sgt G L Bruce	Sgt G George
Flt Lt I S Beeston	Plt Off N W Bayly RAAF	Sgt K E Edwards RAAF
Lt H R L Alder SAAF	Plt Off W J Corbett RAAF	Sgt C G Briggs RAAF
Fg Off J S Muller-Rowland	Plt Off P E Graebner RAAF	Sgt K A Gardiner RAAF
Fg Off J K Edmonds	Plt Off A Hilling	Sgt A King
Plt Off J W Maloney RAAF	Sgt D McK Carew-Reid RAAF	Sgt W R Wilson RAAF
Plt Off D G Eve RAAF	Plt Off G E Kemp RAAF	Plt Off N Bain RAAF
Plt Off F W Guy	Plt Off A H Tidswell RAAF	Plt Off R V Alford
Plt Off P U A Keel	Plt Off L G George RAAF	Sgt W Fylan
Plt Off E G Christensen RAAF	Sgt B Pearce RAAF	Sgt R D Hilditch RAAF
2/Lt F A L DeMarillac SAAF	Sgt R Southorn RAAF	Sgt G A Gowing RAAF
Sgt D J Smyth RAAF	Sgt D A Golder RAAF	Sgt J J Alt RAAF
Sgt R P Curtis RAAF	Sgt L J Charlton RAAF	Sgt J L Brinkley RAAF
Sgt L S Powell RAAF	Sgt L W H Connor RAAF	Sgt J J Eden RAAF
Sgt W M Osborne DFM	F/Sgt R A Turton RNZAF	Sgt A R Field
Sgt F E Thompson RCAF	Sgt J W Watkins	Sgt C H Romans
Sgt A N Huon RAAF	Sgt A Thompson	Sgt R I Clark RAAF
Sgt S A Goss RCAF	Sgt C A Whiteside	Sgt A Murray
Sgt H M P Neil RAAF	Sgt E J Hallett RAAF	Sgt F F Brown RAAF
Sgt H C Jewell	Sgt J R Hurley RCAF	Sgt F G Terry
Sgt C Fryar RAAF	Sgt G A Tibbs RAAF	Sgt G F Williams RAAF

Fig 8.3. *The crews who flew No 45 Sqn's Blenheims from Egypt to Burma in February 1942.*

Seen at Bahrein, 14th February 1942, en route Egypt-Burma. From the left: Flt Lt Philip Butters, Lt 'Gus' Alder, Sgt Frank Brown, Sgt Ernie Hallett, Sgt Max Neil, Sgt Cliff Briggs, Plt Off Bill Corbett, Sgt 'Rusty' Curtis, F/Sgt Dave Cliffe, Sgt Denys Golder and Sgt Doug Smyth. (L E Durrant)

The magnificently moustached Lt Gus Alder SAAF compares facial hair with one of the locals at Sharjah.
(Mrs Daphne Hughes)

since he was able to acquire a Fordson Sussex stores tender which, after boring out the steering lock and a spot of hot-wiring, proved to be a runner and was pressed into service with the Flying Camels.

The transit flight to Burma followed a standard route but the composition of the five formations fluctuated considerably as a result of take off and landing incidents, aeroplanes developing technical problems along the way and

hold ups caused by the weather. As a result there were some temporary depletions in strength which were partly offset by picking up strays from Nos 84 and 211 Sqns who had fallen by the wayside over the previous two weeks. As at 11th February a signal from HQME indicated that the disposition of No 45 Sqn was: three at Bahrein; eight at Habbaniyah; six airborne from Helwan and a further seven expected to leave on the 12th and/or 13th.

The experience of Fg Off Bill Maloney, Sgts Des Carew-Reid and Bill Wilson was typical. With Fg Off Harold Pickering and LAC 'Oscar' Wilde as passengers they left Helwan in Z9821 on February 9th as one of a five-aircraft formation led by the CO's crew in Z7635. The first night-stop was at Habbaniyah where Hedley Jewell's V5495 developed a snag and had to be left behind to join one of the groups following on behind. The second night was spent at Sharjah, reached via a refuelling stop at Shaibah. The next night was spent at Karachi before moving on to Allahabad on the 12th where an aircraft was involved in a landing incident (this was Sgt Prentice of No 84 Sqn[3]). Now down to three, the formation reached Dum Dum on the 13th and the next day staged through Magwe, where another aeroplane dropped out (this was Sgt McNamara of No 211 Sqn[3]), leaving just the CO and Maloney to press on to Rangoon. They landed at Mingaladon airport (about five miles north of the city) at 1835hrs.

Several of the officers were required to attend briefings but those who were not involved were able to slope off to spend a night out in downtown Rangoon. 'Oscar' Wilde remembers that they dined at the *Silver Grill* where they were suitably impressed by the buccaneering style of the pistol-packing pilots of the American Volunteer Guard who seemed already to have cornered the market in attractive oriental ladies! They eventually slept in some discomfort at

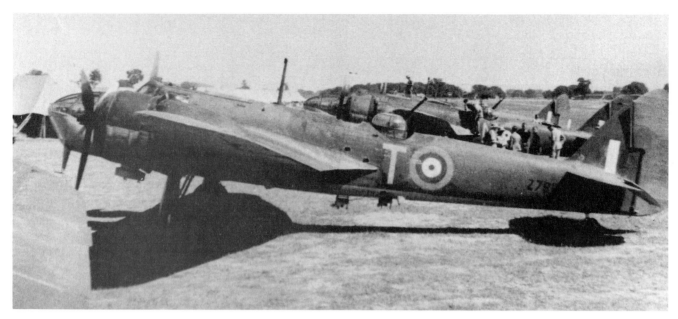

Sgt 'Rusty' Curtis' Z7981/T photographed during a refuelling stop at Allahabad on February 17th. (G A Gowing)

the Mingaladon Golf Club and the following morning, the 15th, the pilots moved their aircraft to Zayatkwin about 20 miles to the north east. Here they were met by another group of recently transplanted 'Desert Warriors' in the shape of No 113 Sqn.

No 113 Sqn's sixteen-aircraft air echelon had left Egypt some six weeks earlier. Like the Flying Camels, their only technical support was provided by the few tradesmen carried on board its aircraft but help was on hand when they reached Rangoon where the aircraft began to arrive from 7th January. The bulk of the resident No 60 Sqn had been away in Malaya when the Japanese first attacked and most of its aircraft had been either lost or absorbed by other units. The squadron's personnel had returned to Rangoon by sea and, since it had few aircraft of its own, No 60 Sqn's airmen were available to assist other units; No 113 Sqn was able to take advantage of this facility and thus acquired a significant ground echelon to sustain its initial activities.

Nine of No 113 Sqn's aircraft (two of them flown by No 60 Sqn crews) opened the RAF's offensive campaign with a raid on Bangkok on the 8th after which the squadron was withdrawn to Lashio for its Blenheims to be given a hurried over-haul. They re-turned to Mingaladon on Jan-

'Tubby' Garfath was not permitted to take his dog on the Orestes *with him so he was flown out to India in a Blenheim. This picture of Sgt Ken Gardiner and 'Tiger' was taken at some stage during the journey. Sadly, 'Tiger' went AWOL when he reached Calcutta, in much the same way as 'Crash' had done in Italy in 1917. (C G Briggs)*

uary 19th and resumed operations. Rangoon was a magnet for Japanese bombers, however, and once its advance party of groundcrew had arrived on the SS *Varsovar* on January 31st, restoring a degree of self-sufficiency, No 113 Sqn moved its HQ north to the relative safety of Toungoo. This boost in manpower also meant that, while never lavish, with the assistance of some of No 60 Sqn's people, No 113 Sqn's technical back-up was always more substantial than that of the Flying Camels. Although help was extended by the other squadrons when it was available, the core of No 45 Sqn's servicing support in Burma remained the handful of tradesmen who had arrived on board its aircraft. On February 6th No 113 Sqn's HQ moved again, across the Pegu Yoma to the civilian aerodrome at Magwe in the Irrawaddy valley. While Magwe was (for the moment) a very secure location, it was too far north to be a satisfactory operating base for the Blenheims and a detachment was based forward at the new airstrip at Zayatkwin. Thus it was that when Wallis and Maloney arrived there on February 15th some of No 113 Sqn's people were on hand to welcome them.

No 45 Sqn promptly set up shop alongside No 113 Sqn's detachment and prepared to commence operations under the operational control of NORGROUP[4] which was located in Rangoon under the command of AVM D F Stevenson CBE DSO MC. Like a number of other RAF airstrips in Burma at that time, Zayatkwin was still under construction. Sgt Geoff Gowing recalls "....hundreds of Burmese civilians, mostly women and girls, carrying baskets of stones on their heads and parties of men squatting breaking up the stones into rubble. When the Japs bombed the strip there were very heavy casualties. The limbs and remains of those who had been killed were simply thrown into a tipper truck and driven away."

The squadron flew its first operational mission in Burma, its aircraft still in their desert colours, on February 16th. At 1435hrs that afternoon, escorted by six Hurricanes, a total of eight Blenheims attacked a paddle steamer at Moulmein. Three of the bombers came from No 113 Sqn, the other five were nominally provided by No 45 Sqn. Wg Cdr Wallis' and Plt Off Maloney's crews definitely took part in this raid and two of the other 'No 45 Sqn' crews are known to have been all-RAAF 'guest' crews (Plt Off A W Pedlar, Sgt M F Roberts and Sgt M Morris of No 84 Sqn in Z9819 and Sgt J C McNamara, Sgt D W Penn and Sgt N A Bruce of No 211 Sqn in Z7892 - see Note 3); the fifth crew has not been identified. Thereafter sorties were flown almost daily, frequently in concert with No 113 Sqn. On February 17th Wg Cdr Wallis led a joint seven-aircraft raid against the Japanese-held aerodrome at Chiang Mai in Siam. No 45

Plt Off Eve's Z7928/D on the last leg into Burma on February 17th. (G A Gowing)

Sqn contributed three of the Blenheims (Wallis, Maloney and McNamara) and No 135 Sqn put up six Hurricanes to meet the formation on its way back and escort it home. The following day the squadron sent six Blenheims, with an escort of five AVG P-40s, to attack troop positions at Pandigon on the Bilin river while six Hurricanes escorted six of No 113 Sqn's bombers on a similar mission to Payinmabinseik.

The squadron's strength was increasing daily and the additional crews which had arrived by the 17th included those of Flt Lt Beeston, Plt Off Eve, 2/Lt DeMarillac and F/Sgt Osborne, some of them shepherding reinforcement Hurricanes into Mingaladon before turning away to land at Zayatkwin. The Blenheims were sometimes dispersed overnight to Mingaladon or a satellite airstrip at Johnny Walker[5], which gave the crews the opportunity to sleep in the relative comfort of the Golf Club.

Hedley Jewell had overcome the technical problem he had encountered on his way to Habbaniyah on February 9th and by the 12th he had reached Karachi. Here his V5495 was taken over by another crew but two days later he was on his way again in V5999. On February 18th his crew set off from Calcutta for the last leg into Magwe. Flying alone, inadequately furnished with maps and unable to raise anyone on the radio, the crew became 'uncertain of their position' and began to run short of fuel. Jewell eventually attempted a wheels-down landing on a level beach on the west bank of the Irrawaddy river near what turned out to be Thayetmyo, about fifty miles south of their planned destination. All went well at first but during the run-out the wheels hit a ridge in the sand and the aeroplane somersaulted onto its back. Sgt

Jack Hurley, the Canadian observer, was thrown out through the nose glazing while Sgt Gordon Terry escaped unhurt via the top (now bottom) hatch. While Hurley limped off to seek help in a nearby village the aeroplane attracted the attention of some orange-robed Buddhist priests who gathered in a silent group to gaze at the wreckage. They offered no practical advice or assistance and were presumably totally absorbed in contemplation of the existential meaning of the event. In the gathering dusk it was quite an eerie and unsettling experience but help arrived in the shape of an expatriate planter from Yorkshire, a Mr Fortescue, who accommodated the crew in his large house for three days until they were able to join the squadron on the 21st via one of the boats carrying refugees upriver from Rangoon while a team of airmen from No 60 Sqn came down from Magwe to salvage what they could from the aeroplane. In his eagerness to get away Gordon Terry left his kitbag behind. It followed him around the air force for the rest of the war and eventually caught up with him at Scampton in 1945!

A second aeroplane had been lost on the 18th when the all-RAAF crew of Plt Offs Dudley Eve, George Kemp and Norman Bain wrote off Z7928, which they had delivered to Zayatkwin only the previous day. Having taken off on their first raid, a fault in their aircraft's hydraulic system prevented its undercarriage from retracting properly and, as a result, one wheel remained firmly locked down while the other swung loose and declined to lock either up or down. There was no telling how the aeroplane would behave if it were to be landed in this condition so, to avoid the risk of damaging any of the several Blenheims parked close to the runway, Eve

Left:- V5999 K on the banks of the Irrawaddy near Thayetmyo on 18th February 1942. Surprisingly, no one was seriously hurt. Right:- Sgts Jack Hurley, Hedley Jewell and Gordon Terry (left to right) with No 226 Sqn in November 1941, shortly before they ferried a Blenheim out to Egypt and joined the Flying Camels. (both F G Terry)

Above:- Sqn Ldr Penny's Blenheim over Akyab on February 19th. (G A Gowing). Left:- Dudley Eve indulges in a spot of submarine salvage on February 19th, having ditched Z7928/D in the Pegu River the previous day. (L E Durrant).

elected to ditch in the nearby Pegu River. He put the Blenheim down successfully but the river was shallow and the aeroplane hit a sand bar which spun the aeroplane around, tearing off both undercarriage legs. The pilot received a blow to the stomach but the other two crew members escaped unharmed. They were treated kindly by the local Burmese and eventually got back to Zayatkwin in a borrowed horse-drawn cart. Early the next day the crew returned to the crash site only to find the aircraft virtually submerged. Having waited for some time for the water to subside a little, they were ferried out to the wreck and, after some difficulty, succeeded in destroying the IFF equipment[6].

The squadron's effective strength was depleted by one more aircraft at about this time. It had damaged a propeller in an argument with a bomb crater at Zayatkwin. Since no spares were available the only options were to abandon the aeroplane or to attempt to fix the prop and hope that the engine would hold together. Using a baulk of timber, a sledgehammer and brute force the propeller, still mounted on the engine, was 'straightened' and the aircraft was flown out, probably to Magwe but eventually to India.

These losses were offset by the steady flow of additional aeroplanes and crews. For instance, Gus Alder, Bill Corbett and Cliff Briggs joined the Zayatkwin detachment in Z9803 on the 18th, arriving just in time to be on the receiving end of a Japanese air raid. Other crews arriving that day included those of Plt Off 'Chris' Christensen with Sgts Beau Pearce and Bob Hilditch, Sgt Arthur Huon with Sgts Albert Thompson and Ron Clark and Sgt Doug Smyth with Sgts Denys Golder and Jeff Alt. Arthur Huon noted in his diary:

> Arrived at Zayatkwin shortly before mid-day and, on reporting to the CO, we were ordered to unload our gear and bomb up the aircraft immediately in readiness to fly an op in the afternoon. We purloined a truck, found the bomb dump, loaded four 250 lb bombs onto the racks, refuelled and had the guns loaded with belts. The operation was scrubbed. We found an open bamboo shed in the scrub, dispossessed three cows, obtained some charpoys (*bed frames*) from stores and set up house.

Sqn Ldr Hughes and his crew, which had included Flt Lt Butters for the duration of the journey, reached Burma on February 19th in V5938. Probably because it was already apparent that Zayatkwin's days were likely to be numbered, they remained at Magwe where they set about establishing a rear HQ. On the same day the operational echelon put up two raids. On the first of these, led by Flt Lt Beeston, the

The technical facilities available to the squadron's handful of airmen in Burma did not permit much routine maintenance, let alone sophisticated engineering. This Blenheim failed to negotiate a bomb crater at Zayatkwin and bent its starboard prop; it is seen here 'under rectification'. Cpl Tommy Cant is on the right in charge of the sledgehammer. Those steadying the baulk of timber are, from the left: LACs 'Junior' Lansley, Doug Huntley, 'Jock' Anderson, Charlie Higgins, 'Oscar' Wilde and 'Jock' Taylor. The aeroplane did fly again, all the way to Calcutta eventually, but it nearly shook itself apart in the process. (L Wilde)

Flt Lt Philip Butters, the Adj, sitting 'up front' alongside Sqn Ldr Hughes during the long flight out to Burma.
(Mrs Daphne Hughes)

Above, Sgt Ron Clark strikes a dignified pose outside his basha (A N Huon) while, below, Sgts Don Page (in topee) and Mac McDade clown for the camera in front of their tent (B T McDade): both pictures were taken at Zayatkwin in February 1942.

squadron contributed seven to a total of twelve Blenheims which, escorted by six Hurricanes from No 17 Sqn, attacked troop positions in the vicinity of Pandigon in two waves. In the evening another four of No 45 Sqn's Blenheims attacked a similar target near Danyingon, cover being provided by six of No 135 Sqn's Hurricanes. By this time the Japanese advance was threatening the army's positions on the Bilin and 17th (Indian) Div had begun to withdraw to the Sittang. This increased the vulnerability of Zayatkwin; it was evident that it too would soon have to be abandoned and before the day was out one of No 113 Sqn's aircraft had moved to Mingaladon while the rest had withdrawn to Magwe. No 45 Sqn's presence also began to thin out from the 20th but the detachment continued to operate from the forward base for two more days.

Despite the tension caused by the imminent withdrawal from Zayatkwin and increasing concern about the proximity of the advancing Japanese army, operations continued with some urgency. On the 20th the squadron mounted sixteen sorties, several crews flying twice, against tactical targets at Bilin, Taungzun, Pagan, Pandigon and Moulmein. This performance was repeated on the 21st. The first of the three missions flown that day was a four-aircraft attack against motorised troops at Kawbein on the Sittang. During a repeat of this strike at about mid-day it was reported that the squadron had actually bombed friendly troops although this was later disputed.

Whatever the truth of this allegation, there is no doubt that the second raid on Kawbein cost the squadron its first combat loss of the campaign; Z7770 was shot down. Having arrived at Zayatkwin on the 16th and flown their first mission two days later, for 2/Lt Freddie DeMarillac and Sgts Ralph Southorn and Geoff Gowing this was their fifth operational sortie in four days. Their aircraft came down on the west bank of the Sittang opposite Kyaikto and, although the pilot and observer had been injured, they all survived. Later that day the CO's crew found DeMarillac's aeroplane and 'Mac'

McDade expended a lot of ammunition in an unsuccessful attempt to destroy it but it declined to catch fire. The pilot and observer of the downed crew had both been knocked about in the crash and a damaged foot made it impossible for Southorn to walk without assistance. They managed to cover about two miles before they were able to commandeer a bullock cart; a little further on they came across some military vehicles and were able to secure a ride to Rangoon whence they were flown up to Magwe in a Blenheim of No 113 Sqn. From there they were evacuated to India via Akyab in DC-2s of No 31 Sqn and by the end of the month all three were safely in Calcutta.

The squadron's third mission on February 21st was a raid by eight aircraft, some operating as singletons, against enemy troops in the vicinity of Bilin. With a total of thirty-two sorties flown in two days the squadron had clearly hit its stride but at the same time it had passed its peak. Logistic problems and inadequate engineering facilities would not permit this pace to be maintained and, even if it had been, it was hardly enough to stop the Japanese army. The steadily mounting total of Blenheim sorties should not obscure the fact that their effectiveness was sometimes limited by a shortage of bombs. There were ample supplies of 250 pounders in Burma but, being heavy and cumbersome, bombs

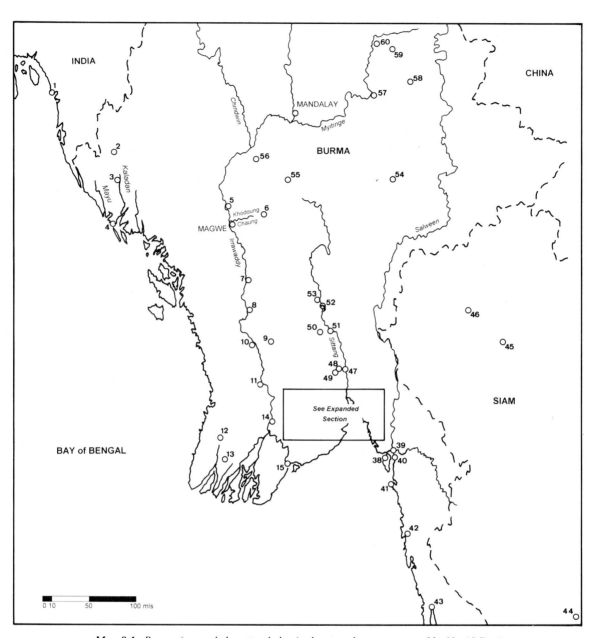

Map 8.1. *Burma (expanded section below), showing the area covered by No 45 Sqn's activities in 1942 and locations mentioned in Chapters 8 and 9.*

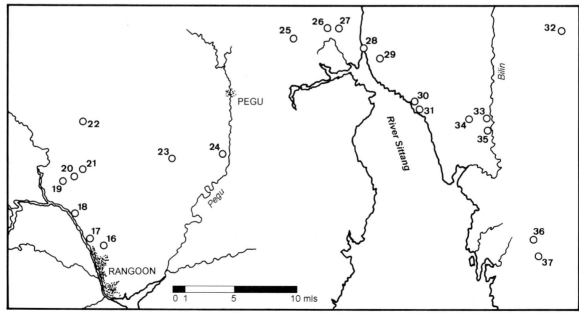

26	Abya	31	Kawbein	33	Pandigon
4	Akyab	29	Kaywe	52	Payagi
41	Amherst	30	Kyaikto	32	Payinmabinseik
12	Bassein	24	Kyauktan	8	Prome/Park Lane
35	Bilin	3	Kyauktaw	13	Pyinbon
46	Chiang Mai	45	Lampang	22	Pyinmadaw
1	Chittagong	59	Lashio	50	Pyu
49	Daik-U	39	Martaban	48	Pyuntaza
34	Danyingon	55	Meiktila	47	Shwegyin
15	Dedaye	16	Mingaladon	37	Taungzun
44	Don Muang	28	Mokpalin	43	Tavoy
6	Gwegyo	51	Mon	36	Thaton
11	Henzada	58	Mong Yai	7	Thayetmyo
19	Highland Queen	40	Moulmein	53	Toungoo
20	Hmawbi	10	Myanaung	25	Waw
17	Insein	57	Namlan	14	Yandoon
18	John Haig	54	Namsang	42	Ye
21	Johnny Walker	60	Namtu	5	Yenangyaung
38	Kalwi	27	Pagan	23	Zayatkwin
56	Kamye	2	Paletawa	9	Zigon

Key to Map 8.1.

are not easy to move about and once local stocks were exhausted re-supply became a major problem as the roads, especially those out of Rangoon, began to fill with refugees. As the makeshift bomb dump at Zayatkwin had begun to run short of weapons a few sorties had had to be flown with the aircraft carrying only 40 pounders and, on one or two occasions, no bombs at all. On the other hand, when bombs were plentiful, the aircraft were loaded with as many as possible and Sgt Norm Bruce's log book notes that on the first of the two raids flown by McNamara's crew on the 21st, Z7892 had been armed with four 250 pounders and eight 40 lb incendiaries while the crew had heaved a further eight 40 lb HE and forty 4 lb incendiaries out of the camera hatch, ie a total of 1,800 lbs, almost twice the normal bomb load of a Blenheim. The availability of bombs was a constant cause of concern to the squadron's executives throughout the campaign and in this context Sqn Ldr Hughes wrote the following in his journal at Magwe on February 20th:

> Any and every kind of bomb is used: 11 sec delays ran out long since; 250 lb GP, ASP and AS have been used up and now 500 pounders are being carried. A load of bombs came up here, was unshipped, put on lorries and had to be reshipped back to Rangoon as an urgent signal came from them. How many we have now I do not know.

The following day Hughes noted that Magwe (which was a commercial and not a military airfield) held a stock of just thirty-two 250 pounders. There were another 1,000 tons of bombs at Mingaladon but there was reported to be a severe shortage of tail units. Despite recurrent crises over the availability of weapons, exacerbated by rumour-inspired alarms, supplies of bombs were available most of the time. To conserve stocks at Magwe, which were slowly being built up by transferring bombs from Rangoon, it became usual for the Blenheims to fly down to Mingaladon or (later) Highland Queen to be armed and/or refuelled prior to flying a mission.

Even without bombs, however, since the Blenheims were generally being despatched to attack troop concentrations, MT vehicles or lightly constructed boats, the machine-gun fire which they could bring to bear could still inflict significant damage on such 'soft' targets, and the very appearance of the Blenheims obliged the Japanese to take cover and thus disrupted their progress. With hindsight it can be seen that a few Blenheim IVF ground-strafers with belly gun-packs might have come in useful but none were available in Burma.

With the south of Burma fast becoming untenable AVM Stevenson moved the core of HQ NORGROUP to Magwe on February 21st, retaining control of bomber operations. On the same date the AOC established 'X' Wg, under Gp Capt N C Singer DSO DFC; it was to remain at Rangoon to direct the efforts of the fighters still attempting to defend the city and to cover the withdrawal of the army. The following day, the 22nd, the SS *Neuralia* docked in Rangoon with No 113 Sqn's main party on board. Presumably in view of the rapidly worsening situation in Burma they were instructed not to disembark and within a few hours the ship sailed for Madras; no reinforcements reached the hard-pressed Blenheim squadrons. The tactical situation indicated that the British would soon have to abandon their line on the Sittang river; they pulled back on the 24th.

Meanwhile No 45 Sqn's withdrawal from Zayatkwin was getting under way. Sgt Huon flew back to Magwe on February 21st with his Z9811 crammed with kit and two airmen passengers. He noted in his diary that he had "....had to pull +9 to get off and the port motor cut, but happily caught again after a brief lapse. Bit sticky for a while." Wg Cdr Wallis led the last crews away on the 22nd, Fg Off Pickering thumbing a lift in Bill Maloney's aircraft. Since they were without an aeroplane, Plt Off Eve's crew made their way to Magwe by road. Dudley Eve drove the CO's car, a Plymouth station wagon, in convoy with a Jeep, a couple of Ford Sedans and an ambulance, the other drivers being George Kemp and Norm Bain, plus two more Australians, Sgts Colin Gerloff and Keith Dumas of No 113 Sqn, and that unit's MO accompanied by a couple of his orderlies. In this context it is interesting to note that the squadron never had too much trouble finding MT in Burma at this stage. Large consignments, much of it American, were arriving at Rangoon and rather than let it fall into the hands of the Japanese it seems that anyone who wanted a truck or a Jeep had only to go and 'sign for one' - so long as he undertook to drive it to Lashio!

By February 23rd most of the squadron was concentrated at Magwe. Sgt Gowing recalls:

> We lived in tents at Zayatkwin; at Mingaladon we were accommodated at the Golf Club but at Magwe we were housed in the jail. They had released the prisoners but the awful smell still remained. We slept in the cells on

The squadron's final convoy pauses on its way from Zayatkwin to Magwe, 22nd February 1942. (D G Eve)

The Zayatkwin rearguard. From the left: two medical orderlies and No 113 Sqn's MO, Sgt Keith Dumas of No 113 Sqn (he would eventually join No 45 Sqn only to be lost on a Mosquito sortie in October 1944); Sgt Colin Gerloff of No 113 Sqn; Plt Off Norman Bain and Plt Off Dudley Eve. Plt Off George Kemp was wielding the camera. (D G Eve)

concrete shelves attached to the walls. They were very hard and uncomfortable but they had at least been constructed with a depression in the middle to stop you falling out!

Geoff Gowing had been particularly unfortunate in his domestic arrangements at Magwe; other aircrew acquired more desirable, if overcrowded, digs in the local school, in the requisitioned houses of various Europeans and in a variety of quite substantial native-style bashas in the vicinity. There were also opportunities to relax at Magwe as a club in Yenangyaung, run by Americans working the oilfields, offered its hospitality to anyone who was able to 'borrow' a vehicle and drive up there. This is not to say that life was a picnic, however, far from it, as Bill Maloney has described it:

> Our short time in Burma was completely chaotic, nothing was organised and communications were non-existent. Crews were accommodated all over the place in houses taken over from the Burmese. Food, most of the time, you had to find yourself.

While the Flying Camels were preoccupied with their withdrawal to Magwe on February 22nd, No 113 Sqn had

This impressive residence, belonging to a European, was one of those commandeered by the squadron to add to its housing stock. Domestic living space was at a premium at Magwe and the situation grew steadily worse as more units pulled back from Rangoon - there were eventually about twenty-five bods living in this particular building. (L Wilde)

put up several sorties. By this time, however, No 113 Sqn was beginning to run short of aircraft and its six-aircraft raid against Kyaikto that day, led by Wg Cdr Stidolph and mounted via Mingaladon, was to be its last major effort. On the other hand, No 45 Sqn was just about at its maximum effective strength and although Blenheims of No 113 Sqn continued to operate for another two weeks, from now on the Flying Camels would increasingly bear the brunt of NORGROUP's offensive effort. Having settled in at Magwe the squadron began flying ops again and Flt Lt Beeston led a five-aircraft attack on the Sittang river bridge at Mokpalin on the 23rd. In most cases the aircraft called at Mingaladon on the outbound leg to be bombed up, and again on the return leg for refuelling so that each mission involved three trips totalling well over four hours flying time.

On February 23rd rumours began to circulate about a withdrawal to either Akyab or China. All available personnel, of all units, were paraded at Magwe that evening and it was announced that everyone was going to Akyab. This decision turned out to be short-lived, however, and the plan changed again; the RAF was to stay put for the time being but all available Blenheims were to continue to move surplus service personnel and civilians to the coast. This operation had begun in earnest on the 22nd when 140 evacuees had been flown to Akyab by a shuttle service mounted by nine Blenheims and this activity became fairly routine for the next couple of weeks. A typical example is provided by the experience of Sgt Max Neil who had reached Magwe in Z7757 on February 19th. Having flown a shuttle bombing mission to Mokpalin via Mingaladon with his crew, Sgts Ernie Hallett and Frank Brown, on the 23rd, he did two solo evacuation sorties to Akyab and back on the 24th and one more in the morning of the 28th. Dudley Eve recalls flying another of these trips:

> 24th February; evacuating people and one pig from Magwe to Akyab. During the take off a petrol bowser drove across in front of me. I had barely enough speed to lift off. I yanked back on the control column, cleared the tanker by inches and touched down again on the other side before finally getting off. At that moment all I could think of was petrol, fire, people and roast pork! To top it off, on landing at Akyab a Burmese woman thanked me and said how wonderful the flight had been. Of course she did not know and could not have seen what had had happened previously as she was jammed somewhere in the fuselage. I thought to myself - this is one case where ignorance is bliss!

The evacuation programme was not a full time activity and ops were still being mounted. On the 24th, for instance, a singleton from No 113 Sqn had flown a reconnaissance sortie while Sgt Huon's crew had carried out a patrol of the Thai border and Sqn Ldr Hughes had led three aircraft of B Flight in an attack against Kyaikto, staging through Mingaladon outbound and nightstopping there on the way back.

Stragglers from Egypt were still arriving in Burma. Sgts Colin 'Rocky' Fryar, Graham Tibbs and Graham Williams were among the last crews to get through, finally reaching Magwe in V6221 on February 23rd, having been delayed at Habbaniyah for a week with a double engine change. On the

25th they flew a reconnaissance sortie to the south and east of Toungoo in Z9801. On the same day the CO led a six aircraft strike via Mingaladon against boats at Kalwi, near Moulmein. A seventh aeroplane, Max Neil's Z5957, developed a fuel leak and turned back to Magwe, which was just as well as the enemy air force was also active that day, mounting two heavily escorted raids on Mingaladon, where the defending fighters of the RAF and AVG were still based. The second Japanese attack, at about 1615hrs, caught the Blenheims on the ground on their way back to Magwe and there were two casualties, both Australians. Sgt Jack McNamara was killed by flying shrapnel and his observer, Sgt Bill Penn, was wounded; their WOp/AG, Sgt Norm Bruce, made his way to Highland Queen whence he was eventually picked up by Plt Off Pedlar who called in to collect him on the 27th on his way back from an attack on the aerodrome at Tavoy. The remaining crews had successfully taken cover and escaped unharmed but only three of the seven Blenheims at Mingaladon at the time survived the attack, Z7892, Z7981 and Z9721; all of those which had been lost (V6221, Z7923, Z9821 and Z9833) had belonged to the Flying Camels. The reports of the pilots of the defending AVG P-40s indicated that they had shot down a remarkable twenty-one of the Japanese raiders which was some compensation but, as was so often the case in the confusion of combat, these claims were wildly optimistic[7]. Nevertheless it was heartening news at the time and was some consolation for the loss of the Blenheims, if not to Eve, Kemp and Bain who had just lost their second aircraft (actually Fryar's V6221) inside a week!

Their Z9821 having been written off at Mingaladon (it had just flown its seventh operational sortie), Plt Off Maloney's crew acquired McNamara's battered but still flyable Z7892 and returned to Magwe the same day. Most of the other aircrew were stranded for the night and were flown back to base in a DC-2 of No 31 Sqn on the 26th but Plt Off Christensen's crew did not get out until the following day. Their aircraft, Z9833, had been another of those which had been written off and they were eventually flown out in a Hudson (V9189) of No 139 Sqn flown by a Sgt White. They had to work their passage, however, and Sgt Bob Hilditch flew as gunner; his log book records: "Left without transport at 'drome: Lockheed leaving, but first did recco to Moulmein, returned over sea; circled over Rangoon then flew to Highland Queen." That evening they were ferried up to Magwe in a Hudson flown by a Sgt Pittman.

Meanwhile, on February 26th the squadron had despatched a total of six aircraft to attack the airfield at Moulmein led by Lt Alder in Z9803. Five took off individually from Magwe and staged through Mingaladon where Sgts Rusty Curtis, Les Charlton and John Brinkley were already positioned, having spent the night there with their Z7981, one of the few Blenheims to have escaped damage during the previous day's Japanese air raid. The aircraft which succeeded in completing the mission returned direct to Magwe from the target but some were caught on the ground at Mingaladon on the outbound leg by another Japanese air raid. As Graham Williams recollects:

The Japs were really hotting things up at this stage and we were caught out nicely when refuelling at Rangoon at an advanced landing ground (*ie advanced with respect to Magwe*). Quite a batch of Japs came over

Above:- Mingaladon, 25th February 1942; smoke billows over the Blenheims caught on the ground by a Japanese air raid. (D G Eve) Below:- One of the five Blenheims lost at Mingaladon on February 25th. (F G Terry)

and bombed the daylights out of the airport with me and others caught in a pill box mid-airfield. One bomb landed about 20 yards away and chewed bits off the pill box galore. The noise was terrific but nobody was hurt. Same didn't apply to the aircraft though, with some on fire and others with holes everywhere, ours included.

William's aircraft was originally Huon's Z9811 which the Fryar crew had "borrowed" for the mission. The damage it had sustained had caused a major fuel leak but there was insufficient engineering support at Mingaladon to rectify the problem. The crew had either to abandon their leaky aeroplane and join the refugees streaming north or risk flying it out. The two Grahams, Tibbs and Williams, persuaded Rocky Fryar to try to fly the aeroplane back to Magwe. They made it, landing in the dark with the aid of vehicle headlights, but the aeroplane was no longer combat worthy (although it did eventually find its way back to India) and the crew was evacuated a few days later.

Having spent February 26th in Rangoon, the CO and his crew flew back to Magwe on the 27th in the only other Blenheim which had escaped damage in the Japanese attacks on Mingaladon (Z9721, probably originally one of No 113 Sqn's aeroplanes). Two raids were flown that day. Five aircraft, three from No 113 Sqn and two from No 45 Sqn, positioned at Highland Queen before taking off to bomb Ye, way to the south, while three more of No 45 Sqn's Blenheims operating from Magwe attacked the Japanese forward positions on the east bank of the lower Sittang at Kaywe. The joint detachment at Highland Queen spent the night at Insein and were joined on the 28th by three more crews (Wallis, Maloney and Curtis) who, accompanied by a pair from No 113 Sqn, attacked Shwegyin before returning to Magwe while each squadron despatched a further pair to the same target without deploying forward. Meanwhile two of

No 113 Sqn's forward crews flew down to Mingaladon to stand by to evacuate some of the remaining HQ staff while the majority of the Blenheim detachments returned to Magwe leaving a small party of No 45 Sqn, including the Maloney crew, in sole possession of Highland Queen.

Although the AOC was now primarily based at Magwe, elements of his staff were still in Rangoon and he had forward detachments operating from airstrips near the city. AVM Stevenson needed to visit these locations periodically, partly to discuss the situation with his army colleagues, partly to familiarise himself with field conditions but, as importantly, just to be seen, to reassure the men under his command that they had not been forgotten and to sustain their morale. On February 24th he had been flown from Mingaladon to Magwe and back again by Sgts Doug Smyth, Denys Golder and Jeff Alt in Z9799. Impressed by this RAAF crew, the AOC had used them again for a round trip from Magwe to Mingaladon and back on the 28th. Doug Smyth was not satisfied with being relegated to providing a taxi service and he said so, both to Brian Wallis and to the AOC himself. But, having now been flown by them twice, Stevenson was content that he had made the right choice and Smyth's crew were obliged to fly the AVM down to Highland Queen and back on March 1st and again on the 4th and then make a courier run to Calcutta between the 5th and 9th. Smyth was determined that his crew should take a full part in the squadron's offensive activities as well, however, and they flew four ops in Z9799 before being shot down on March 11th on their fifth sortie, of which more anon.

By the end of February, although it had thus far sustained no fatalities, No 45 Sqn had lost at least nine aeroplanes in accidents or through enemy action. Several other aircraft were no longer in a fit state for combat and those in dire need of repair were being flown back to India where proper maintenance facilities were available. For instance, Flt Lt Beeston and his crew had taken their aeroplane to Dum Dum on February 24th and, after all its nuts and bolts had been tightened up, they flew it back to Akyab in the morning of the 27th and on to Magwe that evening. In the meantime, in view of the increasing shortage of aircraft, it had been

decided to reduce the number of aircrews in Burma and on February 28th the surplus ones were flown to Akyab to join those who were already there as a result of their involvement in the current operation to evacuate civilians. Some reached Akyab in DC-2s and Valentias of No 31 Sqn, others under their own steam in some of the tattier Blenheims. From there most of the crews made their way to Calcutta by sea on board "a grubby little coaster, the SS *Szechuan*", which sailed at 1900hrs on February 28th and reached its destination at 1700hrs on March 2nd. It appears, however, that there had been considerable uncertainty as to exactly what was happening on February 28th, probably as a result of poor communications. As Arthur Huon recalls:

The night before, at Magwe, we were told we would be ferrying some of our personnel over to Akyab. If anyone knew at that time that it was to be an evacuation, they didn't let on to the NCO aircrew. The next morning, my own aircraft (Z9811) having been bent two days before while under the tender loving care of Fryar, I flew six groundcrew and their gear over to Akyab in Sqn Ldr Austin's aircraft. My crew did not accompany me and I had one 'erk' on the seat alongside me, another at the navigator's work position in the nose and two or three more peering over my shoulder from behind the main spar. On landing at Akyab I expected to return immediately to Magwe and was surprised to be directed to a parking area and signalled to switch off my engines. I was then instructed to await further orders. My crew caught up with me during the day. Late in the afternoon we were directed to adjourn to the wharf where my recollection is that we were to spend the night on the *Szechuan*, moored alongside. We were served with a meal on the wharf before going on board and shortly afterwards the moorings were slipped and we sailed! It is not surprising that many of us were confused and, in the vernacular of the day, brassed off!

It appears that, while the executives back at Magwe no doubt (probably?) knew what was going on, the situation was evidently far less clear at the lower levels of the hierarchy - was this the general withdrawal which had been ordered and then cancelled on February 23rd but had remained a possibility ever since, or was it only a partial evacuation - or what?

Among the crews who left Burma at this time were some of the strays from Nos 84 and 211 Sqns who had failed to get through to Sumatra. Sgt McNamara having been killed a few days before and his wounded observer Sgt Bill Penn already being on his way to Calcutta, that crew's gunner, Sgt Norm Bruce was also evacuated on February 28th. Another of these crews, Plt Off Aubrey Pedlar with Sgts Maxwell 'Lofty' Roberts and 'Morrie' Morris, was flown to Akyab in a Hudson but Max Neil then took the pilot straight back to Magwe in a Blenheim because, as Pedlar has described the episode....

.....another aircraft was considered fit to fly out. I was shown over the machine by the EO. It had many holes in it but the chief point of concern was the damaged main spar in the port wing. I was advised not to fly near other aircraft and to avoid turbulence over the mountains! Another problem was that there were no parachutes left

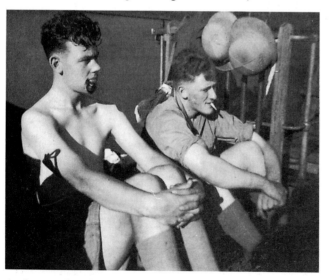

As the squadron began to run out of aeroplanes a number of its aircrew were evacuated to India. Sgts Tony King and Gordon Terry are seen here on board the SS Szechuan *en route Akyab-Calcutta circa 1st March. (F G Terry)*

so I had nothing to sit on. Whilst scrounging around for something to make a seat I was approached by four Hurricane pilots who wanted a lift out. I said that before deciding I would show them the damage to my machine as they might wish to change their minds. Finally they said that if I was going to be stupid enough to fly the wreck they might as well be stupid enough to come with me. Needless to say we made it.

Plt Off Bayly was caught up in the general confusion surrounding the evacuation and, after he and Sgt Ken Edwards had been flown to the coast by Sgt Max Neil in V5495, in the absence of their own pilot, Ivor Beeston, they teamed up with the by now crewless Aubrey Pedlar with his recently acquired, if somewhat beaten up, aeroplane and together they flew it to Dum Dum on March 1st; thus did Gus Alder's Z9803 find its way back to India.

During the first week of March, as the dust settled in Calcutta, the recent evacuees began to realise that a substantial proportion of the squadron was still operating in Burma; several of the crews were most put out about this and pressed to be allowed to go back to Magwe. Among them was Norman Bayly who had inadvertently become separated from his pilot. He immediately set about trying to secure a return passage but it was to be March 9th before he was eventually able to thumb a lift with Sgt Doug Smyth. Another observer who found himself unexpectedly divorced from his crew was Plt Off Alf Hilling, although in his case he was the one still at Magwe while the rest of his team, Fg Off John Edmonds and Sgt Tony King, were now in India.

The *Szechuan* had not been the only means of reaching India from Akyab as a few other crews had been offered the opportunity of flying there in a Blenheim. This was not as attractive a proposition as it sounds, as Dudley Eve was to discover when Sqn Ldr Penny gave him the option of ferrying Jack McNamara's dilapidated Z7892 out to Dum Dum:

> The aircraft had no air speed indicator, no cylinder head temperature gauges, lots of large and small holes all over it and no maps. Hell, I thought, another wonderful choice! It was thought that if I returned it to Calcutta it could be repaired and brought back to Burma (I think it is still there!). I consulted the crew and, having in mind that we would be able to formate on another aircraft to assess our speed, we agreed to take the chance. As soon as the other aircraft had taken off it slewed badly as an engine failed and it promptly landed again. We were stuck up there with no air speed, etc, etc and no maps. As the main risk was going to be landing we thought it would be better to land at Calcutta than return so we headed north, with a great deal of apprehension.

After a nerve-racking flight the aeroplane was successfully delivered to Dum Dum. It was probably at about this time that Paul Keel had a nightmarish trip in another battered Blenheim. There had been no facilities in Burma capable of straightening the prop which had previously been roughly beaten into shape at Zayatkwin and Keel eventually flew the 700 miles back to Calcutta with the Blenheim's out-of-balance starboard engine vibrating so badly that it seemed likely to shake itself loose altogether. According to Sqn Ldr Hughes, the experience so unnerved the pilot that he was unable to fly again for several months!

At Dum Dum in March 1942 after being withdrawn from Burma, from the left: top, Sgt Graham Tibbs RAAF and Sgt Tony King; bottom, Sgt Bill Fylan RAAF and Sgt Jack Hurley RCAF. (F G Terry)

Meanwhile the element of the squadron which was still in Burma and still operational was carrying on with the war. On March 1st Sqn Ldr Hughes led three aircraft in an attack on Abya, routeing via Highland Queen whence at least one of the participating aircraft took off. A pair of No 113 Sqn's aircraft should have joined them but Sqn Ldr Ford crashed taking off from Magwe, delaying his companion, and Plt Off Bassingthwaighte's crew eventually completed the sortie alone some way behind the main formation. Apart from a small detachment of No 45 Sqn which remained at Highland Queen, most of the Blenheims were then withdrawn to Magwe which was fast becoming the RAF's main base in Burma as the RAF and AVG fighters still in the Rangoon area had also begun to move north. At about this time Harold Pickering, No 45 Sqn's Intelligence Officer, was attached to the staff of NORGROUP while its Engineering Officer, Plt Off Arklay, was ordered to start establishing an RSU at Mingaladon, which hardly seemed sensible as Rangoon's days were very obviously numbered.

Having now been operating in Burma without reinforcement for some seven weeks No 113 Sqn was almost a spent force and it was decided to withdraw the unit to India and rebuild it there. On March 2nd, on which date the unit flew no operations, No 113 Sqn's groundcrew began to join the exodus to Akyab.

Although its strength had been significantly depleted the slimmed-down No 45 Sqn was still going strong and, through the efforts of its tiny band of groundcrew, on March 2nd the CO was able to lead nine aircraft in an attack on troops at Mokpalin and Sqn Ldr Hughes led a second six-aircraft strike against Waw, at least three crews flying on both missions. The next day the squadron despatched a total of nine aircraft, accompanied by one from No 113 Sqn, to attack Kyaikto village and transport on the road between Bilin and Thaton.

This action was spread over two hours and involved several formations plus Brian Wallis' crew operating as a singleton, some of the aircraft taking off from Highland Queen and/or landing there to refuel on the return leg. The first raid appears to have alerted the defences as the second formation, led by Sqn Ldr Hughes, ran into a large group of Ki 27s. Having previously observed that the bombers had been flying without escorts for the last three days, Arthur Hughes noted in his journal:

We approached Kyaikto low, pulled up to 1,500' when 4 minutes away and opened up into line astern. When 1 minute away we were promptly jumped by twenty Army 97s. Nos 3 and 4 were already on their way to ground level when I decided to go and we raced for home at +9. I was more interested than scared and, as no fighter actually attacked us, I rather enjoyed it! No 3, Muller-Rowland, had four on him and got twenty holes. No 4 (Flt Lt Lee of 113) is missing and the other one came back with me. So the decree now is: Blenheims must have escorts.

The aircraft which accompanied Hughes was flown by Sgt Curtis. The one which was missing (Z7592) had been shot down. Flt Lt Lee and Sgt Brett were killed; only the gunner, Sgt Walker, survived to rejoin his unit three days later. A pair of No 45 Sqn's aircraft bombed troops at Payagi on the 4th and on a second mission one of No 113 Sqn's few remaining Blenheims accompanied three from No 45 Sqn in a low-level attack against troops at Pyinbon.

In the meantime, the third of the squadron's 'guest' crews, Plt Offs D Mayger and E F French and Sgt Davies, who had reached Magwe in V6328 as early as 17th February (see Note 3), had been shuttling back and forth between Highland Queen, Magwe and Akyab, carrying evacuees in V5422 and Z9573 as well as in their own aeroplane. This crew had not been sent on to India, however, and on 3rd March they flew a long maritime recce from Akyab in V5495. By this time Flt Lt Beeston appears to have come to terms with the fact that he had lost his rear crew so he exercised the privilege conferred by his rank and pinched Mayger's! This scratch crew flew another four-hour patrol over the Bay of Bengal in V5495 on March 4th, debriefed at Akyab and then rejoined the squadron at Magwe, leaving Dan Mayger stranded at the coast.

On March 4th fifteen serviceable Blenheims remained in Burma. Twelve of them belonged to No 45 Sqn, and NORGROUP directed that the squadron was to carry out a maximum effort long-range strike against the Japanese airfield at Lampang in Siam on the 5th. The raid was to be provided with an escort of twelve Hurricanes, fifteen Buffalos and twenty of the AVG's P-40s. In view of the distance involved, however, the mission proved to be a contentious proposition among the fighter fraternity. Wg Cdr Frank Carey (previously OC No 135 Sqn but recently promoted to command No 267 Wg), who had been nominated to lead the operation, is reported to have protested but the AOC was adamant, although it was agreed that Wg Cdr Wallis would lead instead.

It proved to be a somewhat ill-starred mission. Reality had prevailed over wishful thinking by the time it was executed and the force actually fielded had been reduced to eight Blenheims which were to be accompanied by six Hurricanes, four Buffalos and eight P-40s. The fighters moved forward to Namsang where the bombers were to join them. In the event the Blenheims failed to locate the fighters' airfield and landed at Heho to refuel. Most of the formation then returned to Magwe but at least one Blenheim (V5495), flown by Flt Lt Beeston with his borrowed crew of 'Chips' French and 'Taffy' Davies, flew to Namsang, presumably to co-ordinate planning for a re-run the next day. The operation was mounted again on the 6th but shortly after take-off the port engine of Brian Wallis' Z7635 failed and he was obliged to return to Magwe. Twenty-five minutes after landing the crew were airborne again in Z9835, successfully catching up with the rest of the formation at Namsang, which they managed to find this time. The aircraft took off to fly the mission in three groups: the bombers; the Hurricanes (now reduced to four by mishaps on the ground) and the P-40s accompanied by the Buffalos. In the poor visibility, however, the three formations failed to join up. The Hurricanes remained in the vicinity of the airfield, hoping to see something, while the AVG leader took his formation off towards the east. The P-40s and Buffalos pressed on as far as the Salween river but, still not having seen anything of the bombers, they then returned to Namsang where one of the Buffalos was written off in a landing

The Rangoon-based P-40s of the American Volunteer Guard AVG's began to withdraw to Magwe in early March, providing Cpl Hector Sharpe with opportunity to strike this nonchalant pose. (L Wilde)

incident. Brian Wallis and the rest of his bomber crews, having seen nothing of their escort, pressed on alone, eventually dropping their bombs on Chiang Mai before returning to Magwe via Namsang[8].

This dogged, if not entirely successful, attempt at an escorted long-range strike was not the only bomber effort at this time, and the few Blenheims which were not involved continued to operate against the advancing Japanese. On the 5th Sqn Ldr Hughes' crew flew a recce sortie to Yandoon from which they landed at Highland Queen. Late that afternoon they led two other Blenheims to strafe and bomb troop barges at Dedaye while Lt Alder, whose crew had been at Highland Queen since March 1st, accompanied three from No 113 Sqn in a low-level attack on Waw.

By this time things were definitely starting to fall apart and with the minimal support available at Highland Queen missions flown from this forward base were very taxing for the crews. Alder later reported that he, Corbett and Briggs had had to find, fuse and load their own bombs; find oil; fetch and operate a fuel bowser; replace the chain on a starter magneto and carry out their own pre-flight inspection. This experience was not uncommon as Sgt Jeff Alt recalls:

During our stay in Burma we had no air-to-ground or plane-to-plane wireless communication. Consequently I don't ever recall attending any pre-flight briefings; my time was occupied on these occasions by checking guns, turret and ammunition. When doing a bombing op the crew loaded its own bombs - as I was the tallest the bomb was placed between my shoulders whilst Doug Smyth and Denys Golder attached it to the bomb rack. The planes received no maintenance with the crews assisting with the refuelling.

Several of the aircrew who were in Burma (and with whom the author has corresponded) have commented on the lack of servicing provided for their aircraft. This was undoubtedly the case but under the circumstances this was inevitable and these observations need to be seen in a broader perspective. The fact is that, although occasional assistance was provided by other units, No. 45 Sqn had only twenty qualified tradesmen in Burma to look after all of its aeroplanes. Since these men were initially divided between Zayatkwin and Magwe, and odd bodies were detached on occasion to Akyab, Mingaladon, Highland Queen and elsewhere, it is hardly surprising that the aircrew saw little of them; there simply were not that many to be seen. The aircrew, who outnumbered the airmen by two or three to one, were both capable of carrying out routine first-line servicing and qualified to do so. It was therefore appropriate that they should look after these more mundane activities to allow the few available tradesmen to concentrate on rectification where their more specialised skills were essential. In practice the shortage of spares meant that 'rectification' frequently involved salvaging parts from damaged aeroplanes and using them to restore others to flying condition. The available manpower resources clearly precluded the luxury of preventative maintenance and, since there was little capacity to deal with minor battle damage, it became quite normal for aircraft to fly on operations with bullet holes acquired during earlier missions still unpatched. All of this invoked echoes of the helter-skelter scramble around Cyrenaica in April 1941 but, of the aircrew, only

F/Sgt David Cliffe would have remembered that this had required a similar 'all hands to the pumps' approach. In both cases, expedience had to be the order of the day and engineering policy, to the extent that there was one, could be summarised by just two slogans - "If it works, don't fix it" and "If you can do it yourself - do it".

No 113 Sqn's participation in the raid against Waw on the 5th had been its final offensive effort. On the 6th, operating from Highland Queen, it launched its last operational sortie from central Burma, a reconnaissance mission, while No 45 Sqn despatched two aircraft from Magwe to attack troops in the vicinity of Pyinmadaw and another three to bomb Pegu. On the same day the Japanese finally found the previously undetected airstrip at Highland Queen. Arthur Hughes recorded his impressions of the day in his journal:

Spent the night (*of March 5th/6th*) at Insein. Next a.m. at Mingaladon we found some bombs - four here, two there, etc. Loaded them on a truck; went out to HQ and proceeded to bomb up. Previous night they had bombed boats at Dedaye where a recce Blenheim had been fired on by a party of Burmese lead by a Jap. At 1100hrs Lin, Cliffe and I took cover. Bombs fell at 1115. I began to walk back to the aircraft but was chased back to cover again by the return of the force which flew right over again. Giving them plenty of time to get clear, I

LAC Harold Gardner, probably photographed in a Cairo studio circa January 1942. Note that his (army) battledress blouse is decorated with an SS death's head badge, liberated no doubt from Gambut. 'Smokey' Gardner was one of the handful of ground-crew who endeavoured to keep the squadron's Blenheims flying during the Burma campaign. (L Wilde)

Flt Lt Lin Durrant (left) and Sqn Ldr Arthur Hughes squat on a clutch of 250 pounders at Highland Queen while Sgt Dave Cliffe takes a picture before the three of them loaded their own bombs for a mission. (L E Durrant)

returned to the aircraft. About 1145 a Hurricane came round, put his wheels down and proceeded to land. Glancing up idly from my work I saw him making an approach and thought, "H'm, downwind", then in an instant saw five others, also with their wheels down! In two seconds I was in a shallow trench 20 yards away and bullets whistled overhead while the little yellowbellies zoomed and stall turned overhead. The Hurricane was attacked but got away to Mingaladon. I lay there with my face in the dirt trembling and expecting every minute to feel a bullet; I stole glances sideways and each time saw an aircraft about to dive and heard the rattle of guns. I thought, "All right, you've had your fun; now go away, please go away". I dared not move, knowing their penchant for shooting people on the ground and I felt terribly exposed. Finally they began to move off and I got up tentatively and then ran to the culvert Lin had been sheltering under. Those Japs had no opposition and yet in my aircraft, the first they attacked, there were only four bullets, none vital, and only one Blenheim, Gus's, out of all the aircraft there was rendered unserviceable. Nonetheless, there was a scramble to evacuate before they came back and we were sent to do an attack on 2,000 Japs reported 12 miles NE of Highland Queen. Needless to say we saw nothing; you could hide an armoured div in the trees there. So we landed at Mingaladon and then did a recce from Rangoon to Amherst.

Rusty Curtis and his crew landed at Highland Queen just after the Japanese air raid and were directed to fly on down to Mingaladon and collect OC 'X' Wing, Gp Capt Singer. They picked him up and flew him to Zigon as briefed but broke Z7981's stern frame landing on the rough surface of what passed for the 'airstrip'.

The wholesale military evacuation of Rangoon began on March 7th, the local populace having already been streaming north for the previous two weeks. The abandoning of Rangoon put paid to Highland Queen as well and the remnants of the Blenheim detachment withdrew to Magwe, the last crews out being those of Lt Alder and Plt Off Maloney. On the 8th Sgt Powell flew Maloney to Namsang in Z9819, whence the latter returned to Magwe with two passengers in Z9835. That same day the Alder crew flew the CO's unserviceable Z7635 out to Akyab, hoping for an engine change, so Wg Cdr Wallis had to make do with V6128 to carry out a recce down the Prome-Rangoon road to ascertain the whereabouts of the leading Japanese elements. They were fired on by friendly troops (and hit six times) but, since V6128's guns, turret and radio were all unserviceable, 'Mac' McDade could neither fire back nor tell them to stop it! On the 9th, while their pilot was airborne in Z7757, taking part in a raid on Moulmein, Beeston's own rear crew, Bayly and Edwards, returned from India. The following day Bill Maloney used Z7757 to fly French and Davies to Akyab where they were reunited with their own pilot, the Rhodesian Dan Mayger.

No 113 Sqn's withdrawal was now well under way and by the 10th most of its personnel had been evacuated to Akyab whence they sailed for Calcutta. The squadron's last flyable Blenheims left Magwe bound for Dum Dum on March 12th leaving just a handful of the unit's groundcrew to help sustain No 45 Sqn's effort. At this stage the rapidly dwindling RAF resources still remaining in Burma were reorganised again. Following its withdrawal from Rangoon, 'X' Wing had operated its fighters briefly from the primitive airstrip at Zigon but it pulled back to Magwe on the 9th to be dissolved the following day. On March 8th, under the command of the erstwhile OC Mingaladon, Gp Capt H S Broughall MC DFC, Burwing was formed at Magwe to control the operations of Nos 17 and 45 Sqns plus the remaining half dozen P-40s of the AVG, a flight of No 28 Sqn's Lysanders and No 517 AMES' (now mobile) radar equipment[9]. On March 12th, at Akyab, Gp Capt Singer set up Akwing to control the operations of what fighters remained to Nos 67 and 136 Sqns and the Hudsons of No 139 Sqn. On the latter date HQ NORGROUP, which had been concentrated at Magwe since March 10th, was reconstituted in Calcutta and reverted to its original designation of No 221 Group, although AVM Stevenson continued to direct operations from Akyab at first and did not move to his new HQ until the 17th. Another sign of the times was the decision to move No 154 MU from Meiktila to Lashio to keep it out of harm's way and, breaking its journey with an overnight stop at Maymyo, its HQ reached its destination on March 12th.

Another of Len Wilde's stories relates to this period:

One night a parade was called at Magwe to ascertain who was left! In all there were about 250 of us, odd units of a dozen men, 17 Sqn with about thirty, and ourselves, by far the largest, with perhaps sixty. Wg Cdr Wallis marched us on, aircrew and groundcrew all mixed up together. A count was made then remade and then remade again; rumbles of discontent began to break out. "What a load of bull!" came a voice from within our ranks. A young pilot officer from Burwing HQ hurtled over. "Stand out! Stand out the man who said that!" He blanched and slunk away when Sqn Ldr Austin stepped forward and said, "I did!" Our CO then called us to attention and marched us off. He was the senior officer present and quite obviously as cheesed off as the rest of us.

Now representing the RAF's entire strike force in Burma, what remained of No 45 Sqn's operational echelon continued

With its engine cowlings off, V5938/P receives some attention at Akyab on its way back to India on March 8th. Sqn Ldr Arthur Hughes is in the foreground; F/Sgt David Cliffe is working on the aircraft. (D Cliffe)

the fight with an attack by five aircraft on the airfield at Moulmein on the 9th. This mission was slightly different in that it was carried out at 18,000 feet rather than at low level which was the standard tactic for most of the sorties flown in Burma. On the 10th Sgt Rusty Curtis' crew was tasked with an offensive recce down to the Gulf of Martaban in V6328 but experienced engine trouble on the way out and had to put down at Prome. The problem was quickly rectified, however, and the mission was successfully completed later in the day, the crew returning to Magwe to debrief. After first positioning at Prome in Z7579 to be briefed by the GOC's staff, Wg Cdr Wallis, accompanied as always by Sgts Don Page and Mac McDade, flew two more recces on the 10th, one down the Prome-Rangoon road the other covering the Sittang river between Mon and Shwegyin. On landing back at Prome the results were handed personally to Lt Gen Alexander, who had taken over from Lt Gen Hutton on March 4th as the commander of the army in the field. While at Prome some news was gleaned of the adventures of Sqn Ldr Leonard 'Lulu' Penny, who had been attached to 17th Div HQ as RAF Liaison Officer; it appeared that he had been in the thick of it, riding about in a tank, and had established a considerable reputation among the soldiery, both for himself and for the RAF.

Lt Alder and his crew returned to Magwe from Akyab on March 11th in V5422 and promptly joined four other crews in a successful attack on bridges to the south west of Pyuntaza from which all returned safely. That same day Flt Lt Ivor Beeston, by now reunited with his original crew, carried out an uneventful recce of Daik-U but in the course of another solo reconnaissance mission in much the same area the squadron lost an aircraft. Flown by its all-RAAF crew, the 'AOC's taxi', Z9799, was hit by small arms fire and Doug Smyth was mortally wounded by a rifle bullet. Denys Golder and Jeff Alt managed to maintain control of the aircraft and get the unconscious pilot out of his seat. Between them the observer and WOp/AG flew the aircraft back to Magwe, dropped their pilot's body by parachute and then baled out themselves. Because previously published accounts of this incident have differed in detail, the personal recollections of the two survivors are quoted verbatim at Annex I.

It should be noted that during this period, apart from doing their best to stem the Japanese advance, the squadron had still been helping to evacuate military and civilian personnel and casualties from Magwe and Yenangyaung to Akyab. According to Sqn Ldr Hughes' reckoning, something like four hundred people escaped from Burma courtesy of the Flying Camels. Those aircraft in need of overhaul, or repairs which were beyond the capabilities of the primitive technical facilities available at Magwe, were flown out to Dum Dum, often loaded with refugees. As a result the remaining force of Blenheims was slowly dwindling. V5938 was a case in point; it had already been consuming oil at a rate of two gallons per hour when it had left Egypt but with every sortie the problem had grown worse and on March 8th Arthur Hughes with Lin Durrant and Dave Cliffe flew it via Akyab to Dum Dum for an engine change.

The wing commander's crew flew a further recce between Pyuntaza and Daik-U on the 12th, Z9679 collecting two bullet holes in the process, before landing at Toungoo to debrief and then flying back to Magwe. With barely flyable aircraft being evacuated to India and declining serviceability, although a number of recce sorties were flown, the squadron's offensive effort was somewhat curtailed for a few days and only singletons were launched on the 12th, 13th and 14th. In the course of these sorties bombs were dropped on troops at Hmawbi, boats at Yandoon and AA positions at Mingaladon.

The squadron lost a crew on March 14th when Z7899 failed to return from a lone reconnaissance sortie. Sgts Lance Powell, Les Connor and Jim Eden, all Australians, were initially posted missing but when nothing was heard of them it had to be presumed that they had been killed; their bodies were eventually found many years after the war.

Although most of the traffic in Blenheims was now westward, a few more aeroplanes did get through to Burma[10]. As noted above, V5422 (which had been flown to Akyab by Mayger at the end of February) had been brought back by Gus Alder on March 11th. V5957 was another aircraft which returned to Burma, in this case from Dum Dum; there may well have been others. After their somewhat confused evacuation, the slightly bewildered aircrew who had

Wg Cdr Charles Brian Berry Wallis who led the squadron between December 1941 and March 1942, one of the most intensive periods of operations in its entire history. (D Cliffe)

unexpectedly found themselves back in Calcutta in early March were subjected to a further series of conflicting orders. In the end most of them had been packed off to Fyzabad but some were held in Calcutta where they were billeted in the Continental Hotel. On March 15th V5957, having been given a brief overhaul at Dum Dum, became available for further use and it was flown back to Magwe by Max Neil and his crew with Arthur Huon, Albert Thompson and Ron Clark on board. The tension at Magwe had been wound up several notches that day as reports had been received of a Japanese fleet bound for India. The squadron was briefed for a maximum effort, death or glory operation but after a few hours on stand-by the mission had been cancelled - much to the relief of all concerned.

By March 16th the squadron's handful of groundcrew had been able to cobble together some more airframes and sufficient Blenheims, most of them still displaying unpatched bullet holes, were available to permit six to be despatched to attack rivercraft at Yandoon, exploiting the intelligence brought back by the CO from yet another recce sortie which his crew had flown to the south the previous day. Wg Cdr Wallis led the Yandoon attack, which was provided with an escort of five P-40s, and on the way back he flew up the Rangoon-Prome road from Hmawbi to see what was what. There appeared to be a concentration of Japanese MT at Hmawbi and that afternoon a single Blenheim returned to bomb the village, the CO leading four more aircraft back there on the 17th.

Lt Alder's crew also flew on the 17th, an armed recce of Bassein; they were extremely fortunate to make it back to base. On the return leg they were flying up the Irrawaddy at low level when they encountered a cable strung across the river. It was too late to take evasive action and with both engines at full bore they flew straight into it. The cable broke and a length wound itself round the starboard propeller which whipped it across the fuselage, almost severing the nose between the pilot and the observer, sitting up front. Bill Corbett rapidly vacated his precarious perch and moved back to a (slightly) more secure position alongside the pilot. Facing backwards in his turret, Cliff Briggs was able to see the bow wave being created by the Blenheim's tailwheel as it dragged through the water before Alder eventually managed to persuade the stricken aeroplane to keep flying and coaxed it up to a more sensible height. Their problems were not over yet, however, as the slipstream began to tear chunks off the damaged nose and, under the pressure of the 100 mph gale, the fuselage walls began to 'pant'. To relieve the overpressure, Briggs used his pistol to blow out some of the panels of his turret. In this battered condition the aeroplane struggled back to Magwe; it would seem improbable that it ever flew again[11].

There was a two-day lull in offensive tasking after the Hmawbi raid although the odd sortie was still flown. On the 17th for instance the Maloney crew flew to Toungoo in V5495 to position for an offensive reconnaissance sortie, returning to Magwe the next day, and Flt Lt Beeston's crew flew a low-level recce of lines of communication between Myanaung and Henzada on the 18th. There was also a steady demand for priority VIP trips; on March 19th, for instance, Sgts Neil, Hallett and Brown flew General Scott to Toungoo and back in Z9807 and the following day Bill Maloney with Des Carew-Reid and Bill Wilson flew Z9801 to Park Lane (Prome) to collect General Alexander and take him to Mandalay. Offensive operations were resumed on the 20th with a five-aircraft mission. Two of the Blenheims were obliged to return early with engine snags but the others pressed on to Moulmein only to find that their cloud cover disappeared over the Gulf of Martaban. They turned back towards Rangoon, where they saw large numbers of enemy aircraft parked at Mingaladon and on the adjacent landing grounds. The three Blenheims eventually dropped their bombs on Hmawbi and returned safely to base where Flt Lt Beeston reported the large concentration of Japanese aircraft which they had observed. That evening three more Blenheims with an escort of six Hurricanes went to the Sittang valley where they bombed Pyu and strafed the roads leading out of the village.

The slight drop in the sortie rate over the previous few days had permitted the hard-pressed groundcrew to patch up some more aeroplanes and by the 21st the squadron could muster a total of ten aircraft which might be regarded as fit for operations. A reconnaissance flight the previous day had confirmed Ivor Beeston's report of at least fifty Japanese aircraft being concentrated at Rangoon. A planned attack on Henzada was cancelled and a maximum effort raid on Mingaladon was laid on instead. The briefing called for two vics and a box-four in line astern, but in the event one engine of Arthur Huon's aeroplane, which was to have been 'tail-end Charlie', refused to start and, since there was no spare aircraft, only nine Blenheims took off. The crews known to have flown on this mission are listed at Figure 8.4[12]. The bombers had been expecting a close escort of ten Hurricanes, operating from Park Lane (Prome), but the two formations failed to rendezvous as the fighters had gone on ahead. They were just finishing their strafing attacks when the Blenheims arrived at 0850hrs and added 9,000 lbs of bombs to the carnage and confusion which had already been created. The Hurricanes returned to base independently, some of them carrying out further strafing runs on

Pilot	Observer	WOp/AG
Wg Cdr C B B Wallis	Sgt D Page	Sgt B T McDade
Sqn Ldr F J Austin	Plt Off F J Fraser	F/Sgt K Mills
Flt Lt I S Beeston	Plt Off N W Bayly RAAF	Sgt K E Edwards RAAF
Lt H R L Alder SAAF	Plt Off W J Corbett RAAF	Sgt C G Briggs RAAF
Fg Off J S Muller-Rowland	Plt Off P E Graebner RAAF	Sgt K A Gardiner RAAF
Plt Off J W Maloney RAAF	Sgt D McK Carew-Reid RAAF	Sgt W R Wilson RAAF
Sgt F E Thompson RCAF	Sgt J W Watkins	Sgt C H Romans
Sgt H M P Neil RAAF	Sgt E J Hallett RAAF	Sgt F F Brown RAAF
?	?	?

Fig 8.4. Crews of No 45 Sqn who took part in the RAF's last significant offensive air action of the first campaign in Burma, the strike against Mingaladon on 21st March 1942.

the emergency airstrips in the vicinity of Rangoon which the RAF had only recently vacated. In the absence of the Hurricanes, the bombers had picked up an 'escort' of Japanese fighters on the way in and, although their attacks had been a little hesitant at first, once the Blenheims had turned for home the Japanese pilots became more determined.

Norman Bayly later recorded his impression of this raid, from which the following is extracted:

About five or seven minutes out from Mingaladon Japanese fighters came up at us from the other neighbouring 'dromes and then we found more waiting for us over Mingaladon. We were attacked continuously the whole way through for about 25 minutes before we shook them off......Mingaladon aerodrome had diagonally crossed runways, so the leading six went down the runway on which were the heavy bombers. Our aircraft, which was leading the third vic, swung off a mile from the aerodrome and turned down the North-South runway and bombed the fighters parked there. Subsequent PRU photographs revealed that tremendous damage to enemy aircraft had been done......Some of our aircraft used anti-submarine bombs which had a terrific blast and this blast was very effective. As a matter of fact they were better than GP bombs among fighters as they exploded on impact and the blast played havoc among the lightly constructed fighters.......We joined the first formation as we finished our run and the CO, realising the strength of the fighter attack, reduced his speed so that each aircraft had no difficulty in staying right in the formation which was as tight as any I have seen.

During their epic engagement with the Japanese fighters the Blenheims were credited with having definitely shot down two aircraft, with two more being claimed as probables and two as damaged. The confirmed kills were obtained by Sgts Ken Gardiner and Cliff Briggs (who shot one of the wings off his victim) with Sgts Frank Brown and Bill Wilson being other claimants. Gardiner was slightly wounded during the engagement but his pilot, Fg Off Stuart Muller-Rowland, was more seriously injured. No longer able to maintain close formation, he dived his aircraft to low level and returned independently, his precipitate departure probably accounting for the Japanese claiming to have shot one of the bombers down. Since this Blenheim was reported to have had fifty-seven bullet holes in it, they very nearly had! Once down safely the pilot was admitted to hospital in Yenangyaung to have a bullet removed from a buttock, and his crew joined

the growing band of surplus aircrew as the battered bomber fleet dwindled.

The RAF had lost only one Hurricane, although its pilot had survived, and four other fighters had been damaged. In all the Hurricanes claimed to have destroyed or damaged seventeen Japanese aircraft in the air and on the ground, to which must be added No 45 Sqn's two aerial victories and an undetermined amount of damage to installations and parked aircraft caused by the 4½ tons of bombs which the squadron had delivered. As always these were considerable overestimates and post-war analysis of Japanese records reportedly indicates that their losses were actually two shot down and eleven badly damaged. Honours were even in this respect, however, as the Japanese had claimed one Blenheim as destroyed plus three probables whereas none of the bombers had actually been lost, although seven of them had collected bullet holes. Despite these accounting errors, however, the mission had undoubtedly been a major success. But it was to be the RAF's last victory of the campaign.

The Japanese reaction was swift and devastating. Some sources indicate that five more replacement Blenheims had arrived at Magwe during the morning[13]. While these were being prepared for another attack in the afternoon and the groundcrews were trying to make up the numbers from those which had flown the first raid, Magwe was bombed by three waves of enemy aircraft at 1330hrs, 1410hrs and 1430hrs. The total attacking force was reported as having comprised fifty-nine bombers escorted by at least forty-eight fighters[14]. A handful of defenders managed to take off and claimed to have destroyed or damaged five of the raiders but five pilots were wounded and two Hurricanes and two P-40s suffered severe combat damage; on the ground another Hurricane and six Blenheims were destroyed and several other aircraft were rendered unserviceable.

One of the Blenheims which had been destroyed had only arrived at Magwe that day. A batch of six replacement Blenheims had been despatched from Egypt on March 12th. Among them was Z7412, flown by Sgts F Shattock, C Levings and H C Hatherly; they were all RAAF, although Colin Levings was actually a Scot who had been born in India. They had lost a day at Aqir when their aircraft got stuck in soft sand but, apart from that, they made steady progress and finally reached Magwe just as No 45 Sqn's aeroplanes were returning from their last mission. Having delivered their aeroplane, which promptly fell victim to the Japanese bombers, Foster Shattock and his crew reported to Wg Cdr Wallis who gave them the options of being sent back to India or staying in Burma. They chose to stay and were

215

Smoke rising from the airfield at Magwe after one of the Japanese air raids on March 21st. (H C Hatherly)

duly taken under the wing of the Flying Camel. This was a somewhat informal arrangement at first, however; until the bureaucracy managed to catch up and endorse this decision the three men seemed to have disappeared and for a time they were officially listed as missing.

Despite the disastrous effects of the Japanese counter-attack the irrepressible Wilde could still find something amusing in the events of that day, although it probably did not seem very funny at the time:

> During the attack a group of us were in a slit trench firing our rifles at the strafing fighters which were so close that we could clearly see the faces of the Japs who were flying them. A stray bullet hit a hornets' nest which plopped into the trench.   Out came the hornets and attacked us. It was like a slapstick sequence in a film; five of us took off like bats with dozens of hornets in pursuit. I dived through the open window of a basha, got under a mosquito net and spent a painful few minutes pulling off hornets and chucking them out. I had been stung on my arms, legs, face and, most painful of all, in my ears! After the raid we sought the sick bay and stood in a dejected group, very sore and now visibly beginning to puff up. A harassed doctor asked what was wrong with us.   On being informed of our plight, he said, in tones which indicated a rapid loss of patience, 'Look lads, in there I have people with bullet and shrapnel wounds, legs and arms off, so p*** off sharpish before I lose my temper!' We went, but he must have relented because an orderly came running after us with a bottle of meths.

There was to be little respite. The Japanese mounted four more attacks on Magwe on the 22nd. These were reported at the time as: twenty-seven bombers and ten fighters at

0845hrs; twenty-seven bombers and two fighters at 0900hrs; twenty-seven bombers and ten fighters at 1430hrs and ten bombers and ten fighters at 1440hrs[15]. Two Hurricanes, which had taken off before the first attack, engaged and claimed strikes on two enemy aircraft but one of the fighters crashed on landing. This was the only retribution that the RAF was able to exact as no aircraft had been able to get off in time to intercept the second onslaught.

Surprisingly, although a handful of men had been wounded, there had been no fatalities but damage had been extensive; three more Blenheims and three of the AVG's P-40s were destroyed on the ground and the tenuous communications links with No 517 AMES and its radar equipment, which had permitted a semblance of operational control to be maintained, were all severed.   Without an effective warning system and with few serviceable fighters remaining, Magwe was virtually defenceless. All aircraft that could be made airworthy were hastily patched up and flown to Akyab, the Blenheims getting away before the afternoon attacks. In all, six Blenheims and nine Hurricanes succeeded in taking off from Magwe on that dreadful Sunday, although one of the latter failed to make it all the way to the coast. Only three of the Blenheims were flown by pilots of No 45 Sqn, Sqn Ldr Austin, Lt Alder and Plt Off Maloney, and in all three cases (with the apparent exception of Bill Corbett) they left their rear crews at Magwe[16].

Almost inevitably the series of raids on the 22nd sparks another Wilde yarn:

> One of our armourers, Newbould by name, attempted to set up a tripod and Vickers gun to fire at the fighters. One of the Aussie air gunners, Sgt Briggs, threatened to shoot him if he didn't take his sodding gun elsewhere, as

he reckoned it would draw the enemy fighters to us! A furious argument broke out and one of our pilots, Gerry Osborne, threatened to shoot the Aussie if he shot Newbould! We waited for somebody to offer to shoot Gerry, knowing that we would all then shoot him as he was one of our favourite aircrew! At this point a Bofors gun, our sole defence, stupidly sited in the open in the middle of a paddy field, was put out of action by one fighter drawing fire while another attacked it from behind - we had to admit that this did tend to give some substance to the Aussie's point of view![17]

Just as the squadron was being wiped out as an effective fighting force, four of the squadron's crews had been despatched from India as replacements. On March 22nd these twelve men (Osborne, Turton and Field; Goss, Whiteside and Murray; Hockney, Paterson and Gaudet and Armstrong, Gooding and Whittaker) had clambered aboard one of No 31 Sqn's venerable Valentias (K2807) at Dum Dum whence Plt Off Farr flew them to Chittagong and then on down to Akyab. Since the last half-dozen Blenheims had just been withdrawn from Magwe, however, Akyab was now the end of the line.

It was Akyab's turn to be attacked on the 23rd. Sqn Ldr Austin was severely wounded by flying shrapnel and, along with some of the newly arrived reinforcement crews, he was flown out later that day in a Valentia. One of the six refugee Blenheims had been lost during the air raid but the remaining five were able to fly on to Asansol where they were handed over to No 113 Sqn which had begun to reorganise itself there on March 18th. Three more replacement Blenheims had been delivered to Akyab on the 23rd to undertake a projected reconnaissance mission to the Andaman Islands. This never took place. After waiting four hours to be briefed, the crews had still been on the ground when the Japanese air raid had developed. Two of the 'new' Blenheims were lost and F/Sgt Gerry Osborne flew all three remaining crews out in the sole survivor. A Valentia had earlier airlifted Sgts Bob Armstrong, Bert Gooding and George Whittaker as far as Chittagong and two days later they completed their journey by ferrying a stray Blenheim (Z9741) to Dum Dum.

The withdrawal from Akyab effectively ended the Flying Camel's days as an operational Blenheim squadron. Its participation in the Burma campaign was not quite over yet, however, and the adventures of the echelon which had been left at Magwe are recounted in Chapter 9.

While the preceding account of the squadron's operations in Burma is substantially accurate it is, unfortunately, not totally comprehensive. The few surviving official records of the campaign are incomplete, and in places contradictory, so, despite having had access to the flying log books of a number of the squadron's aircrew who flew in Burma, it has not been possible to establish a definitive picture of No 45 Sqn's activities. It appears certain, however, that in the thirty-four days between February 16th and March 21st No 45 Sqn had flown at least 180 offensive sorties. Most of the bomb loads carried had consisted of four 250 pounders but this was not always the case and it is known that lighter loads of 40 lb bombs had been used on occasion and that some of the sorties mounted from Zayatkwin had been flown with guns alone. It follows that the squadron probably delivered

Sqn Ldr Frederick John 'Bunny' Austin, OC A flight from September 1941, was wounded in a Japanese air raid on Akyab on March 23rd. (Mrs Daphne Hughes)

something like 85 short tons of ordnance in a little under five weeks. To this offensive effort must be added numerous reconnaissance missions (at least twenty-five), many non-operational, but vital, flights evacuating service and civilian refugees and several priority sorties conveying senior commanders from place to place.

No 113 Sqn had been running down as No 45 Sqn was building up and, as a result, the RAF's bomber force in Burma had never amounted to more than a single effective squadron and not even that during March. Overwhelmingly outnumbered, the squadron could not hope to do more than delay the inevitable by harassing the Japanese advance. The pressure was sometimes considerable and some crews had found themselves flying their first operational sortie within hours of arriving in Burma after making a six-day intercontinental transit flight. Operating with an absolute minimum of technical support, serviceability was a constant problem and the squadron was hard-pressed to mount raids in substantial numbers but it did what it could whenever it could and, under the circumstances, its substantial total of sorties flown represented a remarkable achievement.

The squadron's experience in Burma had had much in common with the similar episode in Cyrenaica in April 1941. In both cases the squadron was part of a tiny bomber force attempting to blunt a major attack. In both cases, operating under the most trying of conditions, it had continued to fly offensive missions until it was eventually obliged to withdraw to avoid being totally wiped out. Inevitably, both campaigns had ended in defeats but for the Flying Camels they had been glorious ones.

Notes:

1. The situation was evidently confused and, so far as the constitution of the party in Burma is concerned, there are several inconsistencies between the ORB entry for March 26th and those made later on, for instance, 1st April and 6th May. This chronicler has not been able to rationalise all of

these anomalies and, since it has been verified by several of those who were actually in Burma, it is believed that the information contained in this chapter and in Chapter 9 represents a more accurate reflection both of the events that occurred during the Burma campaign and of the personnel who were involved than any other references.

2. Although it had been the intention to establish one, there never was an Air Stores Park as such in Burma. In the autumn of 1941 a unit, No 39 ASP, had been formed to satisfy this requirement and it had sailed from the Clyde on November 11th, accompanied by the nucleus of No 60 RSU. Reaching Bombay on 6th January 1942, No 39 ASP made its way to Calcutta by rail. The unit's personnel sailed for Rangoon on 15th February on the SS *Ellenga* but, once it had been appreciated that they were totally without supplies or equipment and therefore of no practical use whatsoever, the ship was recalled. No 39 ASP, still accompanied by No 60 RSU, disembarked again on the 26th and, after cooling its heels at Bareilly for a few weeks, it eventually set up shop and began trading from Kanchrapara on 9th April.

The main logistic support establishment in Burma was No 154 MU which had been formed from the "Temporary Burma MU" set up in Rangoon in mid-1941. By the end of July it was conducting its business from Mingaladon but in December it moved east to Kyauktan and then, on January 23rd, to Meiktila, which was intended to be its permanent location. Worrall's 'stores park' was probably a detachment of this unit.

3. The order in which the reinforcement squadrons left Egypt was as follows:

a. No 113 Sqn, bound for Burma, in three sections of six, five and five, departing between 30th December 1941 and 1st January 1942.

b. No 84 Sqn, originally earmarked for Singapore but destination changed to Sumatra at about the time of departure, in four sections of six aircraft each, departing on 14th, 15th, 16th and 18th January 1942.

c. No 211 Sqn, originally earmarked for Singapore but destination changed to Sumatra before departure, in four sections of six aircraft each, departing between 25th and 28th January 1942.

d. No 45 Sqn, bound for Burma, in five sections, departing between 9th and 13th February 1942.

e. No 11 Sqn, bound for Ceylon, in four sections of eight, five, three and three, departing on 24th February and 1st, 4th and 10th March. Eighteen of the nineteen aeroplanes involved reached Ratmalana, the last three on 17th March.

None of these units completed their long transit flights without some of their aeroplanes running into problems and the reinforcement route became dotted with stragglers who tacked on to later formations as they came through. In the meantime Japanese paratroops had landed at Palembang on February 14th and within two days Sumatra was being evacuated; thereafter it became impractical for any further Blenheims to proceed beyond Rangoon. It is known that, of the forty-eight crews of Nos 84 and 211 Sqns which had set out from Egypt, a total of ten failed to reach Sumatra for one reason or another. Several of the aeroplanes in which these crews had left Egypt eventually found their way to Burma (see Note 10) but the four crews discussed below are the only ones known to have operated with No 45 Sqn. It is presumed that the remaining stragglers were retained in India, although it is possible that some may have been tacked on to No 113 Sqn.

In this context it is interesting to note that on 20th February Sqn Ldr Hughes recorded in his journal that the local Order of Battle included two Blenheims of No 84 Sqn and one of No 211 Sqn's. Five days later he registered the attachment of ten (unidentified) aircrew of the latter unit to No 45 Sqn. It seems reasonable to assume that these were the crews (plus a spare body) of the three aeroplanes he had noted on the 20th. Hughes' note supports the contention that there were only three stray crews in Burma by this stage but there was evidently some confusion as to which units actually 'owned' them. In fact No 211 Sqn had virtually ceased to exist on February 18th when the remnants of the various Blenheim units in the Dutch East Indies had been pooled under the aegis of No 84 Sqn. Thus, regardless of their origins, all of the stray Sumatra-bound crews which had become attached to No 45 Sqn were thereafter technically on the strength of No 84 Sqn. It is, of course, highly improbable that this would have been appreciated at Magwe at the time and it would have taken the P Staffs several weeks to unravel these developments, to trace all the spare bodies who were scattered about India and Burma and to transfer them to the No 84 Sqn pages of their ledgers. It would seem that they did it, however, as No 45 Sqn's ORB notes on 16th April that, "P/Os French and Mayger and seven aircrew personnel proceeded to rejoin No 84 Squadron, Karachi, on cessation of attachment to this Unit." (Hughes' ten less McNamara? - see below). A brief summary of the activities of the crews who are known to have been attached to No 45 Sqn in Burma follows.

a. Plt Off D Mayger, Plt Off E F French and Sgt Davies had originally been with No 82 Sqn in the UK. Having ferried a Blenheim out from the UK, they arrived in Egypt on 9th January 1942 where they were posted to No 211 Sqn which was preparing to move to the Far East. Flying Z9659, the crew left Egypt on January 27th bound for Singapore as part of the squadron's third wave. They were delayed for a week at Habbaniyah and did not move on until on 5th February, by now in V6328. Further minor delays en route found them travelling in company with No 45 Sqn. They reached Magwe on 17th February but did not fly again until the 26th on which date 'Chips' French's log book notes that he was operating on attachment to No 45 Sqn. The crew became involved in the evacuation shuttle at the end of the month, flying five trips between Magwe, Highland Queen and Akyab but when Flt Lt Beeston found that he had lost his rear crew (see narrative) he co-opted French and Davies and they returned to Burma and flew with him until Beeston's own team were able to find their way back from India. On 10th March Bill Maloney flew French and Davies back to Akyab where they were reunited with Dan Mayger. There they stayed, without an aeroplane, until 26th March when they were airlifted out to Dum Dum by Wg Cdr Jenkins in a DC-2 of No 31 Sqn. This crew remained on No 45 Sqn's nominal strength until April 16th when, by this time evidently regarded by officialdom as rightly belonging to No 84 Sqn, they left to join what had now become their parent unit which was beginning to reform at Drigh Road.

b. When No 84 Sqn moved east Plt Off A W Pedlar RAAF and his crew, Sgt M F Roberts RAAF and Sgt M Morris RAAF, left Egypt on January 18th as part of that unit's fourth and last flight. They were delayed at Habbaniyah for a week and, having switched aircraft from R3733 to Z9542, they ran into trouble again on the Jodhpur-Allahabad leg on January 29th and had to make a forced landing alongside the River Ganges. They eventually reached Dum Dum where they picked up another ex-84 Sqn aeroplane (V5422) which they flew to Magwe on February 10th, still accompanied by Cpl Shand and LAC Dawson who had been with them since leaving Heliopolis. They made two further attempts to proceed south; both had to be abandoned, the first, in V5422 on the 11th, because of engine trouble and the second, in Z9819 on the 14th, because the aeroplane lost part of its cockpit glazing, including the top hatch, and was obliged to return to Mingaladon. The following day the crew moved their aeroplane to Zayatkwin where, as noted in Aubrey Pedlar's log book, they were attached to No 45 Sqn. Between then and February 27th they took part in four bombing raids and flew one reconnaissance and two evacuation sorties, all in Z9819. After being ferried to Akyab on the 28th in Hudson AE540 (piloted by Plt Off P E Springman who, having originally been in Singapore with a detachment of No 53 Sqn, was now in Burma, presumably attached to No 139 Sqn), Pedlar, without his crew, immediately returned to Magwe with Max Neil in V5495. That same day he flew Gus Alder's Z9803 back to Akyab with four refugee Hurricane pilots on board. On March 1st, his own crew having already sailed for Calcutta on the SS *Szechuan*, he picked up Norman Bayly and Ken Edwards of No 45 Sqn and they flew Z9803 on to Dum Dum. For the next six weeks Pedlar remained in Calcutta attached to No 45 Sqn. Anticipating that he would eventually be added to the posted strength of No 45 Sqn, he arranged, on the authority of Sqn Ldr Hughes, to exchange his original rear crew for that of McNamara. They did no flying during this interlude which ended on April 16th when they left to rejoin No 84 Sqn at Karachi.

c. Sgt J C McNamara RAAF, Sgt D W Penn RAAF and Sgt N A Bruce RAAF originally belonged to No 211 Sqn. They left Egypt in Z7892 on January 27th but ran into a heavy sandstorm and, after being obliged to shut down the starboard engine, were forced to land near pumping station H4 (on the oil pipeline from Iraq to Jaffa), collapsing the aircraft's port undercarriage leg in the process. By February 4th a working party from Palestine had patched up the damage and the aeroplane flew on to Habbaniyah. They were delayed further at Shaibah, first by adverse weather and then to await a batch of four eastbound Hurricanes which they were required to shepherd down the Persian Gulf. Thereafter they made steady progress, by this time in company with the first wave of No 45 Sqn's deployment. Z7892 reached Magwe on February 14th accompanied by two of No 45 Sqn's aeroplanes (Wg Cdr Wallis and Plt Off Maloney) but did not fly on to Rangoon until the following day. Too late to proceed to their original destination, Singapore, McNamara's crew was attached to No 45 Sqn (with effect from the 15th, according to a contemporary annotation in Bruce's log book). They flew ops from Zayatkwin on February 16th (twice), 17th, 19th, 20th and 21st (twice). Moving to Magwe on the 22nd they took part in a raid on Moulmein on 25th February but, staging through Mingaladon on the way back, they were caught in a Japanese air raid. John Charles 'Jack' McNamara was killed; David 'Bill' Penn was wounded in the leg, admitted to hospital and then evacuated to India. Norm Bruce was physically unharmed but probably concussed; he found his way to Highland Queen whence he was picked up by Aubrey Pedlar on the 27th and conveyed to Magwe just in time to be caught up in the partial evacuation which took place on the 28th. A Tiger Moth (Z-06) of the Burma Volunteer Air Force flew him to Akyab where he embarked on the SS *Szechuan*, reaching Calcutta on March 2nd to be billeted at Dum Dum. While marking time in India, Penn and Bruce joined Pedlar to make up a notional crew. As noted above, they remained on No 45 Sqn's books until April 16th when they left to join No 84 Sqn.

d. Sgts S J Prentice RAAF, B W Engall RCAF and A Thomas RAAF of No 84 Sqn left Egypt on January 18th in V6128 but, having experienced problems en route, they did not leave Karachi until February 12th, by this time in company with the leading element of No 45 Sqn. Attempting to land at Allahabad in poor visibility they overshot the runway and, to avoid running into the fence and coming to an abrupt halt (Prentice had gashed his face doing this in a previous incident while flying with No 72 OTU), a ground loop was induced and the Blenheim's undercarriage was damaged. It is not known which aeroplane was involved in this incident but V6128 found its way to Magwe and was operating with No 45 Sqn by March 7th. Despite this further delay Jack Prentice, Bill Engall and Alan Thomas eventually got through to Zayatkwin and flew at least one operational sortie (on February 21st) but there the trail goes cold and it is assumed that they must have returned to India at about the time that No 45 Sqn pulled back to Magwe.

4. In an attempt to co-ordinate the disparate responses to the Japanese onslaught a joint controlling organisation, American, British, Dutch and Australian Command (ABDACOM), had been established during January 1942. With his HQ at Bandoeng (Java), Gen Wavell assumed overall command on the 15th. ABDACOM was sub-divided into six regional/functional Groups, that responsible for the defence of Burma being NORGROUP. Although there were a handful of USAAF bombers in India and the AVG had a squadron of Curtiss P-40s at Mingaladon, most of the available air assets in Burma and, more significantly, the only regional controlling organisation belonged to the RAF. With effect from 16th February 1942 HQ 221 Gp adopted the title NORGROUP for operational purposes, although its administrative and support staffs continued to function as a purely RAF formation. While it survived on a nominal basis for some time thereafter, ABDACOM became redundant following the loss of the Dutch East Indies and on March 12th HQ 221 Gp resumed its original designation.

5. The scattering of emergency landing grounds and dispersal airstrips which had been laid out in the vicinity of Rangoon were named after famous brands of spirits - 'Highland Queen', 'Johnny Walker', 'John Haig', 'Dewar', etc.

6. IFF (Identification Friend or Foe) was, and is, a means of identifying friendly aeroplanes by creating a distinctively coded 'paint' on a radar screen. This is achieved through the aircraft's being fitted with a transponder which is triggered by a pulse of energy received from the interrogating radar station. An IFF capability confers a considerable tactical advantage on an air defence system and as a result the airborne devices were highly classified. To ensure that they would not fall into enemy hands, they had either to be salvaged from wrecked aeroplanes or destroyed. They were later fitted with automatic mechanisms which would destroy the circuitry if an excessive g loading was imposed, such as might occur in a crash.

7. Despite the extravagant claims made by the AVG at the time, post war analysis of Japanese records by Yasuho Izawa (see *Bloody Shambles, Vol 2* by Shores, Cull and Izawa) indicates that actual losses amounted to only two Ki 27s. The optimism of the American pilots may not have been unconnected with the fact that they were paid a bounty for each Japanese aeroplane they brought down.

8. Previously published accounts of this mission have presented it from the perception of the participating fighter pilots rather than from that of the bomber crews (see, for instance, *Hurricanes Over the Arakan* by Norman Franks and *Bloody Shambles, Vol 2*) and these have noted the designated target as having been Chiang Mai. Although this is where the Blenheims did eventually drop their bombs, the evidence of the flying log books and journals of various No 45 Sqn aircrew shows that the designated target had actually been Lampang. Curiously, in view of its complexity and the importance which the AOC evidently attached to this long-range mission, this author has been unable to find any reference to it in the surviving records of NORGROUP, HQ 221 Gp or Burwing. This lack of readily accessible

documentation is presumed to be the reason why this particularly significant, if not entirely successful, enterprise is not mentioned in the official history, *The Royal Air Force, 1939-45*.

9. Its radar equipment having begun to function effectively only towards the end of January, No 517 AMES had been withdrawn from Rangoon on February 27th. Reaching Magwe the following day, it had moved on to Yenangyaung on March 2nd where, courtesy of the workshops of the Burmah Oil Company, its vehicles were modified to make the unit and its equipment operationally mobile (as distinct from transportable). The work was completed by the 8th when the unit returned to Magwe and set up shop eight miles north of the airfield near the Khodoung Chaung.

10. The paucity of contemporary documentation has made it difficult to identify all of the Blenheims used by No 45 Sqn during the Burma campaign. From the evidence provided by aircrew log books, however, it is known that the following aircraft were flown out from Egypt by the squadron's crews: V5495 was left at Karachi by Jewell but flown on later by another (unidentified) crew; V5938 by Hughes; V5999 by Jewell (from Karachi); V6221 by Fryar; Z7635 by Wallis; Z7757 by Neil; Z7770 by DeMarillac; Z7899 (probably) by Powell; Z7928 by Eve; Z7981 by Curtis; Z9573 by Austin; Z9799 by Smyth; Z9803 by Alder; Z9811 by Huon; Z9821 by Maloney; Z9833 by Christensen. Other Blenheims which are known to have been flown in Burma by squadron crews included: V5422*, V5957, V6128*, V6328*, V6467 (see Note 11 below), Z7579, Z7859*, Z7892*, Z7916*, Z7923, Z9679, Z9721*, Z9801, Z9807, Z9819*, Z9835. Some of these aircraft will have been among the original twenty-four which the squadron flew out but others were inherited from Nos 84, 113 and 211 Sqns. An asterisk indicates where an aircraft is known to have been 'second hand', eg No 84 Sqn's V5422, having been left behind by Plt Off J H Goldfinch RAAF en route from Egypt, was eventually flown into Magwe by Plt Off Pedlar; V6128 was another ex-84 Sqn aeroplane, which had started out from Egypt on 18th January being flown by Sgt S J Prentice RAAF; V6328 originally 'belonged' to Plt Off Mayger of No 211 Sqn; Z7892 was flown out from Egypt by Sgt J C McNamara RAAF of No 211 Sqn and Z9819 was delivered to Magwe by an unidentified group captain (Gp Capt Singer?) circa 12th February.

11. In his log book, Cliff Briggs records the aircraft involved in the incident on March 17th as '6467', although this number is written in a different coloured ink and *may* have been added at a later date. If it is correct, however, it can only have been V6467, which had certainly been with No 45 Sqn from June 1941 until at least December of that year, but there must be some doubt as to whether this aeroplane was still airworthy on 17th March 1942. Two published references fail to clarify the situation. According to *Air Britain's* painstaking listing of all RAF aircraft by serial number, V6467 crashed on take off from Magwe on 1st March while on charge to No 113 Sqn, although the same source fails to note this aeroplane's previous lengthy service with No 45 Sqn so there must be some doubt as to the accuracy of this particular entry. *Bloody Shambles, Vol 2*, without naming the crew, notes that a Blenheim of No 113 Sqn crashed at Magwe on March 1st but identifies the aeroplane as V6967. This cannot be correct, however, as this serial number was never given to any aeroplane and if it had been it would not have been a Blenheim - V6967 was part of an unalloted block within the series V6533-V7195, which covered a production run of 500 Gloster-built Hurricanes. No 113 Sqn's ORB confirms that an incident took place on 1st March (Sqn Ldr Ford's Blenheim suffered an engine failure and "crashed at the end of the runway", the aeroplane being "considerably damaged", although the crew escaped injury) but, unfortunately, this document does not identify the aeroplane involved. So, if Briggs' log is accepted as being accurate, V6467 did not crash on March 1st or, if it did, the damage proved to be repairable. Alternatively, if the entry in Briggs' log is inaccurate then the identity of the Blenheim in which he flew on March 17th remains a mystery.

Apart from its obvious dramatic content, the nature of the incident on March 17th is interesting as it was widely believed that the Japanese deliberately strung cables across rivers as a disincentive to low-flying aircraft. It would seem equally likely, however, that they were actually electricity supply lines or, even more likely, telegraph wires - in either case their being broken will have been as much of an inconvenience to the Japanese army as it was to the RAF's aircrew. Whatever the motive, there were certainly other instances of damage being caused to aircraft by suspended cables. One which had a tenuous connection with the squadron involved Sqn Ldr Penny, Fg Off Bruce and Sgt Barclay in a Blenheim V (BA611) of No 113 Sqn on 31st October 1942. They were following the Kaladan river downstream from Paletawa when, in the vicinity of Kyauktaw, they hit a cable which led them to make a precautionary landing at Chittagong. The damage proved to have been superficial, however, and they flew back to Asansol the next day.

12. The identity of the ninth crew is problematical. Assuming that they came from No 45 Sqn, the only obvious candidates are those whose names appear in Fig 8.3, however, the whereabouts of all of No 45 Sqn's crews as at 21st March has been established with a high degree of confidence. Apart from those who are listed in Fig 8.4, the other pilots are known to have left Magwe on the following dates.

26th February	DeMarillac.
28th February	Eve, Christensen, Fryar, Jewell, Edmonds and Guy (probably, but in any event he was certainly in Calcutta by 12th March on which date he moved from there to Fyzabad by rail). Neil and Huon had also been evacuated on February 28th but they had returned to Magwe on March 16th.
8th March	Hughes.
11th March	Smyth (killed) and Curtis.
14th March	Powell (killed).

Of the others, Goss and Osborne were probably evacuated at about the end of February, but they were certainly in Calcutta on March 21st as they are known to have flown from there to Akyab on the 22nd; Penny was still attached to HQ 17 Div and Huon was at Magwe with an unserviceable aeroplane. That only leaves Keel, who was in hospital in Poona by March 26th. It is known that he and his crew did fly out of Burma in a Blenheim but not when. However, several of those involved are adamant that only three of No 45 Sqn's pilots flew Blenheims out to Akyab on March 22nd (see Note 16) and, since Keel was not one of them, he must have left before then and he could not, therefore, still have been at Magwe on March 21st.

There would appear to be four possible explanations. First, although ten crews were briefed, only eight actually flew the mission. This cannot be reconciled with the long-accepted belief that there *were* nine aircraft which is supported by the notes and accounts (most of them recorded *at the time* in log books and journals) of various of the participants, eg Bayly, Hallett, Maloney, Huon, McDade and Briggs, who are unanimous in confirming that there were definitely three flights of three.

A second possibility is that the anonymous ninth crew was one of the three strays from Nos 84 and 211 Sqns, but McNamara had been killed at Mingaladon on February 25th and Pedlar had flown a Blenheim back to India on 1st March and he never returned to Magwe. The third of these pilots, Mayger, had been marooned since 3rd March at Akyab where he was joined by his rear crew a week later; they never returned to Magwe either. Prentice is an outsider as he is believed to have been evacuated to India before the end of February; in any case he was well known to several of No 45 Sqn's Australians and had he taken part in the raid it is likely that they would have remembered him.

It is possible that, like Huon's and Neil's, another of the No 45 Sqn crews which had been evacuated earlier had returned to Magwe. The author has corresponded with twenty-five of the squadron's contemporary aircrew (including at least one member of five of the crews of which actually flew on 21st March) and none of them has been able to identify the missing crew. Although due allowance must be made for the effect on memory of a lapse of some fifty years, this does strongly suggest that the ninth crew was at least unfamiliar and thus unlikely to have belonged to No 45 Sqn.

The fourth and last possibility must be that the unidentified crew came from another unit altogether. Candidates might include a crew from Nos 60 or 113 Sqns, another stray crew from Nos 84 or 211 Sqns or a ferry crew who, having just delivered a replacement aeroplane, might have been pressed into service. Of these possibilities, No 60 Sqn's activities have been extensively reconstructed by Sqn Ldr D W Warne, No 113 Sqn's ORB is substantially complete and reasonably comprehensive and No 84 Sqn's history has been researched and published by D Neate; none of these authorities or references indicates that a crew from any of these units took part in a raid from Magwe on March 21st. Of the remaining two options, a ferry crew or one from No 211 Sqn, the former would seem to be the more likely as it is known that a few reinforcement Blenheims were finding their way to Magwe at about this time.

At the time of writing this conundrum has still to be satisfactorily solved.

13. These five aircraft may have been the backmarkers of a group of six Blenheims despatched from Egypt on March 12th, although H C Hatherly (who flew in one of them) stoutly maintains that Shattock's Z7412 was the only one of these aircraft to succeed in reaching Magwe. Accepting that this was the case then the five reported reinforcements (if they existed) must have been drawn from the small pool of Blenheims already in India.

14. According to post-war analysis of Japanese records presented in *Bloody Shambles, Vol 2*, the total force committed on March 21st comprised sixty-two bombers, fifty-two Ki 21s and ten Ki 30s (one other Ki 21 had crashed on take off) and fifty-nine fighters, forty-five Ki 27s and fourteen Ki 43s, plus a handful of Ki 46 reconnaissance/observation aircraft.

15. According to *Bloody Shambles, Vol 2*, the Japanese appear to have actually launched two strikes, each of which evidently either attacked twice or in two waves. The first comprised twenty-four bombers, Ki 48s and Ki 30s, with an escort of sixty-one Ki 27s; the second involved fifty-three Ki 21s and forty-one Ki 27s and Ki 43s.

16. Fig 8.4, as amplified by Note 12, accounts for the ten pilots of No 45 Sqn who were still in Burma on March 22nd. Of these, Muller-Rowland had been wounded and Wallis, Beeston, Penny, Thompson, Neil and Huon are, as described in Chapter 9, known to have remained in Burma. Austin, Alder and Maloney were, therefore, the only squadron pilots available to fly the surviving aircraft. If, as is generally accepted to have been the case, six Blenheims were flown from Magwe to Akyab on March 22nd (and No 45 Sqn's ORB supports his contention, albeit noted in arrears on the 26th) the other three must have been the survivors of the replacements which, according to some sources, had arrived that day. They were presumably flown by their own crews and would have airlifted out the other ferry crews whose aircraft had been lost. Another possibility is that one of these aeroplanes was flown by the unidentified ninth crew who had flown on the previous day's Mingaladon raid.

17. If this incident took place on March 22nd then the pilot involved *cannot* have been Osborne as he was flown from Calcutta to Akyab in a Valentia on that date which precludes his having been at Magwe. It is assumed that either some other pilot was involved or, if it *was* Osborne, that the date is in error and that the incident occurred elsewhere, possibly during one of the earlier air raids on Zayatkwin or a later one at Lashio. Whatever the truth, something fairly entertaining must have happened and it is far too nice a story to disregard. It is, incidentally, probably not without significance that Wyndham McKay 'Gerry' Osborne is the subject of this anecdote as he established for himself something of a reputation as an *enfant terrible* and allegedly had a number of scrapes with authority. Despite his evident indifference to military discipline this was more than compensated for by his aggressive spirit. In less than a week in May 1941, while flying anti-shipping strikes from Malta in Blenheims of a detachment of No 21 Sqn, Osborne had been personally responsible for sinking an Italian destroyer and damaging two other enemy motor vessels; this remarkable achievement was recognised by the award of a particularly well-earned DFM.

Chapter 9. The Flying Camel dispersed; the exodus from Burma and a Diaspora in India.

With no aeroplanes left to fly it was all over at Magwe and Gp Capt Broughall ordered his units to start moving out; their destination was to be Lashio in the Shan Hills of eastern Burma. No 517 AMES and its precious radar equipment had already withdrawn to Yenangyaung on March 22nd and, beginning at 0700hrs on the 23rd, the rest of the RAF began to leave as well, heading in the direction of Mandalay. The bulk of the evacuees comprised HQ Burwing and its staff, the remnants of Nos 17 and 45 Sqns, some bodies belonging to No 154 MU plus an assortment of lost sheep from other units. The personnel of No 45 Sqn known still to have been in Burma at that time included the CO, the Adj, Fg Off Pickering, assorted aircrew - Sqn Ldr Penny (still with 17th Div), Flt Lt Beeston, Plt Offs Fraser, Bayly and Graebner, F/Sgt Mills and Sgts Gardiner, Page, McDade, Bruce, Carew-Reid, Wilson, Neil, Hallett, Brown, Romans, Briggs, Watkins, Huon, Thompson (RAF obs), Thompson (RCAF pilot), Clark, Shattock, Levings and Hatherly - plus the twenty-one NCOs and airmen who had constituted the unit's only groundcrew since it had left Egypt six or seven very long weeks before. Not all of these men stayed until the final

evacuation five weeks later, however, the first to leave the group being Cpl Hector Sharpe who was admitted to hospital in Mandalay as the squadron passed by on its way to Lashio.

OC Burwing, Wg Cdr Wallis and Flt Lt Beeston left early to confer with army HQ at Maymyo, leaving Flt Lt Philip Butters in command of the squadron's convoy which comprised a motley collection of cars and lorries (some military, some requisitioned) plus the odd Jeep. As Arthur Huon recalls:

> My crew and I left Magwe in a commandeered 3-ton Chevy which the MT Section was going to abandon. It had no bonnet and no handbrake; the horn didn't work and the radiator had a six-inch hole, caused by shrapnel, which had been plugged with molten lead. Otherwise it was in excellent condition with only 3,000 miles on the clock. We put a couple of drums of fuel and our personal kit in the back and as Albert (Thompson) couldn't drive he rode in the back with the kit while Ron (Clark) and I shared the driving and travelled in the cab for the whole of the four-day trip. In fact we justified ourselves on the first day by picking up most of the loads from two stores trucks which had broken down.

En route breakdowns such as these prevented the convoy's staying together as a coherent unit and it soon

Above:- The squadron's convoy shortly after leaving Magwe; with his feet up on the Jeep's dashboard is Sgt Mac McDade. (B T McDade). Below:- A group of groundcrew stop for a brew up during the journey to Lashio. From the left: LAC G Bell, LAC G Newbould, LAC Lansley, unidentified, LAC J Morris (bending), LAC D Taylor and LAC D Huntley. The figure that can just be discerned behind the unidentified man is probably Cpl W Worrall. (L Wilde)

One of the squadron's vehicles loaded and ready to leave Magwe on March 23rd. On board are: Sgts Cliff Briggs and Max Neil (backs to the cab); Ron Clark and Ernie Hallett (in front of the petrol drum); Des Carew-Reid (on the right, turned away from the camera); Albert Thompson (on the left, in a topee); Colin Levings (front and centre in a 'Bombay bowler') and Foster Shattock (bottom left). (H C Hatherly)

Left:- Sgt Pete Hatherly with a gruesome find somewhere along the Burma Road. Above:- From the left, Sgts Cliff Briggs, Des Carew-Reid and Pete Hatherly. During the journey to Lashio this group managed to supplement their rations by the acquisition of a sheep which was promptly slaughtered, butchered and cooked. (both C G Briggs)

broke up into smaller sections travelling independently. The majority reached Lashio within three days, most of them having spent intervening nights variously at Kamye, Gwegyo, Maymyo and/or Hsipaw. (*Note: the movements of the party which remained in Burma can be traced by reference to the map at Annex J*).

By March 27th most of the backmarkers had arrived and Burwing and its subordinate units began to settle in at Lashio. They were not to stay together for long, however, and the No 17 Sqn element soon moved on up the Burma Road to Loiwing, just across the Chinese border. A parade was held on March 28th and Gp Capt Broughall announced that No 45 Sqn had been Mentioned in Despatches for the Mingaladon raid on the 21st and that Wg Cdr Wallis had been awarded a richly deserved DSO in recognition of his leadership of the squadron under the most trying of conditions over an exceptionally hectic four months[1]. All personnel were also informed that fifteen people had died of cholera in Lashio and that the town was therefore out of bounds; two days later everyone was given a cholera 'jab'.

Meanwhile, as described in Chapter 8, the bulk of the squadron had recently arrived in India and as it began to reorganise itself a number of changes occurred among its personnel. On March 28th the first replacement aircrew reported to the HQ at Calcutta, Sgts Ross, Edwards and Stone, all of whom were WOp/AGs. Four days later it was learned that several of the squadron's NCO aircrew had been commissioned and that F/Sgt Mills and Sgts Pannifer, Page, and Bruce were all now pilot officers with seniority dating from January 29th; three of these men were at Lashio.

Wg Cdr Wallis was flown out to Calcutta on March 31st and the following day he relinquished command of the squadron to become Station Commander at Aṣansol. Sqn Ldr Hughes, who had been running the India end of the squadron since the sea party had arrived, was made up to wing commander on April 1st to become the next OC No 45 Sqn. With its personnel scattered all over the place, no aeroplanes to fly and an uncertain future, this was quite a daunting proposition, however, especially as the new CO was also expected to act as Wg Cdr Air at HQ 221 Gp. Nevertheless, at that stage it was anticipated that the squadron would soon be re-established and Arthur Hughes was optimistic. To take his place as OC B Flight, Flt Lt Ivor Beeston was also promoted on 1st April but, since he was marooned in eastern Burma, this was a somewhat academic appointment. When Sqn Ldr Penny was posted, along with Plt Off Gordon Bruce (who must have been airlifted out of Lashio at an early stage) to the resurgent No 113 Sqn on April 17th no replacement for him was nominated and C Flight fell into abeyance again, this time (apart from a brief non-flying renaissance in 1956) for good. With Penny's withdrawal from Burma, Sqn Ldr Beeston took over his duties as RAF Liaison Officer with 17th Div, although by then there was not a great deal that the much depleted air force could do to relieve the pressure on the sorely pressed troops. When it was all over, Ivor Beeston was among those who undertook the gruelling and hazardous march out of Burma on foot. His party collected stragglers along the way and the column eventually numbered over 200 men whose survival owed much to his leadership. He finally reported back to squadron HQ in Calcutta on May 29th.

One of the first chores undertaken at Lashio was to send a salvage party all the way back to Magwe to see what they could find. Working in the dark to avoid detection, with few tools and no crane, they did remarkably well to recover nine Mercury engines in a single night. By dawn they were thirty miles away and heading north again. Having trucked these engines all the way to Lashio, when they got there they were simply unloaded and left to rust - the hoped for Blenheims for which they might have been needed never materialised.

In the meantime life had proved to be quite exciting for those who had remained behind as Lashio had been attacked by Japanese aircraft twice on March 31st, twelve civilians being killed at the railway station. Further raids took place on April 1st, 2nd and 3rd. Some damage was done at the airfield, particularly to fuel stocks. There were no military casualties, although there were several more among the local civilian population. In order to provide some regional air defence, seven Hurricanes were flown in from India on March 4th, refuelling at Lashio on their way to Loiwing where No 17 Sqn was now establishing itself. That same day Gp Capt Singer arrived at Lashio in a Blenheim flown by F/Sgts Gerry Osborne and Bert Turton with Sgt Alf Field. On that date No 45 Sqn's strength was reported by HQ Burwing as one serviceable and two unserviceable Blenheims and six crews[2]. On the 6th Gp Capt Singer assumed command of the wing and Herbert Broughall left for Calcutta the next day. To provide Loiwing's fighters with some early warning, No 517 AMES, which had spent a few days at Maymyo, withdrew to Lashio on the 7th but a week later the bulk of the unit moved north to higher ground at Namtu.

Wg Cdr Hughes was flown into Lashio by Plt Off Giles of No 113 Sqn on April 8th to see whether it was possible to get the squadron's people out. Air transport was the only realistic option, however, and there was precious little of that operating. In any case it was still intended to operate Blenheims from Lashio if possible. It was decided that the squadron's detachment would have to stay put for the time being, and on the 14th Arthur Hughes returned to Dum Dum in a civilian DC-3 of the Chinese National Airways Corporation (CNAC). In fact a small bomber force had already begun to take shape at Lashio with Giles' aircraft being joined by four more of No 113 Sqn's Blenheims on the 10th accompanied by a Hurricane and three P-40s. The bombers carried out raids on the 12th and 13th, from the second of which they recovered to Chittagong before returning to Asansol on the 14th. Since the AVG and No 17 Sqn were already operating from Loiwing it began to receive the attentions of the Japanese as well and that airfield was bombed twice on each of 8th and 9th April and once on the 10th.

In preparation for the arrival of the anticipated Blenheim force, Plt Offs Phil Graebner and Norman Bayly set up a briefing and navigation room which was surprisingly well equipped with filing cabinets, planning tables, a stock of charts and wall maps displaying the latest available intelligence information. Having completed the task they decided that it ought to be moved to a site that would be safer from Japanese air attack. A group of NCO aircrew was co-opted and the whole affair was transferred to a basha located in semi-jungle about two miles from the strip. They had no sooner finished the move when there was an air raid which left the basha riddled with holes from flying shrapnel! At this point the two observers gave up and just decided to keep a supply of maps in their rooms in the Mess, just in case anyone ever needed one - which seemed to be increasingly unlikely.

Apart from diversions such as this, the main responsibility for the squadron's aircrew during the month that they were at

Sgt Wyndham McKay Osborne DFM and Sgt Robert Albert Turton RNZAF who, with Sgt Alf Field, flew a Blenheim into Lashio on April 4th. (L E Durrant)

Lashio was keeping the airfield open. This amounted to providing a Duty Crew, day and night, to support any operations which might occur. Pete Hatherly recalls that the night shift involved...

....one person, armed with a Thompson sub-machine gun (which, by the way, was one of the few weapons we had) who was required to sit in the empty hangar from 6pm to approximately 8am the next morning. The only other company you had was an Indian-manned anti-aircraft gun a short distance away. This was not a particularly pleasant duty because after the night had settled in the telephone wires were usually cut by pro-Jap sympathisers and you sat in the corner of the hangar with gun on lap, feeling very lonely and your imagination began to take over.

The huts and bashas available for accommodation at Lashio were adequate but otherwise domestic conditions were not good. Apart from the hazards of cholera, malaria and air raids, food was in short supply and everyone had been on half rations since the evacuation of Magwe. Sgt Cliff Briggs recalls that during the journey to Lashio his group had purchased some rice and a scrawny sheep from some friendly Burmese and with the professional assistance of Hatherly, who had been a butcher before the war, they managed to eat well on that occasion at least. It was something of a paradox that, while life in the arid and barren desert of North Africa had been Spartan and uncomfortable, No 45 Sqn's men had usually had full bellies, even it had only been with hardtack and bully beef; here in the tropical lushness of Burma they had to go hungry.

There was relatively little flying activity at Lashio, just the odd Blenheim or Hurricane calling in to refuel, usually on its way to somewhere else; sometimes a flight of AVG P-40s would stage through on a fighter-bomber mission and there was the occasional CNAC DC-3, the latter usually arriving and departing either at dawn or at dusk to minimise the chance of interference from marauding Japanese fighters.

Cpl Wilf Worrall's hard-worked stores tender overheats during one of the errands it ran from Lashio in April 1942. (L Wilde)

Although Blenheims of No 113 Sqn passed through from time to time, such ops as could be mounted were mostly being flown from Loiwing and there was little for No 45 Sqn's airmen to do in the way of servicing aeroplanes but they were kept busy with other tasks, including administering first aid to civilian air raid casualties.

On April 15th a lone Blenheim from Lashio flew a reconnaissance of the Irrawaddy Front. This sortie is not reflected in the surviving records of No 113 Sqn which suggests that it may have been carried out by one of No 45 Sqn's crews, presumably using the aeroplane which Osborne had brought in on the 4th. The following day another six Blenheims of No 113 Sqn flew into Loiwing whence a few more offensive sorties were mounted. Gerry Osborne and his crew left Lashio on the 19th to convey Gp Capt Singer to Calcutta to confer with the AOC. One of No 113 Sqn's Blenheims having been lost and the pilot of another being sick, the remaining four left Loiwing for Asansol on the 21st, their places being taken by six more later in the day.

At about this time Plt Off Bayly and LAC Wilde were despatched to Namsang to try to locate a mobile signals unit which was supposed to have moved from there to Meiktila but which had failed to contact Burwing for some time. In the course of their adventures, which took from April 18th to the 22nd, they came across a stock of 40 lb bombs at Heho. This find was reported to HQ when they returned to Lashio and a second trip was promptly laid on to collect some of these bombs. This second expedition was a much larger affair and involved a large proportion of the squadron's NCO aircrew, although some had to stay behind to keep the airfield open. Reproduced at Annex J is Norman Bayly's lengthy

This hut at Loiwing belonged to the Burmese Police but, since it had already been vacated, it served as a billet for Sgts Don Page and 'Mac' McDade and others for just one night, 27th/28th April 1942. (B T McDade)

personal account of both of these journeys.

There was a burst of quasi-engineering activity on April 24th when one of No 113 Sqn's Blenheims, operating out of Loiwing, belly-landed at Lashio, its hydraulics having been damaged by machine gun fire. The pilot put his aircraft down alongside the runway but by the time it had come to rest it was squarely in the middle of it. Working with minimal facilities, as always, the squadron's groundcrew hitched a truck to it and, with parties of airmen at the tail and each wingtip to rock the aeroplane and take its weight, they managed to get the runway clear with ten minutes to spare before a DC-3 was due to land. No 113 Sqn lost another Blenheim that day when Z9831 failed to return from an attack on the road between Loi-lem and Hopong. Only the gunner, Sgt Bailes, managed to escape and he turned up at Lashio three days later, just as the airfield was being evacuated.

Gp Capt Singer returned from India on the 25th to find the situation at Lashio becoming increasingly tense. It was difficult to establish a precise picture of what was happening at the Front, which was supposed to be being held by the Chinese VIth Army. Indeed it was not entirely clear where the Front was; what was certain, however, was that it was getting uncomfortably close. No 517 AMES had deployed one of its mobile units forward to Mong Yai, about thirty miles south of Lashio, on April 21st in an effort to increase air raid warning times but three days later they had seen Japanese soldiers in the vicinity and had hastily withdrawn. Len Wilde recalls that by this time elements of the Chinese Army were beginning to trickle into Lashio as they pulled back, "...they were busy thieving anything not battened down. Two of them went swimming in a large tank kept for drinking water. A Chinese officer appeared and had them shot out of hand for polluting the water."

Discipline was harsh in Chiang Kai-shek's conscript army and Cliff Briggs recalls a similar instance of rough justice being meted out:

> While we were with some Chinese troops my flying jacket was stolen and I reported this to an English-speaking officer. Within ten minutes I had it back as he soon discovered that it had been taken by one of his own soldiers. He had the man shot on the spot. Stealing was not tolerated and was punishable by death, he told me - afterwards! I would rather the poor fellow had kept the jacket; he probably needed it more than I did. I've never forgiven myself for mentioning it to the officer.

Two Hurricanes flew tactical reconnaissance missions from Lashio on April 25th in an effort to clarify the situation. Based on the information they brought back, Noel Singer signalled HQ 221 Gp[3] that he was reducing his strength at Lashio to a party of 100 men with sufficient stores to support up to six Blenheims. Orders were issued locally to prepare for a partial withdrawal to Loiwing to begin the following day. Those who were to move early began assembling their belongings but the schedule was advanced and some, including Don Page and Mac McDade, set off at midnight on the 25th/26th. Hampered by heavy rain which turned the road to mud they did not reach Loiwing until 2100hrs on the 26th. That day a No 113 Sqn Blenheim from Loiwing carried out a long range recce and landed at Lashio so that its crew could report its findings directly to OC Burwing. Meanwhile the vital radar set was being moved further north and MT convoys were already shuttling up and down the hazardous hairpin bends of the Burma Road, ferrying stores thirty miles further north to Kutkai while the available stock of bombs was being shifted to Loiwing. No 45 Sqn's groundcrew were fully involved in this operation, many of them serving as MT drivers. It should be recorded that, although many of the squadron's airmen were quite experienced drivers, having picked up the necessary skills in the course of the unit's frequent movements in the Middle East, few of them were actually in possession of such a nicety as a licence. This was hardly the time for formalities, however, and with much grinding of gears they played an active part in the retreat from Lashio. It was during this withdrawal that Wilf Worrall's battered stores truck met its end. It had already survived several scrapes, notably on the way from Magwe when, in an argument with a bridge at Hsipaw, it had lost its roof trying to squeeze under an arch; Len Wilde had tin-bashed a replacement once they reached Lashio. The vehicle finally gave up the ghost en route to Loiwing. Sgt Ted Thompson came back to rescue Worrall and Wilde, and the vehicle was pushed off the road into a chaung (river).

One last Hurricane recce sortie was launched from Lashio in the afternoon of the 27th and confirmed that the advancing Japanese, or possibly the retreating Chinese, were now well north of Namlan, no more than thirty miles away. Whoever they were the situation was obviously becoming increasingly precarious and the partial withdrawal which had been gathering momentum now became a full-scale evacuation.

The last flyable Blenheim at Lashio, hastily patched up after having been damaged by a strafing attack that morning, took off for Chittagong just before mid-day on April 27th as four of the six aircraft of No 113 Sqn at Loiwing were also leaving for India. At 1200hrs Lashio airfield was closed and all but the demolition parties withdrew. Among the last to leave were that day's Duty Crew, Sgts Ernie Hallett and Frank Brown. An account of the departure of No 45 Sqn's convoys and their journey to Loiwing is at Annex J. Beginning at 2359hrs the remaining fuel stocks, all buildings and three grounded aircraft (a Blenheim, a Lysander and a P-40) were destroyed. The demolitions were completed by 0500hrs on the 28th and the last RAF personnel withdrew up the Burma Road towards Kutkai.

Since the radar unit had only just arrived at Loiwing, and had yet not begun operating, there was no early warning for Loiwing and an air raid on the 28th destroyed a Blenheim which had been flown in by F/Sgt Osborne and his crew the day before with a very welcome supply of cigarettes and a batch of mail from home. With no aircraft left to operate, the remaining aircrew were recalled to India. Assembled into small convoys, the squadron's leading party, of about a dozen men, set off in the evening of April 28th and, with the road crowded with refugee vehicles, reached Bhamo at about 0300hrs the following morning. Arthur Huon's diary entry for the next day, April 29th, reads:

> At 1030 am we started for Myitkyina. We are travelling with a convoy from 17 Squadron, but have pushed on ahead since this morning. There are now two 3-ton trucks, a station wagon, an Austin 16 saloon and a jeep in our party (all 45 aircrew) under P/O Graebner. 17 Squadron are carrying rations for us but we have some

Breakfast on the road, probably just north of Bhamo on April 29th. From the left: Sgt Bernard McDade, Sgt Ron Clark, Sgt Max Neil and Sgt Col Levings. (H C Hatherly)

The first river north of Bhamo, the Taping, was crossed using this bridge. It was not very strong and the vehicles crossed one at a time, each one having first been emptied, the loads being carried across by hand. (H C Hatherly)

A picnic lunch in a lay-by somewhere along on the Burma Road. Standing, from the left, Sgt Wilson, Sgt Levings, Sgt Hallett, Sgt Gardiner, next two unidentified, Plt Off Bayly, next two unidentified, and Sgt Shattock on the extreme right. Crouching, Sgts Albert Thompson and Bernard McDade. (H C Hatherly):

food with us (mostly bought ourselves) and are trying to push through quickly to Myitkyina as the dirt road is very bad and the rain has already started. Shortly after leaving the bitumen we came to the first bridge, a rickety bamboo structure, designed for ox-carts and certainly not for 3-ton trucks. We had to unload the vehicles and take them over very gingerly with the bridge undulating and creaking, reloading after carrying the gear across piece by piece. These bridges are washed away every year and are rebuilt after the monsoon.

Having successfully crossed this first river, the Taping, the rest of the journey north was by fairly rudimentary tracks. The next hurdle to be cleared was the Mole Chaung. There was a bridge, but it was even less substantial than the one which had carried them over the Taping and a civilian truck had gone through the decking and rendered it unusable.

Left:- This truck broke through the decking of the bridge over the Mole Chaung. (H C Hatherly). Above:- Sgts Arthur Huon (left) and Des Carew-Reid at the Mole Chaung crossing. (C G Briggs)

Local coolies were mobilised to effect repairs while others laboured against the fast-flowing water to construct a causeway to permit the river to be forded. In the end most of the convoy got across, the trucks by fording and the lighter vehicles via the swaying bridge, but the delay cost them a day (or two days)[4]. The last major water obstacle was the Tabat Chaung. This had no bridge and had to be crossed using a ferry made from three canoes which had been bound together and decked with planking, although the trucks proved to be too heavy and added buoyancy had to be provided by lashing empty oil drums to the structure. It was a laborious do-it-yourself business, as Bernard McDade puts it, "(It) meant paddling up the river for a hundred yards and then letting the current carry you down to the other bank." This obstacle was successfully negotiated by various groups on May 1st and 2nd.

According to 'Mac' McDade's diary the squadron's leading element reached the Waingmaw on the Irrawaddy in the evening of May 1st but their destination, Myitkyina, was on the far bank. The ferry, a passengers-only affair, did not operate after dark and had already completed its last run so the party was obliged to spend the night on the wrong side of the river, finding shelter in a nearby PWD bungalow. The following day the river had swollen and the ferry was unable to operate at first; when conditions did improve it promptly

broke down and the party spent the entire day stranded on the left bank. At about 2000hrs that evening most of the rest of the squadron caught up, along with No 17 Sqn's party. Overnight, in teeming rain, the vehicles were immobilised and personal kit was reduced to about 30 lbs per man. They crossed the river early on May 3rd and were taken to Myitkyina aerodrome by truck.

They found the airfield littered with abandoned possessions and crowded with wounded soldiers and refugees. They also found that their estimate of the baggage allowance had been somewhat optimistic. Rule One was that you could take out what you were wearing; there was no Rule Two. Some of the NCOs volunteered to remain at Myitkyina to assist in the organisation of the evacuation but most of the squadron's aircrew were airlifted out that afternoon, clutching meagre bundles containing a few essentials, perhaps a log book, a toothbrush and the odd flying helmet. Sgt McDade's log book records that he took off at 1330hrs on May 3rd in LR231, a DC-3 bound for Dinjan and flown by OC No 31 Sqn, Wg Cdr H P Jenkins. After landing, each party was provided with a meal and a bottle of beer which, as Arthur Huon recalls, were much appreciated as rations for the previous few days had been reduced to "some oatmeal and some dirty, musty and baggy-smelling rice". From Dinjan the refugees were taken to the railhead at Tinsukia where they boarded a train. The rest of

Negotiating the Tabat Chaung by ferry, one vehicle at a time. (A N Huon)

The 'Air Movements Section' at Myitkyina. From the left: Plt Off Phil Graebner RAAF, Sgt Cliff Briggs RAAF, Sgt Ken Gardiner RAAF and Sgt Bernard 'Mac' McDade. (B T McDade)

their journey was completed by rail and the majority of the squadron's Burma echelon arrived in Calcutta at about 0800hrs in the morning of May 6th.

Back at Loiwing it was obvious that the airfield was rapidly becoming untenable. The convoy system was still running, emptying the temporary dump at Kutkai and moving its contents even further up the Burma Road, first to Milestone 109 (Wan-ting) and then on to Pao-shan, about one hundred miles inside China. By May 1st the site at Kutkai had been cleared.

While all this had been going on it had been decided to set up a formal and permanent RAF presence in China with a view to the possible establishment of a bomber force there or, alternatively, to the provision of temporary operating bases for use during the Indian monsoon season. The nominal establishment of the China echelon was set at twenty-one officers and 350 Other Ranks. These were to be drawn from the units still in Burma in late April which included HQ Burwing, the remnants of Nos 17 and 45 Sqns, the staff of No 517 AMES (all of whom were earmarked for China), the personnel of No 154 MU, the signals people recovered from various scattered W/T outstations and listening posts, those members of the aerodrome parties from Toungoo, Heho, Lashio, Namsang and elsewhere who had not been able to get out by air and assorted strays from other units, mostly groundcrew, including several from Nos 60 and 113 Sqns. From this considerable pool of available manpower it proved possible to identify 348 of the 371 people required to go on into China which left twenty-one officers and 197 NCOs and airmen to be disposed of. This second group included most of the aircrews of Nos 17 and 45 Sqns, who had already set off for India via Myitkyina; the rest, including the few remaining aircrew and the majority of No 45 Sqn's groundcrew element, were now to follow them.

One of No 113 Sqn's last two Blenheims having left Loiwing on April 29th, the remaining crew waited another day for Sgt Bailes to join them before heading for Asansol which they reached on May 2nd. On the 1st HQ Burwing had moved east to Wan-ting while the bulk of the party destined for China continued transferring stores and equipment (mostly bombs) to Pao-shan. Len Wilde again:

> I was given a truck to move 250 lb bombs from Loiwing to about 20 miles inside the Chinese border. At the border Chinese guards halted us - and I had about forty refugees on board in seconds! I walked to the back, showed a guard the bombs under the covers, said "Boom, Boom" to him and I lost my passengers in half the time! When we got back the non-drivers had already left for Chungking. We seven, plus the aircrew, set off for India.

The date would have been 1st May, when the general evacuation of Loiwing was ordered. Now formally divorced from Burwing, the bulk of the party bound for India began the trek to Myitkyina under the overall command of Wg Cdr P K Devitt. They set off in groups of vehicles, two or three at a time, but as the journey proceeded they tended to catch up with each other and form small convoys which became embedded in the flocks of refugees moving north, away from the Japanese. The last to leave was the demolition party. During the day they destroyed the remaining fuel and stores, including the last serviceable Blenheim which had been unable to take off because of the state of the airfield surface.

The last lap - tea and wads during a stop on the train journey from Dinjan to Calcutta. From the left, Sgts Ron Clark RAAF, Colin Levings RAAF, Bill Wilson RAAF and (seated) Sgt Ted Thompson RCAF. (H C Hatherly)

Their work complete they too headed for Myitkyina. As the stragglers set off for India a salvage party from Burwing returned in the evening to pick up anything which might be of use but by midnight on May 1st/2nd Loiwing was deserted.

Wan-ting proved to be an insecure refuge. The fact that the local population were engaged in a hasty evacuation, allied to the sound of distant small arms fire and the unannounced overnight disappearance of the local Chinese army HQ, prompted the RAF to move on as well. Having staged through Che-fang and Lung-ling, HQ Burwing eventually set up shop at Pao-shan on May 5th where it was promptly subjected to an attack by a reported sixty-one Japanese aircraft. It took to the road once more to head deeper into China. By May 9th the leading elements of the convoy had reached Kunming where Gp Capt Singer handed over command to Wg Cdr L V Spencer and left to make his way back to India. From that date Burwing ceased to exist as such and was redesignated as The RAF in China (RAFCHIN). By the 12th all of RAFCHIN was concentrated at Kunming but three days later they set off again in six twenty-five-truck convoys for their final destination at Chengtu which they reached on May 27th. Here they made themselves useful training the Chinese in the use of No 517 AMES' precious radar equipment (which had arrived on the 29th) but the proposed China-based force of British bombers was never established. RAFCHIN was withdrawn to India and disbanded in August 1943. The Burma echelon of the Flying Camels had contributed fourteen men to this rather obscure facet of the RAF's activities in WW II; these were its Adjutant, Flt Lt P P Butters, plus Cpl T J Cant and LACs G Newbould, D Taylor, D Huntley, J Gowers, G R Aldhurst, J Morris, J Flynn, G Adkin, Lansley and Anderson and two unidentified fitters.

In the meantime the parties heading for India had been struggling through to Myitkyina. They experienced the same sort of difficulties as their predecessors; in fact the wear and tear already inflicted on the muddy 'roads' and flimsy bridges by Nos 17 and 45 Sqns, not to mention the stream of civilian refugees, probably made their journey even more difficult. Having encountered similar problems with river crossings, they finally reached Myitkyina airfield on May 5th and were eventually airlifted out to Dinjan.

A group of the squadron's aircrew, cluttering up the entrance to HQ 221 Gp at La Martinière School while waiting for a pay parade; most of these men had just arrived by sea, although a few were evacuees from Burma. The date was either 19th or 21st March 1942. The group on the extreme left, sitting on the steps, are Sgts Jack Nankervis, Jimmy Vernon (with book) and Bob Hilditch. Leaning against the pillar is Sgt Beau Pearce (in slouch hat); sitting, immediately to his left, is Sgt Pat Paterson. The two figures standing on the top step in the centre of the picture (to the right of the pillar) have not been identified. Reading downwards, the three men below the standing figure wearing a topee are all Canadians, Sgts Ted Pulford, Lloyd Butcher and Bob Armstong (in a topee). The four figures sitting on or leaning against the wall are, from the left, Sgts Cyril Hockney, George Whittaker, Bert Gooding and 'Rocky' Fryar. The group of four seated on the steps in the foreground includes Sgt Bill Fylan (on the left in light coloured clothing) and John Kirkpatrick (on the right with his face obscured by his hat); the chap in a topee may be Sgt Henry Garfath and the figure nearest the camera has not been identified. Standing on the right, facing the crowd, is Sgt Dennis Owen.
(D Cliffe)

Having come to the end of the tale of the Burma party, it is necessary to backtrack to pick up the story of the rest of the squadron after it had reached India. The majority of the groundcrew, who, it will be recalled, had been sent to Fyzabad, had stayed there for less than a fortnight. On April 5th they had entrained for Dehra Dun en route No 4 Hill Depot at Chakrata where they arrived five days later. Here, to quote the squadron records, "they completely 'took over' the camp and won all the honours at football and other sports. During their whole stay the football team was unbeaten. A Sports Day held on April 29th was a huge success for the Squadron whose personnel won eighteen out of twenty-one events. Squadron dances were run and were well supported."

Some of the NCO aircrew who had gone to Fyzabad during March had already drifted back to Calcutta before the unit had moved to Chakrata and several of those who did get to the hills were promptly recalled by Squadron HQ so that there was a substantial group of aircrew in town by the middle of April. Although a few of the NCOs had been booked into the relative comfort of, for instance, the Grand and the Continental Hotels, many had initially been billeted in a grim barrack-like establishment on the outskirts of Calcutta. They soon took matters into their own hands and gravitated to the more salubrious surroundings of Talbot House. This was located in Chowringhee and had recently made itself available as a hostel for servicemen. It was run by Canon Bolton and his wife with the able assistance of Mrs Green. Unfortunately, a few days after moving in Sgt Albert Gooding contracted smallpox; he died in the Campbell Fever Hospital on April 12th. Thereafter Talbot House was placed

under quarantine for a time and, since it had never been intended to provide permanent accommodation in any case, the squadron was obliged to make other arrangements. Through the good offices of Mrs Stenton-Dozey, another house was found at No 29 Theatre Road and on May 29th this became No 45 Sqn's Sergeants' Mess - "Quite civilised, although not on a par with TH, but a damned sight better than a hammock on a ship or a hole in the ground in the desert", as Dennis Owen has observed.

Meanwhile most of the squadron's officers were staying in hotels and/or messing with HQ 221 Gp at No 43 Old Ballygunge Road while the majority of the unit's Calcutta-based groundcrew (those attached to HQ and a party

Above:- Killing time at Talbot House, from the left: Sgt John Pannifer, Sgt Jack Kirkpatrick and Sgt Lloyd Butcher. (R J Armstrong). Right:- F/Sgt Dennis Owen and Sgt Jimmy Vernon in the grounds of Talbot House, April 1942. (D A Owen)

The squadron's comfortable Sergeants' Mess at No 29 Theatre Road in Calcutta. (H C Hatherly)

Sgt Dickie Haylock looking after the bar in No 45 Sqn's Sergeants' Mess. (D A Owen)

working on the airfield at Dum Dum) were billeted at No 9 Lower Rawdon Street.

Apart from the administrative staff who were directly involved in running the HQ, productive employment had already been found for many others. On April 1st Plt Off Arklay had been posted to RAF Asansol; he was accompanied by three complete aircrews, all NCOs, who were briefly attached to No 113 Sqn. They were followed a day later by a maintenance team of forty groundcrew. All except Arklay returned to Calcutta ten days later.

There were insufficient aircraft to sustain all the nominal Blenheim squadrons in India at that time and those that were available were being concentrated in Nos 60 and 113 Sqns, which left most of No 45 Sqn's aircrew at a loose end. At first a few flying tasks came the squadron's way (Plt Off John Rowe, Plt Off Ned Hammat and Sgt Arch Fraser delivered a Blenheim to Chittagong on 4th April, for instance, and Plt Off Ed Christensen, Sgt Beau Pearce and Sgt Bob Hilditch flew a couple of communications trips between Asansol, Dum Dum and Kanchrapara on the 4th and 5th) but even these soon dried up. Christensen's sorties were flown in Gus Alder's Z9803; they may have been the last flights made by a No 45 Sqn Blenheim in the hands of its original owners. Left to their own devices, for most of April and May those

aircrew for whom no employment could be found resorted to lotus-eating and became denizens of the luxurious Calcutta Swimming Club by day and Firpo's by night.

Throughout this period people from the squadron's aircrew pool began to be detached to support other units. Among the first to go were Flt Lt Lin Durrant, Plt Off Paul Keel (who had recently been discharged from hospital in Poona but was categorised as unfit for flying duties for a further two months) and Plt Off George Kemp, all of whom were detached on April 17th to Dinjan where they were required to set up an *ad hoc* Movement Control Section to organise the dropping of supplies to the troops still marching out of Burma and to co-ordinate the evacuation of refugees. On June 1st the squadron was to receive a written commendation from OC Dinjan for the contribution they had made to the creation of a form of order out of the prevailing chaos. On April 18th Fg Off Daw was detached to carry out the same sort of duties at Myitkyina. These officers, perhaps unwittingly, will have been instrumental in getting the squadron's operational echelon back to India, since they were among the more than 3,000 refugees who came out of Burma via the airlift between Myitkyina and Dinjan.

Frank Daw, later Wg Cdr F G Daw DFC AFC, has provided a brief impression of his time at Myitkyina:

The odd flying job cropped up for No 45 Sqn's crews after the squadron's withdrawal from Burma, mostly air tests and ferries. This one started out from Dum Dum on April 27th with the intention of delivering Z9669 to No 113 Sqn at Asansol. The port engine cut shortly after take off and Sgt Russell 'Rusty' Curtis, seen walking away on the right, was obliged to put it down in a field three miles north of the aerodrome. Also on board were Sgt Les Charlton and Sgt Colin Gerloff (of No 113 Sqn): they were able to walk away as well. (G A Gowing)

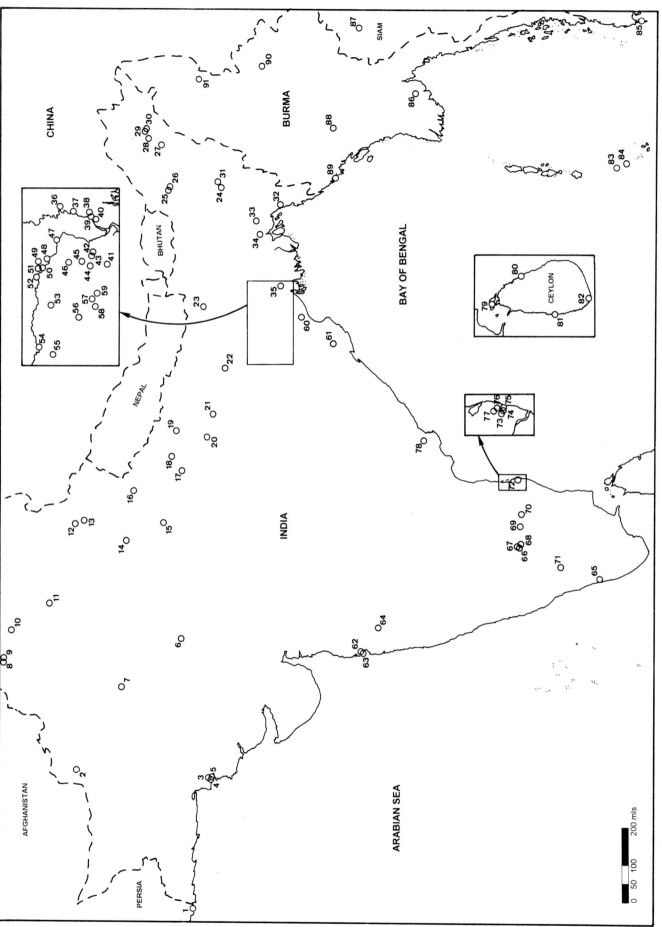

Map 9.1. India and Ceylon showing locations of significance to No 45 Sqn. This map is relevant to Chapters 8 to 13, inclusive, and Chapters 18 and 19.

The airstrip was subject to frequent bombing and strafing which caused many casualties. We had to resort to disposing of the dead in bomb craters; conditions simply did not permit anything more dignified. On one occasion I was within yards of a Dakota, full of wounded, which was machine-gunned by a Zero. After the attack I boarded the aircraft to see what aid I could give - there were no survivors. Shortly afterwards the aircraft was strafed by another Jap fighter which set it on fire. The Dakota burned to a cinder; thus were the dead cremated. More wounded were arriving at Myitkyina all the time

and the scene is difficult to describe. My detachment and I got out on the last aircraft to leave with just the clothes we stood up in. We beat the Japanese by only a few hours.

Myitkyina was not an amusing place in early 1942 but with hindsight there is one aspect that I can recall with a smile, albeit a wry one. About half way through the detachment I was visited by a squadron leader who said he was from Command HQ. He had a good look round and expressed himself well satisfied; indeed, he complimented me on my performance. Then he hopped on the next aircraft out and flew away. Sometime later, back in Calcutta, I was summoned to Group HQ and told that I was required to attend a Summary of Evidence pending the Court Martial of Sqn Ldr X, who had failed to relieve me as Officer i/c Myitkyina!

15	Agra	57	Dalbumgarh	72	Madras
89	Akyab	13	Dehra Dun	88	Magwe
40	Alipore	14	Delhi	27	Mariani
20	Allahabad	28	Dibrugarh	24	Masimpur
60	Amarda Rd	45	Digri	3	Mauripur
70	Arkonam	29	Dinjan	25	Misamari
52	Asansol	4	Drigh Road	91	Myitkyina
68	Bangalore	38	Dum Dum	50	Nadiha
16	Bareilly	19	Fyzabad	81	Negombo
54	Barkakana	22	Gaya	51	Ondal
84	Batti Mali	58	Ghatsila	71	Ootacamund
21	Benares	75	Guindy	48	Panagarh
46	Bishnapur	1	Gwadur	8	Peshawar
63	Bombay	66	Hebbal	85	Phuket
47	Burdwan	56	Jamshedpur	64	Poona
35	Calcutta	6	Jodhpur	73	Poonamallee
83	Car Nicobar	37	Kanchrapara	2	Quetta
17	Cawnpore	79	Kankesanterai	78	Rajahmundry
10	Chaklala	5	Karachi	42	Ramnagar
12	Chakrata	81	Katanayake	36	Ranaghat
59	Chakulia	23	Katihar	55	Ranchi
43	Chandrakona Rd	7	Khanpur	86	Rangoon
53	Charra	41	Kharagpur	76	Red Hills Lake
87	Chiang Mai	82	Koggala	9	Risalpur
80	China Bay	69	Kolar	44	Salbani
32	Chittagong	31	Kumbhirgram	62	Santa Cruz
77	Cholavaram	11	Lahore	74	St Thomas Mount
65	Cochin	34	Lalmai	26	Tezpur
33	Comilla	90	Lashio	30	Tinsukia
39	Cossipore Rd	18	Lucknow	80	Trincomalee
61	Cuttack	49	Madhaiganj	67	Yelahanka

Key to Map 9.1.

Four other No 45 Sqn men were carried to safety on the same Dakota in which Frank Daw left Myitkyina, the last flight out of Burma. Gerry Osborne, Bert Turton, Alf Field and LAC George Bell had planned to fly out from Loiwing but later reported that the last Blenheim had been destroyed by Japanese guerrillas - one is tempted to conclude that in the confusion the 'guerrillas' may actually have been Burwing's demolition party! They had joined a road convoy and made their way to Myitkyina to be flown out to safety. They, the last stragglers of the squadron's Burma echelon, reached Calcutta on 8th May. Some of these refugees were sent on to Chakrata to join the rest of the squadron and to recuperate, although others were retained in Calcutta for a time.

Meanwhile the squadron had begun to divest itself of a number of temporary guests who had taken refuge with the Flying Camels. On April 16th Plt Offs French and Mayger and seven other aircrew "of No 84 Sqn" left for Karachi where their own unit was now reforming (this group is known to have included Sgts Morris, Davies, Bruce, Penn and Roberts plus Plt Off Pedlar - see Note 3 to Chapter 8). Plt Off P Graham and five more unidentified NCO aircrew

A Dakota (strictly speaking a DC-3), LR231 E, loading up with refugees at Myitkyina. This photograph was taken just before the aircraft carried the bulk of No 45 Sqn's aircrew to safety in India on 3rd May 1942. The aircraft was destroyed in a Japanese air raid on Myitkyina two days later, possibly the incident witnessed by Frank Daw. (B T McDade)

who had also found a home with No 45 Sqn in Calcutta were posted to HQ 222 Gp on April 21st. On the same day Fg Off Edmonds, Plt Off Furmage and Sgts Jewell, Hockney, Goss, Armstrong and Taylor left for Drigh Road where they were to collect some B-25s and fly them back to Bengal for use by No 5 PRU[5]. It transpired that only commissioned personnel were required and on the 30th the NCOs were replaced by Plt Offs Pannifer, Christensen, Guy, Reeves and Pailthorpe. On the 26th, with the exception of the MO, the squadron lost all its medical personnel when they were posted to Lahore. Two days later eighteen MT drivers were detached to work with the Indian Army Ordnance Corps at Dehra Dun.

Pilot	Observer	WOp/AG
F/Sgt S A Goss RCAF	F/Sgt C A Whiteside	Sgt A Murray
Sgt W S McLellan RAAF	Sgt J R Vernon RAAF	Sgt J Nankervis RAAF
Sgt F L Butcher RCAF	F/Sgt J A H Kirkpatrick	Sgt R S Stone
Sgt H C Jewell	Sgt J R Hurley RCAF	Sgt F G Terry
Sgt N T Taylor RCAF	F/Sgt J Paterson	Sgt A King
Sgt C G Hockney	Plt Off A Hilling	?
Sgt G W Hartnell RAAF	Fg Off P C Lahey RAAF	Sgt R M Barclay RAAF

Fig 9.1. Aircrew of No 45 Sqn who were attached to No 113 Sqn from May 1942.

The news that the squadron had been hoping for arrived on April 24th. It was to be re-established as a flying unit, initially on a one-flight basis; its Blenheims were to be based at Kanchrapara. Wg Cdr Arthur Hughes, Plt Off Lloyd George (Acting Adjutant since April 21st) and F/Sgt Albert Onions (Equipment) immediately drove up to Kanchrapara to earmark accommodation, reclaim the squadron's stores from No 304 MU and make all the necessary arrangements. Needless to say, most of the squadron's kit had disappeared, including their German bowsers. This burst of activity was to last for only five days, however, for on the 29th the plan was changed and the squadron reverted to its non-operational, non-flying, quasi-existence.

Postings and detachments of personnel continued. Plt Off Bill Maloney and 2/Lt Freddie DeMarillac were posted to fly Valentias with the Air Landing School at New Delhi on April 30th and on May 3rd F/Sgt Leslie with eighteen men began to set up a maintenance facility at Dum Dum while the MO, Flt Lt 'Paddy' Kelly, was detached to No 136 Sqn at Alipore. Being a South African, DeMarillac was soon recalled to the Middle East and by June he was back in Egypt.

The seven crews listed at Figure 9.1 were detached to No 113 Sqn at Asansol on May 9th and shortly afterwards began flying ops. One of them had a nasty scrape not long after joining No 113 Sqn. On May 27th Sgt Bill Hartnell and his crew positioned at Dum Dum in Z7884 to be briefed for a recce mission covering Pakokku and the lower Chindwin. The sortie went well enough until they began to head back towards India and ran into heavy storm clouds. Paul Lahey was still somewhat 'tired and emotional' after his heroic efforts in the bar the night before and the upshot was that with all the twisting and turning to avoid cloud the crew eventually became somewhat uncertain of their position. After having been airborne for five minutes short of seven hours the engines started spluttering as the tanks finally began to run dry; there was nothing for it but to put the aeroplane down as best they could. As Bob Barclay recalls:

> The front guns were jettisoned and down we went to a wheels up landing on the edge of an emerald green lake. The emerald green wasn't grass, of course, but a carpet of weed covering thick black mud. An enormous gout of this stuff splurged through the hole left by the jettisoned guns and literally swamped our nav with a generous coating of goo. Bill and I enjoyed scraping it off with sticks and bits of broken aileron. We all managed a couple of miles walk to a railway siding at Ranaghat and a

freight train took us safely to Calcutta. Our nav weathered the enquiry OK and the radio boys found that my radio was u/s, so all was well.

On May 11th Sgts Bob Armstrong, Colin 'Rocky' Fryar and George Hayley were detached to Dum Dum to serve as Duty Pilots and they continued to carry out this chore until October On the 15th Plt Off Page with Sgts McDade and Pearce were put to work in the Ops Room at Asansol. The squadron also lost all its photographic tradesmen, permanently, on the 15th when they were posted to No 5 PRU. On the 16th Plt Offs Corbett and Rowe were detached to the Aerodrome Siting Board to be followed the next day by Fg Off Muller-Rowland, Plt Off Graebner and Sgt Huon. Thereafter they worked for Wg Cdr Vaughan-Fowler, inspecting possible locations for future airfields which involved travelling extensively throughout Bengal and Bihar.

And so it went on. Plt Off Norman Bain went to Dum Dum on May 17th, to take command of F/Sgt Leslie's set-up, which was now styled the Bomber Rearming and Refuelling Party. This was to be expanded on the 25th when twenty-two more of the squadron's tradesmen were attached to it. Capt Gus Alder, Plt Off Ned Hammat and Sgt Ced Birkbeck went up to Dinjan on May 21st to relieve the original team who had now been there for a month. Acting as Duty Pilots and Movement Control Officers, these replacements were to stay in the north until October, Birkbeck later becoming known around the bazaars as 'Dinjan' Birkbeck - "When I was at Dinjan, etc, etc". 'Doc' Kelly moved again on the 23rd, this time to look after the health of Tezpur, and the squadron's strength was further depleted by the posting of twenty-three airmen to New Delhi. On May 25th a party of twenty airmen was hived off to form an R&R party at Agartala; Plt Off Alan Tidswell, Sgt Rogers and fifteen groundcrew were detached to set up another at Alipore; Plt Off Ken Mills and Sgt Des Carew-Reid were attached to Asansol's Ops Room and Plt Off Jimmy Fraser joined the training staff at HQ 221 Gp. On May 30th Fg Off Culverwell, with Plt Offs Lilly and Wilks, began to move the squadron's main party back from Chakrata to Asansol where they were to take over the servicing of No 113 Sqn's aircraft while their groundcrew went up to No 4 Hill Depot for a rest.

On June 3rd Plt Off Dudley Eve took over command of the R&R Party at Alipore from Tidswell, being relieved in turn by Plt Off Ron Alford on July 10th. Also on the 10th WO George Adam and twenty-five tradesmen, mostly wireless specialists, were detached to No 353 Sqn at Dum Dum.

Despite all the jobs being found for people the squadron still had a surplus of unoccupied and frustrated aircrew and the boredom led a number of them to break the golden rule -

they volunteered. There was a shortage of MT drivers in India at the time and a dozen of the squadron's NCOs (Sgts Bob Hilditch, Geoff Gowing, Pete Hatherly, Ken Gardiner, 'Rusty' Curtis, Denys Golder, Jeff Alt, Les Charlton, Ron Clark, Charlie Romans, Ted Thompson and Arch Fraser) offered their services to help collect a consignment of forty-two new American trucks which had been allotted to No 221 Gp and drive them from New Delhi to Calcutta. With the addition of four of the squadron's MT drivers, the party left Howrah Station for Delhi on May 30th.

Seen just before they started out, seventeen of the forty-odd American trucks which some of the squadron's NCO aircrew volunteered to help drive from Delhi to Calcutta. (H C Hatherly).

They began their return journey on June 4th and, travelling via Agra, Cawnpore, Lucknow, Allahabad, Benares, Gaya and Asansol, they finally reached Calcutta, somewhat the worse for wear, on the 12th. Undertaken in the height of the Indian summer, the trip had been something of an epic. Planning for the expedition could have been a good deal better and, with temperatures often exceeding 120°F, the inadequate provision of rations and water meant that the drivers had had to resort to drinking local cordials and using ice made from untreated water. There were many upset stomachs and cases of heat stroke, four of the latter being fatal. At the outset there had been an officer in charge of the undertaking but he fell by the wayside quite early on and command passed first to Sgt Fraser and then to Pete Hatherly. The latter recalls one particular incident:

> We had to leave (probably at Gaya) another Englishman who was suffering from heat fatigue. This stop caused a bit of a problem because we had to knock over one of the brick pillars to get the truck up to the hospital. I was approached as to who was going to foot the bill for the cost of repairs. I advised them to charge it to the Royal Air Force. I never heard any more about it so I suppose they must have paid up.

No 45 Sqn's contingent did not escape unscathed and after Sgt Fraser had been admitted to hospital in Cawnpore, suffering from heat-stroke, Rusty Curtis became a second casualty. He had taken over a motor-cycle after its original rider had fallen sick. While acting as an outrider for the convoy, clearing the road ahead of pedestrians and bullock carts, he was involved in a collision which resulted in his having to be left at the BMH in Lucknow with a broken leg. This episode had kept people busy for a few days but, apart from stints as Duty Pilot at Dum Dum, there was still a lot of spare time and, as Graham Williams recalls, it was not difficult to find other, less dramatic, ways of getting into trouble:

> Much time was spent at the very beautiful Calcutta Swimming Club where I became friendly with a very nice Eurasian lady. She invited me home to dinner a few times with her Pommy husband who was in charge of waterside coolie labourers and one mean son-of-a-bitch. He

The journey from Delhi turned out to be something of an epic, dogged by both sickness and accidents. When a motor-cycle outrider fell sick Sgt 'Rusty' Curtis took over his machine but eventually lost an argument with a bullock cart, as seen here, and he had to be admitted to hospital in Lucknow with a badly broken leg. (G A Gowing).

couldn't dance and his wife and I would dance on the verandah until he sent their big Airedale dog out to bite me on the bum. One night he showed me his rack of rifles and said he could pick a man off at a thousand yards with one of them - I never went back again - I thought that message came through loud and clear.

The squadron was notified on June 14th that it was to be rearmed with Vultee Vengeance dive-bombers. This caused some initial excitement but it proved to be somewhat premature as it would be nearly Christmas before any aeroplanes arrived. In the meantime, probably to keep them out of trouble, a group of twenty-seven surplus aircrew, most of them Burma veterans, plus some of the airmen who had been with them, were packed off to the cool (and damp - it was often shrouded in cloud) of Chakrata on June 21st; most of them were to remain there for several months.

Two more aircrew had been detached on the 18th, Flt Lt Lin Durrant to Ondal and Fg Off George Kemp to HQ RAF Bengal[6]. Plt Off Norman Bayly was attached to HQ 221 Gp on June 24th to work with the personnel staff and on the last day of the month he was joined there by Plt Off Kenneth

By mid-1942 the squadron had airmen detached all over India, including Dum Dum where the original R&R Party was still operating. This is LAC Dick Holloway with a Mohawk (BB925) of No 5 Sqn. (R T Holloway)

WOp/AGs at Chakrata in July 1942. From the left: Sgt Johnny Brinkley, Sgt Cliff Briggs, Sgt Ken Gardiner and Sgt Jeff Alt. (J J Alt)

Josling who was required at group to act a Field Cashier; he was accompanied by Fg Off Paul Lahey who was needed as a War Room Controller. Lahey was transferred to RAF Dum Dum on September 3rd to work in Bomber Ops. In the meantime there had been a small fillip for morale when, on June 20th, it was learned that Sgt (by now Plt Off) Bert Turton had been Mentioned in Despatches for his efforts in North Africa as had Sqn Ldr Ivor Beeston, although the latter had not been with No 45 Sqn at that time.

On July 4th Plt Off Alan Tidswell joined the team working with the Airfield Siting Board. On the 6th, Sqn Ldr Beeston with Plt Offs Jimmy Fraser and Ken Mills were posted to No 113 Sqn. Two days later one of the detached crews flying with No 113 Sqn was lost on operations; F/Sgts Butcher and Kirkpatrick and Sgt Stone had been posted missing in Z6155. They had crashed in poor weather after flying into a blind valley between Fort White and Stockade No 3. Trapped beneath rock-filled clouds and rising ground and with insufficient space to reverse direction, Lloyd 'Butch' Butcher had eventually put the aircraft down on its belly in a clear patch; it was on an upward slope so steep that the aircraft slid backwards before it finally came to rest. The crew were all pretty badly knocked about, particularly John Kirkpatrick, who had sustained a broken arm and jaw, and Butcher, whose spine had been seriously damaged. Despite his injuries, before the aircraft caught fire, the pilot was able to pull Kirkpatrick out and free Ron Stone, who had been trapped in his turret. Fortunately they were picked up by an army patrol and on July 15th the squadron's HQ at Calcutta learned that they were safe. Bob Armstrong recalls that

Butcher was subsequently encased in plaster from neck to hip and spent several wretched months at Asansol suffering the torments of inaccessible prickly heat which his colleagues tried to relieve by finding air-conditioned theatres to take him to.

It will be recalled that, until their pilot was killed in action on March 11th, the all-RAAF crew of Sgts Doug Smyth, Denys Golder and Jeff Alt had frequently flown AVM Stevenson around his command during the brief campaign in Burma. The AOC had been very impressed with this crew's performance and, having now acquired a Lockheed 12 for his personal use, he arranged for Golder and Alt to be posted to the HQ RAF Bengal Communications Flight on July 9th. Teamed with a new pilot, Fg Off Isaacs, they were to become a full-time VIP crew. Apart from taking the AOC wherever he wanted to go the crew later flew many other prominent personalities, among them Field Marshal Wavell (the Viceroy), Sir John Herbert (Governor of Bengal), Air Marshal Sir John Baldwin, and Lt Gens Irwin, Slim and Hartley.

Sqn Ldr Austin, who was already recuperating at Chakrata along with many of No 45 Sqn's surplus aircrew, was appointed to command No 4 Hill Depot on July 10th but he held this post only until the 23rd when he left for Bombay and the UK. Before departing he threw a memorable farewell party for the squadron's Burma veterans, including the airmen. Plt Off Keel regained his medical category in July and on the 14th he was detached to No 31 Sqn to fly Dakotas. That same day the newly commissioned Plt Off Bill Hartnell was withdrawn from No 113 Sqn and attached to HQ 221 Gp. On the 15th Plt Off Wilks (Cyphers) was

Denys Golder after he had left the squadron to fly on VIP duties and after he had been commissioned as a pilot officer. (Mrs Babs Golder)

The squadron's R&R party at Alipore was redeployed to Feni on 18th July 1942. This photograph shows one of No 113 Sqn's Blenheims, V6456/AD.T, being turned round at Feni; AC1 Gordon Hancox is on the left in a topee. The use of squadron codes was suspended on 26th September so this photograph was probably taken prior to that date. (G J Hancox)

The remains of Blenheim Z7647/MU.Y after a take off accident on 24th July 1942 which cost the lives of Wg Cdr Brian Wallis and Plt Off Don Page and injured Sgt Bernard McDade and two passengers. (I. Wilde)

distinctive spotted green scarf, which the Brian Wallis had usually worn whenever he flew.

By now fully recovered from his wounds, Fg Off Stuart Muller-Rowland had been released from his airfield siting duties along with Plt Off Phil Graebner and, together with their original gunner, Sgt Ken Gardiner, the whole crew was attached to No 60 Sqn on the July 25th for flying duties. On the same day Plt Off Rowe joined No 308 MU at Allahabad as a test pilot. The squadron lost two more of its ground branch officers on the 30th when Fg Off Harold Pickering was transferred to the strength of RAF Asansol and Fg Off Ron Culverwell, who had joined the squadron way back in April 1941, was posted to No 20 Sqn at Jamshedpur. Further written confirmation of eventual re-equipment with Vengeances was received during July along with a policy letter covering the re-training of WOp/AGs as navigators, since the prospective new aircraft were only two-seaters - there was plenty of policy floating about, but there were still no aeroplanes.

No 113 Sqn's groundcrew, now fully refreshed after their two months in the cool of Chakrata, returned to Asansol on August 1st and resumed responsibility for their own aeroplanes. This left No 45 Sqn's people available for other duties and by the end of the month its groundcrew were attached to no fewer than thirty-four separate units while its aircrew were serving with another twelve. Thus, although it was temporarily unable to function as a unit, the squadron's personnel were continuing to make a positive contribution to the war effort. Despite its lack of a tangible existence,

posted to HQ RAF Bengal and Plt Off Page and Sgt McDade were detached to Asansol to rejoin their erstwhile pilot, Wg Cdr Wallis, who had just taken command of No 60 Sqn. Fg Off Eve took over the duties of Acting Adjutant from Fg Off George on the 17th when the latter was detached to No 22 Air Support Control. The following day Fg Off Ron Alford and the Alipore R&R party were redeployed to Feni. The word was now well and truly out that anyone who needed spare bodies could get them from No 45 Sqn and on the 23rd F/Sgts Armstrong and Hayley and Sgt Fryar were detached to Ondal to act as duty pilots.

The following day the squadron was shocked to learn that Brian Wallis had been killed. On July 22nd his crew had flown a solo mission in Blenheim Z7647 against enemy positions on the Mayu river to the north of Akyab after which they had landed at Dum Dum. An attempt to fly back to Asansol the following day was frustrated by the state of the airfield and the aircraft became bogged in the mud. Trying again early on the 24th the aircraft crashed shortly after becoming airborne. Plt Off Don Page was killed outright; Sgt McDade and two passengers (Lt A Dorner SAAF and Sgt N G Whitehead) were all seriously injured. Wg Cdr Wallis emerged from the wreckage, apparently relatively unscathed, and reported the accident personally but shortly afterwards he collapsed; he died in hospital two hours later. Later, in his room at Asansol, Wg Cdr Hughes found the

Taking their ease at Chakrata in July 1942, from the left: Sgt Jeff Alt RAAF, Sgt Denys Golder RAAF, Sgt Hedley Jewell and Sgt Gordon Terry. (G A Gowing)

St Vincent de Paul's School, Asansol. On 16th August 1942 HQ 221 Gp moved to this imposing building and the squadron's HQ element went with it - No 45 Sqn's Orderly Room was somewhere near the middle of the ground floor. The picture was taken from the roof of an adjacent block which housed the Sergeants' Mess and the airmen's accommodation. (D A Owen)

From the left, Sgts Jack Hurley, Gordon Terry and Mac McDade on a balcony at Asansol. (B T McDade)

Seen here at Fayoum on 31st December shortly after they had arrived from Malta, having ferried a Blenheim out from the UK, are, from the left, Sgts Arthur 'Jock' Murray, Charles 'Paddy' Whiteside and Stan Goss. They all died on 18th August 1942 when their aircraft crashed while patrolling a railway line during the "Quit India" campaign. (R J Armstrong)

however, the squadron never lost its identity and the majority of its widely dispersed members remained loyal to it. The squadron's small HQ element at Calcutta kept tabs on everybody in preparation for the great day when the squadron would be reborn - it was all rather reminiscent of the situation faced by Sqn Ldr Summers back in 1927.

On August 4th, the day before he departed for Staff College at Quetta, Wg Cdr Hughes married Miss Daphne Aldridge in Calcutta. This was the second squadron wedding in India, Fg Off Bill Corbett having married Miss Irene Abreu on July 13th. With the departure of Wg Cdr Hughes the duties of CO were assumed by the Acting Adjutant, Fg Off Dudley Eve. Fg Off Geoff Furmage returned from No 3 PRU on the 12th. Two days later Plt Off Bryan Lilly, the last of the squadron's remaining groundstaff officers, was posted to Salbani; a little later he would join No 84 Sqn, serving as its Adjutant until 1945. On August 16th HQ 221 Gp moved to Asansol where an Officers' Mess was established in the Asansol Club while accommodation for its airmen was found in the imposing requisitioned buildings of St Vincent de Paul's School. No 45 Sqn's HQ element (nominally Fg Offs Eve and Corbett and nine airmen) accompanied its Group HQ and shared the same facilities.

Inspired by Gandhi, the Congress party launched its 'Quit India' campaign on 8th August 1942 and the Blenheim squadrons found themselves operating in an internal security role rather than against the Japanese. A particular concern was that the railway network might be sabotaged and patrols were mounted to look out for obstructions and disturbed tracks. These sorties were not without incident and on the 14th, while flying No 60 Sqn's V5692, Fg Off Muller-Rowland had a narrow escape when his aircraft struck a trackside post and lost a substantial portion from one of its wingtips; fortunately he was able to recover the situation and fly the damaged Blenheim back to base. Four days later, while reconnoitring a railway line to the east of Katihar with F/Sgt Charles 'Paddy' Whiteside and Sgt Arthur 'Jock' Murray in Blenheim T2245 of No 113 Sqn, F/Sgt Stan Goss was obliged to crash land. While HQ 221 Gps' ORB states that the pilot (an American from Springfield, Illinois, who

had enlisted in the RCAF) was killed on impact, some accounts maintain that all three members of the crew survived the accident. There is no dispute, however, that those who did survive were quickly surrounded by an angry mob and murdered. On the 29th August news of another death reached the squadron. Fg Off John Rowe had been flying one of a pair of Ryan PT-22s which had crashed near Allahabad; both pilots (the other was the Station Commander, Wg Cdr R B Harvey) had been killed.

Fg Off Geoff Furmage went to Agartala on September 7th to command its R&R party. Jock McCandlish had been there since the detachment had been set up in May and recalls that:

....we all shared the same dining hut, and eventually we got some medical cover. He was an LAC and his sole equipment appeared to be a large bottle of iodine and a gadget for testing the water. There were two F/Sgts in

Fg Off Norman Bayly RAAF chatting with Sgt McDade in the Navigation Office at Asansol. The topic may well have been how to change WOp/AGs into observers to suit them for the forthcoming Vengeances. (B T McDade)

the party, Blasdale-Holmes and Edwards but, apart from the cooks, it was all hands on deck when refuelling and rearming were required. All we had in the way of tools was a long screwdriver to gain access to the fuel tanks and to serve as a dipstick to assess how much fuel was needed. There was no chamois to filter the petrol; they took it neat - it was a very dodgey system.

On September 10th Fg Off Daw, who had previously spent some time with the Airfield Siting Board, was detached to Lucknow to work with the Central Interview Board. An early sign of the squadron's renaissance occurred on the 20th when a new Intelligence Officer, Plt Off J E Arnold, was posted in although he was immediately detached to Group HQ. Flt Lt Durrant completed his stint at Ondal on the 24th but went straight from there to Cuttack to act as Navigation Officer for No 175 Wg. Plt Off Tidswell's work with the Airfield Siting Board had been recognised by a letter of commendation from its CO, Wg Cdr Martin. Since Tidswell was obviously a very capable chap, 221 Gp decided that he

A group of aircrew mugging for the camera at Chakrata. From the left, front row, F/Sgt Dickie Haylock, Sgt Alf Field and Sgt 'Tubby' Garfath; back row, Sgt George Whittaker and F/Sgt Dennis Owen. The Egyptian flag had been 'acquired' by Garfath and Owen during a nocturnal escapade in Cairo in January 1942. (D A Owen)

Surplus RAAF aircrew of No 45 Sqn at No 4 Hill Depot in September 1942. From the left: Sgt Doug Thornton, Sgt Graham Williams, Sgt Ron Clark, Sgt Ralph Southorn, Sgt Frank Brown and Sgt Ernie Hallett. (G A Gowing)

ought to stay among the desk jockeys and he was retained at Lucknow to be employed on further administrative duties. Something a little more enterprising (or daunting) came F/Sgt Gerry Osborne's way at the end of the month when he was attached to the Bengal element of ENSA (the Entertainments National Service Association) as a script-writer and producer. On the same day eight officers and no fewer than fifty-four NCO aircrew of No 353 Sqn were notionally posted onto the squadron's strength; the Flying Camels were now becoming a holding unit!

Two of the crews who were operating with No 113 Sqn had a lucky escape on September 28th. Sgts Wally McLellan, Jimmy Vernon and Jack Nankervis in Z9749 and Sgts Norman Taylor, 'Pat' Paterson and Tony King in Z7639 were taking off from Asansol on an operational sortie when the aircraft collided half way down the runway. Both immediately burst into flames and shortly afterwards exploded, but not before all six men had escaped from the wreckage. Remarkably only Wally McLellan suffered any injuries and, although painful, they were relatively superficial. They were, however, somewhat inconvenient as he had sustained flash burns to his right arm and side which meant that, "I had to do all my drinking left handed."

The squadron lost another man in October. Having been working in the Ops Room at Asansol since May 15th, Sgt Pearce, an observer and one of the squadron's many Australians, flew with No 113 Sqn on an Army Co-operation exercise for the benefit of Asansol's AA gunners on October 11th. The aircraft, Z9598, crashed and 'Beau' Pearce was killed; it had been his first trip since March.

Having been medically downgraded, Dudley Eve left the squadron on 13th October bound for South Africa whence he eventually found his way back to Australia in February 1943. Pending the appointment of a new CO the duties of OC No 45 Sqn were taken over by another Australian, this time an observer, Fg Off Norman Bayly. In the latter half of October another batch of aircrew was attached to No 113 Sqn to join the crews who had already been operating with them on and off since May. This group included Capt Gus Alder, Fg Off Bill Corbett, F/Sgts Graham Tibbs, Bob Armstrong, Ted Thompson, Hedley Jewell, Colin Levings and Ernie Hallett and Sgts Norman Taylor, George Whittaker, Cliff Briggs, Foster Shattock, Max Neil, Charlie Romans, Gordon Terry and Pete Hatherly, but few of them were able to get much flying done before they were recalled again. On the last day of the month one of the crews that was already well-established with No 113 Sqn, McLellan, Vernon and Nankervis, was in trouble again. Taking off from Asansol for an offensive recce in Z9590, the port engine cut and the aircraft finished up on its belly. Once again, although Sgt Vernon had sustained some cuts and bruises, this very fortunate crew walked away from the wreckage.

By this time the arrival of the long-awaited Vengeances was rumoured to be imminent and the posting away of a number of aircrew during October caused some concern at Squadron HQ. This late exodus was, however, actually an indication that something was happening; the personnel staffs were beginning to rationalise the squadron's nominal strength. The Flying Camel's Blenheim era had been stretched into a long, drawn out affair but it was finally about to be brought to a close. Yet, despite having had no aeroplanes of its own for seven months and its personnel having been widely dispersed around India, the sense of loyalty felt by the majority of members had kept the squadron's spirit alive and its identity had never been extinguished.

Before joining No 45 Sqn in the autumn of 1941 as a sergeant, Dennis Owen had flown Blenheims over north western Europe for a year with Nos 57 and 105 Sqns then in Greece and Crete with No 84 Sqn. In 1943 he transferred to No 60 Sqn in India before returning to England in 1944 to fly Stirlings, towing gliders and resupplying Resistance groups. He ended the war as a flight lieutenant. Coming from someone with such a breadth of experience, the following words, written in 1994, are a fine testimonial:

"Of all the squadrons I had served on, 45 had the greatest spirit and camaraderie. Everybody knew everybody else - first name terms. Each aircrew knew his groundcrew, and vice versa. At Fuka and LG 75 we would save up grub and drink and buy in extras when they were available and then have a 'party' in one another's tents in the evening and sit around eating baked beans, bacon and NZ lambs' tongues out of tins. At Chakrata we used to have a football team - captained by Alf Field - and used to play various other units and bodies. Wembley had nothing on us! Every now and again someone would start chanting slowly - forty-one - forty-two - and here the whole squadron gathered round the pitch would join in, ending, in a roar which reverberated around the valley, with:

Forty-Three -

FORTY-FOUR -

FOORRTY-FIIIVE!!!"

Notes:

1. News of Brian Wallis' DSO had reached Magwe as early as 3rd March; he was formally gazetted to the Order on the 24th.
2. While it could arguably muster six notional crews at Lashio (those of Beeston, Huon, Neil, Thompson, Shattock and Osborne) and one serviceable Blenheim (Osborne's), it is difficult to see how the other two aircraft could

The squadron's Chakrata hockey team, 20th August 1942. Left to right, standing: Sgt Bob Hilditch, Sgt Ernie Hallett, Sgt Pete Hatherly, Sgt Geoff Gowing and Sgt Frank Brown. Seated: Deely, Morris, Sgt Graham Tibbs, Sgt John Brinkley, Sgt Graham Williams, Barrow. Deely, Morris and Barrow are assumed to be groundcrew. (E J Hallett)

have actually belonged to No 45 Sqn. It is surmised that they might have been unserviceable aeroplanes that had already been at Lashio for some time. Alternatively they might have been a pair of unflyable, but notionally repairable, aircraft which had been left at Magwe; although this aerodrome had been effectively abandoned, it had not yet been occupied by the Japanese so Burwing may still have harboured hopes of recovering the least badly damaged of the Blenheims.
3. The controlling formations in India had been reorganised the previous day. Possibly originally intended to go to Singapore or the Dutch East Indies, the staff for No 224 Gp HQ began to assemble at Padgate on 3rd February 1942. They reached Bombay on March 8th and by April had begun to set up shop in Calcutta. On the 24th AVM Stevenson took command of HQ 224 Gp which then assumed responsibility for all air defence and fighter ops. This left HQ 221 Gp, now commanded by Air Cdre H J F Hunter CBE MC, looking after the bomber units and directing offensive operations.
4. There is no official record of the journey from Loiwing to Myitkyina. This account of the squadron's adventures is based on information extracted from the contemporary journals kept by Arthur Huon and Bernard McDade, Norman Bayly's formal RAAF debriefing in 1945 (reproduced at Annex J) supplemented by the personal recollections of several others who were there, including Pete Hatherly and Ernie Hallett, and by the squadron's ORB (which only records the dates of arrival in Calcutta). While several of these sources describe similar incidents, the dates on which these were noted as having occurred sometimes differ. In view of the prevailing conditions this is hardly surprising and it must be remembered that the squadron's party did not stay together, so various rivers may well have been crossed by different people on different days. For instance, while Bayly's and McDade's accounts agree that they were only delayed for one day by the collapsed bridge over the Mole Chaung, Arthur Huon is adamant that his party lost two days. Despite these irresolvable differences it is believed that the story of the squadron's exodus from Burma as recounted here and at Annex J is probably as accurate a reconstruction as is reasonably possible after a lapse of more than fifty years.
5. On 28th May 1942 No 5 PRU was redesignated No 3 PRU (India) which, in turn, became No 681 Sqn on 2nd January 1943 .
6. HQ RAF Bengal was a tactical command formation established on 20th April 1942. Its title subsequently changed several times and, since several of these later names also crop up in Chapters 10 and 11, these changes are noted here. HQ RAF Bengal was first renamed in December 1943 to become HQ 3rd TAF. A year later this was changed to HQ RAF Bengal and Burma and in February 1945 it was changed again, for the last time, to HQ RAF Burma.

Chapter 10. The Flying Camel resurgent - Vengeances.

When Britain and her empire had stood alone after the fall of France she had turned to the USA as a production source for additional aircraft to sustain and expand the RAF, and further large orders were placed to supplement those which already existed. Thus it was that the RAF came to acquire large quantities of American dive bombers.

By the late 1930s several air forces were firmly wedded to the dive-bomber concept, notably the Luftwaffe and the naval air arms of Japan and America. The RAF, however, had never viewed dive-bombers with much enthusiasm and neither had France's *Armée de l'Air* until the impact made by the exploits of the *Luftwaffe's* Ju 87s in Spain and Poland led the French to reconsider their previous attitude. By early 1940 the Vultee Aircraft Corporation in the USA was designing a suitable aeroplane to meet a French specification. By the time that France fell in June 1940 the Ju 87 had further enhanced its formidable reputation. Questions were asked in the House as to why the British had no equivalent to this seemingly irresistible German wonder weapon and the RAF overcame its distaste for the concept and took over the French-sponsored project. This was eventually to emerge as the Vengeance. In the fullness of time it became clear that the dive-bomber's remarkable accuracy had been bought at the cost of increased vulnerability. The Battle of Britain was to show that the Stuka was far from invincible when it was confronted by a determined and well-directed air defence system. The RAF's original misgivings had been justified, but it would take time for the lesson to be digested and, in any case, Britain was desperately short of aeroplanes of any kind - the Vengeance project continued.

When they were tested in combat many of the earlier aircraft obtained from America proved to have significant shortcomings and, while the Vengeance was assessed by the A&AEE as having some operational potential, another dive-bomber which had been hastily ordered from America, the Brewster Bermuda, was rejected as being quite unacceptable for squadron service. Vengeances began to roll off the production lines in early 1942, but by that time there could be no question of employing vulnerable dive-bombers in the hotly disputed skies over North West Europe. The RAF looked elsewhere for a theatre of war in which the air combat environment was less intensive and in which clear skies might reasonably be expected - an absence of cloud was another pre-requisite for effective high-dive attacks, a condition which the European climate often denied.

The RAF had been severely mauled in the initial stages of the war in the Far East and it desperately needed aircraft of all types to rebuild its strength. As far as the light bomber force was concerned, of the notional eight squadrons of seriously outmoded Blenheims based in India and Ceylon only four (Nos 11, 34, 60 and 113) were operational in mid-1942. Scattered all over India as it was, the Flying Camels were probably in the worst condition but Nos 82, 84 and 110 Sqns were all at varying states of non-effectiveness as well. Despite the RAF's reservations over the employment of dive-bombers it had been decided to re-equip these four squadrons (and Nos 7 and 8 Sqns of the Indian Air Force) with the Vengeance for operations over Burma. The first of the new aircraft to reach a combat unit were delivered to No 82 Sqn at Cholavaram in the summer of 1942.

On October 30th one of No 82 Sqn's flight commanders was promoted and appointed to command a resurgent No 45 Sqn. Sqn Ldr Anthony Traill stayed where he was at Cholavaram and waited for his new command to come to him. Base Personnel Office (BPO) at Bombay released a signal to all units in India Command on November 2nd recalling all detached personnel of No 45 Sqn. The first to arrive, on November 6th, were Flt Lt Daw, F/Sgt Haylock and Sgt Garfath, all of whom had only recently been detached to No 60 Sqn. Two days later the squadron's small HQ element, three officers, four NCO aircrew and fifteen airmen, left Asansol for the squadron's new base. A group of twelve airmen from Cuttack beat them to it and reached Cholavaram on the 9th. The squadron's renaissance was under way, at last.

The HQ party arrived on November 11th to be welcomed by Tony Traill who, having joined the RAF from Argentina where his family had interests in land and cattle, lent just a touch of Latin American flair to the already cosmopolitan make up of the aircrew contingent. Cholavaram was a reasonably comfortable station, although there were as yet insufficient 'bashas' to accommodate everyone. Until the squadron was able to get itself sorted out it was looked after by the resident No 82 Sqn who provided extensive, and much appreciated, assistance, not least messing for the airmen. On the 17th the large group of No 353 Sqn aircrew who had been nominally attached to the squadron since September were struck off strength. The following day Fg Off Lloyd George returned to the fold along with three NCO aircrew and twenty-two more airmen. Plt Off Bill Hartnell turned up from Asansol on the 19th with three more NCOs and another three airmen and on the same day the squadron acquired a new Adjutant when Flt Lt H H Wilson RAAF was posted in. On the 20th Fg Off Bill Maloney reported back from New Delhi and two more NCOs and three more tradesmen came down from Asansol. Eighteen men from the Dum Dum R&R Party reached Cholavaram on the 23rd to be followed three days later by another twenty-six tradesmen who had been

Taken at Cholavaram in late 1942 this picture shows, standing, from the left: F/Sgt Dave Cliffe; Sgt Ced Birkbeck RAAF; Sgt Bill Wilson RAAF; Sgt Bob Hilditch RAAF; Sgt Ron Clark RAAF; Sgt Ken Edwards RAAF and Sgt Ted Pulford RCAF. Squatting, on the left is Sgt Graham Williams RAAF. (G F Williams)

Hardly of the best quality but this is the only available photograph of one No 45 Sqn's earliest Vengeances. It is seen here at Dum Dum undergoing an al fresco engine change. Coded K (in red?), the aeroplane is wearing the red, white, blue and yellow Type C1 roundels in which it was delivered. Throughout ACSEA these national markings were superseded by blue and white (later pale blue) roundels from June 1943 onwards, which tends to confirm that the photograph was taken earlier in the year. (N Gittins)

working with No 353 Sqn at Cuttack plus seven more or less complete crews who had been released by No 113 Sqn. As all these people were coming in, one went out on November 15th as Plt Off J E Arnold, the Intelligence Officer, began a lengthy attachment to HQ 221 Gp on November 15th.

Despite this steady increase in strength, the general response to the directive ordering the release of the squadron's personnel had been less than adequate. By the end of November only 120 groundcrew had rejoined the unit and some unit commanders had simply refused to release their No 45 Sqn personnel. In the last week of the month Fg Off Bayly went to Bombay to ginger up the BPO people while Fg Off George was despatched on a similar mission to remonstrate with Air Headquarters at New Delhi.

Early in November the squadron had gained access to a Tiger Moth (MA936) and the ex-Blenheim pilots, some of whom had not flown for several months, had begun to refresh themselves on single-engined handling techniques. On December 7th a Harvard (FE415) was delivered and four days later the first two Vengeances (AN845 and AN852) were taken on charge. Throughout their service the Vengeances were camouflaged in Dark Green and Dark Earth with Sky undersides. To begin with the aircraft were delivered wearing Types A2 or C1 roundels but in June 1943 red and yellow were deleted from the national markings of aircraft operating in the Far East. From then until the war's end 'SEAC markings' were in vogue, roundels and fin flashes being in dark blue and white (later pale blue) only. Each of the squadron's aircraft initially carried an individual identification letter in red; these were subsequently repainted in pale grey, along with the squadron's OB code, but not until very late in the Vengeance era.

With the availability of some aeroplanes a type conversion programme was put in hand under the supervision of Sqn Ldr Traill, Fg Off Geoff Furmage and Flt Lt Frank Daw, the latter, for instance, checking out Fg Off Paul Keel (who returned from No 31 Sqn on December 17th), two Canadian flight sergeants, Bob Armstrong and Ted Thompson, and RAAF Sgts Foster Shattock and Max Neil on the Harvard between the 11th and 24th. On December 20th Fg Off Furmage soloed in one of the big single-engined bombers (it was much the same size and weight as a Blenheim I) to become the squadron's first Vengeance pilot (apart from the

Although RAF Squadron Standards were not introduced until mid-1943, and none was actually presented until 1953, this device is remarkably similar to a Standard in its overall design. It was a feature of the Christmas decorations in the Sergeants' Mess at Cholavaram in December 1942. (G A Gowing)

Half-time in an all-ranks football-cum-wrestling match held on Christmas Day 1942. Fg Off Paul Keel is standing between the two vehicles (hand on head); Sgt Bert Turton is sitting at bottom right; next to him is Sgt Bill Hartnell; second from the far left is Fg Off Lloyd George; Sgts 'Tubby' Garfath and (probably) Dickie Haylock are among those in the foreground; Sgt Alf Field is in the centre (wearing a white singlet) and, apparently clutching his leg, is Sgt Bob Barclay. The third head to the left of Field is that of LAC Len Wilde; next to him are LACs 'Smokey' Gardner, Somerville (with a neck garland) and (with their shirts torn off) Sgt Jimmy Toogood and LAC Bert Kingswell. (L Wilde)

CO who was, of course, already qualified on type). He was joined by Flt Lt Daw, Fg Off Maloney and Plt Off Hartnell on the 23rd and WO Hockney on the 24th. Flying was slightly interrupted in mid-December by the demands of Exercise MINX which involved several of the squadron's officers acting as umpires. Fg Off Maloney and Plt Off Hartnell were detached to Arkonam while Fg Off George and Plt Off Fraser went to St Thomas Mount and Plt Off Turton was loaned to Poonamallee; others played their part at Cholavaram. The other significant event in December was monsoon rain - the downpour on the 20th was so heavy that the reputedly blast-proof walls of the bomb dump all collapsed, inspiring little confidence in Indian civil engineering techniques!

In between this activity, and although the squadron was still far from complete, time was found to celebrate Christmas. The 1942 menu, for all three messes, began with tomato soup, followed by fried becti with lime or buttered asparagus tips, a main course of stuffed turkey, roast pork and apple sauce, green peas and roast potatoes, a dessert of Xmas pudding and brandy sauce or blancmange and jelly, with mince pies, coffee, cheese and biscuits, nuts and raisins and fresh fruit to round off. All this was washed down with an extra ration of beer and spirits.

Among those who missed the Christmas festivities was the squadron's chief storeman. Manpower was not the only resource in short supply at the end of 1942; the unit was equally deficient in tools and equipment. F/Sgt Albert Onions was provided with a No 1 Equipment Priority Order, valid throughout the whole of India Command, and, clutching this, he set off on December 19th to pillage the MUs. He returned to Cholavaram on January 7th and was able to report that 80% of the squadron's requirements were now en route. Throughout December old hands had continued to trickle back in dribs and drabs; the MO, Flt Lt 'Paddy' Kelly, returned on the 1st; Fg Off Paul Lahey was released by Dum Dum on the 29th followed by Fg Off Ned Hammat on the 31st. New faces began to appear too: WO G Weedon arrived on the 20th to run the 'discip' side of the squadron and a new Engineering Officer, Plt Off L S Edwards, was posted in on the 31st.

On December 30th Sgt Cooper of No 9 Ferry Unit collected four of the squadron's pilots, Fg Offs Furmage and Maloney, Plt Off Hartnell and WO Hockney and flew them to Karachi in a Hudson (FK497). Here they were to take delivery of four more Vengeances. Their rear crews, Fg Off Lahey and F/Sgts Bob Barclay, Bill Wilson and Tommy Lord respectively, together with a group of tradesmen, travelled by train and reached Karachi on January 3rd. On the 31st the pilots had been presented with five very inadequately prepared aircraft which lacked, among other things, tool-kits and even some flight instruments! Fg Off Furmage flatly refused to accept them, which led to heated confrontations with the local authorities, eventually including the Station Commander; but Geoff Furmage stood his ground. The aircraft were duly brought up to standard and four more were ferried over from Drigh Road but these proved to be unsatisfactory as well. Once they too had been brought up to scratch, the compasses of all nine were swung and test flying began on January 5th. In the meantime a new instruction had been issued to the effect that the aircraft were only to fly 25 hours each before they were to be grounded for an engine change and withdrawn from the squadron's charge, which made it hardly worthwhile ferrying them all the way to Madras just so that they could be flown back to Karachi again. Although some flying was done, on the 11th the expedition was abandoned and a few days later the aircrew departed for Cholavaram by train. The groundcrew remained in Karachi for a time where they were attached to the Vengeance Erection Party to gain experience of working on the aircraft.

The problems being experienced at Karachi did not reflect any fundamental deficiency in the design of the Vengeance so much as the need to adjust to unfamiliar American engineering standards and practices which certainly created some early difficulties. These were not eased by the length of

F/Sgt Albert Onions missed the Christmas celebrations as he was off on a tour of supply depots trying to secure the spares and tools needed to get the squadron functioning again. This picture was taken on the roof of 29 Theatre Road, Calcutta in June 1942. (D A Owen)

Sgt Johnny Brinkley and F/Sgt Dickie Haylock (horizontal) haggle with some youthful fruit vendors at Cholavaram, 20th January 1943. (D A Owen)

To iron the bugs out of the new aeroplanes a dedicated unit was established at Karachi in February 1943. Drawing its manpower from all four squadrons which were then working up on the type, the Vengeance Development Flight took a perverse pride, as seen here, in its abbreviated title of 'VD Flt'. Sixteen of the ground tradesmen and several of the aircrew in this photograph belonged to the Flying Camels. (G J Hancox)

241

Half-time during the semi-final against No 82 Sqn and the teams chat to the 'Red Van Ladies'. Just about everybody on the squadron turned out to support the Flying Camels' team as can be seen from the groups of airmen grandstanding from the tops of trucks. LAC Len Wilde is on the right, hands on hips. (L Wilde)

The Red Van Cup. Winning this trophy marked the re-establishment of the Flying Camels and as such it held great significance for the men of No 45 Sqn in 1943. It is still among the squadron's collection of silver. (No 45 Sqn Archives)

the supply line between the manufacturers in the USA and the users in India as, with the Japanese effectively in control of the Pacific, this had to run the long way round via the Atlantic and Indian Oceans. All of this only served to exacerbate the usual crop of temporary difficulties which accompany the service introduction of almost all new aeroplanes. To identify and solve these problems a dedicated unit, the Vengeance Development Flight, was set up at Karachi under Wg Cdr J H McMichael. Rejoicing in the abbreviation of 'VD Flt', its manpower was to be drawn from all the Vengeance squadrons and No 45 Sqn duly contributed several of its aircrew and a party of thirteen tradesmen under Sgt Hill. The groundcrew team left Cholavaram on February 11th and did not rejoin the squadron until April 24th.

A feature of RAF life in the Madras area at this time was the Madras Hospitality Committee's mobile canteen service which was run on a voluntary basis by a group of local ladies led by the wife of a prominent local mill owner. This much appreciated facility operated from a red van and dispensed the sort of 'tea and wads' that one might have expected from a NAAFI wagon but it also sold khaki cloth from which one could have a reasonably smart uniform made up in place of

the awful kit that was available from Stores. At the end of 1942 these ladies promoted a football competition between all the army and RAF units in the vicinity and generously donated a suitable silver cup as the trophy.

The squadron rose to the challenge. As in Iraq in the 1920s, sport was to provide the glue which would cement the unit together and the squadron's participation in the 'Red Van Cup' was to be a crucial element in re-establishing the squadron's identity and proclaiming its presence to rival units. Since several of the bits of the squadron which had been scattered piecemeal about India in 1942 had formed their own independent '45 Sqn football teams', rather than allowing themselves to be absorbed into those of their various host units, it is evident that many of No 45 Sqn's personnel already displayed strong individual loyalties to the squadron's identity. What was needed was something to rekindle the old corporate spirit which had existed in the desert and to demonstrate to other units that the Flying Camels were back.

The Red Van Cup was taken very seriously by all concerned and tension rose as various teams were knocked out in the early rounds of the competition. The semi-final was played against No 82 Sqn on January 8th and, despite fifteen minutes of extra time each way, resulted in a 1-1 draw. In the replay on the 12th No 45 Sqn won by four goals. The final was played against No 240 Sqn from Red Hills Lake on the 16th and virtually the whole of No 45 Sqn turned out to support their team. The report of the *Madras Times* for 17th January 1943 read:

> Mrs Rene Nuttall kicked off in the all-Air Force Football Final for the Red Van Cup yesterday on the Buckingham and Carnastic Mills ground between two teams of the Royal Air Force, one from Cholavaram and the other from Red Hills. Cholavaram won by five goals to one. At half-time Cholavaram led by one goal to nil, scored by Hardman, outside right. In the second half, Lovett, centre-forward, formerly of Stoke City Reserves, netted the second goal for Cholavaram and Sgt Sharpe, inside-left, performed a hat-trick, all fine goals, two within one minute. Brockett got Red Hills' only goal. Only brilliant goalkeeping by Higgins, a former Scottish Schoolboy International, prevented Red Hills from reducing the margin still further. The match over, Mrs Nuttall presented the Cup to Sgt Sharpe who captained Cholavaram.

The Red Van Cup was never competed for again and it remains in the possession of the squadron. Today it simply represents a reminder of an obscure sporting triumph at some time in the squadron's dimly remembered past, but to those serving with the unit at the time, especially the groundcrew, it symbolised far more; it marked the unit's rebirth. The winning of the Red Van Cup showed all concerned that the Flying Camels were a squadron to be reckoned with. The old *esprit de corps* had been rekindled and thereafter the squadron's spirit was indomitable.

Meanwhile stragglers continued to return to the squadron and during January a total of thirty-three more tradesmen were released from the R&R parties at Agartala, Chittagong and Feni. Despite a shortage of aeroplanes, the conversion programme was making progress and the Harvard flew 30 hours during January while another 75 hours were squeezed out of the Vengeances.

There was to be no repeat of the squadron's experiences in France in 1917 and in Syria in 1941. This time the crews were going to be adequately trained, both individually and as a unit, before the squadron was to be sent into action. This was particularly important since they were going to be operating in a new role, for which no established tactics existed, and on a new type, which would inevitably mean that there would be technical teething troubles to overcome. Eventually No 152 OTU at Peshawar would provide conversion training for Vengeance crews but the squadron was

The winning Red Van Cup Team. Back row, from the left: Cpl 'Half Pint' Hardman, LAC Ken Summers, LAC 'Jock' Roddick, LAC Charlie Higgins, LAC Herbie Kingswell, LAC 'Oscar' Wilde and F/Sgt Hedley Jewell. Front row: LAC Freddie Lovat; Sgt Hector Sharpe, Sqn Ldr A Traill (CO), Cpl 'Jock' (aka 'Donny') Brown and LAC 'Taff' Morgan. (A G McCandlish)

already in being before the OTU started to produce crews so it had to convert itself. The plan then called for tactical training phases to include bombing, aerial gunnery and army co-operation. This was all going to take time and the squadron was not expected to be operational until the summer.

The reconstituted squadron was to be significantly smaller than it had been at the height of the Blenheim era. It was to have only sixteen aircraft instead of twenty-four and, since they were single-, rather than twin-, engined and lacked the complication (or sophistication) of a power-operated turret, the maintenance demands were going to be significantly reduced. As a result some of the old Blenheim tradesmen never did return to the fold.

Similarly a number of aircrew were either posted away or never came back from their detachments. For instance, F/Sgt George Hayley had gone to No 34 Sqn in October and at the same time Capt Gus Alder[1], Fg Off Bill Corbett and Sgt Cliff Briggs had been posted to No 113 Sqn. In January 1943, minus their nav, F/Sgt Des Carew-Reid (who had joined No 167 Wg HQ in October), Fg Off Bill Maloney and F/Sgt Bill Wilson also moved to No 113 Sqn. The attachment to No 60 Sqn of Fg Off Stuart Muller-Rowland[2] and Sgt Ken Gardiner had become a permanent posting in October, although their nav, Plt Off Phil Graebner, had been transferred to No 205 Sqn. Fg Offs Edmonds and Guy and Plt Off Pannifer remained with No 3 PRU flying Mitchells, as did two navigators, Fg Off Reeves and Plt Off Pailthorpe. Sqn Ldr Beeston had returned to the Middle East on December 1st and Flt Lt Daw left the squadron in January and, after a brief attachment to No 173 Wg's HQ, sailed for England where he was eventually to fly Lancasters. Most of the squadron's Canadians had left at the turn of the year, WOs Bob Armstrong and Ted Thompson and Sgt Norman Taylor all having been posted to fly Catalinas with No 413 Sqn on December 28th to be followed by Sgt Ted Pulford on January 16th. Another Canadian, F/Sgt Lloyd Butcher, still had not regained the flying category he had lost as a result of the injuries which he sustained when he had crashed while flying

with No 113 Sqn in the previous July; he was eventually repatriated to Canada where he recovered, only to be killed in a flying accident while towing a drogue at an air gunnery school. On November 9th Flt Lt Lin Durrant's attachment to Cuttack had ceased and he had been posted to Salbani to become No 170 Wg's Navigation Officer; he never rejoined No 45 Sqn but he survived the war and, having transferred to the RNZAF in August 1944, eventually retired in the rank wing commander.

In addition to these recent depletions in strength there had been no replacements for the four men who had been killed during the fighting in Burma in early 1942 or for the six who had died since then. Finally, Sqn Ldr Traill was now the only senior officer on strength whereas a year before there had been Wg Cdr Wallis and three squadron leader flight commanders, Austin, Hughes and Penny; none of these had been directly replaced. Thus natural wastage had significantly reduced the aircrew complement, particularly of

After a year with No 45 Sqn Plt Off Bill Corbett, along with the rest of his crew, Capt Gus Alder and Sgt Cliff Briggs, was posted to No 113 Sqn on 24th October 1942. (C G Briggs)

numbers had been topped up by the posting-in of five (Spitfire-trained!) men from the UK at the end of December: Sgts J H T Hewat, J Hadley, A R Lebans RCAF, L Halley RCAF and C S Matthews RNZAF.

Although there had been a similar wastage of rear crew members, the fact that the squadron was re-equipping with two-seaters inevitably meant that a large number of the squadron's old observers and WOp/AGs were surplus to requirements in any case. In addition to those who have already been mentioned, several others never returned to the squadron from their 1942 detachments and there was a spate of postings between October 1942 and April 1943 which saw the departure of at least twenty-five more of the squadron's Blenheim rear-crewmen:

Navigators. Fg Offs A Hilling, A H Tidswell RAAF, R A Turton RNZAF and G E Kemp RAAF, Plt Off F J Fraser, WOs L J Charlton RAAF and C Levings RAAF, F/Sgts D A Owen, R Southorn RAAF, J A H Kirkpatrick, G A Tibbs RAAF, F W Watkins, F R Haylock, A Thompson and K E Edwards RAAF and Sgt J R Hurley RCAF.

WOp/AGs. Fg Off R V Alford, Plt Offs A A Fraser RAAF and K Mills, F/Sgts D Cliffe, W Fylan, W A Gaudet RCAF and G A Gowing RAAF and Sgts G B Whittaker and A King.

At least thirteen of these men went to the recently formed No 152 (Bomber) OTU at Peshawar, some to serve as instructors while others were recrewed to serve on other Blenheim units.

It will be noted that the above list uses the term 'navigator', which had been in widespread for some time and had formally supplanted that of 'air observer' in July 1942. In September the 'Flying O' brevet, the design of which dated back to the First World War, had been superseded by an 'N' flying badge in the standard single-winged format which had been introduced for all aircrew categories other than pilot in 1939. Only those air observers who had qualified before 3rd September 1939, ie before the declaration of war, were still authorised to wear their old brevet, and only then when they were not directly employed on flying duties; everyone else was required to change his badge. It was easy to make such rules, of course, but enforcing them was another matter. It sometimes proved very difficult to persuade a man who may have been flying in combat as an observer on and off for more than three years that his battle-stained flying badge was no longer valid and that he had to take it off! 'Flying Os' were still stubbornly and proudly, if illegally, being worn by wartime-trained navigators until well into the 1960s[3].

There were four sorts of navigator: the common or garden variety, who drew lines on charts and did mysterious things with a Dalton computer, and Nav(B)s, Nav(W)s and Nav(R)s who were, respectively, additionally qualified as bomb-aimers ('air bombers', to be precise), wireless operators and radar operators (for service in night fighters). It was not unusual for people to be dual qualified so that combinations such as Nav(BW) also began to appear. The breed normally associated with light bombers

A substantial proportion of the squadron's Blenheim aircrew were posted away in early 1943. This is a group of ex-45 Sqn WOp/AGs shortly after they had arrived at No 152 OTU, Peshawar in February 1943. Clockwise from top left: Sgt George Whittaker, Sgt Tony King, F/Sgt Dave Cliffe, F/Sgt Joe Gaudet RCAF and F/Sgt Bill Fylan. (D Cliffe)

Left:- Fg Off Bill Corbett had some skill as an artist and he devised several more aggressive interpretations of the Flying Camel motif. This sketch is believed to date from late 1942 and may well be one of Corbett's designs. (G A Gowing). Right:- A stencil of a 'Dive-bombing Camel' was cut in 1943 and the emblem is said to have appeared on one or two Vengeances but its use on aircraft was very limited. It was also applied to a few vehicles (as seen here) and other items of squadron property. While this emblem was never widely used (apart from anything else the use of squadron badges was prohibited during the war on security grounds), it was still in evidence in early 1945. (N Gittins)

was the Nav(B) and, since most ex-Blenheim observers had attended Bombing and Gunnery Schools, this is how they were automatically regraded. The Nav(B), however, was not entirely appropriate for the Vengeance. As previously discussed, the two-seat dive-bomber was operated only in India and was something of an anomaly in the RAF; it did not fit comfortably into any of the standard operational categories. Although the Vengeance was indisputably a light bomber, its bombs were aimed by the pilot, not the navigator. Furthermore the back-seater needed the skills of a WOp/AG at least as much as those of a nav. Thus it seemed to many in the embryo dive-bomber force that Nav(W)s, additionally qualified in gunnery, would be the most appropriate category. These could be created by teaching the old observers Morse and checking them out in gunnery and/or by training the WOp/AGs in navigation.

There was a prolonged period of confusion between October 1942 and March 1943 during which all the Vengeance squadrons sought clarification from higher authority as to which sort of navigators ought to be occupying the rear cockpits of the new aeroplanes, while simultaneously lobbying for the retention of some of their WOp/AGs. Neither HQ 221 Gp nor Air HQ India was certain what the rules ought to be. But their requests for guidance, which they directed to the Air Ministry, tended to be parried by counter-requests for advice about the unique overseas Vengeance problem which was not clearly understood in London! A compromise was eventually reached and the rear crew establishment was set at a notional seven Nav(B)s and/or Nav(W)s and fourteen WOp/AGs per squadron. Nevertheless, in reality all Vengeance back-seaters, regardless of their trade, needed to be proficient in several roles and all the squadrons had instigated in-house training programmes to create their own hybrid navigator/WOp/AGs.

Based on the guidelines that had originally been published in July 1942, the squadron's RAAF Navigation Leader, Flt Lt Norman Bayly, had set up a suitable *ab initio* nav course for the WOp/AGs shortly after the squadron had begun to reassemble at Cholavaram. The syllabus covered instruction in compasses, maps and charts, meteorology, instruments, photography and, of course, dead reckoning (DR) navigation and plotting techniques. The courses lasted about six weeks; that attended by Sgt Gordon Terry, for instance, running from 1st December 1942 until 15th January 1943. While this course did not warrant a change of flying badge it did serve to qualify a WOp/AG to cope by himself in the back of a two-seater.

In the meantime something similar, if rather less formal, was arranged for the navigators. F/Sgt 'Mac' McDade, having spent five months in hospital recovering from his accident in the previous July, finally rejoined the squadron on January 8th and, after attending a qualification course at Amarda Road, had been appointed as the squadron's Gunnery Leader, a post which he was to hold until the Vengeances were withdrawn in 1944. Under his guidance some conversion training was laid on for the navs, appropriate 'specialist instructors' being co-opted from among the ranks of the groundcrew. Some took great delight in devising hoops through which the officer and NCO navs were obliged to jump, notably Cpl George Brodlie, a

From the left: Flt Lt H H Wilson (Adj), Sgt G A Gowing, Sgt K E Edwards and Sgt C E Birkbeck, all Australians. The date will have been between November 1942, when Herbie Wilson arrived, and April 1943, when Geoff Gowing and Ken Edwards left to fly Liberators with No 159 Sqn. The railway carriage in the background suggests that the occasion may have been the move from Cholavaram to Asansol in February. (G A Gowing)

WOM, who used his expertise to improve their facility with Morse.

By early 1943 No 84 Sqn had begun converting to the Vengeance at Cholavaram, as had No 110 Sqn at Ondal where No 168 Wg had been formed on November 11th to co-ordinate the employment of the new light bomber force. It was decided to concentrate the wing, and Nos 45 and 82 Sqns moved north in February. No 84 Sqn did not join them, however, as it was diverted to Ceylon where it remained for several months to bolster the air defences of that island.

The planned redeployment originally involved No 45 Sqn moving to Panagarh, exchanging its aircraft for new ones at Karachi en route, and on February 9th Fg Offs Furmage and Lahey set off for the new base with an advance party of twenty airmen. Two days later the plan was changed. The squadron was now to retain its present aeroplanes and go to Asansol. The advance party was redirected and arrived at its new destination on the 12th. Since the squadron was now getting into its stride, on the 11th, while he was still in transit, Furmage had been formally designated as a flight commander (at this stage the only one). The move to Asansol proved to be problematical as there was a shortage of rolling stock to convey the main party en masse so a piecemeal transfer began on the 20th when WO Hockney led the first three Vengeances away. By the end of the month three more aircraft had left and a total of seventy men were en route in small rail parties. The advance party found the camp to be in a pretty tatty state. It had been unoccupied for two months and the Care and Maintenance (C & M) Party had done little to look after the site - much of the furniture that still remained was broken; showers and taps had been left running since the previous December and the latrine facilities had not been emptied since then either! Furmage and Co prodded some belated life into the C & M Party and had the camp in a

In March 1943 the squadron moved from Cholavaram to Asansol which involved it in the first of its many long and uncomfortable rail journeys in India. As can be seen here, the only way to travel was stripped to the waist. (G J Hancox)

reasonable state by the time that the bulk of the squadron began to arrive.

Sqn Ldr Traill flew the Harvard up to Asansol on March 1st followed by Fg Off Keel and Sgt Hadley in the last two Vengeances on the 6th. The day before, a road convoy, consisting of ten vehicles and twenty airmen under Sgt Copcutt, had left Cholavaram followed, on the 8th, by the main rail party with the Adj, 'Doc' Kelly and Mr Jones, the civilian representative of the Vultee Aircraft Corporation. On the 12th the move was finally complete and the whole unit was reconstituted at Asansol, apart from Plt Off Edwards and Sgt Worrall (Equipment Assistant in succession to F/Sgt Onions who had been commissioned and posted to No 99 Sqn on 5th February) who were away on a week-long visit to No 312 MU at Cochin on what proved to be a very productive search for Vengeance spares. Despite this prolonged move, training flying, now concentrating on bombing rather than just aircraft handling, had begun on February 25th and gained momentum as additional aeroplanes arrived.

The rail party's trip had not been particularly remarkable, but any journey by troop train in wartime India was a memorable experience; they were invariably long, slow, hot, sticky and uncomfortable. Because the Indian railway network had originally evolved piecemeal under provincial administrations, rather than having been centrally planned, several gauges were in use and whenever the gauge changed everyone and everything had to be offloaded from the original train and reloaded onto a new one. Many Indian rivers were unbridged, which meant that they had to be crossed by ferry, which would involve another offload/reload. Not infrequently, when these changes of train cropped up, there would be no new engine available and the party would be left sweltering until one arrived. Even when a train was under way it would sometimes stop, anywhere, for no apparent reason and remain at a standstill for hours at a time. Other halts were necessary to allow the locomotive's boiler to be topped up from large trackside static water tanks on trestles. Once the engine had been attended to, hordes of naked airmen, armed with pieces of soap, would bunch together in a tight scrum and compete for space under the giant hose as it gushed cool (well tepid) water. On one such occasion the squadron was engaged in these impromptu

ablutions when another troop train pulled up alongside. Its cargo of British nurses declined to join them under the shower and the Flying Camels fled back to their train to hide their - well everything really.

Asansol turned out to be a reasonably comfortable camp once the squadron had settled in, although the weather could be extreme on occasion. Graham Williams, by then a pilot officer, has described one or two incidents:

Ern (*Hallett*) and I and about four others were on a covered verandah during a storm when a lightning strike went through the roof of the next hut and killed a chap. While commenting on how close that strike had been, another one completely demolished the end of our hut about twenty feet away and threw us to kingdom come. We wandered about stunned for about half an hour. Ern had a big burn on his back and his pith helmet pushed down round his ears! We had one massive hail storm with winds up to 90 mph and hail stones like golf balls. We were trying to tie the aircraft down when it struck and we were really thumped until all fourteen of us piled into the CO's station wagon. About ten planes of different types were upended with much damage to them and to our huts. The ground was white, like a snowstorm.

Williams remembers that the wild-life kept people on their toes as well: "There were big monkeys around this camp and we would shoot at them with catapults. In retaliation they would run along branches overhead trying to leak and defecate on us. Can't say I blame them."

The squadron bent its first Vengeance on March 11th when AN978 swung on take-off and finished up in a ditch with a damaged mainplane and oleo leg, although neither of the two Australians on board, F/Sgts Rusty Curtis and John Brinkley, was hurt. Three days later Fg Off Keel was promoted to become a flight commander, re-establishing the squadron on a two-flight basis; Keel had A Flight and Furmage B Flight. On the 16th F/Sgt G Lawrenson (NCO i/c the Armoury) was commissioned and posted to HQ 168 Wg. Sadly he was to die in an aircraft accident at Ranchi on April 24th; a party of twenty-five men from No 45 Sqn attended his funeral the following day.

On March 19th AHQ Bengal signalled that the squadron was to be re-equipped with sixteen new and fully operational Vengeance Mk IAs which were to be collected from No 320 MU at Karachi by squadron crews in batches of four at three-day intervals. Needless to say this plot did not work exactly according to plan and, although the first three aircraft arrived on March 29th (flown in by Plt Off Halley and WO Hallett, Sgts Hewat and Stone and F/Sgt Jewell and Sgt Terry), it was to be late April before the squadron had its full complement of new aeroplanes, and some of them turned out to be Mk IIs. The first two of the aforementioned crews, plus Plt Off Al Lebans and F/Sgt Jimmy Vernon, had actually been at Karachi since early March working with the Vengeance Development Flight.

The receipt of the new aircraft significantly improved serviceability, since the initial batch had suffered quite badly from the anticipated teething troubles. All the Vengeance squadrons had been experiencing problems with hydraulics, fuel pumps and, particularly, with piston rings on the big Cyclone engines. Nos 82 and 110 were somewhat aggrieved when they learned that No 45 Sqn was to be the first to receive fully modified aircraft and the former certainly had a case, since they had been struggling with the older models for much longer. Nevertheless the squadron was allowed to keep its new aeroplanes and the other units received theirs shortly afterwards. Thereafter there were fewer technical problems although difficulties were later experienced with the guns when armament training began.

As delivered, the Vengeance had four fixed forward-firing .30 calibre Brownings, two in each wing, and another pair on a pillar mounting in the rear cockpit. It was found that the front guns had a tendency to move in their mountings, disturbing their harmonisation, while the flexible pair would often jam after having fired only a few rounds. The latter problem was brought into sharp focus when the Vengeance was first committed to combat in March (with No 110 Sqn) and the rear guns were then replaced by the slightly heavier British-standard .303 Brownings which cured the problem. Just how effective a pair of hand-held rifle calibre machine guns would have been in combat is a moot point and it was probably fortunate that the squadron never had to use them to ward off enemy fighters, although they were employed on occasion to spray Japanese ground positions.

Led by Sgt Morris-Owen, No 45 Sqn's armourers were responsible for one innovation which was developed during the work-up phase. There was a requirement for the rear guns to be fitted with a camera for air-to-air practice sorties and LAC Basil Terry was given the job of designing and making a suitable bracket. His prototype was successful and he visited the other squadrons to show them how to make and fit the device which became a standard Vengeance modification, although it is very doubtful whether No 45 Sqn's coffee swindle ever received the royalties which should have been its due.

It is worth pointing out that not all of the technical problems which the groundcrews experienced as they accustomed themselves to the idiosyncrasies of the Vengeance were of a mechanical nature. Shortly after the first aircraft had been delivered, Jock McCandlish recalls being in the rear cockpit working on the radio while his 'Boss', WO Adam, was busy in the pilot's position. Jock could hear the WO talking to him, but he could not make out what he was saying and he was not 'coming through' on the intercom; he eventually climbed out onto the wing and went up front to investigate. George Adam was an old hand who had been brought up on Gosport Tubes and that was what he was using; Jock found him bellowing into the metal 'mouthpiece' of the Pee-tube! WO Adam was commissioned shortly afterwards and he departed for Jodhpur on April 5th.

On April 8th Sgt Jimmy Hadley, with Sgt 'Tubby' Garfath in the back, overshot landing in EZ842 and finished up by standing the aeroplane on its nose, scattering a group of coolies working on the extended runway in the process. Fortunately no one was hurt and the only damage sustained by the Vengeance, which was quite a rugged beast, was a buckled prop. The following day F/Sgt Hedley Jewell, with F/Sgt Jim Vernon in the back, damaged the port wingtip of EZ849 by clipping a tree on Nadiha Bombing Range "whilst flying over the quadrant hut for the purpose of signalling to the range party that bombing practice had been completed for the day". The summary of follow-up action on the relevant Accident Record Card states that, in Tony Traill's opinion,

the accident had been due to "an error of judgement". The Station Commander sternly noted that it had also been a breach of flying regulations but then went on to say, in mitigation, that the pilot was "a keen type" and that appears to have been the end of the matter - those were the days!

The training programme was disrupted somewhat in April by a requirement to check out two pilots from another unit and a commitment to maintain one aircraft on detachment at Alipore for radar calibration work. Another extraneous task was the detachment of three aircraft to Alipore on the 24th and 25th where they were inspected by, and demonstrated to, members of the Indian Defence Council. Other pressures were created by the rotation of parties of airmen to the hill station at Chakrata for a much needed break, the first one departing on April 9th. The consequent shortage of groundcrew was exacerbated by a series of 'backers up' courses which were being run by the Wing HQ; these were intended to get everyone toughened-up in preparation for the harder living conditions they could expect to find when they returned to the Front. Finally Nadiha Range (in the River Damodar) was closed which meant that the only one available was at Silampur which had to be shared with the other two squadrons of the wing, both of which were stationed nearby at Madhaiganj with the Wing HQ (until April 11th when No 82 Sqn moved across to Asansol). The resultant congestion significantly reduced range utilisation. Nevertheless, despite these various adverse factors the squadron flew a respectable 150 training hours during April, not including ferry flights and the like.

There was nearly a nasty accident on April 23rd. The main undercarriage legs of the Vengeance retracted aft into the wing, rotating through 90° so that the wheels lay flat in their wells. Something failed in the mechanical linkage on EZ842 and when Flt Lt Keel touched down the starboard leg had failed to rotate and align its wheel with the fore-and-aft axis. In fact it was not locked at all and on touch down the wheel proceeded to spin, rather like a gyroscope. The aircraft swung violently but the pilot was able to prevent it from ground-looping. The aeroplane came to rest fifty yards off the runway, rocked up onto its nose, teetered there for a moment and then crashed back onto three points. Paul Keel and his nav, Lloyd George, were severely shaken but

A squadron wedding. The marriage of Fg Off Paul Lahey RAAF and Miss Audrey Edgeworth at the Old Mission Church, Calcutta on 28th April 1943. (G A Gowing)

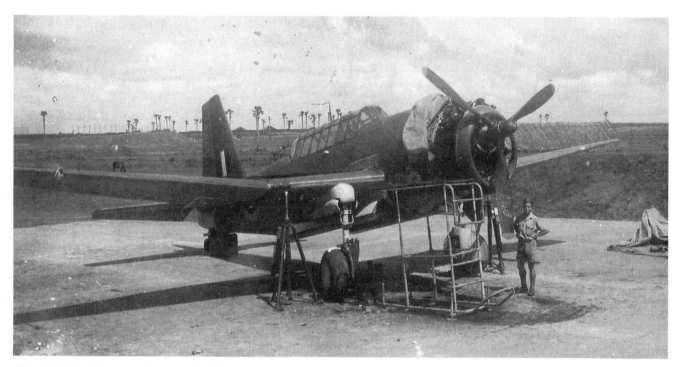

One of the squadron's 'Vengae' on jacks and with its engine cowling disarranged. It has been reported that this photograph was taken at Cholavaram but the fin flashes are of the post-June 1943 variety which, along with the background terrain, suggests that the venue is more likely to have been Digri. (L Wilde)

uninjured.

Two days later there was some more excitement when Cpl Ladd-Thomas and LAC 'Spike' York, with the assistance of two *chowkidars*, arrested ten Indians whom they had disturbed out on the airfield stealing petrol and, it was suspected, attempting to sabotage the aircraft.

A number of the squadron's longest-serving airmen were now coming to the ends of their overseas tours. Sgts Cole and Copcutt and Cpl Inglis, all veterans of North Africa, the Sudan and Syria, departed for the UK in April. They had been preceded in March by another batch of very old timers which had included Sgt Sharpe, who could include active service in Burma among his 'battle honours', Sgt Starr and LACs Jones and Higgins (another Burma veteran). What was of more significance than their campaigning experience, however, was that Sharpe and Higgins had been key members of the victorious Red Van Cup football team; they would be sorely missed, especially as a third team member, Cpl Hardman, was leaving with them.

By this time training was being concentrated on the ten crews who had been selected to form the core of the operational echelon. Bombing training continued during May, as did detachments of airmen to Chakrata, but on the

11th the squadron was warned for a move so that it could embark on the air-firing phase of its work-up. As No 82 Sqn relocated to Salbani, No 45 Sqn began preparing for a move to nearby Digri on the 12th. The eight primary aircraft flew over in two groups of four on the 17th and 19th. The road convoy under Fg Off Edwards arrived the following day, as did the rail party commanded by the MO. Digri turned out to be a generally satisfactory camp and air-firing on Ramnagar Range started on the 21st. On the 24th a party left for Karachi to collect a batch of new Vengeance IIs and on the 27th Sqn Ldr Traill led six aircraft to Alipore for fighter affiliation exercises with the Hurricanes of No 615 Sqn. This exercise was repeated by six aircraft co-operating with Nos 17 and 607 Sqns' Hurricanes on the 28th but a further attempt on the 29th was frustrated by adverse weather. By the end of May the squadron had flown 161 training hours to which could be added 102 hours of extraneous tasking, air tests, radar calibration flights, trips to fetch spares and so on, plus an unrecorded amount of ferry flying.

There were some significant personnel changes during this period. Flt Lt Furmage had been posted to AHQ at New Delhi on May 2nd and was succeeded as OC B Flight by Fg Off George. This was quite an unusual appointment for a navigator in 1943, although, in practice, much of the responsibility for the supervision of aircrew was devolved to his deputy, Fg Off Ed Christensen. On the 13th May Flt Lt Keel went into hospital and A Flight was taken over by his deputy, Fg Off Hartnell. Finally, on June 1st, Plt Off E J Boon arrived to become the squadron's Signals Officer and Flt Lt A A Smith was posted-in to relieve the squadron's long-serving, redoubtable MO, Flt Lt Kelly, who began his journey back to the UK a week later.

The work-up entered its final phase in June. The aircraft began flying with full operational

Patrick Joseph Kelly who, as MO, began administering lotions and potions to the men of No 45 Sqn in Palestine at the end of July 1941. He did the same thing in Iraq, the Western Desert of Egypt, Cyrenaica and at various places in India until 8th June 1943 when he finally left on repatriation to the UK. This photograph was taken in the Middle East, probably at Cairo's Gezirah Club in January 1942. (L E Durrant)

bomb loads; further affiliation exercises were flown with the Hurricane squadrons based around Calcutta and a good deal of thought was devoted to devising the most appropriate for-mations and tactics.

In the meantime the Vengeance had been blooded in action by No 110 Sqn. 14th Division's First Arakan campaign, the objective of which had been to take Akyab, had been blocked at Donbaik. A detachment of seven aircraft of No 110 Sqn had been deployed to Dohazari to contribute to the air offensive which was at-tempting to break the deadlock. They flew the first of five missions on March 19th. In seven days the

Vengeance K tucked up for the night during one of the squadron's two detachments to Ranchi. (W Worrall)

detachment dropped 28,000 lbs of bombs. This was hardly enough to turn the tide, but it was enough to prove that the Vengeance worked and that it could be operated over Burma. So far as accuracy was concerned, the bombing results had fully justified the claims made by the pro-dive-bomber lobby. By early May the ground offensive had failed; the troops began pulling back to a line to the north of Maungdaw and needed air support to hold off the pursuing Japanese. No 168 Wg now had three squadrons of Vengeances ready for action and each in turn was to mount a two-week, eight-aircraft detachment to Chittagong. The first to go were the pioneers of No 110 Sqn who opened the six-week Vengeance campaign with a mission on May 13th. Their detachment returned to Madhaiganj at the end of the month and their place was taken by one from No 82 Sqn. Now it was the Flying Camels' turn and on June 9th HQ 221 Gp signalled that No 45 Sqn was to be "on top line" to take over.

The CO and the squadron's Engineering Officer, Fg Off Edwards, flew to Chittagong on the 10th to spy out the land. As preparations for the impending move gathered speed a modification programme to stop the wing guns moving in their mountings was hastily completed and some test firings on the 17th showed that this had been successful (these guns were still the original .30 calibres which were retained throughout the Vengeance's career). This, the completion of inspections and final 'tweaking' of the aircraft, kept the groundcrew working until late into the night, every night. In the last few days before departure several more exercises were flown to perfect the squadron's tactics, culminating in vertical dives over the runway at Digri to show the squadron's airmen how it was done.

Fg Off Edwin 'Chris' Christensen and F/Sgt Bob Hilditch flew to Chittagong on June 24th to arrange the squadron's reception while the main party of forty-five NCOs and airmen under Fg Off Edwards, plus four spare aircrew, boarded their train at Chandrakona Road. Led by Sqn Ldr Traill, the remaining seven Vengeances left on the 26th. Once they had seen the aircraft off, F/Sgt Edwards and his rear party of twenty-one men boarded a Dakota and followed them to Chittagong, only to find that as soon as they landed they were obliged to become the advance party. The squadron was scheduled to fly its first mission the next day and, since

the bulk of the squadron's personnel had not yet arrived, Edward's team had to arm, refuel and prepare all the Vengeances for their first mission.

The airmen managed, but it was not a good start and was the most unsatisfactory aspect of an otherwise highly successful detachment. Concerned that this sort of thing should not happen again, Tony Traill later pointed out in his formal report that, if a redeploying squadron was required to be immediately available for operations, it was essential that the bulk of its support element be on site before the arrival of its air echelon. While he was about it, he took the opportunity to complain about the "disgusting" conditions under which his men had been obliged to travel:

> The third-class coach provided had very recently been occupied by natives, who had left very definite evidence of their presence in all the lavatories. Not only that, the coach in which the airmen travelled from Calcutta to Chittagong had not been properly cleaned, and on arrival at Chittagong all blankets and mosquito nets were full of bugs. That airmen should have to travel under such conditions is iniquitous, and was a poor start for men who were expected to work at high pressure for two-three weeks.

Back at Digri, Flt Lt Bayly assumed command of the rest of the squadron while responsibility for engineering fell to WO Honeychurch, who had been with the squadron since January. Everyone was on tenterhooks for news as the squadron flew its first operational missions since the attack on Mingaladon on 21st March 1942. Apart from the concern felt for the safety of the aircrew, a considerable competitive spirit had grown up between the three squadrons of No 168 Wg which was felt most acutely by the groundcrews. They were quite confident that the Flying Camels would put up a better show than the other squadrons and waited anxiously for their faith to be confirmed.

There was no feedback from Chittagong until July 1st when F/Sgt Hedley Jewell and Sgt Gordon Terry brought EZ847 back for an inspection. They were mobbed by groundcrew who were clamouring for information and were relieved and exhilarated to learn of operational success and excellent serviceability. Morale soared. Thereafter reports began to filter through by mail and on July 5th the mailplane brought Messrs Jones and Leech, the manufacturer's representatives, back from Chittagong; they too pronounced themselves well content with the performance of the aircraft and were full of admiration for Anthony Traill's leadership. On the 8th WO Gerry Osborne and F/Sgt Alf Field flew back in another Vengeance in need of attention and that evening the pilot gave a presentation in the Airmen's' Recreation Room on the work of the squadron's operational detachment; this was attended by virtually the whole of the base party.

The aircraft returned to Digri on July 14th, the rail party arriving three days later. The airmen's faith in their squadron had been fully justified. It is true that they had had the advantage of going last, and were thus able to build on the experience of the earlier detachments, but this did not detract from the simple fact that the squadron had outperformed its rivals. For the record the key statistics were that No 110 Sqn had flown fifty-one sorties in the course of eleven missions; No 82 Sqn had improved on that with ninety sorties in fifteen missions but No 45 Sqn had topped the unofficial league table with one hundred and two sorties in sixteen missions. The squadron was back in business at last, and very definitely back on form.

Sqn Ldr Traill had personally led all of the missions flown by the Flying Camels. All but two had employed between six and eight aircraft and the total effort had involved 204 operational flying hours. The targets attacked had been at Myohaung, Akyab, Thaungdara, Buthidaung, Maungdaw and Minbya, plus a downed PR Spitfire at Alethangyaw which had been bombed by two pairs on July 9th to prevent its falling into enemy hands. On the second sortie against the Spitfire, Hedley Jewell, carrying four 250 pounders with eleven-second delayed action fuses, put one of his bombs straight through the wreckage. The total weight of bombs dropped was 86,000 lbs; apart from eight 250 pounders used against the Spitfire, all the bombs had been 500 lb GPs. An attack on Akyab on July 10th was notable as it had been an attempt to emulate the recent success of No 617 Sqn in breaching the Möhne dam in Germany. Seven aircraft were despatched with the aim of breaching the lock gates and generation plant associated with the Royal Lake. The attack was executed successfully but, as the 'Dambusters' had discovered, it was not easy to damage such a target. The mission had a mildly exciting aftermath for F/Sgt Matthews and Plt Off Williams in EZ865 as the former has described:

Following massive spouts of water, the gates were still there. However, en route back to base the bomb bay red light was 'on'. Other pilots told me that the doors were not closed properly, so back at Chittagong I made

the best landing of my career and taxied in very carefully. The ground crew announced that there was a live bomb stuck in the door so two brave Colonials promptly did a very smart exit and left them to it.

The weather had been very troublesome throughout the detachment and had prevented the missions launched on July 2nd and in the morning of the 7th from dropping their bombs. Between those dates the weather had been too bad for any operations to be mounted at all. Even on the successful sorties, extensive cloud cover had sometimes dictated that attacks had had to be delivered as shallow dives. Whenever possible, however, the crews had used the preferred high dive delivery as this was far more accurate and rendered the aircraft less vulnerable.

The tactics employed by the squadron during its detachment to Chittagong defined the standard mission profile which remained substantially unchanged throughout the remainder of its period of Vengeance operations. A typical sortie began with transit to the target area at about 185 mph and 10,000 feet in a single group of six or, when eight or twelve aircraft were available, in boxes of four in echelon. Largely dictated by the extent of the cloud cover and the height of the target, the 80° to 90° dives were entered at between 8,000 and 14,000 feet, speed being restrained to no more than 300 mph by the powerful airbrakes which extended from both the upper and lower surfaces of the wings. Aiming corrections applied during the exhilarating two mile plunge could mean that the dive steepened until it was 'past the vertical' which slightly disconcerting situation was easily corrected by rolling the aircraft through 180°. These gyrations must have provided a particularly stimulating experience for the back-seaters, each of whom generally spent most of this critical phase of a sortie effectively lying on his back, gazing at the sky and trusting (hoping?) that his personal 'drivers, airframe' was getting it right! Bombs were released at between 3,000 feet and 1,000 feet with the aircraft then being given its head and, with airbrakes retracting, the recovery was continued down to ground level for an escape at up to 350 mph before reforming for a recovery to base at about 4,000 feet.

All missions had been escorted by between six and twelve Hurricanes drawn from either No 67 Sqn or No 261 Sqn, but no enemy fighters were encountered. Anti-aircraft was variable in intensity, heaviest at Akyab, but the crews felt that the Japanese gunners would have been very lucky to get a hit. None of them was; the only combat damage sustained was a single small-calibre bullet strike on the open bomb doors of EZ865 (Jewell and Terry) on the 9th. On the other hand, two gunners had managed to put bullets through the tail surfaces of their own aeroplanes, Paul Lahey on the 7th (EZ851) and Ernie Hallett on the 8th (AN626). These incidents hastened the incorporation of a modification which was supposed to preclude this possibility.

Fg Off Edwards' subsequent formal report on the remedial action taken on AN626 was short and to the point: "This aircraft was worked on all night. The fin was repaired

One of the squadron's Vengeances at Kumbhirgram. (A N Huon)

and the rudder replaced with one obtained from R & SU". Ernest Henman has a more colourful version. Until a new rudder could be delivered the squadron was going to be one aircraft short. A Vengeance from one of the previous detachments had been forced to land at one of the nearby emergency strips and had been left there to be attended to by an RSU. Since the squadron had just received a request for a crew to test fly this aeroplane it was known that it was about to become serviceable again and it was proposed that it be commandeered. The CO vetoed this suggestion but he was prepared to turn a blind eye to Plan B, which was to pinch its rudder. A night raid was mounted. A set of sheerlegs was knocked up. The pristine rudder, all eight feet of it, was removed and the bullet-riddled unit installed in its place. By dawn the pirated rudder had been fitted to the squadron's aeroplane and there were eight available for ops as usual. Later that morning the NCO i/c the RSU working party contacted the squadron to cancel the request for a crew, explaining that his aircraft appeared to have been damaged by a nocturnal Japanese strafing attack!

Chittagong had relatively primitive domestic facilities, a scattering of bashas distributed about the airfield, but it did at least boast an all-weather runway. This was just as well as the detachment had been mounted during the rainy season which meant that everyone was pretty moist most of the time. The pervading damp had caused several problems. Radios, for instance, could be temperamental, especially in the mornings, and the fuel tanks, which tended to vent in the heat of the day, had had to be constantly topped-up to avoid the contents being contaminated by water from overnight condensation. There had been little in the way of heavy equipment and the 500 lb bombs had had to be manhandled into the Vengeances' relatively small bomb bays. This task had been too much for the armourers alone, and all and sundry had been co-opted into the arming parties. Despite these problems, morale on the flightline had remained high as the groundcrews strove to prove that theirs was the best squadron.

As a result of the sterling efforts of the squadron's groundcrew (who are listed at Annex N), serviceability was excellent throughout the detachment. Only one sortie was lost, on July 10th, when EZ841 developed engine trouble, obliging Arthur Huon and Ced Birkbeck to return to base. The only other snags of any note were bombs which failed to release but there were only three such instances. The original eight aircraft had been AN618, AN621, AN626, EZ843, EZ844, EZ847, EZ848 and EZ850, but, as a result of exchanges with aircraft at Digri, EZ841, EZ849, EZ851, EZ865 also flew operationally with the detachment. The crews who had flown these aircraft and the number of sorties that each crew carried out are listed at Figure 10.1.

The contemporary aircrew complement on the squadron was completed by Flt Lt N W Bayly* RAAF (Navigation Leader) and F/Sgt B T McDade (Gunnery Leader) plus the following: pilots - Fg Off P U A Keel, Plt Offs W S McLellan RAAF, A R Lebans RCAF and A J Lamb, WO F Shattock

RAAF and F/Sgts J Hadley and J Newport and Sgt J Banham; rear crew - Plt Offs J R Vernon* RAAF, R I Clark RAAF, R M Barclay RAAF and J Nankervis RAAF and F/Sgts R Stone, C H Romans and J Paterson* and Sgt H Garfath. Some of these additional personnel were temporarily attached to other units. Others were at various stages of the Vengeance conversion programme; some had almost completed it while others had yet to start. A few would be posted away without ever really getting to grips with the aeroplane.

Those rear crew members whose names are marked in Figure 10.1 and above with an asterisk were navigators; the others were WOp/AGs. It is interesting to note that the end product of the earlier lengthy debates about who ought to be sitting in the back seats of the Vengeances had been settled in favour of the WOp/AGs, the squadron having nine navs and thirteen gunners on its strength. From the proportion of Australians, Canadians and New Zealanders it will also be seen that the strongly international flavour which the squadron had first begun to exhibit in late 1941 was still being maintained and in July 1943 twenty-four of the forty-two aircrew nominally on strength hailed from the Dominions. A certain piquancy was added to this cocktail of nationalities by the presence of the Argentine-connected CO and the Danish Fg Off Keel[4].

While the operational echelon had been away, another Canadian had joined its ranks. Flt Lt J H Stevenson had moved over from No 82 Sqn on July 8th to become a flight commander; his gunner, Sgt S Siddle, followed him on the 19th. The flight commander situation was actually somewhat fluid for the next few weeks. Fg Off Keel had lost his acting flight lieutenancy in June as he had been off sick for several weeks but, since he was posted to the Mauripur Ferry Pool on August 16th, this removed any residual doubt about Bill Hartnell's continuing to run A Flight as a flying officer. In the meantime Flt Lt Stevenson was being given trouble by a Medical Board so Flt Lt George retained nominal command of B Flight. He, however, was being considered for a 'Special Mission' and was away for a series of interview boards so, although Lloyd George did not actually depart to take up his new appointment (which was with Wingate's Chindits) until August 20th, Fg Off Christensen actually ran B Flight between August 2nd and 16th, when Flt Lt Stevenson finally assumed command. Thereafter stability

No	Pilot	Nav or WOp/AG	Sorties
1	Sqn Ldr A Traill	Plt Off D E French*	16
2	F/Sgt H C Jewell	Sgt F G Terry	11
3	Fg Off E G Christensen RAAF	F/Sgt R D Hilditch* RAAF	10
4	Plt Off R P Curtis RAAF	Plt Off J L Brinkley RAAF	10
5	WO C G Hockney	F/Sgt T A Lord RAAF	10
6	WO W M Osborne DFM	F/Sgt A R Field	10
7	Plt Off L Halley RAAF	Plt Off E J Hallett* RAAF	9
8	F/Sgt C S Matthews RNZAF	Plt Off G F Williams RAAF	6
9	Plt Off H M P Neil RAAF	Plt Off F F Brown RAAF	8
10	Plt Off A N Huon RAAF	Plt Off C E Birkbeck* RAAF	6
11	Fg Off G W Hartnell RAAF	Flt Lt P C Lahey* RAAF	7
12	Sgt J H T Hewat	Flt Lt L G George* RAAF	2
Crews 1-8 flew the original eight Vengeances to Chittagong; Crews 9 and 10 travelled with the rail party as spares while Crews 11 and 12 ferried in replacement aircraft.			

Fig 10.1. Sorties flown by participating crews during No 45 Sqn's first operational Vengeance deployment, 26th June-14th July 1943.

was restored.

Flying training had recommenced on July 19th, although it was badly disrupted for the rest of the month by bad weather. A combination of high winds, low cloud and heavy rain meant that the majority of range sorties finished up as low-level attacks, not the preferred option for a dive-bomber squadron. On the 27th WO 'Hock' Hockney with F/Sgt Tommy Lord and Plt Off Max Neil (solo - his gunner, Plt Off Frank Brown, followed on by rail) took two Vengeances to Amarda Road to attend a lengthy course run by the Air Fighting Training Unit (AFTU).

The bad weather continued into August with extensive flooding and on the 7th Fg Off Christensen and F/Sgt Hilditch flew an air search for three men reported missing in a boat in the vicinity of Burdwan; they found nothing. The squadron had been warned for a detachment to Ranchi and on the 10th Fg Offs Hartnell and French (the CO's nav, who had followed him from No 82 Sqn in January) flew there to make contact with the army units with which the squadron was to co-operate and to look into the domestic arrangements. Four days later Fg Off Boon, led off by road with an eight-man advance party. The main party and eight aircraft followed on the 16th. With eight aeroplanes away at Ranchi and two more at Amarda Road, things were a bit quiet at Digri until they all came back on August 23rd and 25th respectively; however, there was enough to keep the base party occupied as both detachments kept sending crews back to pick up replacement aircraft.

Ever since July, when four airmen of No 110 Sqn had collapsed from heat exhaustion, the working day had been adjusted to avoid the 'noon-day sun'. In fact it had probably been at least as hot in Iraq and in the North African desert, but the high humidity of India made the climate even more debilitating and prickly heat was a constant problem for everyone. This hot weather regime was maintained until cooler weather in October permitted work to be resumed immediately after 'tiffin'.

The Ranchi detachment found that, "the camp was in a rather grim state and (that the) billets were in a dirty condition". Life was not made any easier by the domestic accommodation being located some two miles from the aerodrome. Nevertheless, contact was made with the AILO, Capt Darlington; a visit was made to the range and a training

A group of the squadron's Vengeances, probably up from Digri, in the summer of 1943 when there was much discussion over which tactical formation would provide the most effective defence against enemy fighters. (A N Huon)

programme was devised. Flying commenced on the 17th with an attempt to demonstrate target marking. This was frustrated by the weather so the opportunity was taken to give some army officers air experience flights instead. By the 19th the weather had cleared somewhat and three Vengeances, with a four Hurricane escort from No 79 Sqn, were able to carry out successful low-level dummy attacks against a group of Bren gun carriers from the 4/1st Gurkhas. Similar exercises were flown over the next two days and just as things were starting to go with a swing, a signal arrived from HQ 221 Gp recalling the detachment.

Back at Digri there seemed to have been no pressing reason for the detachment's having been cancelled and routine training flying was resumed, with particular emphasis on formation work. After the experience gained from the initial operational detachments to Chittagong, considerable thought was being given to the refinement of tactics and a conference was held at Digri on August 30th at which representatives from HQ 221 Gp, No 168 Wg and Nos 5, 45 and 110 Sqns examined the options and proposed a series of tactical trials. The main conclusion was that, as the Vengeance force had now been successfully blooded, it should aim to operate in larger numbers in future. What remained to be established was how best to handle the larger formations.

On September 1st a fighter affiliation exercise with No 5 Sqn's Hurricanes had to be aborted because of low cloud so the eleven Vengeances that the squadron had put up occupied themselves with formation flying, two boxes of four and a vic. While they were about it a passing USAAF P-38 turned up and made a few attacks, so the aim was partially achieved. Shortly afterwards, however, another casual intruder succeeded in putting the squadron's nose slightly out of joint. While orbiting over Digri prior to landing the vic was 'attacked' again. They did not take exception to this in principle, but it was considered a bit cheeky for a B-24 to have lumbered up and challenged them!

More fighter affiliation was scheduled over the next few days involving groups of up to twelve Vengeances. Sqn Ldr Traill held a squadron wash-up and eventually called for a vote; the available options were three boxes of four, arranged in a vic or stacked up in echelon, or two boxes of six. The pilots favoured the former option, in a vic, while the back-seaters preferred the latter (*which was probably something to do with the rear crew herd instinct - CGJ*). The matter was shelved until more experience had been gained.

September provided little excitement but a good deal of sound consolidation training. Three crews and aircraft left for Amarda Road on the 5th to attend No 4 Bombing and Gunnery Refresher Course which lasted until the 21st. The rest of the squadron carried on with formation flying, fighter affiliation, air-to-air gunnery at Ramnagar Range (with one of the squadron's own Vengeances towing the drogue) and dive-bombing practice, although the weather frequently converted these sorties into low-level attacks. Feedback from No 5 Sqn indicated that Nos 5 and 6 in a six-aircraft box were regarded as being the most vulnerable, so the balance began to tip in favour of operating in fours. Ground training was not neglected and ten full days were devoted to a course on chemical warfare training. Both defensive and offensive techniques were studied, the latter including some training sorties to practise delivery techniques and over a seven-day period a total of seventy-five 65 lb practice bombs was dropped in association with this programme. In the event the Vengeance was never employed operationally in this role but it is interesting to note that in late 1944 No 110 Sqn mounted a lengthy detachment to Takoradi in West Africa where they spent three months spraying pesticides, partly for the benefit of Porton Down's boffins who were interested in quantifying the results achieved by studying the impact on the mosquito population.

Time was also found to resume conversion training in September and Fg Off McLellan and Sgt S O'Connor (a recent arrival from No 215 Sqn) both went solo in the Vengeance during the month. The squadron's own Harvard having been withdrawn in June, both had first had to spend a few days at Kharagpur where they had been checked out courtesy of No 5 Sqn. The personnel kaleidoscope was given a further shake with several more NCO aircrew being commissioned; since its arrival in India in early 1942 the average rank of the aircrew had gone up by about two notches and the majority were now officers. On September 5th F/Sgt Newport, Plt Off Barclay and Sgt Garfath returned to the squadron from Mauripur, where they had been working with the Ferry Pool since May. Old hands continued to drift away: Fg Off Ed Christensen left for Amarda Road, Plt Off Ron Clark went to No 152 OTU and Sgt Ron Stone departed for the UK.

On the last day of September an advance party set off by road under Plt Off Len Halley for another Army Co-operation detachment to Ranchi. Flt Lt Stevenson led off with eight Vengeances the next day, followed by a twenty-man party in a Dakota. The main groundcrew body arrived by road on October 2nd, commanded by the squadron's Intelligence Officer, Fg Off Arnold (who had rejoined the unit from HQ 221 Gp on 20th July). Contact was promptly made with No 168 Wg's AILO, Capt E E Kennington; the range was inspected and flying began on the 3rd. The weather was rather better than on the previous occasion and permitted a number of high-dive attacks to be made using 500 lb bombs. These were all successful in that every bomb fell within fifty yards of the designated aiming points, although no one managed a direct hit. As before, several army officers were taken up for trips, but once again the detachment was cut short by a signal ordering them back to base. Unlike the last time that they had been recalled from Ranchi, however, this time there was a reason. Sadly the detachment came back minus one crew; Sgts Jim Hewat and Charlie Romans had both been killed on the 6th when their aircraft, EZ843, hit a tree while low-flying over Bihar.

Back at Digri the rest of the squadron had been continuing with training flying and on October 6th the CO of No 168 Wg, Gp Capt J B Black DFC, had used one of No 45 Sqn's aircraft to make his first Vengeance solo flight. Two days later the squadron was ordered to prepare to move forward to Assam for operations, this time as a unit, not just a detachment. Most of the aircraft flew back from Ranchi on the 10th and, since the CO was away on leave, 'Steve' Stevenson assumed command. The following day the Acting CO led seven Vengeances to Kumbhirgram followed by a Dakota-load of groundcrew; command of the hive of activity represented by the bulk of the squadron still at Digri fell to

Pilot	Nav or WOp/AG
Sqn Ldr A Traill	Plt Off D E French
A Flight	
Fg Off G W Hartnell RAAF	Fg Off R M Barclay RAAF
Fg Off A N Huon RAAF	Fg Off C E Birkbeck RAAF
Plt Off H C Jewell	Sgt F G Terry
Plt Off L Halley RAAF	Fg Off E J Hallett RAAF
Plt Off A R Lebans RCAF	Fg Off J R Vernon RAAF
WO W M Osborne DFM	F/Sgt A R Field
F/Sgt J Hadley	Sgt A Gebbie
F/Sgt J M Levey RAAF	Sgt H Garfath
F/Sgt S O'Connor	Sgt M Macrae
B Flight	
Flt Lt J H Stevenson RCAF	Sgt S Siddle
Fg Off R P Curtis RAAF	Fg Off J L Brinkley RAAF
Fg Off H M P Neil RAAF	Plt Off F F Brown RAAF
Plt Off A J Lamb	Plt Off R D Hilditch RAAF
Plt Off C G Hockney	WO T A Lord RAAF
F/Sgt J Marshall	F/Sgt J Paterson
F/Sgt C S Matthews RNZAF	Fg Off G F Williams RAAF
F/Sgt W F Tolar	Sgt J Fenwick
Sgt J Banham	Sgt R Sumner

Fig 10.2. No 45 Sqn crew state as at mid-October 1943.

Fg Off Max Neil. Flt Lt Smith (MO) hurried back from a course which he had been attending at AHQ and Capt Kennington was detached from Wing HQ to become the squadron's permanent AILO. Old Vengeances were being flown out and traded-in for new ones which were then ferried up to join the squadron in Assam and a succession of daily Dakotas was loaded with kit and people and despatched to Kumbhirgram. The last of these, on the 15th, had to be shared with No 110 Sqn who were also moving up. The main rail party departed late on the 16th on which date Sqn Ldr Traill resumed command. Excluding officers and WOs, at the time of its move forward the squadron numbered 232 NCOs and airmen plus eight IAF ORs and forty-five Enrolled Followers. The constitution of the air echelon when the squadron deployed to Kumbhirgram is shown at Figure 10.2.

Kumbhirgram had been built in the middle of a tea plantation and construction work was still under way when the squadron arrived. Graham Williams provides the following description:

> They folded the tops of two hills into the valley in between and laid a strip of 2,000 yards of concrete, 60 yards wide with 200 yards of gravel overrun at each end plus more gravel on either side of the runway. This was all done by about 5,000 coolies and 60 elephants; there was practically no mechanical equipment. There were concrete taxiways alongside which were big earth blast pens. Right on the verge of completion, over came the Jap bombers and overnight almost all the coolies and elephants fled the scene.

The squadron's first mission was flown on October 16th when Flt Lt Stevenson led six aircraft to bomb a stores dump and HQ at Kalemyo. The following day the CO and Fg Off French arrived at Kumbhirgram. Poor weather caused a strike against Mawlaik planned for the 17th to be cancelled but it was successfully flown by six aircraft on the 18th. Later that day the CO flew up to Imphal to confer with OC No 170 Wg, Gp Capt Broughall (an old friend of the

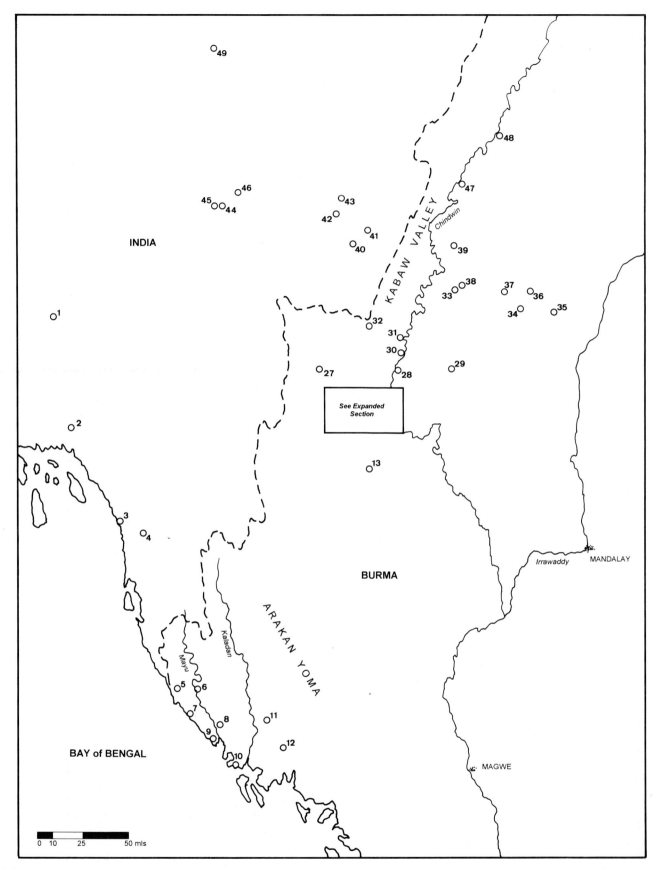

Map 10.1. *Burma - the Arakan and the Kabaw Valley; Vengeance ops 1943.*

1	Agartala	9	Donbaik	38	Kaungkasi	33	Letpangwe	22	Myohla	24	Pyinthazeik	16	Thuklai
10	Akyab	2	Feni	47	Kawya	5	Maungdaw	14	Ngapa	49	Nowgong	45	Silchar West	27	Tiddim
7	Alethangyaw	18	Fort White	32	Kokku	31	Mawku	49	Nowgong	45	Silchar West	42	Tulihal
36	Auktang	25	Hpaungzeik	13	Kontha	30	Mawlaik	40	Palel	21	Stockade 2	41	Wangjing
6	Buthidaung	43	Imphal	46	Kumbhirgram	12	Minbya	29	Palusawa	20	Stockade 3	15	Webula
3	Chittagong	23	Kalemyo	34	Kyaukchaw	17	MS52	37	Pinlebu	8	Thaungdara	35	Wuntho
4	Dohazari	26	Kalewa	39	Le-U	11	Myohaung	48	Pinma	19	Theizang	28	Yazagyo

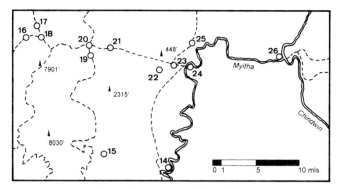

Expanded section of Map 10.1.

squadron from its time in Burma) and to liaise with No 155 Sqn, whose Mohawks were to operate in the pathfinding and target-marking role.

The rail party arrived on the 20th after a relatively smooth journey, despite the inevitable succession of offloads and reloads due to changes in rail gauge, some of these exercises having been undertaken in the dark. The CO led a six aircraft attack on Myohla that day. Thereafter flying took place daily with formation practice being laid on whenever ops were not scheduled. The CO led an attack on Kalewa on October 22nd and Flt Lt Stevenson led another against Pyinthazeik on the 24th; each involved six aircraft. Two more missions were flown on the 25th; in the morning the CO led six aircraft, accompanied by six more from No 110 Sqn, to attack a pinpoint near Stockade No 2 and later in the day Fg Off Hartnell led another six to a target near Ngapa. Both of these attacks were supported by Mohawks as had been those flown on the 20th and 24th. The following day Tony Traill flew up to Imphal with No 110 Sqn's Acting CO, Flt Lt Topley, to discuss with Gp Capt Broughall some problems which had occurred during the first of the missions flown on the 25th. It transpired that both squadrons had bombed very accurately but while No 45 Sqn had hit the markers put down by the Mohawks, No 110 Sqn had aimed at smoke coming from an intense infantry engagement which had involved hand-to-hand fighting. After some discussion it was decided to discontinue the use of the Mohawks.

During a six-aircraft attack on Webula on October 26th, Max Levey, flying with 'Tubby' Garfath in AN656, found that his outer wing guns would not fire. This was duly

recorded in the Consolidated Sortie Report (CSR) submitted that evening by Fg Off Arnold. Alongside the entry noting this failure, an anonymous hand has later pencilled on the file copy of the report the terse comment, "Browning guns fire much better if they are loaded." Further strikes were mounted on the 28th, 29th and 31st (twice) against Theizang, Kokku and Stockade No 3. Apart from the attack on Kokku, in which nine aircraft took part, all of these raids were flown by formations of six; the strike against Theizang had to be aborted as the target was obscured by cloud. Over the entire month, according to No 168 Wg's records, No 45 Sqn flew seventy-five successful sorties and No 110 Sqn contributed a further fifty-nine. Rivalry between the two units, particularly among the groundcrew, was keen, although a modicum of collaboration had to be maintained if for no other reason than that they were obliged to share the same messing facilities. Normally the squadrons would have expected to be entirely self-contained but this was not yet feasible at Kumbhirgram.

There was one other significant event in October. To mark the twenty-fifth anniversary of the formation of the RAF, on 1st April 1943 HM King George VI declared that Standards were to be introduced for RAF squadrons. It was subsequently announced that the basic qualification for such an award was to be the completion of twenty-five years of service, although provision was also made to permit the King to award a Standard to mark his recognition of particularly significant operational actions. Squadron Standards were to take the form of a ceremonial flag, or banner, and were to be presented and consecrated at a suitably formal occasion after the war. Only thirty squadrons qualified for the immediate award of a Standard[5]. They represented the hard core of the RAF. It was their efforts in the 1920s, especially those of the units which had served abroad, which had ensured the RAF's survival as an independent force. No 45 Sqn was one of this select band and on 11th October 1943, the day the unit began its move forward from Digri, it learned that the King had approved the award of its Standard. It was a proud moment

The squadron moved to its forward operational airfield at Kumbhirgram in October 1943. The site was still under construction by an army of coolies. This is one of about sixty elephants which were used to do the heavy work - until the JAAF intervened whereupon a large proportion of the labour force decamped. (G J Hancox)

Plt Off Arthur Huon with EZ841/OB.A shortly after the squadron's arrival at Kumbhirgram in October 1943. The outer yellow ring to the roundel was another variation on the ACSEA theme. The tones in this photograph suggest that the code letters may have been applied in red. (A N Huon)

With a Vengeance under camouflage netting in the background, three of the squadron's aircrew display a nonchalant attitude towards a couple of 500 pounders at Kumbhirgram. From the left: Plt Off Hedley Jewell, Fg Off Al Lebans RCAF and Plt Off Bob Barclay RAAF. After flying with the unit for over two years Hedley Jewell was to be killed on 27th January 1944 on the squadron's final mission with Vengeances. (L Wilde)

LAC's 'Bunny' Warren (in topee) and Frank Whitlock, two of the squadron's medics, find a way to keep cool. The picture was taken at Digri in May 1943. (F Whitlock)

but there was a war to fight and celebration would have to wait.

November continued the pattern established during the previous month. Raids, mostly in sixes and led by either the CO or one of the two flight commanders, were flown almost daily. The targets attacked during the first ten days of the month were at Yazagyo, Le-U, Kawya, Stockade No 2 and Pinma and a pontoon bridge at Hpaungzeik. All of these strikes were successful but an incident on 5th November had dampened the squadron's spirits. While it was being refilled from a fuel dump the pump motor of a petrol bowser backfired and the vehicle burst into flames. Although he had been badly burned by the initial flash, AC1 T F Bamkin drove his blazing bowser away from the conflagration in an attempt to minimise the damage. Despite his efforts the bowser, the fuel dump and a nearby hut which had served as the squadron's armoury were all destroyed, although most of the armoury's contents was saved. 'Doc' Smith did his best for him, calling in a specialist burns team, and one of his orderlies, LAC Frank Whitlock, nursed Bamkin for the next three days. It was to no avail, however, and he died on the 8th. He was buried with full military honours at Silchar the following day.

There was reason to believe that a Japanese air attack was imminent and on November 9th a practice survival scramble was staged, all of the squadron's serviceable Vengeances being airborne within nine minutes of the alarm being given. At 0908hrs on the 11th the anticipated raid took place, but most of the squadron's Vengeances had been able to get away. The Japanese raid, by eighteen bombers with an escort of six fighters, was very successful. The airfield was bombed; three British servicemen and twenty Indian civilians were killed and a total of twenty-seven others were wounded. Some bombs fell in No 45 Sqn's dispersal area but fortunately the squadron sustained no casualties and the only damage inflicted was to one unserviceable aircraft which was hit by bomb splinters.

A second, somewhat bizarre, incident on the same day was to make November 11th one of the more memorable dates in the squadron's entire history. At about 1620hrs and from a height of about 1,500 above the ground, in the course of an air test being flown in F/Sgt Matthews' EZ865, the radio technician in the back seat baled out of the perfectly serviceable aeroplane!

The following account is based on Sgt Jock McCandlish's perception of what had happened as recounted to the author in 1992. The reason that he was in the aeroplane was to diagnose a prevalent fault which was occurring with the IFF boxes at the time. Stray voltages were being induced in the circuitry of the self-destruction devices and, since these were triggered by acceleration switches, it was surmised that this might be due to the high g loadings associated with dive recoveries. The aim of the trip was for Jock to monitor the kit during a dive and pull-out, to see if and when a voltage was registered. The briefing had required just one simulated operational dive and an immediate recovery to base, but Matthews had elected to indulge in a little, unannounced, impromptu 'general handling' on the way home. McCandlish had flown before but he was hardly an experienced aviator and from his point of view, in a relatively unfamiliar airborne environment and with his head 'under the dashboard', these unexpected gyrations could just as well have been symptoms of loss of control. Thereafter the sequence of events took only seconds. From Jock's point of view the exchange went something like: "Bale out!"; "Eh?!"; *"Bale out!!"*, this last being accompanied by a graphic 'abandon ship' gesture with the pilot's thumb! In view of the evident urgency Jock 'hit the silk.' (*Under the circumstances I think I might have done the same! - CGJ*)

'Tua' Matthews concurs with Jock's appreciation but stresses the part played by communications problems[6].

This may be AN626 but the late style of markings suggests that it is more likely to be AN656/OB.H in which Sqn Ldr Traill and Fg Off French lost their lives when it crashed on 27th January 1944. (C E Birkbeck)

Following Sgt McCandlish's test on the IFF I did some weaving through the mountains, more or less in 'no man's land' - a sea of jungle everywhere at about 4-6,000'. I enquired of Jock's health in Kiwi parlance, "Do you feel *theek-hai Hindi*, Mac?" He mumbled something in a broad Scottish brogue to which I responded, "Do you feel OK, Mac?" More mumbles. I gave him a 'thumbs up' and asked again, "OK Mac?!" ⸱ in my *best* Kiwi accent. This is where he understood me to say, "Bale out"! After he had gone I flew low over the jungle and threw out my emergency rations, but he never got them. After this, with darkness coming on, I flew back to base to land downwind (intentionally) amongst a display of vari-coloured lights.

It would seem that this had been a classic case of what George Bernard Shaw might have described as, 'two crewmen separated by a common language'. Jock was picked up by a group of villagers who offered him their hospitality and, as he has recalled, "Suitably refreshed, I noticed that many of the women had babies and were carrying them at their bare breasts, so I did what any self-respecting politician would have done and went around patting the babies' heads." Evidently none the worse for his experience, Jock found his own way back to the squadron two days later.

Operations were resumed on the 12th with two attacks by a total of eleven aircraft against Ngapa. November 13th was a very busy day with both squadrons carrying out three strikes each; No 110 Sqn, incidentally, had received a new CO on the 10th, Sqn Ldr L F Penny DFC, who bore the Flying Camel stamp of approval. Sqn Ldr Traill led the squadron's morning raid which was against Webula. In the afternoon Fg Off Bill Hartnell took six Vengeances to Stockade No 2, followed fifteen minutes later by Flt Lt Stevenson with another four, this second formation being made up to seven by the addition of three more aircraft from

No 110 Sqn. All three attacks were successful but EZ898 failed to return from the last mission. After pulling out from the dive its engine was seen to be coughing and emitting smoke. F/Sgts Bill Tolar, in EZ851, and 'Tua' Matthews, in EZ865, attempted to formate on the stricken aircraft but they were waved away by the pilot. The gunner was seen to be preparing to bale out and shortly afterwards the aircraft dived into the ground and exploded. Only one parachute was seen and it appeared that Sgt Siddle had escaped; Flt Lt Stevenson was posted missing.

There was little time for mourning, however, as November 14th was to be another eventful day. An air raid warning, which turned out to have been a false alarm, disrupted servicing by causing all the Vengeances to scramble. On recovery from this event an hour or so later, Sgt J Banham landed EZ851 with its wheels up and it was two hours before the runway was cleared. Later in the day the CO led four aircraft to attack a point on the track between Stockades 2 and 3. Thirty-two operational sorties had been flown in three days, plus the survival scramble, and the requirement that all aircraft had to be kept in an instantly flyable state between 0700hrs and 1700hrs every day meant that maintenance was a nightmare. By dusk on the 14th the squadron had only six aircraft fit for operations.

Six was enough, however, for the sortie led by Fg Off Hartnell on November 15th. The target had originally been No 3 Stockade but in the middle of the briefing it was changed to Fort White which had been taken by the Japanese during the previous night. As it happened the target was obscured by cloud and the formation was obliged to attack the secondary, the pontoon bridge at Hpaungzeik. Plt Off Cyril Hockney, who had taken over 'Steve' Stevenson's B Flight, led his first attack on the 17th, six aircraft against Fort White, although one had to return to base early with a technical problem.

Two features of domestic life were significant at this

EZ986/OB.V was Sqn Ldr Traill's regular aircraft, although it was also flown on occasion by Bill Hartnell. Faintly visible on the original print is a Saint emblem painted on the side of the fuselage between the cockpit and the engine cowling. By the time the squadron retired its Vengeances this one had flown thirty-four operational sorties. (No 45 Sqn Archives)

period. The tension caused by the recent air raids, real and otherwise, had caused much of the native labour force to decamp and there was a distinct shortage of dhobi-wallahs! On the other hand, a number of local tea planters had decided to 'do their bit' and were offering to put up parties of airmen for forty-eight hour breaks. Not everyone was able to take advantage of this, of course, but it was much appreciated by those who were that lucky.

Snakes were a constant hazard at Kumbhirgram; Graham Williams recalls waking up one night to find one in his bed and desperately trying to throw it out from under the mosquito net. His antics provided much amusement for his colleagues when it became apparent that he was actually trying to throw out his arm which had 'gone to sleep'! On another occasion some of the aircrew caught and killed a sixteen foot long python which they put under the CO's cot with just its head sticking out. "Tony came home tired from an op, thought it was alive and started shooting it up with his pistol - he was very red-faced when we all emerged from hiding, laughing like hyenas".

By this time the Indian Air Force's Vengeance squadrons were just completing their work up and were shortly to become operational. On November 19th two of the squadron's most experienced crews, Fg Offs 'Rusty' Curtis and John Brinkley and WO 'Gerry' Osborne with F/Sgt Alf Field, were posted to Charra to join them. All were veterans of the desert campaign, Osborne having been with the

A group of aircrew trying to think of things to do with a sixteen-foot python - "I know! Let's put it under the Boss's bed. What a merry jape!" (G F Williams)

squadron since Syria. The MO, Flt Lt Smith, also left during November, being posted away on the 26th.

Six aircraft bombed Yazagyo on the 19th and another six attempted an attack on Thuklai on the 20th but found the target obscured. On the 21st separate messing arrangements were finally established for the two squadrons, an arrangement much preferred by all concerned. On the same day the squadron learned that Flt Lt John Stevenson was alive and well, having just made contact with an Army outpost near Tiddim after walking for three days. Two days later he rejoined the squadron at Kumbhirgram. It appears that, when given the order to bale out, Sgt Siddle had rotated his seat, stood up and prepared to go over the side, as had been observed by the other crews. Evidently unable to bring himself to jump, however, Siddle had then resumed his seat. Stevenson had continued to control the aeroplane for as long as he could but it was losing height rapidly and he was eventually obliged to abandon the aircraft. Syd Siddle was posted 'missing presumed killed'; he was the first operational casualty, and only the third fatality, sustained by the squadron since it had started flying Vengeances a year before. While 'Steve' Stevenson was recuperating, Plt Off Hockney retained command of B Flight. Several of his contemporaries have observed, incidentally, that the new Acting OC B Flight was not the tallest man on the squadron and it was said that one could always pick out Hock's aeroplane as a group of Vengeances taxied out as his would be the one without a pilot....

Apart from another survival scramble on November 29th (another false alarm), operations continued for the remainder of the month on a fairly routine basis, culminating on the 29th in the squadron's first attempt at a twelve-aircraft strike. The objective was near Fort White but adverse weather over the target caused this, and an earlier raid on the 25th, to be abandoned. Although neither of these attacks had been successful, they were significant in that they were the first occasions on which the squadron had been armed with 500 pounders with 4½ inch-long rods fitted to their noses. The bombs in use were still of the old GP series and, since their destructive power was considerably reduced if the bombs detonated after they had embedded themselves in the ground, the extended fuses were intended to ensure that the weapons exploded before that to maximise the blast and shrapnel effects. Furthermore, to maintain the pressure on the enemy, most bomb loads carried since November 5th had been salted with a selection of delayed-action fuses set at anything from one to twelve hours.

During the first fortnight of December seven attacks were mounted against targets in the vicinity of Fort White, concentrating on Milestone (MS) 52, about two miles to the north. The only break in this pattern occurred on the 5th when the squadron carried out a particularly successful strike on a Japanese camp alongside the road between Kaungkasi and Letpangwe, the twelve Vengeances being escorted by eight Hurricanes. The dive was carried out from 10,500' down to 2,500' at an average of 80° and 280 mph. Once the twenty-four 500 pounders (half of them with delayed-action fuses) had been released the Hurricanes peeled off to strafe the area while the bombers expended their ammunition attacking river traffic on the Nam Makwin as far as Auktaung on the Chindwin. There was a notable incident three days later, on the 8th, when F/Sgt Marshall became aware that AN711 had developed a fuel leak in the course of a routine air test that he was carrying out. He immediately returned to Kumbhirgram and landed but as he shut down the engine it backfired and the aircraft was rapidly enveloped in flames. Johnny Marshall and his passenger escaped, a trifle singed, but the aircraft was completely burned out, only bits of the tail unit remaining.

The objective of flying larger formations, which had been the aim for some time, began to be realised during December and more than half of the seventeen missions launched that month were flown by ten or more aircraft with the numbers sometimes being doubled by the squadron's missions being co-ordinated with those being undertaken by No 110 Sqn so that up to two dozen Vengeances would be hitting the same target. By the middle of the month the effects of a Vengeance strike had been further enhanced by an increase in the standard bomb load and the aircraft frequently began to carry a 250 lb bomb under each wing in addition to the pair of 500 pounders in the bomb bay; No 45 Sqn dropped its first 250 pounders on December 12th.

IV Corps called for two to three days' maximum effort on the Imphal front on the 11th and the squadron responded by putting up two raids of twelve aircraft on the 12th, one of ten and another of eleven on the 13th and two of six on the 14th. After launching fifty-seven sorties in just three days serviceability had taken a knock, but the groundcrew quickly recovered the situation; two six-aircraft missions were flown on the 14th and on the 18th Plt Off Hockney was able to lead eleven aircraft in a successful strike against Pyinthazeik. The squadron stood by for the next few days but the next mission was not called for until the 22nd when the CO led nine aircraft, plus three from No 110 Sqn, in a strike on Kalemyo.

No 110 Sqn had lost an aeroplane (EZ904) on December 17th when a hung up wing bomb fell off and detonated as the aircraft touched down. Sgt John Scanes, who had joined the Flying Camels only the previous day, recollects that thereafter it became a common practice to attach a generous length of string to each wing bomb so that in flight it could seen streaming out behind the trailing edge of the wing, the idea being to let the pilot know at least that he had a problem should any further hang ups occur.

The brief slack period had been useful to the squadron, since it had allowed the concert party to complete its preparations for its revue, *Just Nuts*, which was staged in front of a sell-out house in the Station Cinema in the evening

AN711/OB.Q with a 250 pounder under each wing, which suggests that the picture was taken very shortly before 8th December on which date this aeroplane was destroyed by fire. (AN Huon)

of the 22nd. Directed by Cpl M D Hull, produced by F/Sgt E Harrison and aided and abetted by the Adj, Herbie Wilson, who had greased many wheels 'behind the scenes', the performance was attended by Gp Capt Black, OC No 168 Wg and Station Commander, plus a variety of local RAF luminaries and guests from many adjacent units. It was a great success and a quite remarkable achievement for a squadron working under operational conditions.

Just Nuts got Christmas 1943 off to an excellent start. There was no operational tasking on the December 23rd, although Fg Off Hartnell led another nine aircraft raid, to which No 110 Sqn again added a further three, on the 24th. No targets were issued on Christmas Day and work ceased at lunchtime. The traditional airmen's dinner was served in the evening with all the officers, from the Group Captain on down, doing the honours; the only significant variation from 1942's menu was that some messes had goose instead of turkey. Towards the end of the meal Sqn Ldr Traill addressed the squadron, conveying his thanks for their efforts and his hopes for the future; he was received with overwhelming applause which reflected not only sympathy with what he had said but also marked the high esteem in which the airmen held him. The celebrations continued with 'open-house' parties in all the messes.

Ernie Henman, by then a flight sergeant and Treasurer of the Sergeants' Mess, recalls that the run-up to Christmas at Kumbhirgram had been full of incident. It appears that the NCOs had planned ahead and had decided to supplement their rations. WO Honeychurch managed to arrange 'a spares run' to Calcutta in an aircraft of a Communications Flight, the crew's co-operation being secured by the promise of a suitable proportion of the consignment of liquid freight which it was planned to collect. He returned, without the vital spares he had claimed to need but with a substantial quantity of booze and two live pigs. The pigs had travelled lying on their sides in individual crates, with their feet projecting through the bars and trussed on the outside. When the livestock was unpacked it was discovered that the lower part of one of the unfortunate animal's front legs had been severed by the lashings. Since Christmas was still a month away the MO was approached to see whether he could arrange a peg-leg. The MO demurred at this suggestion and insisted that the luckless animal be slaughtered. For appropriate recompense, however, (which made further

PROGRAMME : : :

COMPERE : : : ERNIE KIFF

1. Over T'You—ER!	(Overture)	... Swing Trio.
2. Tune In to Forty-Five	...	... Introducing the Cast.
3. Lew Barker	... ...	... Yodel-ay-ee!
4. Andy and Baron	(Anderton & Boscoe)	Two of Our Nuts.
5. "All in Vain" ... SKETCH ... Husband		JIMMY HENDRY
	Doctor	HARRY WHITAKER.
6. Geoffrey Dee	... ...	... Tells us about Sam Small.
7. "Apaches Let Loose" GYMNASTIQUES		RON PALEY AND
		JACK PARTINGTON.
8. 'Art' Smith	... ...	... Clarinet Solo.
9. "Force of Habit" .. SKETCH ... Wife: GEOFFREY DEE		
		Husband: GINGE GITTINS.
		Abdul: JIMMY HENDRY.
10. Male Voice Choir (Directed by Bill Breeze)		

Bert Geddes.   Bill Murray   JACK WALTERS.
Harry Reed   Lew Barker   VIC BROOKE.
Bert Blamires.   Geoffrey Dee   BILL DAVIS.
Dan Neale   Eric Kitching   RAY WARREN.
Harry Whitaker.

INTERVAL.

DURING WHICH THE CURTAIN WILL BE LOWERED FOR
FIFTEEN MINUTES TO DENOTE THE PASSING
OF A QUARTER OF AN HOUR

11. Swing and Jive with Forty-Five	...	Swing Trio.
	Piano	ROY TAYLOR.
	Violin & Clarinet	'ART' SMITH.
	Drummer	STEVE BURTON.
12. Food Review (The Western Brothers at Kumbhirgram)		
		ERIC HARRISON.
		RAY WARREN.
13. Yankee Doodle Dandy	...	ERNIE KIFF AND
		JIMMY HENDRY.
14. Willing Anyway	...	... ANDY AND BARON.
15. Raymond Warren	...	... Will Sing for us.
16. "How Time Flies" ... SKETCH ... Wife		WILLIE RAY.
	Husband	HARRY WHITAKER.
	Newsboy	BILL MURRAY.
17. Geoffrey Dee	...	... Tells us more about Sam Small.
18. "The only Way" ... SKETCH ... Barman		JIMMY HENDRY.
	Customer	MICHAEL HULL.
	Drunk	ANDY.
	Manager	GINGE GITTINS.
19. Roy Taylor	... ...	... Piano Solo.
20. "What the Eye Doesn't See" SKETCH		ANDY
		JIMMY HENDRY.
	Girls:	GEOFFREY DEE
		GEORGE STANLEY.
FINALE.		ENTIRE CAST.

GOD SAVE THE KING.

FORTY-FIVE SQUADRON.

(BY KIND PERMISSION OF
THE OFFICER COMMAN-
DING, SQUADRON LEADER
A. TRAILL.)

— PRESENT —

"JUST NUTS"

DIRECTED BY MICHAEL D. HULL.
PRODUCED BY ERIC HARRISON.

December 22nd, 24th, 26th.

AT

7-30 P. M.

AT THE :—

STATION CINEMA.

The programme for Just Nuts. Not reproduced here is the last page which carried four more credits: Production - Eric Harrison; Stage Direction and Lighting - Michael Hull; Scenery and Curtains - Bill Sheridan and Costumes and Make up - Constance Morley.

inroads into the Mess' liquor stock) arrangements were made to store the butchered joints in a brine bath in the sick bay. Christmas Dinner in the Sergeants' Mess was going to be a novel combination of pork and bacon! A sty was constructed for the surviving animal to grub about in but just before its number came up the pig disappeared; whether it had been liberated by a proto-animal rights activist or had made its own bid for freedom was never resolved. After a fruitless search the NCO aircrew, armed with pistols, were despatched into the surrounding jungle on a search and destroy mission with orders to recover the pig, 'dead or alive'. After a suitable display of firepower the pig gave itself up without a struggle and was led back in triumph. The sergeants dined that Christmas Day off spotless white linen - freshly laundered sick bay sheets, diverted by a co-operative, but thirsty, medical orderly. With all the calls made on the Mess' liquor stocks one can only hope that the illicit Calcutta run had secured adequate supplies.

On Boxing Day the grim business of the war was resumed, the CO leading twelve aircraft in an attack on a Japanese camp at Kontha, one aircraft ('Hock' Hockney and Tommy Lord in AN731) returning with a .50 calibre bullet hole in its starboard flap. It is interesting to note that, despite the modification to prevent the back-seater hitting his own tail, in the course of this same mission Fg Off Sandifer, flying with F/Sgt Carter in AN821, had a runaway gun and the aircraft's fin was damaged. That evening a repeat performance of *Just Nuts* was staged and the cast was entertained in the Officers' Mess. On December 28th 'Hock' Hockney led six Vengeances to Kontha in the morning and in the afternoon Fg Off Bill Hartnell took six more to attack a troop concentration at Palusawa. Both raids were successful, although one crew was obliged to abort the first mission. The last strike of 1943 was flown on 30th December; it was not quite as successful as it could have been. The twelve aircraft were led by the CO and post-strike photographs revealed that the majority of bombs had overshot. The following day Sqn Ldr Traill assembled all the aircrew and firmly reminded them that it was essential for each individual pilot to identify the aiming point positively, and not aim at the leader's, or anybody else's, strike, which is what had happened on the 30th, leading to the creeping overshoot. Fortunately no friendly troops had been in the immediate vicinity on this occasion but the CO stressed that, apart from wasting bombs, the consequences of this practice could be tragic when the bomb-line was close to friendly forces, as it so often was.

1944 opened quietly. Flt Lt Stevenson rejoined the squadron but he had not really recovered from the effects of having to abandon his aircraft and Cyril Hockney continued to lead B Flight. In the meantime Bill Hartnell was finally given his due and promoted to flight lieutenant, seven months after having taking over A Flight! His was not the only promotion that was slow to come through in 1943. F/Sgt 'Mac' McDade's commission had been in the mill since mid-1942 and he had been filling the post of Gunnery Leader since the start of the Vengeance era, yet, although it carried backdated seniority, he was not actually made a pilot officer until 11th November 1943.

No ops were ordered for the next few days and the groundcrews took the opportunity to bring the aircraft up to

A No 45 Sqn Vengeance taxies out at Kumbhirgram. (V A Emson)

scratch while a few AA co-operation sorties were flown. A twelve-aircraft mission was ordered on January 6th, but on that day the monsoon arrived and with 10/10ths cloud from 2,000 feet and heavy rain the operation had to be cancelled. The weather was bad for several days and caused the next planned mission, on the 9th, to be cancelled as well. Twelve aircraft launched on the 10th, the first mission to actually get off the ground in 1944, but cloud over the target prevented the attack from being delivered.

After several more false starts the squadron flew a twelve-aircraft raid against Kyaukchaw on the 17th; this was part of a major effort by both tactical and strategic air forces against a single target in the space of a few hours. The mission planned for the following day was to have involved twenty-four aircraft, twelve from each of the Vengeance squadrons at Kumbhirgram, carrying out a strike against Wuntho. No 45 Sqn took off as briefed, formed up and spent the next forty minutes orbiting while awaiting the arrival of their colleagues. No 110 Sqn had actually taken off only fifteen minutes after the leaders but the extensive cloud prevented the two formations from ever seeing each other to effect a join-up. Eventually the two units proceeded independently. One of No 45 Sqn's aircraft turned back early with a technical problem. The remainder pressed on as far as the Chindwin but the shortage of fuel caused by the prolonged wait for their colleagues had reduced their ability to deal with the weather conditions which had deteriorated to 10/10ths cloud all the way up to 14,000 feet and they too abandoned the mission, one aircraft (F/Sgt Tolar and Sgt Fenwick in AN819) being obliged to divert to Palel. Max

Relaxing at the squadron's dispersal between sorties are, from the left, Fg Off Bill Hartnell, RAAF, Plt Off Hedley Jewell, Fg Off Jim Vernon RAAF and Fg Off Bob Barclay RAAF. (L Wilde)

EZ8?? of No 45 Sqn over the jungle-covered mountains of the border between India and Burma. The Vengeance's wing was set at low angle of incidence which tended to give the aircraft a tail down 'sit' in flight. (V A Emson)

Neil flew one of the squadron's fitters over to Palel on the 20th, returning with Sgt Fenwick, and two days later Bill Tolar brought AN819 back to Kumbhirgram under its own steam.

Twelve aircraft made a successful attack against Mawku on the 19th, this mission being provided with an escort of Hurricanes from No 123 Sqn at Feni. No 123 Sqn escorted the next two raids as well. The first of these, against Pinlebu on the 21st, involved eleven aircraft led by the CO, and was notable for the first employment of 250 lb incendiary bombs. Pinlebu was attacked again on the 22nd by a large joint No 45/110 Sqn formation led by Flt Lt Hartnell, to which the squadron contributed ten aircraft.

News came through on January 24th that the Flying Camels were to be re-equipped with Mosquitos in the near future. This caused great excitement throughout the squadron and the following day the CO and Fg Off French flew to Agartala to try to pin down some more precise details. Poor weather caused the cancellation of a mission planned for the 26th but a message was received that day ordering the CO to fly to Delhi to discuss the forthcoming move and the subsequent re-equipment and conversion programmes. Tony Traill and Doug French took off at 0730hrs on the 27th and headed west; the first planned stop was to be made at Alipore. At 1020hrs the squadron was informed by telephone that their aircraft had been seen to crash in flames near Masimpur; both crew-members had been killed.

In North Africa in 1941, especially during May and November, the casualty rate had been so high that the majority of the squadron's personnel, that is to say its

Regrettably the original of this photograph has been torn but it is still of considerable interest as it shows another of the squadron's Vengeances wearing full codes - AN716 OB.J at Kumbhirgram. (No 45 Sqn archives)

groundcrew, had become rather hardened to the losses. Their very frequency provided a kind of insulation and, more often than not, the crews that went missing had not survived for long enough for their faces to have become too familiar. It had been very different with the Vengeances; apart from one crew killed in a flying accident while on detachment back in June, the only loss had been Syd Siddle and in that case grief had quickly been displaced by relief when it was learned that Flt Lt Stevenson had unexpectedly survived. The squadron was no longer accustomed to tragedy. The CO had been with the squadron ever since it had been re-established in October 1942 and Doug French had been flying with him since their days together on Blenheims in the UK. They were both familiar, popular and much respected figures. Their loss was very deeply felt. But the day was not yet over and there was to be more bad news.

Flt Lt Hartnell assumed temporary command of the squadron and the war went on. The mission cancelled on the 26th had been rescheduled for the 27th and at 1403hrs Fg Off Hockney led ten aircraft off to attack a Japanese position at Mawlaik. It was to be the squadron's last operational mission with Vengeances; it was not a great success. The weather was awful and three aircraft turned back early, one of them jettisoning its bombs. The remaining seven pressed on and, despite the weather, delivered an attack, but the results were inevitably, to quote the ORB, "mixed". The weather prevented the group from reforming and they made their way back in ones and twos. Three got back to Kumbhirgram, although their arrivals were spread over 25 minutes. Three others landed at Palel. Sgt Carter and Fg Off Sandifer elected to stay there for the night but, after refuelling, F/Sgt 'Tiffin' O'Connor and Plt Off Sam Potts took off again and managed to get back to base. Fg Offs McLellan and Nankervis attempted to follow them but were unable to locate Kumbhirgram and were obliged to put down at Silchar West. The seventh aircraft failed to return; Plt Offs Jewell and Bottrill were missing in EZ879.

On January 28th Wally McLellan and Jack Nankervis flew to Delhi to keep the appointment made for the CO. On the same day Sqn Ldr Traill and Fg Off French were buried at Silchar. As a final mark of respect, one minute's silence was observed during that day's pay parade. Throughout the day news was sought of the missing crew; no one could, or would, believe that Hedley Jewell and Keith Bottrill were dead too. That evening it was learned that their aircraft had come down at Nowgong. Fg Off Bottrill had bailed out and was safe. It appeared that the pilot may also have made an attempt to use his parachute but had left it too late and his body was found alongside the wreckage; he was buried at Nowgong on the 31st.

Amid the prevailing gloom, on January 29th, a new CO arrived from Palel to take command. The very experienced Sqn Ldr D S Edwards came from No 189 Wg where he had been Squadron Leader Flying. On the very day that he assumed command the squadron was struck yet another blow. It was informed that, of its current aircrew strength, only those pilots and navigators with previous twin-engined experience were to be retained; all of the others, including all the WOp/AGs, were to be posted - this would leave only two crews (Huon/Birkbeck and Hockney/Paterson) intact! Since the squadron was about to convert to Mosquitos the cold logic of this directive was indisputable. But squadrons are about *esprit de corps* and 'family' as well as logic, or at least No 45 Sqn was. After the stress of the last few days this edict seemed to be the last straw. On the 30th the nominal roles required by Air Command South East Asia (ACSEA) were despatched but Sqn Ldr Edwards followed up with an appeal for the retention of some of the single-engined pilots, on the grounds of their operational experience, and of some of those gunners who had completed a short navigation course.

A mission was ordered for the 31st but later cancelled due to the weather and at dusk the squadron was taken off ops. That morning Fg Offs Arthur Huon and Ced Birkbeck had already left for Yelahanka with a seven-man advance party. On February 2nd ten Vengeances of No 45 Sqn took off together from Kumbhirgram for the last time and Flt Lt Hartnell led them west to Alipore. The following day they flew on to Cawnpore where the aircraft were handed over to No 322 MU. Later that day F/Sgts Marshall and Sumner reached Cawnpore with the eleventh aircraft and Wally McLellan and Jack Nankervis, who were still at Delhi, delivered the squadron's last Vengeance to No 322 MU on the 4th. No 84 Sqn arrived at Kumbhirgram that day to take the place of the Flying Camels and maintain the strength of the Vengeance striking force. The crews who flew the last twelve Vengeances are listed at Figure 10.3. Those whose names are annotated with an asterisk were to leave No 45 Sqn at Cawnpore and report to Base HQ Calcutta for disposal (apart from the three Canadians, Lebans, Halley and Lenney, who were to remain with No 322 MU as test pilots). In the case of the backseaters who were earmarked for disposal, all apart from Dick Sumner were WOp/AGs.

Other aircrew on strength at the close of the Vengeance era were: the new CO, Sqn Ldr D S Edwards; Flt Lt J H Stevenson RCAF; Fg Offs A N Huon RAAF, A J Lamb*, C E Birkbeck RAAF, E L Sandifer, K Bottrill, L A Mears and C G Hockney; Plt Offs R D Hilditch RAAF and B T McDade*; F/Sgts J Newport* and S O'Connor and Sgts Parcell*, M Macrae, A A McKie, F G Terry*, D Carter*, Bliss*, V A Emson*, W Etchells, Hume*, J Scanes* and J Banham*. All of those marked with an asterisk were earmarked for disposal by Base HQ Calcutta and posting to other units. Flt Lt Stevenson, still in hospital when the squadron left Assam, was eventually posted to Poona. Capt E E Kennington ceased his long attachment to No 45 Sqn and rejoined the staff of No 168 Wg. To complete the picture, the squadron's commissioned support staff at the end of the Vengeance era were: Flt Lt H H Wilson RAAF (Adj), Flt Lt R C Witt (MO), Fg Off A E Joyce (Eng)[7], Plt Off R B Serjeant (Int) and Plt Off K D Hoare (Sigs)[7], several of whom were quite recent arrivals.

Aircraft	Pilot	Nav or WOp/AG
EZ847	Flt Lt G W Hartnell RAAF	Fg Off R M Barclay* RAAF
AN818	Fg Off L Halley* RCAF	Fg Off E J Hallett RAAF
EZ841	Fg Off A R Lebans* RCAF	Fg Off J R Vernon RAAF
AN679	Fg Off H M P Neil RAAF	Plt Off F F Brown* RAAF
EZ848	Fg Off W S McLellan RAAF	Fg Off J Nankervis* RAAF
AN731	Plt Off C G Hockney	F/Sgt J Paterson
EZ865	Plt Off S Lenney* RCAF	Plt Off S Potts
EZ896	WO J M Levey RAAF	Sgt H Garfath*
AN772	F/Sgt C S Matthews* RNZAF	Fg Off G F Williams* RAAF
AN821	F/Sgt W F Tolar	Sgt J Fenwick*
AN779	F/Sgt J Hadley*	Sgt A Gebbie*
AN837	F/Sgt J Marshall*	F/Sgt R Sumner*

Fig 10.3. The crews who ferried No 45 Sqn's last twelve Vengeances to Cawnpore for disposal in February 1944.

A statistical summary of the squadron's record on Vengeances is presented on a monthly basis at Annex F but in total it amounted to its having launched 549 operational sorties in the course of which it had dropped some 464,500 lbs of bombs. The most battle-scarred of the squadron's aircraft was EZ865 which had first gone into action with the original detachment to Chittagong in June 1943 and was still going strong right up to the end. By the time that the squadron was taken off ops EZ865 had flown forty sorties; EZ848, another veteran of Chittagong had flown thirty-seven and EZ986, thirty-four.

The Vengeance experience had been a very satisfactory one. The work-up had proceeded at a measured pace. Ample training opportunities had been provided and the bugs had largely been worked out of the new aircraft before operations began in earnest. Most importantly, the authorities had resisted the temptation of throwing the crews into combat just as soon as they could fly their aeroplanes. As a result the transition from training to operations had been untroubled and, under Sqn Ldr Traill's exemplary leadership, the squadron had quickly become highly proficient and had exploited the dive-bomber's inherent accuracy to the full. Often tasked against targets which were alarmingly close to friendly troops, the squadron had established a reputation that was second to none. Officialdom, however, still seemed remarkably reluctant to show any overt signs of acknowledging the squadron's efforts by the award of decorations[8].

From a parochial point of view it had been a hard but a happy period. Living conditions at Kumbhirgram were not easy, especially in the wet season, but shared adversity had only served to strengthen the ties that had been forged in the Desert. The personnel complement of the squadron from the spring of 1943 onwards had remained relatively constant, which had permitted strong personal bonds to develop and the mutual respect, even affection, which grew up between aircrew and groundcrew contributed much to the squadron's exemplary performance. This was equally true of the other Vengeance units, but ample evidence of No 45 Sqn's exceptionally high morale and distinctive unit identity is provided by the initiative and energy they displayed in staging a concert party in the middle of an intensive operational tour. In view of all this it was singularly unfortunate that, just as the squadron's success with the Vengeance had been crowned by the news of its forthcoming re-equipment with

Mosquitos, the atmosphere had to be clouded by the events of January 27th.

In an operational context, the dive-bomber era in the RAF lasted for only a year and, since it was selected to be the first of the light bomber units to be withdrawn to convert to the Mosquito, No 45 Sqn flew the type operationally for less than five months. Only four RAF squadrons flew · the Vengeance in combat and No 45 Sqn left the force just before the intensity of dive-bomber operations rose to a crescendo in the defence of Imphal and Kohima. The dive-bomber was rendered obsolete rather abruptly in mid-1944 by the advent of the Republic Thunderbolt fighter-bomber, these aircraft being able to carry out precision attacks with a 50% saving in aircrew manning while their self-defence capability largely obviated the need for escorts. The RAF had been a late convert to the tactically limited dive-bomber concept and had embraced the role only as a stop-gap shortly before it was rendered redundant by more capable aeroplanes with greater tactical flexibility. Nevertheless, while it may have been something of an anachronism, the dive-bomber was available when it was needed and the Vengeance force made a considerable contribution to preventing the Japanese from continuing their advance into India. Having been one of the RAF's few operational dive-bomber units, the Flying Camels had been members of a very exclusive club and had helped to write a unique chapter in the annals of the service.

Notes:

1. Apart from selected personnel who were seconded to fly with the RAF in other theatres, it was Union policy that South African aircrew should operate only on the continent of Africa (although this was extended in 1943 to include Italy),ideally in SAAF units. The South African pilots who had begun to join RAF fighter and light bomber units in North Africa from mid-1941 were essentially there to gain operational experience before being transferred to new SAAF squadrons as they were formed. When the RAF suddenly redeployed a number of Hurricane and Blenheim squadrons from the Middle East to India in early 1942 those SAAF pilots serving with them were given the option of remaining with their units or of staying in North Africa. Pretoria later recalled most of the men who had gone east to serve in the ever-expanding SAAF in the Mediterranean Theatre. Freddie DeMarillac was back in Egypt by June 1942, leaving Gus Alder as the last of No 45 Sqn's South Africans. After transferring to No 113 Sqn, he remained in India flying ops until as late June 1943 when, by then a major, he too was transferred to the Mediterranean where he was killed in action over Italy on 13th July 1944. He was lost in Marauder FB487 of No 12 Sqn SAAF, one of a dozen carrying out an attack on a road junction at Monteviarchi, while flying as co-pilot to the CO, Lt Col M Barnby DFC. Over the target an adjacent aeroplane in the formation (FB437) exploded and the blast tore the nose section off the leader's aircraft. There were no survivors from either crew.

2. He was to survive the war as Sqn Ldr John Stuart Muller-Rowland DSO DFC* only to be killed on 15th February 1950 during a test flight in the third DH 108 (VW120).

3. The category of navigator was introduced by AMO A.746/42 of 23rd July 1942. The navigator's flying badge and its displacing of the 'Flying O' was authorised by AMO A.1019/42 of 17th September 1942. The wearing of all flying badges is governed by QR 206 which still (1994) refers specifically to the wearing of RFC-style wings; paras 3 and 4 are particularly relevant in this context.

4. Paul Ulrik Axel Keel had been working in Tanganikya in 1940 when he had suddenly found himself cut off from home by the German occupation of Denmark. Unable to rejoin his wife and young son, he had found his way to England where he joined the RAF and eventually finished up back in Africa with the Flying Camels. Sadly, after returning to the UK, he was to be killed in a crash at No 16 OTU on 4th June 1944; he never was reunited with his family.

5. The select group of thirty squadrons which qualified for the immediate award of a Standard in April 1943 were Nos 1, 2, 3, 4, 5, 6, 7, 8, 11, 12, 14, 20, 24, 25, 27, 28, 30, 31, 39, 45, 47, 55, 56, 60, 70, 84, 100, 207, 208 and 216 Sqns.

6. 'Tua' was not, as was widely believed by some of Matthews' contemporaries, a Maori nickname; it was a childhood diminutive of Stuart which stuck for the rest of his life.

7. During the latter part of the Vengeance era the manning situation is none too clear so far as Technical Officers was concerned. It seems certain, however, that the squadron had had to do without a Signals Officer for the three months between the departure of Plt Off Boon at the end of October 1943 and the arrival of Plt Off Hoare late in the following January. On the nuts and bolts side, Fg Off Edwards, who had looked after mechanical engineering since the squadron's renaissance, was posted out shortly before the move to Kumbhirgram. The squadron's records contain just one reference to another Tech(e) officer, Plt Off W R Hughes, which appears in September 1943; it is assumed that he was Edwards replacement and that he served as the squadron's chief 'spanner' until the arrival of Fg Off Joyce just before the withdrawal to Yelahanka.

8. If this was observed upon at all at the time it is probably true to say that the squadron's airmen were far more concerned about this lack of formal recognition than were the aircrew. It is certainly the case that many of the surviving groundcrew from the campaigns in the Desert, Burma and India who have contributed to the compilation of this narrative feel quite strongly that 'their' aircrew were poorly served in this respect.

A pair of No 45 Sqn's Vengeances at dusk, probably at Ranchi. (L Wilde)

Chapter 11. The Flying Camel victorious - Mosquitos.

In early 1944 the Mosquito was still a relatively new type in India. A few had been issued to No 27 Sqn at Agartala in April 1943 but this unit was fully operational on Beaufighters and the object of the exercise had been to assess the response of the Mosquitos' unorthodox form of construction to tropical heat and humidity rather than to fly ops with them. At the end of the year the squadron received a few Mk VI fighter-bombers and one of these flew the first planned offensive Mosquito sortie of the Far Eastern war on Christmas Day 1943. A few more isolated sorties were flown with individual Mosquitos in early 1944 but the squadron much preferred its sturdy Beaufighters and these remained its primary equipment. In March, before any substantial experience of operating the Mosquito in the attack role had been accumulated, No 27 Sqn and its Beaus withdrew to Cholavaram to become a maritime strike unit.

Some of No 27 Sqn's original batch of Mosquitos had been transferred to No 681 Sqn at Dum Dum with whom they were pressed into service in the photographic reconnaissance role. With the arrival of some Mk IXs in the summer of 1943 Dum Dum held sufficient Mosquitos to warrant the establishment of a dedicated unit and on September 29th they were concentrated in the newly formed No 684 Sqn. Thus by the time that No 45 Sqn began to re-equip in the following February there was already some in-theatre Mosquito operating experience, albeit largely in a high-level role. There was also a pool of technical expertise but it was at Calcutta, some 800 miles from Bangalore where the squadron was about to embark on its conversion programme. The Flying Camels were going to have to find out a lot of things for themselves.

Meanwhile the squadron's advance party was on its way south. At one of the watering holes en route the airmen in this group had run into difficulties finding somewhere to eat. There had been little enough for them to spend their money on at Kumbhirgram so they were not short of cash but there appeared to be only one half decent place and this was reserved for officers. It was there or nowhere, however, so Sgt Henderson and Cpls Taylor, Moore and Bergmans slipped makeshift officers' rings onto their epaulettes and brazened it out. Luckily for them, they were not rumbled. The advance party eventually reached Yelahanka on February 4th, just as the bulk of the squadron was setting off from Silchar by train under the command of Sqn Ldr Edwards with WO Hammond riding shotgun. This party numbered one hundred and sixty-five men in all (six officers; 102 British WOs, NCOs and airmen; twenty-one IORs and thirty-six enrolled followers - see Annex N), which was considerably

fewer than it had had in the previous October; it is believed that a substantial number of the experienced Vengeance groundcrew were transferred to various units within No 168 Wg and remained at Kumbhirgram.

The aircrew from Cawnpore arrived at Yelahanka on the 11th and, after spending over a week in transit, the main party reached Bangalore station late on the 12th, one day behind schedule. They spent the night on board the train before offloading the kit and moving it to the airfield the following morning. Flt Lt Herbie Wilson, Fg Off Keith Bottrill and the ten men of the rear party arrived on the 19th.

With the posting of so many of the Vengeance men and conversion to twins the squadron was in need of a lot of new personnel and entitled to a wing commander CO. The new CO was to be Wg Cdr H C Stumm DFC RAAF who had previously commanded No 11 Sqn until it had begun to convert from Blenheims to Hurricanes in August 1943. He arrived at Yelahanka from HQ 3rd TAF on February 10th. When he had learned that he was to command the first Mosquito fighter-bomber squadron in India and that it was going to need an infusion of new crews Wg Cdr Stumm had trawled around the Command to round up a few of his old cronies. This effort had included a visit to Lalmai to see whether any of No 11 Sqn's ex-Blenheim pilots, who were now flying Hurricanes, would like to join him. Before the end of February a total of thirty-three replacement aircrew had arrived at Yelahanka, largely restoring the squadron's strength. Among those recruited personally by Harley Stumm were two navs, Fg Off H J Cargill RAAF, who was to fly with 'the Boss', and Fg Off A McFadzean and four

Fg Off P N Ewing RAAF (left) and F/Sgt R L C C Pinkerton, joined the Flying Camels right at the start of the Mosquito era. This photograph of them perched on top of HR402 OB.C was taken about a month after they had had a narrow escape from an encounter with some Ki 43s on 9th November 1944. Flying temporarily with WO Gordon Ashworth, Bob Pinkerton failed to return from a dawn strike against Heho on 17th February 1945. (A N Huon)

Australian pilots, Fg Off P N Ewing, Fg Off J O Cartledge, Fg Off E L J Anderson DFM and WO H M Nicholls, several of whom were ex-No 11 Sqn. With the appointment of a wing commander as CO, the rank of the flight commanders was restored to squadron leader with Sqn Ldr Don Edwards becoming OC B Flight. Flt Lt Bill Hartnell continued to run A Flight until March 2nd when Sqn Ldr N L Bourke RAAF was posted-in from No 22 Ferry Control to take over.

No 45 Sqn was to spend its time at Yelahanka being taught all about the Mosquito by No 1672 Conversion Unit (CU) which was commanded by Wg Cdr W T Perfect. This unit, initially known as the Light Bomber Conversion Flight, had itself only been formed on 1st February. It had a notional establishment of three dual-controlled Mosquito IIIs, eight Blenheim Vs (Bisleys) and an Anson but on the date that it formed the CU actually had none of these. During the first two weeks of February an Anson and several Blenheim Vs were received (Harley Stumm had delivered one of the latter when he had arrived by air to take up his appointment). By the 15th the CU was in a position to begin the formal conversion programme and flying started two days later.

The aircrew were organised into four sections, two of pilots and two of navs, alternating between flying and classroom work. In general the mornings were taken up with

When No 45 re-equipped with Mosquitos it was decreed that its redundant WOp/AGs were all to be posted away. Three of the RAAF gunners who had been with the squadron since 1941 were determined not to 'leave home', however, and chose to ignore this edict, although, in order to avoid any unseemly confrontations, they did eventually deign to be regraded as navigators. Seen here in late 1944, Jack Nankervis was one of these stalwarts. (A N Huon)

lectures while twin-engined refresher flying took place in the afternoon. There was more to it than just learning to fly all over again, however, and all the aircrew were required to spend some hours at Hebbal Range for instruction in small arms; the pilots each had to complete five hours of cockpit drills and everyone had to learn about the Mosquito's construction and systems. Where the CU lacked the appropriate specialist staff, the squadron's own people were pressed into service as instructors. Thus, for instance, three of the armourers were co-opted to teach the mysteries of the 20mm Hispano cannon while Fg Off Adam McFadzean organised 'dry swims' for the navigators.

As with the conversion to Vengeances, the squadron once again found itself with the wrong sort of rear crews (not strictly 'rear' any longer, as a Mosquito nav sat alongside, rather than behind, his pilot). This time the problem was that many of the navigators, or at least the Vengeance veterans, were Nav(B)s; what was wanted now was Nav(W)s. A programme of signals lectures and Morse practice was laid on to permit the misfits to be recategorised. This activity was supervised by the Signals Officer, Plt Off Hoare, who had been transferred in from No 84 Sqn just as the squadron was leaving Kumbhirgram. By the end of the month he had made good progress and had all the navs ditting and dahing at fourteen words a minute.

In the context of rear crews, Sqn Ldr Edward's appeal on behalf of the 'disqualified' aircrew had fallen on deaf ears and it had been confirmed that there was no question of any of the old WOp/AGs or pilots who lacked twin-engined flying experience being retained. The only hope of any of the former ever returning to the squadron was for them to remuster as navigators. Three of the squadron's stalwart RAAF gunners, Jack Nankervis, Bob Barclay and Graham Williams, had absolutely no intention of being separated from the Flying Camels, however, and although they did eventually go as far as applying for retraining as navigators, that was the only concession they were prepared to make and they simply joined in the conversion programme and began to learn all about Mosquitos.

Before the squadron learned that it was to leave Kumbhirgram, a Farewell Dinner had been planned for some thirty airmen who were approaching the end of their overseas tours. Many of them had spent their whole time with No 45 Sqn and were thus part of the now dwindling band of Desert Warriors. The menu cards, bearing the customary formal acknowledgement of the CO's permission to hold the function, had already been printed and carried the date on which the dinner had originally been scheduled to take place - 6th February 1944. In the event, the bulk of the squadron had spent that night in transit in Calcutta en route to Bangalore. The squadron was not going to be cheated out of its party however, and the dinner was rescheduled for February 24th. It thus served as a welcome to new arrivals and a 'house-warming' for Yelahanka in addition to being a farewell to those who were about to depart. Since they bore the name of Tony Traill, the use of the original menu cards lent a certain poignancy to the proceedings but an insert was also provided which carried the revised menu, Harley Stumm's formal stamp of approval and an apposite quotation from Tennyson, "The old order changeth and giveth place to the new". As always, the application of a little social lubrication served to reassert the unit's corporate identity in its new role and surroundings.

The squadron took delivery of LR250, its first Mosquito VI, on 29th February and it naturally attracted a great deal of interest, not least from the groundcrew who were curious about its unique wooden construction. This aircraft had been issued before repainting and it was flown in the standard European colours of Dark Green and Ocean Grey with Medium Sea Grey undersides and a 'fighter style' Sky band around the rear fuselage. Later aircraft were repainted before (or perhaps shortly after) delivery to the squadron and for the next twelve months the Mosquitos wore the Dark Green and Dark Earth with Medium Sea Grey undersides specified for use in ACSEA. A single aircraft-in-squadron letter was applied but the OB codes were not worn in the early days of the Mosquito era.

The availability of an airframe permitted No 1672 CU's technical NCOs to start the maintenance training programme for the squadron's tradesmen but the demands of the flying programme meant that there was little time for classroom work; 'on the job training' soon took the place of formal lectures. More Mk VIs were delivered in early March and, in the absence of a trainer, conversion flights in the fighter-bombers began with first two trips being flown on the 6th. On March 13th Wg Cdr Stumm became the first of the squadron's pilots to solo on the new aeroplane, followed later in the day by Sqn Ldr Edwards. Night flying began that same evening.

Conversion training now gathered considerable momentum, the peak activity for the month being achieved on March 26th when the squadron flew twenty trips in the Mosquitos, ten with Blenheim Vs and three on the Ansons. By the end of the month all of the pilots had gone solo, taking an average of four hours each. By that time the squadron had eight aircraft on charge. It would have been nine if Fg Off Pete Ewing had not chalked up the squadron's first bent Mosquito on the 20th when he swung on landing from his first solo trip and collapsed the under-carriage of HP868.

Doug Goodrich (then a flight sergeant) recalls some-one, possibly Hockney, doing a wheels-up, in one of the Blenheims at about this time. The cockpit roof had already been jettisoned and after touch down the gun position under the nose collapsed and acted as a scoop; the aero-plane careered across the airfield with a spectacular fountain of earth spewing out of the cockpit. Another com-ment on the Blenheim V has been offered by Arthur Huon who recalls that, while it had substantially the same power as the Mk IV, it was sig-nificantly heavier. "Their per-

FORTY – FIVE
SQUADRON

(BY KIND PERMISSION OF THE
OFFICER COMMANDING
S/L A. TRAILL)

Farewell Dinner

&

Social Evening

" FROM THOSE WHO SERVE
TO THOSE WHO SERVED."
ANON.

SUNDAY, FEBRUARY 6, 1944

SOMEWHERE IN INDIA

The cover of the menu for the Farewell Dinner which had been planned for February 6th, when the squadron was still at Kumbhirgram. In the event the Flying Camels were in transit through Calcutta on that date and the function was eventually held at Yelahanka on February 23rd using the original menus, still bearing Sqn Ldr Traill's name.

On 29th February 1944 LR250/Y became the first Mosquito to be taken on charge by No 45 Sqn. As can be seen from this photograph, which was taken at Amarda Road in May, the aeroplane wore ACSEA-style national markings but was still painted in a European green/grey camouflage scheme complete with a 'day fighter' band around its rear fuselage. (Howard Levy)

267

This photograph of HP941/B taking off from Amarda Road was taken on the same day and from the same position as the previous picture of LR250. A comparison clearly shows the difference in camouflage tones, indicating that HP941 has been repainted in the green/brown scheme then in vogue in India. HP941 flew with the squadron until October 16th when it dived into the ground following a strafing attack on Kadozeik, killing Sqn Ldr Norman Bourke RAAF and Fg Off Keith Dumas RAAF. (Howard Levy)

formance was such that, against the instruction in the Pilots' Handling Notes that the undercart was not to be lowered at speeds in excess of, I think, 175 mph, I felt constrained to write, 'How the hell do you get the speed up to 175 mph?'"

There was some reshuffling of crews during March and April. Four were posted to No 27 Sqn and two more went to No 177 Sqn, all to fly Beaufighters. Since No 27 Sqn were then disposing of the last of their handful of Mosquitos, some of their experienced men transferred to No 45 Sqn, among them Flt Lt A Torrence with Plt Off E D Rainbow and Flt Lt C S Emeny RNZAF with WO J J Yanota RCAF. Flt Lt Freddie Snell was another of the ex-No 27 Sqn pilots; he was not to remain with the Flying Camels for long on this occasion but he returned two years later, by then a wing commander, and for a few weeks was OC No 45 Sqn.

Another aeroplane was damaged on April 3rd when Flt Lt Hartnell collapsed the undercarriage of HP872 after a swing had developed during its take off run. Navigation training flights, on all three types of aircraft in use, began on the 12th and trips began to take up to four hours, rather than the one hour which had sufficed for circuit work. By mid-April most of the pilots had completed the required five hours of solo flying on the Mosquito and, with basic type-conversion and initial familiarisation nearing completion, thoughts turned to the first phase of the tactical training programme. Preparations began for another move. On the 28th, a fifty-six man advance party under Flt Lt J E Turnbull departed by rail to begin a month's detachment to the AFTU at Amarda Road.

The air party, eleven Mosquitos, with additional personnel and kit carried by two Ansons and a pair of Liberators, headed north to Amarda Road on May 1st; three

more Mosquitos followed on the 2nd. The transfer was not entirely uneventful. HJ811 had been suffering from a string of technical problems and, despite the Maintenance Flight's having worked on it overnight, it appears that these had not been cured. As Arthur Huon recollects:

Two hours after take off the starboard engine caught fire and at the same time we lost all of the electrically operated functions. The cockpit of the Mosquito was a pretty tight fit for the pilot and navigator at the best of times. On this occasion we were also carrying a rigger, AC Geoff Dee, as a passenger and I realised that there was no hope of Ced Birkbeck and Dee being able to get at their observer-type parachutes, let alone clip them onto their harnesses. Somehow we had to land. This we were able to do on a half-completed strip about 20 miles behind us (*at Rajahmundry - CGJ*). We got down and the undercart collapsed in the process. We left the aircraft in some haste and managed to distance ourselves by about 30 yards before the starboard inner tank exploded. During our short run on the recently laid concrete strip we had marred its pristine surface with a stream of molten metal and burnt rubber.

Fortunately all three men escaped injury but there was a casualty that day when Fg Off Sandifer managed to burn his foot quite seriously with acid from a fire extinguisher while in transit in another Mosquito.

The object of the squadron's detachment to Amarda Road was to attend No 9 Fighter Refresher Course which was to be run by the AFTU in conjunction with No 22 Armament Practice Camp (APC). These courses were routinely attended by fighter squadrons prior to a tour of operational flying, but No 9 Course was something of an innovation; it was the first to be laid on for what were essentially bomber crews who were now getting their hands on an aeroplane with a significant air-to-air combat potential and who needed some coaching on the best way to use it. Naturally enough, the flying experience of most of the AFTU's staff pilots was largely confined to single-engined fighters so, to give them a feel for the Mosquito, Wg Cdr Stumm and Sqn Ldr Edwards gave several of the instructors familiarisation flights before the course began. To bring the bomber boys up to scratch a pre-course programme of lectures on sighting theory was laid on and these were attended by both pilots and navs. In addition, the pilots indulged in some dual exercises in Harvards to polish up their range estimation and to practise flying curves of pursuit. While the aircrew were thus occupied the armourers were kept busy harmonising the guns.

The formal course began on May 8th. Flying took place daily, in the early morning and late afternoon, with lectures sandwiched in between. Trips were about an hour in duration and each pilot was planned to fly three dual sorties in the Harvard and one in the Mosquito (the squadron had a dual-controlled Mk III (LR521) on charge by this time) before flying up to fifteen hours of solo sorties, involving dummy attacks on USAAF B-25s, live gunnery against a drogue and culminating in a squadron attack on a formation of Mitchells. On the ground the previous day's camera gun films were analysed and mutual debriefs with the bomber crews were laid on. The lecture programme was wide-ranging and, apart from technical lectures on gun sights and guns, many actual combat films from Europe and Burma were shown and analysed. Other topics covered by the syllabus included escape and evasion, aviation medicine, survival techniques, photography and general squadron organisation. It was all very pertinent and very up to date, reflecting the most recent lessons learned by squadrons currently in combat over Burma. The groundcrew did their bit too and there was never any shortage of aeroplanes.

Ever since the squadron had been re-established in India it had tended to fall foul of the irksome regulations on the issue of beer rations. Presumably to prevent supplies being depleted by transients, Canteen Stores Depots, always reluctant to dispense beer, would not issue any at all until a unit had been in residence for a month - 'you can't have any unless you have had some before'. The rationale could be appreciated, but it was a bit hard on a mobile unit like the Flying Camels which tended to move every two or three months. In effect it meant that the squadron spent far too much of its time being 'not entitled'. The legendary ability of the camel to go for long periods without a drink definitely did not extend to the flying variety and this bureaucratic regulation rankled. It was not easy to outflank the system, but it did happen at Amarda Road. The B-25s with which the squadron was working came from the USAAF's 12th Bombardment Group which had recently redeployed from Italy and was completing its in-theatre work-up. F/Sgt Doug Goodrich recalls the American NCOs being most put out when they found that they could not buy a beer in the RAF Sergeants' Mess because they had not been on strength for four weeks! A B-25 was promptly despatched to the USAAF's home base to collect sufficient supplies to lubricate both the Americans and the thirsty men of No 45 Sqn.

The fighter course proceeded apace but it was marred by tragedy. During the afternoon of May 13th Harley Stumm was airborne in HP939 with Flt Lt McKerracher (a staff nav from No 22 APC and a veteran of No 113 Sqn during the initial Burma campaign) carrying out dummy attacks on a B-25. After breaking away from its last pass the Mosquito crashed. Both of the crew were killed. The DeHavilland representative considered that the undercarriage doors had opened under the application of g, become detached and removed the tailplane. This did not convince everybody. 'Tiffin' O'Connor (then a flight sergeant but eventually to retire as Sqn Ldr S O'Connor DFC AFC DFM) was airborne at the time and watched the whole incident. He recalls: "After a quarter attack the aircraft was rolled over and a pull through commenced; as the nose fell the port wing came off and the aircraft spun in. I have always been convinced that it was our first loss due to airframe failure." At the time, however, there was no reason to suspect the integrity of the Mosquito's construction and the official explanation was accepted.

Sqn Ldr Edwards temporarily resumed command of the squadron until Wg Cdr R J Walker arrived to take over on the 25th. In the meantime there had been another accident; LR250, the squadron's very first Mosquito, had been written off on the 16th. Graham Williams had been on board and he describes the incident as follows:

Seen here as a flight lieutenant, Wg Cdr Robert James Walker took command of No 45 Sqn on 25th May 1944, shortly after Wg Cdr Stumm had been killed in a flying accident. (No 45 Sqn archives)

It was as hot as blazes - Joe (*Cartledge*) thought that he had flying speed on take off but we sank back a bit on selecting wheels up and hit the ground, partially buckling one undercarriage. We spent two and a half hours flying around trying to get both wheels down but ended up - one up, one down and no hydraulics to get the flaps down. They told us to land on the grass on the right hand side to avoid blocking the main bitumen runway. We touched down at 150 mph and the right wingtip hit the ground at about 125 mph. The undercarriage came through the cockpit under my feet; the propeller straddled the cockpit and went 100 feet into the air; the pilot's seat and its armour plate broke loose and pinned me in my seat. We spun round and round across the main runway and smashed into the trees. Wow! I don't know where I found the strength but I pushed Joe and his seat off and we both went out the top escape hatch. The aircraft was completely smashed and a write off. Only bruises for both of us.

This happened at 0850hrs. At 1720hrs Cartledge and Williams were airborne again in LR306 on a fighter tactics exercise!

The course ended on May 27th and the squadron was given a farewell address by one of the RAF's most successful fighter pilots of WW II, Wg Cdr Frank Carey DFC DFM, who was then commanding the AFTU. He was a veteran of the Burma campaign during which he had led No 135 Sqn whose Hurricanes had escorted several of No 45 Sqn's bombing raids; some of those ex-Blenheim men were in his audience that day. He pronounced himself well satisfied with the results, "considering that all the crews had been bomber trained," which, from a fighter pilot, was probably the best that they could have hoped for.

Apart from the activity generated by the occasional rotation of aircraft to and from the detachment at Amarda Road, life had been fairly quiet for the rump of the squadron back at Yelahanka. The only event of any significance was the departure on May 6th of Flt Lt Bill Hartnell and Fg Offs Frank Brown and Bob Hilditch, all of whom, were heading home to Australia. Towards the end of the month preparations began for yet another move, this time to Ranchi, a prospect that

Plt Off Don 'Blink' Blenkhorne, RCAF arrived on the squadron in April 1944. He eventually flew fifty-seven operational Mosquito sorties, more than half of them with F/Sgt Alf Pridmore who became his regular nav in January 1945.
(Mrs Faye Blenkhorne)

was not viewed with much enthusiasm by the older hands who had spent a hot season on the plains to the west of Calcutta before. The squadron's Intelligence Officer, Fg Off Arnold, set off with an advance party on the 16th but, shortly after they left, the squadron's destination was switched to Dalbhumgarh. The squadron was not familiar with this location and on the 19th Fg Offs Hockney and Paterson flew up there to have a look at the camp site and the airfield. The 20th was spent packing and loading the kit onto a train and that evening as many people as possible took the opportunity of sampling the delights of Bangalore for the last time. Bangalore may not have been all that strong on fleshpots, but it certainly had more than Dalbhumgarh! Greatly assisted in their final preparations by Yelahanka's staff and the personnel of the resident No 261 Sqn, the squadron train departed on the 21st for the five-day haul to the north.

The train arrived on the 26th and, as had been feared, Dalbhumgarh's climate proved to be hot and sticky. Wisely, the Adjutant declined to force the pace and postponed unloading until the following day. A shortage of transport complicated the issue but with the loan of half a dozen 3-ton trucks from the Public Works Department the task of unloading and ferrying the stores to the camp began. This chore took all day and by the time everything had been transferred to the airfield everyone was exhausted. On the 28th Wg Cdr Walker flew in to make himself known to the half of his new squadron which he had not previously met. Most of the remaining Mosquitos were ferried across from Amarda Road on the 29th.

Following the intensive period of APC flying most of the aircraft were now due for a Minor Inspection so the groundcrew faced a considerable early workload and the heat soon began to cause difficulties. The problem of acclimatisation was aggravated by the fact that Yelahanka had been at a relatively cool 3,000 feet above sea level while at Dalbhumgarh, which was at only 400 feet, the aircraft were too hot to touch at mid-day. Working hours were set at 0715hrs to 1230hrs and 1600hrs to 1800hrs but, despite this, the squadron's first case of heat exhaustion occurred on June 2nd.

Apart from the climate, initial impressions of Dalbhumgarh had been quite favourable but, as the squadron settled in, the limitations and drawbacks of its new abode soon began to manifest themselves. It was a new station and No 45 Sqn was the first unit to use it. The inadequacy of the drainage system quickly made itself apparent; the soakaways had been constructed in rock and they simply could not cope with the effluent generated by over 300 men. An entirely new system had to be constructed. On first arriving at Dalbhumgarh the discovery of a shower block that actually worked had raised the squadron's spirits but they rapidly subsided again when it was discovered that it was about the only thing that did work! Much of the rest of the water supply system was not connected up and, most significantly, none of the messes had running water. The latrines were inadequate and no native labourers ('sanitary sweepers') were available. None of the fire extinguishers was serviceable. The advertised electricity system did not work, although this was not uncommon in India before 1944, and when it did come on-line on June 24th, albeit somewhat hesitantly, it was actually the first time that the squadron had enjoyed such a luxury for many months. Unfortunately the technical site and the domestic site were provided with different supplies (AC and DC) but some ingenuity on the part of the electricians adapted one of the mobile generators to provide a back-up link to ensure that power was available at most places for most of the time.

The supply system, run by the Royal Indian Army Service Corps (RIASC), was dependent upon a depot some 50 miles away and, not being accustomed to having an RAF unit at Dalbhumgarh, there were problems with obtaining rations. This turned out, briefly, to be a blessing in disguise. Only eight miles away there was a USAAF base at Chakulia and, with characteristic American generosity, they were only too happy to provide three days' rations to tide the squadron over. The American supplies were far superior to the British ones but the squadron's efforts to have this ad hoc arrangement made permanent came to nought and, needless to say, the squadron was once again 'not entitled' to a beer ration. Some relief to the problems of daily existence was expected with the delivery of the first batch of MT on June 5th but on inspection these vehicles proved to be in a very tatty condition and, rather than easing the workload, they increased it. The second consignment of MT arrived on the 19th. Like the first lot, it was in a terrible state and every vehicle had broken down en route. Until then flying had been going on without a fire appliance being in attendance and even when one did arrive there was a total lack of the specified fire retardant (*Saponine, extracted from Panama bark, was added to the water to create a foam which could smother fuel fires - not a lot of people know that - CGJ*). This deficiency was finally made good on 9th July.

By this time the system had finally caught up with the squadron's three maverick WOp/AGs who had, as the ORB notes, "been posted away from the unit on several occasions but had never gone." On June 9th Plt Offs Barclay, Nankervis and Williams began a recategorisation course at No 231 Gp's Navigation School in Calcutta. They could not have timed it better. While the rest of the squadron were trying to cope with Dalbhumgarh's domestic and logistic inadequacies and the sweltering heat (still without a beer ration), the three budding navs were able to live it up at Firpo's while sustaining themselves with copious infusions of Pondicherry gin - "Carew's smooth brews for aircrews".

Despite the many technical and domestic problems, flying started on June 8th, with effort now being concentrated on low-level navigation exercises. On the 14th the starboard engine of HP878 failed and WO Bill Tolar was obliged to make a precautionary landing. Unfortunately the undercarriage failed to lock down and the aircraft finished up on its belly. It was not too badly damaged, however, and looked as if it could be repaired but in the attempt to move it from the runway (with a crane borrowed from the USAAF) it was further damaged and it never flew again.

The maintenance teams now began to run into real difficulties. The routine 'Minors' were turning out to require about ten days each, partly as a result of a shortage of spares and partly because of an unforeseen problem. The groundcrew were discovering significant wood shrinkage which meant that all the control surfaces had to be removed so that their hinges could be adjusted and tightened. Tyres were another cause for concern; supplies were arriving but

From the left: Fg Off Merv 'Nick' Nicholls, Fg Off Frank Harper, Fg Off Pete Ewing and Plt Off Max Levey, all of whom were with the squadron from the start of the Mosquito era. The first three survived the war and won DFCs. Max Levey (who had joined the squadron in April 1943) was killed, along with his navigator, Fg Off Harry Cargill, when their aircraft crashed and burned attempting an emergency asymmetric landing at Yazagyo following an attack on Ye-U on 17th December 1944. This photograph was taken on 11th November 1944. (H M Nicholls)

they were of the wrong type and did not fit. Difficulties were also being experienced with the engine exhausts as there was a lack of spares to replace blown manifold joints. A new design of exhaust system was being introduced but, until adequate supplies were available to refit all of the squadron's aircraft, blown manifolds continued to cause problems, especially as the hot gases often damaged ignition harnesses and engine cowlings. Overall serviceability in June averaged only 33% and the groundcrew had been at full stretch to achieve even this.

To offset the shortage of serviceable Mosquitos a request had been submitted to No 231 Gp (now the squadron's controlling authority) for a pair of Harvards and the first of these, FS945, was delivered on June 13th. Meanwhile the available Mosquitos continued to carry out low-level exercises - and "low-level" meant just that. On June 24th Flt Lt Cliff Emeny and WO Johnny Yanota hit a tree in HP867 and wrote the aircraft off in the subsequent crash landing at Bishnapur.

June 27th was a stand down and No 45 Sqn's football team took to its hastily marked out pitch to play a team from the local copper mine at Ghatsila. They beat them 4:0. As a result of this initial liaison the squadron gained access to the copper mine's sports field every Tuesday. The availability of proper facilities for playing football improved morale somewhat, but what most people had wanted, ever since they had arrived at sweltering Dalbhumgarh, was a beer ration. The local Canteen Stores Depot was adamant, however, and the squadron had to do its statutory four weeks before they would issue any. At the end of June the squadron finally became 'entitled' and the Flying Camel was able to quench its thirst again.

By July the squadron had become adjusted to life at Dalbhumgarh and was making the best of it. Serviceability, however, especially the lack of tyres, was now becoming a cause for major concern; by July 7th eight aircraft were grounded for this reason alone and by the 20th the squadron was reduced to just two effective machines. Wg Cdr Walker made this very clear to HQ 231 Gp in his weekly Training Reports. Another of his complaints was that, while his squadron was established for forty-six aircrew, he actually had sixty-six on strength. He pointed out that No 45 Sqn was not a training unit but a fighter-bomber squadron engaged in working up to operational status. In view of the lack of aircraft availability, this was going to be difficult enough to achieve without Group stacking the deck by giving the squadron surplus crews to train. This provoked a satisfactory reaction and several crews were posted away later in the month.

Some initial bombing training was undertaken in July and the average of the first sorties, flown on the 2nd, was a very respectable twenty yards. Since these were academic pilot exercises, the assistance of a nav was not strictly necessary and this permitted a number of the Nav(B)s to spend a couple of weeks at the Navigation School gaining the required formal wireless endorsement which transformed them into Nav(BW)s. Among those who got away to Calcutta at this stage were Fg Offs Keith Dumas, Jim Vernon, Harry Cargill and Ced Birkbeck and Plt Off 'Pat' Paterson. Their absence meant that there were seats available for any airmen who wished to fly on practice bombing trips and, for instance, Fg Off 'Nick' Nicholls took LAC's Boscoe and Strickland up on

Roland John 'Ron' Wilcock joined the squadron in 1944 as a flight sergeant pilot. He flew sixty operational sorties, surviving the entire period of operations with Mosquitos only to be killed, by then a pilot officer, in a crash on 17th June 1945.
(D E Goodrich)

his two trips on July 2nd; his scores, incidentally, were 12 yds and 17 yds. Strickland evidently enjoyed this sort of thing as he was up again the next day with F/Sgt Goodrich. One aircraft suffered a bird strike on the 5th, which threatened to make it unavailable for at least three weeks while the supply system tried to find a new wingtip. This was reduced to a week by salvaging the necessary bits from Emeny's wrecked aeroplane at Bishnapur.

The squadron began to take advantage of the Masaboni Mine's hospitality and a party of airmen were able to enjoy a swim on the 4th while the footballers beat the home team again, this time by six goals to nil. On the 7th there was some depressing news for those approaching their tour expiry date; all repatriation had been temporarily suspended. Most of those concerned accepted this decision philosophically, however, since the reason given was the demand for shipping which had been created by the invasion of Normandy and everyone was able to accept the validity of this.

Night flying training began during July and on one of the first trips, on the 8th, Fg Offs Pete Ewing and Frank Harper, crashed when HP876 suffered an engine failure during an overshoot at Ondal, the pilot suffering leg injuries.

On July 12th a party from No 684 Sqn, the only other Mosquito unit in India with any substantial experience of long-term operation with the type, arrived at Dalbhumgarh to see whether they could offer any assistance. They were led by their CO, Wg Cdr W B Murray, and accompanied by Messrs Myers and Waterhouse, the representatives of DeHavilland and Rolls-Royce respectively. They were all very helpful, and Mr Myers provided much useful technical advice on problems to look out for in the rainy season, but the squadron's fundamental difficulties were to do with spares. Indian stockpiles of the bits and pieces which went to make up a Mosquito were, as yet, simply insufficient to support the user units. Since they had no access to a black market supply of tyres, there was little that the visitors could do that was of immediate practical value. To be fair to the staff of HQ 231 Gp, they had been doing their best and the search for tyres had been widened to include the Middle East. On July 31st a batch of eight tyres was delivered from No 111 MU at Tura (located in caves in Cairo's Moqattam Hills) - they were the wrong size!

The lack of aeroplanes provided more time for football and several matches were arranged with the miners and with No 28 Sqn, who had arrived on July 6th to share the domestic delights of Dalbhumgarh. The latter included the flooding of the Parachute Store after a storm on the 10th, the failure of the main water pump on the 21st and the always intermittent electricity supply. The enforced low rate of flying made it possible to detach parties of airmen to No 4 Hill Depot and many of the airmen were provided with the opportunity to relax in the comfort and comparative cool of Chakrata. The Sergeant's Mess held a party on the 15th to repay the hospitality and support that they had received from the Masaboni Mine and the Americans at Chakulia and on the 28th the officers did their bit by entertaining representatives of the Indian Copper Corporation.

Barclay, Nankervis and Williams completed their course on July 17th and two days later two of them reported back to the squadron, formal confirmation of their new status as Nav(W)s following on 24th August. Bob Barclay was unable

There were several accidents while the squadron was working up on Mosquitos. This one occurred on 16th August 1944 when Fg Off Pete Ewing and WO Bob 'Pinkie' Pinkerton had a problem with the brakes on HP914/H after landing at Dalbumgarh. What appears to be a 'sharksmouth' marking on the nose is actually a gash in the structure. (No 45 Sqn archives)

to rejoin the squadron until July 26th as he was obliged to spend ten days in hospital in Calcutta recovering from injuries he had sustained when he had been assaulted by some Indians on the 16th. Another of the squadron's navs, Fg Off Ced Birkbeck, was recalled from his wireless course at about this time as he had been earmarked for repatriation to Australia along with one of the pilots, Fg Off Ted Anderson. They left on July 19th and Arthur Huon recalls their departure:

> We had a wild night in the Mess and poured them onto the Bombay Express (from Calcutta) at about midnight. Dalbhumgarh was a little wayside stop on that line - certainly not a scheduled stop for the Express. To make sure that it stopped, the Indian Station Master (in what was possibly the greatest event of his life) stood between the rails swinging a lantern. The Express stopped all right, but not in time to avoid killing the poor man, which dampened the proceedings considerably.

With only two aeroplanes available, and those only kept flying by cannibalising the others and playing musical tyres, relatively little flying was done during July although those aeroplanes which were available were flown whenever possible. Unfortunately Sqn Ldr Edwards hit a kite hawk on the 24th which damaged the port main spar of his aircraft and necessitated a precautionary landing at Kanchrapara, whence he returned to Dalbhumgarh by train - that was another pair of tyres out of action! By now the weather was beginning to break and storms caused several trips to be cancelled, although the associated, and very welcome, drop in temperature allowed a more normal working day to be introduced.

The training programme called for the squadron to move to Ranchi in August, which was going to be difficult without tyres as the aircraft could not take off! On the 7th a truck which had been despatched to Digri to collect some tyres became bogged down in the mud but LAC C G Williams managed to dig it out without assistance and returned in triumph with his precious cargo. These tyres were actually intended for Hudsons but they fitted well enough and were pressed into service. With the handful of aeroplanes which the groundcrew were now able to cobble together, the squadron started to fly low-level cross-countries and dummy attacks in formations of up to four, allowing them to indulge in cross-over turns for the first time. Progress was being made, but slowly. In the week ending August 19th only eight sorties were flown, for a total of just over four hours of airborne time. On one of these trips, an air test on HP914 on the 16th, Pete Ewing experienced intermittent engine cutting and, on landing, the brakes faded, resulting in an uncontrollable swing and the undercarriage collapsed. The aeroplane was somewhat the worse for wear but neither Ewing nor his nav, F/Sgt Bob Pinkerton, was hurt. The shortage of equipment was now beginning to affect the

armourers as well, since the next phase of training would concentrate on bombing and gunnery. There was a lack of bomb trolleys and loading hoists and such pieces of kit as were being delivered were all too often found to be incomplete. There was also a need to reharmonise the guns, but the squadron lacked a suitable mobile crane to raise the aircraft into a flying attitude.

Although the pace of training had picked up a little, there was still ample time available to sustain the weekly swimming expeditions and football matches with the miners. On August 1st Fg Off Sam Potts had organised a Squadron Swimming Gala which was held in the Copper Mines' Baths at Ghatsila, LAC Botterell putting up the best individual performance. The prizes were presented at a parade held on the 18th and, since he happened to be visiting the squadron at the time, Bengal Command's senior Accountant Officer, a group captain, was invited to do the honours. This was not as odd as it might seem as he was actually Jim Lambie, an ex-Flying Camel who, it will be recalled, had been the squadron's tame 'acker basher' at Helwan and Nairobi for much of 1933-36. Further light relief was provided by an ENSA concert party which played to a full house in the station cinema (which had never yet shown a film) on 9th August.

Preparations for the move to Ranchi accelerated in late August and on the 22nd, in the nick of time, the long-awaited tyres arrived, proper Mosquito ones this time. An advance party travelling in a convoy of nineteen vehicle under the command of Fg Off Jack Nankervis, who doubled as the squadron's MT Officer, left by road on the 23rd and reached their destination that afternoon.

Flt Lt McFadzean assumed command of the detachment when it reached Ranchi and he reported to the Station Commander to learn that all was ready for the arrival of the squadron. On having a look at what was available, however, he found that this was hardly the case. The facilities at Ranchi had not improved since the squadron had last been there with its Vengeances a year before. The airmen's accommodation was in a poor enough state of repair but the officers' mess was even worse; one of its billets had a collapsing ceiling and was flooded while its cookhouse lacked a roof! This was plainly unacceptable and alternative civilian accommodation for some of the officers was requisitioned outside the camp. The only working administrative and technical facilities offered were an armoury and a block of five small offices; there was a notable lack of furniture. Since the Station Commander appeared to be unable or unwilling to do anything about the latter problem, the squadron decided to 'borrow' the necessary furniture from Dalbhumgarh and even succeeded in rustling up three Dakotas to assist in this nefarious project. In the meantime ten large tents had been acquired and these were erected to supplement the offices that had been earmarked for the squadron. The move to Ranchi was no great distance but the transfer of the squadron was hampered by heavy rain, which also delayed the departure of the aircraft, the fifteen Mosquitos eventually flying over on the 27th.

The squadron had moved to Ranchi to undergo the final phase of its work-up, a three-week course with the Special Low Attack Instructors' School (SLAIS). With the aeroplanes properly shod at last, the CO was eager to press on and training began on the 29th. The remoteness of some of the accommodation complicated matters and put a strain on the available MT resources but the cooler climate (Ranchi is 2,000 feet higher than Dalbhumgarh) and a significant improvement in messing balanced this and the armourers set to with a will, harmonising machine guns, cannons and sights, and interminably belting ammunition.

After some initial sector recces and low-level navigation exercises, air-to-ground gunnery began on September 4th. It rapidly became apparent that the lessons learned at the AFTU and the experience gained at Dalbhumgarh (despite the serviceability problems) had provided a sound foundation. With the intensive flying that was now possible the squadron began to hone its skills. Twenty sorties were flown on the 4th, during which 7,000 rounds of .303 and 1,298 rounds of 20mm ammunition were loosed off. There were a lot of stoppages, however, which kept the armourers busy, readjusting the guns and realigning magazine covers, although it later became clear that most of the problems were due to a poor batch of ammunition which produced insufficient recoil to keep the guns functioning.

As the Low Attack Course proceeded, the tactical low-level routes devised by Flt Lt McFadzean became more intricate. Every sortie was debriefed by the SLAIS instructors who provided advice and guidance on the best techniques to use when attacking specific types of target, bridges, airfields, moving vehicles, trains and so on. By the 7th, when night flying was added to the programme, the Armament Section had solved most of the initial troubles, despite being eighteen men understrength, and the incidence of stoppages had declined markedly. All concerned, not least the aircrew, were becoming increasingly enthusiastic about

When the squadron's small MT column made its way from Calcutta to Kumbhirgram in September 1944 they found that the road had been considerably improved since late 1943. This is the pontoon bridge at Silchar. (D E Goodrich)

the Mosquito's formidable eight-gun weapons fit.

Having just moved, the squadron ran into the perennial beer ration problem again. It was learned, however, that beer was available at Salbani, if the squadron would come and get it. Fg Off Harry Cargill promptly commandeered a truck and drove the 300 mile round trip to provide the airmen with their due.

Low-level bombing practice started on the 9th and the squadron began experimenting with bending the fins of the bombs in an attempt to cut down 'skip' - shades of October 1941! The CO tried it on the Salbani Range on the 10th, but it did not really work, the ORB recording that "some bombs definitely stuck in the target but others still skip for a considerable distance."[1] Night gunnery and bombing exercises began that evening and, while taking off, LR304 developed a swing which Flt Lt Goodwin was unable to control and its undercarriage eventually collapsed. As it careered across the airfield the aircraft clipped the wingtip of one of No 82 Sqn's Mosquitos which had performed a similar manoeuvre that morning. The following day the squadron lost another crew when Fg Offs J H Reeves RNZAF and L G Prout were killed when HP915 dived into the ground while operating over Random Range.

As the intensive armament training programme proceeded the CO began to turn his thoughts to the squadron's next move which would be to the operational area. On the 13th Fg Off Neil flew the Adj to Calcutta to make the arrangements for the redeployment with Movement Control. Two days later Flt Lt Torrence set off with the advance party, bound for the squadron's old stamping ground at Kumbhirgram. At the same time twelve MT drivers left for Comilla to pick up a batch of new vehicles which they were to drive to the new base. Packing started that day, but the squadron's footballers still found time to play a team from SLAIS. Just for once they let the opposition win, although they allowed them only one goal.

On September 17th the squadron was heartened to learn of the award of DFCs to Flt Lt A McFadzean, Fg Off E L J Anderson DFM RAAF and Fg Off C G Hockney. Recognition at last! In all three cases these awards reflected over two years of operational service, with experience stretching back to the Western Desert and Syria. By the time that the awards were gazetted, however, only Adam McFadzean was still on strength. Each of these men had flown over seventy operational sorties, although only Cyril Hockney, who had left for England on August 5th, had spent his whole time with No 45 Sqn.

Jock Torrence and his team reached Silchar on the 18th whence they were trucked out to Kumbhirgram and welcomed back into No 168 Wg, where the Flying Camels were to displace No 60 Sqn's Hurricanes. The remainder of the Wing, which was now commanded by Gp Capt E A Whiteley DFC, comprised Nos 146 and 261 Sqns, both flying Thunderbolts. Plt Off Max Levey and Fg Off 'Joe' Mears flew the first Mosquito over that day, followed by WO Taylor and Fg Off Nankervis in a Harvard, the latter stopping off at Comilla to make arrangements with No 333 MU for the provision of additional MT. Over the next few days batches of airmen were ferried across from Ranchi in Dakotas and the bulk of the Mosquitos were flown to their new base on September 22nd. That same day Fg Off Cargill and three of the MT drivers turned up at Kumbhirgram with a Jeep and three bowsers, the first of the 'new' vehicles which had been collected from Comilla. They observed that many of the intervening rivers had been bridged since the squadron's previous stint in Assam and that, although there were still several ferry crossings to be made, the road journey from Calcutta was now much easier.

The Ranchi camp site was cleared on the 23rd, to make way for the incoming No 27 Sqn, and the main party began its journey back to Assam with its ninety-three packing cases of kit and stores loaded into thirty trucks which had been loaned by the army. The first stage was a 37 mile road trip to the railway station at Barkakana. Once on board the train the trek was prolonged by the inevitable off-loads and on-loads necessitated by changes in railway gauge and the need to take to a ferry to cross the Brahmaputra. They finally reached the railhead at Silchar, the usual one day behind schedule, at 0200hrs on the 29th. Needless to say it was pouring with rain, but everyone buckled down to unloading and, with the establishment of an MT shuttle, by lunchtime the squadron was settling in to its accommodation. Although the site probably seemed pretty Spartan to those who had not seen it before, the Vengeance veterans found that there had been many domestic improvements since February. The bashas were certainly more substantial and, while there were still plenty of duckboards about, many of them had acquired concrete floors.

LAC James Gillan joined the squadron's large team of armourers a few days after the squadron arrived at Kumbhirgram, on transfer from the resident No 146 Sqn. He recalls that malaria was a real hazard:

> Strict precautions were enforced and Mepacrin tablets were handed out daily at mealtimes. Long trousers and long-sleeved shirts buttoned at the neck were worn from just before dusk. Mosquito nets had to be used and we were always supposed to dress and undress under them. At dawn a squad would come round and pump DDT, or something similar, into the billet until the place was full of smog. Not pleasant, but definitely worthwhile.

The Flying Camels' departure from Ranchi almost brought a premature end to the Kiplingesque tale of 'Joey'. The following account is based on the story as recalled by LAC Ray 'Chico' Lea, a bowser driver with the squadron's MT Section from 1943 to 1945. Shortly after the squadron's 350-odd men had arrived at Dalbhumgarh back in May, an itinerant tailor had set up shop in the hope of securing a monopoly on the potential trade which they represented. To fetch and carry for him he had a boy of perhaps seven years of age; whether he was actually an orphan was uncertain but there were certainly no parents in evidence. Joey, as he came to be known, attached himself to the squadron where he became the informal joint responsibility of a group of airmen led by LAC George Hibbert of the MT Section. Deep down, the airmen knew that they could not look after the boy indefinitely so 'Joey's Fund' was established, with the aim of providing sufficient cash to settle him in a mission school when the time came. Generously supported by sundry contributions and profits generated by that mainstay of airmen's entertainment - 'Housey-Housey' - the contingency fund began to grow but, in the meantime, Joey had effectively become a supernumerary member of the squadron and he

moved with it to Ranchi. Here, as before, he lived in one of the billets and his several minders ensured that he was

A typical basha at Kumbhirgram. (N D Murrell)

Taken at Kumbhirgram in March 1945 this photograph shows a very happy and smartly turned out 'Joey' with a group of his minders. Standing immediately behind Joey, with his hands on his shoulders, is LAC Ray 'Chico' Lea; to his left is LAC Dave Leggatt. (D Leggatt)

LAC Ray 'Chico' Lea, one of Joey's minders, seen here on the left, with his colleague, LAC Taffy Thomas, and their refuelling bowser. (R Lea)

entertained, occupied, fed, washed, clothed and generally cared for - and that he said his prayers before going to sleep! In short, in their rough and ready way, they loved him.

The CO had turned a blind eye to the boy's reappearance at Ranchi, but when the squadron was warned to return to the forward area he ruled that it would be inappropriate to take Joey to Kumbhirgram and directed that alternative arrangements would have to be made. When the time came for the Mosquitos to fly out, however, among the party of groundcrew still at Ranchi to see the aircraft off was Joey. The aircrew arrived to board their aeroplanes and the wing commander, not best pleased to find the boy still there, reasserted that there was no way that he was moving up with the squadron. Joey burst into tears. Johnny Walker hesitated for a moment then picked the lad up and heaved him into the nearest Mosquito. Joey flew into Kumbhirgram perched happily on the knee of one of the navigators.

The squadron had fifteen Mosquitos and two Harvards on its charge when it moved back to the operational area. The established forty-six aircrew were crewed into fixed pairs, although, as always, postings and sickness caused occasional shifts in the crew pattern and the exigencies of daily squadron life meant that everyone had to stay flexible and, when necessary, fly with whomever was available. The nominal crew state at the time that the squadron moved to Kumbhirgram (as always, some individuals were temporarily non-effective for various reasons) is listed at Figure 11.1. In addition to these reasonably stable pairs the squadron had one surplus pilot, Fg Off L E Lancaster RNZAF, and a number of spare navs, Flt Lt L S Andrews, Fg Off H J Cargill RAAF and WO F R Kirk (plus F/Sgt Harrison and Sgt Meredith whose trades are uncertain - they may have been groundcrew). The squadron's ground officers were Flt Lt H H Wilson RAAF (Adj), Flt Lt E A Joyce (Eng), Flt Lt G W

Pilot	Navigator
Wg Cdr R J Walker	Fg Off F J Harper
A Flight	
Sqn Ldr N L Bourke RAAF	Plt Off K R Dumas RAAF
Flt Lt V S H Duclos	Fg Off K Bottrill
Flt Lt A Torrence	Plt Off E D Rainbow
Fg Off W S McLellan RAAF	Fg Off J R Vernon RAAF
Fg Off A N Huon RAAF	Flt Lt A McFadzean DFC
Fg Off R K Garnham RNZAF	Fg Off J Nankervis RAAF
Plt Off P N Ewing RAAF	WO R L C C Pinkerton
Plt Off J M Levey RAAF	Fg Off L A Mears
WO J R Wilson RCAF	F/Sgt W J S Hayward
WO S O'Connor	WO A A McKie
WO W G M Taylor RAAF	F/Sgt K Putman
B Flight	
Sqn Ldr D S Edwards	Fg Off E L Sandifer
Flt Lt G H Proctor	Sgt G W Bargh
Flt Lt C S Emeny RNZAF	Plt Off J J Yanota RCAF
Flt Lt C R Goodwin	Fg Off S Potts
Fg Off H M P Neil RAAF	Fg Off E J Hallett RAAF
Fg Off J O Cartledge RAAF	Fg Off G F Williams RAAF
Plt Off H M Nicholls RAAF	Fg Off R M Barclay RAAF
Plt Off D M Blenkhorne RCAF	Plt Off J Paterson
WO N Abbott	F/Sgt W P Edwards
F/Sgt D E Goodrich	F/Sgt S M D Nessim
F/Sgt R J Wilcock	WO N Maddock

Fig 11.1. No 45 Sqn's crew state in late September 1944.

Balfour (MO), Fg Off L S King (Sigs) and Fg Off J E Arnold (Int) who were supported by WOs Hammonds, Fowler and Henman. The rank and file comprised 271 RAF NCOs and airmen (see Annex N) plus six IORs and fifty-five Enrolled Followers.

Having more or less settled in, the first attempt at an operational Mosquito mission was made on September 27th. Wg Cdr Walker and Sqn Ldr Bourke flew to Imphal where they expected to pick up two army officers and take them on an armed recce. In the event the soldiers failed to put in an appearance and the two aircraft returned to base. The mission was rescheduled for the following day and this time the arrangements worked. Sqn Ldr Norman Bourke in HP941 and Fg Off 'Joe' Cartledge in HP884 collected their passengers as briefed and then took them on a reconnaissance of the Shwebo area, dropping a couple of 500 pounders while they were about it. The sortie was uneventful but the squadron was operational again.

To permit the groundcrew to finish unpacking and setting up shop there was no flying on the 29th or 30th; the squadron had, incidentally, been allocated the same dispersal area that they had occupied with Vengeances a year before. By the evening of the 30th the aircraft had all been serviced and armed, with the assistance of the aircrew who had been put to work belting ammunition. The squadron was ready for action.

On October 1st No 168 Wg was renumbered as No 908 Wg but this change of designation had little practical impact on the squadron, which flew its first planned offensive Mosquito missions that day. Flt Lts Emeny and Andrews in HR291 and Plt Offs Blenkhorne and Paterson in HP884 investigated the airfields at Nawnghkio, Onbauk and Ye-U. All three appeared to be overgrown and deserted. The opportunity was taken to strafe a Ki 48 found at Nawnghkio, although it was suspected that this aircraft might already have been damaged. Shortly afterwards another six aircraft carried out what amounted to an extended sector recce, ranging east to the Chindwin river and west to Agartala at low level, in the course of which they attacked what appeared to be the only remaining relatively intact building at Kalemyo with cannon and machine-gun fire. In the evening another pair strafed river traffic on the Chindwin. Ten sorties flown - so far so good.

Four more sorties were flown on October 2nd and on the 3rd three pairs were despatched on offensive recces, one just before dawn, one just after mid-day and one at dusk. HP936 failed to return from the second mission and Flt Lt Gordon Proctor and Sgt George Bargh were posted missing; since the two aircraft had become separated there was no explanation for the loss. There was then a brief pause in tasking, although local flying took place, and on one of these trips, on the 4th, Sqn Ldr Norman Bourke was alarmed to see the leading edge of one of the wings of his Mosquito starting to buckle as he recovered from a dive; he carried out a rapid emergency landing before the failure became catastrophic and the aircraft was handed over to No 143 RSU for a technical investigation to be carried out.

Daily operations were resumed on the 6th and thereafter up to eight sorties were launched each day. At this stage of the war the Japanese were basing most of their aircraft in Thailand and moving them forward to airfields in central

Burma only in preparation for a raid. Many of the Mosquito sorties were patrols to identify which airfields were active. The squadron struck lucky on October 6th when Fg Offs Max Neil and Ernie Hallett in HR291 went to Heho where they found a taxying Ki 46 which they blew up with a strafing attack. The squadron suffered another casualty on the 12th when HP883 was hit by ground fire while strafing Meiktila airfield. Flt Lt Duclos was able to get the damaged aeroplane down at Tulihal but his mortally wounded navigator, Fg Off Keith Bottrill, had already died.

On the 15th the CO took eight aircraft to Chiringa whence they were to participate in Operation LOVE, a large-scale strike against Japanese-held airfields in the vicinity of Rangoon. Plt Off Bill Taylor accompanied them with the Harvard in case it was needed to fetch spares; the required groundcrew were ferried down by Dakota. Gp Capt Whiteley, with Flt Lt Andrews as his nav, joined the detachment later with a ninth aircraft. In addition to mounting this detachment, the balance of the squadron flew four operational sorties from Kumbhirgram that day. On one of these Flt Lt Cliff Emeny and WO Johnny Yanota (HP879) and WOs 'Bud' Abbott and Bill Edwards (HP881) strafed a railway engine near Myitkyina and had the satisfaction of leaving it enveloped in clouds of steam, the first of No 45 Sqn's eventual tally of seventy-one locomotives damaged or destroyed.

Two of the aircraft remaining at Kumbhirgram took off on an offensive recce early on the 16th but adverse weather obliged them to return. The same crews tried again later in the day and were successful but, after a strafing run at Kadozeik, HP941 pulled up sharply, rolled onto its back and dived into the ground. Flt Lt Arthur Huon circled the area twice; the aircraft had not caught fire and he could not even locate the wreckage, but he had no doubt that Sqn Ldr Bourke and Fg Off Dumas could not have survived the impact. No return ground fire had been observed, which left the reason for the crash as something of a mystery. It was conjectured at the time that the most probable explanation was that some cables had sheared resulting in loss of control but, with hindsight, it would seem more likely that the cause was a structural failure.

Operation LOVE was executed on October 18th, spearheaded by a total of twenty-one twin-engined attack aircraft. Twelve Beaufighters of No 901 Wg drawn from Nos 177 and 211 Sqns attacked the airfields at Mingaladon and Hmawbi while No 45 Sqn's nine Mosquitos, plus the Thunderbolts of Nos 146 and 261 Sqns which had accompanied the Flying Camels down to Chiringa, were led against Zayatkwin by OC No 908 Wg. The squadron's strike was very successful, although Wg Cdr Walker's aircraft was hit by defensive fire from the ground and he had to fly back on one engine, the score being evened by a parked 'Dinah' being claimed as damaged. The detachment returned to base later that day leaving Flt Lt Torrence at Chiringa to

bring the CO's aeroplane back once it had been repaired. Two other sorties had been flown from Kumbhirgram on the 18th and four more were launched on the 19th.

Six aircraft operated on the 20th. One pair was obliged to return early as a result of poor weather. As they flew over the aerodrome, HP921 was seen to break up in flight, some reports suggesting that it had run into a flock of kite hawks. The wreckage fell in the jungle a short distance from the airfield. Neither Sqn Ldr Don Edwards (whose AFC was to come through two months later) nor Fg Off Eric Sandifer survived. While a bird strike could be expected to cause some damage it should not have resulted in such a catastrophic airframe failure. As with the loss of HP941, there was no really satisfactory explanation for this crash. While the squadron was eager to carry on, the higher reaches of ACSEA, particularly its engineering staffs, began to express concern about the robustness of the Mosquitos, especially as No 82 Sqn, then working-up at Ranchi, had also lost a crew on the 20th when their aircraft had broken up over Random Range.

The squadron had lost both of its flight commanders in five days. Victor 'Duke' Duclos, who had been made up to squadron leader on the 17th to take over Norman Bourke's A Flight, now transferred to B Flight and Plt Off Max Levey was flown down to Chiringa to relieve Flt Lt Alexander 'Jock' Torrence, who was to become OC A Flight (he was promoted to squadron leader on November 7th).

Eight sorties were flown on the 21st but the following day the squadron was grounded while the cause of the recent losses was investigated. This left No 908 Wg with no aircraft at all as its two Thunderbolt squadrons had moved to Wangjing that day. The remains of three Mosquitos were available for examination: HP919, No 82 Sqn's aeroplane at Ranchi; HX821, which had crashed at Bishnapur on the 10th during a test flight with No 143 RSU[2], and HP921, the aircraft in which Edwards and Sandifer had died. Mr Myers of DeHavillands arrived at Kumbhirgram on 23rd October and after inspecting the wreckage of HP921 and several other aeroplanes he reported that they all displayed similar defects in that there was inadequate bonding between certain components within the wings. That the structural integrity of the Mosquito left something to be desired was beyond doubt,

HP921/O taking off from Amarda Road in May 1944. This aeroplane broke up in flight over Kumbhirgram on 20th October 1944, killing Sqn Ldr Don Edwards and Fg Off Eric Sandifer. This was not the only unexplained recent Mosquito accident and two days later all Mosquitos in India were grounded for inspection. (Howard Levy)

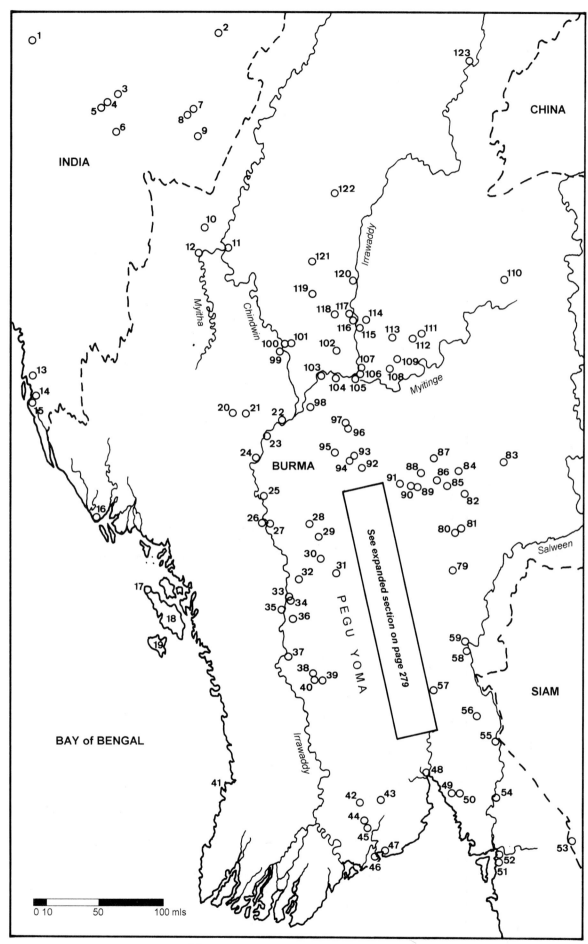

Map 11.1. Burma - Mosquito ops in 1944-45.

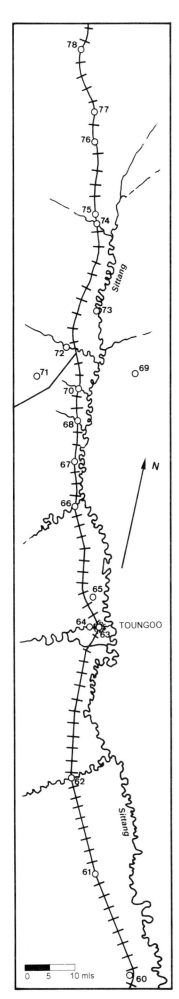

16 Akyab	57 Ketkako	80 Nam Tamhpak Br	37 Shwedaung
34 Allanmyo	98 Kinmagan	82 Namhkok	54 Shwegun
99 Alon	2 Kohima	83 Namsang	86 Shwengyaung
108 Anisakan	114 Kokko	111 Nawnghkio	5 Silchar
90 Aungban	3 Kumbhirgram	104 Ngazun	4 Silchar West
50 Bilin	87 Kunlon	60 Nyaunglebin	115 Singu
24 Chauk	116 Kyaukmyaung	23 Nyaungu	74 Sinthe
19 Cheduba Island	17 Kyaukpyu	117 Onbauk	21 Sinthe LG
13 Chiringa	38 Kyaunggon	22 Pakokku	64 Sinzeik
15 Cox's Bazaar	69 Kywebwe	56 Papun	66 Swa
31 Dalangyun	110 Lashio	59 Pasawng	75 Tatkon
41 Danson Bay	71 Lewe	21 Pauk	65 Tennant
70 Ela	79 Loikaw	40 Paungde	120 Thabeikkyan
32 Gwegyo	85 Loikawng	39 Payangsu	89 Thamakan
88 Heho	27 Magwe	61 Penwegon	47 Thaunggon
81 Hishseng	107 Manadalay	95 Pindale	68 Thawatti
42 Hmawbi	52 Martaban	96 Pontha	35 Thayetmyo
76 Hngetthaik	109 Maymyo	78 Pyawbwe	92 Thazi
84 Hopong	94 Meiktila	72 Pyinmana	101 Thazi LG
112 Hsumhsai	53 Mesoht	97 Pyinzi	93 Thedaw
7 Imphal	26 Minbu	62 Pyu	63 Toungoo
36 Ingon	44 Mingaladon	18 Ramree Island	8 Tulihal
14 Joari	48 Mokpalin	45 Rangoon	9 Wangjing
55 Junction of Salween &	6 Monerkiel	46 Sadainghmut	122 Wuntho
Thaungyin Rivers	100 Monywa	102 Sadaung	77 Yamethin
121 Kadozeik	51 Moulmein	29 Sadongyaung	10 Yazagyo
91 Kalaw	103 Myinmu	105 Sagaing	119 Ye-U
12 Kalemyo	106 Myitinge Bridge	30 Satthwa	25 Yenangyaung
11 Kalewa	123 Myitkyina	113 Sedaw	73 Yezin
49 Kawkadut	67 Myohla	1 Shillong	33 Ywatang
58 Kemapyu	28 Myothit	118 Shwebo	43 Zayatkwin

Key to Map 11.1, including expanded section at left.

but there was soon to be some dispute between the RAF and the manufacturers as to the root cause of the problem[3].

Regardless of what actually lay behind the wing failures, the fact was that the aircraft were suspect. All Mosquitos in India now had to be inspected and the future of the aircraft hung in the balance. The embargo on flying remained in force for several days while each aircraft was examined to determine which, if any, of them could be certified as being fit for operations. The lull in activity provided an opportunity to send a batch of airmen to No 3 Hill Depot at Shillong for a break. There was an interesting project to work on for those who remained behind. No 27 Sqn had been successfully experimenting with the fitting of an F.24 camera in the noses of its Beaufighters and the staff at 908 Wg thought that this might work on the Mosquito too. The groundcrew set to work to design a suitable installation for the Mosquito.

By the 26th the situation had clarified; only eight of the Mosquitos then on charge to the squadron were assessed as being fit for ops and over the next few days ten unserviceable aircraft (HJ833, HP871, HP877, HP881, HP942, HP969, HP971, HP978, LR306 and LR307) were transferred to No 143 RSU. As the moon would be up for the next few days, it was now intended to employ the remaining aircraft at night. The first few attempts were frustrated by the weather but on the 28th five Mosquitos were despatched to attack Japanese airfields, although one had to return early with a fuel-flow problem and another was obliged to divert to Tulihal where it crashed on landing. It transpired that HP883's airspeed indicator had been overreading by a substantial margin and instead of approaching at 140 mph the aircraft was probably only flying at something like 115 mph when it stalled from about 35 feet. It bounced heavily, twice, hit the ground with a wingtip, slewed, and the undercarriage collapsed. Plt Off Max Levey and Fg Off Jim Vernon emerged from the battered aeroplane unhurt. Nevertheless, despite the tribulations suffered by the squadron during its first month of Mosquito operations, it had still managed to make a worthwhile contribution to the war effort mounting seventy-nine sorties for a total of 312 flying hours.

Replacement aircraft began to trickle through in early November. Graham Williams remembers 'Duke' Duclos taking one of them up and giving it a thorough work out over the aerodrome, which successfully dispelled any lingering doubts about the effectiveness of the 'fix' which had been devised. The new aeroplanes required acceptance checks and test flights, however, so the squadron was still significantly

With a 500 pounder under each wing, OB.D emerges from its pen for a sortie in late 1944. Problems with the structural integrity of the Mosquito at this time led to a period of instability during which a number of aeroplanes passed through the squadron's hands, some of them remaining on charge only briefly. As a result four Mosquitos were coded as D during November and December (HP985, HR451, HR447 and HR409, in that order); it is not certain which one of these is shown in this picture. (A N Huon)

below strength. Nevertheless it continued to fly ops with such serviceable aeroplanes as were available and in the first week of the month it put up twenty-six sorties, all of them at night. The objectives were to harass lines of communication along the Chindwin and to attack airfields, Shwebo, Thedaw, Heho, Onbauk and Meiktila all receiving visits, some of them several times. All of these sorties were successful and uneventful, apart from that flown by Max Levey and Joe Mears in HR368 on the 6th. They bombed Yazagyo as briefed but, owing to a navigational error on the way home, they finished up, rather embarrassingly, having to land at Dinjan to refuel.

Two aircraft carried out individual 'rhubarbs'[4] 'n the small hours of November 9th, followed by a dawn raid on Meiktila by seven aircraft. Poor weather prevented the formation from rendezvousing as planned and the strike was eventually delivered piecemeal by only four aircraft, three others electing to attack alternative targets. Those which reached Meiktila encountered spirited resistance from ground fire and, for the first time, Japanese fighters, 'Oscars' and 'Tojos'. Fg Off Pete Ewing sustained some superficial injuries when HR368 was hit by AA fire and shortly afterwards the aircraft was engaged by a Ki 43. His nav, WO Bob Pinkerton, had the hair-raising experience of having his seat pan creased by a machine gun bullet which then passed between his legs, leaving him with bruised buttocks but essentially complete - it could have been so much worse! Not soon enough for Pinkerton, his pilot opened up the taps and the 'Oscar' was, as the ORB puts it, "left standing".

Flt Lt Emeny's aircraft was also hit by ground fire and he called on the R/T that he was having to shut down one engine. At this point he too was engaged by an 'Oscar'. Fg Off 'Nick' Nicholls went to his rescue in HR458 and made two attacks on the Japanese fighter, claiming hits on its wings and forcing it to break off. It was too late for the stricken Mosquito, however, and HR374 crashed, slithered along the ground and burst into flames. Remarkably, although they were badly burned, both Cliff Emeny and Johnny Yanota had survived the crash. With great difficulty and in considerable pain they made their way to a village where they were robbed of what few possessions they had and turned over to the Japanese. They were given no medical attention and held for four days and three nights without food or water. They said nothing and were eventually taken to Rangoon jail where they were to spend the rest of the war. Emeny, who had

been a farmer in New Zealand, had some basic veterinary experience and was able to adapt this to ease the suffering of some of his fellow prisoners. The last crew to arrive over Meiktila on 9th November reported a Japanese aircraft burning on the airfield (it was definitely not the downed Mosquito) so someone had done some damage and, since no one else submitted a claim, it was assumed that it must have been a victim of the attack carried out by Emeny and Yanota.

While the loss of another crew was deeply regretted it was quite evident that this time the Mosquito had been shot down; it had *not* just come apart. In fact the crews' confidence in their aircraft was quite undented, especially after the recent run of successful missions, and there was considerable disappointment on November 10th when the squadron was grounded again. In the first nine days of November, with only half of their established number of aircraft available for use, in only thirty-six sorties the crews had dropped 28,000 lbs of bombs and fired 5,276 rounds of 20mm and 11,103 rounds of .303" ammunition. They had damaged or destroyed one aircraft, two locomotives, thirteen MT vehicles, fourteen rivercraft and eighteen items of rolling stock. It was quite clear that the Mosquitos could be just as potent in the Far East as they were in Europe - provided, of course, that they could be kept in the air.

A second programme of inspections was instigated and the groundcrew spent the 11th opening up the mainplanes to permit examination of the spar attachments. The squadron is known to have had at least fourteen Mosquitos on charge at the time and every one of them, including several which had only recently been acquired, was found to be defective. Eight crews were promptly sent on leave while the others began gingerly ferrying the aircraft to No 1 CMU at Kanchrapara. There was considerable doubt as to whether it would be practical to attempt to repair the faulty aeroplanes and there were rumours, no doubt fostered by the aircrew, that it might be necessary to send the crews back to the UK to pick up new aircraft and fly them out to India. In the event a rectification scheme was devised and six of the condemned aeroplanes (HR368, HR372, HR399, HR401 HR413 and HR455) were eventually restored to service but another eight (HP879, HP884, HP985, HR283, HR291, HR388, HR458 and HR487) were never seen again - not by No 45 Sqn anyway.

Although its future was now somewhat uncertain, in compliance with a new scheme which was being imposed on all tactical units in India, a major restructuring of the squadron began in November. The aircrew were to be divorced from their groundcrew and the latter were to be reorganised into separate units. In the case of the Flying Camels their airmen were to become No 7045 Servicing Echelon (SE). In theory an SE was an independent organisation and could be used to support the aircraft of any unit and even, if necessary, become separated from its associated squadron. In practice this rarely happened; in the case of No 45 Sqn and No 7045 SE they continued to work together much as before and Flt Lt Wilson and his staff continued to provide administrative services for the personnel of both units. The reorganisation involved a significant changeover of tradesmen and as new faces arrived to fill the revised establishment others, who had suddenly become surplus to requirements, were posted away. It was hardly a popular move. It was no doubt done in the name of efficiency but most of the old hands knew where their loyalties lay and the whole business was regarded as something of a cosmetic exercise. The new system was formally introduced on December 1st and on that date No 7045 SE came into being under the command of Flt Lt A E Joyce, who had become the squadron's Engineering Officer towards the end of the Vengeance era. Only sixty airmen remained on the strength of the parent unit by the end of November. The majority of these were awaiting postings and by the end of January this figure had been reduced to just sixteen.

In the meantime, despite continuing hopes of a Blighty trip, the prospect of receiving new aeroplanes in the short term receded and HQ 3rd TAF decided to find some useful employment for the squadron's aircrew, or at least for some of its pilots. On November 22nd Sqn Ldr Torrence with a party of fifteen groundcrew and Fg Offs Garnham, Blenkhorne and McLellan plus Plt Offs Wilson and Taylor and WO O'Connor, left for Cox's Bazaar. On the same day Sqn Ldr Duclos took Fg Offs Neil, Nicholls and Cartledge and another nineteen groundcrew to Imphal. They were to work for HQs 224 and 221 Gps respectively and were expected to be employed flying light aircraft on communications duties. The remaining aircrew, mostly navigators, were left to indulge themselves with sport and cultivating the local tea planters in the hope of securing invitations to play tennis or take part in shooting parties, in which endeavours they were moderately successful.

On December 2nd the first two replacement aircraft, HR390 and HR447, arrived. Ops began again on the night of the 4th with the two new aeroplanes being used to fly three singleton missions against a reported Japanese transit camp north of Monywa. The crews were Wg Cdr Walker and Fg Off Cargill, Flt Lt Goodwin and Fg Off Potts and Plt Off Goodrich and WO Nessim. The last-named was a particularly interesting character. If Paul Keel's Danish contribution to the squadron's efforts in Egypt, Burma and India had been unusual, that of Maurice Nessim was perhaps even more remarkable. Salen Maurice Daoud Nessim was an Arab, an Iraqi to be precise, and his participation in the British campaign against the Japanese in Burma must surely have been unique. There can be no doubt, however, that his contribution was significant for both he and his regular pilot, Doug Goodrich, were to be awarded DFCs in October 1945.

Doug Goodrich (left) and Maurice Nessim, both of whom flew more than sixty operational sorties with No 45 Sqn, nearly all of them as a crew. In October 1945 both were gazetted for DFCs which, since he was an Arab, may have been a unique achievement in Nessim's case. (D E Goodrich)

The squadron's complement of aircraft grew only slowly at first but by the second week of December replacement Mosquitos were arriving at a rate of one or two per day and up to ten daily sorties were being flown against airfields, lines of communication and anything that moved. A pair of railway bridges on the line between Wuntho and Sagaing came in for a lot of attention but it proved to be very difficult to 'drop a span'. On the 8th, for instance, the ORB notes, "The attacks on the first bridge were good, but all bombs skipped and burst some 80 yards away in the paddy and no damage was claimed. The attack on the second bridge was modified in an endeavour to overcome the 'skip'. The aircraft came in a shallow dive from 800 to 50/100 ft but the results were identical to the first attack, although slight damage to the railway track was claimed." The same two bridges were hit again on the 9th. The first attack produced similarly disappointing results but at the second target "...the bridge was hit and a section was destroyed"[5]. Although it was proving to be extremely difficult actually to destroy bridges, the strikes usually left them unusable and most sorties inflicted other damage on the enemy and the squadron's tally of locomotives, rolling stock, MT vehicles and assorted rivercraft grew daily.

Meanwhile the squadron's (or, to be precise, the SE's) indefatigable song-and-dance men, undaunted by the recent tribulations, had put together a concert which they staged to the usual acclaim in the station cinema on December 9th. Stalwart 'showbiz' personalities at this time were Cpl Ernie Kiff (compère), LAC Wally Lindsay (magician), LAC S

"It ain't 'arf 'ot Mum" - the squadron concert party, Christmas 1944. Third from the left may be LAC Cohen. Fourth from the left is Wally Lindsay with Ernie Kiff on his left; third from the right is Geoff Dee. It is not visible in this picture but above the proscenium arch is a late version of the 'Diving Camel' illustrated in Chapter 10, superimposed on the number 45. (G J Hancox)

The squadron's dance band. (N D Murrell)

Cohen (singer), LAC Thomas (comedian), LAC Geoff Dee (monologues) and LACs Edwards, Harper and Regan. The squadron band, which made a crucial contribution to the concert party's success, and also played at the occasional dances organised in the Retreat Club at Silchar, comprised LACs Steve Burton, Roy Taylor and Norridge reinforced by Cpls Burgess and Cuthburtson, who were co-opted from the staff of No 908 Wg. For over a year the band's leader had been LAC 'Art' Smith, who had been a professional clarinettist in civilian life. Unfortunately for the squadron, however, he had been 'talent spotted' and in February 1945 he was 'poached' and posted off to join one of the official Touring Concert Parties.

While the recent enforced lull in operational activity had allowed the concert to be rehearsed and had permitted some more airmen to have a break at Shillong, this had not been the case for the carpenters. With a wooden aircraft that tended to come unstuck they had their work cut out and had been slaving away non-stop ever since the first grounding. Now that some serviceable replacement machines were being received, however, they could afford to relax a little, and Sgt Kemp and his team of 'chippies' were sent off to a planter's bungalow for a week's rest.

The ability to do this on occasion was much appreciated; No 45 Sqn (and the men of many other units) owed a considerable debt to the generosity of the owners and

managers of the local tea plantations in Assam. Many of the squadron's personnel, both aircrew and groundcrew, were able to rest and recuperate under the roofs of these expatriate Britons, and their contribution to the maintenance of morale has rarely been acknowledged. Beyond this, the main sources of entertainment were the station's cinema, which was always well-attended, the squadron's home-grown concerts and the very popular dances at Silchar. The highlights of the entertainment calendar were provided by the occasional visits of professional ENSA concert parties, and many of those who were at Kumbhirgram at the time will recall, for instance, the performance given by Miss Marie Burke on 19th December 1944.

Although there were such lighter moments, the war continued relentlessly. By December 13th the squadron's strength was up to nine aircraft and the number of missions being flown was steadily increasing. One consequence of the rising sortie rate was a corresponding increase in the number of Mosquitos returning to base with battle damage, particularly after strikes against airfields. The bridges between Wuntho and Sagaing were still being attacked and, although they stubbornly refused to collapse, the damage inflicted was more than enough to disrupt the enemy's use of the railway line.

With more aeroplanes becoming available most of the detached pilots had already returned to the squadron from Calcutta but it was now necessary to recall the rest, and the team from Cox's Bazaar arrived back at Kumbhirgram by air on the 18th. As trained fighter-bomber pilots they had initially been somewhat unenthusiastic about being assigned to second-line duties but in the event they had been usefully and intensively employed on casualty evacuation work in the

Fg Off Wally McLellan (left) and Plt Off Bill 'Cobber' Taylor at Cox's Bazaar with a Stinson Sentinel in December 1944. (A N Huon)

Arakan and had found it a most satisfying and rewarding experience. 'Tiffin' O'Connor recalls this interlude:

Pending the arrival of the new aircraft, a small number of aircrew (myself included) and groundcrew was detached to Cox's Bazaar. Using Tiger Moths, modified to carry a casualty strapped-down under the rear fuselage decking behind the front cockpit, and American Stinson Sentinels, which were designed for observation and ambulance work, we were able to fly out casualties and have them in hospital in under two hours, instead of their having to be carried for up to thirty days on stretchers. The flying was demanding in that very short jungle strips were used. These were often very close to the Jap lines and arrivals and departures sometimes provoked enemy action. These flights and flying hours were granted operational status and some of the permanent staff of the unit were, I believe, decorated for their work. After about a month we returned to the squadron.

When its Mosquitos were grounded in November 1944 many of the squadron's pilots were detached to undertake casevac work. This group of pilots of No 224 Gp's Communications Flight at Cox's Bazaar includes: Fg Off Wally McLellan, Plt Off Bill Taylor, Sqn Ldr Jock Torrence, Fg Off Bob Wilson and WO 'Tiffin' O'Connor. Note that the Tiger Moths in the background have had the decking of their rear fuselages modified to provide stowage for a stretcher. (H M Nicholls)

The day before the party from Cox's Bazaar returned, the squadron had lost another crew. On December 17th, whilst over the target during an attack on a military camp at Ye-U, HR453 suffered an engine failure. Plt Off Levey feathered the prop and succeeded in nursing the aircraft as far as Yazagyo but crashed while attempting to land; the aircraft burst into flames. Max Levey and his nav, Fg Off Harry Cargill, were both killed. Ops continued unabated, however; Pakokku was attacked twice on the 18th, four Mosquitos taking part in each strike, and the following day the waterfront at Myinmu received the same treatment. The squadron was given another bridge, at Alon, to have a go at on the 20th. This time they achieved their ambition and had the satisfaction of demolishing one complete span. This mission was not without its drama, however, as HR389 stripped a tyre on take off and its undercarriage would not retract fully. Escorted by their No 2 (WO Ashworth and F/Sgt Smith in HR492) Max Neil and Ernie Hallett jettisoned their bombs, fired off their ammunition and burned off fuel for four hours before attempting a landing which turned out to be quite uneventful.

The squadron's fighting strength was fully restored when the Imphal detachment returned to Kumbhirgram on the 22nd. Flying Sentinels and the odd Tiger Moth, these pilots had been similarly employed to those who had been at Cox's Bazaar. There had been some casualty evacuation work but most of the trips had been in the communications role moving personnel or high priority freight, including such diverse items as a consignment of land mines and an engine for a motor boat. As an example, Fg Off 'Nick' Nicholls' log book shows that during the twenty-one days that he was with "Phantom Flight" he flew a total of thirty-three trips, twenty-eight of them being classified as operational. Among the more prominent personalities whose names appear as passengers in Nicholls' log book are General Slim, Lt Gen Messervy and Brig Dyer. Lesser mortals are identified, with an irreverence that was perhaps characteristic of the wartime RAAF, as 'General Factotum', 'Brigadier Johnny', 'Col Type', 'Lt Col Blimp' and 'Plt Off Prune'.

In the run up to Christmas thoughts had turned to celebrating it properly and it was decided to build a church. LAC Wally Lindsay was among those involved in this

The church that No 45 Sqn built at Kumbhirgram. (J Gillan)

HR526 was one of the replacement Mosquitos which began to arrive in mid-December 1944. Despite its indifferent quality this photograph is worth reproducing as it shows that some Mosquitos were still being issued painted in the European colour scheme of Medium Sea Grey with areas of Dark Green on the upper surfaces and sporting C1 Type roundels. After a coat of Dark Earth had been added to the grey areas of the upper surfaces and the markings had been replaced by the local ACSEA variety, this aeroplane was coded OB.P and remained on the squadron's charge until at least November 1945, by which time it should have been repainted in silver overall. The annotation SNAKE (painted on the fuselage in front of the roundel) had been introduced on 1st May 1943 to identify aircraft specifically destined for India and thus stop a practice common among senior commanders and units in the Mediterranean region who frequently 'hi-jacked' such aeroplanes as they passed through the Middle East. (J Byrne)

project. As he recalls it:

We shared the 'strip with 82 Squadron. There was always a great, but amicable, rivalry between us but I think we got together over the church, although I am sure that it was 45's idea. The prime mover was one of the Chaplains, Sqn Ldr Fr Buckley, the RC Padre. The building was specifically designed and constructed for its purpose but it was, of course, only a standard bamboo basha; it was, however, a very large one and it had a tower! By inter-denominational agreement the church would be 'christened' on Christmas Day when the first service was to be held but Fr Buckley 'pulled a stroke' by craftily nipping in at 0001 hrs on December 25th to celebrate a Midnight Mass. All legal and above board, but regarded by the RCs as a political coup - one up for the Pope! From then on the church was used every Sunday by all denominations working on a rota basis with

A group of the squadron's airmen celebrating Christmas 1944 at Kumbhirgram. (G J Hancox)

the various different services at preallocated times. It was still going strong when we left Kumbhirgram.

Christmas 1944 was made slightly more memorable than usual by an earthquake on December 24th. It was little more than a tremor, but it was startling nonetheless. Fortunately all the buildings were of light bamboo/basha construction so damage was negligible. Six sorties were flown on Christmas Day but, undeterred by this diversion, the cooks, Sgt Sale, Cpl Low and LACs Horwarth and Taylor worked their usual magic and the festive dinner went ahead as planned. The bill of fare was much as was to be expected with the changes being rung by the appearance of roast duck and (as the Airmen's Mess menu had it) "micne" pies. Having assisted with the serving of the meal, Wg Cdr Walker addressed the whole assembly, the squadron and the SE being inseparable, commended them all on their efforts, singling out the carpenters for a special mention, and forecast a tough 1945. The airmen cheered him to the rafters, such as they were.

From December 21st the primary targets had been switched back to airfields and Heho, Thedaw, Namsang and Meiktila were attacked repeatedly for the rest of the month. The most satisfying action was on the 26th when a total of nine aircraft (a formation of four followed by five singletons at hourly intervals) patrolled Heho between dusk and midnight hoping to catch the Japanese in residence. The first

Flt Lt Arthur Huon taxies out in HR451/OB.F, another of the replacement aircraft received late in 1944. This one is already wearing full ACSEA colours, green/brown camouflage with national markings in light and dark blue and squadron codes. (A N Huon)

formation found two aircraft on the ground and Plt Off Ron Wilcock and Flt Lt Leonard 'Andy' Andrews in HR456 had the satisfaction of strafing a 'Dinah' and seeing it burst into flames, although no one managed to hit the accompanying 'Oscar'. Attacks on Japanese airfields were no sinecure and the Mosquitos often encountered very intense AA fire, as they did on this occasion when HR447 was hit in the starboard engine. Fortunately the fire went out and, with the prop feathered, Plt Off Bill 'Cobber' Taylor and WO Ken Putman limped to Kalemyo where the pilot carried out a successful asymmetric landing. Fg Off Rex Garnham and Flt Lt Jack Nankervis had a nasty experience too, as their HR527 suffered a bird strike while they were over the target, although the damage proved to be superficial and they were able to fly back to base.

There another spot of excitement on December 29th when, during an attack on Meiktila, Japanese fighters were encountered again, six Oscars and a Tojo. One of the 'Oscars' attacked HR451 (Sqn Ldr 'Jock' Torrence and Fg Off Ted Rainbow) but WO's Walsh and Orsborn got behind it in HR456 and forced it to break off, claiming it as damaged.

Throughout December, as aircraft availability had improved so the pace of operations had continued to increase and by the end of the month the squadron was once again operating at full steam. From a gradual start with pairs it had finished up launching up to twelve aircraft per day or, when the moon was up, per night. This effort had been complemented by that of No 82 Sqn which had arrived at Kumbhirgram on the 15th, commencing operations four days later. The Wing was finally restored to its full three-squadron strength on December 23rd with the arrival of No 22 Sqn's Beaufighters.

Having begun December with no aeroplanes at all the squadron's strength had grown until, by New Year's Eve, it had sixteen on charge[6]. Several of these aircraft were reissues of the squadron's original airframes after they had been suitably modified. Apart from now being 'guaranteed not to come apart', the new aircraft had significantly

increased capabilities. Good progress had been made with the F.24 camera fit and on December 15th Wg Cdr Walker had used the 'prototype', HR390, to photograph the damage inflicted on the Wuntho-Sagaing bridges. As a result of the success of this trial, F.24s were installed in more of the squadron's aircraft. Even more significant was the fact that the aircraft now on charge had been modified to carry up to 2,000 lbs of bombs. Bomb bay racks were slow in arriving but within a few weeks all of the aircraft would be able to carry four 500 pounders, two internally and one under each wing. Thenceforth each aircraft could deliver twice the load toted by the squadron's earlier Mosquitos, not forgetting the devastating additional firepower represented by the battery of eight guns. Compared to the Blenheims and Vengeances, the Mosquito's destructive power was further enhanced by the fact that the weapons now being carried were Medium Capacity (MC) bombs which produced considerably more blast effect than the old GP series[7].

The Flying Camels had been selected to act as the spearhead of the Mosquito light bomber force in India. The introduction of the type had proved to be unexpectedly troublesome, however, and the squadron's work had been punctuated by the loss of several crews and frustrated by periodic groundings, all due to structural failures. Under the circumstances it would have been quite understandable if morale on the squadron had sunk to an all time low. But the quality of the squadron's leadership and the mutual support engendered by its corporate spirit were more than enough to overcome the setbacks it had experienced. The state of morale on No 45 Sqn is perhaps best reflected by Wg Cdr Walker's personal remarks concluding the ORB submission for December 1944:

The spirit and keenness of the groundcrews is terrific and the rapidity with which the turnround of aircraft is completed shows what a grand effort they are making. The proven structural failures in the Mosquitos in this squadron do not seem to have affected the morale of the aircrews in any way and they are most enthusiastic about

The aeroplane in the background to this picture, HR402 OB.C, was taken on charge on 11th December 1944 only to be shot down by an 'Oscar' on 15th January 1945, with the loss of Flt Lt Goodwin and Fg Off Potts. Thus the date of the photograph can be fixed as being within a few weeks of Christmas 1944. The officers arranged around the bomb trolley are, from the left, Fg Offs Jack Nankervis, Max Neil, Ernie Hallett, Bob Barclay (leaning on the propeller), Rex Garnham (in the slouch hat) and Merv Nicholls with Flt Lt Herbie Wilson standing on the right. (G F Williams)

On 3rd January 1945 a total of sixteen Mosquitos, two of them from No 82 Sqn, attacked the Japanese telephone exchanges at Thazi and Maymyo. This picture shows the latter complex being strafed. (D E Goodrich)

the aircraft. There is a terrific keenness to top the 'ops' sorties and hours each month and a firm hand is needed at times to stop some of the crews from 'punching' too many trips. Taken all round, the aircrew and groundcrews are as keen as mustard and today the command of No 45 Squadron is the finest post in India.

Enough said! - although it is interesting to observe that when he wrote these words, with twenty-one sorties flown, 'Johnny' Walker actually topped the league table himself - so the pot appears to have been calling the kettle black.

New Year's Day 1945 was a stand down and only two sorties were flown on January 2nd, reconnaissances of two targets in preparation for Operation NASTY. NASTY was aimed at Japanese telecommunications and on the 3rd the squadron launched a total of sixteen sorties against the telephone exchange at Thazi and another suspected one at Maymyo. Both were substantially destroyed, although the day's success was marred by the loss of WOs John McQueen and Bill Edwards who were both killed when their aircraft, HR515, developed engine trouble shortly after take off and crashed about five miles from the airfield.

In the meantime there had been another brief grounding when a signal was received on January 2nd calling for an inspection of the joints of the Mosquitos' dinghy stowage. Most of the aircraft were quickly cleared to continue flying but five proved to be faulty and had to be withdrawn and ferried to Kanchrapara, which left the squadron short of aeroplanes again until replacements arrived.

Ops continued at a fairly low intensity for the next few days, not least because of the weather, but on the 8th fifteen aircraft, plus five more from No 82 Sqn, mounted a series of strikes on Sagaing and 'rhubarbed' the Irrawaddy as far down as Chauk. Ten more sorties were flown against targets along the Irrawaddy on the 9th. Two aircraft were hit by fire from the ground and both had eventful landings when they got back to Kumbhirgram. HR526's undercarriage collapsed as the aeroplane touched down, leaving Fg Offs Freddie Fortune and 'Joe' Mears to walk the rest of the way back to the squadron's dispersal area. The damage to the aeroplane seems to have been fairly superficial, however, and it was flying ops again within a few weeks. HR455's undercarriage

Standing, on the left, is WO Bill Edwards and, on the right, WO John McQueen. This picture was taken at Kumbhirgram only a few days before they were killed when one of their Mosquito's engines failed immediately after take off on 3rd January 1945. The third figure has not been identified. (Mrs Mollie Abbott)

would not lower and Plt Off Wilson put the aircraft down on its belly on the 'kutcha' strip alongside the main runway. He and WO Hayward both walked away from this incident but HR455 does not appear to have rejoined the squadron. Sadly, Bob Wilson and Bill Hayward were killed only three days later when an engine cut shortly after they had taken off in HR492. Although their Mosquito came down fairly close to the airfield it was some hours before the wreckage was located by LAC Willoughby who had gone into the jungle on his own initiative to find the crew.

The style of operations now settled down to a routine of a strike against a specified objective followed by strafing of targets of opportunity along lines of communication. A typical example on the 13th involved formations of six and four attacking Sagaing and Monywa and then 'rhubarbing' the Chindwin and Irrawaddy Rivers; twenty-three MT vehicles were claimed as having been destroyed and over one hundred rivercraft, mostly small sampans, had been hit. Night strikes against airfields began again from the 14th and shortly after dawn on the 15th a section of two patrolling over Meiktila airfield was engaged by four 'Oscars'. Flt Lt Goodwin and Fg Off Potts were shot down in HR402, their aircraft bursting into flames on impact about eight miles north of Thedaw.   General Slim's XIVth Army had launched Operation CAPITAL, the retaking of northern Burma, in early December and by the third week in January it had made substantial progress. In the north 2nd and 19th Divs had reached Shwebo and the latter had established footholds on the left bank of the Irrawaddy north of Mandalay at Thabeikkyan and Singu. In the centre 20th Div had taken Monywa and in the south 7th Div was at Pauk. The Japanese XVth Army was retreating to the east as General Katamura withdrew his troops behind the major obstacle represented by the Irrawaddy - Kipling's 'Road to Mandalay'. At this rate of advance it was anticipated that the squadron might soon be required to move forward and on January 17th it was ordered to become tactically mobile.

A selection of demonstration tents was erected for the edification of those whose knees were not yet as brown as those of the dwindling band of 'desert warriors', for whom camping was, of course, old hat. Everyone was issued with 'jungle greens'. Personal effects and kit were limited to 140 lbs for officers and 70 lbs for airmen and the surplus had to be packed in preparation for storage with No 313 MU (Cossipore Road).   Another aspect of this preparatory activity was a major 'jabs' session which kept the doctor happy for several days; the MO was now Flt Lt T H Redfern, who had joined the squadron on 9th November and was to be Mentioned in Despatches on January 17th.

Missions continued throughout the rest of January, these frequently being flown in conjunction with No 82 Sqn's Mosquitos or, less often, the rocket-firing Beaufighters of No 47 Sqn who had arrived in mid-January, displacing No 22 Sqn which had been transferred to the Arakan to join No 901 Wg. Although the Japanese Army Air Force (JAAF) was by now chiefly notable for its absence, this did not mean that combat flying was without incident and defensive fire from the ground could be intense. On January 18th, for instance, three waves of four Mosquitos bombed Kokko and then 'rhubarbed' the river from Mandalay to Chauk, two of these aircraft sustaining damage; HR409 (Walsh and Orsborn) had its starboard outer petrol tank holed and HR462 (O'Connor and McKie) was hit in the starboard flap. The following day HR389, HR390 and HR492 all sustained damage and other aircraft were hit by ground fire on 26th, 29th and 30th. These problems were compounded by occasional technical snags, as on the night of the 20th when HR451 suffered a compass failure while it was on its way back to Kumbhirgram after carrying out a 'rhubarb' in the Myinmu area. In the darkness Flt Lts Wally McLellan and Jimmy Vernon were unable to fix their position until they sighted the Brahmaputra, by which time they were about 100 miles of north of base, and were able to land at Misamari to get the problem sorted out. As with any high-speed low-level flying, there was also a constant risk of bird strikes and it was quite common to find holes in leading edges and small corpses stuck in radiators and air filters during after-flight inspections.

Such were the almost routine occurrences which punctuated the steadily rising intensity of operations.   It should be noted, however, that not all flying was operational, and 97 of the 742 hours flown in January were devoted to training, which included practice bombing on the unfortunately named Pispur Range. Depending on the target and the weather, the Mosquitos used one of three standard attack profiles: glide-bombing from 12,000 feet down to 7,500 feet, shallow glide-bombing from 5,000 feet down to 2,000 feet, and low-level attacks. The published anticipated errors were 200 yards, 175 yards and 25 yards, respectively. The squadron had little difficulty in keeping their bombing, both academic and operational, well inside these limits.

Low-level bombing was always a hazardous affair and there were several instances of self-damage including a very

Fg Offs Graham Williams (standing) and Joe Cartledge gaze in the direction of the Southern Cross and dream of 'Oz': Kumbhirgram circa January 1945. (G F Williams)

Relaxing outside the Officers' Mess at Kumbhirgram, front to rear: Fg Off Pete Ewing, Flt Lt Herbie Wilson, Flt Lt Arthur Huon, Fg Off Merv 'Nick' Nicholls and Fg Off 'Joe' Cartledge. (H M Nicholls)

close run thing on January 18th when the CO and Fg Off Frank Harper were obliged to land at Kalemyo on one engine after they had nearly blown themselves up with their own bombs during that day's strike on Kokko. On most sorties

WO Alf Pridmore joined the squadron at Kumbhirgram in January 1945 as a flight sergeant and crewed up with Don Blenkhorne. This photograph was taken shortly after the squadron had been withdrawn to Cholavaram in May 1945. (A H Pridmore)

The marshalling yards at Thazi on the Toungoo-Mandalay railway. WO 'Tif' O'Connor found four locomotives here on 17th February and burst the boilers of all four. (D E Goodrich)

the bombs were fitted with 11 second delayed-action fuses but they were prone to detonate in rather less than that, which meant that the Mosquito could still be perilously close to its own bombs when they 'went off'. They could be even closer if the bombs skipped, as they often did, and, as Doug Goodrich recalls, "On many occasions bombs were seen to bounce off the ground to a greater height than that of the aircraft which had dropped them." These bouncers often exploded before they had fallen back to earth, resulting in airbursts which, apart from being dangerous, were of real value only when attacking troop concentrations. When such targets were specifically involved, as in Vengeance days, the bombs were often instantaneously fused and fitted with a long spike on the nose to maximise the blast effect by ensuring that they detonated before they bounced or buried themselves in the ground.

At one stage the squadron tried using a barometric fuse which was intended to detonate the bombs at about fifty feet to maximise their blast effect. The problem was that when these were dropped in a stick the first one detonated more or less as intended but the shock wave then set off the others and the explosions climbed up the stick towards the aeroplane! Their use was soon discontinued.

Another recurrent problem with bombs was hang-ups. 'Tiffin' O'Connor recalls:

The problem was not new as it had also occurred with Vengeances but we had several cases on Mosquitos, fortunately always with wing bombs which tended to fall off on the final approach after all previous efforts to dislodge them had failed. Thus we discovered that they fell off when the flaps were lowered - a jettison procedure! All this when the armourers insisted that an 'open hook' hang-up was impossible! I experienced one of these incidents after an attack on an army camp near Sedaw (*in HR462 on 28th February 1945 - CGJ*). My port wing bomb hung-up but fortunately it fell in a ravine on the approach to Kumbhirgram so we escaped the major part of the blast.

The squadron's tasking normally involved its operating in small groups against a variety of targets but there was something a little different on January 29th when a total of twelve Mosquitos was despatched to bomb the Myitinge Bridge. By this time the necessary bomb racks had been delivered and all of the aircraft were able to carry four 500 pounders. These were delivered by moonlight, using a glide-bombing attack from 6,000 feet, the instantaneously-fused bombs being released at 1,500 feet. By operating individually and attacking at roughly thirty minute intervals the defences were kept occupied for over four hours. Although AA fire was disturbingly accurate, only three aircraft actually sustained any damage; this was superficial in each case, however, and all twelve aircraft returned safely to base.

By early February the squadron's Harvards were beginning to earn their keep and, in addition to fetching and carrying spares, they were now delivering mail and dropping newsprint to forward troops to keep them in touch both with home and with events in the wider world. On a more parochial note, to ensure that its groundcrews fully understood the Wing's business and appreciated just how vital a contribution each one of them was making, a major presentation was staged at Kumbhirgram on February 7th.

One of No 45 Sqn's Mosquitos at Kumbhirgram. Interestingly, there is a Saint figure (with a few musical notes beneath it) painted on the entrance door. The fact that Sqn Ldr Traill's Vengeance (EZ986) had also sported a Saint emblem suggests that the crew of this particular Mossie may have been Vengeance veterans but it has not been possible to identify these Leslie Charteris fans. (S J Findley)

The main speakers were the Wing AILO, Capt Dee, and Flt Lt McLellan. Their briefing was illustrated, and ample evidence of the effectiveness of the Wing's activities was provided by a selection of photographs taken by the F.24 cameras fitted in the noses of No 45 Sqn's aircraft. On the same day two replacement airmen arrived on No 7045 SE, two AC1 Bells. They were identical twins and, to complicate the issue, they were joining their brother, Cpl Bell. To the uninitiated, all three were indistinguishable, which provided much scope for mischief.

Most of February's operations were much the same as January's; occasional attacks on bridges, but more usually airfields, and 'rhubarbs' by day and by night routinely involving anything from one to ten sorties generally operating as singletons or in pairs. The airstrips patrolled and attacked during February included those at Kunlon, Anisakan, Hsumhsai, Aungban, Heho, Magwe, Pyinmana, Lewe and Toungoo. The first highlight of the month occurred on one of eight individual night sorties launched against enemy aerodromes in the early hours of February 4th. Fg Off Pete Ewing and WO 'Pinkie' Pinkerton, flying HR404, were on their bomb-run at Heho at dawn when they saw a Ki 21 taking off. The ORB noted: "Switching to guns, the enemy aircraft was attacked at 500 feet, fire being opened at 1,000 yards, closing to 200 yards and the enemy aircraft burst into flames and is claimed totally destroyed". This evened the score for Pinkerton's nasty experience of three months before. The following day this crew and a navigator who had joined the squadron in December, F/Sgt N A Smith, were involved in a serious MT accident. They had been acting as the ground party out on the bombing range and were making their way back to base at the end of the day's flying when their Jeep skidded on loose gravel and fell fifteen feet into a culvert. All three aircrew were admitted to hospital. F/Sgt Smith had been very seriously injured and, despite the efforts of a special surgical team flown over from Imphal, he died on the 6th.

The largest single operation in which the Flying Camels participated during February was mounted on the 8th when each of Kumbhirgram's Mosquito squadrons put up a dozen aeroplanes. This mission was part of an "Earthquake", an intensive forty-eight hour onslaught involving many other aircraft, notably Mitchells and Thunderbolts. The objective was to neutralise the Japanese heavy artillery which was trying to dislodge 19th Div's Irrawaddy bridgehead at Singu.

Led by Gp Capt Whiteley, the twenty-four Mosquitos bombed and strafed the Japanese gun positions to great effect, causing extensive damage and secondary explosions, the group captain remaining in the target area throughout the action to observe results. All of No 45 Sqn's aircraft had carried their maximum load of 2,000 lbs of bombs on this strike.

By the middle of the month XIVth Army had consolidated its position and effectively controlled the right bank of the Irrawaddy from north of Kyaukmyaung to 30 miles below the junction with the Chindwin. In preparation for the next stage of the ground offensive, the squadron began to be routinely tasked against targets as far to the east as the Sittang river. This meant that Kumbhirgram was now so far in the rear that it was often necessary to carry additional fuel in external 'slipper' tanks fitted under the wing leading edges which limited the bomb load to the two internal 500 pounders. In fact from February 9th onwards bombs were carried less frequently and, for a few weeks, the squadron concentrated its efforts on strafing attacks.

The use of deception techniques to confuse the enemy in the European Theatre of Operations has been well publicised but it is probably less widely appreciated that such methods were also employed in Burma. At a tactical level such devices as 'Canned Battle', 'Aquaskit' and 'Parafex' were developed to simulate ground engagements by producing appropriate noise and pyrotechnic effects[8]. The idea was to divert the enemy's attention from the real thrust, if there was one, or to lead him on a wild goose chase and raise his adrenaline level if there was not. These tactics were particularly effective in Burma where jungle or dense scrub limited visibility and thus severely hampered the ability of the Japanese to determine which disturbances were spoofs and which were real. No 45 Sqn was briefly involved in this campaign during February when it took part in Operation CLOAK. It must have been evident to the Japanese that General Messervy's 4th Corps was about to cross the Irrawaddy somewhere to the south of Pakokku; CLOAK was intended to keep them guessing as to precisely where and when by creating a diversion well away from the selected bridgehead. This was eventually established at Nyaungu on February 21st followed by another, by General Stopford's 33rd Corps, at Ngazun early in March.

Four aircraft (HR451, HR526, HR527 and HR567 flown respectively by McLellan and Vernon, Wilcock and Andrews,

Nicholls and Barclay and Walsh and Orsborn) flew a "special mission" on February 10th to drop a total of eight, one- and two-hour delayed, Parafexes on the east bank of the Irrawaddy between Chauk and Yenangyaung. The operation required only that the devices be dropped surreptitiously in the designated positions by aeroplanes apparently on their way to somewhere else. As a result these sorties were curiously bland as they lacked the instant gratification that was normally to be had from a satisfying display of flashes and bangs, although some compensation could be had from the subsequent strafing of lines of communication before heading for home. In the event only six of the Parafexes were dropped as HR567 suffered a total electrical failure and the crew diverted to Onbauk where the aircraft overran the runway on landing, although it sustained only superficial damage.

The squadron flew a second CLOAK mission on February 12th when Fg Offs Garnham and Nankervis in HR451 and Flt Lt Aykroyd and WO Sellars in HR527 dropped four more Parafexes from a height of 2-3,000 feet in the same area as the first lot but this was to be the last time that the squadron was tasked in the deception role. Having delivered their 'secret weapons' both crews indulged in a little ground strafing of roads and railways and took in the Japanese airstrips at Allanmyo and Magwe while they were about it. AA fire was particularly brisk over the latter and both aircraft were hit, obliging Rex Garnham and Jack Nankervis to make a precautionary landing at Kalemyo, but neither aeroplane was seriously damaged and both crews were unhurt. HR451, which had been flying its forty-third operational sortie, was rescued the next day when a 'chippy' from No 7045 SE was flown over to Kalemyo in a Harvard to patch up its perforated wingtip.

The squadron's sortie rate was still increasing and this inevitably produced a corresponding rise in the incidence of bird strikes and small arms damage, resulting in more repair work for the groundcrew and more ferry trips for the Harvard. The next such incident occurred on February 19th when Sqn Ldr Duclos and Flt Lt McFadzean opted to land at Sadaung when HR526 had one of its fuel tanks holed during a sortie on the 19th.

An additional task came the groundcrews' way on February 14th when No 908 Wg set up an Advanced Landing Ground (ALG) at Thazi to provide a staging post between main base and the operational area. By providing an intermediate refuelling point this allowed the aircraft to carry four 500 lb bombs again, since any crews who found themselves short of fuel could land at Thazi to top-up on the way home. The ALG was manned by a joint detachment drawn from the combined resources of Nos 7045, 7047 and 7082 SEs. They were to earn their keep as Thazi was to see a fair amount of use over the next two months.

At about this time the appearance of the squadron's aircraft was radically altered as a result of the promulgation on 15th February of a new colour scheme for some aircraft serving in ACSEA. Henceforth they were to be silver overall, apart from a black recognition stripe on the wings, tailplane and fin. This change conformed to an emerging policy, first introduced by the USAAF in 1944, which was leading to the progressive abandoning of camouflage altogether in the interests of reducing maintenance demands and weight (and thus enhancing performance), and saving both time and money. The RAF was less enthusiastic about this at first but from early 1945 it did go so far as to begin flying some of its American-supplied aeroplanes, notably Thunderbolts (used operationally by the RAF only in ACSEA), in the natural aluminium finish in which they had been delivered. In the specific cases of Mosquitos and Warwicks based in India, however, the adoption of a silver finish had nothing to do with weight-saving; it was an attempt to minimise heat absorption by their wood and fabric coverings (see Annex K).

Wg Cdr Walker had been very disturbed when he had first learned of this proposal during January (at which stage it was apparently the intention to paint the aeroplanes white) and at the end of the month he had written, "I should be impressed if any Mosquito designer can convince me and my crews that a white Mosquito is safe to fly and a camouflaged one is not. From an operational standpoint the proposal is too stupid to warrant comment. To date this development has not been

No wonder the wings came off! B Flight at Kumbhirgram - the figure on the right, picked out by an arrow, is Fg Off Don Blenkhorne. Note the gremlin which had been B Flight's emblem since at least October 1940. Previously only applicable to Thunderbolts, the white identification bands marked on the wings of this aeroplane, HR392/OB.N, were authorised for use on Mosquitos and other types from 1st February 1945. Only two weeks later further instructions were received directing that Mosquitos were to be repainted in silver, with their tactical markings in black; implementation of this change was well advanced by the end of March, although No 45 Sqn was still flying some camouflaged Mosquitos in mid-April. The date of this photograph is probably, therefore, within a few weeks either side of 1st March 1945. (L Wilde)

passed on to the crews." Even after it had been implemented the idea of silver aeroplanes was regarded with a considerable lack of enthusiasm and at the end of March the CO, by then Sqn Ldr Duclos, wrote:

> The increasing number of silver doped Mosquitos is being met with increasing disapproval by the aircrews. Whatever the technical advantages of this scheme may be, and it is believed that they are very limited, the operational disadvantages incurred are considerable. It has been found that the standard camouflage on a Mosquito renders it extremely difficult to spot from above when flying over wooded or scrub country such as is encountered in Burma. The silver ones, however, can hardly be missed as they immediately catch one's eye due to the great contrast. Fortunately, of late, no enemy air opposition has been met but it must be accepted that losses due to enemy fighters will be probable when we come up against them while flying our silver aircraft.

As it happened the squadron was never to be engaged by the JAAF again so the problem went away and by late April most (if not all) of its Mosquitos were silver. By this time the aircraft had already been wearing the squadron's OB code for some months. It is not certain when this had first been reintroduced but it is possible that code letters were first painted on when the squadron moved forward to Kumbhirgram in September 1944; they were certainly being worn by late November. Originally applied in pale grey on the green/brown camouflage, on the new silver finish the codes were in black[9].

There had been several changes in the aircrew complement since the squadron had moved back to the forward area and some of the real veterans had left during February. Fg Offs Max Neil, Ernie Hallett and 'Joe' Cartledge all departed for home that month, the first two having been with the squadron since its days in North Africa; in August all three were to be gazetted for DFCs. A number of new faces had appeared to maintain the squadron's strength and the most recent intake, Flt Lts J McPhee AFC, B V Draper DFC, G O L Dyke and J L Evans DFC, Fg Offs R M Cowley RAAF and D F Kerr and WOs R P Buist and P R James, F/Sgt C J Zussen and Sgt J A Russell, had all checked in during February. Some had arrived virtually direct from the UK while others had come via No 1672 CU, but all were fully Mosquito-qualified and most were flying their first ops within a few days.

Two of the new arrivals were to be lost before the month was out. Two sections of four were tasked with a bombing attack against a concentration of Japanese troops and armour on February 28th. Flt Lt Draper and WO James were killed when HR457 was seen to break up at about 4,000 feet in its dive; no one reported any enemy fire. Another crew had been posted missing on February 17th. WO Pinkerton had been released from hospital after the Jeep accident on the 5th but his usual pilot, Pete Ewing, was still unfit to fly. In his absence, Bob Pinkerton flew a dawn strike against Heho aerodrome with F/Sgt Gordon Ashworth. Their Mosquito failed to return but, as the two aircraft involved had became separated, there was no explanation for HR390's disappearance and its crew was posted missing presumed killed.

XIVth Army started to break out of its bridgeheads in late February and began to advance on Mandalay and Meiktila. Both had fallen by the end of March. No 45 Sqn operated at full stretch in direct support of this campaign and in softening up the area to the south in preparation for the eventual drive towards Rangoon. The events of March 1945, during which it flew an average of more than eleven sorties every day, represent what is arguably the highpoint of the squadron's entire career. It certainly does when measured in purely statistical terms; hours flown, sorties launched and weapons expenditure all exceeded anything that it had ever done before, or has done since.

The first attacks were made by six Mosquitos hitting lines of communication around Mandalay on March 1st, several Japanese tanks being claimed as destroyed. Eight aircraft went further south on the 2nd and disrupted rail traffic around Allanmyo. Fourteen sorties were flown on the 3rd against rail traffic near Magwe. And so it went on. Between the 4th and 7th twenty-two night sorties were flown against the airfields at Toungoo, Heho, Pyinmana and Tennant to prevent the JAAF's interfering with the army's advance and then the campaign switched to bridges until the 11th.

Many of the bridges in Burma had a by-pass which was even more difficult to destroy than the bridge itself. The ORB laments, "By-pass bridges on embankments are heart breaking, for an error of only 5 yards has little or no effect on their serviceability." Up to sixteen sorties a day were flown against bridges at Thawatti, Sinthe, Swa and Pyinmana during this period. Much damage was done and the bridges were certainly rendered unusable but it was a frustrating business. On the 9th, for instance, a total of twelve aircraft attacked the Thawatti main and by-pass bridges in three waves of four. When the first formation withdrew they left a substantial hole in the northern end of the main bridge and thirty yards of adjacent track torn up. The second strike added to the damage and the last formation obtained three direct hits on the embankment of the by-pass and disrupted its approach tracks. The following day three more aircraft attacked the Thawatti by-pass, "of their 12 bombs, 2 registered direct hits and the bridge was seen to break up and the rails to twist, 2 more were seen to burst under the centre section" - but the bridge was still standing. Four more aircraft went back on the 11th and, "2 bombs hit the embankment 10 yards south of the bridge, 2 burst to the north of the bridge centre, 2 were direct hits on the centre of the bridge. The bridge appeared almost destroyed and was

This picture conveys an excellent impression of a railway bridge and by-pass. This one, at Sinthe, was bombed by the squadron on March 10th, 11th, 12th, 16th, 28th and 29th. (D E Goodrich)

leaning to the east at an angle of 30°" - but still it had not actually collapsed. That afternoon, however, three aircraft went for the Pyinmana by-pass bridge and scored five direct hits. A section, sixty feet long, collapsed completely, taking a further twenty feet of trestle with it - it could be done!

On March 12th tasking priority was switched to direct support missions in response to army requests and over the next few days the briefed targets included stores dumps near Pontha and Kalaw and troop concentrations at Pyinzi and Pindale. Attacks against bridges continued, however, and strafing of road, rail and river traffic was a feature of most sorties.

By this time the ALG at Thazi was being used quite frequently both as a staging post and as a bolthole. On March 4th, for instance, WO Stace and Plt Off Kirk had taken off from there in company with Plt Off Goodrich and WO Nessim to 'rhubarb' the railway line between Pyawbwe and Thawatti. Towards the end of their sortie they came across a pair of stationary locomotives and several coaches camouflaged with foliage. Between them the two Mosquitos expended 1,640 rounds of 20mm and 6,500 rounds of .303 ammo and when they left both locos were enveloped in smoke. HR441 had been hit by return fire, however, and had sustained damage to its elevators, starboard outer fuel tank and port engine. Nursing his aeroplane back 'on one', Fred Stace carried out a successful emergency landing at Thazi. Having seen his companion safely down, Doug Goodrich flew on to Kumbhirgram, returning the following day in HR456 to pick up the stranded crew. Less than twenty-four hours later Thazi was to see another drama. Having positioned there during the day WOs O'Connor and McKie were taking off at 0140hrs on the 5th when a water buffalo ran across the runway from left to right! The aeroplane (HR404) stopped somewhat abruptly but the crew were able to walk away from the wreckage - which is more than could be said for the unfortunate buffalo. Although it was the first time that a No 45 Sqn aircraft had been involved in such an

HR462 OB.J taxies in on 11th March 1945 after flying its fiftieth sortie; the crew were WOs O'Connor and McKie. Although a silver finish was now in vogue, this aeroplane is still camouflaged, although the entrance door looks as if it might have been transferred from a silver aircraft. There is personal device painted on the door but it is not possible to make out exactly what it is. Also of interest are the forty-nine mission symbols on the nose and a small glazed panel for an F.24 camera just above the machine gun muzzles. (S O'Connor)

incident it was reported to have happened before at Thazi and it was rumoured that Japanese guerrillas were stampeding the animals onto the runway to hinder operations.

Another aeroplane, HR539, had been damaged during a sortie flown on March 4th and Rex Garnham and Jack Nankervis had also been obliged to return with one fan feathered, eventually landing at Sadaung. Yet another forward strip was to prove its worth on the 15th. That day twenty-four Mosquitos, twelve from each of Nos 45 and 82 Sqns, attacked oil installations at Yenangyaung. No 82 Sqn delivered their weapons in a shallow-dive attack from 12,000 feet while the Flying Camels planned an approach from the east in line abreast at low level. As they converged on the target, with some aircraft drawing ahead of the others, the AA guns opened up. For those at the back of the bunch the problem was not only the flak but the explosions of the delayed action bombs dropped a few seconds earlier by the leaders of the pack. Wally McLellan reckoned he could get away with it but miscalculated; he described what happened next in an account published in 1985[10].

> Over the target the whole ground came up to meet us as the thirty-two 500 lb bombs dropped by the preceding aircraft exploded together. We seemed to be flying through solid earth mixed with all sorts of junk from trees

One of No 45 Sqn's silver Mosquitos, with its bomb bay doors still open, clears the target area at Yenangyaung, probably on 15th March 1945. In the original of this photograph three other Mosquitos can be made out over the trees on the far bank of the river, all flying at a much lower level. (D E Goodrich)

> to 40 gallon drums. The noise was mind bending and holes, large and small, appeared everywhere in the aircraft. A black log, about six feet long, hung suspended perpendicularly in the air in front of me but there was nothing I could do to avoid it. We hit it with a terrific jar which yawed the aircraft. The log jammed in the leading edge of the wing between me and the port motor and stayed there against the main spar. This was not a good thing as the leading edge also contained the oil radiator for that engine and oil was pouring out. At the same time every Jap gun was concentrating on us and we could feel the thuds of hits and hear the explosions. I had accepted that this was the end but I felt quite calm.

Although it soon proved necessary to shut down the port engine, the aeroplane held together but the problem was not made any easier when Jim Vernon reported that they still had one 500 pounder hung-up. With the drag of the log stuck in the wing and a dead engine they could not get the aeroplane above 1,000 feet and an unsuccessful attempt to shake the bomb loose by firing the guns only served to reduce their airspeed and bleed off pneumatic pressure which could not be replenished with the port engine out. Unenthusiastic about the prospect of a parachute descent into Japanese-occupied territory they headed for Kalewa with the operating temperature on the good engine steadily rising. It seems unlikely that they would have made it but, quite by chance and with about 100 miles still to go, they found the newly opened Thunderbolt strip at Sinthe. McLellan landed fast and flapless on the short airstrip and, low on air pressure to

WO Freddie Stace, encumbered with all the paraphernalia of an operational pilot - 'Mae West', pistol, kukri, parachute, etc. With WO Eric Ashton as his nav, Fred Stace flew his first sortie on 8th January 1945. A month later he teamed up with F Sgt Kirk with whom he flew until the squadron was withdrawn to Madras in May by which time he had flown over forty ops. (A H Pridmore)

work the brakes, the aircraft was still doing about 90 mph when it ran off the end of the runway and careered through various storage areas. Eventually the undercarriage collapsed and the aeroplane slid to a halt on its belly. Happily, the hung-up bomb did not explode, but that was the end of the road for HR451. Two other aircraft had sustained damage during the attack and one of them, HR399, also landed at Sinthe. Its arrival was comparatively unspectacular, however, and, having ascertained that their colleagues were substantially intact, Flt Lt Hal Aykroyd and WO Harry Sellars were later able to fly on to Kumbhirgram.

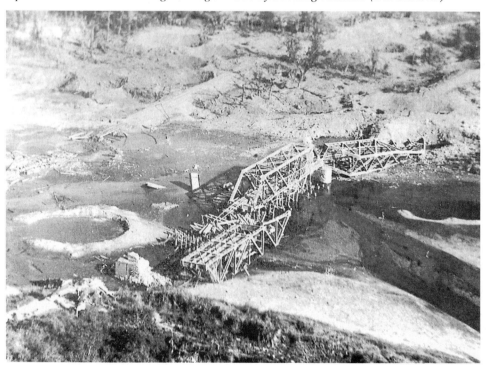

The Thawatti bridge which, along with its embanked by-pass, was attacked by sixteen of the squadron's Mosquitos on 9th March, three more on the tenth, four on the 11th, two on the 16th, two on the 26th and three on the 28th. The date of this picture is not known but the main bridge has been badly damaged and has been propped up from beneath by timbers; furthermore there are no rails on the approach to either end. The bridge was still intact but clearly unusable and it was left like this after every visit but the damage was quickly repaired and on 31st March it was reported to be back in use - bridge-busting could be a frustrating business. (D E Goodrich)

All of the bombs dropped on Yenangyaung had been fused at eleven seconds and the crews insisted that their problems had arisen because premature detonations had not allowed the later aircraft (which were only a few seconds behind) to clear the target. An irate signal was despatched, complaining that some bombs had exploded no more than four seconds after impact. This produced the bland response that an eleven-second setting could produce a delay of, "anywhere between four and twenty seconds" - there was no answer to that!

Some repair work had been carried out on the bridges at Sinthe and Thawatti so ten Mosquitos were despatched to render them unserviceable again on March 16th, four more attacking the Swa bridge in the afternoon. The following day the CO and Frank Harper had to divert to Monywa in HR456 after an attack on Pontha. It was another self-damage incident and at least the third time that this particular crew had nearly been hoist with their own petard - which may well explain why many of the groundcrew referred to Johnny Walker as "the Mad Hatter". The CO was not alone on this occasion, however, as 'Nick' Nicholls and Bob Barclay had picked up a ricochet from one of their own 20mm cannons but the damage to HR526 was sight and they were able to fly back to Kumbhirgram.

Bridges were easy enough to find and to damage but notoriously difficult to destroy. Nevertheless it could be done. This one is the bridge at Swa which was attacked by the squadron on several occasions. (D E Goodrich)

In the afternoon of March 18th twelve aircraft, each loaded with 2,000 lbs of bombs, positioned at Thazi whence they were to carry out individual attacks during the night against enemy positions at a village in the vicinity of Singu. Don Blenkhorne's aircraft developed a glycol leak and he and Alf Pridmore had to be withdrawn from the operation. Although there was a moon, the target proved to be very difficult to find and, in view of the proximity of friendly forces, three of the crews were not convinced that they had identified it correctly and wisely elected not to attack. The other eight were confident that they had the right place and a total of twenty-three 500 pounders and eight 250 lb incendiaries was dropped and by the time that the last aircraft left substantial fires had been started. On the 20th ten aircraft, operating in two groups of five, 45 minutes apart, hit Yenangyaung again, this time using a dive attack. Extensive fires were started and all aircraft returned to base although several had sustained damage from AA fire.

A total of ten aircraft took off together on March 21st and then split up into pairs to 'rhubarb' lines of communication east of the Irrawaddy. The following day two aircraft took off from Thazi for another strafing mission while another eight bombed supply dumps in the vicinity of Ingon. HR567 was hit in the tailplane but Flt Lt George Dyke and F/Sgt 'Joe' Zussen were able to return to Kumbhirgram while the CO and Frank Harper stopped off at Thazi in HR627 to pick up some fuel. Another twelve sorties were flown on the 23rd, eight of them against Loikawng, and the squadron had another go at some bridges on the 24th, four small ones this time, carrying road rather than rail traffic. The squadron attacked in three pairs and a section of three. The bridges at Shwengyaung and Thamakan were near-missed but those near Namhkok and at Hopong both collapsed. The nine crews despatched to tackle the bridges were not the only ones to fly that day, incidentally, a further nineteen sorties being flown in the course of five further missions, several crews flying twice.

On March 25th the CO led seven crews on a long-range strike against the solidly constructed bridge over the Sittang at Toungoo. The bombing was very accurate. Of the twenty-eight bombs dropped, no fewer than sixteen burst *under* the eastern end of the bridge, four *hit* the second pier and four more *hit* the fifth span from the western end (the seventh aircraft's strikes were not observed as the aircraft was itself hit by return fire). Despite this display of outstanding marksmanship, however, the 500 pounders were not really up to the job and the bridge was only damaged, not destroyed. On the other hand, it had been defended and two of the Mosquitos were hit by AA fire.

The aircraft flown by WOs Rollins and Moutrey, HR539, had suffered some damage but the crew were uninjured and they were able to fly it safely back to base. Things were more 'dicey' in HR627, the CO's aircraft, which had been hit in the cockpit area. 'Johnny' Walker had been wounded in the face; his eyesight was badly impaired and shortly afterwards he lost consciousness. Frank Harper succeeded in maintaining control of the aeroplane and when the CO, who was bleeding profusely, came round he rendered first-aid to staunch the loss of blood. Although there was a strip at Meiktila its possession was still being hotly disputed by ground forces and they were refused permission to land. Between them, and escorted by George Dyke and 'Joe'

Fg Off Bob Barclay sits on a 500 lb bomb and contemplates life, the universe and everything while giving himself a manicure with a kukri - that hat has evidently seen some service! (H M Nicholls)

Zussen in HR514, they flew the aircraft to Monywa where, with Harper's invaluable assistance, the CO eventually managed to land off his third approach. Wg Cdr Walker was transferred to hospital in Comilla where the surgeons were able to save both of his eyes, although he was left with permanently impaired vision in one of them and it was obviously going to be some time before the doctors would permit him to fly again. He had already led the Flying Camels for ten hectic months, during which he had flown fifty-three operational sorties - despite the pious observations he had made back in December about the need to prevent people "punching too many trips", it is interesting to note that the CO was still top of the missions-flown league table - and by a comfortable margin too. It was decided that 'Johnny' Walker had done enough and that he was to be repatriated; he began his journey back to the UK on April 21st.

Sqn Ldr 'Duke' Duclos assumed command of the squadron and the following day he flew Fg Off Russ Cowley over to Monywa in HR456 so that the latter could pick up Walker's aeroplane and ferry it back to Kumbhirgram. Another aircraft was lost that day, March 26th, but this time both of the crew were killed. WO Holmes and F/Sgt Austen, who had been with the squadron since January, were in one of a pair of aircraft which had taken off from Thazi to patrol in the vicinity of Toungoo at dawn. Two vehicles were spotted and the Mosquitos turned in to attack. HR527 scored strikes on one of the vehicles but failed to pull out of its dive, flew into the ground and blew up. Doug Goodrich and Maurice Nessim circled the area in HR397 but observed no fire from the ground. Alan Holmes and Bill Austen were to be No 45 Sqn's last combat fatalities during the Second

World War.

As the month drew to a close the intensity of operations continued to rise. The first peak had occurred on the 24th when twenty-eight sorties had been flown but there were others: twenty-one on the 28th; twenty on the 29th; nineteen on the 30th and again on the 31st. Rail and road bridges continued to figure prominently among the assigned targets in late March, among them those at Thawatti, Ela, Sinthe, Pyinmana, Loikaw, Namhkok and over the Nam Tamhpak near Hishseng, the latter being destroyed on the 30th. Only three aircraft sustained any damage as a result of all this activity; on March 26th RF598 (Fg Off Blenkhorne and WO Pridmore) picked up a .50 calibre round, probably fired from Satthwa, and in the course of a four-aircraft strike on a factory in Thayetmyo on March 29th HR567 (Fg Off Ewing and Flt Lt Williams) and HR627 (Sqn Ldr Braithwaite and Fg Off Whitcutt - a recently arrived crew) were both hit by small arms fire but the damage was slight in all three cases.

During March the squadron had mounted 352 sorties and flown 1,501 hours, of which 1,348 had been operational. It had dropped 556,500 lbs of bombs and fired 149,850 rounds of ammunition[11]. This was certainly a 'personal best' for the Flying Camels and very probably also established the monthly record for all RAF attack squadrons during the Far Eastern campaign. The groundcrews had worked miracles. Average serviceability had been a remarkable 87%. The supply of replacement aircraft had dried up towards the end of the month and spares had become a problem but the fleet had been kept in the air by salvaging parts from crashed and damaged aircraft. Even at the end of this most remarkable March there were still thirteen aircraft available for ops. As Sqn Ldr Duclos wrote at the time, "The increased tempo of work proved tiring but the sense of pride in the squadron's achievements has been ample reward, providing personnel with a 'dig' at the other Mosquito squadrons operating from our strip"[12].

It was a source of considerable satisfaction to aircrew and groundcrew alike that several of the squadron's aircraft passed their 'half-century' during March. By the end of the

During March 1945 several of the squadron's Mosquitos racked up their fiftieth operational sorties. This one is HR456/OB.M which notched up its half century on March 13th. It is seen here on that occasion with its crew, Plt Off 'Ron' Wilcock and Flt Lt Andy Andrews wearing suitable crowns, sashes and extravagant medals, and half buried in bouquets. There are many photographs of Luftwaffe units celebrating the passing of significant operational milestones with ceremonies of this nature but there are few showing that the RAF did it too. (D E Goodrich)

month six of them had flown over fifty missions, the top-scorer at that date being HR462/OB.J with a total of sixty-one operational sorties to its credit. The month had also seen some changes among the executive appointments. Sqn Ldr Torrence left on attachment to HQ 221 Gp on the 10th (this arrangement becoming permanent a month later), leaving his flight in the hands of Flt Lt McLellan until the new OC A Flight, Sqn Ldr D A Braithwaite DFC*, arrived from HQ RAF Burma on the 18th. Braithwaite and his nav, Fg Off C G Whitcutt, flew three sorties but at the end of the month he was detached to Ranchi to attend a SLAIS course. In his absence Fg Off R A Whiteside became OC A Flight and, since Sqn Ldr Braithwaite was packed off to Kolar within days of rejoining the squadron in April, Allan Whiteside subsequently retained the post being promoted to flight lieutenant on April 9th. So far as B Flight was concerned, when Sqn Ldr Duclos had been obliged to take over as CO on March 25th, command of his flight had passed to Flt Lt Hal Aykroyd. Both of the new flight commanders had been with the squadron since the previous December. Whether it was by accident or design is uncertain, but the effect of all these changes was to drop the rank of all the senior appointments by one notch. Despite this, their leadership of the squadron during its final months in combat was to result in the award of DFCs to all three on various dates in August and October.

Other notable occurrences among the flying personnel in March were the departures of the squadron's last New Zealander, Fg Off Rex Garnham, and another of the seasoned Australians, Flt Lt Jack 'Nank' Nankervis. On March 26th the squadron learned of the award of a DFC to Fg Off Ewing and, in April, of another to Fg Off Harper. Finally, there was a well-deserved DSO for 'Johnny' Walker who had shepherded the squadron through most of its work up, sustained it during its early set backs and then led it on to its spectacular performance in March 1945.

There had been two notable events in March so far as No 7045 SE was concerned. On the 19th they took delivery of HR627, the squadron's first aircraft fitted for rocket-firing, although rockets continued to be No 47 Sqn's speciality and the Flying Camels never used these weapons in action. The second significant incident concerned the MT Office. This bamboo-built basha had been used by the squadron when it had first been at Kumbhirgram in 1943 (some of the drivers from that era were still on strength) and in its time it had withstood Japanese air attacks, gales, monsoon rains and even an earthquake. On March 21st, for no apparent reason, it just gave up and collapsed.

As is so often the case, so long as the work is perceived to be worthwhile, there seems to be almost no limit to the amount of effort that airmen inspired by unit loyalty will make, and the squadron's outstanding performance in March was due to them just as much as to the aircrew. Despite the notional separation of the groundcrew into No 7045 SE it was still the practice for a pilot and navigator to have a personal aeroplane with its own maintenance team of two fitters and a rigger. This bred close working relationships and an interdependence which inspired mutual trust and respect. Sadly, however, it is difficult to quantify the undoubted value of these commodities, and in an increasingly cost-conscious post-war air force such manpower-intensive

Left:- WO Ken Putman, who first crewed up with Bill Taylor, one of the squadron's many Australians, in the UK in mid-1943. They joined No 45 Sqn in February 1944 and continued to fly together until the end of the squadron's period of ops with Mosquitos. This photograph was taken at Cholavaram circa July 1945. (A H Pridmore). Right:- Flt Lt Hal Aykroyd, F Sgt Harold Sellars and their groundcrew team in March 1945 with a, still camouflaged HR399/OB.R, displaying fifty-four mission symbols. Aykroyd and Sellars flew this aeroplanes on 13th April when it completed its fifty-fifth and last operational sortie, which suggests that this may have been the occasion on which this photograph was taken. (W G A Glaze)

arrangements were soon abandoned.

There is an atavistic desire for any team, however small, to have some sort of identifying symbol or badge and this is particularly strong within the military community. As with many other units, before and since, this took the form of what has come to be called 'nose art' and many of the squadron's Mosquitos sported an individual device painted on the crew entry door. These emblems included the cartoon character *Oor Wullie*, the *Saint*, a maple leaf and the inevitable bathing beauties. Many of these doors appear to have been transferred from aircraft to aircraft as replacements were received and some were still in evidence as late as October 1945 on aeroplanes which had not actually flown in combat[13].

Despite the intensive demands being made on the squadron, time was still found for sport and during March its soccer team had played six matches, five of which they had won. Morale could not have been higher. It is very significant that No 908 Wg's ORB entry for March 1945 observes that the camaraderie between No 45 Sqn and No 7045 SE was still very apparent and stressed how important it was that these two notionally independent units should not be separated.

Meanwhile the war went on. Four aircraft bombed and strafed a bomb dump and troop positions near Yezin on 1st April 1st, nineteen passes being made over the target, while two others damaged the bridge at Yamethin. The squadron was then given a well-earned two-day stand down. Ops resumed on the morning of the 4th with two sections of three attacking bridges near Sadongyaung and Myothit and then 'rhubarbing' along the Irrawaddy. In the afternoon four aircraft staged through Thazi on their way to attack a reported Japanese concentration in the village of Ketkako which they left in flames. Despite having been able to top-up on the outbound leg, WOs Walsh and Orsborn were obliged

to land at Monywa when HR567 ran short of fuel; they were accompanied by Fg Offs Fortune and Mears in HR332 which had an unserviceable ASI. Unfortunately both aircraft were damaged when they overshot the runway. The other pair returned to Thazi whence they flew another mission on the 5th, while another six from Kumbhirgram attacked the railway station at Hngetthaik.

Hngetthaik was hit by another six aircraft on the 6th, while two more went to Dalangyun. On the 7th eight sorties were launched. Six of them, each toting four 500 lb bombs, were tasked against an ammunition dump at Pasawng, on the Salween river, which they hit with what seemed at the time to be only moderate results, although some fires were certainly started. A few days later, however, Intelligence reported that, apart from having destroyed large quantities of petrol and other stores, this attack had accounted for eight MT vehicles and inflicted 180 Japanese casualties.

This remained the established pattern of operations for the remainder of April. Missions tended to be flown in sections of two or three aircraft, but the total number of daily sorties rarely exceeded eight. Many attacks were flown in direct support of the army which was now advancing rapidly southwards down the Sittang with a second thrust later developing down the Irrawaddy towards Allanmyo. In fact Doug Goodrich recalls that the military intelligence network was often hard-pressed to keep the squadron informed as to the exact whereabouts of the forward troops - on occasion the bomb line was plotted from the *Times of India*, since this was the most up to date information available! Targets allocated to the squadron in April were often Japanese troop positions and stores dumps but bridges still figured occasionally as did the fort at Toungoo (on the 14th) and 'rhubarbing' of road, rail and river traffic continued to be a feature of most trips. The squadron's operations were wide-ranging and its targets included Magwe, Myohla, Tatkon,

Minbu, Sinzeik, Namhkok, Kywebwe, Pyu, Ywatang and Penwegon. Occasional use was made of Thazi, Monywa and Kinmagan, either to top up on the way out or to pick up fuel on the way back. No Japanese aircraft were encountered and, compared to a month or two earlier, there was relatively little opposition from ground fire. In fact April was notable for being the first month since the squadron had begun Mosquito operations in which there were no casualties.

The comparative reduction in effort during April was partly due to a lack of aircraft. Replacements were scarce and when they did come through they often seemed to arrive in groups of three, all of which tended to be due for immediate 'Minors'. The implementation of a Special Technical Instruction (STI) on all Merlin engines caused further problems, as a result of which one aircraft was grounded for sixteen days awaiting the delivery of a spare engine. The STI required the valve covers to be removed but no replacement gaskets were available. The ever-resourceful fitters of the SE solved the problem by raiding the map store and making their own out of compressed paper - whether they ever told the aircrew about this is not recorded! The temperature and humidity were rising again and, for the SE's Maintenance Flight, Fg Off Hanslip reintroduced the split working day that had been employed in the hot seasons of 1943 and 1944. There was no relief for the airmen of the turn round teams, however, and they continued to refuel and rearm aircraft as and when required.

On April 18th the squadron was warned for a move to Joari, as was No 82 Sqn, and preparations began immediately. Sqn Ldr Duclos and OC No 7045 SE flew down there on the 20th to discuss the implications of the move with No 224 Gp's Advanced HQ. It transpired that only the Daily Servicing Sections of the SE were to go to Joari, the Repair and Inspection people (and Joey) remaining at Kumbhirgram. The deployment was to support the final assault on Rangoon and on the 24th the squadron was further notified that on May 15th it and the entire SE were to be

Pilot	Navigator
Sqn Ldr V S H Duclos	Flt Lt A McFadzean DFC
A Flight	
Flt Lt R A Whiteside	Fg Off G Lauder
Flt Lt L R Ovenden AFC	F/Sgt A J Walters
Flt Lt G O L Dyke	Fg Off D F Kerr
Fg Off P N Ewing DFC RAAF	Fg Off G F Williams RAAF
Fg Off W G M Taylor RAAF	WO K F Putman
WO P Buist	F/Sgt J A Russell
WO S O'Connor	WO A A McKie
WO H Rollins	WO R E Moutrey
WO B Walsh	WO H Orsborn
B Flight	
Flt Lt H A Aykroyd	WO H Sellars
Flt Lt J McPhee AFC	Flt Lt J L Evans DFC
Fg Off F C Fortune	Flt Lt A Mears
Fg Off H M Nicholls RAAF	Flt Lt R M Barclay RAAF
Fg Off D M Blenkhorne RCAF	WO A H Pridmore
Fg Off R M Cowley RAAF	F/Sgt N Jones RAAF
Plt Off J R Wilcock	Flt Lt L S Andrews
Plt Off D E Goodrich	WO S M D Nessim
WO F J Stace	Plt Off F R Kirk
WO G A McDonald	F/Sgt T H Bartlett

Fig 11.2. No 45 Sqn's crew state as at mid-April 1945.

withdrawn to Chakulia where they both would be rested from operations. On April 22nd two more of the desert veterans, Flt Lts Wally McLellan and Jimmy Vernon, left the squadron and began their journey home to Australia; both were decorated with DFCs in August. Among the aircrew, only Flt Lt Bob Barclay could now shoot lines about the sandstorms at Gambut in 1941.

Over the preceding six months losses and postings had significantly altered the squadron's constitution, less than half of the aircrew who had arrived at Kumbhirgram in the previous September still remaining on strength. The crew state as at mid-April 1945 is shown at Figure 11.2, this pattern remaining substantially unchanged until the squadron was withdrawn from operations. There was, as always, a handful of supernumerary aircrew available who continued to fly as and when required. These included just one pilot, Fg Off A N Huon, and a number of navs whose pilots had either been posted or recrewed: Fg Offs C G Whitcutt, F J Harper and E D Rainbow; WO E Ashton and F/Sgt C J Zussen.

There had already been a number of changes among the incumbents of the various ground appointments and others were about to occur; by the end of the month, only the Adj, Flt Lt Wilson, remained from the original team that had moved in from Ranchi. A new MO, Flt Lt J A Duncan, was about to replace Flt Lt Redfern. Plt Off Arnold had been posted to No 669 Sqn on December 7th and his replacement as Intelligence Officer, Plt Off R B Serjeant, was on the point of leaving for the UK so responsibility for debriefing crews and compiling Operations Reports (OPREP) was now in the hands of Fg Off J L Bonnar. Flt Lt Joyce had transferred to No 7060 SE in January, his successor as OC No 7045 SE being Flt Lt W S E Allen MBE, who had arrived on February 20th, but a month later he had been relieved by Fg Off R L Hanslip who was to look after the squadron's nuts and bolts for the next year. Finally, the squadron's second Signals Officer of the Mosquito era, Fg Off L S King, was about to be replaced by Fg Off J R Halsey.

While packing was getting under way the first Mosquito flew down to Joari on the 24th (Flt Lt Whiteside with Fg Off Whitcutt and Fg Off Halsey) followed by a second (Plt Off Goodrich and WO Nessim) on the 25th. Ops continued while all this activity was going on with six sorties being flown on April 22nd and four on the 23rd, all operating as pairs. These missions were unremarkable apart from HR309's developing an engine problem while operating over Toungoo on the 22nd which led to its crew, Fg Off Fortune and Flt Lt Mears diverting to Thedaw accompanied by their No 2, WO Buist and F/Sgt Russell in HR539. One of the missions flown on the 24th, a strike against a petrol dump at Nyaunglebin was also slightly out of the ordinary as both crews (Goodrich and Nessim, and Cowley and Jones) were required to operate from and recover to Monywa for briefing and debriefing. The squadron flew its last missions from Kumbhirgram on the 25th, seven aircraft in three sections against a cluster of objectives at Payangsu, Kyaunggon and Paungde.

The move to the Arakan involved the transfer of a total of one hundred groundcrew and was carried out by five Dakotas on the 26th and another three on the 27th. At much the same time Flt Lt Duncan, the new MO, and sixteen men returned from Kinmagan where they had been supporting No 908

Wg's Advanced HQ. Eleven Mosquitos flew down to Joari on the 27th, making a total of thirteen, with a few more following over the next few days. In all the squadron used sixteen of its Mosquitos while operating from the Arakan: HR309, HR368, HR372, HR526, HR539, HR573, HR627, HR633, RF585, RF598, RF657, RF660, RF668, RF672, RF679 and RF697.

The squadron was now attached to No 901 Wg which was based at Chiringa with Nos 22, 27, 177 and 211 Sqns (all Beaufighters), while No 110 Sqn (Mosquitos) was forward at Joari where it was now joined by Nos 45 and 82 Sqns. Joari was only a fair-weather strip with a surface of rolled, dry paddy and there was some concern about the ability of the runway to support the operations of three Mosquito squadrons - the staff at Wing HQ prayed that it would not rain. Compared to Kumbhirgram, the new airfield was pretty primitive domestically; there was, for instance, no lighting, no cinema and there were no charpoys! Those with personal camp beds were all right, of course, but everyone else was obliged to make his own bed from bamboo. Conditions were not improved by the climate and, despite being close to the sea, it was even hotter and stickier than it had been in Assam. Some relief could be gained from the occasional swimming trip but even these proved to be something of a mixed blessing as two airmen were incapacitated for a couple of days after an encounter with a sting ray. The squadron had not gone to Joari to enjoy itself, however, but to take part in the recapture of Rangoon. It was the last lap and they could live with a little discomfort; morale remained high and enthusiasm was undented.

The first three-aircraft mission was flown from Joari on April 30th but the monsoon season was opening and deteriorating weather frustrated their attempt to reach the target and the sorties were aborted. That same day OC No 901 Wg, Gp Capt C D Tomalin DFC AFC, and his staff briefed the aircrew on the assault on Rangoon, Operation DRACULA, and Sqn Ldr Duclos later addressed the squadron's groundcrew to keep them in the picture.

On May 1st the squadron put up six aircraft in the morning and another six in the afternoon as its contribution to the wing's sixty-seven sortie effort on the first day of DRACULA. It was something of an anticlimax. Both missions were required to mount 'cab rank' patrols to the west of Rangoon and await tasking by the army. Their help was not called for, however, and when they reached their fuel limit all aircraft deposited their bombs on their designated secondary targets at Thaunggon and Sadainghmut and did a bit of strafing on the way home.

Twelve aircraft were airborne before dawn on the 2nd to patrol each bank of the Irrawaddy in sections of six. Although they made contact with 'Boxwood', their controller on the ground, he had no trade for them so six tons of bombs were dropped on targets of opportunity before the aircraft

The squadron and much of No 7045 SE moved to the coast in May 1945. While domestic facilities were more primitive than at Kumbhirgram, and it was hotter and stickier, there were opportunities for a spot of skinny-dipping in the sea. (A H Pridmore)

turned for home. The recovery meant penetrating a belt of violent electrical storms and most crews experienced some difficulty with the weather. The RAAF crew of Fg Off Russ Cowley and F/Sgt Nev Jones flew on one of these five-hour sorties in HR309; the pilot remembers it well: "....the return trip was the most frightening I have ever experienced. For about an hour I had virtually no control over the aircraft as it was tossed up and down from about 200 feet to 10,000 feet with lightning flashing from all points. The instruments just did not operate. The most amazing thing was that the 'wooden wonder' held together."

Another six-aircraft cab rank was attempted on the 3rd but the crews encountered heavy rain north of Ramree with the storm centred over Cheduba Island. Although they attempted to skirt this obstacle by staying out to sea, the cloudbase was at 500 feet which meant that it was, "on the hilltops 30 miles inland from Danson Bay, visibility nil," as Fg Off Bonnar's CSR put it. The formation was obliged to abandon the mission and bring its bombs back to Joari through steadily deteriorating weather. One crew had a narrow escape as the bomb they were carrying under the port wing of their aircraft lost its safety device in flight. The bomb was therefore 'live' and had the aircraft decelerated

Wearing the later all-silver finish, RF598/OB.M was one of the aeroplanes which operated from the Arakan. (J Gillan)

RF668/OB.J, one of the all-silver Mosquitos which moved to Joari in April 1945 in preparation for Operation DRACULA. (M W Neale)

hard on landing it could have detonated. Rangoon was taken that day without opposition, and subsequent operations were concerned with the pursuit and mopping up of the disorganised and retreating Japanese.

The weather frustrated another six-aircraft mission launched on May 4th but the next day eight Mosquitos attacked a Japanese troop concentration at Kawkadut, each aircraft dropping two 500 pounders and carrying out three strafing runs in the course of which a total of 9,475 rounds of ammunition was expended. On the 6th three out of four aircraft struck at a variety of objectives well to the east of Meiktila, harassing Japanese troops retreating towards the Shan States; the fourth crew (Bill Taylor and Ken Putman in RF668) was obliged to return to Joari with trim problems. The prayers of the wing staff had evidently fallen on deaf ears and that evening the weather forecasters predicted heavy rain so ten of the squadron's aircraft were moved out of Joari to the all-weather strip at Chiringa. Nos 82 and 110 Sqns did the same so there were now seven squadrons squeezed into Chiringa. Space was at a premium but the three visiting squadrons were made very welcome and as comfortable as possible by the residents. Although the weather continued to deteriorate the wing was able to keep flying and the squadron put up eight aircraft from Chiringa on the 7th. All were to bomb Bilin and then split into fours, one to 'rhubarb' between Mokpalin and Moulmein and the other to strafe the roads and tracks between Bilin and Loikaw. The second formation ran into some AA fire and RF585 was damaged; the crew were uninjured, however, and Fg Off Freddie Fortune and Flt Lt Joe Mears diverted to Magwe.

At about this time, as one of the first missions mounted from Chiringa was preparing to take off, a jeep drove down the runway with about a dozen wildly waving men on board. When it drew up at the squadron dispersal it turned out to contain Flt Lt Emeny and Plt Off Yanota. It transpired that the Japanese had withdrawn from Rangoon on April 29th and over the next few days the prisoners released from the jail began to reassert their authority. Their chief, and as it happened well-justified, concern was that the Allies might be unaware that the Japanese had gone and that the assault on the city, which was presumed to be imminent, would still take place. In an effort to avert this they had displayed suitable messages on the roofs of their former prison: "JAPS GONE", "BRITISH HERE" and "EXTRACT DIGIT". Convinced by the unmistakably British character of the last of these notices, Wg Cdr A E Saunders, OC No 110 Sqn, and Flt Lt Stephens had landed their Mosquito at Mingaladon and made their way into the city. Having assessed the situation they proceeded

down river in a small boat and succeeding in preventing the navy from starting their bombardment. Most of the prisoners who were still able to walk had been marched away by the retreating Japanese to serve as hostages but from among the remaining aircrew a small party went out to Mingaladon and began to prepare the airfield for the receipt of relief aircraft. Gp Capt John Grandy flew the first Dakota in on May 5th to be greeted by the 'Station Commander' - an emaciated Cliff Emeny clad in a loin cloth.

As LAC 'Chico' Lea recalls it, the long lost crew arrived still wearing the tattered remnants of the kit in which they had been shot down and although exhausted, very thin, and suffering from sores, they were in high spirits. When he had been on the squadron, in the chill of the early morning Emeny often used to wear his flying jacket until he boarded his aircraft when he would give it to his fitter to look after for him until his return. Almost as if it had been yesterday, instead of eight long and painful months before, Cliff Emeny surveyed the sea of welcoming faces until he spotted LAC Paddy Ewing and demanded to know where his jacket was! After a brief exchange of greetings, preparations for the sortie were resumed. Lea recalls that Emeny drew the formation leader to one side, "Anything you see moving," he said quietly, "hit it - you'll be doing it for me." It was only a brief reunion, however, and the two men soon departed to receive proper medical attention before starting their journeys back to New Zealand and Canada.

There was no operational flying on May 8th while VE Day was celebrated but three pairs operated from Chiringa on the 9th, 'rhubarbing' lines of communication and attacking targets of opportunity to hinder the Japanese as they struggled across the 5,000 feet high range of mountains between the Sittang and Salween rivers in their retreat towards the Thai border. The area covered on the 9th ran from Loikaw, through Kemapyu to the junction of the Salween and Thaungyin rivers and on down to Shwegun, Kawkadut and the Gulf of Martaban. Each of these sorties was successful but the weather was a problem again during the recovery and the squadron's ORB notes that "the last four aircraft were forced to land at Akyab and flew on to Chiringa in the evening." These crews were Flt Lt Aykroyd and WO Sellars in RF672, Fg Off Wilcock and Flt Lt Andrews in RF598, WO Stace and Plt Off Kirk in HR372 and Flt Lt Ewing and Flt Lt Williams in HR633. As Graham Williams remembers it, it was quite an experience:

There was not much room in a Mossie's cockpit but, just for the hell of it, and while we were still over enemy territory, Peter Ewing and I changed seats and I flew the aircraft until we ran into thick cloud. One hell of a job changing back quickly! When we got back to Chiringa there was a massive storm just about to strike. We could see the 'drome about four miles away under low cloud and tried to slip in. All hell broke loose as we were caught in the updraughts and only by putting the nose down and using full throttle were we able to get clear and land at Akyab. Nobody could get through the front and scores and scores of aircraft landed at Akyab which was small and had a linked matting runway. What a shambles! There were masses of Liberators, Spitfires, Hurricanes, Mustangs, DC-3s and goodness knows what else. The Japs could have had a ball if they had known. When the

Aircraft	Pilot	Navigator
HR573/OB.K	Flt Lt L R Ovenden AFC	F/Sgt A J Walters
HR627/OB.A	WO R P Buist	F/Sgt J A Russell
RF672/OB.R	Flt Lt H A Aykroyd	WO H Sellars
RF657/OB.N	Flt Lt J McPhee AFC	Flt Lt J L Evans DFC
RF660/OB.S	Plt Off D E Goodrich	WO S M D Nessim
RF697/OB.L	WO F J Stace	Plt Off F R Kirk

Fig 11.3. The crews and aircraft which flew on No 45 Sqn's last operational mission of WW II, 12th May 1945.

front had passed it was like a crowd scene at the gates of a football match. Everybody was trying to get off at once as it was late in the day and nobody wanted to spend the night in dreary old Akyab.

Again operating as pairs, eight more sorties were flown against river traffic and other targets along the lower Salween on the 10th. The weather intervened again, forcing three more aircraft to land at Akyab, and the storms which hit Chiringa destroyed three bashas. Targets were now becoming hard to find; the three pairs which flew on the 11th did not even carry bombs and only two crews (Aykroyd and Sellars in RF672 and Cowley and Jones in HR309) found anything worth strafing. On May 12th the squadron flew what turned out to be its last operational sorties of the Second World War; the participating aircraft and crews are listed at Figure 11.3. Six aircraft, without bombs, 'rhubarbed' lines of communication between Bilin and Loikaw, Papun and Kemapyu, and Moulmein and Mesoht, the latter being just across the Thai border. No one found any targets of real significance but everyone found something to shoot at and ammunition expended amounted to 735 rounds of 20mm HE, 735 of 20mm SAP, 2,030 rounds of .303" AP and 680 rounds of .303" Incendiary.

Another storm, the big one, hit Chiringa on the night of May 12th/13th. Dawn broke to a scene of absolute devastation. Since the buildings were all of relatively insubstantial basha construction it looked much worse than it really was, but few of the huts had been left undamaged.

The squadron was stood down from operations on the 13th and an initial party of airmen immediately set off for Chakulia. Needless to say this plan was changed and the squadron's destination was switched to Cholavaram. While the advance party was being redirected, the balance of the groundcrew, still split between the operational echelon at Chiringa and the base party at Kumbhirgram, began to pack in preparation for their journeys to Calcutta en route for Madras. Most of the aeroplanes at Chiringa were flown down to Cholavaram via Cuttack on May 17th and 18th while those at 'Kum' followed over the next few days. In the midst of this upheaval, on May 24th, Sqn Ldr Duclos was nominated to command No 47 Sqn, this appointment carrying with it a promotion to wing commander. Although 'Duke' Duclos was to remain on strength for another three weeks, command of the squadron effectively devolved to the senior flight commander. Flt Lt Aykroyd became de facto OC No 45 Sqn, pending the formal appointment of a new CO, while Flt Lt George Dyke succeeded him as OC B Flight.

Although the squadron was relieved to be pulling back, the departure from Kumbhirgram was tinged with regret as it meant parting with Joey who had now been an integral part of the squadron for nearly a year. When the bulk of the

squadron had left for Joari it had known that it would not be returning to Assam and Joey, whose fund now contained a substantial sum, was placed with a school at Shillong. There was tragedy too, since the squadron lost one more crew just as they were withdrawing from the operational area. Fg Offs Freddie Fortune and 'Tiny' Lauder were killed flying from Kumbhirgram when their Harvard, FE614, crashed while making an inverted run over Monerkiel on May 14th.

As a parting gesture, the night before the squadron finally left for Madras a lavatory, a particularly noxious multi-holer which had long been a festering blot on the immaculate landscape of Kumbhirgram, was ceremonially disposed of. It was incinerated. It is understood that this practice subsequently became something of a tradition at Kumbhirgram and that several other such facilities were consigned to the flames as their owners departed. This was actually not the first time that No 45 Sqn had done this and the first known arson attack of this nature had occurred in India as early as 1942 when one of the groundcrew who had been with the squadron in Burma, LAC 'Smokey' Gardner, had made a small reputation for himself by burning down a bog which had become intolerably fly-blown and smelly. Incidentally, he was not called 'Smokey' because of his incendiary tendencies; he was thus named because he used to smoke a form of 'hookah'!

The ruins of the domestic site at Chiringa after the storm of 13th May 1945. (A H Pridmore)

From the left:- Fg Off Don Blenkhorne, Fg Off Russ Cowley and Plt Off Doug Goodrich in the wreckage of their basha after the storm hit Chiringa. (A H Pridmore)

Mention has previously been made of the unstinting hospitality extended by the tea planters in the vicinity of Kumbhirgram. Mr K O Smith (he was always known as 'KO') and his wife had become particular patrons of No 45 Sqn and had rarely been without at least one crew as guests in their house. On May 15th the officers of the squadron who remained at Kumbhirgram gave a farewell party to mark their departure and to repay the generosity which they had received for so long. As this chapter draws to its close it seems appropriate to include a few spontaneous lines of verse written by Olive Smith in pencil on a scrap of paper on that occasion.

Thank you, the boys on '45'

Thank you for the lovely party you threw,
And the invitation to us to share it with you.
The overwhelming welcome with which we were met
At the door of your Mess we will never forget.
We were deeply touched at the way that you showed
Feelings of friendship in the gifts you bestowed.
These were a surprise, in no small measure;
Two beautiful tokens we'll treasure for ever,
Of happy times spent with you all.
Thank you, the boys on '45'.

Thank you for all the pleasure you brought
To two lonely souls who were keen to be taught
The fine points of Poker, Liar Dice, Dealer's Choice.
It wasn't our fault, and we didn't rejoice,
We would hide our wild cards and oft underbid,
Just for the pleasure of seeing you win,
But somehow or other your luck wasn't in.
So we rooked you quite often and now we feel sad,
For we weren't just beginners - you see, you were 'had'.
Thank you, the boys on '45'.

Thank you for coming on visits to us
And being 'at home' without any fuss.
Our big moment on Saturdays was hearing the Jeep
On its way up our hill, grinding gears where it's steep.
And waiting to greet you when you should arrive,
(And trusting you'd get here safe and alive,
Especially when someone was learning to drive!)
It's no use regretting when good times are done,
But we'll think of you often, now you have gone,
And follow your progress with keen interest
And remember you always - the Best of the Best.
The time is now here for saying Good-Byes
And Good Luck to you all - you guys of the skies.
You'll always be welcome; knowing you has been fun.
Do haste ye back often.

Your Favourite Blonde

The operational record of the Flying Camels on Mosquitos had been second to none. Since it is tabulated on a monthly basis at Annex F, it suffices to note here that it had flown 1,260 operational sorties, 303 of them at night, in the course of which it had dropped nearly 800 tons of bombs. The squadron's 'Game Bag' for the period from 28th September 1944 to 12th May 1945 is summarised at Figure 11.4. Since No 45 Sqn had been the first to take the Mosquito into combat over Burma it now had a hard core of

Item	Destroyed	Damaged
MT Vehicles	55	96
Rivercraft	21	409
Locomotives	22	49
Rolling Stock	10	553
Bridges	11	29
Aircraft	4	3
Tanks	0	6

Fig 11.4. No 45 Sqn's Game Bag,
28th September 1944-12th May 1945.

aircrew who were extremely experienced on type. Among those still serving with the squadron when it was withdrawn to India and who had accumulated over fifty operational sorties were: Sqn Ldr Duclos, Flt Lts Mears, Andrews, Whiteside, Ewing, Aykroyd, Barclay and McFadzean, Fg Offs Nicholls, Blenkhorne, Taylor, Lauder and Wilcock, Plt Off Goodrich and WOs O'Connor, Nessim, McKie, Putman and Sellars[14].

Although initially hindered in bringing its full weight to bear by early uncertainties about the Mosquito's structural integrity, once it was given its head the squadron established an enviable record. Its aircrew had fully maintained, even enhanced, the reputation for excellence in combat that had been established by their predecessors on 1½ Strutters, Camels, Vernons, Blenheims and Vengeances. The cost had been high: twenty-one men had died on operational sorties; two had become POWs and six further lives (including Flt Lt McKerracher of No 22 APC) had been lost in accidents. It was tragic that at least four, and very probably several more, of these deaths had been due to structural failures rather than to enemy action but, as the first squadron to fly the Mosquito intensively in India in the attack role, it was inevitable that the Flying Camels would bear the brunt of this problem. This problem had to be revealed before it could be solved, however, and, since the Mosquito did eventually prove its worth in the Far East, the lives lost by squadron crews had not been in vain.

In marked contrast to its experience in the Middle East, the squadron's efforts in India were recognised by the award of a number of decorations. Several of the citations made specific reference to the remarkable lengths of operational service accumulated by the recipients of these awards, particularly by the Australians, so it could be said that some belated acknowledgement of the squadron's contributions in North Africa and on Vengeances had finally been made. Apart from those already mentioned, DFCs were awarded to Flt Lt L S Andrews, Flt Lt G F Williams RAAF, Flt Lt R M Barclay RAAF, Fg Off H M Nicholls RAAF, WO S O'Connor and WO H Sellars before the end of the year and to Sqn Ldr G O L Dyke and Flt Lt W R Peasley in February 1946 (the latter's decoration actually reflecting previous service with another unit).

They did not know it at the time, of course, but when No 45 Sqn withdrew to Madras in May 1945 it had already flown its last operational missions of a war in which it had become one of the very few units which could claim to have fought all three of the major Axis powers and, for good measure, the Vichy French as well. Since the squadron had flown fighters in WW I and light bombers in WW II it is not practical to make a direct comparison of its relative performance in the two conflicts. Even if the exercise cannot be entirely productive, however, it is still of some interest to compare the raw 'profit and loss accounts' of the two wars. Between October 1916 and November 1918 the squadron lost seventy-four men in, or as a result of, combat; eight more died in flying accidents and twelve became POWs. The corresponding figures for the period June 1940 to May 1945 were 109, eight and fourteen. Coincidentally, the numbers of decorations awarded to members of the squadron were virtually identical: two DSOs were won in each war; twenty-five men were decorated with MCs or DFCs in WW I and the same number of DFCs were awarded in WW II, and there was one DCM in 1917 and one DFM in 1940. An examination of the airframes listed at Annex L reveals that the squadron worked its way through over 270 aeroplanes in 1916-18; between 1939 and 1945 more than 320 different aircraft passed through its hands.

Notes.

1.   The reason that the bombs skipped was the forward momentum with which they left the aircraft; the only really effective way to have reduced this would have been to provide some form of airbrake. Modifying the tail units could only have had the effect of making the bombs more unstable in flight. If it induced the bomb to 'tumble' this might, at the expense of some accuracy, have slowed it down a little, but from a low-level release there would have been insufficient time for the consequent drag to have had much effect. The problems inherent in bombing from low-level were not resolved until the introduction of retarding tail units in the 1960s.

2.   It is possible that HX821, which had been briefly on charge to No 45 Sqn, was the aircraft in which Sqn Ldr Bourke had experienced a partial wing failure on October 4th.

3.   The structural problems encountered by the Mosquito in the Far East are not strictly a part of No 45 Sqn's story. Nevertheless, they had a major impact on the squadron and, in view of this, an interpretation of the cause(s) of these problems is presented at Annex K.

4.   'Rhubarb' was an official nickname introduced in late 1940 specifically to cover the operations of UK-based fighter squadrons tasked with ground attack missions over the near Continent as Fighter Command switched to the offensive after the Battle of Britain. The term was subsequently absorbed into the RAF's wartime lexicon, evolved into a verb and became a portmanteau word used to describe ground strafing activities by any tactical aeroplanes, anywhere.

5.   Bridges were (and are) generally easy targets to find but they are notoriously difficult to destroy. Most bridges in Burma were of light trestle construction and were thus an open latticework of timber or steel. As a result they were more space than substance, so there was relatively little to hit and most of the blast of a near miss went 'through the gaps'. Furthermore any bridge is designed to accept considerable vertical loads (that is after all its function) so it is inherently resistant to blast overpressures imposed from above; even a direct hit, while it might damage the trackbed, will rarely collapse the whole structure. The ideal solution in bridge-busting is to detonate the weapon *underneath* the trackbed to force it upwards but, since a single track bridge is only four or five yards wide, that requires extreme accuracy of delivery, especially if the bombs involved are the relatively small 500 pounders.

6.   In fact the squadron did have one aeroplane at the beginning of December, HR372. It was technically unserviceable but the CO was not going to have a squadron with no aeroplanes at all and he steadfastly refused to allow it to go to Kanchrapara until he was satisfied that the replacements were going to work - which took until the 12th.

7.   Depending on the specific Mark, a GP bomb was about 23% (by weight) explosive; the rest was casing. In the MC series the proportion of explosive was increased to about 50%.

8.   'Canned Battle' was a device which reproduced the sounds of an infantry engagement; it was deployed by ground forces. The 'Parafex' was an air-delivered system which did much the same thing, simulating the sounds of small arms fire and the explosions of hand grenades. 'Aquaskit' was activated by water and produced a display of Verey lights; it was air-delivered and presumably intended for use at night.

Thankfully out of focus, this seems to be a suitable illustration to bring this chapter to an end - the 'Khasi of Kum', or one of them. (F Scholfield)

9.   When the squadron had displayed identification letters on its Blenheims and Vengeances they had been applied in the conventional manner with the unit code leading so that they read, for instance, OB.Z on both sides of the aeroplane. While the practice was not unique, it is interesting to note that No 45 Sqn's Mosquitos were unusual in that their codes were always applied with the OB *ahead* of the roundel so that they appeared as OB.Z on the port side but Z.OB to starboard. This form of presentation was retained throughout the Mosquito, Beaufighter and Brigand eras and at least one of the squadron's early Hornets (WB898/OB.A) had its starboard codes applied in this 'backwards' fashion. By May 1952 this style had been dropped, however, and until 1955, when code letters were finally abandoned, all of the squadron's aeroplanes read from left to right on both sides.

10.   The article from which this extract was taken appeared in Vol 14, issue No 1, of the *North West and Hunter Valley Magazine* published on 21st April 1985. Although Wally McLellan registered only thirty-two bombs being dropped, according to the CSR and the subsequent OPREP a total of forty-six 500 pounders was delivered between 1259hrs and 1300hrs; Fred Stace had one hang up and the other was McLellan's own. It is interesting to note that in this instance 'low level', for all but two of the twelve aircraft, meant fifty feet at a speed of between 280 and 300 mph.

11.   An indication of the Mosquito's offensive capabilities can be gained by comparing these figures with those given towards the end of Chapter 10. In just one month of Mosquito ops the amount of ordnance delivered on the enemy by the squadron far exceeded that which it had delivered during its entire period of Vengeance operations.

12.   No 47 Sqn had begun conversion in February and the Wing was virtually an all-Mosquito outfit by the end of March. No 47 Sqn continued to specialise in RP work as it had with its Beaufighters, the last of which were withdrawn in late April.

13.   The author has been told that a 'group photograph' of all of these doors was taken at one time but as yet a print has failed to materialise.

14.   In many cases these fifty-odd Mosquito sorties (Nicholls, Goodrich, Barclay, Nessim, Wilcock and Andrews had all actually flown sixty or more) were only a part of the overall experience which had been accumulated. For instance, several of the pilots had flown operationally on casualty evacuation duties in November-December 1944 and some of these and others, and some of the navs, had flown previous tours. Tif O'Connor, for instance, ended the war with 116 operational sorties in his log book, fifty-six of them on Mosquitos, twenty-one on Vengeances and twenty-one on Tiger Moths and Sentinels (all flown while serving with No 45 Sqn) plus a further eighteen while flying Wellingtons with No 215 Sqn. Bob Barclay is another example; he ended the war with a total of 113 operational sorties to his credit, eleven on Blenheims, thirty-nine on Vengeances and sixty-three on Mosquitos; apart from two Blenheim trips flown while on detachment to No 113 Sqn in 1942, all of these sorties had been flown with No 45 Sqn and he was almost certainly the squadron's 'top-scorer' in this respect.

Chapter 12. The post-war doldrums in India and Ceylon.

When the squadron pulled back to Cholavaram the war was expected to go on for at least another year, possibly longer. Staff planning for the next phase of operations was already well in hand but the details of Operation ZIPPER remained a closely guarded secret. It was fairly obvious to everyone that the next move would be the retaking of Malaya but in the absence of any positive information, the squadron could do little more than listen out for the latest rumour, embellish it and pass it on. In the meantime its immediate task would be to get itself ready for the next call on its services, and wait.

With no technical support available, the aircraft were not flown in late May apart from a couple of air tests, although the aircrew carried out DIs and ran the engines periodically to keep things from seizing up. The bulk of the groundcrew from Chiringa and Kumbhirgram finally reached Madras on June 4th with the heavy kit following a day later. On one of the few trips that the squadron was able to put up during this period Fg Off Ron Wilcock was obliged to divert to Yelahanka when RF598 shed a panel in flight on June 4th. By the 12th everyone had settled in; all eighteen aircraft had been serviced and the squadron was ready to start training flying in earnest.

From a domestic point of view Cholavaram was reasonably convenient and the squadron's personnel were accommodated not too far from their dispersal. On the other hand the accommodation itself left something to be desired. On a fogbound bomber base in Yorkshire, with a pot-bellied stove glowing cherry red and a few old newspapers stuffed into the cracks to keep out the draught, a Nissen hut could provide quite a snug environment. But 'snugness' was the last thing that was wanted in the oppressive heat of southern India! Although some bashas were available many of the billets at Cholavaram turned out to be corrugated iron Nissen huts and, as was only to be expected, they were quite literally like ovens.

Before the squadron had been able to make much progress with a training programme, its plans were thrown completely out of gear. A directive was received early in June which screened from further operational flying all aircrew who had already accumulated more than 200 flying hours with a squadron, and all Empire personnel, irrespective of their experience. At the same time the duration of an overseas tour, which had only recently been shortened to three years and eight months, was reduced by a further four months. Since many of the squadron's airmen had joined the unit at the beginning of 1942, a large proportion of No 7045 SE's personnel immediately became due for repatriation and there was a flood of postings. Among the many officers who left at this stage was Flt Lt Herbie Wilson, the RAAF Adjutant who had shepherded the squadron around India ever since its renaissance with Vengeances. At the same time the last of the really long-term RAAF aircrew went home; Graham Williams, who had joined the squadron at Helwan as a brand new sergeant WOp/AG on 8th January 1942, finally left for Australia on 20th June 1945 as a flight lieutenant navigator with eighty-three operational sorties recorded in his log book and a DFC in the post.

These developments completely knocked the bottom out of the squadron. To preserve airframe hours, flying was immediately restricted to the remaining handful of employable crews and two new crews who had arrived during the squadron's withdrawal to Madras. Since there were now so few aircrew available, the daily requirement for aeroplanes was much reduced and there was insufficient work to keep all the groundcrew fully occupied. This was fortunate, since they were very tired after having maintained the squadron in combat in the field for eight months and the opportunity was taken to give them a break. Parties were organised and groups of airmen, and aircrew were sent off to Ootacamund for a well-earned rest in the cool of the Nilgiri Hills.

Programmed flying training began on June 13th and the two new crews, Flt Lt G J Tonks and F/Sgt G Cook and Fg Off F Scholfield RCAF and Fg Off R W Fussell, were sent off

*Navigator Fg Off R W Fussell (left) and pilot Fg Off F Scholfield RCAF joined No 45 Sqn just as it was pulling back to Madras. They are seen here with RF668/OB.J on 13th June 1945, shortly before taking off on their first trip. The aeroplane displays several interesting features, including underwing tanks, a glazed panel in the nose for an F.24 camera and a personal emblem of some sort on the entrance door - apparently the one previously fitted to HR462, which had also been coded OB.J (see page 292). The inboard upper surfaces of the engine cowlings have been given a roughly applied coat of dark paint to cut down glare.
(F Scholfield)*

together for an area familiarisation trip and a little formation flying. While leading the pair, Geoffrey Tonks in HR372 suddenly broke away, dived to very low level and flew up a river inlet. He failed to clear some cables associated with a viaduct and crashed; he and his navigator were both killed. Four days later the squadron lost another aeroplane. On the 17th Wg Cdr Duclos finally departed to take up his post as OC No 47 Sqn and Fg Off Wilcock flew him up to Kinmagan in HR309. On the return flight the aircraft crashed about twenty miles north east of Kyaukpyu. The pilot and his (possibly unauthorised) passenger were both killed. The site was extremely remote and inaccessible and the wreckage was not recovered so the cause of this accident appears never to have been clearly established.

By the end of June the manpower situation was becoming clearer. No 45 Sqn had been reduced to just six effective crews and a rapidly dwindling base of experienced technical support. In just one month it had been transformed from being what was probably the most effective strike squadron in the India-Burma Theatre to not much more than a cadre, although there was still a hard core of very experienced men who had worked together for a long time and their continuing presence was instrumental in maintaining the camaraderie between aircrew and groundcrew which continued to be very strong. Despite the severe reduction in the squadron's fighting strength, the spirit of the Flying Camels was still very much alive.

No 82 Sqn had moved to Cholavaram with No 45 Sqn and on 1st July they were joined by HQ No 901 Wg, their controlling formation from Chiringa. Within a few days, having travelled via Yelahanka where it had been re-equipped with Mosquitos, No 211 Sqn also rejoined the wing, although it was stationed on the far side of Madras at St Thomas Mount. No 84 Sqn joined them there on July 26th to restore the wing to a nominal strength of four squadrons, although all of these units were suffering to some degree from the recently imposed constraints on available manpower.

To relieve Flt Lt Aykroyd and restore the squadron to its proper status Wg Cdr J H Etherton DFC* was posted-in. He formally assumed command of No 45 Sqn on July 3rd and promptly set about rebuilding it. Richard Whiteside left in July, his place as OC A Flight being taken by Flt Lt Ovenden while George Dyke retained command of B Flight, both flight

RF668/OB.J, in full ACSEA markings, taxying for take off at Cholavaram on 13th June 1945 with Frank Scholfield and Reg ('Taffy') Fussell on board. (F Scholfield)

Flt Lt Geoffrey Tonks in the cockpit of HR372/OB.F; this picture was taken about an hour before his fatal crash on 13th June 1945. (F Scholfield)

commanders being promoted to squadron leader before the end of the month. A flock of new faces began to arrive, five complete crews being transferred from No 84 Sqn as soon as they reached St Thomas Mount, and by early August the fully restored squadron, along with the rest of the wing, was being held at 48 hours notice to take part in Operation ZIPPER - the invasion of Malaya. Les Ovenden recalls a popular story going the rounds at the time to the effect that ZIPPER was

LACs 'Ginger' Lake, 'Blondie' Crawshaw and 'Shiny' Glaze with an unidentified colleague at Cholavaram with RF672/OB.R. Like a number of the squadron's later Mosquitos, this aeroplane has its serial number repeated on its fin. (R Lea)

An unidentified Mosquito with thirty-two mission symbols on its nose and its door propped open to display a Disney-style Big Bad Wolf and the name Tee Emm, provides the background for a photograph of its team. From the left: Sgt Raffel, LAC Waterson(?), Fg Off Don Kerr, Sqn Ldr George Dyke and Cpl White. Of interest is the flat area on the nose, just above the machine guns; this is the glazed aperture for the locally-installed F.24 camera which, in this instance, appears to have been painted over. (M W Neale)

One of a series of group photographs taken at Cholavaram on VJ-Day, this one shows the A Flights of No 45 Sqn and No 7045 SE. Evidently coded F, the aeroplane shown cannot have been the original OB.F (HR372) as this had been lost in an accident on 16th June. The next OB.F, and presumably the one shown here, was RF774, which never flew on ops. Nevertheless, in anticipation of Operation ZIPPER, the aeroplane has been modified to have a nose-mounted F.24 camera and has inherited an 'operational' crew entrance door bearing an Oor Wullie *motif. An earlier photograph (not reproduced here) shows this* Oor Wullie-*door fitted to an unidentified aeroplane with thirty-one mission symbols on its nose. (R Lea)*

so called because it was never properly buttoned up! Rumour had it that the squadron's task would be to mount a 'cab rank' over Singapore and carry out strikes as required as the army moved in. Another rumour maintained that there were two Japanese fighter squadrons based on the island but if they were there the squadron never had to tangle with them. Atomic weapons were detonated over Hiroshima and Nagasaki on August 6th and 9th; on the 16th the Japanese sued for peace. Four days later the squadron put up twelve Mosquitos to take part in a flypast over a Victory Parade held in Madras and on September 2nd representatives of the Japanese administration signed the formal letters of capitulation. The fighting was over. Instead of going to war the squadron held a party.

A modified and scaled-down version of Operation ZIPPER went ahead to re-occupy Malaya but the only contribution required from No 901 Wg was the deployment of No 84 Sqn which set off for Singapore on September 10th, having first transferred to No 45 Sqn five crews who were due for relatively early repatriation. A few weeks later No 211 Sqn was hived off as well, its ultimate destination being Thailand. The groundcrews of No 7211 SE and their kit were loaded into three LSTs and despatched by sea. The aircraft and crews were to remain in India until their SE was ready to receive them and on September 23rd they moved to Cholavaram where they could be looked after by Nos 7045 and 7082 SEs. Now that peace had broken out the flying programme, which had just begun to develop some momentum, was significantly curtailed again and as many people as possible were packed off to the hills of 'Snooty Ooty'. Up until then training flying had produced the usual run of incidents as on July 26th when Flt Lt J H Robertson

Back in the days of Blenheim Is B Flight had adopted a gremlin as its symbol, although it was not applied to its aeroplanes at that time. This motif seems to have lain dormant for a time but it had reappeared by early 1945 and, after the withdrawal to Madras, at least one Mosquito had one painted on its fin. Also of interest is the duplication of the serial number on the fin, a curious feature displayed by a number of aircraft in ACSEA in mid-1945. RF778/OB.T joined the squadron on 14th April 1945 and remained on charge until late 1946. (M W Neale)

got his tail up too high during a formation take off and the tips of RF668's propellers chewed the runway and, on August 26th, when Fg Off George Viner swung on landing in RF584 and collapsed its undercarriage. Since the latter trip had been an air test, one of the squadron's airmen had been

RF953/OB.X was a replacement aircraft taken on charge at Cholavaram in July 1945. (J Byrne)

up for the ride and the experience no doubt provided LAC Waddington with an excellent line to shoot in the canteen.

Air Vice Marshal Bouchier visited Cholavaram on October 2nd and announced that the Wing HQ and Nos 45 and 82 Sqns had been selected to go to Japan as part of the Allied occupation force which he had been nominated to command and which would come to be known as British Commonwealth (Air). Planning for the move was put in hand immediately and it was soon realised that the flying programme would have to be carefully managed as each aircraft would need about 25 flying hours in hand to make the trip. With the intensity of flying training already reduced, however, this was not expected to present too much of a problem. The squadron started packing. The move was postponed. The squadron unpacked again.

By this time POWs liberated from Japanese camps were being repatriated and, as Cholavaram was considered to be more suitable as a staging post, No 901 Wg was transferred to St Thomas Mount. The squadron repacked its kit and on 12th October, by now fully restored to strength, its eighteen Mosquitos flew the short trip to the other side of Madras in two immaculate boxes of nine. But it all went wrong at the end. Red 2 got too close to his leader on the approach and the runway controller fired a Verey light to send him round again. Red Leader thought it was for him and overshot. Red 2 continued his approach through his leader's slipstream, lost control and crashed. Although they both managed to escape, Flt Lt W McCracken and Fg Off R W Fussell were trapped in the blazing wreckage long enough to be severely burned. In hospital both men appeared at first to be recovering well but one of McCracken's legs became gangrenous and, despite its being amputated, he died on the 23rd.

Quickly putting this tragedy behind them the squadron set about making itself at home at its new base, some additional space being created by the departure of No 211 Sqn's air echelon for Akyab on November 2nd, which reduced the wing to a strength of just two squadrons. The airmen were housed in a camp at Guindy while the officers used No 84 Sqn's old accommodation at Adyar until November 16th when they were moved into two Messes on the airfield itself. On that date the squadron was still a very substantial unit with a strength of forty-six officers and 256 NCOs and airmen; this was to decrease markedly over the next six months.

Life was reasonably comfortable at St Thomas Mount. Hill parties continued to be detached to Ootacamund and there was plenty of sport. Madras and its environs offered swimming in the sea from Elliot's Beach or in the large new

pool at Saidapet with its associated tennis courts. In the city itself dances were sponsored by organisations such as the YMCA and the Nurses' Association, and the Connemara Hotel was a popular social rendezvous. The Salvation Army and TocH offered a variety of recreational and cultural facilities and there were theatres, restaurants and, for those

Little Flying Camel badges like this one, about one inch across and made of silver, were certainly worn by squadron members after the squadron's withdrawal to Madras, although some reports suggest that they might first have been introduced at Kumbhirgram. The wearing of jewellery with uniform is normally forbidden but a number of the squadron's airmen recall that this brooch had some form of, at least semi-official, local approval and they wore it on their uniforms while on leave in Calcutta and Ootacamund. (S J Findley)

A view of the fairly comfortable domestic site at Guindy Camp. Front and centre, LAC Stan Findley waiting for the gharry to take him into Madras where he is bound for the Connemara Hotel to celebrate his twenty-third birthday. (S J Findley)

In October 1945 instructions were issued for the wartime ACSEA markings to be replaced by red, white and blue ones. Most units were then heavily preoccupied with running down or disbanding and few made much progress in implementing this directive. By contrast, No 45 Sqn was being maintained at full strength in anticipation of a move to Japan and they repainted all of their aeroplanes, removing the black recognition bands and applying pre-war style Type A national markings as seen here on RF964/OB.Z, which still has its serial number repeated on its fin. In February 1946 this aeroplane, flown by Flt Lt 'Gil' Underwood and Fg Off 'Jock' Haggarty, was one of those which were deployed at short-notice to Santa Cruz when the RIN mutinied. (C Haggarty)

determined to get into trouble, a full range of the less savoury delights that any big city has to offer.

An overt sign of the end of hostilities was the promulgation in October 1945 of an order cancelling the distinctive ACSEA-style national markings and replacing them with more conventional red, white and blue ones. There was no great sense of urgency attached to this order, however, and the new markings were to be applied progressively as aeroplanes became due for overhaul or

Sqn Ldr Ovenden, in RF736/OB.K, leads A Flight's RF668/OB.J and HR633/OB.C, probably on 25th October 1945. The photographic aircraft was being flown by Flt Lt Jackie Lowes. Note the variation in the application of tactical markings. The size and location of the band on the fin is slightly different in each case and comparison with other photographs shows that RF668's band has been slimmed down to permit its serial number to be displayed beneath it. HR633 and RF736 both appear to lack wing bands, perhaps because a start had been made on implementing the recent directive reinstating peacetime markings. (L R J Ovenden)

needed repainting. With most people preoccupied with the prospect of going home and ACSEA's squadrons either disbanding or, pending the re-establishment of French and Dutch colonial administrations, being actively engaged in operations to control emergent nationalist movements in Indo-China and the Dutch East Indies, little progress was made in implementing this directive. In marked contrast to this general trend, No 45 Sqn immediately got stuck into the task. The squadron was still on stand-by to go to Japan and the aircraft were being spruced up so that they would be worthy representatives of Great Britain when they eventually flew to Nippon. Many of the aircrew were co-opted into this programme which involved all the aircraft being given a fresh overall coat of silver paint, obscuring both the old 'blue-only' roundels and the black identification bands carried on the wing and tail surfaces. The new national markings which were applied were pre-war style Type As, with the roundel colours divided into fifths, rather than thirds as was the case with the post-war Type D roundel when it was introduced in 1947. As a result the squadron's aircraft (and probably those of No 82 Sqn as well) presented a rather unusual appearance as very few post-war Mosquitos sported this rather old-fashioned style of marking.

During this early post-war period the dominant feature of squadron life was the fluctuating personnel complement. By the time that the squadron had moved to St Thomas Mount there were only six aircrew left who had flown ops with No 45 Sqn and two of these, WOs G A McDonald and T H Bartlett left on December 1st. The hard core was dissolving fast. Nevertheless, despite these constant changes the squadron kept itself up to the mark and on December 1st it put up a twelve-aircraft formation just to show that it could still do it.

One of the more stable crews at this period was that of Flt Lt G W Underwood and Fg Off C Haggarty who flew together for a year from May 1945. Writing in 1994, the navigator in this partnership evidently adopted a fairly robust attitude towards the contribution that he was supposed to make in determining the whereabouts of his aeroplane:

A typical crew photograph taken in about September 1945 with a very clean and shiny OB.T (RF778) providing the backdrop. From the left LACs Shreeve and Fletcher (port and starboard engine fitters), Flt Lt G W Underwood (pilot), Fg Off C Haggarty (nav) and LAC Hazell (rigger). (G W Underwood)

Photographed with RF947/OB.M at St Thomas Mount circa November 1945, from the left, standing: Fg Off George Viner, F/Sgt Maurice Payne, LAC Grant and LAC Henry (or Hendry?); crouching are LAC's Parr and Buckley. (G Viner)

Christmas 1945, Wg Cdr J H Etherton DFC, OC No 45 Sqn, (left) and Gp Capt C D Tomalin DFC AFC, OC 901 Wg. (D J Clarke)

Gil (*Underwood*) had this irritating habit of always wanting to know where we happened to be during a flight - I mean, how should I know? After all, he was the one driving and looking out of the window. I always minded my own business and hated being interrupted as I studied 'Jane' in the air mail edition of the Mirror; filched I may add from the anteroom of the Mess. (*While, of course, quite unable to condone the deplorable practice of pinching the Mess' newspapers, this chronicler has some sympathy with Jock Haggarty's perspective on aerial navigation! - see Note 5 to Chapter 18*)

As training flying continued, additional aircrew were constantly running up against the 200 hours barrier, which immediately rendered them ineligible for the projected move to Japan, while others became due for repatriation on a time basis as did further batches of groundcrew. The Manning Staffs did their best and replacements were usually found but it meant that there was a constantly shifting population, which fostered an atmosphere of impermanence. These problems, which were shared by all units in India, were inevitable in the early postwar months and only time would resolve them. The squadron soldiered on, buoyed up by the anticipated move to Japan, although there were some among the newer faces, who had arrived in India since VJ-Day, who were less than enthusiastic about this prospect. After all, they pointed out, the war was over now and, since they had only signed on 'for the duration', not unreasonably they wanted to head west, not further east. Throughout ACSEA, demobilisation was becoming an increasingly contentious issue. Repatriation was being conducted as Operation PYTHON but the available transport resources were simply unable to cope with the hundreds of thousands of men suddenly due for repatriation as a result of the shortened overseas tour length. Disaffection can be highly contagious and the squadron's executives made determined efforts to identify and weed out any malcontents before their influence could become corrosive. Fortunately No 45 Sqn's morale was extremely resilient and the situation never became a problem.

In the short term, Christmas provided a spiritual lift for everyone with a stand down, a soccer game with No 82 Sqn (which they won!) and a comic football match to follow. Sgt Kettle's Cooks and Butchers did their stuff; the officers and NCOs served dinner to the airmen; there was a plentiful supply of beer and a good time was had by all.

There was, however, a handful of chaps who, despite the festive season, may well have been a trifle depressed - for the most personal of reasons. With the squadron being stationed

No 45 Sqn's football team at St Thomas Mount, Christmas 1945. From the left, back row: F/Sgt Alastair Russell, WO Maurice Payne, Fg Off H Holder, Wg Cdr John Etherton, LAC Nicholson, LAC Gant and Fg Off H B Deacon. Front row: LAC Bartlett, LAC Sexton(?), LAC Slater, LAC Howell and LAC Crawshaw. Reserve, LAC Byrne, not shown. (R Byrne)

A group of airmen at Guindy circa Christmas 1945. From the left, standing, LACs Clough and Shorter. Seated: LAC Wilkinson, Cpl S C Murrell and LACs Martin and Scott. (N D Murrell)

close to civilisation for the first time in ages and with more free time than before (the peacetime working routine was now a 5½ day week), there were those who sought entertainment at *Madame Jean's* or *Mitchell's* where one could 'catch a dose' for as little as £1. The top rate was about £3; it is assumed that such a substantial sum must have purchased a particularly sophisticated service, but it is not known whether it was accompanied by a correspondingly exotic disease. At the other end of the economic scale, the MO, Fg Off D Hutchinson since the end of the previous May, noted that one enterprising airmen had managed to catch the clap by engaging the services of a coolie labourer for an outlay equivalent to just eight old pence; he certainly got his money's worth! It should be stressed that these were isolated cases. The squadron was not riddled with VD; indeed no new cases were reported at all from February 1946 onwards.

The exigencies of peace meant that a controlling operational formation was now considered to be superfluous and HQ 901 Wg had been disbanded at the turn of the year. Now owing its allegiance to SHQ St Thomas Mount, No 45 Sqn began 1946 with an adequate complement of aircrew in purely numerical terms but so many of them were in a state of pre-release limbo that only eight crews were really effective. These kept themselves current in all the usual skills, including bombing, navigation, photography and ground strafing. In addition there were occasional fighter affiliation exercises; opportunities to indulge in a little air-to-air firing against a drogue pulled by an old Vengeance were laid on from time to

time and, to allow the pilots to indulge themselves in a little aerobatics, there was the odd trip in FT186, the squadron's Harvard.

Despite the shortage of aircrew No 7045 SE was still looking after a full complement of eighteen aircraft when the Mosquito's structural bugbear cropped up again. Someone, inspecting an aeroplane somewhere, had found that the rear web of the rear spar had separated from the edge boom and STI/ACSEA/Mos/13A was issued calling for all aircraft to be examined. Fourteen of No 45 Sqn's were promptly grounded. Monthly serviceability, which, despite the constant turnover of groundcrews, had been running at between 75% and 90% ever since the squadron's withdrawal to Madras, suddenly plunged to 15% but there was little that the groundcrew could do to recover the situation until DeHavillands had devised a repair scheme. There was a bright side to the enforced lull in activity, however, as it enabled the thespians to strike again and during January the squadron staged *Rise and Shine* at the Garrison Theatre in Madras. As ever it was a knock out success.

On one of the relatively few Mosquito trips which could be flown at this time Flt N R Harrison touched down tail first on January 18th and broke off RF947's tailwheel. In mitigation it should be noted that this was the pilot's first trip on the squadron and indeed his first flight for six weeks. He was not alone in having slightly damaged an aeroplane through misjudging a landing; his was just one of a spate of minor landing accidents which occurred from December onwards. The cause was nearly always the same; a combination of inexperience on type and a lack of flying continuity. What was really needed was a dual-controlled Mosquito to provide some coaching in low-speed handling techniques, but the squadron did not have one and the best that could be done was to provide the newcomers with a demonstration flight in a Mk VI and then hope for the best.

The widespread morale problems referred to previously reached a crisis in early 1946. After an initial demonstration at Mauripur on January 22nd, the airmen at a dozen of the larger RAF stations in ACSEA went on strike, the timing of these incidents suggesting to some that this action had been orchestrated[1]. To some extent it had been; there were instances of co-ordinating messages having been relayed around the Command written on the hulls of aeroplanes. Within a day or two the unrest had spread west to units in the Middle East, east to Burma and south to Ceylon, Singapore and Java, although the response was patchy and the airmen at many stations declined to participate at all. The strike was essentially a matter of withdrawal of labour. There were few, if any, instances of violence being offered and officers were not threatened. It was a peaceful protest intended to draw attention to a grievance. It might well have been treated as a mutiny and, since the men involved were refusing duty while on active service, that is probably what it was. That term has very serious implications, however, and is

Seen here shortly after it was acquired by the squadron and still wearing ACSEA markings Harvard FT186 was to remain on the unit's charge until 1949. The apparently dark finish is a result of the type of film used: the aeroplane was actually bright trainer yellow overall. (G W Underwood)

associated with the severest of penalties; in formal discussion it was very carefully avoided and the unrest remained a "strike".

The protest was inspired by a whole range of factors, ranging from ideologically motivated disapproval of British involvement in the re-establishment of European colonial regimes in Indo-China, the East Indies and Malaya, to mundane grouses about food and overcrowding. But these were all peripheral issues; the main sources of discontent were repatriation and demobilisation. Operation PYTHON was proceeding far too slowly and there was a widespread perception that while men were being released from the service in Europe others, many of whom had served for much longer periods but were stationed further afield, were not. Several discontented airmen had already been in touch with their MPs and the unrest attracted the attention of Parliament. The Prime Minister was moved to make a statement to the House on January 29th, by which time he was able to announce that the airmen at eleven of the stations involved had already resumed their duties and that those at the twelfth, and last, would return to work the next day. The disgruntled servicemen had made their point and had gained the attention of the highest authority possible; they had wanted no more and by the end of the month normality had returned.

A handful of extremists was rounded up and court martialled but on the whole there was little attempt on the part of the authorities to exact retribution. Within ACSEA much of the blame was later laid on 'middle management' at station and unit level for not having had their fingers on the pulse. It was recognised that they might not have been able to prevent the strike but it was considered that if there had been more awareness and better communication the problem might have been avoided altogether and, even if not, the authorities would at least have been able to see it coming. The service acknowledged the men's complaints and undertook to examine them, but it insisted that no one would go home any earlier than his scheduled release date; the RAF would not give in to force.

Although the strike had spread rapidly as news of it passed along the grapevine, it elicited little response at the stations around Madras[2]. Writing in 1986, R H Dargue, who was serving there at the time as an NCO, offered several explanations for the lack of participation by the airmen at St Thomas Mount. First, Nos 45 and 82 Sqns had both had strong contingents of airmen who had joined their ranks as long ago as 1942 thus, when the overseas tour length had first been shortened in 1945, many of the veterans had been released and had left India long before the unrest broke out. There were, therefore, relatively few men still on strength who felt overdue for repatriation. Secondly, many of the men had seen the awful condition of the liberated POWs who had passed through Cholavaram and recognised the need for differentials in movement priorities. Thirdly, the officers of

A neat formation by B Flight, probably photographed in October 1945. This picture was used as an insert in the squadron's 1945 Christmas card. From the front the aeroplanes are RF778/OB.T, RF953/OB.X, RF657/OB.N and RF660/OB.S. Note that RF778 lacks the black ACSEA tactical markings (it may never have had them), although the other three aircraft are still wearing them. (L R J Ovenden)

both squadrons had made a positive effort to address the needs of their airmen and to keep them constructively occupied. This was both acknowledged and respected. Fourthly, there was the prospect of both units moving to Japan, or possibly Ceylon, both of which were relatively attractive options for those committed to spending more time 'out east'. Finally, "Quit India" sentiment was less prevalent in southern India at the time so the atmosphere was less inhospitable than it was in, say, the Punjab and the Central Provinces. In this context Dargue did not fail to point out the irony of a situation in which young British servicemen found themselves facing hostile mobs screaming at them in an incomprehensible language to "Go Home!" when that was their most fervent wish too!

The service authorities had ordered the Riot Act to be read at all stations and, although it was hardly necessary, this was duly done at St Thomas Mount. When the Station Commander, Wg Cdr N C Harding DFC, had finished addressing the men, one or two of the more truculent among them promptly left the assembly and the rest followed, rather than allowing the CO to leave first as normal service etiquette would have dictated, but this was as overt as the protest ever became. More constructively, at unit level a concerted effort was made to ascertain the reactions of the airmen. The findings were very reassuring. Many of them regarded the strike as something of a joke. A lot disapproved, some of them quite strongly. Few felt that they had any substantial grounds for complaint and most were confident that their officers and NCOs would conscientiously address their grievances to the extent that they were able. There was no unrest; the squadron's morale was undented[3].

Standing by at Santa Cruz in February 1946, RF957/OB.B totes a three-second fused 250 pounder under each wing. (S J Findley)

As one crisis subsided another arose. As part of the rising tide of protest at the continued British presence in India, the Royal Indian Navy (RIN) mutinied in February 1946. The mutineers seized shore establishments in Bombay and some twenty vessels, the largest a sloop, and threatened to bombard the city. On the 21st No 45 Sqn was ordered to deploy of all its serviceable aircraft to Santa Cruz, fully armed. As a result of the outstanding STI on the wings the squadron could field only five aeroplanes but HQ 225 Gp waived the current technical constraint and the first three aircraft (flown by Flt Lt Roberts with Fg Off Shingler, Flt Lt Leslie with Fg Off Deacon, and Flt Lt Hamilton with Fg Off Davies) left for Bombay at dusk, calling in at Yelahanka en route to be loaded with 250 lb bombs. The next morning these three joined others from No 82 Sqn in mounting a show of force over the ships and the city. Later that day a further eight aircraft, led by Sqn Ldr Dyke, deputising for Wg Cdr Etherton who was in Rangoon at the time, joined the others at Santa Cruz. A ninth Mosquito (RF666 flown by Flt Lt N R Harrison and Fg Off G McMahon) damaged its tailwheel during an intermediate landing at Yelahanka and had to be left behind. A further demonstration was flown on the 23rd as described by Fg Off 'Jock' Haggarty: "...a mock attack was made in squadron formation at mast-top height over the Indian Navy ships and installations with bomb doors open and wing bombs for good measure." Before the day was out the mutineers had surrendered.

The detachment remained on stand-by at Santa Cruz until the 25th and then flew directly back to St Thomas Mount in a

RF672/OB.R having a 250 pounder dismounted after returning to St Thomas Mount following the collapse of the RIN mutiny. (S J Findley)

Balbo of eleven aircraft only to find that civil unrest had broken out in Madras in their absence. It had been a good show by what was by then largely a new air echelon and, moreover, one which had done very little flying for over a month because of the wing problem. The bulk of the groundcrew were equally new and this short-notice operation had been a significant test for them too. Preparing the aircraft had involved repairing all the wings which had been opened up for inspection and removing the slipper tanks and fitting bomb racks in their place. To get the aircraft ready they had worked cheerfully right through the night of 21st/22nd February. If there had ever been any residual doubts about the reliability of No 45 Sqn's groundcrew in the aftermath of the recent strike these must surely have been dispelled by their willing response to this challenge.

Wg Cdr John Etherton left for the UK on March 6th and his place as CO was taken by Sqn Ldr Dyke. He was the last of the squadron's wartime pilots, Sqn Ldr Les Ovenden having left in January, bequeathing A Flight to Flt Lt Springthorpe who was promoted to squadron leader a few weeks later. The other key member of the management team had changed back in November when one of the squadron's very senior navs, Flt Lt Ted Rainbow, had taken over as Adj, his predecessor having been Flt Lt F Pusey who had succeeded Herbie Wilson in May. George Dyke's becoming CO, albeit temporarily, left a vacancy for an OC B Flight but the rate at which people were leaving meant that there could be little continuity in post and the B Flight slot was filled in quick succession by Flt Lt E J Roberts, Flt Lt N R Harrison and Flt Lt A D Wood. Another sign of the times was that the squadron had had no Intelligence Officer since 1st February when Plt Off Weir had been posted to Delhi; he was never replaced.

After months of uncertainty the squadron was finally notified in March that the Japan trip was definitely off. A move did seem likely at the end of the month when, on the 31st, eight aircraft were put on stand-by to deploy to Meiktila but this requirement was cancelled the following day. By this time the instability in Madras was such that the city had been put out of bounds to all squadron personnel.

No 82 Sqn, the Flying Camels' companions-in-arms since the end of 1944, had disbanded on March 15th and ten days later their CO, Wg Cdr F W Snell DFC*, relieved George Dyke, restoring the squadron to its appropriate status and allowing him to resume command of B Flight. Freddie Snell brought with him a handful of aircrew and three of No 82 Sqn's best aeroplanes which gave No 45 Sqn a total of eight quasi-serviceable Mosquitos, although all had to be operated within such stringent g limits that they were effectively confined to straight and level flight. Keeping tabs on the state of the aircraft now became the responsibility of Flt Lt R W Woodcraft, previously OC No 7082 SE, who took over command of No 7045 SE from Flt Lt Hanslip, the squadron's chief "plumber" since March 1945.

The effective fleet was immediately reduced by one aeroplane as the squadron was obliged to detach a Mosquito

Flt Lt Hanslip (right), OC No 7045 SE from March 1945 until April 1946, with F/Sgt L Paxton, an engine fitter who had been with the squadron since mid-1944. (G Viner)

to Santa Cruz where it was at the disposal of HQ 225 Gp for use as a high-speed courier aircraft. Much of the flying involved was associated with courts martial in the wake of the 'strike' and the aircraft flew all over India fetching and carrying witnesses and documentary evidence. Fg Off McCulloch and F/Sgt Booton were the first crew to undertake this duty but several others took a turn over the next few weeks. This provided some flying for the detached crew but if the bulk of the squadron was to maintain any degree of proficiency at all something needed to be done urgently about the current structural problem. Aggravated by the recent burst of flying associated with the RIN mutiny, the state of the rear spars had deteriorated markedly in the two months that had elapsed since the STI had first been issued. The situation was not improved by the arrival of a fresh batch of aircrew in April and a marked increase in the rate of release among the groundcrew. Whether the latter was a consequence of the January strike is debatable but, despite the air marshals' insistence that they would not be blackmailed, the number of men being repatriated had increased perceptibly (on No 45 Sqn at least).

An interesting task cropped up in early May when two aircraft (Sqn Ldr Dyke with Fg Off H B Deacon, and Flt Lt A D Wood with WO J O Paull) were detached to Chaklala for several days from the 10th to carry out some photographic work. Of much greater significance, however, was a change of base. Rumours of a move to Ceylon had been in the wind for some time and it was now confirmed that the squadron was to redeploy to Negombo, their intended destination having been changed from Kankesanterai in April. The squadron began to pack. They had become very adept at this exercise during the war when they had rarely stayed anywhere for more than a few months, often only a matter of days, but with the wholesale changeover of personnel this was a new experience for many of them. The process was interrupted by a fire in the squadron armoury on the night of 21st/22nd May which produced some spectacular detonations (stored gas bottles), a colourful display of pyrotechnics and the occasional broadside of cannon shells and .303 ammo. In the true tradition of all Adjutants, it was alleged that Fg Off Deacon, who had taken over from Ted Rainbow in April, was to be seen dumping files into the blaze. While this may have saved him a good deal of paperwork he must have had to talk fast to explain why he

kept his files in the armoury! Although the fire had caused considerable damage, later assessed as having been worth some Rs60,000, no one had been hurt; the squadron hastily completed its packing and left for Ceylon before the embers had cooled.

An advance party, comprising WOs Fox and Russell and F/Sgt Adamson, arrived in Ceylon by train on May 21st and the air party flew down on the 27th. It consisted of just the eight flyable Mosquitos, the remaining ten being left at St Thomas Mount for disposal. The Harvard was unserviceable too, so FT186 was also left behind, although it was hoped to recover it later. The formation was led by Sqn Ldr Dyke who had again assumed command as Wg Cdr Snell had been posted to join the station staff at St Thomas Mount on 15th May.

Command of B Flight now passed to Flt Lt W Appleby, who had recently joined the squadron on transfer from No 82 Sqn. Accompanied by Fg Off E J Davies and Fg Off J F Umdasch, Appleby's first job was to command the main rail party which left Madras on the 27th to begin an uncomfortable four-day journey to the south. Among the bits and pieces that had been loaded into the train was 'Chopper', a dog of uncertain ancestry but strong character which had been adopted by the squadron at Madras and was to remain 'on the ration strength' for the next ten years. The incendiary proclivities which the squadron had displayed at St Thomas Mount manifested themselves again on the way to Ceylon and there was a fire on board the train. Once again no one was hurt but a significant amount of damage was done.

A classic Indian scene - a group of No 45 Sqn's airmen grab the chance of a shower during one of the many wayside stops on the four day marathon from Madras to Negombo. (S J Findley)

313

The rail party reached Negombo on 31st May but, before the squadron had had time to settle in, George Dyke left for the UK and Sqn Ldr Springthorpe, took his place as CO, Flt Lt D J Clarke becoming OC A Flight. After holding the fort for less than a month Springthorpe departed and on June 28th command passed to Sqn Ldr A J P Marvin who had just been posted-in, notionally as a flight commander. This constant reshuffling of COs and flight commanders, and several organisational changes which were to be implemented during July, created something of a hiatus within the internal structure of what was rapidly becoming a *de facto* one-flight unit commanded by a squadron leader.

All of these changes in command (there had been six COs since early March) were not good for the squadron, especially when aggravated by the upheaval of a major move. Furthermore, shortly after its arrival in Ceylon all of the squadron's Mosquitos were grounded again. The long-awaited 'fix' for the spar problem had now been defined but it required the application of a specially formulated glue, of which none was immediately available. The wing inspection associated with the latest STI resulted in three more aircraft being condemned. Replacements were available at Mauripur but by this time the squadron was down to just four effective crews. Two new aeroplanes had been collected at the end of May while the squadron was moving and six more were ferried down over the next few weeks, the last ones reaching Negombo on July 10th. The pilots involved in this exercise were Flt Lt D J Clarke, Flt Lt W Appleby, Fg Off D Brockett and F/Sgt Sorrell, assisted in various combinations by the following navs; Fg Off E J Davies, Fg Off C Haggarty, WO V D Garner, F/Sgt A Smart and Sgt J Edwards. By the end of July the squadron 'owned' a total of fifteen Mk VI fighter-bombers plus a dual-controlled Mk III and had recovered the Harvard which had been left at Madras - although the latter promptly went unserviceable again as soon as it reached Ceylon. Despite having a fleet of some seventeen aeroplanes

the squadron no longer had anything like this number of crews, which was of little real consequence as few of the aeroplanes were fit to be flown. During July the squadron managed a total of fifty-seven sorties but most of these were ferry trips and air tests and little, if any, productive training flying was done.

The change of base had involved a change of controlling authority from HQ 225 Gp to AHQ Ceylon and this had generated a mountain of official returns and correspondence as the unit was struck off the books of one formation and taken on charge by another. The squadron was by now very short of professional administrative and clerical staff and, with the constant changes of 'Boss', of continuity of supervision too. A number of aircrew stepped into the breach to help out. That they were willing was self-evident and that they were capable goes without saying; but they were also amateurs. They were young aviators who had yet to acquire the deviousness of the seasoned bureaucrat and as a result they made detectable errors. (*From personal experience, one knows that errors made by a* qualified *staff officer are much harder to spot; those made by an* experienced *one are even more so! - CGJ*). These errors generated queries and so the paper-chain lengthened. Still, so long as the bumf kept circulating it seemed to keep the staffs at AHQ Ceylon happy. At least they knew that the Flying Camels had arrived; they were receiving letters from them every day, amending the information they had been sent the day before!

The squadron underwent three major transformations in July 1946. The first of these was a change in role from Light Bomber to Maritime Strike. With no ships to sink, however, its primary task was to be the conduct of twice-weekly meteorological reconnaissance sorties. These began in August when nine such exercises were flown. They followed a triangular route, flown at about 10,000 feet: east to Male, west to Addu Atoll and then back to Ceylon. Each trip took about five hours and could involve a lot of instrument flying in quite lively conditions. The lack of on-board navigation equipment and the absence of any external aids over the ocean meant that the only means of keeping a handle on the aircraft's whereabouts was to carry a manual air plot supplemented by what could be deduced about the wind by constructive use of the drift-sight. Every 30 minutes the crew were required to send a W/T report containing the essential atmospheric data required by the forecasters and eventually the aeroplanes were fitted with special therm-ometers for this purpose.

The aircraft on the right is probably RF679 OB.D which was just about to be used as the backdrop to a formal group photograph; the date is early June 1946. From the left, the first (crouching) figure is the bowser driver, then: Sqn Ldr E Springthorpe, Flt Lt D Hamilton, Flt Lt D J Clarke, Fg Off A Weatherly and Flt Lt Williams: the others are unidentified. (D J Clarke)

While the met recce sorties undoubtedly fulfilled a vital requirement, and were quite demanding for both crew members, they could also be very boring. There was, however, the occasional notable trip, as on July 20th when the squadron put up a formation of four Mosquitos, virtually a maximum effort, to fly in salute over HMS *Victorious* as she left Colombo harbour bound for the UK with the outgoing Governor of Ceylon, Sir Henry Monck Moore, on board. But beyond this, aircraft availability was severely constrained by the Mosquito's continuing wing problems and the shortage of crews; apart from the met recces, the occasional air test and the odd local practice flight, the squadron did relatively little flying during its first few months at Negombo.

The second major change was formal recognition of the *status quo* by HQ ACSEA who, on 3rd July, directed that the squadron was to be reduced to a strength of eight aircraft and organised as an HQ and one flight. AHQ Ceylon implemented this instruction on July 23rd and on the 31st the squadron was formally reduced to cadre status. The Unit Establishment (UE) remained at a notional sixteen fighter-bombers but its in-use strength was to be maintained at only eight. The aeroplanes which were eventually retained were the most recent arrivals and for the next few months the squadron's fleet comprised eight Mk VIs (TE599, TE640, TE796, TE799, TE809, TE811, TE859 and TE879) of which five or six were usually available, plus the Mk III (TW110) and the Harvard (FT186); several more Mk VIs were retained on charge as non-flying reserves. With the squadron reduced to this level, a squadron leader CO was now appropriate. Tony Marvin was confirmed in command and Flt Lt D Brockett became the sole flight commander.

The third major change was implemented on July 30th on which date No 7045 SE was disbanded and reabsorbed by its parent formation. Apart from generating another mountain of paperwork, an early task for Flt Lt D McCowan who had become the Adjutant on 25th July, the demise of the SE was as cosmetic as its creation had been; although the squadron's groundcrew and aircrew had been legally separated, their divorce had never been made absolute.

The merging of the two halves of the unit occurred against a continuing background of instability within the pool of manpower. For instance, in one ten day period in July no fewer than fifty-three men left for the UK and demob, and at the end of that month the total strength of No 45 Sqn was down to just 135 men of whom seven were officers. By early August, although the squadron still had a nominal seven navigators on its books, four of them were categorised as supernumerary and only Fg Offs H B Deacon and E J Davies and F/Sgt G D Thomas were effective; in practical terms therefore the squadron had a working strength of just three crews.

The rapidly dwindling pool of engineering manpower, meant that those who remained had to struggle to keep the whole fleet in working order -

despite the notional reduction in strength to just eight aircraft, the squadron was still technically responsible for all seventeen Mosquitos that were actually on its books. In fact a consignment of the appropriate glue had recently arrived so they had even begun to make inroads into the spar problems. The pressure was relieved somewhat with the receipt of instructions for the disposal of surplus airframes in August but, although a few were allotted away, most were to be broken up and even this task created work. Useable items, engines, instruments, radios and so on, had first to be salvaged and, to make the aircraft safe, fuel tanks had to be drained and systems inhibited. This was enough to keep the depleted numbers of groundcrew, down to just 102 by the end of September, busy for several months.

The reuniting of the squadron with its SE was part of a progressive programme to convert the huge wartime air force into a much smaller peacetime organisation, although it was to differ in many ways from the pre-war RAF. The cumulative results of these changes were permanently to alter the character of most squadrons. Ever since its original formation in 1916, No 45 Sqn (which is considered to have included its SE between 1945 and 1946) had been a more or less autonomous unit with its own organic administrative, catering, medical and logistic support, its own transport and an adequate engineering capability. The degree of sophistication of these facilities varied from time to time but the essential concept of the squadron being a semi-independent entity had prevailed for thirty years. Throughout this period the essential function of a host station (when there was one), backed up by the heavy engineering and supply organisations (the MUs), was to provide the facilities to permit its resident squadrons to do their job, not to tell them how do it.

From now on there was to be a progressive shift in emphasis. Centralisation became the watchword and with it came a steady decline in the independence of squadrons and

20th July 1946 and the squadron pulls the stops out to put up a four-ship, a maximum effort, to overfly HMS Victorious *in salute as she sailed from Colombo with the outgoing Governor of Ceylon on board. The curious protuberance on the starboard side of the lead aircraft's fuselage has not been identified. (S J Findley)*

Seen being refuelled at Negombo, TE879 was one of the batch of replacement aircraft collected from Mauripur during and shortly after the squadron's redeployment to Ceylon. (via A J Thomas)

in the authority of their COs as the balance of power shifted in favour of station staffs. Thus, for instance, the freedom of action of a Squadron Engineering Officer became increasingly subject to the endorsement of the Station Engineering Officer. In No 45 Sqn's case, its reduction in size had meant that the rank of its Engineering Officer had been reduced by one notch in any case. As a result Flt Lt F T Avent, who had relieved Flt Lt Woodcraft on July 15th, soon moved on to be succeeded by Fg Off Nicholson in August. The continuing process of demobilisation meant that he in turn was relieved by Fg Off R J E Walker in October. Another symptom of centralisation and contraction was that the squadron was no longer 'entitled' to have its own MO. 'Doc' Hutchinson had left shortly after the squadron arrived in Ceylon and ever after lumps, bumps and jabs became a

LAC Stan Findley (left) and two other armourers belting ammunition for one of the squadron's Mossies at Negombo. (S J Findley)

station rather than a unit responsibility.

In time the reduced status of the squadron came to be accepted but in mid-1946 the significant inroads being made into the squadron's autonomy came as something of a shock which needed a period of adjustment before an accommodation was reached. No 45 Sqn, which had always taken pride in the way in which it looked after its men, particularly resented having its style cramped by the intrusion of the station's welfare organisation into what it regarded as family business; for a time, for instance, it stubbornly continued to run its own book and gramophone record library facility. It was a losing battle, however, and slowly No 45 Sqn, like all the others, was obliged to come to heel and recognise the inevitability of 'progress'.

The unsettled atmosphere persisted throughout the first few months at Negombo. There was a pervasive sense of aimlessness; people were increasingly 'boat happy' and the aircrew were finding that the squadron's new role provided little professional satisfaction, this being exacerbated by the inadequacy of the equipment-fit in the aircraft. The summer of 1946 was not a very satisfactory period and it probably saw the Flying Camel come as close it ever has to getting the hump. It must be stressed, however, that the symptoms which No 45 Sqn was displaying were those of a sickness with which much of the RAF was afflicted at the time. Although the war had now been over for a year, the service was still manned largely by wartime conscripts and volunteers who wanted to resume (or start) their civilian careers. This situation would improve substantially during 1947, as the manning problem began to resolve itself and an identifiable hard core of professionals emerged to marshal the continuing flow of post-war National Servicemen, and the early tensions of the Cold War started to restore a sense of purpose.

The unhappy state of affairs at Negombo had not gone unnoticed and plans were already in hand to rebuild the squadron on a firmer foundation. A revised establishment was published in September 1946 proclaiming that the squadron was to have sixteen Mosquitos, one Harvard and no fewer than twenty crews. This, however, was going to be difficult to achieve. There were still plenty of Mosquitos scattered about the Far East, although their numbers were rapidly being reduced as they kept coming unglued and, since trying to stick them together again was proving to be an uneconomic proposition, large numbers were being condemned. Even so, aeroplanes were not immediately a limiting factor. Of far greater significance was a severe shortage of aircrews and for the time being the squadron was going to have to soldier on at half-strength.

Contemporary plans envisaged there eventually being a total of three maritime strike squadrons in the Far East (Nos 27, 45 and 84 Sqns). All three were to be equipped with the Bristol Brigand. Unfortunately, the Brigand's development programme was proving to be a protracted affair and ACSEA feared that they might well run out of Mosquitos before any of these new aeroplanes materialised. At the Air Ministry's suggestion it was decided to introduce the Beaufighter as an interim measure. It was planned to re-arm No 45 Sqn with these in January 1947. With some positive developments to look forward to, spirits began to recover and by the end of September the squadron's diarist was able to note that "morale was rising again".

While the prospect of Brigands engendered some early optimism at Negombo it might have caused rather less excitement if people had known just how long it was going to be before any of these aeroplanes were to appear; certainly no one then serving on No 45 Sqn would see a Brigand before he went home to the UK. Nevertheless, in the autumn of 1946 it was expected that Brigands, and crews to fly them, would shortly be forthcoming and, in anticipation of the squadron's early expansion, it was decided to restore it, with effect from November 1st, to a two-flight basis with a wing commander CO. This decision was promulgated by AHQ Ceylon during October in an Organisation Memorandum which had a curious twist to it, of which more anon.

AHQ Ceylon issued a maritime training syllabus in October but there seemed to be little effective staff effort to support it. The increasingly centralised organisation seemed to be long on issuing directives but short on providing the facilities with which to implement them. Left to fend for themselves, the squadron attempted to set up liaison channels with the Sunderlands at Koggala and the RN but experienced a lot of trouble in establishing an effective network through which to arrange co-operative training events. Nevertheless some progress was made and over the next few months a workable system slowly evolved. Another sign of the squadron's gradual recovery was that night flying, an activity which had been allowed to lapse since the move to Ceylon, had been reinstated during September. Furthermore the Harvard at last became serviceable again, which gave the pilots the opportunity to indulge themselves occasionally.

As in 1919, post-war demobilisation had been accompanied by the wholesale disbandment of squadrons; 267 had gone in 1945 and a further seventy-seven disappeared in 1946. The Air Ministry was concerned that the squadron numberplates which remained in use should be those of the units which had already established particularly long and/or distinguished service records. Inevitably, as operational requirements lapsed and units disbanded, the numberplates of some of the more famous squadrons were being withdrawn. These were earmarked for early reuse

when a new squadron was to be formed. In late 1946 a scheme was devised which was intended to give these defunct squadrons a quasi-existence by grafting them onto existing units. Had the author of this concept ever served on a proper squadron he would surely have known that it was not really a practical proposition. The scheme was short-lived and this writer has identified only five instances of its being used; one of them involved the Flying Camels.

No 27 Sqn had been disbanded at Mingaladon on 1st February 1946 but, as it was a long-service 'colonial' unit, it was intended to apply its numberplate to a new maritime strike squadron which was shortly to be formed in Singapore. Unfortunately, the same shortage of crews that had caused the Flying Camels to be reduced to a half-strength cadre prevented No 27 Sqn from reforming at all. In an attempt to give the dormant unit some semblance of life, however, its numberplate was allocated to No 45 Sqn on November 1st, the date on which the latter was to be restored to two-flight status. The relevant Organisation Memorandum required that it was to be brought into use by the host unit as its "B(27) Flight", the ultimate intention being to use this flight to provide the nucleus of a new No 27 Sqn once the necessary crews and aeroplanes became available. They never did, and this artifice was formally terminated on 1st October 1947 when No 27 Sqn's numberplate was withdrawn to the UK for allocation to a newly forming Dakota squadron. Although No 45 Sqn was duly reorganised into two four-aircraft flights in compliance with AHQ Ceylon's directive, it is significant that there is not one reference in the squadron's surviving documentation to its having held No 27 Sqn's spirit in trust and this obligation seems to have been tacitly ignored[4].

As has already been pointed out, the massive turnover of personnel, including frequent changes of CO, progressive reductions in the squadron's autonomy, recent changes of both base and role and inadequate equipment to fulfil the latter, had all had a very unsettling effect and the squadron was, as had been noted in its ORB at the end of August, "suffering from a sense of loss of identity". Any serious

Seen here in mid-1946 wearing its anachronistic pre-war style roundels, TE640 OB.F failed to return from the squadron's last met recce sortie on 5th November; Flt Lt Arthur Proctor and F/Sgt Gordon Thomas were posted missing. Mosquitos in the Far East were all supposed to be painted silver by this time but the aircraft in the background is obviously camouflaged as was at least one more of the squadron's last Mossies. (Author's collection)

The shape of things to come. VA367, one of the two Buckmasters which were expected to herald the early advent of Brigands. (via A J Thomas)

attempt to face up to the implications of dealing with the identity of another (non-existent!) unit as well, would probably have resulted in a terminal case of corporate schizophrenia. While the Air Ministry, seemingly oblivious to the realities of life at unit level, chose to believe that it was adding a year to No 27 Sqn's history, No 45 Sqn simply ignored the pachydermatous cuckoo that was being pushed into its bactrian nest......

The squadron lost a crew on November 5th when Flt Lt A V Proctor and F/Sgt G D Thomas failed to return from a met recce sortie, the twenty-eighth since the squadron had begun the task in August. Based on their W/T reports it was estimated that their aeroplane, TE640, must have gone down in the vicinity of 9°N 85°E. For the next five days the squadron swept the area with five-aircraft formations carrying out parallel track and creeping line ahead searches, but nothing was ever found. This unexplained loss revived lingering doubts about the robustness of the Mosquitos and on the 11th they were grounded for a series of precautionary inspections. These revealed nothing of significance, however, and flying was resumed on the 16th. So many flying hours had been expended on the search for TE640, however, that it was not possible to mount any more met recces in November and the task was withdrawn the following month.

Prior to this, on October 22nd, the squadron had taken delivery of VA366, its first Buckmaster, a second arriving on November 2nd. One of them turned out to have its ASI calibrated in miles per hour while the other's was in knots, which served to keep the pilots on their toes but, despite this minor shortcoming, the arrival of the Buckmasters was regarded as a good omen as it was anticipated that their arrival would be followed by the early receipt of Brigands. Morale continued to improve and an attempt was made to set up an initial tactical exercise with the navy in November. The idea was for the aircraft to rendezvous with HMS *Jamaica*. It could not be said that it worked entirely as planned but it certainly kept the navs busy trying to keep track of where they were, while estimating where the ship ought to be, and then trying to make the two plots converge. They did it; but the ship was not there! (*As any aircrew who have exercised with them will know only too well, the RN is notoriously reluctant to reveal the actual position of its ships, even to the 'good guys' and, since they had been attacked by the Flying Camels in 1941 - see page 164 - they do have a point. On the other hand less charitable aviators maintain that sailors never really know where they are themselves - CGJ*). In an effort to improve the squadron's understanding of naval

procedures, Sqn Ldr Marvin was attached to the RN for a month from November 27th.

The squadron suffered its last Mosquito accident (at least, its last while the type provided its primary equipment) on December 3rd in unfortunate circumstances. Flt Lt E Garland, who had succeeded Flt Lt Brockett as flight commander in October, had flown over to Trincomalee on some errand and after taking off for the return trip he indulged in some unauthorised aerobatics. He evidently lost control of TE811 and the aircraft spun into the sea. The pilot and his navigator, F/Sgt J Edwards, were both killed but at least there was no mystery about the loss of this Mosquito.

By this time, in accordance with the instructions published in October, the squadron was in the throes of reorganising itself into two flights and Flt Lt P W R Varley temporarily took over the vacant flight commander slot. On December 11th a pair of the squadron's aeroplanes made a successful rendezvous with a York with MRAF Lord Tedder on board and escorted it into Ceylon. This was nearly, but not quite, the Mosquito's swansong with No 45 Sqn. The following day all of its aircraft were grounded - again!

Notes.

1. While it is not suggested that there was any co-ordination between the events it is interesting to note that at exactly the same time as the RAF was experiencing an outbreak of indiscipline in the Far East something very similar was happening among American servicemen both in Europe and in the Pacific. The American protest tended to be more overt and at some locations there were riots. The root cause was the same in both cases; the war was over and the men were impatient to go home.

2. Although there was little more than grumbling from RAF personnel based around Madras, there were several later demonstrations by RIAF airmen at Red Hills Lake and No 377 MU. Like the RAF protests they were brief and non-violent. No doubt partly inspired by the RIN mutiny, there was an incident at St Thomas Mount on February 22nd when some 150 IORs, (about 65% of the total) refused duty; no NCOs were involved. They were addressed by their (RAF) officers, who then listened to their grievances and the men returned to work. This protest was not to do with repatriation, of course; the Indian airmen were concerned about conditions of service and certain institutionalised discriminatory regulations, not least rates of pay and travel allowances, which differentiated between British and Indian airmen.

3. In the course of researching this book the author specifically asked several ex-members who were serving with the squadron in early 1946 for their recollections of the strike. Few could recall it at all, which tends to confirm the impression that it was something of a non-event at St Thomas Mount.

4. Although the initial proposal may originate from a Command (as in this case), the ultimate sanction for organisational changes concerning the formation and disbandment of units and the allocation of numberplates rests with the Air Ministry (later MOD) and its decisions are published in the SD (Secret Document) 155. The formal authority for the association of No 27 Sqn's numberplate with No 45 Sqn was contained in SD155/1946 No 2201 and for its withdrawal in SD155/1947 No 997. It is interesting to note that, while several references to this arrangement can be found among the papers of HQ ACSEA and AHQ Ceylon, there is no mention of this totally unrealistic episode in No 27 Sqn's surviving records - hardly surprising really, since the unit has no records for this period as it did not actually exist! Nor is this artificial 'existence' remarked on by Chaz Bowyer in *The Flying Elephants*, his comprehensive history of that unit between 1915 and 1969. It certainly had no impact on the Flying Camels and none of the ex-members contacted by the author, including Gp Capt Key, who was in command for most of the period in question, were even aware of the arrangement. It would seem that the AOC Ceylon, Air Cdre C E Chilton CBE, may have had the wisdom to have appreciated its impracticability and, while obliged to reflect the association in the formal paperwork published by his HQ, he evidently declined to make an issue of it. His successor, Air Cdre A R Wardle CBE AFC, appears to have adopted the same Nelsonian attitude. It was a non-event which had substance only in the files of the Organisation Staffs.

Chapter 13. Things get better with Beaufighters.

As 1946 drew to a close the turbulence of the immediate post-war period continued to subside. With stability returning, the improvement in morale first noted in September was sustained and the squadron's sense of identity began to reassert itself. Surprisingly, since the unit had just been grounded again, things continued to look up in December with the arrival of the new CO. After wartime service in the Burma campaign, latterly as OC No 910 (Thunderbolt) Wg, Wg Cdr G C O Key OBE DFC had been sent back to the UK for a short conversion course on Buckmasters, Beaufighters and Brigands at Kinloss. In the event there had not been any Brigands and he had returned to ACSEA, reaching Ceylon on November 15th and assuming command of No 45 Sqn a week later.

He arrived as the squadron was completing its internal reorganisation. Flt Lt Pete Varley was looking after A Flight, pending the arrival of Sqn Ldr B H D Foster DSO DFC* on 31st December. B Flight, or B(27) Flight as the Air Ministry's 'Organists' liked to think of it, was in the hands of Sqn Ldr Tony Marvin (one hand really, as he spent much of this period with an arm in plaster) and would remain so until his posting to HQ ACFE came through in April 1947[1]. This reshuffle was accompanied by the arrival of the first Beaufighter Mk Xs. Having just flown 40 hours during the transit from the UK, however, the aircraft were immediately seized by the squadron's engineers to be overhauled with the aid of the appropriate 'teach-yourself Beaufighters' handbooks. With the recent grounding of the Mosquitos, the only airworthy aeroplane between December 12th and 19th was a single Buckmaster, but after that the Beaufighters gradually began to become available for conversion flying and before the end of the month three pilots had been checked out by the new CO and Flt Lt Varley had cleared two more.

Wg Cdr Key set about rebuilding the squadron and started by supporting the airmen's plan to run their own bar in the No 45 Sqn Club over Christmas. He also began badgering AHQ Ceylon to find out what had happened to the squadron's silver and to recover it. There was a significant influx of new junior officer aircrew in late 1946/early 1947 and the CO encouraged them to identify themselves with their groundcrew, each billet having an officer appointed to look after its affairs.

The bar of No 45 Sqn's Airmen's Club at Negombo all set for Christmas 1946. The style of the squadron badge and of the Vargas pin-ups give some indication as to the date of this picture, but if it were not for these clues it could have been taken anywhere at almost anytime during the squadron's extensive travels. Wherever and whenever they were (and still are) built, and whatever style of construction is involved, these establishments have a comfortingly similar ambience and a reassuringly familiar appearance; compare this picture with those on pages 134 and 186. (G C O Key)

The wartime prohibition on the display of squadron badges, which had actually been rescinded as long ago as August 1946, finally percolated through to Ceylon and with the AOC's announcement of this on 21st January they soon began to reappear on flying suits and the breast pockets of the odd blazer. These initiatives all helped to foster the squadron's spirit and by early 1947 it had largely recovered from its brief post-war slump.

By comparison with the sleek silver Mosquitos (although some of the later ones had been camouflaged) the chunky new Beaufighters were a sombre lot as they were in warpaint, although there is some uncertainty as to exactly what kind of warpaint this was. Since it was the current vogue for maritime strike aircraft, the colour scheme should have been Dark Slate Grey, possibly with a disruptive pattern of Extra Dark Sea Grey, on top with Medium Sea Grey undersurfaces. On the other hand the aircraft may have had their upper surfaces painted in a tactical temperate scheme of Dark Green and Ocean Grey and the contrasting tones evident in most of the available photographs suggests that the latter was probably the case. Unfortunately, black and white photographs inevitably portray all colours as shades of grey and it is not always possible to draw definitive conclusions. To complicate the issue further, photographs of several aeroplanes taken on charge in 1948 suggest that these had their upper surfaces painted in only one colour, in which case, assuming them to have had maritime origins, it was probably Dark Slate Grey. Finally, one of the initial batch of aeroplanes (and there may have been another) was all-silver, which was very unusual, if not unique, for a Beaufighter on an operational squadron. There is no doubt about the OB codes, however; these were boldly applied in black. As a final touch, most, if not all, of the original batch of Beaufighters sported a white band around the fuselage just ahead of the fin[2].

January 1947 was devoted to conversion flying and consolidation training. The Beaufighters were much

RD830/OB.A at Negombo with the sad remains of a number of Mosquitos in the background. (No 45 Sqn archives)

'meatier' aeroplanes than the Mosquitos and at first some of the pilots missed the latter's lightness of control, but the new aeroplanes were nothing if not robust - and there was no glue to come unstuck. The squadron flew its first formal exercise with its new aeroplanes on February 6th when seven of them co-operated with a detachment of four Lancasters of No 7 Sqn who were in Ceylon for Exercise RED LION, a Bomber Command practice deployment. The bombers' timing was not all that it might have been but the event was at least a qualified success. The idea had been for the Beaufighters to rendezvous with the Lancs over Kankesanterai, then to escort them as far as Madras where they were to participate in a co-ordinated attack on a sea range before returning directly to Negombo while the bombers droned on around southern India on an extended navex.

The day began badly with one of the Lancasters failing to get airborne and finishing up in the overshoot. The other three arrived at the RV thirteen minutes ahead of schedule and decided not to wait. No 45 Sqn's Blue Section pursued them at max boost and just managed to overhaul their charges but Red Section and an independent 'rover', following on a couple of minutes behind, were unable to catch up until they reached Madras. The Beaus then formed up and returned to base in close formation and good order. Despite its not having gone exactly as planned the event had been a good show as far as the Flying Camels were concerned. The groundcrew, now supervised by Fg Off A E Lloyd, who had become the squadron's Engineering Officer on 3rd February, had done particularly well in getting seven

Despite its poor quality this picture is worthy of reproduction as it shows RD776/OB.B in its unusual (for an operational Beaufighter) overall silver colour scheme. (via A J Thomas)

aircraft up as the squadron only had a total of eight on charge. There was another training event later in the month which involved the squadron's intercepting a submarine, HMS *Affray*, and carrying out a co-operation exercise with it. The Flying Camels were now getting into the swing of this maritime business and by the end of February, during which the squadron flew over 190 hours, the aircrew had become quite accustomed to their new mounts and were developing a considerable respect for them.

Apart from the occasional formal exercise, routine flying activities included helping the maritime authorities in Colombo to keep track of shipping by intercepting vessels whose presence had previously been reported by No 205 Sqn's Sunderlands or by the RN. Negombo's primary function, however, was to provide a Staging Post on the route to the Far East and this kept the squadron busy as there was a constant flow of VIPs whose aircraft had to be escorted in and who were then entitled to a Guard of Honour when they deplaned, these guards being furnished by No 45 Sqn. Wg Cdr (later Gp Capt) Gordon Key recollects:

As the VIP Yorks frequently altered course to avoid bad weather, intelligent guesswork was often needed to intercept them. This was usually (if not invariably) successful and the escorts earned much approbation for their skill. I was able to see this for myself when returning as a passenger on one occasion with the CinC. Two pairs of Beaus, not having made the anticipated contact, split up to carry out a square search, intercepted the York's erratic flightpath, reformed and brought it in to Negombo. The CinC was much impressed and made a point of letting the crews know......Despite the grumbles that providing Guards evoked, the airmen derived a certain satisfaction from the credit they earned and the opportunity to see at close quarters the eminent personages involved.

March was another good month for flying, the squadron putting in 166 hours, which beat the target published by HQ ACFE by over 50 hours. This 'flying hours target' was another recent innovation, stemming from greater centralisation and the tighter management of increasingly scarce and expensive resources (*with which present day squadron executives will be all too familiar - CGJ*). While there had always been a need to manage the consumption of airframe and engine hours in the light of known future tasks and to phase the incidence of overhauls, in pre-war and wartime days there had been few absolute limits on the number of hours flown. It was essentially a question of flying as much as was necessary to be proficient or to get the job done, which could be broadly interpreted as, 'as much as you like, at the discretion of the CO'. In 1947 the staffs were still refining the formula used to calculate the appropriate monthly tasking and at first their estimates tended to be wildly off the mark.

The squadron mounts yet another Guard of Honour at Negombo for some unidentified dignitary who just happened to be passing through Ceylon on his way to somewhere else. (G C O Key)

Thus, in March the squadron overflew its first target, while the revised requirement for May (189 hours) was quite unachievable. The wrinkles were eventually ironed out of the system and ever since then, except for periods of operational tasking, the administration of routine flying training at squadron level has been governed by the 'flying hours chart' which decorates every flight commander's office.

Among the many prominent personalities who staged through Ceylon in 1947, one of particular significance to the Flying Camels visited in March, Sir Roderic Hill, who had been the squadron's last CO on Vernons back in 1926. He was now an Air Chief Marshal and Air Member for Technical Services. He flew into Negombo piloting his own personal Mitchell - those were the days! Beyond that, March was pretty routine, the only unusual events being a trip up to Agra to fetch some valves for the Radio SEAC transmitter station in Ceylon while Fg Offs R D Booker and D Wood had the good fortune to spend three weeks detached to HMS *Glory* to see how the FAA played the maritime strike game.

Meanwhile the engineers were kept busy bringing the last six Mosquitos which had not been condemned up to a fully-modded state, and then storing them pending disposal instructions.

It was just as well that the Mossies had been properly looked after, as an STI was issued in April which grounded the Beaufighters; it was engines this time, not airframes, which at least made a change. As it happened the squadron had already been instructed to break out three of the Mosquitos and to make them ready for ferrying to Burma where No 1300 Flt was to use them to fly met recce sorties over the Bay of Bengal. Since they were now serviceable they were flown as much as possible, their availability permitting the squadron to take part in an exercise with the East Indies Fleet on the 23rd and 24th, but the bulk of the crews had to make do with the Harvard and a Buckmaster. On April 25th the three Mosquitos (TE796, TE859 and TE879) left for Mingaladon where, on the 26th, they were handed over to their new owners, now No 18 Sqn which had

RD824/OB.K at Agra in March 1947. It had been flown up there by Fg Offs David Wood and Bill Lyne to collect some radio spares. This aeroplane is wearing a well-defined two-tone camouflage pattern finished off with a white tail band. (D W Warne)

RD777/OB.C sporting a white band around its rear fuselage and sundry splotches of primer where repairs have been made to the tail surfaces. (No 45 Sqn archives)

Wg Cdr Gordon Key presents an award to one of the squadron's locally recruited airmen. Also in attendance, on the left, Sqn Ldr Brian Foster. (G C O Key)

been created by the simple expedient of renumbering No 1300 Flt.

The Hercules STI turned out to require 90 man hours per aircraft and while this work was being done the squadron was also instructed to prepare its remaining three Mosquitos for ferrying to No 18 Sqn. As a result the groundcrew were heavily overtasked and they could provide only one serviceable Beaufighter a day throughout most of May. One of these, RD776, was lost on the 16th when Fg Off R M Currie, making his first solo on type, did not use full power on take off. When one of the engines then failed the aircraft crashed and he was killed. A spare Beaufighter (RD775) was available at Poona and later that month a Buckmaster flew a crew up there to pick it up and ferry it back to Negombo.

Matters improved in June as more Beaufighters began to appear on the flight line and the squadron was able to put in a good month's training flying. Their departure having been postponed from May, the last three Mosquitos, two FB 6s (TE599 and TE809) and the T.3 (TW110) left for Mingaladon on the 14th piloted by Fg Offs R D Booker, A E S McCallum and R T Saunders. They ran into some pretty rough weather on the last leg and beat a hasty retreat back to Dum Dum, not reaching their ultimate destination until the 17th.

Both of the Buckmasters were grounded in July with suspected corrosion in their fuel tanks. Neither ever flew again. That month the squadron flew its longest sorties since re-equipping with Beaufighters when four aircraft carried out a simulated strike on the Maldive and Laccadive Islands.

This sortie involved 7½ hours of flying and was achieved by carrying a 200 gallon auxiliary fuel tank under the belly of each aircraft, extending the Beaufighter's already considerable range to more than 2,000 miles. Trips of this length were a trifle problematical as the squadron had only three navigators on strength as a result of the continuing shortage of these high calibre chaps in the Far East at that time. In fact the squadron ran right out of navs on July 18th when all three were detached to Singapore, leaving the squadron with no crews at all, only pilots. Fg Offs W E Lyne, J E Herridge and W M Drake had been loaned to No 81 Sqn to assist them in carrying out an aerial survey of North Borneo. As Bill Drake notes, "Our PR OTU was ten minutes on the back of a fag packet in the crew room."

From August 8th until September 1st the squadron was detached to Trincomalee (HMS *Bambara*) for an APC. The Perikarachi Range was close at hand, so trips were short and action-packed. A total of 152 sorties was flown, during which the pilots gained their first intensive experience of using the Beau's formidable firepower. The CO recalls this episode:

> The extraordinary success of this detachment was due to a variety of factors. RAF Negombo was set in the middle of a coconut plantation; wherever one looked there were palm trees in dead-straight parallel lines, horizontal, diagonal and vertical, which seen through barred windows (as all of them were) induced a state of 'stratiphobia', ie a morbid impulse to fly off at a tangent. By comparison, the surroundings at 'Trinco' on the eastern seaboard were unparalleled, the scenery attractive, the climate invigorating and our naval hosts exceptionally co-operative, friendly and hospitable to officers and men alike. The large and well-established Base offered every facility for training and for recreation. Our aircraft availability was maintained throughout - with every credit to the men left behind at Negombo who did sterling work in producing replacements as necessary. All the pilots recorded satisfactory results in air-to-air and air-to-ground/sea cannon and RP attacks against fixed targets on the naval ranges and air- or seaborne targets obligingly towed for us by RN aircraft and HM Ships. Even I was able to compete on occasion.

In all, the squadron had loosed off a total of 292 RPs and 10,500 rounds of ammunition in what had been a highly satisfactory camp. Having developed a taste for shooting at things, and being unable to fly long sorties due to the absence of the navs, the squadron concentrated on further weapons training in September and on the 16th they managed to sink a target being towed for them by HMS *Jamaica*.

The squadron was still relatively small. Although the notional UE still stood at sixteen, there were only twelve Beaus actually at Negombo in mid-1947 and, since several of these were held in storage, the unit's effective strength was closer to the eight authorised against its nominal organisation as two four-aircraft flights. The critical factor, however, was not the number of aircraft but the continuing shortage of crews. Even if the engineers had been able to produce all eight aeroplanes at once it is very doubtful whether the squadron could have drummed up eight pilots to fly them; it certainly could not have found eight navs. In fact, despite still being notionally divided into A and B Flights, the squadron had been running pretty much as a one-flight organisation ever since Tony Marvin's departure in April. Being quite small and relatively isolated, the squadron was particularly vulnerable to fluctuations in serviceability and in mid-1947 the engineers frequently had problems keeping the aircraft going; it was often a struggle to meet the monthly flying hours targets being handed down from above. Spares were scarce and when they were available they were all too often found to be corroded when they were withdrawn from storage. The tropical climate provided a pleasant enough living environment, but it was hard on machines - glue came unstuck; wood rotted; metal oxidised.

During 1947 the RAF was progressively reorganising its stations by introducing the 'three prong system' which remains the structure of a typical RAF station today. This innovation had been under discussion at AHQ for some months and the plan was for it to be implemented at Negombo on 1st September. In the event, to ease the transition, it was actually introduced on a partial basis from 1st August. The establishment of Flying, Technical and Administrative Wings further institutionalised the loss of autonomy which the squadron had resented so much when it had first begun to make itself felt a year before. The earlier wounds had largely healed, however, and it was by now more or less accustomed to the newfangled and 'more efficient' ways of operating.

The creation of Tech Wg meant that in mid-September a significant proportion of the squadron's groundcrew, including its entire R&I (Repair and Inspection) Section, were transferred from its strength to that of the station. This reduction in manpower brought several organisational changes in its wake. The smaller numbers meant that the squadron no longer warranted a wing commander CO and on September 22nd Wg Cdr Key left to take command of RAF Katakurunda; it was to be 1972 before the Flying Camels had their next wing commander 'Boss'. The transfer of much of the engineering task to the station meant that the squadron no longer rated its own Engineering Officer either and Arthur Lloyd, who had left for the UK in August, was not replaced. Responsibility for in-house technical matters now became the preserve of F/Sgt Fawcett and thenceforth aircraft maintenance at squadron level continued to be supervised by flight sergeants, and the occasional warrant officer, until the 1960s. At the same time the erstwhile OC A Flight, Sqn Ldr Brian Foster, succeeded to the CO's slot and Flt Lt Birbeck, who had been minding B Flight's store since Tony Marvin's departure, became the sole flight commander. Within a month Mike Birbeck had gone back to

Wg Cdr Key says a few words at a Guest Night in September 1947 shortly before leaving the Squadron. Just discernible on the table are sundry items from the squadron's silver collection which had only recently been recovered from wartime storage - the Flying Camel is on the extreme right. (G C O Key)

the UK to attend a lengthy course, leaving Fg Off Ronnie Booker to take his place. The reversion to a one-flight basis fitted in neatly with the ending of the nominal association with No 27 Sqn whose numberplate was withdrawn on 1st October - no one noticed its departure, however, as no one had known that it was there!

The squadron lost its second Beaufighter on November 4th when one of RD824's fuel tanks ruptured as Fg Off Tommy Saunders was starting up. Although the pilot escaped unhurt, the aeroplane quickly caught fire and was a write off. Following the recent grounding of the Buckmasters with fuel tank problems, this incident pointed to major difficulties which were to emerge in the near future.

Just as the squadron was becoming adjusted to Maritime Strike, had established a working relationship with the Navy and had begun to achieve sound results, the RAF abandoned the role altogether. It would not be resurrected until 1969 when the service picked up some ex-FAA Buccaneers as a windfall when the last of the RN's fixed-wing aircraft carriers

Its white fuselage-band very prominent and with Fg Off David Wood and AC1 Graham on board, RD824/OB.K poses for the camera late in 1947. One of the pictures taken during this session was used for the squadron's 1947 Christmas card but by December the aeroplane had been written off, following a fuel tank explosion on 4th November. (E W Johnson)

was withdrawn from service. In November 1947 No 45 Sqn was redesignated as a Light Bomber unit. This change was accompanied by another change of CO, Sqn Ldr F L Dodd DSO DFC AFC taking over on the 24th. A few days before this the squadron had lost RD782 when one of its tyres burst on take off. The aeroplane was another write-off but Fg Off R A S Bingham was unhurt.

The change of role did not mean a change of aircraft so, pending the receipt of the long-advertised Brigands, the squadron carried on with its Beaufighters which, if a little long in the tooth, were still a capable enough strike aircraft. They needed some minor modifications to adapt them to their new role and in the fullness of time underwing racks for bombs were acquired. Although No 45 Sqn's maritime Beaufighters had all been fitted with the TF 10's prominent nose radome, it appears that they had never been fitted with ASV radar and, since this equipment would have been of little practical value in the bomber role, the nosecones continued to conceal only ballast to maintain the centre of gravity in roughly the right place. Another reason for ballast was the need to balance the navigator in the back seat and, since the squadron was still very short of navs, the aeroplanes were probably all a bit nose-heavy just then. An intake of new back-seaters was urgently needed.

The chronic navigator shortage was resolved before the end of the year by the return of Fg Offs Bill Lyne and Bill Drake from their attachment to No 81 Sqn and the arrival of four new men: N2s J Oliver, A deT Prévost, R Platts and H Handley. The curious-sounding rank of N2 was a consequence of the promulgation, by AMO A.498 of 12th June 1947, of a startlingly new trade structure. Previously all aircrew had been either officers or NCOs. The intention now was to make most aircrew a quite distinct third category. There would still be a few commissioned pilots and navigators, who were to be provided by the RAF College at Cranwell, but the majority of them and all new aviators of all

other trades were simply to be 'Aircrew' and they were to have a unique status all of their own.

Within the new trade structure a man was to be trained as an Aircrew Cadet, become an Aircrew 4 to undergo his operational conversion and reach his first productive unit as an Aircrew 3. Thereafter the progression to Aircrew 2 was based on time and experience, with the final jumps to Aircrew 1 and Master Aircrew being conditional upon both time and selection. These ranks were signified by cloth badges worn on the upper sleeve, in lieu of chevrons, except for the Master's insignia, which was worn on the lower sleeve like that of a Warrant Officer. Trade specialisation was indicated by the appropriate flying badge worn on the left breast. In shorthand these ranks were expressed as P3, N1, E4 or S2, as examples of a pilot, navigator, air engineer and air signaller; Roman rather than Arabic numerals were often used at first. In its fully developed form it was anticipated that separate Aircrew Messes would eventually be provided at every flying station for this new breed, but considerable capital outlay would be necessary to build these and only limited progress was made in this respect. In the meantime Aircrew were treated as quasi-NCOs and became members of the Sergeants' Mess.

It was an extremely unpopular innovation and opposition to it did not subside with time. It provoked a great deal of resentment on two grounds. First it denied most aircrew the opportunity of advancement to a commission and secondly, it meant that a P3, who might be the captain of a Lincoln, had a notional status similar to that of the corporal who ran the bedding store! Both of these anomalies were inherent characteristics of a system which was widely perceived to be unjust, divisive, retrograde, class-ridden and ultimately unacceptable. After four years of undiminishing opposition the scheme was abandoned. The only remnant of this radical experiment is a modified form of the Master Aircrew badge which is still worn today by Airmen Aircrew of Warrant

One of the squadron's longer-serving Beaus, RD805/OB.J was among the original batch delivered at the turn of 1946/47 and it was still going strong in February 1950 when it was finally replaced by a Brigand. (Author's collection)

Officer rank.

Although it was not actually the colour scheme currently specified for bombers, Dark Green and Ocean Grey upper surfaces with Medium Sea Grey underneath was quite appropriate for the squadron's new tactical role and, since most of the aeroplanes were probably already painted this way, there was little change in the squadron's outward appearance when it first reverted to being a bomber outfit. The white fuselage band continued to be worn by at least some aircraft, and code letters continued to be painted in black. Since May 1947 the wartime Type C national markings with their subdued colours and dull finish had been superseded by bright red, white and blue roundels. These were similar to the pre-war Type A but with the proportions of the colours based on thirds, rather than fifths, of the diameter. No urgency was attached to the application of the new Type D roundels, however, and it was probably early 1949 before any appeared on No 45 Sqn's aeroplanes by which time some aircraft had begun to wear their codes in white. By late 1949, however, some of the aeroplanes would finally have begun to appear in the black and Medium Sea Grey scheme which had actually been specified for all bombers in May 1947. Since some of its aeroplanes retained their tactical camouflage to the end of their days while others may still have been in quasi-maritime colours, the Flying Camels seem never to have managed to get all their Beaufighters to look the same.

Before much progress could be made with training in the bomber role the squadron ran out of aeroplanes again. On December 31st an order was received directing that all Beaufighter fuel tanks were to be inspected. On No 45 Sqn, 100% were found to be suffering from crystalline corrosion. Grounded again! And the Harvard had just two flying hours left before a major servicing was due....

There was little option but to begin 1948 with a lot of ground training, and there was no flying at all for the first two weeks of January. Some Harvards were soon transferred from the Station Flight, however, and by the end of the month the squadron had three to fly. In the meantime some new Beaus had been located in the UK and four crews (Fg Offs Wood and Lyne, Fg Off Booker and N2 Handley, P2 Mitchell and N2 Platts, and P2 Whittaker and N2 Oliver)

With most of its Beaufighters temporarily grounded, the squadron had to rely on Harvards for the first few weeks of 1948. A number were acquired from Negombo's Station Flight but this is the squadron's own, FT186, with Flt Lt Bob Stewart in the driver's seat. (No 45 Sqn archives)

were despatched to fetch them. Hopes of an early solution to the problem were raised by the priority transfer of some fuel tanks from Singapore and another batch from the UK. On receipt, however, both consignments were also found to be corroded.

For most of February the squadron had just one airworthy Beaufighter and a notional fleet of seven Harvards, of which four could usually be relied upon, but it still managed to fly over 150 hours, which actually exceeded the monthly target! Towards the end of the month two more Beaus became available. So far as flying training was concerned, with four crews away in the UK, there were only two navs left at Negombo so the Beaufighters were largely dedicated to their need to fly navigation exercises while the pilots made do with the Harvards. Even so, quite a lot of useful training was achieved: formation practice, instrument flying, aerobatics and even a little practice bombing. One particularly productive project was a photographic survey of the Ratnapura district using a hand-held camera to create a composite panoramic oblique from which the local authorities hoped to be able to forecast the size of the annual rubber crop.

The first three replacement Beaufighters arrived from England early in March, which was just as well as by this time several of the defective aircraft had been categorised as being beyond economic repair. Things were pretty much back to normal by the end of April and in May the squadron flew its first exercise in its new role. No 97 Sqn's Lincolns were in Ceylon on Exercise RED LION II and the squadron flew with them twice. On May 5th the Beaufighters acted as pathfinders on an oversea navigation exercise by laying a trail of smoke floats; this was not entirely successful as there was a lot of low cloud and the 'heavies' had difficulty seeing the markers. Two days later the Lincolns flew out to Car Nicobar and on their return No 45 Sqn, controlled by Ceylon's GCI station, acted as an air defence force. A number of successful intercepts was carried out and these developed into a series of spirited quarter attacks accompanied by the expenditure of copious quantities of camera gun film. It was great fun for the pilots but, as

One of the squadron's tradesmen doing something technical to a Beaufighter at Negombo in 1948. Note that the aircraft in the background, RD817, lacks a white tail band and that its upper surfaces appear to be painted in a single dark colour. (No 45 Sqn archives)

No 45 Sqn in April 1948. The aircrew, in the front row, are, from the left: P2 M C B Mitchell. N2 H Handley. P1 M F J Berrey. Fg Off W M Drake. Fg Off D Wood. Flt Lt K W Dalton-Golding.
Sqn Ldr F L Dodd (and 'Chopper'). Flt Lt G T Jones (Adj). Fg Off W E Lyne. Fg Off R D Booker. N2 M Kerr. N3 F Moorcroft and N2 A deT Prévost. (R F G Howard)

Maréchal Bosquet might have said, *"c'était magnifique, mais ce n'était pas le light bombing."* Something a little more appropriate was arranged in June when the squadron contributed six aircraft to a simulated airfield strike laid on for the benefit of a Land/Air Warfare Course.

July got off to a good start with a seven-aircraft formation escorting the SS *Dilwara* on her way back to the UK with a cargo of time-expired troops, some of whom had been Flying Camelmen. Another activity with a nautical flavour was an exercise with HMS *Norfolk* which provided a towed target. Six aircraft took part but the first one shot the target away and the rest had to make do with smoke floats. It was all going very well when another Hercules STI arrived on the 26th and grounded all the aircraft yet again. Three days before this there had been another change of CO when Sqn Ldr E D Crew DSO DFC* had assumed command. In fact Frank 'Dad' Dodd, who was eventually to retire in 1974 as Air Vice Marshal F L Dodd CBE DSO DFC AFC**, had left on 26th June and Flt Lt K W Dalton-Golding, had been Acting CO for a month.

The aeroplanes had all been cleared by August 5th and flying was able to be resumed. This was just as well as a State of Emergency had recently been declared in Malaya and the squadron was called upon to provide a detachment to go to Kuala Lumpur. In preparation for this deployment a hasty programme of shallow dive-bombing was laid on against smoke floats using 250 pounders, the largest bombs that could be found in Ceylon. Fitted with external long-range tanks, three Beaufighters left on August 12th led by the new CO. They landed with over 100 gallons of fuel remaining which would have been enough to have taken them all the way down to Singapore. A support party had left Ceylon the same day in one of No 205 Sqn's Sunderlands. The fortunes of the squadron's operational echelon in Malaya will be dealt with in Chapter 14.

With the 'sharp end' of the squadron now detached, command of the base echelon fell to Flt Lt Ken Dalton-Golding who had relieved Fg Off Ronnie Booker as flight commander in March. The HQ element of the squadron continued with routine training and the conversion of new crews. The only event of any particular note was the squadron's participation in a Battle of Britain flypast on September 15th to which it contributed a vic of three to complement three Harvards from Negombo's Station Flight and three of No 205 Sqn's flying-boats from Koggala.

In November the detached aircrews were rotated and Flt Lt Dalton-Golding took a party of replacements over to Malaya. They were flown across by Sunderland on the 3rd, having been ferried to Koggala in Beaufighters. On one of these trips RD808 burst a tyre on take off and P2 M F J Berrey was obliged to belly-land at Negombo. Much to the relief of N3 A A France, and two other navs who were on board, he made a good job of it. The original batch of crews returned to the squadron on November 11th. On the 30th the squadron lost another aeroplane when Fg Off W E Edwards and N3 P J Lavender crashed on landing in RD775.

Rumours about Brigands had been gathering strength again for some months and these were given substance in December when a batch of Brigand-trained tradesmen arrived on the squadron. The sting in the tail was that the new aeroplanes were not being delivered as bombers after all; they were to be used for meteorological reconnaissance. Exactly who was going to fly them remained a trifle vague but in September the squadron's Flt Lt R C Stewart had gone back to the UK for a conversion course and he was expected to bring the first Brigand out in February 1949 - although by now some people had begun to suspect that the Brigand was a mythical beast, one which was often spoken of but never actually seen.

Although the squadron was now operating in the light bomber role, being based on an island, and with a strong naval presence, most training events still tended to have a distinctly nautical flavour and co-operative exercises with ships of the RN continued to crop up from time to time. The US Navy also put on an occasional appearance in the Indian Ocean, as in March 1948 when the squadron had worked with a Carrier Task Force built around the USS *Valley Forge*, and again in May when it had had co-operated briefly with the carrier USS *Rendova*. A third opportunity to work with the Americans presented itself in early 1949 when, in the course of a world cruise, the aircraft carrier USS *Tarawa* stopped off in Ceylon. When she sailed again on January 3rd the squadron (half-squadron really) took part in an exercise with *Tarawa's* Air Group.

Sqn Ldr Crew returned to Malaya on January 13th, leaving the Ceylon-end of the squadron in the hands of Flt Lt David Wood with the senior nav, Flt Lt N Westby DFC, as flight commander. The very next day another aeroplane was written off when RD825's undercarriage collapsed while Flt Lt K A O Norman and N1 M Kerr were carrying out a practice asymmetric landing. The AOC temporarily cancelled all further single-engined practice flying. This was fully in accord with the views of those who contended (as some still do) that more aeroplanes are bent through practising asymmetric landings than are lost through actual engine failures. It is a moot point; but the Beaufighter had long had a considerable reputation for being a bit of a handful on one engine and in the months to come many of the squadron's aircrew were going to be thankful that the pilots had kept themselves current in single-engined handling techniques.

In 1948 Ceylon had become a self-governing Dominion within the British Commonwealth and the first anniversary of Independence Day was celebrated on 4th February. The big parade in Colombo included a flypast, and three of No 45 Sqn's Beaus flew over in salute accompanied by the usual vics of Harvards and Sunderlands plus four Dakotas.

Although the Kuala Lumpur echelon was flying fewer sorties in early 1949 than it had been six months earlier, it

RD825/OB.A after its undercarriage had collapsed following an asymmetric landing at Negombo on 14th January 1949; Flt Lt Norman and N1 Kerr emerged unscathed. Unless one of the colours has faded badly, which is always possible, the upper surfaces of this aeroplane appear to have been painted in a single dark tone and there is no white band. (No 45 Sqn archives)

was quite evident that the problem in Malaya was not going to be a short-term affair. Since Ceylon was now independent, there was little justification for keeping the squadron there, especially as there was no real work for it to do. As the detachment at Kuala Lumpur seemed to be turning into a permanent fixture it became increasingly likely that the whole squadron would soon be concentrated in Malaya. Its days in Ceylon were rapidly drawing to a close.

When the squadron had arrived at Negombo in 1946, its spirits, like those of much of the RAF, had been at an all-time low. It was difficult to be depressed for long in Ceylon, however, and once the squadron had adjusted to the post-war style of organisation and some stability had been restored to its pool of manpower, morale had recovered rapidly, despite recurrent problems with its aeroplanes. Negombo was without doubt the most comfortable station that the squadron had ever occupied. The NAAFI was a great improvement on the Indian canteens to which the older airmen had been accustomed and the light, airy billets were equipped with radios; luxury indeed in 1946! The station was a little isolated but it offered sailing on the local shallow lagoon and there was a beach. The climate was hot and humid but not nearly as oppressive as it had been in Madras and there were liberty runs into Colombo for those prepared to undergo the uncomfortable fifteen mile ride in a gharry. From time to time nationalist activists provoked civil unrest in the city which resulted in its being temporarily put out of bounds but this was not a permanent situation and it eased considerably once Ceylon had been granted its independence; for those who did make the journey, Colombo offered its own variety of bright lights.

In the latter context, Sqn Ldr Crew later recalled one of the squadron's live-wires, Fg Off Bob Bingham, during one foray into town, diving fully clothed into the swimming pool of the Galle Face Hotel - it was empty! Another memorable feature of social life was the practice of piling dried fronds around the base of a palm tree and setting fire to them; eventually the whole tree would burst into flames and blaze like a giant torch. For the reluctant heroes who were obliged to serve out their wartime engagements in the post-war RAF and for the National Servicemen who followed them, there were a lot worse places than Ceylon to weather the austerity of the late 1940s. The squadron's time at Negombo had turned out, after an uncertain start, to have been a very pleasant interlude.

Ron Jones, then a brand-new AC2 on the squadron, recalls that, despite Ceylon's independence, the mounting of parades to honour the great and good as they passed through Negombo on their way to somewhere else was still a fairly fairly frequent occurrence in 1949. Another regular chore was guard duty, which seemed to come round every four of five days for a junior erk. Before he signed off, one of the unofficial responsibilities of a guard was to use his bayonet to spear a large, juicy bullfrog to take back to the billet where it was served up to the squadron's pet mongoose as its breakfast. This mongoose was a relatively recent addition to the menagerie and as such represented a challenge to Chopper's paramount status within the squadron's quadrupedal hierarchy. The mongoose expressed its bid for supremacy by deliberately teasing the dog, inviting pursuit by

chattering at it and then enraging it further by taking refuge in inaccessible hidey-holes. It eventually overplayed its hand, however, and Chopper exacted his bloody revenge. This event caused a schism within the squadron, with the mongoose fanciers demanding the hound's summary execution while his supporters rallied to his defence; sadly, no one appears to have been prepared to act as spokesman for bullfrogs' rights. Fortunately for Chopper, this division in the ranks was soon forgotten in the upheaval of the move to Malaya and he lived to fight another day.

Routine flying continued without further incident for a while and the next major event was the arrival of a Brigand! Flt Lt Bob Stewart flew the first one in on May 25th, only three months behind schedule. By this time, however, the rump of the squadron had already been ordered to move to Malaya to join the detachment and it was in the final throes of packing. Since the squadron was going to what was little more than a field site, however, the silver, which had been recovered in mid-1947, was put back into store to await the squadron's posting to a relatively civilised location.

With the departure of No 45 Sqn's rearguard on May 29th, the original plan, for the Brigands to be maintained by the squadron's groundcrew, had had to be revised. An independent unit, No 1301 Flt, had been established to carry out the meteorological task on 1st May and on June 8th it was embodied with Flt Lt Stewart as its first OC.

Brigands had been on the cards for No 45 Sqn ever since September 1946. The appearance of one, three days before the rear party left Ceylon, may have convinced the sceptics that such aeroplanes really did exist but there was no prospect of anyone actually flying one as the aircrew had already gone before the first Brigand had landed. The last of the four remaining Beaufighters had headed east across the Indian Ocean on May 16th. FT186, the Harvard which the squadron had first acquired at Cholavaram in 1945, was bequeathed to No 1301 Flt.

Notes:

1. HQ ACSEA, by now at Changi, had been restyled HQ ACFE (Air Command Far East) on 30th November 1946.
2. The reason for the rear fuselage band has not been established. From inspection of photographs it appears to have been some twelve to eighteen inches wide. It was not a standard RAF marking, although the maritime Beaufighters of the Thorney Island-based No 254 Sqn wore a very narrow white band in 1946, so there may be some link there. No 45 Sqn's bands were much wider, however, and more closely resembled the eighteen-inch Sky band used by day fighters in Europe during the war but these had been deleted for aircraft operating on the Continent in January 1945; from March 1945, with the promulgation of general authorisation for day fighters to dispense with camouflage, this marking had become redundant. When post-war colour schemes were formally promulgated in April 1946, well before the squadron received its Beaufighters, there was no mention of Sky bands. In any case, since the Beau never was a day fighter, despite the superficial similarity in appearance, it seems unlikely that the bands carried by the squadron's aeroplanes had any significance in this respect. It has been suggested that they might have been a flight marking but the bands were still evident well into 1949 and the squadron had reverted to a one-flight basis over a year earlier so this also seems improbable. They seem to have gradually faded away in 1949, probably because they were missing from replacement aircraft while others may have been painted out during overhauls. The author would find it very satisfying if it could be shown that the white bands were a unit marking adopted to reflect the original white band worn by the squadron's 1½ Strutters in 1917. Sadly, there is absolutely no evidence to support this surmise and, while attracted to the idea, Gp Capt Gordon Key, the CO for much of this period, can offer no confirmation.

Chapter 14. FIREDOG - the opening rounds in Malaya.

During the war the British had fostered and supplied the Malayan People's Anti-Japanese Army (MPAJA), a small but effective force of predominantly Chinese, jungle-based guerrilla fighters which had coalesced around the Malayan Communist Party. It was formally disbanded in December 1945, but a hard core retained its arms and turned its attention to dislodging the imperial regime which the British quickly re-established. Their early activities concentrated on fomenting strikes and provoking demonstrations and riots. While they had some effect, these tactics were insufficient to overthrow the government of the Malayan Federation, which was established on 1st February 1948, or to dislodge its British sponsors. In early 1948, the more extreme activists decided to remobilise the MPAJA as the Malayan People's Anti-British Army (MPABA) and take more direct action in the form of a guerrilla campaign involving sabotage and murder, ie doing what they had been encouraged, trained and equipped to do by Force 136 during the war. By the middle of the year the degree of unrest which these Communist Terrorists (CT) had succeeded in fomenting was such that the government was forced to react. On 16th June it invoked Emergency Powers and requested military assistance from its British protectors. This was the beginning of the Malayan Emergency, Operation FIREDOG.

Units immediately available to the Air Commander, AVM A C Sanderson CB CBE DFC, were Nos 28 and 60 Sqns (Spitfires), No 84 Sqn (Beaufighters), No 81 Sqn (PR Mosquitos), Nos 48, 52 and 110 Sqns (Dakotas), No 209 Sqn (Sunderlands) and No 656 Sqn (Austers); all were based at various stations on Singapore island. Since insurgent activity could be expected anywhere on the mainland, much of which was beyond the effective range of Singapore-based aircraft, it was decided to set up a forward HQ and operating base at a more central location in Malaya. Although it was rather small, the civil airport at Kuala Lumpur was selected as being the most appropriate airfield as it was also conveniently close to the seat of government.

Kuala Lumpur had been used by military aircraft ever since Operation ZIPPER in 1945 but it had ceased to be an RAF station in November 1947. On 1st July 1948 Wg Cdr H N G Wheeler (Changi's OC Flying Wing) and an advance party were flown up to Kuala Lumpur (KL) in three Dakotas of No 110 Sqn to reopen the airfield to support the operations of an RAF Task Force. The main party and the heavy equipment arrived by road and rail the following day. Three more Dakotas joined the Force on the 2nd as did three Spitfires of No 60 Sqn. Two of these Spitfires carried out the first strike of what was to become a twelve-year campaign on July 6th. Although No 28 Sqn contributed some more Spitfires on the 9th, the Task Force needed a heavier punch and Beaufighters were called forward. The nearest Beaus were those of No 84 Sqn at Tengah, but these could only be an interim solution as the squadron was about to redeploy to the Middle East where it was to convert to Brigands. The only other heavy strike aircraft in the Far East were the Beaufighters of No 45 Sqn, and AHQ Malaya made arrangements to 'borrow' some of these from AHQ Ceylon.

No 45 Sqn's first three Beaufighters flew non-stop to KL on August 12th. Two additional crews accompanied the support party of sixteen tradesmen, led by Sgt R F G Howard, which was ferried over by Sunderland. The aircrews are listed at Figure 14.1.

In the meantime, No 84 Sqn had sent a pair of Beaufighters up to KL on August 10th with a small party of groundcrew in support. The following day, with the

Pilot	Nav
Sqn Ldr E D Crew	Fg Off W E Lyne
Fg Off R T Saunders	N2 H Handley
Fg Off R A S Bingham	N1 M Kerr
Fg Off D Wood	N2 A deT Prévost
P2 M C B Mitchell	N2 R Platts

Fig 14.1. The first five crews of No 45 Sqn to deploy to Kuala Lumpur, 12th August 1948.

RD820/OB.E, one of the three aircraft which were redeployed from Ceylon to Malaya with No 45 Sqn's initial detachment in April 1948. It is seen here on the PSP at KL, toting a full load of rockets and awaiting a task. (Author's collection)

Shortly after the squadron's operational echelon arrived in Malaya it inherited several of No 84 Sqn's Beaufighters which were allocated codes from the 'other' end of the alphabet. This is one of these aeroplanes, RD784/OB.Z, seen here on its way to a target accompanied by RD866, the second OB.K.. Note that the codes on the 'second-hand' OB.Z were painted in white and that the aeroplane lacks a white tail band. (No 45 Sqn archives)

fleet being held in Singapore as a reserve. The acquisition of these aeroplanes introduced another variation in colour schemes as several of them appear to have had their upper surfaces painted in only one colour, possibly Dark Sea Grey. As previously noted, No 45 Sqn's 'own' Beaufighters carried black code letters which ran from A to L. The newly acquired aeroplanes were initially allocated codes from the other end of the alphabet and these were applied in white.

assistance of a No 110 Sqn Dakota, they moved up to Kota Bahru and flew the first Beaufighter strike of the FIREDOG campaign from there on the 12th, the target being a CT camp in a derelict gold mine on the Thai border. On completion of their attack they flew back to KL to meet No 45 Sqn's detachment from Ceylon. While the newcomers were getting their bearings, No 84 Sqn's two aircraft carried out a second strike, against Triang, on the 13th. No 45 Sqn flew some local area familiarisation trips on the 15th and then, led by OC No 84 Sqn (Sqn Ldr S G Nunn), all five Beaus, accompanied by some of No 60 Sqn's Spitfires, attacked a target near Tapah on the 16th. No 84 Sqn led another joint strike against a target near Bentong on the 17th and then withdrew to Tengah to start packing, although they continued to provide what help they could and a small groundcrew party remained at KL to help out until September 25th.

Since No 84 Sqn was disposing of its aircraft, there was a deal of toing-and-froing of Beaufighters for a few weeks, at the end of which the No 45 Sqn detachment finished up with five ex-84 Sqn aircraft immediately available (RD784, RD826, RD836, RD857 and RD858) with the rest of the

From the outset, a notable feature of FIREDOG was the extensive use of transport aircraft to support troops on the ground by dropping supplies, either by parachute or by free-fall, using techniques developed in Burma during the war (although the Flying Camels had been doing this sort of thing in Iraq as early as 1923). This service was also provided for the locally recruited police, who were fully integrated into the anti-terrorist forces, and a number of remote police posts were sustained almost entirely by air. No 45 Sqn suffered its first casualty in Malaya in the course of one such resupply mission when Fg Off Bill Lyne was killed in a Dakota (KJ962 of No 110 Sqn) which crashed on August 19th in the vicinity of the police post at Batu Melintang.

By that time the squadron's detachment had made itself more or less at home at KL. The airfield was fairly rudimentary with a single short, narrow runway (1,600 yds by 33 yds) of crushed laterite with a railway embankment across one end. The latter provided precious little clearance when trying to coax a fully-loaded Beaufighter over it on a hot day - particularly when there was a train passing by. On the other hand, following the railway line provided a useful way of finding the airfield, which was totally lacking in navigation aids. The dispersals, which were perilously close to the runway, were of Pierced Steel Planking (PSP) which, if nothing else, at least prevented the aeroplanes from sinking into the mud.

Domestic accommodation was either in tents or in atap-roofed timber huts built in the local *kadjan* style and located in a nearby rubber plantation; the latter had previously provided shelter for the Japanese occupation forces. There was no running water or electricity. The only flush toilet in the vicinity was in the KL Flying Club's building, but its use

Sqn Ldr Eddie Crew, who commanded the Flying Camels for a year and a half from July 1948. He had had a notably successful wartime career flying with Nos 604, 85 and 96 and was eventually credited with having destroyed twelve enemy aircraft, shared in the destruction of another and damaged five more; in addition he had personally accounted for twenty-one V-1s. (R Jones)

A general view of the camp site at RAF Kuala Lumpur in mid-1949. (M A Clarke)

330

With its starboard engine already turning and the port prop just beginning to move, Fg Off David 'Timber' Wood's RD784/OB.Z starts up prior to a strike. The name on the nose, Winnie the Pooh, is a reference to the pilot's fiancee. The small hole in the nosecone reveals a modification which permitted the carriage of an F.24 camera, emulating the squadron's Mosquitos in 1945. Like the Mosquito fit, the Beaufighter 'mod' was locally devised but, unlike the Mosquito fit, it had no official sponsorship and there was some fluttering of the engineering dovecotes when RD784 was delivered to Seletar for an overhaul! (D Wood)

Seen here in 1949, this is another of No 84 Sqn's hand-me-down Beaufighters, RD836/OB.Y. The white square on the nose suggests that this one may also have had an illicit camera on board. Note that, adhering to the pattern established with the squadron's Mosquitos, code letters were still being applied 'in reverse' on the starboard side of the aircraft. (M A Clarke)

was a jealously guarded privilege of the club's members. Technical and Ops facilities were under canvas. No hangar space was available and all servicing was carried out in the open, which could be a soggy business during the frequent torrential downpours. Since RAF Kuala Lumpur was hardly a full-blown three-wing station, with all the trimmings that went with the new-fangled, so-called "Binbrook system" of organisation, the squadron regained a little of its lost autonomy for a while. A handful of additional personnel was squeezed out of the Establishers to ease the burden of self-administration but the squadron was always short of people, even when the detachment was eventually joined by the rest of the squadron in 1949. Whenever something needed doing

that was awkward or urgent, ie nearly everything, it was a question of all hands to the pump, and that often included the CO. As is always the case, so long as there is plenty of real work to be done and few distractions are available, Spartan conditions are cheerfully accepted; morale was high.

The detachment's operational commitment was to respond to tasking as required by the Joint Operations Centre (JOC) which had been set up at KL as part of AVM Sanderson's HQ. At first the CTs were village-based, but these relatively accessible and substantial settlements were easily policed by the security forces. The Communists were soon obliged to take to the jungle where they set up camps which were supported by sympathisers among the indigenous Chinese population, who were a minority, but a substantial and influential one. In the early days of the campaign the terrorists had some quite large camps with semi-permanent basha structures surrounded by an area of reclaimed jungle under cultivation. These, however, were easy to spot and to attack. By late 1948 the majority of Communists had been obliged to abandoned this style of living too and had been forced to retreat deeper into the jungle and become mobile, although they still received a substantial amount of willing support from fellow-travellers and coerced it from others.

Initially, the squadron's normal posture was to have two aircraft at one hour's readiness but this was progressively relaxed until it had stabilised at four hours by the end of the year. When a task seemed likely, however, the readiness state could be reduced to as little as 30 minutes and, when appropriate, additional aircraft could be generated. Weapon

In the fullness of time all of the aircraft began to wear their codes in white as indicated by this photograph of RD819/OB.F, one of the squadron's original batch of Ceylon-based Beaufighters, still sporting a white, and unusually broad, tail band. It is pictured taking off from KL on an operational sortie. (R A Cook)

loads could include a pair of 500 lb bombs, up to eight 3" (60 lb) RPs and the four 20mm cannon; when supplies of the larger bombs ran short, as they did in 1949, 20 lb bombs were also carried. At first the cupola over the nav's station mounted a .303 Browning but, despite the interrupter gear, someone eventually managed to put several rounds through his own tailplane. This incident confirmed the opinion of many of the pilots that a navigator with a gun was more of a threat to the RAF than to the Communists and these weapons were dismounted in mid-1949.

Operational tasking was only moderate in September so there was no difficulty in finding three Beaufighters to accompany some Dakotas for a Battle of Britain flypast on the 15th. There was more action in October and on the 7th and 8th two maximum effort strikes were mounted against a positively identified camp to the east of Tras. On each occasion all five of No 45 Sqn's Beaufighters and all six available Spitfires participated. Thereafter operations reverted to the normal pair, responding to tasks as required, and planned strikes as ordered. The aircraft which were not on stand-by were available for training and for other productive, if not offensive, flying. Tasks carried out by the squadron's Beaufighters included: conducting anti-shipping patrols and overland reconnaissance sorties, taking photographs with a hand-held camera in either case; dropping leaflets; taking part in 'shows of force'; dropping flares in support of Dakota night ops, and acting as high speed couriers to convey key personnel about the place. The CTs were adept at mounting ambushes and by late 1948 travel by road in single vehicles had become very dangerous in some parts of Malaya. A convoy system was introduced and these were often escorted through insecure territory by armed aircraft, the Beaufighters taking the lion's share of this task because of their excellent endurance. It was very rare for these sorties to produce any trade, but it was also very rare for an escorted convoy to be attacked.

Pilot	Nav
Flt Lt K W Dalton-Golding	N2 A L J Harris
Fg Off R D Booker	N3 A A France
Fg Off R Neil	N3 F Moorcroft
P2 M F J Berrey	N3 J H Lewis

Fig 14.2. The replacement crews who reached Kuala Lumpur on 4th November 1948.

On November 4th the first batch of relief aircrew arrived, Sqn Ldr Crew and the old guard returning to Ceylon on the 11th. The new crews are listed at Figure 14.2.

By this time the rate of tasking had declined significantly but, in between the occasional strikes, co-operative exercises began to be laid on with the navy. The first was on October 25th when the squadron carried out dummy attacks on HMS *Birmingham* and then flew calibration profiles to permit the ship to set up its radar. On November 2nd a pair of the squadron's aircraft worked with HMS *Black Swan* and HMS *Aeneas*, the latter being a submarine. Naval exercises like these became a regular part of the training programme thereafter. More direct air/sea co-operation resulted from the squadron being tasked with periodic 'blue water' reconnaissances, which involved passing to a patrolling frigate details of all shipping observed within eighty miles of the coast. The reduced level of offensive activity also permitted the sportsmen to indulge their taste for football and allowed some time for a little social life. Saturday night squadron parties became a regular fixture at KL and the detachment would repair to its favourite hostelry to indulge itself with Chinese food and *Tiger* beer. Christmas 1948 was particularly memorable as the whole detachment was stood down and flown to Penang for a few days' break.

Ordnance expended in September 1948 had amounted to 37,000 lbs of bombs, 294 RPs and 5,600 rounds of ammunition but the level of operational activity then declined progressively until it reached a low point in April 1949, when the corresponding figures were just 1,500 lbs, twenty-eight rockets and 1,955 rounds. Although operations had reduced in intensity, the period had not been without incident. In January 1949 Sqn Ldr Crew had returned to Malaya with another batch of crews and in February the groundcrew were rotated. The detachment lost its first Beaufighter on February 11th when P2 Berrey crashed while making a single-engined approach to Butterworth in RD858; both he and his nav, N2 Harris, were killed. Mike Berrey had been

RD858 is believed to have been unique in that it carried a squadron badge; it is suspected that it may have been the CO's personal aeroplane until it was written off in a fatal accident at Butterworth on 11th February 1949. (R Jones)

RD816 was the third of the squadron's Beaufighters to be coded OB.D and probably the first of them to wear Type D roundels. It was taken on charge at KL in December 1948 and flown across to Negombo by Flt Lt Dalton-Golding and N2 Prévost on 19th January 1949. Seen here with a long-range fuel tank plumbed-in, the picture was probably taken as the aeroplane arrived in Ceylon. Different tones are evident in the upper surface colour scheme but, perhaps because it was a late arrival on the squadron, this aeroplane lacks the white fuselage band. (Author's collection)

awarded a King's Commendation for Valuable Service in the Air only a few weeks earlier.

There were two more incidents in March. On the 21st, Fg Off Bill Edwards and N3 Johnny Lavender were obliged to make a single-engined landing at Butterworth when RD784 blew an oil seal. Lavender had another rough ride, on the 30th, when RD836 lost an engine on take-off. Fg Off Robbie Neil aborted the run and managed to prevent the aircraft from ground looping but he was unable to avoid clipping the wingtip of a parked Dakota. April was not a busy month from an operational standpoint but it was notable for the award of a BEM to Sgt Ray Howard in recognition of his contribution to the squadron's success by keeping the aircraft flying under very primitive conditions.

By this time the CTs had largely abandoned their relatively vulnerable large camps and were now operating in smaller groups and skilfully camouflaging their presence. As a result clearly identifiable targets became an increasing rarity. Very often a target was simply defined by a set of co-ordinates in a featureless tract of jungle. Sometimes an Auster would be on hand to mark the precise aiming point with smoke, but this presupposed that the intelligence was precise enough to permit the Auster pilot actually to spot what it was that everyone was supposed to shoot at. It was often very difficult to tell what, if any, damage had been inflicted; bombs and rockets sometimes detonated on the forest canopy, which was as much as 200 feet above the ground, or disappeared through it to explode unseen beneath. Often the only indication that a strike had been delivered would be the brief presence of a few wisps of smoke which managed to percolate through the almost impenetrable foliage.

An idea of just how dense the jungle could be can be gained from the fact that it took four days to locate the wreckage of a No 60 Sqn Spitfire which crashed on November 12th, even though it had been seen going in; it was simply swallowed up by the jungle. Later that day a Dakota of No 110 Sqn which had been searching for the lost Spitfire also crashed. Although the wreckage of the Dakota was visible from the air, the going was so hard on the ground that it took the rescue party twelve days to reach the site, bury the crew and march out again. The final stage of the outbound march had covered just 350 yards but it had taken all day. Helicopters would have helped enormously and they were on the way, but they would not become available operationally until 1950.

The Communists' mobility gave them a definite tactical advantage. Once a camp had been located by aerial reconnaissance, by information provided by friendly natives or by foot patrols, there was a significant time lag before this intelligence reached the JOC. Because they could see and hear reconnaissance flights, and had a well established grass roots network of informers to warn them of the presence of patrols, the CTs would often have melted away before aircraft could be tasked and a strike delivered.

Although the security forces were not losing the campaign, they were not winning it either, and it was evident that No 45 Sqn was going to be needed for an indefinite period. It was decided to concentrate the squadron in Malaya and on April 28th four crews were flown back to Negombo to pick up the last Beaus and ferry them across. They were flown over one at a time, staging through Car Nicobar. The aircraft and crews involved are listed at Figure 14.3.

The only aeroplane to have a problem was RD805 which suffered a constant speed unit (CSU) failure and was

Date	Aircraft	Pilot	Nav
3rd May	RD817	Sqn Ldr E D Crew	N2 A deT Prévost
4th May	RD866	Plt Off M M J Robinson	N3 P J Lavender
8th May	RD816	Flt Lt K A O Norman	N3 A A France
16th May	RD805	Flt Lt K W Dalton-Golding	N1 M Kerr

Fig 14.3. Crews and aircraft involved in the final phase of No 45 Sqn's deployment to Malaya in May 1949.

marooned at 'Car Nic' until a replacement unit could be fitted, this aircraft finally reaching KL on the 20th. Once the aircraft had been seen off, the Ceylon echelon packed its kit and, complete with Chopper, boarded a Dakota which flew them to Butterworth. The whole squadron, with a total strength of ten aircraft, was now based at KL.

May had been quite a busy month, as the KL detachment had undertaken an APC at Butterworth which had involved 116 hours of non-operational flying. At the same time the requirement for strikes had suddenly increased again; fifty-six 500 pounders had been delivered, along with 360 RPs and over 12,000 cannon shells. There had been some lively flying incidents too, no fewer than eight single-engined landings having been made, all of them arising from actual engine failures. Fortunately AHQ Ceylon had rescinded the temporary ban which it had imposed on asymmetric flying

There was a complication to staging through Car Nicobar. The runway was too narrow for an aeroplane to turn round under its own steam and someone had to get out to push the tail around. On this occasion in 1949 Cpl Bates drew the short straw but, as seen here, he was able to use his charm to persuade this group of topless ladies to give him a hand. (R F G Howard)

Chopper flew across from Negombo with the rump of the squadron in May 1949. (M A Clarke)

practice following Flt Lt Keith Norman's accident in January. The rate of engine failures was such that it was quite obviously essential for Beaufighter pilots to maintain their proficiency in single-engined handling techniques.

In June a minor diversion was provided by another naval co-operation exercise in which five Beaufighters were to work with HMS *Birmingham*. The aircraft were to rendezvous with the ship after having first carried out a live strike on the mainland. In the event the mission was aborted and, as a precaution, the formation first disposed of its ten 500 pounders. Although they were jettisoned 'safe', every one of them exploded on hitting the sea! Operational tasking continued at a steady rate in July with fourteen strikes being mounted, each involving four to six aircraft. There was some atavistic satisfaction to be had from loosing-off large quantities of high explosive but it remained an essentially frustrating business as few of the nominated targets had specific aiming points and there was rarely any intelligence feedback. For example, on 12th and 13th July the squadron flew 36 hours in the course of Operation PINTAIL, a campaign against a band of 200 CTs reported to be in the valleys of the Sungei Piah and Sungei Par in southern Perak. When the troops eventually moved in they found - nothing.

The majority of FIREDOG missions were not the classic high-speed, low-level approach for a single-pass followed by a twisting, turning escape at maximum boost which the term 'strike' tends to conjure up. There was no hostile air defence system to contend with; in fact the only effective defence available to the CTs was to take cover, although they did have the option of shooting back with rifles - if they could see the aircraft through the jungle canopy and if they could afford the ammunition. FIREDOG sorties were a fairly leisurely affair with transits to and from the target being flown at a comfortable height before dropping to low-level for the initial attack in the hopes of taking the enemy by surprise. Thereafter the strike was continued by setting up what amounted to an academic 'range pattern' with aircraft following each other around the racetrack delivering attack after attack, frequently spending well over an hour over the target. While it had to be accepted that the Beaufighters could not often guarantee to do a great deal of damage, they could certainly do a lot to break the CTs' morale and undermine their resolve by subjecting them to what amounted to a prolonged artillery barrage.

On one such five-aircraft strike, against a target in the Seremban Forest on July 2nd, the squadron came literally within inches of tragedy. Taking his turn on the merry-go-round, as he approached the end of a firing run in RD784, Fg Off L S R Smith suddenly found his windscreen full of Beaufighter. It was Wg Cdr Pike (by then OC Kuala Lumpur) in RD866. Taking avoiding action as best he could, Laurie Smith could not avoid clipping his leader's starboard wingtip with his port prop. Luck was with them, however, and both aircraft returned safely to base.

July 1949 was also notable for the reintroduction of night flying. The limited facilities provided by KL's small and cramped airfield meant that it was unsuitable for this activity and, as they had involved night landings, the last three sorties of Operation PINTAIL had recovered to Butterworth.

Thereafter the maintenance of night currency, which had been allowed to lapse, was reinstated as part of the training routine. Butterworth was used for these exercises at first but later on Tengah became the more usual venue for night flying.

There was another narrow squeak in August when, on the 10th, P3 M A Clarke had a problem with RD866; once again the back-seater was the unfortunate Johnny Lavender. On the way back from a strike near Taiping they left the formation to fly out to sea to try to shake off a hung-up 500 pounder. Clarke succeeded in getting rid of the bomb but, as he resumed heading for home at about 3,000 feet, the port engine stopped and the aeroplane began very slowly to lose altitude. The question was, would they reach KL before the aeroplane ran out of height? They made it, but it was a close

Fg Off Robbie Neil (left) and Flt Lt Ken Dalton-Golding at KL. Next to DG is LAC Bevan and next to him is AC Les Manners; the airmen on the right is unidentified. (R Jones)

run thing and to minimise drag the pilot did not select undercarriage down until he was 'over the hedge.' He touched down hard on the port wheel and bounced, which was just as well as the 'goofers' who had assembled to watch the anticipated crash were all convinced that the starboard leg had not been fully extended; it was by the time the aircraft touched down for its 'second landing'. There were the usual muttered comments about a routine single-engined approach having been turned into a crisis through the pilot's inexperience, which Maurice Clarke, as a relatively new-arrival and a mere P3, had no option but to tolerate. When the engine snag had been sorted out the squadron's senior pilot, Flt Lt Ken Dalton-Golding, announced that he would fly the air test, finishing off with an asymmetric landing to show all concerned how it should be done. Everyone turned out to watch as Ken sank gracefully downwind on one. Before he had turned onto the base leg people were already offering rapidly shortening odds as to whether he was going to make it. Just as everyone had begun to look forward with ghoulish glee to a fairly spectacular arrival, there was a puff of smoke from the dead engine as it started up and the single-engined demonstration was abandoned. Nothing was said, of course, but Maurice felt that his honour had been restored.

While he may have had a problem on this occasion, Ron Jones remembers that the squadron's flight commander had a considerable reputation as a pilot among the squadron's airmen:

His take off routine was legendary. He would lift off the runway, settle down again to within about six feet of the deck, travel the whole length of the runway and overshoot, and then hang the Beaufighter on its props and climb until almost at stalling speed, level out and away. All this with a full load of bombs and rockets. I flew with DG (as he was always known) several times. I particularly remember a flight from Butterworth, near Penang, during a firing exercise. The firing range was a small island off Penang and we flew to it at zero feet all the way, plastered it with 60 lb concrete training rocket heads, then headed back for Butterworth again at zero

In preparation for conversion to the long-awaited Brigand, Buckmaster RP198 was delivered to the squadron. From the absence of OB codes this is evidently an early picture and the Dakotas in the background suggest that it may have been taken during the few days that the aeroplane was operated from KL in August 1949. (M M J Robinson)

feet. On the way we encountered a sampan, DG promptly made straight for it and I can still recall glimpsing three or four crewmen diving over the side in panic as we flashed past. He then climbed to about 5,000 feet, selected wheels down and landed as smooth as silk, taxied to the dispersal, climbed out of the aircraft, gave everyone a huge grin and stalked off. There was sea water dripping from every crevice of the Beaufighter, which had been picked up by his props.

A few days after Maurice Clarke's asymmetric incident the legendary Brigand came a step closer to reality when the squadron's first (third really) Buckmaster overflew KL on its way from Butterworth to Singapore on delivery to the Far East Air Force (FEAF)[1]. On August 18th Dalton-Golding collected it from Seletar and, after the groundcrew had looked it over, he began a conversion programme, Sqn Ldr Crew going solo on the 30th. Having just been ferried out from the UK, however, the aeroplane was short of flying time and the squadron only got 5½ hours out of it before it had to be returned to Singapore for a Minor Inspection. KL's airfield was really far too small for the Buckmaster, especially for conversion work, and it never came back. When it became available for flying again a few weeks later, it was operated from Tengah.

The squadron's aircrew pose for the camera at KL in September 1949. Note that the Beaufighter in the background, RD819/OB.F, has been repainted in the ultimate black and grey 'bomber' colour scheme. From the left, back row; P2 T E Cantwell, P2 B E Stocker, N3 F Moorcroft, N3 P J Lavender, P3 M A Clarke and N2 J H R Flett. Middle row; N2 M Parker, Fg Off M M J Robinson, Fg Off W E Edwards, Fg Off L S R Smith and N3 D L Green, Front row; Flt Lt N Westby DFC, Flt Lt K W Dalton-Golding, Sqn Ldr E D Crew DSO DFC*, Flt Lt A H Fernand DFC and Fg Off R Neil. (M M J Robinson)

In September the squadron's HQ basha was completed, which gave the Flying Camels an air of at least semi-permanence after thirteen months under canvas. By this time a meagre electrical supply was available and each basha boasted a solitary dim light bulb to attract night-flying insects. Otherwise domestic facilities had improved little. There was a wash house with a couple of shower stalls but it was a wise precaution to fill a bowl first as the water was likely to stop flowing once one was well-covered in lather. As Maurice Clarke recalls, the latrines were "bottomless pits with wooden surrounds and a suitably carpentered hole. A torch was essential to check for snakes, large spiders and other creepy-crawlies. A place to avoid at night if it was humanly possible."

Sgt Ray Howard left for the UK to be commissioned at about this time and the task of keeping the Beaufighters going was taken over by F/Sgt R F A Holdaway. In that same month the Brigand, for so long the subject of rumour and speculation, at last took on a tangible form. The first one out from the UK, VS857, landed at KL on September 6th but it took off again on the 8th and disappeared over the horizon bound for Singapore and a sensibly sized airfield. It was to become No 45 Sqn's first Brigand on 21st September when it was officially taken on charge by a detachment of the squadron which had been set up at Tengah to support the introduction of the new aeroplanes.

The squadron had flown a particularly satisfying mission on September 7th when it was called upon to hit some specific huts in a squatter camp on the outskirts of KL itself. Insurgents were known to be hiding in them but it was

10th November 1949; the squadron provides the rearguard to Sir John Slessor's York on its way to Singapore. Eight of No 60 Sqn's Spitfires protect the flanks and half a dozen of No 81 Sqn's Mosquitos joined in before the formation reached Tengah. (No 45 Sqn archives)

obviously vital not to hit the wrong huts. Five Beaus took part in the operation and, although the RAF was not credited with having killed any terrorists, the residents were stampeded into the arms of the waiting security forces. Fifty-six arrests were made and twelve of the suspects were subsequently identified as terrorists. Such positive feedback, however, continued to be the exception rather than the rule.

Eight days later, on the 15th, six Beaufighters and three Spitfires flew a Battle of Britain flypast over Ipoh. This effort was overshadowed, however, by another flypast on November 10th. The CAS Designate, ACM Sir John Slessor, was carrying out a tour of the RAF before taking the helm and as his York flew down the west coast of Malaya on its way to Singapore it picked up an escort. As the York

Better late than never, and very late in the Beaufighter's operational career, a number of them (at least four) were painted in what had officially been the colour scheme for bombers since 1947. This one is RD857/OB.R; a couple of Spitfires and some of KL's tents can be made out in the background. (R Jones)

passed Port Swettenham three of No 45 Sqn's Beaufighters formated on it and a little later they were joined by eight of No 60 Sqn's Spitfires and finally by six Mosquitos from No 81 Sqn, the whole Balbo eventually driving across Tengah airfield in splendid style. That evening three aircraft were tasked with a strike from which they landed back at KL in the dark, although this was still not the normal procedure.

During 1949 the amount of air power on call to sustain the FIREDOG campaign had increased steadily as additional units, some on detachment from the UK, joined FEAF, sometimes being supplemented by the Air Group of one of the RN's aircraft carriers. As a result the air offensive was slowly gaining momentum. On October 21st Operation LEO, involving five Beaufighters, four Spitfires, eleven Fireflies, ten Seafires, four Tempests and a Sunderland, was mounted against a reported CT concentration near Gemas. This was followed, on November 17th, by the biggest all-RAF strike of the campaign so far when Tempests, Beaufighters, Spitfires, Sunderlands and Lancasters of Nos 33, 45, 60, 205, and 210 Sqns, plus some Harvards from the FEAF Communications Sqn, bombarded a CT position in Kelantan. In all thirty-one sorties were flown. Some of these were precision strikes by the tactical aircraft aiming at specific points, while the Lancasters unloaded some 1,000 pounders and the Sunderlands cruised up and down dropping a total of 342 20 pounders at random anywhere within the designated target area. The action went on for nearly five hours with Sqn Ldr Eddie Crew acting as airborne controller throughout.

Nine days later the squadron lost another Beaufighter. It was the old problem of the aeroplane's being unable to maintain height on one engine, let alone climb over the hills that run down the spine of Malaya. Fg Off Smith was airborne in RD866 with N3 Curry and an army cameraman, Sgt Townley, when the port propeller 'ran away'. The pilot shut down the engine, feathered the prop and headed south for Singapore. The aeroplane lost height steadily and Smith

was eventually left with no alternative but to attempt a crash landing near Durian Tipus. At the end of its run the aircraft hit a tree, broke up and caught fire. Laurie Smith, a graduate of the first post-war intake into the RAF College, died, as did Townley. Curry, who had only just arrived in FEAF via a Brigand ferry, survived, although he had been severely burned and was eventually evacuated to the UK.

The rate of tasking, and with it the wear and tear on the now tired aeroplanes, had increased markedly since early October and, with the loss of RD866, the squadron was down to just one flyable aircraft at one stage. A couple of others were unserviceable at KL and the rest of the fleet was in Singapore undergoing repair and inspection programmes which were beyond the squadron's rudimentary up-country engineering capacity. Two more Brigands had reached Singapore in November, however, and the Beaufighter's day was nearly done. Before the month was out some crews had been transferred to Tengah where Ken D-G had started pilot conversion training on the Buckmaster.

The squadron was now ordered to move to Tengah to re-equip. Its last strike from KL, a pair against a target in Perak, was flown on December 2nd and the next day three aircraft were ferried down to Singapore by Flt Lt Dalton-Golding and Fg Offs Robbie Neil and Bill Edwards. Sqn Ldr Crew with most of the remaining aircrew, the bulk of the groundcrew, the more manageable kit and 'Chopper', followed in three Dakotas. The rump of the squadron and the heavy kit travelled down overnight by train under the supervision of Flt Lt Norman Westby. The last Beaufighter was flown out of KL by Fg Off Mike Robinson on December 9th. The following day the Flying Camels mounted their first strike from Singapore when three aircraft attacked a target in the Yong Peng Estate to the west of Kluang.

Notes:

1. ACFE was redesignated as FEAF on 1st June 1949.

Chapter 15. Brigands - formidable but flawed.

In marked contrast to KL, Tengah was a quite sophisticated airfield. It had originally been built for the RAF in 1937 and had been extended during the Japanese occupation. When the British returned in 1945 there were two runways: the pre-war one, which ran NW/SE, and a Japanese addition, which ran NE/SW. Both were a trifle short for post-war high-performance aircraft, however, and the one laid down during the occupation was unusable, as was an extension to the original runway, since the construction of both had been deliberately sabotaged by the POWs who had built them. Japanese prisoners were used in 1946-47 to lay a third runway, 6,000 feet long and running N/S. Complementing the airfield itself there were light, airy barrack blocks (the aircraft control tower being atop one of these), appropriate messes, large permanent hangars,

Home to several generations of airmen of No 45 Sqn, Cheshire Block at RAF Tengah. (C E French)

comprehensive technical facilities, a cinema, a swimming pool and ample sports fields. Further afield there was a yacht club and, for the less athletic (or more jaded?) there were the exotic sights, smells and entertainments of Singapore city.

While Tengah had much to offer, it was short of working accommodation and for a long time most of the squadron's offices were to be under canvas. The CO had the luxury of an office in No 1 Hangar but most activity took place in the tents erected alongside the squadron's dispersal which, for the next two years, was at the south western end of the old 'Jap strip'. The duckboard flooring of the tents provided a potential sanctuary for rats but Chopper soon appointed himself to be in charge of rodent control and this never became a problem. Working conditions such as these were not unusual in the early 1950s, of course, especially on overseas stations, and they were certainly no worse than those to which the squadron had been accustomed at KL. In fact, apart from the two years spent at Negombo, the squadron had not had the luxury of proper offices since it had left Helwan in 1939. Beyond this minor inconvenience Tengah was a very comfortable berth and, since it was to become the squadron's permanent base, the silver and the other assorted bric-a-brac which had been left in store in Ceylon were recovered and brought 'home'.

While Beaufighter ops continued, missions of up to five aircraft at a time being flown, Brigand conversion gathered speed. The first Brigand incident occurred on December 16th when the port engine of Robbie Neil's aircraft had an

Tengah airfield, looking towards the south west (see plan at Annex B). The main runway runs diagonally from top left to centre right. At the beginning of the 1950s No 45 Sqns Brigands were parked at the far end of the 'Jap strip', roughly where the aeroplane's trim tab is. Its Hornets were later parked at the near end of the same unusable runway (near the white markings). In early 1958 the squadron's Canberras used the south eastern end of the pre-war RAF runway (occupied here by No 84 Sqn's Brigands) but they soon moved to a substantial hardstanding in front of No 1 Hangar (where the Lincolns are parked in this picture); No 81 Sqn's Canberras had the near end of the same stretch of concrete. Other notable features which may be discerned are the Aircrew Mess in the centre foreground, the hangars in the middle of the picture and the water tower, barrack blocks and Sergeants' Mess at top left; the Main Guardroom and SHQ are at the extreme left-hand edge of the picture, where two roads converge. The photograph was taken in August 1952. (M Retallack)

overspeeding propeller but he got the aeroplane down safely 'on one'. Three days later the squadron lost one of its pilots in an unfortunate accident when P1 T E Cantwell was killed in a fall from the upper storey of a barrack block.

The Brigand flew its first operational sortie on December 19th when one aircraft accompanied four Beaufighters on a strike to the north east of Kluang. By the end of the month the conversion programme was well established and every pilot except two had flown either the Buckmaster or the Brigand. The Brigand fleet in Singapore numbered six by New Year's Eve, of which five were available to the squadron. Most of the new aircraft had been ferried out by crews who then joined the unit. The latest three had arrived on 13th December (P3 S V Hayler, N3 B A Ellis and S2 P A Weston in RH829), 19th December (Fg Off J Widmer and N3 R Mercer in VS855) and 25th December (P3 J F Austen-Brown, N3 E J Mousdale and S2 L E Howard in VS864).

It is interesting to observe that brand new bombers were being flown about the world by people with virtually the same status and practically the same pay as a corporal cook; furthermore they had to do it on Christmas Day! Or did they? As VS864 was touching down at Tengah most of the squadron's aircrew had just piled into Ken Norman's pre-war Morris Seven tourer at the Officers' Mess and were on their way to the Airmen's Mess where they were going to do the honours and serve lunch. Overflowing with seasonal spirit(s), they followed the Brigand as it taxied in and extended a noisy and fluid welcome to its crew. A trifle wearily, the new arrivals accepted the proffered cold beers. In fact it transpired that there had been no particular pressure to fly on Christmas Day but the crew had elected to do so in an effort to escape from the overgenerous hospitality at Butterworth - out of the frying pan....

The Brigands were delivered in the standard Bomber Command finish of Medium Sea Grey upper surfaces with gloss black underneath and extending up the fuselage sides. In the course of repainting during overhauls in late 1949, at least four of the Beaufighters had appeared in this scheme, which looked most incongruous on a fighter type, even if it was being operated in the light bomber role. Aircraft of both types painted in this scheme wore the squadron's OB code letters in white, which stood out boldly against the black background.

At the end of the war the curious quasi-independent empire which the Brooke family had established in Sarawak was ceded to the British, which had resulted in the territory becoming a crown colony in 1946. This change of status was not universally popular with the local population and there had been increasing unrest which culminated in early December 1949 in the assassination of the Governor, Mr Duncan Stewart. The shock of this action calmed the situation somewhat and there was little likelihood of the CT problem spreading to Borneo as there were relatively few Chinese there. Nevertheless it was considered that a show of force would be in order and four of No 45 Sqn's Brigands

RD805/OB.J was one of the first Beaus to be issued to No 45 Sqn and one of the last three to be struck off its charge on 20th February 1950. By that time it had at last acquired the colour scheme that had been officially in vogue for bombers since April 1947 - but it still looked inappropriate on a Beaufighter. It is seen here at Tengah with the squadron's Buckmaster, by now coded as OB.Z, in the background.
(via A J Thomas)

were despatched to make it, in conjunction with four of No 81 Sqn's Mosquitos. There being no airfield at Kuching, the aircraft flew to Labuan on 13th January 1950 and the next day returned to Singapore, flying down the coast in formation. Unfortunately, while carrying out a formation change to permit the Mosquito leader to inspect fabric reported to be stripping from the wing of one of the aircraft in his flight, Nos 2 and 4 collided over Seria; both Mosquitos crashed and all four on board were killed.

Back at Tengah, strikes continued to be flown throughout January, Brigands contributing eight of the fifty-one sorties mounted, but most effort was devoted to the completion of the conversion programme. This period was punctuated by the usual run of incidents, both Sqn Ldr Crew and Fg Off Edwards being obliged to make single-engined landings in Brigands while the latter also did well to get Beaufighter RD819 down in one piece after it had shed large sections of its port engine cowling in flight.

Early in February the squadron was presented with another opportunity to show off its new aeroplanes when four aircraft were detached to Ceylon to take part in the Independence Day Flypast. Departing on the 2nd and accompanied by a Dakota carrying a ground support party, the detachment made stops at Car Nicobar on both the outbound and the inbound flights. Here, as Ron Jones recalls, "...we had to refuel them (*the Brigands*) from 50 gallon drums - it took two days for the fuel to filter through

VS855/OB.V on the ground at Labuan in early 1950.
(via A J Thomas)

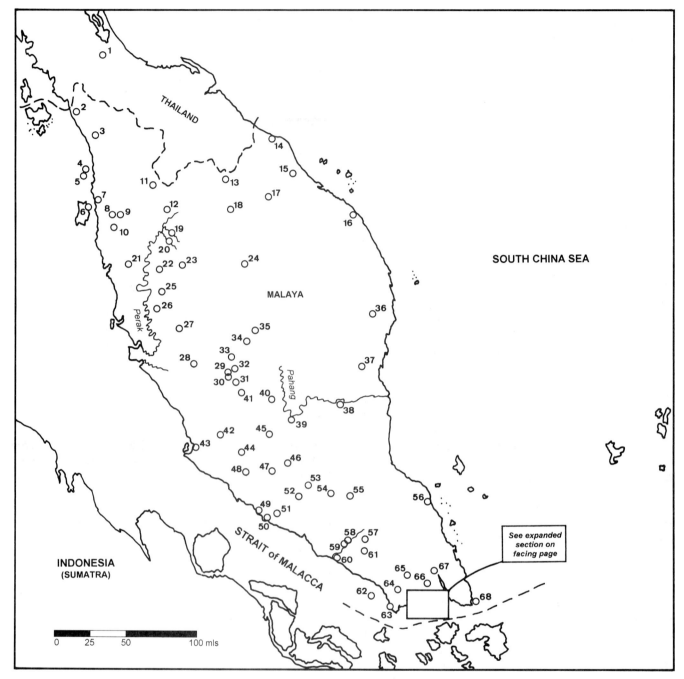

Map 15.1. *Malaya and Singapore. This map is relevant to Chapters 14 to 19 inclusive.*

3	Alor Star	40	Bukit Woh	1	Haad Yai	11	Kroh	76	Paya Lebar	4	Song Song
52	Asahan	7	Butterworth	74	HMS *Terror*	17	Kuala Krai	47	Pilah	20	Sungei Piah
61	Ayer Hitam	78	Changi	25	Ipoh	35	Kuala Lipis	64	Pontian	22	Sungei Siput
46	Bahau	33	Cheroh	69	Johore Bahru	16	Kuala Trengannu	43	Port Swettenham	21	Taiping
13	Batu Melintang	68	China Rock	77	Kallang	37	Kuantan	62	Pulau Pisang	27	Tapah
60	Batu Pahat	45	Durian Tipus	2	Kangar	63	Kukup	31	Raub	71	Tengah
34	Benta	29	Fraser's Hill	26	Kinta Valley	8	Kulim	54	Segamat	49	Terendak
41	Bentong	53	Gemas	42	Kuala Lumpur	55	Labis	75	Seletar	30	The Gap
5	Bidan Island	6	Georgetown	57	Kluang	38	Lake Chini	73	Sembawang	32	Tras
9	Bongsu Forest	15	Gong Kedak	23	Korbu	50	Malacca	48	Seremban	39	Triang
44	Broga	12	Grik	14	Kota Bahru	56	Mersing	28	Slim River	51	Tualang
10	Bukit Relau	24	Gua Musang	67	Kota Tinggi	65	Mount Kulai	59	Sungei Belman	66	Ulu Tiram
72	Bukit Gombak	18	Gunong Inas Forest	70	Kranji	36	Padi	19	Sungei Par	58	Yong Peng

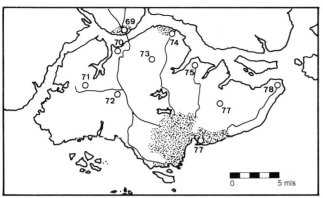

Expanded section of Map 15.1.

the chamois leather." On the day of the flypast itself, Ken D-G had an undercarriage malfunction in VS855 which obliged him to use the emergency system to blow his undercarriage down and lock it. He could hardly take part with his wheels dangling so the squadron's formation turned out to be a vic instead of a box, but nobody noticed. When the detachment arrived back at Tengah on the 7th Mike Robinson had a similar problem and had to use the emergency system on RH832. Such teething troubles were almost inevitable with a new type but they were annoying all the same.

The squadron flew its last Beaufighter mission, a pair against a target near Johore Bahru, on February 7th. This brought to an end the ten-year operational career of one of the classic RAF aircraft of WW II. Relegated to second-line duties, the Beaufighter was to soldier-on for a while yet but the guns which had first been used in anger in 1940 would fire no more. To mark the Beaufighter's honourable retirement from operations, one of the squadron's aircraft was displayed, floodlit, in front of the Officers' Mess at a dance held on 11th February. This sounds easier than it was and manhandling the aircraft up the hill to the Mess had been a considerable feat of civil engineering; a number of trees had to be felled and, to avoid the aircraft disappearing into monsoon drains, several makeshift bridges had been constructed. It was recorded that the 600 yard trip had taken 7 hours and 10 minutes, which was getting a bit close to the Beau's maximum endurance!

On February 17th Sqn Ldr A C Blythe DFC assumed command and Sqn Ldr Crew sailed for the UK on the SS *Dunera*. As the ship left Singapore the squadron flew past in salute with three Brigands, three Beaufighters and the Buckmaster. This was the last time that the Beaus flew with No 45 Sqn, although squadron crews later ferried two of them up to Hong Kong where they became target-tugs. Eddie Crew was subsequently awarded a Bar to his DSO in recognition of his leadership of the squadron throughout a very eventful tour. He retired in 1973 as Air Vice Marshal E D Crew CB DSO* DFC*. F/Sgt Hóldaway left the squadron at much the same time and his stalwart contribution on the engineering side was also recognised by the award of a BEM which was gazetted in March.

A second flag waving trip to Borneo was ordered in February, this time involving only No 45 Sqn. The new CO led five Brigands over to Labuan on February 23rd, returning the next day. The trip had been uneventful, apart from Alec Blythe's having to make a flapless landing - hydraulic problems again. The month was rounded off by a session with a TV film crew which recorded a four-aircraft strike on

VS838/OB.A being refuelled by hand at Car Nicobar while on its way to (or from) Ceylon in February 1950. (R Jones)

On 23rd February 1950 five of the squadrons Brigands were despatched to Labuan to show the flag over Borneo. They are seen here, VS813/OB.Q nearest the camera, forming up for the return run down the coast to Kuching on the 24th. (M A Clarke)

the 28th. It had been a very busy February. The squadron had flown 185 trips with its new Brigands plus nineteen on Beaufighters, twenty on the Buckmaster and thirty-three on Tengah's Harvards.

March 1950 was a period of consolidation flying with only thirteen operational sorties being called for. The CO had a narrow escape on the 13th when, during an attack on the Bentong Gap, one of the delayed-action fused 500 pounders he was carrying detonated shortly after it had been released from VS857; fortunately the damage was only superficial. The month was also significant for the start of Operation MUSGRAVE, the deployment of a succession of Lincoln squadrons from the UK, which was to provide FEAF with a heavy bomber element until April 1951. Another sign of the increase in FEAF's striking power was the return to Tengah of No 84 Sqn. Now fully equipped with Brigands after a protracted work-up at Habbaniyah, they arrived in April for what was initially intended to be a six-month detachment, providing the Flying Camels with some direct, if friendly, competition; something up with which it had not had to put since the disbandment of No 82 Sqn in 1946.

Having virtually completed the squadron's conversion programme, Ken Dalton-Golding's time was up and after two very busy years as the squadron's sole flight commander he left for the UK[1]; his place was taken by Flt Lt L H Clark who had joined the squadron the previous November. As with the Beaufighters, the UE was to remain at ten aircraft and the squadron continued to operate as a one flight organisation throughout the Brigand era. In point of fact it would be late 1951 before the squadron actually had ten aircraft on charge and for most of 1950 its strength was more like seven.

341

A strike briefing at Tengah in mid-1950. In the front row, from the right, Sqn Ldr A C Blythe DFC, Sgt S V Hayler, Sgt J F Austen-Brown and Flt Lt K A O Norman. (No 45 Sqn archives)

On April 4th, five aircraft, each carrying two 1,000 pounders and two 500 pounders, hit a target at Bukit Woh. It was a successful operation and one of the comparatively rare occasions on which the squadron received positive confirmation that its strikes were having an effect; they were credited with having killed six CTs and wounded a further four. This was the squadron's first strike carrying the Brigand's full bomb load and it convincingly demonstrated that the new aircraft had roughly three times the offensive capability of the old Beaus. On the other hand, while the Brigands were more powerful than their predecessors, they were also rather larger and very much heavier. As a result they were less manoeuvrable than the squadron's previous mounts and this needed to be borne in mind, especially when trying to deliver attacks in valleys, as was often the case.

While the new aircraft certainly had a heavy punch, in order to deliver it the aircraft needed to be serviceable, and the groundcrew were fighting an uphill battle. Early Brigand flying was plagued by undercarriages which were reluctant to retract and/or to lower. Once the fault had been traced to perished rubber seals in the high pressure hydraulic system, they were closely monitored and the problem became less prevalent; much later the operating pressure of the system would be reduced, which eased the problem considerably. Another common occurrence, especially in the early days, was overspeeding propellers. Few of these incidents

VS859/OB.G pumps out a cloud of smoke as its port engine fires up. If the engine was overprimed this smoke was preceded by a sheet of flame which saved any members of the groundcrew who were still lurking under the wing from having to pluck their eyebrows. (M A Clarke)

developed into real emergencies, although Flt Lt Norman came too close to one on April 26th when a CSU failed on the way to a target. He jettisoned his weapons and turned back towards base but the propeller declined to feather and with the consequent drag from the windmilling prop he could not maintain altitude. He nursed the Brigand back to Tengah, running out of height just as he arrived. He touched down just five feet short of the runway!

The day after Keith Norman's exemplary display of skilled airmanship the CO had a narrow escape when he had another bomb explode prematurely. He was flying RH832 and, as with VS857 on March 19th, he was able to fly it back for a normal landing. This time, however, the damage was more severe and the aeroplane had to be withdrawn for the attention of the MU. In the fullness of time it was repaired and eventually reissued to No 84 Sqn.

Prior to this there had been one other notable event in April when, on the 15th, the High Commissioner himself, Sir Henry Gurney, had flown with the squadron. This was no "local area famil", however; it was a full blown six-aircraft strike on Broga with Sir Henry riding shotgun in Sqn Ldr Blythe's aircraft.

By June the squadron was routinely contributing heavily to the offensive, despite its continuing technical problems, although the recurrent unserviceabilites were exacerbated by a serious shortage of tradesmen. At this stage the squadron was manned to only 65% of its establishment and postings-out regularly exceeded postings-in. Overcoming its handicaps by hard work on the part of the groundcrew, the squadron flew sixty-four operational sorties that month during which it dropped 190,500 lbs of bombs, fired 404 RPs and 22,985 rounds of 20 mm cannon shells. It was a lot of ordnance, but just how much damage it was all doing was, as usual, never very clear.

By this time the 'Briggs Plan'[2] was well established and well over 400,000 Chinese had been moved and concentrated into new villages where they could be monitored and controlled. This cut off the active terrorists from their grass roots support, aggravated their logistic problems and isolated them from their intelligence sources. Since it was increasingly difficult for the CTs to establish permanent camps the majority of targets continued to be featureless areas of jungle. The initiative was slowly passing to the government forces but the enemy was elusive and could be effectively confronted only by troops on the ground. The RAF's role was largely that of demoralising the CTs and driving them out of an area in which they were known (or believed) to be, so that they could be engaged and mopped up by the army. Even if the tons of explosives being unloaded into the jungle, often it seemed almost indiscriminately, never actually hit anything of military significance, they still made a vital contribution to the offensive. If there were any CTs in the vicinity, even if all the weapons missed, it must have been, at the very least, unsettling to have been on the receiving end of what was by now a very heavy offensive air campaign, especially as a proportion of the bombs were fused with delays of up to 36 hours. No 45 Sqn was not, of course, the only unit involved and its efforts were complemented by those of Nos 33, 60 and 84 Sqns, the Sunderlands and the Lincoln's 'big stick'.

While the CO was content to carry out operational strikes

as briefed, he considered that such missions were insufficiently demanding and that his pilots needed some academic range work to maintain their proficiency. The problem was that the only calibrated range available was over 300 miles away at Song Song, to the north of Penang; nevertheless the squadron began to use it. Attention was also given to navigation training and three aircraft made trips to Labuan and back during June, these flights also serving to 'show the flag'. Another interesting diversion that month was Exercise BLUE ROAD which took place between the 9th and 28th and involved aircraft of Nos 45, 60 and 84 Sqns 'attacking' a flotilla of ships of the Indian Navy.

On the social side, the Squadron was visited by the Inspector General of the RAF, Air Chief Marshal Sir Hugh Saunders, on June 23rd. It will be recalled that he had commanded the squadron in Egypt when it was flying Fairey IIIFs and he spent some time reminiscing with the aircrew before he was obliged to move on and visit some of Tengah's lesser inhabitants.

At about this time Alec Blythe, who had previously spent some time with the Instrument Flying Flight at Changi, was concerned to enhance the squadron's all-weather capability. He introduced the pilots to flying cloud penetrations in the Buckmaster and then graduated them to formation penetrations in the Brigand. He has described the cloud-break technique as follows:

> On approaching the cloud the formation was brought in close, so that each pilot could check his heading with the leader's compass. This was to allow for compass deviation. Then numbers 2 and 3 turned 5° away from the leader for five seconds and climbed 500 feet before returning to the leader's heading. Numbers 4 and 5 turned 10° and descended 500 feet before resuming the leader's heading. The aircraft were carefully trimmed for straight and level flight before entering cloud and once in it were allowed to ride the storm with the minimum of interference from the pilot. All he was required to do was to maintain heading as far as possible without harsh use of the controls.... It was rare for angles of bank to reach 45° and vertical displacement was not really unpleasant once personal fear was overcome and the aircraft was allowed to fly itself.

Maurice Clarke also recalls a spate of cloud flying trials at about this time, probably inspired by the USAF's recent publication of a book on thunderstorm penetrations based on a series of investigative flights conducted in 1948-49:

> The Americans had used Black Widows packed with sophisticated equipment. The Brigand, undoubtedly robust, was FEAF's answer and one was fitted with a five-shilling accelerometer! About three of us flew these storm penetrations as our navs tried to write down all the relevant figures - quite impossible when we were being bounced through a large, or even a small, Cb. We had no oxygen so flight had to be restricted to below 10,000 feet. The biggest problem was the Brigand's large glazed canopy. When the lightning started, and it became almost continuous, everyone on board was flash-blinded. To overcome this we had old maps and sticky tape to try to black ourselves out. I don't think that we got any useful data but the experience taught me a lot about flying in

Post-strike photographs like this one were quite unusual as there was rarely anything very specific to shoot at.
(No 45 Sqn archives)

heavy weather. If we had been able to fly at higher altitude I have no doubt that icing would have created very considerable problems.[3]

The squadron's operational effort continued to increase in July when it flew eighty-one sorties but this achievement was marred by the loss of the first Brigand on the 6th. RH850 hit the top of a hill while carrying out an RP attack near Kuala Lipis and the aircraft crashed with the loss of Fg Off N B Harben, N3 T W Smith and S3 C Lloyd.

A spate of problems with the guns was alleviated in August by a policy of replacing the barrels after every 500 rounds. This significantly reduced the incidence of stoppages and permitted an additional 10,000 rounds to be loosed off compared to July. On the other hand it had been found that carrying two 1,000 lb bombs was cracking the skins of the aircraft behind the nose (the bombs were slung externally under the fuselage, well forward, virtually under the pilot's seat). The underslung load was reduced, first to one 1,000 lb bomb and one 500 lb bomb, and later (in December 1950) to just a pair of 500 pounders. Even so, with another 500 pounder under each wing, this was still twice the load toted by the old Beaufighters and towards the end of 1951 the bigger bombs were reintroduced, albeit on a limited scale.

Four Spitfires had to be delivered to No 28 Sqn in Hong Kong during August and the squadron was required to shepherd them up there via Kota Bahru, Saigon and Tourane. Kai Tak was then a comparatively small aerodrome and before departure Alec Blythe made some practice short take offs to brush up on the technique and succeeded in getting a fully loaded aircraft off in a remarkably short 750 yards. During an en route stop at Saigon on August 14th two of the

No 45 Sqn poses in front of one of its Brigands in December 1950, the picture accentuating the considerable size of these aeroplanes. From the left, back row: LAC B Wright; AC A A C Amos; Cpl K J B Menzies; AC P D Short; LAC D G Rockett; LAC A Clegg; AC P C Smith; Cpl E D Davies; LAC E D Worsley; Cpl G W Ryder; Cpl J Hislop; LAC K P Walpole; LAC F Kent; AC C A Payne; LAC D Rushbrooke; AC W J White; AC M Rea; AC J C Piddington; AC D R Older; AC K E Bingham; AC J Gerrard; AC E Thirkell; LAC E Jenkinson; LAC H Witton; Cpl A Wilkes; AC V J Mortimer; Cpl R Nicholson; LAC J A H McDonald; LAC D C Browne; AC D P Broadwith. Middle row: Sgt S V Hayler; Sgt E Simpson; Fg Off R J Gammans; Fg Off D W Helps DFM; Flt Lt M M J Robinson; Flt Lt L H Clark; Sqn Ldr A C Blythe DFC; Flt Lt K A O Norman; Flt Lt M A Noble; Flt Lt W Edwards; F/Sgt R Holdaway BEM; Sgt P A Weston; F/Sgt W H Burton. Front row: Sgt K Hall; Sgt L S O'Donoghue; Sgt A J Martin; Sgt R E Morling; Sgt R Robinson; Sgt J F Austen-Brown; Sgt F Moorcroft; Sgt B E Stocker; Sgt M A Clarke; Sgt E J Mousdale; Sgt B A Ellis. (H Witton)

Spitfires collided, resulting in the death of Flt Lt Abrey, the pilot of TP383. The CO pressed on with the remaining pair but his Brigand went unserviceable at Saigon on the way back. The Adj, Fg Off Mike Robinson with N3 Moorcroft and S3 Grace as crew, flew the necessary spares up to Saigon on the 19th then carried on to Hong Kong to see the sights themselves before returning to Singapore on the 21st. These two Brigands had been the first of the type to visit the colony and they blazed what was to become a very familiar trail for the Flying Camels of the 1960s. In between shopping trips, and other diversions, the crews had given the operational facilities the once-over and had concluded that, if it ever became necessary, Brigands could be operated from Sek Kong but they were less enthusiastic about Kai Tak. While the squadron had been extending its sphere of influence to include Hong Kong, Flt Lt Bill Edwards had been broadening his personal horizons by spending some time with No 656 Sqn. He returned to the fold on August 28th having flown 80 hours in Austers during the previous seven weeks.

Apart from the odd flying highlight, August 1950 was of particular significance to many of the squadron's aircrew. On the 31st the unpopular Aircrew Trade Structure which had been introduced in 1947 was finally abandoned. Traditional SNCO ranks were reinstated and overnight the alphanumeric soup of P1s, N2s and S3s became sergeants and flight sergeants again. It is interesting to note that Tengah may have been unique among overseas stations in that it had boasted a dedicated Aircrew Mess. This had originally been the airline terminal building but when the runway at Kallang had been sufficiently extended to permit BOAC's and QUANTAS' long-haul types to fly into there, the commercial operators had moved out. The vacant building became the Aircrew Mess. The restoration of proper NCO ranks had little immediate impact on domestic arrangements; the Sergeants' Mess could not cope with the sudden increase in its membership so the old Aircrew Mess remained in use for at least two years and probably much longer.

Ninety-three operational sorties were flown in September, the highest monthly total so far on Brigands. These were complemented by a Battle of Britain flypast to which the squadron contributed six Brigands and the Buckmaster. Two other Brigands, accompanied by one of No 84 Sqn's, flew over to Sarawak on the 26th to participate in the ceremonies marking the opening of an airport at Kuching.

By November a substantial amount of weapons training had been conducted at Song Song but the results were rather disappointing. This was not really the pilots' fault, however, since the Brigand lacked any form of bomb sight. Level bombing was a matter of waiting until the target had disappeared under the nose then counting an appropriate number of seconds, depending on speed and height, before letting the bombs go. Dive-bombing was a little better. As the squadron had found during the war, accuracy increased with the steepness of the dive, but the Brigand was no Vengeance and 90° dives were out of the question.

The main problem was the lack of reliable airbrakes. The system was pneumatic and operated by opening a valve in the leading edge of each wing; the resultant inflow of air was conducted via flexible trunking to a set of bellows which expanded to force the airbrakes out into the slipstream. It worked well enough on the few occasions that they were tried but the trunking and the bellows tended to perish under tropical conditions and this raised the possibility of asymmetric operation. Such an incident had occurred with one of No 84 Sqn's aeroplanes in June and the crew were fortunate to have got away with what could have been a catastrophic accident. The risks were far too great to permit the airbrakes to be used and in July the system had been inhibited. In any case the g limitations of the Brigand's airframe precluded anything too dramatic in the way of a dive recovery. Aiming in a dive, at about 30°, was a matter of lining up on the target with the help of the small metal tube which dispensed de-icing fluid onto the windscreen! It was very much a matter of eyeball and judgement but satisfactory results could be achieved with practice and experience. The aeroplane did have the luxury of a proper gunsight, so cannon and rockets could be aimed with a reasonable chance of getting somewhere near the target - when there was one. While academic range work was definitely improving the squadron's accuracy, the long haul up to Penang and back was onerous, and expensive in flying hours. China Rock Range (just off the south eastern tip of the Malayan mainland) was about to become available, however, and this would significantly reduce transit times.

On December 21st Sqn Ldr Blythe was carrying out a practice asymmetric approach when his undercarriage refused to lock down. He had little option but to select 'wheels up' and belly it in on the grass alongside the runway. When RH829 was hoisted back onto its wheels it did not look too bad but on closer inspection it turned out to have sustained quite a lot of damage. It was taken away to Seletar where it was beaten back into shape and eventually restored to flying

RH829/OB.M was Sqn Ldr Blythe's personal aeroplane and, as such, it had his rank pennant and a small squadron badge painted on its nose. As can be seen from the state of the propellers, this picture was taken shortly after the wheels had been coaxed down again, following the CO's belly-landing on 21st December 1950. (H Witton)

The squadron's Buckmaster, RP198/OB.Z, at Tengah early in 1950. This aeroplane served the squadron well enough during the initial conversion to Brigands but its serviceability became quite troublesome later on and the squadron was sometimes obliged to borrow RP194 from No 84 Sqn to keep abreast of pilot checks. When Tengah's airfield was extensively remodelled ten years later, the substantial hill in the background completely disappeared. (via P H T Green)

condition. At about this time the squadron's Buckmaster began to play up and No 84 Sqn's RP194 had to be borrowed to check out some new pilots.

The pattern of operations established by the Beaufighters in 1948 continued into 1951. Most strikes were pre-planned but aircraft and crews were also held at readiness to respond to short-notice tasking. The normal FEAF requirement by this time was for two light bombers and four fighters to be at 30 minutes' readiness, squadrons taking it in turns to meet the commitment. This situation prevailed throughout 1951-52 but thereafter the at-notice time was progressively relaxed. These were not hard and fast rules, however, and the numbers of aircraft and crews required to be on stand-by, and their readiness state, could be altered at any time in the light of current intelligence. Against the constant background of ops, training continued and China Rock was now in almost daily use for weapons practice. Academic pilot exercises and checks were carried out in the Buckmaster, although much of this was accomplished courtesy of No 84 Sqn whose trainer seemed to stay serviceable far more than the squadron's own RP198 which was becoming increasingly recalcitrant.

Seventy-five operational sorties were flown in the course of thirty-four strikes in January 1951 but a crew was lost on one of these missions. VS838, one of four Brigands taking part in a strike near Ipoh on the 11th, suffered an explosion in its cannon bay; the aircraft caught fire and crashed. None of the crew, Sgts S V Hayler, G A Robinson and K Hall, survived the incident, although the pilot did succeed in baling out. He seemed to have landed safely as he was seen waving to the rest of the formation but, despite knowing his precise location it took five days for the rescue team to cut their way through bandit-controlled jungle to reach him, and by that time he was dead. He was buried on the spot and a year later, when the area had been secured, his body was recovered. It has been suggested that a post-mortem indicated that Sidney Hayler had actually died of poisoning from a *Sakai* (aboriginal) arrow.

Throughout the Brigand era the squadron periodically found itself short of navigators, signallers or both and it often flew with only two-man crews. Since most missions were flown in formations, however, with the leader looking after navigation and communications for everyone, it was not essential for every aircraft to carry a full rear crew and there appears to have been a policy change to endorse the practice of 'flying light'. This was the case on February 15th when VS859 crashed at Pilah on February, killing Sgt Kent and Sgt Ellis. The cause was another explosion in the cannon bay and an immediate embargo was imposed on the further use of guns, pending an investigation. Despite this the squadron continued to fly strikes in formations of up to four aircraft, often accompanied by similar numbers from No 84 Sqn. Targets could be anywhere in Malaya and it was not unusual to be tasked against objectives as far north as Alor Star.

Apart from a sharp drop in tasking during April there were few occurrences of note during the next few months, apart from the comings and goings of new and old crews. The ex-Beaufighter brigade were now in a diminishing minority and among those who left in April was Flt Lt Mike Robinson. He had joined the squadron at Negombo in November 1948 and, while doubling as Adj for much of his tour, had flown 172 operational sorties. He would eventually retire as Air Vice Marshal M M J Robinson CB, another distinguished Flying Camels graduate.

The demand for strikes recovered slightly in May but the CO noted that operations still seemed to consist mainly of delivering large quantities of high explosive to featureless areas of jungle, almost as an act of faith. As always, it was rarely possible to distinguish a specific aiming point. While feedback from a specific sortie remained a rarity, however, the general picture was encouraging. Although they might not be visible, there usually were CTs in the vicinity of the nominated targets. Kept moving by the constant air attacks by day, and deprived of sleep by Sunderlands cruising overhead all night throwing out small but noisy bombs at irregular intervals, terrorists captured by army patrols were often found to be exhausted. There were other positive indicators too. Operating in direct support of 42 Cdo, the squadron had carried out two strikes near Bahau in conjunction with No 33 Sqn on May 13th and 14th. When the Marines moved into the now deserted MRLA[4] camp they found that it contained slit trenches to provide some cover from air attack, so the strikes were evidently having some effect. There were few clear victories directly attributable to air power during FIREDOG, however; it was a matter of applying constant grinding pressure. Progress was being made, but it was a slow process.

The fault with the cannons had by now been diagnosed as being a consequence of their exceptionally long barrels. The Brigand's four Hispanos were mounted in the fuselage, the breeches being well aft of the rear cockpit while the blast tubes were under the pilot's feet. It appeared that, during prolonged firing, ventilation was inadequate and enough hot gases could build up in the barrels to create a back pressure sufficient to cause an explosion. An extended firing trial was arranged on the butts at Tengah and just such an explosion was induced, resulting in buckling of the skin on the underside of the fuselage. This trial had been conducted using only ball ammunition, but operational magazines were loaded with both ball and high explosive (HE) rounds. It was quite evident that if an HE round had been involved the explosion would have been large enough to have damaged the adjacent hydraulic plumbing, causing spillage of inflammable fluid and fire. In effect the Brigands had been shooting themselves down.

In May the embargo on firing the guns was lifted but their use was restricted to short bursts and only ball ammunition was to be employed from then on. The cannon had been restored to use in time for them to be used during Operation WARBLER, a three-day maximum effort against a terrorist band which had been located in Johore. Operating in twos and threes, the squadron flew seventeen strikes for a total of forty-three sorties between June 16th and 18th. WARBLER's success was marred, however, by its being bracketed by two more fatal accidents.

On June 15th the starboard engine of VS857 literally fell off and the aircraft crashed among the mangroves just to the north of Tengah. The signaller, Sgt Weston, initially attempted to bale out but realised that the aircraft was too low. Sgt Martin, hoping that he might reach the runway, had lowered the undercarriage but when it became apparent that they would not make it he selected wheels up again. On impact, with the undercarriage legs still partly extended, the aeroplane somersaulted onto its back and slid along Kranji Creek inverted. The nose cone broke off and the pilot emerged through the hole; the signaller escaped through the lower hatch, which was now the 'upper' hatch. Having first helped the injured Alf Martin to dry land, the signaller realised that their nav was missing. Peter Weston went back to look for him but by this time the aircraft had filled up with muddy water and he could not get back into the crew compartment to attempt a rescue; Sgt V Bowen did not survive the accident.

No 84 Sqn had lost another Brigand on 1st June in what may well have been very similar circumstances and on the 19th the engine fell off another one. With three Brigands having crashed in nineteen days, with the loss of five lives, the fleet was grounded.

When it became apparent that diagnosing and curing this problem might take some time, most of the navs were detached away to keep them flying. Some went to No 110 Sqn to fly Dakotas, others to Seletar on Sunderlands. A third group was attached to No 1 Sqn RAAF whose Lincolns arrived at Tengah in July to take over from the RAF's series of heavy bomber detachments which had ceased in April. During this enforced lull in operations there was another change of flight commander with Flt Lt R Whittam taking over from Flt Lt Clark who moved to the Far East Training Squadron which had just been established at Seletar.

The cause of the recent accidents was eventually traced to the fracturing of the Rotol propellers around the blade roots after about 400 hours of running time. The prop would throw a blade and the consequent vibration would tear the Centaurus engine off its bearers. New engine bearers and

Not a bad job! When VS864's undercarriage declined to lower on 24th July 1951, Sgts Clarke and Smith burned off their excess fuel and then delivered the aeroplane direct to the MU by making a copybook belly-landing alongside the runway at Seletar. (M A Clarke)

new propellers were fitted and the aircraft were restored to use. The squadron flew its first mission with a refurbished aircraft on July 12th when the CO, accompanied by an aeroplane from No 84 Sqn, carried out a strike on the village of Sungei Siput.

Most aeroplanes seem to stay serviceable if they are flown regularly but they tend to sulk if they are not. The Brigands ran true to form and, having stood idle for a month, they were most reluctant to become serviceable again and for some time there were recurrent problems with the electrical and hydraulic systems. Nevertheless, despite Sgts Clarke and Smith having to carry out a belly landing at Seletar in VS864 on July 24th, the engineers had managed to coax five aircraft back on line by the end of the month. Understandably, for a time the prospect of flying them was viewed with a certain lack of enthusiasm by some of the aircrew.

By August things were more or less back to normal, although the month's operational effort amounted to only forty-nine sorties. This decline was solely the result of reduced tasking and was not typical of the remainder of the year. By this time convoy escorts had become a routine addition to the programme of planned strikes and short-notice responses to army requests for direct support. An innovation was introduced in August when the squadron pioneered the operational use of a two-tier rocket mounting, permitting the Brigand to carry and launch up to sixteen 60 lb RPs. This was a timely boost to the Brigand's firepower as the guns had been inhibited again. On August 5th there had been another incident of a gun barrel exploding, this time on one of No 84 Sqn's aeroplanes, and (apart from a few rounds being loosed off in October) the guns were not used again until February 1952.

A new CO, Sqn Ldr I S Stockwell DFC AFC had arrived

VS865/OB.R neatly tucked up for the night at Tengah. (H Witton)

347

In December 1951 the squadron mounted a detachment to Butterworth; this is the palatial HQ facility. (H Witton)

VS855/OB.V having one of its wheels changed at Butterworth in December 1951. (H Witton)

The interior of the squadron's billet at Butterworth in December 1951. Note the rifles stacked in the centre aisle. (H Witton)

at Tengah on August 1st and on the 27th he assumed command. A number of other people were 'tourex' along with Alec Blythe and six of the squadron's NCOs and several of its airmen were with him at the ship's rail to witness the squadron's five-aircraft farewell fly-past over HMT *Empire Fowey* as she sailed for the UK on the 29th. In September Sqn Ldr Blythe was awarded a Bar to his DFC for his leadership of the squadron during a highly successful tour, made exceptionally difficult towards the end by the Brigand's unsatisfactory safety record. At the same time Sgt Nav (by now a pilot officer) Green and Cpl Nicholson were Mentioned in Despatches.

A Singapore Air Day was held at the civil airport on September 1st. The squadron positioned its smartest aeroplane at Kallang for the public to admire and wonder at, while Flt Lt Ron Whittam led three others in an 'attack on a terrorist camp', much as Bert Harris' Vernons had done at Hinaidi back in 1924. Operational tasking declined even further in September, only eleven strikes (thirty-two sorties) being called for. Ian Stockwell, who had participated in five previous strikes, led his first show, against Cheroh, on the 3rd. The other strike leaders at this time were Flt Lts R Whittam, D Helps and B Muth and Sgts M A Clarke and B E Stocker. The relatively little used quick reaction facility was exercised on the 12th when a pilot of No 656 Sqn reported a target near the Sungei Belman in Selangor. The three aircraft on stand-by were quickly despatched and Sgt Stocker landed at KL en route to pick up the Auster pilot so that he could point out the target. Stocker then marked it with RPs and everyone hit it. The camp was destroyed.

The comparatively low rate of tasking was offset by a corresponding increase in training flying, forty-one bombing and thirty-six RP details being flown at China Rock during September. In addition the squadron ran a navigation competition which was won by Bryan Stocker's nav, Flt Lt M A Noble. Academic pilot training continued to be problem, however, the Buckmaster managing to stay serviceable long enough to remain airborne for just 55 minutes during the entire month!

On October 5th three aircraft flew up to Butterworth for a fortnight's detachment in the hopes of finding more trade in the north. They did. The MRLA had stepped up its campaign from mid-1951 and on October 6th, while travelling to Fraser's Hill, the High Commissioner was ambushed and killed by terrorists. The following day No 45 Sqn flew six sorties against targets in the Gap area in pursuit of the assassins. Overall the month produced twice September's operational activity and, even more satisfyingly, many of the targets were clearly identifiable, so there was

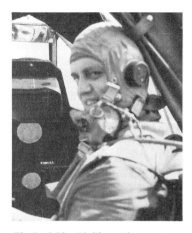

Flt Lt Mike Noble airborne in a Brigand. Above the armoured seat back, Flt Lt Ron Whittam's eyes can be seen peering out of the rear-view mirror. (R Whittam)

Arming a Brigand on the PSP dispersal at Kuala Lumpur in 1952. (L Anderson)

something to aim at for a change. While the detachment was at Butterworth it took advantage of the calibrated range facilities at Song Song to carry out the squadron's first assessed academic bombing and RP details for over a year. Meanwhile, back at Tengah, the squadron succeeded in coaxing nine hours flying out of the Buckmaster, although these were enlivened by three emergency landings, one of them at night, before the aeroplane withdrew its co-operation altogether and retired to its lair in the hangar more or less permanently.

In the wake of the assassination of Sir Henry Gurney there was an unprecedented burst of operational activity in November. The squadron flew forty-one strikes in formations of up to seven aircraft, involving a total of 144 sorties. This was an all time monthly record for the Brigand, and indeed for the squadron, throughout the whole twelve-year FIREDOG campaign. By this time the squadron's strength had risen to a notional ten aeroplanes and throughout November four or five of them were deployed to KL as a forward detachment. The airfield had been having a facelift and No 45 Sqn's Brigands were the first operational aeroplanes to use it for eighteen months. They were kept very busy, flying up to nine sorties a day in formations of up to five aircraft. One particularly successful mission was flown on the 27th when the CO led a strike against a pinpoint target at Alor Star. The camp, probably the HQ of the 8th Regt, MRLA, was destroyed; one terrorist was killed, another was wounded and a third, whom the army described as "bomb happy", surrendered. Back at Tengah the squadron had been visited by 'the Trappers', the Examining Wing of the Central Flying School (CFS) but the lack of a working Buckmaster and the high rate of operational activity frustrated their efforts to find anything seriously amiss.

The squadron's place at KL was taken by a detachment of No 84 Sqn in December but the pace cooled markedly. In search of trade the squadron positioned three aircraft at Butterworth between the 13th and 18th but they only attracted three strikes, most of the available work being allocated to KL. Everyone was back at Tengah in time to attend an all-ranks party in Singapore on the 21st to get the festive season off to a good start.

Although there had been some depressing moments when

crews had been lost, in retrospect 1951 had actually been a very good year. The squadron had flown 815 strike sorties, which was more than any other squadron involved in the campaign, even though it had been grounded for six weeks. Despite its vicissitudes, the Brigand had actually done quite well, but its accident record was such that it was inevitably regarded with deep suspicion by some of those who were obliged to fly in it. The good news was that the squadron was soon to be re-equipped and the aircrew, at least the pilots, were now eagerly looking forward to the arrival of the new Hornets. No 33 Sqn had been the first of FEAF's units to re-equip with these, trading in its Tempests at Butterworth in May 1951 and moving down to Tengah in August to show off its sleek new twin-engined fighters. No 33 Sqn returned to its original haunts in January 1952 by which time enough Hornets had arrived in the Far East to allow Hong Kong's No 80 Sqn to give up its Spitfires. No 45 Sqn also took delivery of the first of its new aeroplanes (WB912) at the beginning of January 1952 but, at first, this one was largely for the benefit of the groundcrew. While the engineers were familiarising themselves with the new aeroplane, Flt Lt Whittam began to devise a ground training programme for those pilots who were to be converted in-house.

Brigand ops continued without respite, however, and the squadron was to fly another 124 sorties in the six weeks or so that remained before the aircraft were finally withdrawn. By this time the detachment at KL had become a more or less permanent commitment for Tengah's squadrons and, it being the Flying Camels' turn again, four aircraft were sent up there on January 11th. The team at KL flew No 45 Sqn's last Brigand strikes on February 7th. Ron Whittam led the first of these, a three-aircraft attack on a target north of Bahau. Once the aircraft had returned and been rearmed Sgt Paddy Turley led the squadron's final mission, a three-aircraft strike against a target near Bentong. The detachment returned to Tengah that day and the squadron flew its last Brigand sortie from there on the 8th - a weather reconnaissance in the Grik area in preparation for Operation HELSBY, the first use of paratroops in FIREDOG. On February 10th the Flying Camels officially ceased to operate the Brigand, although there were one or two more short trips to ferry the odd aeroplane to the MU at Seletar.

The squadron's executives at Tengah in early 1952; the black armbands signify formal mourning for HM King George VI who died on 6th February (and, coincidentally, perhaps for the passing of the Brigand which No 45 Sqn officially ceased to operate four days later). From the left: Flt Lt Ron Whittam, Sqn Ldr Ian Stockwell and Flt Lt Bogdan 'Dan' Muth. As can be seen from the background the squadron was still operating under canvas as it had been since its arrival at Tengah at the end of 1949. Note also the duckboards which were a breeding ground for rats - or would have been had it not been for 'Chopper'. (R Whittam)

The Brigand has gone down in the annals of the RAF as a brute of an aeroplane which was prone to accidents and something of a killer. There is undeniably some truth in this but the aircraft does at least deserve to be seen in perspective. It is true that its hydraulic system had been troublesome, especially in the early days, but its undercarriage could usually be persuaded to come down eventually and, once down, it was a very robust structure. No 45 Sqn actually suffered only two major accidents involving undercarriages during the Brigand era, which compares favourably both with its previous record on Beaufighters (four) and with its subsequent experience with the Hornet (eight). On the other hand No 8 Sqn at Khormaksar suffered four Brigand undercarriage failures in 1951 alone.

While the Brigand had its defects, it must be pointed out that both of its engines used to keep going most of the time and when one did stop there was sufficient power available from the other to keep the aeroplane airborne. This was more than could be said for the Beaufighter and in the squadron's last year of operation with that type it had suffered at least thirty engine failures, two of which had led to fatal accidents which cost the lives of four men; yet the Beau is regarded with affection while the Brigand is not.

All of this needs to be seen in context. The RAF sustained some 270 fatalities in 1951 as a result of flying accidents and incidents which resulted in no fewer than 486 aeroplanes being written off. The figures for 1952 were even worse! Such carnage seems appalling today but it was simply a reflection of the size of the RAF in the early 1950s and the then current state of the aviation art.

Statistics can be manipulated to prove almost any contention but the raw facts clearly show that, while the Brigand went through a bad patch in 1951, its overall accident record was far from exceptional. In FEAF alone in that year No 81 Sqn wrote off six Mosquitos in non-fatal accidents, mostly through undercarriage failures, while No 60 Sqn accounted for four more aeroplanes. What was significant about the Brigand, however, was that in 1951 it was effectively a new type and, like many aeroplanes, when they first enter squadron service, it was prone to unforeseen technical problems which manifested themselves without warning and for which there was no immediate solution. One is reminded of No 45 Sqn's earlier experience with wing failures on the Mosquito, and the fatalities which resulted from runaway tail trimmers in the early days of the Canberra's long service career. It is possible that the Brigand's tendency to reveal its shortcomings so dramatically fostered a considerable respect for the aeroplane because, apart from catastrophic failures, Nos 45 and 84 Sqn's both had remarkably good flight safety records on Brigands. Many flying accidents in the 1950s were attributable to indiscipline or overenthusiasm; this tended not to be the case within the Brigand brigade.

Another factor which inevitably sets the Brigand in a poor light is that it had a three-man crew, inherited from the aeroplane's maritime origins. In this respect it was unique among the RAF's contemporary tactical aircraft and meant that it inevitably built up a disproportionately high tally of fatalities. When a Tempest or a Vampire crashed only one man's life was at risk; with a Brigand the potential casualty

Photographed very late in the Brigand era: (from the left), Sgts R J Gratton, P Holden-Rushworth and G J Taylor. Sgt Gratton was killed when the port wing of Mosquito RR290 became detached in flight on 21st February 1952; Holden-Rushworth was very fortunate to survive this same incident. (R Whittam)

A pleasing study of RH829/OB.M leading a formation over the densely jungle-clad mountains of the Malayan interior. (R Whittam)

figure was automatically trebled.

Having originally been planned to replace the Beaufighter as a torpedo carrier in 1945-46, the Brigand eventually entered service as a light bomber four years later. This is not to say, however, as has been suggested, that the Brigands' problems stemmed from their having spent the intervening years mouldering in MUs. The bombers were not built until 1949 and most were only a few months old when they were delivered. Nevertheless the Canberra entered service in 1951 which made the Brigand, from the outset, something of a piston-engined anachronism in an increasingly jet-powered air force. For all that it was a workmanlike enough aeroplane and it packed a considerable punch. In its two years of Brigand operations, during which the number on charge gradually rose from seven to ten, No 45 Sqn flew more than 3,500 hours on ops and, as indicated at Annex G, carried out well over 1,500 strike sorties. In the course of these it dropped over 3,000,000 lbs of bombs and fired more than 10,000 rockets and 300,000 rounds of ammunition. Of the six types flown by the squadron during FIREDOG, the Brigand's efficiency, in terms of actual weapons effort per sortie, was rivalled only by that of the Canberra, and the inability of the latter's B.2 variant to deliver precision attacks with rockets and guns meant that it was a much less flexible weapons system, despite its greater weight-lifting potential.

Although it actually established a very sound operational record, the Brigand is not often afforded much credit for this. Far more attention is usually paid to its generally unsavoury reputation, and it is true that no amount of rearranging of the statistics will overcome the distaste with which it was viewed by some of those who were obliged to fly in it. But even this may have been exaggerated in later years. The Brigand's crews were, of course, saddened by the loss of colleagues

and there were certainly widespread misgivings at Tengah in July 1951 when five men were killed in less than three weeks, but effective remedial action was taken to restore the situation and both Brigand squadrons were soon back in operation. The aeroplane went on to realise its full potential in November of that year, by which time it was once again being flown with confidence, and No 45 Sqn alone flew a record 144 strike sorties in that one month. All the same, it was with some relief that the squadron began its conversion to Hornets. Sadly, the Brigand had one more fatal trick up its sleeve. In 1952 it began to suffer from wing spar failures and another crew was killed, but by that time the Flying Camels were a fighter squadron and No 84 Sqn had to bear that particular across alone.

Notes:

1.   Ken Dalton-Golding was killed on 25th February 1954 at the end of a pre-delivery test flight from Radlett in WJ622, a Handley Page-built Canberra B.2.

2.   Named for Lt Gen Sir Harold Briggs who had taken over as Director of Operations in late 1949.

3.   It seems to have worked as no one crashed. In later years, however, there were several incidents in FEAF involving aeroplanes suffering severe damage from mega-hailstones and lightning strikes and some unexplained losses which were believed to have resulted from structural failures caused by extreme turbulence. Furthermore, certain types of second-generation gas-turbine engines, eg the Sapphire and Proteus, proved to be susceptible to problems attributed to the high humidity associated with dense tropical cloud. By the 1960s the prevailing doctrine in the Far East was that clouds were only there to be avoided.

4.   In early 1951 the terrorists reorganised and styled themselves as the Malayan Races Liberation Army (MRLA) to reflect more accurately their contention that they were a popularly-based nationalist movement. There was some truth in this but the MRLA continued to be primarily a revolutionary Communist organisation, largely Chinese in its membership, which drew its moral and material support increasingly from Peking, rather than from Moscow.

Chapter 16. Happy days on Hornets.

While the Brigands may have had their drawbacks, they had at least been available to fly. Having disposed of them the squadron found itself distinctly short of aeroplanes as the delivery of Hornets was painfully slow. Since the new aircraft had no two-seat variant, FEAF's Hornet squadrons used dual-controlled Mosquito T.3s for initial conversion and for continuation training. Apart from Chopper, there was now no one left who could recall the squadron's old troubles with the Mosquito, but if there had been he would not have been at all surprised when the first one, RR290, came apart in

Sgt Gratton was killed when Mosquito RR290 crashed on 21st February 1952. He was buried at Tengah the next day. This is his funeral cortège as it moved slowly out of the station entrance on its way to the cemetery; the building in the background is the Main Guardroom. (F G Neale)

flight. While flying over the sea to the west of Tengah on February 21st its port wing came off. Sgt P Holden-Rushworth, who had arrived only a few weeks before, literally fell out and was able to use his parachute but his nav, Sgt R J Gratton, was killed. It was not a promising start to a new era.

Despite this early setback the conversion programme made some headway and by the end of March, by which time the squadron had moved its dispersal to the opposite, north eastern, end of the 'Jap strip', 115 hours had been flown on Hornets and a further twelve on Mosquitos. The first operational sortie was flown that month when F/Sgt A F Craighill mounted an armed patrol over some troops operating in the jungle near Kluang. Although he was not asked to shoot at anything it was at least a sign that the squadron was making positive progress. There was more good news in March with the gazetting of a DFM for Sgt Maurice Clarke, now back in the UK, who had flown 199 operational sorties during an eventful tour.

With conversion to single-seaters in the offing, the rear crew population had begun to thin out from the end of 1951 but the bulk of them were disposed of between February and April 1952. Of the rearguard of navs, Flt Lt Mike Noble had left to join the personal staff of Air Marshal Sir Francis Fogarty at HQ FEAF in December; Fg Off P Gilliat and Sgt A C Smith went to Seletar, as did Sgts N Tennant and L H T Wellard, both of the latter being specifically earmarked for Sunderlands; Fg Off D J Clements went to HQ FEAF and

WB912 was the first Hornet to be formally taken on charge by No 45 Sqn but it was initially used for engineering training and the first aeroplane to become a going concern was this one, WB898, which was collected from Seletar by Sqn Ldr Ian Stockwell on 25th January 1952. This splendid photograph shows WB898 being refuelled at Tengah in April or May, by which time the squadron was operating from the north-eastern end of the 'Jap strip'. Following a precedent established on their Brigands, the Hornets wore their code letters aft of, rather than flanking, their fuselage roundels. Unusually for a Hornet, in the case of WB898 the code on the starboard side was initially applied, à la Mosquito/Beaufighter/Brigand 'in reverse', as A.OB. Clearly distinguishable in this picture are the banded spinners and the red tip to the fin; the underwing rocket rails and faired bomb rack are also clearly visible. It is believed that the five coloured bands on the spinners were supposed to be, from the front, dark blue, red, dark blue, pale blue and dark blue but other photographs reproduced here would suggest that there were several variations on this theme. (No 45 Sqn archives)

A group of pilots who have been rousted out of the Ops Tent to stage an 'impromptu' briefing photograph, circa April/May 1952. From the left: Flt Lt Dennis Helps, Flt Lt Bill Morrison, Sgt Paddy Turley, Flt Lt Ron Whittam, Sgt Phil Holden-Rushworth, F/Sgt Norrie Grove, Sgt Mike Retallack and F/Sgt Red Craighill. (No 45 Sqn archives)

The squadron spent 26th-30th May at Butterworth in a frustrating attempt to complete the weapons training phase of its initial work-up. Seen here during this camp is a group of the squadron's airmen, mostly armourers. (C E French)

F/Sgt R E Morling to the Far East Training Squadron (FETS)[1]. The last four signallers, MSig L Eyre and Sgts R D Tranter, R D Williamson and G J Taylor, were all transferred to No 84 Sqn to persevere on Brigands. By the end of April the only remaining back-seater, a nav, was Flt Lt J R Hill.

Although it was still non-operational, by early May the squadron had been reorganised on a two-flight basis with Flt Lt Whittam commanding A Flight and Flt Lt B Muth DFC running B Flt. With only five Hornets and two rather beaten up Mosquitos on charge, however, Ron Whittam had an uphill struggle trying to complete the in-house conversion programme. There had actually been three Mosquitos available for a short time as VA888 had been borrowed from FETS but during a sortie on May 22nd this aeroplane's rear fuselage began to exhibit a disturbing tendency to move about of its own accord and Whittam flew it very carefully to Seletar. There the tail unit was assessed as having 1½° freedom of movement and the aeroplane disappeared into No 390 MU's workshops for liberal applications of glue, but it found its way back to the squadron in due course.

Having completed the necessary aircraft handling, formation flying and navigation exercises, the squadron spent the end of May up at Butterworth having a go at weapons training. There a variety of factors conspired to prevent the

squadron making as much progress as it would have liked. The biggest problem was still the shortage of aircraft but weapons training was severely constrained in any case by the Song Song's range safety launch's being unserviceable for a week and an embargo on the use of RPs which had been imposed intermittently since February. Nevertheless the squadron did what it could before flying back to Tengah in time to get in some formation practice for the Queen's Birthday flypast which took place on June 5th, Ian Stockwell leading all six of the squadron's Hornets and a dozen of No 60 Sqn's Vampires in salute over the Padang in Singapore.

By this time it had become standard practice for one of the Tengah-based squadrons to maintain a detachment at KL and No 84 Sqn had been up there since February 11th, waiting patiently for the Flying Camels to relieve them. Although it had yet to complete some aspects of its conversion training and still owned only half a dozen aeroplanes, the squadron was declared operational on June 6th and four aircraft were promptly deployed to KL to allow the Brigands to go home. The detachment was not very busy and the first strike was not called for until the 9th when Flt Lts Dennis Muth and Bill Morrison with F/Sgts Norrie Grove and 'Red' Craighill, flying WB956, WB898, WB908 and WB912 respectively, attacked the Gap Road in support of the Suffolks who were pursuing the 'Gurney Gang', the band of CTs who had murdered the High Commissioner in the previous October. In all the detachment flew thirty-six operational sorties in June. The most successful mission was a short-notice response to a call for support from the Malay

No 45 Sqn mounted the first of several operational detachments to Kuala Lumpur between 6th June and 29th August 1952. These were the four aircraft involved in this initial deployment: from the left, WB908/OB.L, WB912/OB.C (lost during the detachment), WF956/OB.M and WB898/OB.A (with its starboard code now applied conventionally so that it reads from left to right). (M Retallack)

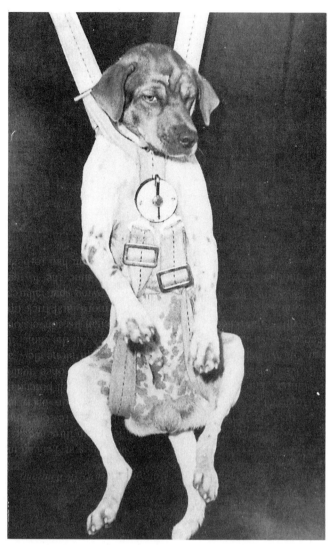

Photographed in 1952, this is not Chopper but 'Hatchet', the product of an encounter between the squadron's amorous hound and No. 48 Sqn's 'Smokey' at KL in 1949. Hatchet was initially looked after by N3 Alf France who brought him down to Tengah when the squadron moved. It is not thought that Hatchet ever actually flew in a Hornet but a trial fitting of a parachute harness was carried out - just in case. The dog's expression invites the reader to write his own caption to this photograph. (C E French)

others wounded.

Back at Tengah the Hornet fleet was growing, but very slowly; by the end of July the total had reached eleven but it was to be October before any more aircraft were received. Since the KL detachment needed the best aeroplanes, the base party was poorly placed for flying, especially as both of the Mosquitos on charge were unserviceable at Seletar. The lack of Mosquitos meant that Instrument Rating Tests (IRT) and the like had to be done on the Station Flight's Harvards. It was not all gloom, however, as the aircraft at KL stayed serviceable and 102 sorties were flown during July, the squadron acquiring a rather macabre trophy as a result of a strike led by Ron Whittam on the 3rd. This was another action flown in support of the Suffolks, Operation CHURCHMAN. This time the troops were after Liew Kong Kim, 'The Bearded Terror of Selangor'. When the troops moved in, following the air strike, they shot Kim, his mistress and one other bandit. In recognition of the squadron's contribution to the success of the operation the battalion presented it with the lady's brassière, which was duly nailed to the door of the CO's office....

The KL detachment flew another 110 sorties in August before it was relieved by No 84 Sqn. As the pace of operations had intensified there had been a corresponding increase in the number of incidents that had inevitably begun to occur. During August two aeroplanes had sustained damage, either from ricochets or from debris thrown up by their own weapons, although neither incident resulted in major problems. On the 2nd, F/Sgt Reeder damaged WB911's props while landing at KL and, during a strafing run on the 14th, Sgt G J Turley lost the panel covering

Regt who had cornered a party of terrorists to the west of Ipoh. Flt Lt Muth led a four-ship strike to flush out the CTs, who were only 500 yards from the friendly troops. The operation worked exactly as planned; in the subsequent ground engagement three terrorists were killed and several

Three of A Flight's Hornets formate on one of No 84 Sqn's Brigands to have their picture taken on their way to target. WB911/OB.B leads WB898/OB.A (nearest to the camera and still wearing its reversed code, which dates the photograph as pre-August 1952) and WB908/OB.L. (R Whittam)

One of the squadron's early Hornets, WB908/OB.L, lines up for take off at Tengah. (No 45 Sqn archives)

WB961's gun installation; in both cases the damage was superficial and quickly repaired. A more serious accident occurred on the 28th when Plt Off R Jackson crashed while carrying out a strafing attack on a target in Seremban. WB912 was destroyed and the pilot was killed. The following day the detachment flew back to Tengah.

The embargo on the use of RPs had been lifted early in August, so the squadron had been able to make full use of the Hornet's offensive capability for the first time. In the course of flying a grand total of 127 operational sorties that month (seventeen of them from Tengah) 97,000 lbs of bombs had been dropped, 259 RPs had been fired and 28,584 rounds of 20mm cannon shells had been expended. Although still below its established strength, it is evident that the squadron was now beginning to fire on all four cylinders again. Much of this success was owed to the engineering efforts of Sgt Simpson. Although Eric Simpson had recently returned to the UK, it was noted with some satisfaction that his contribution had been recognised by the award of a BEM.

Although there was little operational tasking in September, the squadron flew a great deal during the month (285 hours), making extensive use of China Rock and preparing for a forthcoming CFS visit. On September 15th, the squadron put up nine Hornets for the Battle of Britain flypast - 100% of its immediately available strength (if you don't count the Mosquitos). As was becoming usual, the Flying Camels led the formation.

The Duchess of Kent and her son, the Duke, paid a formal visit to Malaya at this time and on 30th September six of the squadron's Hornets rendezvoused with the incoming Royal Flight and escorted BOAC's DC-4M *Argonaut* to within fifty miles of Singapore where six of No 60 Sqn's Vampires joined them and took over the lead, the Hornets dropping back to form a rearguard. During October, the squadron flew two further royal escorts, providing top cover for road convoys. The CFS Examining Wing team arrived in October and, just in time, the trainer decided to become serviceable. Needless to say, some of the squadron's pilots were found to be a little rusty on Mosquito handling! That was the only adverse observation, however, and the squadron was given a clean bill of health.

It was now No 45 Sqn's turn to mount the KL detachment again and six aircraft went up there on October 1st. They attracted a fair amount of trade and, by the time that they returned to Tengah six weeks later bandit activity had increased in the south so the whole squadron had been kept busy. A feature of squadron life at this time was an exchange of pilots with No 80 Sqn who were flying Hornets from Hong Kong. F/Sgt Craighill had been the first to go, back in August, when he had swapped places with Sgt

Parker. In November Fg Off Bruce Lacey went up to Kai Tak, Fg Off Stoppard taking his place at Tengah.

The squadron had received another three aeroplanes in October so it was at last beginning to approach something like its established strength, a notional sixteen, of which twelve were intended to be available for flying while the remainder underwent scheduled maintenance. Having a dozen aeroplanes to fly meant that there were usually about eight on the flightline each day and the squadron was able to push the monthly flying effort up to 401 hours in November, forty-nine of these being flown on the Mosquitos! Strike leaders at this time were usually the CO, Flt Lts Helps (OC A Flight since July), Muth and Morrison and F/Sgt Grove. The squadron was called on to mount two major efforts in November. The first, flown on the 13th, involved an attack by Nos 45, 60 and 84 Sqns against a band of about fifty CTs to the north of Labis, the squadron contributing sixteen sorties. The second was a dummy strike near Kota Tinggi on the 18th, laid on for the benefit of the Jungle Warfare School; this involved the squadron's flying eighteen sorties in one day.

Another notable training event during November was a dummy attack by four-ship formations on HMS *Ceylon*. Having carried out their 'strikes', the Hornets then switched sides, became the ship's defenders and were vectored by the cruiser's radar to intercept incoming Brigands and Lincolns. This whetted the squadron's appetite for air defence and Sqn Ldr Stockwell began to press for formal authority to train in the day fighter role. Technically, the squadron had been classified as a Light Bomber/Day Fighter (Ground Attack) [LB/DF(GA)] unit ever since the Brigands had been withdrawn in February 1952, but the 'LB' was really something of a misnomer, and the training syllabus was long on 'GA' and did not address the 'DF' bit at all.

Since No 45 Sqn was scheduled to cover the KL commitment over Christmas, they had their 1952 party early, while everyone was still together. It was held in the Union Jack Club in Singapore on December 2nd and turned out to be a memorable evening with a number of impromptu turns being staged. The evening's stars included Flt Lt Bill Morrison on ukulele, Plt Offs O'Brien and Cooper on harmonica (one each!), LAC Tichias on piano and AC Ainsley who did his Al Jolson impression. Lubricated by

Changing an engine out on the flightline during one of the squadron's frequent detachments to KL. Sgt C R Everingham on the left (with his arm in plaster) directs operations as the dismounted Merlin from WF956/OB.M is gently lowered onto a makeshift cushion of sandbags. LAC Howard Witton, back to camera, helps to steady the load. (H Witton)

A pair of No 45 Sqn's Hornets share a dispersal with one of No 84 Sqn's Brigands. (M Retallack)

copious quantities of Anchor and Tiger beer, everyone rolled back to base full of the seasonal spirit, only to find that a strike had been scheduled for the 3rd. Nine aircraft were prepared and armed overnight and seven of them took off at dawn, the other two going unserviceable with faults which could not be rectified without spares which the squadron did not hold. In view of the circumstances it had been a very good effort and clearly demonstrated the willingness of the squadron's airmen to work hard as well as play hard.

The detachment left for KL on December 5th and the four aircraft stayed there until January 3rd. With fifteen Hornets on charge, however, mounting the detachment no longer meant that the Tengah echelon had to play second fiddle. Tasking was only moderate during December and most of it (fifty-six sorties) went to the KL detachment including two strikes on Christmas Day; a further twenty-nine sorties were flown from Tengah during the month. A significant event in December was the arrival in Singapore of some USAF B-29s on a liaison visit. Several of the squadron's aircraft picked them up on their way in and escorted them for the last 200 miles, which were flown down Malaya at low level. Flying in close proximity to these big juicy targets raised further hopes that the squadron might be authorised to exploit the Hornet's air combat potential.

By the end of the year the squadron had flown 2,747 hours on Hornets and, without making any allowance for the prolonged conversion period, it had established the best annual serviceability rate of the three Hornet squadrons in FEAF. The Hornet era may have got off to a slow start but by the end of 1952, with the squadron almost at full strength and fully worked up and operational, the Flying Camels had their tails well up again.

Seventy-two operational sorties were flown in January 1953 which was a slight reduction in the previous rate of tasking. In fact FIREDOG had turned the corner by now and the area of Malaya in which the CTs could operate freely was very slowly shrinking. Growing confidence that the campaign would eventually be won permitted the new RAAF AOC, AVM F R W Scherger CBE DSO AFC, to reconsider the conduct of air operations and to introduce a new policy. It was evident that the expenditure of ordnance had been somewhat profligate in the past and the AOC was concerned to restrict the use of aircraft to strikes which had a reasonable expectation of having some positive effect. As a result an increasing number of army requests began to be turned down. The way in which aircraft were being employed had also been

reviewed; it had been concluded that the most effective weapons system available was the Lincoln which continued to be used for area saturation attacks. Rather than allowing the tactical aeroplanes simply to carry on adding their relatively small bomb loads to the general conflagration, however, they began increasingly to be reserved for precision attacks. These sometimes involved dive-bombing, rocketing and strafing the fringes of the swathe of destruction created by the 'heavies' in a planned and co-ordinated assault, but more usually they were held back for precision strikes against specific identifiable or marked targets.

The upshot of all this was that the demand for Hornet strikes was significantly reduced and the overall rate of tasking declined steadily throughout the remainder of the FIREDOG campaign[2]. Paradoxically, this reduction in the overall intensity of air operations was actually a positive sign, as it was symptomatic of a more methodical approach which was in turn an indication that the security forces were gaining the upper hand. Although these forces increasingly held the initiative, the remainder of the campaign was far from being a walkover and it would be 1956 before the number of CT-inspired incidents began to show a marked decline.

On January 13th OC Flying Wing, Wg Cdr Marcus Knight, was shooting some circuits with Ian Stockwell in a Mosquito. During an asymmetric approach RR311 yawed and hit a bulldozer parked close to the runway. The bulldozer won. Neither of the pilots was seriously hurt but the Mossie's flying days were over. Seletar scraped up VT628 as a replacement.

The last Brigands were withdrawn from operations that month which meant that No 84 Sqn was to be disbanded, although it was immediately to be reformed in the Canal Zone as a transport unit. On January 16th the Flying Camels took part in a parade to bid a formal farewell to their comrades and rivals of the last two years. The only other notable event that month was a requirement to provide an escort to General Sir Gerald Templar who was travelling by road and rail from Segamat down to Singapore[3]. This involved the squadron's maintaining a patrol over the route from dawn until dusk.

Despite some temporary problems with serviceability, largely due to shortages of both spares and manpower, the squadron was able to respond to all the tasks that came its way in February. The biggest of these was an operation in support of the 1st/7th Gurkhas on the 19th. An Auster

Although their serviceability often left something to be desired, the squadron always had at least one Mosquito T.3 on charge during the Hornet era. This one is VA888, which gave Flt Lt Ron Whittam a nasty moment on 22nd May 1952 when its back-end started to move about of its own accord. It is interesting to note that the fuselage roundel on this aeroplane was seriously out of proportion - compare the size of the red centre spot with those painted on the wings. (F G Neale)

marked the target with smoke and No 45 Sqn's Hornets hit it with RPs. The area surrounding the target was then plastered by RAAF Lincolns, and the Hornets finished off the attack by raking the area with gunfire. When the Gurkhas moved in they found that the area had been well and truly destroyed but it appeared that the smoke marker had rolled about 50 yards off the target so relatively little damage had been inflicted on the camp. As the camp was found to have been empty, however, this was of little consequence. Such were the continuing frustrations of jungle operations.

Sgt 'Paddy' Turley had a spot of excitement on February 12th when WF967's hydraulic system packed up and the undercarriage declined to respond to the emergency lowering system. He was able to carry out a good belly-landing, however, and in due course the aeroplane was restored to service. By this time the Mosquitos were in trouble again. One was condemned after defective glued joints were found in its wings and the other was grounded due to acid corrosion caused by the explosion of an accumulator battery. As a result nine pilots were overdue an IRT by the end of March.

Despite sixteen of the squadron's airmen being posted out in March and only three replacements being received, serviceability began to improve again and by the end of the month there were usually twelve aircraft on the flightline and eight-ship strikes were not uncommon. Strike leaders by this time were Flt Lts Brittain (OC A Flight in succession to

Helps since November 1952), Muth and Morrison, F/Sgt Grove and Sgts Retallack and Turley.

Tactics were constantly being refined during **FIREDOG** and in March 1953 the squadron began to work in conjunction with helicopters for the first time. Troops pursuing CTs through the jungle on foot sometimes measured their progress in terms of yards per day. Helicopters permitted them to overtake and surround a fleeing band and force a confrontation. On the other hand a hovering helicopter is extremely vulnerable so, to dissuade the CTs from opening fire, the squadron's Hornets were sometimes called upon to mount Combat Air Patrols (CAP) over the Landing Zones, involving flights of up to 4½ hours duration. April was notable for a number of major strikes, joint efforts with No 33 Sqn's Hornets from Butterworth and the RAAF's Lincolns. The first of these was mounted on the 1st when the squadron put up eleven aircraft to hit a target in the Cameron

WF966/OB.N displays a full load of bombs and rockets. (No 45 Sqn archives)

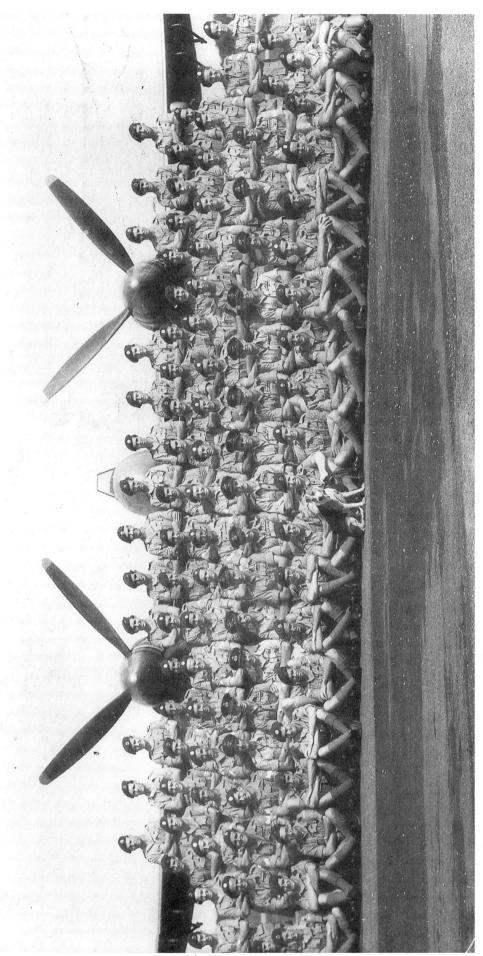

A formal group photograph taken in May 1953. From the left, back row: LAC R J North, SAC P J Jones, LAC J T J Orr, LAC E Garbutt, LAC R T Goodman, LAC B A Chesser, LAC R A Stringer, LAC J W Webber, LAC L Booth, LAC J Redman, LAC R Holmes, LAC C F Gage and ACl D J Amos. Fourth row: LAC R McGowan, LAC C Domm, LAC T Durham, LAC E Leathwaite, SAC F J Pullen, LAC J E Winnard, LAC W A Green, SAC W T Hutchins, LAC D J Starkey, SAC R W Fotherby, SAC J E Hensman, ACl F A Jennings, LAC A K Fisher, SAC E E H Gentry, LAC J M Forsgate, LAC P J Ellis, LAC P Ater, LAC D W Lloyd, LAC M P Stewart and ACl D E Hunnisett. Third row: ACl K Parsons, SAC D J Slatter, LAC J P Hill, LAC J A Ramsden, Cpl D P Watson, Cpl L W Cook, Cpl R Bottle, Cpl D T Walters, Cpl D Liston, Sgt D A E Humfryes, Sgt C R Everingham, Sgt D J Peacock, F/Sgt B Yarnall, Sgt J H Swann, F/Sgt B R Carling, Cpl A J Young, Cpl D F Bond, Cpl D Tomlin, Cpl B F Hardy, Cpl G P C Moore, Cpl D A Goult, Cpl C E French, Cpl H Witton and LAC J Power. Second row: LAC R G Carroll, LAC T Cummings, Sgt G J Turley, Sgt M Retallack, Sgt J A Vigar, Fg Off D H O'Brien, Fg Off I D Pattinson, Fg Off B P H Lacey, Fg Off C E F Cooper, Fg Off J Fraser, Flt Lt H G Brittain DFC AFC, Sqn Ldr I S Stockwell DFC AFC, Flt Lt B Muth DFC, Flt Lt W J O Morrison AFC, Fg Off E A Peters, Fg Off C T Lake, Fg Off J E Bowler, Fg Off J F Alderton; F/Sgt N Grove, LAC N Holmes, LAC J H Smith and LAC J Jones. Front row: SAC T F Jones, LAC W J McIntyre, LAC B Turner, LAC K Abbott, ACl H Smith, AC2 E Shropshire, SAC T C Spargo, SAC J C Barthram, ACl J W Ebdon, LAC R Rowell, MDog 'Chopper', LAC D E N Collins, SAC D S Ackley, SAC A A Calladine, LAC J White, LAC J Ellwood, LAC J A Mitchell, LAC A Barker, LAC E Carmichael, LAC R D Traube and SAC Pickett. (M Retallack)

Highlands. The last was on the 25th when the squadron, operating from Butterworth, where it had positioned the previous day, put up another eleven aircraft. After the strike all the fighters joined up to carry out a spectacular twenty-three Hornet flypast over Penang.

Half of the squadron's Hornets returned to Tengah after the flypast but B Flight stayed on until May 15th to carry out a weapons training programme with No 27 APC. In the process they set new records for accuracy in both air-to-ground gunnery and RP attacks. In fact F/Sgt Grove's accuracy was such that the APC staff described it as "uncanny"; Norman Grove's skills had already been recognised and his DFM had been gazetted on March 6th[4].

The Flying Camels on their Hornet dispersal, the north eastern end of the old 'Jap strip'. This picture was taken in early 1953, before any huts had been built - the tented 'offices' can be seen on the right hand side of the pan. The first four aeroplanes are WF966/OB.N, WF956/OB.M, WF959/OB.K and Mosquito T.3 VA888. The photograph is taken looking down the flightline towards the south west; on the horizon, to the right, is the Officers' Mess and, to the left, a group of pre-war airmen's married quarters. The latter were demolished in the early 1960s to make room for a new runway. (F G Neale)

May 1953 began quietly but the month ended in a crescendo of activity associated with Operation COMMODORE. This operation was intended to eliminate

Cpl Chas French and SAC 'Pat' Moore waiting for their aeroplane to return to Tengah to be refuelled and rearmed between sorties. (C E French)

the State Committee of the MRLA in Johore, which was believed to number several hundred men. The squadron was held on the ground at a high state of readiness awaiting calls for direct air support from the army. On one occasion it had ten aircraft in the air within four minutes of the task being received at Tengah and rockets were hitting the target just twenty-five minutes after the request had first been submitted by the security forces. In the last week of May the squadron flew seventy-six sorties in support of this campaign. All of the targets were in the vicinity of Kluang, the aiming points sometimes being within 400 yards of friendly troops. When it was all over the soldiers moved in; the final body count was just six! Despite this disappointing outcome, which was pretty much par for the FIREDOG course, the squadron had excelled itself. The contribution made by the groundcrew had been crucial and they had responded to the challenge splendidly. There had been very few gun stoppages and more than half of those which had occurred had been due to fractured shell cases, something over which the armourers had no control. No bombs had hung up and the RP failure rate had been a remarkably low 1.7%. It had been a good show all round.

The squadron had lost another aeroplane just before the start of COMMODORE when, on the 21st, Fg Off E A Peters in PX389 swung into a monsoon drain alongside the runway during a stream landing. That particular Hornet never flew again, but Ted Peters did.

Tasking fell right off in June and the squadron flew only three strikes, each of six aircraft. This was perhaps just as well, as the recent burst of activity had consumed a lot of flying hours and several of the aircraft had to be pulled into the hangar for scheduled servicings. Here they joined the hangar queen which had already been lurking there for three months awaiting the delivery of a replacement engine. Enough aeroplanes could be scraped together, however, to put up the customary immaculate formation for the Queen's

Birthday on June 6th.

A Flight flew up to Butterworth on June 29th to see whether they could better B Flight's performance with No 27 APC. Their scores were very respectable but they could not quite match their predecessor's achievements. For A and B Flights respectively, the comparative figures were 9.9 yds and 8.1 yds for RPs, 38.3% and 50.4% hits for air-to-ground gunnery and 25.8 yds and 24.2 yds for bombs.

Sadly, the second detachment was marred by the loss of a pilot. On July 15th Fg Off B P H Lacey was working on Song Song Range in WB898. He had turned in from about 2,000 feet to commence an attack but his Hornet was then observed to dive vertically into the sea. Since the pilot had not called the Range on R/T, as was normal at the start of a live run, and had not transmitted a distress message either, it was assumed that he might have lost consciousness but the precise cause of this accident was never positively established. Two days later A Flight flew back to Tengah.

In the meantime B Flight had been covering the squadron's operational commitment, although tasking amounted to only forty-two sorties for the whole month. Many of these missions had been flown in support of Operation STING which had begun in June and was intended to deny access to crops to CTs operating in the vicinity of Fraser's Hill. The rate of consumption of live ordnance had created a shortage of cannon shells and, to offset this, in July the squadron began to receive batches of ammunition which, although considered safe, were technically categorised as being unserviceable. As was only to be expected, despite individual stripping and cleaning of ammunition belts, round by round, the rate of stoppages began to increase significantly.

The squadron flew its 1,000th operational Hornet sortie during August but rounded off the month with another prang when, on the 28th, Plt Off C A Rogers swung on landing and WF954's undercarriage folded up in protest. The pilot was unhurt and the damage to the aeroplane proved to be repairable. WF954 was duly restored to service but a year later its undercarriage was to collapse again.

In September the RAF resumed the detachment of Lincoln squadrons to FEAF, this time as Operation BOLD. These detachments were in addition to the RAAF's Lincolns, which continued to operate, and thus represented a considerable increase in the available striking power. The first combined operation was flown on the 24th as a maximum effort by Nos 33, 45, 1 RAAF and 83 Sqns. The target was at Kangar on the Thai border and the timing of the attack required No 45 Sqn to take off from Tengah while it was still dark and fly a long transit before delivering its strike and landing at Butterworth. Instead of flying back to Tengah as originally briefed, however, they were then ordered to rearm and carry out a second attack in conjunction with No 33 Sqn, after which they were to return directly to Tengah.

It had been a long day but Sgt Mike Retallack has recalled that it seemed to have been even longer than it actually was as the squadron had had little notice of the operation. In fact they had not expected to be flying at all that day and it had been well after midnight, as a heavy party was drawing to its close, when they first learned of the requirement for an early take off. Getting airborne in fully-armed aeroplanes well before dawn, after only a couple of

hours' sleep, was in itself a somewhat taxing exercise. Everyone managed it successfully, however, and with those pilots who were still a trifle 'tired and emotional' breathing 100% oxygen, the mission went well enough until they landed at Butterworth for breakfast and a much needed snooze. The real problems began when they were roused after only a short kip to be briefed on the second, unanticipated, strike which was then delayed while No 33 Sqn got its act together. By the time that the squadron was heading south again for the long transit flight back to Singapore the previous night's revellers were hard-pressed to stay awake and from time to time people became very drowsy. As odd aeroplanes began to drift out of formation their pilots had to be roused by the shouts of their colleagues over the R/T. It was an exhausted, relieved and somewhat chastened group of aviators that eventually landed back at Tengah. It had been a salutary experience for all concerned - as Wg Cdr Spry would say, "They learned about flying from that."[5]

Yet another new tactic was introduced in September, helicopters spraying herbicidal chemicals to destroy cultivation in the jungle clearings created by the CTs. The first use of this technique was in the Labis/Segamat area and went by the name of Operation CYCLONE. As with all helicopter operations, when the risk to them was assessed as being significant, Hornets flew top cover.

Ever since the demise of No 84 Sqn in February the Flying Camels had had the dispersal all to themselves but, apart from a couple of offices in No 1 Hangar, the squadron's accommodation was still in tents. A building programme had been under way for some months on the dispersal site, however, and some new and fairly substantial huts now became available (to be followed a little later by a proper ATC tower, erected more or less in front of No 1 Hangar, to replace the facility on top of Learoyd Block which had been in use 'temporarily' since 1945). A Flight moved into its new offices on September 26th followed by B Flight on October 1st. Even so many of the squadron's administrative and technical facilities continued to be under canvas for a while yet. September was also notable for the long-awaited authority to start training in the Day Fighter role and the squadron flew its first air-to-air gunnery details that month. As was only to be expected the initial results were somewhat

From the left, AC1 K Parsons, SAC G Ford and LAC G Black checking unused ammunition after a strike. (No 45 Sqn archives)

Sgt Mike Retallack in PX354/OB.S, outbound for a target 30 miles north of Kuala Lumpur on 7th December 1953; it was his 104th operational strike. (M Retallack)

mixed, especially as this was their first experience of this form of training exercise for some of the pilots.

Operational tasking continued to run at a relatively low level in October with forty-eight sorties being flown, some of these being armed escorts to cover Operation CYCLONE and General Templar's movements. The squadron deployed to Butterworth on the 28th for a planned strike but this was cancelled and they flew back to Tengah on the 30th.

While ops had been rather low-key in October there had been some quite interesting training opportunities to compensate for this. First there had been a chance to work with another USAF B-29 detachment, these now rejoicing in the exercise nickname JOSSTICK. After taking off from Clark Field in the Philippines, the three bombers carried out a 'raid' on Johore then flew up to Song Song for a live bombing attack before flying back down Malaya to land at Changi. Tasked in the air defence role for the first time, No 45 Sqn made several interceptions in which No 60 Sqn's Vampires also participated. The second training event was a naval co-operation exercise with HMS *Comus* and HMS *Newcastle*. The month was rounded off with a spot of formation flying on the 31st, the groundcrews doing a grand job by having all twelve Hornets available to fly. Unfortunately one had to return early 'on one'; even more unfortunately it was Ian Stockwell's!

By this time the pilots were regularly flying a very respectable 30 hours per month and air-to-air scores were approaching an acceptable level. Training was not all flying, of course, and as always the routine embraced a range of ground-bound activities which included the periodic renewal of aircrew servicing certificates, dinghy drills and lectures on such topics as airmanship, navigation and the technical aspects of the Hornet's systems. There was a burst of this sort of thing during October as the CFS 'Trappers' were due again in November. Unimpressed by the significance of this forthcoming event, both of the squadron's Mosquitos sat resolutely on the ground throughout October. Fortunately a backlog of IRTs had been cleared in July and August when the trainers had been in a more co-operative mood. The CFS team came, examined, pronounced themselves content and went away to bother another unit.

There was a resurgence of CT activity in November but it generated little tasking for the squadron. Sqn Ldr Stockwell had now completed his tour and on December 15th he handed over to Sqn Ldr V K Jacobs who had recently flown himself out to Singapore in PX385. It will be recalled that Viv Jacobs already had a tenuous connection with the Flying Camels as he had shared the discomforts of the *Orestes* with them in early 1942. That evening the squadron held an all-ranks farewell party in the Buffs' Lodge. Ian Stockwell, who was eventually to retire as Air Commodore I S Stockwell CBE DFC AFC, sailed for the UK on the *Empire Clyde* in January 1954 and the squadron laid on the customary flypast, although this was somewhat hampered by poor weather.

FEAF was still suffering from a shortage of ammunition and, since the idea of using defective rounds had not worked, to conserve stocks the squadron was restricted to the use of only two guns per aircraft from December. This was not terribly significant as the rate of tasking was still declining. In search of trade the squadron had sent four aircraft up to KL for four days from December 31st but no strikes had come their way. A pair went back there in January to provide cover for a continuation of Operation CYCLONE and were called upon to carry out some strafing attacks under the control of an Auster. After two strikes the Auster was reported missing and the Hornets were employed on the subsequent air search. The little aeroplane had been swallowed up by the jungle, however, and eventually the search was called off; the Auster was not found until March 1957.

A Flight spent most of January (2nd to 22nd) at Butterworth with No 27 APC while B Flight (commanded by Flt Lt Bill Morrison since the previous July) had another opportunity to bounce B-29s on JOSSTICK III. The big event of the month, however, was the arrival of the squadron's first jet. The new CO flew WZ521, a Vampire T.11, across from Seletar on the 8th but it promptly went unserviceable and sat on the ground for the rest of the month. Nevertheless it seemed to be a portent of things to come. No 60 Sqn had already been flying Vampires for two years. Was the Flying Camel about to become jet propelled? No, it was not - not yet anyway. Even so, the T.11 would provide some

A major production number from The Flying Camel Revue. *Fg Off Johnny Bowler offers Flt Lt Bill Morrison a steadying hand as he performs the Sleepy Princess from* The Dance of the Hours; *in the left background can be seen the bed, complete with mosquito net, to which the Princess kept retiring. The* corps de ballet *comprises Flt Lt Alan Humphrys, Fg Off 'Chico' Cooper and Fg Off Julian Alderton. A "thinks bubble" might read, "I bet they don't have to do this to get a decent '1369 on 60 Sqn!".*
(V K Jacobs)

jet handling experience which would come in useful one day and before the end of February all of the pilots had flown at least one trip in the new aeroplane. This was just as well as it was about to go back into the hangar again. On March 12th Fg Offs Johnny Bowler and Ted Peters were carrying out some circuit work. Accelerating down the runway after a roller landing, one of them noticed that the flaps were still extended and decided to retract them; unfortunately he pulled the wrong lever and the wheels came up instead. WZ521 slid gracefully along the runway on its belly for about 400 yards before coming to rest. There was some dented pride from which both pilots made a full recovery; damage to the airframe had not been terminal either.

Only four missions came the squadron's way in February 1954 for a total of just nineteen sorties. These were a singleton helicopter CAP on the 3rd flown by Fg Off Ray Cordey; a six-ship area attack at Padi on the 6th and two six-ship strikes on a CT camp at Slim River on the 27th and 28th. This low rate of tasking was not really an indication that the security forces were winning, although they were, slowly. It was more of a reflection of the continuing trend towards the use of heavy bombers in preference to tactical aircraft. Something that the smaller aeroplanes could do well, however, was the mounting of patrols and this was especially true of the Hornets which had an endurance at least three times longer than that of the Vampire. Two such tasks came the squadron's way in February: Operation FLAGWAG, which involved flying up and down the Ayer Hitam-Johore Bahru road, and a periodic requirement to patrol the pipeline which carried Singapore's essential water supply from the Mount Kulai reservoir on the mainland.

Strike tasks in March dropped off to just two, one near Raub, the other in the Korbu area. Operation FLAGWAG continued, however, as did the pipeline patrol so there was plenty to keep the squadron occupied. A one-off task was the provision of an airborne escort to Lady Mountbatten who was flown from Batu Pahat to Kota Tinggi in a Pioneer - not the easiest of aeroplanes on which to keep station! Following

a successful naval co-operation exercise with HMS *Ajax* in February, another was laid on in March with HMS *Defender* and HMS *Newfoundland*. These followed the well-established pattern of the aeroplanes being given the opportunity to beat up the ships at the cost of their then having to fly specified tracks and heights so that the navy could calibrate its guns and radar. This presupposed, of course, that the ships could be found in the first place which proved difficult when another exercise was scheduled with HMS *Comus* in April; she was eventually found some 120 miles from her advertised position! There were further opportunities to work with radars during March as a Sector Operations Centre was being set up in Singapore to provide a coherent air defence system for the island but these early sorties indicated that much progress still needed to be made.

Aircraft serviceability had been declining steadily over the previous three months and by April the new CO was coming to the conclusion that the aeroplanes were simply too old and tired. In view of the low aircraft availability being produced, despite the intensive efforts being made by the squadron's tradesmen, he began to question the Hornets' continued viability. Following A Flight's detachment to No 27 APC in January, it was now B Flight's turn and they were up at Butterworth from March 27th until April 14th. The lack of aircraft and the significant reduction in operational flying had inevitably had an adverse impact on the pilots' skills and, while still creditable, the results of these APCs were not as good as those of a year earlier. The atmosphere was far from gloomy, however, and despite the scarcity of flyable aeroplanes morale was very high as was clearly demonstrated by the squadron's staging of *The Flying Camel Revue* to great acclaim, recreating a concert party tradition first established in 1943.

The aeroplanes were spruced up too and at Viv Jacob's instigation Flt Lt J H W Wilson had designed a more dynamic variant of the squadron's motif; a very distinctive 'Pouncing Camel' now adorned the noses of the Hornets, and even the Vampire when it eventually returned to the flightline. Otherwise the aircraft were still in the overall silver finish in which they had originally been delivered with their code letters in black behind, rather than bracketing, the fuselage roundels and in many cases, as some of the accompanying photographs show, hyphenated. From quite early in the aircrafts' service with the squadron they had had their spinners painted with five alternating bands of (from the front) dark blue, red, dark blue, pale blue and dark blue; these

An innovation during 1954 was the reintroduction of camouflage, the painted aeroplanes being concentrated in A Flight. Seen here are PX353/OB.F and WF967/OB.H. (V K Jacobs)

The 'Pouncing Camel' motif was introduced early in 1954 but it is not easily seen on photographs of Hornets as the nose is often obscured by an engine nacelle. This problem does not arise with the squadron's Vampire. WZ521 is seen here on 18th March 1955 being flown by Fg Off Johnny Bowler with Sqn Ldr D Harrison (not of No 45 Sqn) up for the ride. (V K Jacobs)

continued to be worn and were also applied to the Mosquito T.3s although the latter never acquired the more lively version of the Flying Camel. The only other distinguishing marking had been confined to A Flight which had originally painted the fin tips of its aircraft in red but this practice seems to have lapsed during 1953. WF967/OB.H had become the CO's personal aircraft and it was unique in that, in addition to the highly stylised Camel on the nose, it carried a more traditional rendering of the squadron's emblem on its fin.

In 1954 a camouflaged finish was reintroduced for day fighters and well before the end of the year this fashion had spread to FEAF. Hornets began to appear with Dark Sea Grey and Dark Green upper surfaces while retaining the original silver 'below the Plimsoll line'. This was a progressive programme, however, and none of FEAF's Hornet squadrons appears to have had all of its aeroplanes painted before the type was withdrawn from service. In the case of No 45 Sqn the painted aircraft were concentrated in A Flight while B Flight had all the silver ones.

Another innovation in fighter markings had been introduced in 1950 with the reappearance of the pre-war style of squadron identification markings, worn as a coloured bar flanking the fuselage roundels. These markings, which had last been authorised for use in 1938, displaced the letter codes which were then being withdrawn in any case. The Air Ministry had published an approved list of such markings late in 1950 but, since none of them had been fighter units in the 1930s, this had not featured any of FEAF's squadrons. In the absence of traditional marking Nos 28, 33, 60 and 80 Sqns promptly devised some and, once they had been officially endorsed, began to apply them. For the time being, however, the Flying Camels stuck to their unique nose emblem and continued to use their OB codes, now applied in white on A Flight's camouflaged aeroplanes.

Operational activity remained at a low key in April and the squadron was allocated only one mission. This was flown from Butterworth by five aircraft of B Flight which, accompanied by three Hornets from No 33 Sqn, attacked an alleged MRLA camp at Kangar. The target was marked by an Auster and, although they could see nothing of significance, the pilots duly plastered the smoke; No 45 Sqn's

contribution amounted to ten 500 pounders, twenty 60 lb RPs and 1,203 rounds of 20mm. It appeared to have been just another exercise in dumping HE into the jungle and the formation flew back to Butterworth with no great expectations. This time, however, when the troops moved in they found six dead terrorists and were able to round up and capture several others. One could rarely assess the likely results of jungle strikes in advance but it was heartening to be given confirmation that, at least sometimes, it was all doing some good. Beyond this the only other tasking involved a continuation of the patrol pattern established in February.

As no bombs had been available in April, B Flight had to go back to Butterworth for three days in May to complete the bombing element of their APC. The Station Commander had heard about *The Flying Camel Revue* via the grapevine and requested a performance to show No 33 Sqn how things ought to be done. By some judicious alteration of nominal rolls the appropriate bodies were despatched to Butterworth to support B Flight's detachment and the squadron's strolling players chalked up another success. The APC went well too, with forty-two trips being flown in just two days.

May began with the gazetting, on the 4th, of a DFM for Sgt Gerald Turley and a BEM for the Sgt John Swann, the squadron's senior armourer. Apart from the routine patrols over Johore, however, there was no operational tasking at all during May and the squadron had to content itself with training flying, of which air-to-air gunnery was now an integral part. The usual procedure was for the Beaufighter target-tug to take the banner back to Seletar but from May onwards it was arranged that it would be dropped at Tengah at the end of each sortie so that the squadron's Pilot Attack Instructor (PAI), F/Sgt 'Red' Craighill, could speed up the process of assessing the scores. The highlight of the month was the arrival in Malayan waters of HMS *Warrior* on her way to Korea. Her Air Group flew off to operate from Tengah and on the 25th and 26th Tengah's Hornets and Vampires had great sport defending their airfield against attacks by *Warrior's* Sea Furies and Fireflies. Sadly, however, the squadron's serviceability was now such that it could field only four aircraft each day. Nevertheless it had been a productive exercise for those who had been able to

Viv Jacobs' personal aeroplane for a time was WF967/OB.H. It had the 'Pouncing Camel' on its nose but was unique in that it also had a more reserved representation of the 'Flying Camel' on its fin. It is seen here being flown over Singapore's Keppel Harbour by Fg Off 'Pat' Pattinson in May 1954. (M Retallack)

take part; it was rounded off by a Beating the Retreat ceremony on the carrier's flight deck which many of the pilots were fortunate enough to attend.

Viv Jacobs had been giving much thought to the squadron's poor serviceability and had by now concluded that it was not due to the age of the aircraft after all; the problem lay with the working routine. The standard day involved shift changes which resulted in time being lost during handovers and a degree of duplication of effort. There was no suggestion that the airmen were not working hard enough; the problem was that they were working inefficiently. In times of stress it had been said by the wittier members of No 45 Sqn many times before, and it has been many times since, but there has probably never been a better example of there being "Too much bloody *Ardua* and not enough *Surgo*." The CO began to press for the introduction of a 'tropical working day' with all hands to the pump for one prolonged stint. After some teeth-sucking from the authorities he was given permission to try it. It worked. The system was introduced in June and the squadron was able to put up six aircraft for the Queen's Birthday flypast early in the month. Even the Vampire took to the air again, although it promptly ran up against a scheduled inspection which put it back in the hangar; nevertheless it was serviceable, even if it was not available. By the end of the month the squadron was able to put up a twelve-ship formation which proudly showed the No 45 Sqn flag over KL, Changi and Seletar. The squadron was back in business. The new working routine was from 0700hrs to 1300hrs, which left the rest of the day for sport and recreation. The only adverse aspect of the scheme was that the squadron was still required to take its turn at maintaining a quick response capability, which meant

that a proportion of its pilots and groundcrew had to remain on call during the afternoons in case of a short-notice tasking, but this was a small price to pay for the satisfaction of having the aeroplanes flying again.

The CO had recovered the situation just in time as there was a surge of operational activity in July, the squadron flying fifty-five sorties in the course of nine strikes. During one of the first of these missions, in Johore on the 2nd, the Auster marker aircraft set itself on fire with one of its own flares and the pilot was obliged to crash land in a swamp. No 45 Sqn maintained a relay of armed patrols over the downed pilot for the next 5½ hours until a helicopter could be rustled up to effect a rescue. Activity peaked with Operation TERMITE for which the squadron mounted an eight-aircraft detachment to Butterworth between the 8th and 11th. The target was a 250 square mile area to the south east of Ipoh. Hundreds of soldiers were involved and they were supported by area-bombing Lincolns, precision strikes by Hornets and by Valettas operating in the resupply and paratroop dropping roles. No 45 Sqn flew five strikes, four led by Viv Jacobs and one by Flt Lt 'Brit' Brittain. Some of these missions involved all eight aircraft and, apart from one minor incident, the whole lot remained fully available throughout the detachment, virtually 100% serviceability.

In fact the squadron's extraordinary new level of serviceability was proving to be slightly embarrassing; it now began to find itself in the unusual position of having aircraft standing idle due to a lack of pilots! The annual CFS visit was looming again and the usual programme of preparatory lectures was instigated but, predictably, the Mosquito promptly went unserviceable, just when it was needed to update everyone's IRT. This was partly offset by the availability of the Vampire which was also being used for bombing and RP training, although its guns were inhibited pending the delivery of a new cannon bay fairing. JOSSTICK IV was staged in July. These deployments were becoming increasingly comprehensive training events and this time the squadron spent two days operating with Singapore's GCI radar in the air defence role intercepting B-29 raids.

Only one strike was ordered in August which was otherwise a fairly routine month. The most notable event was a visit by a number of MPs who were touring the Far East and Sir Bob Boothby spent a long time with No 45 Sqn on the 19th, inspecting its aeroplanes and chatting to its young men - which is more than could be said for most of his colleagues, who seemed to be preoccupied by the 'refreshment' facilities being offered by the Officers' Mess. The intermittent exchange of pilots with No 80 Sqn was still going on and during August Flt Lts A H Humphrys and L H Southall went up to Kai Tak, No 45 Sqn receiving Flt Lt Peter Cornish in their stead.

September was full of incident. Against the continuing background of the pipeline patrol, thirty-four strike sorties were flown and the squadron managed to write off the remarkable total of five aeroplanes in one month. Fg Off 'Pat' Pattinson opened the score on the 1st by collapsing WF954's undercarriage while making a heavyweight landing which put paid to that aeroplane's flying career. On the 14th WB911 suffered an hydraulic failure and Sgt Jack Doudy had to make a belly-landing, resulting in terminal damage to the airframe. MPlt R J Buckley swung on landing in WB908 on

the 29th and another undercarriage gave up in protest. The following day Plt Off Julian Greenwood, who had been with the squadron for only four weeks, had an ASI failure in WF956, resulting in a high-speed landing which took him into the overshoot and yet another undercarriage folded up. The fifth aeroplane was VT628, by then the only Mosquito still on charge. This one was not bent; it just came unglued, as Mosquitos were wont to do in the tropics, and it was condemned on the 9th.

Despite all this carnage, no one had been seriously hurt and it had gone some way towards reducing the slightly embarrassing surplus of serviceable aeroplanes! The squadron still had no problem finding six to take part in a Battle of Britain flypast on the 15th and it was joined in this enterprise by numerous Valettas, Lincolns, Vampires and Harvards as they flew over KL in salute.

At the end of September A Flight went up to Butterworth for another APC but were recalled half-way through to take part in Operation WHIP. WHIP was mounted between the 8th and 13th and was another co-ordinated effort, much like July's TERMITE. This time the target area was north east of Kluang where a band of MRLA, who had perpetrated a series of recent incidents, had taken refuge. After the squadron had contributed forty-two sorties A Flight resumed its APC but it remained at Tengah and accepted the inconvenience of the long transit flights to and from Song Song.

The team from CFS did their stuff during October and, in the absence of a Mosquito, they flew with the squadron's pilots in the relatively unfamiliar Vampire. Despite their

The squadron's pilots in late August 1954. From the left, back row: Sgt J C Doudy, Fg Off W J Armstrong, Fg Off R Cordey, Fg Off I D Pattinson, Fg Off J F Alderton, Fg Off E Collier and F/Sgt A F Craighill. Front row: Flt Lt A H P Cornish, Flt Lt C E F Cooper, Flt Lt H G Brittain DFC AFC, Sqn Ldr V K Jacobs, Flt Lt W J O Morrison AFC, Flt Lt J J Connors and Fg Off C T Lake. (V K Jacobs)

fearsome reputation the 'Trappers' were really quite an understanding bunch; due allowances were made and they went on their way content that all was well with the Flying Camels. No sooner had they left than a replacement Mosquito arrived. If there was one thing that could be said about No 45 Sqn's succession of Mosquito T.3s it was that they were never there when they were needed!

It will be recalled that the Flying Camels had been one of the original thirty squadrons to qualify for the immediate award of a Standard when these had first been introduced in 1943 but, as yet, it had still not actually received its banner. In fact none of these Standards was formally presented until April 1953 when No 1 Sqn took possession of theirs. Thereafter they began to be presented to units, broadly in numerical order, at a rate of about one per month. By late 1954 No 45 Sqn's turn was approaching and in November preparations began for the necessary ceremonial parade; thenceforth drill sessions became an integral part of the daily routine. There was not too much operational activity going on to interfere with the marching practice but, unusually, on the 15th the squadron was required to respond to a short-notice task. A truck carrying a platoon of the Fijian Regt had been ambushed near Yong Peng by a band of about thirty CTs; five soldiers had been killed, a further six had been

One of the squadron's groundcrew striking a suitably nonchalant pose before going for a trip in the Mosquito T.3, probably VT586. Note that the aeroplane has banded spinners but lacks the 'Pouncing Camel' badge. (V K Jacobs)

wounded and the terrorists had made off with their weapons and ammunition. Air strikes were called in to pin the CTs down while the army prepared a sweep to round them up. The squadron reacted immediately but was only able to provide three aircraft as most of the fleet was up at Butterworth with B Flight on an APC.

JOSSTICK V took place during December and on the 3rd and 5th most of the squadron's pilots had further opportunities to carry out interceptions and to fly as bomber escorts. This activity was shared by B Flight at Butterworth as well as the rump of the squadron at Tengah. While the B-29s were flying back to Clark Field on the 6th, the squadron bent another Hornet. PX369's undercarriage declined to lower and its pilot was obliged to do without this luxury, but the Hornet was a good belly-lander and, although it did the aeroplane no good at all, Fg Off John Wilson emerged from the incident unscathed. December was also notable for very heavy rainfall which caused extensive flooding in southern Malaya and obliged the MRLA to take to the high ground. The CTs having been concentrated into known areas, several strikes were laid on to make their lives even more uncomfortable, 250 lb bombs being used to conserve stocks of the more usual 500 pounders. Twenty-two sorties were flown on this task in late December but the campaign really took off in the New Year and in January 1955 the squadron added a further ninety-one operational sorties to its now considerable tally.

The Christmas season was celebrated in the traditional fashion with the added bonus of a pantomime. Written and produced by the CO (and 'producing' included the co-opting of those members of the cast who did not willingly volunteer to dress up as fairies!), the squadron staged an extravaganza entitled *Tengarella*, which was presented three times and hugely enjoyed both by its audiences and by all those who took part - even the pressed men.

By now the presentation of the Standard was imminent and it had already been produced by Hobson and Sons of London (Soho), who have made nearly all such banners for the RAF. Squadron Standards are pale blue, heavy silk flags, beautifully embroidered with the squadron's badge and up to eight Battle Honours. The Battle Honours are selected by the unit from a list of those to which it is entitled which is compiled by the Air Ministry. In the case of No 45 Sqn the following options were available, those marked with an asterisk being the ones which were chosen:

Western Front 1916-1917*
Somme 1916
Ypres 1917
Italian Front and Adriatic 1917-1918*
Piave
Independent Force and Germany 1918*
Kurdistan 1922-1924
Iraq 1923-1925
Egypt and Libya 1940-1942*
East Africa 1940*
Syria 1941
Burma 1942*
Arakan 1943-1944*
Burma 1944-1945*

Since no royal visits were scheduled for the Far East at the appropriate time, it was not possible to invite a member

No 45 Sqn's Standard Presentation Parade at Tengah on 9th February 1955. A number of interesting features are visible in the background, including the RAAF Lincoln dispersal and No 1 Hangar (the nearer one) both of which were to become No 45 Sqn's preserve in 1958. In front of the hangar can be seen the new ATC tower; between them, in the distance, is Learoyd Block with the ten-year old 'temporary' ATC facility on its roof. (V K Jacobs)

of the Royal Family to make the presentation. The senior resident representatives of the Crown were the Commissioner for South East Asia and the Governor of Singapore but, although it was considered appropriate for them to attend the ceremony, and both did, the CO preferred not to have a civilian directly involved and asked the AOCinC if he would officiate. Air Marshal F J Fressanges was delighted to accept. The parade, supported by the band of the Far East Air Force and flanked on three sides by immaculate Hornets, took place on the squadron's dispersal on 9th February 1955. The parade commander was Sqn Ldr Jacobs with A and B Flights commanded by Flt Lt H G Brittain DFC AFC and Flt Lt W J O Morrison AFC, respectively. The Standard was borne by Fg Off J H S Greenwood and was consecrated by the RAF's Chaplain in Chief, Canon A S Giles. All the appropriate civilian and military dignitaries were present along with the personal guests of the squadron. It was a splendid occasion, the formalities being rounded off by a reception in the Officers' Mess followed by an all-ranks party at the station swimming pool. Most of the officers attending had a shrewd suspicion that, one way or another, they might be going to get wet - they were quite right![6]

On February 16th PX332's canopy shattered in flight which resulted in terminal damage to the airframe, although John Wilson was able to fly it back for a normal landing. Despite No 45 Sqn's periodic attempts to reduce its front-line strength, FEAF's operational potential continued to grow and in early 1955 there were two significant additions to its Order of Battle. Although No 1 Sqn RAAF continued to commit its Lincolns to FIREDOG for another three years, the RAF had by now virtually withdrawn this type from bomber operations. From March 1955 the detachments of Lincolns under Operation BOLD was superseded by the deployment of Canberra squadrons under Operation MILEAGE, the only difference being that the Canberras generally operated from Butterworth rather than Tengah. The second increment to the strike force was the arrival of No 14 Sqn RNZAF on redeployment from Cyprus. The new squadron's Venoms were to be based at Tengah and the Rt Hon Sidney Holland, Prime Minister of New Zealand, visited the station personally to inspect the accommodation which was to be allocated to

his unit. It was that presently occupied by the Flying Camels, which meant that they were going to have to be evicted. It was clear that Commonwealth defence policy at the highest level was involved here and Viv Jacobs realised that there would be little point in lodging a protest - especially as he was a Kiwi himself and might want to go home to Auckland some day!

By this time the Hornet's days were numbered. Spares were becoming increasingly scarce and there were growing doubts about some aspects of the integrity of their airframes. Plans were already in hand to replace them with Venoms, however, and a start was to be made by gradually running-down the Hornet force. As the first stage in this programme it had been decided to move the Flying Camels up to Butterworth and to amalgamate them with No 33 Sqn. A shot-gun marriage had been arranged and the two units were to be 'linked' as No 45/33 Sqn with Sqn Ldr Jacobs as CO. This was to be the last manifestation of another attempt to keep squadron identities in use by artificial means, much like the business of the Flying Camels having notionally fostered No 27 Sqn's numberplate back in 1947. The Linked Squadron concept had been introduced by AMO A.86 in February 1949 and between then and 1957 thirty-two such combinations were to be formally established. In each case the first of the two designated units in each pair was deemed to be the one which was actually in being but it was supposed to keep alive the spirit and traditions of its *alter ego*. It was another well-intentioned but unrealistic idea; any squadron attempting to grant more than token recognition to its dormant half could only do so at the expense of diluting its own identity. Predictably, the 'other' squadrons in these liaisons rarely received more than scant attention. The merging of Nos 33 and 45 Sqns differed significantly from earlier 'linkings', however, in that it was created from two active units, rather than by grafting a defunct numberplate onto a serving squadron.

After five years at Tengah the squadron had put down deep roots so it took the best part of a month to get it ready to move. The CO wanted to make one last demonstration of the Flying Camels' superiority before they left and he called upon the airmen to get all the aeroplanes up for one last

As a final gesture, before leaving Tengah, the squadron flew one last Balbo over KL and Singapore on 18th March 1955. Seen here are twelve Hornets with Mosquito VT586 bringing up the rear. The photograph was taken from the squadron's Vampire T.11, WZ521. (V K Jacobs)

flypast. They responding willingly and on March 18th the squadron's dispersal was empty while all fourteen aircraft showed off in fine style by flying up to KL and back to Tengah via Changi; twelve Hornets, the Vampire and even the Mosquito!

As FETS was to disband on the same day that No 45/33 Sqn was established, it was quite clear that the Hornet was now living on borrowed time. With the 'Hornet OCU' closed, there could be no more replacement pilots so the new unit was to be quite large to start with and then allowed to

waste away. Even so it was not intended to create a mega-squadron so, to reduce the manpower to a manageable but still generous level, there was a spate of postings from both units, mostly involving the early repatriation of those who were approaching their tour-expiry dates, while a number of No 45 Sqn's airmen remained at Tengah to join other units. One stalwart member of the squadron who did not make the trip up to Butterworth was Chopper. He was still going strong but was now over ten years old, which was not a bad age for a hound of his pedigree in a tropical climate. Having previously established his authority over Negombo and Kuala Lumpur he was now the undisputed canine king of Tengah and it seemed unreasonable to make him face the challenge of

The merging of two active squadrons was inevitably going to produce something of a mongrel and this is well illustrated by this picture of the combined unit's somewhat piebald flightline in April 1955. Shortly after setting up home at Butterworth as No 45/33 Sqn, WF975, an ex-No 33 Sqn aeroplane, was repainted with the prototype of a proposed new No 45 Sqn marking, a white dumb-bell on a red ground with a red/blue Flying Camel at each end, both facing towards the roundel. Events were to preclude any further Hornets having this marking applied but it was to gain official Air Ministry recognition as the squadron's fighter marking and was promulgated as such on 8th November 1955 - although this fact seems to have been overlooked by later generations of Flying Camels. The second aeroplane in this line-up is No 45 Sqn's WF961/D, now camouflaged and devoid of its OB code. Behind that is PX342/W wearing No 33 Sqn's bars. Next is WB879/T, ex-No 45 Sqn, still in silver but again minus its OB code. Of the remaining four unidentified aircraft, one is camouflaged, as is the one on which the photographer was standing. (via A J Thomas)

Although the OB codes were deleted from the ex-No 45 Sqn aircraft after they had moved up to Butterworth, as can be seen from this picture the 'Pouncing Camel' was retained as were the banded spinners. The aeroplane in the back-ground is WF975 with its unique dumb bell marking. (A D Ashworth)

a new territory at his age; Chopper stayed in Singapore.

The squadron began its redeployment on March 21st when five Hornets were flown up to Butterworth. On March 31st No 45/33 Sqn formally came into being. As with the personnel of the two squadrons, their aircraft had been pooled and, although a number of aeroplanes had been despatched to Seletar, the new unit had twenty-two Hornets to start with, of which nine wore the Flying Camel and thirteen No 33 Sqn's bar-style insignia (a red stripe on a pale blue band edged top and bottom in dark blue). There were also two Vampire T.11s (one of which was on loan to the New Zealanders) and a trio of Mosquito T.3s of mixed parentage.

By this time squadron codes were becoming distinctly passé and it was definitely the 'in thing' to have a bar-type insignia. It was decided to resurrect the dumb-bell which had been worn by No 45 Sqn's Camels in 1918. It was to be painted in white on a red ground and applied flanking the fuselage roundels with a miniature representation of the Flying Camel in each of the dumb-bell's discs. A prototype marking was applied to WF975, a camouflaged ex-No 33 Sqn aeroplane, which carried the individual letter N on its fin in white. The strong ex-No 33 Sqn lobby were not over-impressed with the idea of having their markings replaced and there were proposals to have the aeroplanes marked as No 33 Sqn on one side and No 45 Sqn on the other - such are the problems which can arise from daft ideas like 'linked' squadrons. Fate was to intervene before this matter came to a head and the dumb-bell was never applied to any other aircraft.

The personnel complement of the combined squadron was as mixed as its fleet of aeroplanes, nine of the pilots being ex-No 33 Sqn. In total the squadron consisted of twenty-two officers, one master pilot, thirteen SNCOs, twenty-four corporals and ninety-eight airmen. Both of No 45 Sqn's original flight commanders were 'tourex' so their places were taken by Flt Lt R L Maslan as OC A Flight and Flt Lt J J Connors as OC B Flight. A period of accommodation and adjustment began as the two halves of the unit began to get to know each other, to bury hatchets and to try to work out a new corporate identity. As part of this process the reconstituted A Flight embarked on an APC to shake itself down.

The reconstituted unit flew its first strikes on All Fools' Day when a dozen of its Hornets participated in Operation BEEHIVE, most of them landing at Kuala Lumpur before returning to base. The following morning No 45/33 Sqn suffered its first losses. The authorised strength of the squadron was only twenty Hornets so two of those on charge had to be disposed of. Fg Off J E Bowler was on his way back to England and the first leg of his journey was to be undertaken by ferrying one of the surplus aeroplanes, PX350, down to Seletar. Fg Off R J Russell, a relatively new arrival, was to accompany him in the other redundant aircraft, PX362. Most of the pilots, and several wives, were at the airfield to see Johnny Bowler leave. The pair took off and then turned back to make what appeared to be a farewell run across the airfield. In fact Bowler had an undercarriage problem and had called the Tower to let them know that he was planning to make a flypast so that the Local Controller could inspect his aeroplane. His companion, neatly tucked in on his leader's right, appears not to have been aware of this complication, or not to have understood its implications. As they reached the Tower, Bowler banked to starboard to expose the underside of his aircraft and his No 2 flew straight into him. Both aircraft crashed on the airfield; both pilots were killed. The shock of this awful accident was aggravated by the fact that it had been witnessed by a large proportion of the squadron including Mrs Russell. The tragedy did at least serve to unite the new squadron, albeit in shared grief.

The next day, April 3rd, Plt Off Sheppard was taking off in WL654, one of a handful of Vampire FB 9s belonging to the APC, when it lost its brake pressure and he ran off the runway but no major damage was done. A couple of weeks later three of A Flight's Hornets were grounded with serious mainspar defects and the aircraft were condemned. The rest of the Hornets were permitted to continue flying but the original twenty-two aircraft fleet was already down to seventeen. Hampered by the loss of three aeroplanes, A Flight was unable to complete the bombing element of its APC but had done what it could by May 3rd. B Flight began their APC two days later.

Having reconsidered the wing problem, AHQ Malaya ordered the temporary grounding of all its Hornets on May 7th and this edict was promptly endorsed by HQ FEAF and extended to those at Kai Tak. Coincidentally, DeHavillands had been having misgivings too and had just informed the Air

Ministry that in their opinion it was inadvisable to continue to fly the aircraft. With both the manufacturer and the operating authority expressing concern, London confirmed the grounding order which became permanent on May 17th. The Hornets were to fly just one more trip. On the 16th fifteen

This evocative picture was taken after a tropical storm shortly before the last sixteen Hornets were flown away to be scrapped. (A D Ashworth)

Fg Off Julian Greenwood pre-flights PX310 at Butterworth before taking her up on her final flight to the breaker's yard at Seletar on 16th May 1955. (A D Ashworth)

Symbolising the end of an era, not only for No 45 Sqn but for the whole service, one of the RAF's last operational single-seat piston-engined fighters languishes in the scrapyard at Seletar awaiting the breaker's axe. The camouflaged WF961/D is still wearing the 'Pouncing Camel' on its nose but it is no longer coded OB. (D J Carlin)

Hornets were ferried gingerly down to Seletar where they were to be broken up. Two days later Hornet PX293 and Mosquito RR297 followed them to Singapore in the hands of the CO and Sgt Jack Doudy. Since this trip was made one day after the type had been officially grounded, it is quite possible that Viv Jacobs' trip was the last flight ever made by a Hornet. Whether it was or not, his and Doudy's ferries were certainly the last flights ever made by piston-engined aeroplanes of No 45 Sqn.

The period during which No 45 Sqn had flown Hornets had been a memorable one. The aeroplane is a prime contender for the title of the fastest, and possibly the best, piston-engined fighter ever produced and its pilots had certainly enjoyed flying it. Slow delivery of aeroplanes had made the conversion programme a rather protracted affair in 1952 but, once it was up to strength, the squadron became highly successful. During the Hornet era the squadron's role had been expanded and it had become a DF(GA) unit in the fullest sense, providing its pilots with a broad spectrum of flying experience and, since it was on active service, ample opportunity to make lots of very satisfying flashes and bangs. In its primary role of strike the squadron's Hornets had flown a total of 1,657 sorties, dropping 1,226,500 lbs of bombs and firing 5,073 60 lb rockets and 479,746 20mm cannon shells. It had also flown a considerable, but undetermined, number of additional operational missions on such tasks as convoy escorts and patrols.

It was particularly unfortunate that this notably successful chapter in the story of the Flying Camels should have come to such an untidy and precipitate end, leaving the squadron with a confused identity, grounded and non-operational.

Notes:

1. FETS was formed at Seletar on 1st June 1951 to provide what amounted to an Operational Conversion Unit for some of the aircraft types which were being flown exclusively by FEAF. It trained the last few replacement crews for the Brigand but its main function was to turn out pilots for Nos 33, 45 and 80 Sqns once the Hornet Conversion Unit at Linton-on-Ouse began to run down. The course included a weapons training phase and in August 1954 FETS moved to Butterworth to be closer to Song Song Range.

2. Despite its Brigands being grounded twice, No 45 Sqn flew an average of sixty-eight sorties per month during 1951; by 1953 the monthly sortie rate had fallen to fifty-eight. This absolute reduction in the level of activity was considerably greater in relative terms as the squadron had by that time roughly twice as many Hornets as it had had Brigands.

3. Appointed in February 1952, Gen Templar filled both of the senior British executive regional appointments, ie those Director of Operations and High Commissioner. This permitted him to co-ordinate all activities related to FIREDOG, both military and civil, which considerably enhanced operational efficiency.

4. Norrie Grove was to stay in the flying business after leaving the RAF and became Chief Test Pilot to Slingsby Aviation Ltd, his work with the company's Firefly trainer contributing significantly to the considerable commercial success of that project.

5. Something of an oracle, 'Wg Cdr Spry' has for many years been the RAF's in-house commentator on flying accidents, advisor on airmanship matters, promoter of sound flying procedures and all round good thing; his is the corporate voice of the Directorate of Flight Safety.

6. The swimming pool was a common venue for all-ranks parties throughout the squadron's twenty-odd years at Tengah. It was not unusual for the aircrew to finish up in the pool and it was understood, at least it was in Hornet days, that if they had taken the precaution of wearing their swimming kit then they *might* be allowed to undress first. Needless to say, this fine point of protocol was usually omitted from the Arrivals' Briefing offered to new pilots.

Chapter 17. Jets at last - Vampires and Venoms.

The squadron had been proud to fly the Hornet and had established a fine record with it, but there was no avoiding the fact that it was actually a WW II design. By the mid-1950s a self-respecting fighter outfit like the Flying Camels really ought to have been operating jets - as its erstwhile colleagues on No 60 Sqn had frequently pointed out while the squadron had been at Tengah! By this time Nos 28 and 60 Sqns had both been flying Vampires in FEAF for four years and the latter was already in the process of re-equipping with the second-generation Venom. With the recent arrival of No 14 Sqn RNZAF the proliferation of Venoms only served to heighten the contrast between these more modern aircraft and the Flying Camels' stylish but dated mounts[1]. Nevertheless, no one was expecting that the squadron would have to make the transition to jets in quite the undignified manner that circumstances dictated.

When the squadron was suddenly grounded and declared non-operational on 7th May 1955, AHQ Malaya immediately set about devising a rescue plan. The AOC, AVM W H Kyle CB CBE DSO DFC, came to Butterworth in person to let the squadron know what was in store for them. The recovery programme was to have three phases. The priority task was to rustle up as many jets as possible to get the squadron flying again. It would then standardise on No 60 Sqn's hand-me-down Vampires and finally, when sufficient aircraft were available in-theatre, it was to be re-equipped with Venoms.

The first stage was implemented very rapidly, largely at the expense of the staff of the APC at Butterworth, whose small fleet of aeroplanes was handed over to No 45 Sqn along with most of that unit's jet-experienced technicians who were to train the squadron's groundcrew[2]. Before May was out the squadron had acquired a Vampire T.11 from the APC, to complement the one which had been part of No 33 Sqn's dowry; a Meteor T.7 and an F.8 had been provided by Seletar; another T.7 and a pair of F.8s had been transferred from the APC; two Vampire FB 9s had been donated by the Far East Communications Squadron at Changi and the APC had contributed another. Meanwhile a fifteen-sortie jet conversion syllabus was concocted, to be followed by a further thirty sorties of consolidation flying, to include weapons training and tactical indoctrination which was to be accomplished by a formal APC.

Training was well under way by the end of the month with Flt Lt Jimmy Connors and Fg Off Paddy Grogan working the Vampires and MPlt K F Scott (of the APC staff), assisted by Flt Lt Steedman (borrowed from No 101 Sqn who were then the resident Operation MILEAGE Canberra outfit) instructing on the Meteors. The collection of aircraft continued to

expand and by the end of June three more had been taken on charge, one of them a Meteor F.8 which had come all the way from Hong Kong. By working shifts to get the most out of the motley collection of aeroplanes, rapid progress was made and the squadron flew over 400 hours in June. Just to show that they were still in business the squadron even put up the five-aircraft formation at Figure 17.1 to take part in the Queen's Birthday flypast on the 9th. B Flight completed its conversion flying in early July and started its APC on the 15th; by the end of the month it was close to being declared operational.

The newly linked squadron had barely begun to establish a corporate identity when its Hornets had been withdrawn. Morale had faltered at the shock as the ex-No 33 and ex-No 45 Sqn factions both found the ground cut from underneath them. The speed with which AHQ Malaya had reacted had been reassuring however, and the hectic pace at which conversion was being conducted (another 385 trips were flown in July) did much to restore confidence. United in their common aim of regaining operational status, a joint squadron identity soon began to emerge. Everyone responded well to

Aircraft	Type	Pilot
WZ614	Vampire T.11	Fg Off C D Grogan
WR176	Vampire FB 9	Fg Off P R Sheppard
WL564	Vampire FB 9	Fg Off R B Vass
WH379	Meteor F.8	Fg Off A D Ashworth
WA676	Meteor T.7	Fg Off G J Brand

Fig 17.1. *No 45 Sqn's contribution to the Queen's Birthday Flypast, 9th June 1955.*

Unusual in that it was not camouflaged, WR206 was one of the Vampire FB 9s contributed by Seletar in the successful attempt to keep the squadron flying. (A D Ashworth)

Vampire T.11, WZ610, was another of the jets hastily collected to keep the squadron flying after the Hornets' sudden demise. This aeroplane was already at Butterworth on charge to the APC. (A J Thomas)

Fg Off Bob Vass climbing aboard one of the half dozen Meteor F.8s acquired by the squadron. (No 45 Sqn archives)

Fg Off Mike Holmes peeks over the cockpit sill of a Vampire FB 9 just before start up at Butterworth. (No 45 Sqn archives)

what was undoubtedly a considerable challenge; morale recovered rapidly and the unit soon began to find its feet again.

Having been given priority from the outset, B Flight completed its APC on August 15th and was declared operational. With the heat off a little, A Flight, who had been using the Meteors, now began to convert to Vampires. Lots more Vampire FB 9s were arriving by then, a total of eight being formally taken on charge during August, and towards the end of that month it was possible to return to their original owners most of the aircraft that had been on temporary loan. By the end of August A Flight had five FB 9s and a pair of T.11s while B Flight had six FB 9s and one trainer.

The squadron was saddened to learn on August 17th of the death of Flt Lt Brand who had been killed in a flying

accident while on detachment to Leconfield where he had been undergoing a PAI course. There had been another, less traumatic, incident on the 8th when Fg Off Ashworth had undershot the runway in WH379, one of the Meteor F.8s. It was perhaps surprising that this was the only accident of note to occur during the high pressure conversion programme. Arthur 'Kiwi' Ashworth describes his adventure as follows:

In the Hornets we usually did a fast run and break for landing, cutting both throttles on the threshold before doing a continuous turn, dropping gear and flaps and levelling the wings just before touchdown. I attempted the same approach early in my jet flying days and found that the lag in receiving engine power was very real compared to that of the Merlins. I hit in the paddy undershoot with a spectacular splash; continued to the (higher) runway threshold where I left the undercarriage and ventral tank. The canopy failed to jettison so when the aircraft came to rest and started to burn I wound back the hood by hand and left smartly. The incident was looked upon by Higher Authority as inexperience on type and the inevitable result of our limited jet conversion.

The most significant event in August was the squadron's first operational jet strike which was flown on the 30th. Eight aircraft, operating in pairs over a three hour period, carried out attacks in the Gunong Inas Forest, delivering a total of sixteen 500 pounders, thirty RPs and 3,360 rounds of 20mm ammunition. The pilots and aircraft involved, some of the latter flying twice, are listed below.

WL514	Sqn Ldr V K Jacobs
WL554	Fg Off W J Armstrong
WR204	Flt Lt J J Connors
WL513	Sgt J C Doudy
WL514	Fg Off J R J Froud
WR176	Fg Off P L Davies
WR204	Fg Off G H Baker
WL554	Fg Off P R Sheppard

The squadron was now back in business and available for tasking, but there had been a significant reduction in demand for fighter-bomber strikes and for the next several weeks no further ops were called for. September was still busy, however, with a Battle of Britain flypast on the 15th and A Flight embarking on its APC the following day. For the former the squadron put up eight FB 9s and a pair of T.11s. During the month a lecture programme began in preparation for the forthcoming changeover to Venoms, the first four of which arrived at Butterworth on September 21st. As these aeroplanes were destined for No 45 Sqn, Sqn Ldr Jacobs claimed the right to make the first flight in one, this claim being disputed by OC Flying Wing on the grounds that the aeroplane still belonged to the

Meteor F.8 WH379 after 'Kiwi' Ashworth had been caught out by the relatively slow throttle response of its new-fangled jet engines and had wiped off its undercarriage. The black and yellow striped undersides of this aeroplane, which had been donated by Seletar, indicate that it had previously been used for target towing. (A D Ashworth)

station; rank prevailed, of course, and Wg Cdr Gundry-White had that privilege. Viv Jacobs had to be content with making the first Venom flight by a No 45 Sqn pilot on September 30th. On October 13th fate stepped in to rebuke the wing commander's hubris; WR369 lost power during its take off run and Gundry-White was obliged to retract the undercarriage to avoid going off the end of the runway. The aeroplane caught fire and,

WK486 was one of the first four Venoms to be delivered to Butterworth (on 21st September 1955). Shortly afterwards this photograph was taken to be used as an insert in the squadron's 1955 Christmas card. (A D Ashworth)

despite the efforts of the crash crew, sustained some damage, although the pilot emerged unscathed.

The Vampires, after a very intensive period of flying, were now beginning to flag and A Flight had to struggle through its APC with only two serviceable aeroplanes; nevertheless it made it, and by the end of the month both flights were operational. Little progress was made with Venom flying, however, as the aeroplanes had to undergo a prolonged pre-acceptance servicing and only one was made available to the pilots[3]. On October 10th and 11th the squadron took part in an intensive search for a seaman who had fallen overboard from the MV *Astynax* off Penang. Sadly, despite the squadron's flying thirty-six sorties (four of them by Flt Lt Jimmy Connors in WR346, the only available Venom), they did not find the missing sailor.

The uncomfortable 'linked' arrangement was formally terminated on October 15th when No 33 Sqn's numberplate was withdrawn for reallocation to a new squadron which was to form at Driffield with Venom night-fighters. It was something of a relief to have the squadron's identity unambiguously re-established and the residual flickering of schizophrenia quickly died out. The CO thumbed a lift back to the UK in a Canberra of No 617 Sqn, by now the resident Canberra unit, and personally escorted No 33 Sqn's silver back to the UK.

Tech Wg began to pass significant numbers of Venoms to the squadron during November but they were still suffering from the inevitable symptoms of new aeroplane-itis and there were lots of early serviceability problems, mostly to do with the sensitivity of the electrical system to the high humidity, difficulties with the braking system and a problem with wing flutter. Despite these teething troubles, which per-sisted into early 1956, there was only one significant in-cident, on the 7th, when WR353's engine failed on take off causing Fg Off Pete Davis to run off the side of the runway but both he and the aeroplane escaped major dam-age. In this context it is worth pointing out that Butterworth

had been built close to the sea and one end of the east/west runway was virtually on the beach. An abandoned take off or an overshoot on landing could easily result in wet feet. Furthermore, to cope with the frequent torrential rain, in common with most of Malaya's airfields there were deep monsoon drains all over the place, some of them almost capable of swallowing a Venom whole. This meant that going off the side of the runway could be almost as hazardous as going off the end. The runway had ample length, so long as the engine and/or brakes worked, so it was not quite like flying from an aircraft carrier, but it was still quite important to stay on the hard bit. There was a north/south runway as well but this had been built during the Japanese occupation, allegedly on a foundation of tree trunks which were decomposing by the mid-1950s, and its surface was in such a poor state that it was used only rarely.

Apart from the mild idiosyncracies of the aerodrome, as 'Kiwi' Ashworth (one of the ex-No 33 Sqn men) has recalled:

> Squadron life at Butterworth was idyllic for a young man. Apart from the flying we swam at the Penang Swimming Club and played rugby at the Penang Sports Club. Jim Froud and I often dined at the E & O Hotel in Penang on Saturday nights (right out of Somerset Maugham) and then enjoyed taxi-dancing in the none too salubrious atmosphere of the *City Lights*.

Two more Vampire strikes were flown in December, on

No 45 Sqn's interim Vampire FB 9s wore no unit identification markings. This one is WL513, one of No 60 Sqn's hand-me-downs. (No 45 Sqn archives)

This group photograph was taken in about January 1956. It is believed that the Hornet-style 'Pouncing Camel' emblem was never actually painted on any of the squadron's Venoms and those just discernible on the noses of the aircraft flanking this picture are reported to have been paper cut-outs produced for the occasion. Seated in the front row are, from the left: Fg Off H R Walker, Fg Off J R J Froud, Fg Off W J Connors, Fg Off M E Y Holmes, Flt Lt L J Connors, Flt Lt L J Connors, Flt Lt L J Connors, Flt Lt L J Connors, Flt Lt R I. Maslan, Sqn Ldr V K Jacobs, Flt Lt L J Connors, Fg Off J R J Froud, Fg Off W J Armstrong, Flt Lt G H Baker, Fg Off J B Sullivan, (probably) MPlt J C Lloyd, Sgt J C Doudy, an unidentified WO and F'Sgt 'Blondie' Webber. Sgt Arthur Holden is standing at the left hand end of the row and F'Sgt Harry Osborne is at the right hand end. (H Osborne)

Representative seasonal activities at Butterworth, Christmas 1955. On the left, Flt Lt Jimmy Connors serving dinner to the airmen, and on the right, F/Sgt Harry Osborne chatting with Fg Off Harry Walker at a Sergeants' Mess do. (both H Osborne)

the 1st and 6th, totalling twelve sorties in all but this was the only operational tasking. In the meantime Venom flying had advanced to the stage that weapons practice could begin. In summarising 1955 in the Operations Record Book at the end of December, the CO reviewed what had been a very hard nine months and pointed out how apposite the squadron's motto was - it had been "*Per Ardua Surgo* in spades!" Early in the New Year Sqn Ldr Jacobs left for New Zealand on leave and went directly from there to the UK, leaving the squadron temporarily in the hands of Flt Lt Roy Maslan pending the arrival of a new CO, at the same time Flt Lt R T F Plowman took over A Flight.

New Year's Day 1956 was marked by Fg Off John Sullivan's abandoning a take off in one of the squadron's trainers and, after careering across the airfield, leaving it neatly bridging a monsoon drain. Recovering the aeroplane presented the recently arrived F/Sgt Harry Osborne with a considerable problem as the ground was too soft to support a crane. The space underneath the aeroplane had to be filled with ammunition boxes and rubble to create a firm enough base for the Vampire to be towed back onto terra firma on its own wheels. The exercise took two days but WZ509 survived all this rough treatment and eventually resumed its place on the flightline.

The groundcrew began to get the measure of the Venom's idiosyncrasies in January, although the supply system had yet to catch up with the fact that the squadron was operating two types of aeroplane so there were still shortages of spares. Nevertheless, by working hard on the old Vampires (most of which were quite tired after having flown a tour with No 60 Sqn) and by cannibalising the Venoms to keep some going, the flightline looked quite respectable on most days and a lot of flying was done. By this time the pilots were beginning to drop pairs of 1,000 pounders on the range using a steep glide delivery borrowed from the Venom squadrons in MEAF.

Three strikes were put up in January, on the 1st, 2nd and 30th, for a total of twenty-nine sorties. Most were flown by the FB 9s but a T.11 took part in the first attack and Flt Lt Connors flew the squadron's first operational Venom sortie on the 2nd when WR346 took part in an attack on a target in the Bongsu Forest. On the last strike of the month, which

involved eleven sorties against Bukit Relau, four of the participating aircraft were Venoms. Although the Venom was capable of carrying two 1,000 lb bombs, twice the Vampire's bomb load, at first the squadron tended to be tasked with only gun and rocket attacks.

There was a JOSSTICK during January, but most of the activity was concentrated in the Singapore Sector and the squadron was provided with few opportunities to make interceptions. Another extracurricular event was a visit to FEAF by the CAS Designate, ACM Sir Dermot Boyle, for whom a flypast was laid on by four Canberras (by now of No 12 Sqn) to which the squadron added a pair of Venoms and seven Vampires.

Sqn Ldr G S Cooper had arrived in January and on February 1st he formally assumed command of the squadron. Four strikes were carried out that month, fourteen of the twenty-five sorties flown being contributed by Venoms. Three of these operations, two on the Thai border and one near Ipoh, were carried out in conjunction with six-ship Canberra formations from No 12 Sqn and the bombing was left to them.

By the end of the month Butterworth had received fifteen Venoms and, allowing for the one which OC Flg Wg had written off in October, the squadron still had fourteen, which was enough to consider its re-equipment to be substantially complete. The Vampires had begun to disappear in January and by the end of February most of them had been

Fg Off John Sullivan managed to park WZ509, one of the squadron's pair of Vampire T.11s, athwart one of Butterworth's monsoon drains on New Year's Day 1956. (H Osborne)

375

In February 1956 news finally filtered through that the squadron's marking of a white dumb-bell on a red ground had been formally approved and these were promptly painted on the Venoms' tailbooms. The blue and white wingtip tanks with a white bar and a small red Flying Camel, as seen here on WE469/O, were not added until April 1957. (D Brereton)

withdrawn.

The Venoms had been delivered in the standard 2nd TAF colour scheme of Dark Green and Dark Sea Grey camouflage on top with Azure undersides as had most of the Vampires, although one or two of the latter had been in plain silver. The Vampires had carried no distinguishing markings; nor did the Venoms at first. In November 1955, however, the Air Ministry had formally endorsed the white dumb-bell on a red ground, which had been tentatively introduced in the previous April. News of this decision finally percolated down to Butterworth in February 1956 and the new markings soon began to appear on the tail booms of the Venoms. The only difference from the original design was that there were no mini-Flying Camels, policy dictating that the emblem from a squadron's badge was not to be a part of the design.

The squadron celebrated its Fortieth Birthday on March 1st and this auspicious occasion was marked by a suitable party. There was a JOSSTICK that month too and this time the squadron flew ten sorties in defence of Penang, intercepting a Lincoln and a B-29. There was more day-fighter activity later on when the airfield was defended against attacks from the Air Groups of HMS *Centaur* and HMS *Albion*. In addition to these exercises the squadron carried out an air-to-air programme using ciné and operating at heights of up to 30,000 feet. On the ranges it was also experimenting with 60° dive-bombing and achieving very satisfactory results.

Only one strike was called for in March but it provided

WE469/O looses off a practice rocket at Song Song. (D Brereton)

the opportunity for the squadron to drop bombs for the first time, Fg Off Mike Holmes in WE373 and F/Sgt "Z²" Zmitrowicz in WE407 each dropping a pair of 1,000 pounders on the 17th. There was one flying incident during the month when WR346's canopy shattered but Flt Lt Giles Baker was able to get the aircraft down safely. Serviceability dropped sharply in the middle of the month and at one stage all eighteen aircraft were on the ground. Part of the problem was spares but it was compounded by a shortage of SNCOs. F/Sgt Osborne was trying to run both flights and it simply was not possible. The only option was temporarily to suspend the two-flight organisation and centralise the squadron's servicing arrangements. This was done but the absence of the competitive inter-flight spirit was missed. In April F/Sgt 'Spike' Morrell arrived and it became possible to revert to a two-flight organisation; thereafter things quickly began to recover with the specialist engineering teams being supervised by F/Sgt 'Blondie' Webber as senior armourer and Sgt Arthur Holden to look after the engines. To back up the efforts of the groundcrew working on the flightline, a C Flight was also set up on a trial basis to handle rectification. One of the senior pilots, Flt Lt P L Davis MC, was appointed as flight commander with Fg Off A M Eckel, a refugee from Hong Kong after No 80 Sqn's Hornets had been grounded, as his deputy. Mike Eckel recalls: "C Flight was the ground staff flight. Due to a shortage of riggers I found myself, complete with tool box, working on the line and once even in the hangar. I thoroughly enjoyed that!" These arrangements all seemed to work and in April the squadron actually achieved its monthly flying hours target for the first time since Hornet days.

By this time No 9 Sqn was the resident Canberra unit and it had been selected to represent FEAF at an airshow to be held in Manila. In preparation for this they had been working

up their display sequence and No 45 Sqn's fighter pilots had had to put up with the indignity of having to watch the frequent rehearsals of the visiting bombers. On April 10th AVM Kyle came to Butterworth to give his formal approval to No 9 Sqn's routine. Working behind the scenes, Sqn Ldr Cooper had arranged to take the stage immediately after the Canberras with the aim of giving a show-stealing performance to demonstrate that, impressive as the bombers were, a Venom was inherently more agile and thus more exciting to watch than a Canberra could ever hope to be. His performance was cheered by his own groundcrew and, significantly, by those of No 9 Sqn too. The AOC got the point and promised that the next time there was a requirement for FEAF's flag to be waved the Flying Camels would be given the job.

The rest of the month was uneventful, apart from a six-aircraft strike on the 23rd, but there was more activity in May which opened and closed with formation flypasts. The first was a twelve-ship on the 1st in honour of the departing Director of Operations, Lt Gen Sir Geoffrey Bourne. The second was the Queen's Birthday flypast on the 31st when the squadron's Venoms flew over Penang in salute accompanied by No 9 Sqn's Canberras and three of the Station Flight's Harvards.

There was a slight increase in tasking during May and ops were flown on the 18th, 25th and 29th, although each strike called for only four aircraft. They were notable, however, for the squadron's first use of a level-bombing technique; this had been devised by No 60 Sqn to overcome an embargo on 60° dive-bombing due to concerns about a Venom's chances of surviving the dive if one of its bombs were to hang up. The new method involved flying in close formation and simultaneously releasing all the bombs from 2,000 feet on the leader's command. Aiming was simply a question of tracking

The squadron's pilots in June 1956. From the left, back row:- Fg Off M E Y Holmes, Fg Off J H W Wilson, Fg Off J B Sullivan, Fg Off H R Walker, Fg Off D V King, Fg Off W E Close, Fg Off A M Eckel and F/Sgt Z Zmitrowicz. Front row:- Flt Lt G H Baker, Flt Lt P L Davis MC, Flt Lt W Topping, Sqn Ldr G S Cooper, Flt Lt J J Connors, Fg Off J R J Froud and Fg Off W J Armstrong. (W E Close)

"When I say, 'Drop 'em' - Drop 'em!" Level bombing from Venoms was only a problem for the leader; everyone else just punched them off when he did. WR277/S and WE469/O are seen here doing just that. (D Brereton)

towards the target until it passed through a line marked on the windscreen with a grease pencil. Primitive as this was, accuracy was still of the order of 75 yards, about double that of dive-bombing, but this delivery mode had the considerable advantage of being less easily disrupted by cloud.

On the training side there was a memorable incident during May in which the squadron's Venoms got mixed up with No 9 Sqn's Canberras in the circuit at night, which raised the adrenaline level a trifle, the engagement subsequently being refought at some length in the bar! There were two other notable incidents during the month. The first was on the 3rd when Fg Off Holmes was obliged to divert into Ipoh when his cockpit canopy shattered in flight. The second was more serious, SAC Blackmore being killed in a rearming accident on the ground. He was hit by the blast of a rocket motor which he inadvertently fired by connecting up the firing circuits on an armed, but unoccupied, aircraft without having first checked that the cockpit switches were all selected to 'safe'.

Having used only bombs on its operational sorties since March, June was notable for a return to tasking with cannon and rockets as well and for an overall increase in trade. Thirty-six sorties were flown, the largest and most complex strike being that mounted on the 18th which involved the squadron's positioning at Tengah to take part in a major effort against a target near Kluang in conjunction with Nos 9,

Although there was only one aircrew fatality during the squadron's time on Venoms, accidents were not infrequent. This is WR304/A looking somewhat the worse for wear after Fg Off Dave Proctor's abandoned take off on 6th August 1956. (H Osborne)

60, 1 RAAF and 14 RNZAF Sqns. June was a good month with lots of ops and plenty of flying; spirits were high and Fg Off King and F/Sgt Osborne organised an all ranks party, just to celebrate the fact that the squadron was feeling good. As a prelude to the serious drinking, there was an aircrew v groundcrew football match which the pilots allowed the airmen to win 5:1.

The Venom routine was well-established by now and although operational activity declined from the June level there was sufficient to keep a hard edge on the squadron's expertise in weapons delivery. The embargo on dive attacks had been lifted again (at least it had for small practice bombs) and there was a concentrated session of 60° dive-bombing practice in July during which, in a total of forty-four sorties, the squadron kept all of its bombs within fifty yards of the target. The squadron also had a go at live air-to-air gunnery - for the first time in over a year, and it showed. If nothing else, this exercise demonstrated quite conclusively that it was necessary to keep one's hand in if one expected to be able to hit the flag - at all!

After this the squadron experienced a run of bad luck. There were four incidents in five weeks which resulted in the loss of three aeroplanes and one pilot. The first incident, a relatively minor one, occurred on July 17th when WE465's nosewheel collapsed on landing. The damage was repairable and Flt Lt Wally Close was unhurt.

The second accident was much more serious. On July 24th WE373 made a high-speed run across the Range at an estimated height of about 50 feet before pulling up sharply. During the subsequent climb, which took the aeroplane up to about 4,000 feet, the pilot radioed that the aircraft was out of control and it was seen to be pitching violently and shedding pieces of debris. Fg Off F W T Hobson had undoubtedly overstressed his aircraft and he died when it crashed into the sea about 1,500 yards off Bidan Island. Although the squadron was saddened by this unnecessary loss, it would prove to be the only flying fatality that it suffered during its whole time on Venoms and, with hindsight, there was some comfort to be drawn from that.

The third incident occurred on August 6th when WR304's wingtip touched the ground just after it had become airborne; the aircraft careered across the airfield, writing itself off in the process. Fortunately it stayed in one piece and the pilot Fg Off Dave Proctor was able to walk away from it.

A third aeroplane was lost on August 21st when WE382 shed its canopy during a take off run. Fg Off P J Brockson abandoned the take off but the brakes could not cope and the aircraft overshot the runway into the sea. Harry Osborne, who was off duty at the time, was the first on the scene and he plunged into the sea to render assistance; he was relieved shortly afterwards to meet Brockson swimming in the opposite direction. Surveying the scene a little later the Station Commander, Gp Capt R E Baxter DFC, was alleged to have observed acidly that it was a "damned silly place to park an aeroplane."

Although it had not involved a Venom, this run of bad luck had actually begun on July 7th when a squadron pilot had had a very frightening experience in WL180, one of the Station Flight's Meteor F.8s. Dave Proctor had been flying inverted when the ejection seat drogue gun had fired of its

The squadron's original pair of trainers were replaced in late 1956. This is one of the new ones, B Flight's XH359/X, complete with dumb-bells. (No 45 Sqn archives)

own accord. This had fractured the canopy but the drogue had become entangled with the tail unit and, not having developed properly, had failed to fire the main seat gun. Proctor carried out a hasty landing with the drogue 'chute still wrapped around the Meteor's tail!

While ops continued at a moderate level, the next event of note was a Battle of Britain flypast over KL on September 15th which was flown by eight of the squadron's Venoms after which the CO did his solo aerobatics display. AVM Kyle carried out his Annual Formal Inspection in October and, as he was about to leave the station, the squadron put on a show. They flew past first in a diamond nine then did it again in a vic of three vics before running in for a third time in three echelons of three, line astern, for a break into a stream landing. It was very pretty and the AOC delayed his departure to offer his personal congratulations - or perhaps he had to as ATC would not let his aeroplane take off through the Venomous overcast! With all this formation flying and the CO's solo routine an aerobatic team was definitely in the offing.

Although the intensity of ops was nothing like it had been a few years earlier, the squadron was still committed to respond to short-notice tasking when necessary, and on October 13th it was. The requirement, which was received at Butterworth at 1000hrs, was for four aircraft which had to be prepared, armed and flown down to Tengah whence they were to fly a strike before returning to base. To be on the safe side, five aircraft were generated and despatched. The mission was flown as briefed and the last Venom landed back at Butterworth at 1915hrs where the groundcrew were waiting to put it to bed. It had been a long day - and a Saturday to boot!

Operation MUSKETEER, the Suez campaign, was launched at the end of October 1956 and the squadron was agog for news of how the MEAF Venom squadrons had fared, hoping to learn something from their experience, but beyond this the Egyptian fracas had little impact in distant Malaya. A far more pressing local matter was a visit to Butterworth on 31st October by the Duke of Edinburgh, hosted by the AOCinC, Air Marshal Sir Francis Fressanges. The squadron mounted an immaculate Guard of Honour, commanded by Flt Lt Baff, which provided an opportunity to parade the Standard. While all the marching about was going on, the rest of the squadron was hard at it preparing aeroplanes and later in the day a joint formation of sixteen Venoms drawn from the Flying Camels and the Tengah-based Kiwis flew in salute over the Royal Yacht *Britannia*. Since the station had had only forty-eight hours notice of HRH's visit it had been a good show all round.

A batch of new pilots arrived during November. Serviceability was particularly good in late 1956 so aeroplanes were plentiful and the newcomers had a very satisfactory introduction to the squadron. As it happened, a concentrated programme of day fighter activity had been planned with No 487 SU, so the new pilots were given an early and thorough grounding in interception techniques before working up to full-scale dogfights. All of this was supervised by the CO, along the lines taught at the Day Fighter Leaders' School (DFLS), ably assisted by Flt Lt Ron Plowman who had recently completed the DFLS course at West Raynham. So far as check rides were concerned, the new arrivals also had the luxury of being able to use the pair of replacement Vampire T.11s, XH359 and XD398, which had been taken on charge in September and October. These were the latest de luxe models, boasting such features as ejection seats and (almost) frameless 'see-through' canopies.

C Flight, the experimental rectification team, was disbanded on November 5th and its personnel were absorbed back into A and B Flights which continued to be run by F/Sgts Osborne and Morrell. The engineering side of the squadron was now running very smoothly and the outstanding aircraft availability was largely due to the efforts of the two flight sergeants. The squadron hit its peak in November 1956 when it flew just five minutes short of 573 hours. This was an all-time monthly record for the squadron's twenty-two years in Malaya and was all the more remarkable for having been achieved with such short-endurance aeroplanes. Feeling justifiably pleased with themselves again, the officers and NCOs took themselves off for a day out on Bidan Island where they defuelled a barrel or two of *Tiger*.

Two more aeroplanes were written off at about this time. In a very similar incident to Brockson's in August, WE465's

The squadron's first, and only, aerobatic team was up and running by early 1957. (No 45 Sqn archives)

canopy opened on take off on November 15th. Fg Off D V King retracted the undercarriage and brought matters to an abrupt halt; he was unhurt but the aeroplane was somewhat the worse for wear[4]. On December 3rd the recently arrived Plt Off G H Haddock sank back onto the runway immediately after take off, slithered off the end and finally came to rest in a paddy field, which put paid to WR281's flying career. Sadly it put paid to Haddock's as well. The AOC had been disturbed by the accident rate on his three Venom squadrons and decreed that the next person to bend one through pilot error would be on the next boat home; he was as good as his word[5].

To end the year with a bang there was a burst of air-to-air gunnery in December. Some 23,387 rounds were loosed off for an overall squadron average of 21.4% hits, the stars being Fg Off Bob Vass with 35% and the Boss with 30%. This added the final touches and the squadron ended 1956 in as sound a state as it had ever been. It was now regularly meeting its monthly flying targets; all of its pilots were rated and all were current in all weapons delivery modes and tactics. Even more satisfying was the fact that the squadron was now actively working up an aerobatic team, the first in the Flying Camels' long history.

With the security forces now gaining the upper hand, the air offensive had begun to wind down and when No 101 Sqn had returned to the UK in September 1956, after their second stint in Malaya, detachments under Operation MILEAGE had ceased. From 1957 the Canberras' place was taken by the occasional appearance of detachments of V-Bombers under Operation PROFITEER but they were far from being a permanent presence in FEAF and, although notionally available for tasking, they were never directly employed on FIREDOG ops. The big stick was now reduced to the ageing, but still very effective, Lincolns of No 1 Sqn RAAF.

WE475/F is seen here being refuelled on the new concrete pan which became available to the squadron at the beginning of 1957. As can be seen from the hangar going up in the background, there was a great deal of construction work going on at Butterworth at the time. (No 45 Sqn archives)

The aerobatic squad, from the left: Flt Lt W E Close, Flt Lt R N Baff, Fg Off K R Curtis, Sqn Ldr G S Cooper, Flt Lt F J Barrett, Fg Off C R Bainbridge. (W E Close)

As a result of the decline in activity, No 45 Sqn had flown no ops for two months, but this was made up for in January 1957 when the squadron flew twenty-eight sorties in the course of five strikes. It should be noted that since mid-1956 some of the squadron's operations had actually been 'pseudo-strikes'. MRLA-related incidents were now so infrequent that there were prolonged periods during which little air support was called for. When this occurred, to keep the squadrons (and the whole tasking chain from the foot patrol in the jungle up to the JOC and back down to the flying units) in practice, dummy strikes were occasionally mounted against targets of no direct significance, such as an old CT camp or an abandoned cultivated clearing. Apart from serving to keep the CTs' heads down, there was little chance of inflicting any real damage on the MRLA on these sorties but, this aside, the whole procedure was conducted as a genuine operation, including the use of live weapons.

There were some noteworthy changes in the squadron's organisational and domestic arrangements during January 1957, starting with Flt Lt John Barrett's taking over A Flight from Ron Plowman and Flt Lt Bob Baff succeeding Jimmy Connors as OC B Flight. Since 1956 the engineers of the RAAF's No 2 Airfield Construction Squadron had been working at Butterworth to transform it into a modern airfield which was eventually to be transferred to Australian administration. This programme involved considerable refurbishment and extension of the paved surfaces and in January 1957 a new concrete hardstanding was brought into use. It was a little cramped at first as the contractors had yet to complete the finishing touches but, having worked from PSP ever since the squadron had arrived at Butterworth, it was a luxury for the groundcrew to be able to work on a proper dispersal.

With so little trade in the strike game, the squadron's efforts were increasingly concentrated on air defence and the training routine, in conjunction with No 487 SU, consisted largely of broadcast control exercises, high-level ciné attacks and tactical intercepts with No 60 Sqn. As an indication of the level of activity, the squadron carried out 131 practice interceptions (PI) in March. Led by Bob Baff, the aerobatic team was making good progress too and by this time it had finalised its display sequence and had been cleared down to 3,000 feet.

Exercise TRADEWIND took place in April and on the 17th the squadron defended Butterworth against attacks by the Gannets of HMAS *Melbourne*. The intruders were all intercepted and 'shot down' about thirty miles out but the Aussies pressed on regardless and the groundcrew were treated to the spectacle of their Venoms harassing the enemy as they flew across the airfield.

A bit more colour was added to the Venoms in April. To complement the red and white markings on the tailbooms, the wingtip tanks were painted blue, with the noses and tails in white connected by a white bar, ie as close to a dumb-bell as the tank's shape would permit. In the middle of the bar, the classic Flying Camel motif made its reappearance in red. By this time the aeroplanes had all been allocated an individual code letter which was painted on their fins in white. The aeroplanes now looked very smart and the squadron was ready for the display season. The air display circuit in the 1950s was nothing like as intensive as it is today, however, and in the Far East it was almost non-existent. In fact there was only one venue in 1957 and that was to be at Brunei where a new airport was to be opened. The AOC kept the promise he had made a year before and gave the display task to No 45 Sqn, so the CO and the team leader flew to Labuan and back between 4th and 6th April to carry out a recce and set up the arrangements.

Under the overall command of Gp Capt Ronnie Baxter, the fifteen-man groundcrew support team plus Flt Lt Proctor, as reserve pilot/commentator, and an air traffic controller, left for Tengah on May 6th and flew on to Labuan via Kuching courtesy of a Valetta of No 110 Sqn and a Bristol 'Vibrator' of No 41 Sqn RNZAF. On the 7th the five primary aircraft

Aircraft	Pilot	Remarks
WR300/H	Sqn Ldr G S Cooper	Solo
WR277/S	Flt Lt R N Baff	Team Leader
WR350/Q	Flt Lt W E Close	
WK476/E	Flt Lt F J Barrett	
WK486/N	Fg Off K R Curtis	

Fig 17.2. No 45 Sqn's contribution to Brunei airport's opening ceremony, 8th May 1957.

In June 1957 the availability of a vast stretch of concrete provided the opportunity to recreate the clockface first portrayed by the squadron's Fairey IIIFs in 1930, thereby establishing a tradition that has been maintained ever since. (No 45 Sqn archives)

listed at Figure 17.2 flew to Labuan, also staging through Kuching. A sixth aeroplane and pilot (WE449 and Fg Off C R Bainbridge) remained at Tengah as a reserve.

As Brunei's runway was not cleared for jets, Labuan was to be the operating base for the detachment. After a shortrehearsal by two aircraft on the afternoon of the 7th, the formal display was carried out on the 8th before HH the Sultan of Brunei and a small but admiring public. It began with eleven minutes of formation aerobatics culminating in a 'bomb-burst'. This was immediately followed by Geoff Cooper's four minute solo demonstration which included a symbolic touch-and-go to christen the runway. The CO then joined up with the team and all five Venoms signed off by smoking across the airfield in a high-speed run. The display was a great success, the local press making reference to the watching crowds having been "enthralled" and the CO's display having been "breathtaking". The pilots were subsequently flown back to Brunei in the RNZAF Freighter to be entertained by the Sultan that evening, eventually being returned to Labuan in his private yacht. The detachment returned to Butterworth on the 9th, flying all three stages in a single day. Almost as impressive as the display itself had been the performance of the groundcrews in keeping the aeroplanes going; all five had flown seven sorties in four days with limited back-up and no failures, in fact the two aircraft used for the rehearsal had each flown eight times.

The month was rounded off by a live strike on the 27th, the first for some time. It was a short-notice affair, a party of

WK486/N being refuelled at Kuching on its way to Labuan, 7th May 1957. (H Osborne)

about fifty CTs having been spotted about to cross the border into Thailand at Kulim. Seven Venoms were en route to the target area within an hour of the task having been received.

Apart from two more strikes, June 1957 seems to have consisted largely of demonstration flights. AVM Kyle relinquished his post as AOC Malaya that month and, as he left Butterworth on the 6th at the conclusion of his final formal visit to the station, the squadron provided him with a twelve-aircraft flypast. When he sailed from Singapore on the SS *Canton* a day or two later, another farewell flypast was laid on by units based on the island. This was neat enough, if a trifle pedestrian, and 'Wally' Kyle advised his companions to wait until they were a little further north. The Flying Camels had their turn as the ship approached Penang on the 12th. As Geoff Cooper describes it:

The squadron gave him the full treatment with a

The squadron provided many flypasts with its Venoms. Here they are seen starting up on 12th June 1957 to salute the departing AOC No 224 Gp. (No 45 Sqn archives)

flypast of nine in a diamond formation followed by a quick individual and formation aerobatics sequence finishing with a 'bomb-burst' over the ship. The pilots went aboard in the evening for a farewell drink - draught English beer for a change - and the AVM admitted that, although he had told his fellow passengers to expect something worth seeing, he had not bargained on quite such a spectacular show!

The Queen's Official Birthday was celebrated the next day and nine of the squadron's Venoms rendezvoused with another nine from No 14 Sqn RNZAF over Port Dickson so that Sqn Ldr Cooper could lead the whole lot in a high-speed flypast across a parade at KL at 0804hrs. They were next required to be over Georgetown (on Penang Island) at 0830hrs as their parade began. A second formation comprising four more of No 45 Sqn's Venoms, plus one of their Vampire T.11s and three Meteors from the Station Flight, flew over the Georgetown parade again at 0840hrs. The specified timing accuracy had been +/-5 seconds throughout; all the appointments were kept exactly as

Venom swansong: the squadron's second generation aerobatic team "slips the surly bonds of Earth on laughter silvered wings" in October 1957. Leader - Sqn Ldr G S Cooper; No 2 - Flt Lt T F Copleston; No 3 - Fg Off B E StClair; No 4 - Fg Off K R Curtis. (No 45 Sqn archives)

scheduled. The final flypast of the month took place on the 25th when five aircraft were put up in honour of a visit by the AOCinC; that was an easy one.

The security forces now definitely had the upper hand but the CTs were nothing if not dogged and the pressure had to be kept on. All thirty-eight operational sorties flown during July were to harass groups of the MRLA withdrawing towards the Thai border. Operation FIREDOG was to smoulder on for another three years and by the time that it ended the squadron would have been re-equipped yet again. In July it was learned that re-equipment was to be handled rather differently this time. Rather than converting the existing aircrew, as had been done in the past, an entirely new air echelon was to be formed at Coningsby with Canberras. They would then fly the squadron's new aeroplanes out to Tengah, where the reconstituted squadron was to be based. None of the Venom pilots would be staying but most of the current groundcrew were to remain on board, which would mean moving them down to Singapore. From now on the squadron could expect to have its Venoms progressively withdrawn, and there would be no more new pilots.

The slow run-down of the squadron began in August and, on the 28th, Flt Lt J H Badham made his personal contribution to reducing the size of the Venom fleet when WK477's brakes failed on landing and he was obliged to retract its undercarriage to persuade it to stop. The pilots began to thin out too. Flt Lt C A Charman and Fg Off A C Grafham were the first to go, being transferred to the Far East Transport Wing at Changi. Flt Lt Baff was posted to the Far East Communications Squadron as a CIRE, Flt Lt T F Copleston taking over B Flight. Flt Lt Wally Close also left in August, returning to the UK 'tourex', accompanied by Fg Off Colin Bainbridge who was to attend a PAI course. Another sign of the times was the granting of full independence to Malaya whose freedom was proclaimed on August 31st. Since FIREDOG meant that there was still such a strong British presence as to be potentially embarrassing to the newly independent nation, however, it was considered inappropriate to overstress this and military participation in the celebrations was kept at a discreet level; there were no flypasts.

One strike was ordered in September but poor weather intervened and it was cancelled. Pilots continued to drift away; Flt Lt R T A Innes returned to England and Flt Lt Barrett transferred to No 60 Sqn to fill a flight commander slot. This left Flt Lt Trevor Copleston as the sole flight commander to co-ordinate the day-to-day activities of the rapidly dwindling squadron. During October the Venom fleet shrank to nine aeroplanes, two of the others having been withdrawn when they reached the end of the Venom's notional lifespan of 750 flying hours[6]. F/Sgt R G Ferrier and three tradesmen left Butterworth that month to start setting up the new squadron at Tengah.

Despite the steady erosion of its strength, the squadron kept on flying and training. Eighteen operational strike sorties were flown in October and, during a session of live air-to-air gunnery at 20,000 feet, Fg Off B E StClair notched up the remarkable score of 45% hits against a twenty-five foot banner. On the 18th, the new AOC, AVM V E Hancock, paid his first visit to Butterworth. The heady days of twelve-ship Venom formations were now over but the squadron still managed to field eight, to which were added the squadron's Vampire and another from the Station Flight plus a Meteor T.7 and an F.8 from the same source - it was a bit "Pick 'n' Mix", but the AOC got his due.

The squadron went out with a bang, not a whimper, flying nine operational sorties on the 4th and 11th Nov-ember. In the course of these it dropped sixteen 1,000 pounders and fired 950 cannon shells. In fact, with just seven available aircraft, against a target of 110 hours, the squadron flew 157 hours in its last two weeks. No 45 Sqn's

WR353/T cruises over an area of paddy to the east of Butterworth; note the abrupt change to dense forest at the edge of the cultivated area. (No 45 Sqn archives)

Venoms made their last flights on 15th November 1957. In the morning Flt Lt Coplestone led a farewell formation over HQ 224 Gp at KL[7]. That afternoon the squadron treated Butterworth to one last aerobatics demon-stration; the pilots were the CO, Flt Lt Coplestone and Fg Offs Curtis and StClair.

On November 22nd the bulk of the squadron's groundcrew boarded a Hastings and two Valettas to be flown down to Tengah where they were welcomed by the Station Commander, Gp Capt R J F Prichard OBE DFC. A handful of married men, earmarked to remain with the squadron, stayed on at Butterworth to await the availability of married quarters in Singapore and another small group, comprising two SNCOs and twenty-four corporals and airmen, were transferred to Technical Wing and left the squadron. Of the remaining aircrew, Sqn Ldr Cooper went to HQ 224 Gp (he was eventually to retire as Air Commodore G S Cooper OBE and was for eleven years thereafter the air correspondent of the *Daily Telegraph*); Flt Lt Coplestone and Fg Offs Curtis, StClair, McGregor and Badham were posted to No 60 Sqn while Flt Lt Proctor and Fg Offs Jude, King, Franks and Baxter remained at Butterworth pending their return to the UK.

The Venom era had been a very satisfactory one. Since Sqn Ldr Jacobs had made its inaugural Venom flight in September 1955 the squadron had flown a further 6,975 trips totalling 7,747 flying hours. In addition to the weapons expended on ops (see Annex G) the squadron had dropped 2,691 25 lb practice bombs and fired 2,166 concrete-headed RPs and 125,371 rounds of 20mm ammunition during training flights.

It would have been difficult to have devised a more difficult start to the squadron's initial experience with jets, but under Viv Jacobs it had overcome the divided loyalties which had been an inevitable result of the misguided idea of marrying two active squadrons and then expecting the unit to reflect two identities. He had also seen the squadron through its conversion from piston-engines to jets in time to hand over to Geoff Cooper, who had then built the squadron up on

Venoms to a peak of efficiency. It seemed a shame to run the unit down again but the Venom's airframe had a relatively short life and there were no more available. It had to be.

Notes:

1. It is interesting to note that when No 45 Sqn began to receive its Hornets in February 1952 it was the last squadron in the RAF to re-equip with piston-engined single-seat fighters. Since it was also the last squadron to fly propeller-driven fighters it can claim the distinction of having added at least a couple of significant footnotes to the overall history of the service. It had embodied the end of an era.

2. No 27 APC had effectively been run in conjunction with FETS, its major customer, since the latter's transfer to Butterworth from Seletar in August 1954. When FETS closed down on 31st March 1955, No 27 APC was disestablished as well, only to re-emerge the following day redesignated as APC (Butterworth). It operated as such until it too closed down on 1st May 1956. Thereafter each station assumed direct responsibility for providing weapons training for its resident squadrons, using the Ranges at Song Song and China Rock and the facilities offered by the Target-Towing Flight based at Seletar (later Changi).

3. Only four of the Venoms issued to the squadron could be regarded as having been new when they were taken on charge. Most had already seen service with a variety of units, including the CFE and Nos 6, 16, 32, 73, 98, 118 and 266 Sqns, and had been operated from West Raynham, and a variety of bases in Germany, Malta, Cyprus, Jordan and Iraq.

4. After leaving the RAF, Fg Off Dave King pursued a successful career in commercial aviation and became managing director of his own aircraft brokerage firm of DK Aviation.

5. The author recalls spotting a stranger wearing a squadron tie in the bar of the Officers' Mess at Tengah in 1964. On being challenged he explained that he was a fighter controller from Bukit Gombak but that he had previously been a pilot with the squadron at Butterworth. He recounted a graphic tale about a less than successful take off in a Venom which had finished up slithering across a paddy field and bisecting a buffalo with which a local peasant farmer had been ploughing his watery furrow. It was a colourful yarn, which may have gained a little in the time that had elapsed since the incident had occurred, but it was universally agreed to be worth a beer and to entitle the teller to wear his tie.

6. An aeroplane's lifespan is virtually infinite if sufficient resources are invested in maintaining it and in replacing components as they become time-expired. To the RAF, however, the Venom had never been more than an interim type and with the Hunter becoming available in large numbers in the late 1950s there was little to be gained from diverting cash and effort into sustaining a fleet of obsolescent aeroplanes. The Swiss saw it differently, however, and by paying meticulous attention to maintenance and restricting utilisation, the Flugwaffe kept its Venoms flying until well into the 1980s.

7. AHQ Malaya had been redesignated HQ 224 Gp on 31st August 1957.

Chapter 18. The Silver Fleet - Canberra B.2s.

While the Flying Camels were running down as a Venom squadron in the sunshine, heat and humidity of Malaya, a new No 45 Sqn was beginning to take shape in the fog, cold and damp of Lincolnshire under the leadership of Sqn Ldr C C Blount MVO. To supplement the ex-Venom groundcrews, who were then moving from Butterworth to Tengah, a small group of Canberra-trained technicians began to assemble at Coningsby during November 1957. The first four complete aircrews were formally taken on strength on November 18th and, pending receipt of sufficient bombers, they kept their hands in on the Canberra T.4s of the Bomber Command Holding Unit. The squadron's first B.2, WJ983, was taken on charge on November 20th and the plot was for each of the first four aeroplanes to be flown for ten hours to iron out any wrinkles before they set off together for Singapore.

Enough aircrew had arrived to permit a second flight to be formed on December 2nd. Their aeroplanes were due to be delivered on the 9th and they were scheduled to follow the first team on the 16th but the programme soon began to slip. One of the second batch of aeroplanes, WH874, was already at Coningsby, but needed a new cockpit canopy before it could be accepted, and there were delays in the delivery of the rest. The next one, WH646, did not arrive from Colerne until December 16th to be followed by WH665 from Aston Down on the 20th and WJ567 from Colerne on the 30th.

In the meantime the first flight was ready to go and it left Coningsby on December 9th; its composition is listed at Figure 18.1. One additional pilot, Fg Off K A Ball, accompanied this first team, hitching a ride in WH853. Their route took them via Idris, Akrotiri, Bahrein and Karachi to Katunayake (the squadron's old base of Negombo which had since reverted to its original name). Here, on the 13th,

WH853 was delayed for twenty-four hours. The others pressed on but as they crossed the Indian Ocean WJ983 developed an oxygen leak and WJ570 a fuel leak. All three aeroplanes diverted into Butterworth to top up with fuel so that they could fly the final stage down to Tengah at a reasonable height. As they approached Singapore the formation entered cloud and WJ983 and WH882 collided. Sqn Ldr Blount and Fg Off Buchan ejected and escaped with only superficial injuries but Flt Lt Hall, Flt Lt Hartley, MNav Brown and F/Sgt Stevens were all killed. The wreckage of both aircraft fell near Pontian. It was a tragic beginning to a new era.

Back in the UK the second flight, composed as at Figure 18.1, finally had all its aeroplanes in working order and they set off for sunnier climes on 11th January 1958. They had a trouble-free passage and reached at Tengah on the 16th. In the meantime flying had already begun in Singapore using a T.4, WH706, and the first of the surviving pair of the original B.2s. This aeroplane emerged from its post-ferry servicing on January 8th to be joined by its companion two days later. By the end of the month the balance of the squadron had been 'trooped out' from the UK by air and its strength stood at twenty-one officers and airmen aircrew, eight SNCOs and eighty corporals and airmen, the majority of the latter being the ex-Butterworth brigade. The immediate aim was to have the squadron fully acclimatised and worked up by 1st May on which date it was to be declared operational.

FEAF had not had Canberras permanently on its strength before and it been well over a year since the last of the Operation MILEAGE detachments had returned to the UK, so the squadron needed to establish the best way of employing their aircraft themselves. By this time No 1 Sqn RAAF had accumulated over seven years of experience of bomber operations in support of FIREDOG but their Lincolns were shortly to be withdrawn so, before they left, several of the squadron's aircrew flew with them and picked their brains for any tactical tricks that they might usefully be able to play with their rather different aeroplanes.

Strikes were frequently flown in conjunction with No 656 Sqn and several of the squadron's aircrew accepted the offer of a trip in their Auster AOP 6s. One or two of the Canberra men felt that they were lowering themselves a little by going for a ride in these very basic little aeroplanes but by the time that they landed after an exhilarating low-flying trip they had the deepest respect for the capabilities of the pilots of the Army Air Corps. Flt Lt Chris Webster recalls that in a long flying career the hair on the back of his neck literally stood up only twice. One of those occasions was during a flight with No 656 Sqn when the pilot, flying his aeroplane only just

The second flight of Canberras parked on the ramp at Idris on 11th January 1958 on their way out to Singapore. (No 45 Sqn archives)

Aircraft	Pilot	Nav	Nav
Crews and aircraft of the first flight to leave the UK, 9th December 1957.			
WJ983	Sqn Ldr C C Blount MVO	Flt Lt H Hartley	Fg Off F N Buchan
WH882	Flt Lt L G Hall	MNav D M Brown	F/Sgt E E Stevens
WJ570	Flt Lt M R Bishop	Fg Off P J Rourke	Fg Off R J Marchant
WH853	Fg Off J Hardstaff	F/Sgt T Robinson	Sgt P B Nowell
Crews and aircraft of the second flight to leave the UK, 11th January 1958.			
WH665	Flt Lt R E Abbott	Flt Lt R C W Stokes	Flt Lt C M F Webster
WH874	F/Sgt A Ross DFC	F/Sgt J R Denney	F/Sgt L A C Kennedy
WH646	Fg Off I Bashall	Flt Lt S D Rogers	Fg Off A L Leslie-Miller
WJ567	Fg Off R J Oltmann	Fg Off I D Symonds	Sgt M Oxley

Fig 18.1. The original eight Canberra B.2s of No 45 Sqn and the crews who ferried them from the UK to Singapore.

above the surface of a river, continued to follow it upstream as it narrowed and the jungle closed in from each side. Eventually they were flying through a green tunnel with the sky above obscured. Whether this was sensible is debatable, but there is no doubt that it was impressive.

Formation flying began in February and the first practice bombing mission was flown on the 7th. The available fleet was temporarily reduced by one aeroplane on February 12th when Fg Off Hardstaff switched WJ570's Master Safety Switch 'on' without having first checked that the groundcrew had left all the tits and knobs 'off'. Unfortunately they hadn't and there was a loud bang as the explosive bolts jettisoned the canopy! Despite this minor setback, a week later the squadron flew its first full-scale dummy FIREDOG mission, complete with an Auster target marker. On the 28th it flew all six of its Canberras in concert with the Venoms of Nos 14 Sqn RNZAF and No 60 Sqn in an 'attack' on some RN ships. This event proved to be rather more exciting than had been anticipated. The navy was firing break-up shot but as the bombers ran in the colour of the smoke changed. The formation leader called the flotilla on the safety frequency, just to check that all was in order. It wasn't. Some live ammunition had been fed into the hoists in error and, since the shells were short-fused, the ships were being peppered with their own shrapnel. In fact the problem was already being sorted out and the rest of the 'engagement' took place without incident, the only damage being some chipped paintwork on one or two of Her Majesty's Ships.

By this time the squadron was settling in well. It was organised on a two-flight basis; Flt Lt Abbott commanded A Flight and ran the flying side of the unit while Flt Lt Bishop had B Flight and was responsible for the unit's airmen. The squadron had not had an Engineering Officer of its own since 1947 and the advent of the relatively large and complex Canberra made no difference. For deep servicing the aircraft were passed to Technical Wing or to No 389 MU but day to day engineering matters were supervised by F/Sgt Tam Ferrier. By the end of the month a new Flying Camel identity had clearly begun to emerge and this was advertised by the appearance of the squadron's motif on the fins of its aeroplanes in the form of a classic red-winged blue camel on a white disc. This camel, which always faced forwards, was quite a graceful beast and most closely resembled in style the original version as used on the Vernons in the 1920s. At first the emblem was relatively small but it grew steadily and by 1960 the pale blue-outlined white disc was occupying as much of the fin as was practical. Otherwise the aircraft were in the then standard bomber scheme of High-Speed Silver overall.

Most of the aircrew were already experienced on type and many knew each other from previous tours. This helped the shake-down programme to proceed both rapidly and smoothly and encouraged the warm 'family' atmosphere which soon developed. A curious feature of the squadron's first batch of Canberra men was that they were unusually tall, with Ian Bashall being a veritable giant at 6'7". Out of

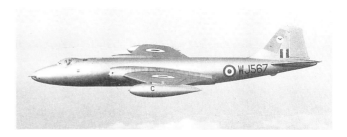

WJ567 at altitude over Malaya wearing the original small version of the squadron's badge on its fin. (No 45 Sqn archives)

curiosity, they arranged themselves by height one day and Chris Webster, at a respectable 5'11" was surprised to find himself only twelfth in line. A particularly useful member of the community was Fg Off Fred Leslie-Miller. As a child he had been in Sumatra when the Japanese invaded and his parents had been interned for the duration. Fred lived with local villagers and virtually 'went native'. As a result he spoke fluent Malay and when out on the town in Singapore he would sometimes startle a truculent waiter who had muttered some epithet by rounding on him and firing a broadside of gutter invective in his own tongue.

To begin with, the squadron's dispersal was at the south-eastern end of the long-disused pre-war runway. Apart from the CO, who lived in No 1 Hangar, the squadron's line huts and offices were a bunch of tents and some fairly dilapidated buildings alongside the aircraft parking area. The dispersal was rather cramped and whenever one of the Canberras was attempting to manoeuvre its way in or out, the huts tended to be blasted by the efflux from the engines, redistributing any loose papers and shaking down all manner of lizards, spiders and creepy-crawlies from the atap roofs.

A notable characteristic of the Canberra B.2 was that, when fully fuelled and loaded with bombs, it was only just balanced; it was quite possible to lift the nosewheel off the ground with one hand. As a result one could often see daylight under the nosewheel if an aeroplane taxied too fast on an uneven surface; harsh braking also needed to be avoided as the recoil from an overcompressed nosewheel oleo could also lead to problems with a heavily laden aeroplane. This delicacy of balance meant that it was essential to ensure that the fuel tanks, which were in the upper fuselage above the bomb bay, were always filled

Arming Canberras of No 45 Sqn for a strike in mid-1958. This picture was taken on the squadron's initial temporary dispersal at the south east end of the old pre-war runway; some of the tented 'offices' can be seen in the background. (No 45 Sqn archives)

starting from the front. Starting from the back with No 3 would inevitably result in the aeroplane's tipping gracefully back onto its tail bumper. Although this rarely did any real damage, it could be relied upon to create lots of fuss and was, to say the least, highly embarrassing for those concerned. All of this is not to say that the Canberra was a problem on the ground, only that it needed to be treated with a reasonable degree of respect. Tail-sitting Canberras were hardly an everyday sight at Tengah - but it did happen at least once. There was a variation on this theme early in the B.2 era when an aeroplane had a starter cartridge explode on start-up. Shrapnel punctured the No 1 tank and fuel began to drain out. As the tank emptied, the centre of gravity shifted inexorably backwards and the aeroplane very gently sat back on its tail. This left the groundcrew with an aeroplane with six live bombs in its belly, parked with its nose in the air in a lake of AVTUR. Not a bad tactical problem and the squadron's redoubtable aviators withdrew to a safe distance to watch the groundcrew solve it.

The squadron did not need all the time that it had been allocated to become fully operational and during a detachment to Butterworth between 17th and 22nd March it began to fly live FIREDOG strikes. The first mission, Operation GINGER, was led by the CO on the 18th and involved four aircraft, each of which dropped six 500 lb bombs. By the end of the month the squadron had racked up forty-three operational sorties during which it had delivered 110,000 lbs of bombs.

Conversion to Canberras had significantly increased the squadron's striking power. Its new aeroplanes could lift a considerable weight of bombs, carry them a long way, fly very high and go very fast. For all that, however, a Canberra crew could no more see terrorists in the jungle than those flying Beaufighters had been able to ten years before. Apart from visual aiming, which was rarely employed as targets were rarely discernible, the squadron employed three basic methods of bombing.

The first was the Flare Datum Technique. This required the crews to measure the precise track and distance to be flown between the known position of a party of soldiers on the ground and the target. Neither was likely to be visible but this was overcome by the soldiers igniting a flare at a predetermined time. This would provide the crews with something to aim at. The idea was to cross this datum already on track at the required bombing height, and with the bomb bay doors open. Thereafter no corrections could be made and it was simply a matter of maintaining heading, speed, height and attitude as accurately as possible for a precalculated time and then releasing the bombs into the jungle. Bombs were usually delivered from about 12,000 feet so the weather was a factor as it was necessary to be able to see the flare. The system was inherently inaccurate and was of real use only against area targets, the bombers flying on slightly diverging tracks to scatter the bombs within a one kilometre square.

A more accurate method of assisted bombing employed a Target Director Post (TDP). A TDP was based on a gun-laying radar adapted from its original role to work in the reverse sense - instead of aiming at the aeroplanes it was used to guide them[1]. Knowing both its own position and that of the target, the TDP was able to project a narrow beam of energy across the aiming point. The bomber would be flown over the transmitter at about 12,000 feet and then continue outbound towards the target. Knowing the aircraft's speed and height, and after making appropriate adjustments for the wind and the ballistic characteristics of the bombs, it was possible for the TDP to 'aim off' the beam, to allow for cross-trail, and calculate the forward throw of the weapons and thus the release point. Maintaining the prebriefed speed and height, the pilot followed heading corrections passed from the ground to keep the aircraft 'on the beam'; when the release point was reached the bombs were dropped in response to an instruction from the TDP. From the pilot's point of view it was much the same as following the bomb-aimer's instructions on a visual bombing run, the only difference being that the bomb-aimer was not in the aeroplane.

There were only two such radars in Malaya but their range and mobility was such that a blind bombing service could be provided virtually anywhere. The only significant drawback was that, if it was necessary to move the TDP, it could be slow to respond. The radar was a relatively cumbersome piece of kit and, depending on the distance involved, it could take up to two days to reach its new location, survey the site, set up the transmitter and then go through the process of levelling, tuning and calibration to achieve the desired accuracy. Nevertheless this system permitted reasonably accurate attacks to be carried out against unseen targets and it was independent of the weather.

A well-known picture of WH853 dropping four 500 pounders. The aeroplane was being flown by Fg Off Ian Bashall who, at 6'7", may well have been the RAF's tallest pilot at that time (No 45 Sqn archives)

388

This four-ship, comprising WH853 (nearest the camera), WH667 (leading), WH874 and WH665 (in the box) was flown on 1st July 1958 to mark No 45 Sqn's taking over the role of FEAF's primary strike unit from the Lincolns of No 1 Sqn RAAF. (No 45 Sqn archives)

The third and most exciting method of bombing was Auster marking. The bombers would fly to a prearranged Initial Point (IP), ideally sufficiently far away to be out of earshot of the CTs to preserve the element of surprise, and co-ordinate the final details of the attack with the Auster over the radio. The Auster, whose pilot already knew the precise location of the target, quite possibly having located it himself on a previous reconnaissance sortie, would be orbiting at another prebriefed position. Allowing for the differences in speed between the Auster and the Canberras, the aircraft would leave their respective positions and head for the target, the idea being to arrange matters so that the Auster flew across the target at about 90° to the bombers' track a few seconds before the latter arrived, marking the target with smoke as he passed. The trick was to spot the Auster on its run in and then aim for the point at which it pulled up after dipping its nose to drop the marker. With luck, smoke would begin to percolate through the trees in time for last minute adjustments to made but, if not, the bottom of the Auster's dive trajectory served as a makeshift point to aim at. Auster marking was quite a demanding exercise for all concerned and as a result was very satisfying. It permitted precision surprise attacks to be carried out at fairly short notice against targets that would otherwise be invisible to the bombers, but it required reasonable weather as it was necessary to be able to see the target from a typical bombing height, when delivering 500 pounders, of about 4,000 feet.

April 1958 was significant for the squadron's first participation in a SEATO[2] training event, Exercise VAYABUT. VAYABUT involved the detachment of four aircraft to Don Muang (Bangkok) from 21st to 26th April. Finding four aeroplanes might have been a problem had the squadron not already received WH667 and WJ632 as replacements to restore its strength to eight B.2s. By this time FIREDOG ops had become routine, a further thirty sorties being flown during April. Some of these missions were slightly unusual in that they were not planned as precision strikes. Operation BINTANG on April 30th, for instance, was not intended to kill CTs so much as to harass them, which involved six aeroplanes, operating as singletons at half-hourly intervals, dropping bombs in the Tualang area.

The receipt of Avro Triple-Carriers in May permitted the squadron to start carrying 1,000 pounders and training with these began almost immediately, seventy-two being dropped while a further 36,000 lbs of 500 pounders were dropped on operational missions. The squadron was effectively taken off ops in the middle of May to complete its final work-up before it formally relieved No 1 Sqn RAAF which was scheduled to be withdrawn from operations in July. To emulate the Lincolns meant flying in somewhat unwieldy five-aircraft formations and some time had to be spent perfecting this technique. A few trial sorties demonstrated that doing this in the dark was an unrealistic proposition and to achieve a satisfactory bombing concentration by night the squadron eventually elected to fly in line-astern at 30 second intervals. All this formation practice was useful preparation for the Queen's Birthday Flypast which was to be flown in conjunction with Venoms of No 60 Sqn and Meteors of No 81 Sqn but, although the rehearsal went well enough, poor weather on June 12th meant that the actual event had to be cancelled.

The Lincolns flew back to Australia as planned in July and No 45 Sqn took their place as FEAF's 'big stick'. They were formally reassigned to FIREDOG ops and, thenceforth were required to maintain five crews at six-hours' readiness. To mark the squadron's assuming the role of the primary strike unit, a four-ship formation (Sqn Ldr Blount - WH667; Fg Off Bashall - WH853; Fg Off Oltmann - WH874 and Flt Lt Abbott - WH665) was put up on the 1st for an air-to-air photography session with a Vampire T.11. The departure of the Australians permitted the squadron to take over their far more satisfactory facilities. The unit's offices were now in newer and more substantial huts than those with which it had originally had to make do and its aircraft were parked on the broad expanse of concrete which had previously been the Lincoln flightline.

Although No 1 Sqn had gone home, as had No 14 Sqn, the 'ANZACs' had not withdrawn from FIREDOG, or from their obligations to SEATO. The original squadrons were to be replaced by two more units, No 2(B) Sqn RAAF and No 75 Sqn RNZAF. The former was to be stationed at Butterworth[3] with Australian-built Canberra B.20s while the latter was to operate from Tengah with Canberra B.2s leased from the UK. During July and August the Flying Camels spent some time liaising with the advance parties from the new squadrons to show them the ropes.

Forty-nine sorties were flown in July but this dropped off sharply to just five in August and the intensity of tasking remained at a similarly low level for the rest of the year. In fact the squadron had hit its stride with Canberras just as FIREDOG was entering its terminal phase. As a result the squadron's staple activity became practice bombing. Some of the squadron's earliest bombing practice had been carried out on Raffles Range, a naval off-shore gunnery facility to the south of Singapore, but this had proved to be unsatisfactory as there was little room for manoeuvre without infringing Indonesian airspace. Song Song Range became available to Canberras in August and the squadron used it for the first time on the 6th. It was still a long haul up to Penang and back, however, even in a Canberra, and most academic bombing practice and bomb sight calibration was carried out at China Rock. Apart from bombing there was a steady demand for the squadron to participate in ceremonial flypasts and on August 31st the squadron put up a five aircraft formation over KL to mark the first anniversary of Malaya's independence - Merdeka Day.

With the significant decline in the intensity of FIREDOG ops it was no longer crucial for HQ 224 Gp to be at KL and, since Malaya had now been independent for a year, it was considered to be politically tidier for the HQ to be withdrawn to Singapore, which was still a British colony. Despite the inevitable upheaval caused by this move the AOC, AVM V E Hancock CBE DFC RAAF, found time to come to Tengah on 11th August to review a formal parade and beating of the retreat to mark No 45 Sqn's completion of ten consecutive years of FIREDOG operations. In his subsequent address the AOC acknowledged the considerable contribution that No 45 Sqn had made to the long drawn out campaign and made brief reference to the squadron's forthcoming new role. On September 20th the squadron was required to stage a six-ship flypast over the Governor's Residence and five of them went on to repay the AOC's compliments by flying in salute over his new HQ at Seletar.

The new role of which the AOC had spoken was the reassignment of the squadron from local tactical operations to more broadly-based strategic deterrence. The three Canberra squadrons available to FEAF were to form the core of the Commonwealth Strategic Reserve, the creation of which was an indication that, with the parochial FIREDOG campaign virtually over, the wider implications of the Cold War in the Far East were beginning to take precedence.

Led by the Flying Camels, No 2(B) Sqn RAAF flew its first FIREDOG mission, against a target near Ipoh, on 3rd September. On the 30th, in conjunction with both No 45 Sqn and the Australians, No 75 Sqn RNZAF flew its first strike, the target being in northern Perak. The Strategic Reserve was now up and running. Although all three bomber squadrons could still be tasked with FIREDOG missions when required, the demand for short-notice anti-CT work was now so small that it was sufficient for just one squadron to be held at readiness and from then on the three squadrons took it in turns to be on stand-by on a monthly rota.

It is interesting to note that during September 1958 the squadron had dropped sixty 1,000 pounders but that this had involved only ten sorties. It is a measure of the considerable increase in offensive capability conferred by the Canberra that to have delivered 60,000 lbs of bombs would typically have required sixty Hornet sorties, thirty by Venoms or twenty by Brigands.

The squadron lost an aeroplane on 18th November when one of WH853's engines failed shortly after take off and the pilot was obliged to ditch in Kranji Creek, just to the north of the airfield. Only Fg Off Ivan Symonds, one of the navs, survived. His colleague, Fg Off Brian Casling was killed by the impact; the pilot Flt Lt John Rolfe, appears to have survived and to have vacated the wreck but, with both ankles broken, he subsequently drowned. This highlighted a significant inadequacy in the Canberra's safety equipment. It had ejection seats, but they were of an early model and their operating envelope did not permit them to be used when the aircraft was low or slow. Seats capable of being used at ground level were becoming available at this time but it was to be several years before they were installed in Canberras.

The widening of the squadron's horizons was marked by an increase in the number of long-range navigation exercises being flown and from September these began to include occasional landaways at Labuan. In November the squadron mounted its first ever trip to Australia when Flt Lts Bashall and Cullum and Fg Off Rourke flew down to Darwin via Labuan on the 26th, returning via Changi the following day. Lone Rangers[4] were introduced in December, the usual destinations being either Katunayake or Kai Tak. The first Hong Kong trip was undertaken in the T.4 which flew via Clark Field in the Philippines. WH706, which had been flown up on 11th November by Wg Cdr A E Cross AFC RAAF (Wg Cdr Ops/Trg at HQ FEAF) and Fg Offs P deA Atkinson and G W Pollard, promptly went unserviceable and the crew managed to prolong their jaunt until the 18th before flying back minus the wing commander who had already returned to Singapore by other means. In fact serviceability was beginning to be a problem back at Tengah too as the squadron was running about 20% light on groundcrew. Nevertheless it had been able to fly one operational mission, a joint No 45/2(B)/75 Sqn affair on 8th December against one of the few remaining bands of terrorists in hiding in northern Selangor.

The wreckage of WH853 following an engine failure shortly after take off on 18th November 1958. Fg Off Symonds survived but Flt Lt Rolfe and Fg Off Casling were both killed.
(No 45 Sqn archives)

By January 1959 the squadron was fully engaged in training for its strategic role and the routine consisted of navexes, lots of high-level bombing, air defence exercises for the benefit of the fighters plus the occasional Ranger. In February a Canberra was flown down to Wigram to assess the feasibility of adding New Zealand to the squadron's list of possible destinations. Although

In February 1959 WH665 was flown down to New Zealand to investigate the possibility of its becoming a regular destination for overseas training flights; it is seen here at Wigram. (No 45 Sqn archives).

WH665 was one of No 45 Sqn's aeroplanes the crew was rather a job lot, only the pilot, Flt Lt Abbott, actually belonging to the squadron. The other two crew members were Wg Cdr E Garrad-Cole from HQ 224 Gp's Air Staff and Flt Lt J I Davies, Tengah's Station Navigation Officer. They were away from the 6th to the 18th and shortly after they returned, on the 23rd, the T.4 was used to fly Wg Cdr Cross up to Kai Tak again. Unfortunately for the crew, this time the aeroplane kept going and it was back at Tengah on the 25th.

There was a spot of excitement in February when, at 0200hrs on the 3rd, the Orderly Officer was woken to be informed that an emergency consignment of drugs was on its way to Tengah and that they were to be flown to Ceylon as soon as possible. F/Sgt Ferrier was called out and within half an hour he had nine men preparing an aircraft. The drugs were delivered to Tengah at 0415hrs and twenty-five minutes later Flt Lts Abbott, Rourke and Marchant were airborne in WJ981, next stop Katunayake.

There were a number of demands for flypasts at this time and the squadron participated in three in early 1959. The first two were station affairs (Nos 45, 60, 81 and 75 RNZAF Sqns) for a visit by the CAS, MRAF Sir Dermot Boyle on January 16th and for HRH the Duke of Edinburgh on February 23rd. The third was an all-Canberra formation when three aircraft from each of the three squadrons flew over the harbour in salute as the Duke sailed from Singapore on the Royal Yacht *Britannia*.

On March 1st three aircraft were detached to Don Muang for nine days to participate in SEATO's Exercise AIR PROGRESS. It went well enough apart from a sortie on the 4th when one of WJ981's main undercarriage legs declined to lower. It was flying with only a two-man crew, Sqn Ldr Blount and Flt Lt Pordham, and the CO elected to make a belly landing which turned out to be as uneventful as such an incident can be. Once the aircraft had been jacked up and its reluctant wheel

pumped down, the damage appeared to be fairly superficial and largely confined to the bomb-bay doors. After a judicious application of 'speed-tape' the CO eventually flew the aeroplane back to Singapore. Here it was ascertained that the aeroplane had been rather more badly bent than had been immediately apparent; it was passed to No 389 MU who took several months to beat it back into shape but in the fullness of time WJ981 reappeared on the squadron's flight line at Tengah. This aeroplane was unusual for a B.2 at that time, and unique in FEAF, in that it wore a tactical Dark Green and Dark Sea Grey camouflage scheme rather than being silver like the rest of the fleet.

The RAF/USAF liaison programme which had begun in the days of Hornets and B-29s was still running and still using the nickname JOSSTICK. Now that the squadron had some long-legged aeroplanes, however, it was able to play away for the first time and on April 1st four aircraft were detached to Clark Field in the Philippines. Here they spent ten days working alongside the USAF, which included flying several practice bombing sorties on the Crow Valley Range. Clark Field was an immense base and the Americans employed some of the indigenous Negrido Indians to police its perimeter. These aboriginal tribesmen were armed with their own primitive weapons which they used, on occasion with lethal effect, to deter intruders. At one of the many social gatherings during the detachment the Americans presented the squadron with an Indian bow and arrow as a memento of their visit. As they left the hostelry at the end of a very convivial evening, Chris Blount, who evidently fancied

WJ981, parked rather embarrassingly in the middle of Don Muang's runway by Sqn Ldr Chris Blount, after its undercarriage had malfunctioned on 4th March 1959. This aeroplane was one of relatively few B.2s to wear a tactical camouflage scheme; it was the only one on No 45 Sqn. (No 45 Sqn archives)

The squadron's aircrew as at 17th May 1959. From the left, front row: Flt Lt P J Rourke, Flt Lt J M Cole, Flt Lt E Pordham, Flt Lt R J Oltmann, Flt Lt I Bashall, Flt Lt J Hardstaff, Flt Lt G Dack DFC, Sqn Ldr C C Blount MVO, Flt Lt C H F Webster, Flt Lt R C W Stokes, Flt Lt A D Ashworth, Flt Lt F N Buchan, Fg Off K A Ball, Fg Off G W Pollard and Flt Lt V K Metcalf. Back row: MPlt A Ross DFC, F/Sgt M Oxley, Sgt P Elton, Flt Lt S D Rogers, Fg Off J Cumming, Flt Lt R J Marchant, Fg Off A L Leslie-Miller, Flt Lt J H Bosher, F/Sgt T Robinson, Sgt P B Nowell, F/Sgt D Irwin and F/Sgt E R Culley. (A D Ashworth)

himself as some kind of oriental Robin Hood, used the bow to 'shoot' a stag featured in a decorative painting. He was compounding the damage by trying to retrieve his arrow when the manager turned up. At this point his excessively-Merry Men rapidly melted away into the darkness giggling, leaving the CO to talk his way out of that particular corner alone.

Shortly after their return to Tengah a group of aircrew were playing with the bow outside the crewroom but it had a remarkable pull and no one was able to flex it more than about 18 inches. Not to be outdone Dick Oltmann lay on his back and by using his feet managed to flex the weapon to its full extent. Inevitably, someone fitted the arrow and it was let fly. It soared into the air and disappeared from sight to fall to earth they knew not where. They soon found out, however, when the telephone rang. At the other end was an aggrieved voice with a strong New Zealand accent which complained, "Hey! Tell your blokes to stop shooting arrows at our blokes!" The arrow had come down some 400 yards away, narrowly missing a group of airmen working on No 75 Sqn's flightline. Since Oltmann was a South African, most of the squadron put the whole business down to a display of colonial immaturity - but they never got their arrow back.

Apart from these diversions some productive training was also carried out in April including participation in Exercise SEA DEMON which involved the squadron being held at a high state of readiness and then being scrambled to mount dummy attacks on a combined RN/RAN/USN Task Force.

There was a concerted effort to enhance the squadron's bombing during May. In general new crews started bombing at 20,000 feet and then worked upwards in increments of 5,000 feet. This involved a number of landaways and night-stops at Butterworth while Song Song Range was given a fairly comprehensive working over. Despite the whole Canberra fleet's being grounded for several days while an elevator problem was investigated and resolved, the squadron ended the month with one crew cleared to bomb from 40,000

feet and two others at 35,000 feet.

The last Lone Rangers had been to Ceylon in January and Hong Kong in February but after that they had dried up. Possibly as a subtle hint to remind HQ 224 Gp that the Canberra could go quite a long way, MPlt Ross flew an endurance trial in June and managed to stay airborne for five hours and seventeen minutes, which was not at all bad for a B.2. It is not known whether this actually did the trick but in July Don Muang was added to the list of possible destinations. Although they were better than nothing, the crews felt mildly short-changed by these Bangkok trips as they were only landaways, not nightstops, and thus did not afford time for the delights of that city to be explored. There was another JOSSTICK in July. This time the squadron played host to the B-57s of the USAF's 13th Bombardment Squadron (BS) which flew down from Japan. As well as providing frequent opportunities for 'exchanges of operational views' in suitably convivial surroundings, a certain amount of training flying was also carried out and many of the navs were able to fly in each other's aeroplanes.

A ferry programme began in July when the first aircraft was flown back to the UK for a partial refit which included the installation of Godfrey air coolers in an attempt to improve the cockpit environment. They were not much help. The problem was that the Canberra's large canopy acted rather like a lens and, once the door was shut and the locally-produced bamboo and canvas sunshades had been removed, the cockpit temperature rapidly rose well above the already high ambient temperature. Even when the new air coolers became available they were really only effective when the engines were running at high rpm, which did not occur until the aeroplane began its take off run and by that time the crew was already drenched with sweat. If the ensuing trip was flown at high-level, the usual case until 1962, the cabin temperature would rapidly fall to well below zero; the rubber bladder, which acted as the ejection seat cushion and contained an emergency water supply, soon froze and the

One of those unavoidable chores, the AOC's Annual Formal Inspection, in this case at Tengah in 1959. AVM V E Hancock CBE DFC RAAF, shakes hands with Fg Off Roger Marchant; Fg Off John Cumming is on the left and Flt Lt Arthur Ashworth on the right. On the extreme right of the picture is OC No 45 Sqn, Sqn Ldr Chris Blount. 'Kiwi' Ashworth was one of a mere handful of people who have managed to do two stints with the squadron; he first became a Flying Camel at Butterworth in May 1955, on transfer from No 33 Sqn, and flew Hornets, Vampires, Meteors and Venoms until the end of that year then, after a tour on Canberras in the UK, he flew with the squadron again from October 1958 until March 1961. (A D Ashworth)

high humidity caused a frost to form all over the inside of the cabin. After an hour or two of sitting on blocks of ice (which tended to substantiate the rumoured high incidence of piles among Canberra crews!) the aircraft would commence its descent towards Tengah. As it lost height the temperature rose, the frost melted and it 'rained' all over the crew, especially the navs.

At intervals throughout the Canberra era 'flying doctors' from the Institute of Aviation Medicine at Farnborough visited and flew with the squadron, sometimes togged up in outlandish outfits incorporating a variety of thermometers which measured the temperature of the body in all sorts of intimate places. Clutching their sets of Noritake china and camphorwood chests, they always returned to the UK tut-tutting and looking concerned but the problem was never really solved. Canberra flying in FEAF was always a hot, cold, wet and sticky business.

Another innovation introduced in July 1959 was the installation of modified, windowless, hatches for the navigators' compartment which were equipped with a mounting for periscopic sextants. These did not last too long, however, as one of these hatches, which were frangible to permit ejection through them (rather than having to jettison them first), partially imploded in 1961. Although alarming, the incident was not critical and the aeroplane flew back to base with a somewhat concave roof in place of the normally convex variety. The original metal hatches, which had two small windows, were reinstalled[5].

Mention of sextants raises the question of navigation in the Canberra. The early versions of the aircraft were equipped for Bomber Command operations in the European theatre and their primary navigation and bombing aids were GEE and GEE-H, respectively. The necessary ground installations to support these systems did not exist in the Far East, however, so high-level navigation consisted of an air plot, monitored by bearings from the Marconi radio compass (or 'Cunim Homer') and ranges from REBECCA/EUREKA, using the handful of beacons which were scattered thinly around the region. It was also possible to request bearings from a few airfields, but only if the aircraft did not venture too far from land as the B.2 had only VHF radio which was limited in range and once the aircraft disappeared 'over the horizon' it was out of radio contact in any case.

Some use was made of astro but, as the aircraft lacked an autopilot, and its inst-rumentation did not permit the accurate assessment of speed and heading changes, it was not possible to calculate acceleration errors, which began to become significant at the Canberra's operating speed. The acquisition of periscopic sextants improved matters slightly for a while, but when these were withdrawn again the navs had to revert to taking sights with a hand-held bubble sextant while crouching beneath the pilot's canopy with its highly distorting double-glazing. This was hardly a satisfactory arrangement although it sufficed for heading checks. At one stage a concerted effort was made to calibrate the canopies of all the aircraft by taking a series of simultaneous shots on the ground with one nav inside the aircraft and one outside. At the end of the exercise everyone repaired to the Nav Office to plot out the results. The average of all the sights taken conclusively proved that Tengah was actually some twenty-four miles away from the position indicated on what had previously been considered to be quite reliable charts.

Many of the navigators found a 'dangleometer' (a home-made device which, combined with a knowledge of the aircraft's altitude, permitted an assessment of range from an identifiable object on the ground) a very useful adjunct to the navigation suite. All things considered, apart from the speeds and altitudes involved (and the cramped accommodation), a Wellington navigator in 1942 would not have been too unfamiliar with the navigation techniques employed twenty years later by No 45 Sqn on its Canberra B.2s - such is progress[6].

Whatever it had been, the problem that had caused the recent interruption in the allocation of Lone Rangers seemed to have been solved by August and two crews were able to get away to Katunayake. August was also notable for the squadron's flying its first FIREDOG strikes since the previous December. Although the campaign would not be formally terminated for another year, these sorties would turn out to be No 45 Sqn's last contribution to it, joint missions being flown with the Australians and New Zealanders on the 13th and 17th. The alleged camps were hit, No 45 Sqn alone

Aircraft	Pilot	Nav	Nav
WH646	Sqn Ldr C C Blount	Flt Lt R C W Stokes	F/Sgt M Oxley
WJ570	Flt Lt G Dack	Flt Lt J H Bosher	Flt Lt P G Hannam
WH874	Flt Lt V K Metcalf	Flt Lt J M Cole	MNav E R Culley

Fig 18.2. The aircraft and crews which, on 17th August 1959, flew No 45 Sqn's last Operation FIREDOG mission.

delivering a total of 36,000 lbs of bombs, but there had been no sign of the CTs being in residence. The participants in the Flying Camels' last operational FIREDOG mission are listed at Figure 18.2.

In September an STI called for the undercarriages of the entire Canberra fleet to be subjected to an X-Ray examination. Three of the squadron's aeroplanes proved to have cracks in the so-called 'Epstein forging' and this kept them on the ground for the next four weeks. Despite the temporary shortage of aeroplanes, the squadron was still able to participate in a major air defence exercise during which it was intercepted by Venoms from Tengah, Sabres from Butterworth and Sea Hawks from HMS *Centaur*. The Canberra's ceiling was considerably in excess of that of all these aeroplanes so they could easily have avoided interception by 'attacking' at well above 40,000 feet. But air defence exercises are usually arranged by the air defence staff who have a vested interest in demonstrating the effectiveness of their system. As a result the flight profiles for bombers participating in FEAF's ADEXs always stacked the cards so that the fighters could at least reach the intruders and the Canberras were usually required to drone in at altitudes as low as 28,000 feet.

A significant symptom of the new deterrent role of FEAF's bomber squadrons was the introduction in October 1959 of a Bomber Command-style crew classification scheme. Under this system a crew was expected to be rated as 'Combat' within three months of arrival. Thereafter it would progress through 'Combat*' (expressed as Combat Star), 'Select' and, possibly, reach 'Select*' towards the end of its tour. Each upgrade required the fulfilment of a specified training quota within a six month period, progressively higher standards of accuracy in navigation and bombing being demanded at each stage. In a burst of initial enthusiasm it was decided to hold an inter-squadron competition in November to sharpen up the bombing. Each crew was actually to bomb from its maximum classified height but the results would then be factored by the air staff at Group, who claimed to know how to do such things, to present the results at a common standard of 30,000 feet. The Flying Camels won the three-cornered contest, the best individual crew being Sqn Ldr Blount, Flt Lt Webster and Flt Stokes whose stick of six 1,000 pounders neatly straddled China Rock.

With the demand for FIREDOG ops now virtually non-existent, HQ 224 Gp introduced occasional dummy missions to ensure that the system did not fall into decay, in much the same way as they had done during lulls in tasking when the squadron had been flying Venoms. These practice sorties were flown very much as the real thing and the first, on November 6th, involved the squadron putting up two waves of four aircraft each, each carrying six 500 pounders. There was another one on December 17th when three aircraft each dropped six 1,000 lb bombs, but thereafter even practice missions ceased.

It had been a long time since the squadron had celebrated the wedding of one of its officers so the festive season was given a good start when Fg Off E G Rivers married Miss Maureen Stevenson on December 20th. To supplement the traditional Airmen's Christmas Dinner and the various Mess functions, the aircrew awarded themselves a squadron party in the Chicken Inn in Singapore and there was an all-ranks barbecue as well.

By early 1960 training had become a routine with the highlights being provided by the continuing UK-ferry programme, day trips to Don Muang and weekend Rangers to Kai Tak which was reached via a refuelling stop at Clark Field. In fact the squadron was settling down to what was to become a prolonged stint of 'garrison duty' and, in essence, the 1960s at Tengah were to be very similar to the 1930s at Helwan. The squadron was required to maintain proficiency in its role, to show the flag around the region (via Lone Rangers and participation in SEATO exercises), to provide ceremonial flypasts and to react to local disturbances as and when they occurred. All of which is exactly what they had done with their Fairey IIIFs.

The first local disturbance to occur was self-inflicted; the airfield underwent a major facelift. Beginning in 1960 a large-scale civil engineering programme was put in hand that would take well over a year to complete. The most significant feature would be the remodelling of the airfield itself, which involved the levelling of a fairly substantial hill to the north west. What had originally been the main north/south runway was to become merely a part of the parallel taxi-track to a new 3,000 yard long V-bomber class runway. Accompanying this was a considerable upgrade in the domestic and support facilities including new bomb storage facilities, a new Operations Block, a new Air Traffic Control tower, a new church, additional accommodation and even, on a selective basis, some air conditioning. Perhaps surprisingly, all of this was done with the squadrons still in residence and using the original runway as the new one took shape alongside it (see plan at Annex B).

There were two major air/sea exercises in early 1960. The first, Exercise JETEX on February 16th, involved two attacks against HMS *Centaur* and HMS *Belfast*, which were defended by the carrier's Sea Hawks and Sea Venoms. The squadron's initial attack was carried out at a relatively high level and was successfully intercepted by the defenders but they got through at low-level on their next attempt. The second maritime event, Exercise SEA LION, was flown on May 11th and involved the squadron attacking a

WJ630 displays the later, and much larger, Flying Camel which was progressively introduced during 1960. (via P H T Green)

large group of ships including the carriers HMS *Albion*, HMAS *Melbourne* and the USS *Bon Homme Richard* which were accompanied by a number of transports and screened by a covering force of destroyers.

The squadron took part in several flypasts early in the year. The first, on February 10th, involved three aircraft from each of the three Canberra squadrons and was to celebrate the coronation of the Sultan of Johore. The second, on April 3rd, was a larger affair, led by Sqn Ldr Blount with three of No 45 Sqn's aircraft, to mark the death of the nominal King of Malaya, the Yang di Pertuan Agong. In 1960 Hong Kong celebrated the Queen's Birthday on its true date (21st April) and four aeroplanes were detached to Kai Tak on the 19th to lend some weight to the proceedings. The Canberras flew back to Tengah on the 22nd but, as it had proved impossible to lay on a dedicated Hastings to recover the accompanying party of groundcrew, they had to endure the hardship of an enforced week's stopover in Hong Kong before being flown back to Singapore in a scheduled Transport Command aircraft.

The only other events of note in the first half of the year were an aerial recce of Kuantan airfield in February and some early exploratory work on low-level bombing techniques, including shallow-dive attacks, in April. In May the squadron's maintenance system was converted to 'progressive servicing' as a result of which, after a gap of some thirteen years, it acquired its own engineering officer again. In fact the status of the senior 'spanner' had already been raised from flight sergeant to warrant officer when WO E B Jane had succeeded Tam Ferrier in November 1959. The first incumbent of the newly re-established officer post was Fg Off P T E Ryans who was posted in from Seletar. A warrant officer remained on strength for sometime thereafter, however, and between 1960 and 1963 these were successively WOs Swift, Thompson and West.

Chris Blount had now been in command for over two years and it was time for him to hand over to his successor; on May 26th Sqn Ldr J W Valentine became CO. The flight commander had also changed, Flt Lt D A V Clark now occupying that slot. June 11th was the Queen's Official Birthday and a squadron contingent paraded at Seletar while the usual trios of Canberras from each squadron flew over in salute with the Flying Camels in the lead.

The exploratory flight to New Zealand, which had been carried out as long ago as February 1959, had finally born fruit and it had been agreed that Combat* crews could undertake New Zealand Lone Rangers (NZLR). From then onwards an NZLR was regarded as the best perk of a tour with No 45 Sqn. Because the squadron's aircrew had all arrived together, however, it had been necessary to shorten some people's tours and lengthen those of others to avoid everyone having to be replaced at once. The instability which this had caused had prevented much progress being made with the classification scheme and as at the end of June the squadron had just one Combat* crew; five others were Combat and three, which were either newly arrived or had been reconstituted, were unclassified. The squadron's first NZLR was flown by its only qualified crew, Flt Lts V K Metcalf, E Pordham and J M Cole, in WJ567 between 6th and 15th July. The route to Ohakea involved intermediate stops at Darwin and Amberley; the trip was made in company

The impressive outcrop of Lion Rock dominates the Kai Tak flightline and four of No 45 Sqn's Canberras, WJ567, WJ648, WD948 and WJ632. The date was 21st April 1960 and the occasion: the flypast for the Queen's Birthday. The first Canberra of No 45 Sqn to visit Hong Kong had arrived in November 1958, thereafter it became an increasingly frequent port of call until it almost became a second home in 1969. (via P H T Green)

with single aeroplanes from Nos 2(B) and 75 Sqns, with the Australians leading the way as the RAAF's B.20s were fitted with a doppler radar (GREEN SATIN) which enabled them to determine an accurate wind velocity and relay it to the crews of the B.2s over the radio.

The State of Emergency in Malaya was declared to be over on 31st July 1960 and with it Operation FIREDOG virtually came to an end[7]. Early the following day the squadron sent four aeroplanes up to Butterworth where they later took part in a flypast by seventy aircraft of the RAF, RAAF, RMAF and RNZAF to mark the occasion. No 45 Sqn was the only unit to have been committed to FIREDOG in an offensive role from start to finish and over the twelve years it had flown 4,335 sorties[8]; there could be no doubt that the Flying Camels had earned their place in the formation.

WJ667 exhibited a classic Canberra fault on August 2nd when its undercarriage retraction mechanism malfunctioned, permitting one mainwheel bay door to close before the wheel was in place, leaving the leg folded but jammed outside the aeroplane. There was no answer to this one and Fg Off M Randle had the dubious honour of carrying out No 45 Sqn's first belly-landing at night for many years, a feat which he

Lone Rangers to New Zealand were introduced in 1960 and by the end of that year three had been flown. This picture shows F/Sgt Doug Irwin, Sgt Pete Elton and MNav Ed Culley after landing back at Tengah following one of these productive and intensive training events (or jaunts). (No 45 Sqn archives)

pulled off with considerable success.

Having begun with a spot of excitement, the rest of August proved to be quite busy too. On the training side there was an interesting ADEX, which involved HMS *Eagle's* Air Group and there were three landaways, including a Bangkok Ranger and another to Hong Kong; sadly the latter got stuck at Clark Field and eventually had to return from there directly, without the crew's having done its shopping.

The third overseas trip was on the 27th when the CO flew down to Darwin with Fg Off Neil McFarlane and Flt Lt Peter Ryans, the squadron's 'plumber', to spy out the land for a forthcoming exercise which was to be held in Australia. This was the first time that one of the squadron's aeroplanes had ventured away from base with a bomb bay tank fitted. Pete Ryans recalls that this created a potentially sensitive situation as the tank made it necessary to carry a pair of 1,000 pounders to keep the aircraft's CofG within reasonable bounds. The transit flight was largely through Indonesian airspace and, since diplomatic relations with Sukarno's regime were only lukewarm, there was no telling how the local authorities might have reacted to the presence of an armed British bomber if the crew had been obliged to divert; fortunately, the trip was uneventful so they never found out. Interesting as the prospect of an exercise in Australia was, however, of the activities undertaken during August those having the greatest long term significance were the squadron's first experiments in sustained low-level operations.

Within the RAF the concept of the unarmed bomber, largely dependent for its survival on its high performance, had been introduced by the Fairey Fox and this philosophy had subsequently been sustained by types such as the Hart, the Mosquito, the Canberra and the V-bombers. Incremental increases in performance and the addition of electronic countermeasures had enabled the bomber to maintain an edge over defensive fighters since 1945 but a new weapon system, the surface-to-air missile (SAM), which had the potential to shift the balance permanently in favour of the defence, had been under development over the same period. The shooting down of Gary Powers' U-2 over the USSR on 1st May 1959 represented a very public proclamation that the SAM had finally matured and was now a real threat to prospective intruders. It was no coincidence that, a year later, Flt Lt Collins and Flt Lt Utton were examining the implications of operating No 45 Sqn's Canberras at low level over Malaya.

The West had, of course, been well aware of the progress being made by the Soviets and in the same timeframe had begun to deploy their own first-generation SAMs, Bloodhound, Thunderbird and Sea Slug in the British case. It had also long been appreciated by the RAF that the best way to avoid detection by radar was to operate at low level but now that radars had effectively been given teeth this was no longer an option; it was essential. Low-level trials with Canberras had begun as early as 1952 and had led to the entry into service of the interim B(I) 6 variant in 1955 and the definitive B(I) 8 the following year. These, however, were essentially low-level interdictors in the tradition of the Boston and Mosquito and as such their introduction was hardly an innovation. What was revolutionary was the wholesale adoption by 1963 of low-level tactics by the RAF's entire

strike/attack force, strategic as well as tactical. Bomber Command's rapidly shrinking force of Canberras had begun to adopt low-level tactics from 1958 and by 1960 the new gospel was spreading eastward to Cyprus and Singapore. What was needed, however, was a rather more capable Canberra than the B.2, with a beefed up airframe to withstand the buffeting of low-level flight and, hopefully, something useful in the way of a navigation fit. This need was to be satisfied by the B.15 and B.16 variants which were to emerge in 1961 but, in the meantime, the overseas squadrons were tentatively seeing what they could do with their old B.2s and B.6s.

The latter part of 1960 was a very satisfactory period for the Flying Camels. To begin with, the squadron flew 325 hours in September; the first time it had exceeded its monthly task for over a year. On the 3rd it contributed four aircraft to a flypast over KL on the occasion of the State Funeral of the Yang di Pertuan Agong. Rangers were now a frequent feature of the flying programme and before the year was out there had been two more NZLRs, four crews had had weekends in Kai Tak and several more had been able to snatch a hasty lunch in the airport terminal at Bangkok. JOSSTICK VII had taken place at Tengah between 23rd and 31st October with the squadron playing host to the B-57 crews of the 8th BS.

The most significant event, however, was Exercise NIGHTGLOW which took place at Darwin from 7th to the 21st November. This was a joint affair with each of FEAF's Canberra squadrons fielding three aircraft. No 45 Sqn's groundcrew party and a fourth crew were flown down and back in a Britannia. It was quickly discovered that Darwin was not the most comfortable of bases in the early 1960s. Most of the buildings were raised on stilts to provide a suitable habitat underneath for all manner of nasty creatures, which temporarily included some of the squadron's detachment! The more fortunate ones were under canvas. Nevertheless, despite these privations, the exercise, which was essentially a period of concentrated bombing training, was considered to have been both enjoyable and a success.

The first notable event of 1961 was a brief grounding of the aeroplanes while a malfunction in the circuits controlling the jettisoning of the nav's hatch was sorted out. Sitting on the ground in the high humidity did the aeroplanes no good at all and once they were cleared to fly again they exhibited the inevitable list of electrical snags which disrupted planned flying for a while.

Tengah's new runway became available for use in March and the Station Commander, Gp Capt J E S Morton, christened it on the 11th by making the first take off. As was only right and proper, he chose to fly an aircraft from the station's best squadron to make this inaugural trip; lest there be any doubt, this was a Canberra of No 45 Sqn. Four days later the squadron made its usual three-aircraft contribution to an all-Canberra flypast over Paya Lebar airport on the occasion of the Singapore Air Show.

The last few days of April 1961 were quite hectic. With the airfield reconstruction programme approaching completion HQ Flying Wing moved into its palatial new air-conditioned Ops Block. This left the offices along the front of No 1 hangar empty and these were taken over by the squadron's aircrew, permitting the groundcrew to spread

The squadron's officers and aircrew in April 1961. From the left, front row: Fg Off L C Warren, Fg Off G D Armitage, Flt Lt P T E Ryans (EngO), Flt Lt D T A Lansley, Flt Lt D A V Clark, Sqn Ldr J W Valentine, Flt Lt K H Utton, Flt Lt D Collins, Flt Lt J J Walker, Flt Lt G Thompson and Flt Lt J T Miles. Middle row: Flt Lt E G Rivers, Fg Off P Langdown, Flt Lt K Allsop, Fg Off B A Balding, Flt Lt A S Wotherspoon, Flt Lt M J Dawson, Fg Off M J Moy, Flt Lt A R Pinches, F/Sgt J E Cochrane and F/Sgt P Mountain. Back row: Fg Off N McFarlane, Sgt P Elton, MNav T F Gostelow, Flt Lt E B C Gwinnell, Fg Off M Randle, Fg Off K C Carter, Fg Off D J Milne, F/Sgt D Irwin, Mnav G D Ross and MNav E B Culley. (No 45 Sqn archives)

themselves out a bit in the original hutted accommodation. The Queen's Birthday was celebrated on the 21st by a ceremonial flypast over Seletar, the standard three vics of Canberras being joined this time by Meteor NF 14s of No 60 Sqn and some RAAF Sabres from Butterworth. On the 25th the squadron took part in Exercise PONY EXPRESS with the RN and the next day four aircraft set off on a JOSSTICK.

The squadron's opposite numbers in the USAF were the Yokota-based B-57s of the 3rd Bombardment Wing (BW), two of whose constituent units, the 8th and 13th BSs, had already visited Tengah. Unfortunately treaty provisions precluded RAF combat aircraft from landing in Japan itself so the venue for JOSSTICK VIII was to be Kadena Air Base (AB) on Okinawa. The squadron was to be hosted by the third of the 3rd BW's units, the 90th BS, which sent a detachment down to join them. Since both squadrons were effectively playing away, the locally based 67th Tactical Fighter Squadron (TFS) extended its hospitality to both units which included the provision of some rides in their F-100Fs. After a thoroughly enjoyable stay the groundcrew were collected by a pair of Hastings and the whole detachment was back at Tengah by May 5th, several of the aircrew ostentatiously sporting 'Mach Buster' pins on their flying suits.

It is interesting to note that the process of centralisation which, so far as the Flying Camels was concerned had begun back in 1946, was still going on. In June 1961 the squadron numbered thirty-one officers and airmen aircrew but its groundcrew strength had declined to just seven SNCOs and fifty-seven corporals and airmen; only 72% of its strength when the squadron had first begun flying Canberras only three years before. Fortunately, although Tengah had several squadrons, they all flew different types so No 45 Sqn escaped

the ultimate degradation which was inherent in the plans of the centralisers[9].

There was another ADEX in June and the squadron was given the opportunity to attack HMS *Victorious*, which provided them with their first confrontations with the FAA's smart new Sea Vixens and Scimitars. No 60 Sqn to be re-equipped with Javelins at about this time and its new aeroplanes were to be flown out from the UK. To provide navigational assistance to the fighters, two of No 45 Sqn's aircraft, WH874 and WJ567, left for Karachi on June 28th. They got back to Tengah on July 13th; just in time for their crews to attend a particularly memorable squadron barbecue, an 'all-ranks-with-wives' affair which was held on Changi Beach the following evening. Operation GILMER, the support of the Javelin ferry programme, was to become a regular commitment over the next few months; Flt Lt (later Wg Cdr) Mike Dawson took part in the second deployment and describes what was involved:

We left Tengah on 28th July, reaching Karachi on the 29th (overnighting in Rangoon). We stayed there for three days until the Javelins arrived and then departed on August 1st. The fighters had to make frequent refuelling stops but it was so arranged that the Canberras only landed at alternate stops - in other words the two Canberras leapfrogged each other down the route. According to my log book, my aircraft progressed as follows: 1st August - Karachi to Delhi; 3rd August - Delhi to Benares to Calcutta; 5th August - Calcutta to Rangoon; 6th August - Rangoon to Bangkok and 7th August - Bangkok to Butterworth to Tengah. On the 5th, just after we had left Calcutta, one of the Javelins crashed in the Ganges delta. We got caught up in that

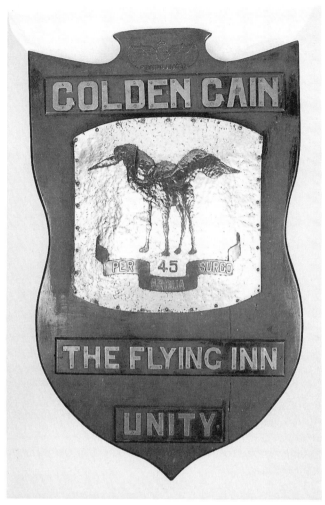

Ian Matheson's splendid memento of Vernons which was acquired by the squadron in August 1961. (No 45 Sqn archives)

Fg Off A R Pinches, Flt Lt E B C Gwinnell and Flt Lt M J Dawson in the spring of 1961. On 27th November Mike Dawson was made up to squadron leader and became OC No 45 Sqn - the first navigator to be formally appointed to command the Flying Camels - and thus far the only one. (M J Dawson)

incident forming a radio link with a British Airways (as was) aircraft.

By late August No 60 Sqn's conversion was sufficiently advanced for them to start participating in exercises. ADEXs were now a regular fixture on the training calendar, cropping up at roughly two-monthly intervals, and the Flying Camels encountered Javelins for the first time during an exercise held on the 29th. Although the flow of Javelins was drying up by this time, the squadron was now required to provide a similar service for batches of Hunters which were being flown out to equip No 20 Sqn which was to be reformed at Tengah on September 1st. On August 28th two Canberras were sent up to Calcutta to await the first group.

It will be recalled that when Ian Matheson left the squadron in 1924 he had taken with him the nameplate and the aluminium and copper Flying Camel badge from *Golden Gain* plus the nameplates from *Flying Inn* and *Unity*. These, all mounted on a wooden shield, eventually resurfaced in Matheson's cottage at Nigg in 1960 and passed into the hands of Mr Stout, the landlord of the St Duthus Hotel in Tain, for use as a pub decoration. The Deputy Assistant Provost Marshal for that part of Scotland, Sqn Ldr Graves, spotted the shield and suspected that it probably originated with an RAF unit. Mr Stout, being ex-RAF himself, was sympathetic and amenable to releasing his recently acquired artefact provided a more appropriate home could be found for it. Sqn Ldr Graves contacted the *RAF News* which agreed to carry the story and 'Jock' Valentine quickly claimed the shield for the squadron. It arrived at Tengah in August 1961 and this splendid memento has been among the squadron's most prized possessions ever since.

Three aircraft were detached to Darwin between 18th and 29th September to take part in Exercise NIGHTGLOW II. This allowed the participating crews to catch up on their bombing but problems with range availability in Malaya meant that most of the others were well behind with their weapons training. The situation was exacerbated by the frequent commitment of two aeroplanes, a quarter of the squadron's total strength and about half of that which was routinely available, to Operation GILMER. This ferry-support programme, which had been running since June, would not finally end until the last pair of Canberras returned to Tengah in November.

On October 26th a stream of Canberras at ten-minute intervals flew up to Song Song Range for a night bombing exercise. On the way the leader reported over the radio a rapidly building 'cunim'. Ten minutes later No 2 confirmed this report, adding that the cloud's top was almost at his cruising height of some 40,000 feet. When No 3, one of No 75 Sqn's aeroplanes, reached the area he reported that the top of the cloud was above him. Nothing more was heard from this aircraft and it failed to return to base. A search was mounted for the wreckage which was not found for five and a half days. The aircraft had entered the cloud which had proved to be extremely turbulent and control had been lost. There were only two men on board and both had ejected. The pilot eventually walked out of the jungle but the navigator had been killed. From then on cloud was treated with the greatest respect in FEAF, by all aircrew, not just those on Canberras, and, where large cunims were involved, the standing brief was to go around them or turn back.

Although it had been an essential task, participation in the search for the missing New Zealanders had created yet another diversion from the routine business of training. The upshot was that, while a great deal of productive flying had been done since June, much of it had been against priority tasks and relatively little training flying had been carried out. No crews had succeeded in raising their classification during this period and several had been unable even to complete the formal training requirement.

There was some improvement in October with an ADEX and an exercise with HMS *Victorious* but, just as things were beginning to look up, the T.4 went u/s and spent the whole of December on the ground which inevitably caused problems with instrument ratings and pilot proficiency checks. In the meantime Sqn Ldr Valentine had been posted rather suddenly and, since there were no spare squadron leaders immediately available within the Canberra system, Flt Lt M J Dawson was promoted from within the squadron to became CO on November 27th, suddenly finding himself having to solve the kind of intractable problems which, during his time as Adj, he had previously been able to pass up the chain to the Boss. Apart from a month in 1942, when Norman Bayly had been de facto CO, Mike Dawson was the first navigator to command the Flying Camels. In its forty-fifth year No 45 Sqn had finally reached full maturity and had at last become an 'equal opportunities employer'.

To round off the year and to provide a sound basis for the Christmas season, JOSSTICK XI[10] took place between 7th and 14th December giving the 90th BS an opportunity to visit Singapore. They brought five B-57s with them, but this time there was to be no flying.

While the squadron may not have made a great deal of progress with the classification scheme in 1961 it had certainly been a busy year. It may have fallen short of its brief in terms of maintaining its proficiency but it had excelled itself in showing the flag! At various times Canberras wearing the insignia of the Flying Camel had graced the flightlines at Ohakea, Amberley, Darwin, Kadena, Clark Field, Kai Tak, Karachi, New Delhi, Benares, Calcutta, Mingaladon and Don Muang. Although they were really outside its sphere of influence, the odd UK ferry trip had meant that the squadron's aeroplanes had also been seen at Luqa, Akrotiri, Nicosia, Meherabad and Muharraq as well.

The RNZAF had recently taken delivery of its own Canberras, probably the best equipped and most effective variant of all, the B(I) 12. Since FIREDOG was over, however, these were to be based at Ohakea with No 14 Sqn, although they would still be committed to the Commonwealth Strategic Reserve and to SEATO and the unit would be at permanent notice to fly up to Singapore in the event of a regional crisis. In line with this policy, No 75 Sqn handed its B.2s back to the RAF in January 1962, some of them later appearing in No 45 Sqn's colours, and a parade was held at Tengah on the 27th to mark the formal standing down of the New Zealand squadron. An airborne farewell salute was provided by a box of Canberras, two each from Nos 45 and 81 Sqns, followed by four of No 60 Sqn's Javelins and four Hunters of No 20 Sqn.

By this time No 45 Sqn had been notified that it was shortly to be re-equipped with B.15s and a series of preparatory lectures on the new model was laid on in

A flypast by Tengah's Canberras, Javelins and Hunters on 27th January 1962 to the mark the departure of No 75 Sqn RNZAF. If it were not for the fact that two of the Canberras were provided by No 81 Sqn this photograph would represent the three squadrons of RFC's 11th Wg in the summer of 1917 when Nos 20, 45 and 60 Sqns had been based together at Ste-Marie-Cappel.
(No 45 Sqn archives)

January. At the same time the squadron began to adapt itself to the low-level environment with a programme of navigation exercises and some shallow-dive bombing. The following month the new CO, accompanied by Flt Lt Johnny Walker, spent four days in Cyprus visiting No 32 Sqn, the first unit to receive the B.15, to see what they could find out about the new aeroplane.

In FIREDOG days there had been little trouble in gaining access to 500 lb and 1,000 lb bombs but since the campaign had ended they had suddenly become scarce. The armourers hoarded their stocks and the squadron had only a limited allocation for training use. There was never a problem with the availability of 25 lb practice bombs but the heavier, and much more expensive, weapons were now doled out very sparingly as 'treats'. The squadron mounted its first concentrated bombing period in March 1962 when most crews were given the opportunity to drop live 1,000 pounders on a range at Batti Mali in the Nicobar Islands. To have flown the round trip from Tengah would have been stretching the B.2's fuel somewhat so the squadron was detached to Butterworth on the 4th and stayed there until the exercise was completed on the 9th. At the same time an attempt was made to take part in a SEATO naval exercise but this was not a very satisfactory enterprise. SEATO's communications were nowhere near as sophisticated as those of NATO and position reports on ships were often hours, sometimes even days, old. This was the case on this occasion and the exercise turned out to be a game of hunt the ships. The squadron never found them, so the exercise was a failure - unless, of course, that had been the idea all along, in which case the sailors had won and the event had been a resounding success.

The summer of 1962 - one of the interminable games of volleyball on the grass in front of the squadron's offices in No 1 Hangar. From the left:- Fg Off 'Digger' Balding, Fg Off Neil McFarlane, Flt Lt John Miles, Fg Off 'Loz' Warren, Fg Off Jimmy Milne (in singlet), M Nav Geordie Ross, Fg Off Tony Golds and Flt Lt Frank Pearson. (M J Dawson)

Most of the squadron went up to Kadena on March 15th for JOSSTICK XII. This time there was some flying and after being shown around the local area by the residents the squadron carried out some medium-level bombing on Pork Chop Range before returning to Singapore on the 23rd. A new weapons range had recently become available in Malaya and the squadron used it for the first time at the end of March. Ranges are usually located on the coast, like those at China Rock and Song Song, and their targets are relatively easily seen. Asahan Range, which was inland, was to be used for tactical exercises in the forthcoming low-level era and the targets were quite difficult to spot. Exercise DAYGLEAM was held on March 30th. Six of the squadron's Canberras participated, all operating at low-level; three carried out level attacks while the rest did shallow-dive deliveries.

The squadron was able to provide six Canberras for an ADEX, the thirty-seventh in the series, on April 12th but the groundcrew had excelled themselves and the Flying Camels actually had nine aeroplanes serviceable, seven B.2s and a pair of T.4s. The opportunity was too good to miss so before the exercise participants set off on their briefed sorties the squadron put up a nine-ship formation.

Four days later WJ605 crashed killing Fg Offs M J Moy and D T A Lansley. The aircraft had been one of two carrying out a low-level academic bombing detail at China Rock. After five uneventful bomb runs the aircraft was proceeding outbound before turning-in again. Debris was seen to fall from the port side followed by a brief ball of fire. The aeroplane then broke up and fell into the sea. A search

A couple of the squadron's 'intellectuals' pass the time with a game of chess. The player on the left is Flt Lt Wally Wotherspoon; his opponent is Flt Lt Fred Pinches and Sqn Ldr Mike Dawson, the CO, is acting as umpire. (M J Dawson)

was made but insufficient wreckage was recovered for the cause of the accident to be firmly established. The most likely explanation appeared to have been a catastrophic engine failure. There was some talk of sabotage but this could not be substantiated. Another possibility was airframe fatigue as a result of the stresses being imposed by the recently introduced low-level training. As a precaution, HQ FEAF restricted the squadron's aircraft to flight at not above 250 knots and not below 2,000 feet and, without special authorisation, this had to suffice as 'low-level' pending delivery of the B.15s.

By mid-1962 there were indications that the precarious political stability of the Far East might be about to overbalance. For the British the 1960s was a decade of hasty (and sometimes undignified) withdrawal from Empire. Singapore had had a high degree of autonomy since 1959 and was eager to gain its full independence by a union with Malaya. The government in Kuala Lumpur was concerned at the possibly adverse (for the indigenous Malays) political and economic implications of adding the predominantly Chinese population of the island to Malaya's racial cocktail. The Malayan Prime Minister, Tunku Abdul Rahman, had proposed in May 1961 that the British throw in the predominantly Malay Crown Colonies of Sarawak and North Borneo as well, plus the Sultanate of Brunei. Whitehall had agreed to this neat solution and initial plans envisaged the new state of Malaysia being established in August 1962. The idea was not universally popular, however, and domestic dissent and opposition from neighbouring states delayed implementation of this plan.

Further north, the withdrawal of the French from Indo-China and the partitioning of Vietnam in 1954 had not been followed by the promised elections. Ho Chi Minh was still determined to unite the country under a communist administration, however, and, denied access to the ballot box, he resorted to subversion and guerilla warfare in an attempt to topple the corrupt regime in the south. Early American efforts to stave this off by supporting Ngo Dinh Diem had not had the desired effect and the US was gradually increasing its direct involvement. When President Eisenhower had left office in January 1961 there had been 650 US military advisers in the South; a year later, under President Kennedy, there were already 4,000, and the figure was still rising.

In Laos the weak pro-Western government was under increasing pressure from the communist Pathet Lao which was causing alarm in neighbouring Thailand. As Thailand was a member of SEATO, this might have been an opportunity for the organisation to show its teeth but the Alliance elected to do nothing, unless or until one of its members was actually attacked. Instead the USA entered into a bilateral defence agreement with Thailand which outflanked and undermined the already weak Alliance. American troops were deployed to Thailand in May 1962. They were not alone, however, as the British and Australian governments were also concerned over the perceived threat to Thailand because of its long-term implications for Malaya, and ultimately for Australia, in the context of the then fashionable 'domino theory'. In May 1962 a detachment of Sabres of No 77 Sqn RAAF (later redesignated as No 79 Sqn) moved to Ubon while No 20 Sqn's Hunters were deployed to Chiang Mai.

The Hunter deployment, which went by the name of Operation BIBBER, was supported by No 45 Sqn whose Canberras flew from Tengah to Don Muang and/or Chiang Mai twelve times during May. Apart from acting as shepherds to the single-seaters, the squadron was used to carry urgent spares and to convey key personnel, not least Wg Cdr Ian Pedder who was in the throes of setting up the Offensive Support Wing at Tengah to co-ordinate the operations of Nos 20 and 45 Sqns. BIBBER was not the squadron's only escort duty at this time as No 28 Sqn at Kai

The crewroom coffee bar. Flt Lt Johnny Walker (with shirt) and Fg Off Neil McFarlane (without) usurp the place of 'Kassim', the squadron's cleaner who usually occupied this space.
(M J Dawson)

Tak began to replace its Venoms with Hunters during May and they too needed to be shepherded up to Hong Kong by Canberras, which involved staging through Labuan and Clark Field.

Despite these extraneous tasks the squadron had made significant headway in catching up on its classification training and by the end of June it had one crew cleared to bomb at 45,000 feet, one at 40,000 feet and four at 35,000 feet with the two most recent arrivals still at 25,000 and 20,000 feet. The 50% average of all bombs dropped from high level during the month was 195 yards while for First Run Attacks (FRA) it was 175 yards. Of more significance for the future was the fact that the squadron had begun to record its low-level bombing scores for the first time and these were 53 yards for all bombs and 47 yards for FRAs.

There were several more long-range trips in the summer of 1962. A T.4, WD963, was flown back to the UK in May and when its replacement, WH706, was brought out in June it was accompanied by a pair of Meteor F.8s bound for Seletar. In July two Meteors were escorted up to Kai Tak. There was a change of flight commander in July with Flt Lt R C E Duke taking over from Dave Clark. Almost as soon as he had arrived Dicky Duke was 'trooped' back to Cyprus with the first two ferry crews to spend a week at Akrotiri, being checked out on the peculiarities and capabilities of the B.15 in preparation for the forthcoming re-equipment programme. By August some replacement aeroplanes were ready for collection and the first pair of B.2s to be traded in, WH739 and WK102, set off for the UK on the 20th.

With the Hunters now well-established at Chiang Mai, on August 18th an air show was laid on to publicise their presence. The squadron sent WJ632 up to take part, the crew being Fg Off Jeff Thomas, Flt Lt Neil McFarlane and Fg Offs 'Digger' Balding and Malcolm Clark. On an occasion such as this Jeff Thomas liked to hold the aeroplane down "really low" after take off to build up speed; not for the last time, when he brought it back to Tengah it was found to have scuff marks on the outer walls of its mainwheel tyres!

Two months later Operation BIBBER was wound up and, escorted by one of No 45 Sqn's gradually diminishing fleet of Canberra B.2s, No 20 Sqn returned to Tengah on November 16th. In the meantime substantial progress had been made with the ferry programme and by the end of

November 1962 seven B.15s had reached Tengah. A new and more turbulent era was about to begin.

Notes:

1. Similar radars were in widespread use in the UK until the 1970s with a number of Radar Bomb Scoring Units (RBSU). In this instance they were adapted to work in a third mode, tracking the bomber until it signalled electronically that it had 'released' a notional bomb. Knowing the precise position of the aeroplane at its release point, the RBSU applied all the necessary correction factors to predict the point of impact of the weapon. Using this means, V-bombers, and others, were able to attack truly representative targets all over the UK, avoiding both the expense and the artificiality inherent in academic live bombing ranges.

2. SEATO (the South East Asia Treaty Organisation) was an anti-Communist alliance of eight nations, broadly similar to CENTO (the Central Treaty Organisation) in the Middle East and the more familiar NATO. Established in 1955, in the hope that it might preserve the neutrality of the Indo-China settlement which had been agreed at Geneva the previous year, SEATO was a far less substantial arrangement than NATO, since it had no forces assigned to it in peacetime. It did, however, have a permanent multi-national HQ located in Bangkok. The chief functions of the HQ's staff were to devise contingency plans, to sponsor exercises, to foster commonality of operating procedures and to encourage standardisation of equipment. Primarily, however, the Alliance was intended to symbolise democratic solidarity and resolve in the Cold War. The UK was a full member as were the USA, Australia, New Zealand, the Philippines, Thailand, France and Pakistan but, significantly, Malaya was not.

3. Butterworth, which had been considerably redeveloped and now had a V-bomber class north/south runway some 9,000 feet long, was transferred from RAF to RAAF administration on 1st July 1958 and eventually became home to Nos 2, 3 and 77 Sqns RAAF, although RAF units continued to be based there as well.

4. 'Lone Ranger' was a term borrowed from Bomber Command. It covered the practice of crews taking aeroplanes away to remote locations, often over a weekend. The exercise gave the crew valuable practical experience of planning and executing an international flight which provided excellent training in captaincy and airmanship and fostered their self-reliance. At the same time it was a break from the routine, a few days in a different environment and an opportunity to do some shopping and/or to get into trouble.

5. The small windows in the roof of the Canberra let in a little natural light but, unless the aeroplane was flying upside down, provided no view of the outside world other than of the sky. The only other window in the nav's compartment was at desk level on the port side but, since it was only about nine inches square, this provided only a very restricted and oblique view of the ground. This appeared to be symptomatic of a post-war Air Ministry policy which required that, whenever possible, navigators were to be buried in the bowels of an aeroplane and denied any external visual reference. This was in sharp contrast to the opposition's practice; the navigator's station on a typical Soviet bomber had generously-glazed bay windows, providing a magnificent panoramic view. The ultimate expression of the British philosophy was manifested in the V-bombers whose navs were required not only to work in the dark, but to sit facing backwards, leading to spatial disorientation and providing bags of scope for misunderstandings as to whether a left turn meant "my left, or yours?" The basic rules of the game were simple - navigators were supposed to estimate where the aeroplane might be and every now and then announce this to their pilots, who would then look out of their windows and award the guess marks out of ten. This policy prevailed for many years and even the designers of the TSR2 seemed to have been persuaded that glass was a strategic commodity which was in short supply. By the 1960s, however, the navigators' union had finally begun to gain some influence within the Operational Requirements Branch and they began actively lobbying for 'windows for navs'. Their case was strengthened by the acquisition of some second-hand Buccaneers from the FAA and the purchase of Phantoms from the USA which clearly demonstrated that the fears of pilots (presumably that their omnipotence might be in some way called into question if their back-seaters were able to see what they were up to) were groundless. Reassured, the pilots eventually acceded to the Tornado specification which provided the nav with an adequate view. This may be a fanciful interpretation but it is a fact that for many years this particular navigator flew over much of the world, courtesy of the RAF, but actually *saw* very little of it!

6. For the cognoscenti it is worth noting that, since most flights were carried out within a few degrees of the equator, there was no perceptible difference between a Lambert's and a Mercator's projection and the navs were, therefore, untroubled by the esoteric complications in plotting caused by convergence and conversion angle. Even better, Variation was almost zero, so there was virtually no difference between True and Magnetic North.

7. Although they had been defeated as an effective fighting force, the remnants of the MRLA with their leader, Chin Peng, had taken refuge across the border in Thailand whence, to the embarrassment of the Thai government, the CTs made sporadic incursions back into Malaya for many years, obliging No 81 Sqn to fly occasional FIREDOG-related sorties to keep an eye on them. The dissidents were nothing if not tenacious and the diehards hung on for almost thirty years - until the collapse of the USSR. Chin Peng had been chief liaison officer between Force 136 and the Malayan Resistance during the war and the valuable service that he had rendered had been recognised by the award of an OBE; he had marched through London in the Victory Parade in 1946. Having successfully dislodged a Japanese imperialist regime, however, he was implacably opposed to the re-establishment of a British one and from 1947 onwards he had masterminded the Communist insurrection. In late 1989, still with over 1,000 devoted followers, Chin Peng emerged from hiding in the jungle and surrendered. On December 3rd, at Haad Yai in Thailand, he signed a Treaty with Malaysian and Thai military representatives; the insurgents finally laid down their arms of their own free will and the Communist Party of Malaya was formally disbanded.

8. In 1959 a series of photographs was taken to celebrate the squadron's "6,000th sortie"; some of these later appeared in the Press. While this exercise obviously produced valuable publicity, it is not known how the total of 6,000 was derived, but it would seem to have been something of an exaggeration. The author's figure of 4,335 sorties, as presented at Annex G, has been extracted from a variety of contemporary official documents and is believed to be substantially correct.

9. It is (probably) a trifle far-fetched but it is not too difficult to interpret centralisation as a sinister left-wing plot, as follows: "Those who advocated a Marxist approach to RAF management had been spreading their dogma since the middle years of the war and the establishment of No 7045 SE at the end of 1944 had been just one early indication that their propaganda was having the desired effect. With the advent of the Cold War, however, the influence of the hardliners declined and they realised that they could no longer achieve their aims through stealthy encroachment; a more overtly revolutionary approach was necessary - only full-scale 'collectivisation' would suffice. A new campaign was launched, the agitators achieving their greatest success in the 1960s when they succeeded in suborning the main bulwark of the service, the V-Force, by imposing upon it wholesale centralised servicing. Under the new regime, the Marxist slogan of "From each according to his ability" was used to justify the virtual emasculation of the old ruling class, the squadron commanders, by taking away their aeroplanes and their airmen - *all* of them. The corresponding, "To each according to his needs", was a matter for the Station Politburo to decide, and aeroplanes were allocated to crews by a kind of People's Committee drawn from the prominente of Engineering and Operations Wings. The Flying Camel had not appreciated the temporary loss of its airmen in 1944, or the inroads which had been made into its traditional autonomy in 1946/7. What No 45 Sqn's old COs of the 1920s and 1930s thought about the ultimate effects of these developments is probably unprintable. Surely none of *them* could have been among the generation of air marshals who had been seduced into promoting the 'worker's paradise' which centralisation represented - or could they? Fortunately there was a bourgeois counter-revolution in the corridors of power in the 1970s, when many squadrons had their aeroplanes and most of their airmen restored. Sadly, these reforms did not extend to the larger transport and maritime stations where the Marxist-Leninist philosophy had been more rigorously imposed during the Great Patriotic War of 1941-45. They still continue to function as colourless, amorphous state collectives. Even here, however, the spark of individualism still flickers; on occasion a Nimrod or a Hercules can be seen briefly displaying a unit badge or daubed with a slogan marking the anniversary of some event in the half-forgotten past. These grafitti represent coded signals to the rest of the air force that the spirit of the old squadrons still survives, awaiting the day of liberation. But help never comes. The protests are ruthlessly suppressed by the MOD's Thought Police and the aeroplanes quickly revert to their customary anonymous, drab appearance."

10. JOSSTICKs were not the exclusive preserve of the Flying Camels, hence the gap between Exercise XI and the previous one noted which had been JOSSTICK VIII. Although No 45 Sqn was the only unit able to participate in away fixtures, Tengah's other squadrons also had the opportunity to host visiting USAF detachments and F-101s, F-105s and even US Navy A-3s were occasionally to be seen in Tengah's circuit.

Chapter 19. Canberras in warpaint - the B.15.

The first of the Flying Camels' Canberra B.15s, WH969, arrived at Tengah on September 2nd flown by Flt Lt Dickie Duke; his crew for the delivery flight had comprised Flt Lts Ken Utton and Don Sleven, who were, respectively, the squadron's Navigation and Bombing Leaders. Unfortunately the aeroplane was promptly declared to be unserviceable and it remained on the ground for the rest of the month. Apart from a lack of spares for the new aeroplane it was found to have swarf in its fuel system, a problem that had first come to light while the second B.15 was still on its way out to Singapore crewed by Fg Off Gus Ross, Flt Lt Wally Wotherspoon and Flt Lt Fred Pinches. The latter recalls that...

....we left Lyneham in WJ766 on 4th September bound for Akrotiri. We reached Karachi on the 5th and the following morning lined up for take off; at full throttle, just before releasing the brakes, both engines cut out - swarf! We were stuck in Karachi for a double engine change which took until the 30th. Our diplomatic clearance for India had now lapsed and the authorities in Pakistan would not permit us to fly an unscheduled air test sortie so we had to reroute via Ceylon and check out the engines on the way to Katunayake. We finally got back to Tengah on October 1st.

Despite the delays caused by this defect, three more B.15s reached Tengah during October and towards the end of the month a start was made on an operational conversion programme, although this was seriously hampered by a number of factors: the continuing lack of spares; a total absence of certain key role equipment in the new aeroplanes; the absence of several crews at any one time on ferries and the need to make fairly frequent trips to Chiang Mai to take important bits of Hunter up to No 20 Sqn.

FEAF, being at the far end of the supply line from the UK, had long been the elephants' graveyard for the RAF's combat aeroplanes. The Beaufighter, Spitfire, Mosquito, Tempest, Brigand, Hornet, Vampire, Venom, Sunderland and the PR and NF variants of the Meteor had all ended their days as first-line types in the Far East, several of them in the hands of No 45 Sqn. This pattern was to be maintained with, for instance, the Valetta, Beverley, Javelin and

Belvedere. The same fate was to befall the Canberra and No 45 Sqn had the dubious honour of operating (in their intended role as bombers) the RAF's last B.2s. As a result, it had been the last squadron to re-equip with the B.15 - it was to be the last to fly those too.

The B.15s were not new aeroplanes. They were refurbished B.6s and, as No 45 Sqn had never had any of this intervening variant, the contrast with the B.2s was quite marked. The squadron's new mounts had the significantly more powerful Avon Mk 109 engines, with the luxury of a three-shot starting capability in place of the B.2's single cartridge. They also had the integral wing fuel tanks of the B.6 and were thus much longer-legged than the squadron's original Canberras[1]. In addition the airframes had been strengthened to make them more tolerant of the stresses of low-level operations. The most significant difference, however, was the major increase in operational flexibility conferred by the B.15's avionic fit and its range of weapon options.

Although the Marconi radio compass and REBECCA had been retained, these were all that remained of the original equipment fit. The Air Position Indicator had been removed and replaced by a Ground Position Indicator driven by a BLUE SILK Doppler radar which provided a reasonably accurate and self-contained means of navigation. There was also a tail-warning radar, ORANGE PUTTER (although this particular navigator never actually saw anything on it). A radio altimeter was another useful addition for low-level operations. The communications fit had been extensively revised and in addition to the original VHF radio the new aircraft had UHF and HF as well. The vertically mounted F.24 camera aft of the bomb bay had been retained from the B.2 but this had been supplemented by a G.45 gun camera in the leading edge of the starboard wing and an optional F.95 which could be mounted in the nose in lieu of the bombsight; not exactly a comprehensive PR fit but more than adequate for taking tactical snaps. The only thing that seemed to have been overlooked was safety equipment and, despite the fact that the B.15s (and the similar B.16s) were specifically intended for low-level operations, the opportunity had not been taken to upgrade the ejection seats to provide the crew with the ground-level/90 knot capability which was widely

WH963 taxies out with a pair of Microcell rocket pods under its wings. This picture shows how well the badge on the fin stood out against the B.15's camouflage, and the early style of serial numbers in large white characters. The four black-finned silver aeroplanes in the distance are PR 7s of No 81 Sqn. (D Pells)

Seen here taxying out for a sortie, WJ766 was the second B.15 to reach the squadron. In the background is No 60 Sqn's Javelin T.3 on the engine running pan. (Author's collection)

available by the early 1960s.

The B.2's original high-level bombing capability, carrying up to six 1,000 lb bombs internally, was unimpaired but the new variant also had a pylon under each wing, each of which could take another 1,000 pounder. In practice the squadron never exercised this option, although later on the pylons were used to carry 25 lb practice bombs when toss-bombing was added to the range of attack options. More routinely each pylon could be fitted with a Microcell pod containing thirty-seven 2" RPs giving the potential to fire a salvo of up to seventy-four which, since this did not interfere with the ability to carry bombs in the bomb bay, provided the aircraft with a pretty devastating ground attack capability.

Significant as all these enhancements were, the most obvious indication that the squadron had been re-equipped was in the appearance of the aircraft. In place of the silver finish sported by the B.2s, the B.15s were camouflaged in Dark Green and Dark Sea Grey with silver undersides, although a little later the silver began to be replaced by Light Aircraft Grey, first appearing in 1964 on those aircraft which were overhauled and repainted under civilian contract by the Hong Kong Aircraft Engineering Co (HAEC) at Kai Tak. Serial numbers were worn in large white characters on the rear fuselage and the fins were soon adorned with a B.2-style Flying Camel on a white disc, which appeared to be even larger against the dark background of the camouflage.

By November the first B.15s were beginning to venture further afield and Flt Lts Duke and Utton were despatched to Hong Kong with Sqn Ldr Dawson, the latter holding a substantial portion of the Officers' Mess' funds with which to purchase prizes for the impending Christmas Draw. Having completed their weekend shopping expedition, they began their return flight which, owing to a fuel problem, had to be via Clark Field. On landing and opening WH969's bomb bay doors they found that the contents of the freight panniers were soaked in AVTUR. Although the goodies were spread out on the pan to dry in the tropical sun, bemusing a number of passing USAF personnel, there was a still a distinct whiff of the flightline in the Mess when the function took place a month or so later.

On December 4th one of No 60 Sqn's crews operating over Malaya was obliged to abandon their Javelin after its Sapphire engines had blown up as a result of centre-line closure - a phenomenon induced by the cooling effect of the

high humidity associated with tropical clouds. Both men ejected successfully and descended into the jungle some distance apart. Unfortunately, both had been issued with SARAH location beacons operating on the same frequency which complicated and prolonged the business of finding them[2]. A major search operation ensued to which No 45 Sqn contributed a Canberra to act as an airborne radio relay between the aircraft directly engaged in the search and the Rescue Co-ordination Centre in Singapore. Several sorties were flown before both men were located and picked up.

With seven B.15s at Tengah by the beginning of December some progress had been made with the conversion programme but the squadron was far from being operational when a crisis occurred. Britain's efforts to implement the Tunku's 1961 proposals for uniting Malaya with Singapore and the territories of northern Borneo had fallen well behind schedule. Opposition had come from many quarters. First, since Kalimantan, the southern portion of the island of Borneo, was already a part of Indonesia, President Sukarno had raised a counter-claim, for sovereignty over the Crown Colonies of Sarawak and British North Borneo and responsibility for the Protectorate of Brunei to be transferred to Djakarta's jurisdiction rather than to that of Kuala Lumpur.

President Macapagal of the Philippines had presented a second, Fortinbras-like claim to the territories of North Borneo, maintaining that his state also had "some rights of memory in this kingdom". The waters were further muddied by Macapagal's active promotion of his concept of 'Maphilindo', a proposed confederation of all the Malay states, ie Malaya, Borneo, the Philippines and Indonesia.

Thirdly and, initially at least, more significantly a variety of home-grown nationalist movements emerged in northern Borneo. Strongest in Brunei, but also present in the northern Divisions of Sarawak, there were several factions and these had disparate aims. Common among these aims, however, were support for British withdrawal and opposition to the shotgun marriage with Malaya. Most activists advocated independence followed by self-determination of the destiny of the new state, the most popular options on offer being continuation of the proposed merger with Malaya, a merger with Indonesia or self-sufficiency under the leadership of the Sultan of Brunei. Many of these factions had a strong left-wing bias and there were ties, especially among the Chinese population, with the powerful Communist Party of Indonesia. Among these particular groups there was strong opposition to the involvement of the autocratic Sultan.

The Sultan was the fourth major player in the Borneo game. The exploitation of the oil resources of the tiny state of Brunei was in the process of making the Sultan into possibly the richest man in the world; money is power, and it also talks so the Sultan had a very loud voice. He knew that union with Malaya, or anywhere else, would dilute his personal authority and mean that Brunei's (ie his) resources would be siphoned off to underwrite the development of the rest of whatever new state emerged. He preferred the status quo, independence under British protection.

The initiative was seized by the Borneo Liberation Army in the small hours of 8th December 1962 when, led by Sheikh Azahari, it launched a revolution in Brunei. The British reacted instantly and before the day was out troops from

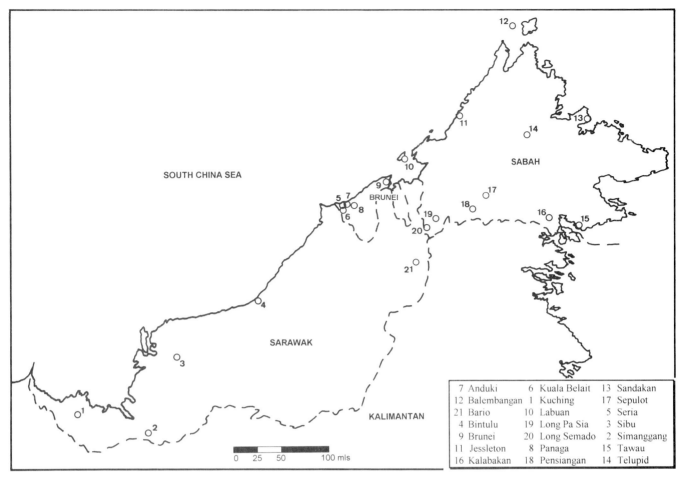

7	Anduki	6	Kuala Belait	13	Sandakan
12	Balembangan	1	Kuching	17	Sepulot
21	Bario	10	Labuan	5	Seria
4	Bintulu	19	Long Pa Sia	3	Sibu
9	Brunei	20	Long Semado	2	Simanggang
11	Jessleton	8	Panaga	15	Tawau
16	Kalabakan	18	Pensiangan	14	Telupid

Map 19.1. Northern Borneo.

Singapore were landing at Labuan and at Brunei, where a company of Gurkhas secured the vital airfield which had been ceremonially opened by No 45 Sqn's Venoms only five years before. Elements loyal to the Sultan had already regained control of several of the key installations that the rebels had seized in Brunei town. The remainder were flushed out on December 9th but they still held some rural police stations and Shell Company installations in the oilfields of Seria further down the coast.

Although the RAF was heavily committed to moving troops about and resupplying them, this was to be an army rather than an air campaign and there was little demand for offensive air support. Nevertheless, No 45 Sqn was soon called upon to provide a high speed taxi service. The first such trip was flown on December 8th when Fg Offs L C Warren and R A M Burr, flew to Labuan carrying Maj Waterton and Mr Pumphrey. Leaving their passengers there, the crew brought the aeroplane back to Singapore early the next day. It was promptly turned round again so that Flt Lts Dicky Duke and Ken Utton could ferry Brig Jack Glennie (who was to begin setting up a Joint Force Headquarters in Brunei the following day) and Capt Whitehead over to the crisis area. The aeroplane was back at Tengah by nightfall, ready for its next task.

WH969 made its third trip to Labuan on the 10th. This time the crew was Fg Off Jeff Thomas and Flt Lt Don Sleven, accompanied by AVM Headlam and Wg Cdr Pedder. Having dropped off the AOC, two hours later the crew, including Ian Pedder, were airborne again to carry out a reconnaissance of the Seria-Anduki area. The following day they flew a second sortie, this time without the wing commander, to cover Seria and Kuala Belait. After debriefing at Labuan the aircraft and all three crew members returned to Singapore.

Although the crew had not realised it at the time, their first recce mission had had a significant tactical impact. The rebels had been talking to the Shell representatives at Seria by telephone and threatening to use the hostages which they had already taken as a shield in an attack on the police post at Panaga. At that point the Canberra roared over; a new voice promptly came on the line and promised that the hostages would come to no harm. The mere presence of the aeroplane had been sufficient to induce a considerable change in the aggressive attitude of the rebels.

On December 12th, Flt Lt Johnny Walker and MNav Tony Gostelow flew across to Labuan in XK641. After refuelling they carried out a shipping recce and, following a local debriefing, returned to Tengah. This was the last operational mission that came the squadron's way but several more special flights were laid on to take key personnel across to 'Lab'. On December 14th Flt Lt Pete Blewitt and Fg Off Baz Webb used XK641 to deliver Maj Allen; the next day Fg Offs Gus Ross and Tony Golds flew Air Marshal Sir Hector McGregor and AVM Headlam to and from Labuan in WJ766; Flt Lt 'Rick' Rickards and Fg Off Roy Quarrell did a similar round trip in XK641 on the 20th, carrying Vice Admiral Dyer and Captain Leach while Dicky Duke and Ken Utton flew Gen Poett and Maj Kenyon back and forth in WJ766 on the 27th.

The squadron had done all that was asked of it but it was probably just as well that it had not been required to do more, as the crisis could hardly have caught the squadron at a worse moment. Although it had by then received most of its new B.15s, some of the later arrivals were still undergoing post-ferry servicings, and spares continued to be scarce. Some progress had been made with pilot proficiency checks and a start had been made with low-level navigation exercises but few (if any) bombing details had been flown, so none of the aircraft had calibrated bomb sights and, since no gunsights had yet been delivered, it had been impossible to do anything about introducing RP work. To cap it all, the squadron had been in the throes of a change of command, Sqn Ldr J B Carruthers formally taking over from Mike Dawson on 17th December.

Had the squadron been called upon to mount any offensive sorties, it would no doubt have muddled through somehow but fortunately this had not happened. In fact the only offensive air action taken before the revolution was quashed was by a Hunter, one of a flight of four, carrying out a dummy attack on a rebel-held police post near Seria on December 12th. The aircraft loosed off a single warning burst of cannon fire and shortly afterwards the position was successfully stormed by the Queen's Own Highlanders, resulting in the freeing of forty-six hostages without any casualties; the rebels fled.

It seems probable that FEAF never really considered it likely that the Canberras would be required to operate in an offensive role as the last two B.2s, nominally the only calibrated bombers in the Command, had been allowed to depart for the UK on December 10th. Although notionally capable of being used, these two aeroplanes, WH667 and WJ986, were the tattiest of the old fleet. In fact several bits of WJ986 had flown home already as they had been removed to make other B.2s fit for the trip. It had been the 'hangar queen' for some time and Flt Lt Hancock, who had been the squadron's engineering officer since July 1962, had been hoping that it would be necessary only to patch it up so that it could make the hop to Seletar where it could have been

quietly put out to grass. Authority decided otherwise, however, and a great deal of effort had to be expended on preparing WJ986 for the long trip back to the UK.

These endeavours were only partially successful. On the Calcutta-Karachi leg one engine stopped suddenly, precipitating the aeroplane into a steep spiral dive, accompanied by the broadcasting of a MAYDAY message. Several thousand feet lower down the driver, Flt Lt Stuart Pearce, announced that he had the situation under control again and cancelled the emergency, but it took all of his persuasive skills and the passage of a respectable period of time before he was able to convince his navigators, Flt Lt Phil Mason and this writer, that normal service really had been resumed. After some embarrassing confusion as to precisely which of Karachi's several airfields was supposed to be their destination (navigator finger trouble), they picked the right one and returned to earth without any further crises. The aeroplane proved to have an unserviceable fuel pump which took two days to rectify. Thereafter the trip went as planned until the last leg, from Malta to the UK. Shortly after take off Stu Pearce's WJ986 lost its only radio and, having used frantic hand signals to explain the situation to the pilot of the accompanying aeroplane, Flt Lt Rupert Butler led the transit across France and into Lyneham with WH667 doing the honours for both aeroplanes[3].

The last of the original batch of B.15s, WH958, arrived at Tengah on 13th January 1963. It had flown direct from Delhi, cutting out the planned intermediate stop at Mingaladon (much to the annoyance of the resident Air Attaché) which was an indication of the increased range capability of the new variant. By this time the conversion programme had gained considerable momentum and a great deal of weapons training was carried out in January 1963, mostly at Song Song where Fg Off Peter Sykes was detached to act as Range Safety Officer (RSO). Most crews flew double sorties, dropping a total of sixteen bombs. After a low-level cross-country to the range to drop the first eight, they would land at Butterworth, grab a steak sandwich and a Coke in No 2(B) Sqn's crewroom, move the spare eight bombs forward to the live carriers and repeat the sortie in reverse to land back at Tengah. In the course of January 366 25 lb practice bombs were dropped and the squadron's original bombing capability had been largely restored. The gunsights arrived in February and Flt Lt Neville Whittaker, who had arrived in October to become the squadron's first PAI since Venom days, was able to start checking out the pilots in the techniques of RP work, initially using a 20° dive attack, firing at 1,500 yards.

Now that the squadron was functioning fully again it began to familiarise itself with the operational techniques which went with its newly acquired Close Air Support role. Prominent among these were Forward Air Control (FAC) procedures and, once the basics of RP work had been buttoned up, attention turned to developing this aspect of the squadron's role. Before attempting any live shoots, however, some initial 'dry' FAC exercises were laid on with army controllers operating at Ulu Tiram, which was conveniently located some twenty miles north of Singapore, between Johore Bahru and Kota Tinggi. This activity, along with a good deal of low-level navigation training and experimentation with a variety of low-level attack profiles, kept the

A typical squadron crew of the B.15 era, all first tourists. From the left, Fg Off Deryk Butler, Fg Off Peter Sykes and Fg Off 'Jeff' Jefford. The aeroplane is WT209. (Author's collection)

crews happily occupied for much of the early part of the year.

Meanwhile it was becoming evident that the political situation was still highly unstable. Although the Brunei Revolution itself was virtually over by December 20th, mopping up was to take several more weeks and its after effects were to rumble on for more than three years. The rebellion had received enthusiastic verbal support from Djakarta and, despite its rapid failure, President Sukarno continued to provide aid and comfort to the rebels. He offered sanctuary to dissidents and set up camps in Kalimantan to harbour those who succeeded in escaping. Sukarno intended to train and equip these expatriate malcontents (or nationalist freedom fighters, depending upon your point of view) and then infiltrate them back across the border to mount a guerrilla campaign. It was not yet clear whether a FIREDOG II was about to start but it was evident that the UK was going to have to maintain a much stronger military presence in northern Borneo than it had in the past. To support this, a number of new RAF posts, mostly as shift-working Operations Officers, were created and these had to be manned, to begin with at least, from FEAF's pool of manpower. This meant that, like other local units, No 45 Sqn had to start detaching aircrew to fill these appointments. First to go, to Brunei in January 1963, was Fg Off Mason who was relieved a month later by Fg Off Jefford; others went to Labuan and to HQ Far East Land Forces (FARELF) at Phoenix Park in Singapore. Obligations such as these, which considerably disrupted the constitution of crews, did little to help the squadron settle down with its new aeroplanes.

Despite these problems, the squadron made substantial progress with training and by mid-February it was well able to respond when ordered to prepare to take part in a full scale strike. Sheikh Azahari was still at large with a small band of followers and had been confined in a tract of swamp by army patrols. On the 19th the army called for an air strike to flush them out. Acting on the instructions of HQ 224 Gp, Operation COLD SHOWER, a combined effort by the Offensive Support Wing, was planned. The force was to comprise four Canberras, each carrying six 1,000 pounders, and eight Hunters. The aircraft had been fuelled and armed and the crews were briefed and in flying kit, awaiting only the appointed take-off time, when the mission was suddenly cancelled. It seemed that HQ FEAF had got wind of Group's enthusiastic response to the army's request and wiser councils had vetoed the idea - or so it was rumoured at the sharp end.

Despite this disappointment there was some excitement in February when, on the 28th, WH963's port undercarriage malfunctioned. The pilot tried all the usual tricks, including bouncing the aeroplane down the runway on its starboard wheel, but the port undercarriage leg stubbornly refused to come down and he was committed to jettisoning his tiptanks, burning off fuel and making a belly landing. There was considerable concern that the aeroplane would eventually slew off to the left and fall into the deep monsoon drain which ran parallel to the runway. The left hand side of the runway was liberally coated with fire retardant foam and Fg Off 'Loz' Warren eventually landed on the dry side, holding the port wing up until his speed decayed and he was obliged to let it drop onto the runway. It must have been the first

such landing by a Canberra with underwing pylons. Much to everyone's surprise (and at least half of the station's personnel had come out to watch the show), the geometry of the situation was such that the wingtip never actually touched the ground and, instead of slewing off to the left, the aeroplane ran straight on with the underwing pylon acting rather like an ice skate. The aircraft never left the runway and the only damage was to the port flaps which had been ground away where they had come in contact with the concrete. The aircraft was jacked up, the undercarriage was lowered and, after a rigging check, WH963 was flying again in a matter of days.

By March the squadron's routine was pretty much back to normal, although this now involved a much broader range of activities. The Ranger programme was resurrected too, Ohakea receiving its first visit from the Flying Camels since the previous July and two other crews undergoing the rigours of weekends in Hong Kong. The B.15's increased fuel tankage meant that it was no longer necessary to stage through the Philippines to get to Kai Tak and the route was now more or less direct, overflying Saigon. From then on it was only necessary to call in at Clark Field if the T.4 was used or if the Canberra was escorting a Hunter. The squadron was also called upon to fly a formation around northern Borneo in March to show the flag and there were still occasional demands for senior officers to be flown to Labuan or for priority spares to be taken across to stranded aeroplanes. In the course of these courier duties Canberras of No 45 Sqn landed six times at Labuan and once at Kuching during the month.

On the training side the squadron received its first allocation of 1,000 lb bombs since re-equipping with B.15s and sixty-three of them were dropped at Batti Mali between March 13th and 16th. This time, however, the increased range capability of the new aeroplanes meant that it was no longer necessary to set up a detachment at Butterworth and all sorties were flown from Tengah. Best of all was a JOSSTICK mounted as an away fixture. Five B.15s, supported by a Beverley and a Hastings, flew to Kadena on the 20th. As on previous occasions, a detachment from the 3rd BW came down from Yokota to join them, co-ordination being provided this time by the locally-based 15th TFS who took it upon themselves to ensure that a good time was had by all. The squadron returned to Singapore on the 29th.

Intensive training was resumed during April. The pattern now tended to be a low-level navex to Song Song for a lengthy academic weapons detail involving eight 25 pounders and eight rockets, followed by a crewroom lunch at Butterworth before flying a low-level cross-country down to China Rock to drop another eight bombs[4]. By this time most of the pilots had been checked out on FAC work with 'dry runs' at Ulu Tiram and April also saw the squadron undertaking its first controlled live shoots on Asahan Range.

There was more of the same in May although progress was still being hampered by the detachment of aircrew, the squadron having four men away, filling slots with HQ FARELF and at Labuan, Brunei and Kuching. Interesting as these jobs were for junior officers, the detachments prolonged the process of consolidation with the new aeroplanes and the constant disruption of crews prevented a great deal of progress being made with the classification

Acting as RSO at one of the weapons ranges was a regular chore. This is Fg Off Jeff Jefford exploring the beach at China Rock during a lull between range slots. The corporal is examining a flare which has been washed ashore. (Author's collection)

scheme which was still technically in force although it was becoming increasingly moribund.

Another, more or less constant, diversion of effort is worthy of mention. There were no permanent RSOs established for the Air Weapons Ranges in Malaya and they were manned by the squadrons which used them. During the B.2 era most of the navs (and even the odd pilot) had spent a week up at Song Song but by the mid 1960s it was more usual for the Australians from Butterworth to look after 'their' range and China Rock became the Flying Camel's more regular commitment. The routine was much the same in either case. One left, accompanied by two or three airmen assistants, in an RAF launch early on a Monday morning. A couple of hours later the expedition was deposited on the beach with a week's supply of rations and the boat drove away, leaving the party marooned until about tea time on Friday. The RSO would already have a copy of the week's range bookings (or 'dream sheet') and the first tasks, made easy by a well-thumbed check list, were to fire up the pre-positioned Landrover and have both quadrant huts manned and the radios working in time for the first scheduled bombing detail. Thereafter the routine consisted of: clearing aeroplanes on and off the range; ensuring that they were

conforming to approved range patterns while delivering their weapons, and remonstrating with the crews if they were not; plotting the bearings of each strike as measured from the two quadrant huts; converting their intersection into a range and bearing from the target and, after encryption, passing this to the aeroplane by radio. In between bombing details and in the evenings the party was free to swim and explore the shoreline and hinterland. The third range, Asahan, which was some seventy miles north of Singapore (about three hours drive), was not permanently active and when it was, the chore of providing the RSO generally fell to No 20 Sqn, although the odd No 45 Sqn man could be seen there too from time to time.

There was another diversion in May, to which no one objected, when the 3rd BW sent a detachment down to Tengah on a JOSSTICK. Opportunities were provided for the navs to swop seats and it was an eye-opener to fly in the B-57. The cockpit was roomy, comfortable, and provided tandem seating (with built in ashtrays!) under a clear canopy, permitting a panoramic view of the outside world - for the navs to see out of the RAF's Canberras they had either to perch on a fold-out occasional seat next to the pilot or lie in the bomb aimer's position wearing a neck-cricking bone dome; in either case this involved abandoning the security offered by their ejection seats. Even better, the B-57 could be taxied with the lid open and when it was closed prior to take off the air conditioning was instantly effective and the cockpit momentarily filled with fog as the moisture was rapidly condensed out of the air. The RAF navs were all eager for a second trip but the Americans, when they emerged, sweat-soaked and gasping for a cheroot, from the dark cubbyhole which provided the working environment for their British counterparts, seemed curiously unenthusiastic about the prospect. Despite having inflicted this experience on the American back-seaters, cordial relations were sustained and shortly before they left the 3rd BW presented the squadron with a large carved wooden eagle, very much in the heroic style of the Third Reich school of art. They said it was their 'mascot'. It may well have been but it seems likely that they thought that it ought to be someone else's! At any rate the squadron accepted the gift with profuse thanks and it remains among the collection of artefacts which the squadron has accumulated over the years.

Another extraneous task cropped up in May when the squadron was required to fly several sorties to calibrate No 61 SU's new radar at Bukit Gombak. In view of the crucial role that this installation would have to play if Indonesia decided to attack Singapore, this job, mundane as it was, was afforded a high priority. As yet President Sukarno had not taken any overt action but he was becoming increasingly outspoken in his opposition to the British plans for the creation of Malaysia which were now proceeding apace.

There was a JOSSTICK in May 1963 during which the squadron put up three of its B.15s to fly this 'mixed six' with three of the 3rd Bomb Wing's B-57s. (No 45 Sqn archives)

The situation in Indo-China was also slowly deteriorating and SEATO decided to exert itself by mounting a major exercise in June 1963 to remind everyone that it was there. For Exercise DHANARAJATA, which was to be held in Thailand, No 14 Sqn RNZAF flew up to Tengah with its shiny silver B(I) 12s and No 20 Sqn's Hunters went back up to Chiang Mai on June 7th, for which deployment No 45 Sqn provided a weather recce aircraft to lead the way. The exercise opened with a fire power demonstration on Pulone Range on the 13th; No 45 Sqn fielded three B.15s, each of which fired two full pods of RPs which provided quite a spectacle. The tactical phase lasted from the 14th to the 19th and the Flying Camels were fully involved although, like the New Zealanders, they continued to be based at Tengah. Simulated hi-lo sorties were flown with the aircraft either turning round at Don Muang to repeat the trip in reverse or landing at Chiang Mai to spend the night before flying a lo-hi sortie back to Tengah the following day. All such transits involved transmitting a position report shortly after entering Thai airspace which invariably sparked intensive discussion within the crew as to the correct pronunciation of the name of the designated reporting point - Phuket - it is unlikely that many crews got it right.

The termination of Exercise DHANARAJATA on 24th June was marked by a ceremonial flypast over Bangkok; this had all the makings of a potential disaster. It was to include aeroplanes of every type and every nation involved. This covered a spectrum ranging from RNZAF Bristol Freighters through French Vautours to USAF F-101s. At the briefing it quickly became apparent that the Thai group captain in charge was having difficulty working in English and Wg Cdr G W Johnson, Tengah's OC Ops Wg and leader of the Commonwealth contingent, offered to help out. It was a masterly display of impromptu hot planning. The wing commander first divided the assembly into those with propellers and those without, then sub-divided them again into groups which might reasonably be expected to be able to keep up with each other. Each group had then to agree on the speed at which it would make its flypast and select a suitable Initial Point (IP). Johnson decided the order of the procession, slowest first, fastest last, and gave each formation a height to fly and a time to be over the reviewing stand. It was rough and ready but, if not entirely smoothly, it worked.

The jets were to assemble in three groups, Thais, Commonwealth and USAF, then join up before making their final run over the city together. The selected IP was a pagoda and the Commonwealth formation, nine Canberras, British, Australian and New Zealand, eight RAAF Sabres and eight Hunters, arrived first as had been agreed and set up an orbit beneath scattered cloud at about 2,000 feet. As the time to leave the IP approached there was still no sign of the Thais, who were supposed to be leading. A call on the radio

An informal group during the May 1963 JOSSTICK. From the left, standing:- Fg Off Rupert Butler, USAF, Fg Off Geoff Say, Fg Off Jeff Thomas, Maj Jimmy James (GLO), Fg Off Phil Mason, Flt Lt Frank Pearson, USAF, Fg Off Gus Ross, Fg Off Tony Golds, Fg Off Malcolm Clark, two USAF men, Flt Lt Don Sleven and another American. Kneeling:- Fg Off Baz Webb, Fg Off Jimmy Milne, USAF, Sqn Ldr Brian Carruthers and two more USAF aviators. (No 45 Sqn archives)

revealed that the sixteen F-86s were there too, but above cloud. Their leader cheerfully announced that they were coming down, immediately! Johnson rapidly led his formation out of the way to avoid this Kamikaze attack. By the time that Johnson had tacked on behind the Sabres the formation was late and it set course for the parade at, for the Canberras, a rivet-popping 400 knots, instead of the 300 knots that had been negotiated. The Americans arrived at the IP late and had to use afterburner to catch up! As always happens, the gaggle sorted itself out for the final run across the reviewing stand as the last of the heavy prop jobs cleared the area. But there was one more surprise in store. As the formation thundered up Bangkok High Street, the air seemed to be full of smoke trails and fluttering leaflets which were being liberally distributed by a flock of Thai Army L-19s - of which not a word had been said at the briefing! Fortunately the pilots of the Bird Dogs appeared to be aware of what was going on and they stayed below the flypast aircraft. Once across the city the formations broke up into their constituent sections and dispersed to their various operating bases under private arrangements. No 45 Sqn's three aeroplanes were safely on the ground at Don Muang in time to see the RAF's heavy transport element, a Beverley and two Hastings, which had entered enthusiastically into the spirit of the thing, rejoin the circuit in echelon for a lumber in and break.

The presence of No 14 Sqn at Tengah provided an opportunity to compare tactical notes informally and these discussions provided an interesting commentary on the state of low-level bombing in the mid-1960s. The New Zealanders were practising straight-in attacks at 250 feet. When it was pointed out that their bombs would almost certainly skip and go off underneath them, they countered that this would not be the case if the bombs were retarded. This was true but, although retarded tail units were just beginning to become available, there were none in the Far East. Unperturbed, the Kiwis wanted to be ready for when they did arrive and anyway, they said, it was more fun. The Australians at Butterworth favoured a low-level approach and a pop-up to 2,000 feet. This would certainly reduce the incidence of bombs skipping but, using 1,000 pounders, there was a significant risk of self-damage and at this relatively low altitude the aircraft would be very vulnerable to the target's defences, including small arms fire. As No 2(B) Sqn had only eight aeroplanes, it was questionable whether *any* such risks were affordable. At this time No 45 Sqn was advocating a pop-up to 7,000 feet which would guarantee the bombs' staying put where they hit, eliminate any risk of self-damage and avoid the threat from all but AA guns, with which the Indonesians were not well provided (and in the mid-1960s they totally lacked any form of SAM). On the other hand, bombing accuracy degraded with height and there was a significant chance that the aeroplane would climb into cloud.

It should be stressed that none of the squadrons practised one tactic to the total exclusion of all others; nevertheless they all tended to have different starting points in crewroom discussions. Theoretically, as the controlling formation, HQ 224 Gp should have laid down the law but the wide range of prevalent opinion was symptomatic of the fact that wholesale low-level tactics had been introduced only recently and, in the absence of appropriate low-level weapons, everyone was still groping for the best interim solution. In 1963 there were many alternative approaches to the problem, but there was no right answer. Despite the passage of over twenty years, in practical terms, little had changed since 1941 when the Flying Camels had first begun to worry about the best way to deliver 250 pounders at low level without blowing up their Blenheims and themselves in the process.

The rest of the summer of 1963 settled into a comfortable routine which was to prove to be the lull before, if not a storm, at least a very unsettled period. There was a change of Engineering Officer in June when Flt Lt Hancock was promoted to squadron leader and posted to Seletar; his replacement was Fg Off C P Gilding. In July and September extensive use was made of Asahan Range where further live exercises were held with army FACs, several of whom were given bumpy rides over the range in Canberras and in No 20 Sqn's Hunter T.7s. Beyond this, however, there were few untoward events.

It is convenient to mention here that, while most of the RAF had given up week-end working some years before, FEAF, always the last to hear of such developments, was still regularly working on Saturday mornings, although there was rarely any flying. About once a month there was a full-scale station parade but otherwise these occasions provided an opportunity for the squadron's executives to deal with their paperwork, for the groundcrew to catch up on servicing backlogs, for the aircrew to carry out compass swings and for people to complete a variety of ground training requirements. Ground training included periodic small arms practice and riot control drill for everyone, and sundry specialist training sessions for the aircrew. The latter included the inevitable lectures on topics such as safety equipment, aircraft recognition, jungle survival and aircraft systems; a modicum of 'target study', renewal of aircrew servicing certificates and wet dinghy drills in the station pool.

Once in a while dinghy drills would be conducted in the sea, courtesy of Seletar's Marine Craft Unit and a Whirlwind helicopter which would provide a 'wet-winching'. For the really adventurous, a tour in FEAF also offered the opportunity to participate in the 'Changi Splash'. This involved a couple of days of parachute training at Seletar, culminating in a live jump into the sea from about 800 feet. Members of the squadron volunteered for this curious activity several times but there was tendency for the exercise to be cancelled at the eleventh hour due to the Beverley's being diverted to a priority task. Nevertheless, a few people did occasionally manage to throw themselves out of perfectly serviceable aeroplanes, just for the hell of it.

Ground training Saturdays had their lighter moments and the writer recalls taking part in a memorable golf competition between the aircrews of Nos 45 and 60 Sqns. This took place on the station course, which encircled the Officers' Mess, and invoked echoes of the squadron's epic cricket match against the New Zealanders at Ma'adi in 1940. The rules required that each foursome was to include a player and a novice from each squadron. A 'cool box' was positioned at each hole and the losers were required to drink a can of *Tiger*. This was a great leveller and as the tyros' confidence grew so the experts' edges were dulled; the upshot, of course, was that within a short time divots were flying in all directions. As the greens were in danger of being irreparably damaged, a distraught club secretary intervened and managed to get the game called off after nine holes. The outcome of the golf was ruled to be have been a draw and the rest of the day was devoted to a tie-breaking drinking session.

In October the squadron began to use the Low Altitude Bombing System (LABS) for the first time. This was yet another approach to the problem of low-level bombing. An easily identifiable IP was selected and the aircraft began its run towards the target from there at 250 feet and 420 knots, starting an automatic timer as it passed overhead. After a predetermined interval, which had been calculated at the planning stage and preset, the timer prompted the pilot to begin a 3g pull up; at this point the aircraft would still be some two miles short of the target. At a preset climb angle the bomb was automatically released and continued to fly in an upward and forward parabola towards the target while the aeroplane continued its looping manoeuvre which culminated in a roll off the top, by which time it was at about 7,000 feet, followed by a rapid descent to low level to escape on a reciprocal heading. It took a lot of practice to achieve accuracy with this method but it did ensure that the bomb would not ricochet and, so long as the cloud base permitted flight at 250 feet, it was relatively free from weather interference. It did expose the attacker to the defences, but only relatively briefly, and the bomb(s) would almost certainly have been released before the aircraft could be engaged. Most importantly, it more or less guaranteed that the aircraft would escape the effects of its own weapons, including even the most powerful ones.

The introduction of LABS complicated training as the crews were now required to be proficient in this technique as well as conventional low-level and high-level bombing, RP attacks and high and low-level navigation. This was a much wider range of activities than had been required a year before and the problem was exacerbated by the need for slightly different aircraft fits to execute some of these roles. With one aeroplane usually away on a Ranger or a Borneo run there were rarely more than four aeroplanes available for routine training and this was insufficient to provide the necessary flexibility to permit crews to do what they liked when they liked. To manage this problem a system of phased training soon evolved under which the squadron tended to operate at high level for a couple of weeks, then spend a fortnight on intensive RP work, then a period of LABS and so on. This way a crew would be pretty good at what it was presently doing and it ought to be no more than about six weeks since it had had a go at everything else. It was a very satisfactory compromise and this cyclic approach to training remained in vogue until 1970.

Meanwhile, despite Indonesian opposition, the Anglo-Malayan plan for the establishment of Malaysia (minus the Sultanate of Brunei) had come to fruition. On 16th September 1963 Britain relinquished her imperial authority over the Crown Colonies of Singapore, Sarawak and British North Borneo, the latter thenceforth being known as Sabah. The UK retained close ties with Malaysia, however, and remained responsible for its defence. As part of the celebrations, and to underline the continuing British presence, the squadron contributed five aircraft to a major flypast over Paya Lebar airport on September 14th.

In the months leading up to the creation of the state of Malaysia President Sukarno had begun to promote what came to be known as 'Confrontation', a state of armed political and economic hostility, sometimes including direct military involvement, but stopping short of outright war. From mid-1963, bands of guerrillas had begun to make incursions across the border from Kalimantan and the frequency of these increased in the autumn. It was not known how far President Sukarno would go but the possibility of a direct attack could not be ruled out. While the army established forward posts in Borneo and began patrolling the border, the British government began to reinforce its forces in the Far East.

As part of this overall pattern it was decided to investigate the possibility of using Kuantan as a dispersal airfield. Plans for this had been in the mill for some time and from as early as August crews had been carrying out the occasional roller landing there. The squadron mounted Exercise MERRYDOWN, a full-scale deployment to Kuantan with all eight (and that was eight out of eight!) of its B.15s, between 2nd and 8th October 1963. Beyond a runway, some frying-pan dispersals, a bulk fuel installation

Canberras parked on the frying pans at Kuantan, October 1963. (Author's collection)

and an ATC shack, Kuantan boasted few other facilities and those that did exist were off-limits. The squadron pitched its tents on the airfield, dug its latrines, set up its field kitchen and operated in much the same way as its predecessors had done at Fuka and Kumbhirgram. It was a very successful

In days of yore the squadron had its own MO but ever since 1946 it has had to borrow them from the station. This is Flt Lt John 'Doc' Rollins, on the right, supervising the construction of the shower facility erected at Kuantan for Exercise MERRYDOWN. It was furnished with a trailer of water each day from which a galvanised header tank was filled via a hand-operated pump. The rules required everyone to top up the header tank after use - having worked up a sweat using the hand pump one was ready for another shower! (No 45 Sqn archives)

A general view of the domestic site at Kuantan during Exercise MERRYDOWN. (Author's collection)

exercise, crews often flying two sorties in a day, and a considerable amount of weapons training was carried out, mostly at China Rock. It was convincingly demonstrated that it was perfectly feasible to operate a light bomber squadron from this relatively primitive site.

As part of his Confrontation campaign President Sukarno had closed Indonesian airspace to RAF aircraft which made it difficult to get down to Australia. The British could not allow themselves to be thwarted, however, and alternative routes were established via the Pacific Islands to the east or via Cocos Island and Perth to the west. Canberras used the western route and NZLRs continued to be flown, the first to go the long way around being mounted in November.

The squadron hosted another JOSSTICK in November which provided a few lighter moments but the following month the tension increased perceptibly with the declaration of a full-scale security alert. This diverted the squadron's airmen to guard duties, disrupting engineering work, but whatever had caused the alarm proved to be short-lived and after a few days the readiness state was relaxed.

Indonesia's air force, the AURI, had several Tu-16 bombers and a number of MiG fighters of various models but they also continued to operate a significant force of WW II-vintage B-25 Mitchells, B-26 Invaders and P-51 Mustangs. Despite their age, all of the latter were still very effective ground attack aircraft and they were considered to represent the greatest potential threat. The AURI had begun to probe Malaysian airspace over Borneo in September and during November nine such incursions were reported, several of them by the old piston-engined types. This led the British to establish an Air Defence Identification Zone (ADIZ) over Borneo which meant that it had to deploy detachments of Hunters and Javelins to Kuching and Labuan to patrol it. This wound up the tension another notch and increased the demand for No 45 Sqn's Canberras to run urgent spares and key personnel to and from Borneo as and when required. These tasks even began to encroach on the sanctity of the traditional weekend - always a bad sign - although it also meant that Saturday morning parades became a thing of the past.

The proximity of Indonesian airspace, only fifteen miles from Tengah, precluded the mounting of long-range fighter patrols or the stationing of radar picket ships to the south, and low-level radar cover from Bukit Gombak was limited. As a result Singapore was quite vulnerable to a surprise air attack and as an initial measure to counter this a survival scramble plan was devised. On December 5th it was practised for the first time when the AOC, AVM F Headlam CBE RAAF, gave the signal and everything that could fly flew. Once airborne the aeroplanes dispersed to take part in an ADEX, the fighters setting up patrols while the bombers flew outbound before turning back to 'attack' the airfield.

Christmas was celebrated in the traditional manner with each unit's airmen building a bar where they held open house and Christmas Dinner was served by the officers in the approved fashion. Serviceability was excellent in the early part of 1964 and a lot of training flying was accomplished, including several sessions of FAC work at Asahan. There was a major ADEX on 21st February, Exercise GOLFCLUB, during which the fighters tried a new tactic. For the purposes of the exercise the air defence sector was effectively rotated through 90º so that the target became China Rock rather than Singapore, with the threat axis coming from the east instead of the south. The fighters operated in pairs, a Javelin at low level with its radar looking upwards, accompanied by a Hunter at 1,500 feet which could be vectored towards incoming targets by the two-seater. To make this work, the bombers were required to drone in at 1,000 feet so that they could be seen. Needless to say they were all intercepted, but it was not clear exactly what this had proved. Had the Canberras approached at *low* level, as any self-respecting attacker would have done, it is highly unlikely that they would have been detected, either on radar or visually, until it was too late to carry out an interception. It was rather reminiscent of the artificiality imposed on the high-level ADEXs run in the B.2 days. The air defenders evidently drew much the same conclusions as this tactic did not appear to be persevered with. Once they had passed China Rock, the bombers had been allocated specific military installations to 'attack' in Singapore. This provided a rare opportunity to low-fly over the island to exercise the local defences and, presumably, to reassure (or frighten) the population.

There was another chance to drop live 1,000 pounders at China Rock from late February, this programme culminating in Exercise JET TRAIN on March 4th when the target was Batti Mali. On one of these sorties the CO's aircraft developed both a fuel leak and an oxygen leak. Initial hurried calculations indicated that the aeroplane would have insufficient oxygen to get back at high level and insufficient fuel to make it at low level. Brian Carruthers wisely decided that he did not need two tons of extra weight and directed Fg Off Burr to get rid of the four bombs they were carrying. The switches having been set to ensure a safe release, the bombs were jettisoned into the sea from 40,000 feet. Bob Burr continued to watch after they had disappeared from sight and eventually observed four bursts of fire as the bombs detonated on the surface of the sea. After reassessing the situation, the crew concluded that they could safely make it back to Tengah after all and an armament officer was requested to meet the aircraft. From the position of the cockpit switches and the absence of the safety lanyards in the bomb bay the latter was able to confirm that the bombs had been jettisoned 'safe'. When informed that they had in fact gone off, he pondered for a moment then opined that, since many of the bombs were quite old stocks which had been cooking in the bomb dump since Lincoln days, it was possible that they were so unstable that they might well explode under extreme conditions. Not overimpressed with this, the CO asked what would happen if the bombs were dropped via the Pilot's Emergency Jettison facility in the event of an engine failure on take off. The armourer thought it "unlikely" that they would explode under those circumstances - but he would not recommend it!

To support the fighter detachments policing the Borneo ADIZ the MU at Seletar had, almost literally, cobbled together two surveillance radars from redundant parts and spares and these had been set up at Labuan and Kuching. Fg Offs Sykes, Jefford and Butler were detached to Bornco in WT209 to calibrate them, flying five sorties between 9th and 12th March and giving the AOC a lift back to Singapore on the return flight. There was an ADEX involving attacks on HMS *Centaur* towards the end of the month. Extrapolating from the most up to date information available to the Canberra crews as to the position, speed and heading of the carrier, it appeared that, by the time of the proposed strike, it would be somewhere in southern Cambodia. Needless to say, the ship escaped detection.

The squadron found itself being drafted to help the air defences during March. The plan for the air defence of Singapore went by the name Operation FRANCISCAN and involved Javelins being held on Quick Reaction Alert (QRA) and occasional patrols by Hunters or Javelins, usually at dawn and dusk, which were considered to be the most likely times for an Indonesian air strike. Mounting these patrols, while also sustaining the detachments at Labuan and Kuching, was beginning to overstretch the fighters. To relieve this pressure, on several occasions Canberras armed with full pods of RPs took part in FRANCISCAN patrols, although the idea of using No 45 Sqn as a fighter squadron never really caught on - shades of Blenheim IVFs over Crete in 1941!

The BLUE SILK radar was the key element in the B.15's navigation fit and it developed a problem in March. There was a risk of one of its pressurised 'black boxes' exploding and until the problem could be resolved, which took several months, the aircraft were restricted to flight below 10,000 feet. Since the aircraft operated almost constantly at low-level and frequently remained below 1,000 feet from take off until they rejoined the circuit prior to landing, this had little practical impact on routine training. On the other hand, when it was necessary to climb to height, as on a Ranger, then the suspect unit had to be removed and the Doppler was inhibited. This really was something of an inconvenience and it threatened to compromise the NZLRs as they involved a very long sea leg from the northern tip of Sumatra down to Cocos Island, for which the Doppler radar was deemed to be essential. Pending a solution to the BLUE SILK snag, the problem of NZLRs was solved by mounting trips to Ohakea in pairs, with the B.15 flying in tandem with one of No 81 Sqn's PR 7s, the latter's GREEN SATIN being unaffected by the problem.

There was another chance to work with the navy in April when Exercise HIGH UP called for FEAF to carry out hi-lo strikes against HMS *Centaur* and HMS *Victorious* in the South China Sea. To circumvent the problems previously experienced in finding ships the Navy laid on a Gannet AEW 3 which stationed itself over the coast at the end of the Canberras' initial overland low-level route and vectored them towards the ships. This did the trick, but HIGH UP was a relatively small scale event compared to a SEATO exercise which ran for the whole of the last week of April. Still

*Clark Field, in the Philippines, was a fairly frequent port of call for No 45 Sqn's Canberras and several crews spent a fortnight there in April 1964 to take part in Exercise LIGTAS. These four navs, from the left, Fg Off Baz Webb, Fg Off Roy Quarrell, Flt Lt Mike Doyle-Davidson and Fg Off Deryk Butler, have just emerged from Clark's BX, clutching recently acquired bargains (or are they just looking for somewhere to stow their sick bags?).
(D J Butler)*

determined to demonstrate its solidarity and resolve, the Alliance sponsored Exercise AIR BOON CHOO. No 20 Sqn was too busy to take part this time but No 45 Sqn participated, although there were no night stops this time, the aeroplanes turning round at either Don Muang or Udorn Thani.

Flying an exercise sortie out of Don Muang could be an interesting experience This very busy airfield, which served as a major Thai air force base *and* as Bangkok's international airport, had two parallel runways, both of which seemed to be under the control of one ATC officer who, understandably, sometimes lost count of whether an aeroplane was number sixteen or seventeen to land. Once on the ground, visiting military aircraft were given no special treatment and were simply parked facing the main passenger terminal in vacant slots on the bustling main ramp between DC 8s, Boeing 707s and other commercial types. Two squadrons of Thai F-86s lived at one end of this stretch of concrete and from time to time half a dozen of these would taxi at high-speed to the end of the runway, scattering the neat crocodiles of fare-paying passengers as they were being shepherded to or from their aeroplanes.

After a hurried mission brief under the wing, getting airborne on an exercise sortie could be quite exciting. Reaching the end of the runway was done by emulating the Sabres and a request for permission to enter the active runway was usually answered with an immediate take off clearance. Fg Off Paddy Langdown received one of these automatic responses on one occasion but took the precaution of looking before he moved forward, which was just as well as the runway happened to be occupied by a pair of F-102s which had just been scrambled from the opposite end! AIR BOON CHOO ended with a flypast over Bangkok on May

1st, to which the squadron contributed four aircraft, and the following day three more took part in a flypast over Paya Lebar to mark the opening of the airport's new terminal building, the latter event being something of an anti-climax by comparison.

SEATO sponsored another major exercise in early June, this time in the Philippines. Exercise LIGTAS was essentially an amphibious assault on the island of Mindoro mounted from a fleet of seventy-five ships which included two British and two American aircraft carriers. When the main assault went in it resembled, from the air, a re-enactment of D-Day in 1944. Having just run AIR BOON CHOO, SEATO had called for only token air participation in LIGTAS, but even so this ran to some 300 aircraft. The RAF needed to be seen as players in this event and among its participating units was No 45 Sqn which detached four aircraft to Clark Field on 28th May. As the formation approached Clark the leader called up and requested guidance as to where he should park his aeroplanes - after all he had a whole half squadron here. He was advised to put them at the end of the B-57 line. This turned out to be about sixty aeroplanes long, which rather put things in perspective.

The B-57s were the squadron's old friends of the 3rd BW from Yokota. They had been on the point of flying back to the USA to re-equip with F-4s when they were diverted to the Philippines to await developments in Vietnam. Air participation in Exercise LIGTAS ended on June 9th and the squadron's detachment returned to Singapore. LIGTAS turned out to have been SEATO's swansong. The Alliance survived until 1977 but, increasingly divided over the conflict in Indo-China, it lacked cohesion. American preoccupation with Vietnam and the increasing commitment of ANZUK forces to Confrontation also weakened the Alliance and precluded the mounting of any more major exercises.

On August 2nd an incident involving the USS *Maddox* in the Gulf of Tonkin led to the 3rd BW's deployment to Bien Hoa two days later. Here they were subjected to a damaging Viet Cong mortar attack before they were finally cleared to open an interdiction campaign in February 1965, B-57s dropping the first bombs from a jet aircraft during America's war in South East Asia. Sadly, all this meant that JOSSTICKS were a thing of the past, at least they were so far as mutual exchanges between the British and American Canberra units were concerned. Another effect of the deteriorating state of affairs in South Vietnam was that Hong Kong Rangers no longer overflew Saigon on their way to Kai Tak and from then on aeroplanes always skirted round Vietnam, staying well clear of the coast.

Back at Tengah training was resumed in July with a period of LABS work and the development of a combined strike with No 20 Sqn. Using four Canberras and two four-ships of Hunters, various combinations were tried, but a typical strike would involve the Canberras plastering the area with a barrage of 296 2" RPs followed by the two sections of Hunters with their heavier 60 lb rockets. As the last of these cleared the area the Canberras ran back in to drop 24,000 lbs of bombs and the Hunters then returned to rake the target with cannon fire. It was tried out with considerable success on Exercise RAVEN at Asahan on July 19th.

While Tengah's Offensive Support Wing was busily raising a lot of dust at Asahan, simmering inter-racial tension in Singapore erupted into violence and in the course of several days of bloody rioting twenty-two people died and several hundred were injured. The assistance of British troops was offered but the local authorities, led by Lee Kuan Yew, preferred to deal with the problem themselves which they did most effectively, chiefly by the imposition and enforcement of a curfew. Nevertheless it was considered necessary to increase security at Tengah and to mount patrols around the enclaves of off-base housing where many families lived. This was essential to reassure heads of families that their dependants were safe, but the diversion of airmen to these duties considerably disrupted routine engineering work.

In addition to the implications of the steadily deteriorating political situation, daily life was further complicated by a widespread drought which affected much of the south east Asia for several uncomfortable weeks in the summer of 1964. Singapore's reservoirs were almost dry and virtually all of its water was being pumped in from Johore via the pipeline which the squadron's Hornets had spent such a lot of time patrolling. Throughout the island the mains water supply was cut off apart from a period of about four hours in the evening. During this period Tengah was able to refill its storage tanks but prudence dictated that, in order to maintain an adequate reserve, water was only made available overnight, between about 1900hrs and 0800hrs. Off camp, long queues waited all day at the stand pipes which had been installed in the villages. Despite the restrictions on the use of water on camp, the rate of consumption did not appear to decrease, much to the puzzlement of the resident civil engineers. Assuming that there had to be a major leak, the station's water supply was turned off on a selective basis to isolate the offending area. It turned out to be on the western side of the camp; but it was not a leak. Unbeknown to anyone, an adjacent village was served by a pipeline spur tapped into Tengah's water supply; the arrangement of valves and stopcocks was such that the villagers still had access to water all day and they were doing a roaring trade selling it by the bucketful.

The squadron lost its first aeroplane for some time when WH958 ingested a bird into an engine intake at Kai Tak on August 17th. Too slow to take off and too fast to stop, the aeroplane belly-flopped off the end of the runway into the sea. The crew, Flt Lt Robin Renton, Fg Offs George Wade and Malcolm Clark and Sgt Ian Ramsay were all unhurt and one of the Wanchai-Kowloon ferries diverted to pick them up.

By this time, as well as sponsoring dissident groups from the north, Indonesia was committing its own troops to operations in northern Borneo. Encouraged by the recent rioting in Singapore and believing that this had been inspired by, or could be converted into, anti-Malaysian sentiment, Djakarta raised the stakes by launching incursions into Western Malaysia, ie Malaya, for the first time. On August 17th about 100 Indonesian regulars were landed by boat at three places near Pontian on the west coast of Johore. On the 27th there was a commando attack on an oil installation on one of the small islands to the south of Singapore and that same night a Malaysian patrol boat was engaged by several

WH958 was fished out of the sea following its rather spectacular failure to get airborne after ingesting a bird on 17th August 1964. Its fairly substantial remains graced a quiet corner of Kai Tak for some months thereafter. (D J Butler)

Indonesian craft. On September 1st/2nd two, out of a planned four, Indonesian C-130s carried out an ill-advised and only partially successful night operation in the course of which ninety-six paratroops were scattered in the vicinity of Labis. The following day British Intelligence was unable to account for the whereabouts of one of the AURI's Hercules. One possibility was that it might have landed on the Indonesian-administered Natuna Islands, about 150 miles north of Kuching. Sqn Ldr Carruthers was despatched, with Flt Lt Jack Richardson and Fg Off Mal Gaynor, to carry out a low-level recce of the largest of these islands and its small airstrip but they saw nothing of significance. It was later concluded that the Hercules had crashed somewhere in the South China Sea.

Although mopping up the incursions took time and effort, none of these Indonesian actions had much real military significance. The infiltrators were certainly not given the warm welcome from the Malayan people that they had been led to expect. There was another wave of communal violence in Singapore between September 2nd and 7th, which may well have been stirred up Indonesian *agents provocateurs*, but this was contained as efficiently as July's unrest had been.

While these Indonesian initiatives had all been speedily contained they had succeeded in markedly increasing the prevailing degree of tension. Air raid precautions were implemented at military installations on Singapore island and all sections at Tengah built makeshift shelters. Most of these were based on the many monsoon drains which criss-crossed the camp. These drains were home to some really nasty creatures and the idea of sharing their habitat was regarded with some trepidation by those who had taken the time to pay a visit to the Station Hygiene Section, where preserved examples of the biggest and ugliest creepy-crawlies were kept. Another argument put forward by the anti-drain brigade was that there was a risk of their filling up with water; this was countered by the contention that if it was raining that heavily then the weather would be too bad for an air raid. Somewhat reassured by the poor weather rationale, the critics' distaste for snakes, spiders and leeches was ultimately overcome by their even greater lack of enthusiasm for Plan B - which was actually to dig real trenches!

In the event a few proper trenches were excavated, but most of the station's air raid shelters were constructed by selecting a convenient length of monsoon drain, roofing it with timber or purloined PSP and then stacking generous layers of sandbags on top. Fortunately this programme was undertaken during the school holidays and with flocks of children out from the UK there was no shortage of youthful volunteers to help fill the bags.

The station was also provided with an active defensive system in mid-1964 and Tengah soon boasted two sets of AA guns, an outer ring of radar-laid guns operated by the RA and an inner ring of RAF Regiment-manned 40 mm Bofors within the airfield perimeter. In addition to these, a few 20mm Oerliken cannons had been sited at random locations for use by anyone in the mood to engage the enemy.

The more aggressive stance being adopted by the Indonesian military in the west increased the possibility that the AURI might attempt an air strike and this led to concern about the arrangements for parking aeroplanes on the increasingly congested airfield. It was feared that with all the aeroplanes operating from their own dispersals there was a distinct possibility that all the aircraft of a given type might be neutralised in a single strafing run. For a time the aeroplanes were all mixed up so that a dispersal might contain two or three Hunters, a couple of Canberras, a Victor, a Javelin and the odd Britannia or Hastings that was passing through. It proved to be quite impractical as the increased demand for MT simply could not be sustained. If a fitter needed to collect a grommet or a widget, the squadron's Stores was no longer just across the pan. It was now likely to be a couple of miles away on the far side of the busiest runway in the RAF which could only be crossed during rare intervals in the intensive flying programme. The alternative meant going off camp through one gate and in through another, which involved laborious security checks, and then retracing one's steps. Minor engineering snags could take hours to clear. There were even cases of aeroplanes being 'lost' for hours because they had been parked on a different dispersal from the one from which they had taken off! After a few days of this the aircraft all returned to their own pans but, where space permitted, they were no longer parked in neat rows but staggered, with some aircraft being pushed right back onto the grass.

Another sign of the times was a change in the appearance of the squadron's aeroplanes as they were 'toned down' to render them less conspicuous. In September the large (twenty-four inches high) white serial numbers were repainted in black but only a short time later they were replaced by eight-inch characters. The large white disc on the fin was even more of a give-away and these too were painted out. For a few weeks the aircraft wore no unit markings but by the end of October they had reappeared. The squadron's new emblem was a rather cheeky little red and blue Flying Camel which now appeared on both sides of the fin and on the starboard side of the nose just ahead of the entrance door. This new camel, which was loosely based on the College of Heralds' rendering on the official badge, was always portrayed proceeding from right to left.

Indonesia's raising of the stakes in August had provoked a rapid build up of British forces in the Far East and by September Tengah had become very crowded. FEAF had had a virtually permanent detachment of V-bombers since December 1963, initially Victor B.1s and, although they later moved up to Butterworth, Victors and Vulcans continued to be frequent visitors at Tengah. Treaty arrangements precluded FEAF's having more than one all-weather fighter unit so No 60 Sqn had been progressively expanded until it had become the biggest squadron in the air force with thirty aircraft on strength; this situation was rationalised diplomatically in 1965 and with the arrival of No 64 Sqn a more manageable arrangement was possible. Photo-reconnaissance capacity had been enhanced since June by the reinforcement of No 81 Sqn; the first incoming detachment being provided by No 58 Sqn from the UK. No 14 Sqn RNZAF, its Canberras now sporting camouflage, was on its way up from Ohakea. No 73 Sqn was coming in from Akrotiri and a composite squadron of B(I) 8s was being prepared to deploy from Germany. In addition some RAAF Sabres were about to be detached from Butterworth to take a turn at standing QRA to maintain the FRANCISCAN alert. HMS *Victorious* had been recalled from Australian waters and, after a dramatic passage of the Lombok Straits with armed Sea Vixens on her catapults, she flew off her Air Group to join the mass of combat aeroplanes being concentrated at Tengah. Domestic accommodation was at a premium and people were doubled up everywhere; two Sea Vixen crews were even sleeping in hammocks in the shed which normally housed the golf course's lawnmowers.

A general state of emergency was declared in mid-September and the Flying Camels were ordered to exercise their dispersal option. On the 17th all eight of the squadron's bombers, half of them loaded with 1,000 pounders and the others with RPs, their crews packing sidearms, deployed to

WJ766, fully-armed and on stand-by, at Kuantan in September 1964. The squadron badge has been obliterated and the large serial numbers have been repainted in black. (D J Butler)

Kuantan. The advance party had already erected the tents but had not yet had time to dig trenches so this task became the first order of priority. An unenthusiastic start on this chore had already been made when a group of Gurkhas was spotted doing something industrious in a remote corner of the airfield. They were probably signallers laying a cable but, whatever they were, they had a trench digging machine. Putting on his best public school accent, the better to communicate with the British officer in charge, Fg Off Sykes went off to parlay and

A mobile crane picking over the crumpled and burnt out wreckage of WT370 after it had come down in a rubber plantation about a mile from Kuantan airfield on 23rd September 1964. Fg Offs Sykes and Jefford were very fortunate to have got away with this one relatively unscathed. (Author's collection)

returned shortly afterwards with the machine and its operator and the trenches were dug in no time. Several of them contained what appeared to be shards of pottery, although little significance was attached to these archaeological curiosities at first. They turned out to be the shattered remains of the pipes which drew off and dispersed storm water from the main monsoon drains running alongside the runway. This became only too apparent after the first heavy rains as the trenches promptly filled up with water!

Like Tengah, Kuantan had also sprouted some 20mm Oerlikens, drawn from naval stocks and now mounted on concrete plinths in the vicinity of the camp site. One of the navs, Flt Lt Don Gibbons, appeared to know how these things worked and, shortly after the arrival of the air echelon, he checked out all the aircrew on the complexities of the harness and the cocking and firing procedures. That evening the CO briefed the squadron on the likelihood of a dawn strike by the AURI and explained that if this happened the duty crew would sound the alarm by banging on a steel triangle hanging outside the Ops Tent. The first men to reach them were to take over the guns; everyone else was to take cover in the trenches. At dawn the next morning the alarm sounded and everyone dived into a trench. Sqn Ldr Carruthers exhorted his troops to man the guns but was confronted only by rows of heads sticking out of the ground like so many vegetables. Once they had been reassured that this was only a drill there was no shortage of volunteers willing to pose out in the open with a machine gun, like so many pale imitations of Burt Lancaster in *From Here to Eternity*, but it had been an illuminating practical demonstration of the instinct for self-preservation at work.

The squadron was held at a high state of readiness from dawn to dusk for the next few days and no flying was permitted. During this interval an Intelligence Officer joined the squadron from the UK. He had been one of two qualified linguists who had been ordered to report to Lyneham with their tropical kit and prepared for an indefinite overseas detachment at an unspecified location. As their Britannia staged its way eastwards they had enquired at each stop whether anyone wanted them. One was expected at Khormaksar where he was to assist in the Radfan campaign; the other was awaited at Changi. He was promptly given a

pistol and put on the daily resupply Hastings which delivered him to Kuantan. It had been an impressive demonstration of the RAF's stand-by system in operation. The only problem was that the chap who had stayed in Aden spoke Malay while the one at Kuantan spoke Arabic. Close!

Brian Carruthers had been nagging HQ 224 Gp for permission to do at least some flying from Kuantan and eventually authority was granted to have one aeroplane airborne at any given time. The squadron had recently acquired a single B.16 which differed from the B.15 in being fitted with a sideways looking radar, BLUE SHADOW. As a result it had only two ejection seats, one of the navs having to make do with a loose parachute. When this aeroplane, WT370, appeared on the flying programme on 23rd September the parachute turned out to be overdue for servicing. There was a brief inter-nav squabble which Fg Off Deryk Butler lost and he had to stay on the ground. After a short low-level navex the two-man crew returned to Kuantan for some circuit work. On the first overshoot the starboard engine failed to respond and by the time that the pilot had ascertained that it was not simply a surge, to which the Canberra's Avons were prone, especially if roughly handled, the aeroplane was too low, too slow and no longer aligned with the runway. Avoiding the temptation to increase power on the good engine, which would only have rolled the aeroplane onto its back, Fg Off Sykes kept it airborne as long as he could before crashing, fully stalled but wings-level, into a rubber plantation. The aeroplane broke up and burst into flames but both he and his nav, Fg Off 'Jeff' Jefford were fortunate to escape with only back injuries from which both subsequently recovered. Like most Canberras, the aircraft had still been fitted with Mk 1 scats and the crew had never had the option of ejecting.

The squadron was withdrawn to Singapore on October 9th, their place at Kuantan being taken by the composite squadron of Canberra B(I) 8s which had finally arrived from Germany. Tension was still high and flying continued to be restricted, which was just as well as there was a considerable backlog of scheduled servicing to be attended to. From the 19th the squadron spent several days on stand-by at a very high state of readiness but nothing dramatic happened. It was time for a show of force, however, and on the 28th a large flypast was mounted over an aircraft carrier which was cruising to the east of Singapore with much of the Malaysian leadership on board. While this display was primarily intended to reassure Britain's allies it could be seen as clearly from the Indonesian-held Riau Islands just to the south of Singapore and it contained an equally powerful message for the administration in Djakarta. Almost all of the participants took off from Tengah which meant that there were several more short-term detachments for the station to handle. All went well until the recovery, when a sudden tropical storm flooded the runway. With light fuel loads there was little scope for people to hold off but most aircraft managed to land at Changi or Tengah while one or two made it up to Butterworth. The storm took its toll, however, and several aircraft had aquaplaning incidents which caused burst tyres and one aeroplane finished up in the arrester barrier. No 45 Sqn had contributed four aeroplanes to this event but all succeeded in landing safely.

In December the squadron was committed to action. A group of Indonesians had landed on Kukup Island, off the south western tip of Johore, and Operation BIRDSONG was mounted to winkle them out. The first sortie was flown by Flt Lt 'Rick' Rickards (who had succeeded Dickie Duke as Flight Commander in October), Flt Lt Ken Cringle and Fg Off John Oxley who carried out simulated strikes on the 23rd but failed to dislodge the infiltrators. The next day Flt Lt Stu Pearce with Fg Offs Phil Mason and Bob Burr repeated the exercise but the Indonesians still declined to give themselves up. On Boxing Day the CO and his crew, Flt Lt Richardson and Fg Off Gaynor, assisted by an airborne FAC in a Whirlwind helicopter, loosed off some live rockets which did the trick.

December ended with Flt Lt Rickards' crew being detached to Labuan to carry out patrols of the border between Malaysian Sarawak and Sabah, and Indonesian Kalimantan, the aim to reduce the demands being made on the Hunter and Javelin detachments by exploiting the Canberra's considerable endurance at low level. The border was an ill-defined line running along a range of rugged jungle-covered mountains, reaching in places to heights of well over 6,000 feet. No 81 Sqn's repeated attempts to

Operating from Labuan's PSP dispersals proved to be quite hard on the tyres. (No 45 Sqn archives)

complete the aerial survey of Borneo, which had been under way for years (it will be recalled that No 45 Sqn's navs had been drafted to assist in this project as long ago as 1947), had been constantly frustrated by the fact that much of the rain forest covering the high ground of the interior was almost permanently shrouded in cloud. As a result, some of the remoter areas were still very poorly surveyed and such detail as did appear on available charts was largely based on travellers' tales and the reports of explorers. Such information was inevitably imprecise and reports were often conflicting; some maps showed such improbable features as rivers that apparently ran uphill. Over the previous two years, however, the daily flights of the transport and helicopter squadrons resupplying jungle forts and patrols had built up a substantial amount of local knowledge among the aircrew community. Particularly distinctive features had by now been located with some precision, permitting maps to be amended by hand.

The other significant feature of December 1964 was the acquisition of some low-level bombsights and the squadron began to familiarise themselves with their use but, as there were still no low-level bombs, this was a somewhat academic activity. At much the same time the squadron also adopted as an additional attack option a level delivery of RPs as advocated by the Akrotiri-based Canberra operators.

At the beginning of 1965, apart from those belonging to the visitors from Cyprus, FEAF had ten B.15s on strength. No 45 Sqn was supposed to have eight of these on charge at any one time, the others being held in reserve at the MU. In practice, depending on circumstances and the demands of major servicings, the squadron could have anywhere from seven to nine bombers on its books, plus the T.4. Because of the prevailing state of tension the squadron was overstocked with aeroplanes in early 1965 and, although this increased the workload for the groundcrew, it had the advantage of ensuring that there were sometimes more aeroplanes than crews available to fly them. Thus, if an aeroplane 'went u/s' on start up, there was very often a reserve available and the sortie was not lost. In January the squadron was able to accumulate a very respectable 343 flying hours, handsomely beating its published task for the first time in months. A fair proportion of this flying was done in Borneo where it had now become the practice for a Canberra to be stationed more or less permanently, five crews sampling the Labuan experience during the month. The main task was to fly border patrols but there were also ample opportunities for exercising with FACs as far to the east as Tawau; by February such exotic names as Long Pa Sia, Bario, Kalabakan and Pensiangan were being nonchalantly dropped by the Borneo veterans during crewroom discussions.

The pattern of one crew being detached to Labuan and lots of flying being done, both there and at Tengah, continued for the next two months. After two years of high-intensity Confrontation operations, however, Tengah's runway was now in urgent need of repair and it was necessary to reduce the numbers of aircraft movements to allow the contractors access to the airfield pavement. The Flying Camels were required to move out at the end of April. Just before this occurred there was another change of CO with Sqn Ldr A G Skingsley taking over on the 23rd. The following day the squadron flew a box-four over Paya Lebar as Brian

The bulk of the squadron spent two months at Labuan in 1965 to permit essential repair work to be carried out on Tengah's runway. Four of its aeroplanes are seen here over the coast of Sabah in June, shortly before the detachment returned to Singapore. (No 45 Sqn archives)

Carruthers boarded the aeroplane that was to fly him back to the UK where, as a wing commander, he was to join the directing staff of the Staff College at Andover. Three days later the squadron flew to Labuan. Six aircraft made the move. One of them, WT206, was a B.6 which had recently been taken on charge for a special task.

To permit training to continue, an Air Weapons Range had been laid out and surveyed at Balembangan Island (off the northernmost tip of Sabah) early in April and this was quickly licensed for use. The squadron soon settled in at Labuan and established a training routine which began with a period of concentrated pop-up bombing. Variety was provided by the continuing requirement to fly border patrols as required by Major General Walker and his staff at HQ COMBRITBOR. An unusual task cropped up in Hong Kong in May and between the 19th and 25th WT206 and WT208 were detached to Kai Tak where they flew twenty sorties in support of Operation MONOMANIA.

The squadron was holding a beach party on an off-shore island on June 11th when a signal arrived, urgently recalling two of the squadron's aircraft to Singapore. The message was relayed to Tony Skingsley by helicopter and just one hour and forty-five minutes after the signal had been received at Labuan the two aeroplanes were airborne. The following day the CO led a vic of Canberras and a vic of Hunters in a flypast over Brunei to mark the Queen's Birthday. On the 28th the detachment was wound up and the aircraft returned to Tengah. Here the CO found that several new crews had arrived in the squadron's absence and were waiting to embark on the in-house role conversion programme. There

was a further slight delay before a substantial start could be made on this, however, as the squadron's heavy kit was coming back by sea. The situation was further complicated by the fact that the contractors who had been giving the offices a facelift while the squadron was away had not yet finished, so temporary accommodation had to be brought into use for a while. There was one other notable event in June when Fg Off W A M Tait took an aeroplane up to Thailand to take part in the ceremonial opening of a new airport at Leong Nok Tha.

The next few months were unremarkable from the squadron's parochial point of view, the only significant event being a change of flight commander when Flt Lt Ron Miles took over from Flt Lt 'Rick' Rickards in August when the latter returned to the UK. There was, however, a political development which could have had a considerable impact in the context of Confrontation. Experience had shown that the incorporation of Sarawak and Sabah into Malaysia had been insufficient to constrain the growing political and economic influence of the dynamic and industrious urban society of Singapore. The temperamental incompatibility between the island's predominantly Chinese population and that of the mainland Malays had already bred the resentment which had given rise to the previous year's riots, and the Tunku was fearful of further social and political instability in the future. Sadly, the incorporation of Singapore within Malaysia was proving to be a threat to the cohesion of the Federation and, with regret, Lee Kuan Yew agreed to its amicable withdrawal. On 9th August 1965 Singapore became an independent state.

To mark the squadron's 50th birthday, the clockface was recreated with five B.15s and a T.4. (No 45 Sqn archives)

This could have prompted the collapse of the whole Malaysian edifice had Djakarta moved to exploit the situation but the initiative had slipped from Sukarno's grasp. In protest at Malaysia's taking a seat on the Security Council in January 1965, he had effectively withdrawn Indonesia from the United Nations. Sukarno had hoped to rally support within the Third World against what he claimed to be the British neo-colonial regime being established on his northern border. In the event he was increasingly viewed as a trouble-maker and Indonesia began to become diplomatically isolated. Sukarno turned to Peking for aid, which inspired the Indonesian Communist Party to attempt a coup on 1st October 1965. This was bloodily suppressed and a wholesale massacre of Indonesian Communists ensued. Sukarno's popular stature was sufficient to ensure his personal survival and even the retention of his nominal appointment as President but his influence diminished rapidly as power passed into the hands of a group of right-wing generals. The new leaders were more concerned with domestic affairs, the re-establishment of internal stability and economic development, than in pursuing "Bung Karno's" expansionist aim of annexing northern Borneo. There was no immediate overt change of policy, however; the rhetoric of Confrontation was maintained by the new rulers and cross-border incursions from Kalimantan continued to occur, now increasingly involving the use of regular troops in place of guerrillas but, with its instigator now marginalised, the campaign slowly began to run out of steam.

The Americans were far from winning their struggle in Vietnam but their military strength in the theatre was now so massive that they were once again able to spare aeroplanes to undertake training detachments. No 45 Sqn participated in JOSSTICK 3/65 between September 18th and 24th when they played host to the 12th TFS from Kadena, ten of the squadron's aircrew being treated to rides in the two-seat version of the visitors' very impressive F-105s. Towards the end of the month the squadron co-operated with No 205 Sqn on Exercise SHAVING BRUSH. This was a trial to establish the feasibility of carrying out both bombing and rocket attacks at night by the light of flares dropped from Shackletons. It worked, and the trials were extended into October to refine the techniques.

Although the bulk of the squadron had been back from Labuan since June, the requirement to keep one aeroplane there at the disposal of COMBRITBOR had continued, the commitment changing in October to one of having three aeroplanes at Kuching, but over the weekends only. In the meantime, however, Indonesian interest in pursuing Confrontation was waning fast. The last Canberra detachment returned to Tengah on November 8th and from then on the squadron was required to do no more than respond if the commitment were to be reinstated. Towards the end of November the squadron sent a small detachment to Hong Kong to provide the garrison with an opportunity to carry out some FAC work with aeroplanes other than the resident Hunters of No 28 Sqn.

Akrotiri's four Canberra squadrons had been taking it in turns to be detached to FEAF ever since September 1964 but, in view of the relaxation of tension, this commitment was now terminated and No 32 Sqn was not replaced when it flew back to Cyprus in December 1965. Although FEAF's reinforcements were now beginning to be withdrawn, its area of responsibility was still far from stable and it was essential for its permanent squadrons to maintain a high state of operational efficiency. Tengah's resident units continued to train hard and as part of this programme the Canberras and Javelins mounted Exercise CONGER EEL during December. In a reversal of its role in SHAVING BRUSH, this time it was No 45 Sqn which dropped the flares, the aim being to provide intra-red targets to permit No 60 Sqn to carry out some live Firestreak firings. To keep the Canberras up to the mark, HQ 224 Gp gave the squadron some 1,000 pounders for Christmas and these were dropped on First Run Attacks at Balembangan in sticks of six, aeroplanes and crews being refuelled at Labuan before returning to Singapore.

The squadron's bombing campaign against Balembangan continued into the New Year of 1966 which turned out to be the start of a period of relative stability. As Confrontation continued to ease, the 'pre-war' pattern of routine training was re-established and over the next few months the squadron settled down to a cyclic training programme during which it practised LABS deliveries (quite intensively at first to regain proficiency in this role), shallow dive-bombing, dive and level rocket attacks and pop-up bombing to 800, 3,500 and 7,000 feet using China Rock, Song Song and Asahan Ranges. It is notable that the requirement for medium and high-level bombing, although still notionally within the squadron's capabilities, was now very much on the back burner. Variety was provided by the occasional Hunter escort trip to Borneo or Kai Tak, radar calibration sorties and FOTEXs (Flag Officer Training Exercises) with the RN who could usually be prevailed upon to tow a splash target for the pilots to shoot at.

By this time there had been another change of Engineering Officer and the task of trying to outguess the Boss and produce the right number of aeroplanes in the right fit was now in the hands of Flt Lt P Miller, Chris Gilding having returned to the UK at the end of 1965.

There was brief flurry of activity in Borneo at the beginning of 1966 and Fg Off J A Barnes with Flt Lt G M Perrin and Fg Off A G Stevenson were detached to Labuan with XK641 on January 28th. They flew some border patrols in the Central and Eastern Brigade areas and carried out some FAC training at Bario and Tawau before returning to Tengah on the 31st. Over the next few months there were several more such calls for the squadron to send aircraft to Labuan at short notice in response to Indonesian incursions. There they were at the disposal of COMAIRBOR, who just happened to be Air Cdre Eddie Crew, the squadron's last CO in its Beaufighter days. Having paid a visit to the squadron at Tengah, he was flown across to Labuan in a Canberra on 5th March. In the course of some of these Borneo detachments the Canberras delivered live weapons. On 15th May, for instance, six 1,000 pounders were dropped in the Central Brigade area and the following day two aircraft dropped bombs in Eastern Brigade's area.

March 1st was the squadron's 50th Birthday and it put up a five aircraft formation to let everyone know, Kuching being included in the itinerary. That evening an all-ranks dinner was held at the New Straits View Hotel, across the causeway in Johore Bahru. The occasion was also marked by a commemorative photograph of the squadron's aeroplanes

On 1st March 1966 the squadron put up a five-aircraft formation to celebrate its 50th birthday. Three of these aircraft are seen here overflying Kuching. (No 45 Sqn archives)

posed in a clockface *á la* Fairey IIIF and Venom, although aircraft availability and the size of the Canberra meant that it had to be done with only six, rather than twelve, aeroplanes. The photograph was taken by No 81 Sqn, who could not resist taking the opportunity to 'bomb' the squadron with toilet rolls while they were about it.

There was an interesting diversion at this time when the squadron mounted a three-week field expedition to Lake Chini. There were ancient tales of a legendary 'Lost City of Pahang' and, exploiting the RAF's traditional support for such enterprises, a team from the squadron decided to go and look for it. Whilst possibly making some permanent contribution to Malayan history, the expedition would also provide an opportunity to collect samples of local flora and fauna while, and this was the RAF's real interest, providing good character-building experience of prolonged living in a jungle environment. Flt Lt J D H Price was in overall charge of the party but the designated leader was Fg Off D McL Paton; the rest of the team comprised Fg Off P J Ford and six ground tradesmen. Two more officers, Flt Lt P D Stonham and Fg Off D Walder acted as drivers to take the party up to Lake Chini on April 2nd and to recover them on the 23rd.

The expedition was very successful. Traces of several buildings were discovered and, after some excavation, the dimensions of the largest of these were estimated to have been some thirty feet by twenty feet. Several interesting artefacts were found; these and some building bricks were removed from the site and eventually passed to the museum authorities in Kuala Lumpur. The initial interpretation was that the site was at least 500 years old, possibly much older, and that it showed evidence of Thai culture. The expedition had been strongly supported by the Station Commander, Gp Capt Hawkins, who found the time to have himself flown up to the camp in a Belvedere to pay the team a personal visit on April 20th. Most gratifyingly, from HQ FEAF's point of view, this RAF activity also stimulated a considerable amount of public interest and attracted extensive Press coverage, both locally and in the UK.

Sadly this success had been marred by tragedy. On 4th

April, shortly after the expedition had established its camp, a pair of the squadron's Canberras overflew the site while carrying out a low-level navex to pay their respects to the explorers[5]. While still in the vicinity of Lake Chini XK641 was seen to roll over and crash into the jungle. Sadly there were no survivors from the crew of Fg Off Rufus Redley, Fg Off Phil Harrison and Flt Lt Colin Cooke.

The late-series Canberra .was already a very flexible attack aeroplane but it was to have one last shot added to its locker, an air-to-surface missile. Rumours that the squadron was to be armed with the French-built Nord AS 30 had begun circulating as early as 1964 but in the event the Akrotiri-based No 73 Sqn was to be the first to introduce them into service, spending most of 1965 working up on the system before conducting its first live firings in November. No 32 Sqn was next to get missiles and the Flying Camels did not receive their first aircraft modified to carry AS 30s until June 1966. This aeroplane, WH977, and a ground simulator permitted a start to be made on training with the new system but the supply of further aircraft was slow and the squadron still had only three AS 30-capable Canberras (WH961, WH977 and WT213) by the end of the year.

On 30th June 1966 the squadron took part in Exercise LONG HOP which provided an opportunity to attack HMS *Eagle* and HMS *Albion*. This turned out to be a most successful training event, especially as the squadron considered that it had won the engagement - it is not known what the RN's view was. Between 6th and 13th July there was another detachment to Hong Kong where the Canberras supplemented No 28 Sqn's Hunters in their routine patrolling of the border. They also carried out some FAC training with

No 45 Sqn's Lake Chini Expedition Team in April 1966. From the left, standing, are SAC Pollard, Cpl Sprinks, Flt Lt John Price, SAC Mills and Sgt Hamilton. Squatting: Fg Off Phil Ford, J/T Thompson, Fg Off Don Paton and SAC Duckworth. (No 45 Sqn archives)

WT211 in 1966 showing the toned-down Confrontation colours - small emblem on the fin; small black serial numbers. Note the bamboo and canvas sunshade over the cockpit and the absence of tip tanks which, apart from Lone Rangers, were rarely fitted to the B.15s. (MAP)

the garrison, indulged in some air combat manoeuvring with the resident fighters and found time to fire off some rockets on Port Shelter Range.

There was another opportunity for the squadron to demonstrate its expertise with RPs on July 21st when a major firepower demonstration was laid on at China Rock; in fact they proved to be a little too good. A surplus LST had been coaxed out of the navy and moored in the bay to serve as a target which the combined efforts of FEAF would be called upon to sink with a spectacular expenditure of live weapons. To ensure that everyone was familiar with the revised range layout, the participants were permitted to have a practice run on the 20th. Tony Skingsley led three crews across to the range, each aeroplane being armed with two 2" rockets and a single 25 lb practice bomb. The rocket attacks were delivered first and the second crew actually hit the LST, which subsequently filled up with water and disappeared beneath the waves. To have sunk a quite substantial vessel with just one, or at best two, small rockets was quite an achievement, but 'their airships' seemed curiously unimpressed, particularly when the navy declined to offer up any more spare boats on the grounds that they did not have any and, even if they had, they would prefer to sink them themselves, thank you very much!

The sinking of the LST had not been the only unforeseen event. Another star turn was to have been a Victor delivering a stick of thirty-five VT (ie radar) fused 1,000 pounders. These fuses turned out to be as oversensitive as those that the squadron had frightened themselves with in 1945. On the rehearsal day the first half-dozen bombs airburst just above the sea, as planned, but the rest of the stick detonated sympathetically while it was still falling, resulting in a vertical, rather than a horizontal, line of explosions which climbed up towards the bomber, although it never actually reached it. Fg Off Don Paton was RSO at the time and he recalls having been deeply impressed by the fiery spectacle which was

unfolding no more than a mile from his quadrant hut, and even more so by the rapidly advancing tidal wave caused by the first few explosions. Not knowing what other surprises might be in store, the entire range party promptly took to their heels! Despite these hiccups, FEAF still had plenty of firepower to display; the full-scale demonstration went ahead more or less as planned, accuracy no longer being a problem as the tactical target was now just a particular bit of sea.

Throughout the previous year the state of armed hostility had continued but Indonesian incursions into Western Malaysia had long since ceased. Border-crossings were still occurring in Borneo, however, and although these tended to be on a much larger scale, as time passed their frequency steadily decreased. The Commonwealth troops were now very firmly established, in considerable strength, well armed and amply supplied, almost entirely by air. There were still occasional firefights but the Indonesian troops scored very few successes. By mid-1966 power in Indonesia was firmly concentrated in the hands of the army. Confrontation had been 'Bung Karno's' idea and with his eclipse it had lost its

Sqn Ldr Geoff Wallingford, OC No 14 Sqn RNZAF, and Sqn Ldr Tony Skingsley, OC No 45 Sqn, share a convivial moment out on the pan shortly before the Kiwis returned to New Zealand in November 1966. The picture provides a good impression of the rather jaunty 'Confrontation Camel' which was introduced in the late summer of 1964. (No 45 Sqn archives)

423

momentum. Djakarta began to make diplomatic evertures in May 1966 and these eventually led to a conference in Bangkok where a peace treaty was signed on 11th August. Confrontation was over.

Flying training was constrained by a patch of poor serviceability during September, this being compounded by the ferry programme associated with the provision of further AS 30-equipped aeroplanes, which was running late. Things were beginning to quieten down in any case. The reinforcement of No 81 Sqn ceased in August 1966 and in November No 14 Sqn flew back to New Zealand. Apart from the continued presence of a second Javelin outfit, No 64 Sqn, Tengah began to look much as it had done in 1962, except that the return to a relatively normal routine no longer included working on Saturday mornings.

In October/November the CFS 'Trappers' materialised in the Far East and the Flying Camel was put through its paces. Based on its recent experience, No 45 Sqn's contribution to the next edition of the *Tengah Times* first suggested that a Trappers' visit was a good time to go on leave or to report sick; the squadron's scribe then offered.....'the following list of instant excuses and answers, without prejudice and free of charge, to help embarrassed pilots after substandard manoeuvres:

1. a. 'I feel sick.'
   b. 'The navigator feels sick.'
   c. 'You feel sick.'
2. Substitute, as applicable, 'My arms/legs/stomach/liver suddenly felt weak.'
3. 'I've always been taught to do it that frightening/dangerous/suicidal way.' Use the same adjective as the Trapper for maximum effect.
4. 'My attention was distracted by....'
   a. Javelin pilot - '...the flashing red light.'
   b. Hunter pilot - '...MiG-21, high, 6 o'clock, 10 miles, closing left to right, Asian eyes under the visor!'
   c. Canberra pilot - '...the navigator screaming in terror.'
5. If asked how you got through flying training, try:
   a. 'You were my instructor.'
   b. 'My father is an air vice marshal.'
   c. 'I went to Cranwell.'
   d. 'What?'

e. 'They didn't have it when I joined.' - only applicable to Javelin pilots.
6. As a last resort try offering a blank cheque."

Apart from the presence of the CFS team, November 1966 proved to be a busy month. The Javelin boys wanted to fire some more Firestreaks so the squadron obliged with another Exercise CONGER EEL and dropped some 4.5 inch flares for them. There was another opportunity to drop 1,000 lb bombs at Balembangan in Exercise JETEX II/66 and there were two joint army/RAF counter-insurgency exercises staged near Terendak and Batu Pahat, WINGED HAGGIS and STRAIGHT FLUSH. Both were useful for the soldiers but neither produced sufficient trade to satisfy the squadron. One aircraft and crew were dedicated to the first exercise and held at a high state of readiness throughout the ten days, awaiting short-notice tasking. This yielded just eight hours of actual flying; for the rest of the time the aeroplane just sat on the ground and rusted. The second event was a little better, but even then it was not until well into the second day before the squadron was required to participate actively. Nevertheless, despite these adverse influences, the squadron still managed to fly 256 hours during the month which, with an average daily availability of only three aeroplanes, was quite a respectable figure. November was also notable for a change of flight commander, Flt Lt John Price taking over from Ron Miles who was now 'tourex'.

Now that No 14 Sqn had returned to Ohakea, NZLRs reappeared on the programme and the first one for about three years was flown in February 1967. Thereafter there were few events of great note until 3rd May when the squadron participated in Exercise ALGUM. This involved two pairs of Canberras flying independently to northern Malaya where they joined up before rendezvousing with six of No 20 Sqn's Hunters, the whole Balbo then proceeding to Gong Kedak to carry out a co-ordinated dummy strike. Having comprehensively 'destroyed' the target, all the aircraft landed on it to join their groundcrew who had been flown up in advance. The joint detachment then operated from Gong Kedak, mounting attacks on Singapore until May 9th, when it flew back to Tengah.

Three aircraft, one of them a B.6 which had been delivered as long ago as April 1966, were detached to Kai Tak from 23rd to 25th June to take part in Operation TENNON. Four days later the squadron lost an aeroplane.

Distinguishable by the absence of an HF 'washing line' aerial and its modified wingtip tanks, this is one of two B.6s flown by No 45 Sqn. Seen here towards the end of its time with the squadron, WH976, was on charge from April 1966 until April 1967. (MAP)

Two of the squadron's aeroplanes, WH956 (nearest the camera) and WH974, at Labuan for Exercise HOTSHOT in August 1967. (Author's collection)

Fg Offs I D Hill and T V Hudson (a South African) had just taken off from Tengah in a T.4, WD963, when it suffered a double flame-out. With insufficient height to relight they were obliged to eject at 650 feet. Fortunately, most Canberras had by then been retrofitted with ejection seats with a low-level capability and the crew survived with relatively little damage.

The missile conversion programme began to gain momentum in early August and the navs fired a dozen SS 11 wire-guided missiles from Whirlwind helicopters of No 103 Sqn before five aircraft deployed to Labuan on the 22nd for Exercise HOTSHOT. Before they returned to Tengah on the 31st they had fired twenty AS 30s of which eight malfunctioned to some, in most cases only minor, degree. Despite this, the 50% error for all twenty was still an impressive twenty-four feet.

In September there was another opportunity to fire SS 11s at China Rock, followed by another JETEX, dropping 1,000 pounders at Balembangan and turning round at Labuan. By this time relations with Indonesia had improved to the extent that it was no longer necessary to make the long detour via Cocos and Perth and the first NZLR to fly the original direct route, through Darwin, was flown between 6th and 13th September by Fg Off Paton, Flt Lt Morley and Flt Lt Gibson with Fg Off Morgan of No 20 Sqn as a passenger.

Sqn Ldr Tony Skingsley had now done his time with the squadron and he handed over the reins on November 7th to pursue a highly successful career in other fields. He was eventually to retire as Air Chief Marshal Sir Anthony Skingsley GBE KCB, his final appointment being within NATO's integrated command structure as DCINCENT. His successor at Tengah was Sqn Ldr W J A Innes who would turn out to be the sixth and last CO of the Canberra era. Within a month the squadron was on the move again with a six-aircraft detachment to Kai Tak. Hong Kong's Hunters had been withdrawn in January 1967 when No 28 Sqn had been disbanded; since then the only RAF aeroplanes in the colony had been transients, mostly transport types, and there was a need both to show the flag and to provide the garrison's troops with continuation training in FAC work. This was to become a regular and welcome commitment for No 45 Sqn for the next two years. The first detachment, christened Exercise SHARPSHOOT, took place between 5th and 13th December.

Christmas came and went and then, on 1st February 1968, the squadron bent another aeroplane when Fg Offs Hill, Head and Godfrey were obliged to land without the benefit of an undercarriage as a result of a massive hydraulic leak, which meant that frantically waggling WT209's emergency hand pump served only to empty the hydraulic reservoir without doing anything positive about coaxing the wheels down. The problem had cropped up during a four-ship practice dusk strike and by the time the aircraft had returned to Tengah and burned off fuel it was completely dark. A film was being shown in the Officers' Mess at the time and this was interrupted while everyone moved out onto the balcony to watch with the usual sense of ghoulish anticipation. They were to be disappointed, however; 'Geordie' Hill pulled off an exemplary 'wheels-up' and once it was clear that there

This photograph of an AS 30 being loaded onto WH961 at Labuan shows the bulky additional pylon which was part of the kit. (No 45 Sqn archives)

425

The officers of No 45 Sqn in September 1968. From the left, front row: Fg Off M K Steel, Flt Lt L E White, Flt Lt J F Schofield, Sqn Ldr P D Stonham, Sqn Ldr W J A Innes, Flt Lt R S Williams, Flt Lt D E Betts, Flt Lt P N Thorpe and Flt Lt A L Wall. Middle row: Flt Lt C Harrison, Flt Lt T P Burns, Fg Off P J Somerfield, Fg Off G A Brady, Fg Off B G L Burnett, Fg Off R A Head, Flt Lt P A Walliker, Fg Off J Vinales, Fg Off J S F Kitchen, Flt Lt D G Watkins and Flt Lt D G M Hughes. Back row: Fg Off W B Harrison, Fg Off M R L McDougall, Flt Lt S B Cox, Fg Off C J Yeo, Fg Off J M Ravenhall, Fg Off A Threadgold, Fg Off A T Hine, Fg Off P R Lea, Fg Off M Ingham and Plt Off M R Cann. (No 45 Sqn archives)

426

Five Canberras lined up at Lab during HOTSHOT 2, April-May 1968. (No 45 Sqn archives)

would be no fireworks, the audience quickly lost interest and the film was restarted. Although Canberras were often returned to service after this sort of treatment, the aeroplane was now approaching the end of its front-line service and WT209 was eventually assessed as being beyond economic repair and scrapped. This was to be No 45 Sqn's last serious Canberra incident. It had occurred just as the squadron was changing its Engineering Officer for the last time. Flt Lt Pat Miller returned to the UK in February, bequeathing custody of the unit's nuts and bolts to Fg Off Brian Crockford with WO Hill remaining on hand to provide continuity.

The only out of the ordinary activities over the next couple of months were a spate of calibration sorties for the Bukit Gombak radars controlling No 65 Sqn's Bloodhounds and a burst of RP work against a splash target. To help celebrate the Fiftieth Anniversary of the foundation of the service, three aeroplanes flew up to Hong Kong on March 28th but it rained on the RAF's parade; the flypast was cancelled and the detachment returned to Tengah on 1st April. Back in Singapore the weather had been kinder and three more B.15s, with one of No 81 Sqn's PR 7s to make a box-four, had led a formation of thirty-two aircraft which had toured all the airfields on the island (the other participants were: four Canberras of No 14 Sqn RNZAF, back in Singapore for the occasion; eight of No 20 Sqn's Hunters; four Javelins of No 60 Sqn; four Lightnings of No 74 Sqn; four Mirages of No 75 Sqn RAAF from Butterworth and four Meteors of Changi's No 1574 Flt).

The remainder of 1968 was chiefly notable for the number of detachments mounted by the squadron. The first was to carry out another session of AS 30 firings, Exercise HOTSHOT 2, at Balembangan between April 26th and May 6th, for which the squadron deployed to Labuan. Between 14th and 29th August six aircraft were based at Kai Tak for Exercise SHARPSHOOT 2. This detachment was interrupted by Hurricane SHIRLEY and the aeroplanes beat a hasty retreat to Tengah on the 20th, returning to Hong Kong on the 23rd after the typhoon had moved on.

While the unscheduled flights to and from Singapore had disrupted the detachment's social routine, this transit flying was actually a blessing in disguise. While a SHARPSHOOT was a highly enjoyable experience for all who participated it did tend to create problems for the squadron's executives.

One of the participating crews in HOTSHOT 2. Flt Lt Adrian Wall, Flt Lt John Schofield and Fg Off Simon Kitchen at Labuan in June 1968. (No 45 Sqn archives)

Despite the operating constraints imposed by the confines of Hong Kong's limited airspace, there was still a need to satisfy the unremitting demands of the 'Flying Hours Graph', which assumed that every trip would involve something like two hours' flying time. The problem was that it was difficult to find two hours' worth of constructive things to do while flying from Kai Tak, especially now that there no longer any Hunters to play with. Nevertheless, by firing RP details at Port Shelter, carrying out some FAC work with the garrison, flying border patrols and shooting some circuits in between the airliners using Kai Tak's startlingly unique air traffic pattern (which involved a curved approach seemingly *between* high rise apartment blocks) a SHARPSHOOT could usually amass a respectable amount of flying time.

In October the squadron mounted a detachment in Australia to participate in Exercise SHADOW, a close support exercise involving FAC work. Four aircraft flew down to Amberley on the 4th offering to fly up to two missions per aircraft per day. In the event only thirty-five tasks were allocated to the squadron, of which thirty-two were successfully completed. On completion of the exercise, on October 15th, only two of the aircraft returned to Singapore. The other pair flew across to Woomera. Here they joined two others which had come down from Tengah on the 9th and 11th; all four were to take part in another AS 30 shoot - HOTSHOT 3.

A DX47 airborne missile simulator had been introduced at Tengah a month before and one of the aims of HOTSHOT 3 was to complete the evaluation of this device by assessing whether the three crews who had been trained on it showed any improvement in performance when compared with their less fortunate predecessors. Before it flew back to Tengah on the 28th the squadron had loosed off forty rounds, of which eleven had scored direct hits. One aeroplane, WT213, had to be left behind at Woomera, pending an engine change, and it did not get back to Tengah until November 4th. Analysis of the exercise results indicated that a novice crew probably was more likely to be successful in their first live shoot if they had been trained on the airborne simulator; the difference was not great, however, and this small advantage had to be set against the considerable expense of the device (it was said to cost three times the price of a live missile) and the fact that it created its own set of sometimes intractable logistic and maintenance problems.

In the meantime there had been another change of flight commander when Flt Lt R S Williams had succeeded to the appointment during October; he was to be the last man to fill it, his predecessor, Pete Stonham having been in the chair

Flt Lt Don Betts does his stuff in WH974 during the Open Day held at Tengah on 2nd November 1968. The Officers' Mess can be seen in the background. (No 45 Sqn archives)

since January 1968 (as a squadron leader since May) when he had taken over from John Price.

On November 2nd, Tengah had held its first ever Open Day, Flt Lt D E Betts doing the honours for the squadron by displaying the Canberra's remarkable manoeuvrability. Exercise SHARPSHOOT 3 took the squadron back to Kai Tak on December 6th whence they returned to base on the 20th in good time for the seasonal festivities.

By this time the writing was clearly on the wall for FEAF. Since 1945 Great Britain been embroiled in many campaigns in an effort to sustain her global status, to retain her imperial influence and to honour her post-colonial obligations. Confrontation was not the last of these but it had been the biggest and probably the most expensive. It had driven home the lesson first taught by Suez, that Britain was fighting above her weight; the UK was seriously overextended and needed to reduce its commitments to match its military and economic capacity. There was a major Defence Review during 1966, the findings of which were reflected in the following year's White Paper which announced a 50% reduction in Britain's military presence in the Far East by 1971. On further reflection it was concluded that even this swingeing cut was insufficient. Despite the intensity of the war in Vietnam, and the perceived risk to the rest of South East Asia and Australia if the Americans should fail in their endeavours to hold the ring, and Britain's commitments to SEATO, the 1968 White Paper on Defence announced that Britain would withdraw virtually all of its forces from the region by 1971, with the exception of those stationed in Hong Kong. Her remaining regional defence obligations were to be met by a small residual contribution to a joint ANZUK Force and even this was withdrawn in 1976 to be replaced by occasional exercise deployments.

In the wake of these announcements, No 64 Sqn had been disbanded in 1967 to be followed by No 60 Sqn in May 1968. The two Javelin squadrons had been replaced by No 74 Sqn whose Lightnings were destined to remain until September 1971 to provide air defence cover in the event of anything untoward occurring during the British withdrawal, but Tengah's other long-term residents were all earmarked for disbandment.

Although the squadron had only a year left to live, there was no relaxation in the training schedule during 1969 and the Ranger programme ensured that the Flying Camels' continuing presence was advertised throughout the region from New Zealand to Hong Kong and from the Philippines to Gan, where the squadron occasionally sent an aeroplane to provide a met recce for incoming squadrons on reinforcement exercises. In addition Sqn Ldr Bill Innes finally succeeded in persuading HQ FEAF that they ought to extend the duration of a Bangkok Ranger to permit a weekend stopover.

Since the Canberra's days were now numbered, there was less need to conserve airframe hours and by March the squadron had nine B.15s on charge, mostly AS 30-capable and all in sound running condition. Just to show the other outfits what 100% serviceability looked like, on March 27th the squadron put up a diamond nine, with the T.4 airborne as well, as whipper-in[6].

All four strike squadrons of Akrotiri's Canberra Wing had recently been disbanded and a few of NEAF's redundant AS 30 carriers were flown out to Tengah, the arrival of WH966

27th March 1969. Nine out of nine, and the T.4 was up as well! (No 45 Sqn archives)

and WH968 in March 1969 permitting the squadron to dispose of WJ766, its last non-AS 30 aircraft. Several more of Akrotiri's second-hand aeroplanes (and a few 'used' navs) found their way out to FEAF, not as reinforcements but simply to sustain No 45 Sqn's strength. After several years of quite punishing low-level flying in the turbulent tropical air, cracks were now beginning to be discovered in the Canberra's wing centre section forging. WT213 was the first aeroplane to display these symptoms and it was grounded in March 1969. WH959 and WH961 were diagnosed as suffering from similar problems in May, both of these aeroplanes being flown back to the UK for rectification. Two more ex-NEAF missile-firers, WH948 and WH981, were ferried out to Singapore as replacements and taken onto the squadron's charge in June[7].

In the meantime the squadron had returned to Woomera on 9th April for yet another session of AS 30 firings. Since it was now the sole remaining missile-firing Canberra unit, it was permitted to dispose of a substantial quantity of the remaining stock and, in conjunction with the staff of the WRE, to experiment with delivery methods. The AS 30 was normally fired at about 3½ miles from its target and it rapidly accelerated to near supersonic speed. This meant that the controller had a very short time in which to 'capture' the missile, by making radio contact with it and establishing that it would respond to his demands, and then guide it to its target. This in turn meant that the target had to be distinct enough to be visible at the time of launch and that the aeroplane had to be high enough to permit it to be seen. The usual technique involved a low-level approach, followed by a pop up to about 1,000 feet for launch and a gradual descent during the guidance phase. A significant drawback with this first generation missile was the necessity for the launch aircraft to follow the missile until its impact, which involved flying very close to the (presumably defended) target.

During the squadron's second Woomera deployment a number of variations were tried. One involved ultra-low level approaches at 50 feet with a pop up to only 250 feet, which was only practical with a very clearly defined target. Another

experiment involved multiple launches from as many as four aircraft flying line abreast. In an attempt to overcome the need for the launch aircraft virtually to overfly the target, some launches were carried out with two aircraft in tandem about 3½ miles apart. The first aeroplane launched the missile and, having 'captured' it, control was then passed to the second aircraft, permitting the Leader to turn away and leaving his No 2 to complete the terminal guidance phase from a relatively long range, ie a safe distance. Some success attended these experiments but it was found that the No 2 could have difficulty in identifying the target at this distance and the missile was even harder to pick out, despite the flares carried by the latter to the make it more visible. Nevertheless, much useful data was accumulated and the WRE's boffins were able to add substantially to their fund of practical knowledge of missile guidance.

In addition, an RAF Regiment team happened to be at Woomera at the time, developing operational tactics for the Rapier point defence missile system. They too were able to take advantage of the AS 30s firings which provided them with many opportunities to deal with very small, high speed targets, although no live engagements were attempted. By the time the squadron returned to Singapore on 24th April it had loosed off another forty-eight missiles and its crews were far and away the most experienced exponents of the art of live missile-firing in the RAF.

There had been one other notable event during the Woomera detachment. While the squadron was there the experimental establishment fired a Skylark atmospheric sounding rocket - and lost it. The Flying Camels were asked to help find the nosecone with its valuable instrumentation package and its recorded data. The locals forecast the most promising search area but the squadron's Nav Leader, Flt Lt Dave Castle, did his own analysis of the available data and came up with a different answer. He and his crew, Flt Lt Paul Coulson and Fg Off Trevor Marks, backed their hunch and on 22nd April they found the missing nosecone more or less where they had predicted that it would be.

On June 5th the squadron was honoured by a visit from one of its most eminent Old Boys, Air Chief Marshal Sir Basil Embry GCB KBE DSO DFC AFC, the erstwhile captain of the Vimy Ambulance in 1925, who was now farming near Perth. He was escorted by the Air Commander, Air Marshal Sir Neil Wheeler KCB CBE DSO DFC AFC. In the course of an informal crewroom chat, Sir Basil recalled that during his time on the squadron discipline had been very strict and life had been quite hard for a junior officer. Sir Neil agreed enthusiastically, recollecting an instance from his own youth when, for the infringement of some obscure minor regulation, he had been made to run around his aerodrome wearing a parachute. Quick to regain the initiative, Sir Basil

During his visit to Tengah in June 1969 Air Chief Marshal Sir Basil Embry, the erstwhile captain of No 45 Sqn's Vimy Ambulance, was presented with a squadron plaque by Sqn Ldr Bill Innes. (No 45 Sqn archives)

observed airily that in his day they had not had parachutes. Touché!

Exercise SHARPSHOOT 4 was mounted between 1st and 17th August with six aircraft being deployed to Kai Tak. Back at Tengah routine training continued for the rest of the summer, with a distinct 'end of term' atmosphere beginning to develop as the time for disbandment drew nearer. Towards the end of the year the squadron laid on several Exercise FIREFLASHES. Similar in concept to the CONGER EELS that used to be run for the Javelins, a FIREFLASH involved dropping Lepus flares for No 74 Sqn's Lightnings to practice live infra-red missile firings. In November the squadron went back to Hong Kong for the last time, for SHARPSHOOT 5, and the following month Exercise FINAL FLING provided one last opportunity to destroy China Rock with 1,000 pounders. The squadron had chipped quite a few bits off this little island over the previous twenty years but it had resisted their best efforts thus far and it continued to do so. China Rock won - it is still there; the squadron has gone.

No 81 Sqn disbanded on 16th January 1970 and on February 18th Nos 20 and 45 Sqns followed them into limbo. This sad occasion was marked by a parade held at sunset. The Reviewing Officer, most appropriately, was Sir Basil Embry who had very strong connections with both units; his service with No 45 Sqn as a flying officer in Iraq had earned him an AFC in 1925 and, as a squadron leader in India he had commanded No 20 Sqn in 1937-38. Six aeroplanes from each squadron flew past in salute and the ceremonial ended with the two Standards being marched off into the gathering

WH948 turning in for a run on the Port Shelter Range during Exercise SHARPSHOOT 5 in November 1969; the last of many visits to Hong Kong by No 45 Sqn's Canberras. Note the double pylons, the outer ones being fairings to cover the gubbins associated with the carriage of AS 30s. (No 45 Sqn archives)

Exercise FINAL FLING at China Rock in December 1969. WH948 releases the last stick of 1,000 pounders to be dropped by a Canberra of No 45 Sqn - and probably the last by any RAF Canberra. (No 45 Sqn archives)

dusk. It was a moving sight and symbolic of more than just the sun setting on two proud squadrons; it also marked the late evening of Britain's once powerful empire in the Far East. By the end of 1971 HQ FEAF would have gone and with it most of its remaining squadrons. By 1972 all that would be left would be a small Shackleton (later Nimrod) detachment and the Wessex helicopters of No 103 Sqn based at Tengah, which by then belonged to the Singapore Air Defence Command. Three years later even these remnants would have disappeared.

The Flying Camels had been a permanent feature of the RAF scene in Malaya and Singapore since 1948 and, apart from a couple of years at Butterworth, the squadron had been based at Tengah since 1950. For the last twelve of these years it had flown the Canberra, a fine aeroplane, even if it was fast approaching obsolescence by 1970. The Canberra's reliability, and the operational flexibility conferred by the wide range of weapon options offered by the B.15 variant, had provided the squadron's crews with plentiful flying experience which was both varied and stimulating. Although the Canberra era had begun with a tragedy, the squadron had recovered quickly from this initial setback and there can be few who served with the Flying Camels between 1958 and 1970 who do not look back on their experiences with affection. A tour in Singapore was in itself probably the most sought after posting in the RAF of the 1960s; participation in squadron exchanges and SEATO exercises, along with practice deployments and training detachments, plus the mounting of Lone Rangers all provided frequent opportunities for travel throughout South East Asia and Australasia. There had been a slightly sticky patch during Confrontation but the increased tension which this had involved, and the odd associated burst of excitement, had provided challenges which the Flying Camel had taken easily in its stride.

FEAF had always had a comprehensive range of operational capabilities but it tended to have only one squadron operating in each role. Thus, throughout the 1960s, the Flying Camels had filled a unique niche as FEAF's only long-range strike/attack unit. It has been suggested that there was some disadvantage in this as the spur of competition was lacking. On the other hand, had there been two or more bomber squadrons at Tengah, there is little doubt that they would have fallen prey to the machinations of 'the centralisers' and their identities would inevitably have been diluted, as had happened in Cyprus in 1966 when all four of Akrotiri's Canberra squadrons were stripped of their groundcrews and obliged to pool their aeroplanes. No doubt this had made NEAF's striking force cheaper and (possibly) more efficient, but whether these advantages had actually added up to its being *better* is highly debatable. It was certainly an unpopular innovation at unit-level and did nothing for morale and *esprit de corps*, vital commodities with which No 45 Sqn was richly endowed. During its last year, however, even Tengah had fallen victim to a degree of centralisation and, although it retained a handful of airmen to work on the flightline, the bulk of its groundcrew were drafted into Engineering Wing to labour on PR 7s or B.15s, which technically speaking were much the same.

As the squadron began to disperse, the silver, the albums and all its other mementoes were packed and despatched to the UK for storage. The aeroplanes were ferried home and the Standard was conveyed to the RAF College where it was to reside pending the squadron's reformation. There had been a No 45 Sqn since before there had been an RAF. It was now among the most senior and longest-serving of the service's fighting formations. It was unthinkable that the RAF would not need it again. It could only be a matter of time before the squadron would be recalled to the line.

Notes:

1. All Canberras had the ability to carry fuel in jettisonable wingtip tanks which could be temperamental and sometimes failed to feed, especially after they had just been fitted. These tanks created quite a lot of drag and, although they theoretically provided a significant increase in range, this was only the case if the fuel in them was consumed first and the empty tanks were then jettisoned. This was not a viable option in peacetime so the tanks stayed on and the cost of carrying them about was something like 70% of the fuel that they contained. The integral wing fuel tanks meant that a B.15 without tip tanks already had a longer range than a B.2 with them; in general, the squadron dispensed with the drop tanks on its B.15s and they tended only to be fitted for specific long-range trips, like Rangers.

2. A SARAH (Search And Rescue And Homing) beacon was a small, battery-operated radio transmitter which, if the aerial was kept more or less vertical, permitted a search aircraft to pinpoint a survivor's location with considerable accuracy by flying towards the signal and finding the overhead 'null'. If two transmitters were operating on the same frequency, however, their polar diagrams merged and, while it was still possible to narrow down their general location, the mutual interference made it impossible to distinguish their individual positions.

3. Having delivered it to Lyneham, the squadron's responsibility towards WJ986 was at an end and it was to be collected and taken away. Once they had looked the aeroplane over, the ferry crew from the MU decided to make the next trip as brief and uncomplicated as possible and the short hop to Wroughton was flown without tempting fate by retracting the undercarriage. Since he had flown home in it, this writer was curious to discover what fate ultimately befell WJ986. Despite its superficially tatty condition, once it had been given a respray and been fitted with a few value-enhancing accessories, it proved to be a sound runner and a second-hand bargain. It eventually found its way to No 360 Sqn with whom it ended its days, by then a T.17, as late as 28th October 1994 - which just goes to show that first impressions can be deceptive.

4. The Microcell rocket pods carried by the Canberra B.15 and B.16 could be fired in quadrants. If only one rocket was loaded into each quadrant it was possible to make eight passes firing a single RP each time. This was excellent for improving a pilot's accuracy but it was never the intention to employ these weapons individually on operations. A single 2" RP lacked punch and the system achieved its effect by firing all seventy-four in a salvo to carpet an area about the size of a football pitch.

5. It was a long-standing practice for squadrons based in Malaya and Singapore to pay a flying visit to any of their personnel who were operating 'up country'. This occurred most frequently at about Friday lunchtime on the second week of a long Jungle Survival Course. Attendance at this course was mandatory within three months of arrival for aircrew permanently assigned to FEAF. The second week was spent living in the jungle. On completion of this phase the crews emerged and rendezvoused on a bridge over a river a few miles to the south of Mersing on the east coast of Malaya. Since the courses were drawn from many different units the bridge attracted aeroplanes from all squadrons like bees to a honeypot. Concerned at the collision risk, HQ FEAF established a Prohibited Area within a two mile radius of the bridge on these occasions. It may have been the most infringed piece of Restricted Airspace in the world! The only aeroplane permitted to enter it was a Pioneer of No 209 Sqn which always dropped a couple of cases of Tiger beer to the tired and thirsty 'survivors', who would then be gambolling naked in the stream - much to the amusement of the occasional passing busload of locals - to remove five day's worth of sweat and grime (and in some cases the RAF-issue condom which was alleged to prevent too intimate an acquaintance with leeches - the author could never decide whether this was a real risk or a private joke for the benefit of the staff of the Survival School; in any event it was a severe test of manhood for those who attempted to maintain an adequate state of excitement for five consecutive days!).

When the author was at the bridge in 1962 he was treated to low passes by a Canberra B.2 and a PR 7, a Hunter, a Beverley, a pair of Javelins (which ruffled the reeds) and one of No 1574 Flt's target-towing Meteors, which was *not* pulling a drogue at the time. Some of these aircraft followed the road while others flew up and/or down the river. Although a few surreptitious telephone calls were sometimes made between neighbouring units to co-ordinate their efforts, no one dared to broadcast his illegal intentions openly over the radio and it could hardly be claimed that these activities on converging headings had been adequately deconflicted. There was a very real risk of a collision, but it never happened.

6. No 73 Sqn had done this at Tengah in late 1964. At the time the Flying Camels had only recently returned from their detachment to Kuantan and, with a hefty backlog of servicing to catch up on, they were in no position to compete. Much to their chagrin, they could only bite their collective lips while the visitors queened it over their preserve. On closer examination, however, various of the eight visiting aeroplanes turned out to be wearing the badges of *all four* of Akrotiri's squadrons. The detachment had evidently been mounted on the eight, of Akrotiri's total fleet of thirty-two, aeroplanes that were considered to be least likely to break down. The ninth aircraft in the formation was actually one of No 45 Sqn's which had been borrowed for the occasion. The Cypriots' performance in 1964 may have been a trifle embarrassing for No 45 Sqn but, having been backed by the resources of no fewer than five squadrons, as an achievement it hardly compared to the Flying Camels' home-grown nine out of nine in 1962 or its ten out of ten in 1969.

7. One of the pilots involved in this enterprise was Fg Off C J Yeo. Having attended the Empire Test Pilots' School, Chris Yeo left the RAF as a squadron leader in 1978 and joined British Aerospace. He became Director of Flight Operations in 1988 and on 6th April 1994 he piloted the UK-prototype of the Eurofighter 2000 on its first flight.

Chapter 20. The Hunter Era.

Britain's substantial withdrawal from empire during the 1960s, accompanied by ever-increasing financial stringency, had led to further reductions in the overall size of the RAF, continuing a trend that had begun in 1957. In the course of this prolonged retrenchment some of the old and famous squadrons which had formed the core of the service in the even leaner, but for the RAF crucial, years of the 1920s had disappeared. At this stage, however, the responsible MOD staffs still understood the symbolic significance of these key units and in an effort to sustain some of their identities several of their numberplates were applied to flying units which had not had such an exalted status in the past, notably the regional communications squadrons. By this means Nos 26, 32, 60 and 207 Sqns were saved from obscurity and kept flying, albeit in a less glamorous role than those with which they had previously been associated. Unfortunately, No 45 Sqn was among the last of the old guard to be disbanded and by that time the service had run out of suitable second-line units to redesignate.

For the first time since 1921 the RAF was without the Flying Camels and it seemed at first as if there might be no place for them in the RAF of the 1970s. In the expectation that the squadron would eventually be reformed, however, its Standard hung beneath the rotunda of Cranwell's College Hall along with the banners of a number of other dormant units. Within two years a new role was found for the squadron; the camel was to fly again after all.

Although it may never have been a published policy, the practice throughout the late 1950s and the 1960s had been for those newly qualified pilots and navigators who had been earmarked for high performance aircraft to spend their first tours in Germany, Cyprus, Aden or Singapore flying Hunters or Canberras. If they managed to survive this experience without dunking their aeroplanes in the Rhine or wrapping them around a sand dune or a rubber tree (or at least not too often) they would return to the UK as relatively competent aviators with several hundred hours of flying in their log books to be converted onto more complex, and much more expensive, V-bombers and Lightnings. This is not to say that all 'first-tourists' were denied the opportunity of proceeding directly to the RAF's most advanced aeroplanes but the route described above was certainly that followed by the majority of young 'fast jet' aircrew at that time.

By 1972 the British withdrawal from 'east of Suez' and the replacement of the Akrotiri Wing's Canberras by Vulcans meant that the squadrons on which the previous generation of young pilots had cut their teeth had gone, taking with them their relatively cheap and cheerful aeroplanes. All Hunters and most Canberras had been withdrawn from front-line service and replaced by Phantoms, Harriers and Buccaneers and the Jaguar was scheduled to join these types in the near future. Experience was already showing that there was a real need to provide a period of consolidation flying before newly qualified aircrew got to grips with the more demanding aeroplanes now equipping the operational squadrons. Apart from this, the training system was producing a surplus of pilots at that time and they were starting to queue up to enter the OCUs - the perennial problem of the training backlog[1]. There was nowhere to send these spare bodies where they could be usefully occupied while they waited, and in the meantime they inevitably began to lose their tenuous grip on their recently acquired skills. After spending several months in limbo (a not infrequent occurrence) it was deemed essential for them to be given a flying refresher course before they could safely be put back into the system, this serving only to lengthen further, and to increase the cost of, the training sequence. It was decided to solve both of these problems by inserting a constructive interim flying stage between graduation from FTS and reporting to an OCU, particularly for pilots earmarked for the forthcoming Jaguar. To fill this gap the recently retired Hunter was to be reinstated in squadron service and the unit was to be allocated the numberplate of the senior inactive squadron - No 45 Sqn.

The idea was to create what would in reality be a post-graduate training unit but one which would function as a fully operational DF/GA squadron. Its core was to be provided by a group of pilots with substantial flying experience who would supervise and coach the tyros while they became accustomed to flying relatively high performance, if somewhat dated, Hunters in the low-level environment and became familiar with ground attack procedures and air combat tactics. The 'core' pilots could expect to do a full two to three year tour while the 'trainees' would be on strength for perhaps six months, although this period could be adjusted in the light of an individual's performance and the

Humble beginnings - the Line Hut at West Raynham in July 1972. (D Ketteringham)

A Hunter T.7 undergoing a 'primary'. XL613 was the first of three two-seaters to serve with No 45 Sqn; it was the only one without a camouflage finish and was on charge only while the squadron was at West Raynham. (D Ketteringham)

varying demands and capacities of the overall training machine.

The new No 45 Sqn was to operate from Wittering but, as the runway there was being worked on, the squadron began to assemble at West Raynham during July 1972. It was formally embodied on 1st August under the temporary command of Sqn Ldr W T Willman, pending the arrival of Sqn Ldr M E Kerr who was posted-in ten days later. Wittering eventually declared itself able to accept its new inmates and with ten Hunters (nine FGA 9s and a T.7) the squadron flew across to its permanent base on September 29th. The very experienced Wg Cdr T A Hastings arrived to take command on October 16th and the two squadron leaders became his flight commanders, Wally Willman having A Flight and Calum Kerr taking B Flight.

The squadron was in the rather unusual position of having no formally designated war role; nor was it assigned to NATO. On the other hand, it did have a significant combat potential and was required to be fully operational and thus available to meet any unforeseen contingency. With the experience level on the unit there was no problem in achieving this aim and No 45 Sqn was added to the Order of Battle of No 38 Gp, at that time the RAF's tactical 'fire brigade' organisation.

The aeroplanes were camouflaged in the Dark Green/Dark Sea Grey scheme that had been standard for Hunters for the previous twenty years. Nevertheless the aircraft looked a little odd at first until it was realised that the paint now had a matt rather than a gloss finish; that the undersurfaces were painted in Light Aircraft Grey, rather then being in silver and that the roundels were the recently reintroduced Type B which omitted the white circles. The overall effect was that, until the eye adjusted to these changes, the reincarnated Hunter force looked strangely unfamiliar.

The ownership of the aeroplanes was proudly proclaimed by squadron markings applied on either side of the nose and these had already been emblazoned on the aircraft by the time that they flew over from West Raynham. These markings consisted of a white disc containing a red and blue Flying Camel (always travelling from right to left) flanked by a dark blue bar carrying red diamonds, the whole being thinly outlined in pale blue. This device had been the outcome of a competition held at West Raynham when the squadron had

The leading lights among the engineering fraternity partake of a flute of champers to celebrate the squadron's safe arrival at Wittering. From the left Flt Lt T W Mould, Flt Lt M J Murphy, WO Small, F/Sgt McRoberts and Ch/Tech Clarke.
(D Ketteringham)

What a bunch of poseurs! The air echelon shortly after the Hunters had landed at Wittering on 29th September 1972. From the far left: Flt Lt Mike Murphy (JEngO), Flt Lt Cyd Sowler, Flt Lt Mike Fernee and Flt Lt Mike Crook. Front and centre is Sqn Ldr Callum Kerr, then, moving to the right, Fg Off Dave Farqharson, Sqn Ldr Wally Willman, Flt Lt Wyn Ward, Fg Off Roger Hyde and Fg Off Jerry Barnett with Flt Lt Jim Giles in the box. (M E Kerr)

first begun working up (Cpl Keith Stott is believed to have been the winner). It is perfectly understandable, of course, that the men of the newly formed unit might not have been aware that it already had an officially registered and recognised fighter marking. It is, however, less easy to understand why the authorities whose responsibility it was to know such things, appeared to not to have been aware of this either[2]. The new design was submitted for approval and duly endorsed. Despite its being something of an anomaly, the new style of marking certainly made generous use of the squadron's traditional colours and it quickly became a familiar sight around East Anglia and further afield. All the same it seems a pity that the opportunity to sustain the squadron's traditional fighter marking was missed.

So far as the composition of its groundcrew complement was concerned the new squadron was quite a distinctive unit, some might have said they were a trifle maverick! As the RAF had run down its once substantial Hunter force in the 1960s the technicians who had looked after its aeroplanes had moved on to newer and better things. From this large pool of dispersed manpower about seventy NCOs and airmen, many of them very experienced on type, had been selected and posted to form a new Hunter squadron in that aeroplane's twilight years. Sleek as it was there was no denying that by 1972 the Hunter was an obsolescent type and the resident No 1 Sqn with their new-fangled Harriers took every opportunity to stress this point - It was suggested, for instance, that No 45 Sqn's motto of *Per Ardua Surgo* was a

A nice portrait of XG130/A providing a clear impression of the marking devised for the squadron's Hunters. (T A Hastings)

reference to the Hunter's lack of VTO capability! The (mostly) good-natured banter between No 1 Sqn and the Flying Camels continued throughout the squadron's time at Wittering and was a constant feature of crewroom chaffing and barrack block humour. As they were never allowed to forget that they were operating second-class aeroplanes, however, the airmen treated the ribbing as a spur and produced a first-class squadron.

To advertise the Hunter's return to front-line service the squadron heralded the New Year by flying a ten-ship formation over Chivenor which, as host to No 229 OCU, had been the Hunter's spiritual home for many years. By this time the last of its initial allocation of aeroplanes had been delivered to Wittering and the squadron boasted a total of fifteen Hunters, of which two were trainers. All the single-seaters were FGA 9s but the squadron also held four modified nose sections, which could be switched between aeroplanes with relative ease; each contained a single F.95 camera rigged to take oblique photographs. This installation was hardly comparable to that of the Hunter FR 10 but it worked well-enough and it permitted the squadron to offer an introduction to tactical recce techniques. At first the aircrew were accommodated an inconvenient quarter of a mile or so from the flightline (not far enough to warrant a crew coach but too far to walk in the rain) but on 9th February 1973 they were able to move into their new

purpose-built offices which were much closer to the aeroplanes.

Peter Stevenson, an MOD photographer, had visited and flown with the squadron in December and some of his pictures were used to give the squadron a burst of publicity to celebrate its reincarnation. The February 1973 issue of *Air Clues*[3] sported a No 45 Sqn Hunter on its cover and contained an illustrated feature article. As *Air Clues* said, "The squadron's training programme is well under way. The syllabus includes high and low level battle formation flying, low-level strike, FAC, reconnaissance and gunsight handling. The weapons work to date has included air-to-ground SNEB and gun attacks. Additional attack profiles, including dive and level bombing, are to be included."

The Flying Camels were back in business and, by now comfortably established at Wittering, they began to broaden their horizons, mounting a five-day detachment to Kinloss in February and a four-day one to Valley in March. Since it was now firing on all four cylinders it was time to reclaim the Standard and this was recovered from the RAF College with due ceremony on March 9th. At much the same time the squadron arranged a dozen Hunters in a circle and had the now traditional clockface photograph taken.

In its four years on Hunters the squadron lost only two aeroplanes, the first of them on 6th April 1973. As they were turning onto final approach for Wittering, the experienced Flt Lt Hyde, flying as No 2, reported signs of fire from the aircraft in front, XG135. In view of the low-speed, low-altitude situation, Roger Hyde advised the Leader to abandon his aircraft. Flt Lt Grant McLeod made a successful ejection and the aeroplane crashed about two miles to the east of the airfield. There were more positive aspects to April, however, as it saw the posting of the squadron's first 'graduate', who departed to convert to Phantoms, and the squadron's first overseas deployment when it mounted a brief detachment to Sola in Norway.

Maintaining the tradition, the squadron produced a full clockface of Hunters in March 1973. (No 45 Sqn archives)

The training syllabus was further expanded in June with the addition of

Dissimilar Air Combat Training (DACT) with Phantoms, Lightnings and Harriers. This activity was of mutual benefit to the squadron's tyros and to the pilots of the other aircraft, particularly those of the Harrier persuasion as they were then experimenting with the use of thrust vectoring in flight ('Viffing') to assess its potential as an air combat tactic. In fact the Flying Camels became directly involved in No 1 Sqn's 'Viffing' trials. One of its FGA 9s was temporarily rigged with a forward-facing G.90 camera mounted on the tip of its fin. It would fly in line astern with the Harrier and record the remarkable antics which resulted when its nozzles were rotated.

The squadron took part in a DATEX, a recurrent air defence exercise sponsored by the French Air Force, on 26th June. The low-level sortie around northern France went well enough but the recovery to the UK turned out to be even more exciting. As Alan Hastings recalls:

A neat line-up of eight FGA 9s outside the squadron's hangar at Wittering. The groundcrew are assisting the pilots to strap in prior to a formation sortie, circa December 1972. (T A Hastings)

> On our return, the designated recovery airfield, Thorney Island, became clamped and we made for our planned diversion at Boscombe Down where a very surprised air trafficker was obliged to control a recovery with equipment which seemed to be on the blink. During the 'pairs in trail' let-down, the second pair was lost on radar and some fairly hectic turns were demanded in thick turbulent cloud to ensure separation. As a result, my wingman, Flt Lt Jerry Barnett, became detached and made his own way to the airfield at low level without any further assistance from the ground. He subsequently found that he had flown around a high point near Boscombe Down in cloud some 200 feet below the height of the summit and had then landed downwind to the detriment of both mainwheel tyres. I, as the erstwhile Leader of the second pair, had meanwhile assessed that

some barbed wire fencing and grazing cattle, observed at close proximity as the aircraft broke through the very low cloud base, were unlikely to be part of the airfield facilities and rapidly climbed for a second, and more accurate controlled descent and GCA from which I landed with very little fuel remaining.

A detachment to Leuchars the following month to take part in an exercise resulted in some productive flying but proved to be less demanding on the adrenal glands.

When the original announcement of the re-establishment of an operational Hunter force had been made to the House of Commons on 22nd June 1972 it had indicated that it was to consist of two squadrons. It was now time to form the second of these. This proved to be an exercise in politician puzzling. It is doubtful whether the MPs ever realised it but they were short-changed as they only really got two half-squadrons! On 1st August 1973 No 45 Sqn was split in two. Alan Hastings retained command of the parent unit while

This photograph of XG261/C shows well the recently introduced matt finish and the toned-down national markings which contrasted sharply with the previous gloss paintwork and bright red, white and blue roundels and made the rejuvenated Hunter force seem oddly different at first. (MAP)

XK137/D climbs away from Wittering. (T A Hastings)

Calum Kerr used the 'other bit' to set up No 58 Sqn pending the arrival of Wg Cdr D C Whitman who was posted-in a month later.

The pilots who constituted the slimmed-down No 45 Sqn were Sqn Ldr Willman, as flight commander, Flt Lt J J Barnett, Flt Lt M R W Crook, Flt Lt D C Dalgliesh, Flt Lt M F Fernee, Flt Lt J A Giles, Flt Lt R W Hyde, Flt Lt D J Keenan, Flt Lt G McLeod, Fg Off S H Bedford and Fg Off A J Wilson. The aeroplanes were divided between the units (see Annex L), No 45 Sqn retaining XE582, XG130, XG252, XG261, XK137, XK138, XK151 plus XL619 as its trainer and a promise that a replacement would eventually be forthcoming for XG135. Flt Lt Trevor Mould stayed with the parent unit to oversee the maintenance of this reduced fleet. The remaining aeroplanes were given No 58 Sqn's owl motif, the red diamonds of the flanking bar marking being repainted in green, and were looked after by No 45 Sqn's erstwhile JEngO, Flt Lt Mike Murphy.

Although this exercise served to satisfy the originally announced intention, created a flying appointment for another wing commander and kept another squadron numberplate going, in practical terms not a great deal changed. The two Hunter squadrons shared the original accommodation and its assorted communications and 'Ops' facilities. On the technical side, even as the fleet was being notionally divided, it was decided to pool resources and to continue to operate as a single unit for engineering purposes. Between 6th and 17th August the two squadrons carried out their first joint training programme, an intensive APC based on

Despite its poor quality, this picture, which was taken in Denmark in November 1973, has several significant features. First, it shows the snow which caused some minor ground-handling problems during the squadron's detachment to Karup. Secondly, it illustrates the introduction of two-digit codes in place of the previous single letters which began in late 1973; previously 'C', this is XG261 displaying its new identity as '64'. Finally, the discontinuity in the lower edge of the camouflage line and the camera window shows that this aeroplane is wearing one of the squadron's interchangeable 'photo-noses'. (D Ketteringham)

Theddlethorpe Range. Life went on much as before except that both squadrons already knew that their days were numbered. The reformation of No 58 Sqn had been accompanied by the depressing news that both units were to be disbanded in 1976.

In the meantime there was plenty of varied activity to keep the squadron(s) busy. In September four aircraft were deployed to Gardermoen for a week to participate in Exercise BOWLER HAT while three more were detached to Lossiemouth. Later in the month a Forward Air Control Exercise (FACEX) was flown from Wittering. There was a formal parade on October 31st to mark the reformation of No 58 Sqn and, between 5th and 23rd November, both units carried out another APC involving dive and retard bombing, rocket (SNEB) and gun attacks.

There was another overseas trip in late November when, on the 24th, Flt Lt Mould took a party of thirty-five groundcrew across to Karup where they were joined by four Hunters two days later. The detachment was to take part in Exercise OCEAN SPAN, the squadron's task being to mount raids against targets in the UK to test the air defence system. This it did, but not without some difficulty as the weather conditions in Denmark were abnormally severe; six inches of snow fell and the temperature dropped at one point to a remarkable -18°C! This produced some interesting operating problems. It was, for instance, difficult for the wheels of the aeroplanes to gain traction when attempting to taxi from a standing start on an iced up dispersal. It proved necessary to have an airman on each wingtip to prevent the aircraft from slipping sideways and to keep them pointing in the right direction until some forward momentum had been built up. This provided at least a semblance of directional control which sufficed while the aircraft skated their way to the properly cleared parts of the airfield pavement where they were able to gain a surer footing. Despite the weather, the squadron fulfilled its commitment and the detachment returned to Wittering on the 30th.

Although neither of Wittering's Hunter squadrons was assigned to NATO, No 1 Sqn was, which meant that it was subject to periodic assessments of its operational capability. In order to ensure that all units declared as being available to him in wartime were able to meet certain operational criteria, SACEUR (Supreme Allied Commander Europe) required that they were to undergo Tactical Evaluations (TACEVAL) to demonstrate their readiness and their ability to operate to predetermined standards under simulated wartime conditions. In preparation for these assessments, some of which took place without prior notice, Station Commanders sponsored similar events, MINEVALs and MAXEVALs, at their own discretion. Despite their not really being required to participate in these activities, to avoid disrupting the station's 'wartime' routine, the Hunter squadrons always played along, although they were not subjected to direct assessment. The first such exercise involving the Flying Camels, a MINEVAL, took place on 6th December 1973. Along with the rest of Wittering the Hunter squadrons reacted to the early morning call-out and within a few hours had ten fully-armed aircraft ready for operations. Since they were given no exercise sorties to fly the Hunter units ran their own programme and fired off their weapons at Holbeach, Wainfleet and Cowden.

By this time the consequences of the OPEC-instigated

'Oil Crisis' of late 1973 were being felt throughout the UK. The RAF was not insulated from this and the situation was aggravated by a spate of industrial unrest. January 1974 brought short working weeks and short working days to minimise the consumption of fuel for lighting and heating. For a while the RAF was required to operate within a severely constrained allocation of fuel[4]. Fortunately for No 45 Sqn, the Harriers happened to be suffering from an engine-related problem at the time and Wittering's Hunter community was able to siphon off the surplus from the relatively generous allocation of fuel earmarked for the gas-guzzling 'jump jets'. As a result the Flying Camels were able to conduct an almost normal flying programme at the expense of their technically advanced but groundbound neighbours and honour an undertaking to provide the Phantoms of No 228 OCU with some DACT between 9th and 11th January. Nevertheless, even the Hunters were subject to some constraints, and the New Year saw rather more lectures and ground training than was usual. The fuel situation began to moderate in February, however, and the Hunter squadrons were able to fly at about their usual rate, ie about 300 hours per month, from within their own fuel allocation, although it still proved necessary to cancel a planned detachment to Lossiemouth.

Activity throughout the spring was fairly routine with a staple diet of low-level navigation exercises, weapons details on the east coast ranges and intermittent FAC and DACT sorties. Something a little out of the ordinary came the squadron's way in late April when four aircraft took part in another DATEX. As before, this involved attempting to evade the air defences while penetrating to a target about 100 miles inside France and then flying back across the Channel to land at Thorney Island to refuel before returning to Wittering. This time it all went as planned.

May 1974 was very busy with the first stage of Wittering's formal TACEVAL beginning on the 6th. This was the no-notice element in which the station was required to demonstrate its ability to recall and arm all its personnel, generate its aircraft for operations and adopt a fully prepared wartime posture, all within a specified time. Both Hunter units participated on a 'voluntary' basis which created a brief hiatus in the middle of a concentrated weapons training programme which took place between 2nd and 23rd. In addition the Hunters found time to provide aircraft to take part in Exercises PRIORY and FOREGROUND.

In the 1970s it was the practice for students of the Royal College of Defence Studies (RCDS) to spend a week with the RAF which culminated in an impressive major display, mounted in co-operation with the aircraft industry, of the latest and best in British aeroplanes, weapons and equipment. Wittering, home of the still very novel Harrier, drew the short straw in 1974 and was nominated as the host base for this event. The early-1950s

Wg Cdr Alan Hastings straps on XG130/A prior to a training sortie. (T A Hastings)

vintage Hunters hardly represented the leading edge of technology, however, and in any case their dispersal would be needed for the extensive static display. Nos 45 and 58 Sqns were invited to make themselves scarce and on June 14th their aircraft were flown over to Cottesmore. Since this was only a few miles away, however, the squadron still continued to live at Wittering and simply operated as if its aeroplanes were on a particularly remote dispersal. The first sorties were flown from Cottesmore on the 17th and the squadron promptly lost its second Hunter when XG130 had to be abandoned after its pilot had become disorientated in cloud. Flt Lt I C Firth (who was technically on the books of No 58 Sqn) made a successful ejection and landed safely, the aeroplane crashing close to the mouth of a railway tunnel near Melton Mowbray. Since XG130 had been the CO's 'personal' aeroplane, Wg Cdr Hastings was not best pleased.

While the basing of the aircraft at Cottesmore was a little inconvenient, not least for the groundcrew, it had no major impact on training; flying continued much as before with emphasis being given to DACT, exercises of this type being flown with Phantoms, Harriers and Lightnings during this period. On July 10th Wittering was honoured with a Royal visit, Flt Lt Mould and C/Tech A J J Inkersole preparing an extensive exhibition of the unit's history for Princess Anne's delectation. The day was rounded off by a flypast, led by Sqn Ldr Willman, the Hunters arranged in a unique 'A' formation

Sqn Ldr Kerr ripples off a SNEB pod at Theddlethorpe in June 1974. It is an indication of the joint nature of Wittering's two Hunter units that Calum Kerr was by this time on the strength of No 58 Sqn but the aeroplane he was flying, XG261/64, nominally belonged to No 45. (T A Hastings)

Ch/Tech Dave Ketteringham interfering with the fixtures and fittings in the cockpit of one of the squadron's Hunters. (D Ketteringham)

in the Princess' honour. The last of the VIPs having departed, the following day the Hunters were permitted to return to their roost.

There were two events of note in August 1974. The first was an international Tactical Fighter Meet, hosted by Leuchars, where the squadron mounted a detachment from the 3rd to the 16th. This produced some interesting training flying and extensive 'exchanges of operational views' in the bar.

The second event was a change of command and a revision of the unit's structure. It had now been a year since the Flying Camel had spawned No 58 Sqn and a move was made towards rationalising what was in many ways already a joint unit. It was decided to acknowledge the *status quo* and effectively to run the unit as a two-flight squadron under the command of a single wing commander. To sustain the two squadron numberplates, however, the overall structure had to be termed a wing. By this time Alan Hastings had completed his two years in command of No 45 Sqn so it was convenient to effect the restructuring from his departure. He left on August 24th, bound for Salalah where he was to take command of the Strike Wing of the Sultan of Oman's Air Force.

Its title having already been common currency for some time, Hunter Wing was formally established on 2nd September 1974. Its CO was Derek Whitman, previously OC No 58 Sqn. His place was taken by Sqn Ldr W L Norton and command of No 45 Sqn fell to Sqn Ldr M J Gibson with Flt Lt M R W Crook as flight commander. At the same time the overall size of the combined unit was slightly reduced and

XL619 was the squadron's two-seater for almost the whole of the Hunter era. Seen here late in its career it has acquired a couple of 'zaps' on its nose; one of them a chequerboard, probably applied by No 63(R) Sqn. (MAP)

it was destined to be allowed to run down further through natural wastage. All of the groundcrew were transferred to the strength of the wing but organised into two 'shifts' under separate engineering officers. For disciplinary purposes one of these 'shifts' came under OC No 45 Sqn, the other under OC No 58 Sqn, thus sustaining at least a semblance of there still being two squadrons. As before, peacetime flying continued to be carried out on a fully integrated basis with Mike Gibson running routine activities, in effect acting as Flight Commander Training, while Bill Norton looked after operational readiness and exercise participation, fulfilling the role of Flight Commander Ops. There were, however, contingency plans which would have permitted each of the nominal squadrons to have operated autonomously in wartime if required.

Thereafter it is increasingly difficult to distinguish the activities of the individual squadrons as they no longer operated as such. Hunter Wing despatched a six-aircraft detachment to Brüggen on September 6th to take part in Exercise CRACK FORCE. Towards the end of the month, operating in formations of up to six aircraft, the squadron participated in Exercise NORTHERN MERGER. Mike Gibson recalls an incident which occurred during one of his sorties:

> Over the four days this exercise involved a total of nine missions, flying out low-level over the North Sea for up to 150 miles then returning, still at low level, to test the air defence system and 'attack' defended targets in the UK. On a sortie flown on September 24th, Flt Lt N J Day's aircraft suffered engine vibration which caused a high pressure fuel pipe to burst, leaving a plume of fuel in the aircraft's wake. He pulled up to 6,000 feet but found that he could not maintain height on the limited thrust available to him. However, the fuel leak was so great that he needed to retain his drop tanks for as long as possible, otherwise he would have had no chance of reaching land. He slowly descended towards the sea until, at below 1,000 feet, he jettisoned the tanks, the reduction in weight now allowing him to coax his aircraft slowly back up to 3,000 feet. He just made it into Leconfield where the engine seized on touchdown. There was only a bucketful of fuel left in the aircraft.

For his exemplary airmanship in saving his aeroplane (XJ688, which was on temporary loan from Brawdy) Nigel Day was awarded a Queen's Commendation for Valuable Service in the Air in December.

After two more preparatory MINEVALs, Wittering underwent the second, and longer, part of its formal TACEVAL between 20th and 24th October. This was the operational phase which was pre-planned to the extent that it did not involve a no-notice call-out; the game was simply restarted from the position that had been reached at the end of the generation phase which had taken place in May. As before, Hunter Wing, still lacking a war role, was not formally tested but it played along all the same, not least because it provided valuable experience for its junior pilots who would shortly have to do this sort of thing once they had reached their ultimate destinations. The Hunters were prepared for ops and dispersed to remote corners of the airfield where they were placed under guard, the unit's personnel becoming involved in several ground defence incidents. There was some flying too as the Hunters were periodically sent off to return and make 'attacks' on Wittering to simulate enemy air raids.

The TACEVAL concept developed progressively over the following fifteen years and as it did so these events tended to become increasingly demanding and sophisticated. For the rest of its time on Hunters the squadron often found itself co-opted to overfly other stations which were being evaluated. Apart from simulating an enemy air raid the aircraft used would often be fitted with one of the recce noses and the resultant photographs were used by the Evaluation Team to assess the effectiveness of air raid precautions, camouflage measures, on-base aircraft dispersal plans and so on.

For the remainder of 1974 training flying continued without undue disturbance. There was a concentration on DACT, by now including Jaguars, and FACEXs on the ranges at Sennybridge, Castle Martin and Stamford. Something a little out of the ordinary took place on December 13th when Hunters were used to photograph inflatable decoys which were then being developed to disguise the presence of real tanks. That month Hunter Wing flew its 10,000th flying hour since the reformation of No 45 Sqn in 1972. This milestone was passed on the 13th in the course of an eight-ship air combat exercise, led by Flt Lt Roger Hyde who was flying his last trip before leaving the air force to return to New Zealand.

The reduction in strength that had accompanied the establishment of the wing was now beginning to make itself felt. By November the aircraft fleet had begun to dwindle and, although some people had already left, by February 1975 there was a significant surplus of ground personnel awaiting posting.

The highlight of March 1975 was an 'attack' on Brüggen as a contribution to that station's TACEVAL and in May Wittering inflicted another MINEVAL on itself. Hunter Wing dutifully prepared for war again and took itself off to a remote dispersal whence it flew CAPs over the airfield and mounted 'missions' against Holbeach, ie it carried out its normal training sorties within the overall structure of the exercise. DACT continued to be a major feature of the flying programme, mostly with the Phantoms of No 228 OCU from Coningsby.

In June the wing mounted a detachment to Laarbruch for several days in the course of which XG261 suffered a bird strike and had to divert to Oldenburg. C/Tech Dave Ketteringham took a hastily organised recovery team to the *Luftwaffe* base and after a spot of panel beating and the judicious application of 'speed tape' the aircraft was soon flying again. The weather was good throughout July and the wing took advantage of this to fly 432 hours, not a bad total for what was now a relatively small unit. This effort had included participation in no fewer than eight exercises of varying importance and complexity and a CFS visit which took place between July 21st and 25th. The 'Trappers' found little to complain about and, with all of its pilots night current (always a problem with short summer nights), Hunter Wing ended the month in fine fettle.

The Hunter celebrated its 21st year of RAF service in 1975 and, since Hawker Siddeley had presented a barrel of beer to mark the occasion, the wing held a Hunter Birthday

The old brigade. From the left: SAC Al Jewkes, Ch Tech Dave Ketteringham, Ch Tech Tony Slingsby, SAC Tony Clarke, Cpl John Simpson, SAC Brian Hawkes, WO Ben Corlette, Cpl Al Groves, SAC Keith Preston, Ch Tech 'Nick' Nicolle, Cpl 'Willy' Williams, Cpl Keith Stott and LAC Pete Farley. Seen here in August 1975, all of these men had been with the squadron since its formation three years before: five still would be when it finally disbanded a year later. (D Ketteringham)

Party on 1st August at which to consume it. The unit was visited by Air Cdre Ian Pedder during the month, thus renewing an old acquaintance from the early 1960s when he had frequently flown with No 45 Sqn in the early days of the Indonesian Confrontation in his capacity as OC Tengah's Offensive Support Wing.

In early September the wing staged some quite complex training sorties with pairs flying Hi-Lo-Hi missions to Scotland while one or two other Hunters lurked somewhere around the route and attempted to bounce them. The month ended with a detachment to Wildenrath on the 29th for Exercise HIGHWOOD, the aircraft returning to Wittering on October 3rd.

Flt Lt Mike Bull assumed responsibility for supervising aircraft maintenance in December when Flt Lt Trevor Mould BEM, who had been the squadron's, and latterly the wing's, SEngO since its formation, retired after thirty-eight years of service. His association with the Flying Camels predated 1972, however, as he had looked after No 20 Sqn's Hunters in the mid-1960s when that squadron had frequently flown with No 45 Sqn's Canberras in at least a semblance of co-operation. The family tie was even stronger as Trevor's daughter, Lesley, had married into No 45 Sqn when she had wed Flt Lt Mike Doyle-Davidson in 1965.

Hunter Wing became directly involved in an operational detachment in January 1976 when, following an initial deployment of some of No 1 Sqn's Harriers to Belize in November 1975, the wing was required to supply experienced officers to supplement HQ 38 Gp's staff in the Tactical Operations Centre which had been set up in-theatre. For a period of six months there was always at least one of the wing's pilots detached to Belize and Sqn Ldr Gibson did a spell as Deputy Air Commander there in early 1976. This depletion in its effective strength added to the gathering momentum of the wing's run down, early departures being Flt Lts Firth and Elsdon who left to fly Jaguars in February. Nevertheless training continued apace and March 1976 was quite busy with an APC at Holbeach during which all pilots qualified in weapons deliveries to NATO standards. There was also some FAC work in Devon and Exercise CLARION

CALL at Stamford. To cap it all SHAPE (Supreme Headquarters Allied Powers in Europe) called an Exercise ACTIVE EDGE to which Hunter Wing responded by producing the required ten fully-armed aeroplanes well within the time allowed.

May was another hectic month with a detachment to Leuchars for a session of DACT with Phantoms and another to St Mawgan for a FACEX. The wing also took part in four formal exercises, a DATEX over France, YETI'S PAW, HARD POUNDING (FAC work on Salisbury Plain) and, via another short detachment to Aalborg, a BLUE MOON during which the Hunters found themselves under seemingly constant attack by RDAF F-104s. Finally the wing took part in a trial programme held on Salisbury Plain to assist in the development of the Blowpipe hand-held surface-to-air missile. Despite being smaller, the Hunter outfit was still going strong, but it was all to no avail and before the end of the month its imminent demise had been confirmed.

As the trickle of postings swelled to a flood in June the wing began to melt away. At the end of May it had still had a dozen FGA 9s and a pair of trainers on strength. Three of the fighter-bombers had gone by the end of June, but these were enough to allow participation in Exercise CLOUDY CHORUS over Holland and another BLUE MOON. On the evening of July 3rd the officers attended a final formal Dinner Night, after which both squadrons' silver and other memorabilia were packed for storage. The wing's final participation in a NATO exercise was on July 5th when four Hunters flew over to Gütersloh for another CLOUDY CHORUS. A disbandment parade was held on July 23rd, the reviewing officer being AVM P G K Williamson CBE DFC, AOC No 38 Gp. Sqn Ldr Slade led a four-aircraft flypast in salute as the Squadron Standards were marched off; they were both subsequently restored to their places in College

Hall at Cranwell to await another call to arms.

The last training sorties had been flown on July 19th and on the 26th both squadrons ceased to exist. Most of the Hunters which had already been withdrawn had been passed to Brawdy and the rest of the fleet, down to just three FGA 9s when the lights finally went out, now followed them. At the time of its disbandment there remained a hard core of eight men who had served first with No 45 Sqn and then with Hunter Wing ever since the former had begun to assemble at West Raynham in 1972. They were Ch Tech Nicolle, Sgt Booth, Sgt Parkinson, Cpl Groves, Cpl Hawkes, Cpl Stott, J/T Watson and LAC Farley. The squadron's last CO on Hunters, who was to retire as Air Vice Marshal M J Gibson CB OBE, and five other pilots were posted to form the nucleus of a new Jaguar squadron in Germany which turned out to be No 20 Sqn, the Flying Camel's old sparring partners from Ste-Marie-Cappel and Tengah.

No 45 Sqn had been reformed to provide young pilots with a short intermediate tour of post-graduate flying so that they could be passed on to the fast-jet OCUs with a substantial background of flying experience in the low-level tactical environment and already qualified to lead pairs. Using a quasi-operational squadron to support this concept had never been more than an interim solution, however, and when No 229 OCU finally closed at Chivenor in September 1974 its Hunters had been used to establish a dedicated training school, the Tactical Weapons Unit (TWU), at Brawdy. It was the creation of this unit which had led to the initial reduction in size of Nos 45 and 58 Sqns and their effective amalgamation within Hunter Wing at that time. So long as there was a backlog of junior pilots in the system, however, Wittering's Hunters could still fulfil a useful function but as the surplus slowly reduced throughout 1975 and 1976, so the TWU became increasingly able to take on

The disbandment parade on 23rd July 1976. Sqn Ldr Mike Gibson leads No 45 Sqn past the dais and AVM P G K Williamson returns the squadron's salute. On the AOC's left is the Station Commander, Gp Capt L A Jones. The Standard Bearer is Fg Off Roger White, escorted by Sgt Garth Cleaver (nearest the camera) and Sgt Dave Booth. Completing the Standard Party is the Flying Wing Adjutant, WO Carruthers. (No 45 Sqn archives)

the whole burden and the need for the interim squadrons evaporated.

In four years the Hunters had accumulated 15,900 flying hours in the course of which the wing and its predecessors had trained fifty-one junior pilots. Although primarily intended to produce Jaguar-drivers, in the event the output had been fairly evenly distributed between Jaguars, Phantoms, Buccaneers and Harriers with just a few being siphoned off to Canberras or Hercules or for secondment to the Sultan of Oman's Air Force. The squadron had made a very valuable and necessary contribution to maintaining the efficiency of the RAF during one of its frequent periods of readjustment to changing defence policy. It had been a particularly happy unit and twenty years later many of its groundcrew still rate their days at Wittering as having been among the most enjoyable and satisfying of their service careers.

As indicated earlier in this chapter the ageing Hunters were regarded with some disdain by Wittering's Harrier community and both teams spent a good deal of time trying to strike sparks off each other. In the July 1976 edition of *Wittering View*, the station magazine, the Hunter fraternity had the last word. The editorial contained the following anonymous lines:

'You are old Hawker Hunter,'
The young man said,
'And your paintwork is no longer bright,
Yet I see that you constantly stagger aloft,
Do you think at your age that it's right?'

'Yes, I'm old', smiled the Hunter,
'As you observe.
Yet you're missing the pertinent thought,
Were it not for its age no antique would deserve
All the money for which it is bought.'

'But you're old AND outdated,'
The young man frowned,
'And your instruments ancient and plain.
Tell me, how can you navigate close to the ground
Without using a digital brain?'

'In my youth,' yawned the Hunter,
'Pilots could fly
Using stopwatch and compass and map,
And I'm teaching them still to be Kings of the Sky,
Now be off....while I'm taking a nap.'

Notes:

1. Backlogs have been an almost permanent feature of RAF flying training since the late 1950s. It was not a new phenomenon even then; the earliest official correspondence relating to this topic of which this author is aware was written in 1915! The root of the problem is a mismatch between the timing of changes in manpower requirements and the ability of the training system to respond to them. It takes well over two years for a modern pilot to progress from his initial military induction training to his graduation from an OCU, nearer three if recourses are involved or if there are holding periods between courses. If the recruiting and selection phase is added to this pattern then it will be seen that a notional pilot can be 'in the training pipeline' for as long as four years. Policy decisions affecting the size and shape of the RAF occur at random and at relatively short notice, rarely more than two years, often only a matter of months, and they have usually meant reductions in strength. Although the input to 'the pipeline' can be adjusted fairly promptly, it already holds more pilots (and navigators) than will be needed but in whom much time, effort and money have already been invested (and to whom an obligation has been given). The system therefore continues to train

A gentle formation break at altitude, just for the photographer. Nearest the camera is XK140/P; next is XF519/F with XE651/M lifting away to follow XG207/R.
(T A Hastings).

the surplus but, as its capacity contracts to match the reduced end-user requirement, backlogs inevitably occur which take time to absorb. This backlog problem is periodically exacerbated by other unforeseen circumstances as when an aircraft type is delayed in entering service (like the Jaguar), or experiences problems early in its career (like the Phantom), in mid-career (like the Buccaneer), or prematurely ends it career (like the Valiant). Unpredictable complications of this nature inevitably result in the cancellation of long-planned and carefully phased OCU courses, but the aircrew to fill these slots will have entered 'the pipeline' two or three years earlier and, until the problem is resolved, they represent another 'bulge' in the system. A large air force has many hidey-holes in which employment can be found for such spare aircrew. If it contracts, however, such places become fewer. Management of its increasingly complex and expensive training machine becomes more, not less, difficult as the RAF continues to shrink.

2. Air Ministry letter C34842/DDOps(AD) of 8th November 1955 formally authorised the 'second series' of fighter squadron markings, superseding the 'first series' which had been promulgated on 20th October 1950. The 1955 letter covered a full-colour representation of the approved markings for *all* fighter squadrons, portrayed in the classic format of roundel-flanking bars. Although the style in which these markings have been applied in later years has sometimes undergone considerable adaptation, and they have appeared on some distinctly unfighter-like aeroplanes, eg Shackletons of No 8 Sqn, Belvederes of No 26 Sqn, Sycamores of No 118 Sqn and Twin Pioneers of No 152 Sqn, the basic designs and colours have always stayed the same. Since No 45 Sqn's white dumb-bell on a red ground had been approved by DDOps(AD)'s 1955 letter, it is something of a mystery as to why the diamond marking was ever sanctioned for use on its Hunters. One is tempted to surmise that the AD staff at MOD must have 'lost the Policy File' by 1972 and thus endorsed a new marking by default. Through such oversights is history made - or tradition confounded.

3. *Air Clues* is the RAF's professional house magazine.

4. The overwhelming, and by 1973 traditional, influence of the 'Flying Hours Graph' on routine squadron training was referred to briefly in Chapter 13. For a time in 1974, however, it was eclipsed by the 'Fuel Consumption Graph' and this became the crude yardstick by which success or failure was measured. There have been other variations on this theme, airframe fatigue, for instance. All aeroplanes have a calculated lifespan; this used to be expressed simply as a finite number of flying hours but today it tends to be measured in terms of the amount of 'fatigue' that the aeroplane has experienced so that, depending upon how they have been flown, two aircraft of the same basic type can differ significantly in their longevity, although efforts are made to rotate aircraft between units to spread the consumption of fatigue evenly across the fleet. As a type approaches the end of its life, if no replacement is in prospect and there are no funds to underwrite a refurbishment programme, the aircraft have to be flown very carefully to avoid inflicting excessive fatigue on them and thus to prolong their active lives. In such circumstances the 'Fatigue Index Consumption Graph' becomes the overriding preoccupation of squadron executives.

Chapter 21. Shadow status with Tornados.

Most people's awareness of the RAF is probably confined to its operational squadrons but they are actually only the tip of a very large iceberg; there is a great deal of additional combat potential embedded within the training units which support the front line. In the past, when circumstances have dictated, the service has drawn upon this reserve of fully operational aeroplanes and their experienced instructor crews and, on occasion, has even committed them to action. Early examples of such measures being taken include the earmarking of fighter OTUs for use in the event of a German invasion in 1941, the defence of Habbaniyah by No 4 FTS in the same year and the participation of bomber OTUs in the 1,000-bomber raids of 1942.

As the Cold War intensified the RAF again looked to its training units to reinforce the front line in the event of hostilities and in 1956 the numberplates of several defunct squadrons were allocated to elements of the Central Fighter Establishment (CFE). These were not permanent designations, however, and they were for use only when these units participated in operational exercises, but there were plans for them to be fully embodied as additional squadrons in the event of general mobilisation being ordered. This principle was gradually extended to embrace a number of OCUs and other training units which maintained a secondary operational capability, and these potential front-line units came to be known as 'shadow' squadrons. By the 1970s many of these units had come to identify very closely with the traditions of their *alter egos*. Typically, they had taken possession of the squadron's silver and memorabilia; they sometimes hosted reunions of ex-members; their aeroplanes permanently displayed the appropriate markings and their aircrew wore the squadron's badge on their flying suits. Despite this outward show, however, they remained essentially second-line units and, although some periodically took part in exercises under their pseudonyms, they did *not*

formally assume their operational identities until an appropriate stage in the transition from peace to war - and thus far this has never happened[1].

The practice of earmarking training units to reinforce the front line had begun under entirely national auspices but as NATO evolved into an increasingly integrated multi-national force so it became necessary to rationalise these arrangements within the framework of the Alliance. To permit SACEUR to plan for the defence of Europe, SHAPE needed to know precisely what resources were available to him - and when. A squadron 'declared' to NATO as being operational was required to be fully manned and equipped and able to adopt a high state of readiness in a matter of hours. Once assigned to SACEUR under these terms all such units were subject to TACEVALS as described in Chapter 20. There were, however, a number of lesser categories of 'declaration' which permitted the UK (and other nations) to commit remotely located or second-line units to NATO within defined timescales which permitted them to be brought fully up to strength and preparedness and, if necessary, redeployed during a period of tension before operational control over them was formally transferred to SACEUR. Although the popular label of 'shadow squadron' remained in widespread use, the official designation of RAF units with such an emergency war role was 'reserve squadron'. Such units were not normally vulnerable to TACEVALs, which would have been too disruptive of their primary peacetime activities, but their phased commitment allowed SHAPE to develop plans for the progressive reinforcement of the front line in a methodical manner.

By the early 1980s the steady decline in the front-line strength of the RAF had meant that the number of squadron numberplates in use had grown progressively smaller. As they affected No 45 Sqn, examples of attempts to sustain the identities of defunct squadrons in the 1940s and 1950s have

Seen here at an air display in 1991, ZA368 was one of the aeroplanes on charge to the TWCU when it became No 45(R) Sqn in 1984. It is wearing on its nose the Hunter-style Flying Camel flanked by red diamonds on a blue bar. The location of this marking meant that the roundel had to be moved from its standard position and reapplied on the intake trunking. Just visible on the fin is the original TWCU emblem of a crown, crossed arrows and a sword. (MAP)

Not long after being allocated No 45 Sqn's numberplate the TWCU arranged a dozen of its aeroplanes for the squadron's traditional clockface photograph. (No 45 Sqn archives)

been discussed in Chapters 12 and 16 and the later broadening of the interpretation of squadron status to permit the allocation of numberplates to communications squadrons was referred to in Chapter 20. Despite innovations such as these the Ministry of Defence had, since 1976, been unable to preserve the identity of the Flying Camels, one of the RAF's longest serving and most distinguished squadrons. It was, however, to be given a quasi-existence in 1984 by allocating its numberplate as the 'shadow' identity of the Tornado Weapons Conversion Unit (TWCU).

The Panavia Tornado had been developed as an Anglo-German-Italian joint venture and this international flavour was maintained by the setting up of a joint conversion school at RAF Cottesmore - the Tri-national Tornado Training Establishment (TTTE). The air forces of all three nations sent their crews to the TTTE for an initial type conversion course but thereafter they dispersed to national units to complete their operational training. The RAF's tactical training school was the TWCU which began to form at RAF Honington with the arrival of the first two nominated staff crews on 1st August 1980. It was formally established on 8th January 1981 and opened for business with the commencement of No 1 Course four days later. The RAF's first operational Tornado unit, No 9 Sqn, formed at Honington on 1st June 1982 and thereafter the TWCU's output was geared to permit the formation of further squadrons at a planned rate of about one every six months.

Since the Tornado was a new aeroplane there were at first few crews experienced on type to man the TWCU and most of the initial batch instructors was drawn from the Buccaneer and Phantom forces with a number of additional pilots coming from Jaguar squadrons. By 1984, however, the first graduates of the school were beginning to complete their operational tours and some were being posted back to the TWCU as instructors, bringing with them a sound background of experience on type. This meant that the TWCU was now sufficiently well established to make it a

potential additional operational squadron in a crisis and on 1st January 1984 it became No 45 (Reserve) Sqn. On the 19th the Station Commander and Wg Cdr D A Griffith, OC TWCU, collected the Standard from the RAF College and brought it back to Honington. It was tacitly understood that, since the squadron did not technically exist, the Standard should not be paraded in public, although it was accepted that it could be displayed in the privacy of the Officers' Mess on appropriate formal occasions.

By the time that the TWCU became No 45(R) Sqn it had already provided sufficient crews for four Tornado squadrons and was training those destined for the fifth, No 16 Sqn. No 17 Course was in residence as was No 5 Qualified Weapons Instructors' (QWI) Course and No 1 Electronic Warfare Instructors' Course was about to start. The unit's staff comprised twenty pilot and fourteen navigator instructors, plus four pilots and four navs to run the flight simulator. The aircraft complement varied, but on average there were some twenty-three Tornados on strength. To maintain the unit's aircraft there were three engineering officers and 193 technicians, organised into two flights. Finally there was an Adjutant who doubled as Intelligence Officer. It was a big outfit and a busy one; on 21st March 1984 it flew its 10,000th Tornado flying hour.

The TWCU's Tornados already carried a unit emblem on their fins but this was quickly supplemented by a No 45 Sqn marking which appeared on either side of the nose. The opportunity to resurrect the traditional dumb-bell was missed again, however, and the Tornados carried the Hunter-style bar of red/blue diamonds instead. Since the bar flanked a representation of the Flying Camel, rather than the roundel, the latter was displaced from its normal location and repainted on the side of the intake trunking, which was something of an innovation.

Since the student crews arriving from the TTTE were already qualified to fly the Tornado, the course they were to undergo at Honington concerned itself only with tactics and weapons delivery techniques. The first week was spent in the groundschool and the flight simulator. The flying phase began with a couple of familiarisation trips followed by a series of exercises concentrating on low-level terrain-following navigation culminating in laydown and loft delivery of bombs, all of which are heavily dependent on the Tornado's on-board radar and computing systems. Laydown bombing involves a very fast, very low approach with the aircraft eventually passing directly over the aiming point. In a loft delivery the aircraft still approaches fast and low but, about three miles short of the target, the aircraft is pulled up into a climb and 'tosses' the bomb forward[2]. The crews also practised the classic shallow dive attack and strafing, neither of which would have been unfamiliar to the squadron's Mosquito crews of forty years before. Having mastered all these techniques, and the reversionary procedures to be used in the event of equipment failures, both pilot and navigator were given check rides before practising them by night. On completion of the weapons delivery phase of the course, crews progressed to Air Combat Training (ACT), the aim of which was to master evasive manoeuvres, although the opportunity to claim a 'kill', using either Sidewinder missiles or guns, was not to be ignored. In the final stages of the course, all of these techniques were brought together in a series of increasingly complex simulated combat missions, the last of which was flown as the leader of a pair, with a staff crew, or crews, lurking in ambush around the route to 'bounce' the formation.

During the Tornado's service new weapons were introduced, eg the JP 233, and delivery techniques were progressively refined and updated with, for instance, the addition of laser-assisted aiming and medium-level bombing. As innovations such as these were introduced so the TWCU course was adapted to embrace them, to reflect feedback from the front-line squadrons and to incorporate lessons learned during the Gulf War of 1991. Despite these changes, however, the core of the syllabus remained much the same providing both pilots and navs with about 35 hours in the air,

of which about half was flown with instructors and the remainder as a crew.

Although No 45(R) Sqn was earmarked for SACEUR, the terms of its assignment meant that it would not be transferred to his operational control until a comparatively late stage of pre-hostilities tension. Nevertheless, to maintain their operational 'edge' the TWCU's staff crews occasionally took part in NATO and national exercises as in March 1984 when some flew on an Exercise DATEX with the French Air Force, which involved landing away at Landivisiau, and others participated in a BLUE MOON with the Danes, which required a landing at Schleswig.

Like all RAF units the squadron had a variety of additional tasks to keep it occupied. Prominent among these was the hosting of a constant stream of visitors, keen to see the still very new aeroplane; especially as it was hoped that one or two of them might even buy some. In an increasingly commercially competitive world, by the 1980's the RAF was very much a division of 'UK Ltd' and Honington was often required to act as a shop window for the British aviation industry's latest and best product. The most promising sales prospect was the Royal Saudi Air Force (RSAF) and in August 1984 Honington received the first of several delegations which came to examine the aeroplane and the infrastructure necessary to support its operation. Negotiations were protracted and involved the station, and not least No 45(R) Sqn, in a great deal of what was, from a strictly parochial point of view, diversionary effort over a period of several months. Ultimately, however, the RSAF was to place a very substantial order for Tornados - so the end had justified the means.

Another symptom of the need to keep the Tornado, and the RAF, in the public eye manifested itself in a requirement to demonstrate the aeroplane to the taxpayer. To this end the squadron had a nominated crew to show the aircraft off during the 1984 display season; Sqn Ldr N J Slater and Flt Lt C C Edmonds gave their first displays in May, participating in events at Innsworth, Staverton and Manchester (Barton).

ZA408 served with No 45(R) Sqn for only six weeks. Taken on charge at the end of May 1984 it was lost in a mid-air collision with a Jaguar on 12th July; Sqn Ldr Boxall-Hunt and Flt Lt Cave both ejected successfully. (MAP)

No 45(R) Sqn lost an aeroplane on 12th July when ZA408 was involved in a collision with a Jaguar near Sheringham: Sqn Ldr Boxall-Hunt and Flt Lt Cave both ejected successfully, as did the Jaguar pilot.

Honington sponsored an exercise during September as a rehearsal for an anticipated TACEVAL. An operational unit can afford to stop its routine training activities for a time, convert itself to a war footing and practise alert and readiness procedures, ground defence and the like; indeed, it is essential that a squadron should do this to rehearse these aspects of its role under operational conditions. For a second line unit, however, such exercises are of only secondary significance and for the TWCU to have participated in them would have disrupted the continuity of training. With the build-up of the front-line Tornado GR 1 force still only half complete in 1984, the priority was to maintain the impetus behind the formation of further operational units and any interruption in the planned output of students would not have been acceptable. On the other hand, if No 9 Sqn and the rest of the station were going to batten down and 'go to war', it was not possible for the TWCU to carry on as if everything was normal so No 45(R) Sqn decamped to Marham for the duration. The following month the formal TACEVAL took place and, again, the squadron removed itself. This time it went to Machrihanish, whence it carried out its training task from the 7th to the 14th of October.

No 22 Course graduated in November. Among its students was Wg Cdr G L McRobbie, who had already lived with the aeroplane for several years and had previously overseen its service introduction from behind the desk of the Tornado Project Officer at HQ Strike Command. On November 11th he succeeded Duncan Griffiths as OC TWCU and thus also became OC No 45(R) Sqn.

The weather intervened in January 1985 and on the 17th several of the squadron's aeroplanes were diverted to Machrihanish. As conditions remained poor in East Anglia the squadron stayed put and flew from its temporary Scottish base until the 25th. There were more station exercises in January and April but the squadron remained at Honington and operated as best it could within the constraints which these imposed. It was inevitable that there would be some short-term disruption of training but it proved possible to make up most of the lost time later. In any case, it was already known that the timing of courses was to be significantly revised in July, when the whole training pattern was going to be rescheduled to improve the dovetailing of TWCU courses with the output from the TTTE, and any necessary adjustments could be made then.

Activities in support of the prospective RSAF order for Tornados were revitalised at short notice in August 1985; the squadron was obliged to devote several days to this task which included the provision of seven demonstration flights for RSAF personnel. It was a busy month as the TWCU was also launching its first course for Instrument Rating Examiners at the same time. In all the unit flew 662 hours in August, a performance worthy of its Fairey IIIFs - although it had had only a dozen of those!

Honington was subjected to another TACEVAL in October and the TWCU moved out again, taking fourteen of its aeroplanes back to Machrihanish. Even so the TACEVAL had an impact on training as the unit was obliged to provide chase aircraft to follow some of No 9 Sqn's aeroplanes as they flew their simulated war missions. No 45(R) Sqn was required to report back to the assessors on how closely No 9 Sqn's crews had conformed to their planned and briefed mission profiles - a particularly appropriate task for a 'shadow' squadron.

With the formation of No 14 Sqn in November 1985, the initial build up of the RAF's nine-squadron force of Tornado bombers was complete. From then on the TWCU's task was to be one of maintaining the strength of the front line rather than of creating it. Many of the first generation crews on the operational squadrons were now completing their initial tours but a substantial proportion of them remained within the Tornado force for a second stint. Nevertheless there was still a significant overall wastage rate as people were transferred to ground appointments, staff duties or instructional tours. Spread across the whole Tornado community, this amounted to something like the loss of a complete squadron's complement of aircrew over a six month period so the size of the TWCU's training task remained much the same, although there was a detectable easing of pressure. On the other hand, the Saudi order for Tornados was in the bag by this time and No 1 RSAF Course began in January 1986, running in parallel with the RAF's No 32 Course, which meant that the unit was still very busy.

No 45(R) Sqn was nominated to provide a display crew again for the 1986 season and in February Sqn Ldr Pete Chandler and Flt Lt Nigel Nickles began to work up their routine. 1986 was the 70th anniversary of the squadron's original formation and to celebrate this event the TWCU hosted a reunion at Honington on May 9th which was attended by a number of ex-members.

With the Tornado force now complete, No 45(R) Sqn found time to indulge in some of the more exotic training activities which had previously been the preserve of the operational units. The first of these was an exchange with the Tornados of JaboG 38. Sixty-seven *Luftwaffe* personnel were hosted at Honington while fifty-nine of No 45(R) Sqn's spent August 11th to 21st at Jever. While they were there the squadron's crews were able to participate in some buddy-buddy refuelling training with the German Tornados, exploring a corner of the aircraft's potential which the RAF did not really begin to exploit until 1994.

Since No 9 Sqn was about to depart from Honington, leaving the TWCU as the only resident flying unit, it now fell to the squadron to represent the station on ceremonial occasions and in September they furnished a contingent for a Battle of Britain parade in Thetford and four of its aircraft flew in salute over Bury St Edmunds on the 14th.

At the beginning of October, No 9 Sqn moved to Germany where it was to join the Brüggen Wing, leaving its hardened dispersal facilities at Honington unoccupied. Some consideration was given to transferring the TWCU's activities to this accommodation but, despite wearing No 45 Sqn's markings, the TWCU was still essentially a training unit and its style of operation was more suited to an Aircraft Servicing Platform (ASP). In any case, the unit was far too big to fit comfortably into the hardened site and to have divided it between the 'hard' and 'soft' sides of the airfield would have required additional MT and manpower, both of which, particularly the latter, were becoming increasingly scarce and expensive. The TWCU stayed put, although it familiarised itself with the hardened facility so that it could move over there should the squadron ever be formally embodied in its operational guise.

Although it was still not assigned to SACEUR as an immediately available operational unit and retained its reserve status, No 45(R) Sqn was now formally 'declared' at a higher state of readiness than had originally been the case. By this time, of course, all of its aircrew instructors and the majority of the ground tradesmen on the unit were veterans of at least one tour on an operational squadron, so everyone was familiar with NATO operating procedures. Nevertheless there was a need to maintain currency and the squadron began to take an increasing part in exercises and to indulge in Overseas Training Flights (OTF), so long as these did not detract from the primary task of maintaining the flow of new and recycled crews to the squadrons[3]. In October No 45(R) Sqn took part in an Exercise BLUE MOON for the first time in two years, detaching a small party of airmen to Aalborg for several days to turn the aeroplanes around.

Gordon McRobbie left to take over the RAF Presentation Team in November 1986 and on the 28th command of the squadron passed to Wg Cdr A V B Hawken. That month was also notable for the despatch of a small detachment of airmen to RAF Leuchars. Leuchars was a popular airfield for intermediate landings by Tornados of both the TTTE and the TWCU flying training sorties over Scotland during the winter months but previous experience had shown that this overstretched the host station's handling capacity. From 1986 onwards the two Tornado training units maintained a small joint groundcrew detachment at Leuchars in the winter to turn their own aircraft round.

The squadron lost its second Tornado on December 1st when Sqn Ldr E Wyer and Flt Lt J Magowan experienced a major systems failure in ZA555. The crew had no alternative but to abandon their aeroplane and they ejected successfully in the vicinity of Diss, although both sustained some injuries.

The squadron's display crew for the 1987 season was Flt Lt MacDonald and Flt Lt Middleton, backed up by Flt Lt Dobb and Flt Lt Davies. They began to work up the routine in April. April is also the start of the 'building season' and Honington was scheduled to have its runway resurfaced in that year. Although arrangements can usually be made to permit the odd aeroplane to land and take off while a runway is being worked on, it is not feasible to operate at normal intensity and the squadron was required to use Marham as a 'bolthole'. On April 24th twenty-two Tornados of No 45(R) Sqn redeployed to what was now a very crowded airfield, since it already housed Nos 27 and 617 Sqns with Tornados and the Victor tankers of No 55 Sqn. Honington was close enough to permit its ground training, support and technical facilities to be used, however, although time lost in the constant toing and froing had to be compensated for by a temporary, but significant, increase in the number of airmen on strength.

Despite playing away, the squadron was still expected to represent Honington when appropriate and on May 30th it provided a four-aircraft flypast over the town to mark the Freedom of Bury St Edmunds which had been granted to the station some years before[4]. On 3rd June a third Tornado was lost when ZA366 suffered a systems failure and fire; Wg Cdr

A V B Hawken and Wg Cdr N Irving (of No 53 Course) ejected successfully near Manby.

Moving to Marham did not mean that the squadron had escaped the disruption caused by MINEVALs and MAXEVALs and the unit was effectively grounded between the 13th and 16th September while their temporary base rehearsed for its formal TACEVAL. This did not affect everyone, however, as the resident QWI course had taken five aeroplanes and a party of groundcrew to Sardinia on the 7th. This was the first time that No 45(R) Sqn had used the Air Combat Manoeuvring Installation (ACMI) at Decimomannu but when the detachment returned on the 16th they reported positively on its value and such training events became regular, if infrequent, activities from then on. Prior to this the unit had taken part in Exercise BOTANY BAY, an air/sea exercise, which had involved four aircraft landing away at Eggebeck.

There were several interesting events over the next two months. There was another short detachment to Aalborg to support participation in an Exercise BLUE MOON in October, followed by a missile firing camp at Valley, and between the 19th and 21st eighteen of the unit's Tornados operated from Wattisham to escape yet another station exercise at Marham. In November two TWCU aeroplanes participated in a flypast over London on the occasion of the Lord Mayor's Show and, while Marham underwent its formal TACEVAL between the 16th and 19th, eighteen of the TWCU's Tornados went back to Wattisham to keep out of the way.

The refurbishment of Honington was virtually complete by now and the bulk of No 45(R) Sqn flew back there on November 24th. The initial wave comprised thirteen aircraft which flew past in formation before breaking off to carry out a mock attack on the airfield to let everyone know they were back. Unfortunately this display of noisy exuberance disturbed some of the local residents who had grown accustomed to the relative peace and quiet while the runway had been out of action!

By 1988 the Tornado was firmly established in the bomber business and the first of two dedicated reconnaissance units was formed in September, the crews for No 2 Sqn passing through the TWCU throughout the year. They did much the same course as the bomber crews, the 'black arts' of recce being taught in-house on the squadrons. As an indication of the length of time that the aeroplane had now been in service, in February five of the unit's officers, Sqn Ldrs Corney, Monk, Waddington and Watts and Flt Lt Dobb, celebrated having flown 1,000 hours on type, although not all with No 45(R) Sqn.

1988 was a relatively quiet year, the highlights being two QWI Course detachments to Decimomannu, one in March and one in November. Honington held a station exercise in April and this time, rather than decamping as in the past, No 45(R) Sqn was fully involved, exercising its ability to meet the increased state of operational readiness which was now required of it. The squadron prepared the required number of its aeroplanes 'for war' within the prescribed time limits and transferred its operations from the hangar and its adjacent dispersal to No 9 Sqn's vacant hardened site. The squadron took part in BLUE MOONs in August and October and in MALLET BLOWs in March and July. The latter were national, rather than NATO, exercises (although foreign participation was involved) based on the Otterburn Range in Northumbria. They provided high value training, involving penetration of 'enemy' airspace defended by fighters and missiles and culminating in live attacks against a variety of difficult ground targets in a hostile electronic environment. In September the squadron laid on a four-ship flypast over Bury St Edmunds to commemorate Battle of Britain Day, and the following month a pair spent the weekend at Akrotiri on an OTF, the furthest from home that the unit had flown thus far. As had become the norm the unit had had a display crew for the 1988 air show season, the honour falling to Flt S Dobb and Flt Lt S Hughes.

All of the TWCU's Tornados wore their 'last three' on their fins. This is ZA545 with the last two digits suitably stressed. This aeroplane served with No 45(R) Sqn from 28th August 1986 until it was lost in a mid-air collision with another Tornado (ZA464 of No 20 Sqn) on 12th July 1984. The crew, Maj Wise USAF and Flt Lt Bowles, were both killed. (MAP)

1989 was notable for some opportunities to drop live 1,000 pounders at the Garvie Island Range off the north western tip of the Scottish mainland. There was the usual crop of BLUE MOONs and MALLET BLOWs and, in March, the squadron participated in a Forward Air Control exercise (FACEX) for the first time. This took place at Sennybridge Range in Wales and involved the use of laser target marking to assist in the accurate delivery of 3 kg practice bombs. None of this was new to the unit's staff crews, of course, since they were by now all experienced men who had completed one or more operational tours on type, but the more extensive participation of the TWCU in such events was another symptom of the increased operational status of No 45(R) Sqn.

Perhaps even more enjoyable than exercise participation was an increase in the unit's allocation of OTFs. Airfields visited in 1989 by Tornados wearing the Flying Camel insignia included Lechfeld, Laarbruch, Terrejon, Villafranca, Ghedi, Zweibrücken, Aalborg, Decimomannu (another QWI Course), San Xavier, Pisa, Limoges and Brüggen.

The squadron fielded two display crews in 1989, Flt Lts James and Hughes and Flt Lts Riley and Smith, who performed at a variety of venues throughout the air show season. The unit also contributed four aircraft to a set-piece airfield attack at Mildenhall on May 27th and 28th. This was a co-ordinated effort involving several of No 1 Gp's units and proved to be a major feature of that year's USAF Air Day. In June the TWCU hosted the No 45 Sqn Reunion Association, as it had in May the previous year, and in July there was another change of command, Tony Hawken handing over to Wg Cdr M Prissick.

Towards the end of 1989 there were two liaisons with other air forces. The first involved the Italians, who had been invited to take part in the USAF's Exercise RED FLAG in Nevada. RED FLAG was one of the most demanding live air training events yet devised and participating units from European air forces always invested in an intensive work-up phase prior to setting off across the Atlantic. Between August 30th and September 9th, nine Italian Tornados were based at Honington to use the RAF's training ranges in the UK and, as the only resident flying unit, it fell to No 45(R) Sqn to host them. The second event was a 'private' bombing

competition between the TWCU's Tornados and the F-111s of the USAF's 493rd TFS from Lakenheath. Each unit fielded four aircraft. No 45(R) Sqn took the first four places.

In 1990, the TWCU's cumulative total of Tornado flying hours passed the 45,000 mark. Some of this time was spent on OTFs and during the year aircraft of No 45(R) Sqn visited Aviano, Getafe, Aalborg, Murcia, Leeuwarden, Montijo, Elefsis, Villafranca, Twenthe and Ghedi. The squadron suffered its fourth, and last, Tornado flying accident on August 14th when ZA545 collided with another aircraft over Spurn Head. Sadly this accident was fatal and Maj Dennis Wise USAF and Flt Lt John Bowles lost their lives as did the navigator of the other aircraft, Tornado ZA464 of No 20 Sqn.

The unit's display crew for 1990 was Flt Lt D Reid and Flt Lt I Brunning. The theme of that year's air show season was the commemoration of the 50th anniversary of the Battle of Britain, the climax being a spectacular flypast over London by 168 aircraft. Honington's units contributed a formation of sixteen Tornados, twelve of them from No 45(R) Sqn and four from No 13 Sqn the latter having been formed in January as the second of the dedicated recce units. Planning for this event had begun several months before and, although it did eventually take place as scheduled, its execution had been put in jeopardy by events in Kuwait, Operation GRANBY having begun in August 1990. The initial RAF deployments to Saudi Arabia were managed with relative ease but, as tension continued to increase, so the size of the RAF's commitment grew; the detachments lengthened and the demand for additional men and equipment began to make itself increasingly felt across the whole service.

The TWCU was not immune to the steady shift of the RAF's centre of gravity towards the Middle East. One of its navigators, Sqn Ldr Tony Francis, was detached to Riyadh to work with the Joint Planning Staff, and a pilot, Flt Lt Ian McLean, joined him in Saudi Arabia to act as liaison between the HQ staff and the crews of the Tornado reconnaissance detachment. Fifteen of the unit's tradesmen, six of them armourers, were also sent out to the Gulf to reinforce the various operational detachments. The demands of the Gulf were also making themselves felt back at Honington, not least because priority for the use of the flight simulator had to be given to the recce crews of No 13 Sqn and, as a result,

1991 was the seventy-fifth anniversary of the squadron's original formation and to mark the occasion the display aircraft, ZA606, was given a special paint scheme. The whole of the fin and the rear fuselage was in dark blue with a large red diamond containing a Flying Camel. The underside of the tailplane was in pale blue, edged in dark blue, and there was a dark blue flash running most of the length of the underside of the fuselage with its centre picked out in pale blue. Best of all, on this aeroplane, the red/blue diamond marking was replaced (at last!) with a white dumb-bell on a red ground; this flanked a white disc with a pale blue silhouette of a Flying Camel superimposed on a red '75'. The names painted on the cockpit sill read: Wg Cdr M Prissick and Flt Lt Guy Riley. (British Aerospace, Kingston)

TWCU courses began to run late. As a second-line unit, however, No 45(R) Sqn did not become directly involved in the Gulf War in its own right and its contribution was confined to responding to requests for assistance and pressing on with training as best it could.

Following the remarkably brief and successful execution of Operation DESERT STORM in February 1991, the Arabian detachments were progressively withdrawn and there was a major reshuffle of the entire Tornado fleet as aeroplanes with similar modification states were concentrated on various bases. This involved a good deal of ferrying to and fro, and TWCU crews became involved in this programme, some of them being flown out to Muharraq to bring aeroplanes back to the UK.

Things slowly began to return to normal during 1991 and the OTF programme was resumed, giving crews the opportunity to visit Rivolto, Valkenberg, Karup, Colmar, Twenthe, Aalborg, Ghedi and Bad Sollingen. The TWCU was again required to provide a solo display crew for that year's season and Flt Lt Riley and Flt Lt Kinnaird duly obliged Since 1991 was the 75th anniversary of the squadron's formation, the display aircraft was given a spectacular colour scheme involving generous applications of the squadron's blue and red colours and, better late than never, the reappearance of the white dumb-bell painted, Venom-style, on a red background on either side of the nose in place of the red and blue diamonds.

By 1991 the TWCU's personnel identified very closely with the history and traditions of the Flying Camels but they were about to be sharply reminded of the squadron's true

Another picture of ZA606 showing the underside of its 'birthday suit'. (British Aerospace, Kingston)

status. In May RAF Honington exercised its traditional rights as holders of the Freedom of Bury St Edmunds by holding a parade in the Abbey Gardens and marching through the town. The Standards of both Nos 13 and 45 Sqns were paraded. A photograph of this event appeared in the *RAF News* of 14th June, artfully captioned to identify the banners as being those of No 13 Sqn and "the TWCU". This was noted by an ex-member of the Flying Camels (Sgt A G 'Jock' McCandlish, last mentioned in this narrative in Chapter 10) and he wrote to the editor in mild protest at the failure to identify No 45 Sqn as such. His letter was published on 12th July and this minor flurry of publicity caught the attention of 'the Staff'. The unfortunate consequence was that Honington was reminded that it was considered inappropriate for the Standard of a reserve squadron to be paraded in public. The TWCU was directed to return the banner to Cranwell where it was once again lodged beneath the cupola of College Hall - but see Chapter 22.

In September there was a squadron exchange with EC 2/13 of the French Air Force, some of whose Mirages visited Honington while six Tornados and a support party went to Colmar from the 16th to the 23rd.

The fifth, and last, CO of No 45(R) Sqn was Wg Cdr A T Hudson who was appointed to command the TWCU in succession to Mal Prissick at the end of January 1992. By this time most of the dust of the Gulf War had settled and the impact of the end of the Cold War was making itself increasingly felt. With the reduction in east-west tension, it was inevitable that the government would seek to reduce defence expenditure and a number of units had begun to disband from mid-1991 onwards, beginning with the residual Phantom force. As part of this programme the RAF's presence in Germany was to be considerably reduced and three of its Tornado units were earmarked for early disbandment. In an attempt to soften the blow it was decided that the identities of these squadrons, all of which had recently been engaged in the Gulf War, were to be preserved. They were Nos 15, 16 and 20 Sqns.

While it may not have been a surprise, it was nevertheless with some dismay that the TWCU's personnel learned that they were to lose the numberplate with which they had identified for more than eight years. They were to assume the identity of No 15 Sqn which had disbanded at Laarbruch on 31st December 1991. Appeals were voiced by the unit itself and by Air Cdre Dennis Rixson on behalf of the Reunion Association, but they were to no avail. The Flying Camel was going to have its wings clipped again, and this time it would probably be for good[5]. The date of its demise was to be 31st March 1992. Sqn Ldr Keith Hargreaves, who had previously organised reunions in 1990 and 1991, arranged a final gathering of ex-squadron members at Honington on March 28th.

When the squadron's identity was withdrawn No 112 Course was in residence. Since it had assumed No 45 Sqn's identity in 1984 the TWCU had trained and/or refreshed 410 pilots and 385 navigators on its Main Courses in addition to training thirty-eight aircrew for the RSAF. The QWI Courses had trained fifty-five pilots and forty-eight navs; seventeen pilots and ninety-eight navs had qualified as Electronic Warfare Instructors and five IREs had been certified as competent on the Tornado.

The last flight made by a Tornado of No 45(R) Sqn was a night training sortie in ZA602 on 31st March 1992. It was a 'competent to instruct' sortie with Keith Hargreaves checking out a new instructor, Flt Lt 'Tommy' Tank. At the post-flight debrief the latter airily observed that it had been rather quieter than his last night trip as there had been no Iraqi flak - a line like that was undoubtedly worthy of an instructor and he duly joined the TWCU staff.

Notes:

1. It is an indication of the insubstantial nature of a 'shadow' squadron that time spent with this status does not count towards the accumulation of the

twenty-five years of service which is the basic qualification for the award of a Standard.

2. Loft bombing was the ultimate development of the LABS technique as used by the squadron during the latter part of the Canberra era and it had the same aims - avoiding penetration of the target's defensive perimeter and escaping the effects of the bomber's own weapons. The main difference was that, whereas a LABS delivery took the aircraft up to some 5,000 feet in a loop with a roll off the top, a loft manoeuvre permitted it to turn away and descend much earlier, thus minimising the time that the attacker was exposed to the defences.

3. An OTF was '1980s-speak' for the Lone Rangers which the squadron had flown in its Canberra days. The objective was the same - to give a crew the responsibility for planning and executing an international flight to an unfamiliar airfield. This provided valuable training in airmanship and captaincy, broadened the base of the crew's experience and fostered their self-sufficiency. It also provided a weekend's relaxation in different, if not always exotic, surroundings and an exercise in ingenuity in finding places to stow the 'duty frees' in what was quite a small and densely-packed airframe.

4. RAF Honington had been granted the Freedom of Bury St Edmunds on 25th April 1972 and thereafter the station normally exercised its rights with an annual parade, sometimes accompanied by a flypast.

5. The decision (which is understood to have been directly attributable to the Secretary of State for Defence) to sustain the identities of the squadrons which had participated in the Gulf War, was questionable, or ill-advised, on several grounds:

a. The ruling took no account of the loyalties felt by members of a unit to its unique identity. While the men of No 15 Sqn at Laarbruch no doubt felt strong ties to their unit's history and traditions, the fact was that their squadron was to be disbanded and as individuals they were to be dispersed. The corporate contemporary identity of No 15 Sqn was thus going to be irretrievably lost. It only exacerbated the problem to require the personnel of No 45(R) Sqn to abandon *their* unit's identity as well. Overnight they were supposed to ignore the significance of the artefacts, trophies and photographs which had adorned the squadron's offices and crewrooms for the previous eight years; abandon the active links they had developed with their predecessors in the Reunion Association; erase the Flying Camel insignia from their aeroplanes and remove the squadron badges from their flying suits. They were to redecorate their accommodation with the bric-a-brac of an entirely different unit, repaint their aeroplanes, sew on new badges and carry on as if nothing had happened. It was both unrealistic and unnecessary; they did as they were told, of course, but with little enthusiasm.

b. The decision ignored the long-established policy governing the selection of squadron numberplates which, in essence, requires that priority be given to sustaining those units which already have the longest accumulation of service (see the Epilogue). It is notable in this context that, although the term 'reserve squadron' was not then in use, No 15 Sqn had actually spent the ten years from 1924 to 1934 as a trials unit attached to the A&AEE with a very similar status to that of No 45 Sqn while it was 'shadowing' the TWCU. If appropriate allowance is made for this then No 45 Sqn was still senior to No 15 Sqn in terms of *active* service accumulated. Furthermore, and perhaps even more significantly, its Standard had been awarded six years before that of No 15 Sqn. No 45 Sqn's identity was to be obliterated in favour of that of a unit that was its junior.

c. By effectively making participation in the Gulf War the overriding qualification for a squadron's numberplate being retained the decision appeared to afford the brief campaign against Iraq greater significance than the First and Second World Wars or, alternatively, it implied that history began in 1991 and that all previous events were of no account.

d. The RAF's participation in the Gulf War was peculiarly notable for the extensive use of 'composite' squadrons. Thus, for instance, while No 15 Sqn was nominally at Bahrein from November 1991 it included a substantial contingent of personnel from No 17 Sqn from the outset and was later reinforced by elements of Nos 27 and 617 Sqns as well. On this basis there were few RAF units which did *not* take part in the Gulf campaign! Even the TWCU had made its contribution but, since the emergency had not been sufficient to cause No 45 Sqn to be embodied, this evidently did not count. No 45 Sqn did not exist, so it could not have been in the Gulf, so its identity was forfeit.

Chapter 22. Pilot training.

When No 45(R) Sqn had had its identity abruptly snuffed out at the end of March 1992, as a casualty of yet another round of defence cuts, it had seemed improbable that it would ever be reformed. But the spate of disbandments, which stemmed from the 'Options for Change' study in the wake of the collapse of the USSR and the Warsaw Pact, caused the MOD to reconsider the question of sustaining unit identities. In an attempt to prolong at least a semblance of the existence of selected units, several of the numberplates of disbanding squadrons were to be reallocated to OCUs which had not previously been so honoured, and even to FTSs. This change in policy suddenly meant that the Flying Camels were once again considered to be worthy of representation. It was announced that the Multi-Engine Training Squadron (METS) of No 6 FTS at Finningley was to become a new No 45(R) Sqn on 1st July 1992.

Prior to 1960 most RAF pilots were trained to 'wings' standard on single-engined fixed-wing aeroplanes, most recently via the classic Provost/Vampire sequence, but in that year 'streamed' training was introduced. Thenceforth only the basic Jet Provost course would be common to all pilots and, depending upon the aptitude of the individual and the immediate needs of the service, students were to complete their advanced flying training on jets, twins or helicopters. The first twin-engine courses were run at Valley, but from 1963 this became the exclusive task of No 5 FTS at Oakington. In 1972 twenty-six Jetstreams were ordered to replace the venerable Varsities in the pilot training role and they began to enter service from June 1973. Before all of the new aircraft had even been delivered, however, it was foreseen that there would be little need for additional pilots to fly multi-engined types in the near future as a further round of defence cuts was forecast. In late 1974 multi-engine advanced flying training ceased altogether; No 5 FTS closed and the new Jetstreams were put into storage at St Athan. The 1975 White Paper on Defence confirmed the anticipated reduction in strength, and eight squadrons of 'heavy' aircraft were disbanded over the next two years[1]. As a result the RAF found itself with a large surplus of redundant qualified pilots and, until they could be disposed of or absorbed, the small amount of residual multi-engine training that was still required, mostly refresher flying, was contracted out to the College of Air Training at Hamble.

By 1976 the temporary 'bulge' in the availability of pilots qualified on 'heavies' had begun to subside and it became necessary to start feeding new pilots into the system again to restore the balance of age and experience within the overall manning pattern and career structure. Meanwhile some of the Jetstreams had been diverted to the RN for observer training but another eight were broken out of store and the first of these was delivered to Leeming in November 1976. Here METS began to work up under the aegis of No 3 FTS until its official formation date of 9th May 1977. On 23rd April 1979 METS moved to Finningley where it became an element of No 6 FTS, which was otherwise responsible for the training of all aircrew other than pilots.

METS has changed little since its inception, apart from having grown slightly so that it had a fleet of eleven aeroplanes when it assumed the alternative identity of No 45(R) with Sqn Ldr David Piper as its first CO. The unit is divided into three flights. A and B Flights (commanded in 1992 by Flt Lt 'Rolly' Hendry and Flt Lt Craig Campbell, respectively) handle flying training, employing a total of about a dozen Qualified Flying Instructors (QFI) between them. The only permanent member of C Flight is its OC (Flt Lt David 'Syd' Bowsher in 1992) as this element serves as a holding unit for post-graduate students awaiting courses at OCUs. In addition to these aviators, there is a Chief Ground Instructor (Sqn Ldr Ian Welch in 1992) with a staff of three classroom instructors, and a Synthetic Training Section whose two operators run the flight simulator. METS' throughput of students can be variable, depending on the flow through the overall training machine, and a selection of courses is offered to cater for a variety of different kinds of student.

The core function of METS is to operate as an Advanced Flying Training School and the twenty-week AFTS Course represents the backbone of its flying task. There are seven overlapping courses per year, each capable of handling up to nine students, all of whom are graduates of the Basic Flying Training Schools where they had previously flown Jet Provosts or, more recently, Tucanos. On completion of their Jetstream course the students are awarded their wings.

Since the AFTS Course is METS' mainstay it is of interest to consider the broad content of its syllabus. In all a student pilot can expect to fly some 50 hours while he is at Finningley, covering general handling, night and instrument flying and navigation, the latter

One of the squadron's Jetstreams demonstrating that it can do it on one - XX482/J with its starboard prop feathered. (METS)

including airways procedures and at least one overseas landaway. Over 80% of the flying is dual. In addition to the airborne work there is a considerable amount of simulator time and there are the inevitable classroom sessions to learn about the construction and operation of the Jetstream's airframe, engines and systems. Finally, since the students have yet to complete their formal officer training, there is a generous allocation of syllabus time dedicated to General Service Training which aims to develop their skills as junior officers, to increase their awareness of their responsibilities, and to broaden their understanding of the wider implications of service in the RAF and the many functions that the service fulfils.

The Jetstream's flightdeck - where it all happens. Flt Lt Rolly Hendry, right, and Sqn Ldr Dave Lee about to start the starboard engine. (METS)

METS' other major commitment is the Multi-Engine Cross-Over Course (MEXO). This caters for *ab initio* students who may have faltered during advanced training on the Hawk or on helicopters and/or for experienced pilots who are transferring to heavy aircraft after a period of productive service on other types. This ten-week course is run up to six times per year with three or four students per intake.

There are two other courses. For pilots with previous experience on 'heavies' who are returning to flying after a ground appointment there is a five-week Multi-Engine Refresher Course. This is run up to eight times per year, each course having up to five students. Finally there is the Tristar Enhancement Course which is run on an 'as and when required' basis to satisfy the peculiar demands of No 216 Sqn whose aeroplanes are unusual among heavy RAF types in that they do not carry navigators. This course serves to prepare pilots for the additional duties which they will have to carry out in the unique operating environment of the Tristar's flightdeck.

Jetstream QFIs are homegrown at Finningley but not by METS, although METS' aeroplanes are used. This responsibility lies with the Multi-Engine Standards Squadron which runs four twelve-week QFI Courses per year, two students per course being sufficient to satisfy the demand.

If all courses are running to capacity, at peak loading there can be well over thirty students in residence, which makes METS a busy unit. In practice the population is usually well in excess of this as a proportion of graduates tends to remain on strength, marooned in one of the recurrent training backlogs caused by the progressive contraction of the front line. While holding at Finningley most of them continue to fly and thus to build up their First Pilot hours, ideally on the unit's Jetstreams but often on other types. A snapshot of this situation as at mid-July 1993 showed that METS had twenty-eight supernumerary pilots nominally on its strength. Nine were at a variety of stations, giving ATC cadets rides in Chipmunks; thirteen were detached elsewhere about the RAF; two had been 'on hold' for so long that they were then undergoing a Refresher Course prior to joining an

The squadron's Jetstreams range far and wide on their training and occasional light transport sorties. This one is seen at Keflavik on 10th March 1993 with Sqn Ldr Dave Lee (on the left) and Flt Lt Rolly Hendry - looks as if they might be there for another night. (R Hendry)

OCU, and four were attached to C Flight flying Jetstreams.

Throughout the late 1980s and early 1990s the majority of flying units in Support Command were 'civilianised' and Finningley was no exception[2]. The effect is that, apart from the aircrew and a few servicemen filling key executive or support appointments, the day to day running of the station is largely in the hands of a civilian contractor. Thus the blue-overalled groundcrew who tend METS' Jetstreams are not airmen but civilian tradesmen employed by the contractors, Short Bros. In most cases, however, they are ex-RAF or ex-RN technicians who are very familiar with service procedures and attitudes. For the moment this system seems to work well enough and it is considered to be very cost effective. Contracting-out aircraft engineering at most training airfields has, of course, significantly reduced the requirement for uniformed groundcrew, which has in turn enabled the RAF to make considerable savings by permitting it to cut back on the numbers of tradesmen which it needs to train. It remains to be seen, however, what the long-term financial consequences of this concept will be when the supply of ex-RAF airmen dries up in a few years' time. If the RAF continues to shrink until it finally disappears altogether there should be no problem. If, on the other hand, this process is halted but the service continues to train only sufficient tradesmen to man its front-line squadrons, then someone else will have to start

The Flying Camel as worn on the squadron's Jetstreams. The Camel is in the traditional dark blue, highlighted in white; the wings are red and the frame is in pale blue. (MAP)

training groundcrew for the various civilian contractors to employ on the second-line units. These costs will inevitably be passed on to the customer, the RAF. If (or when?) that happens, it would seem that this policy will have gained a relatively short-term financial saving at the cost of a permanent loss of flexibility; one cannot draft contracted civilian employees to trouble spots and the pool of available manpower which used to be represented by the airmen on the strength of the MUs and FTSs has largely dried up - as became all too apparent during Operation GRANBY.

The Jetstream was originally designed as a commuterliner and as such it is a very efficient light transport aircraft. As employed by the RAF, however, the focus of interest is very much the flightdeck, and the aeroplane's significant passenger and/or freight carrying capacity is of only secondary importance. Nevertheless METS is often called upon to act as a communications squadron and, when the overriding priorities of flying training permit, its aircraft frequently operate in the light transport role. A typical task might involve taking a party of groundcrew and spares to a Tornado that has developed a problem and has diverted, perhaps to an airfield in Norway, bringing the stranded crew back to the UK on the return flight and then repeating the process a few days later to collect the rectification party and deliver a new Tornado crew to ferry the repaired aeroplane back to its base. Although tasks of this nature are outside the unit's true remit, when the capacity exists and it can be shown that using a Jetstream would be cheaper than other means of transport, they are often undertaken. For METS to fly such support missions has the additional advantage of providing a worthwhile consolidation sortie for a recently qualified pilot, especially when it involves an international flight, airways procedures and a foreign landaway, all of these activities representing very valuable experience for a prospective Hercules captain. Such tasks are generally handled by the floating population of C Flight under the direct supervision of a QFI. The intensity of tasking in this secondary role varies but has tended to increase to such an extent that it has been suggested that the acronym METS actually stands for METS' Executive Taxi Services!

Having been allocated No 45 Sqn's identity, METS lost little time in maintaining a squadron tradition by creating this Jetstream clockface. This picture was taken in October 1992. (No 45 Sqn archives)

It is in this light transport role that METS would be required to operate in a time of tension. This has long been the unit's designated wartime task and it did just that during the Gulf Crisis of 1990-91, when its contribution won a commendation from the AOCinC. Although this planned function had not been considered to warrant such an accolade in the past, this is the justification for the unit's being allocated a formal identity as a reserve squadron and it has given the Flying Camel another lease of life.

Very shortly after being designated as No 45(R) Sqn the unit began to advertise its new identity on its aeroplanes and a Flying Camel motif soon appeared on either side of the nose with a row of red diamonds on a blue bar across the tips of the fins - that new-fangled Hunter marking again! The silver and the squadron's other memorabilia were collected from Honington, and METS' crew rooms and offices were soon decorated with photographs of bygone days.

The RAF celebrated its seventy-fifth birthday on 1st April 1993 and to mark the occasion a new Queen's Colour was to be presented at a major celebration to be staged at Marham. The Standards of all extant squadrons were to be paraded in a proud and colourful display. By this time, however, the RAF had been reduced to just fifty-two numbered squadrons with this figure likely to fall to about forty-five within the decade. The last time that the RAF's permanent Order of Battle had numbered only forty-five squadrons had been as long ago as 1926 and it must be pointed out (again) that at that time the Flying Camels had been among the select band of units which had constituted the front line. Despite the professed concern of the RAF's leadership for preserving the heritage of the service, it is a mute comment on the lack of rigour applied to the implementation of this policy that No 45 Sqn has not had a substantive existence since 1976.

The plan to parade all available Standards at Marham may not have been unconnected with a timely change in policy which, from June 1992, permitted reserve squadrons not only to take possession of their Standards but to parade them in public as well. It can surely have been no coincidence that, as a direct result of this change, an additional eleven banners could be fielded at Marham, a 21% increase, creating at least the illusion of a still substantial air force.

Only a year before METS had become No 45(R) Sqn, the TWCU had had its metaphorical knuckles rapped for parading No 45 Sqn's Standard in public, and had been obliged to take it back to Cranwell. The reversal of policy meant that it could be recovered yet again and on 22nd July 1992 a Standard Party collected the banner from College Hall in a joint ceremony with No 60 Sqn which had also recently been reformed, but in their case as an operational helicopter unit. The arrival of No 45 Sqn's Standard at Finningley was marked by a brief but formal ceremonial which was witnessed by the Station Commander and the personnel of No 45(R) Sqn.

A squadron's Standard is a splendid symbol of a unit's past achievements but, as an artefact, it is rather delicate. It does not have an infinite life and, despite the care with which

Another overseas training sortie; although lacking the refinement of a row of red/blue diamonds on the tip of its fin, XX492/A still adds a considerable splash of colour to the ramp, at North Front, Gibraltar on 11th September 1993. (METS)

453

it is always handled and stored, it can withstand only so much exposure, particularly on parades when it is subjected to the stresses of sun, wind and rain. In 1993 the Standard of the Flying Camels was still the original example which had been presented in 1955. It had spent the first fifteen years of its life in the demanding climate of Singapore and after a further twenty-three years it was showing its age quite badly. When the Standards were inspected at Marham prior to the Royal Review it was considered that if No 45 Sqn's were to be paraded there was a significant risk that it might well part company with its staff. It was decided, with regret, that if the parade took place as planned No 45 Sqn's Standard would not appear. As it happened the weather intervened, causing the scheduled flypast to be cancelled and the presentation ceremony took place in a hangar. Thus, rather than being paraded, all the Standards were displayed statically to provide an impressive and colourful backdrop to the ceremonial and the Flying Camels' venerable banner was able to take its place with those of all the other units represented.

In normal circumstances a Squadron Standard has an

No 45(R) Sqn was presented with a new Standard at a ceremony held at Finningley on 4th October 1994. Flt Lt G D Edwards is seen here receiving the Standard from ACM Sir Andrew Wilson, assisted by Gp Capt D J G Wilby. (No 45(R) Sqn

lifespan of about twenty-five years after which it is replaced. A Queen's Colour, which is displayed more frequently, has a life of only fifteen years, hence the Marham event which was to provide the venue for the replacement of the Colour which had been presented on a similar occasion held at Finningley in 1978. In view of the age and condition of No 45 Sqn's banner enquiries were made about arranging for it to be replaced. This proved to be a little complicated. Technically a reserve squadron does not assume its operational identity until a specific stage in the conversion of the RAF from a peacetime to a wartime footing. Since it was peacetime, No 45(R) Sqn did not really exist; could it therefore be presented with a new Standard? With the recent proliferation of reserve squadrons, however, and the revision of policy concerning the display of their Standards this problem had already been addressed and in 1992 the Air Force Board had ruled that such presentations could be made. After all, if the RAF wanted to be able to parade the banners of all of its squadrons, including those of its reserve units, then it would have to ensure that they were all presentable. A new Standard was authorised for the Flying Camels in 1993 and the following year it was ready for collection from Hobsons of London (although now actually located at Thundersley in Essex rather than in Soho) who had made the original article in 1954.

The date fixed for the ceremony was 4th October 1994, but there was a problem. The mounting of a respectable parade requires something like a hundred men, and when a Standard is formally paraded it is always provided with an armed close escort. If the proceedings are to make any real sense then both the escort and the supporting flights ought to be drawn from the unit's own ranks[3]. Unfortunately METS had no 'ranks'. Having been largely civilianised, the station had precious few either but, as the training school for loadmasters, air engineers and air electronics operators, Finningley did have a substantial number of airmen aircrew. Most of these were pressed into service and, with some additional assistance from No 100 Sqn, it proved possible to stage a suitable event - although few Standards can have been supported by quite so many SNCOs. With the assembly flanked by a pair of gleaming Jetstreams and with the RAF Museum's Sopwith Camel providing an appropriate backdrop to the spectacle, the parade commander, Sqn Ldr Piper, ordered the old Standard to be marched off into honourable retirement. The new one was then consecrated by the Chaplain-in-Chief, the Venerable B H Lucas, before being formally presented to the squadron by the Reviewing Officer, Air Chief Marshal Sir Andrew Wilson, the Air Member for Personnel and AOCinC Personnel and Training Command. It was then ceremonially trooped in front of the parade before being marched off to face a rather uncertain future. The parade was witnessed by Air Cdre Ian Stockwell, President of the Reunion Association, supported by a substantial contingent of ex-squadron members, including Viv Jacobs, who had commanded the squadron when the original Standard had been presented in 1955.

The award of a new Standard brings the story of the Flying Camels up to date and brings this narrative to a close. It remains to be seen how long No 45 Sqn will survive in its present form. At the time of writing, economic imperatives continue to exert an unremitting pressure on the Defence

Budget. Finningley has been earmarked for early closure and its resident units are to be moved elsewhere. At the time of writing METS is expected to go to Cranwell in October 1995, but its long-term future is somewhat uncertain.

A start has already been made on civilianising some of the RAF's flying activities, including primary flying training, radar calibration and electronic warfare training. It is possible that this policy might be extended to include advanced flying training. Rather than attending a METS course, in 1994/5 a small batch of student pilots was trained by a civilian contractor in Canada. It will take a while for the results of this trial to become clear and in the interim the existence of No 45(R) Sqn seems to be assured, but it is quite possible that its task may be contracted out to a commercial flying school in the not too distant future. If this does happen it seems highly improbable that a unit manned entirely by civilians could still be regarded as an RAF squadron, even a reserve squadron. If the Flying Camel were to end its days being ordered about by a man in a business suit Bert Harris would surely turn in his grave.

Notes:

1. The eight squadrons which were disbanded were: Nos 36 and 48 Sqns (Hercules); No 46 Sqn (Andovers); No 53 Sqn (Belfasts); Nos 99 and 511 Sqns (Britannias); No 203 Sqn (Nimrods) and No 216 Sqn (Comets).
2. Support Command ceased to exist with effect from 1st April 1994 when its responsibilities were divided between two new formations, Logistics Command, and Personnel and Training Command. Flying training units, like METS, were taken over by the latter.
3. The inability of a unit to provide an appropriate escort for its own Standard is hardly a new phenomenon. It was one of the many improvements introduced by 'the centralisers'. In the 1960s, for instance, when the Standards of V-bomber squadrons were paraded, the supporting flights were entirely composed of aircrew officers but the armed escorts had perforce to be drawn from station resources since, beyond a SNCO administrative assistant, the squadrons themselves had no personnel of the appropriate ranks. This is not to say that the warrant officers and sergeants who were involved were not willing, even proud, to be personally associated with these Standards and all that they represented, but it is another reflection of the increasingly ambivalent attitude of the RAF towards the status of its squadrons.

This night shot of XX500/H seems to be a particularly appropriate picture with which to conclude this account of No 45 Sqn's history.

Epilogue

Having come to the end of the story of the Flying Camels, it is worth reflecting on the significance of the absence of such a long-serving unit from the RAF's permanent Order of Battle. Does it matter? Does it matter *which* squadrons constitute the front line?

This book appears in print as the British military establishment is implementing yet another in what seems to have become an unceasing round of defence cuts in the wake of the Cold War. As the RAF continues to contract in the later 1990s its personnel will become an increasingly select group, much like the RAF of the 1920s. One of the ties with the potential to unite them is the common heritage represented by the history of the service.

Over time, contributions to this corporate history have been made by all of the personnel, of all ranks and trades, who have ever served with the RAF; by the image created by the aeroplanes which they flew, maintained or supported; by the operations in which they participated and by the many organisations which have been a part of the RAF's structure. Of these, the men, the machines and the events are to a greater or lesser degree ephemeral; even the units are periodically reorganised and restructured to cater for changing circumstances. In the RAF of the 1990s only the Central Flying School and the squadrons can claim an unbroken line of descent from 1918. Since it is both its traditional fighting unit and its basic organisational formation, it is the squadron which is at the RAF's core and which therefore best represents the unique personality of the "Third Service". The attention previously given to the preservation of a particular group of squadrons indicates that their individual contributions to this corporate identity are considered to have been of great significance - or at least that *used* to be the case. So, demonstrably, it certainly used to matter *which* squadrons constituted the RAF's front line. Since some squadron numberplates evidently do have a particular resonance, why is this so? How did they gain this distinction and how has their existence been prolonged?

Following the massive demobilisation of 1919 it was necessary to identify the units which would constitute the peacetime RAF. It was decided to preserve the numberplates of the half-dozen squadrons with which the RFC initially went to war plus a selection of others chosen to represent all the theatres of war in which the RFC/RNAS/RAF had fought and the variety of roles in which they had operated. Where a number of units were eligible for selection General Higgins recommended that seniority, rather than excellence, should be the deciding factor and General Trenchard broadly concurred. It had been agreed that the peacetime RAF was initially to comprise thirty-four operational squadrons, all but two of which were to be established by the spring of 1920. They were to be Nos 1, 2, 3, 4, 5, 6, 14, 20, 24, 25, 27, 28, 30, 31, 39, 47, 55, 56, 60, 70, 84, 100, 202, 203, 205, 207, 208, 210, 216, 230, 238 and 267 Sqns, these identities being approved on 8th December 1919 by CAS (who made three changes himself, deleting the proposed Nos 8, 186 and 201 Sqns in favour of Nos 208, 210 and 203 Sqns respectively). The two units needed to make up the authorised total, Nos 8 and 45 Sqns, were nominated on 26th August 1920, Trenchard personally selecting the latter in preference to the staff recommendation, No 151 Sqn (representing the night fighter role in France). Apart from the early demise of several of the 200-series numberplates, Trenchard's selected units constituted the core of the RAF during the 1920s while the case for a separate air force was tested and proved. They therefore represent the cornerstone on which the service was built, hence their very special significance.

Demobilisation after WW II led to a second exercise in number selection. Length of active service was the primary consideration this time, their now considerable seniority automatically guaranteeing the continuance of most of the numberplates endorsed by Trenchard, including that of No 45 Sqn. The selection problem was less acute in 1946 than it had been in 1919, however, as the RAF's strength never fell much below 150 squadrons, allowing plenty of scope for the preservation of unit identities. Despite this, it was felt in some quarters that some deserving numberplates were being omitted and, while the idea did not attract universal support at the highest levels, 'Linked Squadrons' were introduced in 1949 in an attempt to preserve even more squadrons.

The next numbering crisis occurred in the wake of the 1957 White Paper on Defence as a result of which the RAF was to lose more than seventy squadrons; it was appreciated that hard choices would have to be made this time and it was decided to adopt a more formal approach. Squadron numbering policy is the responsibility of the Air Member for Supply and Organisation, then Air Chief Marshal Sir Donald Hardman, and, having first solicited the views of the individual Commanders-in-Chief, he appointed a Working Party to devise a system which would identify the most significant numberplates while embracing certain constraints imposed by the Air Council, specifically including the rejection of the unrealistic concept of 'linked' squadrons.

Led by Mr J C Nerney, the Head of the Air Historical Branch, the Working Party reported on 16th October 1957, having devised an objective system which awarded each unit points based on a number of pertinent factors. The three most important of these were:

a. Most credit was to be given for overall length of service; one point per year in peacetime and three points per year in wartime.

b. Additional credit was to be given for participation in specified campaigns (essentially those which earned a Battle Honour) and an inevitably, and admittedly, subjective attempt was made to weight these to reflect their relative importance.

c. Further points would accrue from "special distinctions", such as the winning of a VC by a squadron member and participation in certain post-war campaigns.

There was one overriding consideration. Reflecting another Air Council dictum, regardless of how many points it scored, the numberplate of any squadron which had already been awarded a Standard was sacrosanct; there were at that time sixty-three such squadrons.

The 1957 system was used to establish a 'pecking order' which was fair, reasonable and paid due regard to the length and nature of each unit's service. Its implementation governed the wave of disbandments and renumberings which occurred in 1958 and it subsequently guided the staffs in their recommendation of numberplates for retention in later force reductions. It could be seen at work, for instance, when the decision was made to give numberplates to the regional communications squadrons in 1969, the identities allocated being selected from among those of the most senior dormant squadrons. Again, when it became politically necessary to disband two of the six Hercules squadrons in 1976 (although there was no reduction in the size of the Hercules fleet), the four numberplates which were retained were those of the squadrons having the longest records of service.

By the 1980s many more Standards had been awarded but so many more units had been disbanded that there were now more Standards than active squadrons. The logical extension of the existing seniority-based policy would have been to apply its principles to Standards so that the oldest of these would continue to fly. Sadly, this step appears not to have been taken and it is clear that in recent years the highly objective rationale underlying the 1957 policy has been increasingly set aside and more superficial considerations have come into play - to No 45 Sqn's cost.

During 1983 a requirement emerged for two numberplates to be brought back into use in 1984. One was for a new front-line Phantom squadron; the other was to become the 'shadow' identity of the quasi-operational TWCU. Since No 45 Sqn's was the senior numberplate not currently in use, it was surely the most appropriate one to be applied to any new front-line squadron. It was not, however, and the Phantoms went to a reformed No 74 Sqn. Without belittling in any way the honourable record of No 74 Sqn, the fact remains that there were available for reformation at that time many inactive squadrons with equally distinguished and far longer histories. No 45 Sqn, for instance, had, at that time, seen eighteen years more service than the 'Tigers' and its Standard was senior to that of No 74 Sqn by sixteen years. Furthermore, if an identity with a fighter tradition was considered essential for the Phantom unit then No 45 Sqn's exemplary record in that role could have met that criterion too. By any objective method of assessment the new Phantom squadron should have been the Flying Camels. That it was not, suggests that some other, more subjective, factor must have been involved.

No 45 Sqn became the *alter ego* of the TWCU instead and was thus relegated to reserve status. Thereafter, since it was notionally in use, No 45 Sqn's numberplate appears to have been ineligible for selection on the few subsequent occasions that the RAF found itself in need of a new squadron identity. The Flying Camels, one of Trenchard's chosen few, had been marginalised while other units, and most significantly units which had made no contribution to the struggle for the preservation of an independent air service during the 1920s, replaced them in the front-line.

In this context it must be asked, for instance, what compelling reason there could have been for selecting No 78 Sqn for reformation in 1986, at a time when the numberplates of so many far more senior squadrons were available? Furthermore, if the fact that a numberplate has been applied to a reserve squadron means that it cannot then be used when a new number is required, as precedent would suggest, then the outlook for Nos 19, 56, 74, 92 and 208 Sqns (all recently relegated to reserve status) would appear to be bleak. It will be interesting to see whether what now passes for policy is revised yet again to satisfy their lobbyists when the Eurofighter 2000 enters service.

Senior RAF officers have always professed to place great store by the history of the service and in the fostering of its traditions. But both history and tradition are to do with continuity and longevity, which is precisely why the 1957 policy and its predecessors gave such weight to length of service. Of late, however, it would appear that, despite the sometimes lofty rhetoric employed, this principle has been either discarded or circumvented. As discussed in Footnote 5 to Chapter 21, it is difficult to discern any substantial rationale behind the decision to afford priority to sustaining the identities of the units which happened to have participated in the brief Gulf War of 1991, apart from its being a short-term public relations exercise to put some political sugar on the bitter pill of a defence cut so soon after a successful campaign. But history is not a *short*-term affair. Sadly, this was not the first, only the most recent, decision to suggest that since 1980 the selection of . squadron numberplates has become almost entirely arbitrary - unless, of course, patronage has become the driving force. Could it be that erstwhile squadron commanders, filling senior appointments later in their careers, have exerted their influence to ensure that their old units have survived? If so, this would hardly be surprising, as it would be no more than a manifestation of squadron spirit - but the system should be robust enough to resist such a partisan approach. For it to be unable to do so is surely a careless and unworthy response to the challenge of how best to preserve the RAF's heritage.

The past achievements of the RAF are a firm foundation on which to build its future. These foundations were laid in the 1920s. The squadrons which served during that crucial decade, the units which proved the case for an independent air force, were the creators of the RAF's ethos. They fostered the innovators who understood and exploited the potential of air power, many of these men later becoming the great British air commanders of the Second World War. Post-war economic and political circumstances have led to a progressive reduction in the size of the RAF, but if contraction was inevitable it was surely appropriate that its remaining squadrons should have been those which in the 1920s had fought and won the crucial battle for the service's very survival. Most of these units do still serve but there has been a notable gap in the ranks since 1976 when No 45 Sqn was last embodied as a fully-fledged unit.

It is something for No 45 Sqn to have a nominal existence as a reserve unit, but its prolonged relegation to second-line status is a poor reflection of the RAF's regard for its own history. Like the service itself, No 45 Sqn has had its successes and its failures, its victories and its defeats and these have combined to form a coherent pattern. Until 1976 the story of the Flying Camels was an almost unbroken thread which was inextricably woven into the history of the RAF itself. Since then, its absence from the front line has meant that the historical fabric of the whole service has been significantly weakened.

If the RAF's history matters at all then it does matter *which* squadrons are kept in being, and it matters very much that No 45 Sqn is no longer a part of the permanent Order of Battle.

Annex A. Commanding Officers.

The decorations shown below represent those which had already been awarded to an officer prior to the date of his appointment as OC No 45 Sqn or which were gazetted while he was still in post. There may, however, be some instances where the early notification of an award, carrying the authority for the recipient to wear the appropriate ribbon, is not reflected here. There are certainly cases where awards were not formally promulgated until after the recipient had relinquished command. Wg Cdr Walker and Sqn Ldr Crew, for example, were both appointed to the DSO (for a second time in Crew's case) shortly after relinquishing command and

Capt Dawes, Capt Jones, Sqn Ldr Duclos and Flt Lt Aykroyd were all decorated with DFCs in recognition of their achievements while serving with No 45 Sqn, although it is doubtful whether any of them would have worn their ribbons while they were acting as CO. A list of all awards and decorations won by squadron members is at Annex D.

This list includes a number of officers who acted as OC No 45 Sqn on a temporary basis, either because of the sudden death of the appointed CO or because of a significant gap occurring between the departure of a CO and the arrival of his successor.

Commanding Officer	Date of Appointment
Capt C E Ryan	20 Mar 16
Maj L A Strange	27 Mar 16
Maj W R Read MC	24 Apr 16
Maj H P Van Ryneveld MC	24 Apr 17
Capt A T Harris	18 Aug 17
Maj A M Vaucour MC* DFC	24 Aug 17
Capt R J Dawes	16 Jul 18
Capt N C Jones	23 Jul 18
Maj J A Crook MC	28 Jul 18
Maj A M Miller DSO	21 Oct 18
Capt J W Pinder DFC*	3 Feb 19
?[1]	26 Sep 19
Disbanded	31 Dec 19
Sqn Ldr E M Murray DSO MC	2 Apr 21
Sqn Ldr A T Harris AFC	20 Nov 22
Sqn Ldr R M Hill MC AFC	14 Oct 24
Sqn Ldr J K Summers MC[2]	25 Apr 27
Sqn Ldr F J Vincent DFC	15 Nov 28
Sqn Ldr H W L Saunders MC DFC MM	13 Feb 32
Sqn Ldr A R Churchman DFC	14 Sep 35
Sqn Ldr N V Moreton	14 May 37
Sqn Ldr E B Webb	1 Mar 39
Sqn Ldr J W Dallamore	20 Apr 40
Flt Lt P P Troughton-Smith	2 Oct 40
Sqn Ldr V Ray	5 Nov 40
Wg Cdr J O Willis DFC	21 Mar 41
Sqn Ldr F J Austin	22 Nov 41
Wg Cdr C B B Wallis DSO	26 Nov 41
Wg Cdr A Hughes DFC	1 Apr 42
Fg Off D G Eve RAAF[3]	5 Aug 42
Fg Off N W Bayly RAAF[3]	3 Oct 42
Sqn Ldr A Traill	1 Nov 42
Sqn Ldr D S Edwards	29 Jan 44
Wg Cdr H C Stumm DFC RAAF	10 Feb 44
Sqn Ldr D S Edwards	13 May 44
Wg Cdr R J Walker	28 May 44
Sqn Ldr V S H Duclos	25 Mar 45
Flt Lt H A Aykroyd	24 May 45
Wg Cdr J H Etherton DFC*	3 Jul 45
Sqn Ldr G O L Dyke DFC	6 Mar 46
Wg Cdr F W Snell DFC*	25 Apr 46
Sqn Ldr G O L Dyke DFC	13 May 46
Sqn Ldr E Springthorpe	4 Jun 46
Sqn Ldr A J P Marvin	28 Jun 46
Wg Cdr G C O Key OBE DFC	22 Nov 46
Sqn Ldr B H D Foster DSO DFC*	22 Sep 47
Sqn Ldr F L Dodd DSO DFC AFC	24 Nov 47
Flt Lt K W Dalton-Golding	26 Jun 48
Sqn Ldr E D Crew DSO DFC*	23 Jul 48
Sqn Ldr A C Blythe DFC	13 Feb 50
Sqn Ldr I S Stockwell DFC AFC	27 Aug 51
Sqn Ldr V K Jacobs	15 Dec 53
Flt Lt R L Maslan	6 Jan 56
Sqn Ldr G S Cooper	1 Feb 56
Sqn Ldr C C Blount MVO	18 Nov 57
Sqn Ldr J W Valentine	26 May 60
Sqn Ldr M J Dawson	27 Nov 61
Sqn Ldr J B Carruthers	17 Dec 62
Sqn Ldr A G Skingsley	23 Apr 65
Sqn Ldr W J A Innes	7 Nov 67
Disbanded	18 Feb 70
Sqn Ldr W T Willman	1 Aug 72
Sqn Ldr M E Kerr	11 Aug 72
Wg Cdr T A Hastings	16 Oct 72
Sqn Ldr M J Gibson	24 Aug 74
Disbanded	26 Jul 76
Wg Cdr D A Griffiths AFC	1 Jan 84
Wg Cdr G L McRobbie	9 Nov 84
Wg Cdr A V B Hawken AFC	28 Nov 86
Wg Cdr M Prissick	19 Jul 89
Wg Cdr A T Hudson OBE	31 Jan 92
Disbanded	31 Mar 92
Sqn Ldr D Piper	1 Jul 92

Notes:

1. Capt Pinder was posted on 26th September 1919. It is not known who (if anyone) acted as CO of what was left of the squadron's cadre for the remaining three months of its nominal existence.

2. Sqn Ldr Summers had previously commanded the residual No 45 Sqn when the unit was reduced to a strength of one flight (parented by No 70 Sqn) on 1st November 1926. He remained in command from 17th January 1927, when the squadron was reduced to cadre status, until its re-establishment in Egypt on 27th April 1927.

3. When Wg Cdr Hughes left to attend Staff College at Quetta command of the squadron's small HQ staff fell first to Fg Off Eve and then to Fg Off Bayly. Thus, although neither was formally appointed as such, they were both in turn *de facto* OCs No 45 Sqn.

Annex B. Squadron Locations.

A unit rarely moves from one base to another in a single day, even when the two locations are fairly close together. A change of aerodromes generally involves advance, main and rear parties whose departures are at least a day apart and the journey itself can take anything from a few hours to several weeks, depending on the distance involved and the mode of transport used. These complexities are dealt with in the main narrative; the table below is intended to do no more than provide reasonable working dates for quick reference. The dates listed generally reflect the movements of the squadron's operational echelon rather than of its HQ and/or base party; again, a more comprehensive account appears in the body of the book. Finally, the detachments noted here are generally confined to those which were undertaken during wartime or which had an operational significance in peacetime; for instance, periods spent on APCs at Butterworth in the 1950s are included, as these detachments remained available for tasking and sometimes flew operational strikes while at camp.

Date	Base	Detachment Dates From - To
1 Mar 16	Formed at Fort Grange, Gosport	
2 May 16	Thetford	
21 May 16	Sedgeford	
15 Oct 16	Fienvillers	
5 Nov 16	Boisdinghem	
4 Dec 16	Ste-Marie-Cappel	
16 Nov 17	Fienvillers	
18 Dec 17	San Pelagio	
26 Dec 17	Istrana	
16 Mar 18	Grossa	
22 Sep 18	Bettoncourt	
22 Nov 18	Le-Hameau	
19 Jan 19	Liettres	
5 Feb 19	reduced to cadre	
15 Feb 19	Rendcomb	
15 Oct 19	Eastleigh	
31 Dec 19	Disbanded	
1 Apr 21	Reformed at Helwan	
11 Jul 21	Almaza	
20 Apr 22	Hinaidi	
	det Mosul	24 Jan 23-20 May 23
	det Diwaniyah	29 Nov 23-23 Dec 23
	det Kingerban	26 May 24-29 May 24
17 Jan 27	reduced to cadre	
11 Feb 27	Heliopolis	
25 Apr 27	re-established	
21 Oct 27	Helwan	
	det Ramleh	15 Mar 28-10 Apr 28
	det Amman	26 Mar 28-10 Apr 28
	det Ramleh	27 Aug 29-8 Dec 29
	det Amman	10 Nov 29-14 Nov 29
	det Nairobi	25 Sep 35-15 Dec 36
16 Jan 39	Ismailia	
4 Aug 39	Fuka	
18 Jun 40	Helwan	
	det El Daba	26 Jun 40-6 Jul 40
	det Erkowit	29 Jul 40-21 Aug 40
	det Summit	9 Sep 40-26 Sep 40
27 Sep 40	Wadi Gazouza	
4 Dec 40	Helwan	
8 Dec 40	Qotafiyah	
11 Jan 41	LG 81	
17 Jan 41	Menastir	
9 Feb 41	Helwan	

Date	Base	Detachment Dates From - To
4 Apr 41	Derna	
6 Apr 41	Gazala	
7 Apr 41	Gambut	
	det Tobruk	8 Apr 41-ca 22 Apr 41
9 Apr 41	Qasaba	
13 Apr 41	Fuka	
4 Jun 41	Wadi Natrun	
22 Jun 41	Aqir	
	det Ramleh	22 Jun 41-1 Jul 41
	det Muqeibila	5 Jul 41-17 Jul 41
10 Aug 41	Habbaniyah	
27 Sep 41	LG 16 (Fuka Satellite)	
14 Nov 41	LG 75	
18 Dec 41	Gambut	
2 Jan 42	Helwan	
	det Bu Amud	25 Jan 42-6 Feb 42
Feb 42	to Far East by air and sea	

	Air Echelon	Base Echelon
15 Feb 42	Zayatkwin	
22 Feb 42	Magwe (Ops from Mingaladon & Highland Queen)	
17 Mar 42		*arrives Calcutta*
18 Mar 42		*majority to Fyzabad*
26 Mar 42		*HQ Established in Calcutta*
28 Mar 42	Lashio	
10 Apr 42		*majority to Chakrata*
27 Apr 42	Loiwing	
3 May 42	Myitkyina	
6 May 42	Calcutta	
30 May 42		*most personnel to Asansol*
Jun 42	HQ remains at Calcutta, personnel dispersed on a detached basis among numerous units at many different locations	
16 Aug 42	HQ to Asansol	
2 Nov 42	all detached personnel recalled	
11 Nov 42	HQ to Cholavaram	
20 Feb 43	Asansol	
17 May 43	Digri	
	det Chittagong	26 Jun 43-14 Jul 43
	det Amarda Road	27 Jul 43-23 Aug 43
	det Ranchi	16 Aug 43-25 Aug 43
	det Ranchi	1 Oct 43-10 Oct 43

11 Oct 43	Kumbhirgram			
4 Feb 44	Yelahanka			
	det Amarda Road	1 May 44-29 May 44		
29 May 44	Dalbumgarh			
27 Aug 44	Ranchi			
22 Sep 44	Kumbhirgram			
	det Chiringa	15 Oct 44-18 Oct 44		
27 Apr 45	Joari			
6 May 45	Chiringa			
17 May 45	Cholavaram			
12 Oct 45	St Thomas Mount			
	det Santa Cruz	21 Feb 46-25 Feb 46		
29 May 46	Negombo			
	det Kuala Lumpur	12 Aug 48-28 May 49		
28 May 49	Kuala Lumpur			
5 Dec 49	Tengah			
	det Kuala Lumpur	1 Nov 51-29 Nov 51		
	det Butterworth	13 Dec 51-18 Dec 51		
	det Kuala Lumpur	11 Jan 52-7 Feb 52		
	det Butterworth	26 May 52-30 May 52		
	det Kuala Lumpur	6 Jun 52-29 Aug 52		
	det Kuala Lumpur	1 Oct 52-7 Nov 52		
	det Kuala Lumpur	5 Dec 52-3 Jan 53		
	det Butterworth	24 Apr 53-15 May 53		
	det Butterworth	29 Jun 53-17 Jul 53		
	det Butterworth	28 Oct 53-30 Oct 53		

	det Kuala Lumpur	31 Dec 53-3 Jan 54
	det Butterworth	2 Jan 54-22 Jan 54
	det Butterworth	27 Mar 54-14 Apr 54
	det Butterworth	5 May 54-9 May 54
	det Butterworth	29 Aug 54-14 Sep 54
	det Butterworth	15 Nov 54-? Dec 54
21 Mar 55	Butterworth	
31 Mar 55	linked as No 45/33 Sqn	
15 Oct 55	link with No 33 Sqn terminated	
18 Nov 57	UK echelon forming at Coningsby	
22 Nov 57	Tengah (arrival of ex-Venom groundcrew)	
	det Butterworth	17 Mar 58-22 Mar 58
	det Kuantan	17 Sep 64-9 Oct 64
27 Apr 65	Labuan	
28 Jun 65	Tengah	
18 Feb 70	Disbanded	
1 Aug 72	Reformed at West Raynham	
29 Sep 72	Wittering	
26 Jul 76	Disbanded	
1 Jan 84	Reformed at Honington as a reserve squadron	
31 Mar 92	Disbanded	
1 Jul 92	Reformed at Finningley as a reserve squadron	
Oct 95	Cranwell	

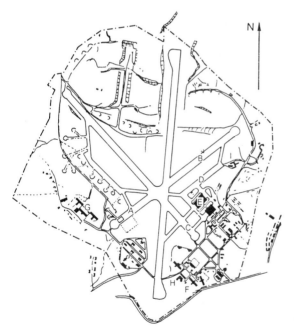

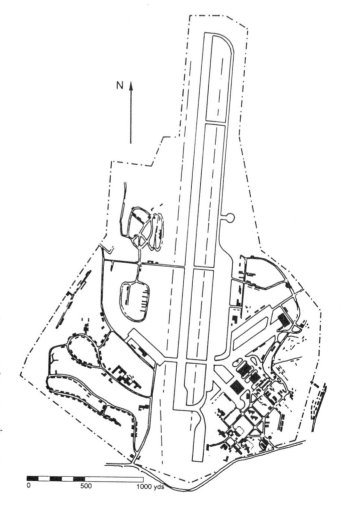

During its long history No 45 Sqn spent far more time based at Tengah than anywhere else and this airfield might therefore be considered as its spiritual home. The plan above provides an indication of the layout of Tengah when the squadron arrived at the end of 1949 (a parallel taxitrack to the east of the main N/S runway was added later) while that on the right, which is to the same scale, shows the remarkable changes that had occurred by the time the squadron disbanded in 1970, most of the expansion and rebuilding having taken place in 1960-61. Points of particular significance are indicated as follows:- A: Beaufighter/Brigand dispersal. B: Hornet dispersal. C: early Canberra dispersal. D: permanent Canberra dispersal. E: No 1 Hangar. F: Cheshire Block. G: Officers' Mess. H: Sergeants' Mess. I: Aircrew Mess.

Annex C. Roll of Honour.

The names listed below are of those members of No 45 Sqn who lost their lives in, or as a direct result of, confrontation with the enemy on operations. Many more were wounded in action or taken prisoner, sometimes both; others were killed or injured in accidents in both peace and war. Their names have been recorded in the main narrative.

In some cases the ranks given in this Annex differ from those in the main text. Where this is the case the narrative generally reflects the rank recorded in contemporary squadron documentation while that noted below has been taken from subsequent casualty reports which were sometimes adjusted to take account of post-dated seniority.

Name	Date	Aircraft
Sopwith 1½ Strutter		
Capt Leslie Porter[1]	24th October 1916	7777
2/Lt George Bernard Samuels	22nd October 1916	7777
2/Lt Oliver John Wade	22nd October 1916	7786
2/Lt William Johnson Thuell	22nd October 1916	7786
Sgt Percy Snowden	22nd October 1916	A1061
2/Lt William Francis Hannan Fullerton	22nd October 1916	A1061
2/Lt James Vernon Lyle	23rd January 1917	A1078
A/Bdr Alfred Harrison	23rd January 1917	A1078
F/Sgt Walter George Webb	26th January 1917	A1074
Cpl Robert Dick Fleming	26th January 1917	A1074
2/Lt Edward Eustace Erlebach	7th February 1917	7789
2/AM Frederick James Ridgway	7th February 1917	7789
2/Lt Denys Edward Greenhow	6th March 1917	A1072
Capt Hon Eric Fox Pitt Lubbock	11th March 1917	A1082
Sub Lt John Thompson	11th March 1917	A1082
2/Lt Horace George Cecil Bowden	11th March 1917	A1071
2/Lt Douglas Baptiste Stevenson	11th March 1917	A1071
2/Lt John Arthur Marshall	6th April 1917	A1093
2/Lt Francis George Truscott	6th April 1917	A1093
2/Lt Colin St George Campbell	6th April 1917	A2381
Capt Donald William Edwards	6th April 1917	A2381
2/Lt James Edward Blake	6th April 1917	7806
Capt William Stead Brayshay	6th April 1917	7806
2/AM Burnaby George Perrott	30th April 1917	A1080
Lt William Longley Mills	9th May 1917	7803
Lt Joseph Senior	9th May 1917	A8226
Capt Christopher Hutchinson Jenkins[2]	23rd May 1917	A8246
Capt Lawrence William McArthur	27th May 1917	A8226
2/Lt Allan Stewart Carey	27th May 1917	A8226
2/Lt Edward Denison Haller	3rd June 1917	A8272
2/Lt Frank Hawley Foster	3rd June 1917	A8272
2/AM Stanley Thompson	5th June 1917	A8280
2/Lt Robert Smith Bennie	5th June 1917	A1925
Lt Thomas Arthur Metheral	5th June 1917	A1925
Sgt Ernest Albert Cook	5th June 1917	A8268
2/AM Harry Victor Shaw	5th June 1917	A8268
2/Lt Arthur Edward John Dobson	7th June 1917	A8296
2/Lt Gwynonfryn Albert Haydn Davies	7th June 1917	A8296
2/Lt Robert Sherwin Watt	12th June 1917	A8244
2/AM Walter Pocock	12th June 1917	A8244
Rfn Percy Clarence Hammond	15th June 1917	A1019
2/Lt Toby St George Caulfield	16th June 1917	A381
Rfn George Edwards	16th June 1917	A381
Rfn Edward Sydney Henry Sharp	27th June 1917	?
L/Cpl Fred Russell	2nd July 1917	?
Lt Thomas Hewson	7th July 1917	A1029
Lt Frederick Carl Henry Snyder	7th July 1917	A1029
2/Lt John Victor Ariel Gleed	7th July 1917	A8281

Lt John Beveridge Fotheringham	7th July 1917	A8281
2/Lt Robert Hartley Deakin	22nd July 1917	A1032
2/Lt Reginald Hayes	22nd July 1917	A1032
2/Lt James Harold Hartley	22nd July 1917	A1036
2/Lt Henry Neville Curtis	25th July 1917	A1020
Sgt William Stanley Wickham	25th July 1917	A1020
Lt George Henderson Walker	28th July 1917	A1031
2/Lt Benjamin George Beatty	28th July 1917	A1031
Dvr William Fellows[3]	29th July 1917	A8766
2/Lt Edward John Brown	17th August 1917	A8771
2/Lt Claude Murray Ross	19th August 1917	A8298
2/Lt John Orr Fowler	19th August 1917	A8298

Sopwith Camel

Lt Aubrey Talley Heywood	3rd September 1917	B3917
Lt Robert Leslie Clegg	3rd September 1917	B2306
Lt William Shields	5th September 1917	B3838
Lt Alister Orr MacNiven	5th September 1917	B3863
Lt Oscar Lennox McMaking	11th September 1917	B6236
Lt Basil Raymond Davis	20th September 1917	B6205
2/Lt Clifford Fraser Risteen	26th September 1917	B2374
Capt Horace Bertram Coomber	12th October 1917	B2375
2/Lt Kenneth Hugh Willard	12th October 1917	B2386
2/Lt Cecil Ivor Phillips	27th October 1917	B2382
2/Lt Douglas William Ross	11th January 1918	B2436
Lt Donald Gordon McLean	4th February 1918	B2494
Maj Awdry Morris Vaucour MC* DFC	16th July 1918	D8102
Lt Alfred John Haines	10th August 1918	D9412

Bristol Blenheim I

Sgt Peter Bower	11th June 1940	L8476
Sgt Stanley George Fox	11th June 1940	L8476
AC1 John William Allison	11th June 1940	L8476
Sgt Maurice Cresswell Thurlow	11th June 1940	L8519
Sgt Bernard Alfred Feldman	11th June 1940	L8519
AC1 Henry Robinson	11th June 1940	L8519
Fg Off John Scott Davies	13th June 1940	L8524
Sgt Geoffrey Edward Negus	13th June 1940	L8524
LAC John King Copeland	13th June 1940	L8524
Sqn Ldr George Justin Bush	30th September 1940	L6665
Sgt John Charles Usher	30th September 1940	L6665
Sgt James Corney	30th September 1940	L6665
Sqn Ldr John Walter Dallamore	2nd October 1940	L8452
Sgt Myles Broughty Ferry Mackenzie	2nd October 1940	L8452
Fg Off Gordon Cyril Butler Woodroffe	13th October 1940	L8463
Sgt Eric Bromley Ryles	13th October 1940	L8463
Sgt Albert Alfred Meadows DFM	13th October 1940	L8463
Plt Off Laurence Stewart Roberts	13th October 1940	L8463
Plt Off George Angus Cockayne	13th October 1940	L8502
Sgt Trevor Ascot Ferris	13th October 1940	L8502
Sgt Robert William Reader	13th October 1940	L8502
Plt Off Patrick Collimore Traill-Smith	12th December 1940	L8465
Plt Off Vincent Dennis Fry	12th December 1940	L8465
Sgt Tom Osborn Liggins DFM	12th December 1940	L8465
Fg Off Peter James Bingham Griffiths	3rd January 1941	L8479
Sgt Arthur Charles Tadhunter	3rd January 1941	L8479
Sgt Colin Blackshaw	3rd January 1941	L8479
Sgt Harry Cecil Thomas Holmans	4th February 1941	L8538
Sgt Colin Pryce Edwards	4th February 1941	L8538

Bristol Blenheim IV

Fg Off Francis Godfrey Collins	18th April 1941	V5438
Sgt Eric John Street	18th April 1941	V5438
Sgt Robert Herbert Charles Crook	18th April 1941	V5438
F/Sgt William Beverley	22nd April 1941	V5625
Sgt Ronald William Gentry	22nd April 1941	V5625
F/Sgt Victor William Joseph Harrison	22nd April 1941	V5625
Plt Off Bruce Cartwright de Gardanne Allan	28th April 1941	Z5898
Sgt Leonard Woolford Morling	28th April 1941	Z5898
Flt Lt Anthony Cluse Huxtable Haines	16th May 1941	V5817
Sgt Stanley Christopher Cordy	16th May 1941	V5817
Fg Off John Beveridge	18th May 1941	T2056
Plt Off Allan Herbert Wise RNZAF	18th May 1941	T2056
Sgt Victor James Griffiths	18th May 1941	T2056
Plt Off David Carter[4]	19th May 1941	T2179
Sgt Henry John Cassar	19th May 1941	T2179
Plt Off Paul John Vincent	23rd May 1941	V5624
Plt Off Stuart Charles Niven RNZAF	23rd May 1941	V5624
F/Sgt Oswald Burnell Thompson	23rd May 1941	V5624
F/Sgt Neville Headley Thomas	26th May 1941	T2339
Sgt Geoffry Runell Adams	26th May 1941	T2339
F/Sgt George Kenneth Grainger	26th May 1941	T2339
Sgt Wilfred Bernard Longstaff	26th May 1941	T2350
Fg Off Norman Wilfred Pinnington	27th May 1941	Z5896
Plt Off Howard Fleming Irving RNZAF	27th May 1941	Z5896
Sgt Richard John Martin[5]	10th June 1941	Z5896
F/Sgt John Bullock	27th June 1941	V5968
Sgt John Edward White	4th July 1941	V6503
Sgt John Collard Wimhurst	10th July 1941	Z6433
Sgt Douglas John Lowe	10th July 1941	Z6433
Sgt Guy Mitton Hardy	10th July 1941	Z9547
Sgt John Newhouse	10th July 1941	Z9547
F/Sgt Kenneth Rupert Cornford	10th July 1941	Z6455
Sgt William Donald Capewell	10th July 1941	Z6455
Sgt Gwilyn Enrie Sully	3rd November 1941	V6143
Sgt Joseph Roy Mansfield	3rd November 1941	V6143
Plt Off Eric Albert Magor RAAF	19th November 1941	Z7510
Plt Off Alexander John Cain RAAF	19th November 1941	Z7510
Sgt Thomas Scott MacLiver RAAF	19th November 1941	Z7510
Wg Cdr James Owen Willis	22nd November 1941	Z6439
Plt Off Laurence Philip Bourke RNZAF	22nd November 1941	Z6439
Sgt Michael Francis Carthy	22nd November 1941	Z6439
Sgt Charles Edward O'Neill	22nd November 1941	Z7686
Sgt Lionel Smith	22nd November 1941	Z7686
Sgt Kenneth John Chapman	22nd November 1941	Z7686
Plt Off James Henry Tolman	4th December 1941	V5991
Fg Off Antony Woods Hutton	4th December 1941	V5991
Sgt Douglas Stephen John Harris	4th December 1941	V5991
F/Sgt John Burns	20th December 1941	V6132
Sgt Roy Edwin James Reeves	20th December 1941	V6132
Sgt James Edward Wilcock	20th December 1941	V6132
Sgt Douglas James Smyth RAAF	11th March 1942	Z9799
Sgt Lance Sydney Powell RAAF	14th March 1942	Z7899
Sgt Les William Higgs Connor RAAF	14th March 1942	Z7899
Plt Off John Jerram Eden RAAF	14th March 1942	Z7899
F/Sgt Stanley Arthur Goss RCAF[6]	18th August 1942	T2245
F/Sgt Charles Alexander Whiteside[6]	18th August 1942	T2245
Sgt Arthur Murray[6]	18th August 1942	T2245

Vultee Vengeance

Sgt Sydney Siddle	13th November 1943	EZ898
Plt Off Hedley Charles Jewell	27th January 1944	EZ879

DeHavilland Mosquito

Flt Lt Gordon Hayter Proctor	3rd October 1944	HP936
Sgt George Willliam Bargh	3rd October 1944	HP936
Fg Off Keith Bottrill	12th October 1944	HP883
Sqn Ldr Norman Leslie Bourke RAAF	16th October 1944	HP941
Fg Off Keith Russell Dumas RAAF	16th October 1944	HP941
Sqn Ldr Donald Stuart Edwards AFC	20th October 1944	HP921
Fg Off Eric Leonard Sandifer	20th October 1944	HP921
Fg Off James Maxwell Levey RAAF	17th December 1944	HR453
Fg Off Harry James Scutchings Cargill RAAF	17th December 1944	HR453
WO John Sawers McQueen RNZAF	3rd January 1945	HR515
WO William Prince Edwards	3rd January 1945	HR515
Plt Off John Robert Wilson RCAF	12th January 1945	HR492
WO William James Sidney Hayward	12th January 1945	HR492
Flt Lt Charles Ronald Goodwin	15th January 1945	HR402
Fg Off Samuel Potts	15th January 1945	HR402
F/Sgt Gordon Herbert Ashworth	17th February 1945	HR390
WO Robert Leonard Cecil Conrie Pinkerton	17th February 1945	HR390
Sqn Ldr Bryan Vincent Draper DFC	28th February 1945	HR457
WO Peter Roesch James	28th February 1945	HR457
WO Alan Holmes	26th March 1945	HR527
F/Sgt William Arthur Austen	26th March 1945	HR527

Bristol Brigand

Fg Off Norman Brian Harben	6th July 1950	RH850
N3 Tom Walter Smith	6th July 1950	RH850
S3 Clifford Lloyd	6th July 1950	RH850
Sgt Sidney Vincent Hayler	11th January 1951	VS838
Sgt George Albert Robinson	11th January 1951	VS838
Sgt Kenneth Hall	11th January 1951	VS838
Sgt William Kent	15th February 1951	VS859
Sgt Bruce Augustien Ellis	15th February 1951	VS859

DeHavilland Hornet

Plt Off Robert Jackson	28th August 1952	WB912

Notes:

1. Died from wounds sustained on 22nd October 1916.
2. Died from wounds sustained on 20th May 1917.
3. Died from wounds sustained on 28th July 1917.
4. A Free Belgian whose real name was George Henri Mathieu Reuter.
5. Died from wounds sustained on 27th May 1941.
6. While flying on attachment to No 113 Sqn.

Annex D.   Decorations and Awards won by members of No 45 Sqn.

The decorations listed below are those awarded to personnel on the strength of No 45 Sqn or in recognition of their service with that unit. In several cases these awards were made some time after the individual concerned had left the squadron.   The dates tabulated below are those of the London Gazettes in which the awards were formally promulgated, although in many instances the wearing of the appropriate ribbon will have been authorised prior to this. Regrettably, a list such as this is inherently imperfect in that it excludes people whose awards were not made until after they had left the squadron.   For example, Sqn Ldr Leonard Penny's DFC was awarded while he was serving with another unit but his previous lengthy service with No 45 Sqn undoubtedly contributed to the earning of his decoration.

Conversely, while Flt Lt Adam McFadzean rendered sterling service during his time with No 45 Sqn, his DFC was awarded quite early in his tour and really acknowledged the record he had previously established while flying with No 11 Sqn. Similarly, while Flt Lt Peasley's DFC was promulgated while he was serving with No 45 Sqn he did not actually join the unit until after it had been withdrawn to India in 1945 and he never flew with it on operations; again, this award reflects his service with another squadron. It should also be noted that the Italian awards made to Capts Carpenter, Williams and Montgomery and to Lt Drummond reflected their overall campaign service in Italy, some of which was spent variously with Nos 28 and 66 Sqns.

Distinguished Service Order

Capt Matthew Brown Frew MC*	4th March 1918
Capt Cedric Ernest Howell MC DFC	2nd November 1918
Wg Cdr Charles Brian Berry Wallis	24th March 1942
Wg Cdr Robert James Walker	9th June 1945
Sqn Ldr Edward Dixon Crew DSO DFC*	10th March 1950

Military Cross

Lt James Dacres Belgrave	18th July 1917
2/Lt Geoffrey Hornblower Cock	26th July 1917
Lt Dudley Charles Eglington	16th August 1917
2/Lt Matthew Brown Frew	18th October 1917
Lt Edward Denman Clarke	17th December 1917
2/Lt Matthew Brown Frew MC	17th December 1917
Capt John Charles Bradley Firth	18th February 1918
Capt Norman Macmillan	18th February 1918
2/Lt Kenneth Barbour Montgomery	18th February 1918
2/Lt Peter Carpenter	4th March 1918
Lt Cedric Ernest Howell	16th September 1918
2/Lt Henry Michael Moody	16th September 1918
2/Lt Thomas Frederic Williams	16th September 1918

Distinguished Flying Cross

Maj Awdry Morris Vaucour MC*	3rd June 1918
Capt Richard Jeffrey Dawes	21st September 1918
Lt Alfred John Haines	21st September 1918
Capt Cedric Ernest Howell MC	21st September 1918
Capt Norman Cyril Jones	21st September 1918
Capt Jack Cottle	2nd November 1918
Lt Mansell Richard James	2nd November 1918
Lt Alan Rice-Oxley	2nd November 1918
Capt Earl McNabb Hand	1st January 1919
Lt James Henry Dewhirst	3rd June 1919
Capt John William Pinder DFC	3rd June 1919
Wg Cdr James Owen Willis	30th May 1941
Flt Lt John Mervyn Dennis	10th October 1941
Flt Lt Adam McFadzean	16th September 1944
Fg Off Edward Leslie James Anderson DFM RAAF	16th September 1944
Fg Off Cyril Garbutt Hockney	16th September 1944
Fg Off Peter Norman Ewing RAAF	6th April 1945
Flt Lt Frank James Harper	9th June 1945

Flt Lt Leonard Stanley Andrews	17th August 1945
Flt Lt Robert Montrose Barclay RAAF	17th August 1945
Flt Lt Ernest James Hallett RAAF	17th August 1945
Flt Lt Walter Scott McLellan RAAF	17th August 1945
Flt Lt Hugh Maxwell Paton Neil RAAF	17th August 1945
Flt Lt James Reginald Vernon RAAF	17th August 1945
Flt Lt Graham Frederick Williams RAAF	17th August 1945
Flt Lt Richard Allen Whiteside	17th August 1945
Fg Off John Owen Cartledge RAAF	17th August 1945
Fg Off Horace Mervin Nicholls RAAF	17th August 1945
WO Sinclair O'Connor	17th August 1945
Wg Cdr Victor Sidney Henry Duclos	2nd October 1945
Flt Lt Harold Allan Aykroyd	20th October 1945
WO Harold Sellars	20th October 1945
Fg Off Douglas Erich Ward Goodrich	30th October 1945
WO Salen Maurice Daoud Nessim	30th October 1945
Sqn Ldr George Oswald Leonard Dyke	29th January 1946
Flt Lt Wilfred Robert Peasley	29th January 1946
Sqn Ldr Alexander Conway Blythe DFC	18th September 1951

Distinguished Conduct Medal

Pnr William Thomas Smith MM	22nd October 1917

Meritorious Service Medal

CMM P Smyth	31st December 1918

Distinguished Flying Medal

AC1 Albert Alfred Meadows	19th July 1940
Sgt Maurice Archibald Clarke	21st March 1952
F/Sgt Norman Grove	6th March 1953
Sgt Gerald Joseph Turley	4th May 1954

Member of the British Empire

Flt Lt Frederick Lionel Rippingale	1st June 1945

British Empire Medal

Sgt Raymond Frederick George Howard	26th April 1949

F/Sgt Ralph Fraser Aldridge Holdaway	10th March 1950
Sgt Eric Simpson	29th August 1952
Sgt John Harry Swan	4th May 1954
Sgt William Ronald Curtis	13th June 1959

French Croix de Guerre with Palme

Lt James Henry Dewhirst	2nd November 1918
Lt Ernest Harold Masters	2nd November 1918

French Croix de Guerre

2/Lt Earl McNabb Hand	21st September 1918

Italian Silver Medal for Military Valour

Capt Matthew Brown Frew DSO MC*	12th September 1918
Capt Jack Cottle DFC	2nd November 1918
Maj Awdry Morris Vaucour MC* DFC	2nd November 1918

Italian Bronze Medal for Military Valour

Capt Peter Carpenter DSO MC*	2nd November 1918
Capt John Charles Bradley Firth MC	2nd November 1918
Capt Thomas Frederic Williams MC	2nd November 1918
Lt Malcolm David George Drummond	2nd November 1918

Italian Croce di Guerra

Capt Kenneth Barbour Montgomery MC	8th February 1919

Belgian Chevalier de l'Ordre de la Couronne

Lt William Alan Wright	24th September 1917

Belgian Croix de Guerre

Capt William Alan Wright	11th March 1918

The award of a DSO and two MCs made Captain Matthew Brown Frew one of No 45 Sqn's two most decorated pilots. (J A Brown)

2/Lt Peter Carpenter, who won an MC while flying with No 45 Sqn, poses for the camera atop B3929/L at Istrana. (G Muir)

Seen here as flying officers at Kumbhirgram in late 1944, Max Neil (nearest the camera) and Bob Barclay both earned DFCs after flying with No 45 Sqn for more than three years. (A Huon)

466

Annex E.   Victories claimed by No 45 Sqn during WW I.

The terminology used to classify victories in aerial combat during WW I was a little different from the, perhaps more familiar, labels which were applied in WW II. In both conflicts independent confirmation of a claim was normally required, this generally being provided by a third party or by location of the wreckage. The WW I-term 'Driven Down Out of Control' (OOC) was broadly equivalent to WW II's 'Probable' while 'Driven Down' equated to 'Damaged', and that term was itself also used occasionally in WW I. Although the classification of aerial victories was broadly similar in the two wars, even if the terms used differed, there was a major difference in the way in which scores were represented. Within the British services during WW II it was normal to confine quoted victory scores to confirmed kills, claims for 'probables' and 'damaged' being afforded far less prominence. By contrast, in WW I it was conventional to include both confirmed and probable victories in a single tally - the point being to reflect whether the engagement had been won. This convention has been reflected in the following tabulation. Confirmed kills, including instances where an aeroplane was forced to land in Allied territory, have been indicated by the abbreviation 'Dest', or 'Dest(F)' where the victim was reported to have fallen in flames. 'Probables', including instances where aeroplanes were forced to land in enemy territory, have been indicated by the term 'OOC'.

Another procedural difference between WW I and WW II concerned the treatment of shared claims. In WW II shared claims were often credited to the junior pilot involved otherwise the claim was apportioned as a half or even a third. This was not the practice in WW I and where two or more pilots participated directly in shooting down the same enemy aeroplane it was usual for both, or even all three, of them to be credited with the victory. In the tabulation below, to allow individual scores to be assessed, the participants in known shared claims have been identified but the running total in the left hand column has been adjusted to avoid duplication.

Awarding credit for claims by two-seater crews is obviously a difficult and potentially contentious topic. Early in 1918 the Air Ministry advised that both crew members were to be credited with any claim allowed, regardless of whose gun(s) had actually inflicted the damage. Thus individual scores would be equally distributed between pilots and observers. In order to avoid duplication, however, when *unit* totals were called for these were confined to the sum of the claims accredited to pilots. This ruling was made in the era of the Bristol Fighter and it is doubtful that any serious attempt was ever made to revise earlier claims made by two-seater squadrons in 1915-17. In the tabulation below, where the Combat Report (Army Form W3348) permits a reasonable assessment to be made, an asterisk has been applied to indicate whether the victim claimed is more likely to have fallen to the pilot's or the observer's gun.

In recent years researchers have done a great deal of work in attempting to correlate claims with actual losses. As in WW II this has indicated that claims, although made in good faith, were sometimes overoptimistic. For instance, we now know that Macmillan's two OOC claims on 11th September 1917 were both made against Werner Voss in the prototype Fokker Triplane and that the aircraft actually escaped without damage. Similarly, in an engagement with a number of Albatros scouts on 19th June 1918 the squadron claimed a total of seven victories: Dewhirst - three destroyed;

The problem of how to apportion victories to two-seater crews was eventually resolved by ruling that both crew members were to have equal credit, regardless of whose guns did the damage. Lt James Frederick Scott, a Canadian, never actually claimed a victory during the less than two months that he served with No 45 Sqn but he did find time to take these interesting photographs during his first operational patrol over Ypres, probably flown on 27th March 1917 with Lt Philip Newling in A1093. Above, the view over the port tailplane and, below, looking forwards and to the right towards the starboard wingtip. (Geo H Williams)

A "Berg Scout" (more precisely an Aviatik D.1 Srs 138.27) flown by Korporal Andras Kulczar was shot down by Bush and Williams on 2nd February 1918. The aeroplane was later salvaged and its wings are seen here at Fossalunga. (via J A Brown)

467

Howell - two destroyed; Masters - one destroyed and another OOC. Subsequent research has revealed that the Austro-Hungarian unit concerned, Flik 9J, lost only two pilots that day, Fldw Messner and Zgsf Cerda. Ltn Hessenberger's aircraft was also damaged but succeeded in regaining its base. Having established what damage was actually inflicted does not, however, determine which pilot's claims ought to be disallowed, especially as it is probable that all of the pilots involved inflicted varying degrees of damage on the three victims.

Although no attempt has been made to revise long-standing claims in the light of later information it has been considered necessary to make some adjustments for other reasons. For instance, on 6th March 1917, a three-aircraft patrol of 1½ Strutters drove an aircraft down OOC but it is not clear from the Combat Reports who had done the damage, since at least four guns had been brought to bear. Curiously, the RFC's War Diary gives the credit to Mackay and Greenhow, although the latter was killed early in the engagement and the pilot's report makes no claim. This victory is allocated below to the other two crews who took part in this engagement.

Anomalies of this kind were not, of course, peculiar to No 45 Sqn and an in-depth analysis of the claims made by any unit, including those of other air forces, both friend and foe, will reveal many instances such as these. It is undeniably a function of an historian to establish the facts but, in the context of writing a unit's history, this chronicler is not persuaded that the pursuit of truth should be carried to the lengths of iconoclasm. The claims listed below are intended

Representative of the 114 confirmed kills credited to No 45 Sqn during its time in Italy is this "two-seater Aviatik" which was shot down by Lt Charles Catto on June 7th. The aeroplane actually turned out to be this Brandenburg C.1 Srs 61.5 flown by Zgsf Alois Gnamusch and Ltn Rudolph Huss. (Geo H Williams)

to reflect the position as it was understood at the time and upon which the reputations of both the unit and of its individual members were built. Although some refinements have been made, causing the listing to differ in minor detail from some others which have appeared, there has been no serious attempt to rationalise the squadron's 'Game Book' in the light of subsequent information.

No	Date	Crew	Serial	Type	Location	Claim
1	22 Oct 16	2/Lt H H Griffith & Lt F Surgey	A1066	?	Bapaume	OOC
2	23 Jan 17	Capt W G B Williams & Lt J Senior	A1083	Halb D	Menin	OOC
3	7 Feb 17	Capt E F P Lubbock & 2/Lt F H Austin	A1084	Alb DIII	Menin	OOC
3	7 Feb 17	Capt J E Mackay & 2/Lt F G Truscott	7800		as above (shared claim)	
3	7 Feb 17	Lt J D Belgrave & Sub Lt J Thompson	7775		as above (shared claim)	
4	6 Mar 17	Capt J E Mackay & 2/Lt D E Greenhow	A1072	SS DI	Langemarck	OOC
4	6 Mar 17	Capt E F P Lubbock & Sub Lt J Thompson	A1082		as above (shared claim)	
4	6 Mar 17	2/Lt J A Marshall & 2/AM B G Perrott	A1086		as above (shared claim)	
5	18 Mar 17	Lt J D Belgrave* & 2/Lt F G Truscott	A2384	2-seater	Ploegsteert Wood	Dest(F)
6	6 Apr 17	2/Lt G H Cock & 2/Lt J T G Murison*	A1075	Alb DIII	Lille	Dest
7	6 Apr 17	Lt P T Newling & 2/AM B G Perrott*	?	Alb DIII	Lille	OOC
8	5 May 17	Lt J D Belgrave & 2/Lt C G Stewart	A2382	Alb or Halb	Becelaere	OOC
9	7 May 17	Lt J D Belgrave* & 2/Lt C G Stewart	A2382	Alb DIII	Lille	Dest(F)
10	7 May 17	2/Lt G H Cock* & Lt J T G Murison	A8620	SS DI	Lille	OOC
11	7 May 17	2/Lt C W Carleton & 2/Lt J A Vessey*	A8216	?	Lille	OOC
12	7 May 17	2/Lt H Forrest & Gnr F A R C Lambert*	A1075	2-seater	Dickebusch Lake	OOC
13	9 May 17	2/Lt G H Cock* & Lt J T G Murison	A8260	Alb DIII	NW Seclin	Dest
14	9 May 17	2/Lt G H Cock & Lt J T G Murison*	A8260	Alb DIII	NW Seclin	Dest
14	9 May 17	2/Lt W A Wright & Lt E T Caulfield-Kelly*	A8225		as above (shared claim)	
15	9 May 17	2/Lt J Johnstone & 2/AM T M Harries*	A963	Alb DIII	W Menin	Dest(F)
16	12 May 17	2/Lt R S Watt & Lt G W Blaiklock	A8173	Alb DIII	E Armentières	Dest(F)
16	12 May 17	Capt C H Jenkins & Lt D C Eglington	A8246		as above (shared claim)	
16	12 May 17	2/Lt J Johnstone & 2/AM T M Harries	A963		as above (shared claim)	
17	12 May 17	2/Lt J Johnstone & 2/AM T M Harries*	A963	Alb CV	E Armentières	Dest
18	20 May 17	Sgt E A Cook* & Lt G W Blaiklock	A8268	Alb DIII	Lille	Dest(F)
19	20 May 17	Sgt E A Cook & Lt G W Blaiklock*	A8268	Halb D	Lille	Dest(F)
20	20 May 17	Capt C H Jenkins* & Lt D C Eglington*	A8246	Alb DIII	Lille	Dest
21	20 May 17	2/Lt G H Cock* & 2/Lt A S Carey	A8226	Alb DIII	Lille	OOC
22	24 May 17	2/Lt W A Wright & Lt E T Caulfield-Kelly*	A8269	Alb DIII	Zonnebeke	Dest(F)
23	24 May 17	2/Lt W A Wright & Lt E T Caulfield-Kelly*	A8269	Alb DIII	Zonnebeke	OOC
23	24 May 17	Lt P T Newling & Lt W E Holland*	A1095		as above (shared claim)	
23	24 May 17	Lt J D Belgrave* & 2/Lt C G Stewart	A8223		as above (shared claim)	
24	25 May 17	Capt G Mountford* & 2/Lt J A Vessey	A1099	Alb DIII	Dadizeele	OOC
25	25 May 17	Capt G Mountford & 2/Lt J A Vessey*	A1099	Alb DIII	Dadizeele	OOC
26	27 May 17	Lt J D Belgrave* & 2/Lt G A H Davies	A8280	Alb DIII	Roulers	OOC

27	27 May 17	Capt G H Cock* & Lt E T Caulfield-Kelly	A1016	Alb DIII	Menin	OOC
28	27 May 17	2/Lt H E R Fitchat* & 2/Lt R Hayes	A1099	Alb DIII	Roulers	Dest
29	27 May 17	Capt G Mountford* & 2/Lt J A Vessey	A8299	Alb DIII	Roulers	OOC
30	27 May 17	Sgt E A Cook & 2/AM H V Shaw*	A8268	Alb DIII	N Menin	OOC
31	28 May 17	2/Lt W A Wright & Lt E T Caulfield-Kelly*	A8269	Alb DIII	Comines	Dest(F)
32	28 May 17	Capt G H Cock & 2/Lt W G Corner*	A1095	Alb DIII	Menin	Dest(F)
33	31 May 17	Capt G Mountford & 2/Lt J A Vessey*	A8299	Alb DIII	Comines	OOC
34	31 May 17	2/Lt R M Findlay* & Lt G W Blaiklock*	A8295	Alb DIII	Comines	OOC
35	3 Jun 17	2/Lt R S Watt & Cpl T M Harries*	A8244	Alb DIII	SE Quesnoy	Dest
36	3 Jun 17	2/Lt H E R Fitchat & 2/Lt R Hayes*	A1093	Alb DIII	SE Quesnoy	OOC
37	5 Jun 17	2/Lt M B Frew & 2/Lt M J Dalton*	A8279	Alb DIII	Menin	Dest(F)
38	5 Jun 17	2/Lt M B Frew* & 2/Lt M J Dalton	A8279	Alb DIII	Menin	OOC
39	5 Jun 17	2/Lt N Macmillan & 2/Lt P F H Webb*	A8281	Alb DIII	Menin	OOC
40	16 Jun 17	Capt G H Cock* & Lt J T G Murison	A1016	Alb DV	Warneton	OOC
41	16 Jun 17	Capt R M Findlay* & Lt G W Blaiklock	A8295	Alb D	nr Comines	OOC
42	16 Jun 17	Lt G H Walker & 2/Lt J W Mullen*	A8308	Alb D	nr Comines	OOC
43	16 Jun 17	2/Lt M B Frew & 2/Lt M J Dalton*	A8790	Alb DIII	nr Comines	OOC
44	16 Jun 17	Capt W T Wood & Lt C T R Ward*	A8789	Alb D	nr Comines	OOC
45	16 Jun 17	Sgt R A Yeomans & Rfn P Davis	A8782	Alb D	nr Comines	OOC
46	5 Jul 17	Capt A T Harris* & 2/Lt P F H Webb	A8792	Alb D	NE Ypres	OOC
47	6 Jul 17	Capt G H Cock* & Lt C T R Ward	A1016	Alb DIII	NW Comines	OOC
48	6 Jul 17	Capt R M Findlay* & Lt M Moore	A8295	Alb DIII	Menin	OOC
49	7 Jul 17	Capt R M Findlay & Lt M Moore*	A8295	Alb DIII	Menin	OOC
50	7 Jul 17	Lt E F Crossland & Lt G W Blaiklock*	A1031	Alb DIII	Menin	OOC
51	7 Jul 17	Capt A T Harris* & 2/Lt P F H Webb	A8792	Alb DIII	Comines	Dest
52	7 Jul 17	Sgt R A Yeomans & Cpl T M Harries*	A8292	Alb DIII	Wervicq	Dest(F)
53	7 Jul 17	Sgt R A Yeomans & Cpl T M Harries*	A8292	Alb DIII	Wervicq	OOC
54	7 Jul 17	Sgt R A Yeomans & Cpl T M Harries*	A8292	Alb DIII	Wervicq	OOC
55	7 Jul 17	Capt G H Cock & Lt C T R Ward*	A8298	Alb DIII	Wervicq	OOC
56	7 Jul 17	Lt G H Walker & 2/Lt J W Mullen*	A8295	Alb DIII	Wervicq	OOC
57	12 Jul 17	Lt R Musgrave & Cpl A Jex*	A1038	Alb D	Kortewilde	Dest(F)
58	12 Jul 17	Capt A T Harris* & 2/Lt P F H Webb	A8792	Alb C	Kortewilde	OOC
59	12 Jul 17	Lt G H Walker* & 2/Lt J W Mullen	A1031	Alb D	NE Armentières	OOC
60	12 Jul 17	Lt O L McMaking & 2/Lt L M Copeland*	A8315	Alb DIII	E Messines	OOC
61	12 Jul 17	Lt J C B Firth & 2/Lt J H Hartley*	A1036	Alb DIII	E Messines	OOC
62	13 Jul 17	Capt G H Cock* & 2/Lt V R S White	A1016	Alb DIII	E Polygon Wood	OOC
63	13 Jul 17	2/Lt K B Montgomery* & Sgt W J Wickham	A970	Alb DIII	E Polygon Wood	OOC
64	16 Jul 17	2/Lt M B Frew & Lt G A Brooke*	A1020	Alb DIII	Polygon Wood	Dest(F)
65	16 Jul 17	2/Lt R H Deakin & Capt J W Higgins*	A8292	Alb DIII	Polygon Wood	OOC
66	16 Jul 17	2/Lt K B Montgomery & 2/Lt R C Purvis*	A8298	Alb DIII	Polygon Wood	Dest(F)
67	20 Jul 17	Lt R Musgrave & Cpl A Jex*	A8315	2-seater	Houthem	OOC
68	20 Jul 17	Lt A E Charlwood* & Lt A S Selby	B2569	D-type	NW Warneton	OOC
69	22 Jul 17	Lt J C B Firth* & 2/Lt J H Hartley	A1036	Alb DIII	Menin	OOC
70	22 Jul 17	Lt E F Crossland & Lt G W Blaiklock*	A8304	Alb DIII	Menin	OOC
71	22 Jul 17	Capt G H Cock* & Lt M Moore	B2576	Alb DIII	Warneton	Dest(F)
72	28 Jul 17	2/Lt M B Frew* & Lt G A Brooke	A8228	Alb DIII	S Comines	Dest
73	28 Jul 17	Sgt R A Yeomans & Dvr W A Fellows	A8766	Alb C	Polygon Wood	OOC
74	9 Aug 17	Capt A E Charlwood & 2/Lt M J Dalton*	A1064	?	Warneton	OOC
75	10 Aug 17	Capt R M Findlay & 2/Lt J W Mullen*	A1056	Alb DIII	E Menin	Dest
76	10 Aug 17	2/Lt M B Frew & Lt G A Brooke*	A1013	Alb DIII	E Comines	OOC
77	10 Aug 17	Lt O L McMaking & Cpl A Jex*	B2569	Alb DIII	Zandvoorde	OOC
78	11 Aug 17	Lt O L McMaking & Cpl A Jex*	?	Alb D III	Deulemont	Dest(F)
79	11 Aug 17	Capt I McA M Pender & Pnr W T Smith*	A5244	Alb D	Deulemont	Dest
80	11 Aug 17	2/Lt K B Montgomery & 2/Lt R C Purvis*	A1053	Alb DIII	Comines	OOC
81	21 Aug 17	2/Lt E A L F Smith & Pte H Grenner*	A1056	Alb D	SE Ypres	Dest
82	21 Aug 17	2/Lt N Macmillan & 2/Lt R S V Morris*	B2583	DFW C	Ploegsteert Wood	Dest(F)
83	23 Aug 17	2/Lt E D Clarke & Lt G A Brooke*	A1048	Alb DV	Bellewerde Lake	OOC
84	23 Aug 17	2/Lt K B Montgomery & 2/Lt R C Purvis*	A1053	Alb DV	Bellewerde Lake	OOC
85	25 Aug 17	2/Lt N Macmillan	B3917	Alb DIII	Polygon Wood	OOC
86	27 Aug 17	Capt A T Harris	B3875	Alb DV	Moorslede	OOC
87	3 Sep 17	Capt A T Harris	?	Alb DV	Dadizeele	Dest(F)
88	3 Sep 17	Lt W C Moore	?	Alb D	Dadizeele	OOC
89	3 Sep 17	Lt O L McMaking	?	Alb D	Dadizeele	OOC
90	3 Sep 17	2/Lt E D Clarke	B2327	Alb DIII	Zandvoorde	Dest(F)
91	3 Sep 17	2/Lt M B Frew	B3871	Alb D	Zandvoorde	OOC
92	3 Sep 17	2/Lt N Macmillan	B6205	Alb D	Tenbrielen	Dest(F)
93	4 Sep 17	2/Lt M B Frew	B3871	Alb C	NE Comines	OOC
94	4 Sep 17	2/Lt M B Frew	B3871	Alb C	NE Comines	Dest
95	4 Sep 17	2/Lt H M Moody	B6238	Alb C	NE Comines	OOC
96	5 Sep 17	Capt W A Wright	B3903	DFW C	NE Comines	OOC
97	5 Sep 17	Lt O L McMaking	B2314	Alb DIII	Comines	OOC
98	9 Sep 17	2/Lt E A L F Smith	B3791	Alb C	Comines	Dest(F)
99	9 Sep 17	2/Lt E A L F Smith	B3791	Alb C	E Ypres	OOC
100	10 Sep 17	2/Lt R J Brownell	B2323	DFW C	Houtholst Forest	Dest(F)
101	10 Sep 17	2/Lt N Macmillan	B6236	DFW C	Houtholst Forest	OOC
102	10 Sep 17	2/Lt E A L F Smith	?	Alb DIII	Houtholst Forest	OOC

103	11 Sep 17	2/Lt H M Moody	?	DFW C	Westroosebeke	OOC
104	11 Sep 17	2/Lt M B Frew	?	DFW C	Kortewilde	OOC
105	11 Sep 17	2/Lt J E Child	B2328	Alb D	Hooge	OOC
106	11 Sep 17	Capt W A Wright	?	2-seater	SE Moorslede	OOC
107	11 Sep 17	2/Lt N Macmillan	?	Fok DrI	E Langemarck	OOC
108	11 Sep 17	2/Lt N Macmillan	?	Fok DrI	E Langemarck	OOC
109	14 Sep 17	2/Lt E D Clarke	B2327	Alb DV	E Merckem	OOC
110	20 Sep 17	2/Lt E D Clarke	B2327	Alb DV	Passchendaele	Dest
111	20 Sep 17	Capt W A Wright	B3903	2-seater	Westroosebeke	Dest
112	20 Sep 17	2/Lt K B Montgomery	B3871	Alb DV	Westroosebeke	OOC
113	20 Sep 17	2/Lt P Carpenter	B2314	Alb DV	E Ypres	OOC
114	20 Sep 17	2/Lt R J Brownell	B2323	2-seater	Passchendaele	Dest(F)
114	20 Sep 17	2/Lt H M Moody	B6238		as above (shared claim)	
114	20 Sep 17	2/Lt E A L F Smith	B3791		as above (shared claim)	
115	21 Sep 17	2/Lt M B Frew	B3871	Alb D	Comines	Dest(F)
116	21 Sep 17	2/Lt E A L F Smith	B3791	Alb DV	Passchendaele	OOC
117	22 Sep 17	2/Lt K B Montgomery	B2376	Alb DV	Quesnoy	OOC
118	25 Sep 17	Lt J C B Firth	B2374	Alb C	Passchendaele	OOC
119	26 Sep 17	Lt E D Clarke	B2327	Alb C	E Zillebeke	Dest
120	26 Sep 17	Lt J C B Firth	B2350	Alb D	Passchendaele	Dest
121	1 Oct 17	2/Lt R J Brownell	B2323	Alb DV	Quesnoy	OOC
122	1 Oct 17	Capt W A Wright	B3903	Alb DV	Polygon Wood	Dest
123	1 Oct 17	2/Lt E A L F Smith	B2375	Alb DV	Quesnoy	OOC
124	10 Oct 17	2/Lt M B Frew	B6372	Alb D	Dadizeele	Dest
125	10 Oct 17	2/Lt M B Frew	B6372	Alb D	Dadizeele	OOC
126	15 Oct 17	2/Lt K B Montgomery	B2393	2-seater	Houtholst Forest	Dest
127	15 Oct 17	Capt N Macmillan	B6383	2-seater	Houtholst Forest	OOC
128	20 Oct 17	Capt N Macmillan	B6382	Alb DV	Kastelhoek	Dest(F)
129	20 Oct 17	Lt E D Clarke	B2327	Alb DV	Kastelhoek	OOC
130	20 Oct 17	2/Lt R J Dawes	B6412	Alb DIII	Kastelhoek	OOC
131	20 Oct 17	2/Lt R J Brownell	B2376	Alb DV	Kastelhoek	OOC
132	21 Oct 17	2/Lt P Carpenter	B2388	Alb DV	Lille	Dest(F)
133	21 Oct 17	2/Lt M B Frew	B3903	Alb DV	Lille	OOC
134	24 Oct 17	2/Lt T F Williams	?	Alb DV	Coucou	Dest
135	26 Oct 17	2/Lt K B Montgomery	?	Ju JI	Houtholst Forest	Dest
135	26 Oct 17	Capt M B Frew	B6372		as above (shared claim)	
136	27 Oct 17	Capt M B Frew	B6372	Alb DV	NE Comines	Dest
137	27 Oct 17	Capt M B Frew	B6372	Alb DV	Moorslede	Dest(F)
138	27 Oct 17	Capt J C B Firth	B6354	Alb DIII	NE Comines	Dest(F)
139	31 Oct 17	Capt J C B Firth	B6354	2-seater	E Quesnoy	Dest
139	31 Oct 17	2/Lt P Carpenter	B5182		as above (shared claim)	
140	5 Nov 17	Capt J C B Firth	B6354	Alb DV	Poelcapelle	OOC
141	8 Nov 17	2/Lt J E Child	B2443	Ju JI	Westroosebeke	Dest
142	8 Nov 17	2/Lt P Carpenter	B5182	Alb C	S Passchendaele	Dest
143	8 Nov 17	2/Lt T F Williams	B6282	Alb DV	Westroosebeke	Dest(F)
144	8 Nov 17	2/Lt T F Williams	B6282	Alb DV	Houtholst Forest	OOC
145	8 Nov 17	Capt J C B Firth	B6423	Alb D	Houtholst Forest	Dest
146	9 Nov 17	2/Lt K B Montgomery	B3929	2-seater	S Becelaere	OOC
147	13 Nov 17	2/Lt T F Williams	B6282	Ju JI	Westroosebeke	OOC
147	13 Nov 17	2/Lt H M Moody	B6238		as above (shared claim)	
148	15 Nov 17	2/Lt P Carpenter	B5182	Rumpler C	Houtholst Forest	Dest
149	15 Nov 17	2/Lt K B Montgomery	B3929	Alb DV	Langemarcke	Dest(F)
150	15 Nov 17	2/Lt E McN Hand	B2430	Alb DV	Poelcappelle	OOC
151	15 Nov 17	Capt J C B Firth	B6423	Alb DV	E Comines	OOC
152	31 Dec 17	2/Lt R J Brownell	B2430	Alb DIII	Pieve di Soligo	Dest
153	31 Dec 17	2/Lt H M Moody	B6238	Alb DIII	Pieve di Soligo	OOC
154	31 Dec 17	2/Lt R J Dawes	B6412	Alb DIII	Pieve di Soligo	OOC
155	31 Dec 17	2/Lt H M Moody	B6238	Alb DV	Paderno	Dest
155	31 Dec 17	2/Lt R J Brownell	B2430		as above (shared claim)	
156	1 Jan 18	2/Lt G H Bush	B6354	Rumpler C	Moriago	Dest
157	1 Jan 18	Capt N Macmillan	B6383	Alb DIII	San Fior	OOC
158	2 Jan 18	Lt H T Thompson	B4609	Aviatik C	Conegliano	Dest(F)
158	2 Jan 18	Capt J C B Firth	B6423		as above (shared claim)	
159	3 Jan 18	2/Lt K B Montgomery	B3929	Alb DIII	Corbolone	Dest
159	3 Jan 18	Capt M B Frew	B6372		as above (shared claim)	
160	10 Jan 18	2/Lt P Carpenter	B3929	Alb DIII	Ceggia	Dest
161	10 Jan 18	2/Lt R J Brownell	B2430	Alb DIII	Portobuffole	Dest
162	10 Jan 18	2/Lt D W Ross	B2436	Alb D	Portobuffole	OOC
163	10 Jan 18	2/Lt T F Williams	B6282	Alb DIII	Portobuffole	OOC
164	11 Jan 18	Capt M B Frew	B6372	Alb DIII	Motta di Livenza	Dest
165	11 Jan 18	2/Lt H M Moody	B6383	Alb DIII	Corbolone	Dest
166	11 Jan 18	2/Lt R J Brownell	B2430	Alb DIII	Santo Stino di Livenza	Dest
167	11 Jan 18	2/Lt T F Williams	B6282	Alb DIII	Vittorio	OOC
168	11 Jan 18	Capt J C B Firth	B6423	Alb DIII	Vittorio	OOC
169	11 Jan 18	2/Lt E McN Hand	B6238	Alb DIII	Vittorio	OOC
170	11 Jan 18	2/Lt E McN Hand	B6238	Alb DIII	Vittorio	OOC

171	11 Jan 18	Lt H T Thompson	B2494	Alb C	Vittorio	Dest
172	14 Jan 18	2/Lt C E Howell	B4609	Alb DIII	Cimetta	Dest(F)
173	14 Jan 18	2/Lt R J Dawes	B6412	Alb DIII	Borgo	Dest
174	15 Jan 18	Capt M B Frew	B6372	Alb DV	Vazzola	Dest(F)
175	15 Jan 18	Capt M B Frew	B6372	Alb DV	Vazzola	Dest
176	15 Jan 18	Capt M B Frew	B6372	DFW C	Vazzola	Dest(F)
177	15 Jan 18	2/Lt P Carpenter	B3929	Alb DIII	Vazzola	Dest
178	26 Jan 18	2/Lt P Carpenter	B3929	Alb DIII	Noventa	Dest
179	26 Jan 18	2/Lt C E Howell	B4609	Alb DIII	Sette Casoni	Dest
180	26 Jan 18	2/Lt T F Williams	B6282	Alb DIII	Roncade	Dest(F)
181	27 Jan 18	Capt M B Frew	B6372	Alb DIII	Conegliano	Dest(F)
182	27 Jan 18	2/Lt R J Dawes	B6412	DFW C	Conegliano	OOC
183	30 Jan 18	2/Lt R J Brownell	B6383	DFW C	Saletto	Dest(F)
184	30 Jan 18	Lt M D G Drummond	B2426	DFW C	Ormelle	Dest
185	30 Jan 18	2/Lt E McN Hand	B4609	DFW C	Ormelle	Dest
186	30 Jan 18	2/Lt H M Moody	B4609	Alb DIII	Susegana	Dest
187	2 Feb 18	2/Lt G H Bush	B6423	Alb DIII	Il Montello	Dest
188	2 Feb 18	2/Lt G H Bush	B6423	Berg DI	Il Montello	Dest
188	2 Feb 18	2/Lt T F Williams	B3887		as above (shared claim)	
189	4 Feb 18	Capt M B Frew	B6372	Alb DV	Collalto	Dest
190	4 Feb 18	Lt H D O'Neill	B3862	Alb DV	Marcatelli	Dest
191	4 Feb 18	2/Lt A J Haines	B5182	Alb DV	Susegana	Dest
192	4 Feb 18	Lt D G McLean	B2594	Alb DV	Susegana	Dest
193	4 Feb 18	Capt M B Frew	B6372	Alb DV	Susegana	OOC
194	22 Feb 18	2/Lt J E Child	B2443	Alb DIII	Salgareda	Dest(F)
195	22 Feb 18	Lt H D O'Neill	B6372	Alb DIII	Vazzola	Dest
196	22 Feb 18	2/Lt G H Bush	B3887	Alb DIII	Grassaga	Dest
197	22 Feb 18	2/Lt J R Black	B3862	Alb DIII	Negrisia	OOC
198	22 Feb 18	Lt H T Thompson	B6354	Alb DIII	San Nicolo	OOC
199	27 Feb 18	Maj A M Vaucour	B6354	Alb DIII	Oderzo	Dest
200	27 Feb 18	Maj A M Vaucour	B6354	Alb DIII	Oderzo	OOC
201	10 Mar 18	2/Lt R J Dawes	B6412	DFW C	SE Salgareda	Dest
201	10 Mar 18	2/Lt J Cottle	B6354		as above (shared claim)	
202	24 Mar 18	2/Lt J P Huins	B2379	Alb DIII	Val d'Assa	OOC
203	24 Mar 18	2/Lt J H Dewhirst	B6282	Berg DI	NW Asiago	OOC
204	27 Mar 18	2/Lt T F Williams	B3887	Alb DIII	Ceggia	Dest(F)
205	27 Mar 18	Capt J C B Firth	B6423	Alb DIII	Ceggia	OOC
206	27 Mar 18	Lt H T Thompson	B7307	Alb DIII	Ceggia	OOC
207	17 Apr 18	Capt R J Brownell	B3872	Alb DIII	Oderzo	OOC
208	18 Apr 18	Capt R J Brownell	B3872	KB	Piave River	Dest
209	23 Apr 18	2/Lt E McN Hand	B2430	Alb DIII	N Levico	Dest
210	23 Apr 18	2/Lt C E Howell	B5238	Alb DIII	N Levico	Dest
211	2 May 18	Lt E McN Hand	B2430	Alb DIII	Monte Chiesa	Dest
212	4 May 18	Lt J H Dewhirst	B6282	Berg DI	W Feltre	Dest
213	9 May 18	Lt E McN Hand	B2430	Alb DIII	Vazzola	Dest
214	13 May 18	Lt C E Howell	B5238	Alb DIII	Coldarco	OOC
215	13 May 18	Lt C E Howell	B5238	Alb DIII	Coldarco	Dest
216	13 May 18	Lt C E Howell	B5238	Alb DIII	Costa	Dest
217	13 May 18	Lt C E Howell	B5238	Alb DIII	Rocca	Dest
218	13 May 18	Lt E H Masters	B2379	Alb DIII	Costa	Dest
219	13 May 18	Lt E H Masters	B2379	LVG C	Frisoni	Dest
219	13 May 18	Lt F S Bowles	B2426		as above (shared claim)	
220	18 May 18	Lt J Cottle	B5181	Alb DIII	Roncegno	Dest
221	19 May 18	Lt C G Catto	B6412	Aviatik C	Mel	Dest(F)
221	19 May 18	Capt N C Jones	B6372		as above (shared claim)	
222	20 May 18	Capt N C Jones	B6372	Alb DIII	NE Asiago	Dest
223	21 May 18	Lt H D O'Neill	B7381	Alb D	Salgareda	OOC
224	22 May 18	Capt G H Bush	B3887	LVG C	Lavarda	Dest
224	22 May 18	Lt C G Catto	B6372		as above (shared claim)	
225	1 Jun 18	Capt N C Jones	B6372	Alb DV	Feltre	Dest(F)
226	1 Jun 18	Lt J H Dewhirst	B7360	Alb DV	S Feltre	Dest
227	3 Jun 18	Capt R J Dawes	B6412	Alb DV	Caupo	OOC
228	3 Jun 18	Lt M R James	B3872	Alb DV	Arten	Dest
229	7 Jun 18	Capt N C Jones	B6372	DFW C	Arsiero	Dest
230	7 Jun 18	Lt A J Haines	D1975	Alb DIII	Arsiero	Dest(F)
231	7 Jun 18	Lt A J Haines	D1975	Alb DIII	Caldonazzo	Dest(F)
232	7 Jun 18	Lt G McIntyre	B2443	DFW C	Folgaria	OOC
233	7 Jun 18	Capt R J Dawes	B6412	Alb DIII	Piovene	Dest
234	7 Jun 18	Lt M R James	D8102	Alb DIII	San Marino	Dest
235	7 Jun 18	Lt M R James	D8102	Alb DIII	Collicello	Dest
236	7 Jun 18	Lt C G Catto	B3872	Brand C	Collicello	Dest
237	8 Jun 18	Capt C E Howell	D9394	Phönix DI	Monte Tomba	Dest
238	8 Jun 18	Capt C E Howell	D9394	Berg DI	Monte Tomba	Dest
239	8 Jun 18	Lt J P Huins	D1910	Berg DI	Monte Tomba	OOC
240	8 Jun 18	Lt H B Hudson	D1974	Aviatik C	Monte Tomba	OOC
241	8 Jun 18	Lt H D O'Neill	B7381	Alb DIII	Feltre	OOC

242	15 Jun 18	Capt R J Dawes	B6412	Aviatik C	Poselaro	Dest
243	15 Jun 18	Lt F S Bowles	B5181	DFW C	Ponte di Piave	OOC
244	15 Jun 18	Lt C G Catto	D9392	Aviatik C	Poselaro	OOC
245	15 Jun 18	Maj A M Vaucour	D9394	DFW C	Susegana	Dest(F)
246	19 Jun 18	Capt C E Howell	D9394	Alb DV	Camporovere	Dest
247	19 Jun 18	Capt C E Howell	D9394	Alb DV	Monte Meatta	Dest
248	19 Jun 18	Lt E H Masters	D1974	Alb DV	Monte Meatta	Dest
249	19 Jun 18	Lt E H Masters	D1974	Alb DV	Asiago	OOC
250	19 Jun 18	Lt J H Dewhirst	D1910	Alb DV	Monte Verena	Dest
251	19 Jun 18	Lt J H Dewhirst	D1910	Alb DIII	Monte Verena	Dest
252	19 Jun 18	Lt J H Dewhirst	D1910	Alb DIII	Asiago	Dest(F)
253	19 Jun 18	Maj A M Vaucour	D1975	2-seater	Postioma	Dest
254	20 Jun 18	Lt C G Catto	D9392	Alb DIII	Montello	OOC
255	25 Jun 18	Maj A M Vaucour	D1910	Brand C	E Treviso	Dest
256	28 Jun 18	Capt N C Jones	D8169	Alb DIII	W Padavena	Dest
257	5 Jul 18	Lt J Cottle	B7360	LVG C	Pederiva	OOC
258	7 Jul 18	Lt J E Child	D1975	LVG C	Val d'Assa	Dest
259	12 Jul 18	Capt C E Howell	D9394	Alb DV	Feltre	Dest
260	12 Jul 18	Capt C E Howell	D9394	Phönix DI	Feltre	Dest(F)
261	12 Jul 18	Capt C E Howell	D9394	Berg DI	Feltre	Dest(F)
262	12 Jul 18	Capt C E Howell	D9394	Phönix DI	Feltre	OOC
263	12 Jul 18	Capt C E Howell	D9394	Berg DI	Feltre	OOC
264	12 Jul 18	Lt A Rice-Oxley	D8240	Phönix DI	Astico	Dest
265	12 Jul 18	Lt A Rice-Oxley	D8240	Berg DI	Feltre	Dest
266	12 Jul 18	Lt J Cottle	D8113	LVG C	Cismon	Dest
267	14 Jul 18	Lt E H Masters	D1974	D-type	Cismon	Dest
268	14 Jul 18	Capt C E Howell	D9394	Alb DIII	Tresche	Dest
269	14 Jul 18	Lt A Rice-Oxley	D9392	Alb DV	Cogollo	Dest
270	15 Jul 18	Capt C E Howell	D8113	Phönix DI	Costa Alta	Dest(F)
271	15 Jul 18	Capt C E Howell	D8113	Phönix DI	Monte Forcellona	Dest
272	15 Jul 18	Lt J P Huins	D1910	D-type	Monte Forcellona	Dest
273	15 Jul 18	Lt A Rice-Oxley	D1975	Phönix DI	Costa Alta	Dest(F)
274	15 Jul 18	Lt A Rice-Oxley	D1975	Phönix DI	Monte Forcellona	OOC
275	20 Jul 18	Lt M R James	D8211	Alb DV	Feltre	Dest
276	20 Jul 18	Lt M R James	D8211	Alb DV	Feltre	Dest
277	20 Jul 18	Lt F S Bowles	D1975	Alb DV	Feltre	Dest
278	20 Jul 18	Lt F S Bowles	D1975	Alb DIII	Cesana	Dest
279	23 Jul 18	Lt A J Haines	D9412	Aviatik C	Grigno	Dest
280	29 Jul 18	Capt N C Jones	D8169	Alb DIII	Brugnera	Dest
281	29 Jul 18	Lt A J Haines	D9412	Phönix DI	Prata di Pordenone	Dest
282	29 Jul 18	Lt A J Haines	D9412	Phönix DI	Prata di Pordenone	Dest
283	31 Jul 18	Capt J Cottle	D8237	Phönix DI	Fontane	Dest
284	5 Aug 18	Capt J Cottle	D8237	D-type	Monte Grappa	Dest
285	5 Aug 18	Lt F S Bowles	D9392	D-type	Monte Grappa	OOC
286	5 Aug 18	Lt C G Catto	D8243	D-type	Monte Grappa	Dest
287	5 Aug 18	Lt M R James	D8211	AEG C	Porteghetti	Dest
288	6 Aug 18	Lt M Gibson	B5181	Aviatik C	Segusino	Dest
289	6 Aug 18	Lt M R James	D8211	Alb DV	Segusino	Dest
290	6 Aug 18	Lt M R James	D8211	Alb DV	Segusino	OOC
291	6 Aug 18	Lt M R James	D8211	Alb DV	Segusino	OOC
292	10 Aug 18	Lt E H Masters	C54	LVG C	Fodatti	Dest
293	20 Aug 18	Capt J Cottle	D8237	2-seater	Loncon	Dest
294	20 Aug 18	Capt J Cottle	D8237	2-seater	S Asiago	Dest
295	20 Aug 18	Lt E H Masters	C54	2-seater	S Asiago	Dest(F)
296	21 Aug 18	Capt N C Jones	C3284	Alb DV	Piavon	Dest
297	21 Aug 18	Capt N C Jones	C3284	Alb DV	Piavon	OOC
298	22 Aug 18	Capt A Rice-Oxley	E1500	2-seater	San Nazario	Dest
299	31 Aug 18	Capt J Cottle	D8237	Alb DIII	Peralto	Dest
300	31 Aug 18	Capt J Cottle	D8237	Alb DIII	Arsiero	Dest
301	31 Aug 18	Capt J Cottle	D8237	Alb DIII	Posina	Dest
302	31 Aug 18	Lt M R James	D8211	Alb DIII	Monte Seluggio	Dest
303	31 Aug 18	Lt M R James	D8211	Alb DIII	Arsiero	Dest
304	31 Aug 18	Lt R G H Davis	D9386	Alb DIII	Monte Campomolon	OOC
305	31 Aug 18	Capt J Cottle	D8237	2-seater	Val Sugana	OOC
306	9 Oct 18	Capt J W Pinder	D8240	Rumpler C	Xaffévillers	OOC
307	10 Oct 18	2/Lt L B Irish	D8237	Rumpler C	Erbéviller	OOC
308	23 Oct 18	Capt J W Pinder	E7244	Alb C	S St Die	OOC
309	23 Oct 18	Capt J W Pinder	E7244	Rumpler C	Fraize	Dest(F)
310	23 Oct 18	Lt E H Masters	E7212	Rumpler C	Coincourt	OOC
311	23 Oct 18	Lt H T Thompson	D8240	Rumpler C	Montonoy	OOC
312	28 Oct 18	Capt J W Pinder	E7244	Rumpler C	W Corcieux	Dest(F)
313	3 Nov 18	Capt J Cottle	D8211	Fok DVII	Erbéviller	OOC
314	5 Nov 18	Capt J W Pinder	E7244	Rumpler C	N Parroy	Dest
315	5 Nov 18	Lt J H Dewhirst	E7204	Fok DVII	N Parroy	Dest
316	5 Nov 18	Capt J Cottle	D8237	Rumpler C	E Dieuze	Dest

No 45 Sqn's Aces.

By popular consensus an Ace is considered to be the victor of at least five aerial engagements. Based on the tabulations above, No 45 Sqn produced the remarkable total of thirty-two pilots who claimed to have shot down, or to have shared in the shooting down of, five or more enemy aircraft. To these may be added two observer/gunners who claimed five victories in their own right. It is conventional for the pilot of a two-seater to be credited with a victory whether the victim fell to his own gun or to that of his observer. This factor is reflected in the scores of several of No 45 Sqn's Ace pilots. If the principle is reversed, ie if observers are credited with victories which fell to the guns of their pilots (as became the standard practice in 1918), then three further observer/gunners qualify as having taken part in at least five successful combats and should thus also be considered to have achieved the status of being Aces. The thirty-seven aircrew of No 45 Sqn who participated in at least five victorious engagements are listed below; the ranks shown in each case are the highest held while serving with No 45 Sqn.

Ace	Score (with No 45 Sqn)	Remarks
Capt M B Frew	25	Includes four claims by observers.
Capt C E Howell	19	
Capt J Cottle	14	
Capt G H Cock	12	Includes three claims by observers.
Capt J C B Firth	12	Includes one claim by an observer.
Capt R J Brownell	11	
2/Lt K B Montgomery	11	Includes three claims by observers; one later claim with No 66 Sqn.
Capt M R James	11	
Capt N Macmillan	10	Includes two claims by observers.
Lt T F Williams	9	Plus six later claims with No 28 Sqn.
2/Lt P Carpenter	8	Plus sixteen later claims with No 66 Sqn.
Capt R J Dawes	8	Plus one claim with No 28 Sqn.
Capt N C Jones	8	Plus one earlier claim with No 28 Sqn.
Lt C H Masters	8	
Capt H M Moody	8	
Capt W A Wright	8	Includes four claims by observers.
Lt G W Blaiklock	7	Observer. Includes at least two claims by pilots.
Lt J H Dewhirst	7	
Cpl T M Harries	7	Observer (at least six to his own gun) plus five with No 24 Sqn.
2/Lt E A L F Smith	7	Includes one claim by an observer.
Lt J D Belgrave	6	Plus twelve later claims with No 60 Sqn.
Lt C G Catto	6	
Lt E D Clarke	6	Includes one claim by an observer.
Lt A J Haines	6	
Capt A Rice-Oxley	6	
Lt F S Bowles	5	
Capt G H Bush	5	
Lt E T Caulfield-Kelly	5	Observer. Includes one claim by a pilot.
Capt E McN Hand	5(7)	Two OOC claims on 11/1/18 were not ratified.
Capt A T Harris	5	
Lt O L McMaking	5	Includes three claims by observers.
Lt J T G Murison	5	Observer. Includes three claims made by pilots.
Capt J W Pinder	5	Plus twelve earlier claims with Nos 9N, 13N and 213 Sqns.
Lt H T Thompson	5	
Maj A M Vaucour	5	Plus three earlier claims with No 70 Sqn.
2/Lt J A Vessey	5	Observer. Two claims by pilots.
Sgt R A Yeomans	5	At least three claims by observers.

Annex F.   A summary of No 45 Sqn's operational effort in WW II.

Blenheim I.

So far as can be ascertained from surviving records, the squadron flew at least 398 sorties on Blenheim Is. These can be broken down as shown at Figure F.1.

The nominal offensive load of the Blenheim was 1,000 lbs. Classically this consisted of four 250 lb GP bombs. No 45 Sqn certainly carried such loads in its Blenheim Is on occasion but they tended to be the exception rather than the rule in the earlier months of the war. Comprehensive details of all of No 45 Sqn's missions are lacking but for the sorties flown in June 1940 bomb loads were chiefly made up of 40 lb GP bombs leavened with 4 lb and 25 lb incendiaries, 20 lb fragmentation bombs and only the occasional 250 pounder. It should be appreciated, however, that even when smaller bombs were carried the total load was still approximately 1,000 lbs. A typical example from the East African campaign is provide by the three-aircraft attack against Asmara on 14th September 1940. Each Blenheim was loaded with twelve 40

Period	Theatre	Sorties
June 1940	North Africa	23
July-August 1940	the Sudan	21
September-December 1940	the Sudan	142
December 1940-February 1941	North Africa	212

Fig F.1. Number of sorties known to have been flown by No 45 Sqn's Blenheim Is, June 1940-February 1941.

pounders, twelve 20 pounders and four 25 lb and sixty 4 lb incendiaries - a total load of 1,060 lbs per aeroplane. Mixed loads continued to be delivered after the squadron's return to the Western Desert, as on 24th December when the three aircraft which attacked Tmimi carried six 40 pounders, twenty-four 20 pounders and forty 4 lb incendiaries - a total of 880 lbs each; and on 18th January when Tobruk was attacked by three aircraft loaded with a pair of 250 lb bombs and twenty-four 20 pounders for a total of 980 lbs each. The range of weapon options was completed by the 500 pounder, and a few of these were reportedly manhandled into the Blenheims' bomb-bays in late 1940 when the squadron was flying in support of Operation COMPASS. Ideally the composition of the bomb load should have been that considered most likely to cause the maximum damage to the specified target but the availability of stocks, during what was often a fast moving campaign, frequently precluded the luxury of any kind of choice. Some allowance must also be made for two other factors. First, several of the sorties flown while the squadron was based in the Sudan were tasked as unarmed reconnaissance missions during which no weapons were delivered and, secondly, some bombing missions were unsuccessful, resulting in the weapon loads being brought back. In all, it is estimated that the squadron probably delivered at least 380,000 lbs of bombs while flying Blenheim Is.

Blenheim IV in the Middle East.

In the ten months that the squadron operated long-nosed Blenheims under HQME it flew at least 899 operational sorties (the most uncertain period being April-May 41). These can be broken down as shown at Figure F.2.

Specific bomb loads are not always detailed in the squadron's records. The Mk IVs probably carried the classic four 250 lb GP bombs more frequently than had been the case with the Mk Is but, depending on the nature of the mission, it

Period	Theatre	Sorties
April-May 1941	North Africa	277
June-July 1941	Syria	172
August 1941	Iran	39
September-1941-January 1942	North Africa	411

Fig F.2. Number of sorties known to have been flown by No 45 Sqn's Blenheim IVs in the Middle East.

was still not unusual for them to carry mixed loads of lighter bombs. The average bomb load of the squadron's Blenheim IVs will probably have been much the same as that of its Mk Is, ie about 950 lbs. Not all of the sorties flown with Mk IVs were bombing raids, however; a number of the attacks mounted in May 1941 delivered 'spikes' rather than bombs, for instance, and the majority of the raids flown over Iran carried leaflets. Furthermore, as the Mk IVF's bomb bay was occupied by a pack of four .303 Brownings, its bomb load on offensive sorties was restricted to what could be carried on an external rack under the rear fuselage, usually four 40 lb GPs, and even these would not have been carried on the fighter patrol missions flown over Crete in May 1941. Bearing these constraints in mind, a reasonable guesstimate might be that the squadron delivered at least 800,000 lbs of bombs during its time on Blenheim IVs in the Middle East.

Blenheim IV in Burma.

Official records for the campaign in Burma in 1942 are even more sparse than for those in the Middle East. So far as it has been possible to establish, and ignoring the many reconnaissance, evacuation and communications sorties which it flew, the squadron mounted at least 180 bombing sorties between 16th February and 21st March 1942. As in the Middle East, the standard bomb load was four 250 lb bombs, although 40 lb bombs are known to have been carried and

there is anecdotal evidence to suggest that some 500 pounders may also have been used. Although depleted stocks occasionally meant that sorties had to be flown with guns alone, at other times up to 1,800 lbs of bombs were carried, so it would seem likely that the average bomb load would have been about 1,000 lbs. On that reasonable assumption it is probable that the overall weight of bombs delivered was at least 180,000 lbs.

Total Blenheim Effort.

Bearing in mind the caveats qualifying the above figures, the squadron's total effort on Blenheims amounted to at least 1,477 offensive sorties. In flying these it is unlikely to have delivered less than 1,360,000 lbs of bombs. No figures recording the expenditure of gun ammunition appear to have survived for the Blenheim era.

Vengeances.

The squadron's records for the Vengeance period are comprehensive and well-preserved, although figures are lacking for the expenditure of gun ammunition during the initial deployment to Chittagong. The following statistics are largely confirmed by those of No 168 Wg but, where differences do occur, the squadron's accounts have been accepted as, being 'first hand', they are considered to be more likely to have been accurate. A digest of the squadron's operational effort on Vengeances is tabulated at Figure F.3.

Month	Missions	Sorties	Bombs (lbs)			Rounds Fired	
			500 lbs	250 lbs	Total	0.30"	0.303"
June 1943	4	28	28,000	0	28,000	?	?
July 1943	12	74	56,000	2,000	58,000	?	?
October 1943	12	75	57,500	0	57,500	10,260	8,120
November 1943	21	132	102,000	0	102,000	11,490	9,380
December 1943	17	161	70,500	76,250	146,750	6,210	8,440
January 1944	7	79	44,500	27,750	72,250	3,980	2,430
Total	**73**	**549**	**358,500**	**106,000**	**464,500**	**31,940+**	**28,370+**

Fig F.3. Sorties flown and operational weapons expenditure by No 45 Sqn while flying Vengeances, June 1943-January 1944.

Mosquitos.

The squadron's operations on Mosquitos were well recorded. Apart from the ORB, most of the OPREPs and CSRs have also survived and the summary at Figure F.4 has been distilled from the contents of all of these documents.

Month	Sorties		Bombs (lbs)			Round Fired	
	Day	Night	500 lbs	250 lbs	Total	20mm	0.303"
September 1944	2	0	1,000	0	1,000	?	?
October 1944	98	7	17,500	0	17,500	?	?
November 1944	8	28	28,000	0	28,000	5,276	11,103
December 1944	96	63	234,500	0	234,500	23,709	50,089
January 1945	153	64	310,500	0	310,500	65,000	140,175
February 1945	95	76	161,500	0	161,500	34,955	53,690
March 1945	287	65	549,000	7,500	556,500	55,675	94,175
April 1945	136	0	213,000	15,000	228,000	29,910	98,910
May 1945	82	0	57,000	0	57,000	10,146	17,375
Total	**957**	**303**	**1,572,000**	**22,500**	**1,594,500**	**224,671+**	**465,517+**

Fig F.4. Sorties flown and operational weapons expenditure by No 45 Sqn while flying Mosquitos, September 1944-May 1945.

Total.

So far as it has been possible to establish, the squadron's total offensive effort during WW II amounted to *at least* 3,269 sorties in the course of which it must have dropped at least 3,419,000 lbs of bombs and fired an undetermined quantity of ammunition (but it can hardly have been less than a million rounds). Owing to incomplete data being available for the period prior to 1943, if these figures are significantly in error they will be underestimates.

Air Combat Victories.

The crediting of aircraft destroyed to bomber crews is a contentious topic. At several places within the main narrative reference has been made to attacks on airfields, particularly in North and East Africa, in the course of which aircraft on the ground were reported to have been destroyed or damaged. It is unclear to what extent these claims were accepted and where two or more aircraft were involved in the action, as was usually the case, it is impossible to attribute the damage caused to any particular crew. The specific claims listed below appear to have been fairly well substantiated, however, and those listed during the Mosquito era reflect the squadron's recognised 'game book' as recorded in its ORB and endorsed in that of its parent wing.

No	Date	Crew	Aircraft	Type	Location	Claim
1	27 May 41	Lt D N Thorne SAAF Plt Off L P Bourke RNZAF Sgt Grant	T2243	Ju 88	Crete	Dam
2	29 May 41	Sgt J McLelland Sgt H Vipond Sgt J McGurk	T2252	Ju 88	Crete	Dest
3	19 Nov 41	2/Lt H R L Alder SAAF Plt Off W J Corbett RAAF Sgt C G Briggs RAAF	T2393	CR 42	Sidi Rezegh	Dest
4	20 Dec 41	Sqn Ldr A Hughes DFC Plt Off L E Durrant F/Sgt D Cliffe	V6180	Bf 109F	Ghemines	Prob
5	21 Mar 42	Fg Off J S Muller-Rowland Plt Off P E Graebner RAAF Sgt K A Gardiner RAAF	?	Ki 27	Mingaladon	Dest
6	21 Mar 42	Lt H R L Alder SAAF Plt Off W J Corbett RAAF Sgt C G Briggs RAAF	Z9807	Ki 27	Mingaladon	Dest
7	21 Mar 42	Sgt H M P Neil RAAF Sgt E J Hallett RAAF Sgt F F Brown RAAF	Z7981	Ki 27	Mingaladon	Prob
8	21 Mar 42	Plt Off J W Maloney RAAF Sgt D K Carew-Reid RAAF Sgt W R Wilson RAAF	V5495	Ki 27	Mingaladon	Prob
9	1 Oct 44	Flt Lt C S Emeny RNZAF Flt Lt L S Andrews	HR291	Ki 48	Nawngkhio	Dam
9	1 Oct 44	Plt Off D Blenkhorne RCAF Plt Off J Paterson	HP884	as above (shared Claim)		
10	6 Oct 44	Fg Off H M P Neil RAAF Fg Off E J Hallett RAAF	HR291	Ki 46	Heho	Dest
11	9 Nov 44	Flt Lt C S Emeny RNZAF WO J J Yanota RCAF	HR374	?	Meiktila	Dest
12	26 Dec 44	Plt Off R J Wilcock Flt Lt L S Andrews	HR456	Ki 46	Heho	Dest
13	29 Dec 44	WO B Walsh WO H Orsborn	HR456	Ki 43	Meiktila	Dam
14	3 Feb 45	Fg Off P N Ewing RAAF WO R L C C Pinkerton	HR404	Ki 21	Heho	Dest

Annex G. No 45 Sqn's operational effort during Operation FIREDOG.

Apart from the footnoted exceptions, the figures tabulated below have been extracted from the squadron's own Operations Record Book supplemented, where necessary, by those of AHQ Malaya, RAF Tengah, RAF Butterworth and RAF Kuala Lumpur.

The figures presented here suffer from the inconsistencies which were introduced by periodic changes in the contemporary interpretation of precisely what constituted an 'operational' sortie, eg did an armed convoy escort or a pre-strike met recce count, and should the occasional dummy strikes flown in the eras of the Venom and Canberra be included? Without first ironing out anomalies such as these, which will affect the records of all units which took part in

FIREDOG, any attempt to evaluate the comparative performances of the various squadrons would be invalid and no such comparison is attempted here. Despite their inherent limitations, the figures tabulated below (which are believed to reflect only strike sorties) were those submitted to, and accepted by, higher authority at the time and they stand as the formal contemporary record of No 45 Sqn's contribution to Operation FIREDOG. Although several other FEAF units served alongside the squadron for the duration of the twelve year campaign, the Flying Camels were unique in that they were the only squadron to have operated in an offensive role throughout.

Month	Type	Sorties	Bombs				RPs	20 mm
			1,000 lb	500 lb	250 lb	20 lb		
Aug 48	Bfr	5	-	6	-	-	29	900
Sep 48	Bfr	11	-	24	-	-	109	4,830
Oct 48	Bfr	30	-	74	-	-	294	5,600
Nov 48	Bfr	18	-	35	-	-	141	4,895
Dec 48	Bfr	28	-	10	-	-	204	9,118
Jan 49	Bfr	11	-	12	-	-	24	2,920
Feb 49	Bfr	9	-	18	-	-	69	3,480
Mar 49	Bfr	7	-	8	-	24	70	3,275
Apr 49	Bfr	5	-	3	-	24	28	1,955
May 49	Bfr	85	-	56	-	203	360	12,322
Jun 49	Bfr	36	-	33	-	187	189	10,910
Jul 49	Bfr	54	-	53	-	167	341	16,790
Aug 49	Bfr	40	-	86	-	166	322	15,560
Sep 49	Bfr	47	-	76	-	40	358	14,000
Oct 49	Bfr	79	-	151	-	48	609	22,975
Nov 49	Bfr	74	-	137	-	-	571	20,651
Dec 49	Bfr/Bgd	33/1[1]	-	53/2	-	-	254/6[2]	9,800/330[2]
Jan 50	Bfr/Bgd	43/8[1]	-	80/15[3]	-	-	333/48[3]	12,900/2,720
Feb 50	Bfr/Bgd	2/9[1]	-	4/16[3]	-	-	16/5[3]	610/3,700
Mar 50	Bgd	13	8	45	-	-	68	3,649
Apr 50	Bgd	72	32	256	-	-	423	23,750
May 50	Bgd	53	84	82	-	-	243	22,972
Jun 50	Bgd	64	128	125	-	-	404	22,985
Jul 50	Bgd	81	130	135	-	-	462	22,030
Aug 50	Bgd	76	39	249	-	-	446	32,540
Sep 50	Bgd	93	32	293	-	-	512	38,050
Oct 50	Bgd	36	29	139	-	-	301	24,810
Nov 50	Bgd	63	54	165	-	-	309	18,715
Dec 50	Bgd	45	25	166	-	-	280	18,800
Jan 51	Bgd	75	-	292	-	-	433	20,746
Feb 51	Bgd	70	-	265	-	-	402	11,830
Mar 51	Bgd	74	-	236	-	-	475	-
Apr 51	Bgd	51	-	212	-	-	307	-
May 51	Bgd	97	-	388	-	-	552	-
Jun 51	Bgd	98	-	391	-	-	589	14,020
Jul 51	Bgd	25	-	96	-	-	141	4,190
Aug 51	Bgd	49	-	170	-	-	260	650
Sep 51	Bgd	32	-	128	-	-	200	-
Oct 51	Bgd	63	64	127	-	-	370	250
Nov 51	Bgd	144	24	446	-	-	946	-
Dec 51	Bgd	37	52	28	-	-	481	-
Jan 52	Bgd	83	26	134	-	-	1,189	-
Feb 52	Bgd	41	-	150	-	-	130	4,185
Mar -May 52			Non-operational during conversion to Hornets					
Jun 52	Hnt	36	-	50	-	-	-	9,806
Jul 52	Hnt	102	-	112	-	-	-	28,726
Aug 52	Hnt	127	-	194	-	-	259	28,584

Sep 52	Hnt	20	-	40	-	-	77	8,045
Oct 52	Hnt	95	-	128	-	-	269	22,859
Nov 52	Hnt	101	-	164	-	-	390	42,215
Dec 52	Hnt	85	-	149	-	-	312	26,557
Jan 53	Hnt	72	-	104	-	-	249	30,106
Feb 53	Hnt	78	-	80	-	-	290	30,457
Mar 53	Hnt	49	-	48	-	-	98	11,155
Apr 53	Hnt	64	-	88	-	-	157	17,120
May 53	Hnt	81	-	74	-	-	336	34,435
Jun 53	Hnt	18	-	36	-	-	69	8,080
Jul 53	Hnt	42	-	84	-	-	165	17,260
Aug 53	Hnt	59	-	116	-	-	231	16,925
Sep 53	Hnt	75	-	84	-	-	225	17,670
Oct 53	Hnt	48	-	88	-	-	174	15,705
Nov 53	Hnt	51	-	76	-	-	167	10,952
Dec 53	Hnt	55	-	82	-	-	167	11,772
Jan 54	Hnt	29	-	51	-	-	88	4,990
Feb 54	Hnt	19	-	34	-	-	72	4,592
Mar 54	Hnt	14	-	12	-	-	46	2,519
Apr 54	Hnt	6	-	10	-	-	20	1,203
May 54				No ops tasked				
Jun 54	Hnt	16	-	30	-	-	59	4,394
Jul 54	Hnt	55	-	90	-	-	198	7,131
Aug 54	Hnt	4	-	8	-	-	16	840
Sep 54	Hnt	34	-	67	-	-	131	8,301
Oct 54	Hnt	42	-	84	-	-	168	9,975
Nov 54	Hnt	11	-	5	-	-	43	4,150
Dec 54	Hnt	22	-	18	20	-	84	5,446
Jan 55	Hnt	91	-	134	2	-	326	24,619
Feb 55	Hnt	31	-	54	-	-	110	8,955
Mar 55	Hnt	13	-	24	-	-	52	2,600
Apr 55	Hnt	12	-	24	-	-	25	1,602
May-Jul 55			Non-operational during jet conversion					
Aug 55	Vpr	8	-	16	-	-	30	3,360
Sep-Nov 55				No ops tasked				
Dec 55	Vpr	12	-	10	-	-	20	4,784
Jan 56	Vpr/Vnm	24/5[1]	-	-	-	-	89/20	6,427/1,339
Feb 56	Vpr/Vnm	11/14[1]	-	-	-	-	40/52	3,845/4,895
Mar 56	Vnm	6	4	-	-	-	15	734
Apr 56	Vnm	6	12	-	-	-	-	-
May 56	Vnm	12	22	-	-	-	-	-
Jun 56	Vnm	36	28	-	-	-	48	8,003
Jul 56	Vnm	8	16	-	-	-	-	1,250
Aug 56	Vnm	10	16	-	-	-	-	748
Sep 56	Vnm	16	16	-	-	-	23	1,230
Oct 56	Vnm	21	34	-	-	-	-	1,595
Nov-Dec 56				No ops tasked				
Jan 57	Vnm	28	30	-	-	-	26	5,589
Feb 57	Vnm	4	8	-	-	-	-	1,080
Mar 57	Vnm	4	6	-	-	-	-	810
Apr 57	Vnm	4	8	-	-	-	-	1,080
May 57	Vnm	11	22	-	-	-	-	2,081
Jun 57	Vnm	20	32	-	-	-	15	2,160
Jul 57	Vnm	38	16	-	-	-	112	7,082
Aug 57	Vnm	8	16	-	-	-	-	-
Sep 57				No ops tasked				
Oct 57	Vnm	18	16	-	-	-	40	3,455
Nov 57	Vnm	9	16	-	-	-	-	950
Dec 57-Feb 58				No ops tasked				
Mar 58	Can	43	-	220	-	-	-	-
Apr 58	Can	30	-	179	-	-	-	-
May 58	Can	12	-	72	-	-	-	-
Jun 58	Can	4	16	-	-	-	-	-
Jul 58	Can	49	50	330	-	-	-	-
Aug 58	Can	5	-	30	-	-	-	-
Sep 58	Can	10	60	-	-	-	-	-
Oct 58				No ops tasked				

Nov 58	Can	14	-	66	-	-	-	-	-
Dec 58	Can	2	-	12	-	-	-	-	-
			No further ops until						
Aug 59	Can	6	36	-	-	-	-	-	-

Figure G.1 summarises the above tabulation to present the overall weapons expenditure figures by aircraft type.

Type	Sorties	Nos of bombs				RPs	20mm
		1000 lbs	500 lbs	250 lbs	20 lbs		
Beaufighter	617	0	919	0	859	4,321	173,491
Brigand	1,553	727	4,751	0	0	10,031	290,922
Hornet	1,657	0	2,442	22	0	5,073	479,746
Vampire	55	0	26	0	0	179	18,416
Venom	278	318	0	0	0	351	44,081
Canberra	175	162	909	0	0	0	0
Total	4,335	1,207	9,047	22	859	19,957	1,006,656

Fig G.1. Weapons expenditure by each aircraft type flown by No 45 Sqn during Operation FIREDOG.

From Figure G.1 it is possible to derive an average weapon load per sortie for each type of aircraft as shown at Figure G.2. It should be stressed, however, that Figure G.2 does not represent a true comparison of each type's full potential. For instance, the Brigand's relatively poor figures for cannon resulted from a design defect which led to an embargo on the use of its guns for one third of the type's period of service with the squadron. Similarly, the Hornet's potential performance was artificially degraded by a ban on the use of RPs early in its career, by shortages of weapons which led to 250 lb bombs being substituted for 500 pounders for a time and by a period during which, for the same reason, only two guns were loaded. Then again, the Venom's comparatively poor figures for gunnery resulted from a decrease in the demand for gun attacks and do not represent that type's full capability either. Nevertheless, Figure G.2 does reflect what was actually achieved.

Type	Weapons per sortie		
	Bombs (lbs)	RPs	20mm
Beaufighter	773	7.01	281
Brigand	1,998	6.46	187
Hornet	740	3.06	290
Vampire	236	3.25	335
Venom	1,144	1.26	159
Canberra	3,523	0	0

Fig G.2. Average weapon load per sortie by aircraft type.

It may be of some interest to consider No 45 Sqn's contribution as a proportion of the overall offensive effort involved in Operation FIREDOG. Although they are known to contain some errors and omissions, the most reliable statistics available are those in Annex R of the official history (*Operation Firedog*, HMSO). Figure G.3 has been constructed from these official figures and those tabulated above (weight of bombs dropped by No 45 Sqn has been converted into short tons, ie 2000 lbs/ton). To keep these figures in proportion, it should be noted that, despite the prodigous efforts of the tactical squadrons, nothing could compare to the Lincoln when it came to piling up statistics and, according to one published Australian source, No 1 Sqn RAAF alone delivered more than 85% of the total bomb tonnage dropped during FIREDOG. It is very likely to have topped the table for ammunition expended as well.

	Offensive Sorties	Bombs (tons)	RPs	Gun Ammunition
Total	23,004	34,500	74,159	9,809,000
No 45 Sqn	4,335	2,876	19,957	1,006,656
% of total	18.8%	8.3%	22.9%	10.3%

Fig G.3. No 45 Sqn's contribution as a proportion of the overall offensive effort during Operation FIREDOG.

Notes:

1. It has been possible to establish the number of sorties flown by each type during the periods of Beaufighter/Brigand and Vampire/Venom conversion but surviving records give weapons consumption only as totals. In these cases the total ordnance expended has been divided proportionally, making some allowance for the likely differences in weapon loads between the types.
2. The figures actually submitted by the squadron for expenditure of RPs and gun ammunition in December 1949 were 436 and 14,508 respectively. Compared to the number of operational sorties flown that month, both of these figures are too large to have been correct and probably reflected all of the ordnance expended, including that fired on training sorties. The figures entered above are estimates based on the average contemporary rate of operational expenditure. There is some evidence to support the contention that the squadron was reporting incorrect figures at about this time as AHQ Malaya admonished the squadron for submitting excessively high returns for gun ammunition in February 1950; the figures tabulated for February have been taken from the revised return which was resubmitted in arrears.
3. Although the number of sorties flown in January and February 1950 can be established, no figures are available for weapon expenditure other than for gun ammunition. For these two months the figures presented for bombs dropped and RPs fired are estimates based on average rates of consumption while those for gun ammunition are the actual totals divided proportionally between the two aircraft types.

Annex H. A personal account of No 45 Sqn's final desert deployment, 26th January-5th February 1942.

The following account was written by Sqn Ldr (later Gp Capt) Arthur Hughes DFC while attending the Joint Services Staff College at Latimer and is dated 26th January 1950. It is reproduced verbatim:

"The ability to muddle through has long been a British boast but one which the increasing complexity of modern warfare is rapidly rendering unreliable. Personal participation in one unsuccessful improvisation brought home to me forcibly that unless sufficient attention is paid to the administrative factors a unit cannot function effectively.

My unit, a light bomber squadron equipped with Blenheims, was withdrawn to the Delta in mid-January 1942 to be re-equipped prior to leaving for Burma where the Japanese, in the unlikely event of the fall of Singapore, might prove something of a nuisance. About a week later, at half-past nine in the evening, I received instructions from the CO to collect twelve complete crews and report with them by ten o'clock. The location of 36 officers and NCOs on the loose in Cairo presented something of a problem, but a judicious use of applied psychology and some rapid walking enabled me to round them up from the Continental, Groppi's and Tommy's Bar, and we duly assembled in the lounge of the Hotel de Paris.

The news that Rommel had attacked and driven our forces from Benghazi was received with equanimity, rudely shattered when the CO explained that the squadron was to assist in holding his advance by sending a detachment back to the Desert as 'tank-busters', with fighter Blenheims mounting one 20mm cannon and five machine-guns.

That no pilot had received any instruction, let alone practice, in the technique of ground strafing appeared to leave the authorities unruffled. To deepen our gloom, only a nucleus of our own servicing personnel was to be taken, and we were to depend for all other necessities on the good offices of two squadrons already located at Bu Amud which was to be our base.

Our forebodings were not lessened next day when, arriving at Wadi Natrun to collect our twelve "new and operationally serviceable" aircraft, we found them to be battered, dirty and suffering from prolonged exposure to wind and sand. Selecting those which appeared least likely to let us down, we set out in two flights for Libya. The lack of adequate meteorological facilities (normal at that period) nearly led to immediate disaster as the forward areas proved to be covered by an extensive sand-storm, and I barely succeeded in leading my flight back to Ma'aten Bagush before petrol ran out. Of the other flight, one aircraft

Arthur Hughes' Z6094, one of the squadron's cannon-toting Blenheims. (Mrs Daphne Hughes)

Left to right: Plt Off Lin Durrant, Sqn Ldr Arthur Hughes and F/Sgt David Cliffe. The picture was taken circa November 1941 in front of V5967/V, which was not one of the cannon-toting Blenheims. (Mrs Daphne Hughes)

returned to Wadi Natrun with elevator flutter, one made a forced landing at an airfield en route with engine trouble, one crashed at Bu Amud where the pilot was compelled by engine failure to attempt a landing, and one made a precautionary landing beside the coast road owing to petrol shortage.

Two days later, by which time eleven aircraft had gathered at Ma'aten Bagush, the sand cleared and we left for Bu Amud. Wing Headquarters, who had expected a fully operational fighter squadron ready to be thrown immediately into the fray, were no little perturbed to receive nine aircraft (two had been unable to get off from Ma'aten Bagush) manned by bomber crews and showing symptoms of advancing senility such as defective instruments, leaking hydraulic and pneumatic systems, flat accumulators, and high oil consumption. Moreover, although the aircraft bristled with a ferocious display of guns, it was found that neither the special tools nor experienced armourers for the maintenance of the cannon were available. Hurried consultations produced the promise of tools by the next day, and a 48 hour training period was arranged after which we were expected to find no more difficulty in picking off tanks than clay-pigeons.

Messing and accommodation presented few difficulties, thanks to the whole-hearted co-operation of our sister squadrons. In the provision of tools, equipment and spares, however, they were able to offer less assistance, owing to shortages and to preoccupation with their own intensive operations. We succeeded in 'scrounging' two 30 cwt Chevrolets of doubtful reliability and an Italian lorry and were able by this means to transport our fuel and ammunition. Next day we set out to learn the new role assigned to us, using burnt-out MT on the Trigh Capuzzo for targets; results were disappointing, as on three aircraft none of the guns would fire and only one cannon fired 6 rounds and then jammed.

A lecture on the art of ground strafing by a fighter expert improved our theoretical competence, but practical efficiency did not follow. We continued our determined assault on the fortunately inoffensive relics of recent battles but despite the utmost efforts of our technical personnel no cannon could be induced to fire more than 6 rounds in any one sortie. Common sense dictated the view that .303 machine guns would be ineffective against tanks, and operational employment was therefore postponed. On 1st February came the order for the three squadrons to retire to a landing ground south of Sidi Barrani.

Despite our ineffective armament, however, we were ordered to remain at Bu Amud on stand-by lest the situation should become desperate. Unfortunately the authorities appeared to have over-looked our administrative dependence on the other squadrons: we were left for nearly 24 hours after their departure without rations or water, spares or fuel (other than that already in the tanks) before we too received instructions to leave. Our departure, as our arrival, was shrouded in sand and all but three aircraft failed to locate the right landing ground and came to earth at various airfields between there and the Delta. Needless to say the landing-ground proved to be devoid of any facilities, and food and accommodation could only be had by a two mile walk through the sand-storm to a neighbouring strip. Our ground party arrived next day, the Italian truck towing one of the Chevrolets which had given up the ghost.

At this new location, even graver difficulties were encountered. Only one squadron was now based with us at LG 76, and their resources were inadequate to meet all our needs in addition to their own. We were moreover further from the rations, ammunition and petrol dumps than we had been and this meant increased demands on the limited MT available to them. Naturally enough their own requirements received priority and Wing Headquarters began, under pressure of urgent representations by our Detachment Commander, to appreciate that in these conditions we could never become an effective fighting force. Whether some inspired solution would have been found to turn this fiasco into triumph I do not know. The problem was fortunately resolved by a "Deus ex Machina" in the shape of our squadron commander who arrived bearing orders from Headquarters Middle East for our immediate withdrawal. We left on 6th February[1]; on 9th February the first echelon set course from Helwan for Burma.

Those members of the squadron who had taken part in this abortive operation congratulated themselves on this release from chaos. In the light of subsequent experience, these congratulations were perhaps premature.....but that is another story."

Note:

1. Although Sqn Ldr Hughes noted February 6th as the date of the detachment's return to Helwan in this post-war account, it would seem that, as with most unit deployments it actually took place over several days. For example, while Hughes' log book records his own flight back as having been made on February 5th, Sgt McDade, who flew with the CO, notes the return trip on the 6th. Some crews, for instance those of Plt Off Eve and 2/Lt DeMarillac, did not leave LG 76 until the 7th. The squadron's ORB, which makes only brief reference to the detachment, records its return to Helwan on the 7th, which was presumably the date of the return of the last stragglers.

Annex I. Two first hand accounts of the loss of Blenheim Z9799 on 11th March 1942.

In Melbourne on 28th May 1945 Flt Lt D A Golder was debriefed on his wartime experiences by Flt Lt N K Welsh at HQ Southern Area RAAF. The following passage, which reads as if it was taken down in shorthand and then typed more or less verbatim, is extracted from the report which resulted:

"On the 11th March we were not needed by the AOC so the CO briefed us for a low level reconnaissance of Nyaunglebin, Daik-U, Kaywe and Myitkyo for enemy troops on the move, and if we saw any, we had orders to strafe them.

We saw quite a lot of Japanese troops on the move and strafed them. We then carried out a reconnaissance of the various places, and then we decided to go back to the first place - I cannot recall the name but they were all together - and see if there were any more troops because they had scattered when we had started strafing them. Suddenly we saw a lot more Japs on the road and we began strafing them. Then there was a yell over the inter-com, "I'm hit." I was in the nose of the Blenheim at the time, strafing some Japanese troops on the Nyaunglebin-Daik-U road, and we were only 50 feet high. I rushed to the pilot who was flopped over the controls, apparently trying to hold them. I made a dive and pushed the stick back as we were going 'down hill' rapidly. As it was we nearly hit the trees. I don't know why we didn't.

I yelled out through the inter-com to the gunner to come as the pilot was shot. The opening between the turret and the pilot's cabin is very narrow but within a minute, Alt had managed to get through. That in itself was a good feat. He lifted the pilot away from the controls and I got into the seat.

I had done no piloting other than nine hours as an air cadet in a Moth. At the time Smythe[1] was shot, we thought he had been a victim of fighters - at least I did - so I concentrated on getting away, so for the next 20 minutes I flew due north for roughly 50 miles. Then we began to realise that it was ground strafing that had killed the pilot. During this time we had been flying due north so obviously no navigation had been done, and we only had a rough idea where we were.

I reckoned that if we turned west we must hit the Irrawaddy River so we turned west. We were then flying at about 1,000 feet and we suddenly found that ahead of us were mountains 3,000 feet high, so we had to spend half an hour gaining height. Not knowing enough about flying, I would nearly stall the aircraft trying to gain height, and then have to put the nose down and lose a lot of the height we had gained.

At this stage Alt realised that Smythe was dead - he had examined him and told me he was dead - so he took up a map and tried to do some navigation. When we reckoned we

On 11th March 1942 this RAAF crew was flying an operational sortie in Z9799 when it was hit by fire from the ground. The pilot, Sgt Douglas James Smyth, seen here on the left, was killed. The observer, Sgt Denys Golder (centre) and WOp/AG, Sgt Jeff Alt (right) managed to fly the aeroplane back to Magwe where they dropped their pilot's body by parachute before baling out themselves. This picture was taken at Nakuru in October 1941. (J J Alt)

were high enough to get over the hills we turned west for the Irrawaddy. We passed over some of the hills with two feet to spare and finally came across the Irrawaddy and followed it up to Magwe.

When we got to Prome, Alt took over the controls - the only piloting he had done was on the way out from Cairo when the pilot had given him an hour at the controls - so that I could write out a report of the trip. At that stage we intended attempting to land the aircraft, and we realised that we might get 'wiped off' but we wanted them to have a report of the trip. At the end of the report I said that if they did not want us to land but to bale out, to fire a red Verey light, but if it was OK to attempt to land, to fire a green Verey light.

On reaching Magwe, I took over the controls and dropped the report from about 1,200 feet. This was too high to drop a message, but because of my inexperience of flying, I was not prepared to go low. Although I was inexperienced I know I could have got the aircraft down. We would have landed with the wheels up. I could see some DCs lined up for evacuees, and it is difficult for an inexperienced man to prevent an aircraft from swinging. A DC was worth three Blenheims and it was better to wipe off a Blenheim than a DC.

We circled for a long time and there were some of our own fighters in the air. We waited for the message in reply to our report but did not get one, so dropped another repeating the former message. Some time later we received a red Verey light which we understood to mean bale out. It transpired subsequently that the red Verey light indicated that we were to wait until the Hurricanes had landed. Not until the next day did they pick up our message which had drifted a couple of miles away.

We then went up to 7,000 feet and I told Alt to tie a rope on the ripcord of the pilot's 'chute and drop him out through the main hatch. We did this so that the body could be retrieved rather than leave it in the aircraft. Accordingly, Smythe's body was released through the front hatch, and when it was examined by the squadron medical officer, he confirmed our belief that death had been instantaneous when Smythe was shot. Smythe did not utter another word after he had called out through the inter-com, "I'm hit".

We then tied the rudder controls to ensure that the aircraft would fly well away from the 'drome before crashing. Alt then baled out and I did a circuit and watched him go down. Then I jumped and I can remember the rip-cord coming away in my hand and then there was a perfect blackout.

When I regained consciousness, some Burmese had me and were giving me a drink of water. I had landed in the main street of a native village some three miles from the aerodrome.

The CO (W/Cdr Wallis) arrived half an hour later and took me back to the camp in a Jeep. Large bruises under the chin and a very stiff neck suggested that I had been rendered unconscious by the opening of the 'chute. I was kept in hospital for a night for observation whilst Alt was interrogated and commended by General Alexander, General Officer Commanding 14th Army[2], who had witnessed the baling out.

When Alt was about 500 feet from the ground, our aircraft, which had gone into a flat spin when abandoned, was going straight for him, and that, he told me was the worst part of the whole trip. The aircraft crashed 500 yards from him and he landed three miles from the aerodrome."

Nearly half a century later, on 15th September 1993, J J Alt provided the following recollection of the same incident:

"In order to get to the front of the plane from the turret, I had to divest myself of my parachute harness to squeeze through over the bomb well. Doug Smythe had died instantly, so it was with great difficulty that I managed to get him from the pilot's seat, whilst Denys Golder struggled to prevent us from crashing - as it was low level recco, and we were also returning fire; the ground was very close at times. After stabilising the aircraft we flew east (sic) to the Irrawaddy, thence to Magwe. En route Golder made out a recco report - told them of our predicament - asking for a flare if they didn't want us to land. Over the runway I shot off a flare to attract attention, and dropped a recco report. During the flight back I returned to the back of the plane for my parachute harness. After baling Doug Smythe's body out of the front hatch I followed suit. Then Golder followed after seeing my chute open - we had some doubts (about them) after the treatment they had received on the way out from Egypt. It was in later years that Golder told me he intended to belly land in a paddy field had my chute not opened - I thanked him appropriately. Incidentally, Denys was knocked out when his chute opened and he landed unconscious in a native village.

Notes:

1. The pilot's name appears as 'Smythe' in the originals of both of the accounts reproduced above. Elsewhere in this book, however, it is rendered without the final 'e', which is the way his name appeared in contemporary documentation, including both Alt's and Golder's flying log books.
2. Strictly speaking Lt Gen Alexander was, at this time, GOC Burma; XIVth Army was not established until 15th October 1943.

Annex J. A personal account of two expeditions undertaken from Lashio and of the withdrawal to Myitkyina, covering the period 18th April-3rd May 1942.

To record his wartime experiences, Sqn Ldr Norman Bayly was first interviewed by Flt Lt N K Nash of the RAAF's War History Section at Asansol in April 1943. Over a three day period in April/May 1945 the process was repeated in greater depth and the original report was considerably amplified. The following extract is drawn from the final version. It has been lightly edited by this chronicler to standardise the spelling of place names.

"On the morning of 18th April, while we were at the range of the Burma Rifles practising with our pistols and .303s, I was called to the office of the CO of Burwing and detailed to make a trip, starting after lunch, in search of a forward signals unit which had been ordered to move from Namsang to Meiktila. This move necessitated their crossing the area towards which the Japanese were proceeding and no word had been received from them since they left Namsang.

I was given a Buick-8 sedan and took with me a young driver from 45 Squadron, with provisions, a tommy gun, pistol etc. We set out late in the afternoon and took the eastern road to Ke-hsi Mansam, about 75 miles away. Nothing of interest happened en route and we arrived at the Dak bungalow at about 1830 hours[1]. We endeavoured to buy some fresh food in the village, but although we knew the usual ways of approach, the feeling was decidedly against us and made us feel that we were by no means welcome. However, the bearer at the bungalow appeared on our return and soon obtained chicken, butter, and eggs for our breakfast in the morning.

Early next morning we set off again for Namsang and this route led us through hills for some 60 miles of very winding track to Loi-lem. At Loi-lem, again we found difficulty in obtaining food as nearly all the shops had been closed and what was left for sale was guarded for special use, mainly for the local people. Bananas were about the only reasonable food we were able to obtain so we continued on towards Namsang which we reached early in the afternoon. This road is one of the most winding I have ever driven over. I consider the turns were only an average of 30 yards apart for about seven miles of the route.

As a result of doing most of the driving myself, I ended up the day with corns on my hands, such as I have never known.

At Namsang, about 25 miles east of Loi-lem, we found an almost deserted aerodrome. Whilst looking for the detachment in charge of the maintenance we noticed a fighter aircraft coming over, and an AVG pilot landed and taxied up to the hangar. The maintenance crew came out to refuel his aircraft, which was a Kittyhawk, and we contacted them regarding the movement of the Signals Unit. We found that the unit had moved two days previously with the intention of spending the night at Heho and continuing on to the Meiktila aerodrome.

While we were discussing this, a Jap plane came over and we very hurriedly pushed the Kittyhawk into the hangar where I also put my car. The Jap circled several times at a considerable height and eventually made what appeared to be a photographic run before coming low to thoroughly inspect

the aerodrome. In the meantime, we took cover in the nearest slit trench anticipating a machine-gun attack, but he flew away in the direction of Heho without paying us any further attention.

The AVG pilot was very interested in what stocks of 40 lb bombs and detonators were on the drome and spoke of the AVG using this drome as an advance base. I knew nothing official of this and could not give him any satisfactory information, but made a note to pass the information on to Burwing. This drome was in excellent condition, although it had been bombed, and it seemed a great pity that we had not the aircraft to make use of it and the store of bombs and fuel located there. However, we had other worries at that time and it was not my concern.

After the usual cup of char back at the maintenance party's hut, we continued on our way through Loi-lem to Heho. This was quite a hilly drive, taking us across the Hopong Valley to Taunggyi, which, the previous day, had been raided by the Japs. We realised the futility of trying to obtain food in this area unless we could speak the language, so kept going, though it was after 2020 hours when we reached this town. About 30 miles further on we came to Heho aerodrome which we located by the Sikh guards who stopped us on the main road at 2146 hours.

I was amazed to find these Indian soldiers, for whom I always had the highest regard as well-trained men, were not only unruly and irresponsible, but several of them were drunk on duty. Possibly the recent bombing of Taunggyi had, in some way, accounted for the liquor which they had obtained but on reaching the aerodrome and expressing my views about these men, I was told that this was by no means an uncommon occurrence with these Sikhs. From further experience with Indian soldiers in India, I have come to the conclusion that these were possibly some of the hurriedly trained men which India was endeavouring to supply for her local defence.

At Heho, we found the CO at 2230 hours, and eventually had a good meal and were given accommodation for the night. I was awakened next morning, shortly after daylight, by the CO calling me by name, and upon my appearing at the end of the ante-room of the mess, he brought me to my senses by shouting, "Hurry, they're here again". I wasted no time throwing on a few clothes and rushed outside to find him waiting in a slit trench, covered all but the entrance, over which he held back a sheet of tin until my arrival. I clambered down to find a thick, muddy mess, about two inches deep at the bottom of the slit trench, and we waited for the fighters to arrive. Within a couple of minutes, three enemy fighters were shooting up the drome and for about a quarter of an hour, they continued their raid on the perimeter and billets. One small fire was started near a petrol dump but otherwise, only a few windows had been broken in some of the more permanent billets.

It was still pre-monsoon weather, but even so, the slit trenches were a most unpleasant alternative to staying above the ground, and some of the airmen had become very careless as a result of these regular morning raids having caused no casualties for some time. One airman, in particular, this

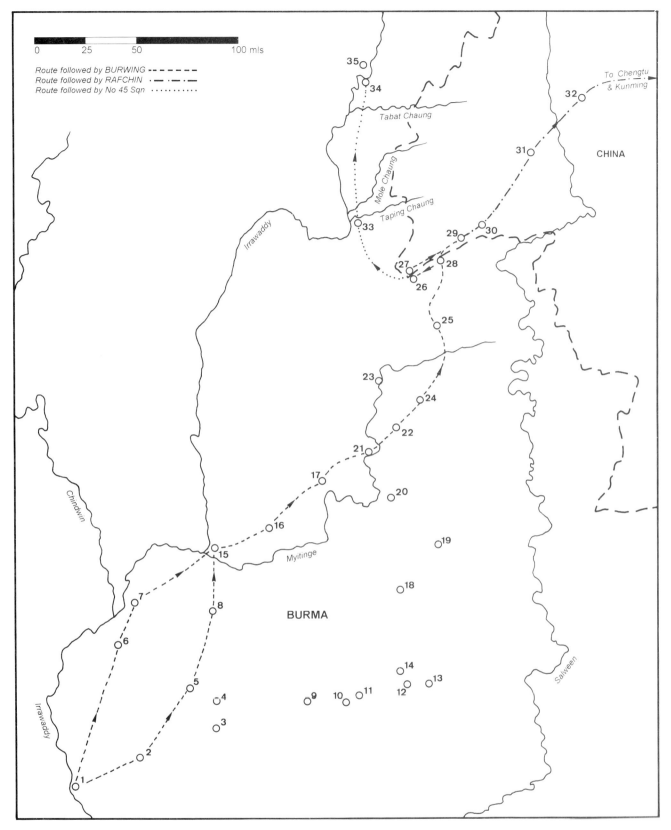

Map J.1. *Burma - the way out.*

33 Bhamo	6 Kamye	1 Magwe	35 Myitkyina	32 Pao-shan
30 Che-fang	19 Ke-hsi Mansam	15 Mandalay	8 Myittha	3 Pyawbwe
17 Gokteik Gorge	25 Kutkai	16 Maymyo	26 Namhkam	22 Se-en
2 Gwegyo	24 Lashio	5 Meiktila	20 Namlan	10 Taunggyi
9 Heho	12 Loi-lem	18 Mong Kung	13 Namsang	4 Thazi
11 Hopong	27 Loiwing	28 Mu-se	23 Namtu	34 Waingmaw
21 Hsipaw	31 Lung-ling	7 Myingyan	14 Nawngmong	29 Wan-ting

morning had remained in his billet and calmly proceeded to dress while the enemy attacked. To his amazement and good fortune, a bullet fastened the foot of his stocking, which he was putting on, to the leg of his charpoy (bed).

The fire near the petrol dump was quickly extinguished by a fire party from the camp and everything returned to normal in a very short time. However, as warning systems were absolutely nil in this area, all people moving about on any work had to do so very promptly and with a watchful eye on the horizon. This made all activity on the aerodrome extremely troublesome, in that one had to be continuously looking for cover for vehicles.

We left Heho about 0845 hours after refuelling and proceeded on towards Meiktila. All along this road, after coming out of the hills, we came in contact with small sections of the Chinese Army and as usual, we found these people looking more as though they were on a picnic than having any interest in the war. It is astounding how so many of these Eastern people appear to totally relax in every way and carry on what appears to be a normal civil life almost ten minutes after they have left an active area.

At Thazi we endeavoured to buy some food but once again it was being kept mainly for the Burmese and we were unable to succeed in purchasing anything of any use to us. The Chinese had, in many places, obtained fowls, but even these were very limited, although normally fowls are almost part of the Burmese' staple diet.

The general attitude of the people here was immediate evacuation, and the Chinese soldiers appeared to thoroughly sympathise in their attitude. It made us think several times as to the possibility of our meeting Japs before turning north at Meiktila, but although we had no definite information, we felt confident that some of the Army Headquarters was still at Pyawbwe, a few miles south of Thazi.

We proceeded to Meiktila, a town which I had previously visited on our trip north, and where I knew a few of the residents. It was a very deserted and uninviting place when we arrived there, and rather than seek assistance from civilians, I hoped to purchase some food in the town. We drove straight into the centre of the town where we were confronted by an impassable mass of rubble and bombed buildings on the intersection of five roads. Being in a large car it was much easier to continue forward, if possible, than endeavour to turn in such narrow village streets, and we endeavoured to find our way out by a narrow lane taking us away from the obstruction. The noise of the car had attracted the attention of many unseen looters who stealthily came to doorways and peered through partially open doors at the car. More by good luck than good management, the lane led us into a clear thoroughfare, and though we had the protection of the tommy gun and pistol, it was a great relief to get away from the eerie silence and most unpleasant feeling of being watched from all angles by people who were definitely not friendly.

There was no active opposition or any sign of Japanese personnel around Meiktila but our imagination was quite sufficient to cause us to make a hasty retreat towards the north.

It was quite obvious that our Signals Unit was not in the town itself and once again we headed out along the main road where the main aerodrome is situated about a mile from the town on the eastern side. At this time the strip was barely completed and could only be used for emergency purposes. We expected to find the Signals Unit close to this drome but there appeared to be no sign of life or any of our equipment around it. By this time another Jap reconnaissance plane had come over and was hovering above Meiktila as though waiting to spot some activity in the area. We parked the car under the trees on the road and waited for some time for the plane to disappear. After half an hour I decided to walk over to the centre of the strip. There appeared to be no activity whatever, not even local farming within sight, and upon returning to the car, we continued north towards Mandalay hoping to find some sign of the signals unit in that direction.

By this time - about 1400 hours - we were decidedly hungry but could do very little about it. However, about eight miles up the road we found the trailer of the unit parked on the side of the road and in contact with Burwing. A little further on, there was a Dak bungalow at which the signals personnel were living. Here I contacted their CO who immediately arranged for some food for us. I mentioned to him the enemy aircraft which was still hovering over Meiktila, and he smiled as he told me how the Japs had followed them from the time the unit left Namsang. They did not attempt to set up their unit as ordered on this new strip at Meiktila, but had stopped just outside of the town for half a day whilst scouting around for a suitable location in hiding.

The road from Meiktila up to the Dak bungalow being tree lined nearly all the way, it had given him easy cover and up to this time they had not been detected nor attacked. A u/s vehicle from a dump nearby had been pulled into the position in which the signals trailer had been standing outside Meiktila, and it seemed that the Japanese did not realise the difference.

My trip had not really been necessary, as later on in the afternoon I had left Lashio (18th April), the unit had contacted Burwing from its new position. However, I was able to collect considerable information in writing and continued within an hour towards Lashio.

At Mandalay (20th April) we found the town burnt out after its big raid earlier in the month. Actually, this raid was not so big or successful as it appeared when one saw the remains. So much Fifth Column activity had been combined with this raid that areas which were hundreds of yards away from the bombed parts were set alight almost simultaneously. Burmese were openly throwing oiled rags among the tatti and wooden huts. This was told to me by people who were in Mandalay at the time of the raid and who were evacuating north.

We did not go into the centre of the town as one could see at a glance that there was nothing to be obtained in the shopping area nor had I any other interests there. We proceeded straight on to Maymyo which we reached about 1700 hours. We had to spend the night here owing to being unable to obtain petrol immediately. The Burma Rifles Officers' Mess gave me accommodation. Although they had not actually prepared for an evacuation, they were all obviously aware that there was no alternative and that the war was now really at their front door. I say this because on my previous trip through to Lashio at the end of March, the general attitude at the Maymyo Club and amongst the few people I met was that Maymyo, being Army Headquarters,

One of the squadron's convoys climbing out of the Gokteik Gorge during the trip up the Burma Road from Magwe to Lashio. (H C Hatherly)

was at least the safest spot in Burma. Possibly the bombing of Mandalay had convinced them of similar possibilities at Maymyo and everything was definitely on a war-time basis.

After a very acceptable night's rest, we were able to get petrol early in the morning and left for Lashio about 0830 hours. We had scarcely left Maymyo when I found one of our squadron trucks on the side of the road in trouble. The repair situation of our vehicles was becoming more critical almost daily, due to the lack of spares, and we had to take the greatest care of the few vehicles we had left in good condition. In consequence, I spent most of the morning endeavouring to obtain the required parts to repair the damage and did not set out on our track to Lashio again until the afternoon.

For the second time we crossed the Gokteik Gorge, one of the most difficult parts of the road to Lashio, and which I think, is one of the most vulnerable spots of the Burma Road in Burma. From here we made good time to Hsipaw and were well on our way to Lashio when the car developed ignition trouble. It was a very unpleasant end to our trip, as after considerable urging and fiddling about with the engine on the part of my driver, who was a Fitter IIE, and myself, we spent the night in this car some 15 miles out of Lashio. About 2300 hours, a passing vehicle stopped and we sent word to the squadron headquarters, but the breakdown van did not come out until the following morning (the 22nd) when we were towed into Lashio.

On reporting to the CO of Burwing, I was told that I would, in all probability, be going south in a few days to collect petrol and small bombs from Heho. The information I brought back was of little use, unfortunately, as the signals unit had already given all that was required of the more important details. However, it was decided that we could well afford to assist the AVG with our 40 lb bombs if they required them.

On the evening of the 23rd April, it was decided that a convoy of 45 squadron vehicles should go immediately to Heho to collect 40 lb bombs and as many detonators as we could carry, to be brought back and taken north to Loiwing where the AVG were situated. Most of the aircrew of 45 Squadron were detailed to assist and a few groundstaff. Flt Lt Gardiner RAF was in charge of the convoy with Phil Graebner and myself and two other junior officers assisting. We left with about 27 vehicles soon after breakfast on the 24th April, and Flt Lt Gardiner decided to bring up the rear so as to hasten any breakdowns that might occur. I was left

in charge to carry on as far as possible that day and make camp for the night. We took the western road past Ke-hsi Mansam and continued on to Mong Kung where we stopped a while to collect the convoy together, and to eat some food.

We moved on again until we reached Nawngmong where we found a considerable number of Chinese Army people breaking camp. By this time it was after 1800 hours. As we could not find any suitable camping spot near the town, we continued on across a few miles of swampy area to the nearby hills and stopped the convoy on the first reasonably clear part of the slopes. As soon as we had settled, I sent a couple of trucks back to Nawngmong with those who wished to buy something or supplement their rations.

They returned about 1930 hours and were quite agitated as to the situation of the Japanese. In Nawngmong they had heard that the Japanese were now in the Hopong Valley which ran parallel with our road about 30 miles to the west. There was nothing authentic on which to act and I was unable to make any immediate decision as to what should be done. Phil Graebner and I discussed the matter and we were still doing so when the Maintenance Party from Heho came along the road. They had just a short time before left Loi-lem and told us that the Japanese had cut the road from Loi-lem to Taunggyi along which we would have to go to reach Heho. This confirmed the previous report, and in view of the value of our trucks which were the only reasonable means of retreat from the Japanese at any speed, I decided immediately to turn the convoy back to Lashio.

Unfortunately, at this time, Flt Lt Gardiner was somewhere north of us on the road and we could not contact him, other than by finding him. I took the risk of doing so at night and the convoy set out on its return to Lashio at 2200 hours. In the event of us missing the OC of the convoy, I detailed one party to sleep beside the road about 25 miles north of our starting point so as to stop Flt Lt Gardiner from continuing south. Unfortunately, we did miss him and he passed our rear party also with the result that he reached Loi-lem and discovered that we had not passed through that town. Fortunately Loi-lem had not fallen into the hands of the Japs nor was the road cut before he could return that afternoon (the 25th April).

We continued driving all night and I preceded the convoy to Lashio, leaving the repair lorry in charge of two of our capable NCOs to bring in any break downs. On arriving at Lashio about 0530 hours on the 25th, I counted in all but three of our vehicles by 0700 hours. The remainder came in about 0900 hours and the party left at the rear followed about midday. On my reporting to the CO, I received a very cool reception and he was considerably amazed at my return. Apparently no news had, at that time, been received at Lashio of any Jap advance north of Taunggyi, and from all information that he could gain immediately from local sources, the roads were still open to Heho and Namsang. As a result I was told immediately to collect the convoy and set out once more for Heho at 1330 hours. This was quite a problem for me as all the vehicles had been travelling all night and still the rear party had not arrived at Lashio.

However, the order was later changed in the morning to setting out at about 1600 hours and proceeding to Se-en, about 25 miles south of Lashio, on our road. Here we had petrol and bomb dumps and were ordered to collect sufficient petrol for our trip and spend the night in between Se-en and Hsipaw in the best position we could find. On arrival at Se-en, we organised a routine for re-fuelling with 40-gallon drums and had nearly completed this when I received orders by telephone from the CO to remain at Se-en and to await orders for my future movements within a few hours. While the re-fuelling was taking place, F/Lt Gardiner arrived from Loi-lem.

No further message came from the CO that night nor could I get any information from Lashio on inquiry. At about 0700 hours on the 26th April, we were told we must not proceed south but to await further orders. About 0900 hours we were instructed to load all vehicles with 40 lb bombs and detonators and to proceed to Lashio with sufficient petrol to take us on to Loiwing, a distance of approximately 120 miles through mountain country. A few vehicles went straight on to Loiwing after they had reported to Lashio, but it was soon realised that the Jap approach was too speedy for us to consider anything but our evacuation at the same time, with the result that the convoy was held up until evening when it left in charge of Phil Graebner.

At this time, most of the officers of Burwing had gone forward to Loiwing and only three of us remained in our billet that night. It was a very uneasy Mess when we sat down to dinner and it was difficult to joke about the situation which was so uncertain. An incident about which I had been doubtful on the previous evening, was confirmed when an Army officer living with us told us that two Japanese had been captured at Hsipaw. On the previous evening (25th), while we were at Se-en two trucks, which had been detailed to collect bombs lying at the Hsipaw railway station, were returning to the supply dump when two officers, who appeared to be Chinese, standing by a jeep on the side of the road, hailed them as they came along. The first truck, which was well in advance of the other, almost stopped before the driver realised that one of the officers held a pistol in his hand. On second thoughts he changed down and opened the throttle to avoid being stopped. The result was that he was fired on by these officers.

The driver of the following truck heard the shots and happened to see the activity as he was turning a corner further back, so was prepared on his arrival at the jeep. Likewise, he slowed down and on being hailed endeavoured to push the men off the road as he opened up.

Both drivers reported this with great indignation and were very annoyed at the "Chinese" taking such action. They were totally unaware of the fact that these people were not Chinese. We were shocked that these men had obtained a jeep south of Loi-lem and driven unmolested this far before running out of petrol. You can imagine our feelings with regard to any intrusion or unexpected noises around our mess on this night of the 26th April, and we went to bed with a very uneasy feeling.

In the early hours of the morning (27th April), we heard terrific explosions in the direction of Namtu where I had spent, some time previously, a very enjoyable weekend with Mr Espie, formerly of Adelaide, who was managing director of the Burma Corporation Silver Lead Mine. We had no idea of the cause of these explosions, but would have believed anything had we been told that the Japanese had done it.

The first thing we were told in the morning was that some of the bridges on the Namtu road had been demolished the previous night, and we were relieved to know that it was the work of the Allies and not the Japanese.

Hasty preparations were made for our evacuation, and I was appointed OC the convoy of as many squadron vehicles as we could make serviceable, to leave the same evening for Loiwing.

We left Lashio about 1930 hours on the night of the 27th April. The Chinese Army were digging themselves in and rumours were going about that some Japs were only a mile away from the town. The convoy consisted of two parties - the larger one comprising Burwing Headquarters, and the smaller one 45 Squadron. The CO of Burwing was W/Cdr Peter Devitt RAF[2], and the acting CO of 45 Sqn was F/O Fraser RAF and Adjutant (F/Lt Butters). The 45 squadron convoy, being the smaller, was appointed to leave from Lashio town itself so as to facilitate the order of departure. About 7 o'clock the first vehicles were sent from the camp and half an hour later I left with the last five. Our acting CO and party later left in the early hours of the morning rather hurriedly after doing demolitions.

I arrived at Lashio to find that the Chinese were guarding the entrances to the town with about half a dozen bren guns, and about two dozen soldiers with rifles, all dug in at the side of the road. The officer-in-charge stopped me at the point of his pistol and refused to let me pass. I got out of the jeep and tried to indicate that with my Air Force emblems that I was friendly and must pass, but the more I tried, the more active their fingers seemed to be around the triggers, and as their voices became high pitched, I beat a retreat as dignified as possible. I then came to the conclusion that the boys I had sent on previously had not passed this barricade so I immediately set out for Old Lashio, about a mile and a half away along the road running north, in the hopes of finding them waiting at the side of the road for me. However, I found no one of my convoy there, but there seemed to be a tremendous number of evacuees and Chinese Army people in trucks, ready to depart on the northern road, so I carried on with my five transports behind us and hoped for the best - that my convoy would be somewhere ahead as I had orders to proceed immediately.

Bit by bit, as we moved along the road, I found my vehicles held up by Army or evacuee congestion. These re-assured me that my convoy must be in front of me, so I left one of the senior Aircrew NCOs in charge of the vehicles I had so far collected, and hastened on in my jeep in the hopes of getting to the head of my convoy before it had got too far out of control.

The terrain was very mountainous, and this gave me a considerable advantage in my jeep in overtaking most of the other vehicles on the road with the result that I had picked up all but about half a dozen of the convoy of 35 within two hours.

It was an exceedingly slow trip owing to the terrific congestion in many parts of the road due to the Chinese Army trucks trying to go in both directions, and the great number of evacuees heading towards China and Northern Burma.

After we had been climbing on one particular section of road for nearly an hour, I came to a very sharp corner where one of our trucks had become stuck as a result of a case of

Some of the Burma party taking the opportunity to clean up in a mountain stream, possibly a few miles north of Kutkai on 28th April. (H C Hatherly)

condensed milk having bumped off the previous vehicle and become squashed under the wheels of the following one, with the result that it was unable to grip the road, and with each new effort to turn the corner had slid sideways towards the precipice of some 2,000 feet drop. To add greatly to this confusion, all the following vehicles for some two to three miles back were blocked on the road, various ones trying to pass others for better positions. Likewise, Chinese Army vehicles coming down the hill in the opposite direction persisted in trying to make their way past the blocked convoy.

Having a jeep enabled me to pass these vehicles on the corner and after blockading the road for some quarter of a mile further up the mountain, with the aid of torches and two or three of our Australian aircrew, we managed to indicate to the Chinese that they could not pass until the road was cleared. In the meantime, several of my senior NCOs had a party working with their hands, digging loose gravel from the sides of the hill and with the aid of many more from the following vehicles of our convoy, were able to get the three-ton wagon safely around the corner, and cleared the way making it safe for vehicles to follow on.

This was the first night out from Lashio and when we saw our milk go down, our thoughts went down too.

Anyone who has heard Chinese talking can just imagine the noise and confusion that went on when there were English speaking personnel, Chinese and Burmese, all endeavouring to explain matters to one another in their own particular tongue. This was 11 pm and we were half way up this mountain on the western side of the Shan Hills.

This holding up of the Chinese vehicles going south enabled the convoy to open out to sufficient distance to disentangle itself in the quarter of a mile road which had been kept clear of traffic.

About another 15 miles further on, outside Kutkai, we found the last of our vehicles that had preceded us, parked by a creek with all the crew climbing into bed under their mosquito nets and nicely settled for the night. When I arrived I had to make them continue their journey.

At Kutkai we found the Wing Convoy having a rest and preparing some food. At the house taken over by the CO I was instructed to carry on with my convoy immediately.

At 0030 hours on the 28th we started out again and continued until 0530 hours when most of us were too tired to continue driving. We rested until 0730 hours and moved on again to a small river where we removed most of the grime of

the previous night's trip and enjoyed quite a reasonable breakfast made from the provisions we carried.

At this stage, the convoy was somewhat broken, due to the various troubles on the road, and being ahead of the Wing convoy, we left the stragglers to follow with the aid of break-down gangs who operated at the tail of the convoys.

We continued all that day to the border of China at Mu-se when we branched off the Burma road and headed for our destination - Namhkam, which is in Burma but adjacent to Loiwing which is in China. We arrived here about 1730 hours after many stops on the road, due to having taken cover from several downpours and Japanese reconnaissance planes. We were very relieved to reach somewhere where we thought we could relax and make ourselves temporarily comfortable, but on arriving at the RAF Mess, I was instructed that I would be leaving at 2115 hours with all of our aircrew personnel who were at that time in camp, and No 17 Squadron, for Myitkyina via Bhamo. The idea was to split our squadron into two, the aircrew personnel going to Myitkyina with 17 Squadron to be flown out, and the remainder to go into China to represent the RAF there.

At this stage, we realised we would have to limit our baggage considerably, and once again, as we had at Zayatkwin, Magwe and Lashio, we discarded all we considered as surplus kit.

I slept most of the way and arrived at Bhamo in the early hours of 29th April, where we had quite a reasonable rest for some four or five hours, in a huge hall, divided into three rooms. Facilities were available here for good cooking and we had a very welcome breakfast about 0900 hours, and immediately packed up our few belongings in the vehicles and started off for Myitkyina.

As 45 Squadron section of this convoy was much smaller than 17 Squadron, consisting of about 23 aircrew personnel only, in cars and station wagons, we were granted permission to lead the convoy, after having made very slow progress in our position in the convoy up to the first bridge, about 20 miles out from Bhamo. This gave us the advantage of considerable speed over the others, and as a detachment of the convoy we remained ahead of them, reaching the Irrawaddy River at Myitkyina a good 24 hours in advance of them on 1st May, a total travelling time of four days from Lashio.

This route took us through considerably hilly country over roads which could scarcely be called tracks in many parts, and which wound precipitously around jungle clad slopes with only sufficient room for one way traffic.

By this time, the pre-monsoon storms had thoroughly soaked the ground, although fortunately insufficient rain had fallen to raise the level of many of the tributaries of the Irrawaddy. Climbing the hills was as much good luck as good judgement, and on many occasions it was a case of a wild scramble to stop a car from skidding over the side of the road or to help it up a hill when the rear wheels could not grip sufficiently to stop sliding backwards. The tyres on our wagon were desert tyres which would not grip muddy roads.

In the light of evacuation this was not exactly a picnic, but nowhere did I see any panic nor did the general spirit of the fellows become depressed in any way when obstacles appeared unsurmountable at the moment. It is amazing what ingenuity can come from such difficulties. It was most

Local labour at work on the bridge over the Mole Chaung, trying to free the truck which had gone through the decking, while others were mobilised to reinforce the causeway; a truck can be seen climbing out of the river on the far bank

The bridge over the Mole Chaung after traffic had begun to flow again. (H C Hatherly)

noticeable that the Australians almost invariably were first with practical ideas and had their hands on the job.

This brings to my mind the tremendous feeling of assurance I had in depending on several of our Australian senior NCOs, in particular the late Col Levings and his crew colleagues, Fos Shattock and Peter Hatherly, although it seems unfair to single out any particular individuals when I consider the excellent work done by the others. On one occasion, Ern Hallett and a colleague went forward into Myitkyina, went round the place and bought several dozen loaves of bread at about 9d each and 4x6x2½ inches in size and then raced back to the convoy to deliver this food. However, the whole lot worked as a grand team and all took their opportunities of displaying initiative and resource-fulness.

On the second night out from Loiwing (29th April), we found a Dak bungalow empty. This bungalow had a couple of bedrooms and was principally for the use of Government officials and for Europeans travelling around the country. We slept in the bungalow and its environs and in the motor vehicles, and were glad of protection against the rain which fell during the night.

As we had been carrying almost all our food with us, we had no fresh meat or vegetables, so two of the party set out in a 7-seater Austin in the dark in search of any fresh food that might be available in the nearby village. After waiting for about three-quarters of an hour in vain, we sent out a search party to hasten matters. Much to our regret we found that the Austin had broken a front axle on a caved-in culvert across the road, and we had to abandon the car when we left in the morning. This seriously increased our load in the remaining vehicles and once again we reluctantly parted with a few more of our valued possessions.

We pushed on early in the morning (30th April), making slow progress owing to the number of bridges which were almost in a state of collapse, or having to make detours through fords to avoid those which had already collapsed. After what seemed quite a long journey, but which was actually only 30 miles or less, we came to a long line of cars parked on the road. We pulled up behind them and walked along the road for some half a mile past vehicles of all sorts with evacuees - British, Indian and Burmese - all living beside their vehicles on the road, until we reached the head of the column which was at the edge of a river. In front of us was a typical native-built bridge which had collapsed in one section

under the weight of an overloaded truck which was still half way through the decking of the bridge. No one was doing anything about repairing it at the time, but we discovered that a party of Chinese had been engaged to effect repairs. This was about midday and some people on the road had been living there for the past five days.

Prospects of having to do likewise did not appeal to us so we endeavoured to hasten repairs by approaching the supervisor of the Chinese gang. Once again, the language question was rather difficult, and though we had very good and earnest intentions, we could do nothing but sit down and wait for the "East" to take its time. Fortunately for us, all preparatory arrangements had been made. The offending vehicle was removed that afternoon and the new timber hauled onto the bridge for the reconstruction, with the result that we were only held up until the following afternoon.

We came back from the bridge to our cars to prepare some food. Somebody had already thought of this idea and not knowing how to cook rice, had half filled a petrol tin with the grain and added water for cooking. In about 20 minutes boiled rice was being supplied to anyone in the neighbourhood who would accept it, and still the tin seemed to be full. However, we were very grateful for something to eat, and with a few tins of fish, it made a very palatable luncheon which was eaten in drizzling rain. Towards the evening, the rain cleared off and we put out our beds on whatever flat space we could find between the vehicles and the edge of the road, usually not more than three feet away.

As far as I can remember, we all enjoyed a very pleasant night's rest until the rain awakened us about 6 o'clock in the morning when the lazy ones merely pulled their ground sheets over on top and turned over. Later in the day, we were told that it was a well known spot for hunting tigers and leopards - in fact most wild life.

As the bridge was finished about 12 noon on the 1st May, we moved off at about 1400 hours, being 60th in the line. We were across the bridge and on our way with no further incident. Once again we found that we were faster than almost all others on the road and soon reached the front line of evacuees. Rain teemed down for the rest of the day but we made fair progress up to Waingmaw on the eastern bank of the Irrawaddy almost opposite Myitkyina. We arrived there about 1900 hours and found the Dak bungalow almost

Almost the last lap - the passenger ferry across the Irrawaddy between Waingmaw and Myitkyina. (H C Hatherly)

Safe at last. Sgt Des Carew-Reid, Sgt Ken Gardiner, Sgt Albert Thompson and Plt Off Phil Graebner while away the time with a hand of cards during the train journey from Dinjan to Calcutta. (A N Huon)

filled. However, owing to the emergency, people slept on the floor in all the rooms, and with the aid of a few ground sheets which we still had, we were all able to find cover for the night.

On the 2nd May, the advance section of 17 Squadron arrived with W/Cdr Devitt[3], and we crossed to Myitkyina on the ferry, leaving all our vehicles on the eastern bank.

While waiting for the people to come off the ferry, I was amazed to still find Chinese women with their feet bound so that they wore tiny shoes only five inches long.

In Myitkyina we were told at RAF Headquarters that we had been expected there several days before, and that planes from Assam were evacuating people continually from the aerodrome.

I came out with the first party on the afternoon of the 3rd May, being flown to Dinjan, and left that night by train from Dibrugarh, nearby, for Calcutta. A few of the senior NCOs volunteered to remain behind to help control the evacuation by air, and some came out in the last British 'plane from Burma."

* * *

The 'young driver from 45 Squadron' referred to early in Sqn Ldr Bayly's account was 649123, LAC Wilde, L G. While his rank gave him a slightly different perspective, 'Oscar' Wilde's recollections of the events which occurred during their journey from Lashio to Heho and back tally closely with those of Bayly, although they were not committed to paper until many years later. The only significant difference is that Wilde remembers coming across a stranded captain of the Burma Rifles somewhere in the vicinity of Mandalay and towing his car to Maymyo for him. It was this grateful captain who provided the air force with accommodation that night in his bungalow.

As Norman Bayly suggests, the war was getting close to Maymyo by this time and expedience was evidently beginning to overcome the formal demands of protocol, even among the soldiery, and the unexpected guests had to be fed, regardless of rank. The following extract from Len Wilde's memoir adds a certain something to the foregoing:

"I had the honour to be invited to the Officers' Mess. His (the captain's) colonel greeted me and I sat down at the top end of a table bedecked with regimental silver. The only dissenter was the chief bearer, a Kachin, who hobbled around the mess on a crutch. He knew that I wasn't a pukka sahib and glowered at me for tainting his beloved mess. After dinner I excused myself as previously instructed and retired to the captain's bungalow. He'd left a bottle of gin and some limes, so I proceeded to sort that out.

After breakfast I was outside the guardhouse, waiting for my officer to appear. I sat on the verandah and my attention was attracted by about six KOYLIs who were inside making dumb smoking signs. When the guard's back was turned I skidded a packet of fags under the bars. They vanished like lightning and matches were requested. On receipt of these they all made silent salaams and I made myself scarce."

Notes:

1. A Burmese Dak bungalow was in much the same tradition as an English coaching inn or a Malayan rest house. They had originally provided shelter for travellers using a Dak route (a kind of oriental imperial pony express). Their upkeep was the responsibility of the colonial administration and in later years they continued to provide overnight accommodation for District Officers and the like as they went about their business.

2. Burwing was actually commanded by Gp Capt Noel Singer who was presumably on his way to, or already at, Loiwing by this time, leaving Wg Cdr Devitt in command of the rear echelon.

3. HQ Burwing's ORB for April 29th records the departure of No 17 Sqn from Loiwing but it does not mention Wg Cdr Devitt in this context, or No 45 Sqn; the latter is hardly surprising as most of No 45 Sqn's aircrew were only at Loiwing for a matter of hours. The ORB entry for May 1st, however, specifically states that the bulk of the party bound for India left Loiwing at 1100hrs that day commanded by Wg Cdr Devitt. They are subsequently reported as having reached Myitkyina at 1300hrs on May 4th and having been flown out that evening. It is difficult to rationalise these reported movements with Sqn Ldr Bayly's account. It would appear either that Devitt travelled with No 17 Sqn and had therefore left Loiwing two days before the ORB specifically states that he did, or that he made extraordinarily good speed and reached Myitkyina in a little over 24 hours (and two days ahead of the party he was commanding) or that this part of Sqn Ldr Bayly's account contains an element of hearsay or hindsight, rather than of personal recollection.

Annex K. An assessment of the Mosquito's structural problems.

Six Mosquitos, three Mk IIs and three Mk VIs, were delivered to India in April/May 1943. They were allotted to No 27 Sqn at Agartala as the first examples of the type to be issued to a squadron in the Far East. The Mk IIs were intended for "operational trials and familiarisation" while the Mk VIs were to be used for weathering trials during the forthcoming rainy season. It had already been anticipated that the casein glue normally used to bond the Mosquito's structure might not stand up to tropical conditions and in the trials Mk VIs this had been replaced by a formaldehyde adhesive. The trials were to be supervised by Mr F G Myers, DeHavilland's technical representative in India. Despite the somewhat experimental nature of these aeroplanes it was decided that the aircraft could also be used to supplement the squadron's Beaufighters on intruder operations[1]. In the event only three offensive sorties were mounted before the five surviving Mosquitos were sent to Kanchrapara where they were adapted for reconnaissance duties and issued to No 681 Sqn at Dum Dum.

Despite these aircraft having been exposed to high temperatures and humidity, no significant deterioration of the adhesive seemed to have occurred so, in August 1943, approval was given for the delivery of more Mosquitos to India. The PR aircraft were concentrated in No 684 Sqn, which formed at the end of September 1943, and the Mosquitos proved to be so effective and trouble-free that, by January 1944 the Air Ministry was planning to equip no fewer than twenty-two bomber and strike squadrons in the Far East with Mosquito VIs, using them to replace Vengeances and some Beaufighters[2]. DeHavillands were accordingly instructed to begin the manufacture of replacement airframe components at Karachi.

No 1672 (Mosquito) Conversion Unit was established at Yelahanka in early 1944 to introduce the type into service in the attack role. No 45 Sqn was the first operational unit to be re-equipped, flying its first operational mission on 28th September. No 82 Sqn began its conversion in July and No 47 Sqn in October with Nos 110 and 84 Sqns following a few weeks behind and it appeared that No 684 Sqn's effort was going to produce a record photographic coverage in November. The type's prospects were thus looking very bright when all Mosquito flying in India came to an abrupt stop following a series of fatal accidents.

On September 13th the crew of HP886, a Mk VI of No 82 Sqn, had been killed when their aeroplane crashed while making dummy attacks on another aircraft; the CO thought that a gluing fault might have caused a failure of the wing or tail[3]. Then, on October 4th, the wing leading edge of one of No 45 Sqn's Mosquitos began to buckle in flight, although Sqn Ldr Bourke RAAF was able to land safely. On October 10th, HX821 crashed near Bishnapur killing the pilot, Flt Lt Campbell RCAF, and No 143 RSU's Chief Technical Officer, Flt Lt Rimmel.

Sqn Ldr C J Chabot was despatched from HQ Base Air Forces South East Asia (HQ BAFSEA) on October 11th to investigate the recent spate of accidents. On the 20th two more Mosquitos crashed with the loss of four more lives; HP919 of No 82 Sqn lost a wing while on a practice bombing sortie from Ranchi and No 45 Sqn's HP921 broke up over Kumbhirgram. Pending a diagnosis of the problem, flying was suspended the following day. Mr Myers was already studying the available wreckage and he arrived at Kumbhirgram on 23rd October to inspect No 45 Sqn's aircraft. An initial analysis indicated that the accidents had been caused by glue failure; it was believed that within the wings of aircraft which had been parked in the open, "extreme heat has caused the glue to crack and the upper surface to lift from the spar"[4]. It soon began to become apparent, however, that the adhesive was not the real cause of the trouble. Worse, it would also emerge that the problem was not confined to India.

As early as March 1944 production of the first batch of Australian-built Mosquitos had been disrupted when it was discovered that some components of the wing's internal structure were failing to mate. Gaps had appeared in the glued joints between the main spar and the plywood skin and, under flight loading, the upper surface could become completely detached, leading to the potential collapse of the box-section spar assembly. The first fifty sets of wings had to be modified, delaying the aircraft's entry into service by several months[5]. In the UK a series of fatal flying accidents between 5th April and 30th October, involving eighteen Mosquitos of various marks, had also been attributed to failure of the wing structure[6]. Furthermore HQ No 8 Group had expressed concern over nine accidents in a ten-week period in June-September, some of these also being put down to wing failures.

In an initial report dated 26th October 1944, Myers noted that his examination of the wreckage of HP919 had indicated that the front spar had "broken away clean at the scarfe (*sic*) joint adjacent to the fourth rib from the wingtip. On careful examination it was discovered that there was no evidence of any glue on either of the surfaces of the scarfe (and that) further examination of the parts of this wing have shown that there is a very great lack of glue in many places....in some cases leaving a gap of up to 0.25 inches." Examination of another aircraft, HP976, again revealed, "no evidence of any glue between the spar sections."[7]

On completion of its initial investigation into the spate of local accidents HQ BAFSEA reported their findings to the Air Ministry in signal T.397 which was released on 28th October 1944[7]. The main conclusions were that there had been failures of glued joints between the spar web, the spar boom and the packing block on the front mainplane spar and further failures of a glued joint in the top boom splice at Rib 12. Other problems were identified with tailplane structures, particularly in the vicinity of the elevator hinge attachments. Eight of the eighteen Mosquitos held by No 45 Sqn had been found to be defective. At this early stage the incidence of failures appeared to be most common with aircraft which had undergone a prolonged period of outdoor storage in India.

This last observation suggested that there might be some justification for believing that the glue had broken down under tropical conditions, a possibility that had been feared ever since the Mosquito had first been introduced in India and the experience of No 45 Sqn while it had been at Dalbhumgarh had provided some support for this theory. The squadron's Training Report for June 1944 had complained that, "A great deal of trouble was experienced with wood shrinkage due to heat and every aircraft had to have its control surfaces checked and the main connections to the spars connected up." But was shrinkage pulling the components apart or a lack of glue allowing this to occur? Myers had little doubt that it was the latter. He had refined his initial report but in a letter to BAFSEA dated 31st October he still maintained that "...there was no trace of cement on either of the surfaces forming the splice", and that, "the whole of the structure examined showed a general low standard in the quality of the cementing."[7]

On November 1st the text of BAFSEA's signal of 28th October was relayed to DeHavillands from the Ministry of Aircraft Production (MAP) with a request that DH's representative visit No 45 Sqn and make his own inspections. The MAP convened a meeting in London on November 2nd to discuss the problem but there was insufficient data available to draw positive conclusions. It was agreed, however, that there was cause for concern over quality control at Standard Motors, who had built the wings of the aircraft exhibiting the defects. On November 4th Myers submitted a report on No 45 Sqn's HP914 which had been dismembered for inspection. This report again included observations such as "no cement or adhesion" between certain components.[7]

Meanwhile Myers had been inspecting other aircraft in India and on November 5th he sent BAFSEA a further report (originally including photographs which are, unfortunately, no longer on file) on a number of other aircraft which had been opened up. Several of these had been in India for only a few weeks yet they already displayed deficiencies similar to those which had crashed. This tended to undercut the theory that the problem was due to lengthy tropical exposure and thus strengthened Myers' contention that the wings were inadequately constructed in the first place. To settle this point, the oldest Mosquito wing in India had been examined. This belonged to HJ730 which, as one of the original six aircraft delivered in April/May 1943, had been in use more or less continuously with Nos 27, 681 and 684 Sqns ever since it had arrived. Myers reported that this machine was "in perfect condition throughout", and therefore concluded that the problem "could in no way be attributed to weathering conditions in this Command, but only to faulty workmanship in the original manufacture of the components."[7]

BAFSEA released a further signal to the Air Ministry on November 8th reporting that all aircraft that had been in India for more than three months had now been inspected. All but one of the twenty-four aircraft involved had been found to have a defective splice, ie the scarf joint, adjacent to Rib 12. Two days later another signal was released grounding all Mosquitos in India pending further inspections. The effects of this were far-reaching. The planned manufacture of components at Karachi was stopped and the ACSEA re-equipment programme, which was just beginning to gain momentum, was suspended. DeHavillands, still maintaining that the failures in India resulted from climatic conditions, ordered the destruction of components bonded with casein glue. BAFSEA sent a further message to London on the 13th, listing the serial numbers of the twenty-three defective aircraft[7]. Curiously this included HJ730, to which Myers had given a clean bill of health only a few days before. It began

to appear that, apart from there still being different interpretations of the cause of the problem, there were also differences of opinion as to what precisely constituted a defective wing.

No 684 Sqn evidently had no doubts about the reason for the grounding. On 12th November 1944 their diarist wrote: "Section of wingtip splicing on some aircraft found to be defective due to inferior workmanship at the factories producing these components."[8]

Early conclusions, that the faults occurred only with Mk VI wings built by Standard Motors at Canley, soon proved to be premature and a further signalled report to the Air Ministry, released by BAFSEA on November 17th, listed more aircraft with a wing fault adjacent to Rib 12, about six feet in from the wingtip[7]. This list covered Mk IIIs, VIs, IXs and XVIs, and included some which had been built by the parent company at Hatfield.

Led by Major Hereward DeHavilland, the manufacturer's investigation team arrived in India from the UK on November 26th. A week later they concluded that the accidents were not caused by deterioration of the glue but by extensive shrinkage of the airframes in monsoon conditions, but Chabot and Myers remained convinced that the problem definitely arose from faulty manufacture. Myers signalled, "Defects not due to climatic conditions. The standard of gluing leaves much to be desired."

On the day that Major DeHavilland's team had reached India, HQ BAFSEA signalled a situation report to the Air Ministry from which the following is extracted[9]:

> You will by now have received a signal from this HQ explaining briefly the reasons for grounding Mosquitos. There are, unfortunately, at the present time rumours going around various units that large numbers of Mosquitos have broken up. The facts concerning the Mosquito are set out below:-
> There have been three serious accidents attributable to faults in the wing spar manufacture. It cannot be definitely stated that these are due to faulty manufacture or to glue deterioration but the evidence goes to show that there are errors in the shaping of the wood making up the spar assembly. A common fault running through one series of Mosquitos coming mainly from one factory is that pieces of wood are so shaped that, when assembled, essential elements do not make surface contact and no adhesion takes place. Ban on flying Mosquitos will be lifted when we can be certain through which series the fault runs.

By late November there appear to have been at least five possible explanations under consideration: deterioration of the glue; lack of glue; wood shrinkage; incorrectly shaped components and, as an outsider, insect infestation. There were signs of a broad dispute emerging between the manufacturers, who favoured an environmental explanation, and the RAF in India who, initially at least, tended to accept local advice that the aircraft were inadequately constructed.

On December 4th the Chief Technical Officer (CTO) at Air HQ India prepared a lengthy and measured appreciation of the problem of wooden aircraft (not only Mosquitos) in India and sent it to the MAP[10]. He first explained that there had been early concern about the effects of "decay, fungus (*or*) bugs" but then went on to write: "I think we have formed a false idea of how wooden aircraft stand up to the Indian climate. Reports on Mosquitos and gliders give an optimistic picture." He went on, however, to consider the effects of damp and painted a pretty gloomy picture: "In general the condition of all types I have examined is alarming, and I think the RAF will need all the help either we or the constructors can give them if they are to maintain a reasonable standard of serviceability on any wooden aircraft in this theatre." In the specific case of the Mosquito, he went on to summarise the faults found in India on all available variants up to the Mk 32, identifying two main types of serious defect. One concerned the scarf joints, the other the failure of the joints between the spar edge booms and various plywood members, including the wing skin.

The CTO recognised that in the case of the scarf joints, while there had been some deterioration of the glue and/or wood shrinkage, neither of these was the root cause of the problem which was due solely to "faulty assembly". Some 75% of the aircraft inspected in India had exhibited this defect and it was anticipated that it would found to be equally prevalent among those in the UK. On the other hand it was acknowledged that Major DeHavilland had succeeded in convincing all concerned that this defect was probably not as critical as had initially been thought.

The second problem concerned the adhesion between the spruce spar booms and various plywood components. Although there was some evidence of inadequate gluing in these cases, which were far less prevalent, it was concluded that the cause was "probably due to swelling of the top skin" causing the securing screws to pull through.

On balance it now appeared, in the case of the Mosquito, that both the manufacturer and the weather had contributed to the failures but it was now beginning to be appreciated that, in the latter case, the shrinkage which had led to separation of components was not so much a cause as an effect; the real damage mechanism was swelling.

Apparently acting on this information, the MAP issued a Servicing Instruction to all Mosquito operators on December 6th calling for the wing skins to be examined for signs of lifting from the front spar adjacent to Ribs 11 and 12 on the next and all subsequent daily inspections[11]. Defford promptly reported that inspection of the six different marks of Mosquito they had in service, all built by the parent company at either Hatfield or Leavesden, revealed that several suffered from "defective wing spar glued joints" (this is understood to have referred to the scarf splices)[11]. While this appeared conclusively to exonerate Standard Motors as being the sole culprits, it did little by itself to support the environmental lobby as none of these UK-based aeroplanes had been exposed to monsoon conditions, and they certainly had not been attacked by termites.

Pursuing CTO BAFSEA's forecast that defective scarf joints would be found throughout the fleet, some sixty wings in the hands of various repair contractors in the UK were examined during December. The findings were submitted to MAP on 28th December. While in some instances the joints were "not entirely satisfactory", the incidence was nothing like the 75% reported in India and there was no associated lifting of the wing skins[11]. This report, combined with that from Defford, clarified the position somewhat. The detection

of some defective scarf joints in the UK tended to confirm that there was a manufacturing problem but the much higher incidence of this fault in India indicated that environmental conditions had exacerbated it considerably. The absence of any observations on lifting skins in the UK, compared to India where this symptom was common, provided further strong evidence to support the contention that the Mosquitos' problems arose from dampness.

These emergent conclusions were confirmed at an MAP meeting on 1st January 1945 which heard an explanation of the Mosquito's defects from Maj DeHavilland who had now returned from India. He was able to report that the manufacturer had conducted strength tests on the suspect scarf joint using partially glued specimens and these had shown that the strength factor in that region of the wing was adequate; surprisingly this was even the case when *unglued* samples were tested. The more critical failures were those concerning the mutual adhesion of spar booms (particularly the front ones), spar webs and wing skins. The trouble was "attributed to water soakage in conjunction with differential shrinkage and some unsatisfactory initial gluing."

The company undertook to improve manufacturing techniques among the contractors building Mosquito components which would take care of the inadequate "initial gluing" problem entirely. The "differential shrinkage" aspect was less easily resolved. The root cause of this was considered to be the ingress of water and it had become apparent that a major factor here was the deterioration of dope and sealant on the upper surfaces of the aircraft; a factor which had not been widely reported at first. Repair of defective aircraft, of which there were about fifty in India, would involve replacement of the entire front spar and leading edge assemblies. Prevention of future occurrences was to be achieved by applying a plywood strip spanwise along the entire wing to seal the whole of the upper skin joint which ran the length of the front spar. This was subsequently introduced as Modification (Mod) 638. Surprisingly, since it altered the aerofoil section, Mod 638 appears to have had no adverse effect on either performance or handling. Finally, to improve the protective finish further, Major DeHavilland reactivated an earlier proposal that reflective silver paint be introduced. Although this had previously been ruled out on tactical grounds it was agreed that the suggestion would be re-examined and on 14th February 1945 a silver finish was authorised for all Mosquitos based in India.

In the meantime No 45 had been issued with new aircraft and had resumed operations in early December, being joined by No 82 Sqn before the end of the month. At the same time the stalled re-equipment programme was restarted, Nos 47, 84 and 110 Sqns eventually joining the Mosquito force a few weeks before the fall of Rangoon. ACSEA's original plans for the large-scale introduction of the Mosquito had lost too much momentum, however, and although Nos 89, 176 and 211 Sqns also converted to the type they did not become operational until the war in Burma was virtually over.

The Mosquito remained in service in the Far East after the war and Nos 47, 82, 84 and 110 Sqns all saw some action against Indonesian nationalists in the Dutch East Indies in 1945-46, but operations were hampered by the discovery of further faulty wing structures. Plagued as it was by periodic groundings and flying restrictions, the Mosquito was now of doubtful value and before the end of 1946 the type had been withdrawn from service in the attack role in the Far East. Ironically its successor was to be the Beaufighter, the type which the Mosquito had been intended to replace.

DeHavillands had, at first, been understandably reluctant to acknowledge that their construction techniques were lacking but there seems little doubt that this had been the case in 1944, although this was a problem of quality control rather than a fundamental fault in the Mosquito's design and seems in any case not to have been critical. There is little reason to doubt, however, that the aircraft's greatest deficiency was the inherent inability of its wooden structure to stand up to the demands of the tropical climate and it appears to have been impossible to make the aeroplane waterproof. While Mod 638 may have been sufficient to keep the rain out in Europe, continuing post-war problems with late-build Mosquitos would indicate that it evidently failed to do the job in southern Asia.

With the advantage of hindsight an additional contributory factor suggests itself. It seems likely that the inherent tendency for the integrity of the Mosquito's wing to become degraded under tropical conditions was exacerbated by the stresses imposed by low-level attack operations. This conclusion is based on the fact that, although inspection of No 684 Sqn's reconnaissance aircraft had revealed that they were suffering from the same defects as the fighter-bombers in late 1944, that squadron appeared not to have experienced any catastrophic failures. Furthermore, despite continuing problems with the wing structures of Mosquitos operating in the attack role in the Far East, which led to their early post-war withdrawal, the type continued to give safe and relatively trouble-free service with No 81 Sqn, which operated Mosquitos from Singapore on (mostly) high-level PR and survey work until as late as 1955.

Having drawn this tentative conclusion, however, there must remain a lingering doubt over the fate of some of the aircraft which simply 'went missing' during the war. At the time it was naturally assumed that such losses had been due to enemy action but there is evidence to suggest that this may not always have been the case. In the course of the War Graves Commission's painstaking post-war work of locating the remains of lost servicemen and removing them to military cemeteries, two "Unknown British Airmen" were reburied in Taukkyan War Cemetery in 1953[12]. Although they could not be positively identified, the date and location of their bodies leaves little doubt that they were Fg Off E A Fielding and Fg Off R A Turton RNZAF (previously of No 45 Sqn). They had been flying a reconnaissance mission over Rangoon on 2nd November 1943 when their aircraft, Mosquito II DZ697 of No 681 Sqn, was seen to disintegrate; eyewitnesses made no observations of any enemy involvement. DZ697 had been one of the first batch of Mosquitos to reach India and, prior to being adapted for PR work, it had been one of those issued to No 27 Sqn on a trials basis. The loss of DZ697, due to what would appear to have been a catastrophic structural failure, pre-dates the general alarm over this phenomenon by a year and it must leave an unanswered question as to how many of the other Mosquitos which were reported missing actually came apart rather than being shot down.

In conclusion, while stories of the glue 'breaking down' circulated widely both during and after the war, and there was some factual basis for these, this was not the root cause of the Mosquito's problem. It is true that there were some early manufacturing deficiencies and joints did tend to come apart but the real problem lay in the swelling and/or shrinkage of the wooden structure, rather than simply inadequate adhesion - although the end result was the same. Despite the remedial action that was implemented, silver painted, late-series Mosquitos, complete with Mod 638, were still being grounded for "defective glued joints" in Singapore as late as 1954, eg VT628 of No 45 Sqn. But was it really defective glue, or a defective joint, or a well-glued well-made joint which had pulled apart through wood shrinkage? It seems evident that, regardless of the type of glue employed, the colour of the paintwork and the incorporation of Mod 638, the Mosquito was simply unable to stand up to prolonged exposure to the high ambient temperature and humidity of the tropics.

The assistance of Mr G J Thomas in compiling this account of the sometimes troubled career of the Mosquito in the Far East is gratefully acknowledged.

Notes. The last of the following references originated with the Commonwealth War Graves Commission; the others are related to files held in the Public Record Office at Kew or are drawn from *Mosquito* by C Martin Sharp and M J F Bowyer (Faber & Faber, 1967) :

1. Letter dated 2nd April 1943 in AIR23/5107.
2. *Mosquito*, page 261.
3. With hindsight it seems likely that the same thing might well have occurred in May when No 45 Sqn's HP939 had broken up at Amarda Road in very similar circumstances, costing the lives of Wg Cdr Stumm and Flt Lt McKerracher. The possible connection does not seem to have been noted at the time, however, and the original diagnosis, that an undercarriage door had come off and carried away the tailplane, does not appear to have been reviewed.
4. ORB entry for No 45 Sqn, dated 23rd October 1944, in AIR27/457.
5. *Mosquito*, page 111.
6. From a report on Mosquito accidents on file AVIA15/2605. The figures were: April - two; May - five; June - five; July - one; September - one; October - four.
7. Copy on file AVIA15/2605.
8. ORB entry for No 684 Sqn, November 1944, in AIR27/2213.
9. Copy of a letter on file AIR23/4350.
10. Report on file AVIA15/2606.
11. Copy on AVIA15/2606.
12. Graves Concentration Report BUR/140, dated 5th March 1953.

Annex L. Aircraft known to have been used by No 45 Sqn.

This Annex records all the individual airframes which have been positively identified as having been on charge to No 45 Sqn at some time.

The initial date given below is generally that on which an aircraft was taken on charge by the squadron. The final date given is that on which each aircraft ceased to be effective because it had been lost, either in combat or as a result of a flying accident, scrapped or transferred to another unit. The precision with which these dates are expressed depends on the reliability of the source from which they were obtained. From the 1950s onwards, official records (Aircraft Movement Cards) frequently note an aeroplane's disposal as being to the "Deposit Account" or "Main Base". When this occurred (perhaps for the duration of a modification programme or while repair work was carried out on-site by a contractor's working party or pending transfer of the aircraft to an MU), although the aeroplane concerned was no longer officially on charge to the squadron it may well have lingered on its dispersal or in its hangar. If such aircraft were eventually flown away the trip would often be undertaken by

a squadron pilot, so it is quite possible for flying log books to record a ferry flight, perhaps preceded by one or more air tests, in an aeroplane several weeks after the final date shown below.

It has been possible to identify almost all of the individual aeroplanes which have ever been on charge to No 45 Sqn but surviving official records do not always permit specific periods of service to be traced; this is particularly true of the inter-war period. The annotations 'in use' or 'at least' associated with the dates given below indicate that they have been extracted from documents, often Aircrew Flying Log Books, which confirm the presence of the aircraft from, to or between the dates noted, but do not necessarily reflect its entire career with the squadron.

Crew names are always given in the order: pilot; observer/navigator; gunner/signaller. Where no indication is given as to the fate of the crew it can be assumed that they survived the incident without significant injury.

Where known, an aircraft's individual identity within the squadron has been noted.

March 1916-October 1916

The aircraft listed below have all been identified as having been on charge to No 45 Sqn at some time between March and October 1916 while the squadron was functioning as a training unit in the UK prior to its deployment to France; regrettably, this list is not comprehensive.

RAF BE 2B

2179	18/4/16-5/16

RAF BE 2C

1659	in use 6/16-7/16
1761	30/3/16-?
2062	30/3/16; damaged in forced landing at Burnham Market, 25/6/16: 2/Lt Turner-Bridger
2069	30/3/16; to Reserve Aircraft Park 20/4/16
2073	30/3/16; written off 8/4/16
2081	in use 7-8/16
2712	in use 6/16
4567	in use 7/16
4473	20/4/16-?
4474	in use 6/16-8/16
5403	in use 6/16

Avro 504   All 504As, apart from 793 which was a 504D.

793	30/3/16-?
2890	30/3/16-?
4047	30/3/16-?
4048	30/3/16-?
4052	30/3/16; wrecked circa 14/4/16
4065	4/4/16-?
4066	4/4/16-?
4069	20/4/16-?
4074	20/4/16-?
4759	30/3/16-?

Bristol Scout C

5294	30/3/16; to No 1 Reserve Sqn 11/4/16

Martinsyde S.1

5442	30/3/16; wrecked circa 14/4/16

RAF FE 2B

6957	in use 7/16 (with No 64 Sqn by 9/16)

Henri Farman F.20

7408	in use 7/16
7412	in use 7/16

Sopwith 1½ Strutter

7762	22/7/16-? (went to France but not *with* No 45 Sqn)
7763	22/7/16-?
7764	22/7/16-?
7765	22/7/16-?
7774	by 12/9/16-to France with No 45 Sqn
7786	1/10/16-to France with No 45 Sqn

October 1916-September 1917

Sopwith 1½ Strutter. Fourteen of the aeroplanes listed below are annotated 'ex-UK', followed by a date. This is the date on which each of these aircraft arrived at Fienvillers; all were actually taken on charge in England a few days, or in a few cases weeks, before this, eg 7786 was collected from Farnborough by 2/Lt Cock on 1/10/16.

Between 3/6/17 and 18/6/17 the squadron was rearmed, its 110hp Clerget-powered aircraft being replaced by new ones with 130hp Clegets. The first replacement aircraft were A8272 and A8293.

Incidents noted are usually the last, not necessarily the only, identified event which occurred while each aeroplane was with No 45 Sqn. Wrecked aircraft were often rebuilt and may well have had several leases of life with this or other units. For instance, A1064, which accompanied No 45 Sqn to France, was crashed at least twice but, after being rebuilt by No 1 Aircraft Depot at St Omer, it was redelivered to the squadron on 13/4/17 and again on 5/8/17; hence its apparent longevity.

7762	7/4/17; forced to land Marckeghem, 19/4/17: 2/Lt A E J Dobson and 2/AM S Thompson
7774	ex-UK 16/10/16; wrecked, 13/4/17: Sgt E A Cook (solo)
7775	ex-UK 15/10/16; returned to No 1 AD 19/4/17
7776	ex-UK circa 17/10/16; wrecked at Bertangles 18/10/16: 2/Lts E E Glorney and J A Vessey
7777	ex-UK 14/10/16; lost 22/10/16: Capt L Porter and 2/Lt G B Samuels (both killed)
7778	ex-UK 14/10/16; wrecked 21/10/16: 2/Lts M J Fenwick and G H Bennett (both injured)

7779 circa 18/10/16; wrecked (by ?) and passed to No 1 AD 21/10/16

7780 ex-UK 14/10/16; stalled after take off Hazebrouck, 10/2/17: Lt J B Fenton and 2/Lt D B Stevenson

7782 ex-UK 14/10/16; damaged on landing, 6/3/17: 2/Lts G H Cock and C G Stewart

7783 ex-UK 15/10/16; forced to land 2 mls east of Boisdinghem, (engine failure), 8/11/16: 2/Lts H G P Lowe and W Jordan (both killed)

7786 ex-UK 14/10/16; lost 22/10/16: 2/Lts O J Wade and W J Thuell (both killed)

7788 ex-UK 15/10/16; forced to land Hazebrouck, 29/1/17: 2/Lt W O Phillips and Gnr F A R C Lambert

7789 14/11/16; lost 7/2/17: 2/Lt E E Erlebach (killed) and 2/AM F J Ridgway (POW, died of injuries)

7790 28/10/16; wrecked on landing, Ste-Marie-Cappel, 11/12/16: 2/Lts H H Griffith and W G Scotcher

7792 15/11/16; wrecked (engine failed after take off), 3/4/17: 2/Lt G B Barker (injured) and Lt A S Selby

7793 6/11/16; forced to land 3 mls south west of Poperinghe, 8/1/17: F/Sgt W G Webb and Cpl R D Fleming

7794 6/11/16; returned to No 1 AD 20/4/17

7800 16/12/16; damaged on landing, 23/3/17: Lt P T Newling (solo)

7803 3/4/17; lost 9/5/17: Lt W L Mills (killed) and 2/AM J W Loughlin (POW - wounded))

7806 circa 1/2/17; lost 6/4/17: 2/Lt J E Blake and Capt W S Brayshay (both killed)

A381 12/6/17; lost 16/6/17: 2/Lt T S Caulfield and Rfn G Edwards (both killed)

A963 7/4/17; lost 25/5/17: 2/Lts J Johnstone (wounded) and T S Millar (both POWs)

A970 28/6/17; forced to land 5 mls north east of Poperinghe, 17/7/17: Lts W R Winterbottam and C T R Ward

A977 3/7/17; forced to land near Nieppe,11/7/17: Sgt R A Yeomans and Rfn P Davis

A991 7/4/17; undercarriage collapsed on landing, 3/6/17: 2/Lt R S Bennie and Lt T A Metheral. (NB This was the fourth incident involving this aircraft since 18/5/17)

A992 7/4/17; forced to land Béthune (engine failure), 28/4/17: 2/Lt R M Findlay and 2/AM T M Harries

A996 5/8/17; forced to land near Woesten, 8/8/17: 2/Lts A Champion and H Dandy

A1004 9/8/17; fuel tank holed, forced to land Kemmel, 10/8/17: 2/Lts C StG Campbell and A E Peel (wounded)

A1008 30/4/17; wrecked 3/5/17: 2/Lt J Johnstone and Lt E F Crossland

A1013 17/6/17; wrecked on take off, 19/8/17: Lt E C Stringer (solo)

A1016 26/5/17; forced to land Kemmel, 15/7/17: Capt G H Cock and 2/Lt F E White

A1017 28/5/17; forced to land near Caestre, 15/6/17: Sgt R A Yeomans and Lt R Hayes

A1019 5/6/17; lost, east of Ypres, 16/6/17: Capt I G Elias and Rfn P C Hammond (both wounded, Hammond fatally)

A1020 5/6/17; lost 25/7/17: 2/Lt H N Curtis and Sgt W S Wickham (both killed)

A1021 6/6/17; forced to land Bailleul, 16/6/17: 2/Lt W A Wright and Lt D C Eglington

A1022 28/7/17; wrecked landing, 15/8/17: 2/Lts H M Moody and T W McLean

A1023 6/6/17; lost wheel on take off from Bailleul, wrecked on landing at base, 6/7/17: Lts R Musgrave and F C H Snyder

A1027 18/6/17; forced to land Droglandt (weather), 27/6/17: Lt G H Walker and 2/Lt J W Mullen

A1029 26/6/17; lost 7/7/17: Lts T Hewson and F C H Snyder (both killed)

A1030 21/6/17; wrecked on landing, 7/8/17: 2/Lt C M Ross and Pnr W T Smith

A1031 28/6/17; lost 28/7/17: Lt G H Walker and 2/Lt B G Beatty (both killed)

A1032 26/6/17; lost 22/7/17: 2/Lts R H Deakin and R Hayes (both killed)

A1033 23/6/17; wrecked on take off, 27/6/17: 2/Lts W E Nicholson and R Hayes

A1036 7/7/17; forced to land Bailleul, 22/7/17: Lt J C B Firth and 2/Lt J H Hartley (killed)

A1038 10/7/17; damaged on landing, 13/7/17: Lt R Musgrave and Cpl A Jex

A1044 28/7/17; damaged in combat, forced to land Bailleul 13/8/17: Capt A T Harris and 2/Lt P F H Webb (wounded)

A1048 20/8/17; returned to No 1 AD 30/8/17

A1051 16/8/17; returned to No 1 AD 1/9/17

A1053 18/8/17; returned to No 1 AD 1/9/17

A1056 7/8/17; forced to land Bailleul, 21/8/17: 2/Lt B Smith and Pte H Grenner (wounded)

A1061 ex-UK 17/10/16; lost 22/10/16: Sgt P Snowden and 2/Lt F Fullerton (both killed)

A1064 ex-UK 15/10/16; wrecked landing Bailleul, 15/8/17: 2/Lt J C Lowenstein and Lt A J F Bawden (both injured)

A1066 ex-UK 15/10/16; forced to land near Bryas, 22/10/16: 2/Lt H H Griffith and Lt F Surgey (wounded)

A1069 ex-UK 22/10/16; damaged at Clairmarais on arrival and transferred to No 1 AD: 2/Lt L F Jones and A/Cpl S Betts

A1070 ex-UK 25/10/16; forced to land Ostrohove Camp (near Boulogne), 28/11/16: Lt L W McArthur and 2/Lt J A Vessey

A1071 26/10/16; lost (Ypres moat), 11/3/17: 2/Lts H G Bowden and D B Stevenson (both killed)

A1072 12/11/16; forced to land Abeele, 6/3/17: Capt J E Mackay (OK) and 2/Lt D E Greenhow (killed)

A1074 24/1/17; lost (in flames) Halluin, 26/1/17: F/Sgt W G Webb and Cpl R D Fleming (both killed)

A1075 16/12/16; crashed Ouderdom (tail controls severed by friendly AA), 7/5/17: 2/Lt H Forrest and 1/AM F A R C Lambert

A1076 16/12/16; returned to No 1 AD 19/4/17

A1077 16/12/16; forced to land Steenwerke, 6/4/17: 2/Lt R M Findlay and Lt M Moore

A1078 11/12/16; lost 24/1/17: 2/Lt J V Lyle and A/Bdr A Harrison (both killed)

A1080 30/3/17; forced to land near Robecq, 30/4/17: 2/Lt W A Wright and 2/AM B G Perrott (killed)

A1082 9/2/17; forced to land Railway Wood (near Ypres), 11/3/17: Capt E F P Lubbock and Sub Lt J Thompson (both killed)

A1083 11/12/16; returned to No 1 AD 12/5/17 (unfit for further operational service)

A1084 11/12/16; tail partially collapsed in combat, forced to land Chateau Louvie, 9/2/17: Capt E F P Lubbock and 2/Lt F H Austin

A1086 13/2/17; crashed on landing, 28/3/17: 2/Lt H B Evans and 2/AM B G Perrott

A1092 24/3/17; wrecked on landing, 13/5/17: 2/Lt B Smith (solo)

A1093 11/3/17; lost 6/4/17: 2/Lts J A Marshall and F G Truscott (both killed)

A1095 11/2/17; returned to No 1 AD 1/6/17 (unfit for further operational service)

A1099 11/3/17; returned to No 1 AD 8/6/17 (unfit for further operational service)

A1100 16/8/17; returned to No 1 AD 18/8/17

A1925 4/6/17; lost 5/6/17: 2/Lt R S Bennie and Lt T A Metheral (both killed)

A2381 5/12/16; lost 6/4/17: 2/Lt C StG Campbell and Capt D W Edwards (both killed)

A2382 12/3/17; wrecked on take off, 21/5/17: 2/Lts B Smith and F H Austin

A2384 12/3/17; forced to land off aerodrome, 25/5/17: Lt E F Crossland and 2/Lt F H Foster

A2385 1/2/17; wrecked on take off, 12/5/17: Lt J C B Firth (solo)

A2412 18/6/17; forced to land Vieux-Berquin, 25/6/17: 2/Lt C A Hargreaves and Capt J W Higgins

A2413 21/5/17; forced to land 2 mls east of Steenevoorde, 25/5/17: 2/Lt A E J Dobson and 2/AM S Thompson

A5244 25/7/17; forced to land near Poperinghe, 11/8/17: Capt I McA M Pender (wounded) and Pnr W T Smith

A5245 13/7/17; damaged by AA, 22/7/17: Lt O L McMaking and Sgt W S Wickham

A8173 27/4/17; wrecked on landing, 3/7/17: Sgt R A Yeomans and Cpl T M Harries

A8216 6/5/17; wrecked on landing, 21/5/17: 2/Lts R S Watts and T S Millar

A8218 4/5/17; forced to land Bailleul, 27/5/17: 2/Lt C W Carlton and 2/AM W Pocock

A8220 5/8/17; returned to No 1 AD 22/8/17

A8222 28/5/17; wrecked on take off, 2/6/17: 2/Lts R S Bennie and L

M Copeland

A8223	6/5/17; forced to land near Bailleul, 4/6/17: 2/Lt A E J Dobson and Lt C T R Ward
A8225	6/5/17; wrecked on landing,12/5/17: 2/Lts W A Wright and E T Caulfield-Kelly
A8226	6/5/17; lost 27/5/17: Capt L W McArthur and 2/Lt A S Carey (both killed)
A8228	16/7/17; wrecked on landing (undercarriage damaged by AA), 28/7/17: 2/Lt M B Frew and Lt G A Brooke
A8239	1/5/17; wrecked on take off, 5/5/17: Lt W L Mills and 2/AM S Thompson
A8244	1/5/17; wrecked in collision with A8299, 12/6/17: 2/Lt R S Watt and 2/AM W Pocock (both killed)
A8246	circa 7/5/17; forced to land near Neuve-Église, 20/5/17: Capt C H Jenkins (wounded) and Lt D C Eglington
A8260	13/5/17; wrecked on landing, 26/5/17: Lt J C B Firth and 2/Lt J H Hartley
A8261	7/7/17; wrecked on take off, 7/8/17: 2/Lts S Waltho and T W McLean
A8268	13/5/17; lost 5/6/17: Sgt E A Cook and 2/AM H V Shaw (both killed)
A8269	13/5/17; forced to land near aerodrome, 5/6/17: 2/Lt R S Bennie and Lt T A Metheral
A8272	3/6/17; lost 3/6/17: 2/Lts E D Haller and F H Foster (both killed)
A8273	8/6/17; wrecked on landing, 11/6/17: 2/Lt H N Curtis (solo)
A8278	28/5/17; wrecked on landing, 21/6/17: 2/Lt M P Lewis (solo)
A8279	10/5/17; wrecked on landing, 5/6/17: 2/Lts M B Frew and M J Dalton
A8280	14/5/17; lost 5/6/17: 2/Lt B Smith and 2/AM S Thompson (both POWs, Thompson died of wounds)
A8281	12/5/17; lost 7/7/17: 2/Lt J V A Gleed and Lt J B Fotheringham (both killed)
A8282	14/5/17; wrecked on take off, 20/5/17: 2/Lts B Smith and F H Austin
A8289	18/6/17; wrecked on landing, 22/6/17: 2/Lt K B Montgomery and Lt C T R Ward
A8290	9/6/17; wrecked on landing, 9/8/17: Lts W R Winterbottom and C T R Ward
A8291	27/5/17; forced to land St-Sylvestre-Cappel, 5/6/17: Lt J C B Firth and 2/Lt J H Hartley
A8292	8/6/17; forced to land Dunkirk (weather), 4/8/17: 2/Lts A Champion and H Dandy
A8293	3/6/17; forced to land Westouter, 5/6/17: Lt P T Newling and 2/Lt W G Corner (both wounded)
A8295	26/5/17; forced to land near la Crèche, 27/7/17: 2/Lt A Champion and Lt G W Blaiklock
A8296	5/6/17; lost 7/6/17: 2/Lts A E J Dobson and G A H Davies (both killed)
A8297	12/6/17; forced to land Wormhoudt, 17/6/17: Lts R Musgrave and F C H Snyder
A8298	17/6/17; lost 19/8/17: 2/Lts C M Ross and J O Fowler (both killed - probably hit by a British artillery shell)
A8299	26/5/17; wrecked in collision with A8244, 12/6/17: Capt G Mountford and 2/Lt J A Vessey (both killed)
A8300	10/8/17; returned to No 1 AD 26/8/18
A8302	29/7/17; wrecked on take off, 31/7/17: 2/Lt M B Frew and Lt G A Brooke
A8304	17/6/17; collided with Camel B3871 on landing, 28/7/17: Capt R M Findlay and Lt G W Blaiklock
A8307	5/6/17; wrecked on landing, 9/6/17: Lts W R Winterbottom and C T R Ward
A8308	13/6/17; wrecked on landing, 16/6/17: Lt G H Walker and 2/Lt J W Mullen
A8314	11/7/17; wrecked on take off, 14/7/17: 2/Lt H D Lysons and Rfn P Davis
A8315	10/7/17; wrecked on landing, 24/7/17: Lt R Musgrave and Cpl A Jex
A8334	17/6/17; forced to land, 9/7/17: 2/Lt C M Ross (solo)
A8338	22/7/17; crashed on take off, 9/8/17: 2/Lts A V Campbell and A E Peel
A8750	9/5/17; wrecked on landing, 11/5/17: Sgt E A Cook and 2/AM E J Hale
A8766	15/7/17; fuel tank holed, forced to land Bailleul, 28/7/17: Sgt R A Yeomans (OK) and Dvr W Fellows (fatally wounded)
A8771	22/7/17; forced to land 1½ mls south east of Poperinghe,

	17/8/17: 2/Lts E J Brown (killed) and L Cann (wounded)
A8782	13/6/17; wrecked on landing,17/6/17: Lt E F Crossland and Capt J W Higgins
A8783	4/6/17; wrecked on landing, 9/6/17: Capt I G Elias and Cpl F A R C Lambert
A8788	5/6/17; wrecked on landing, 7/6/17: Lts W R Winterbottom and C T R Ward
A8789	9/6/17; wrecked on landing, 17/6/17: Capt W T Wood and L/Cpl F Russell
A8790	5/6/17; wrecked on landing, 25/6/17: 2/Lt M P Lewis and Rfn E S H Sharp
A8792	19/6/17; forced to land 1½ mls south east of Poperinghe, 5/8/17: Capt I McA M Pender and Pnr W T Smith
B2559	16/8/17; returned to No 1 AD 30/8/17
B2560	14/8/17; forced to land near Estaires, 16/8/17: Lt A T Heywood and Pte W Whittington (wounded)
B2569	10/7/17; returned to No 1 AD 23/8/17
B2576	15/7/17; lost 22/7/17: Capt G H Cock (wounded) and Lt M Moore (both POWs)
B2579	7/8/17; forced to land near Steenwerke (AA damage), 10/8/17: 2/Lt E J Brown and Pte F A Tappin
B2581	22/7/17; undershot landing, 27/7/17: Lt R Musgrave and Cpl A Jex
B2583	7/8/17; returned to No 1 AD 30/8/17
B2596	19/8/17; returned to No 1 AD 1/9/17

April-May 1917

Nieuport 20. Interim equipment only.

A6731	13/4/17; returned No 1 AD 6/5/17
A6732	22/4/17; wrecked on take off 26/4/17: 2/Lt J H Forbes and Lt E T Caulfield-Kelly
A6735	20/4/17; returned No 1 AD 6/5/17
A6736	19/4/17; damaged landing 21/4/17: 2/Lt J H Forbes (solo)
A6740	20/4/17; returned No 1 AD 6/5/17
A6741	20/4/17; returned No 1 AD 6/5/17
A6742	13/4/17; returned No 1 AD 6/5/17

July 1917-January 1919

Sopwith Camel. As with the 1½ Strutters, wrecked Camels were frequently rebuilt and reissued, eg B2379 was wrecked on 7/11/17 but, after repair, it was redelivered on 6/2/18 and flew on for another four months.

While it was stationed in Italy, the squadron's 130hp Clerget-powered Camels were progressively replaced by aircraft with 140hp Clergets. The first of the new aircraft, D1910, was received on 13/5/18 and the squadron was fully equipped with the more powerful variant by 1/8/18. In fact one or two 130hp machines lingered on until the squadron withdrew to France, eg B2430 and B6233 were taken on charge as late as 11/8/18 and 21/8/18 respectively, although their use was largely confined to training flying.

B2306	1/9/17; crashed Bailleul, 3/9/17: Lt R L Clegg (killed)
B2311	10/8/17; forced to land Poperinghe, 22/10/17: 2/Lt J E Child
B2314	10/8/17; wrecked on landing, 20/9/17: 2/Lt P Carpenter
B2320	19/9/17; forced to land, 21/9/17: 2/Lt H M Moody
B2321	1/9/17; '5'; wrecked near Zillebeke, 26/9/17: 2/Lt G H Bush
B2323	5/9/17; damaged on landing, 17/10/17: 2/Lt J R Aikins
B2327	1/9/17; lost near Roulers, 26/10/17: Lt E D Clarke (wounded)
B2328	5/9/17; wrecked on take off, 22/9/17: 2/Lt P Carpenter
B2329	31/8/17; wrecked on landing, 19/9/17: 2/Lt K B Montgomery
B2338	12/9/17; wrecked on landing, 18/9/17: Lt B R Davis
B2350	11/9/17; dived in from 3,000', 29/10/17: 2/Lt G Pearson (killed)
B2363	23/9/17; damaged by AA, 26/9/17: 2/Lt K B Montgomery
B2374	21/9/17; lost south west of Passchendaele, 26/9/17: 2/Lt C F Risteen (killed)
B2375	21/9/17; 'E'; lost near Houtholst Forest, 12/10/17: Capt H B Coomber (killed)
B2376	19/9/17; 'E'; damaged landing, 14/1/18: Lt M D G Drummond
B2379	22/9/17; returned to No 7 AP 2/6/18
B2381	22/9/17; forced to land in fog, Oost Cappel, 25/9/17: 2/Lt F A W Mann
B2382	27/9/17; lost 27/10/17: 2/Lt C I Phillips (killed)
B2386	26/9/17; lost 12/10/17: 2/Lt K H Willard (killed)
B2388	23/9/17; wrecked on take off, 29/10/17: 2/Lt G Pearson
B2393	26/9/17; 'M'; wrecked on landing, 12/11/17: 2/Lt H J Watts
B2400	circa 18/11/17 en route Italy; 'R'; wrecked in forced landing,

	25/2/18: 2/Lt H J Watts
B2426	18/1/18; 'E'; damaged on take off, 16/5/18: Lt F S Bowles
B2430	27/10/17; 'B'; to No 28 Sqn 13/9/18
B2436	7/11/17; lost 11/1/18: 2/Lt D W Ross (killed)
B2443	24/10/17; 'K'; forced to land, 15/6/18: Lt A J Haines
B2446	24/10/17; damaged on take off, 28/10/17: 2/Lt P Carpenter
B2460	27/10/17; damaged on landing, 13/11/17: 2/Lt W F R Robinson
B2494	circa 18/11/17 en route Italy; 'S'; lost (hit by artillery shell), 4/2/18: Lt D G McLean (killed)
B3755	24/7/17; wrecked in forced landing close to Ste-Marie-Cappel, 27/7/17: Lt J C B Firth
B3775	10/8/17; lost 11/9/17: 2/Lt E B Denison (POW)
B3791	27/7/17; forced to land, 9/10/17: Capt H B Coomber
B3792	22/8/17; wrecked on take off, 25/8/17: Maj A M Vaucour
B3838	31/8/17; lost 5/9/17: Lt W Shields (killed)
B3862	15/11/17; 'J'; forced to land Monastier di Treviso, 1/5/18: Lt H D O'Neill; returned to No 7 AP 6/5/18
B3863	31/8/17; lost 5/9/17: Lt A O MacNiven (killed)
B3871	27/7/17; forced to land Bailleul, 18/8/17: Maj H A Van Ryneveld (wounded) [aircraft was damaged, but remained in service until wrecked on landing by 2/Lt M B Frew 5/10/17]
B3872	1/3/18; 'A'; returned to No 7 AP 14/7/18
B3875	28/7/17; crashed on landing, 21/9/17: 2/Lt C F Risteen. Subsequently reissued 6/4/18, returned to No 7 AP 19/7/18
B3887	18/1/18; 'P'; crashed north of Castelfranco Veneto, 16/6/18: Lt H B Hudson
B3903	26/8/17; crashed on landing, 21/10/17: 2/Lt M B Frew
B3914	12/8/17; lost 21/9/17: 2/Lt E A Cooke (POW)
B3917	12/8/17; lost 3/9/17: Lt A T Heywood (killed)
B3929	1/11/17; 'L'; forced to land near Grossa, 17/4/18: 2/Lt A F Lingard
B4609	27/10/17; 'F'; forced to land Villa Dona, 1/2/18: Capt N C Jones
B5152	14/10/17; 'M'; lost 27/10/17: 2/Lt E A L F Smith (POW - wounded)
B5158	circa 18/11/17 en route Italy; 'M'; returned to No 7 AP 21/1/18
B5163	14/10/17; forced to land Westouter, 22/10/17 by Maj A M Vaucour but remained with squadron until returned to No 2 AD, 16/11/17
B5175	28/10/17; crashed behind enemy lines, 5/11/17: 2/Lt R G Frith (POW - wounded)
B5176	22/6/18; returned to No 7 AP 26/6/18
B5181	25/2/18; 'C'; damaged on landing, 6/8/18: Lt M Gibson
B5182	29/10/17; 'G'; returned to No 7 AP 17/6/18
B5238	3/2/18; 'F'; damaged on landing, 10/7/18: Lt E H Masters
B5403	3/6/18; crashed near Riese, 15/6/18: Lt J H Dewhirst
B5626	25/1/18; damaged on landing 5/5/18: Lt H J Andrews
B6205	23/8/17; lost 20/9/17: Lt B R Davis (killed)
B6207	23/8/17; forced to land near Coppernollehoek, 16/10/17: 2/Lt R J Dawes
B6214	16/5/18; damaged on landing Malcontenta, 9/7/18: Lt M Gibson
B6233	4/9/17; forced to land south of Ypres, 20/9/17: Lt E F Crossland. 21/8/18 reissued; returned to AEP 13/9/18
B6235	21/9/17; forced to land near St-Sylvestre-Cappel, 26/10/17: Lt E F Crossland
B6236	31/8/17; lost 11/9/17: Lt O L McMaking (killed)
B6238	4/9/17; 'C'; wrecked 22/2/18: Capt R J Brownell (slightly injured)
B6273	21/9/17; forced to land Audricq, 13/11/17: Lt H T Thompson

B6282	1/11/17; 'O'; crashed in River Brenta near Bessano, 24/5/18: Lt H J Watts (injured)
B6354	26/9/17; 'N'; returned to No 7 AP 20/4/18
B6372	8/10/17; 'H'; to No 7 AP 24/6/18
B6383	12/10/17; 'A'; damaged on landing, 26/2/18: 2/Lt E McN Hand
B6412	18/10/17; 'D'; to No 7 AP 9/7/18
B6423	8/11/17; 'T'; lost 1/6/18: Lt E McN Hand (POW - wounded)
B7307	27/2/18; 'R'; lost 1/6/18: Lt F J Jones (killed)
B7360	20/4/18; 'N'; wrecked on take off, 9/8/18: Lt J R O'Connell
B7381	4/4/18; 'J'; forced to land Capo Sile, 5/7/18: Lt G McIntyre, returned to No 7 AP 17/7/18
C54	21/7/18; collided with E1500, 24/12/18: Lt E H Masters (killed)
C55	21/7/18; returned to AEP 13/9/18
C3284	16/8/18; returned to No 3 ASD 6/11/18
D1910	13/5/18; crashed on landing, 12/9/18: 2/Lt A V Green
D1974	2/6/18; crashed on landing, 19/7/18: Lt E L Milborrow
D1975	28/5/18; 'K'; returned to No 3 ASD 20/10/18
D8102	2/6/18; 'F'; shot down in error by Italian Hanriot, Monastier di Treviso, 16/7/18: Maj A M Vaucour (killed)
D8104	18/6/18; crashed on landing, 1/11/18: Lt E G Nuding
D8113	12/6/18; to No 151 Sqn 19/1/19
D8169	16/6/18; night flying crash, 15/8/18: Lt J R Black (injured)
D8211	circa 27/6/18; to No 151 Sqn, 19/1/19
D8237	6/7/18; 'D'; to No 151 Sqn, 19/1/19
D8238	13/7/18; 'W'; night flying crash, 16/8/18: Capt W C Hilborn (fatally injured and died 26/8/18)
D8240	10/7/18; crashed 22/11/18
D8243	9/7/18; 'E'; to No 151 Sqn, 19/1/19
D9386	16/6/18; 'A'; to No 151 Sqn, 19/1/19
D9392	5/6/18; 'B'; crashed landing Maisoncelle, 6/1/19: 2/Lt A V Green injured
D9394	17/5/18; to No 151 Sqn, 19/1/19
D9412	15/6/18; shot down by AA, Monte Asolone, 10/8/18: Lt A J Haines (killed)
D9430	by 2/12/18; to No 151 Sqn, 19/1/19
E1500	9/8/18; collided with C54, 24/12/18: Lt E L Milborrow (injured)
E1501	18/7/18; crashed, 22/11/18
E1539	1/1/19; to No 151 Sqn, 19/1/19
E1580	3/9/18; to No 151 Sqn, 19/1/19
E7168	by 7/9/18; lost 3/11/18: Lt F S Bowles (POW)
E7204	21/10/18; crashed landing Béthencourt, 6/1/19: Lt J H Dewhirst
E7212	by 25/9/18; to No 151 Sqn, 19/1/19
E7230	11/1/19; to No 151 Sqn, 19/1/19
E7244	by 26/9/18; to No 151 Sqn, 22/1/19
F3979	15/11/18; crashed, 22/11/18
F6200	by 2/12/18; to No 151 Sqn, 19/1/19
F6225	by 2/12/18; to No 151 Sqn, 19/1/19
F6281	1/1/19; to No 151 Sqn, 19/1/19
F6443	9/11/18; to No 151 Sqn, 19/1/19
F6497	12/1/19; to No 151 Sqn, 19/1/19

October 1918–January 1919

Sopwith Snipe. Two aircraft only.

E8017	31/10/18; delivered to Marquise 21/1/19
E8081	30/10/18; wrecked 10/11/18: 2/Lt C A Robertshaw

July 1921–April 1922

Vickers Vimy. No 45 Sqn flew the Vimy as interim equipment pending the

Some of A Flight's Camels lined up at Istrana. From the left: B6412/D, B2430/B, B2426/E and B6383/A. This picture is particularly interesting as it clearly shows B2430's serial being worn on its fin, whereas the photograph on page 38 shows it marked on the rudder. (No 45 Sqn archives)

delivery of Vernons. Those listed below are known to have served with the squadron; there may well have been others.

F9191	in use 7/21
F9192	in use 3/22
F9194	
H653	
H654	crashed on take-off (engine cut), 28/3/22: Flt Lt H W R Banting

February 1922-January 1927

Vickers Vernon. The listing of the squadron's Vernons below as Mk I, II or III reflects their status as originally delivered. During their careers, however, several of these aircraft were rebuilt to later standards, which in the case of the Mk Is meant replacing the original Rolls-Royce Eagle engines with Napier Lions.

Most of No 45 Sqn's Vernons were given individual names. Where these can be linked with a specific aircraft they have been noted below. Other names known to have been used included *Vaivode, Vendetta, Vampire, Unity, Ajax, Anceus, Daedalus, Awana, Claribel, Flying Inn, Argo* and (possibly) *Vakrode*.

A number of **Bristol Fighters**, eg D8055, D8095, D8099 and F4928, were flown by the squadron's pilots during the Vernon era, particularly in 1924-25, but these were actually on charge to Hinaidi's AD rather than to the squadron.

Vernon I

J6864	
J6865	crashed on take-off Kirkuk, 4/10/22: Flt Lt A L Messenger, AC1 A A Milne and Flt Lt R C Holme (pax) all killed.
J6866	*Aurora*, 3/22-?
J6867	
J6868	*Stormcock*; in use 3/22-7/24
J6869	in use 12/23-4/24
J6870	in use 2/23-9/24
J6871	in use 12/22-7/24
J6872	9/3/22-10/26
J6873	in use 2/23-8/24
J6874	*Assyrian*; in use 2/23-11/24
J6875	in use 5/23-6/24
J6876	*Pelican*; in use 4/23-5/24
J6877	in use 2/23-7/24
J6878	
J6879	in use 2/23-5/24
J6881	in use 9/23
J6882	*Golden Gain*; in use by 2/23; crashed en route Kirkuk-Serkhuma, 28/4/23: Flt Lt I M Matheson
J6883	in use 7/22-7/24

Vernon II

J6889	
J6891	in use 10/23
J6977	in use 12/23-12/26
J6978	
J6979	in use 1924
J7133	
J7134	*Valkyrie*; 12/5/24-9/26
J7135	*Vagabond*; in use 7/24-9/26
J7136	
J7137	*Vesuvius*; in use 8/24-12/26
J7138	*Morpheus*; in use 10/24-4/25
J7139	*Venus*; in use 3/25; crashed on take off, Hinaidi, 19/7/26; Fg Off J S Dick. Repaired and air tested 6/12/26
J7140	in use by 8/24 when it was crashed at Sulaimaniyah by Sqn Ldr J K Summers; rebuilt; in use again 4/25-9/26
J7141	*Aurora*; in use by 8/24; accident at El Lyssen, 10/25: Fg Off J V Kelly; Eventually written off in night landing accident 9/26
J7142	in use 1/8/24-11/25

Vernon III

JR6904	in use 1926
J7143	crashed into No 1 Sqn's hangar, Hinaidi, 26/7/26. Fg Off O K

Stirling-Webb and six passengers killed; Fg Off G P Mee and LAC Henderson injured

JR7144	in use 1925 (it has not been confirmed that the 'R' was actually incorporated into the serial number after modification to Vernon III standard)
J7539	in use 2/25-1/27
J7544	in use 10/25-10/26
J7545	in use 10/26
J7547	in use 1926; written off 9/26 following landing accident at night

Vimy Ambulance. The Vimy Ambulance was an Eagle-engined military variant of the original Vimy Commercial. Four were built, three of them serving with No 45 Sqn; all three were later converted to Vernon III standard.

J6904	in use 1923; rebuilt as Vernon, JR6904
J7143	in use 3/25; rebuilt as Vernon, JR7143 (but serial did not incorporate the 'R')
J7144	in use 1925; rebuilt as Vernon, JR7144 (serial may not have incorporated the 'R')

April 1927-September 1929

DeHavilland DH 9A

E917	in use 8-9/29
ER8642	flew into the ground in fog after take off, Helwan, 20/11/29
H118	in use 12/28
HR3501	'3'
H3545	in use 9/28
H3636	in use 1928
J7086	in use 11/28-2/29
JR7093	'2'; in use 11/28
JR7339	'B'; forced to land in desert and dismantled 1928
J7823	'6'; crashed at some time while with No 45 Sqn
J7829	in use 9/29
J7831	'1'
J7832	'1'; in use 5/28-9/29
J7840	in use 10/28
J7841	crashed and burned 19/7/27
J7860	in use 12/28; undercarriage collapsed in landing accident at Helwan, 18/1/29
J7874	in use 8/29-9/29
J8098	in use 11/28-12/28
J8118	'2'; crashed 30/1/28
J8138	'6'
J8139	in use 4/29-5/29
J8178	in use 11/28
J8186	in use 4/29-9/29
J8188	in use 12/28-9/29
J8189	'4'; in use 12/28-9/29
J8198	in use 12/28
J8199	in use 1/29
J8202	in use 8/29-9/29
J8203	in use 6/28-7/28
J8206	in use 7/28-10/28

September 1929-December 1935

Fairey IIIF Mk I

S1141	12/28-1/29 only, for familiarisation
SR1171	'N2'; in use 10/29-11/29; flew 1929 West African cruise
SR1172	'N3'; in use 10/29-1931; flew 1929 West African cruise
SR1174	'N1'; in use 10/29-1931; flew 1929 West African cruise
SR1175	in use by 1/34; crashed El Arish 30/6/34; rebuilt but crashed again 19/11/35 with B Flt at Nairobi
S1176	
S1178	in use 11/29
SR1178	in use 1932
S1179	'N1'; *reported by Air Britain but use not confirmed*
S1180	'N3'; *reported by Air Britain but use not confirmed*
S1181	'N3'; *reported by Air Britain but use not confirmed*
SR1183	in use 12/33-1/35
S1197	in use 11/29
S1204	in use 1931

SR1204   in use 1936; engine cut, abandoned, 8/2/36

Fairey IIIF Mk IVM

JR9138	in use 6/31-5/32
J9153	in use 1932
J9160	
JR9162	in use 1932
J9164	in use 12/31 for trials with long range fuel tanks; modified to standard and still in service in 4/35
J9640	'4'; 15/9/29; crashed at Famagusta, 27/10/31 (shipped back to Egypt and restored to use after repair)
JR9640	1/2/34; hit tree on take off, Wajir (Kenya), 4/1/36: Fg Off C S Byram
J9641	'2'; 8/9/29-10/30
JR9641	in use 6/33-8/33 and 1937
J9642	8/9/29-7/31
J9643	15/9/29-8/30
J9644	in use 9/29-4/31
JR9644	in use 3/33-10/33
J9645	'3'; 8/9/29-1931
J9648	in use 11/30-3/32; undercarriage damaged in single-wheel landing, nosed over, Helwan, 1932: Sgt D J Pitcher
J9650	'9'; in use 4/30-10/30
J9652	'5'; in use 1930-1931
JR9652	in use 7/31-11/32
J9653	'10'; in use 2/30-7/31
JR9653	in use 6/32-3/33
J9654	'6'; in use 1930
J9655	'7'; in use by 4/30-1933
J9656	'9'; in use 1930
JR9656	in use 5/34-7/35
J9657	'2'; in use 1932
J9658	in use 1930
JR9658	in use 6/32-11/32
J9659	in use as '3', 6/30-12/30
JR9659	in use as '9', 3/33-5/34
J9660	'1'; in use 1930
J9662	'11'; in use from 10/29; spun and abandoned, 18/5/31: Sgt D J Pitcher and LAC W R Fraser baled out
J9663	
J9677	'9'; in use 1933
JR9677	'9'; in use 2/34-7/35
JR9793	by 2/34; crashed on take off , Lilongwe, 6/4/34: Plt Off D R Evans and Cpl Hamlin
J9805	in use 4/31
J9808	in use 10/9/30-12/31
JR9812	in use 3/33
JR9815	in use 5/31-12/31
J9817	in use 6/31; landed in sewage pit, overturned 5/12/36
JR9818	in use 7/35-1936
JR9826	in use 9/34-6/35
J9827	in use 7/31-11/32
JR9827	in use from 6/35; spun in from steep turn at 300' near Nairobi, 29/12/35: Fg Off C C Francis and Cpl Bryant both killed
J9828	in use 9/31-11/31
JR9828	in use 8/32; force landed and overturned near Helwan, late 1932: Sgt Shearsmith; stripped and burned on site
J9831	in use 12/31
JR9831	in use 3/33-5/35
JR9862	1935-36
K1701	'1'
K1702	'2'
K1703	'1'; flew 1931 West African cruise
K1704	'2'; flew 1931 West African cruise
K1705	'3'; flew 1931 West African cruise
KR1705	in use 7/35
K1708	in use 7/33
KR1708	in use 7/35
K1709	in use 2/34
K1713	'4'; flew 1931 West African cruise
KR1713	'5'; in use 1/35-7/35
K1715	reserve for 1931 West African cruise; transferred to No 47 Sqn 10/31
K1716	caught in downdraught from hills, crashed 25/11/35: Plt Off

C L Gomm

K1728

January-December 1936

Fairey Gordon. Primarily replacements for the Fairey IIIFs of B Flight at Nairobi but also used by D Flight at Helwan and a few were retained for use as target-tugs until as late as 1938.

JR9656	in use 1936
K1162	in use 7/38
K1710	in use 1936
K2617	in use at Helwan 1937
K2618	in use 1936
K2745	taxied into Wellesley K7774, Helwan, 1/9/38: Sgt W Nicholls; still flying 12/38

September 1935-January 1936

Hawker Hart. Six Harts are believed to have been used by No 45 Sqn's D Flight prior to its being transferred to No 6 Sqn. To date the only Hart reported to have had a possible association with No 45 Sqn is K4460.

November 1935-December 1937

Vickers Vincent. Specific details of the Vincent's service with No 45 Sqn are sparse. Known incidents have been noted below, but few will have resulted in the aircraft's being written off and none are known to have involved serious injury to the crew.

K4616	in use 3/38
K4617	21/6/37-10/12/37
K4663	
K4664	port tyre punctured, stood on nose on landing, Heliopolis, 23/10/36: Fg Off C L Gomm
K4665	hit pot-hole landing, port undercarriage sheared off, Kolundia, 1/8/36: Sgt J D T Taylor-Gill
K4666	by 2/37-30/12/37
K4667	
K4668	
K4669	
K4670	
K4671	pulled up to avoid leader during formation take off, stalled and crashed, Aboukir, 24/3/36: Sgt R C Hyett
K4672	
K4673	in use 5/37
K4674	fitted with Fairey-Reed 3-blade prop
K4675	ran into soft sand on landing, stood on nose, Muharraq, 18/1/37: Sgt T D Dixon
K4676	in use 4/37; retained as squadron hack until at last 7/38
K4677	in use 4/37-11/37
K4678	in use 5/37-12/37
K4679	
K4680	
K4681	in use 11/37
K4682	
K4683	
K4684	
K4685	

Refuelling complete, A Flight's Fairey IIIFs lined up at Aswan during the 1929 Lloyd Reliability Trophy winter run; the date will have been 14th or 16th December. Fg Off Patch is standing in front of the centre aircraft, J9641; the aircraft on the right is J9642. (R Grinter via J Grech)

Although it is slightly out of focus, this picture of K4666 is still of interest. It was taken during the India-reinforcement exercise in early 1937 and the original is clear enough to show that by that time the badge on the fin was contained within a grenade-shaped frame. Just distinguishable is the silhouette of a Flying Camel on the port side of the nose; comparison with the roundel shows that this was definitely not blue which suggests that this emblem may have been applied in flight colours - B Flight yellow would be appropriate in this case. (No 45 Sqn archives)

K4686	
K4700	by 2/37; stalled on landing (first solo on type), Helwan, 22/7/37: Sgt S A G Abbott
K4701	22/7/37-11/37
K4702	9/7/37-?
K4704	in use 2/37-10/37
K4709	in use 6/37

November 1937–June 1939

Vickers Wellesley. As with the Vincent, beyond photographs and aircrew flying log books, relatively little information has survived to amplify the following list of serials. Known incidents have been noted but few will have resulted in the aircraft's being written off and none are thought to have resulted in serious casualties.

K7731	in use 5/39
K7742	in use 3/39
K7750	
K7756	
K7758	in use 3/39; heavy landing Ismailia, 23/6/39: APO L J Joel
K7760	
K7773	in use 11/37-2/39
K7774	'45.U'; in use by 2/38; taxied into by Gordon K2745, Ismailia, 1/9/38: Sgt P Bower. Held off too high and stalled, Ismailia, 7/6/39: APO W J Mulholland
K7775	in use 2/38-5/39
K7776	in use 2/38-18/7/39
K7777	wheels would not lock down, landed on nacelles, Helwan, 26/3/38: Sgt I D F Grant. Hit ridge between old LG and new extension and undercarriage collapsed, Helwan, 11/7/38: Plt Off S G Soderholm
K7778	16/12/37; floated on landing, stalled and undercarriage collapsed, Ramleh, 18/8/38: Plt Off S G Soderholm. Taxied into L2678 (taxying with rudder locked) Helwan, 15/11/38: Sgt E R Andrews. Swung on landing undercarriage collapsed, Ismailia, 9/3/39: Sgt G J C P Bateman
K7779	14/12/37; '45.C'; 5/39
K7780	18/12/37-5/39
K7781	by 3/38; '45.L'; forced landing, Toshka, 9/7/38: Sgt S A G Abbott, engine changed on site and recovered
K7782	in use 4/38-6/39; '45.M' and 'DD.M'
K7783	in use 3/38; inadvertently selected undercarriage up after night landing, Helwan, 15/9/38: Fg Off G J Bush. Still in use 6/39
K7784	'45.D'; in use 7/38; landed before undercarriage fully locked down, Helwan, 11/10/38: Plt Off C W S Thomas and AC 1 Turner
K7785	12/27-8/39
K7786	12/37; damaged in landing accident at Wadi Halfa, 4/2/38: Plt Off H P Pleasance, LAC Charnley and AC1 Beer.

K7788	
K7791	in use 2/39-6/39
L2640	in use 10/38; sustained lightning strike 6/4/39: Plt Off A S Smith. Forced to land El Simbillawen, 26/4/39: Plt Off C W S Thomas and AC1 Cooper - no damage
L2650	'45.G'; in use 7/38-5/39
L2651	undercarriage collapsed after hitting rough patch, Helwan, 22/11/38: Plt Off G C B Woodroffe
L2658	in use 7/38; '45.O'; landed short, undercarriage collapsed, Helwan, 11/11/38: Sgt M C Thurlow
L2659	in use 6/38; landed short, undercarriage collapsed, Helwan, 14/11/38: Plt Off C W S Thomas and AC 1 Carter
L2662	in use 4/39; inadvertently selected undercarriage up after landing, Ismailia, 11/7/39: Sgt I D F Grant
L2674	
L2675	
L2676	
L2677	
L2678	in use 7/38; taxied into by K7778, Helwan, 15/11/38; still flying 2/39
L2683	
L2684	
L2685	
L2686	
L2687	
L2694	in use 9/38-6/39
L2696	'45.R'; in use 11/38-6/39
L2698	in use 11/38-6/39
L2699	in use 2/39-5/39
L2700	27/10/38; undercarriage not fully locked down, collapsed on landing, Helwan, 5/1/39: Sgt R T Shaw. Flying again by 18/1/39, still in use 2/3/39
L2701	16/9/38-6/7/39
L2702	28/9/38-4/39 at least
L2703	17/10/38-5/39 at least
L2709	30/9/38-?
L2710	
L2711	
L2712	
L2713	
L2714	
L2715	

Vickers Vildebeest IV

K8087	in use 2-3/39, probably in connection with desert compatibility trials with Bristol Perseus engine

June 1939-February 1941

Bristol Blenheim I

L1492	in use 15/12/40-5/1/41
L1534	by 5/40; 'OB.K'; wheels up at Sidi abd el Raniman after raid on Menastir, 9/12/40: Flt Lt J Paine and Sgts Chaplin and Edwards
L4923	6/39; left with No 52 RSU in Sudan 27/11/40
L4924	6/39-?
L6628	6/39-?
L6629	6/39-?
L6631	22/1/41-2/41
L6663	7/39; *The Chequers*; damaged by CR 42s in attack on Menastir, 9/12/40: Plt Off C W S Thomas, Sgt R Dodsworth, Sgt Fisher; still in use 2/41
L6664	6/39; hit mast of felucca while low flying from Helwan, 23/8/40: Plt Off R W A Gibbs; left with No 52 RSU in Sudan 27/11/40; in use again by 28/1/41
L6665	7/39; lost (to CR 42s?) during raid on Gura, 30/9/40: Flt Lt G J Bush and Sgts J C Usher and J Corney DFM all killed
L8362	engine failure, crashed on take off, Fuka, 3/6/41: Sgt S F Champion (and ?)
L8385	1/41-2/41
L8390	24/1/41-2/41
L8445	7/39-5/1/41
L8452	by 7/40; shot down by CR 42s, Mai Edaga, 2/10/40: Sqn Ldr J W Dallamore and Sgt M B F McKenzie both killed, Plt Off A G Sheppard POW
L8461	in use 9/39-11/40

L8463   by 9/40; lost Gura, 13/10/40: Fg Off G C B Woodroffe and Sgts E B Ryles and A A Meadows plus Plt Off L S Roberts, all killed

L8464   by 10/40; ran out of fuel, forced landed El Daba, 10/12/40 (possibly no longer with No 45 Sqn)

L8465   12/40; shot down in raid on Sollum, 12/12/40: Plt Off P C Traill-Smith, Plt Off V D Fry and Sgt T O Liggins all killed

L8466   by 5/40; single-engined wheels-up forced landing 50 mls west of Sidi Barrani, 11/6/40: Fg Off A J H Finch, Sgt R Dodsworth and AC1 Fisher

L8467   in use 6/40-2/41

L8469   in use 5/40-12/40

L8472   by 11/39; forced to land El Qatara, 9/5/40: Fg Off C W S Thomas, Sgt S Davies and AC1 C Richardson

L8473   by 10/39-24/1/41

L8475   6/39; left with No 52 RSU in Sudan 27/11/40

L8476   7/39; shot down in flames into sea off Tobruk, 11/6/40: Sgts P Bower and S G Fox and AC1 J Allison all killed

L8477   6/39; ran out of fuel, force landed near Gazai station, 10/12/40 (possibly no longer with No 45 Sqn)

L8478   6/39; tyre burst on take off, landed wheels up, Helwan, 8/7/40: Fg Off J H Williams, Plt Offs G A Cockayne and A G Sheppard and AC1 R W Reader

L8479   7/39; shot down by CR42 near Gazala, 3/1/41: Plt Off P J B Griffiths and Sgts A C Tadhunter and C Blackshaw all killed

L8481   7/39; 'OB.X'; 2/41

L8482   7/39; crash landed in sandstorm, Fuka, 19/2/40: Flt Lt G J Bush

L8500   6/39; swung on landing Amman, 10/7/39, undercarriage collapsed: Plt Off R W A Gibbs (and ?)

L8502   by 5/40; lost Gura, 13/10/40: Plt Off G A Cockayne and Sgts T A Ferris and R W Reader all killed

L8510   in use 1/41-2/41

L8519   by 5/40; crash landed Sidi Barrani and burned, 11/6/40: Sgts M C Thurlow and B A Feldman and AC1 H Robinson all killed

L8520   6/39-?

L8524   18/7/39; lost Giarabub, 13/6/40: Fg Off J S Davies, Sgt G E Negus and LAC J K Copeland all killed

L8525   in use 7/40-2/41

L8537   in use 7/40-12/40

L8538   by 6/40; shot down by CR 42s, Barce, 4/2/41: Flt Lt J Paine baled out and returned but Sgts H C T Holmans and C P Edwards both killed

L8667   17/1/41-19/1/41 at least

February 1941-April 1942

Bristol Blenheim IV. An asterisk indicates that the aircraft is known to have flown with the squadron as a Mk IVF; those used in May-June 1941 had the four-gun bomb bay pack of the standard 'fighter' while those taken on charge in early 1942 had this plus a 20mm cannon in the nose.

*N3581   25/1/42; 'J'; damaged undercarriage landing in sandstorm, Sidi Bu Amud, 26/1/42: Plt Off E G Christensen RAAF, Sgt B Pearce RAAF and Sgt R D Hilditch RAAF

R3733   in use 4/41; 'OB.F'

R3777   7/12/41-3/1/42

T1817   3/41-17/5/41

*T1823   3/41; taxied into obstruction before take off 26/4/41: Sgt W Bain. Still in use 27/5/41 but withdrawn 6/41; reissued 25/1/42-5/2/42

T2049   in use 11/4/41-10/41

T2056   4/41; shot down during raid on Derna, 18/5/41: Fg Off J Beveridge, Plt Off A H Wise RNZAF and Sgt V J Griffiths all killed

T2124   7/41; 'F'; tail damaged by AA during raid on Sidi Rezegh, 18/11/41 (Sgts F N Scott, R Jackson and D Catty) but remained in use until 5/2/42

T2170   3/41; forced to land 3 mls south of Mersah Matruh returning from night raid on Derna, 24/4/41: Fg Off F W Chadwick and Sgts Burns and T Turnbull

T2174   24/3/41; lost prop and forced to land 3 mls west of Mersah Matruh returning from night raid on Capuzzo, 28/4/41: Lt E Jones SAAF, Plt Off L P Bourke RNZAF and Sgt S B Whiteley

*T2179   24/4/41; shot down in strafing attack on Capuzzo, 19/5/41: Plt Off D Carter and Sgt H J Cassar killed, Sgt G W Swanbo POW

T2185   4/41; 'N'; hit obstruction on night take-off Fuka (no flarepath) belly landed, 3/11/41: Sgt P Bartlett

*T2243   10/5/41-6/41

T2248   25/2/41; ferried to Greece 26/4/41

T2249   by 1/4/41-4/41

*T2252   15/5/41-12/6/41

T2318   7/41; 'H'; shot down by Bf 109s near El Adem, 22/11/41: Sgt C Melly, Plt Off F L Rippingale and Sgt J Halsall all POWs

T2339   19/3/41; shot down by Bf 109s, Crete, 26/5/41: Sgts N H Thomas, G R Adams and G K Grainger all killed

T2345   26/4/41; ran out of fuel after night attack, landed 21 mls south of El Alamein, 28/4/41: Sgts P Naldrett-Jays, J R Prockter and A W Dann

*T2349   in use 1/1/42-7/2/42

T2350   4/41; crew got lost after raid on Crete, baled out over Cyrenaica, 26/5/41: Plt Off J Robinson and Sgt A F Crosby picked up but Sgt W B Longstaff was not found

T2389   4/41-20/5/41

T2393   4/11/41; 'P'; damaged by AA, 29/11/41: Sgt J Robinson wounded, Sgts J Paterson and W A Gaudet RCAF uninjured; to Fayoum 13/1/42

T2428   4/41; 'P'; 11/41

*T2429   3/41-20/5/41

V5422   3/41-9/41; passed to No 84 Sqn but became unserviceable at Magwe 11/2/42 and re-acquired by No 45 Sqn along with its crew (Plt Off A W Pedlar RAAF, Sgt M F Roberts RAAF and Sgt M Morris RAAF) circa 16/2/42-17/3/42 at least

V5425   in use 9/41

V5435   7/41; 'W'; tyre burst, crashed on take off LG 53, 1/11/41: Plt Off R A Brown, Fg Off J Wright and Sgt Jenkins

*V5436   25/1/42-7/2/42

V5438   3/41; shot down over Cyrenaica, 18/4/41: Fg Off F G Collins and Sgts E J Street and R H C Crook all killed

V5440   20/6/41; tyre hit by EA on recce over Syria, swung on landing Aqir, 23/6/41: Plt Offs S F Champion, L P Bourke RNZAF and Sgt J Bullock.

V5495   9/2/42-21/3/42 at least

V5509   24/3/41-?

V5573   23/3/41; single wheel landing, Fuka North, 6/5/41: Lt D Thorne SAAF, Plt Off D Brooks and Sgt M Grant

V5586   3/41; 'C'; 11/41

V5587   25/6/41; 'E'; 1/42

V5592   by 2/4/41; shot down by Bf 109s, Crete, 26/5/41: Fg Off T F Churcher and Plt Off R D May POWs; Sgt H C Langrish baled out and evaded

V5624   3/41; lost on attack on Maleme, 23/5/41: Plt Offs P J Vincent and S C Niven RNZAF and Sgt O B Thompson all killed

V5625   3/41; shot down in attack on Benghazi, 22/4/41: F/Sgt W Beverley, Sgt R W Gentry and F/Sgt V W J Harrison all killed

*V5817   10/5/41; shot down by Bf 109s in sea off Tobruk, 16/5/41: Flt Lt A C H Haines and Sgt S C Cordy killed

V5899   7/41; 'U'; 1/42

V5926   25/6/41; belly-landed Muqueibila after damage by D.520s over Hammana, 10/7/41: Sgts W M Osborne DFM, Martin and H Garfath

V5938   by 13/12/41; 'P'; 8/3/42

V5943   by 14/10/41; crashed near Sidi Omar, 19/11/41: Sqn Ldr A Hughes DFC, Plt Off L E Durrant and F/Sgt D Cliffe all reached British lines

V5948   20/6/41; 'X'; shot down by Bf 109s south of Barce, 20/12/41: Sgts G T Bennett, H C Nullis and H W Twydell evaded successfully

V5957   30/1/42; 'M'; 15/3/42 at least

V5967   26/6/41; 'V'; 1/42

V5968   20/6/41; two hang-ups fell off at 50' on approach to Muqueibila, 10/7/41; aircraft severely damaged but Sgts Stewart, Colway and Catton not seriously injured

V5991   21/6/41; 'B'; collided on take-off with Lorraine Sqn Blenheim, LG 75, 4/12/41: Plt Off J H Tolman, Fg Off A W Hutton and Sgt D S J Harris all killed

V5992   26/6/41; 'L'; 29/10/41 at least

Blenheim IV V6467/G flew with No 45 Sqn from June to December 1941 and possibly for longer, as it may have met its end in Burma in the following March being flown by a squadron crew (see Note 11 to Chapter 8), but whether the aeroplane was still on charge to No 45 Sqn or had by then been transferred to the books of No 113 Sqn is not clear. (L EDurrant)

V5999   2/42; 'K'; landed short of fuel near Thayetmyo and somersaulted, 18/2/42: Sgts H C Jewell, J R Hurley RCAF and F G Terry

V6128   left Egypt 18/1/42 with No 84 Sqn but at Magwe with No 45 Sqn by 7/3/42-16/3/42

V6132   2/9/41; 'R'; shot down by Bf 109s south of Barce, 20/12/41: F/Sgt J Burns and Sgts R E J Reeves and J E Wilcock all killed

V6143   9/41; 'T'; hung up bomb exploded on landing at LG 53, 3/11/41: Sgt F Scott injured, Sgts G E Sully and J R Mansfield both killed

V6149   7/41; 'A'; 3/1/42 at least

V6180   7/41; 'Q'; forced to land by weather 40 mls south of Burgh el Arab, 31/10/41: 2/Lt H R L Alder SAAF, Plt Off W J Corbett RAAF and Sgt C G Briggs RAAF all picked up. Same crew lost prop 3/1/42 and forced to land near Wadi Natrun

V6221   10/2/42; destroyed on ground at Mingaladon 25/2/42 after raid on Moulmein

V6328   originally of No 211 Sqn but attached to No 45 Sqn with its crew (Plt Off D Mayger, Plt Off E F French and Sgt Davies) 17/2/42 -11/3/42

V6461   2/11/41-7/11/41

V6467   27/6/41; 'G'; hit by AA over Derna, 12/12/41: Plt Off P U A Keel and Plt Off L G George RAAF both OK; Sgt J F Jennings RAAF wounded. Reportedly flew into cables near Bassein, 17/3/42: Capt H R L Alder SAAF, Plt Off W J Corbett RAAF and Sgt C G Briggs RAAF

V6490   7/12/41-6/2/42 at least

V6503   27/6/41; damaged in combat with three MS 406s over Aleppo, 4/7/41: Sgts J Burns and J A H Kirkpatrick unhurt, Sgt J E White killed

V6505   6/41-6/41

*Z5766   5/41; crash landed at night 1 ml south of Sidi Barrani, 24/5/41: Sgts J McClelland, H Vipond and J McGurk

*Z5864   25/1/42-7/2/42

Z5866   20/2/41; hit tar barrel on take-off (no flarepath), jettisoned bombs in sea, crash landed Maaten Bagush Satellite, 13/4/41: Fg Off F W Chadwick and Sgts Burns and Turnbull

Z5886   3/41; 'OB.C'; 4/41 - also in use 12/41

Z5888   4/41; 'OB.A'; engine failure, swung on take off at Habbaniyah, 5/9/41: Sgt C Melly, Plt Off F L Rippingale and Sgt J Halsall

Z5892   4/41-6/41

Z5894   3/41; crashed landed Fuka (undercarriage damaged by EA and lost in sandstorm), 12/4/41: Plt Off P J Vincent

Z5896   5/41; crashed on take-off Fuka, 27/5/41: Fg Off N W Pinnington and Plt Off H F Irving RNZAF both killed; Sgt R J Martin died of injuries 10/6/41

Z5898   22/3/41; shot down by Bf 109s off Tobruk, 28/4/41: Plt Off B CdeG Allan, Sgt L W Morling and five passengers all killed (see narrative)

Z5979   3/41-4/41 at least

Z5980   4/41; forced to land 2 mls east of Burgh el Arab, 6/5/41

*Z6094   25/1/42-7/2/42

Z6155   7/41; 'K'; 19/10/41 at least

Z6156   27/6/41; engine fire, forced to land near Lake Urmia (Iran), 29/8/41: Flt Lt L F Penny unhurt but Sgts J A H Kirkpatrick

and G George both injured

*Z6374   25/1/42-7/2/42

Z6433   27/6/41; shot down by D.520s near Hammana, 10/7/41: F/Sgt L T Wilton-Jones POW; Sgts J C Wimhurst and D J Lowe both killed

Z6439   6/41; 'Y'; shot down by Bf 109s near El Adem, 22/11/41: Wg Cdr J O Willis DFC, Plt Off L P Bourke RNZAF and Sgt M F Carthy all killed

Z6440   7/41; 'Z'; damaged by Bf 109s near El Adem, 22/11/41: Sgt J E Pannifer, Sgt C E Birkbeck RAAF and Sgt E B Pulford RCAF

Z6446   8/11/41; take off incident at LG 75, 4/12/41: 2/Lt A D Allen SAAF, Plt Off E L Hammat RAAF and Sgt G A Gowing RAAF, repaired by No 51 RSU 6-18/12/41; to No 51 RSU 2/1/42

Z6455   2/7/41; shot down by D.520s near Hammana, 10/7/41: Sgt D A Cawthen POW, Sgts K R Cornford and W D Capewell both killed

Z7412   arrived Magwe 21/3/42 and destroyed in air raid that day

Z7509   7/9/41; 'S'; crashed landed Fuka at night, 30/9/41: Fg Off J K Edmonds, Plt Off L E Durrant and Sgt K J Chapman

Z7510   11/41; 'C'; shot down in raid on Sidi Rezegh, 19/11/41: Plt Off E A Magor RAAF, Fg Off A J Cain RAAF and Sgt T S MacLiver RAAF all killed

Z7579   in use 10/3/42

Z7588   6/12/41; 'H'; crashed on take off Heliopolis, 4/1/42: Plt Off C W Head RAAF (solo) killed

Z7635   25/11/41; 'Y'; 8/3/42 at least

Z7686   14/11/41; shot down by Bf 109s near El Adem, 22/11/41: Sgts C E O'Neill, L Smith and K J Chapman all killed

Z7709   in use 22/11/41-25/11/42

Z7757   11/2/42-20/3/42 at least

Z7770   11/2/42; shot down near Kyaikto, 21/2/42: 2/Lt F A L DeMarillac SAAF and Sgt R Southorn RAAF both wounded, Sgt G A Gowing RAAF OK

Z7892   originally of No 211 Sqn but attached to No 45 Sqn with its crew (Sgt J C McNamara RAAF, Sgt D W Penn RAAF and Sgt N A Bruce RAAF) 15/2/42. Ferried Akyab-Dum Dum 1/3/42 by Plt Off D G Eve RAAF, Plt Off G E Kemp RAAF and Plt Off N Bain RAAF

Z7899   1/42; shot down near Mingaladon, 14/3/42: Sgts L S Powell RAAF and L W H Connor RAAF and Plt Off J J Eden RAAF all killed

Z7913   18/1/42; crashed on take off Lydda, 14/2/42: Sqn Ldr F J Austin, Plt Off F J Fraser and Sgt K Mills

Z7916   in use 11/3/42-15/3/42

Z7923   in use 25/2/42 when destroyed at Mingaladon after raid on Moulmein

Z7928   10/2/42; 'D'; forced to land in Pegu River, 18/2/42: Plt Off D G Eve RAAF, Plt Off G E Kemp RAAF and Plt Off N Bain RAAF

Z7981   16/1/42; 'T'; 21/3/42 at least

Z9534   9/41-9/41

Z9546   in use 7/7/41-11/7/41 at least

Z9547   2/7/41; shot down by D.520s near Hammana, 10/7/41: Sgts G M Hardy and J Newhouse killed; Sgt R Waddington POW

Z9573   5/12/41-1/3/42 at least

Z9590   15/11/41-1/42

Z9607   11/41-11/41 at least

Z9609   by 6/11/41; shot down by Bf 109s near El Adem, 23/11/41: Sgts R Wood (POW), R A Turton RNZAF (evaded) and S B Whiteley (POW)

Z9620   23/11/41-1/42

Z9656   12/41-1/42

*Z9658   25/1/42-7/2/42

Z9668   7/12/41; 'N'; 5/2/42

Z9679   2/42-23/3/42

Z9721   in use 27/2/42

Z9799   1/42; hit by small arms fire 11/3/42: Sgt D J Smyth RAAF killed; Sgts D A Golder RAAF and J J Alt RAAF baled out over Magwe

Z9801   in use 25/2/42-20/3/42

Z9803   12/2/42; 'W'; 5/4/42 at least

Z9807   in use 19/3/42-21/3/42 at least

Z9811   24/1/42; 'N'; damaged at Mingaladon by Japanese air raid, 26/2/42

Z9819	delivered to Magwe 12/2/42, absorbed by No 45 Sqn; 8/3/42 at least
Z9821	13/1/42; 'H'; lost on ground at Mingaladon 25/2/42
Z9833	1/2/42; lost on the ground at Minagaladon 25/2/42
Z9835	in use 14/1/42-22/3/42

November 1942-February 1944

Vultee Vengeance I

AN845	11/11/42-23/12/42 at least
AN852	11/11/42-?
AN904	by 27/2/43-3/43
AN925	18/9/43-10/43
AN943	2/43; accident Asansol 12/3/43, repaired by 24/6/43
AN978	11/1/43; swung on take-off Asansol and undercarriage collapsed, 11/3/43: F/Sgts R P Curtis RAAF and J L Brinkley RAAF
AN983	in use 25/2/43-23/3/43
AN999	in use 2/43-3/43
AP103	2/43-23/3/43
AP107	in use 3/43
AP122	by 20/2/43-3/43
AP134	29/5/43-5/43

Vultee Vengeance IA

EZ825	6/8/43; 'D'; 1/10/43
EZ828	4/43-10/43
EZ830	5/11/43-?
EZ835	6/8/43-10/43
EZ839	in use 17/12/43; 'D'
EZ841	30/3/43; 'A' & 'OB.A'; to No 322 MU 3/2/44
EZ842	30/3/43; overshot Asansol, 8/4/43 and hit a car and a heap of sand: Sgt J Hadley and H Garfath. Tipped on its nose when taxying at Asansol 23/4/43: Fg Offs P U A Keel and L G George RAAF
EZ843	29/3/43; 'M'; hit tree low flying from Ranchi, 6/10/43: Sgts J H T Hewat and C H Romans both killed
EZ844	29/3/43; 'Q'; 28/7/43 at least
EZ845	in use 8/43
EZ846	1/4/43-19/5/43 at least
EZ847	4/43; 'C' & 'OB.C'; to No 322 MU 3/2/44
EZ848	in use 10/4/43; 'E' & 'OB.E'; to No 322 MU 3/2/44
EZ849	30/3/43; 'J' & 'OB.J'; hit tree low flying over bombing range, 9/4/43: F/Sgts H C Jewell and J R Vernon RAAF; in use until 12/43
EZ850	4/43; 'Y'; 1/12/43
EZ851	29/3/43; 'T'; undercarriage collapsed landing, Kumbhirgram, 15/11/43: Sgts J Banham and R Sumner
EZ852	4/43; to No 320 MU 4/9/43
EZ855	4/43-5/43
EZ865	4/43; 'OB.N'; to No 322 MU 3/2/44
EZ879	3/11/43; 'OB.L'; abandoned out of fuel Nowgong (Assam) following attack on Mawleik. 27/1/44: Plt Off H C Jewell killed; Plt Off K Bottrill baled out
EZ898	8/43; 'S'; lost following an attack on Kalemyo 13/11/43: Flt Lt J H Stevenson RCAF baled out; Sgt S Siddle killed
EZ900	4/43; 'L'; 2/12/43
EZ904	8/43-?
EZ986	10/43; 'OB.V'; to No 322 MU 3/2/44

Vultee Vengeance II

AN617	14/10/43; 'OB.Z'; 1/44
AN618	5/5/43; 'V'; to No 326 MU 14/9/43
AN621	by 21/4/43; 'Z'; to No 326 MU 14/9/43
AN625	18/10/43; 'OB.R'; 1/44
AN626	2/5/43; 'H'; to No 326 MU 14/9/43
AN628	4/43-?
AN656	15/10/43; 'OB.H'; dived into ground near Masimpur, 27/1/44, possibly attempting forced landing: Sqn Ldr A Traill and Fg Off D E French both killed
AN679	22/12/43; 'OB.T'; to No 322 MU 3/2/44
AN710	by 5/12/43; 'OB.M'; 22/1/44 at least
AN711	20/10/43; 'OB.Q'; fuel leak on air test, engine backfired on

shut-down and caught fire, Kumbhirgram 8/12/43: F/Sgt J Marshall and unidentified (airman?) passenger slightly burned

AN716	2/12/43; 'OB.J'; 1/44
AN731	15/10/43; 'OB.C'; to No 322 MU 3/2/44
AN734	5/12/43-12/43
AN772	2/12/43; 'OB.Y'; to No 322 MU 3/2/44
AN779	9/1/44; 'OB.R'; to No 322 MU 3/2/44
AN796	1/44; 'OB.Z'; 1/44
AN818	11/12/43; 'OB.C' and 'OB.J'; to No 322 MU 3/2/44
AN819	23/11/43; 'OB.X'; 27/1/44 at least
AN821	9/12/43; 'OB.O'; 19/1/44 at least
AN824	24/11/43; 'OB.T'; 12/43
AN837	by 15/11/43; 'OB.F'; to No 322 MU 3/2/44

DeHavilland Tiger Moth

| MA936 | 11/42-12/42 |

North American Harvard II

FE413	in use 22/1/43
FE415	7/12/42-17/6/43
FE416	in use 16/12/42

February-April 1944

While flying with No 1672 CU during the initial conversion to Mosquitos the following aircraft were among those used for twin-engined refresher flying and navigation training:

Bristol Blenheim Vs: BA408, BA452, BA598, BA601, BA618, BA654, BA689, BA979, EH387, EH400 and EH473

Avro Anson Is: LT542 and LT579

February 1944-June 1947

DeHavilland Mosquito VI

HJ739	26/10/44; to Kanchrapara 2/11/44
HJ811	3/44; engine cut, crash landed Rajahmundry, 1/5/44: Fg Offs A N Huon RAAF and C E Birkbeck RAAF
HJ833	6/10/44-circa 27/10/44
HP867	5/3/44; 'F'; hit tree low flying & belly landed Bishnapur, 24/6/44: Flt Lt C S Emeny RNZAF and WO J J Yanota RCAF (burned out but crew unharmed)
HP868	3/3/44; swung on take-of, undercarriage collapsed, 20/3/44: Fg Off P N Ewing RAAF (solo)
HP871	by 21/4/44; 'F'; circa 27/10/44
HP872	by 22/3/44; swung on take off, undercarriage collapsed, Yelahanka 3/4/44: Flt Lt G W Hartnell RAAF (solo)
HP876	3/44; 'D'; engine cut, overshot night landing, Ondal, 8/7/44: Fg Offs P N Ewing RAAF and F J Harper
HP877	by 24/3/44; 'E'; circa 27/10/44
HP878	by 28/4/44; 'C'; engine coolant leak, undercarriage not fully down, crash landed Dalbumgarh, 14/6/44: WO W F Tolar and ? (aircraft damaged beyond repair during salvage)
HP879	11/10/44; 'X'; circa 15/11/44
HP881	13/9/44; 'R'; circa 27/10/44
HP883	10/44; damaged over Meiktila, 12/10/44: Flt Lt V S H Duclos (OK) and Fg Off K Bottrill (killed). Stalled landing at Tulihal (ASI overreading), 28/10/44: Plt Off J M Levey RAAF and Fg Off J R Vernon RAAF
HP884	by 22/8/44; 'Y'; 13/11/44
HP914	3/44; 'H'; brakes failed, swung on landing Dalbumgarh, undercarriage collapsed, 16/8/44: Fg Off P N Ewing RAAF and WO R L C C Pinkerton
HP915	by 8/5/44; 'P'; dived into ground, Random Range, Ranchi, 11/9/44: Fg Offs J H Reeves RNZAF and L G Prout both killed
HP921	3/44; 'O'; broke up in air Kumbhirgram, 20/10/44: Sqn Ldr D S Edwards and Fg Off E L Sandifer both killed
HP936	11/6/44; 'K'; missing on sweep, Meiktila, 3/10/44: Flt Lt G H Proctor and Sgt G W Bargh both killed
HP939	3/44; broke up over Amarda Rd, 13/5/44: Wg Cdr H C

Stumm DFC RAAF and Flt Lt W J McKerracher DFM RAAF (of No 22 APC) both killed

HP941   3/44; 'B'; dived into ground after attack near Kadozeik, 16/10/44: Sqn Ldr N L Bourke RAAF and Fg Off K R Dumas RAAF, both killed

HP942   26/6/44; 'Z'; circa 27/10/44

HP969   18/8/44; 'H'; circa 27/10/44

HP971   14/7/44; 'D'; circa 27/10/44

HP978   14/7/44; 'A'; circa 27/10/44

HP985   20/10/44; 'D'; circa 14/11/44

HR283   21/10/44; 'L'; circa 15/11/44

HR291   by 11/9/44; 'T'; circa 15/11/44

HR309   by 7/4/45; 'OB.Y'; crashed 21 mls north east of Kyaukpyu, 17/6/45, cause unknown: Fg Off R J Wilcock and one (unauthorised?) passenger both killed

HR332   5/1/45; 'OB.T'; overshot landing, undercarriage collapsed, Monywa, 4/4/45: Fg Offs F C Fortune and L A Mears

HR368   by 28/10/44; 'OB.X'; 20/7/45 (at least)

HR371   5/1/45; 'OB.K'; 1/45

HR372   3/11/44;'OB.A' and 'OB.F'; hit wires, crashed 35 mls north of St Thomas Mount, 13/6/45: Flt Lt G J Tonks and F/Sgt G Cook, both killed

HR374   27/10/44; 'Z'; shot down by Ki 43 near Meiktila, 9/11/44: Flt Lt C S Emeny RNZAF and Plt Off J J Yanota RCAF both POWs

HR388   3/11/44; 'N'; circa 15/11/44

HR389   17/12/44; 'OB.T'; 21/12/44 at least

HR390   2/12/44; 'OB.B'; missing from attack on Heho, 17/2/45: F/Sgt G H Ashworth and WO R L C C Pinkerton both killed

HR392   7/12/44; 'OB.R' and 'OB.N'; 5/45

HR393   7/45; 'OB.M'; 8/45

HR397   by 9/1/45; 'OB.S'; 12/4/45 at least

HR399   7/11/44; 'OB.R'; 15/5/45

HR401   4/11/44; probably withdrawn shortly after delivery but reissued later; swung on landing Cholavaram, undercarriage collapsed, 25/9/45: F/Sgt R H Scott (and ?)

HR402   11/12/44; 'OB.C'; shot down by Ki 43s near Thedaw, 15/1/45: Flt Lt C R Goodwin and Fg Off S Potts both killed

HR404   28/12/44; 'OB.C'; hit water buffalo on take off from Thazi, 5/3/45: WOs S O'Connor and A A McKie

HR406   28/12/44; to No 82 Sqn 28/12/44

HR409   24/12/44; 'OB.D'; 5/45

HR413   21/10/44-1/45

HR415   14/12/44; 'OB.R'; 1/45. Reissued by 12/45; 'OB.H'; scrapped 29/8/46

HR437   23/12/44-12/44

HR441   18/1/45; 'OB.X'; 31/5/45

HR447   2/12/44; 'OB.Y' and 'OB.D'; engine fire, landed Kalemyo, 26/12/44: Plt Off W G Taylor RAAF and WO K Putman

HR451   11/12/44; 'OB.D' and 'OB.F'; port engine damaged by bomb blast and debris, crash-landed Sinthe, 15/3/45: Flt Lts W S McLellan RAAF and J R Vernon RAAF

HR453   13/12/44; 'OB.L'; crashed landing asymmetric, Yazagyo, 17/12/44: Plt Off J M Levey RAAF and Fg Off H J Cargill RAAF both killed

HR455   3/11/44; 'OB.H'; damaged by AA fire, wheels up, Kumbhirgram, 9/1/45: Plt Off J R Wilson RCAF and WO W J Hayward

HR456   by 20/12/44; 'OB.M'; 27/5/45

HR457   13/12/44; 'OB.H'; broke up in dive attack, 40 mls south east of Mandalay, 28/2/45: Flt Lt B V Draper and WO P R James both killed

HR458   4/11/44; 'M'; 15/11/44

HR459   12/44-12/44

HR462   by 15/12/44; 'OB.J'; 7/5/45

HR487   11/44; 'OB.C'; 17/11/44

HR491   23/12/44; 'OB.X' and 'OB.B'; 8/45

HR492   14/11/44; 'OB.Y'; engine cut on take off (water in fuel?), crashed near Kumbhirgram, 12/1/45: Plt Off J R Wilson RCAF and WO W J Hayward both killed

HR493   28/12/44; passed directly to No 82 Sqn

HR497   28/12/44; passed directly to No 82 Sqn

HR498   3/45-4/45

HR514   23/12/44; 'OB.T' and 'OB.C'; 28/5/45

HR515   21/12/44; 'OB.Z'; engine cut on take off, crashed near Kumbhirgram, 3/1/45: WOs J S McQueen RNZAF and W P

Edwards both killed

HR526   18/12/44; 'OB.P'; damaged by AA fire, undercarriage collapsed on landing, Kumbhirgram, 9/1/45: Fg Off F C Fortune and Fg Off L A Mears. Repaired; in service until 7/5/45

HR527   8/12/44; 'OB.X', 'OB.L' and 'OB.Y'; hit ground attacking MT, Irrawaddy Valley, 26/3/45: WO A Holmes and F/Sgt W A Austen both killed

HR539   2/45; 'OB.H'; 8/45

HR541   in use by 9/45 as 'OB.A' until 12/45 at least

HR563   3/45-4/45

HR566   20/1/45; 'OB.A'; 3/45

HR567   by 18/12/44; 'OB.D' and 'OB.F'; overshot runway, undercarriage collapsed, Monywa, 4/4/45: WO B Walsh and WO H Orsborn

HR573   by 7/3/45; 'OB.K'; 20/7/45 at least

HR574   17/1/45; not accepted by sqn

HR627   19/3/45; 'OB.A'; 27/7/45 at least

HR633   4/45; 'OB.C'; 11/45 at least

HR638   in use 7/45

HR642   9/45; 'OB.P'; 10/1/46 at least

HX815   14/6/45-?

HX820   30/5/45-?

HX821   by 19/4/44; 'M'; 10/44 (possibly the aircraft which had suffered a partial structural failure on 4/10/44; while being flown by Sqn Ldr Bourke and Fg Off Dumas; it crashed during a test flight with No 143 RSU on 10/10/44)

HX822   by 25/3/44; 'T'; 31/5/44 at least

LR250   29/2/44; 'Y'; port undercarriage leg jammed up - belly landed, Amarda Rd, 18/5/44: Fg Off J O Cartledge RAAF and Fg Off G F Williams RAAF

LR304   3/44; 'R'; swung on take off, undercarriage collapsed, Ranchi, 9/9/44: Flt Lt C R Goodwin and Fg Off S Potts

LR306   4/44; 'N'; circa 27/10/44

LR307   by 5/4/44; 'C'; circa 27/10/44

LR309   30/6/44-?

LR310   18/6/44; 'X'; 9/44

RF584   29/3/45; swung on landing - undercarriage collapsed, Cholavaram, 26/8/45: Fg Off G C Viner and LAC Waddington

RF585   4/45; 'OB.T'; scrapped 11/10/45

RF598   24/3/45; 'OB.M'; scrapped after losing a panel in flight, landed Yelahanka, 4/6/45: Plt Off R J Wilcock and ?

RF657   5/45; 'OB.N'; 11/45 at least

RF660   26/3/45; 'OB.S'; scrapped 25/4/46

RF666   21/3/45; ASI u/s, stalled on landing, broke off tailwheel, Yelahanka, 22/2/46: Flt Lt N R Harrison and Fg Off G P McMahon; scrapped 8/10/46

RF668   1/4/45; 'OB.J'; props struck ground during formation take off, Cholavaram, 26/7/45: Fg Off J H Robertson and ?; scrapped 8/10/46

RF672   10/4/45; 'OB.R'; 3/46 at least

RF679   by 19/4/45; 'OB.D'; scrapped 8/10/46

RF697   21/4/45; 'OB.L'; crashed, St Thomas Mount, 12/10/45: Flt Lt H W McCracken and Fg Off R Fussell both injured; pilot died 23/10/45

RF736   25/7/45; OB.K; 11/45 at least

RF761   15/3/45; 'OB.D'; scrapped 29/8/46

RF774   by 7/45; 'OB.F'; scrapped 8/10/46

RF778   14/8/45; 'OB.T'; scrapped 8/10/46

RF785   3/5/45; 'OB.V'; 29/3/46

RF792   15/3/46; 'OB.X'; scrapped 8/10/46

RF947   20/8/45; 'OB.M'; touched down tail first, tailwheel unit broke off, St Thomas Mount, 18/1/46: Flt Lt N R Harrison and ?; scrapped 8/10/46

RF953   25/7/45; 'OB.X'; scrapped 5/6/47

RF957   15/9/45; 'OB.B'; scrapped 8/10/46

RF962   in use 14/5/46-27/5/46

RF964   10/9/45; 'OB.Z'; scrapped 5/6/47

TE599   9/10/45; 'OB.L'; to No 18 Sqn 17/6/47

TE619   1/7/46-2/7/46 (ferried Mauripur-Negombo)

TE640   27/6/46; 'OB.F'; missing on met recce, Bay of Bengal, 5/11/46: Flt Lt A V Proctor and F/Sgt G D Thomas both killed

TE796   11/7/46; 'OB.P'; to No 18 Sqn 26/4/47

TE799   11/7/46; scrapped 5/1/47

TE809	11/7/46; 'OB.N'; to No 18 Sqn 17/6/47
TE811	28/5/46; spun in during unauthorised aerobatics, Trincomalee, 3/12/46: Flt Lt E Garland and F/Sgt J Edwards both killed
TE857	by 7/46
TE859	11/7/46; 'OB.C'; to No 18 Sqn 26/4/47
TE879	11/7/46; 'OB.B'; to No 18 Sqn 26/4/47

DeHavilland Mosquito III

LR521	by 1/4/44-14/11/44 (to No 1672 CU)
LR558	17/10/46; scrapped 31/12/46
TW110	25/7/46; to 18 Sqn 17/6/47

North American Harvard II. The Harvards specifically on charge to No 45 Sqn are listed below but while the squadron was attending No 9 Fighter Refresher Course at Amarda Road during May 1944 a number of the AFTU's aircraft were used for academic gunnery training exercises. Although these Harvards did not actually belong to the squadron it may be of interest to note that they included FE606, FE704, FE772, FE955, FE957 and FS704.

FE426	by 14/11/44-16/2/45 at least
FE614	?/45; crashed inverted from low run near Kumbhirgram, 14/5/45: Fg Offs F C Fortune and G Lauder both killed
FS925	7/44-31/8/45
FS929	11/44-30/5/46
FS945	13/6/44-27/9/45
FT186	by 8/45-14/6/49 (to No 1301 Flt)

November-December 1944

Although not on charge to No 45 Sqn, the following aircraft are known to have been flown by the squadron's pilots who were detached to Imphal (22 Nov 44-9 Dec 44) and Cox's Bazaar (22 Nov 44-18 Dec 44) while their Mosquitos were grounded.

No 221 Gp Comm Sqn, Imphal. **Stinson L-5 Sentinels** including KJ408, KJ414, KJ415 and KJ427 and **Tiger Moths** including DG542 and NL721.

No 224 Gp Comm Sqn, Cox's Bazaar. **Stinson L-5 Sentinels** including KJ411, KJ412, KJ420, KJ423, KJ425 and KJ426 and **Tiger Moths** including T6038, DE732, EN951, EM978, EM979, LV764 and NL811.

December 1946-February 1950

Bristol Beaufighter TF 10

RD760	20/12/49-20/2/50*
RD766	3/12/46; 'OB.D'; scrapped 12/2/48 (beyond economic repair due to corrosion)
RD775	5/47; 'OB.H'; crashed on landing, Negombo, 30/11/48: Fg Off W Edwards and N3 P J Lavender
RD776	12/12/46; 'OB.B'; crashed asymmetric, Negombo, 16/5/47: Fg Off R M Currie killed
RD777	31/12/46; 'OB.C'; scrapped 12/2/48 (beyond economic repair due to corrosion)
RD782	13/3/47; 'OB.L'; tyre burst on take off - belly-landed, Negombo, 11/11/47: Fg Off R A S Bingham
RD784	3/9/48; 'OB.Z', *Winnie the Pooh*; 20/9/49
RD785	16/1/47; 'OB.G'; scrapped 12/3/48 (beyond economic repair due to corrosion)
RD786	16/1/47-1/9/48
RD789	27/3/47; 'OB.B'; 26/8/48
RD805	1/4/; 'OB.J'; 20/2/50
RD808	3/3/48; 'OB.D'; tyre burst on take off - belly-landed, Negombo, 2/11/48: P2 M F J Berrey and N3 A A France
RD816	1/12/48; 'OB.D'; 18/1/50
RD817	1/3/48; 'OB.C'; 9/2/50
RD819	1/47; 'OB.F'; lost port engine cowling, emergency landing Tengah, 18/1/50: Fg Off W Edwards
RD820	1/47; 'OB.E'; 18/1/50
RD824	2/47; 'OB.K'; fuel tank exploded on start-up, Negombo, 4/11/47: Fg Off R T Saunders
RD825	1/3/48; 'OB.A'; undercarriage collapsed on practice asymmetric landing, Negombo, 14/1/49: Flt Lt K A O

	Norman and N1 Kerr
RD826	2/9/48; 'OB.X'; 8/12/49
RD830	12/12/46; 'OB.A'; scrapped (beyond economic repair due to corrosion), 12/3/48,
RD836	4/9/48; 'OB.Y'; 18/1/50
RD852	20/9/49-20/2/50*
RD857	9/8/48; 'OB.R'; 18/1/50
RD858	20/8/48; 'OB.R'; crashed on approach to Butterworth, 11/2/49: P2 M F J Berrey and N2 L J Harris killed
RD866	28/7/48; 'OB.K'; engine cut, crashed 7 mls south of Durian Tipus, 26/11/49: Fg Off L S R Smith and Sgt Townley (Pax) killed; N3 L W Curry severely burned,

*Either RD760 or RD852 was coded OB.P; it was one of the aircraft which had been repainted in the late black/grey colour scheme by the time it was finally retired.

Bristol Buckmaster T.1

VA366	22/10/46; 'OB.FA'; 14/7/47 grounded (corroded fuel tanks)
VA367	2/11/46; 'OB.FB'; 14/7/47 grounded (corroded fuel tanks)

North American Harvard T.2

FE609	29/1/48-1/6/48 (from/to RAF Negombo)
FE959	29/1/48-1/6/48 (from/to RAF Negombo)
FS795	29/1/48-25/3/48 (from RAF Negombo; scrapped)
FS952	29/1/48-1/6/48 (from/to RAF Negombo)
FT100	29/1/48-1/6/48 (from/to RAF Negombo)
FT186	by 8/45-14/6/49 (to No 1301 Flt)
KF141	21/7/49-22/8/49

September 1949-February 1952

Bristol Brigand B.1

RH755	9/12/51; 'OB.G'; 15/2/52
RH756	28/4/51-15/2/52
RH776	18/9/51-18/2/52
RH829	13/12/49; 'OB.M'; belly-landed, Tengah, 21/12/50: Sqn Ldr A C Blythe. Repaired and restored to use until 15/2/52
RH832	13/1/50; damaged by premature explosion of 500lb bomb, 27/4/50: Sqn Ldr A C Blythe
RH850	4/5/50; 'OB.U'; crashed during attack in Kelantan, 6/7/50: Fg Off N B Harben, N3 T W Smith, and S3 C Lloyd all killed
RH851	19/4/51-12/2/52
VS813	6/1/50; 'OB.Q'; 15/2/52
VS838	14/11/49; 'OB.A'; cannon exploded, fire, crashed near Ipoh, 11/1/51: Sgt Nav G A Robinson and Sgt Sig K Hall killed; Sgt Plt S V Hayler baled out but died from injuries
VS855	19/12/49; 'OB.V'; 10/3/52
VS857	21/9/49; 'OB.K'; lost prop, engine fell out, crashed Kranji Creek, 15/6/51: Sgt Plt A J Martin injured, Sgt Nav V Bowen killed, Sgt Sig P A Weston escaped
VS859	25/11/49; 'OB.G'; cannon exploded, crashed Pilah, 15/2/51: Sgt Plt W Kent and Sgt Nav B A Ellis killed
VS863	12/1/51; 'OB.L'; 15/2/52
VS864	29/12/49; 'OB.N'; wheels up at Seletar, 24/7/51: Sgt Plt M A Clarke and Sgt Nav A C Smith
VS865	7/7/50; 'OB.R'; 26/2/52
VS868	22/2/51; 'OB.A'; 18/2/52

Bristol Buckmaster T.1

RP198	18/8/49; 'OB.Z'; 5/2/52

Bristol Brigand Met 3. Official records note the three aircraft listed below as having been on charge to No 45 Sqn at Negombo between the dates shown. In view of these dates, however, these can have been no more than paper transactions as the squadron's rear party left Ceylon for Malaya on May 28th, a fortnight before the last of these aircraft arrived. All three were passed to No 1301 Flt.

VS821	27/5/49-14/6/49
VS822	25/5/49-14/6/49

VS824   10/6/49-14/6/49

DeHavilland Hornet F.3.   The aircraft marked with an asterisk were actually built as Hornet F.4s.

PX289   ex-33 Sqn 25/3/55; 'T'; scrapped 26/4/55
PX293   ex-33 Sqn 25/3/55; 'V'; to Seletar 18/5/55
PX306   ex-33 Sqn 25/3/55; to Seletar 16/5/55
PX310   4/12/54; 'OB.M' and 'M'; to Seletar 16/5/55
PX312   19/10/54; scrapped 26/4/55
PX328   ex-33 Sqn 25/3/55; 'X'; scrapped 28/4/55
PX332   21/1/55; canopy shattered, written off at Tengah, 16/2/55: Fg Off J H W Wilson
PX335   ex-33 Sqn 25/3/55; 'A'; to Seletar 16/5/55
PX342   ex-33 Sqn 25/3/55; 'W'; to Seletar 16/5/55
PX346   ex-33 Sqn 25/3/55; 'Y'; scrapped 26/4/55
PX348   ex-33 Sqn 25/3/55; 'G'; to Seletar 16/5/55
PX350   3/12/54; 'OB.S'; collided with PX362, Butterworth, 2/4/55: Fg Off J E Bowler (killed)
PX352   1/12/52; 'OB.R' and 'R'; to Seletar 16/5/55
PX353   20/10/52;'OB.F'; to Seletar 25/3/55
PX354   5/1/53; 'OB.S' and 'S'; scrapped 2/5/55
PX362   8/10/54; collided with PX350, Butterworth, 2/4/55: Fg Off R J Russell (killed)
PX367   24/9/53; sank back after take off, undercarriage collapsed on landing, Butterworth, 26/4/55: Fg Off P J Walsh
PX369   24/3/53; undercarriage jammed - belly landed, Tengah, 6/12/54: Fg Off J H W Wilson
PX384   ex-33 Sqn 25/3/55; 'E'; to Seletar 16/5/55
PX389   20/10/52; swung into monsoon drain on landing, Tengah, 21/5/53: Fg Off E A Peters
PX391   10/5/55; to Seletar 16/5/55
WB875   22/7/53; 'OB.N'; to Seletar 27/7/54
WB876   3/7/52; 'OB.O' and 'OB.E'; to Seletar 25/3/55
WB877   ex-33 Sqn 25/3/55; 'B'; to Seletar 16/5/55
WB879   24/4/55; 'OB.T' and 'T'; to Seletar 16/5/55
WB883   3/7/52; to Seletar 6/4/55
WB898   28/1/52; 'OB.A'; dived into sea, Song Song Range, 15/7/53: Fg Off B P H Lacey killed
WB908   28/2/52; 'OB.L'; swung on landing - undercarriage collapsed, Tengah, 29/9/54: MPlt R J Buckley
WB911   28/2/52; 'OB.B'; hydraulic failure, belly landed, Tengah, 14/9/54: Sgt J C Doudy
WB912   1/1/52; 'OB.C'; hit trees recovering from attack, Seremban, 28/8/52: Plt Off R Jackson killed
WF954   20/10/52; 'OB.Q'; swung on landing - undercarriage collapsed, Tengah, 25/8/53: Plt Of C A Rogers. Heavyweight landing - undercarriage collapsed, Tengah, 1/9/54: Fg Off I D Pattinson
WF956   1/5/52; 'OB.M'; no ASI, ran into overshoot and undercarriage collapsed, Tengah, 30/9/54: Plt Off J H S Greenwood
WF957   ex-33 Sqn 25/3/55; 'H'; to Seletar 16/5/55
WF959   1/2/52; 'OB.K' and 'K'; to Seletar 16/5/55
WF961   5/7/52; 'OB.D' and 'D' to Seletar 16/5/55
WF966   5/7/52; 'OB.N'; to Seletar 3/4/55
WF967   20/12/52; 'OB.H'; hydraulic failure, wheels-up landing, Tengah, 12/2/53: Sgt G J Turley. Repaired and restored to use; to Seletar 25/3/55
*WF970   ex-33 Sqn 25/3/55; to Seletar 16/5/55;
*WF973   ex-33 Sqn 25/3/55; 'O' to Seletar 16/5/55
*WF975   ex-33 Sqn 25/3/55; 'N'; dumb-bell marking; to Seletar 16/5/55

DeHavilland Mosquito T.3

RR290   14/1/52; lost port wing, broke up, 24 mls north of Tengah, 21/2/52: Sgt P Holden-Rushworth baled out, Sgt Nav R J Gratton killed
RR297   ex-33 Sqn 25/3/55-18/5/55
RR308   15/3/52-3/7/52
RR311   1/2/52; 'OB.X'; yawed on asymmetric approach and hit bulldozer, Tengah, 13/1/53: Sqn Ldr I S Stockwell and Wg Cdr M W B Knight
RR312   ex-33 Sqn 25/3/55-27/5/55
VA888   13/9/52-13/3/53 (also in use earlier on loan from FETS)
VT586   29/10/54-18/5/55

VT590   11/6/53-28/12/53
VT628   19/1/53-9/9/54 (scrapped - defective glued joints)

DeHavilland Vampire T.11

WZ521   7/1/54; undercarriage retracted on take off 12/3/54: Fg Off J E Bowler and Fg Off E A Peters. Repaired; passed to No 14 Sqn RNZAF, 26/4/55

The aircraft listed immediately below are the assortment of jets which were hastily collected and issued to the squadron to keep it flying after the sudden grounding of its Hornets. The notation 'APC' indicates that the aircraft concerned were transferred to and/or from the squadron's charge from and/or to that of the collocated APC Butterworth.

DeHavilland Vampire T.11

WZ610   ex-APC 17/5/55; to APC 24/10/55

Gloster Meteor T.7

WA676   ex-Seletar 3/6/55; to APC 29/8/55
WA683   ex-APC 17/5/55; to APC 29/8/55
WG976   ex-Seletar 27/5/55; to Seletar 15/6/55

Gloster Meteor F.8

WA761   ex-Seletar 16/6/55; to APC 29/8/55
WH379   ex-Seletar 18/5/55; undershot, Butterworth, 8/8/55: Fg Off A D Ashworth
WH410   ex-APC 17/5/55; to APC 29/8/55
WK649   ex-Seletar 1/7/55; to APC 29/8/55
WL171   ex-Kai Tak 3/6/5; to APC 29/8/55
WL180   ex-APC 17/5/55; to APC 29/8/55

DeHavilland Vampire FB 9

WG878   ex-60 Sqn 3/8/55; to Seletar 16/5/56
WG888   ex-60 Sqn 2/8/55; to Seletar 10/2/56
WL511   ex-60 Sqn 2/8/55; to Seletar 10/2/56
WL513   ex-60 Sqn 2/8/55; to Seletar 1/3/56
WL514   ex-60 Sqn 2/8/55; to Seletar 29/2/56
WL554   ex-60 Sqn 19/8/55; to Seletar 27/1/56
WL555   ex-60 Sqn 25/8/55; to Seletar 18/2/56
WL564   ex-APC 17/5/55; to APC 18/1/56 (actually retained by No 45 Sqn until serviceable and not returned until 26/3/56)
WR176   ex-Far East Comm Sqn 21/5/55; to Seletar 28/2/56
WR204   ex-Far East Comm Sqn 21/5/55; to Seletar 17/5/56
WR206   ex-Seletar 26/8/55; to Seletar 27/1/56

DeHavilland Venom FB 1

WE373   23/2/56; 'C'; broke up in air near Song Song Range, 24/7/56: Fg Off F W T Hobson (killed)
WE382   24/10/55; 'P'; lost hood on take off and overshot into sea, Butterworth, 21/8/56: Fg Off P J Brockson
WE387   27/8/56; 'R'; 13/9/57
WE403   15/5/56; 'R'; 22/6/56
WE407   27/2/56; 'D'; 1/7/57
WE449   17/9/56; 'P'; 2/10/57
WE450   12/9/56; 'A'; 2/12/57
WE465   17/2/56; 'E'; nosewheel collapsed, Butterworth, 17/7/56: Fg Off W E Close. Panel opened on take off - undercarriage raised, Butterworth, 15/11/56: Fg Off D V King
WE469   30/4/57; 'O'; 22/11/57
WE473   17/9/56; 'C'; 22/11/57
WE475   28/1/56; 'F'; 12/6/57
WK420   17/12/56; 'O' & 'F'; 23/12/57
WK476   17/12/56; 'E'; 4/11/57
WK477   28/1/56; 'G'; brakes failed on landing - undercarriage raised, Butterworth, 28/8/57: Flt Lt J H Badham
WK483   3/1/56; 'R'; 8/3/56

For its ferry flight back to the UK in February 1970, the last T.4, WH706, was emblazoned with CAMEL AIR *on its forward fuselage and another (indecipherable) slogan on its tip tanks; it was also the only Canberra to wear a dumb-bell. (MAP)*

WK486	21/9/55; 'N'; 13/9/57
WR277	5/3/57; 'S'; 4/12/57
WR281	23/1/56; sank back on runway on take off, Butterworth, 3/12/56: Plt Off G H Haddock
WR300	23/3/56; 'H'; 11/6/57
WR304	3/2/56; 'A'; wing hit ground on take off, Butterworth, 6/8/56: Fg Off D A Proctor
WR310	1/3/56; 'B'; 26/7/57
WR312	17/7/57; 'D'; 2/10/57
WR346	21/9/55; 'S'; 20/12/56
WR350	23/1/56; 'Q'; 10/12/57
WR353	24/10/55; 'T'; 12/11/57
WR359	21/9/55; 'V'; 26/11/57
WR369	21/9/55; lost power on take off - wheels raised, Butterworth, 13/10/55: Wg Cdr I M Gundry-White (OC Flg Wg)

DeHavilland Vampire T.11

WZ509	3/6/55; landing accident, Butterworth, 1/1/56: Fg Off J B Sullivan. Repaired and retained until 3/9/56
WZ614	ex-33 Sqn 25/3/55-15/11/56
XD398	11/10/56; 'J'; 1/9/57
XH359	4/9/56; 'X'; 30/11/57

November 1957-February 1970

English Electric Canberra. The dates given below are generally confined to those on which each aircraft was initially taken on charge by, and finally struck off the charge of, No 45 Sqn. Note that in the case of the B.2s there was some short-term interchanging between No 45 Sqn and No 75 Sqn RNZAF, and that T.4s were often 'loaned to' and 'borrowed from' No 81 Sqn but, unless these transfers were of significant duration, they have not been reflected here. Similarly, most aircraft, of all variants, were periodically passed to No 389 MU at Seletar or to the Hong Kong Aircraft Engineering Company (HAEC) for major servicing or rectification. Since these aircraft generally returned to the squadron the dates of these essentially administrative transfers have not been shown. On the other hand, the ferrying of aircraft to and from the UK was in itself a significant event (if only for the crews involved) and, since these transfers were usually associated with a major modification programme which took the aircraft out of service for several months, they have been annotated '(to UK)'.

English Electric Canberra B.2

WD948	8/4/58-3/11/59 (to UK) 23/2/60-29/1/62
WH646	16/12/57-26/4/60 (to UK) 11/6/61-8/1/62
WH665	20/12/57-26/3/60 (to UK) 4/8/60-30/12/61
WH666	19/8/58-10/10/58 (to No 75 Sqn RNZAF) 23/3/59-22/4/59
WH667	12/3/58-13/1/60 (to UK) 25/3/60-10/12/62
WH739	29/1/62-20/8/62
WH853	14/12/57; engine cut on take off, crashed 2½ mls north of Tengah, 18/11/58: Flt Lt J I T Rolfe and Fg Off B S Casling both killed; Fg Off I D Symonds slightly injured
WH874	25/11/57-21/1/60 (to UK) 17/5/60-27/10/62
WH882	28/11/57; collided with WJ983 over Pontian, 13/12/57: Flt Lt L G Hall, M Nav D M Brown and Flt Sgt E E Stevens (all killed)
WH922	8/7/59-25/2/60 (to No 75 Sqn RNZAF) 14/10/60-13/2/61
WJ567	30/12/57-4/4/59 (to UK) 11/1/60-17/4/62
WJ570	22/11/57-25/9/59 (to UK) 22/3/60-3/1/62
WJ605	26/2/62; broke up over China Rock Range, 16/4/62: Fg Off M J Moy and Flt Lt D T A Lansley both killed
WJ630	10/1/62-20/9/62
WJ632	21/4/58-13/8/59 (to UK) 29/1/60-14/9/62
WJ648	16/10/59-9/8/60
WJ727	10/8/59-21/10/60
WJ981	10/10/58-4/3/59 (under repair with No 389 MU following wheels-up landing at Don Muang by Sqn Ldr C C Blount and Flt Lt E Pordham) 2/1/60-7/3/60 (to UK) 23/6/60-10/3/62 (to No 389 MU) 28/9/62-19/10/62
WJ983	20/11/57; collided with WH882 over Pontian, 13/12/57: Sqn Ldr C C Blount and Fg Off F N Buchan ejected; Flt Lt H Hartley was killed
WJ986	5/12/61-10/12/62
WJ988	5/1/62-12/11/62
WK102	15/3/62-24/8/62

English Electric Canberra T.4

WD963	1/3/62-28/5/62 (to UK) 24/6/66; double flame-out, abandoned 2 mls south of Tengah, 29/6/67: Fg Offs I D Hill and T V Hudson ejected
WH651	16/9/63-1/12/69
WH706	26/11/57-19/1/62 (to UK) 20/6/62-7/12/63 (to UK and No 81 Sqn) 1/12/69-19/2/70
WH847	16/11/61-15/10/63

English Electric Canberra B.6

WH976	26/4/66-4/4/67
WT206	10/2/65-10/8/65

English Electric Canberra B.15. Those marked with an asterisk were AS 30 capable.

*WH948	6/6/69-19/2/70
*WH955	26/10/67-19/2/70
*WH956	8/5/67-15/7/69
WH958	13/1/63; bird strike on take off and overshot into sea, Kai Tak, 17/8/64: Flt Lt R A Renton, Fg Offs G N Wade and M S Clark and Sgt I A Ramsay
*WH959	30/6/64-13/8/65 (to UK) 25/7/67-16/5/69
*WH961	28/11/66-16/5/69
*WH963	5/12/62-12/9/66 (to UK) 25/7/67-19/2/70
WH965	11/1/63-25/4/67
*WH966	12/2/69-19/2/70
*WH968	12/2/69-19/2/70
WH969	3/9/62-25/7/67
*WH974	17/7/67-19/2/70
*WH977	13/6/69-19/2/70
*WH981	6/6/69-19/2/70
WJ766	2/10/62-14/4/69
WT208	19/11/62-14/12/66
WT209	8/10/62; hydraulic failure - wheels up, Tengah, 1/2/68: Fg Offs I D Hill, R Head and S Godfrey
WT211	10/10/62-14/2/68
*WT213	30/11/66-17/3/69
XK641	6/11/62; rolled and crashed, Lake Chini, 4/4/66: Fg Off M W Redley, Fg Off P Harrison and Flt Lt C Cooke killed

English Electric Canberra B.16

WT370	9/5/64; engine failed on overshoot, crashed off airfield, Kuantan, 23/9/64: Fg Offs P H Sykes and C G Jefford both injured

August 1972-July 1976

Hawker Hunter. The allocation of Hunters to No 45 Sqn was a slightly diffuse arrangement as half of the squadron's aircraft were allotted to No 58 Sqn when that unit was formed in August 1973. This situation was further complicated when, a year later, the fleet was pooled again under the aegis of Hunter Wing. The dates shown below are those on which the listed aircraft were formally transferred to and deleted from the specific charge of No 45 Sqn; between these dates most (if not all) will have worn the Flying Camel motif. Note that several of the aircraft were actually transferred to the squadron before its official reformation date of 1st August 1972. Note also that No 45 Sqn's pilots may well have flown some of these aircraft *after* the last date shown, ie when they were nominally on charge to either No 58 Sqn or Hunter Wing. Furthermore, other aircraft, for instance XJ686 (which was on charge to Hunter Wg between 13/10/75 and 29/6/76), may well feature in a No 45 Sqn pilot's flying log book; such aircraft are not listed below, however, as they were never, strictly speaking, Flying Camel airframes.

The squadron's Hunters were originally identified by an individual code letter, worn on the fin in white. Those which were transferred to No 58 Sqn retained their individual letters at first but all of the aircraft were subsequently recoded with two-digit numbers. Later still, possibly when the fleet was pooled, at least some of these numbers were changed. The individual identities noted below are those known to have been displayed by aircraft wearing No 45 Sqn's colours; there may have been others.

Hawker Hunter FGA 9

XE582	10/7/72; 'F' & '70'; 16/1/75 (to Hunter Wg via No 71 MU)
XE651	26/10/72; 'M'; 1/8/73 (to No 58 Sqn)
XF419	7/9/72; 'L'; 1/8/73 (to No 58 Sqn)
XF431	17/5/74; 'B' & '62'; 26/3/76 (to Hunter Wg)
XF519	6/9/72; 'N'; 1/8/73 (to No 58 Sqn)
XG130	20/6/72; 'A' & '61'; abandoned in cloud near Melton Mowbray, 17/6/74: Flt Lt I C Firth (of No 58 Sqn) ejected
XG135	8/11/72; 'B'; fire warning, abandoned on finals, crashed 2 mls east of Wittering, 6/4/73: Flt Lt G McLeod ejected
XG207	15/10/72; 'R'; 1/8/73 (to No 58 Sqn)
XG252	30/8/72; 'H' & '73'; 27/7/76 (to TWU)
XG261	8/6/72; 'C', '64' and '40'; 29/6/76 (to TWU)
XG264	26/6/72; 'J'; 1/8/73 (to No 58 Sqn)
XG291	27/6/72; 'K'; 1/8/73 (to No 58 Sqn)
XJ695	22/3/73; 'Q'; 1/8/73 (to No 58 Sqn)
XK137	6/11/72; 'D', '66' and '42'; 18/7/76 (to TWU)
XK138	23/10/72; 'E' & '67'; 29/6/76 (to No 71 MU)
XK140	9/8/72; 'P'; 1/8/73 (to No 58 Sqn)
XK151	4/6/73; 'G' & '71'; 28/1/76 (to Hunter Wg via No 71 MU)

Hawker Hunter T.7

XF310	15/8/72; 'T'; 1/8/73 (to No 58 Sqn)
XL613	10/7/72; 30/8/72 (to No 4 FTS)
XL619	7/9/72; 'S' & '77'; 6/2/75 (to Hunter Wg); 28/7/76 (to TWU)

January 1984-March 1992

Panavia Tornado GR 1

ZA322	23/6/88-3/3/89
ZA357	11/6/91-1/8/91
ZA358	22/11/89-9/5/91
ZA360	27/11/89-4/9/91
ZA362	18/12/89-22/1/91
ZA365	1/1/84-24/7/84 & 12/9/86-6/2/87
ZA366	1/1/84; major systems failure near Manby, 3/6/87: Wg Cdr A V B Hawken and Sqn Ldr N Irving ejected
ZA367	1/1/84-30/3/84 & 23/6/86-10/12/90
ZA368	1/1/84-30/3/84 & 6/3/86-17/10/91
ZA369	1/1/84-1/12/86
ZA370	1/1/84-1/10/86
ZA371	26/3/84-23/6/86
ZA372	1/1/84-12/1/89
ZA373	1/1/84-5/11/86
ZA374	1/1/84-27/11/89
ZA375	1/1/84-23/11/89
ZA393	1/1/84-18/12/89
ZA397	3/1/84-11/8/86
ZA398	2/12/85-1/12/87
ZA399	4/3/85-18/7/85
ZA400	1/1/84-31/3/87
ZA401	31/7/84-21/8/86
ZA402	1/1/84-29/3/84
ZA404	1/1/84-1/12/88
ZA405	1/1/84-21/8/87
ZA406	1/1/84-11/3/88
ZA407	1/1/84-4/2/92
ZA408	29/5/84; mid-air collision with Jaguar XZ393 near Sheringham, 12/7/84: Sqn Ldr E A Boxhall-Hunt and Flt Lt Cave ejected
ZA409	24/11/87-16/10/91

ZA410	27/3/85-16/9/85 & 7/1/86-5/3/86
ZA411	6/3/85-17/9/85 & 13/1/86-6/5/86
ZA447	16/11/87-20/11/87
ZA464	17/5/86-17/6/86
ZA466	15/9/88-14/11/88
ZA540	9/12/87-20/12/88
ZA541	21/12/87-24/5/90 & 25/10/91-31/3/92
ZA542	7/1/91-11/4/91
ZA543	7/3/85-11/3/92
ZA544	1/1/84-8/9/87 & 16/3/92-31/3/92
ZA545	28/8/86; mid-air collision with Tornado ZA464 near Spurn Head, 14/8/90: Maj D Wise USAF and Flt Lt J Bowles; both killed
ZA547	7/1/91-30/4/91
ZA548	15/5/87-31/3/92
ZA549	16/10/84-20/2/87 & 28/2/91-31/3/92
ZA551	1/1/84-8/9/86 & 1/6/87-30/7/87 & 22/5/89-31/3/92
ZA552	1/1/84-19/2/88
ZA555	1/1/84; major systems failure near Diss, 1/12/86: Sqn Ldr E Wyer and Flt Lt J Magowan ejected
ZA556	1/1/84-31/3/92
ZA557	5/6/90-31/3/92
ZA559	8/10/86-22/4/87 & 28/2/90-31/3/92
ZA562	1/1/84-27/6/84
ZA564	18/9/86-24/4/87
ZA585	19/3/91-31/3/92
ZA587	12/12/86-26/1/89
ZA588	29/10/86-5/12/89
ZA589	5/1/87-15/1/90
ZA590	17/3/87-31/3/92
ZA591	22/10/86-18/3/88
ZA593	29/8/85-30/8/85 & 9/9/86-15/12/86
ZA594	1/1/84-23/6/87 & 22/2/91-31/3/92
ZA595	2/4/84-24/3/92
ZA596	17/10/86-31/3/92
ZA598	2/4/84-12/2/88
ZA599	1/1/84-30/3/84 & 8/6/87-24/6/88 & 21/3/91-31/3/92
ZA601	22/10/91-31/3/92
ZA602	16/1/92-31/3/92
ZA604	13/8/84-31/3/92
ZA606	10/4/89-7/1/92
ZA607	19/3/91-31/3/92
ZA608	29/10/91-31/3/92
ZA612	2/7/84-7/12/87 & 17/10/91-31/3/92
ZA613	24/2/86-19/3/86 & 7/1/91-15/7/91
ZA614	3/2/92-31/3/92
ZD713	24/4/87-15/11/90
ZD738	29/5/86-30/5/86
ZD743	22/8/85-5/9/85 & 7/1/88-12/12/90
ZD842	3/2/88-27/10/91
ZG705	4/3/91-15/3/91 & 31/10/91-1/11/91
ZG708	1/12/89-8/1/90 & 30/5/91-18/6/91
ZG709	3/1/90-5/11/91
ZG710	8/11/91-5/2/92
ZG711	7/12/90-21/3/91
ZG713	19/3/92-24/3/92
ZG725	16/3/91-18/3/91
ZG726	8/10/91-15/10/91
ZG727	22/2/91-31/3/92
ZG750	12/9/91-31/3/92

June 1992 to date

British Aerospace Jetstream T.1

XX482	1/6/92; 'J'
XX491	1/6/92; 'K'
XX492	1/6/92; 'A'
XX493	1/6/92; 'L'
XX494	1/6/92; 'B'
XX495	1/6/92; 'C'
XX496	1/6/92; 'D'
XX497	1/6/92; 'E'
XX498	1/6/92; 'F'
XX499	1/6/92; 'G'
XX500	1/6/92; 'H'

Annex M. Officers and aircrew of No 45 Sqn, 1916-76.

This annex lists all of the officers and aircrew who have been identified as having served with No 45 Sqn. Regrettably, it is incomplete. The information is presented in two blocks, reflecting the squadron's two continuous periods of front-line service, 1916-19 and 1921-76.

1916-1919

The WW I section relies heavily on notes originally made by Norman Macmillan, these having been amended and refined by this writer as and where considered necessary. Macmillan's data was almost certainly extracted from No 45 Sqn's Daily Routine Orders, covering the period 16th October 1916 to 11th February 1919, which were at one time preserved by the Air Ministry's Air Historical Branch under file references 204/151/2 and 204/151/13. It has been suggested that both of these files may at one time have subsequently been available in the Public Record Office but they are not currently catalogued and, sadly, they no longer appear to exist.

The information shown comprises, where known, the individual's name and initials, the junior and senior ranks that he held while serving with No 45 Sqn and the dates defining his time on the unit's strength. Space does not permit the inclusion of much additional data and this has been confined to noting losses and casualties, although in many cases some additional amplification will be found in the main narrative.

Information relating to the squadron's earliest members is particularly sparse and it should be noted that, although they are listed here as 'aircrew', few were certified as such when they arrived; Lubbock, for instance, joined the squadron in April 1916 but he did not actually gain his wings until July. Only a handful of the original batch of pilots became permanent members of No 45 Sqn; many, eg Pralle, Beanlands and True, spent a couple of months collecting the necessary ticks in boxes to qualify in 'Higher Aviation' before being posted to a mobilising unit or to a formed squadron already in France.

The considerable length of the following list could create a false impression of the overall size of the squadron and a few words of explanation may be advisable. From December 1916 onwards the squadron's established fighting strength was eighteen crews/pilots, plus the CO and the three flight commanders. During the 1½ Strutter era in particular, however, there was a very rapid turnover of personnel as a result of heavy combat losses. Although replacements generally arrived fairly promptly, many of them failed to make the grade and left again after only a few weeks, even days. Most rejected pilots, for instance 2/Lts Burdekin, Evans, Fenton and Harriman, were sent away, usually to Home Establishment (HE), ie back to the UK, to receive further training. On the other hand, many of the observers and gunners who failed to make satisfactory progress (and others who elected to do so at their own request) returned to their original units, for instance 2/AM Hale, Dvr Newton, 2/Lt Scott, Lt Shaver, Lt Sorton and 2/Lt Westerman. The overall picture is further distorted by an occasional inter-squadron trade in back-seaters between Nos 20 and 45 Sqns which was

presumably operated to their mutual convenience to dispose of temporary surpluses and/or to make up for shortfalls. Such arrangements were generally of short duration, as when 2/Lt Flynne and Pte Grenner were attached from No 20 Sqn on 19th August 1917; Flynne returned to his own unit the next day but Grenner was wounded on the 21st while flying a sortie with a No 45 Sqn pilot.

Sickness also helped to sustain the rapid throughput of personnel, since the RFC generally attempted to maintain the effective strength of its units in the field; if admission to hospital was likely to be of significant duration, the patient was often struck off the strength of the squadron to make room for a replacement. Apart from the normal incidence of ailments, a number of the aircraft accidents listed at Annex L led to people being withdrawn from flying duties, although they were not formally categorised as having been wounded or injured and did not therefore feature in casualty returns; such cases included 2/Lt Forrest and Gnr Lambert and, probably, Capt Mackay and 2/Lt Cann; there were almost certainly others.

Apart from casualties and sickness, people also left the squadron for more positive and/or administrative reasons. A few observers, for instance, were sent home for pilot training; Pte Gagne left on commissioning; Lt Musgrave was considered to be too tall to convert to Camels and was posted to fly DH 4s with No 57 Sqn and a number of notably successful pilots, eg 2/Lts Montgomery and T F Williams, were upgraded to Flight Commander status and posted to other units to fill flight commander appointments as captains. As a result of these and numerous other considerations the number of personnel who passed through No 45 Sqn's hands was considerably in excess of that necessary merely to make up for losses - the same was true of every other squadron in the RFC/RAF at the time.

The abbreviations used in the following tabulation are:

A	Acting, as in A/RO - Acting Recording Officer
AEO	Assistant Equipment Officer
AG	Air Gunner
AO	Armament Officer
circa	used to indicate a probable but unconfirmed date
EdO	Education Officer
IFA	Injured in Flying Accident
KFA	Killed in Flying Accident
KIA	Killed in Action
MIA	Missing in Action, later presumed or confirmed to have been killed
O	Observer
P	Pilot
POW	Prisoner of War
RO	Recording Officer
WO	Wireless Officer
WIA	Wounded in Action

Name and rank (s)	Trade	Dates		Notes
		From	To	
J R Aikins, 2/Lt	P	13/10/17	24/10/17	
G Alchin, Lt	O	15/4/16	circa 7/16	
V B Allen, Lt	P	by 9/16	26/10/16	
H J Andrews, Lt	P	1/5/18	2/6/18	

511

Name		From	To	Note
D V Armstrong, 2/Lt	P	19/3/16	circa 5/16	
N G Arnold, 2/Lt	O	19/7/16	8/1/17	
J G Aronson, 2/Lt	P	4/16	circa 7/16	
F H Austin, 2/Lt	O	19/7/16	24/5/17	WIA
F C Axford, Pte	AG	29/6/17	27/8/17	
J N Baker, 2/Lt	P	circa 8/16	circa 10/16	
C A Barber, 2/Lt	P	1/7/17	6/8/17	
J H Baring-Gould, 2/Lt	O	7/5/17	10/5/17	
G B Barker, 2/Lt	P	23/3/17	3/4/17	IFA
A J F Bawden, Lt	O	30/7/17	15/8/17	WIA
P Beanlands, 2/Lt	P	19/3/16	circa 7/16	
B G Beatty, 2/Lt	O	22/7/17	28/7/17	MIA
L Beer, 2/Lt	O	circa 8/16	circa 10/16	
J D Belgrave, Lt	P	30/11/16	1/6/17	
A N Benge, Capt	P	4/6/17	15/6/17	
G H Bennett, 2/Lt	O	by 9/16	21/10/16	WIA
R S Bennie, 2/Lt	P	11/5/17	5/6/17	MIA
H T Birdsall, 2/Lt	AEO	28/3/16	4/11/16	
W Birkett, Lt	O	28/4/17	10/5/17	
J R Black, 2/Lt	P	26/11/17	15/8/18	IFA
G W Blaiklock, Lt	O	22/4/17	1/9/17	
J E Blake, 2/Lt	O	2/2/17	6/4/17	MIA
H G C Bowden[1], 2/Lt	P	26/10/16	11/3/17	KIA
F S Bowles, Lt	P	1/5/18	3/11/18	POW
W S Brayshay, Capt	O	17/2/17	6/4/17	MIA
G A Brooke, Lt	O	18/6/17	1/9/17	
E J Brown, 2/Lt	P	1/8/17	17/8/17	KIA
R J Brownell, 2/Lt-Capt	P	4/9/17	21/4/18	
W E G Bryant, Lt	RO	2/11/16	27/9/17	
R Buck, Lt	AO	1/12/17	5/2/19	
J Burdekin, 2/Lt	P	17/7/17	26/7/17	
G H Bush, 2/Lt-Capt	P	10/9/17	2/6/18	
K L Caldwell, 2/Lt	P	3/16/16	22/7/16	
S J E Callcott, 2/Lt	P	29/9/18	1/1/19	
A V Campbell, 2/Lt	P	23/7/17	18/8/17	
C StG Campbell, 2/Lt	P	7/12/16	6/4/17	MIA
L Cann, 2/Lt	O	30/7/17	17/8/17	WIA
A G Cardwell, 2/Lt	O	circa 8/16	circa 10/16	
A S Carey, 2/Lt	O	19/7/16	27/5/17	MIA
C W Carleton, 2/Lt	O	29/1/17	17/6/17	
P Carpenter, 2/Lt	P	14/9/17	27/2/18	
C G Catto, 2/Lt-Lt	P	16/3/18	2/19	
T StG Caulfield, 2/Lt	P	6/6/17	16/6/17	MIA
E T Caulfield-Kelly, 2/Lt-Lt	O	7/4/17	28/5/17	WIA
L A Chamier, Lt	P	by 9/16	27/10/16	
A Champion, 2/Lt	P	23/7/17	3/9/17	
W Chandler, Pte	AG	by 10/16	28/11/16	
A E Charlwood, Lt-Capt	P	23/2/17	1/9/17	
J E Child, 2/Lt-Lt	P	6/9/17	29/7/18	
E D Clarke, 2/Lt-Lt	P	12/8/17	26/10/17	WIA
R L Clegg, Lt	P	15/8/17	3/9/17	KIA
G H Cock, 2/Lt-Capt	P	25/7/16	22/7/17	POW
E A Cook, Sgt	P	10/4/17	5/6/17	MIA
E A Cooke, 2/Lt	P	18/9/17	21/9/17	POW
H B Coomber, Capt	P	30/9/17	12/10/17	MIA
L M Copeland, 2/Lt	O	17/5/17	1/9/17	
W G Corner, 2/Lt	O	24/5/17	5/6/17	WIA
J Cottle, 2/Lt-Capt	P	16/11/17	31/1/19	
F T Courtney, 2/Lt-Capt	P	23/11/16	30/4/17	
G B Craig, 2/Lt	P	19/9/17	3/10/17	
J A Crook, Maj	P	27/7/18	21/10/18	
E F Crossland, Lt	O	2/5/17	11/17	
C M Crowe, Capt	P	18/4/16	5/16	
H F Crowe, Lt	P	12/6/18	31/1/19	
H N Curtis, 2/Lt	P	7/6/17	25/7/17	MIA
R V Curtis, 2/Lt	A/AEO	10/2/19	2/19	
M J Dalton, 2/Lt	O	17/5/17	1/9/17	
H Dandy, 2/Lt	O	22/7/17	1/9/17	
G A H Davies, 2/Lt	O	24/5/17	7/6/17	MIA
B R Davis, Lt	P	6/9/17	20/9/17	MIA
P Davis, Rfn	AG	31/5/17	4/8/17	
R G H Davis[2], Lt	P	9/6/18	21/9/18	
R J Dawes, 2/Lt-Capt	P	22/8/17	29/7/18	
R H Deakin, 2/Lt	P	8/7/17	22/7/17	MIA
H D W Debenham, 2/Lt	O	circa 8/16	circa 10/16	
E B Denison, 2/Lt	P	1/9/17	11/9/17	POW
J H Dewhirst, 2/Lt-Lt	P	10/2/18	25/1/19	
A E J Dobson, 2/Lt	P	13/4/17	7/6/17	MIA
M D G Drummond, Lt	P	24/11/17	11/2/18	
J W G Dunne, 2/Lt	O	23/7/17	24/8/17	
D W Edwards, Capt	O	17/2/17	6/4/17	MIA
G Edwards, Rfn	AG	18/5/17	16/6/17	MIA
D C Eglington, Lt	O	7/4/17	26/7/17	
I G Elias, Capt	P	6/6/17	15/6/17	WIA
C S Emery, 2/Lt	O	19/7/16	26/4/17	
E E Erlebach, 2/Lt	P	30/11/16	7/2/17	MIA
H B Evans, 2/Lt	P	25/3/17	11/4/17	
G Exley, Lt	P	10/9/18	31/1/19	
T Falconer, Gnr	AG	1/17	1/17	
F H Favell, 2/Lt	O	30/7/17	23/8/17	
M A H Fell, Lt	AO	24/5/17	10/17	
W A Fellows, Dvr	AG	16/7/17	28/7/17	WIA[3]
J B Fenton, 2/Lt	P	30/1/17	24/2/17	
M J Fenwick, 2/Lt	P	by 9/16	21/10/16	WIA
C H Ferme, 2/Lt	O	circa 8/16	circa 10/16	
S K Fey[4], 2/Lt	P	25/8/18	23/10/18	
R M Findlay, 2/Lt-Capt	P	1/2/17	1/9/17	
J C B Firth, Lt-Capt	P	3/5/17	10/4/18	
H E R Fitchat, Lt	P	21/4/17	20/6/17	
R D Fleming, Cpl	AG	by 8/16	26/1/17	MIA
J P Flynne, 2/Lt	O	19/8/17	20/8/17	
J H Forbes, 2/Lt	P	2/4/17	30/4/17	
H Forrest, 2/Lt	P	2/4/17	10/5/17	
F H Foster, 2/Lt	O	17/5/17	3/6/17	MIA
J B Fotheringham, Lt	O	22/4/17	7/7/17	MIA
J O Fowler, 2/Lt	O	23/7/17	19/8/17	MIA
M B Frew, 2/Lt-Capt	P	28/4/17	10/2/18	
R G Frith, 2/Lt	P	13/10/17	5/11/17	POW[5]
D J Fryer, Lt	RO	4/7/18	9/2/19	
F Fullerton, 2/Lt	O	by 10/16	22/10/16	MIA
J Gagne, Pte	AG	10/16	25/11/16	
F G Garratt, 2/Lt	P	23/11/16	1/5/17	
M Gibson, Lt	P	12/6/18	31/1/19	
J V A Gleed, 2/Lt	P	28/6/17	7/7/17	MIA
E E Glorney, 2/Lt	P	by 10/16	25/10/16	KFA
A V Green, 2/Lt	P	6/8/18	7/1/19	IFA
D E Greenhow, 2/Lt	O	19/7/16	6/3/17	KIA
H Grenner, 2/AM	AG	19/8/17	21/8/17	WIA
C S J Griffin, Lt	P	6/16	27/3/17	
G T Griffith, 2/Lt	P	4/10/17	11/10/17	
H H Griffith, 2/Lt	P	by 9/16	13/12/16	
A J Haines, 2/Lt-Lt	P	16/11/17	10/8/18	KIA
E J Hale, 2/AM	AG	26/4/17	11/5/17	
E D Haller, 2/Lt	O	26/5/17	3/6/17	MIA
J G H P Hamel, 2/Lt	P	4/9/17	11/9/17	
E V C Hamilton, Lt	P	22/12/16	19/3/17	
P Hammond, Rfn	AG	26/5/17	15/6/17	WIA[6]
E McN Hand, 2/Lt-Lt	P	20/10/17	1/6/18	POW[7]
S G Hardy, Pte	AG	circa 8/17	8/8/17	
C A Hargreaves, 2/Lt	P	14/6/17	7/7/17	
T M Harries, 2/AM-Cpl	AG	8/3/17	16/7/17	
C H Harriman, 2/Lt	P	30/3/17	11/4/17	
A T Harris, Capt	P	18/6/17	8/10/17	
A Harrison, A/Bdr	AG	1/17	23/1/17	MIA
E Harrop, L/Cpl	AG	16/7/17	6/8/17	
J H Hartley, 2/Lt	O	17/5/17	22/7/17	KIA
L F Hawley, 2/Lt	P	23/10/18	31/1/19	
R Hayes, 2/Lt	O	14/4/17	22/7/17	MIA
L H D Henderson, 2/Lt	P	5/16	circa 7/16	
T Hewson, Lt	P	15/6/17	7/7/17	MIA
A T Heywood, Lt	P	28/7/17	3/9/17	MIA
J W Higgins, Capt	O/RO[8]	11/6/17	18/6/18	
H V Highton, 2/Lt	P	9/10/17	15/10/17	
W C Hilborn, Capt	P	13/8/18	16/8/18	IFA[9]
O S Hinson, 2/Lt	O	15/8/17	15/8/17	
W T H Hocking, 2/Lt-Lt	AEO	3/3/17	28/2/18	
W E Holland, Lt	O	17/5/17	14/6/17	
C E Howell, 2/Lt-Capt	P	28/10/17	9/8/18	
H B Hudson, 2/Lt	P	30/5/18	29/7/18	
R M Hughes, Lt	P	27/5/18	31/1/19	
J P Huins, 2/Lt-Lt	P	6/11/17	30/8/18	
L B Irish, 2/Lt	P	9/8/18	31/1/19	

Name	Role			
G R James, 2/Lt	P	14/9/17	9/17	
M R James, 2/Lt-Capt	P	12/2/18	5/2/19	
C H Jenkins, Capt	P	9/4/17	20/5/17	WIA[10]
R C Jenkins, Cpl	AG	21/12/16	31/1/17	
A Jex, Cpl-Sgt	AG	28/6/17	9/10/17	
H Johns, 2/Lt	O	circa 8/16	circa 10/16	
J Johnstone, 2/Lt	P	28/4/17	25/5/17	POW[11]
F J Jones, Lt	P	22/4/18	1/6/18	KFA
L F Jones, 2/Lt	P	by 9/16	24/10/16	
N C Jones, Capt	P	30/1/18	1/9/18	
W Jordan, 2/Lt	O	by 9/16	8/11/16	KFA
J D F Keddie, Lt	P	25/11/16	22/12/16	
A W Keen, Lt-Capt	P	31/10/16	3/12/16	
C F King, 2/Lt	AEO	20/2/18	2/2/19	
H Kirby, 2/Lt	P	29/4/17	4/5/17	
F A R C Lambert, 1/AM-Cpl	AG	12/16	24/6/17	
Lawford, F/Sgt	P	4/16	circa 7/16	
R L H Laye, 2/Lt	P	19/3/16	5/16	
H S Lees-Smith, Capt	P	circa 8/16	circa 10/16	
B C Lester, Lt	AO	30/10/17	20/11/17	
M P Lewis, 2/Lt	P	17/6/17	3/7/17	
A F Lingard, 2/Lt-Lt	P	11/2/18	28/1/19	
R Loraine, Capt	P	23/3/16	4/16	
J W Loughlin, 2/AM	AG	30/4/17	9/5/17	POW[12]
H G P Lowe, 2/Lt	P	by 5/16	8/11/16	KFA
J C Lowenstein, 2/Lt	P	8/8/17	15/8/17	WIA
Hon E F P Lubbock, Lt-Capt	P	20/4/16	11/3/17	KIA
J V Lyle, 2/Lt	P	21/12/16	23/1/17	MIA
H D Lysons, 2/Lt	P	5/7/17	24/7/17	
L W McArthur, Lt-Capt	P	29/4/16	27/5/17	MIA
D W Macintosh, Lt	A/RO	7/6/18	21/7/18	
G McIntyre, 2/Lt-Lt	P	8/3/18	31/1/19	
J S Mackay, 2/AM	AG	26/8/17	2/9/17	
J E Mackay, Capt	P	21/12/16	9/3/17	
D G McLean, Lt	P	23/1/18	4/2/18	KIA
T W McLean, 2/Lt	O	29/7/17	1/9/17	
S McLure, 2/Lt	P	4/16	circa 7/16	
O L McMaking, Lt	P	21/5/17	11/9/17	MIA
J McMechan, Gnr	AG	19/8/17	22/8/17	
N Macmillan, 2/Lt-Capt	P	31/3/17	28/1/18	
A O MacNiven, Lt	P	18/8/17	5/9/17	MIA
Malcolm, Sgt	P	by 10/16	11/16	
F A W Mann, 2/Lt	P	22/9/17	5/10/17	
E G Manuel, 2/Lt	P	19/3/16	27/10/16	
E Mark, 2/Lt	P	4/16	circa 7/16	
J A Marshall, 2/Lt	P	9/12/16	6/4/17	MIA
R H Martin, Capt	P	9/9/17	15/9/17	
E H Masters, 2/Lt-Lt	P	10/3/18	24/12/18	KFA
J C S Masters, 2/Lt	P	23/10/18	27/1/19	
T A Metheral, Lt	O	31/5/17	5/6/17	MIA
E L Milborrow, 2/Lt-Lt	P	12/6/18	24/12/18	IFA
T S Millar, 2/Lt	O	18/5/17	25/5/17	POW
A M Miller, Maj	P	21/10/18	3/2/19	
W L Mills, 2/Lt	P	13/3/17	9/5/17	MIA
K B Montgomery, 2/Lt	P	17/6/17	4/1/18	
M V Morgan, 2/Lt	P	circa 6/16	circa 8/16	
P C Morgan, 2/Lt-Lt	P	19/3/16	circa 6/16	
R C Morgan, Lt	RO	by 9/16	3/11/16	
R S V Morris, 2/Lt	O	22/7/17	1/9/17	
H M Moody, 2/Lt-Capt	P	1/8/17	2/6/18	
M Moore, Lt	O	26/10/16	22/7/17	POW
W C Moore, Lt	P	19/8/17	25/11/17	
G Mountford, Capt	P	21/4/16	12/6/17	KFA
J W Mullen, 2/Lt	O	17/5/17	10/8/17	WIA
M P Mullery, 2/Lt	AEO	16/12/16	27/2/17	
J T G Murison, 2/Lt	O	4/2/17	4/7/17	
R Musgrave, Lt	P	6/6/17	31/7/17	
P T Newling, Lt	P	17/2/17	5/6/17	WIA
C B Newton, Dvr	AG	13/8/17	3/9/17	
W Nicholls, 2/Lt	P	circa 8/16	circa 10/16	
W E Nicholson, 2/Lt	P	18/6/17	29/6/17	
T F Northcote, 2/Lt	O	26/10/16	32/1/17	WIA
E G Nuding, Lt	P	9/8/18	28/1/19	
J R O'Connell, Lt	P	6/8/18	28/1/19	
H D O'Neill, Lt	P	22/10/17	29/7/18	
F H Oxley, Lt	P	22/4/18	10/8/18	
J H Parry, 2/Lt	P	19/3/16	circa 6/16	
E Pearson, 2/Lt	P	19/3/16	circa 6/16	
G Pearson, 2/Lt	P	28/10/17	29/10/17	KFA
A E Peel, 2/Lt	O	31/7/17	10/8/17	WIA
I McA M Pender, Capt	P	24/7/17	11/8/17	WIA
B G Perrott, 2/AM	AG	2/17	30/4/17	KIA
W G L Peters, 2/Lt	P	10/3/18	16/3/18	
C I Phillips, 2/Lt	P	27/9/17	27/10/17	MIA
W O Phillips, 2/Lt	P	15/1/17	2/2/17	
J W Pinder, Capt	P	25/9/18	26/9/19	
R Platt, Lt	EdO	3/1/19	12/1/19	
W Pocock, Cpl	AG	13/2/17	12/6/17	KIA
W A Porkess, 2/Lt	P	4/16	circa 7/16	
L Porter, Capt	P	circa 7/16	22/10/16	MIA
P Pralle, 2/Lt	P	19/3/16	circa 6/16	
R C Purvis, 2/Lt	O	27/6/17	1/9/17	
N H Read, 2/Lt	P	circa 10/16	19/11/16	
W R Read, Maj	P	24/4/16	24/4/17	
C H Readman, Capt	P	20/8/18	14/9/18	
R R Renahan, 2/Lt	P	12/1/18	9/2/18	
A Rice-Oxley, Lt-Capt	P	9/7/18	30/10/18	
F J Ridgway, 2/AM	AG	1/17	7/2/17	POW[13]
C F Risteen, 2/Lt	P	21/9/17	26/9/17	MIA
C A Robertshaw, 2/Lt	P	29/9/18	28/1/19	
G M Robertson, 2/Lt	P	6/4/17	3/5/17	
W F R Robinson, 2/Lt	P	9/11/17	22/11/17	
G L Rodwell, Lt	P	circa 10/16	27/10/16	
C M Ross, 2/Lt	P	8/7/17	19/8/17	MIA
D W Ross, 2/Lt	P	13/10/17	11/1/18	MIA
G Ross-Soden, 2/Lt	P	circa 8/16	circa 10/16	
F Russell, L/Cpl	AG	4/6/17	2/7/17	WIA[14]
C E Ryan, Capt	P	19/3/16	27/4/16	
G B Samuels, 2/Lt	O	circa 10/16	22/10/16	MIA
W L Scandrett, 2/Lt	P	19/3/16	7/16	
W G Scotcher, 2/Lt	O	21/10/16	23/3/17	
J F Scott, Lt	O	10/3/17	3/5/17	
A S Selby, Lt	O	9/2/17	11/8/17	
J Senior, Lt	O	26/10/16	9/5/17	WIA[15]
E S H Sharp, Rfn	AG	3/6/17	27/6/17	KIA
W W Shaver, Lt	O	12/3/17	24/4/17	
H T Shaw, Lt	P	19/3/16	circa 6/16	
H V Shaw, 2/AM	AG	15/2/17	5/6/17	MIA
W Shields, Lt	P	1/9/17	5/9/17	KIA
R Slaughter, L/Cpl	AG	12/7/17	11/8/17	
B Smith, 2/Lt-Lt	P	11/5/17	5/6/17	POW
E A L F Smith, 2/Lt	P	12/8/17	27/10/17	POW[16]
W T Smith, Pnr	AG	1/6/17	19/8/18	
P Snowden, Sgt	P	by 9/16	22/10/16	MIA
F C H Snyder, 2/Lt	O	11/6/17	7/7/17	MIA
H P Solomon, 2/Lt	P	2/12/16	5/4/17	
T R Sorton, Lt	P	12/3/17	1/5/17	
J Sowrey, 2/Lt	P	19/3/16	5/16	
C W Sowter, 2/Lt	P	27/12/17	6/1/18	
D B Stevenson, 2/Lt	O	3/2/17	11/3/17	KIA
C G Stewart, 2/Lt	O	15/1/17	24/5/17	WIA
L A Strange, Maj	P	27/3/16	18/4/16	
E C Stringer, Lt	P	16/8/17	12/9/17	
F Surgey, Lt	O	by 9/16	22/10/16	WIA
W A Tait, Lt	P	12/6/18	26/6/18	
F W Talbot, 2/Lt	O	15/8/17	15/8/17	
F A Tappin, Pte	AG	29/6/17	27/8/17	
M L Taylor, 2/Lt	P	19/3/16	circa 8/16	
P S Taylor, Sgt-2/Lt	O	circa 9/16	22/12/16	
H T Thompson, Lt	P	1/11/17	18/12/18	
J Thompson, Sub Lt (RNVR)	O	28/10/16	11/3/17	KIA
S Thompson, 2/AM	AG	13/2/17	5/6/17	POW[17]
W J Thuell, 2/Lt	O	by 9/16	22/10/16	MIA
R True, 2/Lt	P	4/16	circa 8/16	
F G Truscott, 2/Lt	O	26/10/16	6/4/17	MIA
Turner-Bridger, 2/Lt	P	circa 5/16	circa 8/16	
H A Van Ryneveld, Maj	P	20/4/17	18/8/17	WIA
A M Vaucour, Maj	P	22/8/17	16/7/18	KIA
C W Verity, 2/Lt	P	25/10/18	circa 2/19	
J A Vessey, 2/Lt	O	19/7/16	12/6/17	KFA
O J Wade, 2/Lt	P	by 9/16	22/10/16	MIA
G H Walker, Lt	P	14/6/17	28/7/17	MIA

L W Walsh, 2/Lt	P	1/9/17	26/9/17	
W J Walsh, 2/Lt	O	15/8/17	15/8/17	
S Waltho, 2/Lt	P	30/7/17	18/8/17	
C T R Ward, Lt	O	31/5/17	1/9/17	
H C G Watney, 2?lt	P	19/3/16	circa 6/16	
R S Watt, 2/Lt	P	2/5/17	12/6/17	KIA
H J Watts, 2/Lt-Lt	P	1/11/17	26/6/18	
P F H Webb, 2/Lt	O	17/5/17	13/8/17	
W G Webb, F/Sgt	P	4/16	26/1/17	MIA
J Westerman, 2/Lt	P	26/7/17	6/9/17	
T M Wheeler, Lt	AEO	11/16	13/12/16	
F E White, 2/Lt	P	14/9/17	17/9/17	
V R S White, 2/Lt	O	18/6/17	1/9/17	

W Whittington, Pte	AG	5/7/17	16/8/17	WIA
W S Wickham, Sgt	AG	4/7/17	25/7/17	MIA
K H Willard, 2/Lt	P	9/10/17	12/10/17	KIA
J C Williams, 2/Lt	P	25/10/18	27/1/19	
T F Williams, 2/Lt-Lt	P	24/9/17	30/5/18	
W G B Williams, Capt	P	12/16	30/1/17	
W R Winterbottom, Lt	P	1/6/17	10/8/17	
W T Wood, Capt	P	9/6/17	19/7/17	
L R Wright, 2/Lt-Lt	WO	by 7/16	30/10/16	
W A Wright, 2/Lt-Capt	P	9/4/17	24/10/17	
G F Wyatt, 2/AM	AG	21/8/17	2/9/17	
R A Yeomans, Sgt	P	12/6/17	28/7/17	
H F Young, 2/Lt	O	15/8/17	15/8/17	

1921-1976

Perhaps surprisingly, while the nominal role of aircrew who flew with the squadron during the First World War is essentially complete, this cannot be said for its second and much longer period of service. It is suspected that the following list contains about 95% of the names which ought to be included and that the information which is provided is about 95% accurate. The most significant omissions are the NCO pilots and airmen gunners who flew with the squadron between 1925 and 1939, since very few of their names appear in contemporary documentation. Other periods for which information is known to be incomplete are mid-1945 to 1947 and 1973-76.

The readers attention is drawn to the following limitations regarding the tabulated data.

a. A substantial proportion of the squadron's aircrew and most of its ground branch officers spent much of the latter part of 1942 attached to other units, notably Nos 60 and 113 Sqns. These attachments are not reflected below but most are noted within the main narrative.

b. Where a date is quoted to an accuracy of a day, it has been extracted from an official document, usually the Air Force List, the ORB or a log book. It should be appreciated, however, that such dates often reflect formal appointments to established posts and are not necessarily the actual dates of arrival and/or departure. For the 1921-39 period, for instance, the departure dates given below are generally those of each officer's appointment *to* his next unit; allowing for the journey from the Middle East to the UK and (usually) a period of disembarkation leave, this could well be as much as six weeks after the individual had actually been struck off the strength of No 45 Sqn. Such mismatches can appear during any period; for example, Flt Lt J H Stevenson was posted from No 82 Sqn to No 45 Sqn with effect from 8/7/43 but he did not actually check in until 19/7/43. Similarly, while Plt Off Vinson was posted to No 45 Sqn from the Middle East Reserve Pool at Ismailia on 4th October 1940, it took him until the 10th to find his way down to Wadi Gazouza.

The abbreviations used in the following tabulation are:

AcO	Accounts Officer
Adj	Adjutant (including Assistant Adjutant/Admin Officer)
AG	Air Gunner - used to denote those airmen known to have flown with the squadron as gunners and/or wireless operators who were not qualified according to the standards introduced from January 1939. Where such an individual later remustered as a WOp/AG he is shown as such, the fact that he had flown before being denoted by the inclusion of a rank less than that of sergeant.
AILO	Air Intelligence Liaison Officer
circa	used to indicate a probable but unconfirmed date
CyO	Cypher Officer
D	Died, other than in a flying related incident
EngO	Engineer (or Technical) Officer
EqO	Equipment Officer (post 1936)
IFA	Injured in Flying Accident
IntO	Intelligence Officer
KFA	Killed in Flying Accident
KIA	Killed in Action
MO	Medical Officer
N	Navigator
O	Air Observer
P	Pilot
POW	Prisoner of War
S	Air Signaller
SigO	Signals Officer
StO	Stores Officer (pre 1937)
WAG	Wireless Operator/Air Gunner
WIA	Wounded in Action

Name and rank(s)	Trade	Date From	To	Notes
N J Abbott, WO	P	9/9/44	12/44	
R E Abbott, Flt Lt	P	16/1/58	6/6/59	
S A G Abbott, Sgt	P	by 7/37	1938	
G R Adams, Sgt	O	11/4/41	26/5/41	KIA
J M Adams, Flt Lt	AcO	6/1/28	26/3/28	
R J Aherne, Flt Lt	MO	3/3/22	1/9/22	
Ainslie, Sgt	P	7/41	1/42	
H R L Alder, 2/Lt- Capt, SAAF	P	20/10/41	24/10/42	
J F Alderton, Fg Off	P	17/12/52	31/3/55	
F E G Aldous, Plt Off	Adj	28/10/41	18/11/41	
R V Alford, Plt Off-Fg Off	WAG	12/41	circa 2/43	
H Alger, Sgt	P	8/24	1926?	
B CdeG Allan, Plt Off	P	16/10/40	28/4/41	KIA
A D Allen, 2/Lt, SAAF	P	4/10/41	1/42	
W R P Allen, Flt Lt	StO	23/11/27	28/3/28	
W S E Allen, Flt Lt	EngO	20/2/45	18/3/45	
J W Allison, AC1	AG	1939	11/6/40	KIA

K Allsop, Flt Lt	N	20/5/60	10/62	
J J Alt, Sgt, RAAF	WAG	1/42	9/7/42	
E L J Anderson, Fg Off, RAAF	P	16/3/44	19/7/44	
W F Anderson, Flt Lt	P	23/3/21	22/11/22	
E R Andrews, Sgt	P	1938	1939	
L S Andrews, Flt Lt	N	24/8/44	3/6/45	
W Appleby, Flt Lt	P	7/4/46	18/7/46	
G Archer, Fg Off	P	20/5/21	14/10/23	
J T Arklay, Plt Off	EngO	1/42	2/4/42	
G D Armitage, Fg Off-Flt Lt	N	20/5/60	10/62	
W Armour, Sgt	WAG	28/6/41	6/10/41	
R J Armstrong, Sgt-WO, RCAF	P	1/42	28/12/42	
W J Armstrong, Fg Off	P	12/4/54	6/56	
J E Arnold, Plt Off-Fg Off	IntO	20/9/42	7/12/44	
E Ashton, WO	N	3/44	6/4/45	
A D Ashworth,[18] Fg Off	P	1/4/55	18/12/55	
A D Ashworth,[18] Flt Lt	P	2/10/58	13/3/61	
G H Ashworth, F/Sgt	P	circa 12/44	17/2/45	KIA
D D Atkinson, Plt Off-Fg Off	P	18/6/34	8/12/36	

Name	Role	From	To	Note
H A C Atkinson, Fg Off	P	23/2/23	18/10/24	
P d'A Atkinson, Fg Off-Flt Lt	P	3/58	3/5/60	
E H Attwood, Fg Off-Flt Lt	P	23/11/23	13/12/26	
W A Austen, F/Sgt	N	1/45	26/3/45	KIA
J F Austen-Brown, P3/Sgt	P	25/12/49	1952	
F J Austin, Flt Lt-Sqn Ldr	P	17/9/41	23/7/42	
F T Avent, Fg Off-Flt Lt	EngO	15/7/46	2/47	
H A Aykroyd, Flt Lt	P	8/12/44	circa 7/45	
J H Badham, Plt Off-Fg Off	P	18/5/57	15/11/57	
R N Baff, Flt Lt	P	6/56	31/8/57	
Bailey, F/Sgt	P	1936	1938	
N Bain, Plt Off-Fg Off, RAAF	WAG	22/11/41	circa 8/42	
W Bain, Sgt	P	4/9/40	18/6/41	
C R Bainbridge, Fg Off	P	7/56	7/57	
Baker, Flt Lt	N	20/4/46	13/6/46	
A R Baker, Fg Off	N	6/64	3/12/66	
G H Baker, Fg Off-Flt Lt	P	1/4/55	6/56	
B A Balding, Fg Off	N	3/61	8/63	
S A Baldwin, Fg Off	N	8/64	6/2/67	
G W Balfour, Flt Lt	MO	12/9/44	9/11/44	
G D Ball, Plt Off	P	6/4/44	circa 7/44	
K A Ball, Fg Off	P	18/11/57	7/12/59	
H S Ballentyne, Flt Lt	StO	23/4/29	21/12/29	
J Banham, Sgt	P	by 10/43	2/44	
H W R Banting, Fg Off	P	13/12/22	23/1/26	
R M Barclay, Sgt-Flt Lt, RAAF	WAG/N	25/11/41	5/45	
G W Bargh, Sgt	N	3/9/44	3/10/44	KIA
F W Barkley, Fg Off	P	18/9/24	17/10/25	
E C Barlow, Flt Lt	P	14/4/34	20/4/36	
J A Barnes, Fg Off-Flt Lt	P	8/65	4/68	
J J Barnett, Fg Off-Flt Lt	P	7/72	5/11/73	
R A Baron, Fg Off	P	16/10/74	1975?	
D J Barradell, Plt Off-Fg Off	N	10/63	1/66	
F J Barrett, Flt Lt	P	9/56	9/9/57	
R Barrett, Plt Off-Fg Off	P	30/9/24	21/6/25	
Barry, Sgt	?	circa 6/40	circa 8/40	
P Bartlett, Sgt	P	7/41	circa 10/41	
T H Bartlett, F/Sgt-WO	N	5/3/45	1/12/45	
I Bashall, Fg Off-Flt Lt	P	16/1/58	1960?	
G J C P Bateman, Sgt	P	1938	1940	
Bax, Sgt	P	by 1/31	?	
G E W Baxter, Fg Off	P	18/5/57	15/11/57	
N W Bayly, Plt Off-Flt Lt, RAAF	O/N	4/10/41	circa 8/43	
G R Beamish, Flt Lt	P	12/11/34	15/11/36	
H I T Beardsworth, Fg Off-Flt Lt	P	10/8/21	18/10/24	
F W L C Beaumont, Fg Off	P	12/12/25	7/2/27	
S H Bedford, Fg Off	P	2/73	14/10/74	
D K Bednall, APO-Fg Off	P	27/5/38	6/40	
I S Beeston, Flt Lt-Sqn Ldr	P	1/42	1/12/42	
J C Belford, Flt Lt	P	27/7/31	13/5/32	
R N Belgrove, APO-Plt Off	P	10/4/37	7/1/38	
Bennet, Sgt	P	by 9/26	1927	
A W Bennett, Plt Off	Adj	by 2/41	28/8/41	
G T Bennett	P	circa 8/41	1/42	
M F J Berrey, P1	P	4/48	11/2/49	KFA
K H Berry, Fg Off	P	10/64	1967?	
D E Betts, Flt Lt	P	18/6/68	18/2/70	
J Beveridge, Fg Off	P	22/4/41	18/5/41	KIA
W Beverley, Sgt	P	by 7/40	22/4/41	KIA
A W Bilbie, Fg Off	P	3/48	11/10/48	
R A S Bingham, Fg Off	P	2/47	26/11/48	
M Birbeck, Flt Lt	P	12/46	24/12/47	
S G Birch, APO-Fg Off	P	19/4/34	22/5/37	
C E Birkbeck, Sgt-Fg Off, RAAF	O/N	17/10/41	19/7/44	
Bishop, Sgt	WAG	15/12/40	1941	
M R Bishop, Flt Lt	P	18/11/57	1/10/58	
Bissett, Sgt	O	24/4/41	30/10/41	
S C Black,[18] Fg Off	P	22/6/21	27/4/22	
S C Black,[18] Fg Off-Flt Lt	P	18/11/27	18/11/28	
Blackmore, WO	?	1/47	8/47	
C Blackshaw, AC1-Sgt	WAG	1939?	3/1/41	KIA
D M Blenkhorne, F/Sgt-Fg Off, RCAF	P	12/4/44	17/7/45	
P J Blewitt, Flt Lt	P	10/62	4/65	
Bliss, Sgt	?	circa 12/43	2/44	
O H D Blomfield, Plt Off	P	5/9/35	21/3/36	
C C Blount, Sqn Ldr	P	18/11/57	31/5/60	
A C Blythe, Sqn Ldr	P	13/2/50	27/8/51	
A L Bocking, APO-Plt Off	P	1/2/36	1/3/37	
W Bond, N3	N	3/9/48	17/1/49	
J L Bonnar, Fg Off	IntO	3/45	circa 7/45	
R D Booker, Fg Off-Flt Lt	P	9/46	29/1/49	
E J Boon, Plt Off-Fg Off	SigO	1/6/43	29/10/43	
R Booton, Sgt-F/Sgt	N	by 10/45	1946	
J H Bosher, Flt Lt	N	12/58	1960?	
M J Bosomworth, Sgt	?	2/47	3/47	
J Boston, Plt Off-Fg Off	P	9/12/30	3/2/35	
J E W Bott, Plt Off	O	8/7/41	16/7/41	
K Bottrill, Plt Off-Fg Off	N	16/12/43	12/10/44	KIA
L P Bourke, Plt Off, RNZAF	O	21/4/41	22/11/41	KIA
N L Bourke, Sqn Ldr, RAAF	P	2/3/44	16/10/44	KIA
C C Bousfield, Fg Off	P	17/2/22	14/1/23	
Bowdler, F/Sgt-WO	P	by 10/45	19/3/46	
Bowen, Sgt	P	by 1929	?	
G Bowen, Flt Lt	P	20/5/21	19/12/21	
V Bowen, Sgt	N	17/11/50	15/6/51	KFA
P Bower, Sgt	P	1938	11/6/40	KIA
J E Bowler, Fg Off	P	6/10/52	2/4/55	KFA
M W J Boxall, Fg Off	P	22/9/25	18/1/27	
Bradford, Sgt	O	7/41	9/41	
H J Bradley, Fg Off	P	20/5/21	6/2/23	KFA
G A Brady, Fg Off	N	21/2/67	18/2/70	
D A Braithwaite, Sqn Ldr	P	8/3/45	12/6/45	
G J Brand, Fg Off	P	1/4/55	8/55	
J P Brazil, Flt Lt	MO	12/5/41	25/6/41	
P Breslain, Fg Off	P	11/2/55	31/3/55	
E T StM Brett, Fg Off	P	4/6/25	15/10/26	
Brien, F/Sgt	?	1946?	10/46	
C G Briggs, Sgt, RAAF	WAG	20/10/41	24/10/42	
J L Brinkley, Sgt-Fg Off, RAAF	WAG	22/11/41	19/11/43	
H G Brittain, Flt Lt	P	22/11/52	31/3/55	
Broadhurst, F/Sgt	P	1939?	1940	
D Brockett, Fg Off	P	8/3/46	10/46	
P J Brockson, Plt Off	P	8/56	1957	
H F Bromwich, APO-Plt Off	P	20/4/36	15/7/37	
Brooks, Sgt	?	1/47	1947	
D Brooks, Plt Off	O	21/4/41	9/6/41	
E Broughton, Fg Off	N	23/7/45	28/3/46	
D M Brown, MNav	N	18/11/57	13/12/57	KFA
F F Brown, Sgt-Fg Off, RAAF	WAG	12/41	6/5/44	
R A Brown, Plt Off	P	26/6/41	1/42	
G L Bruce, Sgt-Plt Off	O	10/41	14/12/42	
F N Buchan, Fg Off-Flt Lt	N	18/11/57	3/60	
R J Buckley, M Plt	P	31/8/54	3/55	
F R Bugler, Fg Off	P	8/47	11/47	
R P Buist, WO	P	14/2/45	circa 7/45	
M Bull, Flt Lt	EngO	12/75	26/7/76	
J Bullock, Sgt	WAG	9/9/40	27/6/41	KIA
F R Bullot, Plt Off	P	19/6/39	1939	
R Bultitude, Sgt	WAG	26/6/41	7/41	
K W Burlton, N1	N	4/50	13/6/50	
B St L Burnett, Fg Off	N	circa 1/67	18/2/70	
Y W Burnett,[19] Plt Off-Fg Off	P	30/9/24	2/1/27	
Y W Burnett,[19] Fg Off	P	27/4/27	14/5/28	
Burns, Sgt	O	circa 4/40	circa 6/41	
J Burns, Sgt	P	28/6/41	20/12/41	KIA
T P Burns, Flt Lt	N	7/9/68	18/2/70	
R A M Burr, Fg Off	N	7/62	1/65	
G J Bush,[18] Plt Off-Flt Lt	P	4/12/35	20/5/40	
G J Bush,[18] Flt Lt-Sqn Ldr	P	4/9/40	30/9/40	KIA
E R Butcher, Plt Off	EngO	by 3/41	8/9/41	
F L Butcher, Sgt-WO, RCAF	P	1/42	1/3/43	WIA
Butler, Sgt	WAG	22/11/41	1/42	
D J Butler, Fg Off	N	11/8/62	2/65	
R L S Butler, Fg Off- Flt Lt	P	3/62	9/64	
P P Butters, Flt Lt	Adj	3/8/41	1/5/42	
V Buxton, Flt Lt	P	23/11/27	11/7/28	
C S Byram, Fg Off	P	26/4/35	17/8/36	
C S Cadell, Flt Lt	P	1/6/36	2/10/36	
A J Cain, Plt Off, RAAF	O	7/11/41	19/11/41	KIA
M R Cann, Plt Off-Fg Off	N	7/9/68	18/2/70	
W J R Cann, Fg Off-Flt Lt	AccO	28/3/36	10/5/38	
T E Cantwell, P1	P	16/7/49	19/12/49	D

Name		Date	Date	
W D Capewell, Sgt	WAG	24/4/41	10/7/41	KIA
D McK Carew-Reid, Sgt-F/Sgt, RAAF	O	7/11/41	26/10/42	
H J S Cargill, Fg Off, RAAF	N	8/2/44	17/12/44	KIA
J B Carruthers, Sqn Ldr	P	17/12/62	24/4/65	
D Carter[20], Plt Off	P	16/5/41	19/5/41	KIA
D Carter, Sgt	P	16/12/43	2/44	
K C Carter, Fg Off	N	29/3/60	6/63	
R H Carter, Fg Off-Flt Lt	P	1/9/28	5/12/29	
M F Carthy, Sgt	WAG	6/41	22/11/41	KIA
J O Cartledge, Plt Off-Fg Off, RAAF	P	23/2/44	11/2/45	
M J Carver, Fg Off-Flt Lt	P	9/6/67	18/2/70	
P J Carver, Fg Off	P	circa 11/54	12/55	
W H Casley, Flt Lt	N	20/4/46	13/6/46	
B S Casling, Fg Off	N	19/8/58	18/11/58	KFA
H J Cassar, Sgt	O	16/5/41	19/5/41	KIA
G Castell, Fg Off	N	5/5/69	18/2/70	
D J D Castle, Flt Lt	N	1968?	18/2/70	
Catton, Sgt	WAG	7/41	1/42	
D Catty, Sgt	WAG	7/41	circa 12/41	
D A Cawthen, Sgt	P	7/41	10/7/41	POW
F W Chadwick, Plt Off	P	21/8/40	10/6/41	
S F Champion, Sgt-Plt Off	P	24/4/41	circa 8/41	
Chaplin, Sgt	O	10/10/40	circa 12/40	
K J Chapman, Sgt	WAG	26/6/41	22/11/41	KIA
Charlton, Sgt	WAG	9/9/40	circa 1/41	
L J Charlton, Sgt-WO, RAAF	O/N	22/11/41	20/4/43	
C A Charman, Fg Off	P	2/5/57	19/8/57	
W G Cheshire, Plt Off	P	17/9/27	19/1/28	
T F C Churcher, Fg Off	P	16/5/41	26/5/41	POW
Cheesewright, Sgt	P	by 1934	?	
E G Christensen, Plt Off-Fg Off, RAAF	P	1/1/42	23/9/43	
A R Churchman, Sqn Ldr-Wg Cdr	P	24/8/35	16/5/37	
G L Clack, Plt Off	WAG	11/9/40	circa 9/40	
C C Clark, Flt Lt	P	23/3/21	18/4/22	
D A V Clark, Flt Lt	P	7/11/59	5/62	
L H Clark, Flt Lt	P	14/11/49	4/6/51	
M S Clark, Plt Off-Fg Off	N	3/62	circa 7/64	
R I Clark, Sgt-Plt Off, RAAF	WAG	1/42	1/9/43	
C J Clarke, Fg Off	P	circa 9/45	28/11/45	
D J Clarke, Fg Off-Flt Lt	P	8/45	18/7/46	
M A Clarke, P3-Sgt	P	21/6/49	23/1/52	
D J Clements, Plt Off-Fg Off	N	6/3/51	7/4/52	
D Cliffe, Sgt-F/Sgt	WAG	circa 8/40	13/2/43	
W E Close, Fg Off-Flt Lt	P	1/4/55	22/8/57	
B A Cochrane, Plt Off	P	1952	1952?	
J E Cochrane, F/Sgt	N	11/59	5/62	
Hon R A Cochrane, Flt Lt	P	7/1/22	13/10/23	
G A Cockayne, Plt Off	P	31/1/40	13/10/40	KIA
L Code-Lewis, Plt Off	IntO	by 2/41	9/41	
J M Cole, Flt Lt	N	3/6/58	12/60	
W I Collett, Plt Off	P	8/1/36	21/4/37	
E Collier, Fg Off	P	circa 1/54	3/2/55	
R T Collier, APO-Plt Off	P	10/4/37	29/4/38	
Collins, Sgt	WAG	10/10/40	circa 12/40	
D Collins, Flt Lt	P	6/1/60	6/62	
F G Collins, Plt Off	P	19/7/39	18/4/41	KIA
F Collinson, Fg Off	N	3/62	12/64	
R W Collinson, Fg Off	AccO	11/4/30	21/2/32	
Colway, Sgt	O	7/41	1/42	
A R Combe, Plt Off-Fg Off	P	3/6/28	15/12/31	
A E Connolly,[18] Fg Off	P	5/9/24	1/1/26	
A E Connolly,[18] Fg Off	StO	9/10/29	5/11/30	
L W H Connor, Sgt, RAAF	O	12/41	14/3/42	KIA
J Connors, Fg Off	?	10/5/46	11/46	
J J Connors, Flt Lt	P	17/5/54	1/57	
C Cooke, Flt Lt	N	26/6/65	4/4/66	KFA
G Cooke, F/Sgt	N	circa 10/45	13/6/45	KFA
Cooper, LAC-Sgt	WAG	1939	9/40	
C E F Cooper, Plt Off-Flt Lt	P	13/8/52	31/3/55	
G S Cooper, Sqn Ldr	P	1/2/56	15/11/57	
J K Copeland, LAC	WAG	1939?	13/6/40	KIA
T F Copleston, Flt Lt	P	31/5/57	15/11/57	
W J Corbett, Plt Off-Fg Off, RAAF	O	20/10/41	24/10/42	
Corcoran, Sgt	WAG	4/9/40	circa 6/41	
R Cordey, Plt Off-Fg Off	P	28/2/53	31/3/55	
S C Cordy, Sgt	WAG	9/9/40	16/5/41	KIA
R M Corker, Flt Lt	MO	30/4/44	5/44	
J Corney, Sgt	WAG	4/9/40	30/9/40	KIA
K R Cornford, F/Sgt	O	7/41	10/7/41	KIA
A H P Cornish, Flt Lt	P	30/7/54	3/55	
J M Cottle, Flt Lt	P	14/9/23	22/10/23	
P Coulson, Flt Lt	P	7/67?	17/11/69	
R M Cowley, Fg Off, RAAF	P	21/2/45	7/45	
S B Cox, Flt Lt	N	21/2/68	18/2/70	
A F Craighill[18], F/Sgt	P	23/7/45	1946?	
A F Craighill[18], F/Sgt	P	circa 4/52	19/10/54	
E D Crew, Sqn Ldr	P	7/48	17/2/50	
K Cringle, Flt Lt	N	5/63	8/65	
B W Crockford, Fg Off-Flt Lt	EngO	4/2/68	18/2/70	
M R W Crook, Flt Lt	P	7/72	1976?	
R H C Crook, LAC-Sgt	WAG	1940	18/4/41	KIA
A F Crosby, Sgt	WAG	16/5/41	circa 6/41	
P Crossley, Plt Off	WAG	3/10/43	1943	
G L Cruickshanks, Fg Off	P	23/3/37	26/6/37	
C W Cudemore, Fg Off	P	14/9/22	8/3/25	
J Cullerne, Fg Off-Flt Lt	P	9/64	4/11/66	
E R Culley, F/Sgt-MNav	N	3/59	10/61	
R D Culverwell, Fg Off	EqO	4/41	30/7/42	
J Cumming, Fg Off	N	22/5/58	1960?	
R M Currie, Fg Off	P	2/47	16/5/47	KFA
L W Curry, N3	N	14/11/49	26/11/49	IFA
K R Curtis, Fg Off	P	1957?	15/11/57	
R P Curtis, Sgt-Fg Off, RAAF	P	22/11/41	19/11/43	
G Dack, Flt Lt	P	12/58	1961?	
H R Dale, Fg Off	P	21/6/33	24/2/35	
I G E Dale,[18] Fg Off	P	29/7/30	22/9/30	
I G E Dale,[18] Flt Lt	P	18/2/33	1/1/34	
D C Dalgliesh, Flt Lt	P	10/72	14/8/74	
J W Dallamore, Sqn Ldr	P	15/4/40	2/10/40	KIA
E H Dally, APO-Plt Off	P	10/4/37	9/2/38	
K W Dalton-Golding, Flt Lt	P	3/48	4/50	
W A K Dalzell, Flt Lt	P	30/3/23	18/10/24	
A W Dann, Sgt	WAG	4/41	30/10/41	
G M Darling, Fg Off	EqO	by 9/40	12/40?	
E B Davidson,[18] Plt Off	O	11/9/40	9/40	
E B Davidson,[18] Fg Off	O	16/10/41	1/12/41	
E J Davies, Fg Off	N	circa 8/45	12/46	
J E Davies,[18] Plt Off-Fg Off	P	3/10/25	1/2/27	
J E Davies,[18] Fg Off	P	1/6/27	27/10/27	
J S Davies, Plt Off-Fg Off	P	30/4/38	13/6/40	KIA
S Davies, Sgt	O	26/4/40	6/41	
P L Davis, Flt Lt	P	1/4/55	11/56	
J Davison, Fg Off	StO	22/9/25	2/1/27	
F G Daw, Fg Off-Flt Lt	P	16/2/42	3/43	
M J Dawson, Flt Lt-Sqn Ldr	N	7/60	12/62	
N J Day, Flt Lt	P	2/74	14/10/74	
V Day, Sgt	WAG	7/41	1/42	
C P F Daymon, Fg Off	P	13/5/74	1975?	
H B Deacon, Fg Off	N	circa 8/45	2/47	
F P C deBeer, Fg Off-Flt Lt	N	9/64	1967	
F A L DeMarillac, 2/Lt, SAAF	P	1/42	30/4/42	
J E Dennant, Plt Off	P	10/9/38	19/4/39	
J R Denney, F/Sgt	N	16/1/58	6/60	
J M Dennis, Plt Off-Flt Lt	P	31/1/40	14/10/41	
T J Desmond, Flt Lt	P	25/11/32	18/11/33	
J S Dick, Plt Off-Fg Off	P	30/9/24	1/11/26	
T C Dickens, Flt Lt	P	16/11/36	27/4/37	
R F L Dickey, Flt Lt	P	13/12/22	30/8/24	
Dingwall, Sgt	P	by 9/26	1927	
P S Dixon, Flt Lt	P	10/72	9/5/73	
T D Dixon, Sgt	P	1936	1937?	
F L Dodd, Sqn Ldr	P	24/11/47	23/7/48	
R Dodsworth, Cpl-Sgt	O	1938	11/6/40	KIA
M V Doherty, Flt Lt	P	1967	1969	
K J Dorricott, Fg Off	N	8/4/44	circa 7/44	
J C Doudy, Sgt	P	12/4/54	10/7/56	
J T Downing, Fg Off	N	circa 8/45	30/11/45	
R D Downs, Plt Off	P	10/56	1957	
M J S Doyle-Davidson, Fg Off-Flt Lt	N	10/62	4/65	
J E L Drabble, Flt Lt	P	1/11/29	24/11/30	
W M Drake, Fg Off	N	4/2/47	16/7/48	
B V Draper, Flt Lt	P	19/2/45	28/2/45	KIA

Name	Role	Date 1	Date 2	Status
G G H DuBoulay, Fg Off	P	18/11/25	17/10/26	
V S H Duclos, Flt Lt-Sqn Ldr	P	13/2/44	17/6/45	
A G Dudgeon, Flt Lt-Sqn Ldr	P	7/8/40	1/10/40	
R C E Duke, Flt Lt	P	5/62	10/64	
K R Dumas, Plt Off-Fg Off, RAAF	N	16/2/44	16/10/44	KIA
J A Duncan, Flt Lt	MO	4/45	25/6/45	
L E Durrant, Plt Off-Flt Lt	O	26/6/41	9/11/42	
G O L Dyke, Flt Lt-Sqn Ldr	P	17/2/45	4/6/46	
E C Eaton, Plt Off	P	18/2/36	30/5/36	
A M Eckel, Fg Off	P	11/5/55	9/56	
Eden, Sgt	WAG	9/40	9/40?	
J J Eden, Sgt, RAAF	WAG	12/41	14/3/42	KIA
J K Edmonds, Plt Off-Fg Off	P	26/6/41	24/4/42	
Edwards, Sgt	WAG	26/3/42	7/5/42	
C C Edwards, Fg Off	P	3/2/29	6/10/29	
C P Edwards, Sgt	WAG	9/40	4/2/41	KIA
D S Edwards, Sqn Ldr	P	29/1/44	20/10/44	KIA
J Edwards, Sgt-F/Sgt	N	1946?	3/12/46	KFA
K E Edwards, Sgt-F/Sgt, RAAF	WAG	4/10/41	22/4/43	
L S Edwards, Plt Off-Fg Off	EngO	31/12/42	13/9/43	
P G C Edwards, Flt Lt	P	20/12/66	4/68	
W E Edwards, Fg Off-Flt Lt	P	7/48	17/12/50	
W P Edwards, F/Sgt-WO	N	circa 2/44	3/1/45	KIA
W J H Ekins, Flt Lt	P	9/12/36	11/5/38	
Eldred, Sgt	P	1925	1926	
C N Ellen, Fg Off	P	1/4/21	11/2/22	
B A Ellis, N3-Sgt	N	14/12/49	15/2/51	KIA
H Ellis, LAC-Sgt	O	1939	circa 9/41	
T N C Elsdon, Flt Lt	P	1973?	2/76	
P Elton, Sgt	N	3/59	10/61	
W N Elwy-Jones, Fg Off	P	28/2/33	14/3/34	
B E Embry, Fg Off	P	14/9/22	1/12/25	
C S Emeny, Flt Lt, RNZAF	P	23/3/44	9/11/44	POW
V A Emson, Sgt	P	16/12/43	2/44	
T Etchalls, Sgt	P	16/12/43	2/44	
J H Etherton, Wg Cdr	P	3/7/45	6/3/46	
D R Evans, Plt Off-Fg Off	P	28/2/33	25/11/35	
H A Evans, Sgt-MSig	S	23/5/51	27/8/51	
J L Evans, Flt Lt	N	19/2/45	circa 6/45	
T C Evans, 2/Lt, SAAF	P	4/10/41	1/42	
D G Eve, Plt Off-Fg Off, RAAF	P	22/11/41	13/10/42	
J E Everington, Sgt	O	9/40	circa 6/41	
P N Ewing, Fg Off-Flt Lt, RAAF	P	15/2/44	20/6/45	
L Eyre, MSig	S	28/5/51	18/2/52	
G Fachiri, Plt Off-Fg Off	P	2/7/28	23/12/30	
L N Faffard, Flt Lt, RCAF	P	circa 6/45	28/6/45	
D I Fairbairn, Fg Off	P	7/4/46	13/6/46	
D Farquarson, Fg Off	P	7/72	9/5/73	
B A Feldman, Sgt	O	circa 4/40	11/6/40	KIA
J Fenwick, Sgt	WAG	16/12/43	2/44	
A H Fernand, Flt Lt	N	6/7/49	27/6/50	
M F Fernee, Flt Lt	P	7/72	14/8/74	
T A Ferris, AC-Sgt	O	by 5/38	13/10/40	KIA
P deC Festing-Smith, Flt Lt	P	1/11/31	24/10/32	
G M Fidler, Plt Off-Flt Lt	P	24/8/35	29/8/38	
Field, Capt	AILO	10/41	11/41?	
A R Field, Sgt-F/Sgt	WAG	7/41	19/11/43	
A J H Finch, Plt Off-Fg Off	P	1940	circa 6/40	
I C Firth, Flt Lt	P	10/72	31/7/73	
Fisher, F/Sgt	N	circa 8/45	7/11/45	
Fisher, AC1-Sgt	WAG	pre-war	circa 6/41	
J F Fisher, Flt Lt	P	7/9/68	18/2/70	
D M Fleming, Flt Lt	P	29/12/33	2/10/35	
E Fletcher, Sgt	WAG	circa 4/40	circa 6/41	
J H R Flett, N2	N	21/6/49	1950?	
E R Floyd, Sgt	WAG	17/8/43	1943	
B P Foley, Fg Off	N	6/65	2/66	
F C Fortune, Fg Off	P	25/11/44	14/5/45	KFA
P J Ford, Fg Off	N	12/64	25/6/67	
G D Forder, Sgt	P	16/10/40	circa 6/41	
B H D Foster, Sqn Ldr	P	31/12/46	11/47	
M G Fountain, Plt Off	SigO	22/3/43	12/6/43	
R G Fox, WO	?	by 5/46	10/46	
S G Fox, Sgt	O	circa 4/40	11/6/40	KIA
F V W Foy, Sgt	P	by 1929	?	
A A France, N3	N	7/48	17/12/50	
C C Francis, Plt Off-Fg Off	P	9/4/35	29/12/35	KFA
T R Francis, Fg Off	P	6/64	27/11/66	
J G Franks, Flt Lt	P	8/1/36	17/6/36	
J N Franks, Plt Off-Fg Off	P	28/3/57	15/11/57	
A A Fraser, Sgt-Plt Off, RAAF	WAG	12/41	2/3/43	
F J Fraser, Plt Off-Fg Off	O	circa 10/41	15/10/42	
J Fraser, Fg Off	P	circa 4/53	21/7/53	
R W Freeman, Fg Off	AcO	2/9/24	20/10/26	
D E French, F/Sgt-Fg Off	N	1/1/43	27/1/44	KFA
D P Frost, Fg Off	P	11/10/36	15/12/36	
J R J Froud, Fg Off	P	1/4/55	5/56	
Fry, Sgt	O	6/41	circa 10/41	
F Fry, Sgt	P	8/24	1926?	
V D Fry, Plt Off	O	11/40	12/12/40	KIA
C Fryar, Sgt-WO, RAAF	P	8/1/42	5/6/43	
G G Furmage, Plt Off-Fg Off, RAAF	P	25/11/41	6/43	
R W Fussell, Plt Off	N	14/5/45	12/10/45	IFA
W Fylan, Sgt-F/Sgt	WAG	by 11/41	19/2/43	
J O Gainford, APO	P	27/5/38	20/6/38	
R J Gammans, Fg Off	P	20/11/50	28/6/52	
G L Gandy, Fg Off	P	14/3/26	28/9/26	
K A Gardiner, Sgt, RAAF	WAG	20/10/41	25/11/42	
H Garfath, Sgt	WAG	7/41	2/44	
E Garland, Flt Lt	P	9/46	3/12/46	KFA
V D Garner, F/Sgt-WO	N	23/7/45	circa 7/46	
R K Garnham, Plt Off-Fg Off, RNZAF	P	2/44	6/3/45	
W A Gaudet, Sgt-F/Sgt, RCAF	WAG	17/10/41	19/2/43	
M A Gaynor, Fg Off-Flt Lt	N	9/63	1/66	
A Gebbie, Sgt	WAG	6/10/43	2/44	
D H Geeson, Fg Off	P	17/3/23	17/10/25	
R W Gentry, Sgt	O	9/9/40	22/4/41	KIA
A H R George, Lt (SAAF?)	Adj	1/5/41	6/41	
G George, Sgt	WAG	7/41	14/12/42	
L G George, Plt Off-Flt Lt, RAAF	O/N	8/12/41	20/8/43	
Gibb, WO	N	circa 8/45	1945?	
D G Gibbons, Flt Lt	N	12/62	6/65	
R W A Gibbs, Plt Off-Fg Off	P	21/12/38	6/41	
H D Giblett, Fg Off	StO	1/3/28	27/5/29	
A Gibson, Flt Lt	P	1/10/74	1976?	
M J Gibson, Sqn Ldr	P	19/8/74	26/7/76	
R H Gibson, Fg Off-Flt Lt	N	11/65	5/6/68	
N A Gidney, Plt Off	P	19/6/39	1939	
R H Gidman, Plt Off-Flt Lt	P	6/3/51	5/7/52	
C P Gilding, Fg Off-Flt Lt	EngO	6/63	12/65	
J A Giles, Flt Lt	P	9/72	14/1/74	
P Gilliat, Fg Off	N	15/9/51	20/3/52	
S J G Godfrey, Fg Off	N	15/9/66	30/12/68	
D A Golder, Sgt, RAAF	O	1/42	9/7/42	
A F Golds, Plt Off-Fg Off	N	7/61	11/63	
C L Gomm, APO-Fg Off	P	1/10/34	30/3/37	
T Gomm, Sgt	O	15/12/40	6/41	
H K Goode, Flt Lt	P	22/7/27	30/12/29	
A F Gooding, Sgt	O	1/42	12/4/42	D
D E W Goodrich, F/Sgt-Fg Off	P	7/2/44	7/45	
C R Goodwin, Fg Off-Flt Lt	P	15/2/44	15/1/45	KIA
A R Gosling, F/Sgt	N	circa 8/46	11/46	
S A Goss, Sgt-F/Sgt, RCAF	P	1/42	18/8/42	KIA
T F Gostelow, MNav	N	9/60	1/63	
G A Gowing, Sgt-F/Sgt, RAAF	WAG	4/10/41	20/4/43	
R P Grace, S4-Sgt	S	14/11/49	20/8/51	
P E Graebner, Plt Off-Fg Off, RAAF	O	20/10/41	22/10/42	
A C Grafham, Fg Off	P	7/56	6/8/57	
H R Graham, Fg Off-Flt Lt	P	28/2/33	7/12/36	
G K Grainger, Sgt	WAG	11/4/41	26/5/41	KIA
I D F Grant, Sgt-F/Sgt	P	by 12/37	19/1/41	
M Grant, Sgt	WAG	21/4/41	circa 6/41	
R J Gratton, Sgt	N	12/10/51	21/2/52	KFA
R J Grayson, Plt Off-Fg Off	N	10/64	4/3/67	
D L Green, N4-Sgt	N	16/7/49	26/11/50	
M Greenhow, Flt Lt	N	6/65	1967	
Greenwood, Sgt	WAG	7/41	circa 9/41	
E Greenwood, Flt Lt	MO	13/4/44	30/4/44	
J H S Greenwood, Plt Off-Fg Off	P	31/8/54	5/55	
C B Greet, Flt Lt	P	15/4/30	16/4/32	
Griffiths, Sgt	WAG	by 9/41	circa 1041	
P J B Griffiths, Plt Off	P	18/8/40	3/1/41	KIA

Name	Role	From	To	Status
V J Griffiths, Sgt	WAG	22/4/41	18/5/41	KIA
Grocott, Sgt	O	9/9/40	1940	
C D Grogan, Fg Off	P	1/4/55	10/55	
N Grove, F/Sgt	P	15/9/51	circa 10/53	
F W Guy, Plt Off	P	12/41	30/4/42	
E B C Gwinnell, Fg Off-Flt Lt	P	25/8/59	2/62	
G H Haddock, Plt Off-Fg Off	P	6/56	3/5/57	
J Hadley, Sgt-F/Sgt	P	30/12/42	2/44	
C Haggarty, Fg Off	N	4/5/45	18/7/46	
A C H Haines, Fg Off-Flt Lt	P	12/9/40	16/5/41	KIA
Hall, Sgt	P	by 4/33	1936	
Hall, Sgt	WAG	circa 11/40	circa 12/40	
Hall, Sgt	O	circa 9/41	circa 9/41	
F O Hall, Flt Lt	AcO	16/3/28	10/4/30	
K Hall, S4-Sgt	S	1950	11/1/51	
L G Hall, Flt Lt	P	18/11/57	13/12/57	KFA
P A Hall, Flt Lt	MO	1/9/22	1/3/23	
M D Halls, Fg Off	N	7/61	11/63	
E J Hallett, Sgt-Fg Off, RAAF	O/N	11/41	2/2/45	
L Halley, Sgt-Fg Off, RCAF	P	30/12/42	7/2/44	
J Halsall, Sgt	WAG	28/6/41	22/11/41	POW
J R Halsey, Fg Off	SigO	4/45	19/7/46	
Hamilton, Flt Lt	P	circa 9/45	circa 7/46	
N I Hamilton, Fg Off	N	29/3/66	26/9/68	
E L Hammat, Plt Off-Fg Off, RAAF	O/N	4/10/41	8/2/43	
C E Hamshire, Flt Lt	N	1/47	3/47	
E J Hancock, Flt Lt	EngO	7/62	6/63	
H Handley, N2	N	11/47	mid 1948	
P C Hannam, Flt Lt	N	12/58	12/60	
R L Hanslip, Fg Off-Flt Lt	EngO	20/3/45	17/4/46	
N B Harben, Plt Off-Fg Off	P	circa 3/50	6/7/50	KIA
R S E Harding, P3	P	14/11/49	3/50	
J Hardstaff, Fg Off-Flt Lt	P	18/11/57	11/8/59	
G M Hardy, Sgt	P	7/41	10/7/41	KIA
Harley, Sgt	P	circa 11/40	19/1/41	
F J Harper, Fg Off	N	by 5/44	1/5/45	
A L J Harris, N2	N	30/10/48	11/2/49	KFA
A T Harris, Sqn Ldr	P	20/11/22	18/10/24	
D S J Harris, Sgt	WAG	26/6/41	4/12/41	KIA
C Harrison, Flt Lt	N	22/6/68	18/2/70	
J A P Harrison, Fg Off-Flt Lt	P	6/10/29	24/9/32	
N R Harrison, Flt Lt	P	16/1/46	6/4/46	
P A Harrison, Fg Off	N	2/64	4/4/66	KFA
V W J Harrison, Sgt-F/Sgt	WAG	circa 10/40	22/4/41	KIA
W P Harrison, Fg Off	N	1968?	18/2/70	
Hartley, Sgt-F/Sgt	N	circa 9/45	28/3/46	
H Hartley, Flt Lt	N	18/11/57	13/12/57	KFA
G W Hartnell, Sgt-Flt Lt, RAAF	P	25/11/41	6/5/44	
A Hassall, Plt Off	CyO	16/10/41	circa 1/42	
T A Hastings, Wg Cdr	P	10/72	24/8/74	
H C Hatherly, Sgt, RAAF	WAG	21/3/42	circa 2/43	
H E Hawkins, WO	P	9/4/34	1936?	
S V Hayler, P3-Sgt	P	14/12/49	11/1/51	KIA
G F Hayley, Sgt	P	circa 12/41	22/10/42	
F R Haylock, Sgt-F/Sgt	O/N	12/41	19/2/43	
Haynes, WO	N	circa 9/45	1945	
W J S Hayward, F/Sgt-WO	N	2/44	12/1/45	KIA
C W Head, Plt Off, RAAF	P	22/11/41	4/1/42	KFA
R A Head, Fg Off	N	23/8/66	30/12/68	
D W Helps, Fg Off-Flt Lt	P	16/8/50	20/1/53	
M F Hempstead, Fg Off	P	11/54	3/55	
J R Henderson, APO-Plt Off	P	20/4/36	3/7/37	
J E Herridge, Fg Off	N	2/47	11/47	
J H T Hewat, Sgt	P	30/12/42	6/10/43	KFA
F P Hewitt, Fg Off	P	13/9/30	30/11/31	
D K Hewson, Plt Off	P	14/7/27	21/9/27	
A J Hicks, Plt Off-Fg Off	P	11/3/32	29/4/35	
D C Hide, Fg Off	N	circa 1/67	18/2/70	
R D Hilditch, Sgt-Fg Off, RAAF	WAG	1/1/42	6/5/44	
Hill, Sgt	P	1933	1935	
Hill, Cpl-Sgt	WAG	by 3/38	1940	
I D Hill, Fg Off	P	circa 2/66	22/8/68	
J R Hill, Plt Off-Fg Off	N	20/12/50	12/6/52	
R M Hill, Sqn Ldr-Wg Cdr	P	18/9/24	30/11/26	
L H Hillier, Fg Off-Flt Lt	StO	5/12/24	30/10/25	
A Hilling, Plt Off-Fg Off	O/N	1/42	14/2/43	
A T Hine, Plt Off-Fg Off	N	27/8/68	18/2/70	
K D Hoare, Plt Off	SigO	24/1/44	2/8/44	
F W T Hobson, Fg Off	P	6/56	24/7/56	KFA
C G Hockney, Sgt-Fg Off	P	7/41	5/8/44	
C A Hodder, Cpl-Plt Off	O	by 4/38	27/6/41	
S W Hodge, Plt Off	CyO	10/9/40	19/10/41	
M W Hodgson, Fg Off	N	19/8/58	2/61	
K G Hodson, Sgt	O	28/6/41	6/10/41	
J Holdaway, Sgt	O	9/9/40	6/41	
P Holden-Rushworth, Sgt	P	17/12/50	1/6/53	
H Holder, Fg Off	N	circa 9/45	10/5/46	
H C T Holmans, Sgt	O	circa 9/40	4/2/41	KIA
A Holmes, WO	P	1/45	26/3/45	KIA
M E Y Holmes, Plt Off-Fg Off	P	31/8/54	10/56	
C E Horrex, Fg Off-Flt Lt	P	27/11/24	19/12/26	
J F Horsey, Fg Off	P	24/11/21	17/5/23	
Horton, Sgt	P	by 8/29	1930?	
B R Hoskins, Flt Lt	P	10/72	31/7/73	
L E Howard, S2-Sgt	S	25/12/49	23/1/52	
L R W Howell, Sgt, RNZAF	P	28/6/41	6/10/41	
C V Howes, Plt Off-Fg Off	P	12/6/29	2/3/31	
Hoyle, Sgt	O	9/9/40	circa 12/40	
Hubbard, Sgt	P	by 5/32	1935	
T V Hudson, Fg Off	N	1966	1968?	
A Hughes, Flt Lt-Wg Cdr	P	25/8/41	5/8/42	
D G M Hughes, Flt Lt	N	22/3/68	18/2/70	
R Hughes, F/Sgt	N	circa 9/45	7/12/45	
W R Hughes, Plt Off	EngO	9/43	circa 2/44	
Hume, Sgt	P	circa 1/44	2/44	
L F Humphry, Sgt	P	by 2/29	1931?	
A H Humphrys, Flt Lt	P	17/2/54	15/8/54	
N R G Hunter, Plt Off	P	18/11/29	26/1/30	
T B Hunter, Plt Off	P	5/9/35	6/1/36	
A N Huon, Sgt-Flt Lt, RAAF	P	circa 1/42	6/45	
J R Hurley, Sgt, RCAF	O/N	1/42	5/3/43	
Hutchings, Fg Off	P	circa 9/45	30/11/45	
D Hutchinson, Fg Off	MO	27/5/45	circa 7/46	
A W Hutton, Plt Off-Fg Off	O	26/6/41	4/12/41	KIA
I J Huzzard, Fg Off	P	2/73	31/7/73	
R W Hyde, Flt Lt	P	1973	10/12/74	
R C Hyett, Sgt	P	by 3/36	1937?	
Inganni, Sgt	WAG	9/9/40	9/6/41	
N Ingham, Fg Off	N	13/2/68	18/2/70	
R T A Innes, Flt Lt	P	5/56	9/57	
W J A Innes, Sqn Ldr	P	11/67	18/2/70	
R Ireland, WO	?	17/5/46	18/7/46	
H F Irving, Plt Off, RNZAF	O	21/4/41	27/5/41	KIA
D Irwin, F/Sgt	P	3/59	10/61	
F J Islip, Fg Off	P	20/5/21	15/2/23	
R Jackson, Plt Off	P	7/6/52	28/8/52	KIA
R G Jackson, Sgt	O	11/41	29/12/41	
V K Jacobs, Sqn Ldr	P	26/10/53	1/2/56	
P R James, WO	N	14/2/45	28/2/45	KIA
R E Jaquest, Fg Off	P	2/47	4/47	
J K A Jeakes, Fg Off	P	20/5/21	14/10/23	
C G Jefford, Fg Off	N	11/8/62	6/11/64	
Jenkins, Sgt	P	by 8/30	?	
Jenkins, Sgt	WAG	circa 8/41	1/42	
E J Jenkins, Flt Lt	MO	15/10/27	9/3/28	
J F Jennings, Sgt, RAAF	O	8/12/41	12/12/41	WIA
H C Jewell, Sgt-Fg Off	P	1/42	27/1/44	KIA
L J Joel, APO	P	19/6/39	1939?	
E Jones, Lt, SAAF	P	21/4/41	6/41	
G D Jones, Flt Lt-Sqn Ldr	P	12/5/41	6/41	
G F Jones, Sgt, RNZAF	O	24/4/41	11/41	
G T Jones, Flt Lt	Adj	1/48	5/48	
J W Jones, Sqn Ldr	P	10/10/36	15/11/36	
M S Jones, Fg Off	N	8/64	1967	
N Jones, F/Sgt, RAAF	N	5/3/45	circa 6/45	
T H Jones, Fg Off	EngO	5/10/41	1/42	
K J W Josling, Plt Off	CyO	24/10/41	30/6/42	
A E Joyce, Fg Off-Flt Lt	EngO	1/44?	1/45	
R A Jude, Fg Off	P	8/56	15/11/57	
H L Karl, Fg Off	P	11/72	31/7/73	
G C Kay, Fg Off	N	14/2/69	18/2/70	
Keating, Sgt	WAG	7/41	30/10/41	

Name	Role	From	To	Status
T L Keddie, Fg Off	N	4/5/45	1945	
P U A Keel, Plt Off-Flt Lt	P	8/12/41	16/8/43	
D J Keenan, Flt Lt	P	10/72	13/6/74	
G B Keily, Flt Lt-Sqn Ldr	P	2/12/36	1/4/38	
P J Kelly, Fg Off-Flt Lt	MO	31/7/41	8/6/43	
J V Kelly,[19] Fg Off	P	5/2/25	28/1/27	
J V Kelly,[19] Fg Off	P	27/4/27	30/1/28	
G E Kemp, Plt Off-Fg Off, RAAF	O/N	22/11/41	8/3/43	
Kemsley, Sgt	P	1931	1932	
L A C Kennedy, F/Sgt	N	16/1/58	7/60	
E E Kennington, Capt	AILO	12/10/43	2/44	
W Kent, Sgt	P	12/49?	15/2/51	KIA
M Kerr, N2	N	3/48	1949	
D F Kerr, Fg Off	N	17/2/45	16/5/46	
M E Kerr, Sqn Ldr	P	7/72	31/7/73	
G C O Key, Wg Cdr	P	28/11/46	22/9/47	
C A Kidd, Fg Off	N	8/2/44	7/44?	
A King, Sgt	WAG	1/42	13/2/43	
D V King, Fg Off	P	1/56	15/11/57	
G S King, Fg Off	P	4/7/30	7/9/31	
L S King, Fg Off	SigO	17/9/44	4/45	
F R Kirk, F/Sgt-Plt Off	N	circa 9/44	circa 6/45	
B C Kirkpatrick, Fg Off	P	31/8/54	3/55	
J A H Kirkpatrick, Sgt-F/Sgt	O/N	28/6/41	22/4/43	
Kirlew, Sgt	P	by 8/29	?	
C J Kirlew, Plt Off	Adj	16/7/40	10/7/41	
J S F Kitchen, Plt Off-Fg Off	N	circa 7/67	18/2/70	
Knights, Sgt	P	by 12/31	?	
R Kyle, WO	P	10/1/34	1936?	
B P H Lacey, Plt Off-Fg Off	P	7/6/52	15/7/53	KFA
P C Lahey, Plt Off-Flt Lt, RAAF	O/N	25/11/41	18/9/43	
C M Laing, Flt Lt	P	18/9/24	28/3/26	
C T Lake, Plt Off-Fg Off	P	7/6/52	2/10/54	
J R Lake, Flt Lt	N	2/47	8/47	
A J Lamb, Plt Off	P	1/5/43	2/44	
J Lambie, Fg Off-Flt Lt	AcO	15/2/33	6/3/36	
L E Lancaster, Fg Off, RNZAF	P	24/8/44	15/11/44	
P Langdown, Fg Off	P	1/61	7/63	
H C Langrish, Sgt	WAG	16/5/41	31/7/41	
D T A Lansley, Flt Lt	N	9/5/60	16/4/62	KFA
F J O Lasbrey, Plt Off-Fg Off	P	8/1/36	1/5/37	
G Lauder, Sgt	N	10/11/44	14/4/45	KFA
P J Lavender, N3	N	5/9/48	1949?	
E W Lawrence, Flt Lt	StO	16/10/30	11/12/31	
P R Lea, Fg Off	P	29/6/68	18/2/70	
A R Lebans, Sgt-Plt Off, RCAF	P	30/12/42	7/2/44	
A Lees, Flt Lt-Sqn Ldr	P	14/9/23	21/11/26	
E F Legg, F/Sgt	N	23/4/46	11/46	
S Lenney, Fg Off	P	16/12/43	7/2/44	
I Leslie, Flt Lt	P	by 8/45	circa 3/46	
A L Leslie-Miller, Fg Off	N	16/1/58	circa 9/59	
J M Levey, Sgt-Plt Off, RAAF	P	30/4/43	17/12/44	KIA
C Levings, Sgt, RAAF	O/N	21/3/42	13/2/43	
J H Lewis, N3	N	7/48	1949?	
W W Lewis-Jones, Fg Off	P	9/9/39	25/11/39	
Lidbury, Sgt	WAG	9/9/40	circa 10/41	
R C Lidstone,[20] Sgt	O	1940	30/6/40	POW
T O Liggins, Sgt	WAG	by 11/40	12/12/40	KIA
B Lilly, Plt Off	Adj	12/12/41	14/8/42	
E S Lindsell, Fg Off	P	7/2/44	1944	
A E Lloyd, Fg Off	EngO	3/2/47	8/47	
C Lloyd, S4-S3	S	3/50	6/7/50	KIA
J C Lloyd, MPlt	P	1/4/55	circa 2/56	
W L V Logan, Plt Off	CyO	1/5/41	10/6/41	
W B Longstaff, Sgt	O	16/5/41	26/5/41	KIA
T A Lord, Sgt-WO, RAAF	WAG	1/12/42	2/44	
D J Lowe, Sgt	WAG	7/41	10/7/41	KIA
J Lowes, Flt Lt	P	circa 8/45	1945?	
T C Luke, Flt Lt	P	23/11/27	1/11/29	
H G Lusher, Fg Off-Flt Lt	P	12/11/73	4/11/74	
A Lussey, MNav	N	12/62	6/65	
A N Luxmoore, Flt Lt	P	5/9/35	6/1/36	
F L Luxmoore, Flt Lt	P	13/12/22	26/3/23	
W E Lyne,[22] Fg Off	N	10/46	19/8/48	KFA
W M Lyons, Fg Off	AcO	12/10/36	15/12/36	
A G S McCallum, Fg Off	P	9/46	8/47	
E W McClelland, Sgt	P	circa 3/41	30/10/41	
G B McCormack, Flt Lt	P	by 9/45	1945	
D McCowan, Flt Lt	Adj	25/7/46	6/47	
H W McCracken, Flt Lt	P	circa 7/45	23/10/45	KFA
McCulloch, Fg Off	P	circa 9/45	20/5/46	
B T McDade, Sgt-Plt Off	WAG	26/11/41	14/2/44	
G A McDonald, WO	P	5/3/45	1/12/45	
M R L McDougall, Fg Off	N	circa 4/68	18/2/70	
A McFadzean, Fg Off-Flt Lt	N	2/44	circa 6/45	
N McFarlane, Fg Off	N	29/3/60	10/62	
K M McGregor, Plt Off-Fg Off	P	9/56	15/11/57	
J McGurk, Sgt	WAG	circa 10/40	circa 8/41	
McIver, WO	?	1946?	10/46	
A F McKenna, Plt Off-Fg Off	P	13/5/31	4/2/34	
McKenzie, Flt Lt	?	29/10/40	circa 11/40	
I K McKenzie, Flt Lt	MO	19/2/38	11/5/38	
M B F Mackenzie, AC-Sgt	WAG	by 4/38	2/10/40	KIA
D P McKeown, Fg Off	P	8/1/36	26/3/36	
W D McKeown, Flt Lt	MO	6/3/28	10/4/30	
A A McKie, Sgt-WO	N	circa 12/43	6/45	
J S McLaren, Sgt	WAG	9/9/40	circa 9/41	
W S McLellan, Sgt-Flt Lt, RAAF	P	22/11/41	22/4/45	
G McLeod, Flt Lt	P	2/73	17/4/74	
T S MacLiver, Sgt, RAAF	WAG	7/11/41	19/11/41	KIA
G P McMahon, Fg Off	N	16/1/46	17/5/46	
D R McMillan, S4/Sgt	S	14/11/49	20/8/51	
J McPhee, Flt Lt	P	19/2/45	circa 6/45	
J S McQueen, WO, RNZAF	P	30/10/44	3/1/45	KIA
M Macrae, Sgt	WAG	21/9/43	2/44	
McWhirter, Flt Lt	MO?	1940	4/9/40	
N Maddock, Sgt-WO	N	1/44	15/12/44	
E A Magor, Plt Off, RAAF	P	7/11/41	19/11/41	KIA
B S Mahaffey, Flt Lt	P	7/1/74	4/11/74	
P E Maitland, Flt Lt	P	7/1/23	24/11/25	
A Malone, Plt Off-Fg Off	P	23/11/23	26/6/25	
J W Maloney, Plt Off-Fg Off, RAAF	P	7/11/41	27/1/43	
J R Mansfield, Sgt	WAG	7/41	3/11/41	KIA
McD B Manson, Fg Off	EqO	28/1/38	1/4/38	
R J Marchant, Fg Off-Flt Lt	N	18/11/57	11/8/59	
W H Markham, Fg Off	P	14/5/21	25/7/22	
T J Marks, Fg Off	N	6/8/67	18/2/70	
A H Marsack, Plt Off-Fg Off	P	16/10/31	24/7/35	
D H Marsack, Plt Off-Fg Off	P	16/10/31	8/10/35	
Marshall, Cpl-Sgt	WAG	by 4/38	1939?	
A B Marshall, Flt Lt	MO	24/6/36	1/12/37	
H Marshall, Sgt	WAG	4/41	6/41	
J Marshall, Sgt-F/Sgt	P	30/4/43	2/44	
Martin, Sgt	O	7/41	6/10/41	
A J Martin, Sgt	P	17/11/50	7/8/51	
H H Martin, Flt Lt	P	1/8/32	27/4/34	
R J Martin, Sgt	WAG	21/4/41	10/6/41	KIA
A J P Marvin, Sqn Ldr	P	15/6/44	4/47	
R L Maslan, Flt Lt	P	1/4/55	2/56	
P J Mason, Fg Off	N	7/62	1/65	
I M Matheson, Flt Lt	P	13/12/22	1/11/24	
C S Matthews, Sgt, RNZAF	P	30/12/42	2/44	
R D May, Plt Off	O	16/5/41	26/5/41	POW
F C Mays, Flt Lt	P	3/9/49	22/11/49	
A A Meadows, AC1-Sgt	WAG	1939	13/10/40	KIA
L A Mears, Fg Off-Flt Lt	N	16/12/43	circa 6/45	
G P Mee, Plt Off-Fg Off	P	12/3/26	17/10/26	IFA
P Meehan, Fg Off	N	31/5/45	23/8/46	
C Melly, Sgt	P	28/6/41	22/11/41	POW
D Menzies, Plt Off-Fg Off	P	28/10/28	12/6/29	
R Mercer, N3	N	20/12/49	4/50	
J H Merry, Plt Off	N	27/3/44	19/4/44	
A L Messenger, Flt Lt	P	17/2/22	16/10/22	KFA
N J Metcalf, Fg Off	P	18/11/74	1975?	
V K Metcalf, Flt Lt	P	3/6/58	12/60	
J T Miles, Flt Lt	N	7/11/59	5/62	
R Miles, Flt Lt	P	9/64	21/2/67	
P C Miller, Flt Lt	EngO	11/65	2/68	
Millington, Sgt	P	circa 1/53	1953	
G O Mills, Flt Lt	P	23/9/39	1/8/40	
K Mills, Sgt-Plt Off	WAG	9/9/40	24/2/43	
D J Milne, Fg Off	N	3/61	8/63	

Name	Role	Start	End	Note
M C B Mitchell, P2	P	1/47	21/12/48	
F Moorcroft, N3/Sgt	N	4/48	1950	
C S Moore, Plt Off-Fg Off	P	29/4/32	22/10/34	
R J Moore, Fg Off	P	9/60	1/61	
N V Moreton, Sqn Ldr	P	1/5/37	29/3/39	
P A Moritz, Fg Off	P	17/2/30	1/9/30	
B G Morley, Flt Lt	N	2/64	7/8/66	
D Morley, Fg Off	N	15/2/69	18/2/70	
L W Morling, Sgt	WAG	9/9/40	28/4/41	KIA
R E Morling, F/Sgt	N	1951?	18/2/52	
H Morris, Sgt	P	1936	1937	
W J O Morrison, Flt Lt	P	5/3/52	3/55	
N R Moss, Fg Off	P	8/47	2/48	
T W Mould, Flt Lt	EngO	8/72	12/75	
L H Moulton, Sgt	P	1938	1938?	
P Mountain, F/Sgt	N	9/59	3/62	
E J Mousdale, N3/Sgt	N	25/12/49	27/8/51	
R E Moutrey, WO	N	10/3/45	circa 6/45	
Moxham, F/Sgt-WO	N	9/46	11/46	
M J Moy, Fg Off	P	7/60	16/4/62	KFA
S Muir, Sgt	P	8/24	1926?	
W J Mulholland, Plt Off	P	10/5/39	25/9/39	
J S Muller-Rowland, Plt Off-Fg Off	P	20/10/41	25/11/42	
G Munson, LAC-Sgt	WAG	1939?	circa 10/41	
M H Munt, Flt Lt	N	26/9/66	29/11/67	
A Murray,[21] Sgt	WAG	1/42	18/8/42	KIA
E M Murray, Sqn Ldr-Wg Cdr	P	23/3/21	20/11/22	
L C Murray, Sgt	WAG	circa 4/40	6/41	
M J Murphy, Flt Lt	EngO	8/72	31/7/73	
F L E Musgrove, Flt Lt	MO	circa 12/40	5/4/41	
B Muth, Flt Lt	P	4/6/51	26/9/53	
P Naldrett-Jays, Sgt	P	4/41	30/10/41	
J Nankervis, Sgt-Flt Lt, RAAF	WAG/N	22/11/41	24/3/45	
G E Negus, Sgt	O	circa 5/40	13/6/40	KIA
H M P Neil, Sgt-Fg Off, RAAF	P	12/41	2/2/45	
R Neil, Fg Off	P	13/6/48	1950	
Nelson, Sgt-F/Sgt	N	1/44	7/44	
S R C Nelson, Flt Lt	MO	14/11/37	16/3/38	
S M D Nessim, F/Sgt-WO	N	7/2/44	6/45	
R T Nevill, Flt Lt	EngO	20/5/21	15/9/21	
J W New,[19] Fg Off	P	8/11/26	2/1/27	
J W New,[19] Fg Off	P	27/4/27	9/8/27	
R D Newbury, Fg Off	N	26/6/65	1/12/67	
J Newhouse, Sgt	O	7/41	10/7/41	KIA
J Newport, F/Sgt	P	30/4/43	2/44	
T H Newton, Flt Lt	P	23/2/23	1/6/23	
H M Nicholls, WO-Fg Off, RAAF	P	23/2/44	circa 6/45	
Nicholson, Fg Off	EngO	8/46	10/46	
I Nichol, Fg Off	N	1964?	1/2/67	
W Nicholls, Sgt	P	1938	1938	
S C Niven, Plt Off, RNZAF	N	4/41	23/5/41	KIA
C J Nobbs, Fg Off	StO	9/11/31	24/7/32	
M A Noble, Flt Lt	N	10/8/50	10/12/51	
A P Norman, Flt Lt	P	12/49	29/8/50	
K A O Norman, Flt Lt	P	7/48	8/2/51	
F E North, Fg Off	P	3/10/25	18/1/27	
P B Nowell, Sgt	N	18/11/57	9/60	
H C Nullis, Sgt	O	circa 12/41	1/42	
D H O'Brien, Plt Off-Fg Off	P	13/8/52	6/9/53	
P O'Brien, F/Sgt	N	8/2/44	1944	
S O'Connor, Sgt-WO	P	5/9/43	6/45	
L S O'Donough, S4/Sgt	S	1/50?	20/8/51	
C E O'Neill, Sgt	P	7/41	22/11/41	KIA
J Oliver, N2	N	11/47	1948	
R J Oltmann, Fg Off	N	16/1/58	3/60	
H Orsborn, F/Sgt-WO	N	circa 12/44	1/6/45	
W M Osborne, Sgt-WO	P	7/41	9/11/43	
G R O'Sullivan, Fg Off	P	20/5/21	27/3/23	
P A Ostle, Plt Off	P	10/9/38	19/4/39	
L R J Ovenden, Flt Lt-Sqn Ldr	P	5/3/45	18/12/45	
W Overell, F/Sgt	P	15/12/40	26/4/41	
D A Owen, Sgt	O/N	4/10/41	13/2/43	
Owens, Sgt	P	by 11/30	1932	
J F Oxley, Fg Off	N	5/63	8/65	
M Oxley, Sgt	N	16/1/58	7/12/59	
D Page, Sgt-Plt Off	O	26/11/41	15/7/42	
F Page, Sgt	P	8/24	1926	
L G Paget, Flt Lt	P	23/2/23	5/12/26	
C D Pailthorpe, Plt Off, RAAF	O	25/11/41	30/4/42	
J Paine, Flt Lt	P	23/10/40	circa 2/41	
L G Palmer, Fg Off	N	1/47	5/47	
J E Pannifer, Sgt-Plt Off	P	17/10/41	30/4/42	
Parcell, Sgt	?	circa 12/43	2/44	
A H Parker, Sgt-F/Sgt	N	circa 8/45	11/46	
M Parker, N2	N	30/10/48	1950	
H L Patch, Fg Off	P	30/3/28	4/3/30	
J Paterson, Sgt-Plt Off	O/N	17/10/41	5/11/44	
M Patterson, Fg Off	N	4/65	1967	
I D Pattinson, Fg Off	P	15/11/52	3/55	
C A Patton, Fg Off	P	3/11/28	1/7/29	
D McL Paton, Fg Off	P	26/6/65	1/12/67	
F McB Paul, Fg Off-Flt Lt	P	15/10/21	23/12/23	
J D Paull, WO	N	23/7/45	circa 5/46	
M Payne, F/Sgt-WO	N	23/7/45	12/6/46	
B Pearce,[21] Sgt-F/Sgt, RAAF	O	1/1/42	11/10/42	KFA
S G Pearce, Fg Off-Flt Lt	P	7/62	1/65	
F J C Pearson, Flt Lt	N	8/61	6/64	
W R Peasley, Flt Lt	N	7/45	24/11/45	
D E W Pells, Fg Off	N	4/65	16/12/67	
G M Pendlebury, Plt Off	P	10/56	4/57	
L F Penny, Fg Off-Sqn Ldr	P	8/7/41	14/12/42	
Percival, Sgt	P	7/41	1/42	
K A Perkin, Plt Off	P	1/42	1/42	
G M Perrin, Flt Lt	N	8/65	4/68	
E A Peters, Fg Off-Flt Lt	P	13/8/52	22/8/54	
B Philbey, Flt Lt	N	circa 8/60	1960?	
A W Phillips, Sgt	WAG	24/4/41	6/41	
H W Pickering, Plt Off	IntO	22/11/41	30/7/42	
P B Pickersgill, Plt Off	P	19/6/39	1939	
A R Pinches, Fg Off-Flt Lt	N	1/61	7/63	
R L C C Pinkerton, Sgt-WO	N	1/44	17/2/45	KIA
N W Pinnington, Fg Off	P	21/4/41	27/5/41	KIA
D J Pitcher, Sgt	P	by 9/30	1933?	
R J Platts, N2	N	11/47	1/12/48	
H P Pleasance, APO-Flt Lt	P	10/4/37	9/39	
P G D Plomer, F/Sgt-WO	N	23/7/45	19/4/46	
R T F Plowman, Flt Lt	P	1/56	15/11/57	
G W Pollard, Fg Off	N	3/58	8/60	
W H Poole, Flt Lt	P	23/3/31	19/9/31	
E Pordham, Flt Lt	N	3/6/58	12/60	
B L Porter, Flt Lt	P	29/3/66	27/3/67	
D V Porter, Flt	MO	7/2/44	1944	
A J Potter, Fg Off	P	2/73	31/7/73	
L L Potter, Fg Off	P	22/9/25	9/10/26	
S Potts, Plt Off	N	16/12/43	15/1/45	KIA
L S Powell, Sgt, RAAF	P	12/41	14/3/42	KIA
Pratt, F/Sgt	N	9/46	1946?	
J E Preston, Fg Off	P	1/3/28	24/9/28	
A deT Prévost, N2	N	11/47	16/9/49	
Price, Fg Off	N	1/47	3/47	
C A Price, Sgt	P	1928	1930	
J D H Price, Flt Lt	P	4/65	30/1/68	
T B Prickman, Fg Off-Flt Lt	P	27/10/28	5/6/31	
A H Pridmore, F/Sgt-WO	N	12/12/44	8/45	
Pritchard, Sgt	?	7/41	circa 10/41	
J R Prockter, Sgt	O	4/41	4/41	
A V Proctor, Flt Lt	P	circa 9/46	5/11/46	KFA
D A Proctor, Fg Off-Flt Lt	P	5/56	15/11/57	
G H Proctor, Flt Lt	N	3/9/44	3/10/44	KIA
L G Prout, Fg Off	N	19/8/44	11/9/44	KFA
E B Pulford, Sgt, RCAF	WAG	17/10/41	16/1/43	
G A Pulman, Fg Off	N	12/64	15/5/67	
F Pusey, Flt Lt	Adj	circa 9/45	9/11/45	
K Putman, F/Sgt-WO	N	2/44	circa 7/45	
C D Pyne, Fg Off	P	20/5/21	1/10/21	
R A Quarrell, Fg Off	N	3/62	9/64	
Rae, Sgt	?	9/40?	1/10/40	
R L Ragg, Fg Off	P	13/12/22	11/9/24	
E D Rainbow, Plt Off-Flt Lt	N	6/4/44	10/5/46	
K J Rampling, Plt Off	P	5/9/35	6/1/36	
I A Ramsey, Sgt	N	9/63	1966	
M Randle, Fg Off	P	29/3/60	11/61	

Name	Role	From	To	Status
E G Rands, APO-Plt Off	P	27/5/38	17/4/39	
J E Ravenhall, Flt Lt	P	21/1/68	18/2/70	
V Ray, Sqn Ldr	P	15/10/40	1/4/41	
R W Reader, AC1-Sgt	WAG	1939?	13/10/40	KIA
T H Redfern, Flt Lt	MO	9/11/44	11/4/45	
M W Redley, Fg Off	P	2/64	4/4/66	KFA
W S Reed, Plt Off-Fg Off	P	13/4/32	15/8/32	
A Reeve, Sgt	P	8/24	1926?	
J H Reeves, Fg Off, RNZAF	P	19/8/44	11/9/44	KFA
R E J Reeves, Sgt	O	circa 9/41	20/12/41	KIA
R H Reeves, Plt Off	O	22/11/41	30/4/42	
Reid, F/Sgt	O	1/42	1/42	
R A Renton, Fg Off-Flt Lt	P	9/63	2/66	
M L Restell-Little, Plt Off-Fg Off	P	25/8/27	28/4/29	
M Retallack, Sgt	P	19/3/52	19/6/54	
A J Reynolds, Plt Off-Fg Off	N	29/6/68	18/2/70	
D Rhodes, Sgt	O	14/4/41	9/6/41	
C S Riccard, Flt Lt	P	11/8/28	6/4/29	
C Richardson, AC1-Sgt	WAG	1939	6/41	
C deW Richardson, Plt Off	P	by 7/40	1/10/40	
J F Richardson, Flt Lt	N	9/63	11/65	
F B Rickards, Flt Lt	P	9/62	8/65	
A I Riley, Fg Off	P	23/11/27	5/5/28	
F L Rippingale, Plt Off	O	28/6/41	22/11/41	POW
J M Ritchie, Flt Lt	MO	29/3/30	10/2/33	
E G Rivers, Fg Off-Flt Lt	P	12/9/59	3/62	
D F Rixson, Plt Off-Flt Lt	P	30/4/38	2/41	
E J Roberts, Flt Lt	P	circa 7/45	28/3/46	
L S Roberts, Plt Off	IntO	2/2/40	13/10/40	KIA
J H Robertson, Fg Off	P	23/7/45	1946?	
G A Robinson, N3-Sgt	N	14/11/49	11/1/51	KIA
H Robinson, AC1	WAG	1939?	11/6/40	KIA
H Robinson, Sgt	?	1950	1951	
J Robinson, Sgt	P	17/10/41	29/11/41	WIA
J Robinson, Plt Off	P	16/5/41	26/5/41	
M H Robinson, Fg Off-Flt Lt	StO	2/10/33	5/9/36	
M M J Robinson, Plt Off-Flt Lt	P	30/10/48	12/4/51	
T Robinson, F/Sgt	N	18/11/57	8/60	
R J Rodwell, Fg Off	P	20/5/21	14/10/23	
C A Rogers, Plt Off	P	14/7/53	21/10/53	
J Rogers, Fg Off	?	8/2/44	21/2/44	
S D Rogers, Flt Lt	N	16/1/58	10/7/59	
J I T Rolfe, Fg Off	P	15/9/58	18/11/58	KFA
H Rollins, WO	P	10/3/45	circa 6/45	
C H Romans, Sgt	WAG	1/42	6/10/43	KFA
Ross, Sgt	WAG	28/3/42	7/5/42	
A Ross, F/Sgt-MPlt	P	16/1/58	7/60	
A J Ross, Plt Off-Flt Lt	P	7/61	10/63	
G D Ross, MNav	N	9/60	2/63	
P J Rourke, Fg Off-Flt Lt	N	18/11/57	24/6/59	
J H Rowe,[23] Plt Off-Fg Off, RAAF	P	12/41	29/8/42	KFA
A W Rule, Fg Off	StO	20/7/32	28/1/34	
Russell, Flt Lt	P	circa 7/45	24/11/45	
J A Russell, Sgt-F/Sgt	N	14/2/45	circa 7/45	
R J Russell, Fg Off	P	11/2/55	2/4/55	KFA
A D Rutherford, WO	P	8/3/33	1935?	
Rutter, Sgt	?	8/40?	2/9/40	
P T E Ryans, Fg Off-Flt Lt	EngO	5/60	7/62	
W H Ryder, Plt Off	P	23/11/23	17/3/24	KFA
E B Ryles, Sgt	O	circa 4/40	13/10/40	KIA
W L Salmon, F/Sgt-WO	P	23/7/45	circa 11/45	
E L Sandifer, Fg Off	N	16/12/43	20/10/44	KIA
R H M S Saundby, Flt Lt	P	17/2/22	24/3/25	
H W L Saunders, Sqn Ldr	P	8/1/32	11/11/35	
R T Saunders, Fg Off	P	9/46	circa 5/49	
G A Say, Fg Off	P	3/62	12/64	
J Scanes, Sgt	P	16/12/43	2/44	
A A Schimmel, Flt Lt	P	8/4/74	4/11/74	
J F Schofield, Flt Lt	N	7/6/67	3/70	
F Scholfield, Fg Off, RCAF	P	12/5/45	6/8/45	
E V G Scoones, Plt Off-Fg Off	P	31/1/40	circa 2/41	
L E H Scotchmer, Flt Lt	P	12/46	2/47	
F Scott, Sgt	P	7/41	1/42	
F N Scott, Sgt	P	28/6/41	12/41	
R H Scott, F/Sgt-WO	P	8/45	12/45?	
H S Scroggs, Flt Lt	P	6/12/21	28/12/24	
J Sears, Sgt-Plt Off	O	circa 4/40	6/41	
S Segal, Flt Lt	MO	22/4/41	28/6/41	
H Sellars, F/Sgt-WO	N	12/44	6/45	
R B Serjeant, Plt Off	IntO	7/12/44	2/4/45	
R Shalom. Sgt	P	24/4/41	27/6/41	
F P Shattock, Sgt-WO, RAAF	P	21/3/42	late 43	
G M E Shaw, Fg Off	P	28/4/26	14/2/27	
R T Shaw, Sgt	P	by 1938	1939	
Shearsmith, Sgt	P	1931	1933?	
H Shelton, F/Sgt-WO	P	circa 9/45	12/45?	
R D Shepherd, Plt Off	P	19/6/39	1939	
A G Sheppard, Plt Off	O	3/5/40	2/10/40	POW
P R Sheppard, Fg Off	P	1/4/55	17/5/57	
R A Shingler, Fg Off-Flt Lt	N	circa 8/45	22/4/46	
S Siddle, Sgt	WAG	19/7/43	13/11/43	KIA
G A D Simpson, Flt Lt	N	9/63	6/64	
J B Sims, Fg Off	P	23/2/33	20/7/34	
G E Singleton, Plt Off	P	10/6/28	27/10/28	
A G Skingsley, Sqn Ldr	P	23/4/65	7/11/67	
D M Sleven, Flt Lt	N	11/61	7/64	
P J Slingsby, Flt Lt	N	1/48	6/48	
A Smart, Sgt-F/Sgt	N	8/45	10/46	
Smith, Sgt	?	1940	6/9/40	
Smith, F/Sgt-WO	P	circa 8/45	1946	
A A Smith, Flt Lt	MO	1/6/43	26/11/43	
A C Smith, Sgt	N	9/3/51	26/2/52	
A S Smith, APO-Plt Off	P	27/5/38	24/4/39	
A W Smith, Sgt	O	9/9/40	5/41	
F J Smith, Fg Off	SigO	1/47	7/47	
J P Smith, Fg Off	N	circa 4/67	18/2/70	
L Smith, Sgt	O	circa 11/41	22/11/41	KIA
L S R Smith, Plt Off-Fg Off	P	30/10/48	26/11/49	KFA
N A Smith, F/Sgt	N	12/44	6/2/45	D
R J D Smith, Fg Off	N	6/64	9/12/66	
R M Smith, Fg Off	P	22/8/33	17/2/34	
S B S Smith, Flt Lt	MO	6/2/33	2/7/34	
S W Smith, Fg Off	P	24/2/22	21/11/23	
T W Smith, N3	N	circa 3/50	6/7/50	KIA
D J Smyth, Sgt, RAAF	P	12/41	11/3/42	KIA
F W Snell,[18] Flt Lt	P	2/4/44	circa 5/44	
F W Snell,[18] Wg Cdr	p	25/4/46	13/5/46	
S G Soderholm, APO-Plt Off	P	27/5/38	27/4/39	
P J Somerfield, Fg Off	N	1967?	18/2/70	
Sorrell, F/Sgt	P	by 5/46	10/46	
L H Southall, Flt Lt	P	circa 1/54	15/8/54	
R Southorn, Sgt-F/Sgt, RAAF	P	1/42	1/3/43	
D J Sowler, Flt Lt	P	9/72	31/7/73	
R Sparks, Sgt, RAAF	WAG	1/42	3/42?	
H W C Springham, Fg Off	EqO	10/10/36	22/2/38	
E Springthorpe, Flt Lt-Sqn Ldr	P	4/5/46	28/6/46	
B E StClair, Fg Off	P	1/4/57	15/11/57	
F J Stace, F/Sgt-WO	P	circa 11/44	6/45	
G N J Stanley-Turner, Fg Off-Flt Lt	P	12/5/29	10/4/30	
F E Starkey, Flt Lt	N	11/62	4/65	
M K Steel, Fg Off	N	5/66	4/11/68	
J A Steff-Langston, Fg Off	P	7/48	5/11/48	
G Stephens, Fg Off	N	1/47	4/47	
E E Stevens, F/Sgt	N	18/11/57	13/12/57	KFA
P C Stevens, Flt Lt	N	27/10/59	16/5/60	
A G Stevenson, Fg Off	N	9/65	30/3/68	
J H Stevenson, Flt Lt, RCAF	P	8/7/43	13/11/43	WIA
Stewart, Sgt	P	7/41	1/42	
I M Stewart, Flt Lt	P	11/72	31/7/73	
R C Stewart, Fg Off-Flt Lt	P	11/47	8/6/49	
O K Stirling-Webb, Fg Off	P	29/1/26	26/7/26	KFA
B E Stocker, P4/Sgt	P	23/7/49	1951	
I S Stockwell, Sqn Ldr	P	28/7/51	1/54	
R C W Stokes, Flt Lt	N	16/1/58	30/11/59	
R S Stone, Sgt	WAG	26/3/42	21/9/43	
P D Stonham, Flt Lt	P	1/1/66	1/10/68	
Stratton, Sgt	P	1929	1931	
Stratton, F/Sgt	M	9/46	1/47	
V C F Streatfeild, Flt Lt	P	7/9/35	15/11/36	
E J Street, Sgt	O	circa 8/40	18/4/41	KIA
P R Stroud, Fg Off	P	15/5/27	10/3/28	
A Strudwick, LAC-Sgt	O	1938	6/41	

Name		From	To	Status
H C Stumm, Wg Cdr, RAAF	P	10/2/44	13/5/44	KFA
J B Sullivan, Fg Off	P	11/54	2/57	
G E Sully, Sgt	O	7/41	3/11/41	KIA
G L Sulman, Sgt	P	14/4/41	9/6/41	
J K Summers, [19]Flt Lt-Sqn Ldr	P	14/9/23	14/2/27	
J K Summers, [19]Sqn Ldr	P	27/4/27	23/12/28	
A L Sumner, Fg Off	IntO	6/43	7/43	
R Sumner. F/Sgt	N	16/12/43	2/44	
G W Swanbo, Sgt	WAG	16/5/41	19/5/41	POW
W J Swire-Griffiths, APO-Fg Off	P	17/2/38	16/3/40	KFA
P H Sykes, Fg Off	P	11/8/62	4/65	
Symonds, Sgt	P	1930	1931	
I D Symonds, Fg Off	N	16/1/58	3/60	
A C Tadhunter, Sgt	O	circa 4/40	3/1/41	KIA
K J Tait, Fg Off	P	12/64	14/6/67	
W A M Tait, Fg Off	P	10/63	1966	
J B Tatnall, Plt Off-Fg Off	P	14/9/30	21/8/33	
G J Taylor, Sgt	S	17/12/50	18/2/52	
J Taylor, Flt Lt	N	7/60	2/61	
N T Taylor, Sgt, RCAF	P	1/42	28/12/43	
W G M Taylor, WO-Fg Off, RAAF	P	7/2/44	20/8/45	
J D T Taylor-Gill, Sgt	P	1936	?	
J Tennant, N2/Sgt	N	27/9/50	28/4/52	
F G Terry, Sgt	WAG	11/41	1/44	
M R N Tew, Flt Lt	P	13/8/73	2/9/74	
D Thacker, Sgt	WAG	14/4/41	9/6/41	
C W S Thomas, APO-Flt Lt	P	27/5/38	11/6/41	
G D Thomas, F/Sgt	N	13/12/45	5/11/46	KFA
G W Thomas, Fg Off	P	31/8/54	3/55	
J A Thomas, Fg Off-Flt Lt	P	1/62	7/64	
N H Thomas, Sgt	P	11/4/41	26/5/41	KIA
R G D Thomas, Fg Off	AcO	18/7/22	19/9/24	
S M Thomas, Fg Off	P	23/11/27	10/3/28	
A Thompson, Sgt	O	1/42	5/3/43	
F E Thompson, Sgt-WO, RCAF	P	25/11/41	28/12/42	
G Thompson, Flt Lt	N	22/9/59	3/62	
O B Thompson, F/Sgt	WAG	4/41	23/5/41	KIA
D Thorne, Lt, SAAF	P	21/4/41	9/6/41	
D Thornton, Sgt, RAAF	WAG	25/11/41	1942	
P E Thorpe, Flt Lt	N	1968?	1/3/69	
R Thorpe, Flt Lt	MO	17/5/34	24/6/36	
A Threadgould, Fg Off	P	27/2/68	18/2/70	
M C Thurlow, Sgt	P	by 10/38	11/6/40	KIA
G A Tibbs, Sgt-F/Sgt, RAAF	O	8/1/42	13/2/43	
A H Tidswell, Plt Off-Fg Off, RAAF	O	12/41	23/4/43	
C H Tighe, Flt Lt	P	10/10/33	16/11/34	
W F Tolar, F/Sgt	P	16/12/43	circa 7/44	
J H Tolman, Sgt-Plt Off	P	26/6/41	4/12/41	KIA
Tompkins, Sgt-F/Sgt	P	1931	1932	
G J Tonks, Flt Lt	P	5/45	13/6/45	KFA
Topping, Sgt	O	7/41	30/10/41	
W Topping, Flt Lt	P	1/4/55	6/56	
A Torrence, Flt Lt-Sqn Ldr	P	12/4/44	8/3/45	
B A Towler, Fg Off	N	5/66	27/9/68	
Tozer, Sgt	O	circa 8/41	circa 10/41	
A Traill, Sqn Ldr	P	1/11/42	27/1/44	KFA
P C Traill-Smith, Plt Off	P	23/10/40	12/12/40	KIA
R D Tranter, Sgt	S	9/3/51	18/2/52	
M C Trench, Fg Off	P	1/4/21	21/10/22	
Tribe, Sgt	P	1929	1931	
P P Troughton-Smith, APO-Flt Lt	P	10/4/37	22/10/40	
Tugdale, Sgt	WAG	circa 11/41	1/42	
G J Turley, Sgt	P	2/10/51	circa 1/54	
Turnbull, Sgt	O	4/9/40	circa 6/41	
J E Turnbull, Flt Lt	P	8/2/44	30/7/44	
T Turnbull, Sgt	WAG	circa 10/40	6/41	
A J Turner, Fg Off	N	9/64	1967	
W H N Turner, Plt Off-Fg Off	P	28/2/33	16/6/35	
R A Turton, Sgt-Fg Off, RNZAF	O	2/7/41	13/2/43	
H W Twydell, Sgt	WAG	circa 8/41	1/42	
J F Umdasch, Fg Off	N	by 10/45	2/47	
W Underhill, Flt Lt	P	9/12/24	21/9/25	
G W Underwood, Flt Lt	P	4/5/45	20/5/46	
J C Usher, Sgt	O	4/9/40	30/9/40	KIA
K H Utton, Flt Lt	N	20/5/60	6/63	
J W Valentine, Sqn Ldr	P	20/5/60	27/11/61	
P W R Varley, Fg Off	P	9/46	12/46	
R B Vass, Fg Off	P	1/4/55	17/5/57	
J R Vernon, Sgt-Flt Lt, RAAF	O/N	22/11/41	22/4/45	
M Verrill, Fg Off	P	23/8/66	22/12/67	
J A Vigar, Sgt	P	16/1/52	circa 6/53	
J Vinales, Fg Off	N	21/2/67	18/2/70	
F J Vincent, Sqn Ldr	P	30/10/28	14/5/32	
P J Vincent, Plt Off	P	7/4/41	23/5/41	KIA
G Viner, Fg Off	P	23/7/45	23/1/46	
R A Vinson, Plt Off	P	10/10/40	1940?	
H Vipond, Cpl-Sgt	O	1939?	6/41	
R Waddington, Sgt	WAG	7/41	10/7/41	POW
Wade, F/Sgt-WO	P	circa 9/45	circa 12/45	
G N Wade, Fg Off	N	10/63	2/66	
D T Walder, Fg Off-Flt Lt	N	11/65	10/8/68	
H E Walker, Flt Lt	P	6/10/30	16/2/33	
H R Walker, Fg Off	P	1/4/55	circa 11/56	
J J Walker, Flt Lt	P	7/60	1/63	
R J Walker, Wg Cdr	P	28/5/44	25/3/45	WIA
R J E Walker, Fg Off	EngO	10/46	5/11/46	
A L Wall, Flt Lt	P	9/6/67	18/2/70	
J Wallace, Plt Off	P	19/6/39	1939	
W F Wallas, Fg Off	P	23/3/21	20/8/21	
Waller, Fg Off	N	circa 8/45	20/10/45	
P A Walliker, Fg Off	N	13/12/66	1969	
C B B Wallis, Wg Cdr	P	26/11/41	1/4/42	
W H Walmsley, Flt Lt	P	1/4/55	5/55	
B Walsh, WO	P	circa 12/44	1/6/45	
P J Walsh, Fg Off	P	1/4/55	circa 1/56	
A J Walters, F/Sgt-WO	N	5/3/45	12/6/46	
R C Wansborough, Plt Off	P	13/12/22	15/4/23	
Ward, Sgt	P	1926	1926?	
A A Ward, Flt Lt	P	21/5/26	21/12/26	
K E Ward, Flt Lt	P	1/6/26	22/2/27	
W Ward, Flt Lt	P	8/72	31/7/73	
L C Warren, Fg Off	P	3/61	8/63	
C Warsow, Fg Off	P	15/5/27	3/11/28	
D G Watkins, Flt Lt	N	26/8/68	18/2/70	
F W Watkins, Sgt-F/Sgt	O	1/42	13/2/43	
F J H Watson, Flt Lt	N	10/63	2/66	
A Weatherly, Fg Off	P	circa 8/45	1945	
B J Webb, Plt Off-Fg Off	N	10/63	6/64	
B W Webb, Fg Off	N	3/62	9/64	
E B Webb, Sqn Ldr	P	4/2/39	20/4/40	
T M Webb, Flt Lt	P	22/5/73	31/7/73	
C H F Webster, Flt Lt	N	16/1/58	10/12/59	
Weir, Plt Off	IntO	circa 8/45	1/2/46	
L H T Wellard, Sgt	N	12/10/51	28/4/52	
N Westby, Flt Lt	N	7/48	circa 9/50	
P A Weston, S3/Sgt	S	14/12/49	1951	
C G Whitcitt, Fg Off	N	24/3/45	23/7/46	
J E White, Sgt	WAG	28/6/41	4/7/41	KIA
L E White, Flt Lt	N	1967?	18/2/70	
M G F White, Flt Lt	P	11/2/74	1975?	
R White, Fg Off	P	1976?	26/7/76	
E R Whitehouse, Flt Lt-Sqn Ldr	P	22/9/25	18/1/27	
S B Whiteley, Sgt	WAG	21/4/41	22/11/41	POW
C A Whiteside,[21] Sgt-F/Sgt	O	1/42	18/8/42	KIA
R A Whiteside, Fg Off-Flt Lt	P	7/11/44	7/45	
R Whittam, Flt Lt	P	4/6/51	26/7/52	
G B Whittaker, Sgt	WAG	1/42	13/2/43	
G H Whittaker, P2	P	11/47	1948	
N S Whittaker, Flt Lt	P	10/62	11/65	
T Whittaker, Maj	AILO	7/41	8/41	
C E G Wickham, Flt Lt	MO	5/9/40	circa 11/40	
S C Widdows, Fg Off	P	28/2/33	18/11/33	
J Widmer, Fg Off	P	20/12/49	14/2/50	
A J O Wigmore, Sqn Ldr	MO	1/6/21	26/4/22	
J E Wilcock, Sgt	WAG	2/7/41	20/12/41	KIA
R J Wilcock, F/Sgt-Fg Off	P	2/44	17/6/45	KFA
P H Wilcox, Flt Lt	P	19/9/74	1976?	
C Wilks, Plt Off	CyO	circa 1/42	15/7/42	
Williams, Sgt	O	7/41	circa 11/41	
Williams, Flt Lt	?	13/12/45	13/6/46	
G F Williams, Sgt-Flt Lt, RAAF	WAG/N	8/1/42	20/6/45	
H A Williams, Fg Off	StO	22/6/21	20/1/25	

J H Williams,	P	30/4/38	10/8/40	
R S Williams, Flt Lt	P	12/12/67	18/2/70	
R D Williamson, Sgt	S	15/9/51	18/2/52	
J O Willis, Sqn Ldr-Wg Cdr	P	15/3/41	22/11/41	KIA
R J Willits, APO-Plt Off	P	27/5/38	24/4/39	
W T Willman, Sqn Ldr	P	8/72	1974?	
A J Wilson, Fg Off	P	2/73	7/10/73	
H H Wilson, Flt Lt, RAAF	Adj	15/11/42	circa 4/45	
J H W Wilson, Fg Off	P	16/2/54	16/2/57	
J R Wilson, WO-Plt Off, RCAF	P	circa 2/44	12/1/45	KIA
R C Wilson, Fg Off	P	27/9/27	5/2/30	
W R Wilson, Sgt-F/Sgt, RAAF	WAG	7/11/41	27/1/43	
L T Wilton-Jones, F/Sgt	P	7/41	10/7/41	POW
J C Wimhurst, Sgt	O	7/41	10/7/41	KIA
C P Wingfield, Fg Off	P	14/9/23	18/10/24	
L P Winters, Fg Off	P	5/2/25	22/6/25	
A H Wise, Plt Off, RNZAF	O	22/4/41	18/5/41	KIA
E M Withy, Fg Off	P	12/10/36	15/12/36	
R C Witt, Flt Lt	MO	2/2/44	circa 9/44	
C G C B Woledge, Fg Off	P	22/2/26	23/10/26	
F L Woledge, Fg Off	P	15/5/27	17/6/27	
A D Wood, Fg Off	P	23/7/45	1946?	
D Wood, Fg Off	P	10/46	1949	
J L Wood, Fg Off	P	1945?	13/6/46	
R Wood, Sgt	P	2/7/41	22/11/41	POW
R W Woodcraft, Flt Lt	EngO	16/4/46	15/7/46	
G C B Woodroffe, APO-Fg Off	P	17/2/38	13/10/40	KIA
Woodward, Sgt	O	circa 11/41	circa 1/42	
C Wordsworth, Cpl-Sgt	O	by 5/38	circa 7/41	
P L Wort, Flt Lt	N	10/64	11/3/67	
A S Wotherspoon, Flt Lt	N	5/61	7/63	
C L Wright, APO-Fg Off	P	17/2/38	circa 7/40	
J Wright, Plt Off-Fg Off	O	26/6/41	1/42	
S C Wyatt, Flt Lt	AcO	7/11/31	1/3/33	

R C Wylde, Flt Lt	N	3/58	5/59	
J J S Yanota, WO, RCAF	N	2/44	9/11/44	POW
T B J Yarrow, Flt Lt	P	18/11/74	1976?	
C J Yeo, Fg Off	P	22/3/68	18/2/70	
R H Young, Fg Off	P	7/9/35	9/11/36	
C J Zussen, F/Sgt	N	2/44	26/6/46	
Z Zmitrowicz, F/Sgt	P	1/4/55	3/57	

Notes:

1. 2/Lt Bowden was non-effective sick 30/10/16-13/2/17.
2. Lt Davis also briefly attached to No 45 Sqn 31/5/18-7/6/18.
3. Dvr Fellows died, 29/7/17.
4. 2/Lt Fey was non-effective sick 22/9/18-20/10/18.
5. 2/Lt Frith was also WIA.
6. Rfn Hammond died the same day.
7. Lt Hand was also wounded (burned).
8. Capt Higgins was RO from approx 27/9/17.
9. Capt Hilborn died of his injuries, 26/8/18.
10. Capt Jenkins died 23/5/17.
11. 2/Lt Johnstone was also WIA.
12. 2/AM Loughlin was also WIA.
13. 2/AM Ridgway was also WIA; he died the same day.
14. L/Cpl Russell died the same day.
15. Lt Senior died the same day.
16. 2/Lt Smith was also WIA.
17. 2/AM Thompson was also WIA; he died the same day.
18. Served with the squadron on two distinct occasions.
19. Nominally on the strength of No 47 Sqn during intervening period.
20. Real name G H M Reuter, a Free Belgian.
21. Died while flying on attachment to No 113 Sqn.
22. Died in a Dakota crash.
23. Died while flying on attachment to No 308 MU.

A large proportion of No 45 Sqn's contemporary aircrew photographed at Gambut, Christmas 1941. Numbering from the left, those who have been identified are, standing: (1) Plt Off P U A Keel, (2) 2/Lt T C Evans, (3) Plt Off L G George, (4) Sgt A Field, (5) Sgt E B Pulford, (6) Plt Off G E Kemp, (8) 2/Lt H R L Alder, (9) Plt Off W J Corbett, (10) Sgt J E Pannifer, (11) Sgt W Fylan, (12) Sgt K Mills, (13) Plt Off F J Fraser, (14) (almost hidden), (15) Sgt D Page, (16) Sgt C G Briggs(?), (17) Plt Off P E Graebner, (18) Plt Off J S Muller-Rowland and (19) Sgt F R Haylock. In front: (21) 2/Lt A D Allen, (24) Sgt C E Birkbeck, (25) Sgt W A Gaudet, (26) Sgt K A Gardiner (27) Sgt B T McDade, (28) Sgt J Paterson, (29) Sgt K E Edwards and (31) Sgt C G Hockney. (D Cliffe)

Annex N. Non-commissioned technical and support personnel known to have served with No 45 Sqn during the two World Wars.

While the author has been able to list nearly all of the officers and most of the NCO aircrew who have served with No 45 Sqn (see Annex M), it has not been practical to do this for its groundcrew. Sufficient documentation survives to identify a significant number of those who served with the squadron during the Great War, although the roll is probably incomplete. Several hundred NCOs and airmen will have been carried on the squadron's books between 1921 and 1939 but information relating to them is extremely sparse. There are few references to groundcrew personalities in the squadron's routine reporting of events during the Second World War but copies of a few Movement Orders still exist and these effectively represent periodic nominal rolls. Pre-war practice was resumed after 1945 and, apart from a brief period in the early 1950s when the comings and goings of most NCOs and airmen were noted, the majority of the squadron's post-war groundcrew are as anonymous as their inter-war pre-decessors, although most of those who were on the squadron in 1950 and 1953 are named in the captions to the group photographs on pages 344 and 358.

For obvious reasons the two World Wars are the most significant periods in the history of any combat squadron. The following lists represent a series of 'snapshots' of No 45 Sqn's ground echelon; they are included to reflect, albeit incompletely and therefore inadequately, the contribution made by the squadron's wartime groundcrews and support personnel. It is regretted that so many names will have been omitted.

The continuity which existed within the composition of the squadron's wartime ground echelon is very apparent from the content of the lists covering WW II. This was a notable characteristic of units which served abroad, many airmen spending their whole time overseas with a single squadron, joining it as a brand new AC2 and leaving four years later, often wearing two, or sometimes three, stripes. This pattern was mirrored by the aircrew and several of those who were fortunate enough to survive flew with the squadron for more than three years. It was this very continuity which gave No 45 Sqn the strong sense of identity which enabled it to

Beyond fading snapshots like this one, little remains in the accessible public domain to record the many groundcrew who served with No 45 Sqn between the wars. Taken at Helwan circa 1930, this picture shows, from the left, Louwdes, Rose, Greenwood, Spaull, Grinter, King and one other unidentified airman of A Flight. (R Grinter via J Grech)

maintain its morale in the face of periodic setbacks and sometimes heavy operational losses.

Inevitably, there will be some errors in the following lists. Most of the information has been taken from second or third carbon-copies or from mimeographed sheets printed on poor quality paper and, apart from numerous typographical errors, in many cases the typist failed to cut through the stencil, leaving many characters indistinct or completely illegible. Furthermore, it is evident that the admin office was uncertain as to the correct spelling of some names. As a result of these and other problems some of the Service Nos quoted below may well be incorrect and there must be doubt over the rendering of names which vary in spelling from one list to another, eg Hardwick may be Hardwicke and Somerville could be Sommerville. Other examples include York/Yorke Hillyard/Hildyard, Gleason/Gleeson and Heseltine/Hezeltine.

Groundcrew known to have served with No 45 Sqn, 1916-19.

Most of the names which follow have been extracted from Daily Routine Orders published by 7th and 14th Wgs and the surviving pages of the Daily State returns which were rendered by No 45 Sqn between its arrival in Italy in late December 1917 and its reduction to cadre in France in early February 1919. Since many personnel remained on the strength of the squadron throughout its existence, the following list is believed to include most of the men who maintained the 1½ Strutters and quite possibly all of those who served in Italy. On the other hand, some of those who joined the squadron at Gosport (and more than forty of these are listed below) may already have left the unit before it moved to France and they will not, therefore, have seen active service with it. A number of points are offered in amplification of what follows.

a. Those NCOs and AMs who flew with the squadron

as gunners are included in Annex M, although some of them were previously (or subsequently) also numbered among its groundcrew.

b. In July 1918 a new and complex rank structure was introduced for RAF NCOs and enlisted men. This survived only until the end of the year when it was replaced by the ranks which, with a few embellishments, are still in use today. Some additional information on this topic is provided at Note 1; suffice to say here that some individuals carried three ranks during their final year on the squadron, eg Morton was a Flight Sergeant who became a Chief Mechanic and then reverted to Flight Sergeant while Frost began 1918 as an Air Mechanic First Class, became a Clerk 1 and finished up as a Leading Aircraftman. In neither case was there any change in status, only in nomenclature. These redesignations could be even more tortuous for those who were promoted and/or remustered from one trade to another. No attempt has been made to reflect these changes as they affected each individual. The rank shown in each case was definitely applicable at some stage, but most people will have had one, and many two, changes in nominal rank. Where promotions were involved the ranks indicated are believed to be the senior ones held.

c. There was some redesignation of trades *circa* July 1918, eg MT Drivers became Drivers/Petrol (to distinguish them from Drivers/Horse and Cart?) which term remained in the RAF's vocabulary until 1941 when it was changed to Driver MT (DMT). The only significance of this here is that those who are designated below as MT Drivers were definitely on strength before this change occurred (it does not follow that those designated as D/Ps were necessarily latecomers, only that their names do not crop up in surviving documents until after July). It is also worth noting that several men changed their trades while serving with the squadron, eg Smith (454) switched from Sailmaker to Upholsterer and Ince, originally an MT Driver, was regraded as a Fitter with effect from 11th February 1918.

d. Those noted below as Ambulance Drivers were not RFC/RAF men but soldiers detached from the Army Service Corps. Similarly, those noted as RAMC were detached personnel serving as Medical Orderlies. At least one other attached 'proper' soldier is included in the list, Pte Bye, who is believed to have been a Pioneer as his parent unit was the 111th Labour Coy. There was at least one other 'cuckoo', who has not been listed below, Sgt Marsala of the 6th Italian Balloon Group, who was attached to No 45 Sqn from May 1918 to act as its official interpreter.

d. Also worthy of note is the incidence of four-digit Service Numbers, indicating pre-war enrolment in the RFC. There are even three examples of the fabled three-digit numbers, Sergeant Major Baker (169), Cpl Ashby (506) and 1/AM Edwards (689), all of whom will have joined or transferred to the Corps during the first few months of its formation, certainly before the end of 1912.

Name	Rank	Trade	Service No	Name	Rank	Trade	Service No
				Clements, L	Clk/1	Clerk	19141
				Cload, G W	2/AM	Sailmaker	10127
Abernathy, D	Cpl Mech	D/P	7269	Close, R T	2/AM	Instrument Repairer	52683
Abrahams, H	Pte/1	Fabric Worker	111922	Coker, B H	Cpl Clk	Clerk	25835
Ames, L	2/AM	Armourer	11649	Collins, H	AC1	Cook	139952
Anderson, M	Pte	Ambulance Driver	M2/078972	Cook, C T	2/AM	Sailmaker	31149
Angell, A G	1/AM	Rigger	29650	Cooper, H	F/Sgt	Rigger	5243
Armfield, E	1/AM	Armourer	15681	Coultate, P	Sgt Mech	D/P	SR10[2]
Ashby, S	Cpl	Sailmaker	506	Craven, P	2/AM	Rigger	86453
Atkins, M	3/AM	Carpenter	112240	Cripps, F	1/AM	Electrician	18832
Avery, F	1/AM	Turner	38708	Daden, W H	1/AM	Batman	79393
Babes, W	3/AM	Rigger	188632	Deakin	2/AM	?	?
Badams, R M	2/AM	Rigger	86458	Dingwall, J	1/AM	Carpenter	14453
Baker, G	SM1	Discip	169	Dixon, W	Pte/1	Batman	21702
Barnes, E C	Cpl	M/Cyclist	17188	Dodwell, W	1/AM	Fitter	17017
Bartaby, E E	1/AM	MT Driver	16829	Doonan, H E	F/Sgt	Fitter	40119
Barton, N H	2/AM	Rigger	12583	Dowie, J	Cpl	Blacksmith	18139
Beech, E	2/AM	MT Driver	64757	Draycott, T E	3/AM	D/P	54690
Beeching, C H	Pte/2	Batman	40971	Drayne, E A	3/AM	D/P	13469
Bendall, W	Sgt Mech	Fitter	27136	Dunster, L	1/AM	D/P	21060
Bennett, H	1/AM	M/Cyclist	17899	Edney, W G	2/AM	Armourer	88429
Betts, S	1/AM	Electrician	14342	Edwards, C	1/AM	Fitter General	689
Biggs, C B	2/AM	M/Cyclist	52559	Edwards, L F	2/AM	Fitter	23035
Blakeman, J W	2/AM	Batman	24001	Evans, S	2/AM	MT Driver	21074
Bland, A T	1/AM	MT Driver	17805	Farrow, W G	SM2	-	148614
Blease, A	2/AM	M/Cyclist	67708	Ferguson, W	2/AM	Fitter	23166
Bloxham, S (F?)	Cpl	Fitter	46374	Fisher, J R	2/AM	MT Driver	21047
Bolland, H	3.AM	Coppersmith	46013	Fletcher, C	2/AM	D/P	64228
Boulton, J	2/AM	Rigger	18795	Francis, F M	Pte/1	Batman	??690
Bozman, D W	1/AM	Fitter	13902	Franklin, W	2/AM	Armourer	29720
Brown, P J	2/AM	Fitter	23254	Frost, A A	Clk/1	Clerk	18248
Buckley, C	2/AM	Batman	43314	Fruin, A H	1/AM	Fitter	38706
Bucknell, W S	2/AM	Carpenter	14409	Fry, P J	1/AM	MT Driver	17161
Butler, W P	2/AM	MT Driver	30919	Gardener, C	2/AM	Cook	24919
Butterworth, H H	3/AM	Rigger	151336	Gaukrodger, W E	1/AM	Electrician	17514
Bye, W R	Pte	(Pioneer?)	66061	Godden, J S	Sgt Mech	Carpenter	14379
Campbell, C	1/AM	Carpenter	18439	Godfrey, H C	2/AM	?	21534
Campbell, P	3/AM	Instrument Repairer	95215	Godfrey, J	2/AM	Fitter	112343
Carter, A J	Cpl	Clerk	18953	Gooding, F	Cpl Mech	D/P	24855
Challen, J W	1/AM	Rigger	26498	Goodwin, A	2/AM	MT Driver	17044
Chamberlain, F E	3/AM	D/P	22647	Gravenor, N	2/AM	Fitter	17028
Charteris, J	1/AM	Rigger	3518	Green, A	1/AM	Fitter	17104
Cheetham, G	3/AM	Fitter	29343	Green, W	Cpl Mech	Carpenter	5574
Cherry, W	2/AM	Fitter	17858	Gridley, E J	Pte/1	Cook	31684
Childs, L	Cpl	Fitter	1590	Griffin, G F	2/AM	Rigger	80546
Clark, R	2/AM	MT Driver	17005	Grimmitt, H W	Cpl	Fitter	14390
Clarke, F	Cpl Mech	Fitter	2688	Gronow, D	2/AM	Rigger	12629
Clarke, H	2/AM	Armourer	18872	Hain, G	2/AM	Fitter	17682
Clarke, H	3/AM	Armourer	94412	Hamblett, P	Cpl Mech	Carpenter	4984
Clarke, J W	2/AM	Carpenter	97670	Hamilton, J R	1/AM	Fitter	29290
Clegg, H	2/AM	Fitter	47810	Hammond	2/AM	Coppersmith	12239

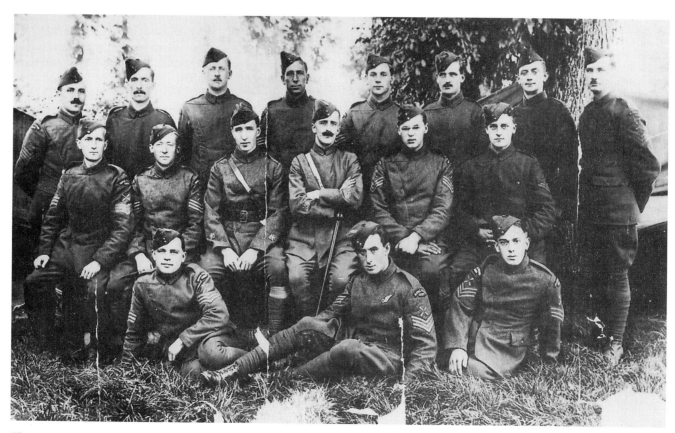

This picture was taken at Sedgeford in the late summer of 1916; it shows most of the WOs and NCOs who moved to France with No 45 Sqn, several of them remaining on strength until 1919. From the left, back row:- Sgt R J Wyatt (C Flight), F/Sgt W J Ryman (HQ Flight - Fitter), F/Sgt J A Morton (A Flight), F/Sgt A Mockford (C Flight), Sgt J Thomasson (HQ Flight - Transport), F/Sgt D McCutcheon (B Flight), Sgt T McNally (HQ Flight - Armourer) and Sgt W Bednall (B Flight). Middle row:- Sgt A High (A Flight), Sgt G Smith (C Flight), Sgt Maj P Smyth (HQ Flight - Technical), Sgt Maj G Baker (HQ Flight - Discip), F/Sgt T A Simkins (HQ Flt - Stores), F/Sgt H Cooper (B Flight). Front row:- F/Sgt W Holmes (HQ Flight - Carpenter), (probably) Sgt P S Taylor (observer) and F/Sgt E G A Newby (HQ Flight - Admin). (Imperial War Museum)

Hansell, M C	1/AM	Rigger	15955	Knight	1/AM	Rigger	3546
Harmon, E	1/AM	MT Driver	17039	Knight, A	2/AM	Fitter	17432
Hart, A	1/AM	Rigger	32254	Lambert, F A	Sgt	Armourer	65200
Haston, T	1/AM	D/P	7126	Laughland, J	1/AM	Fitter	18487
Heald, H	Sgt	Rigger	32251	Lee, A S	2/AM	Armourer	87325
Hedderwick, T	Cpl	Rigger	18608	Lee, R H	Sgt Mech	Electrician	14311
Heley, A	Pte/2	Batman	P/4489	Long, A V	Pte/2	M/Cyclist	75706
Hemphill, R J	Cpl	MT Driver	14701	Lowe, H E	Sgt Mech	Rigger	32257
Henderson, J W	Clk/1	Storeman	11573	Lowrie, J	2/AM	Fitter	17883
Henry, C J	1/AM	Fitter	17928	Lynch, A R	2/AM	MT Driver	28626
High, A	Sgt Mech	Rigger	?3376	Mackenzie	1/AM	?	?
Higham, J	Cpl	RAMC	19027	Macmaster, A	2/AM	Rigger	18503
Hill, H	1/AM	Rigger	32253	McCutcheon, D	F/Sgt	Fitter	18511
Hitchin, F	1/AM	Fitter	26493	McGarva, J	Pte	Ambulance Driver	347316
Hodson, E	1/AM	MT Driver	16493	McLachlan, A	2/AM	Fitter	40077
Holden, J	1/AM	Coppersmith	12314	McNally, T	Sgt	Armourer	34997
Hollyman, E S	2/AM	Electrician	?0094	Macey, H	2/AM	D/P	26589
Holmes, W	F/Sgt	Carpenter	4335	Maddock, F	1/AM	Rigger	18502
Horner, C	Pte/1	Batman	79390	Maidment, C	Cpl	Fitter	18870
Horswell, D E	3/AM	Wireless Op	92914	Marsh, J W	2/AM	MT Driver	21551
Howard, J	Pte/2	Batman	105775	Martin, A G	3/AM	Instrument Repairer	21001
Hyde, E	1/AM	MT Driver	17020	Mawby, F	Sgt	Storeman	?
Ince, R	2/AM	Fitter	37862	Mitton, F	Pte/1	M/Cyclist	58867
Irwin	2/AM	?	3389	Mockford, A	CM	D/P	26322
James, A	3/AM	Rigger	??632	Moir, J M	Pte	Ambulance Driver	181856
James, H	Pte	RAMC	39792	Molyneux, H M	1/AM	Armourer	35816
Jenkins, E J	Pte	Ambulance Driver	346735	Morton, J A	CM	Fitter	16949
Jenner	1/AM	Cook	5907	Moyse, G	Pte/1	Cook	??291
Jones, S W	AC2	Rigger	109859	Munden, F	1/AM	Carpenter	19000
Kellythorne, J	1/AM	Rigger	18768	Narborough, N	2/AM	Rigger	19060
Kemp, C	Pte/2	Batman	25804	Nelson, G H	2/AM	Fitter	12494
Kenshole, C T	Pte/1	M/Cyclist	18610	Newby, E G A	Flt Clk	Clerk	9575
Kiely, T	Pte/2	M/Cyclist	??312	Newham, H	3/AM	Acetylene Welder	404364
Kinley, J	2/AM	Armourer	51756	Nichols, C E	2/AM	Instrument Repairer	51909

526

Name	Rank	Trade	Service No		Name	Rank	Trade	Service No
Noon, W R	3/AM	Wireless Op	97331		Spenceley, P J	Sgt	Discip	3966
Northcote, R A	2/AM	Clerk	17668		Spencer, A E	2/AM	Electrician	45442
Nuttall, J N	2/AM	Storeman	2990		Spencer, H	1/AM	Fitter	40279
Osborne, F S	1/AM	Fitter	35829		Stevens, S	2/AM	Rigger	19068
Owens, T	2/AM	Fitter General	33223		Strachan, L W	3/AM	Instrument Repairer	278108
Page, A W	2/AM	Carpenter	83454		Stratton, W	2/AM	M/Cyclist	28600
Parry, J T S	1/AM	D/P	13878		Strong, E W	3/AM	Wireless Mechanic	53917
Parsons, L	Cpl Mech	Carpenter	12689		Swindells, F	Cpl Mech	Vulcaniser	24727
Payton, J F	Pte/1	Batman	41160		Tarrant, R E	Cpl	Clerk	76254
Peters, W H	Pte/2	Batman	290798		Taylor, M	2/AM	D/P	64137
Poulter, W	Pte/2	Batman	53724		Taylor, W A	2/AM	Rigger	38386
Powell, G	1/AM	Acetylene Welder	7120		Tetlow, H B	1/AM	Fitter	42573
Price	2/AM	Turner	13736		Thomasson, J	Sgt	Fitter?	?
Radford, W	2/AM	?	?		Thornton, A W	2/AM	D/P	17015
Rainbird, T	Cpl	Fitter	14391		Tomlinson, E R	2/AM	M/Cyclist	61774
Rich, H B	Cpl	M/Cyclist	17190		Tompkinson, H	1/AM	Fitter	19674
Ritchie, W	1/AM	Coppersmith	26141		Turner, C R	2/AM	MT Driver	50418
Robinson, W J	1/AM	Rigger	18897		Valentine, G	Pte	Ambulance Driver	346721
Rodber, W G	Pte	RAMC	4531		Van Coevorden, E M	2/AM	Rigger	32225
Rollo, A S	Sgt	Fitter	18542		Voysey	1/AM	?	?
Ross, W	2/AM	MT Driver	16948		Wallis, A	3/AM	Fitter MT	192387
Rowe, W T	1/AM	Upholsterer	12150		Walsh	Sgt	Fitter	1365
Ruddock, W	1/AM	Instrument Repairer	17119		Walters	Sgt	Rigger	2478
Ryman, W J	F/Sgt	Fitter	14047		Walton, J	AC1	Blacksmith	28299
Sampson, H	2/AM	Fitter	3853		Ward	Cpl	?	?
Saunders, A	1/AM	Fitter General	14400		Warren, G	Sgt	Fitter	17267
Saxton, J W	2/AM	Electrician	88054		Wasley, W	Pte/2	Batman	290834
Scott, D	1/AM	Rigger	12711		Weston, H	2/AM	Rigger	80633
Sergeant, J	2/AM	Armourer	69038		Wetherall, B W	2/AM	Carpenter	21245
Shevill	2/AM	Batman	11302		Whicker, A E	3/AM	Fitter MT	198331
Shrimpton, L P	AC2	Fitter	142496		White, A	1/AM	MT Driver	28255
Simkins, T A	F/Sgt	Storeman	5480		White, F E	Pte/2	M/Cyclist	63004
Slaney, W	Pte/1	M/Cyclist	17959		White, V J	2/AM	D/P	22876
Slevin, W R	2/AM	Fitter	6432		Whitlam, A	2/AM	Carpenter	14436
Smith, A	Pte/1	Batman	57325		Whittaker, E	2/AM	Fitter	56856
Smith, F N	Sgt	Clerk	9712		Wigley, H	Cpl Mech	Fitter	38968
Smith, G	Sgt	Rigger	4177		Wilkinson, J J	2/AM	Rigger	??413
Smith, H	Cpl	Sailmaker	10454		Wilks, G	2/AM	Batman	21628
Smith, H	Pte/1	Batman	57146		Williams, G C	Cpl	Sailmaker	16569
Smith, W	2/AM	MT Driver	17041		Williams, W	1/AM	Fitter	78690
Smith, W	2/AM	Armourer	44645		Withers, L F	2/AM	M/Cyclist	59093
Smyth, P	CMM	Tech	3187		Wright, J M	2/AM	Rigger	35470
Snelling, W	1/AM	Fitter	17266		Wright, P	2/AM	Rigger	19617
Sparks	1/AM	Rigger	5978		Wright, S W	Sgt Mech	Fitter	4266
Speed, J S	2/AM	Fitter	21758		Wyatt, R J	Sgt Mech	Fitter	4265

Groundcrew noted as being on strength in late November 1940.

The following list, which is not 100% complete (eg AC Holloway was left behind in hospital), is taken from a Movement Order raised to cover the squadron's return to Egypt from the Sudan. Of particular interest is the significant number of very junior airmen with 'foreign' names and Service Nos beginning 774 or 775. The 774 series was opened in November 1939 to cover personnel recruited from, for instance, Malta and Cyprus. The 775 series followed in July 1940 to cover further local recruiting, including manpower drawn from Palestine; it is suspected that many of the men with German or East European names were Jewish refugees from Nazi Germany who would have entered Palestine (legally or otherwise) during the late 1930s.

Some brief explanatory notes on some of the now long-foregotten groundcrew trades listed here are included at the end of this Annex as Note 3.

Name	Rank	Trade	Service No		Name	Rank	Trade	Service No		Name	Rank	Trade	Service No
					Bates	F/Sgt	F1	362782		Brickell	AC2	ACH	912287
					Baxter	LAC	N/Ord	637805		Brock	F/Sgt	Armr	508432
Abelsky	AC2	ACH/DP	774978		Beer	LAC	F2	566778		Brooke	LAC	ACH	549373
Abraham	AC2	ACH	774811		Bell	LAC	F/M	537182		Brooks	LAC	ACH	540506
Adair	Cpl	ACH	520820		Bennett	AC1	ACH	616793		Brown	LAC	Armr	629052
Adams	Cpl	M/R	533844		Bennett	AC2	ACH	912349		Buchanan	LAC	M/W	522365
Ainsley	AC1	F/M	651902		Benzur	AC2	D/P	774681		Burns	LAC	WEM	550009
Aldhurst	AC1	F2E	649318		Bergmans	Cpl	ACH/SP	912290		Burns	AC1	ACH	617544
Alper	AC2	ACH	774817		Bida	AC2	ACH	775089		Burr	Cpl	?	?
Anderson	Cpl	F2	566155		Bifield	LAC	ACH	533640		Burridge	AC1	ACH	546356
Anderson	AC1	F/M	649351		Blackshaw	LAC	W/Op	612284		Campbell	LAC	Photo	550336
Appleton	Cpl	ACH	528089		Boakes	LAC	W/Op	522728		Cant	LAC	FAE	545815
Armstrong	Sgt	N/Ord	510895		Bolderson	AC1	ACH	617108		Carpenter	AC2	ACH	912346
Azouz	AC2	ACH	774809		Bonell	Cpl	W/Op	521708		Carter	LAC	Armr	530344
Baggott	AC1	ACH	912353		Boot	LAC	F/M	649383		Chambers	F/Sgt	F1	370864
Bailey	AC2	ACH	906894		Brand	AC2	ACH	774812		Chapman	Sgt	Armr	523900
Ballott	AC1	F/R	649162		Braund	Sgt	Photo	355229		Charles	AC1	F/M	651898

527

Name	Rank	Trade	Service No	Name	Rank	Trade	Service No	Name	Rank	Trade	Service No
Clarke	LAC	Photo	551899	Hodkinson	Cpl	F2	566358	Price	Cpl	Armr	523645
Coad	Cpl	ACH/SP	522105	Hogarth	AC1	E2	634837	Pugh	LAC	W/Op	613310
Cole	LAC	M/R	539699	Hoggard	LAC	F2A	535975	Rankin	AC1	F/Armr	569855
Conway	AC2	ACH	912289	Hopper	Cpl	Clerk GD	590972	Reader	LAC	W/Op	548784
Copcutt	LAC	F/Armr	568283	Hornstein	AC2	D/P	774661	Readman	LAC	F/R	536980
Coughlin	AC1	ACH	546515	Hughes	Cpl	M/R	521171	Reid	AC1	F/M	649365
Covo	AC2	ACH/DP	774699	Huntley	AC1	F/R	648861	Reisenfeld	AC2	ACH	775216
Cowburn	Cpl	ACH/SP	533900	Ince	LAC	E/Asst	971007	Reynolds	Cpl	N/Ord	531189
Cowell	AC1	F/M	649319	Inch	LAC	F/M	649301	Richardson	AC1	ACH	628010
Cowles	AC2	ACH	912347	Inglis	LAC	F/R	541244	Rix	AC1	F/R	648177
Cozens	AC1	ACH	627898	Jacob	AC2	ACH/C&B	775101	Rosenblum	AC2	ACH	775095
Crook	LAC	W/Op	549463	Johnson	AC1	F/M	649333	Rossiter	Cpl	E/Asst	519720
Davidson	LAC	E/Asst	610693	Jones	LAC	E2	540997	Rowe	Cpl	ACH	528545
Davis	LAC	F/Armr	569971	Jones	LAC	F/M	651833	Rushton	AC1	ACH	616384
Daxon	AC1	E2	635992	Katz	AC2	ACH/C&B	774835	Sacks	AC2	ACH/C&B	774806
Day	AC2	ACH	912292	Kearney	AC1	ACH	617536	Scott	LAC	ACH	533503
Dean	LAC	E2	541079	Kelly	AC1	ACH	627055	Sharpe	LAC	F/M	522445
Dean	LAC	F2A	535373	Kemp	AC1	F/M	642281	Sharpe	LAC	F2A	542066
Deaville	LAC	F2A	542082	Kerr	AC2	ACH	912355	Sheppard	LAC	C&B	617732
Dueck	AC2	ACH	774035	Kohn	AC1	C&B	774341	Sheridan	Sgt	Armr	519785
Dunlop	LAC	E/Asst	610827	Laham	AC2	ACH	774815	Sim	AC1	ACH	616264
Dunn	LAC	M/R	539726	Lampshire	AC1	ACH	546381	Simmons	AC1	C&B	644272
Durling	AC1	I/R	622261	Leslie	Cpl	C/R	358638	Skinner	AC1	F/R	648995
Dwyer	F/Sgt	ACH	512396	Levinas	AC2	ACH	774818	Smith	LAC	F/M	649287
Eades	Cpl	F2	566792	Loveday	LAC	D/P	530932	Smith	AC1	ACH	626889
Easingwood	LAC	M/R	534487	McAnallen	AC1	Elect	632212	Somerville	LAC	F2	566863
Evans	Cpl	Armr	550241	McAusland	Cpl	F2	566789	Spiteri	AC2	D/P	776691
Exton	AC1	ACH	626985	McConnon	AC1	ACH	617122	Starr	LAC	F/M	537024
Finlayson	AC1	I/R	622032	McCord	LAC	ACH	536289	Stevens	AC2	ACH	912288
Firth	Cpl	W/Op	525459	McGregor	AC1	W/Op	639349	Stone	AC1	F/M	649248
Flinders	LAC	E2	628488	McHugh	AC1	ACH	611274	Summers	AC1	Armr	967021
Freeman	LAC	Photo	551153	McKillop	LAC	F/R	530184	Sumpf	AC2	ACH	775158
Frost	LAC	Photo	551740	McLaughlin	LAC	Armr	529851	Swain	AC1	C&B	628632
Gatcombe	LAC	Photo	551916	McLennon	AC1	ACH	616685	Swann	AC1	F/M	649240
Geary	LAC	F/M	649381	McNichol	AC1	I/R	622403	Szkarlat	AC2	ACH	775087
Gibli	AC2	ACH	775086	Mable	AC2	ACH	912345	Szyftman	AC2	ACH	774805
Gibson	Sgt	ACH	532407	Mapstone	LAC	CGD	638919	Tann	AC2	ACH	911741
Giles	AC1	ACH	616676	Marshall	AC1	WOp	639163	Taylor	LAC	Armr	530192
Giles	LAC	F/M	649330	Maryon	Sgt	F1	561811	Tokely	AC1	WOp	639663
Gluck	AC2	ACH	774289	Milford	Cpl	F2	566203	Toogood	LAC	F2E	543540
Gouge	LAC	F2	566680	Mills	AC2	ACH	912351	Tue	AC2	ACH	912348
Graupe	AC2	ACH	775097	Moger	AC2	ACH	912350	Turnbull	Sgt	C&B	528098
Green	AC1	ACH	616624	Montak	AC2	ACH	775088	Turnbull	AC1	F/M	649340
Griffiths	Cpl	F1	563643	Moon	LAC	Mate	538253	Turner	Cpl	WEM	566749
Gruft	AC2	ACH/C&B	774579	Moore	LAC	C&B	629683	Vassallo	AC2	D/P	776692
Gursztel	AC2	ACH	774087	Morris	AC2	ACH	906897	Vigrow	AC1	ACH	947178
Gwyther	Sgt	F1	351144	Morris	AC2	ACH	853889	White	LAC	F/M	541721
Hall	Cpl	ACH	529256	Moxhay	LAC	Mate	529295	White	LAC	Photo	551420
Hammett	Cpl	Photo	517519	Newbould	AC1	Armr	701630	White	LAC	Carpenter	638567
Hammond	AC1	ACH	628354	Norman	LAC	ACH	532738	White	AC2	ACH	912354
Hammond	AC1	ACH	627655	Nutt	Cpl	F2	566325	Wigham	LAC	Mate	530702
Hanchett	Cpl	ACH	529900	O'Keefe	LAC	Accts	540388	Wilde	LAC	F2E	649123
Hardwick	LAC	F/R	542081	O'Meara	AC1	ACH	616369	Willcocks	Cpl	M/W	529294
Harris	AC1	F/M	649283	Osborne	AC2	ACH	900624	Williams	LAC	WOp	536842
Harris	LAC	CGD	614368	Parker	AC1	ACH	626529	Williams	LAC	E/Asst	616405
Harrison	AC1	ACH	617576	Parkin	LAC	F2A	526303	Williams	AC1	ACH	616467
Hartley	AC2	ACH	907694	Parsons	F/Sgt	WEM	364387	Woolaston	AC1	F/W	747300
Hellin	AC1	F/M	649295	Parvin	LAC	FAE	540905	Worrall	LAC	E/Asst	616923
Herstzberg	AC2	ACH	775214	Peacock	Cpl	ACH	523440	Wray	AC1	F/R	648811
Higgins	LAC	F/M	541691	Pellow	Cpl	F2	566798	Wright	Cpl	F2	566429
Higgins	AC2	N/Ord	638197	Podjarsky	AC2	ACH	774158	Wylie	LAC	F2E	541863
Hill	LAC	F2A	525375	Pownall	LAC	I/R	621889	Zimer	AC2	ACH	775092
Hillman	Cpl	WEM	566764	Prais	AC2	ACH	775090	Zimmern	AC2	ACH/C&B	774564

Groundcrew known to have been on strength in August/September 1941.

The following list has been compounded from the two Movement Orders which covered the squadron's deployments to and from Iraq in 1941. As a result the list covers a period of nearly two months and some of those whose names are included were not on strength for the entire period as they arrived or departed while the squadron was stationed at Habbaniyah. Ranks were not static either, eg O'Keefe was made up to corporal at Habbaniyah and Hesketh went to Iraq a corporal and returned to Egypt as a sergeant; where known, the senior rank is shown below.

Name	Rank	Service No	Name	Rank	Service No	Name	Rank	Service No
			Abel	AC1	930334	Adams	F/Sgt	5?2251
			Adams	AC1	576396	Adams	AC1	1014172
Abbott	AC2	1360431	Adams	Cpl	533844	Adkin	LAC	944553

Name	Rank	Number	Name	Rank	Number	Name	Rank	Number
Ainsley	LAC	651902	Cowles	LAC	912347	Hillyard	AC1	1018696
Aldhurst	AC1	649318	Cozens	LAC	627898	Hodkinson	Cpl	566358
Aldridge	LAC	905733	Crawshaw	LAC	574705	Hogarth	LAC	634837
Allen	LAC	909773	Cross	AC1	907007	Holloway	LAC	701642
Alston	AC2	983425	Crowe	LAC	1006197	Hornstein	AC1	774661
Ambler	AC1	1197185	Curtin	Cpl	519721	Hughes	Sgt	521171
Anderson	LAC	652925	Cushing	LAC	?	Huntley	AC1	648861
Anderson	LAC	992184	Davidson	Cpl	610693	Hyatt	F/Sgt	?
Anderson	LAC	649351	Davies	Cpl	?	Hyden	AC1	545682
Anderson	AC1	1014183	Dawson	LAC	644763	Ilott	AC2	916831
Anderson	AC1	948914	Dawson	LAC	574497	Ince	LAC	971007
Anderton	AC2	1055706	Daxon	LAC	635992	Inglis	LAC	541244
Ardis	LAC	1007116	Day	AC1	912292	Jackson	LAC	636548
Arnold	LAC	534761	Dean	LAC	541079	Jackson	AC1	1119593
Ashton	LAC	617707	Dean	Cpl	535373	James	AC2	985125
Atherton	AC1	927760	Deaville	Cpl	542082	Jasper	LAC	610621
Atkinson	AC1	1110085	Dickinson	AC2	1016052	Johnson	LAC	914438
Badger	AC2	1072695	Dixon	Cpl	536485	Johnstone	LAC	542913
Baggott	LAC	912353	Dueck	AC1	774035	Jones	AC1	651833
Bailey	LAC	906894	Dunbar	AC1	969703	Jones	Cpl	554918
Baillie	LAC	1002928	Dunlop	LAC	610827	Jones	LAC	540997
Bairstow	AC	641087	Dunn	LAC	1004344	Kearney	Cpl	617536
Ballott	LAC	649162	Dunn	LAC	636700	Keeney	Cpl	643444
Banfield	AC2	9?4268	Dunn	Cpl	539726	Kellen(?)	AC2	1072789
Barnett	LAC	914669	Durling	LAC	622261	Kelly	LAC	634322
Baxter	LAC	637805	Dwyer	WO	512396	Kelly	AC2	966897
Bell	AC1	967216	Eades	Sgt	566792	Kemp	LAC	642281
Bell	LAC	537182	Easingwood	Cpl	534487	Kerr	LAC	912355
Bennett	Cpl	616793	Edwards	LAC	914486	King	Sgt	52?3??
Bennett	LAC	912349	Edwards	AC2	1178153	Knowles	AC1	1132561
Benzur	AC1	774681	Evans	LAC	930880	Knowles	Cpl	542858
Bergmans	Cpl	912290	Exton	LAC	626985	Lampshire	LAC	546381
Berry	LAC	1253488	Fairfield	AC2	1131230	Lansley	AC1	574665
Bifield	Cpl	533640	Farebrother	LAC	931041	Lawrence	LAC	930848
Birch	AC1	642103	Finlayson	LAC	622032	Leslie	Sgt	358638
Bishop	Sgt	625720	Firth	Cpl	525459	Leslie	AC1	969677
Bolderson	LAC	617108	Flannigan	AC1	575697	Loveday	Cpl	530932
Boot	LAC	649383	Flinders	LAC	628488	Mackay	LAC	969448
Booth	AC1	1009970	Frankfurt	AC1	775313	Macrae	AC1	637618
Boscoe	AC2	969912	Frost	LAC	551740	McAnallen	AC1	632212
Braund	F/Sgt	355229	Gardner	AC1	1283861	McAndrew	AC2	1018686
Brickell	LAC	912287	Gatcombe	Cpl	551916	McAusland	Cpl	566789
Bridge	AC1	969591	Geary	LAC	649381	McCandlish	AC2	573675
Brocklesby	LAC	539868	George	LAC	934787	McClennan	LAC	616685
Brooks	LAC	549346	Giles	Cpl	616676	McConnon	LAC	617122
Brooks	LAC	540506	Giles	LAC	649330	McCord	Cpl	536289
Brown	AC1	643959	Ginsberg	AC2	774610	McCulley	AC1	652576
Brown	LAC	629052	Gleeson	AC2	900964	McGrann	AC1	633007
Bruce	LAC	998788	Gowers	AC2	573250	McGregor	AC1	639349
Brunt	AC1	958034	Grant	LAC	993716	McHugh	Cpl	611274
Burns	Sgt	550009	Green	Cpl	616624	McLaughlin	Cpl	529851
Burns	LAC	617544	Griffiths	LAC	?63825	McNichol	LAC	622403
Burridge	Cpl	546356	Griffiths	Sgt	563643	Mable	LAC	912345
Burridge	Cpl	546356	Guthrie	AC1	969674	Marsh	Cpl	567287
Burrows	AC2	966913	Hall	Sgt	755387	Martin	AC2	1107013
Bush	AC1	947477	Hammond	LAC	628354	Maryon	F/Sgt	561811
Butterfield	F/Sgt	3?4518	Hampton	AC1	1159468	Melville	AC1	973108
C-Stevens	AC1	774067	Hanchett	Cpl	529900	Metcalfe	Cpl	527096
Cameron	Cpl	519512	Hardman	LAC	541658	Milford	Cpl	566203
Campbell	Cpl	550336	Hardwick	LAC	542081	Miller	AC2	971974
Cant	Cpl	545815	Harris	LAC	649283	Mills	AC1	1166261
Carpenter	LAC	912346	Harrison	AC2	1010350	Moger	LAC	912350
Carter	Cpl	530344	Harrison	Cpl	617576	Montgomery	Cpl	521324
Chambers	F/Sgt	370864	Harrison	LAC	848346	Moon	LAC	538253
Chilman	Sgt	902861	Hartley	LAC	907694	Moore	LAC	629683
Chippington	Cpl	6?947?	Harwood	AC1	943943	Morley	LAC	756030
Clark	LAC	551889	Haselhurst	AC2	13842?8	Morrice	LAC	914448
Clarke	Cpl	636519	Hatson	AC1	911386	Morris	AC1	853889
Clarke	LAC	6?0?84	Hellin	LAC	649295	Morris	LAC	906897
Cole	LAC	539699	Henderson	LAC	636620	Mortimer	LAC	552954
Conlan	AC1	1356382	Hendry	AC2	1018369	Moxhay	Cpl	529295
Constable	AC1	?54422	Hesketh	Sgt	535319	Nathan	Sgt	548973
Cooper	LAC	998861	Higgins	LAC	541691	Newbould	LAC	701630
Copcutt	Cpl	568283	Hill	Cpl	525375	Newton	LAC	990250
Coughlin	LAC	546515	Hillier	LAC	10?205	Nichols	Cpl	912595
Cowell	LAC	649319	Hillman	Sgt	566764	Norman	Cpl	532738

Name	Rank	Service No		Name	Rank	Service No		Name	Rank	Service No
Norton	LAC	556683		Scott	Cpl	533503		Thompson	AC2	969309
Norton	Cpl	538161		Scott	Cpl	528728		Tilsey	AC1	973116
Nutt	Cpl	566325		Selby	AC1	1009643		Tokely	LAC	639663
O'Keefe	Cpl	540388		Sharpe	Cpl	542066		Toogood	LAC	543540
O'Meara	Cpl	616369		Sharpe	LAC	522445		Took	LAC	983352
Onions	Sgt	?		Shrubsole	AC1	756307		Tue	LAC	912348
Osborne	LAC	900624		Shute	LAC	972548		Tufnell	AC1	755313
Parker	LAC	519540		Silber	AC2	775625		Turnbull	F/Sgt	528098
Parker	LAC	626529		Simmons	LAC	644272		Turnbull	AC1	649340
Parkin	LAC	526303		Skinner	LAC	648995		Turner	Cpl	615960
Parsons	AC1	654258		Smith	LAC	1019809		Turner	Sgt	566749
Parvin	Cpl	540905		Smith	Sgt	363740		Vassallo	AC1	776692
Pattison	LAC	990272		Smith	LAC	649287		Vigrow	LAC	947178
Peacock	Sgt	523440		Smith	AC2	953784		Wade	AC2	1176629
Peacock	AC1	1171837		Smith	AC2	920005		Warren	AC2	1256703
Pellow	Cpl	566798		Smith	LAC	635664		Webster	AC2	1018241
Peters	AC1	627994		Smith	LAC	626889		Wells	AC2	1006402
Phillips	AC2	1109120		Somerville	AC1	999058		White	LAC	912354
Pidduck	LAC	???667		Spiteri	AC1	776691		White	LAC	551420
Pownall	LAC	621889		Staley	AC1	904816		White	LAC	638567
Pugh	Cpl	613310		Stanley	LAC	547074		Whitehead	AC2	801393
Purchase	AC2	935559		Starr	Cpl	547024		Whybrow	AC2	1152059
Raine	Cpl	531047		Stevens	AC1	774?57		Wigham	Cpl	530702
Rankin	LAC	569855		Stevens	AC1	912288		Wilde	LAC	649123
Ravenscroft	AC2	1175777		Stone	LAC	649248		Williams	LAC	616405
Rayson	AC1	1160251		Such	AC1	651935		Williams	AC2	1313314
Rees	AC2	1062815		Summers	LAC	967021		Williamson	AC2	1026231
Reeve	LAC	928913		Summerville	Cpl	566863		Williamson	LAC	546832
Reid	LAC	649365		Swain	LAC	628652		Wilson	AC1	744889
Reynolds	Cpl	531189		Swann	LAC	649240		Wilson	LAC	749971
Richardson	LAC	1005356		Sweeney	AC2	1019678		Wilson	LAC	817249
Roberts	Sgt	565786		Tann	AC1	911741		Woolaston	LAC	747300
Roddick	AC2	986550		Tatt	LAC	1163922		Worrall	Cpl	616923
Rogers	Cpl	568417		Taylor	Cpl	530192		Wright	Sgt	566429
Roper	LAC	546892		Taylor	AC2	977223		Wylie	Cpl	541863
Rowley	LAC	994408		Taylor	LAC	614674		Yeates	AC2	1253312
Rumsey	LAC	647019		Thomas	AC	940632		Yelland	AC1	1171843
Ryan	AC2	1261073		Thomas	AC2	574806		York	AC1	652511
Ryder	Cpl	938598		Thomas	AC2	???353				
Scott	LAC	935781		Thompson	AC1	972464				

The groundcrew element of No 45 Sqn's Chittagong detachment, June/July 1943.

The seventy-one personnel listed below are those who travelled to Chittagong to support No 45 Sqn's first operational use of its Vengeances, between 26th June and 14th July 1943.

Name	Rank	Trade	Service No		Name	Rank	Trade	Service No		Name	Rank	Trade	Service No
Ainsley, W	Cpl	F2E	651902		Ewing, F	AC1	FMA	1123611		Murray, W	LAC	ACH/GD	1029468
					Fieldhouse, L	LAC	FME	954789		Paley, R	LAC	CS&MW	1254853
Aldridge, B	LAC	F2A	905733		Fitzmaurice, G	AC1	Arm (B)	1438340		Parsons, R	LAC	FMA	654258
Anderson, D	LAC	FME	649351		Forrester, E	LAC	F2A	964641		Partington, J	AC1	F2E	642541
Anderton, W	LAC	FME	1055705		Fuller, L	LAC	DMT	1263864		Pitman, H	LAC	Arm (G)	1175293
Anstey, G	LAC	E2	1251670		Gleason, K	LAC	FMA	900964		Ravenscroft, R	Cpl	F2A	1175777
Barlow, W	AC1	FMA	1124092		Hall, J	LAC	Arm (G)	1096637		Shaw, R	LAC	I/Rep	771666
Bassett, D	AC1	Gunner	1115047		Harwood	Cpl	F2A	943943		Sheridan, W	AC1	Arm (G)	1144363
Bell, G	LAC	F2E	967216		Hellin, E	LAC	FME	649295		Simonite, F	Cpl	DMT	870246
Bell, J	LAC	FME	9922268		Hendry, J	AC1	F2E	1018369		Smith, H	LAC	F2A	944577
Bennett, A	LAC	Arm	912349		Henman, E	F/Sgt	WEM	761385		Sommerville, R	LAC	E2	999058
Birch, G	Cpl	WOM	642103		Heseltine, J	Cpl	Arm	545265		Stanley, G	LAC	F2A	547074
Bond, A	LAC	DMT	1198350		Hogarth, J	Cpl	E1	634837		Sutton, E	LAC	F/Arm(B)	1477906
Breeze, W	LAC	FME	1276704		Horton, F	LAC	FME	1296072		Tann, C	Cpl	E/Asst	911741
Brooks, F	LAC	DMT	1185096		Kemp, G	Cpl	F2E	642281		Thompson, P	Sgt	F2A	533817
Brown, D	Cpl	Arm	629052		Kerry, B	LAC	F/Arm(B)	1501238		Tucker, K	LAC	Cook	1043487
Brown, S	Cpl	WOM	643959		Low, G	Cpl	Cook	983293		Turnbull, J	Cpl	F2E	649340
Bush, A	LAC	Arm	947477		McAndrew, A	LAC	Arm (B)	1018686		Wade, J	LAC	W/Op	1176629
Chick, S	Cpl	Clk/GD	1391239		McKillop, J	LAC	MTM	1105672		Walters	AC1	I/Rep	637366
Clements, D	AC1	FMA	1124107		Madden, H	AC1	ACH/GD	989838		Williamson, M	LAC	Arm	1026231
Cribbes, J	LAC	Gunner	988178		Martin, J	LAC	Arm (B)	1107013		Wilson, O	Sgt	F2E	548459
Daxon, W	Cpl	E1	635992		Miller, J	LAC	E2	971974		Worthington, C	AC1	Arm (G)	1143619
Drabble, J	LAC	W/Op	1360799		Moore, W	Cpl	Arm	620319		York, J	LAC	FMA	6525111
Edwards, R	F/Sgt	F2	569135		Morris-Owen, H	Sgt	Arm	551174					
					Muggleton, J	LAC	F2E	1170937					

The NCOs and airmen who travelled from Silchar to Bangalore in February 1944,

The following personnel are those whose names appear on the Movement Order covering the squadron's withdrawal from Kumbhirgram on 4th February 1944, bound for Yelahanka where the squadron was to convert to Mosquitos.

The list therefore provides a fair indication of the constitution of the squadron at the end of the Vengeance era. Where known an individual's "last three" has been included.

In addition to the listed RAF personnel the party included the following IORs (Indian Other Ranks); all were AC2s: Bhomick, Bouthanayangam (702), Campos, Deka, Hirlekar (837), Hari Singh (349), Joseph (608), Joseph (662), Juda, Koruthupaily (692), Krishnamurty, Lall (774), Madhavannayar (300), Nair (743), Param (606), Phillip (725), Phillip (741), Pillai (645), Pillai (745), Proshad (057), Santhsnam (441), Simpson (311), Singh (706) and Soldman (607). There were also thirty-six Enrolled Followers.

Name	Rank	Name	Rank	Name	Rank	Name	Rank	Name	Rank
		Dawson	Sgt	Harwood (943)	Sgt	May	LAC	Smith	Sgt
		Daxon (992)	Sgt	Haselhurst	LAC	Mitchell	Cpl	Smith (321)	LAC
Adlam	Sgt	Dee	AC2	Hazell (592)	AC1	Mitchell	LAC	Smith (577)	Cpl
Aldridge (733)	LAC	Dobson (874)	AC1	Hellin (295)	LAC	Moore (319)	Cpl	Smith (809)	LAC
Allard	AC1	Dolan	LAC	Henderson (620)	Sgt	Moore (683)	Cpl	Somerville (058)	LAC
Ambler	LAC	Duerden	LAC	Hendry (369)	LAC	Moore (801)	AC1	Spence	Cpl
Anderson	Cpl	Dunigan	LAC	Henman (385)	WO	Morgan	Sgt	Stanley (074)	LAC
Anderson	LAC	Dunn	LAC	Herbert	LAC	Morris-Owen	Sgt	Stow	LAC
Armour	AC1	Duthie	LAC	Heseltine (265)	Cpl	Moss	AC1	Swain (652)	Cpl
Bailey (894)	LAC	Eastwood	AC1	Hill	Sgt	Mullen (630)	LAC	Taylor (131)	Cpl
Ballott (162)	LAC	Edwards	LAC	Hill (094)	Cpl	Murray (468)	LAC	Taylor (149)	LAC
Bassett (047)	AC1	Edwards (135)	F/Sgt	Hillier (205)	Cpl	Neale	LAC	Taylor (664)	AC1
Bell (216)	LAC	Evans	LAC	Hills	LAC	Nicholas	Sgt	Terry (238)	AC1
Bell (268)	LAC	Everitt	Cpl	Hillyard (696)	LAC	Nicholls	AC1	Thomas (196)	Cpl
Bergmans (290)	Cpl	Ewing (611)	LAC	Honeychurch	WO	Norridge	AC2	Thomas (353)	LAC
Birch (103)	Cpl	Finch	AC2	Honner	AC1	O'Toole	LAC	Thompson (464)	LAC
Blackburn	LAC	Fitzmaurice (340)	AC1	Horton (072)	AC1	Oldland	Sgt	Thompson (817)	Sgt
Booth (970)	Sgt	Forder	LAC	Hull	Cpl	Ollson	Cpl	Thornton	AC1
Boscoe (915)	LAC	Forrester (641)	LAC	Humble	AC1	Orrock	LAC	Tilley	Cpl
Botterill	LAC	Fowler	WO	Huntley (861)	LAC	Paley (853)	Cpl	Tompkins	LAC
Boucher	AC2	Funnell	Cpl	Ilott (831)	LAC	Parkinson	LAC	Tucker (487)	LAC
Boughen	LAC	Gaisford	AC1	Irvine	Cpl	Parsons (258)	AC1	Turnbull (340)	Sgt
Bradshaw (602)	LAC	Gallagher	LAC	Jackson	Cpl	Partington (541)	LAC	Vincent (103)	AC1
Brodlie	Cpl	Gardner (365)	Cpl	James	Cpl	Pennington	LAC	Walters (366)	LAC
Brook	LAC	Geddes	LAC	Kemp (281)	Cpl	Phillips (320)	LAC	Walters (695)	AC2
Brooks (096)	LAC	Gittins	LAC	Kiff	Cpl	Pitman	Cpl	Wells (402)	LAC
Buckley	AC1	Gleeson (964)	LAC	Kingswell (836)	LAC	Proctor	LAC	Whitehead (314)	Cpl
Budge	LAC	Glen (227)	LAC	Kitchen	Cpl	Raper	Cpl	Whitlock	LAC
Burns	AC1	Godbold	AC2	Kitching	AC1	Ravenscroft (777)	Sgt	Wilde (123)	Cpl
Burton	LAC	Grant	AC1	Knox	LAC	Ray	Cpl	Wilkinson (344)	AC2
Castle	Cpl	Green	AC2	Latner	AC2	Redhead	AC1	Wilkinson (479)	LAC
Chalmers	Sgt	Griffiths (822)	LAC	Law	Sgt	Reed (998)	Cpl	Williams	LAC
Charters (932)	LAC	Grimwood	AC2	Lea	AC1	Reid (365)	LAC	Wilson (459)	Sgt
Chick	Cpl	Guthrie (674)	LAC	Leathley	AC2	Roberts (058)	AC1	Wiltshire (566)	AC1
Collins	LAC	Hales (225)	AC1	Lee	LAC	Robinson (985)	LAC	Wood	Cpl
Cook	AC2	Hall (637)	LAC	Leggatt	LAC	Roddick (550)	Cpl	Wood	LAC
Cookson	Cpl	Hammonds	WO	Life	AC2	Roper (892)	AC2	Woodley	LAC
Cowles	Sgt	Hancox	LAC	Love	AC2	Ryder (598)	Cpl	Woodward	Sgt
Cox	AC1	Harm (821)	LAC	Low (293)	Cpl	Scrimshaw	AC1	Worthington (619)	AC1
Crawford	AC2	Harper	AC2	Mackay	Sgt	Seed	LAC	Wright (566)	AC1
Cross	AC2	Harris (283)	LAC	McCandlish (675)	Sgt	Shaw (666)	LAC	York (511)	AC2
Daffy	AC1	Harrison	Cpl	McFarlane (176)	LAC	Sheridan (363)	AC1		
Dancy	AC1	Harrison	F/Sgt	McHaffie	Cpl	Sleet	AC2		

The groundcrew on strength in late September 1944.

The following NCOs and airmen were listed on a Movement Order covering the squadron's return to Kumbhirgram at the end of September 1944 as its Mosquitos became operational. In addition to the listed RAF personnel there were six IORs, including AC2s Hirlekar and Krishnamurty, and fifty-five Enrolled Followers.

Name	Rank	Name	Rank	Name	Rank	Name	Rank	Name	Rank
		Boscoe	LAC	Castle	Cpl	Cull	Cpl	Edwards (152)	LAC
		Bosher	LAC	Chalmers	Sgt	Curran	LAC	Edwards (399)	LAC
Aldridge	LAC	Botterill	Cpl	Chick	Cpl	Cutting	F/Sgt	Evans	LAC
Allard	LAC	Boughen	LAC	Chisholme	AC1	Daffy	LAC	Everett	Cpl
Allison	LAC	Bradshaw	AC2	Clough	LAC	Danby	LAC	Ewing	LAC
Allway	Cpl	Brady	Cpl	Cogbill	LAC	Dancy	LAC	Fairey	Cpl
Ambler	LAC	Brodlie	Cpl	Cohen	AC1	Dawson	Sgt	Fenton	AC1
Anderson	Cpl	Brooks	Cpl	Collins	LAC	Dee	LAC	Finch	LAC
Ashton	AC2	Brown	LAC	Cook	AC1	Dennehy	LAC	Fitzmaurice	AC1
Barber	LAC	Buck	AC2	Cookson	Cpl	Desmond	LAC	Forder	LAC
Bates	AC2	Buckley	LAC	Corbridge	F/Sgt	Dick	AC1	Foster	LAC
Beeson	Cpl	Budge	Cpl	Coulson	LAC	Dives	LAC	Foulkes	LAC
Bell (216)	Cpl	Burrows	AC1	Cox	LAC	Dobson	LAC	Funnell	Cpl
Bell (268)	Cpl	Burton	LAC	Cracknell	Cpl	Donovan	Cpl	Gaisford	LAC
Bellamy	AC1	Calderwood	AC1	Crawford	AC1	Duerden	LAC	Gallagher	LAC
Booth	Sgt	Calvert	LAC	Crawshaw	AC1	Duthie	LAC	Gant	LAC
Booth	Cpl	Cartwright	LAC	Cross	AC1	Dyke	LAC	Gardner	Cpl

Name	Rank	Name	Rank	Name	Rank	Name	Rank	Name	Rank
Garrod	AC1	Hill	Cpl	McFarlane (176)	LAC	Reed	LAC	Taylor (149)	LAC
Geddes	LAC	Hill	Sgt	McGinley	Cpl	Rees	LAC	Taylor (684)	LAC
Gittins	LAC	Hillier	Cpl	McInnes	LAC	Reeve	LAC	Thomas (196)	LAC
Glaze	LAC	Hills	LAC	Martin	LAC	Roberts	LAC	Thomas (353)	LAC
Gleeson	LAC	Hillyard	LAC	Merrifield	AC1	Robinson (252)	Cpl	Thompson	Sgt
Glen	LAC	Hilton	LAC	Mitchell	LAC	Robinson (985)	Cpl	Tilley	Cpl
Godbold	LAC	Honer	Cpl	Mitchell	Cpl	Roddick	Cpl	Titterton	LAC
Goodswen	LAC	Horton	LAC	Moore	LAC	Roper (372)	AC2	Trew	AC1
Green	LAC	Hoyes	Cpl	Mudie	AC1	Roper (662)	LAC	Tucker	LAC
Greenall	AC1	Ilott	Sgt	Mullen	LAC	Rowe	LAC	Vincent	LAC
Greeves	AC1	Ives	AC1	Mundy	LAC	Sale	Sgt	Wade	LAC
Griffiths	LAC	Jackson	Cpl	Murray	LAC	Scott	LAC	Waite	LAC
Grimwood	LAC	James	Cpl	Murrell	Cpl	Scott	Cpl	Walker	Sgt
Grimwood	AC1	Jarvis	LAC	Neale	AC1	Scrimshaw	LAC	Walker (679)	LAC
Guthrie	LAC	Jones (280)	LAC	Nicholls	LAC	Seed	LAC	Walker (917)	LAC
Haines	AC1	Jones (483)	LAC	Nicholson	AC1	Shaw	Cpl	Walters (366)	LAC
Hales	LAC	Jones (681)	LAC	Norridge	LAC	Sheridan	LAC	Walters (695)	AC1
Hall	LAC	Kemp	Sgt	O'Toole	LAC	Sime	AC1	Walters (892)	LAC
Hancox	LAC	Kemp	Cpl	Oldland	Sgt	Simpson	LAC	Warren (431)	LAC
Harle	AC1	Kennaugh	AC1	Orrock	LAC	Sleet	LAC	Warren (708)	LAC
Harper	AC1	Kiff	Cpl	Ottman	LAC	Sloan	LAC	Wells	LAC
Harris	AC1	Kingswell	LAC	Owen	Cpl	Smart	LAC	Wheeler	Cpl
Harrison (226)	AC1	Kirkham	LAC	Paley	Cpl	Smethurst	Sgt	White	LAC
Harrison (416)	AC1	Kitchen	Cpl	Parkinson	Cpl	Smith (001)	AC1	Whitehead (314)	LAC
Harrold	Sgt	Kitching	LAC	Parr	AC1	Smith (038)	LAC	Whitehead (836)	LAC
Hart	AC1	Kitchingman	LAC	Parsons	AC1	Smith (321)	LAC	Wilkinson (344)	AC1
Harwood	Sgt	Lambert	AC1	Parsons	LAC	Smith (432)	Cpl	Wilkinson (479)	LAC
Hayes	AC1	Langley	AC1	Partington	LAC	Smith (502)	Cpl	Williams	LAC
Hayes	Cpl	Langridge	LAC	Paxton	F/Sgt	Smith (577)	Cpl	Willoughby	LAC
Hayman	LAC	Law	Sgt	Pennington	LAC	Sommerville	LAC	Willson	Sgt
Haywood	AC1	Lea	LAC	Phillips (320)	LAC	Sowerby	LAC	Wilson	Sgt
Hazell	LAC	Leathley	AC1	Pitman	Cpl	Spence	Cpl	Wiltshire	LAC
Hazell (592)	AC1	Lee (574)	LAC	Porter	Cpl	Stallan	Cpl	Woodley	LAC
Hendry	LAC	Leggatt	LAC	Price	LAC	Stanley	LAC	Woodward	Sgt
Herbert	LAC	Lindsay	LAC	Proctor	LAC	Stow	LAC	Worthington	LAC
Hewitt	LAC	Low	Cpl	Pulman	LAC	Strickland	LAC	York	LAC
Hezeltine	Cpl	Mackay	Sgt	Raffel	Sgt	Tasker	AC1		
Hibberd	LAC	McFarlane	AC1	Redhead	LAC	Taylor (131)	Cpl		

Notes:

1. Following the creation of the RAF, it was decided to introduce a revised rank/trade structure to reflect the peculiar demands of the newly independent air service. This was to be effective from 2nd April 1918, although the details were not generally available until the publication of Air Ministry Weekly Order No 607 of 10th July 1918 (as amended on the 18th) but from then onwards the new ranks came into daily use. Presumably because it proved to be unnecessarily complicated, this system was short-lived and on 1st January 1919 it was superseded by a single set of ranks, applicable to all trades (Sergeant Majors 1st and 2nd Class, Flight Sergeant, Sergeant, Corporal, Leading Aircraftman and Aircraftman 1st and 2nd Class). The interim structure is represented by the following table.

TECHNICAL GROUP	NON-TECHNICAL GROUP	CLERKS & STOREMEN
Warrant Officers, Class I		
Chief Master Mechanic	Sergeant Major, Cl I	Master Clerk
Warrant Officers, Class II		
Master Mechanic	Sergeant Major, Cl II	-
Non-Commissioned Officers		
Chief Mechanic	Flight Sergeant	Flight Clerk
Sergeant Mechanic	Sergeant	Sergeant Clerk
Corporal Mechanic	Corporal	Corporal Clerk
Other Ranks		
Air Mechanic 1st Class	-	Clerk 1st Class
Air Mechanic 2nd Class	Private 1st Class	Clerk 2nd Class
Air Mechanic 3rd Class	Private 2nd Class	Clerk 3rd Class

2. Sgt Coultate's unusual Service Number indicated that he was one of a small group of Special Reservists earmarked for the RFC on its formation in 1912. All twenty-five were called up "for the duration" on 6th August 1914.

3. Ever since 1918 the RAF's trade structure has been repeatedly revised and updated to reflect the changing demands of contemporary technology and engineering practice. It is not intended to present a comprehensive review of these developments here but the following may help to make sense of some of the abbreviations used in the WW II section of this Annex.

ACH - Aircraft Hand (generally unskilled personnel, available for employment on any task from peeling potatoes to acting as runners)

C&B - Cook and Butcher

CS - Coppersmith

D/P - Driver/Petrol

E - Electrician, later specialised as E1 and E2

E/Asst - Equipment Assistant (ie a storeman)

F - Fitter. There was a hierarchy of Fitters which became increasingly complex as aviation technology advanced and the time available for training reduced. In brief, a pre-war Fitter 1 had done three years at Halton and a further year at Henlow making him competent to deal with virtually all aspects of both airframes and engines. A pre-war Fitter 2 lacked the post-graduate year at Henlow. The rate at which the RAF expanded from the mid-1930s onwards did not permit the luxury of a three/four-year, multi-skill course for the majority of airmen, however, and most technically competent recruits were given shorter courses specialising in particular fields. This approach produced a series of annotations denoting varying degreees of trade proficiency, eg FAE (Fitter Aero-engines), F2A (Fitter 2 Airframes), F2E (Fitter 2 Engines), Fitter MT and F/Arm (Fitter Armourer). Specific qualification on bombs and/or guns was later introduced for Armourers resulting in the annotations Arm(B) and Arm(G).

F/M - Flight Mechanic (also FMA and FME - Flight Mechanic Airframes or Engines)

F/R - Fitter/Rigger

I/R - Instrument Repairer

Mate - an unskilled mechanic

M/R - Metal Rigger

MTM - MT Mechanic

M/W - Metal Worker

N/Ord - Nursing Orderly

SP - Service Policeman

WEM - Wireless Electrical Mechanic

W/Op - Wireless Operator

WOM - Wireless Operator Mechanic

Annex O. Squadron Heraldry.

Following wartime use of two simple geometric designs, No 45 Sqn adopted a Flying Camel as its emblem in 1922; in various forms this has decorated many of its aeroplanes ever since. Some inter-war photographs suggest that this motif may sometimes have been applied in flight colours but positive evidence is lacking; the now familiar red/blue colouring was adopted following approval of the official badge in 1936. Code letters, DD initially but soon superseded by OB, were introduced in 1939 and worn by all types until 1955.

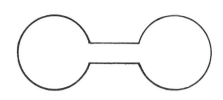

Having first used a white (and sometimes coloured?) band around the fuselage of its 1½ Strutters the squadron's identification marking was changed to a dumb-bell in August 1917 and this was carried by its Camels until 1919.

Devised in 1922, the Flying Camel marking was carried on Vernons, in beaten copper on an aluminium shield, and painted on the tails of Fairey IIIFs, probably in pale blue.

A variation on the Flying Camel theme as worn on the squadron's DH 9As; it is thought to have been painted in pale blue.

Despite the recent approval of the official College of Heralds' design, the original Vernon-style motif continued to be used in silhouette on the noses of Vincents and in the new badge frame, although here the red/blue colouring was adopted. The grenade frame was also used on Wellesleys and a few early Blenheim Is but the style of the badge it contained is not known.

Dive-bombing Camels like this one were evident in 1943-45 but it is unlikely that any ever appeared on an aeroplane. Details of colouring are lacking

The Pouncing Camel, on a white disc outlined in pale blue, was introduced in early 1954 and adorned the squadron's Hornets for just over a year.

A prototype white dumb-bell on a red bar marking was applied to a single Hornet in April 1955. The design was officially sanctioned in the following November; later embellished by blue tip-tanks with a white bar and a silhouette of a Flying Camel in red, it was used for the remainder of the Venom era,.

Between 1958 and 1964 the squadron's Canberras reverted to a red/blue Vernon-style Flying Camel carried on the fin on a white disc outlined in pale blue.

All markings had to be toned down during Confrontation; the squadron adopted this jaunty miniature Flying Camel, thinly outlined in white, in 1964 and it identified its Canberras until 1970.

Since an official marking had been approved in 1955 it is not clear why the MOD endorsed a new one in 1972; nevertheless it did and these red diamonds on a blue bar flanking a Flying Camel, all three elements of the design being outlined in pale blue, were worn by Hunters and Tornados until 1992.

This very stylised Flying Camel is carried on the noses of No 45(R) Sqn's Jetstreams, with a band of red/blue diamonds across the tip of the fin.

Sources and Bibliography

Primary Sources.

Among the documents held by the Public Record Office (PRO) at Kew, the following contain the surviving official returns raised by No 45 Sqn, including the crucial Army Forms W3343 and W3348, and the RAF Forms F.540 and F.541: AIR 1/1786-1789 inclusive, AIR 27/455-458 inclusive and AIR 27/2416, 2615 and 2778. Unfortunately, the AIR 1 series is incomplete; when it was held by the Air Ministry it had originally consisted of fourteen consecutively numbered files but Nos 2, 8 and 10-13 inclusive are not held at Kew, although there is reason to believe that at least some of them were at one time in the possession of the PRO. Other PRO documents examined in the course of preparing this chronicle included the following: AIR 1/173, 692, 804, 818, 845-852, 865, 867, 911, 914, 928-929, 965, 967-968, 984, 989-991, 1000, 1007, 1013-1015, 1022, 1049, 1117, 1130-1131, 1150, 1184-1185, 1266-1267, 1269-1272-1273, 1286, 1395, 1532, 1560, 1563-1565, 1572, 1575-1578, 1664, 1750-1751, 1778-1779, 1827-1828, 1830, 1853-1854, 1867-1868, 1900-1901, 1903, 1957, 1961-1962, 1988, 2002-2003, 2041, 2127-2128, 2209, 2215, 2371, 2388-2389 and 2392. AIR 2/106, 119, 758, 1524 and 8029. AIR 4/111. AIR 5/2, 207, 314, 344, 375, 820, 1219-1220, 1237-1243, 1253-1254, 1287-1291, 1291, 1379, 1434 and 2353. AIR 6/21. AIR 8/6, 72, 655 and 662. AIR 9/13-14. AIR 10/1468, 1481, 1495, 1990 and 2090. AIR 20/93, 540-551, 613, 2121, 2124, 2158 and 6929. AIR 22/256-257. AIR 23/1036, 4350, 4405, 4411, 4653-4654, 4656, 4680, 5107, 6090, 7659 and 6445. AIR 24/362-363, 472, 1051-1054, 1066, 1072, 1085-1091, 1189, 1237, 1259, 1270, 1278-1280, 1662, 1743, 1745-1746, 1752, 1757 and 2404-2405. AIR 25/801-803, 815, 909, 911, 929-930, 4653, 4656, 4680 and 4962. AIR 26/246-247, 350-351, 353, 355, 362-363, 492 and 499. AIR 27/157-158, 173, 193-194, 263, 267, 327, 373, 407, 562, 613, 630, 638, 682-684, 693-694, 696-697, 700-702, 859-861, 864-865, 878-880, 1198, 1302-1303, 1311, 1807, 2213 and 2438. AIR 28/1, 143, 350, 679, 966, 1064, 1088-1089, 1189, 1427 and 1462-1463. AIR 29/7-8, 180, 197, 403, 433, 459, 472, 485, 488-489, 493, 511, 602, 614, 685, 703-704, 708, 778, 779, 787, 782-783, 802-806, 808, 820, 844, 879, 895, 1035-1038, 1040, 1054, 1073, 1075, 1077-1081, 1276-1278, 1573, 2372 and 2416. AIR 29/2372. AVIA 10/225-226. AVIA 15/2605-2607. AVIA 18/258, WO 369/133 and ZJ 1 (various, in search of gazetted information on squadron members).

Miscellaneous.

Other sources consulted included numerous editions of the Air Force List, Hansard, Aircraft Movement Cards (Air Ministry Form 78), Accident Record Cards (Air Ministry Form 1180) and the papers of various ex-squadron members which have been deposited with the RAF Museum, the Imperial War Museum, the Public Record Office and/or the squadron itself; these documents include the Aircrew Flying Log Books of MRAF Sir Arthur Harris, AM Sir Robert Saundby, AVM D R Evans, AVM P E Maitland, Gp Capt G H Cock, Wg Cdr W R Read, Wg Cdr N Macmillan, Wg Cdr J O Willis, Sqn Ldr King, Flt Lt E H Attwood, Lt G Exley, 2/Lt K L Caldwell, Cpl J H Sephton and LACs R Grinter, W R Fraser and R Porton. In addition, the flying log books and journals of many of those listed in the Preface to this book were examined; they were invaluable in establishing information which would otherwise have been lost.

Publications:

Above the Lines: Norman L R Franks, Frank W Bailey & Russell Guest; Grub Street, 1993

Above the Trenches: Christopher Shores, Norman Franks & Russell Guest; Grub Street, 1990
The Aeroplanes of the Royal Flying Corps (Military Wing): J M Bruce; Putnam, 1982
Air Aces of the Austro-Hungarian Empire 1914-1918: Dr Martin O'Connor; Flying Machines Press, 1986
Air Power and Colonial Control: David E Omissi; Manchester University Press, 1990
Australia in the War of 1939-45; The Air War Against Japan: G Odgers; Australian War Memorial, 1957
Australia in the War of 1939-45; The Air War Against Germany and Italy, 1939-43: J Herington; Australian War Memorial, 1954
Baghdad Air Mail: Roderic Hill; Edward Arnold, 1929
Bamboo Workshop: R S Sansome; Merlin, 1995
Bloody Shambles, Vols 1 & 2: Christopher Shores, Brian Cull & Yasuho Izawa; Grub Street, 1992-3
Bomber Command Losses of the Second World War, 1941: W R Chorley; Midland Counties, 1993
'Bomber' Harris: Dudley Saward; Cassell, 1984
Bombs Gone: Wg Cdr J A MacBean & Maj A S Hogben; Patrick Stephens, 1990
Cross and Cockade International Journal, various issues
Customs and Traditions of the Royal Air Force: P G Hering; Gale and Polden, 1961
Eastward: Air Chief Marshal Sir David Lee; HMSO, 1984
Flight Path: F T Courtney; Kimber, 1973
The Flying Elephants: Chaz Bowyer; MacDonald, 1972
From Khaki to Blue: R J Brownell; Military History Society of Australia, 1978
The Hawk Journal, 1928. Two articles: *No 45 Sqn in Iraq, 1922* by Sqn Ldr R H M S Saundby and *No 45 Squadron, 1916-1917* by Flt Lt M Moore
Hurricanes over the Arakan: Norman Franks; Patrick Stephens, 1989
Into the Blue: Wg Cdr Norman Macmillan; Jarrolds, 1969
Mission Completed: Basil Embry; Methuen, 1957.
Mosquito: C Martin Sharp and Michael J F Bowyer; Faber and Faber, 1971
New Zealanders with the Royal Air Force, Vol III: J M S Ross; War History Branch, Department of Internal Affairs, New Zealand, 1959
Offensive Patrol: Wg Cdr Norman Macmillan; Jarrolds, 1973
Operation Firedog: Malcolm R Postgate; HMSO, 1993
RAF Operations 1918-1938: Chaz Bowyer; Kimber, 1988.
RAF Serials; various volumes in the Air Britain series: Air Britain
RAF Squadrons: Wg Cdr C G Jefford; Airlife, 1988
The Rats of Rangoon: Lionel Hudson; Leo Cooper (Heinemann), 1987
Royal Air Force 1939-45, Vols I, II & III: Denis Richards and Hilary St G Saunders; HMSO, 1954
Royal Australian Air Force 1939-42: Douglas Gillison; Australian War Memorial, 1962
Royal New Zealand Air Force: J M S Ross; War History Branch, Department of Internal Affairs, New Zealand, 1955
Scorpion's Sting: D Neate; Air Britain, 1994
A Short History of the Royal Air Force (Air Publication 125): Air Ministry, revised edition 1936
Sun on my Wings: Dundas Bednall; Paterchurch, 1989
Vengeance: Peter C Smith; Airlife, 1986
Wings Over Africa: AVM Tony Dudgeon; Airlife, 1987
Withdrawal From Empire: General Sir William Jackson ; Batsford, 1986
Articles in various aviation periodicals, notably: those by Christopher Shores and Frank F Smith in *Air Pictorial*.

Abbreviations and Glossary of Terms

AA	Anti-Aircraft
A&AEE	Aircraft and Armament Experimental Establishment
AB	Air Base (USAF)
ABDACOM	American, British, Dutch and Australian COMmand
AC	Aircraftman (1 or 2)
ACFE	Air Command Far East
ACM	Air Chief Marshal
ACMI	Air Combat Manoeuvring Installation
ACSEA	Air Command South East Asia
AD	Aircraft Depot, later Air Defence
AdlA	*Armée de l'Air* (French Air Force)
ADC	Aide de Camp
ADEX	Air Defence Exercise
ADIZ	Air Defence Identification Zone
AEP	Aircraft Erecting Park
AFCENT	Allied Forces Central Europe
AG	Air Gunner
AFTS	Advanced Flying Training School
AFTU	Advanced Flying Training Unit
AHQ	Air Headquarters
AILO	Army Intelligence Liaison Officer
Air Cdre	Air Commodore
ALG	Advanced Landing Ground
AM	Air Mechanic (1st or 2nd Class)
AMES	Air Ministry Experimental Station (early cover name for mobile radar stations which remained in use throughout the war)
AMO	Air Ministry Order
AMSO	Air Member for Supply and Organisation
AMWO	Air Ministry Weekly Order
AO	Air Organisation memorandum (later Air Order) issued by the Director of Air Organisation in the approximate period 1914-1930
AOC	Air Officer Commanding (a Group or AHQ)
AOCinC	Air Officer Commanding-in-Chief (of a Command)
AP	Aircraft Park or Armour Piercing, depending upon the context
APC	Armament Practice Camp (may be a unit or an event depending upon the context)
APO	Acting Pilot Officer
ARS	Aircraft Repair Section
ASD	Aircraft Supply Depot
ASI	Airspeed Indicator
ASP	Air Stores Park, later (post WW II) Aircraft Servicing Platform
ASV	Air-to-Surface Vessel (radar)
ATC	Air Traffic Control *or* Air Training Corps, depending upon context
AURI	Angkatan Udara Republik Indonesia (Indonesian Air Force)
AVG	American Volunteer Group
AVM	Air Vice Marshal
AVTUR	AViation TURbine fuel
AWOL	Absent Without Leave
BAFSEA	Base Air Forces South East Asia
Bde	Brigade
Bdr	Bombardier
BG	Bombardment Group (USAAF and/or USAF)
BHQ	Base Headquarters
BIB	Baby Incendiary Bomb
BMH	British Military Hospital
BOAC	British Overseas Airways Corporation
BPO	Base Personnel Office
Brig	Brigadier
BS	Bombardment Squadron (USAAAF and/or USAF)
BX	(USAF) Base Exchange
C&M	Care and Maintenance (Party)
CAP	Combat Air Patrol
Capt	Captain
CAS	Chief of the Air Staff
Cb	Cumulo-nimbus (ie storm) cloud
Cdo	Commando
CENTO	Central Treaty Organisation
CFE	Central Fighter Establishment
CFS	Central Flying School
Ch Tech	Chief Technician
CinC	Commander in Chief
CIRE	Command Instrument Rating Examiner
CIGS	Chief of the Imperial General Staff
CMM	Chief Master Mechanic (see Note 1 to Annex N)
CMU	Civilian Maintenance Unit
CNAC	Chinese National Airways Corporation
CO	Commanding Officer
Col	Colonel
COMBRITBOR	Commander British Forces in Borneo
Comm	Communications
Coy	Company
Cpl	Corporal
CRO	Community Relations Officer
CSR	Consolidated Sortie Report - brief summary of the results of a mission giving up/down and strike times and estimates of damage caused and sustained
CSU	Constant Speed Unit
CT	Communist Terrorist
CU	Conversion Unit
DCINC	Deputy Commander-in-Chief as in DCINCAFCENT
DDOps(AD)	Deputy Director of Operations (Air Defence)
DF/GA	Day Fighter/Ground Attack
DFLS	Day Fighter Leaders' School
DFW	*Deutsche Flugzeug-Werke*
DI	Daily Inspection
Dvr	Driver
EA	Enemy Aircraft
ENSA	Entertainments National Service Association
ERS	Engine Repair Section
EWI	Electronic Warfare Instructor
FAC	Forward Air Control(ler)
FACEX	Forward Air Control Exercise
FARELF	Far East Land Forces
FEAF	Far East Air Force
FETS	Far East Training Squadron
FF	Free French
Fg Off	Flying Officer
Fldw	*Feldwebel* (sergeant)
Flik	*Fliegerkompagnie* (WW I Austro-Hungarian 'aviation company', roughly a squadron)
Flt	Flight
Flt Lt	Flight Lieutenant
FOTEX	Exercise sponsored by Flag Officer Training
FRA	First Run Attack
F/Sgt	Flight Sergeant
FTS	Flying Training School
GCI	Ground Controlled Interception
Gen	General
GHQ	General Headquarters
GLO	Ground Liaison Officer
Gnr	Gunner
Gp	Group
Gp Capt	Group Captain
GP	General Purpose (category of bomb)
HA	Hostile Aircraft
HAEC	Hong Kong Aircraft Engineering Co
HE	High Explosive
HF	High Frequency (radio)
HMAS	His/Her Majesty's Australian Ship
HMS	His/Her Majesty's Ship
HMSO	His/Her Majesty's Stationery Office
HMT	His Majesty's Troopship
Hpt	*Hauptmann* (Flight Lieutenant)
HQME	Headquarters Middle East Command
IAF	Indian Air Force
IOR	Indian Other Rank(s)
IP	Initial Point
IRBM	Intermediate Range Balistic Missile
IRE	Instrument Rating Examiner
IRT	Instrument Rating Test
JAAF	Japanese Army Air Force
JaboG	*Jagbombergeschwader* (post-war German fighter-bomber wing)
Jasta	*Jagdstaffel* (WWI German fighter squadron)
JEngO	Junior Engineer Officer
JFHQ	Joint Force Headquarters

535

JG	*Jagdgeschwader* (German fighter group)	RE	Royal Engineers
JOC	Joint Operations Centre	REAF	Royal Egyptian Air Force
J/T	Junior Technician	Regt	Regiment
KAR	King's African Rifles	RFC	Royal Flying Corps
KB	Kite Balloon	Rfn	Rifleman
KL	Kuala Lumpur	RHA	Royal Horse Artillery
KOYLI	King's Own Yorkshire Light Infantry	RIF	Royal Inniskilling Fusiliers
LAC	Leading Aircraftman	RIAF	Royal Indian Air Force
L/Cpl	Lance Corporal	RIN	Royal Indian Navy
LG	Landing Ground	RMAF	Royal Malayan/Malaysian Air Force
Lt	Lieutenant (2/Lt - Second Lieutenant)	RNAS	Royal Naval Air Service
Lt Col	Lieutenant Colonel	RNZAF	Royal New Zealand Air Force
Ltn	*Leutnant* (Pilot Officer)	ROTB	"Roll on That Boat"
LVG	*Luft-Verkehrs-Gesellschaft*	RP	Rocket Projectile
Maj	Major	RSAF	Royal Saudi Air Force
MAP	Ministry of Aircraft Production	RSO	Range Safety Officer
MAXEVAL	see TACEVAL	RSU	Repair and Salvage Unit
MC	Medium Capacity (category of bomb)	R/T	Radio Telephony, ie speech
ME	Middle East	SAAF	South African Air Force
MEAF	Middle East Air Force	SAC	Senior Aircraftman
METS	Multi-Engine Training Squadron	SACEUR	Supreme Allied Commander in Europe
MEXO	Multi-Engine Cross-Over Course	SAM	Surface-to-Air Missile
MINEVAL	see TACEVAL	SAP	Semi-Armour Piercing
MO	Medical Officer	SARAH	Search And Rescue And Homing radio beacon fitted to life saving jackets in the 1950s and 60s
MOD	Ministry Of Defence		
Mod	Modification	SASO	Senior Air Staff Officer
MPABA	Malayan People's Anti-British Army	SE	Servicing Echelon
MPAJA	Malayan People's Anti-Japanese Army	SEAC	South East Asia Command
MRAF	Marshal of the Royal Air Force	SEATO	South East Asia Treaty Organisation
MRLA	Malayan Races' Liberation Army	SEngO	Senior Engineer Officer
MT	Motorised Transport	Sgt	Sergeant
MU	Maintenance Unit	SHAPE	Supreme Headquarters Allied Powers in Europe
MV	Motor Vessel		
NATO	North Atlantic Treaty Organisation	SHQ	Station Headquarters
NCO	Non-Commissioned Officer	SLAIS	Special Low Attack Instructors School
NEAF	Near East Air Force	SNCO	Senior Non-Commissioned Officer
NZLR	New Zealand Lone Ranger	SOC	Sector Operations Centre
Obfw	*Oberfeldwebel* (Flight Sergeant)	Sqn	Squadron
Obltn	*Oberleutnant* (Flying Officer)	Sqn Ldr	Squadron Leader
OC	Officer Commanding	SS	Steam Ship
OCU	Operational Conversion Unit	SSW	*Siemens-Schuckert Werke*
OOC	Out of Control (ie a 'Probable' in WW I)	Staffel(n)	Squadron(s) (German WW II)
OPREP	OPerations REPort - follow up to a CSR containing details of ordnance carried and expended	Stfw	*Stabsfeldwebel* (Staff Sergeant)
		STI	Special Technical Instruction
		SU	Signals Unit
OR	Other Rank(s)	Sub Lt	Sub Lieutenant
ORB	Operations Record Book (RAF Form 540)	SWO	Station (in this book more usually Squadron) Warrant Officer
OTF	Overseas Training Flight		
OTU	Operational Training Unit	TACEVAL	Formal TACtical EVALuation by an authorised external NATO assessment team. MINEVAL and MAXEVAL: similar events but conducted within a unit at the CO's discretion and on his authority.
PAI	Pilot Attack Instructor		
PC 10	Protective Covering No 10 (the standard camouflage finish applied to the upper surfaces of most RFC aeroplanes from 1917 onwards)		
		TAF	Tactical Air Force
PI	Practice Interception	TDP	Target Director Post
Plt Off	Pilot Officer	TFS	Tactical Fighter Squadron (USAF)
Pnr	Pioneer	TTTE	Tri-national Tornado Training Establishment
POW	Prisoner of War	TWCU	Tornado Weapons Conversion Unit
PR	Photographic Reconnaissance	TWU	Tactical Weapons Unit
PRU	Photographic Reconnaissance Unit	UE	Unit Establishment
PSP	Pierced Steel Planking	Uffz	*Unteroffizier* (Corporal)
PTC	Personnel Transit Centre	UHF	Ultra-High Frequency (radio)
PWD	Public Works Department	USAF	United States Air Force
PX	(USAAF) Post Exchange	USAAF	United States Army Air Force
QFI	Qualified Flying Instructor	USN	United States Navy
QR	Queen's Regulation(s)	VHF	Very High Frequency (radio)
QRA	Quick Reaction Alert	VIP	Very Important Person
QWI	Qualified Weapons Instructor	Vzfw	*Vizwfeldwebel* (Sergeant Major)
RA	Royal Artillery	WEM	Wireless Electrical Mechanic
RAAF	Royal Australian Air Force	Wg	Wing
RAFME	Royal Air Force Middle East	Wg Cdr	Wing Commander
RAMC	Royal Army Medical Corps	WO	Warrant Officer
RAN	Royal Australian Navy	WOM	Wireless Operator Mechanic
RASC	Royal Army Service Corps	WOp	Wireless Operator
R&R	Refuelling and Rearming (Party)	WOp/AG	Wireless Operator/Air Gunner
RBSU	Radar Bomb Scoring Unit	W/T	Wireless Telegraphy, ie Morse
RCAF	Royal Canadian Air Force	WW	World War (I or II)
RDF	Radio Direction Finding, ie 'radar'	ZG	*Zertsörergeshwader* (German eavy fighter group)
RDAF	Royal Danish Air Force	Zgsf	*Zugsführer* (WW I Austrian rank, roughly Sergeant)